1-2-3® Release 3.4:
The Complete Reference

1-2-3® Release 3.4: The Complete Reference

Mary Campbell

Osborne **McGraw-Hill**
Berkeley New York St. Louis San Francisco
Auckland Bogotá Hamburg London Madrid
Mexico City Milan Montreal New Delhi Panama City
Paris São Paulo Singapore Sydney
Tokyo Toronto

Osborne **McGraw-Hill**
2600 Tenth Street
Berkeley, California 94710
U.S.A.

For information on software, translations, or book distributors outside of the U.S.A., please write to Osborne McGraw-Hill at the above address.

1-2-3® Release 3.4: The Complete Reference Series

Copyright © 1993 by McGraw-Hill, Inc. All rights reserved. Printed in the United States of America. Except as permitted under the Copyright Act of 1976, no part of this publication may be reproduced or distributed in any form or by any means, or stored in a database or retrieval system, without the prior written permission of the publisher, with the exception that the program listings may be entered, stored, and executed in a computer system, but they may not be reproduced for publication.

1234567890 DOC 99876543

ISBN 0-07-881900-8

Acquisitions Editor Jeff Pepper	**Copy Editor** Mark S. Karmendy	**Computer Designer** Fred Lass
Associate Editor Vicki Van Ausdall	**Proofreader** Mick Arellano	**Illustrator** Marla Shelasky
Project Editor Mark S. Karmendy	**Indexer** Elizabeth Reinhardt	**Cover Designer** Bay Graphics Design Associates Mason Fong

Information has been obtained by Osborne **McGraw-Hill** from sources believed to be reliable. However, because of the possibility of human or mechanical error by our sources, Osborne **McGraw-Hill**, or others, Osborne **McGraw-Hill** does not guarantee the accuracy, adequacy, or completeness of any information and is not responsible for any errors or omissions or the results obtained from use of such information.

Contents at a Glance

Part 1 1-2-3 Worksheet Reference   1

1 An Introduction to 1-2-3 3
2 The Access System, Display, and Keyboard 21
3 Entering Data in 1-2-3's Worksheet 45
4 Changing the Appearance of the Worksheet Display 75
5 Basic Worksheet Commands 145
6 Printing with 1-2-3 and Wysiwyg 229
7 1-2-3's Built-In Functions 305
8 Working with Files 431

Part II 1-2-3's Advanced Features 487

- 9 Data Management 489
- 10 Using Data Management Features in the Worksheet Environment 559
- 11 Working with 1-2-3's Graphics Features 613
- 12 Keyboard Macros 687
- 13 Command Language Macros 731
- 14 Using 1-2-3's Built-In Add-Ins and Icons 809
- 15 Using the Wysiwyg Add-In 863

Part III Appendixes 955

- A Installing 1-2-3 957
- B The SmartIcons 969
- C LMBCS Codes 977

  Index 993

Contents

PART I
1-2-3 Worksheet Reference

1
An Introduction to 1-2-3 3
- A Product Designed to Utilize Your Hardware Effectively ... 4
- New 1-2-3 Release 3.4 Features ... 4
- Worksheet Options 4
  - 3-D Worksheets 5
  - Multiple Files 6
  - File Links 7
  - Automatic Format 7
  - Expanded Name Support 7
  - Search 8
  - Map 8
- @Functions 10
- Undo 10
- Printing 10
  - Release 3's Print Features 11
  - Support for Printing Graphs Within 1-2-3 11
- Data Management 11
  - /Data Query and /Data Sort 12
  - /Data Fill 12
  - /Data External 13
  - Data Tables 13
- Graphs 14
  - The Graph Window 14
  - Graph Features 15
- Macros 16
- The Wysiwyg Add-In 17
- Network Support 18

2
The Access System, Display, and Keyboard 21
- The Lotus Access System 22
  - 1-2-3 23

Translate	24
Install	24
Exit	24
The Display	25
The Control Panel	25
The Worksheet	28
The Status Line	29
The SmartIcons	31
Help Features	31
The 1-2-3 Menu	32
The Wysiwyg Menu	33
The Keyboard	33
The Mouse	40

3

Entering Data in 1-2-3's Worksheet ... 45

The Worksheet	46
Types of Entries	47
Label Entries	49
Value Entries	52
Correcting Errors in Entries	68
Ranges	70

4

Changing the Appearance of the Worksheet Display ... 75

Global, Range, and GROUP Changes	76
Worksheet Changes	79
Undoing Worksheet Changes	79
Insert Commands to Add Rows, Columns, or Sheets	80
Deleting Rows, Columns, or Sheets	85
Window Perspective Command	87
Column Commands	88
Hiding Sheets	95
Global Commands	96
Range Format Commands	102
Using SmartIcons to Change the Numeric Format	105

Numeric Format Options	105
Fixed Format	107
Scientific Format	107
Currency Format	108
Comma Format	109
General Format	109
+/− Format	111
Percent	112
Date/Time Format	112
Text Format	113
Hidden Format	115
Other Formats	116
Wysiwyg Format Options Accessible with the SmartIcons	118
Enlarging the Font Size	120
Adding Bold	121
Adding Underline	121
Outlining	121
Shading Cells	121
Advanced Features	122
Other International Format Options	122
Clock Display	125
/Range Justify	126
Command Reference Worksheet Display	129

5

Basic Worksheet Commands ... 145

Working with Ranges	146
Methods of Specifying Cell Ranges	146
Naming Cell Ranges	150
Using Filenames and Wildcard References with Range Names	156
Creating and Using Range Name Notes	157
Practical Applications for Range Names	157
Transposing Data	158
Converting Formulas to Values	164
Changing the Justification of Labels	166

Erasing Cell Ranges	167	Command Reference	
Protecting Worksheet Cells	168	Basic Worksheet	211

6

Deciding What Cells to Protect	170	Printing with 1-2-3 and Wysiwyg	229
Enabling Worksheet Protection	170	The Print Menus	230
Specifying an Input Range	171	Print Destination	232
		Background Printing	234
Sealing the Worksheet	172	Print Range	235
Cutting and Pasting	172	Changing the Print Range	239
Moving Information	173	Printing Multiple Ranges	239
Duplicating Existing Entries	176	Controlling the Printer from 1-2-3's Print Menu	239
Copy Options	176		
Copying Formulas	181	Printing Options	241
Using SmartIcon Options for Copying in Release 3.4	188	Creating Headers and Footers	241
		Margins	244
Using 1-2-3's Search and Replace Features	190	Borders	246
		Page Size	250
Using Search	191	Wysiwyg Printing Features	254
Using Replace	191		
Making Other Worksheet Changes	192	Adding Manual Page Breaks	254
Changing Default Label Justification for the Worksheet	193	Previewing Your Printed Output	256
		Compressing Your Printout	256
Erasing the Worksheet	193	Restoring Default Print Layout Settings	257
Controlling the Beep Option	194		
Recalculating the Worksheet	194	Creating a Layout Library File	258
Default Recalculation Settings	195	Setting Printer Configurations	258
Changing the Recalculation Settings	196	Print Settings	261
		1-2-3's Printing Features	263
Modifying the Screen Display	198	Page Breaks	263
		Other Options	263
Freezing Titles	200	Saving Print Settings	266
Adding a Second Window	203	Using Printer Features	266
Using the Map Option to View Worksheet Information	207	Clearing Print Settings	268
		Selecting a Printer	269
Displaying the Current Status of Worksheet Options	208	Global Printer Defaults	270

Command Reference

Printing 275

7

1-2-3's Built-In Functions 305

Date and Time Functions 312
- @D360 312
- @DATE 313
- @DATEVALUE 315
- @DAY 316
- @HOUR 318
- @MINUTE 318
- @MONTH 319
- @NOW 321
- @SECOND 322
- @TIME 322
- @TIMEVALUE 324
- @TODAY 325
- @YEAR 326

Financial Functions 327
- @CTERM 328
- @DDB 329
- @FV 330
- @IRR 331
- @NPV 333
- @PMT 335
- @PV 337
- @RATE 338
- @SLN 339
- @SYD 340
- @TERM 341
- @VDB 343

Mathematical Functions 344
- @ABS 345
- @ACOS 346
- @ASIN 348
- @ATAN 349
- @ATAN2 349
- @COS 350
- @EXP 351
- @INT 352
- @LN 354
- @LOG 354
- @MOD 355

- @PI 356
- @RAND 356
- @ROUND 357
- @SIN 359
- @SQRT 360
- @TAN 361

Logical Functions 362
- @FALSE 363
- @IF 363
- @ISERR 366
- @ISNA 367
- @ISNUMBER 368
- @ISRANGE 369
- @ISSTRING 370
- @TRUE 371

Special Functions 372
- @@ 372
- @CELL 374
- @CELLPOINTER 377
- @CHOOSE 378
- @COLS 380
- @COORD 381
- @ERR 382
- @HLOOKUP 383
- @INDEX 387
- @INFO 389
- @NA 390
- @ROWS 391
- @SHEETS 393
- @VLOOKUP 393

Statistical Functions 397
- @AVG 397
- @COUNT 398
- @MAX 399
- @MIN 400
- @STD 400
- @STDS 402
- @SUM 403
- @SUMPRODUCT 406
- @VAR 407
- @VARS 409

String Functions 411
- @CHAR 412
- @CLEAN 412
- @CODE 413

@EXACT	414
@FIND	415
@LEFT	416
@LENGTH	417
@LOWER	418
@MID	419
@N	420
@PROPER	422
@REPEAT	422
@REPLACE	424
@RIGHT	425
@S	426
@STRING	427
@TRIM	427
@UPPER	428
@VALUE	429

8

Working with Files	431
Naming and Using Files	432
Filenames and File Types	432
Subdirectories	433
The File Menu Options	434
Saving a File to Disk	434
Retrieving a File from Disk	436
Using Passwords with Files	439
Combining Information from Two Files	440
Saving Part of a Worksheet	446
Erasing Files from the Disk	448
Determining What Files Are on Your Disk	449
Adding Text Files to the Worksheet	451
Changing the Current Directory	454
Working with Multiple Files	454
Opening and Closing Multiple Files	454
Using Multiple Files in Commands	457
External File Links	457
Other Ways to Work with Files	459
Creating a Worksheet File That Loads Automatically	459
Changing the Default Directory Permanently	459
Changing the Default Directory for Temporary Files	460
Setting the Default File Extension	460
Using Operating System Commands	461
Translating Files from Other Programs	461
Command Reference Files	467

PART II
1-2-3's Advanced Features

9

Data Management	489
The 1-2-3 Database	490
Setting Up a Database	492
Choosing a Location for the Database	492
Entering Field Names	492
Entering Information	493
Making Changes	494
Sorting Your Data	494
Determining What Data to Sort	495
Specifying the Sort Sequence	495
Starting and Stopping the Sort	498

Starting Over	498
Sorting with the SmartIcons	498
Generating a Series of Values	499
Adding Record Numbers for Sorting Records	500
Using /Data Fill with Dates and Times	502
Searching the Database	505
Telling 1-2-3 Where Your Data Is Located	505
Specifying the Desired Records	505
Highlighting Selected Records	512
Writing Selected Records on the Worksheet	513
Adding Selected Records to the Database	519
Deleting Selected Records from the Database	521
Resetting Selection Options	521
Quitting the Query Menu	521
Adding a Second Database	522
External Databases	522
Opening an External Database	523
Listing Information About External Databases	525
Using External Databases	526
Closing an External Database	527
Creating an External Database	527
Deleting External Database Tables	531
The Database Statistical Functions	531
@DAVG	532
@DCOUNT	533
@DGET	533
@DMAX	534
@DMIN	535
@DQUERY	535
@DSTD	537
@DSTDS	538
@DSUM	538
@DVAR	539
@DVARS	540

Command Reference

Data Management	541

10

Using Data Management Features in the Worksheet Environment	559
Performing Statistical Analyses with /Data Commands	560
Sensitivity Analysis	560
Using Labeled Data Tables in Sensitivity Analysis	568
Regression Analysis	579
Frequency Distribution	583
Matrix Arithmetic	585
Splitting Long Labels into Individual Cell Entries	590
Sequencing Worksheet Data	593

Command Reference

Data Analysis	599

11

Working with 1-2-3's Graphics Features	613
Creating an Automatic Graph	614
Viewing Graphs and Worksheets Simultaneously	616

Creating Graphs 618
   Selecting a Graph Type 619
   Labeling the X Axis 619
   Selecting Data for a
      Graph 625
Enhancing the Basic Graph
      Type 627
   Setting the Orientation of
      the Axes 627
   Stacking the Data
      Ranges 627
   Displaying Data Ranges As
      Percentages 629
   Using Two Y Axes 631
   Changing the Appearance
      of Graph Elements 632
   Adding a Data Table 634
   Changing the Frame's
      Appearance 634
Using the QuickGraph Icon 635
Enhancing the Basic Display 636
   Pie Chart Options 636
   Selecting Colors for Graph
      Ranges 639
   Selecting Hatch Patterns for
      Graph Ranges 639
   Adding Descriptive
      Labels 640
   Adding Grid Lines 644
   Choosing Line and Symbol
      Options 646
   Choosing Color or Black
      and White 647
   Selecting Scaling Options 647
   Using Data to Label Your
      Graph 650
   Resetting Graph
      Options 650
Storing and Using Graphs ... 651
   Naming Graphs for Later
      Use 652
   Deleting Graphs 653
   Saving Graphs to an
      External File 653

Quitting the Graph Menu 654
Printing Graphs 654
   Selecting Graphs to
      Print 655
   Print Menu Commands for
      Graphs 655
   Printing Selected
      Graphs 658
   Moving Beyond 1-2-3's Graph
      Features 658
Command Reference
   Graphics 661

12

Keyboard Macros 687
   Types of Macros 688
   Keyboard Macros 688
      Recording the Keystrokes 690
      Typing a Keyboard Macro 695
      Using the Keystroke
         Recorder Feature 696
      Naming Your Macro 698
      Documenting Your
         Macro 699
      Executing Your Macro 700
      Assigning Macros to User
         Icons 701
      Defining a User Icon from
         Keyboard 702
      Define a User Icon's Macro
         with Stored
         Keystrokes 703
      Modifying the Definition of
         a User Icon 703
      Debugging a Macro
         Assigned
         to a User Icon 704
   Creating a Macro Library 704
   Debugging Macros 705
   Automatic Macros 706
      Creating an Automatic
         Macro 706
      Disabling Automatic
         Macros 707

Ready-to-Use Macros	707
Worksheet Macros	707
Range Macros	714
File Macros	715
Print Macros	719
Graph Macros	723
Data Macros	724

13

Command Language Macros .. 731

Differences Between Command Language Macros and Keyboard Macros	732
Constructing and Using Command Language Macros	733
Planning Command Language Macros	734
Strategies for Designing Complex Macros	736
Entering Command Language Macros	739
Creating Interactive Macros	742
Documenting Command Language Macros	742
Testing Command Language Macros	743
Executing Command Language Macros	744
Macro Commands	745
Syntax of Macro Commands	745
Conventions for Macros in This Chapter	746
Macro Commands that Affect the Screen	746
Interactive Macro Commands	758
Macro Commands that Affect Flow of Execution	776
Macro Commands that Manipulate Data	788
Macro Commands that Handle Files	799

14

Using 1-2-3's Built-In Add-Ins and Icons 809

Activating the Add-In Menu	810
Other Add-In Menu Commands	811
The Viewer Add-In	812
The Auditor Add-In	815
Using the Auditor Add-In	815
The Backsolver Add-In	820
The Solver Add-In	821
Entering The Basic Problem	823
Invoking Solver	826
Creating a Solution	827
Solver Report Options	828
The @SOLVER Add-In Function	836
Using Macros with 1-2-3 Add-Ins	836
SmartIcons	838
Using the SmartIcons	839
Modifying the Custom Palette	839
User Icons	842

Command Reference

Add-In Menu	845

15

Using the Wysiwyg Add-In 863

The Wysiwyg Interface	864
Improving the Appearance of Worksheet Entries	867
Using Different Fonts	867
Adding Boldface	871
Adding Italics	871
Adding Underlining	872
Adding Lines	872
Adding Color	874
Adding Shading	875

Removing Formats 876
Using Named Format
  Styles 876
Using Text Ranges and
  Adding Formats
  to Text 877
  Entering and Editing a Text
    Range 877
  Changing the Alignment of
    a Text Range 878
  Reformatting a Text
    Range 881
  Adding Formats to Text in
    Entries 882
  Removing a Text Range ... 884
Copying, Moving, and
  Importing Formats 884
Changing Column Widths and
  Row Heights 887
Changing the Wysiwyg
  Display 888
  Graphics Versus Text
    Mode 888
  Changing Colors 889
  Zooming In and Out 890
  Setting the Appearance of
    the Cell Pointer 890
  Setting the Appearance of
    the Worksheet Frame ... 891
  Showing Grid Lines 892
  Showing Page Breaks 893
  Setting the Display
    Intensity 893
  Setting the Directory
    Containing Font
    Files 893
  Setting the Display
    Default 893
Using Wysiwyg for Your
  Graphs 894
  Adding and Removing
    Graphs 894
  Changing the Graph
    Settings 896
  Viewing Graphs 898

Making Enhancements to
  Graphics 898
Printing with Wysiwyg 906
  The Basic Print Process 907
  Adding Page Breaks 909
  Layout Options 910
  Changing Printing
    Configuration
    Options 912
Wysiwyg and GROUP
  Mode 915
Using Macros with
  Wysiwyg 915
Command Reference
  Wysiwyg 917

PART III
Appendixes

A
Installing 1-2-3 957
  Your Equipment 958
    Monitors 958
    Printers 959
  Installing 1-2-3 959
  Using Install After Installing
    1-2-3 962
  Creating More Than One
    Driver Set 962
  Modifying the Current
    Driver 963
  Changing Wysiwyg
    Options 965
  Installing 1-2-3 with
    Windows 965

B
The SmartIcons 969

C
LMBCS Codes 977
  Creating LMBCS Codes 978
  Creating LMBCS Characters 978

Index 993

Acknowledgments

I would like to thank the following individuals who contributed much to this revision: Gabrielle Lawrence and Elizabeth Reinhardt, who explored all the new features of Release 3.4 in detail and made all the necessary manuscript changes; Jeff Pepper, acquisitions editor, who coordinated the resources necessary to provide a quality product in a timely manner; Mark Karmendy and Mick Arellano, who handled the editorial and proofreading tasks for the book; to the many, many individuals at Lotus who offered help in different ways, with special thanks to Candice Clemens and Mike Dinwitty.

Mary Campbell

Preface

Although 1-2-3 has been available for many years, it is still one of the best-selling microcomputer software packages. Individuals who are new to computing will gain the same benefits that longtime users have realized from the package. Organizations that have been using 1-2-3 for years will benefit from improvements offered by Release 3.4.

The introduction of Release 3.4 adds many new features to the package. In addition to the three-dimensional spreadsheets, external databases, and expanded graphics added with Release 3.0, Release 3.4 now offers a full set of worksheet publishing features. Wysiwyg commands allow you to customize worksheet fonts and screen colors. You can add lines, shading, boldface, and italics to any location that you want. You no longer need to print text and graphics on different pages; you can create professional-looking output that combines numbers, text, and graphs on the same page. Release 3.4 provides full mouse support to make all of your work with 1-2-3 easier. Release 3.4 also includes SmartIcons that you can select to perform the most frequently used commands.

About This Book

1-2-3 Release 3.4: The Complete Reference is designed to serve the needs of both new and experienced 1-2-3 users. If you are using Release 3.0 or 3.1, this reference is also for you, since all of the features of Release 3.0 and 3.1 are incorporated into Release 3.4. Novice users should start at the beginning of the book and work through the first six chapters. After reading these chapters, they may want to enter some of the examples into their systems for practice. Users already familiar with 1-2-3 basics will want to review the table of contents and focus on topics with which they are less familiar, such as data management features, keyboard alternative macros, and command macros.

Experienced users will also find this volume to be a valuable reference tool, describing all of 1-2-3's many features in detail. Each topic has practical examples in addition to a description of specific features. Boxes in the text summarize important information, and a thorough index will help you find the precise topic you are looking for. Reference sections at the end of many of the chapters provide a quick alphabetical guide to commands. In addition to covering all of the 1-2-3 features, this book provides information on the SmartIcons and the add-ins included with 1-2-3. These add-ins include the Auditor, the Backsolver, the Solver, and the Viewer.

Organization of This Book

This book is divided into three parts. Part One covers the worksheet and all the commands you need to create efficient worksheet models. Part Two focuses on advanced features like database, graphics, macro, and add-ins. Part Three consists of three appendixes that offer supplemental information on installation, the SmartIcons, and the Lotus LMBCS codes. You will also find the inclusion of the command card to be very useful. An outline of the chapters follows:

- Chapter One, "An Introduction to 1-2-3," will get you started with the 1-2-3 package. It provides an overview of all the Release 3.4 features.

- Chapter Two, "The Access System, Display, and Keyboard," provides an overview of the package by introducing you to some of its most important features. You will learn all about 1-2-3's display in this chapter.

- Chapter Three, "Entering Data in 1-2-3's Worksheet," gets you started in creating worksheet models. You will learn all about the types of entries that can be made on the worksheet.

- Chapter Four, "Changing the Appearance of the Worksheet Display," introduces you to the flexibility 1-2-3 allows in formatting data. You will learn how to override the default display characteristics to create the exact display you want, as well as how to take advantage of new formats in Release 3.4. You will use 1-2-3's formats as well as basic Wysiwyg options.

- Chapter Five, "Basic Worksheet Commands," covers all the command options pertaining to the worksheet. You will learn how to determine the worksheet status and change options to suit your needs.

- Chapter Six, "Printing with 1-2-3 and Wysiwyg," provides explanations and examples of all 1-2-3 and Wysiwyg printing features. It shows you how to do everything from printing formulas to adding borders to a printed report. You will learn about all the Release 3.4 and Wysiwyg features that fully utilize the features of your printer.

- Chapter Seven, "1-2-3's Built-in Functions," lists and describes each of 1-2-3's built-in functions. You can read about the ones you are interested in or survey them all to discover new uses for the package.

- Chapter Eight, "Working with Files," covers everything you will need to know to save and retrieve files. You will also learn how to link files and save just a section of your worksheet.

- Chapter Nine, "Data Management," introduces you to the sort and query features of 1-2-3. You will learn how to sequence data in any order and extract particular data for any purpose.

- Chapter Ten, "Using Data Management Features in the Worksheet Environment," introduces you to the power that the data management features can add to worksheet models. You will learn about the tools needed to perform a sensitivity analysis, generate matrices, and sort formula entries.

- Chapter Eleven, "Working with 1-2-3's Graphics Features," provides examples of graphic display for your data. You will learn how easy it is to change numeric data into graphics and charts.

- Chapter Twelve, "Keyboard Macros," shows you how to save keystrokes for menu selections and other activities in worksheet cells. These keystrokes can then be reused at will.

- Chapter Thirteen, "Command Language Macros," covers the powerful command language available in Release 3.4. Each macro command is described and illustrated with an example.

- Chapter Fourteen, "Using 1-2-3's Built-In Add-Ins and Icons," describes the Add-In menu and most of the add-ins that accompany Release 3.4. These add-ins include the Auditor add-in that follows the effects of formulas, the Backsolver add-in that calculates the initial value that creates the desired result, the Solver add-in that finds sets of values that meet limits, and the Viewer add-in that lets you select the file to work with by looking at its contents. This chapter also covers working with the SmartIcons to select which icons appear on the first palette and how the user-defined icons appear on the palette.

- Chapter Fifteen, "Using the Wysiwyg Add-In," covers this add-in, which provides worksheet publishing capabilities to 1-2-3.

- Appendix A, "Installing 1-2-3," explains everything you need to know to install the package successfully.

- Appendix B, "The SmartIcons," lists the available Release 3.4 SmartIcons and the features they represent.

- Appendix C, "LMBCS Codes," provides the representation for each of the Lotus LMBCS codes.

Conventions Used in This Book

Several conventions used in this book should make your task of learning about 1-2-3 Release 3.4 easier:

- Command sequences are shown with initial letters in uppercase (as in /Worksheet Erase).

- User input is indicated in **boldface**.

- Small capital letters have been used for the names of function keys (as in ALT-F4).

- @Function keywords are shown in uppercase, although you may use either upper- or lowercase when making entries.

- Filenames are shown in uppercase.

- The term Release 3 includes Releases 3.0, 3.1, and 3.4. In other cases, specific release numbers indicate that release which introduced the described feature.

Preface

Why This Book Is For You

If you are a typical business user, your time is limited. You don't want to read three books to find the information you need to use a particular feature of your spreadsheet. This book is designed as a one-stop source for every command and feature of 1-2-3 Release 3.4, Release 3.1, and Release 3.0. It is an eay-to-use yet comprehensive guide to every possible option offered by the package, including the automatic Wysiwyg interface.

The organization of *1-2-3 Release 3.4: The Complete Reference* helps you quickly locate features you want to review—from creating basic worksheets to integrating graphics and using the new spreadsheet publishing features of Wysiwyg. If you are a new user you will find this book an excellent teacher, since it presents the information in a logical easy-to-understand manner. Unlike a very basic book that covers only a few features, however, the usefulness of this book will grow with your knowledge. As you become more familiar with the basic operations of the product, you can rely on the command reference sections at the back of each chapter to quickly refresh your memory or provide you with a specific piece of information you need to know quickly.

If you are a Lotus 1-2-3 Release 3.4, 3.1, or 3.0 user at any level, the information in this comprehensive, yet easy-to-use volume will make spreadsheet production, financial analysis, and production of professional looking documents much simpler and faster.

THE COMPLETE

PART ONE
1-2-3 Worksheet Reference

CHAPTER 1

An Introduction to 1-2-3

1-2-3 is one of the most popular products ever introduced for microcomputers. Since its first introduction it has set the standard for spreadsheet product offerings on both mainframes and microcomputers. Release 3.4 includes all the features contained in previous releases of 1-2-3 as well as a new feature, the SmartIcons palettes that make tasks selectable with pictures. This chapter is an introduction to 1-2-3, providing an overview of its major features. With the features mentioned, as with the rest of the book, Release 3 includes Releases 3.0, 3.1, and 3.4.

A Product Designed to Utilize Your Hardware Effectively

If you have invested in 286 and 386 computers, you will want to use programs that utilize the power of these machines effectively. 1-2-3 Release 3.4 offers full support for both expanded and extended memory. It provides its own operating system extenders, so you can even utilize your equipment without upgrading to OS/2. Release 3.4 automatically attaches the Wysiwyg add-in for spreadsheet publishing features and provides palettes of icons that let you complete tasks with a single mouse click.

New 1-2-3 Release 3.4 Features

The most significant enhancement to 1-2-3 Release 3.4 are the SmartIcon palettes that appear whenever Wysiwyg is attached. You can use the 81 predefined icons that are assigned to specific 1-2-3 tasks, as well as define twelve user icons to do whatever you want. You can select these icons with a mouse or the keyboard to complete tasks quickly.

Other additions to 1-2-3 Release 3.4 include:

- performance enhancements to existing features
- new print drivers
- new settings sheets for printing and graphs
- a new macro debugging capability
- the ability to display a graph that you have created as 3-D
- landscape printing for dot matrix printers
- expanded translate features
- ability to erase a cell by pressing the DEL key.

Worksheet Options

The basic worksheet options that allow the recording of numbers, labels, and formulas in 1-2-3's electronic spreadsheet still exist in Release 3.4. Release 3 introduced the ability to directly enter dates and times, which 1-2-3 converts into the appropriate date and time serial number that the program uses to store them. The package continues to be an ideal tool for tasks like budgeting, forecasting, and sales projections—for large and small companies alike. The wide range of 1-2-3's formats and other features allows it to be used in applications as diverse as manufacturing, architectural planning, hospital management, and education. Now new features extend both the range and size of applications that are possible.

3-D Worksheets

The 3-D worksheet features allow you to have up to 256 worksheets in one worksheet file. Each sheet has the same 256 columns and 8192 rows as the first sheet presented. This capability finally allows you to create applications that parallel your work environment, including the multiple products, subsidiaries, and regions that are part of your overall picture.

Each sheet can contain different types of information, or match other sheets exactly. The GROUP mode allows you to insert rows and columns, change column widths, and alter formats for one sheet or all the sheets at once.

Figure 1-1 gives you a look at a three-dimensional worksheet; it is a perspective view that splits the screen to show three different sheets at one time.

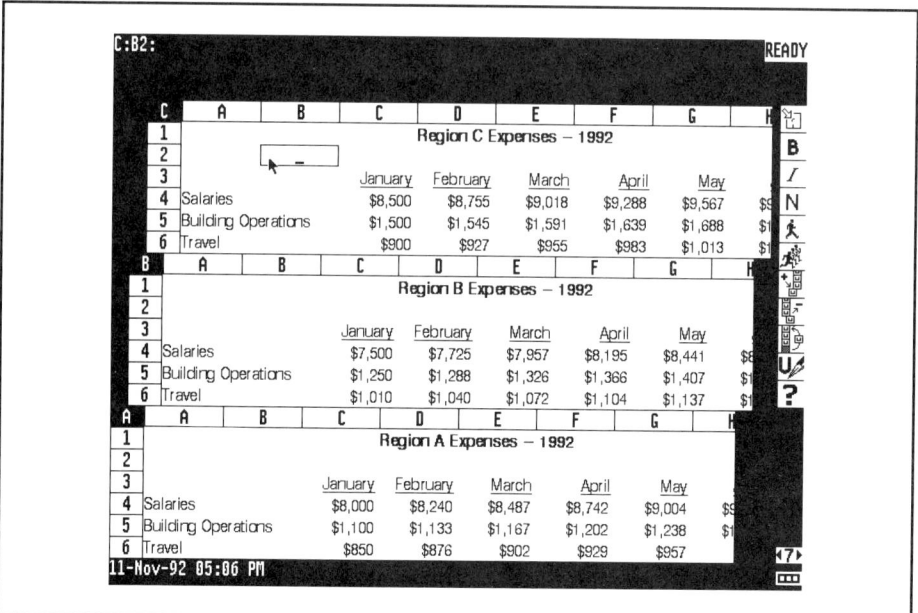

Figure 1-1. *Perspective view of three sheets from a worksheet file*

Each sheet displays a level indicator in the upper left corner that allows you to distinguish it from other worksheets. The three sheets shown are all part of one worksheet file—making it possible to create a consolidation of the data shown, with a simple formula in the same file as the detail.

Multiple Files

With 1-2-3, you have always been able to create multiple files for different types of worksheet information. The difference with Release 3 is that you can bring more than one file into memory at a time. You can have a total of 256 sheets in memory, depending on the size of the sheets and the amount of memory in your system. Some of these sheets can be part of a multiple-sheet file, and others can be separate files.

Figure 1-2 shows a perspective window with information from three different files. The file is active, since it contains the cell pointer. The first sheet contains information on current customer purchases. The second file contains a discount table used in computing discounts on all orders based on the amount and the purchase type. The third file contains additional information on the vendors used by the company. The information in this file would be helpful in

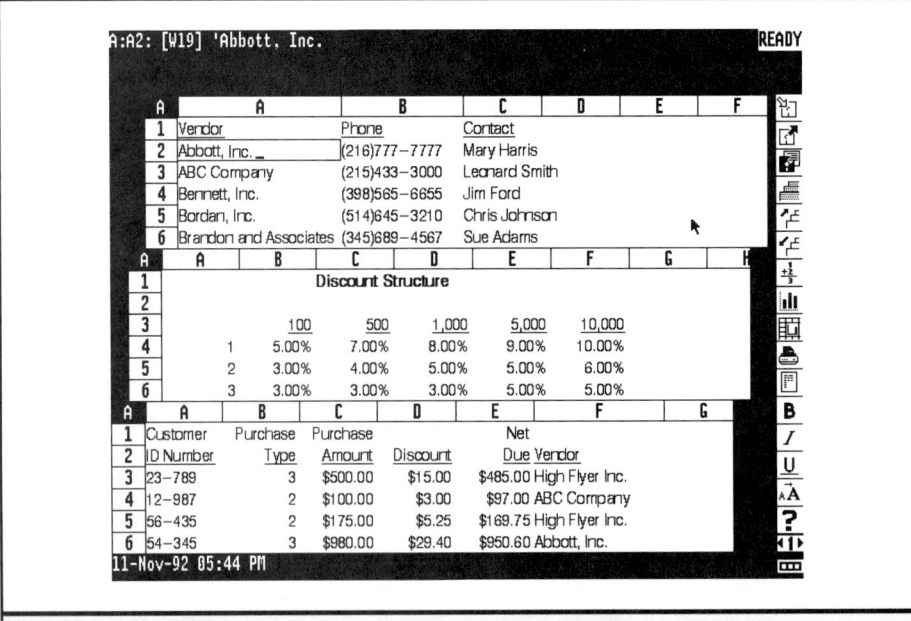

Figure 1-2. Perspective view of sheets from three different files

negotiating a large order, since it may be possible to obtain price concessions or custom features from a vendor if the size of the order is sufficient. Although the screen may look very similar to the multiple-sheet view, you can see that each of the sheets has an A for its level indicator, indicating that it comes from a different file.

File Links

File links are normally used in multiple-file applications. These links can be to other files in memory or on disk. You can use a link to bring information from a cell into the current cell, or data in the linked cell or range can be an integral part of a calculation stored in the current cell.

Once linked, you can control when the links are updated. If the files that you are linking are shared files on a network, you will want to refresh the entries as part of a decision-making cycle, and definitely before printing the current entries.

Automatic Format

Automatic format takes the work out of making many entries. Instead of typing a number and selecting the proper format, you can format a range of cells as Automatic. This format is temporary and will be replaced by a more appropriate format once you make an entry. The Automatic format supports Date, Time, Percent, Scientific, Currency, Label, Comma, and Fixed formats.

Figure 1-3 shows a worksheet that was created after selecting an Automatic format for cells in the range A4..E13. The entry 04/06/92 was placed in A4. Since this entry is a valid date entry, 1-2-3 converted the cell format to Date 4. The control panel, which shows the current stored contents of the cell, indicates that a date serial number was created for the entry. The entries in the other columns were also made while Automatic was in effect. Column C entries were entered with a % sign. The $ was used with the currency entries in column D. Automatic is a much quicker method than having to apply four different formats to four columns.

Expanded Name Support

1-2-3's range name features offer you the ability to assign names to one or more worksheet cells. You can use these names anywhere a range address is acceptable, and you will find that they make your formulas much easier to understand. Release 3 features include the ability to assign notes to range names.

```
A:A4: (D4) 33700                                                    READY

     A       A         B         C         D          E      F    G    H
     1              CD Report For The Week Of April 6, 1992
     2                                            Years To
     3            Date      Time     CD Rate   Amount   Maturity
     4          04/06/92  09:00 AM   7.50%     $5,000     10
     5          04/06/92  12:00 PM   7.00%     $5,000     20
     6          04/07/92  09:00 AM   7.12%     $5,000     15
     7          04/07/92  12:00 PM   7.12%     $5,000     10
     8          04/08/92  09:00 AM   7.10%     $5,000     20
     9          04/08/92  12:00 PM   7.10%     $5,000     25
     10         04/09/92  09:00 AM   7.12%     $5,000     15
     11         04/09/92  12:00 PM   7.14%     $5,000     20
     12         04/10/92  09:00 AM   7.15%     $5,000     10
     13         04/10/92  12:00 PM   7.12%     $5,000     15
```

Figure 1-3.   *Worksheet created with Automatic format*

You can also create tables of range name notes that contain all the information of range name tables, plus the notes attached to them. In Release 3, range names can be used in formulas before they are defined. Although the formula will initially read ERR, the formula can still be finalized.

Search

Release 3 includes search and replace features that are effective in label and formula entries. You can use them to locate a particular entry like a last name or part number, or to change a phone number or an address.

Figure 1-4 shows several worksheet entries. The /Range Search command was used to locate entries for part number 56-435. 1-2-3 locates the first occurrence of the part number entry and highlights it, as shown in the figure. With the Find option you have the option of continuing the search to look for additional matching entries or to end the search. With the Replace option, you have the additional options of replacing the current instance of the string, or all instances of the string, with another string you have already entered.

Map

You can create a map window for any worksheet. This window lets you look at an overview of the worksheet entries. Different symbols are used to mark labels, numbers, and formulas. You can use this view to identify number entries that

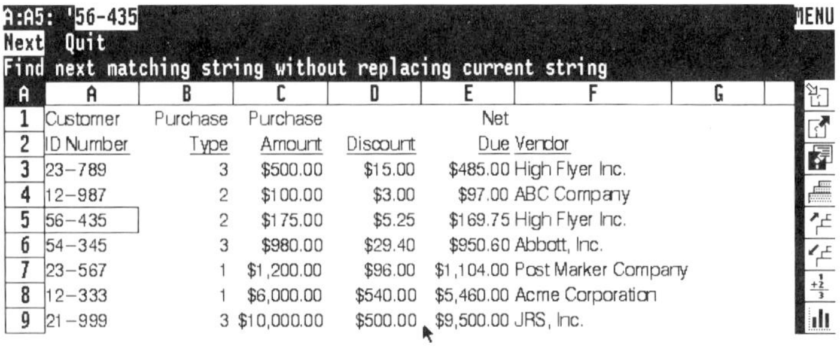

Figure 1-4. Using /Range Search to find a part number

should be formulas, or other problems in the worksheet structure. When you request a map window, 1-2-3 automatically narrows the columns and displays more columns, as shown in Figure 1-5. The pound symbols (#) represent numbers, quotation marks (") represent labels, and plus signs (+) represent formulas.

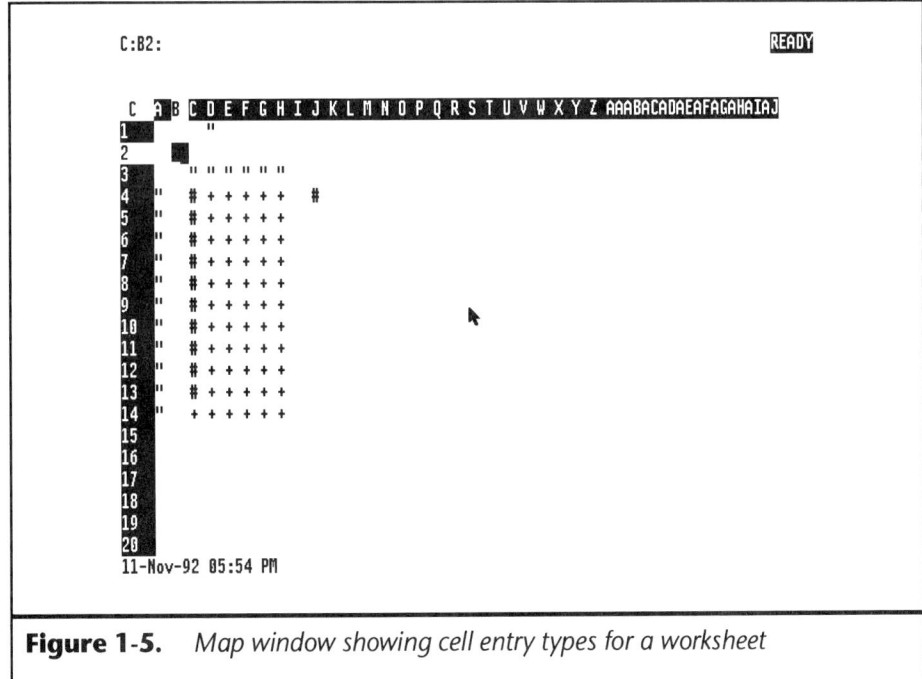

Figure 1-5. Map window showing cell entry types for a worksheet

@Functions

The Release 3 family of spreadsheets provides 13 new @functions, plus expanded capability for 3 existing @functions to support the three-dimensional ranges. You can now sum a range across pages, or reference function arguments on other sheets or even in external files. The new functions are @COORD, @DGET, @DQUERY, @DSTDS, @D360, @DVARS, @INFO, @ISRANGE, @SHEETS, @STDS, @SUMPRODUCT, @VARS, and @VDB. The existing functions that have been improved are @CELL, @CELLPOINTER, and @INDEX.

Undo

In early releases of 1-2-3, once you invoked a command, a permanent change was effected. There was no way to undo the result of the command unless you had the last version of the model stored on disk and available for retrieval. In some cases changing your mind was easy without a disk version, since a change to one format could be altered by the entry of another format command. Other commands that erased data or changed the sequence of the worksheet entries were not as easily undone.

Release 3's Undo feature can be turned on and off through menu selections. When Undo is enabled, any command that does not affect an external device like the disk drive or printer can be undone. The secret is not to execute any intervening commands before attempting to undo the action of a command. With Wysiwyg, you can also use Undo to remove the effect of the changes you make through the Wysiwyg menus. In 1-2-3 and Wysiwyg, the Undo feature undoes most changes since 1-2-3 was last in the READY mode.

Printing

1-2-3's print features have always been easy to use. They provide basic support for printing spreadsheet data; however, in the past you needed to use the PrintGraph program to print a graph. PrintGraph is no longer required, since graph printing support is available from the Print menu and Wysiwyg. Print features extend well beyond the basics, with the Release 3.1 and 3.4 options that support use of most printer features, including different fonts and other customization options for both text and graphs. The new Wysiwyg add-in that is included with Releases 3.1 and 3.4 provides additional print features that you can use in place of the 1-2-3 Print menus.

Release 3's Print Features

A significant addition to 1-2-3's print features is the availability of background printing. You no longer need to sit and wait for a worksheet to print before continuing with your other tasks. You can send many print jobs to the queue, and specify print priorities of default, high, or low. The main Print menu, which used to limit you to a choice of only Printer or File, now provides the additional options Encoded, Suspend, Resume, Cancel, and Quit. The Encoded option allows you to write formatted print output to a file for later printing from the operating system. The file will include all the selected options like colors and fonts. The Suspend option allows you to temporarily stop a print job; Resume allows you to start it again. Cancel eliminates all the print jobs from the queue, including the job currently printing.

The new Options Advanced menu selection allows you to enhance your print output in many ways. You can now change the print device directly from the Print menu, rather than having to modify the default setting. You can change the character size, line spacing, and print orientation without the need for setup strings. Fonts can be changed for the header, footer, border, or frame.

With Releases 3.1 and 3.4 you can also use print setting names. You can assign a name to a set of printer options and change all of the print settings at once. When you select the name, 1-2-3 changes all of the current print settings to the print settings assigned to the name.

With Release 3.4 you are able to use landscape printing with 1-2-3 without the addition of a special utility. Release 3.4 also offers a new print setting sheet as well as improved print drivers and background printing.

Support for Printing Graphs Within 1-2-3

You no longer need to save 1-2-3 graphs for later printing with PrintGraph. With the new /Print Printer Image option, 1-2-3 will print the current graph or any named graph. Image options on the Options Advanced menu allow you to rotate the graph, change the image size, or change the print density of the graph.

Data Management

1-2-3's data management features support the creation of data tables. You can use these features to create a database of client information, or an invoice database. A wide variety of other data management features, in addition to basic query and sort features, include more sophisticated data analysis and the generation of data values.

/Data Query and /Data Sort

1-2-3 supports the creation of databases on the worksheet. The rows of a sheet are the records, and the columns are used for each field. /Data Query features allow you to extract records that match specific criteria, and /Data Sort options allow you to resequence records in any order. Release 3.1 expanded the Sort key features beyond the two-key limit of Release 2, to allow unlimited sort keys. A new Modify option added to /Data Query allows you to extract records in a database table, modify them, and return the modified records to the database.

The three-dimensional features of 1-2-3 expand practical applications, allowing you to use the full 8192 rows for the data table. Criteria and an output area can be defined on other sheets as shown in Figure 1-6, where data from sheet A is extracted using the criteria in sheet B and written to the output area in sheet C. Your databases can contain as many as 256 fields.

/Data Fill

1-2-3's /Data Fill command allows you to generate a series of evenly spaced numbers. You can use it to generate invoice numbers, purchase orders, or day

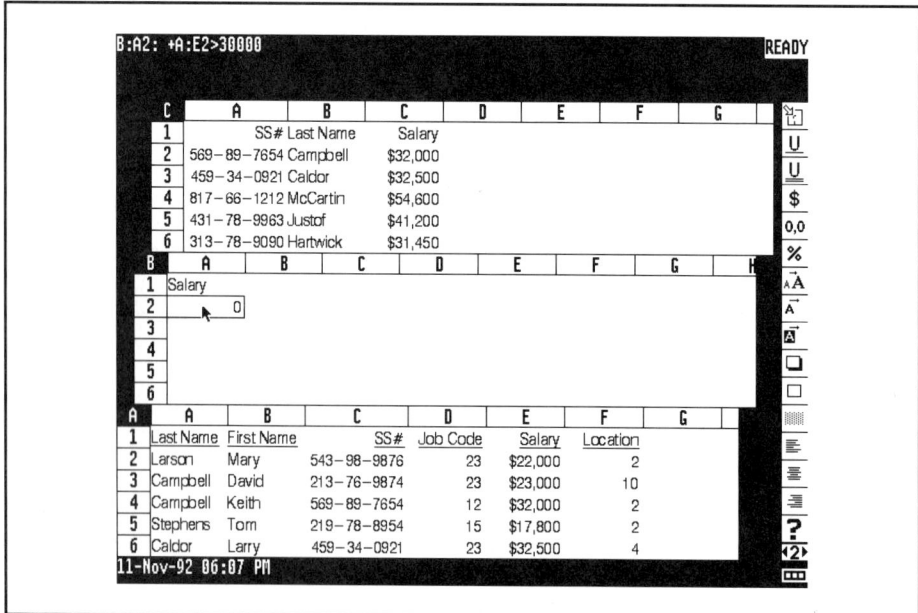

Figure 1-6. Defining criteria and output areas on other sheets

numbers. In Release 3 you will find many new options for this command that allow you to generate date and time serial numbers. You can space dates in increments of a week, a month, a quarter, or a year; you can space times in increments of minutes, hours, or seconds.

/Data External

The /Data External commands were added with Release 3. You can use them to exchange information between 1-2-3 and an external database, like dBASE, if you have a DataLens driver file for the database package. The 1-2-3 package provides sample DataLens drivers for dBASE III, Paradox, and SQL server.

After establishing a connection with the external file, you can add records to it using your 1-2-3 information. You can also add information to your 1-2-3 file from records in the external database.

Other commands allow you to list tables in an external database or to delete a table. You can also use features that update /Data Query operations or /Data Table commands. Functions and commands that are part of the database program can also be executed, even if you do not have a copy of the database program on the computer. Your requests are handled by the DataLens driver for the database program.

Data Tables

1-2-3's /Data Table commands have allowed you to conduct sensitivity analyses or automated "what-if" analyses for your models. With /Data Table 1 you can modify the values for a variable in the model and review the effect of each change on as many formulas as you wish. /Data Table 2 lets you vary two variables within the model, to see which one affects the model the most. With a Data Table type 2 you can only examine the effect on one formula.

Release 3 added the features of /Data Table 3. You can now systematically vary the values in each of three variables. One set of values is placed down a column, the second set is placed across a row, and the third set is placed across sheets. As with /Data Table 2, only the effect on one formula can be evaluated.

The /Data Table Labeled command added with Release 3 allows you to create /Data Table 1, 2, or 3 options. /Data Table Labeled offers much more flexibility than the predefined options, allowing you to use more variables or to tailor other entries. Labeled data tables let you evaluate the effect of changing variables on multiple formulas. You can also change more than three sets of values. You can add blank rows to a table and include formulas within the data table cells. Figure 1-7 shows a table created with the /Data Table Labeled features.

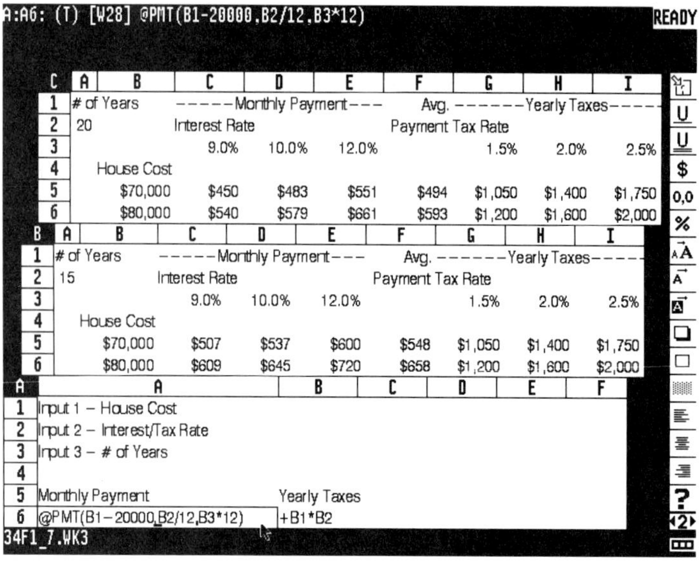

Figure 1-7. /Data Table Labeled

Graphs

Graphs present visual images of the information contained in a worksheet. With the visual appeal of graphs, you can often communicate information that would require considerable time to synthesize from the raw worksheet data. Release 3.1 and 3.4 added many new graph options which dramatically improve the quality of graphics output.

The Graph Window

1-2-3 now allows you to view both a graph and a worksheet on the screen at the same time. The /Worksheet Window Graph command allows you to split the screen in half, with the worksheet data displayed in one half and a graph displayed in the other half. 1-2-3 makes assumptions about how the data in the current area of the worksheet should be graphed and uses default options to create a graph for you automatically. As you make changes to your worksheet data you will be able to see the effect immediately in the graph on the screen. Figure 1-8 is an example of this split screen display.

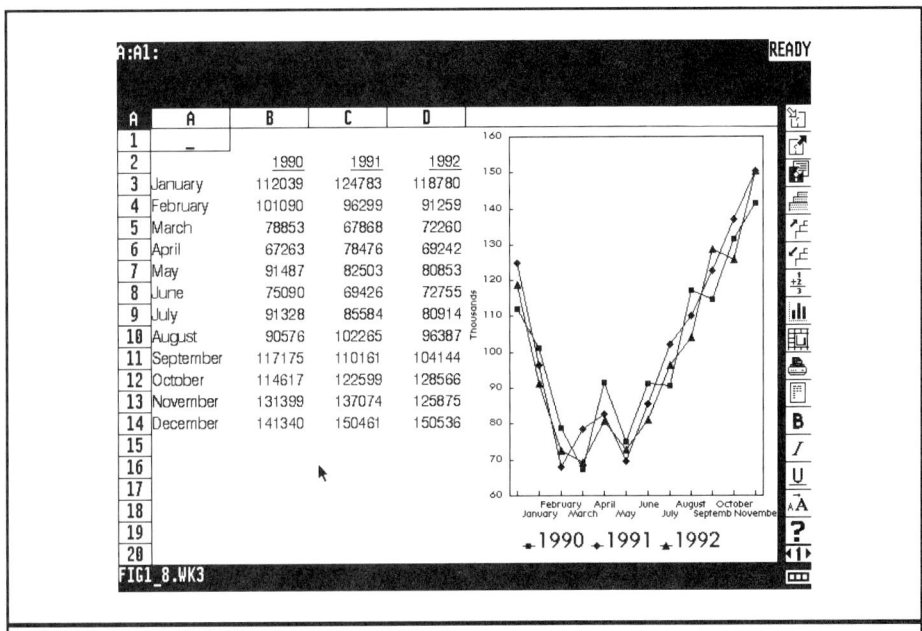

Figure 1-8. Worksheet entries and graph window

Graph Features

Releases 3.1 and 3.4 offer several new graph types and many new graph options. The new High-Low-Close-Open (HLCO) graphs allow you to track quantities that vary periodically. You might use these graphs to show tides at a particular time of day, along with the high and low tides. Wind speeds, temperature, and barometric pressure can also be shown on these graphs, although stock market prices are normally the data for which HLCO graphs are used (see Figure 1-9).

The new Mixed graph type allows you to combine line and bar graphs. Up to three sets of bars and lines can be shown on each mixed graph. You may choose to show expenses in the bar graph, and use a line graph to show revenues for the same periods.

The options for graphs have increased dramatically. You can now have two different y-axes on a graph, allowing you to show data with two different scales. Other options let you set the colors or hatch mark patterns for the graph. Text can be customized with color and font changes. You can also display each of the data points as a percentage of the total of all the data points—without the need for adding formulas to the worksheet. A 100% option will automatically compute the correct amount for each data point. Other graph enhancements are available through the Wysiwyg add-in.

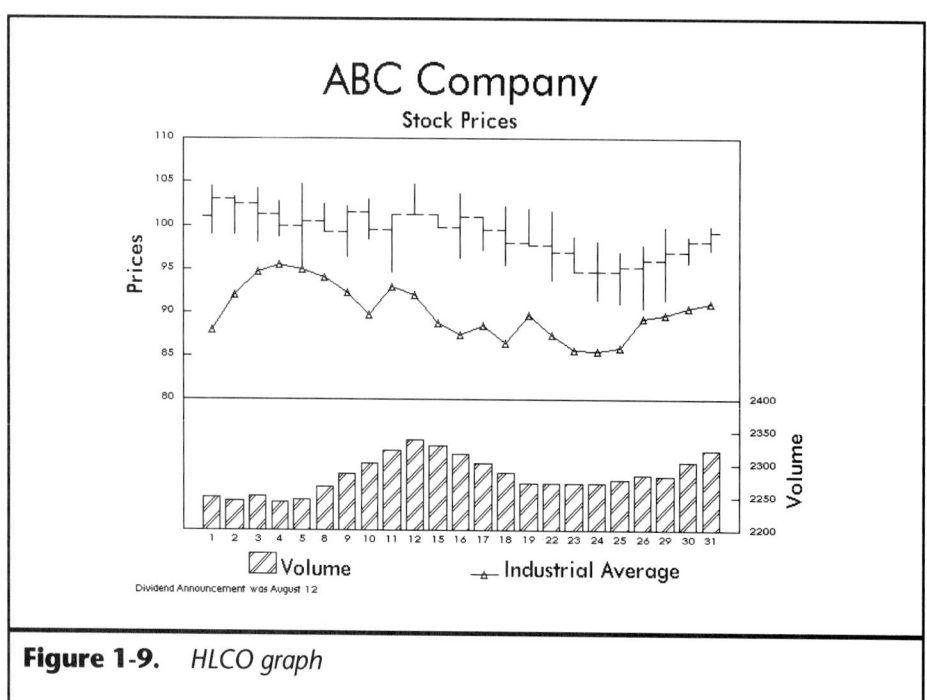

Figure 1-9. HLCO graph

A feature unique to 1-2-3 Release 3.4 is the ability to make any graph 3-D. All you need to do after defining your graph is to use the /Graph Type Features 3D to give a dramatic appearance to any graph. Release 3.4 also offers an improved setting sheet for graphs that makes option selections easier to keep track of.

Macros

1-2-3 macros allow you to automate all types of 1-2-3 tasks. You can use two different types of 1-2-3 macros, the keyboard alternative macro or command language macro. Keyboard alternative macros are nothing more than specially named label cells that contain the letters and symbols representing the keystrokes you would normally type from the keyboard for menu selections and data entry. Command language macros are also labels cells, but they can also contain commands from 1-2-3's macro command language. This language has commands that allow you to duplicate actions of a programming language, like testing conditions, or executing instructions repeatedly. New macro command language commands offer important advances, like the ability to create data entry forms. However, the most significant macro enhancement in Release 3.1

was the addition of an automatic keystroke recorder. With Release 3.4 you can watch the macro execute code at the bottom of the screen with TRACE mode on.

The keystroke recorder is always enabled. This means it records everything you type without any special action on your part. The keystroke recorder allows you to access 512 characters of recorded entries. You can copy these entries to a cell and use them as a macro. You can also "play them back" for repetitive tasks that you need temporarily.

Figure 1-10 shows some of the keystrokes captured by the recorder. The Record menu option, Copy, has already been selected in this example; Copy lets you highlight the keystrokes you want to place on a worksheet. Note that the entries enclosed in curly braces, like {U}, indicate cell pointer movement keys such as the UP ARROW key. This abbreviated form used by the recorder maximizes the number of entries that can be stored in 512 characters.

The Wysiwyg Add-In

A new feature of Release 3.1 was the Wysiwyg add-in, which comes with 1-2-3 and is part of the 1-2-3 installation process. The Wysiwyg add-in provides spreadsheet publishing capabilities that were formerly available only through typesetting. With Wysiwyg, you can change the appearance of text using boldface, underline, italics, and fonts. Wysiwyg can add boxes, lines, and shading to your 1-2-3 data. You can also change row widths and column heights. You can add graphs to the worksheet to print them with spreadsheet data. Additional options let you create graphics and use graphic images stored in 1-2-3 graph files and metafiles. Figure 1-11 shows a worksheet that uses several of the Wysiwyg features. Printing with Wysiwyg provides more options than the 1-2-3 Print menu. Wysiwyg also lets you use a mouse with 1-2-3.

```
A:A5: [W21]                                                    EDIT
Press TAB to anchor cursor, then highlight keystrokes to play back:
/WCS20~{D 5}/RFT{R}~/WCS28~{U}{D}/FS~R/FR{D 9}{U}{D}{R}{L}~/FR{D 9}{R}~{ESC}{GOT
O}B1~{ABS}{R 2}~/M~{D}~{D}{ABS}{R 2}~{GOTO}A1~{GRAPH}{ESC}/W{ESC}GA..{D}~B..{D}~
C..{D}~Q{GRAPH}{ESC}/FS{CE}C:\123R34\DATA\34f1_8~/FR{NAME}{D 27}{U 3}{D}{U 30}{D
 4}{L 3}{R}~{GRAPH}{ESC}/FR{NAME}{D 12}{U 8}{L}~{GRAPH}{ESC}/FR{NAME}{D 5}{U}~{G
RAPH}{ESC}/FR{NAME}{D 5}{U}{R}~{GRAPH}{ESC}fr{ESC 3}/FR{NAME}{D 5}{U}{R 2}~{GRAP
H}{ESC}/FR{NAME}{D 6}{U}{L}~{GRAPH}{ESC}/FR{NAME}{D 8}{U 3}~{GRAPH}{ESC}{U}/RFH{
END}{D 4}~{U 2}{ESC}{ADDIN}R~Q_
```

Figure 1-10. *Keystrokes captured by the keystroke recorder*

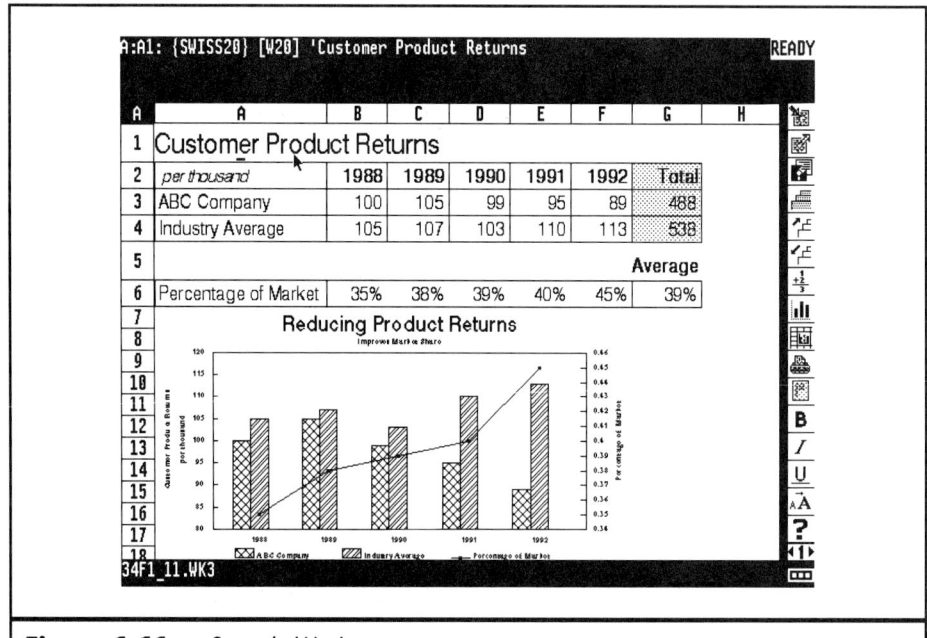

Figure 1-11. *Sample Wysiwyg screen*

Network Support

Lotus has made a commitment to fully support the use of 1-2-3 within a networking environment. In addition to the single user version of the product, 1-2-3 is also packaged in several popular combinations; you can purchase additional workstation copies, or a LAN package containing several copies. The LAN package includes a network administrator's guide, in addition to authorization for the use of 1-2-3 on several machines.

The new 1-2-3 commands in support of a network environment have been added to the File menu structure. Available options allow you to reserve and release files. You can also create a table of file information including the reservation and modification status of files. You can use the new options to refresh the links to files that may have been modified by another user. You can use the /File Admin Seal option to seal a file's reservation setting or the entire file.

CHAPTER 2

The Access System, Display, and Keyboard

This chapter will cover the Lotus Access System, your entry into everything 1-2-3 has to offer. It will also take a look at the screen display and the keyboard in some detail. Although this chapter will not require you to type any 1-2-3 commands, you should become comfortable with the keyboard and the information provided by 1-2-3's display as soon as possible. They are designed to assist you in your work with the package.

The Lotus Access System

The Lotus Access System ties together the different programs in the 1-2-3 system. You can use it to enter 1-2-3 and begin working with a worksheet. You can also use the Access System to change your installation selections, or translate another data file into a format that is usable in 1-2-3. The main menu for the Access System contains the options 1-2-3, Install, Translate, and Exit. You can choose an option from this menu by typing the first character of the desired selection or by highlighting the desired choice and pressing ENTER.

TIP: Highlighting alone does not select a menu option. To avoid a common mistake made by new users, remember to press ENTER after highlighting your desired selection.

Just as with any program, you will have to load the operating system before accessing any of the 1-2-3 programs. You will also want to activate the directory containing the 1-2-3 program files. For example, if your 1-2-3 files are stored in the directory 123R34, type **CD\123R34** and press ENTER to make the directory active. You can then access any program directly, or you can type in **Lotus** and press ENTER to load the Access System. From the Access System you can select the options 1-2-3, Translate, Install, or Exit.

If you wish to use a driver configuration file other than 123.DCF, you will need to specify the filename when you load Lotus. For example, if you wanted to use a driver configuration file called OFFICE.DCF, you would type **Lotus Office** and then press ENTER.

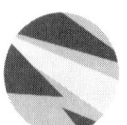

TIP: You can create a number of driver configuration files. You can use several driver configuration files to establish primary printer or screen displays. Rather than using the menu to change the printer after starting 1-2-3, you can choose the active printer by selecting the .DCF file that is appropriate.

Using the Access System makes it easy to transfer from program to program, since you will be returned to the Access System after working with each program. Because Release 3 requires a hard disk system, you can switch from program to program without having to switch floppy disks, as you may have done with earlier releases.

*TIP: Conserve memory requirements by loading only the program you need. If you have limited memory on your system, you will want to load the program you need, rather than using the Access System. To load the Worksheet program, type **123** and press ENTER. To load Translate, type **Trans**; and to load the Installation program, type **Install**.*

Now let's review briefly each of the choices on the Access System menu. Most of the attention in this book will focus on the 1-2-3 option, since that is the main part of the package. The Translate program will also receive additional coverage later in the book; you'll see how it can save valuable time when you want to transfer data between 1-2-3 and another program.

1-2-3

1-2-3 is the main option on the Access System menu for all releases of Lotus. You can enter 1-2-3 from the Access System menu, or by typing **123** from the operating system once you have activated the 1-2-3 directory. This latter approach will save a little memory, since the Access System routines will not have to be loaded into memory.

However you elect to load 1-2-3 into memory, you will need to have the operating system active in the system before you begin. To fully utilize the power of the package, you will want to respond to the operating system date and time prompts with the correct information if your system is not set for the proper date and time. Each file you create will then automatically have the current date and time in its directory entries. These entries will be taken from the system clock at the time each file is created. In addition, you can both date- and time-stamp your worksheet with the @NOW and @TODAY functions, described in Chapter 7, "1-2-3's Built-In Functions."

The Wysiwyg add-in is automatically attached in Release 3.4. Wysiwyg offers spreadsheet publishing features to create professional looking spreadsheets and makes the SmartIcons palette available to perform tasks with a quick mouse selection. This add-in is very useful and you will want to keep it attached unless you are creating a large worksheet on a machine without expanded memory. You can check the available memory by selecting /Worksheet Status. If only limited memory is available, you will want to save the worksheet with /File Save, then clear the add-in from memory with ALT-F10 Clear. If you have several add-ins attached and want to remove only Wysiwyg, you can use /Add-In Detach and select Wysiwyg; however, you may also want to clear any other loaded add-ins.

You can use the menu and features of 1-2-3 to build spreadsheet models, construct databases, and display graphs on your screen through a series of nested menus. Most of the work you do with the package will be done through the 1-2-3 program. The other Access System features are designed to handle more specialized needs, such as translating data and customizing installation settings.

Returning to the Access System after working with 1-2-3 is easy. Simply type **/Q** from 1-2-3's main menu to quit; then type a **Y** to confirm that you wish to exit. With Releases 3.1 and 3.4, you have built-in protection from accidentally forgetting to save a file. If the current worksheet contains changes that have not been saved, 1-2-3 will display a second prompt before quitting—letting you choose whether or not you wish to save the worksheet. If you initially entered 1-2-3 from the Access System, you will be returned to the Access System menu after quitting 1-2-3. If you entered 1-2-3 directly from the operating system, the operating system prompt, C>, will appear on your screen.

Translate

The Translate program permits data interchange between 1-2-3 and other programs by translating files from other programs into a form 1-2-3 can handle, or by translating 1-2-3 files into a variety of other data formats. If you want to access Translate directly, type **Trans** and press ENTER.

Once Translate is loaded, you will see a menu. This menu will allow you to translate from such formats as DIF (Data Interchange Format), Symphony, or dBASE III, into 1-2-3 Release 3, or to translate from a Lotus Release 3 format into one of the other formats.

The process has been made very simple with the Release 3 version of Translate. First, select the type of source file you plan to use as input for translation from the list of products in the left column. After you make this selection, 1-2-3 lists the target file types available for translation of the source file type that you selected. If you select DIF from the first menu, for example, the only target file type available is a 1-2-3 Release 3 file. On the other hand, if you select a 1-2-3 Release 3 file for the source file, you can choose to translate the worksheet file into 1-2-3 Release 1A, Release 2, dBASE, DIF, or another format. This option is useful if you have 1-2-3 data that you want to use with other programs. Translate is discussed further in Chapter 8, "Working with Files."

Install

The Install program is discussed in detail in Appendix A, "Installing 1-2-3." You can enter the program from the Access System menu by selecting Install. If you wish, you can enter Install without the Access System by typing **Install**. If the Install program is not on your hard drive, insert the Install/Setup disk and transfer to that drive before attempting to access it.

Exit

When you finish with one of the Access System options, you will be returned to the Access System menu. To return to the operating system, use the Exit option.

Chapter 2: The Access System, Display, and Keyboard

The Display

1-2-3's screen display is divided into four areas: a control panel at the top of the screen, a worksheet area in the middle, a status line at the bottom, and the SmartIcons palette at the right side of the screen. A border containing the column names separates the control panel from the worksheet portion of the display. The status line area appears at the bottom of the screen below the display of the last row number. Figure 2-1 shows a screen display with all four of the areas labeled.

The Control Panel

Each of the three lines in the control panel has a specific purpose. The second and third lines will be discussed under "The Menu," later in this chapter. In Chapter 3, "Entering Data in 1-2-3's Worksheet," you will learn that long cell entries will cause the control panel area to expand and display the entire cell entry, up to the maximum of 512 characters. This expanded control panel display will limit the worksheet display to 14 rows.

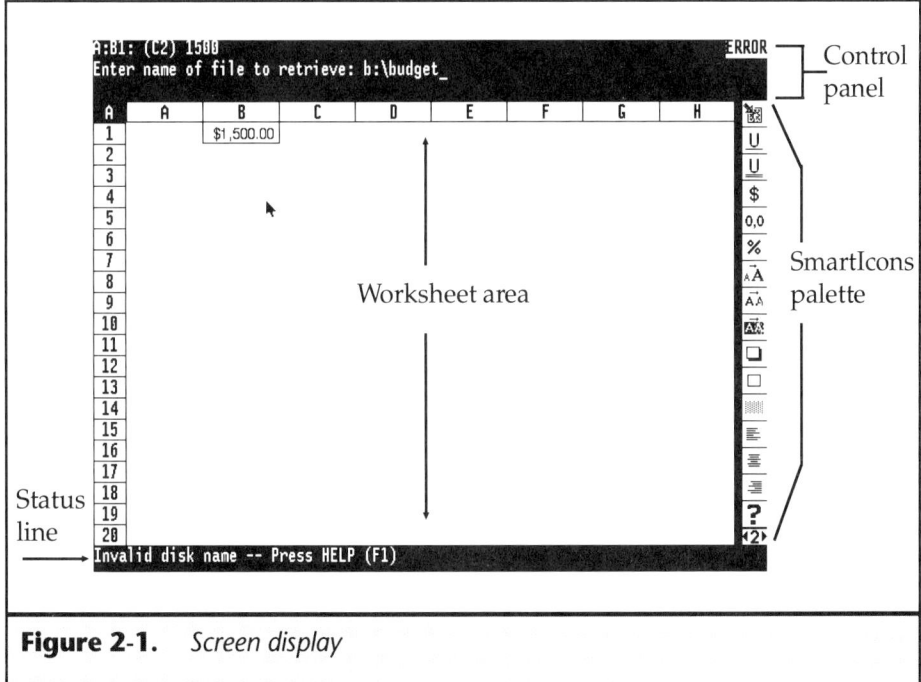

Figure 2-1.   *Screen display*

The top line provides the greatest number of individual pieces of information. At the far left corner you will find the current location of the cell pointer; that is, the highlighted bar visible on the worksheet. In Releases 3, this location gives the worksheet level and the specific location of the cell pointer in the current worksheet.

Release 3 supports the use of as many as 256 worksheets within one worksheet file. Release 3 also allows a number of open worksheet files in memory, as long as the total number of worksheets in all files does not exceed 256. For now, let's focus on the first worksheet, which is automatically available and referred to as worksheet A. The A indicates the worksheet level and is followed by a colon and the address of the worksheet cell that contains the cell pointer. In Figure 2-1 the cell pointer is in cell B1 (the intersection of column B and row 1), so the location reads "A:B1".

Immediately to the right of the cell pointer location, in parentheses, you will see any special display attributes assigned to the cell. Abbreviations for Wysiwyg formats will appear after any 1-2-3 formats. Most of these formatting options are indicated with curly braces ({ }) and text that describes the formatting. 1-2-3 allows you to display numbers as currency, percents, and other special formats. Each assigned format has a special code representing the format, such as C for Currency, and this code will appear in the control panel for a cell that has a special format assigned to it. In Figure 2-1, the Currency format with two decimal places has been assigned to the cell, so you see (C2). The C represents Currency, and the 2 shows the number of decimal places. Other commonly used formats are , for Comma, F for Fixed, P for Percent, G for General, and T for Text.

Release 3 also provides information on the protection status of a cell, and the column width if it is different from the default assigned to the columns in the worksheet the cell is in. These features are also represented by special character codes, which will be discussed in Chapter 4, "Changing the Appearance of the Worksheet Display."

To the right of the format code are the contents of the cell as they were entered. Suppose, for example, that you entered 514.76. If you are displaying the entry as currency with zero decimal places, you will see $515 on the worksheet; but in the control panel you will see your original entry.

On the top line at the far right, in a highlighted area, you will find the mode indicator. This indicator tells you what 1-2-3 is doing, and what it expects from you. It can instruct you to wait, correct an error, point to a worksheet location, or tell 1-2-3 what to do next.

Table 2-1 lists the mode indicators and their meanings. For example, as soon as you begin a cell entry by typing a number, 1-2-3's mode indicator changes from READY to VALUE. If you activate 1-2-3's menu, the mode indicator changes to MENU. Once 1-2-3 is in a certain mode, you have to either follow along with its plans or find a way to change the indicator. For example, if the mode indicator reads LABEL, you will not be able to enter a value entry until you find a way to change the indicator. In some cases this means eliminating your previous selections and starting over. Many of a new user's frustrations come from not understanding and watching the mode indicator. In order to maintain a smooth working relationship with 1-2-3, you must stay "in sync" with 1-2-3's mode indicators.

TIP: When 1-2-3 does not respond as you expect, check the mode indicator first. If the indicator contains anything other than READY, you cannot start a new request. You might think you are in the middle of making menu selections; but if you check the indicator and see ERROR, you will remember to press ESC to acknowledge the error condition.

Indicator	Meaning
EDIT	Cell entry is being edited. EDIT can be generated by 1-2-3 when your entry contains an error and 1-2-3 wants you to edit it. It can also be generated by pressing the F2 (EDIT) key to change a cell entry or by typing an entry in response to a command prompt.
ERROR	1-2-3 has encountered an error. The problem is noted in the lower left corner of the screen. Press ESC to clear the error message, and then correct the problem specified in the error message.
FILES	1-2-3 wants you to select a filename to proceed. This message also appears when you request a list of files on your disk with /File List.
FIND	The /Data Query Find command is active.
HELP	A Help display is active.
LABEL	1-2-3 has decided that you are making a label entry.
MENU	1-2-3 is waiting for you to make a menu selection.
NAMES	1-2-3 is displaying a menu of range, print, or graph names.
POINT	1-2-3 is waiting for you to point to a cell or range. As soon as you begin to type, POINT mode will change to EDIT mode.
READY	1-2-3 is currently idle and waiting for you to make a new request.
STAT	Worksheet status information is displayed.
VALUE	1-2-3 has decided that you are making a value entry.
WAIT	1-2-3 is processing your last command and cannot begin a new task until the WAIT indicator disappears.

Table 2-1. *Mode Indicators*

Wysiwyg Mode Indicator

If you are using Release 3.4, Wysiwyg is already attached for you. This means that you will be able to type a colon (:) from 1-2-3's READY mode to display the Wysiwyg menu. Once you begin to use Wysiwyg, the mode indicators in the upper right corner are Wysiwyg mode indicators. Table 2-2 displays the Wysiwyg mode indicators and what they mean.

The Worksheet

The worksheet occupies most of your display screen. This area serves as a window that allows you to look at the information stored in memory in an orderly format. In earlier releases, one worksheet mapped the entire contents of memory. With Release 3, you can have one or more worksheet files in memory at the same time. A single worksheet file may consist of up to 256 separate sheets that have the same row and column orientation as the sheet you see when you first start 1-2-3. This worksheet layout serves as your access to all worksheet entries, and allows you to look at any section you choose on any open worksheet.

Think of the memory in your computer as similar to the workspace on the top of your desk. Just as different sized desks may hold different numbers of file folders or other information, the varying amounts of memory within various computers control the amount of worksheet data they store. You can use the top

Mode	Meaning
COLOR	Displays when you are selecting a color for a graphic that you are editing.
CYCLE	Displays when you are cycling through objects on a graph to select one.
DRAG	Displays when you are adding a rectangle or ellipse in the graphics editing mode.
PAN	Displays when you select View Pan when editing a graphic.
SELECT	Wysiwyg is waiting for you to select a font, graph, or printer.
SIZE	Transform was selected while editing a graphic.
TEXT	Text Edit was selected.
WYSIWYG	Displays when a Wysiwyg menu is active.

Table 2-2. *Wysiwyg Mode Indicators*

of your desk for one file of information or many files. A file may contain one large sheet of paper or many smaller sheets. It's the same with Release 3: you can read one or more files into memory, and each of these files can contain entries on one or more worksheets. The total number of worksheets that may be in memory at one time is 256—regardless of whether they are all in one file or from different files. The size of the worksheets and the amount of memory in your system will determine how close you come to this upper limit.

The worksheet has an orderly arrangement of rows and columns. The row numbers and column letters appear in a different color on the screen, unlike Figure 2-1. Since you can have many worksheets within a single 1-2-3 file, the upper left corner of the row and column labels provide the current worksheet level. Later you will learn about an option that allows you to see three worksheets at one time.

Every entry you make on a worksheet will be in a specific cell address uniquely identified by the file in which it is stored, its worksheet level, and the row and column location that make up the actual cell address. Cell entries can be numbers, labels, and formulas. You will learn more about the specific worksheet options in Chapter 3, "Entering Data in 1-2-3's Worksheet."

The Status Line

The status line, occupied by a date/time display in early releases, can now be used for either a filename or the date and time. The default is to show the filename of the current worksheet if it has been stored on disk. Before a worksheet is saved, this area shows the date and time display. You may choose an option that changes the default, and displays the date and time in this location at all times. If you elect to display the date and time, it is constantly updated as your screen is refreshed.

Regardless of which display you choose, it will be temporarily suppressed as needed to display error messages such as "Disk Full," "Printer Not Ready," or "Disk Not Ready." Whenever an error message is displayed here, the mode indicator at the top right corner will contain ERROR. To proceed, you must press ESC to eliminate the error message and the ERROR indicator.

Descriptions will also appear in this bottom area to let you know when certain keys have been pressed or when certain other settings for the package are in use. The seven key indicators and their meanings are as follows:

CAP	The CAPS LOCK key is depressed. When the CAP indicator is on, the alphabetic keys will produce capital letters.
END	The END key was pressed and 1-2-3 is waiting for you to press an arrow key.

FILE	The FILE key (CTRL-END) was pressed to move to another file in memory.
NUM	The NUM LOCK key was pressed. This key allows you to enter a number from the numeric keypad.
OVR	The INS toggle was pressed, allowing keyboard entries in Overstrike mode rather than Insert mode.
SCROLL	The SCROLL LOCK key was pressed; this controls the way information scrolls off your screen. SCROLL LOCK toggles the effect of the arrow keys between moving one row or column in any direction, and shifting the entire screen one row or column in the direction of the arrow. When the SCROLL indicator is on, the entire window will shift when the arrow keys are pressed.
STEP	The STEP mode is in effect for macro execution. This mode is activated by pressing ALT-F2. STEP is discussed further in Chapter 12, "Keyboard Macros."

Nine additional indicators signal more than just one key press. These indicators and their meanings are as follows:

CALC	The worksheet needs to be recalculated. Changes have been made to the data that are not yet recalculated in the screen display. You will see this indicator when recalculation is set to manual, and will need to press F9 to begin recalculation. When set to automatic, the entire worksheet is recalculated as soon as a change is made; however, you will still see this indicator while background recalculation to update the worksheet display is taking place.
CIRC	The worksheet contains a circular reference, that is, a cell that refers back to itself. Release 3 provides special help to locate the defective entry with the /Worksheet Status command.
CMD	Appears during the execution of a macro.
GROUP	The current file is in GROUP mode, causing some commands to affect all the worksheets in the file.
MEM	Less than 32K of memory remains.
PRT	1-2-3 is printing something in the background while you continue using other 1-2-3 features.
RO	The status of the current file is Read-only. This means that you will not be able to save any of your changes to the current file.

Chapter 2: The Access System, Display, and Keyboard

SST   This is the macro indicator that appears during single-step execution for a macro. The STEP indicator will change to SST when the execution of a macro begins. SST is discussed further in Chapter 12, "Keyboard Macros."

ZOOM   You pressed ALT-F6 to zoom in for a full-screen view of a perspective view of the worksheet, or a worksheet with multiple windows.

The SmartIcons

If you are using Release 3.4, icons will appear to the right of the worksheet area whenever Wysiwyg is attached. Their appearance depends on the resolution of the monitor that you are using. These icons are ideally designed for use with a mouse, although you can also access them with the keyboard after pressing CTRL-F10 (Select Icons). You can carry out 1-2-3 and Wysiwyg tasks with these icons.

These icons are arranged into SmartIcons palettes. You can choose which palette to use and can even customize the first palette or attach macros to a user palette. The number for the currently selected palette appears at the bottom right corner of your screen.

You can hide these icons, either by pressing CTRL-F9 (Display Icons) or by clicking on the small box at the bottom of the icon palette. When you do so, a new selection of icons, which can only be selected with a mouse, appears. These icons are used to move the cell pointer, or to invoke the Help feature.

Help Features

You can change your screen to an online reference source at will. All you have to do is press the F1 (HELP) key. 1-2-3 will guess at what your question might be and supply information based on your current task. If you want additional help or help with a different subject, you can use the Help index or ask for one of the other topics listed at the bottom of the Help screen.

Figure 2-2 shows the help that 1-2-3 provides for entering a value or formula in a cell. 1-2-3 recognized that a value or formula entry had been started and selected this help topic in case additional information on entering a formula or value was needed. When ENTER is pressed, additional detail for the highlighted choice is displayed. If none of the topics meet your needs, you can access the main Help index by highlighting the "Help Index" entry at the bottom of the screen and pressing ENTER.

The 1-2-3 Menu

Lines 2 and 3 of the control panel can be transformed into a menu of 1-2-3 command selections by pressing the slash key (/). When you type /, 1-2-3 displays this menu:

```
A:A1:                                                          MENU
Worksheet Range Copy Move File Print Graph Data System Quit
Global    Insert  Delete  Column  Erase  Titles  Window  Status  Page  Hide
```

Menus are the backbone of the 1-2-3 program and are your way of accessing all its features. You can make them available at will with the slash key, but they will not clutter the screen when you do not need them.

1-2-3's menus offer an advantage over some earlier spreadsheet programs in that they are self-documenting. The line beneath the individual menu options reflects a description of the current menu selection. You can point to different menu items (in line 2) with the cell pointer movement keys on the keypad. As you move from item to item, the description line (line 3) changes accordingly. For instance, when you point to the Worksheet option in the menu, the second line will list all the specific Worksheet options: Global, Insert, Delete, Column, Erase, Titles, Window, Status, Page, and Hide. These are not completely descriptive of the functions provided, but they will serve as reminders once you learn the commands.

To select a menu item you can either type the first letter of the menu item (for example, **W** for Worksheet) or point to the item with your cell pointer and press

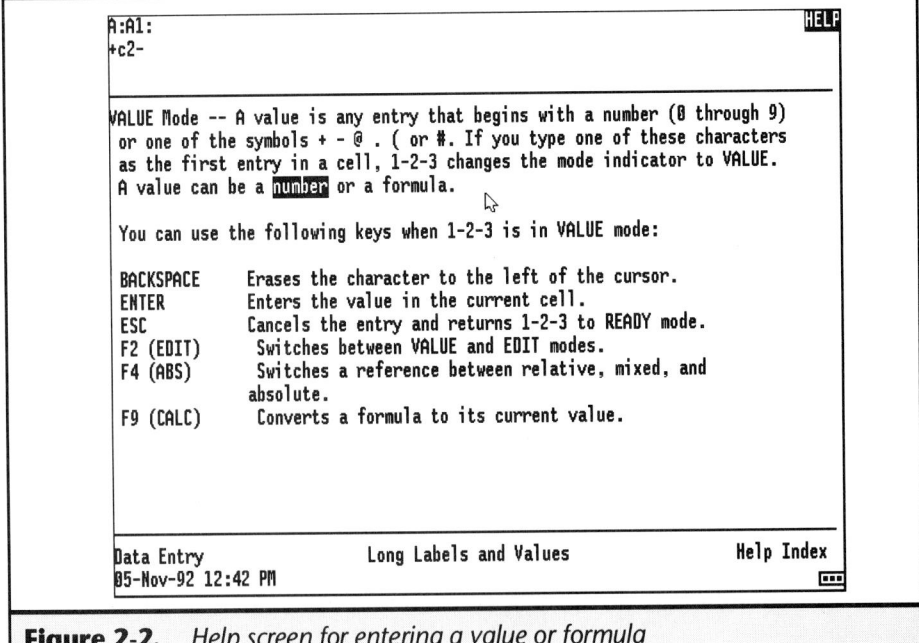

Figure 2-2. *Help screen for entering a value or formula*

ENTER. Either method invokes the selected command or present a menu for further selections.

Each subsequent menu level is selected in the same manner as the previous selection, with each level refining your choice further. If you choose a menu item in error, you can back out to the previous level by pressing ESC once. Each time you press ESC, you retreat to the next higher menu level until you are eventually back at READY mode.

The Wysiwyg Menu

Wysiwyg is an add-in program that supplements 1-2-3 features by adding spreadsheet publishing tasks to existing 1-2-3 capabilities. The letters in WYSIWYG stand for What You See Is What You Get, meaning that what displays on your screen is exactly what will print. When you start 1-2-3 Release 3.4, the Wysiwyg add-in is automatically loaded into memory and attached to 1-2-3. With earlier releases you must use ALT-F10 Load before you can use Wysiwyg. Once Wysiwyg is attached you can type a colon (:) to access its menu shown here

```
A:A1:                                                              WYSIWYG
Worksheet Format Graph Print Display Special Text Named-Style Quit
Column Row Page
```

You may be surprised to see that some of the Wysiwyg menu options are represented by the same commands as 1-2-3's menu commands. Different features are offered by the menu even though there seems to be duplication at first glance. Keep in mind that 1-2-3's basic purpose is to make 1-2-3 entries and provide basic formatting. Wysiwyg offers significant appearance improvements and lets you integrate text and graphics on one printed page. After activating the Wysiwyg menu you make selections the same way that you make selections from 1-2-3's menu, either by highlighting the desired selection and pressing ENTER, or by typing the first letter of the desired selection. Like 1-2-3, Wysiwyg uses settings sheets with some menus to allow you to view the settings you are making with that menu. You will learn more about Wysiwyg throughout this book.

The Keyboard

You will begin using the keyboard in the next chapter as you make entries in worksheet cells. This section focuses on the keyboard for the IBM PS/2. The same keyboard configuration is used for the IBM AT and many IBM-compatible computers. There are some differences between these and keyboards of other popular systems that work with 1-2-3. These differences will not require changes in the installation of 1-2-3 or limit your use of the program, but they may affect the keys you use to access 1-2-3's features.

If you are using a different style of keyboard, you will want to identify where each of the keys mentioned is located on your own keyboard. For example, some keyboards have only one set of cursor movement keys. On these keyboards, you must press the NUM LOCK key every time you want to switch between using the keys in the keypad for numbers and for cursor movement.

All keys will be covered in this chapter to provide a single reference source for all keyboard functions. Individual features will be pointed out again in later chapters where they will be helpful, so you do not have to worry about absorbing all of this information now.

The IBM PS/2 keyboard has three basic sections, as shown in Figure 2-3. The keys at the top of the screen are the function keys. These keys are made available to software developers for program-specific use, so there is little consistency between programs in the way function keys are used. Lotus has assigned these keys the special functions shown in Table 2-3. Pressing any of these keys causes 1-2-3 to take the requested action when the system is in READY mode. The only exceptions are F3 (NAME) and F4 (ABS), which function in other modes. Several of the function keys may be used in combination with the ALT or CTRL keys to perform additional tasks.

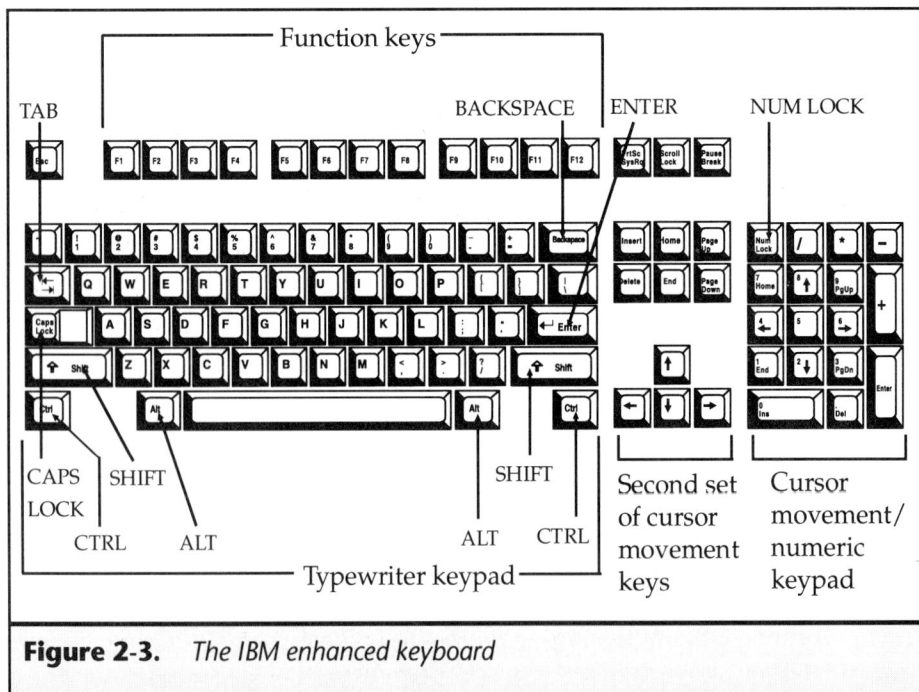

Figure 2-3. *The IBM enhanced keyboard*

Function Key	Assignment
F1 (HELP)	Provides context-sensitive help.
F2 (EDIT)	Allows you to alter the contents of the current cell without reentering all the information. You can add or delete just a few characters if you wish.
F3 (NAME)	Displays a list of your range names, the function names, or macro commands, depending on your prior entry. This key also changes a list of range names, filenames, function names, or macro commands from using only the top of the control panel to using the full screen.
F4 (ABS)	Toggles from a relative address to an absolute or mixed address for a cell or range.
F5 (GOTO)	Moves your cell pointer to the range or address you enter after pressing the key.
F6 (WINDOW)	Functions as a toggle, moving you into the next window when there are several windows.
F7 (QUERY)	Repeats the last query operation.
F8 (TABLE)	Repeats the most recent table operation from the Data menu option.
F9 (CALC)	Recalculates the entire worksheet. Useful when recalculation of the worksheet is set at manual.
F10 (GRAPH)	Redraws the most recent graph.
ALT-F1 (COMPOSE)	Used when creating international characters.
ALT-F2 (RECORD)	Causes macros to execute a step at a time, or allows you to use a 512-byte buffer for recording keystrokes.
ALT-F3 (RUN)	Runs a selected macro.
ALT-F4 (UNDO)	Undoes the effect of all actions since the last READY indicator if Undo is enabled.
ALT-F6 (ZOOM)	Toggles the current window between its current size and full screen size.
ALT-F7 (APP1)	Starts an add-in application.
ALT-F8 (APP2)	Starts an add-in application.
ALT-F9 (APP3)	Starts an add-in application.
ALT-F10 (ADDIN)	Displays the Add-in menu.
CTRL-F9 (DISPLAY ICONS)	Hides or displays the SmartIcons.
CTRL-F10 (SELECT ICONS)	Activates the SmartIcons so that one may be selected using the keyboard.

Table 2-3. *Function Key Assignments with 1-2-3*

Keys	Action
HOME	Moves the cell pointer to A1 of the current worksheet.
UP ARROW	Moves the cell pointer up one cell on the worksheet.
DOWN ARROW	Moves the cell pointer down one cell on the worksheet.
RIGHT ARROW	Moves the cell pointer one cell to the right.
LEFT ARROW	Moves the cell pointer one cell to the left.
PGUP	Moves the cell pointer up 20 rows.
PGDN	Moves the cell pointer down 20 rows.
END followed by one of the arrow keys	Moves the cell pointer to the end of your entries in the direction indicated by the arrow key when the cell pointer is on a cell containing an entry. When the cell pointer is on a blank cell, takes the cell pointer to the next cell in the direction that has an entry.
CTRL-RIGHT ARROW or TAB	Moves your window into the worksheet a full screen to the right.
CTRL-LEFT ARROW or SHIFT-TAB	Moves your window into the worksheet a full screen to the left.
CTRL-HOME	Moves the cell pointer to A:A1 in the current worksheet.
END CTRL-HOME	Moves the cell pointer to the last non-blank cell in the current file.

Table 2-4. *Numeric Keypad Functions*

The keys to the far right serve a dual purpose: they make up the numeric keypad/cursor movement keys. Table 2-4 explains where each of these keys will move the cell pointer. You will notice that these keys also have direction arrows and other writing on them. This shows their normal function in 1-2-3 when they are used for cell pointer movement. If you depress the NUM LOCK key, you can also use these keys for numeric entries. Like the CAPS LOCK key, it toggles each time it is pressed. Fortunately, keyboards like the one on the PS/2 have a second set of cursor movement keys. This allows you to turn on NUM LOCK and use the numeric keypad exclusively for the entry of numbers, while the second set of cursor movement keys is used to change your location on the screen.

Let's look at an example of the use of these keys. A screen display from 1-2-3 is shown in Figure 2-4. The cell pointer or highlighted area is found in location C3, as shown by the row and column designators at the side and top of the display, or at the upper left corner in the control panel. Using the keypad keys will move the cell pointer to new locations. The following table shows the new location of the cell pointer if the listed keys are pressed when the cell pointer is in location C3.

Key Sequence	New Cursor Location
LEFT ARROW	B3
RIGHT ARROW	D3
UP ARROW	C2
DOWN ARROW	C4
END followed by DOWN ARROW	C5
END followed by UP ARROW	C2
END followed by RIGHT ARROW	G3
END followed by LEFT ARROW	B3
PGUP	C1 (cell pointer cannot move up 20 rows from its present location)
PGDN	C23
HOME	A1
CTRL-RIGHT ARROW	I3
CTRL-LEFT ARROW	Beeps, since it cannot scroll screen to the left

The function of these keys will become clearer in the next chapter when we put them to work in a worksheet example. There are also keys that allow you to access other levels within the current worksheet, as well as additional files that you might have open in memory.

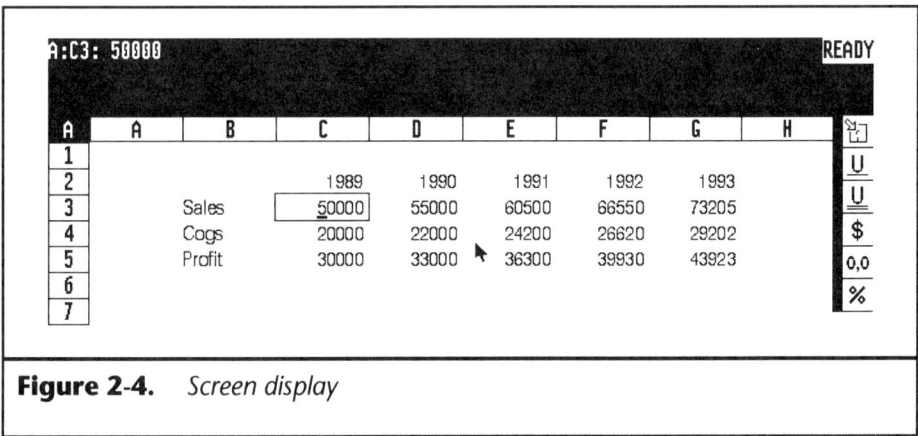

Figure 2-4. *Screen display*

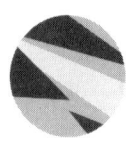

TIP: Focus first on the basic keys for cell pointer movement. There are many keys that allow you to make your way around a worksheet efficiently, but it can be difficult for a novice to remember all the options. Five basic entries are all you need to get started. Press the HOME key to move to A1, and use the arrow keys to move in other directions. If you hold down the arrow keys, they will repeat and move you around very quickly.

Multiple worksheets and files offer you a considerable amount of flexibility. There are special keyboard options that allow you to move with ease from sheet to sheet and from file to file.

Table 2-5 lists the keys that allow you to move between worksheets. As an example, assume that you have four worksheets in the current worksheet file, and worksheet C is active. The cell pointers within each worksheet are in these locations: A:C3, B:B4, C:A1, and D:B3, as shown in Figure 2-5. The following table indicates which worksheet is made active when you use the listed keyboard options while in worksheet C:

CTRL-PGDN	B:B4
CTRL-PGUP	D:B3
END CTRL-PGDN	A:A1
END CTRL-PGUP	D:A1

Keys	**Action**
CTRL-PGUP (Next Sheet)	Moves the cell pointer to the next worksheet.
CTRL-PGDN (Previous Sheet)	Moves the cell pointer to the previous worksheet.
END CTRL-PGUP (End Next Sheet)	Functions similar to the END key, except moves across sheets from the current sheet toward the last sheet. The cell pointer remains in the same location as in the present worksheet, except that the current worksheet becomes the worksheet with a nonblank entry at an intersection of blank and nonblank cells.
END CTRL-PGDN (End Prev Sheet)	Functions similar to the END key, except moves across sheets toward the first sheet. The cell pointer remains in the same location as in the present worksheet, except that the current worksheet becomes the worksheet with a nonblank entry at an intersection of blank and nonblank cells.

Table 2-5. *Keys for Moving Between Worksheets*

Chapter 2: The Access System, Display, and Keyboard

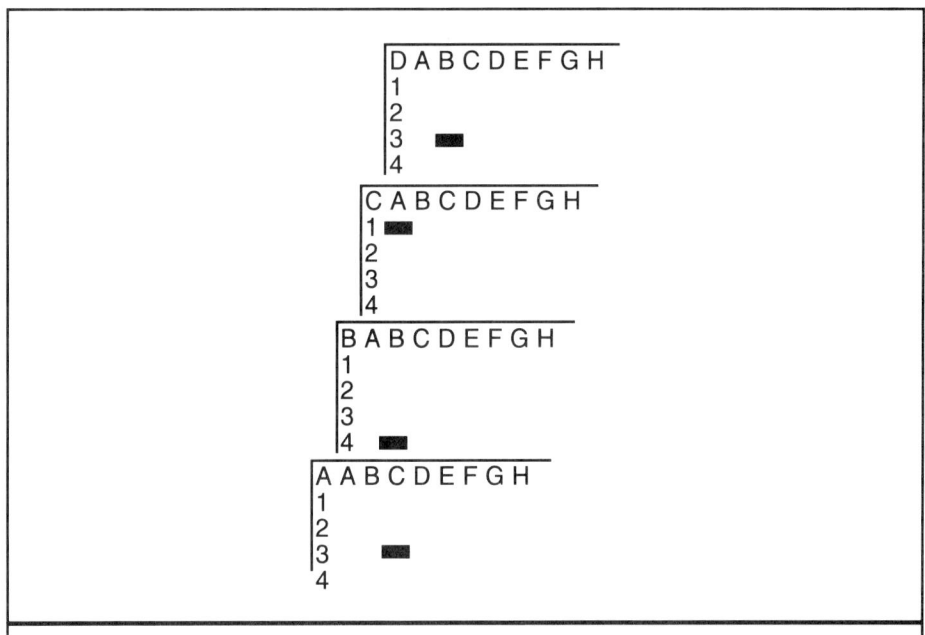

Figure 2-5. *Multiple sheets in one file*

Since you can work with a number of files in memory at one time with Release 3, you will want to move between them effectively. You can use the keys in Table 2-6 to change the active file. Assume that five files are placed in memory

Keys	Action
CTRL-END CTRL-PGUP (Next File)	Moves to the next file and places the cell pointer in the cell that was active in that file when it was last accessed.
CTRL-END CTRL-PGDN (Prev File)	Moves to the previous file and places the cell pointer in the cell that was active in that file when it was last accessed.
CTRL-END HOME (First File)	Moves the cell pointer to the cell last highlighted in the first file.
CTRL-END END (Last File)	Moves the cell pointer to the cell that was last highlighted in the last file.

Table 2-6. *Keys for Moving Between Files*

with the /File Open After command in the following order: Budget, Expenses, Tax, Vendors, and Employ. The Tax file contains six worksheets. If you could look into memory and see the worksheets, they would look like Figure 2-6. If the first worksheet in the Tax file is currently active, the following table shows the effect of pressing the various keys while in the first Tax worksheet:

Key Sequence	New File Location
CTRL-PGUP	Moves to the second sheet in the Tax file
CTRL-PGDN	Moves to the Expenses file
CTRL-END HOME	Moves to the Budget file
CTRL-END END	Moves to the Employ file
CTRL-END CTRL-PGUP	Moves to the Vendors file
CTRL-END CTRL-PGDN	Moves to the Expenses file

Commands for adding and removing files from memory are covered in detail in Chapter 8, "Working with Files."

The keys in the center of your keyboard are in most cases identical to the key assignments on a regular typewriter. Table 2-7 lists some of the special keys and additional uses for the regular typewriter keys.

The Mouse

With Release 3 and the Wysiwyg add-in, you can use the mouse to make selections in 1-2-3. In Release 3.4, Wysiwyg is automatically loaded into memory, along with 1-2-3. For Release 3.4, you can load the Wysiwyg add-in by pressing ALT-F10, selecting WYSIWYG.PLC, and No-Key as described in Chapter 14.

The SmartIcons are displayed at the right edge of the screen. You can carry out a number of 1-2-3 and Wysiwyg commands by selecting an icon with the mouse. The arrow in the center of the worksheet is the mouse pointer and indicates the object the mouse is pointing to. There are several palettes of SmartIcons, the number depending on the type of display driver you are using. To select another palette, click the left mouse button while pointing to the number found in the box at the bottom of the palette. To select an icon, click the left mouse button while pointing to the icon. If you need a description of the kind of action that the icon will carry out, you can press the right mouse button with the mouse pointer on the appropriate icon. Some icons will change the position of the cell pointer in the worksheets or start the help feature.

Chapter 2: The Access System, Display, and Keyboard

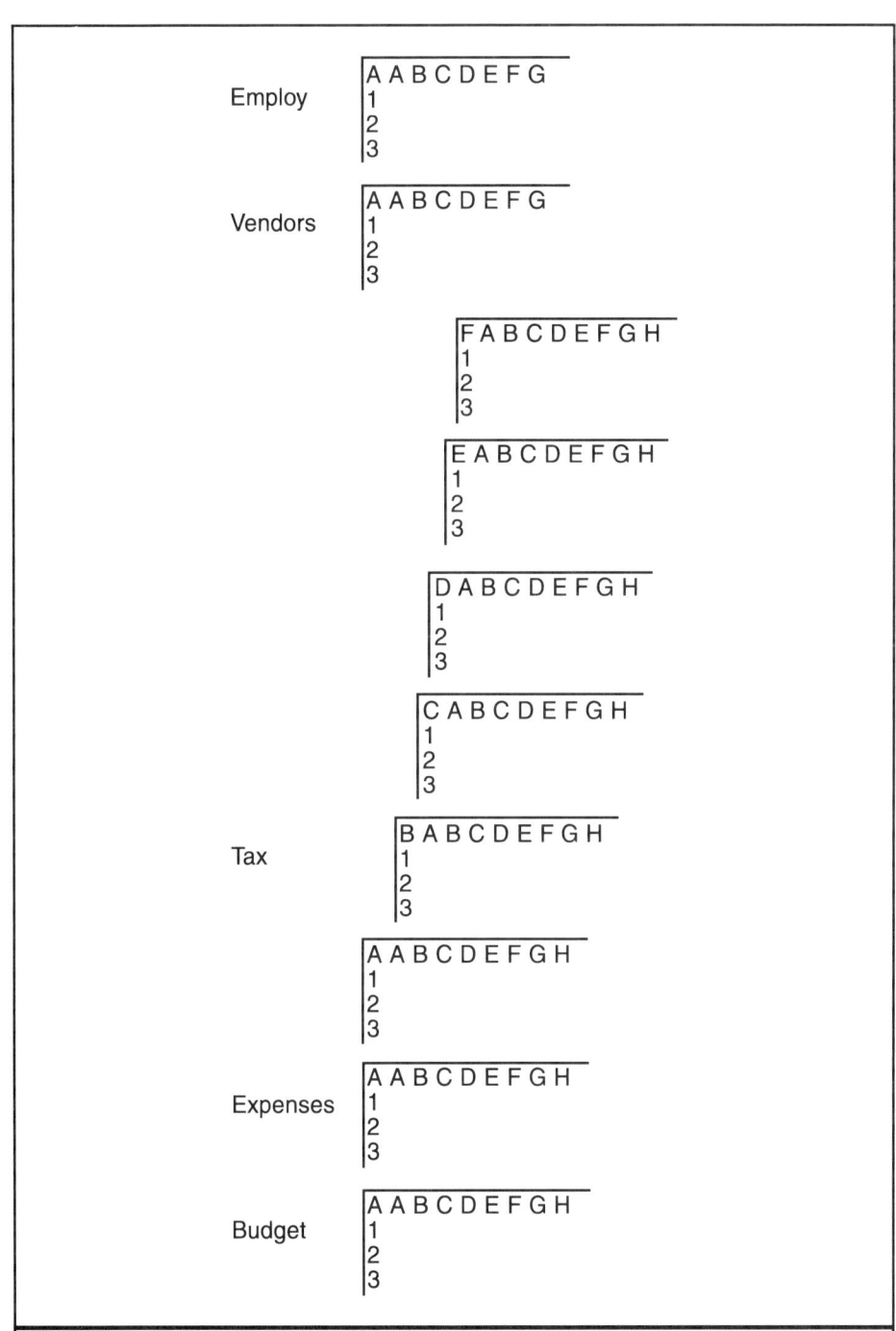

Figure 2-6. *Multiple worksheet files in memory*

Keys	Action
ESC	Cancels the last request.
CTRL-BREAK	Places you in READY mode, canceling one or more selections. Equivalent to pressing ESC enough times to return to READY mode.
TAB	Equivalent to CTRL-RIGHT ARROW; shifts the display an entire screen to the right. SHIFT-TAB shifts the screen window an entire screen to the left; equivalent to CTRL-LEFT ARROW.
CTRL	Used only in combination with other keys.
SHIFT	Causes letter keys to produce capitals. Allows you to access all the special symbols at the top of the keys. Sometimes called the CAPS key, but it differs from CAPS LOCK.
ALT	Used only in combination with other keys.
BACKSPACE	Deletes the last character entered (destructive backspace).
ENTER	Finalizes the last entry made.
PRTSC	Used with the SHIFT key to print the current screen.
CAPS LOCK	Produces all capitals. Toggles each time it is pressed. Does not affect the number keys at the top of the keyboard or any of the special symbols at the tops of keys. (SHIFT must be used to access these.)
INS	Toggles between Insert and Overstrike mode.
NUM LOCK	Toggles numeric keypad between cell pointer movement and numeric entries.
SCROLL LOCK	Toggles scroll display between scrolling a line of the display every time an arrow key is pressed, and just moving the pointer on a stationary display.

Table 2-7. *Special Key Combinations*

If the mouse is connected, the SmartIcons are hidden, and the software for the mouse is running, the top half of the worksheet will look like Figure 2-7. The right side of the screen contains the icon panel. The icon panel uses the solid arrows (◄, ►, ▼, ▲) to represent the arrow keys. Clicking one of these arrows performs the same action as pressing the arrow key. The other up and down arrows in the icon panel switch between worksheets. The last symbol, a question mark, is the same as pressing F1 (HELP). This icon panel is less powerful than the SmartIcons, but maybe more familiar to users of previous releases.

Chapter 2: The Access System, Display, and Keyboard

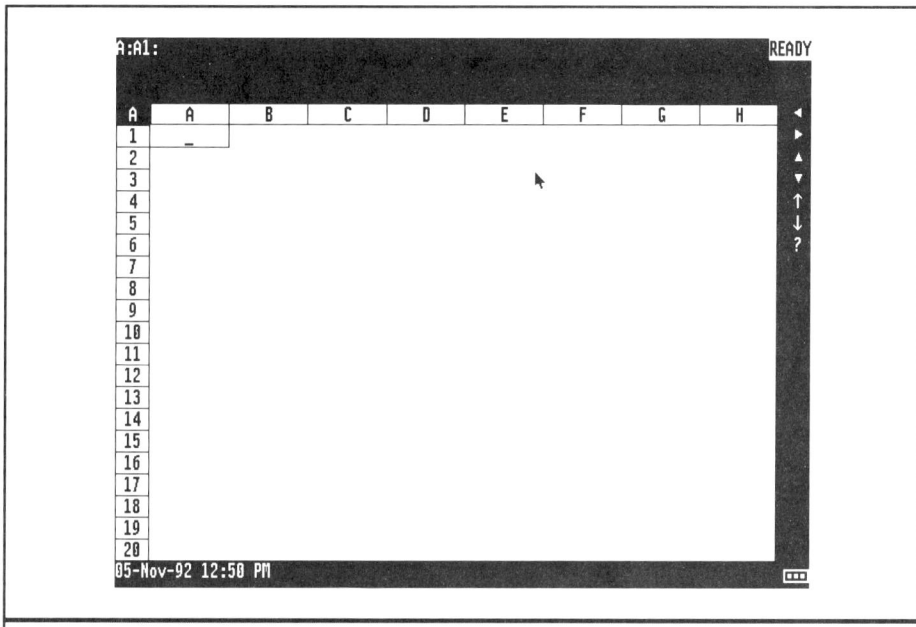

Figure 2-7. *Worksheet display screen with Wysiwyg and Display mouse*

Besides using the symbols in the icon panel or the SmartIcons, you can also move to a cell by pointing to it and clicking the cell with the left mouse button. If the cell you want does not appear on the screen and is on the current worksheet, hold down the left mouse button and move the mouse in the direction you want the worksheet window scrolled. This is called *dragging* the mouse.

To use the menu with the mouse, move the mouse pointer into the control panel. When you move the mouse pointer here, the 1-2-3 or Wysiwyg menu appears (whichever one you used last). You can switch between the 1-2-3 and Wysiwyg menu by pressing the right mouse button. You can also highlight a menu item by moving the mouse pointer to the one you want. You won't be able to select the menu item until you click and release the mouse button.

When you use the mouse, the left mouse button represents ENTER and the right mouse button represents ESC. If your mouse has three buttons, 1-2-3 and Wysiwyg do not use the middle button. This means that to select a menu item from the control panel, you point to it and click the left mouse button.

These directions for the mouse use a right-handed orientation for the mouse. You can change the functions of the two mouse buttons so that you can press the right mouse button for ENTER and the left mouse button for ESC. To make this change, leave Wysiwyg and 1-2-3 and start the Install program. From Install's main menu, select the Wysiwyg Options, Switch Mouse Buttons and Right. Press the right mouse button when the directions indicate left and the left mouse button when the directions indicate right.

CHAPTER 3

Entering Data in 1-2-3's Worksheet

Learning how to make entries on 1-2-3's worksheet is one of the most important steps in gaining full use of the package's features. Everything you do with 1-2-3 depends on the entries you make in worksheet cells. These entries will be the basis for financial models and projections. They will also be the basis for files used in the data management environment, since data records are nothing more than a special organization of data entered into worksheet cells. Furthermore, these entries will be the basis for the graphs you create, because graphs are created by referencing entries in your worksheet.

The Worksheet

The discussion in Chapter 2, "The Access System, Display, and Keyboard," of the worksheet display focused on the visible upper left corner of the worksheet. The 8 columns and 20 rows you saw on the screen are a very small part of the whole sheet. In its entirety, the worksheet has 256 columns and 8192 rows. The entire worksheet, though not visible all at once, is organized just like the small section you examined.

Release 3 also supports the use of multiple sheets in one worksheet file, with each sheet arranged like the first sheet. The only difference between the first sheet and any others you add is the sheet level indicator at the intersection of the row and column labels. The letters assigned to sheets always start with the initial A level that is present in every worksheet file. Subsequent sheets are assigned letters that are incremented sequentially as you insert sheets. The letters B through Z are assigned first, followed by AA through AZ, BA through BZ, and so on, until the 256th level (IV) is assigned.

Additional sheets are never added to a worksheet automatically. You must use the command /Worksheet Insert Sheet to add worksheets after the A level sheet. It is unlikely that you will need to use all the levels in one worksheet file. Moreover, you may be limited to far fewer than 256 sheets by the memory in your computer.

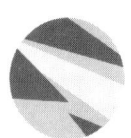

TIP: In similar applications, use sheets consistently. If you create multiple-sheet worksheets, try to establish a pattern for your entries. Don't use sheet A for the consolidated information one time and sheet D the next time. The same advice is true for the location of macros, data criteria entries, and an extract range. It will be easier to find your entries in any application if you follow guidelines that apply to all your applications.

Since the worksheet is a replacement for green-bar columnar pads, it may be interesting to make a size comparison. The space for one entry on a green-bar sheet is about 1 1/8 inches by 1/4 inch. If you multiply this area by the number of cells in the 1-2-3 worksheet, you will find that the equivalent of your electronic sheet would require a piece of green-bar paper over 23 feet wide and 170 feet long! Release 3's multiple sheet capability actually provides 256 of these sheets. The electronic version is certainly more practical in the space it requires for storage, and it offers the added advantage of automatic recalculation.

Figure 3-1 shows the layout of the electronic worksheet. You can use the screen as a window into any part of a worksheet you wish to see. If you have multiple sheets in a file, you can use the special key combinations in Chapter 2, "The Access System, Display, and Keyboard," to move to any of these sheets. It is as if all the sheets are stacked in memory.

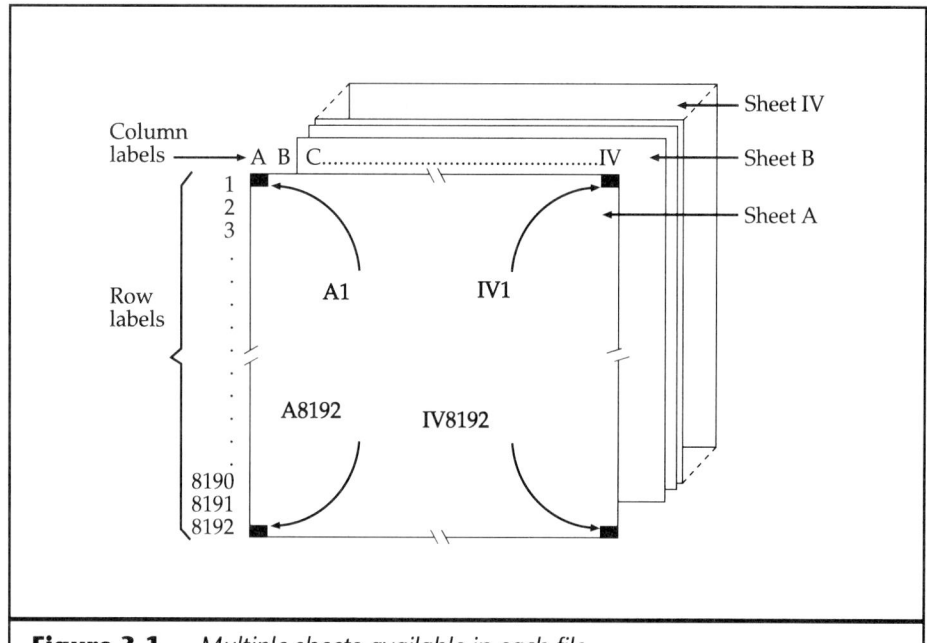

Figure 3-1. *Multiple sheets available in each file*

If you have multiple files in memory, you can also use special keys to change the worksheet displayed on the screen to a sheet within one of these other files. These sheets are also stacked in memory. Unlike moving from sheet to sheet in one file, however, as you move from sheet to sheet in several files you will see the filename change in the status line. Since each worksheet file begins with a level A sheet, you will find that the same level indicators may appear more than once.

You can make entries in any of the cells on any sheet, within the memory limitations of your system. Each cell can contain only one entry at a time, however. If you make a second entry in a cell that already contains information, the existing information will be replaced by the new information.

Types of Entries

1-2-3 categorizes entries as either label entries or value entries. These two entry types serve as the building blocks for both simple and sophisticated worksheet models. *Label entries* contain at least one text character. Examples include Accounting, Sales, John Smith, 111 Simmons Lane, and 456T78. Even the last example, which is composed mostly of numbers, has one letter character and therefore is categorized as a label entry. Label entries cannot be used in arithmetic operations. *Value entries,* on the other hand, are either numbers or formulas. Most value entries can be used in arithmetic operations.

TIP: You will learn more about files in Chapter 8, but for now you will want to select /File Save periodically to save the entries that you make on the worksheet. After the first save operation you will need to confirm that you want to replace the existing copy with a new copy. The first icon in each SmartIcons palette will request a save operation if you select it. You can access any worksheet file stored on disk with /File Retrieve. This operation will replace the worksheet in memory with the requested file from the disk.

1-2-3 determines the type of entry for a particular cell by reading the first character you type in the cell. Once 1-2-3 determines the entry type, the only way you can change its mind is by either pressing ESC and starting a new entry in the cell, or editing the cell to remove or add a label indicator. A *label indicator* is a single character that appears at the front of each label entry and tells 1-2-3 how to display the entry in the cell. You can enter a label indicator or have 1-2-3 generate one for you.

TIP: Learn to check the mode indicator as you perform data entry. You will save yourself considerable time and frustration as you start using 1-2-3 if you watch the mode indicator. One quick look will tell you whether 1-2-3 is treating your entry as a number or a label, and allow you to make a quick correction if you need to before completing the entry.

As you make an entry into a cell, 1-2-3 displays the entry on the second line of the control panel at the top of your screen. This line is referred to as the Edit line. A sample entry in the Edit line looks like this:

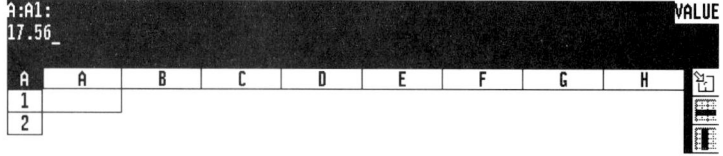

In Release 3, as soon as your entry fills the first Edit line, the control panel expands to give you six and one-half lines for the Edit area. This allows you to make an entry containing as many as 512 characters and to view and edit your complete entry.

Once you finish your entry and review its contents in the Edit lines, you can *finalize* it by pressing ENTER or by moving to a new cell with one of the cell pointer movement keys. This causes the entry to appear in the worksheet cell, as shown here:

```
A:A1: 17.56                                           READY
  A    A      B    C    D    E    F    G    H
  1    17.56
  2
```

TIP: Use the cell pointer movement keys to finalize your entry. You can save a keystroke on most entries if you finalize by moving the cell pointer rather than pressing ENTER and then moving to a new cell.

When the entry is a formula, the results of the formula's calculation will appear on the worksheet. For example, if cell A1 contains 10 and A2 contains 5, entering the formula **+A1/A2** in cell A3 will cause a 2 to appear in A3 on the worksheet. Otherwise, the entry will appear as typed, except that the current format option will be applied. For example, if you enter **.4** and the format is Percent, your entry will display as 40% in the cell. In the top line of the control panel, however, the entry will appear exactly as you typed it.

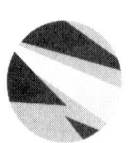

*TIP: Use the special keys or mouse introduced in Chapter 2, "The Access System, Display, and Keyboard," to position the cell pointer for an entry. Although the arrow keys will move you to any location on the worksheet, there are some shortcuts. You can press the F5 (GOTO) key, type an address like **D3** or **C:F2**, and 1-2-3 will immediately position the cell pointer in the new address. The END HOME key sequence is another useful combination; it takes you just beyond the last entry on the current worksheet.*

Label Entries

You will use label entries whenever you want to enter text or character data into a worksheet cell. Labels can contain descriptive information, as well as character data. There are no restrictions on the characters that can be entered within a label.

1-2-3 supports the full set of LMBCS characters, including numbers and symbols. LMBCS codes are the full set of characters that can be represented by Release 3; they provide access to international symbols and many special characters not directly accessible from the keyboard. These characters are listed in Appendix B, "LMBCS Codes."

A special character can be entered with the @CHAR function described in Chapter 7, "1-2-3's Built-In Functions," or through the Compose key sequence. To use Compose, press ALT-F1 and type the two-character Compose sequence. An alternative is to press ALT-F1 twice, type either a **0** or **1** for the code group, a hyphen, and then the key combination representing the desired character. For example, to generate an uppercase E with a circumflex, you could use

@CHAR(210); or press ALT-F1 twice and type 0, a hyphen, and 210. In either case, the special E circumflex character would display (Ê).

Some of the key rules concerning label entries are summarized in the box called "Rules for Labels." 1-2-3 will display as much of the label as possible in the cell you use for the entry. If the label is longer than your cell width and the cells to the right are empty, 1-2-3 will borrow space from them to permit the complete display of the label. If the adjacent cell is not empty, 1-2-3 will truncate the display at the number of characters that will fit. The extra characters are not lost; they are stored internally and will be displayed if the cell is widened or the contents of cells to the right are erased.

As descriptive information, a label might be a report heading containing the company name placed in a cell near the top of the worksheet. Labels can also be column headings indicating the months of the year, row headings indicating account names, or descriptors placed anywhere on the worksheet.

Label entries can also record text data anywhere on the worksheet. Part numbers, employee names, sales territories, and warehouse locations are all examples of data containing text characters. A worksheet to project salaries might contain employee names as label entries. Worksheets that deal with suppliers, inventory items, product sales projections, and client accounts are all likely to have some label entries.

When you type a letter as the first entry in a cell, 1-2-3 will generate a default label indicator that establishes the entry as a label and controls the display of the entry within the cell. If a label begins with a number, you must enter a label indicator before you type that first number in the label entry, since 1-2-3 determines the type of an entry by the first character entered in a cell. However it is generated, the label indicator will appear in the top line of the control panel but will not show in the worksheet cell. Only the effects of the indicator appear on the worksheet.

Rules for Labels

Labels cannot be longer than 512 characters.

An entry is automatically recognized as a label if the first character is an alphabetic character, or any character other than 0 through 9, or any of the following: . + – $ (@ or #

Any entry that contains alphabet letters or editing characters is considered a label, even if it also contains numbers. When a label begins with a numeric digit or symbol, a label indicator must be typed before the label.

Labels longer than the cell width will borrow display space from the cells to the right if those cells are empty.

TIP: Spaces and special characters (such as £) are treated as labels. If you start an entry with a space or a non-numeric character, you can save a keystroke by not entering the label indicator. 1-2-3 will automatically generate it for you.

You can use label indicators to control placement of an entry in a cell. 1-2-3 provides three placement label indicators for this purpose, as the box called "Label Indicators" shows. The apostrophe is the default label indicator, that is, the one 1-2-3 generates for you when you enter character data. It causes an entry to be left justified within the cell. You must type the apostrophe yourself if your entry begins with a number, or begins with a number but contains text—for example, '134 Tenth Street or '213-78-6751. (The hyphens in this latter entry count as text.)

If you do not enter the label indicator, 1-2-3 will not let you finalize the first example (the address) in a cell. The second example (the social security number) can be finalized without a label indicator, but it will not appear as a social security number. 1-2-3 will interpret the hyphens as minus signs and perform two subtractions, resulting in an entry of – 6616. If you edit the cell containing this erroneous entry by pressing F2 (EDIT) and moving to the front of the entry, you can type a label indicator, instructing 1-2-3 to treat the minus signs as hyphens and display the entry as a social security number.

The other two label indicators that can be used for entry placement are the double quotation mark (") and the caret (^). The double quotation mark causes label entries to be right justified, while the caret causes entries to be centered within the cell.

Let's look at a few examples of label entries, to clarify the differences shown in the entries here:

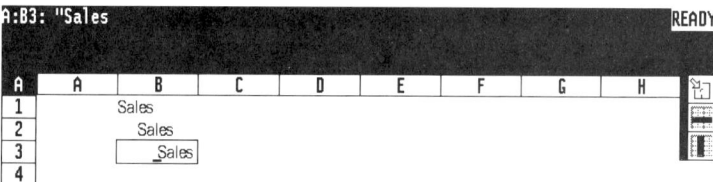

1. The word **Sales** was entered in B1. As soon as the **S** was entered, 1-2-3 changed the READY mode indicator to LABEL. When the entry was completed, the top line of the control panel showed 'Sales, since 1-2-3 generated an apostrophe. The entry was left justified in the cell and appeared without the apostrophe.

2. **^Sales** was typed in B2. The caret (^) caused the entry to be centered in the cell.

3. **"Sales** was typed in B3. This caused the entry to be right justified in the cell.

> ### Label Indicators
>
> The label indicator can be changed with a menu command or SmartIcon (see Chapter 5) or by typing a different indicator at the beginning of the label entry. The label indicators and their effects are as follows:
>
> - '   Left justified—the default setting
> - "   Right justified
> - ^   Centered
> - \   Repeats the characters that follow until the cell is filled
> - |-   Contains a non-printing label that is frequently used to send codes to the printer

In Chapter 5, "Basic Worksheet Commands," you will learn how to alter the default label indicator with /Worksheet Global Label. For now, though, if you want something other than left justification, enter the appropriate label indicator before you start typing your entry.

Two additional label indicators perform special functions. The backslash (\) causes the characters that follow it to be repeated until the entire cell is filled with this pattern. For example, entering \- will fill the cell with dashes. Figure 3-2 shows how * has been used to enter asterisks in all the cells in one row of the worksheet to serve as a dividing line between the worksheet assumptions and the calculation section. You can also use the \ to make multiple characters repeat: \+– would result in a pattern of + and – symbols repeated for the width of the cell.

Labels provide readability to a worksheet and allow you to enter text data. Since a worksheet is primarily involved in projections and calculations, however, you clearly also need a way to deal with numeric entries.

Value Entries

Value entries are treated as numeric entries by 1-2-3. They must follow much more rigid rules than label entries. There are two basic types of value entries: *numbers* and *formulas*. Like labels, numbers are constants; they do not change as the result of arithmetic operations. Formulas are not constants, since the results they produce depend on the current values for the variables they reference. We will examine each category separately, because 1-2-3 handles each differently.

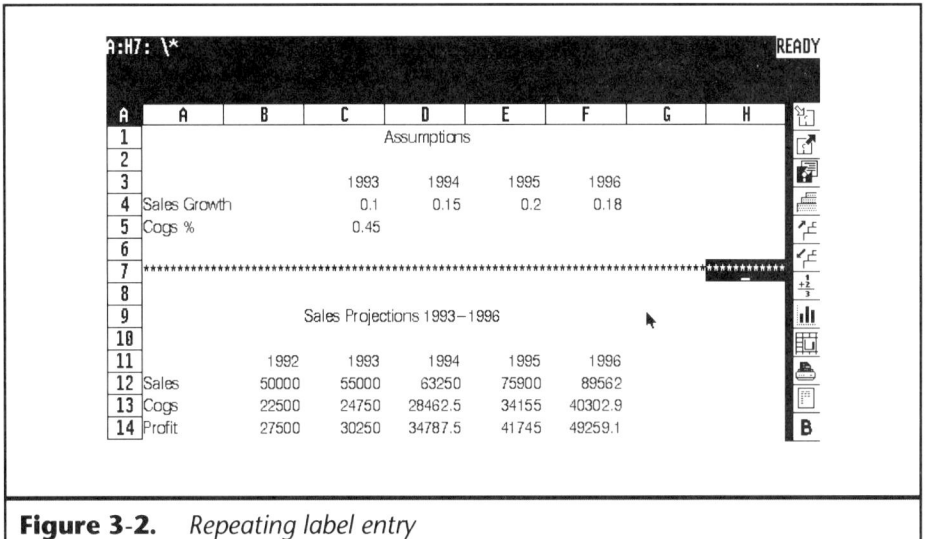

Figure 3-2. *Repeating label entry*

Numbers

The rules for entry of numeric constants are summarized in the box called "Rules for Numbers." Numeric entries do not have a special beginning indicator like labels, but numeric entries can contain only certain characters.

SIZE Numbers can be as large as 10^{99} or as small as 10^{-99} (that is, 10 raised to the 99th power or 10 raised to the –99th power). 1-2-3 can use numbers between 10^{308} and 10^{-308} in its own calculations. Up to 512 characters can be used to represent the numbers, although you must still adhere to the numeric limits of the package.

If you wish, you can use the Scientific notation to enter large numbers. Scientific notation is a method of entering a number along with the power of ten that it will be multiplied by. In this format, the letter E (either E or e may be used) separates the number from the positive or negative power of 10 that will be used. (The number that follows E must be between –99 and 99.) This kind of notation offers the advantage of representing very large or very small numbers in a minimum of space. The following examples should help clarify Scientific notation:

9.76E+4 = 97,600
6.543e+5 = 654,300
6.71E – 02 = .0671
3.86e – 5 = .0000386

> **Rules for Numbers**
>
> Numbers cannot exceed 512 characters; however, the limitation for decimal accuracy and significant digits is 18.
>
> If the first key you press is a number (0-9) or one of the acceptable symbols (+ – .($ @ or #) the entry will be treated as a number.
>
> Only the following symbols can appear in a number entry:
>
> 0 1 2 3 4 5 6 7 8 9 . + – # $ @ ( ) E ^ %
>
> The last four of these cannot begin a numeric entry.
>
> Only one decimal can be used.
>
> Spaces and commas can only be entered as part of a numeric entry with automatic formats, or when you have changed the international punctuation settings.

TIP: Entries you think of as numbers may be labels to 1-2-3. It is common to refer to social security numbers, phone numbers, part numbers, and purchase order numbers. Although these entries are called numbers, they may not be considered number values to 1-2-3 due to the presence of alphabetic characters or special symbols. They must be entered as labels in 1-2-3.

ENTRY   In one sense, entering numbers is easier than entering labels, since all you do is make your entry using the allowable characters and then press either ENTER or an arrow key. You do not need a special character at the beginning of a numeric entry.

As soon as you type any of the allowable characters, the mode indicator will change from READY to VALUE. Once 1-2-3 has determined that you are entering a value, you must continue entering only allowable characters. If you attempt to finalize an entry containing disallowed characters, 1-2-3 will place you in EDIT mode so that you can make necessary corrections. If you realize your error before trying to finalize the original entry, you can use BACKSPACE to remove the incorrect characters, or press ESC to eliminate the entire entry. Later you will learn other error correction methods to save time.

Looking at these numeric entries may clarify the entry process and the way 1-2-3 displays such entries in a cell:

1. With the cell pointer on C1, **.0925** was entered, and the cell pointer was moved to C2 to finalize the entry.

2. **51279** was entered in C2.

3. **4.35E+05** was entered in C3.

Notice that 1-2-3 converted the third entry to 435000, since the number was not too large for decimal display. The first two entries were displayed just as entered, except that a zero was added in front of the decimal in C1. There is no consistency in the number of decimal places displayed because the General format is in effect. General format is the default format for all new worksheets. In Chapter 4, "Changing the Appearance of the Worksheet Display," you will learn how to change the format so that entries are displayed as currency, percentages, or with a consistent number of decimal places. In the next section of this chapter you will get a closer look at the display with the General format in effect.

ENTERING DATES AND TIMES Dates and times are special types of values. Rather than storing 12-Jun-92 or 12:57 P.M., 1-2-3 stores dates and times as numeric values called *date and time serial numbers.* Dates are recorded as the number of days since December 31, 1899. This means that a date of 12-Jun-92, which has a date serial number of 33767, is 33,767 days away from December 31, 1899. Using date serial numbers allows you to use dates in calculations. For example, by adding 90 to 33767, you can calculate the date serial number of a day 90 days after 12-Jun-92. 1-2-3 can handle dates between January 1, 1900 and December 31, 2099.

1-2-3 records times as the fraction of the day. For example, noon is halfway through the day, so it is represented as .5. Using time serial numbers also lets you use times in calculations so that you can calculate the difference between times.

To enter dates or times, enter them as you expect them to appear. (For example, to enter 12-Jun-92, type **12-Jun-92**.) When you finalize the entry, 1-2-3 will convert your entry into the time or date serial number your entry represents. Dates can be entered in the formats DD-MMM-YY, DD-MMM, or the long version of the international date format (initially set to MM/DD/YY). The DD represents the day of the month, the MMM represents the three-letter abbreviation of the month, the MM represents the two-digit number of the month, and the YY represents the last two digits of the year. When you do not include the day, 1-2-3 assumes the first day of the year. When you do not include the year, 1-2-3 assumes the current year.

For times, you can use the formats HH:MM:SS AM/PM, HH:MM AM/PM, or the two international date formats (initially set to HH:MM:SS and HH:MM). The HH represents the hour of the day, the MM represents the minutes in the hour, and the SS represents the seconds in the minute. Even though your entries will not initially appear as the dates and times they represent, you can use them in calculations. To display the date and time serial numbers as the dates and times they represent, you must change the format of the cell containing the date and time serial numbers. Changing the display format is covered in Chapter 4, "Changing the Appearance of the Worksheet Display."

DISPLAY The numbers you enter are shown both in the control panel and in the worksheet. They are also stored internally. The form of the numbers may be slightly different in each case. Internally 1-2-3 can store up to 18 significant digits for an entry. If you enter a number with more than 18 significant digits, the display of the number will be rounded to fit within the 18-digit limitation. The display on the worksheet will depend on the format for the cell and the length of the number in relation to the cell width.

When 1-2-3 displays a number in a cell, it will display all the digits up to one less than the cell width. Numeric entries which are longer than this limit are not handled by borrowing space from cells to the right, as is done with labels. The entries are either shown in Scientific notation, a rounded form, or as asterisks representing an overflow situation. The cell format and the composition of the number determines the display.

If the General format is in effect, 1-2-3 will display the number as you have entered it if at all possible. If the integer portion of the number is too large, 1-2-3 converts the display to Scientific notation if the General format is in effect. If the integer portion of the number fits but some or all of the decimal digits do not, the cell value will be rounded to fit within the display. In both cases when the General format is not in effect, 1-2-3 displays the number as a series of asterisks. The default cell width is nine characters, so you can see that long numbers will not fit unless you expand the width of the column or use Wysiwyg to reduce the size of the characters. You will learn how to do that in Chapter 4, "Changing the Appearance of the Worksheet Display."

How 1-2-3 reacts to long numeric entries is shown here:

```
A:C5: 9578000000                                                    READY

    A        B          C        D     E     F     G     H
1         Sales      0.0925
2         Sales      51279
3         Sales      435000
4                    1.3E-10
5                    9.6E+09
```

1. **.000000000134** was entered in cell C4. The worksheet display changed this to Scientific notation and displayed it as "1.3E–10."

2. **9578000000** was entered in C5. 1-2-3 performed another conversion and shows the entry as "9.6E+09" in the cell. The entry appears in its original form in the control panel.

You have no control over format in the control panel or the internal storage of a number. In both cases 1-2-3 will retain as much accuracy as possible (18 decimal digits maximum for the control panel and internal storage). You can control the accuracy of the number that appears on the worksheet by selecting a format. You will learn how to do this in Chapter 4.

Formulas

Formulas are the second type of value entry. Unlike number and label entries, they produce variable results depending on the numbers they reference. This ability makes formulas the backbone of worksheet features. They allow you to make what-if projections and to look at the impact of changing variable values. To produce an updated result with a formula, you do not need to change the formula. Simply change one of the values the formula references, and the entire formula can be recalculated for you. Formulas follow the same basic rules as numbers in terms of allowable characters. In addition, formulas also support the use of cell references, range names assigned to a group of cells, and operators that define specific operations to 1-2-3. 1-2-3 has three types of formulas. These formulas are summarized in the box called "Formula Types."

A few rules pertain to all formulas:

- Formulas cannot contain spaces, except for the spaces in range names or string variables.

- The first character of a formula must be one of the following:

    + − (@ # $. 0 1 2 3 4 5 6 7 8 9

- Formulas contain special operators to define the operation you wish performed. Operators are assigned priorities (the order in which 1-2-3 calculates them), as shown in the box called "Operation Priorities."

- Formulas can also contain numeric constants or string constants (such as 77 or "sales total"), cell references (such as F4 or Z3), special built-in functions (such as @MIN), or range names (such as TOTAL).

ARITHMETIC FORMULAS Arithmetic formulas calculate numeric values. These formulas are built with *arithmetic operators* and references to values in other cells in the current worksheet file, or to values in other worksheets. The value references are to either the cell address in the current sheet (such as A1 or Z10), cells in other sheets within the current file (such as B:A1 or D:F10), cells in other files on disk, or a name that has been assigned to a cell or cells (such as Cash or Interest). For now, you will concentrate on references to cells in the current file, using both the current worksheet and other sheet references.

> ## Formula Types
>
> 1-2-3 provides three types of formulas for your use: arithmetic formulas, logical formulas, and string formulas.
>
> Arithmetic formulas involve constants, cell references, and the arithmetic operators (+ − * / ^). Arithmetic formulas calculate the formula entered and return its result. Examples are A2*A3, or Sales-Cogs (where Sales and Cogs are names of cells that contain numerical data).
>
> Logical formulas involve cell references, constants, and comparison operators (<> = <= >= < >). These formulas evaluate the condition listed to determine whether it is true or false. If the condition is false, the formula returns 0; if true, a 1 is returned. An example of a logical formula is +C2<=500.
>
> String formulas join two or more character strings. The concatenation character (&) can be used to join string variables or constants—for example, +"Sales for the "&"Midwest "&"Region".
>
> Functions provide predefined formulas for a variety of calculations, including mathematical formulas, financial calculations, logical evaluations, statistical computations, and string manipulation. Functions have a unique appearance: they begin with the @ symbol and contain a list of specific values for arguments within parentheses.

Linkages to external files are covered in Chapter 8, "Working with Files." You will learn how to assign range names in Chapter 5, "Basic Worksheet Commands."

TIP: Blank cells have a zero value. If you reference a blank cell in a formula, the result is the same as referencing a cell that contains a zero. Thus, +A1*A2 equals zero if either A1 or A2 contains a zero or is blank.

The *arithmetic operators* used in 1-2-3 are + for addition, − for subtraction, / for division, * for multiplication, and ^ for exponentiation. An instruction to multiply 3 times 4 would be written as 3*4. These operators are listed in the "Operation Priorities" box.

TIP: Ignoring 1-2-3's operator priorities will result in incorrect formula results. You must use parentheses to group references if you do not want to use the established priorities. A difference in the order of operations can cause a dramatic difference in results.

There are some things to keep in mind when entering cell references. Cell references without sheet letters preceding them are assumed to reference cells on the sheet where the formula is being entered. You cannot reference cells on sheets

Operation Priorities

1-2-3 has a variety of operators for arithmetic, logical, and string formulas. Often more than one operator is used in a formula. In this situation it is important to know which operation 1-2-3 will evaluate first. This table provides the priority order for each operation within 1-2-3, with the highest number being the highest priority. If several operators in a formula have the same priority, they will be evaluated from left to right.

Priority	Operator	Operation Performed
8	(	Parenthesis for grouping
7	^	Exponentiation
6	+ –	Positive and negative indicators
5	/ *	Division and multiplication
4	+ –	Addition and subtraction
3	= <> < > <= >=	Logical operators
2	#NOT#	Complex not operator
1	#AND# #OR# &	Complex and, complex or, and string operator

that you have not added to the current file. For example, the entry +B:C1+D:F10 cannot be finalized unless the current file has four sheets.

In examining the sample formulas, you may have wondered why a plus sign was placed at the beginning of the formula. If you want to multiply the current contents of C1 by the contents of C2, you might think that entering **C1*C2** would seem logical. This will not work, however. The problem here is the initial C. As soon as 1-2-3 realizes a C has been entered, it flags the cell as a label entry. It will show the entry as a label on the worksheet, rather than giving the result of the formula calculation.

You need a formula indicator, and the + is the logical choice, since it requires only one additional keystroke and does not alter the formula. (Actually any numeric character that does not affect the formula result is acceptable.) Therefore, place a + at the front of all formulas that begin with a cell address, as in **+C1*C2**.

Parentheses in arithmetic expressions are the only option for changing the order of operations. Otherwise, operators in formulas will be evaluated according to the priority list, proceeding from left to right within the expression if there is more than one operator at the same level. For example, 3+4*5 equals 23, but (3+4)*5 equals 35. In the first expression, multiplication has a higher priority than addition, so it will be carried out first. This produces the expression 3+20, which is equal to 23. In the second expression, the parentheses take priority. Therefore, 3 will be added to 4 first, making the expression 7*5, or 35.

1-2-3 allows many sets of parentheses in one expression, so you can use them liberally to override the natural priority order. With nested parentheses, the priority sequence will apply within each set of parentheses. Here is an example of priority order within nested parentheses:

$$4*((1+2)*2)/2+3$$

$$\begin{array}{cccc} \uparrow & \uparrow & \uparrow & \uparrow \\ 3\text{rd} & 2\text{nd} & 5\text{th} \\ & 1\text{st} & 4\text{th} & \end{array}$$

You have learned how to build a formula by typing cell addresses and arithmetic operators. This method will work well if you are good at remembering the cell addresses you want to use and do not make mistakes in typing. However, a second method of formula construction can alleviate both these potential problems. This method lets you point to the cell references you wish to include in the formula and then type only the arithmetic operators. After you type an operator, simply move your cell pointer to the cell whose value you wish included in the formula. Watch the mode indicator change from VALUE to POINT as you move your cell pointer. To finalize the selection of the cell reference, either type the next operator or, if you have reached the end of the formula, press ENTER. If you type another operator, the cell pointer returns to the formula's entry cell, and 1-2-3 then waits for you to move your cell pointer to a new location.

Here is a sample worksheet that was developed using this method:

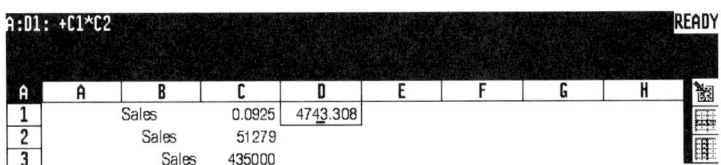

To produce this example, the cell pointer was moved to D1, and a + was typed. Then the cell pointer was moved to C1, putting 1-2-3 in POINT mode. An asterisk for multiplication was then typed, causing the cell pointer to return to D1. The LEFT ARROW and DOWN ARROW keys were used to move to C2. Finally, pressing ENTER caused the formula to appear in cell D1, as shown in the example. You can use the pointing method to select any cell from any open worksheet file.

This may seem like a lot of work compared to typing in cell references. However, once your worksheet becomes large or you are using a number of sheets, the pointing method can save considerable time. It speeds up the testing and verification process for your model, because it forces you to visually verify cell references and therefore eliminates many formula errors that could result from incorrect cell or sheet references.

TIP: Make the pointing method mandatory for all your formulas that reference other sheets. Otherwise, you are using guesswork. It is too easy to type in an incorrect reference. The effects of errors in worksheet entries can be devastating if they are not recognized until after decisions have been made.

LOGICAL FORMULAS Logical formulas use the *logical operators* to compare two or more values. Such formulas can be used to evaluate a series of complex decisions or to influence results in other areas of the worksheet. As noted in the "Operation Priorities" box, the *logical operators* are = for equal, <> for not equal, < for less than, > for greater than, <= for less than or equal to, and >= for greater than or equal to. The logical operators all have the same priority and will be evaluated from left to right in an expression. All the logical operators are lower in priority than the arithmetic operators.

Logical formulas do not calculate numeric results like arithmetic formulas. They produce a result of either zero or one, depending on whether the condition that was evaluated is true or false. If it is a true condition, 1 will be returned; if the condition is false, 0 will be returned. For example, if C1 contains .0925, the logical expression +C1>=500 will return 0, since the condition is false.

1-2-3 also has a few *compound operators*. These operators are used either to negate a logical expression or to join two logical expressions. The negation operator #NOT# has priority over the other two compound operators, #AND# and #OR#. These latter operators can join two expressions, as in C1>=500#AND#C2=50. In this example the expression will return a 1 for true only if both conditions are true.

The function of #NOT# is to negate an expression. For instance, the formula #NOT#(A1=2#AND#D2=1) will return a 1 for true if either the contents of cell A1 are not equal to 2, or those of cell D1 are not equal to 1, since the statement in parenthesis would then be false. (If #OR# replaced #AND# in this formula, the formula would be true if cell A1 were not equal to 2, and cell D2 were not equal to 1.) For practical purposes, you are more likely to use the not equal logical operator, <>, than the more cumbersome #NOT# operator. The formula A1<>2#AND#D2<>1 is easier to read than is #NOT#(A1=2#OR#D2=1), and its meaning is identical.

One application of logical operators in a worksheet might be the calculation of a commission bonus. Figure 3-3 shows a calculation on a worksheet to determine the quarterly commission check for salesperson John Smith. The calculation has two components: the regular commission, and a bonus for meeting sales quotas.

The regular commission is 10% of total sales. The bonus is calculated by product. Each salesperson has a $50,000 quota for each of three products. A bonus of $1000 is given for each product for which the sales quota is met. A salesperson could thus gain $3000 by meeting the quota for all three products.

Let's look at the steps taken to build the model shown in the figure. First a number of labels are entered in cells B2 through A7. Next, **John Smith** is entered

```
A:D14: +C10+C11                                          READY

     A        B           C         D       E      F     G     H
 1
 2             Commission Calculation
 3
 4  Employee:            John Smith         Quotas Met
 5  Sales Product A:        56000              1
 6  Sales Product B:        45000              0
 7  Sales Product C:         3000              0
 8                         104000              1
 9
10  Commission:             10400
11  Bonus:                   1000
12
13
14  Total Commission Plus Bonus:      11400
```

Figure 3-3. *Total pay calculation*

in C4; and **56000**, **45000**, and **3000** are entered in C5 through C7. These numbers are totaled in C8 by entering the formula **+C5+C6+C7** in that cell. The label **Quotas Met** is entered in E4.

The logical formula **+C5>50000** is now entered in E5. When ENTER is pressed, if sales of product A are greater than 50,000, a 1 will be returned, but if they are equal to or less than this number, a 0 will be returned. Similarly, **+C6>50000** is entered in E6, and **+C7>50000** is entered in E7. Pressing ENTER produces the result of the logical formula in both cases. The total formula, **+E5+E6+E7**, is placed in E8 to determine the number of bonus categories.

Additional labels **Commission:** and **Bonus:** are entered in A10 and A11. **+C8∗.1** is then entered in C10, and **+E8∗1000** is entered in C11. A label for total commission is placed in A14, and the final formula is entered in D14 as **+C10+C11**.

STRING FORMULAS   String or text formulas allow you to join or concatenate two or more groups of characters. This allows you to access and manipulate character data to build headings, correct errors, and convert text formats to a satisfactory format for reporting. There is only one operator for string formulas, the ampersand (&). If you want to join the string John with the string Smith, you could enter the string formula **"John"&"Smith"** to produce JohnSmith, or **"John"&" "&"Smith"** to produce John Smith.

String formulas let you alter data previously entered in a worksheet, so you can use them to correct errors or change formats. For example, if names have been entered in a worksheet with the last name first, and you wish to reverse the sequence, you can combine string functions such as @RIGHT, @LEFT, and @MID to produce that result. (String functions are explained in Chapter 7, "1-2-3's Built-In Functions.") String formulas also offer a creative approach to producing new reports by providing an opportunity to join data from two or more locations on your worksheet. For instance, string formulas can be used in combination with cell references to produce flexible report headings.

Figure 3-4 shows a report heading created by combining string constants and variables. There are three string constants in this formula: "Monthly Statistics for the "," ", and "Warehouse". The constants were enclosed in quotation marks and entered into the formula. The variables are references to cell addresses that contain text data. The two variables here are D5 and D4, which contain Dallas and Timber, respectively.

TIP: String references to blank cells result in ERR. Since blank cells are equivalent to zero, referencing a blank cell in a string formula returns ERR, indicating an error in the formula. You cannot combine numbers and strings in a formula, although 1-2-3 has @functions that can convert numbers into strings and strings containing digits into numbers.

The & operator, along with #AND# and #OR#, have the lowest priority of all the operators. This does not diminish the usefulness of these operators; it just means they are the last operators to be evaluated in an expression.

FUNCTIONS   1-2-3's built-in *functions* are a special category of formulas. They can be used alone or as part of a formula you create. The entire algorithm or formula for the calculations represented in a function have been worked out, tested, and incorporated into the package features. 1-2-3 will supply all the

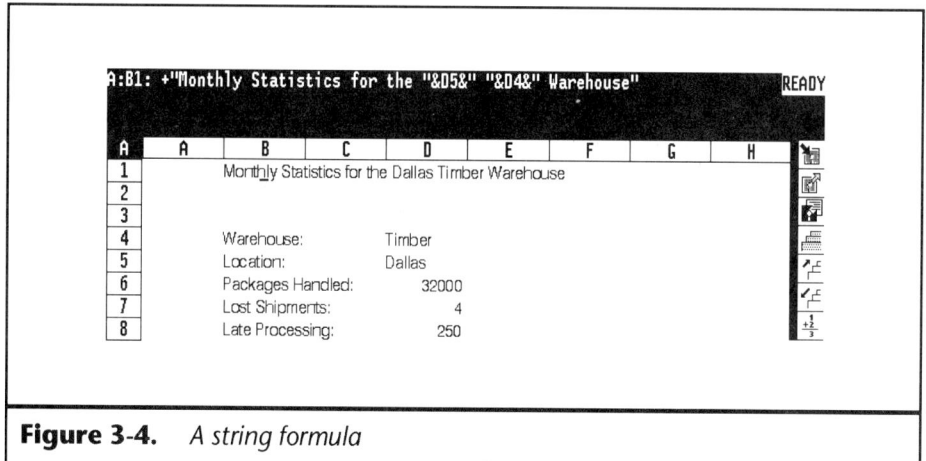

Figure 3-4.   *A string formula*

operators for a function; all you need to supply are the values that the operators work with. There are functions to perform arithmetic operations, string manipulation, logical evaluation, statistical calculations, and date and time arithmetic. They all have the same general format and must abide by the same rules. Regardless of the function type, all are regarded as value entries because they are formulas.

Functions all start with an @ sign. This is followed by a function keyword, which is a character sequence representing the calculation being performed. The keyword is followed by arguments enclosed in parentheses. The arguments define the function's specific use in a given situation. Here are a few of 1-2-3's functions:

@MAX	Calculates the maximum value
@SUM	Calculates a sum or total
@ROUND	Rounds a number to a certain number of decimal places
@NPV	Calculates the net present value

Release 3 of 1-2-3 has over 100 of these built-in functions, spanning calculations in financial, mathematical, logical, statistical, string, and other applications. Functions will be covered thoroughly in Chapter 7, "1-2-3's Built-In Functions."

Figure 3-5 shows an example of the use of the @SUM function to produce a total. After entering appropriate numbers and labels, the sum formula was entered in A:G3 by typing **@SUM(**. The cell pointer was then moved to A: C3 (the beginning of the range to be summed), and this reference was locked in place as the beginning of the range by typing a period. The cell pointer was next moved to the value in A:F3. As a last step, the closing parentheses) was entered, and ENTER was pressed to produce the sum shown in the figure. The @SUM function totals all the values between A:C3 and A:F3. It is the same as the formula +A:C3+A:D3+A:E3+A:F3.

The @SUM function can also be used across sheets of the same file. The numbers that you see in columns C through F on sheet A are the totals of the sparklers, rockets, and fountains sold shown in sheets B and C. For example, the formula in A:C3 is @SUM(B:C3..C:C3). To create this formula, move the cell pointer to A:C3. Type **@SUM(**. Press CTRL-PGUP to move to B:C3. Type a period to anchor the first cell that you want to add. Press CTRL-PGUP again and type **)** to finish the @SUM function. Press ENTER to finalize the formula. The other formulas in columns C through F are created in the same way. 1-2-3 will not let the range of cells you select span beyond the sheets of the same file. For example, if there was another worksheet from another file after sheet C, 1-2-3 would not let you include it in the range with B:C3..C:C3.

If you are using Release 3.4 you can use the SmartSum icon from one of the SmartIcons palettes to sum a preselected range as long as the last cell in the row or column is blank. You can also create a sum without selecting a range by making the current cell the cell where you want the sum. The SmartSum icon is

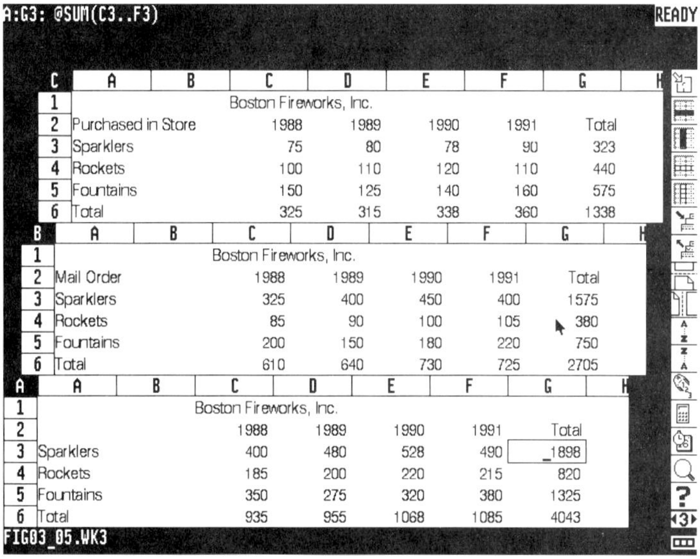

Figure 3-5. *Using @SUM*

available in the first palette as well as other palettes. It is the icon that adds 1 + 2 to total 3 and looks like this:

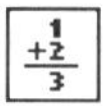

To sum A:C3 through A:F3 with this approach, you would move the mouse to A:C3, press the left mouse button and hold it down while dragging to A:G3. Remember, this extra cell is necessary to leave a place for the @SUM entry. Click the SmartSum icon in the SmartIcons palette and 1-2-3 will place @SUM(A:C3..A:F3) into cell A:G3.

Using the other approach you could click A:G3 to make the cell active then click the SmartSum. Unless you need to sum multiple rows or columns, this latter approach is actually easier. Like the first option, it places the formula @SUM(A:C3..A:F3) into cell A:G3.

A second SmartSum icon, shown here, enables you to sum values from multiple worksheets:

Using this icon with a cell or range highlighted in a multi-worksheet file totals the values in the same cell on the lower level worksheets, and puts the total in the highlighted cell or range.

To sum the values from the B and C worksheets to total on the A worksheet in cells A:C3 through A:F6, you would highlight all of these cells, and then select the second SmartSum icon. The values of the lower worksheets would be totaled. The formula placed in cell A:C3 by this action is @SUM(B:C3..C:C3).

HOW 1-2-3 TREATS FORMULAS You need to know some facts about formulas beyond the procedure for their entry. 1-2-3 offers a number of recalculation options that affect the timeliness of recalculation and the order of formula evaluation. You will probably begin your use of the 1-2-3 package with the default settings, but you should be aware that other alternatives can enhance your use of the package when you begin to build models with greater sophistication.

With the default settings in Release 3, minimal intelligent background recalculation is used. This string of adjectives means a much more efficient method of dealing with recalculation than earlier releases offered. 1-2-3 now has the intelligence to determine which cells require recalculation, and it recalculates only this minimum number of cells rather than the entire worksheet every time you change a variable on a sheet. Even this more efficient recalculation is accomplished in the background, thereby allowing you to continue with additional worksheet entries. Instead of the WAIT mode indicator that you saw during recalculation for past releases, you will see the CALC indicator at the bottom of the screen until the background recalculation is completed. Unless your worksheet is very large, you will hardly notice the amount of time required to perform these calculations. 1-2-3 is one of the fastest spreadsheet packages marketed.

Release 3 offers further processing efficiency for users who have 80287 or 80387 math coprocessor chips installed in their systems, because it can automatically recognize and use these chips. The math coprocessor provides noticeable speed improvements for worksheets with many calculations.

In addition to fast recalculation, 1-2-3's speed in format changes, cell pointer movement, window switching, and copying functions sets standards for the other spreadsheet packages. This is not to say that you will never become impatient with the package, since most users want no delay at all. At these times you can take comfort in knowing that 1-2-3 is using the features of your computer to the fullest. Furthermore, as you will learn in Chapter 5, "Basic Worksheet Commands," there is a method to temporarily turn off recalculation when you have data entry tasks to perform.

REFERENCE TYPES The cell address references in 1-2-3's formulas can be relative, absolute, or mixed. These three reference types will be covered in detail

Reference Types

1-2-3 has three different reference types. These types do not affect the original formula, but do affect Copy operation. You can type the $'s where required or add them with the F4 (ABS) key when you are in POINT mode. The mixed reference type actually has a number of forms, depending on which parts of the address are held constant and which are allowed to change. See Chapter 5.

```
Relative references: A:A2, A:B10, A:Z43
```

Absolute references: $A:$A$2, $A:$B$10, $A:$Z$43

in Chapter 5, "Basic Worksheet Commands," in connection with the /Copy command. They are mentioned here as well, however, because references must be entered in one of the three formats when you type in your original formulas, even though the reference type does not have any effect on the original calculation. The "Reference Types" box provides examples of the three reference type formats.

You will notice that the mixed type addresses have several different options, since mixed is a combination of relative and absolute. Only portions of the address are absolute; the other part of the address may vary depending on the location to which it is copied. It is important to know that the way you enter cell references in your original formula can have long-term and widespread consequences if the formula is copied.

Adding Notes to Formulas

With Release 3 you can annotate formulas with text to describe your entry. This feature allows you to describe the logic behind a formula. You enter the number or formula followed by a semicolon (;). Then type the text for the note after the semicolon, up to the maximum length of 512 characters for a cell entry. You can see the note in the control panel, but when the entry is finalized only the result of the formula displays in the cell as shown here:

You can print the note along with the numbers or formulas entered in the cells if you use the /Print Printer Options Other Cell-Formulas option covered in Chapter 6, "Printing."

Correcting Errors in Entries

1-2-3 offers a variety of error correction techniques. They are summarized in the "Error Correction Methods" box. The method you use will depend mostly on whether the entry to be corrected has been finalized (by pressing ENTER or one of the arrow keys).

When an entry is short and has been finalized, retyping is a good correction method. This will replace the incorrect contents of the cell with your new entry. If the Undo feature is active, you can press ALT-F4 (UNDO). This will eliminate the effect of your last entry. (If Undo is currently disabled, you can use /Worksheet Global Default Other Undo Enable to activate Undo for subsequent use, although it will not help in eliminating the current entry.)

Error Correction Methods

If data is in the control panel but not yet entered in the cell:

Use the ESC key to erase the entire entry.
Use the BACKSPACE key to delete one character at a time until the erroneous character has been eliminated.
Press F2 (EDIT); then use HOME, END, RIGHT ARROW, and LEFT ARROW to move within the entry. Use BACKSPACE to delete the character in front of the cursor. INS can be used to toggle between Insert and Overstrike modes.

If data has already been entered in the cell:

Retype the entry; the new entry will replace the old.
Press F2 (EDIT); then use HOME, END, RIGHT ARROW, and LEFT ARROW to move within the entry. Use BACKSPACE to delete the character in front of the cursor, and DEL to erase the character above the cursor. INS can be used to toggle between Insert and Overstrike modes.

If the Undo feature is enabled, press ALT-F4 (UNDO). This will eliminate the entry only if there have been no intervening actions.

A quick-fix option for an unfinalized entry is pressing ESC, which will make your entire entry disappear. However, if you have not finalized an entry, the most common error correction technique is to use the BACKSPACE key. It functions as a destructive backspace, deleting the previous character each time you press it. This approach is ideal when you realize that the last character you typed was incorrect.

Placing yourself in EDIT mode by pressing the F2 (EDIT) key is a good way to correct errors in entries that have been finalized. When this key is pressed, the mode indicator in the upper right corner of the screen changes to EDIT, and a small cursor will appear at the end of the entry in the Edit line of the control panel. This small cursor marks your place in the entry as you move within it and make changes. EDIT mode is also a good solution for long, incomplete entries where the error is near the beginning of the entry.

The cell pointer movement keys take on new functions in EDIT mode, as follows:

- HOME moves you to the first character in your entry—not to A1 as it does outside of EDIT.

- END moves you immediately to the last character in your entry. You do not have to press an arrow key to have END take an action, as you do in READY mode.

- The RIGHT ARROW and LEFT ARROW move you one character at a time in your entry.

- BACKSPACE still performs its destructive function.

- DEL also eliminates characters from entries. Rather than deleting the previous character, DEL removes the character above the small Edit cursor.

If you have left out a character in an entry, move the cursor to the character that follows the desired location, and type the character you wish to add. It will be inserted, as long as you have not changed the default setting of Insert mode. (If you should want to change this setting, so that what you type will overlay an existing character rather than be inserted, you can press INS. To change the setting back again, just press INS again; this key functions as a toggle switch.)

Let's look at a brief example using EDIT mode to make a correction. In this situation, **sales** has been entered in B1 and finalized. To change the first letter of **sales** to a capital, follow these steps:

1. Move the cell pointer back to the cell containing the error, B1.

2. Press F2 (EDIT) to place 1-2-3 in EDIT mode.

3. Use HOME to move to the beginning of the entry, and then RIGHT ARROW to move under the *s* (the extra character at the front of the entry is the label indicator).

4. Press the DEL key to remove the *s*, leaving the cell pointer under the *a*.

5. Type **S**; then press ENTER to finalize your corrected entry.

You can also use the error correction techniques to change the justification of a label entry by altering the label indicator that appears at the beginning of the entry. Simply press F2 (EDIT) and then HOME to move to the front of the entry. Press DEL to remove the label indicator; then type a caret (^). When ENTER is pressed, this entry will be centered. This same approach works with long label entries and complicated formulas.

Errors can be frustrating, but having several options makes the correction process as painless as possible.

Ranges

Most of the formulas discussed in this chapter have operated on individual cells—for example, +C1*C2 or +B:C2+D:F2, where the value in one cell was multiplied by the value in another cell, or the values in two cells were added. The one exception was the use of a *range* of cells in the @SUM function example (Figure 3-5). When using 1-2-3's built-in functions and other commands, you will often work with more than one cell at a time. This is not difficult as long as the range of cells forms a contiguous rectangle. Figure 3-6 presents examples of valid and invalid ranges. The examples on the left are invalid because the cell groups do not form one contiguous rectangle. Ranges can be large rectangles of cells, or they can be as small as a single cell.

A range specification always includes two cell addresses separated by periods. If you are typing a range address, you only need to type one period; 1-2-3 will supply the second one. If you are specifying a range address by pointing, and if the address already appears in a range format with two addresses separated by a period, you can use the arrow keys to enlarge or contract a range.

The entries B1..B10, F2..F2, and A3..C25 are all examples of range specifications. Any single cell address can be changed to a range reference in POINT mode by typing a period after pointing to the first cell of the range. For example, an entry of B1 will appear as B1..B1 if you type a period after pointing to B1. With @SUM, type **@SUM(**; then point to B1 and type a period; then type **)**. The entry will read @SUM(B1..B1). To expand the range, move the cell pointer down or to the right before typing the closing parenthesis.

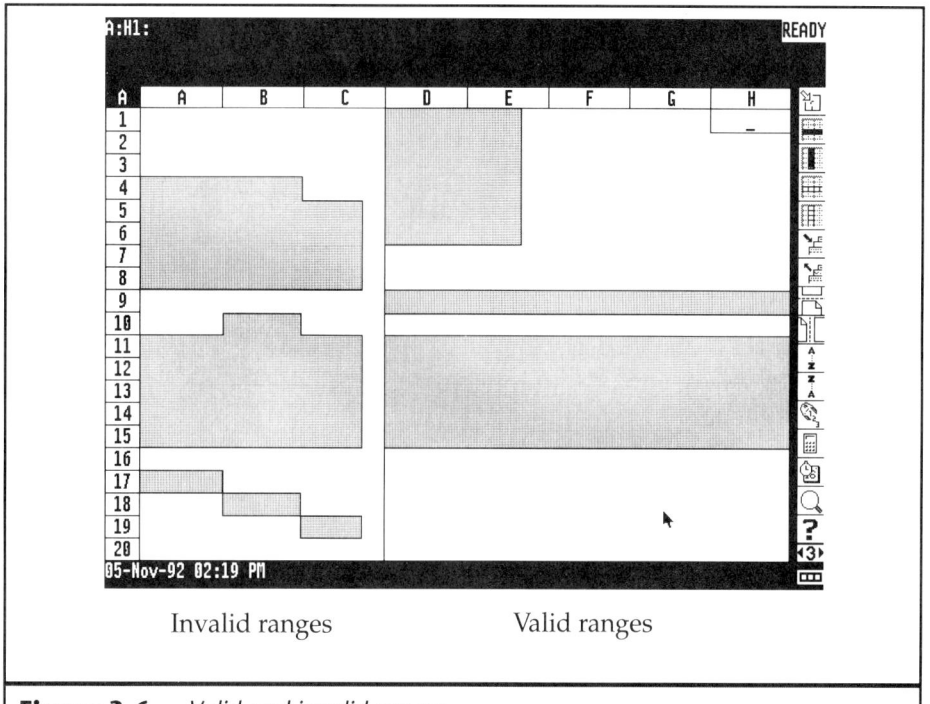

Figure 3-6. *Valid and invalid ranges*

Range addresses can be typed in just like a single address, highlighted with your cell pointer, or specified with a range name (explained in Chapter 5, "Basic Worksheet Commands"). To specify the cells of a range, use the cell names of two diagonally opposite corners of the rectangle, separated by one or two periods. For example, the range shown in Figure 3-7 can be specified as B4.C8, B4..C8, B8..C4, B8.C4, C8..B4, C8.B4, C4..B8, or C4.B8. However, the most common way to represent a range is by specifying the left uppermost cell first and the right lowermost cell last. Also since 1-2-3 will supply the second period, you might as well save a keystroke and just type **B4.C8**.

TIP: Type a decimal point to change the orientation of a range. If you have a range highlighted and need to expand or shrink it from the beginning rather than the end, one option is to press ESC and start over. A better approach is to press the period. This changes the orientation; it makes a different corner of the current range active and allows you to use the arrow keys to push and pull on the range from this corner. For example, the range A1..D10 initially has D10 as the active corner. The first time you press the period, A10 is active; the second time A1; and the third time D1.

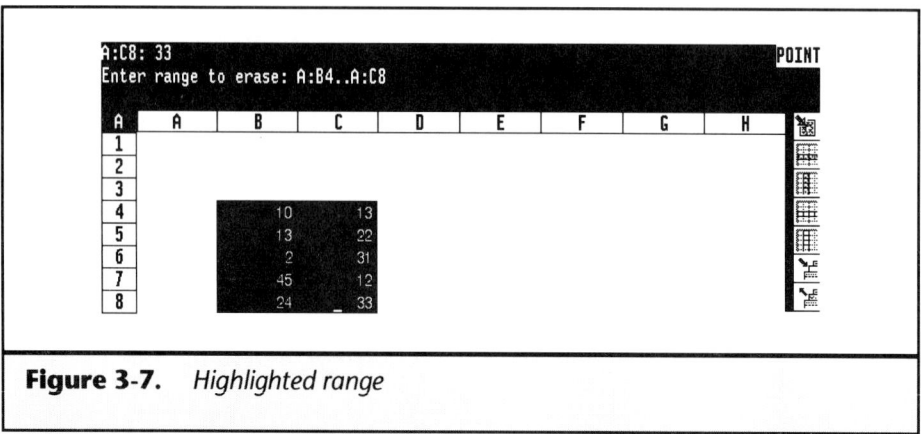

Figure 3-7. Highlighted range

Ranges in Release 3 can also span sheets in a file. You saw one example of this with the @SUM function used to consolidate sales. When specifying ranges across multiple sheets, you must choose diagonally opposite corners for the range on the first and last sheet in the range. Figure 3-8 shows a valid range that spans sheets in a multiple-sheet file. The size of the range in each sheet is always the same.

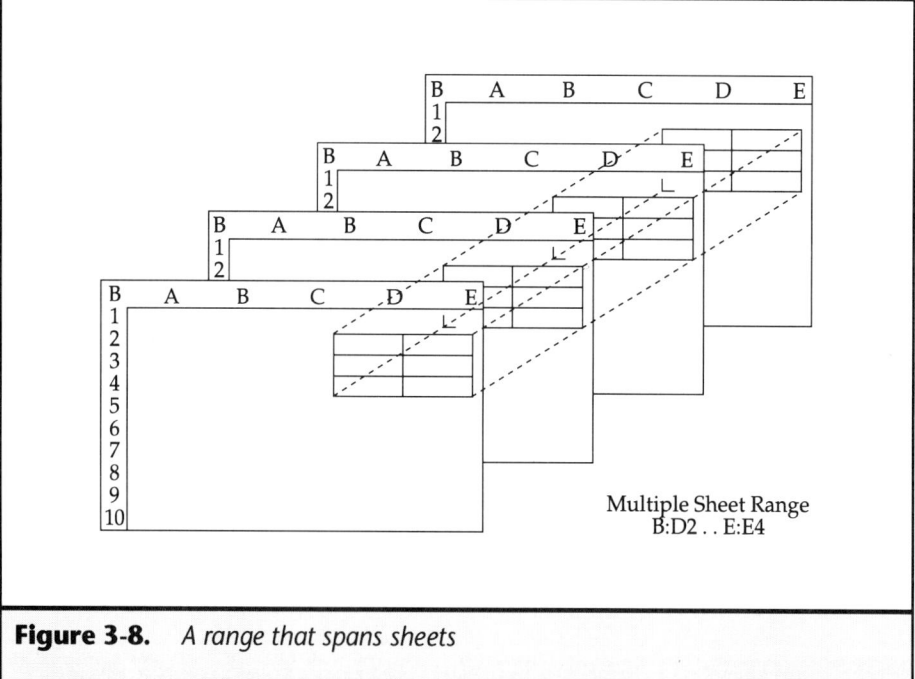

Figure 3-8. A range that spans sheets

When specifying a range encompassing multiple cells on each sheet, you can specify all the cells in the range on the first sheet (as in B:D2..B:E4) and then use CTRL-PGUP to extend the range to other sheets like C, D, and E, with a final range specification of B:D2..E:E4. Another approach to specify this same range is to start with the cell pointer in B2 of sheet B, and extend the range to the remaining sheets so that it reads B:D2..E:D2; then extend the range on the last sheet. Both methods produce the same range.

CHAPTER 4

Changing the Appearance of the Worksheet Display

Using what you have learned up to now, you can make entries on the worksheet that convey useful information. The format of the numeric portion of this information, however, probably is not as attractive as you would like. It has no dollar signs, commas, or aligned decimal points. 1-2-3 can provide these special edit characters for you. The only time you will enter the edit characters yourself is when you are using Release 3's Automatic format. In this case, the special edit characters will be the clue that tells 1-2-3 what type of format you want for the cell.

This chapter describes the features 1-2-3 provides for formatting your worksheet. It will demonstrate global and range formatting options, which give you a choice in the design of all or just a portion of your worksheet. It will teach you commands to change the width of your worksheet columns when the formats you have chosen require additional display space. This chapter will introduce you to the power of Release 3's GROUP mode, which allows you to affect all the sheets in the current worksheet file as you make changes to the current sheet. It will also describe some advanced ways to change 1-2-3's default display options. You will learn how to add and delete rows, columns, and sheets. For an overview of the commands covered in this chapter, see the command map at the start of the Worksheet Display Command Reference section.

Although the details of Wysiwyg are reserved for Chapter 15, you will get a brief glimpse of a few Wysiwyg options here so you will know if you want to skip ahead and make additional format improvements.

Global, Range, and GROUP Changes

1-2-3 has several menu commands for improving the appearance of your worksheet. These commands can work their magic globally, changing the entire worksheet at once, or they can affect only a single range of cells. Moreover, if you turn on the GROUP mode, your entries will affect either the current range on every sheet in the current file, or the entire file—depending upon whether or not your changes are range or global changes. The /Worksheet Global Format command changes the appearance of the entire worksheet from the global setting of General to another display format. If GROUP mode is on, every sheet in the file will have its global format altered. Global changes like the ones made with the commands available in the Worksheet Global menu affect all cells in the worksheet by either altering them or setting the default.

The /Range Format command changes the appearance of just the cells within a specified range. Again, the range affected is in the current sheet, or, with GROUP mode on, the same range in all sheets. If you make changes with the /Range command rather than with a global format change, the results are the same. Without GROUP mode, formatting a range in sheet A would have left the other worksheets in the file unaffected. The same change with GROUP mode on would apply to every sheet in the file. Range commands like the /Range Format command only alter a selected range of cells.

A Range Format option has priority over a Worksheet Format option. This means you can select a Worksheet option that matches your needs for most of the worksheet cells, and still tailor individual cells to have a different appearance. In Figure 4-1 the /Worksheet Global Format command was used to set the overall

Chapter 4: Changing the Appearance of the Worksheet Display

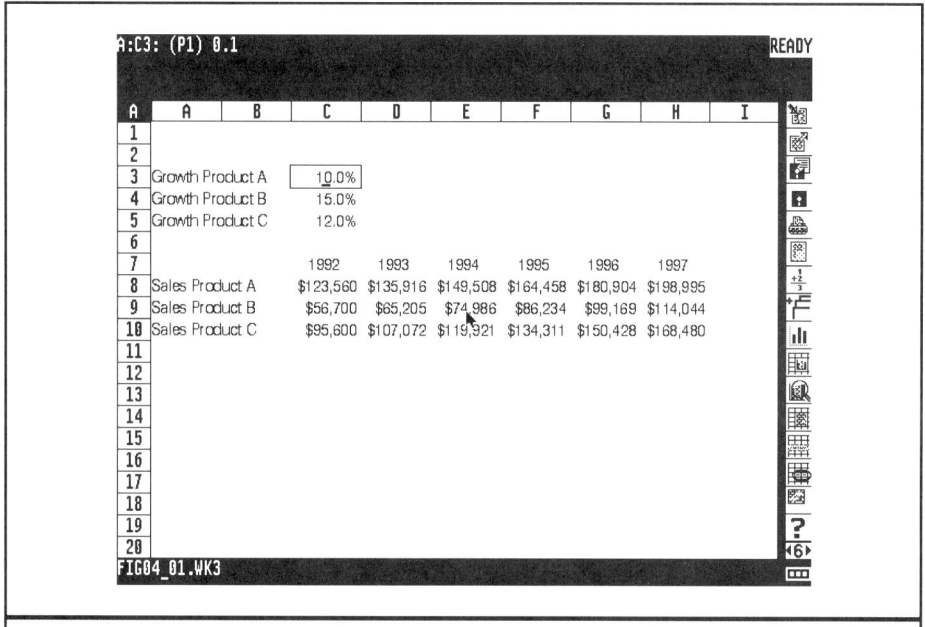

Figure 4-1. Combining global and range formats

format to Currency, and then /Range Format was used to change C3..C5 to Percent format. Changing the global format again would change every numeric worksheet cell except C3..C5. Those cells would not be affected by a worksheet format change because a range format instruction was previously applied to them, and the range format has priority.

If you were using six sheets in one file and wanted all but one sheet to have a global format of Currency, you could turn GROUP mode on (with /Worksheet Global Group Enable), enter **/Worksheet Global Format Currency**, and press ENTER to accept two decimal places. This action formats all the sheets as Currency, including the sheet that you want to show in a different format. Next, turn GROUP off (with /Worksheet Global Group Disable) and then use /Worksheet Global Format Percent, or another desired format on that sheet. Similarly, if you want several cells on one worksheet to use a different format from all the other cells, you can use the /Range Format command after GROUP mode is disabled. Be careful: if you accidentally turn GROUP mode back on at a later time, you will find that the active sheet's range and global settings at the time you invoke GROUP mode will be applied to all the sheets. For this reason GROUP mode is best reserved for the beginning of your worksheet design or for models where all the sheets have identical formats.

In Release 3.4, the SmartIcons let you format a range of cells with either a numeric or Wysiwyg format. The cells to be affected must be preselected before choosing the icon to change their format. Wysiwyg must be attached to utilize the SmartIcons palette options that will be discussed in a separate section later in this chapter.

Before making a change to your worksheet, you should always determine the extent of the change you wish to make. You can then select the command that makes just the amount of change you need. This chapter will look separately at global changes and range changes, and take an in-depth look at each format option that 1-2-3 provides, both for global and range applications. Since the GROUP mode option can affect both range and global options, its coverage will be integrated with options in both sections. The GROUP mode does not affect worksheet entries; it only affects commands that change the appearance of the worksheet.

In addition, GROUP mode moves you from sheet to sheet, keeping the cell pointer on the same column and row. This means if you are in cell A3 on Sheet A when you press CTRL-PGUP, you will still be in cell A3, but on Sheet B. Without GROUP mode, CTRL-PGUP would have placed you in the cell that was active the last time you used Sheet B.

You will need to be especially careful with GROUP mode, unless your sheets are identical for different products or subsidiaries. A GROUP mode indicator appears in the bottom status area when GROUP mode is active. Changes will take place as soon as you activate GROUP mode, based on the settings for the current sheet. All sheets in the file will assume the range format, range and worksheet protection status, worksheet column settings, labels, titles, and zero settings from the current worksheet. All worksheets are affected if you use any of these commands with GROUP on:

/Range Format
/Range Label
/Range Prot
/Range Unprot
/Worksheet Column
/Worksheet Global Col-Width
/Worksheet Global Format
/Worksheet Global Label
/Worksheet Global Prot
/Worksheet Global Zero
/Worksheet Insert Column or Row
/Worksheet Delete Column or Row
/Worksheet Page
/Worksheet Titles

Chapter 4: Changing the Appearance of the Worksheet Display

Worksheet Changes

All the /Worksheet commands are accessed through the Worksheet option on the main menu, which looks like this:

```
Worksheet Range  Copy   Move   File   Print  Graph  Data   System Quit
Global    Insert Delete Column Erase  Titles Window Status Page   Hide
```

Select Worksheet either by pressing ENTER while the command is highlighted, or by typing **W**.

This chapter will discuss the Worksheet menu options that are found under Insert, Delete, Column, Hide, and Global on the Worksheet submenu. In addition, some of the Worksheet Window options will be introduced.

If you make a series of mistakes and wish to eliminate all the entries on your worksheet, you can use /Worksheet Erase Yes. This command makes the ultimate change in worksheet appearance: it clears the screen. Since it also eliminates all the underlying data, affecting more than the display, it is covered in Chapter 5, "Basic Worksheet Commands." A similar command, /Range Erase, clears a range on one or more worksheets; it is also covered in Chapter 5, since it affects the cell entries rather than the display format. You can also use the delete key or trash icon to delete the contents of the current cell.

Undoing Worksheet Changes

Release 3 provides a powerful Undo feature that can return a worksheet to its former status. When Undo is enabled, pressing ALT-F4 (UNDO) and typing a **Y** to confirm that you want to undo your last action will reverse (undo) all the actions taken since the last time 1-2-3 was in READY mode. Pressing ALT-F4 (UNDO) when Undo is disabled has no effect. The Undo option will also have no effect on eliminating a series of actions if another series of actions are executed before you press ALT-F4 (UNDO). In Release 3.4, you have the option for undoing the effect of your last actions by using the Undo SmartIcon that looks like this:

Like the ALT-F4 (UNDO) option, the effectiveness of this command depends on having Undo enabled.

You can use Undo to eliminate format changes, worksheet insertions and deletions, sorting, the effects of macros, and most other changes that affect the worksheet. Most changes made with Wysiwyg (covered in Chapter 15) can also be undone by pressing F4 (UNDO). External activities like printing or saving a file cannot be undone with Undo.

To enable Undo, use /Worksheet Global Default Other Undo Enable. To eliminate Undo's actions, use /Worksheet Global Default Other Undo Disable.

When Undo is enabled, the amount of memory required for 1-2-3 is increased. The exact requirements are determined by the type of command that you are undoing. For example, undoing a cell format requires a minimum of additional memory, whereas undoing a sort of a large database can require extensive storage space.

Insert Commands to Add Rows, Columns, or Sheets

The /Worksheet Insert command adds blank rows, columns, or sheets to a worksheet. The addition of sheets works a little differently from the addition of rows and columns. Adding rows and columns is a little like cutting rows and columns from the end of the sheet and pasting them back at another location, since the full complement of both rows and columns are in a sheet from the beginning. With sheets, only the first sheet is part of a new worksheet file. Subsequent sheets must be added before or after the first sheet up to a total of 256 sheets.

You can use inserted rows and columns to add a heading for a report, or to include new or unexpected information. Adding blank rows and columns can also improve your worksheet design by making it more readable. Adding sheets offers an opportunity for restructuring your entire worksheet. You might choose to use a sheet for each product line or department. You can also store tables and macros on separate sheets from the main model components.

The /Worksheet Insert command is position-dependent, in that rows and columns can be added at the cell pointer location if you position it before entering the command. New sheets can be added before or after the current sheet.

Inserting Rows and Columns

With rows and columns you need not make a second menu choice to indicate the position of the new row or column. Position your cell pointer in the *column to the right* of where you wish to insert, or in the *row below* where you wish to insert. 1-2-3 always inserts columns to the left of the cell pointer, and rows above the cell pointer. After you enter **/Worksheet Insert**, 1-2-3 will ask whether you want to add rows, columns, or sheets. Make the appropriate selection. 1-2-3 will then ask for the range you wish to insert, if you have chosen row or column. You can expand your cell pointer across columns or down rows, covering the number of rows or columns you wish to insert. If you forget to position your cell pointer prior to entering the command, you can always type in the range, or use ESC to free the beginning of the range so you can move it.

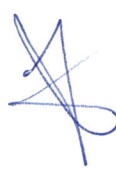

Chapter 4: Changing the Appearance of the Worksheet Display

Release 3.4 provides icons, found in the third icon palette, for inserting rows or columns. The icon for inserting rows looks like this:

If you select a single cell and click this icon, a blank row is inserted above the selected cell. If you select several cells in the same column and click this icon, the number of blank rows will be equal to the number of cells selected in one column.

The icon for inserting columns looks like this:

If a single cell in a column is selected before clicking the icon, one column is inserted to the left of the selected cell. If multiple cells across a row are selected, the number of columns inserted will be equal to the number of columns in the selected range.

REMEMBER: You can also select the SmartIcons by pressing CTRL-F10, *highlighting the icon with the* ARROW *keys, and pressing* ENTER.

Figure 4-2 presents a worksheet that needs the insertion of additional blank spaces to improve its appearance. To make the insertions, move the cell pointer to A1 to insert blank columns to the left, enter **/Worksheet Insert Column**, and then move the cell pointer to expand the range to B1. When you press ENTER, two new columns will be inserted to the left of column A. Next, enter **/Worksheet Insert Row**. Move the cell pointer down three rows and press ENTER to add four rows. The final version of the worksheet, after the insertion of both rows and columns, is shown in Figure 4-3.

When rows, columns, or sheets are inserted in the middle of a range, the range is automatically expanded to allow for the insertions. This applies to range names that have been assigned, and to ranges used in formulas. For example, Figure 4-2 shows an @SUM formula for departmental expenses. When two additional rows are inserted in the middle of the range, as shown in Figure 4-4, the formula is automatically adjusted to include two extra cells so cell F19 contains formula @SUM (F7..F18).

When insertions are made before the first entry or after the last entry, no adjustment is made to the range. Whenever you wish to expand a range, therefore, pick a spot somewhere in the middle for your insertion.

Inserting Sheets

Each new worksheet file automatically provides sheet A. If you were to use the /Worksheet Window Perspective command (described later in this chapter), you

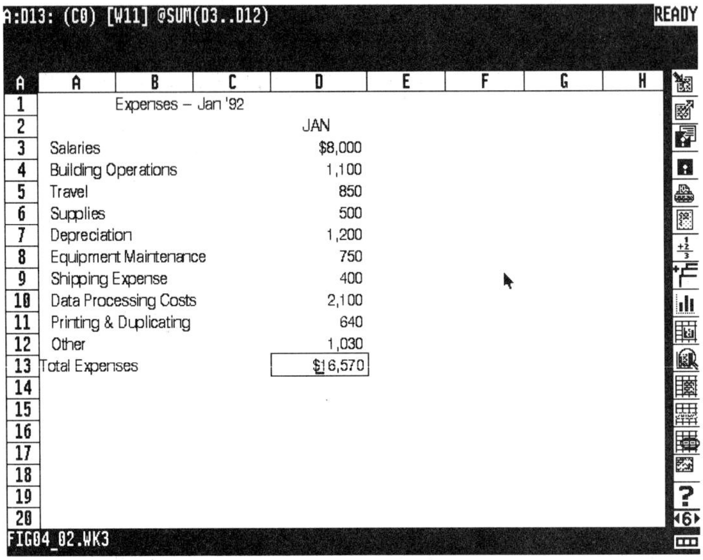

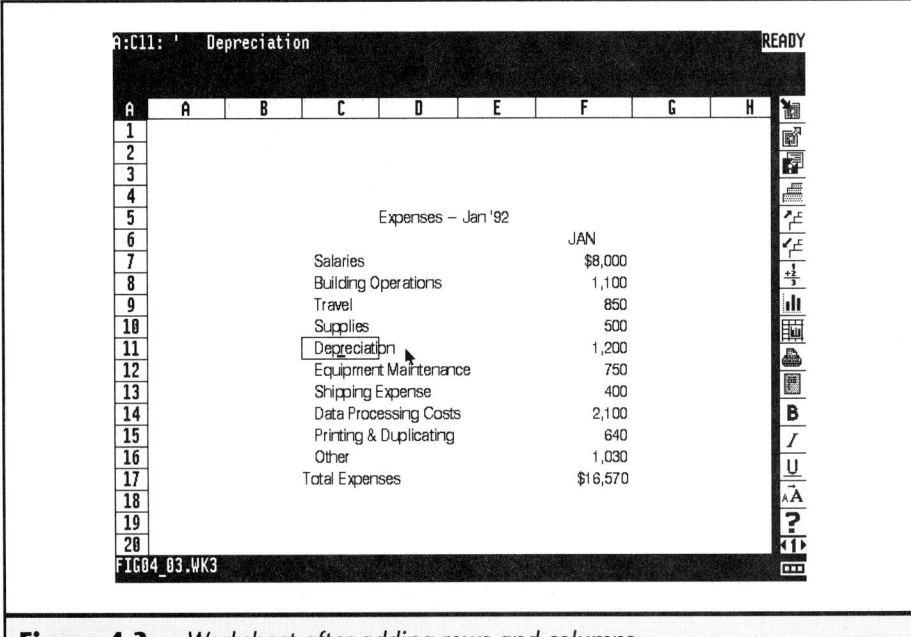

Figure 4-2. Sample worksheet

Figure 4-3. Worksheet after adding rows and columns

Chapter 4: Changing the Appearance of the Worksheet Display

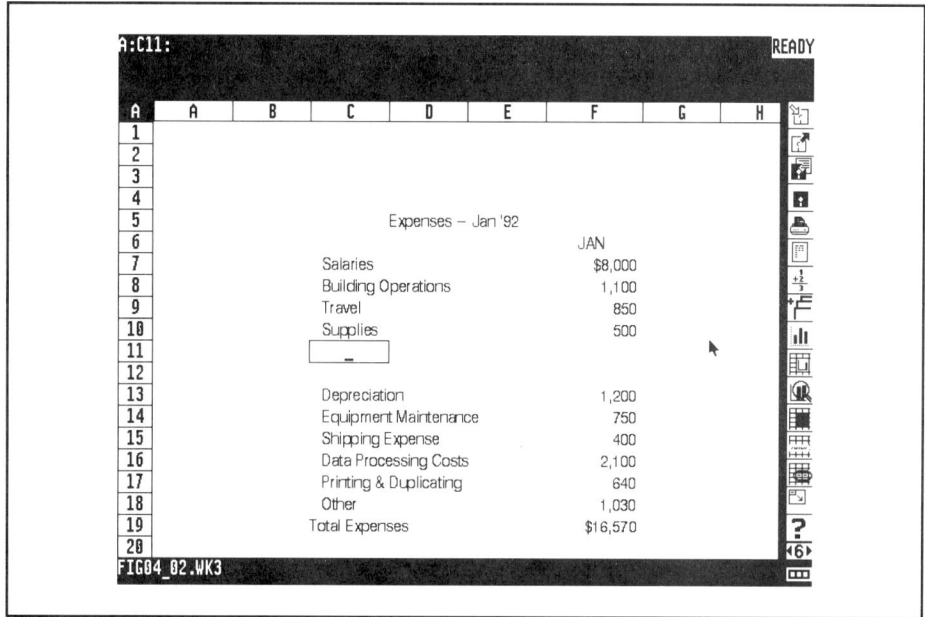

Figure 4-4. *Worksheet after adding two rows*

would see a perspective view of three sheets—but only the first would contain a sheet, as shown in Figure 4-5.

To expand the file to contain multiple sheets using the menu, choose /Worksheet Insert Sheet. The next step is deciding whether the new sheets should be inserted before or after the current sheet. 1-2-3 prompts for the number of sheets to insert.

To insert two sheets after sheet A, enter **/Worksheet Insert Sheet After**. Type a **2** in response to the prompt for the number of sheets to insert. The perspective window will change to match Figure 4-6. Notice that the cell pointer is positioned in the first new sheet (level B). If you want to add a new sheet before sheet A, you first need to move to sheet A with CTRL-PGDN. Next, enter **/Worksheet Insert Sheet Before** and type a **1** in response to the prompt for number of sheets.

With Release 3.4's SmartIcons, you can insert a single sheet (which will be behind the current worksheet) by selecting the insert sheet SmartIcon shown below.

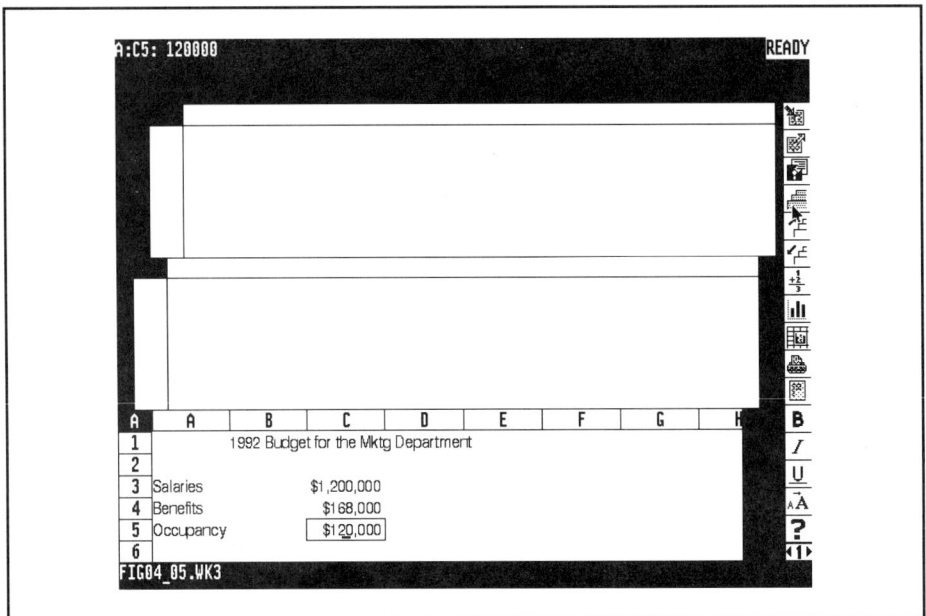

Figure 4-5. A perspective window for a file with only one sheet

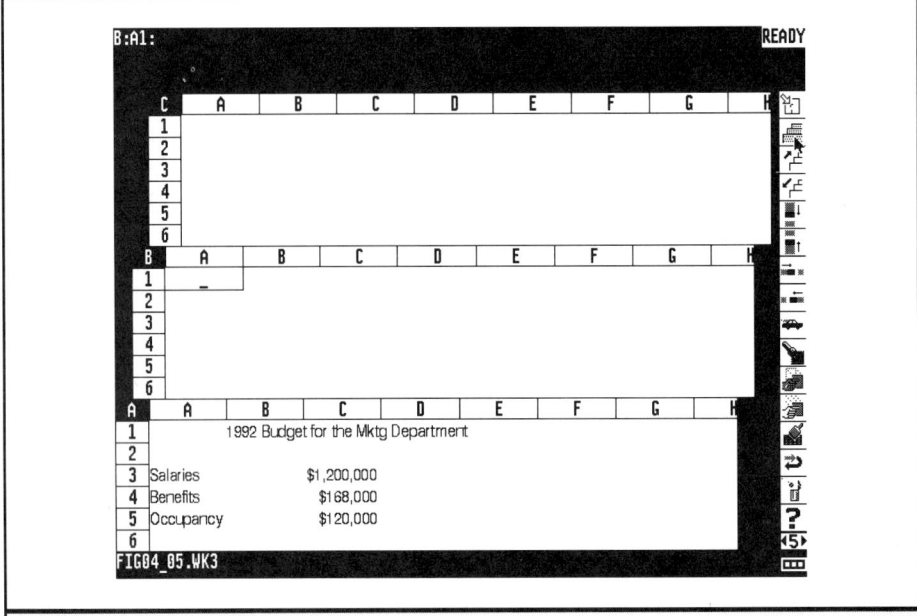

Figure 4-6. Worksheet after adding two sheets after the current one

Deleting Rows, Columns, or Sheets

1-2-3 also provides a command that will delete complete rows, columns, or sheets that are no longer required. Just as with the Insert command, it is easiest to use the Delete command when you position your cell pointer prior to execution. If you are deleting rows, place the cell pointer in the uppermost row to be deleted. If you are deleting columns, the cell pointer should be in the leftmost column to be deleted. If you are deleting sheets you should have the pointer in the first sheet you wish to delete. Note that protected cells cannot be deleted when worksheet protection is enabled.

The rows, columns, or sheets deleted can be blank, or they can contain worksheet data, including formulas. When deleting rows or columns, be sure that the formulas and data in them are not referenced by other worksheet cells. If such references exist, incorrect data may be referenced after the deletion, or an error condition may occur if the new cells are no longer numeric. Figure 4-7 shows the change in a formula when a critical column is accidentally deleted. Before making large-scale deletions, you will want to save your worksheet to disk or make sure that the Undo command is enabled. (To enable Undo when it is off, enter **/Worksheet Global Default Other Undo Enable**.)

Figure 4-8 presents a worksheet with extraneous blank columns in locations A through C. To delete these columns, move the cell pointer to A1 and enter **/Worksheet Delete Column**. Extend the cell pointer to column C by pressing RIGHT ARROW twice, and then pressing ENTER. All three columns are deleted with this one command.

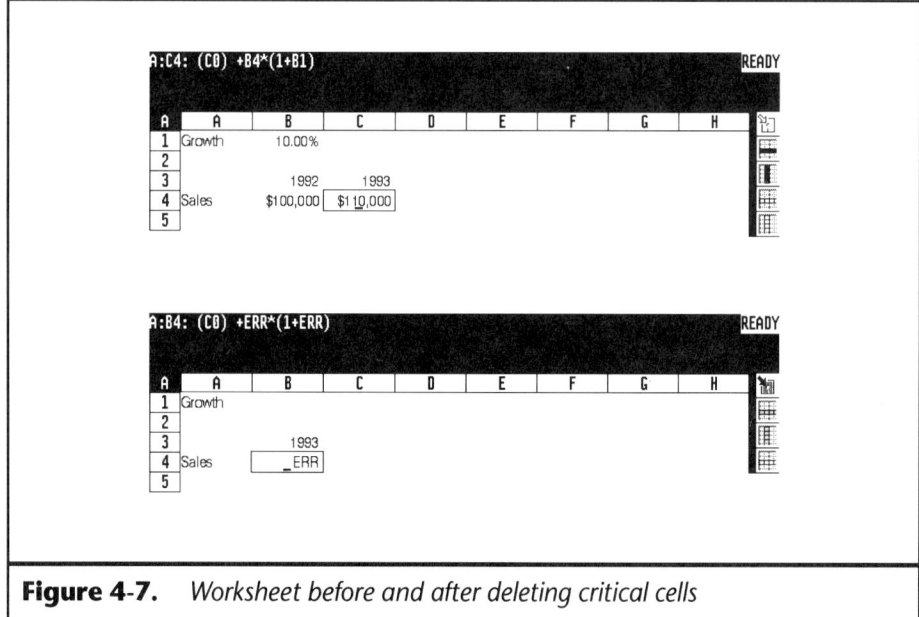

Figure 4-7. Worksheet before and after deleting critical cells

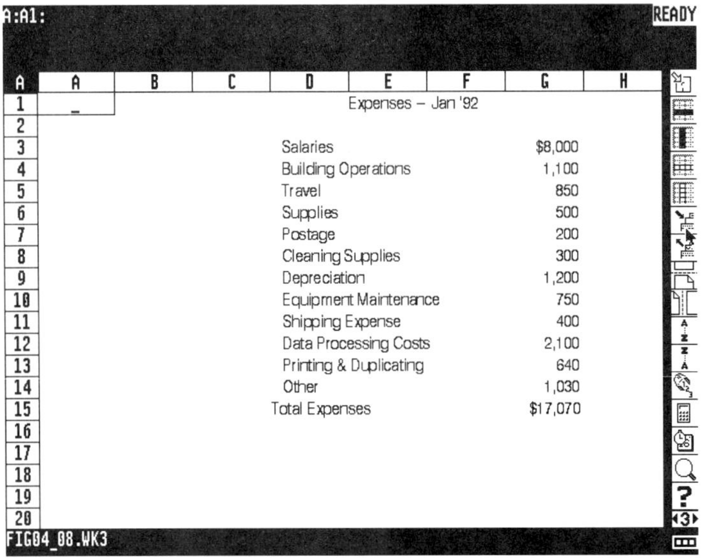

```
A:A1:                                                    READY

    A       B      C      D       E         F       G      H
 1                              Expenses – Jan '92
 2
 3                          Salaries                    $8,000
 4                          Building Operations          1,100
 5                          Travel                         850
 6                          Supplies                       500
 7                          Postage                        200
 8                          Cleaning Supplies              300
 9                          Depreciation                 1,200
10                          Equipment Maintenance          750
11                          Shipping Expense               400
12                          Data Processing Costs        2,100
13                          Printing & Duplicating         640
14                          Other                        1,030
15                          Total Expenses             $17,070
16
17
18
19
20
FIG04_08.WK3
```

Figure 4-8.   *Worksheet with extra columns*

Deleting rows is just as easy. For example, you can delete the row containing the building operations expense in row 4. Move the cell pointer to that row, enter **/Worksheet Delete Row**, and press ENTER to delete just that one row. The altered worksheet is shown in Figure 4-9. 1-2-3 is able to adjust the @SUM function, since the deleted row was taken from the middle of the range.

You can delete entire sheets full of entries with the /Worksheet Delete Sheet command. Be cautious; since 1-2-3 does not verify the deletion first, making file backups or the Undo feature are the only recovery means available. After entering the command, specify the range of sheets that you wish to remove.

With Release 3.4 you can delete rows, columns, and sheets with the SmartIcons. You will preselect a cell in one or more rows, columns, or sheets, then select one of the following icons from the third icon palette.

Chapter 4: Changing the Appearance of the Worksheet Display

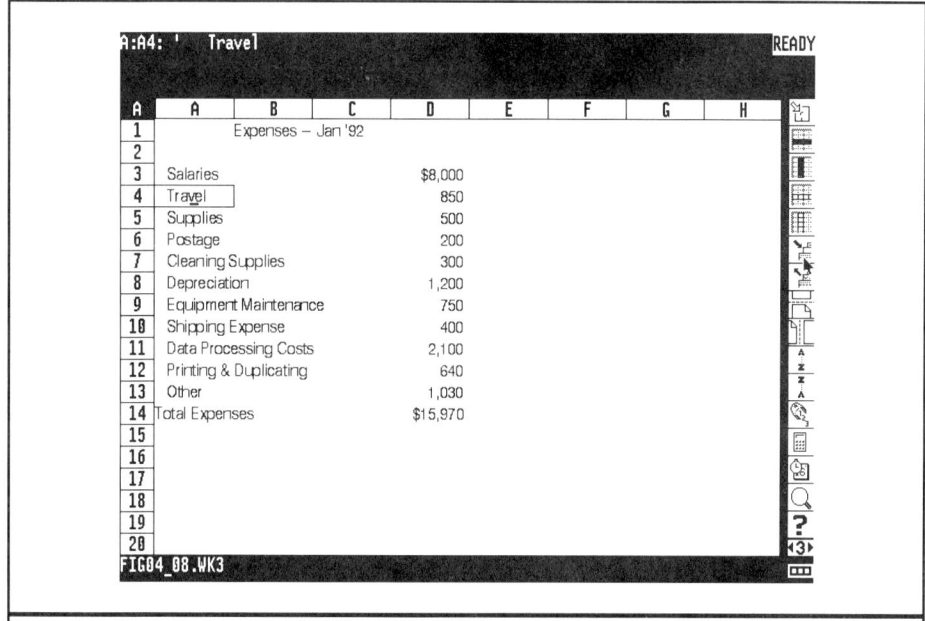

Figure 4-9. *Worksheet after deleting extra row and columns*

TIP: Save the file before deleting entire sheets. Deleting the wrong sheets can quickly destroy an afternoon's work if you have not saved your file. You will want to save your work frequently in case you request the /Worksheet Delete Sheet command by accident.

Window Perspective Command

1-2-3 provides a number of Window commands that allow you to change your view of the worksheet data. One of these commands is covered here so you can learn how to view more than one sheet on the screen at a time. You will be introduced to additional Window options in Chapter 5, "Basic Worksheet Commands."

To view the worksheet with a perspective view of three sheets, shown in some of the earlier examples in this chapter, use /Worksheet Window Perspective. 1-2-3 uses the current sheet as the first sheet, and shows you the two following sheets if they exist. If there are no additional sheets in the file, 1-2-3 still displays three worksheet areas, but only the first area is used.

When working with Release 3.4, you can select this perspective icon from the first or fifth SmartIcons palette, rather than using the menu command to switch to perspective view. Selecting the icon while in perspective view toggles the display back to normal.

If you want a close-up look at the active screen in a perspective view, you can press ALT-F6 (ZOOM). Pressing it a second time returns you to the three-sheet perspective. To eliminate the perspective view and return to a single-sheet view on a permanent basis, use /Worksheet Window Clear.

Column Commands

The /Worksheet Column menu looks like this:

The first two options, Set-Width and Reset-Width, change the width of the column where the cell pointer is located. You will therefore want to position your cell pointer before requesting the command. The Column-Range option also changes the column width, but allows you to affect more than one column at a time. With Column-Range, you also specify whether you want to set or reset width. Instead of assuming the current column is to be changed, 1-2-3 will ask you to specify the affected range.

Set-Width

Every column on a new worksheet is the same width. Unless you change the default width, each column is nine default characters wide. This means that labels with nine characters, or numeric entries with eight digits can be entered in the cell. (Numeric entries are always restricted to one digit less than the cell width.) With Release 3.4, the Wysiwyg add-in is automatically loaded and attached. When Wysiwyg is attached, more characters may appear in a cell than the cell width would suggest, since the default Wysiwyg font is narrower than the default 1-2-3 font. The width of the column, however, is still measured by the width of the characters of the default 1-2-3 font.

When you enter labels that are too long for this width, they are truncated for display if the cells to their right are not empty. If the adjacent cells are empty, 1-2-3 borrows space from them to show the complete label entry. Numbers that are too long are either rounded to fit the cell width or displayed as asterisks, depending on the format in effect for the cell. In earlier releases of 1-2-3 the

Chapter 4: Changing the Appearance of the Worksheet Display

General format truncated numbers without rounding. Release 3 follows these rules governing the General default display of numbers:

- 1-2-3 attempts to display your entry as you enter it.
- If the integer portion of the entry exceeds the cell width, 1-2-3 switches to Scientific notation.
- If the integer portion fits within the cell width but the decimal portion does not, 1-2-3 rounds the value.

Figure 4-10 shows account names that were entered in column A but are too long to display in that column's default width of 9. The entries could be allowed to borrow space from adjacent columns, or column A's width could be changed with Set-Width, so that the entries could be shown in that column. This option is especially useful if you have an entry in column B, and therefore the label in column A is being truncated. First, make sure your cell pointer is in column A. Then invoke the command by entering **/Worksheet Column Set-Width**. Next, you can either enter the desired number of characters and press ENTER; or you can press the RIGHT ARROW and LEFT ARROW keys until the column is the desired width, and press ENTER. The latter method is best, since guessing wrong about the desired number of characters means you have to start over with /Worksheet Column Set-Width. Figure 4-11 shows column A widened to 17 so the long labels fit within the column width.

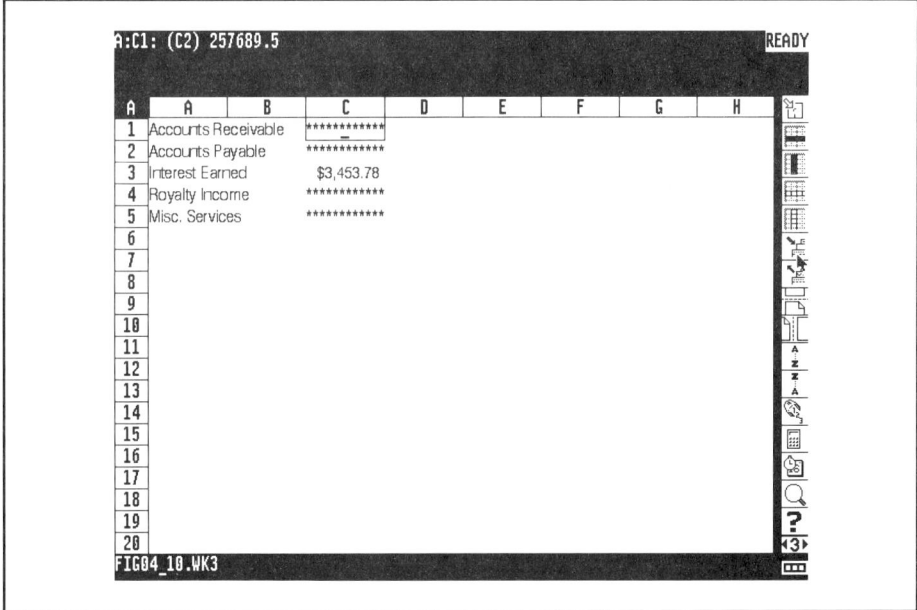

Figure 4-10. *Currency format with entries that will not fit in cell*

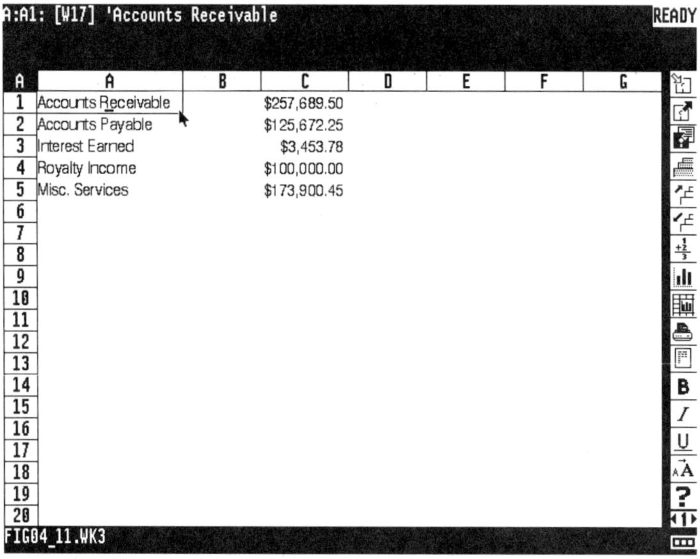

```
A:A1: [W17] 'Accounts Receivable                                    READY

         A              B         C         D      E      F      G
  1  Accounts Receivable      $257,689.50
  2  Accounts Payable         $125,672.25
  3  Interest Earned            $3,453.78
  4  Royalty Income           $100,000.00
  5  Misc. Services           $173,900.45
  6
  7
  8
  9
 10
 11
 12
 13
 14
 15
 16
 17
 18
 19
 20
FIG04_11.WK3
```

Figure 4-11.   *Column C widened to 12 to show numbers*

The Set-Width option can also be used when numbers are too large to display in the default column width. In Figure 4-10, numeric entries were made for the account balances in column C. These cells are formatted as Currency with two decimal places, meaning that 1-2-3 added a $, and a comma after the thousands position. (To produce this format, type **/Range Format Currency**, press ENTER, type **C2..C6**, and press ENTER again.) The asterisks appear in these cells because the values they contain are too large for the cell width once the dollar sign and comma are added to the existing digits. This column can be widened sufficiently by typing **/Worksheet Column Set-Width** and moving the RIGHT ARROW three times before pressing ENTER. Figure 4-11 shows the display after the cells were changed to a width of 12.

When the width of a column is changed with /Worksheet Column Set-Width, that width is conveniently displayed in the control panel for each cell in that column. In other words, if you place your cell pointer on any cell in a column where a special width has been used, you will see the width in brackets in the command line (the top line) of the control panel. For example, [W8] means width 8, [W4] means width 4, and [W25] means width 25. Widths from 1 to 240 can be assigned to any column.

Chapter 4: Changing the Appearance of the Worksheet Display

Reset-Width

Once you have used /Worksheet Column Set-Width to change the width of a column, its width will be different from its neighbors'. If that width ceases to be useful, you can return the column to the global column width with the Reset-Width command. In Figure 4-11, placing the cell pointer in column D and entering **/Worksheet Column Reset-Width** will return the column to a width of 9, causing the asterisks to reappear.

If you are uncertain of the current global width, you can make a quick check by typing **/Worksheet Status**. A display similar to Figure 4-12 will appear, allowing you to review the status information; you can return to your model by pressing ESC to return to READY mode.

Hidden Columns

/Worksheet Column Hide allows you to eliminate individual columns from the display. In effect, it cuts a section of the worksheet temporarily. You can use this option to eliminate confidential or proprietary information from the display. Hidden sections can be restored to the display at any time, since the data has not

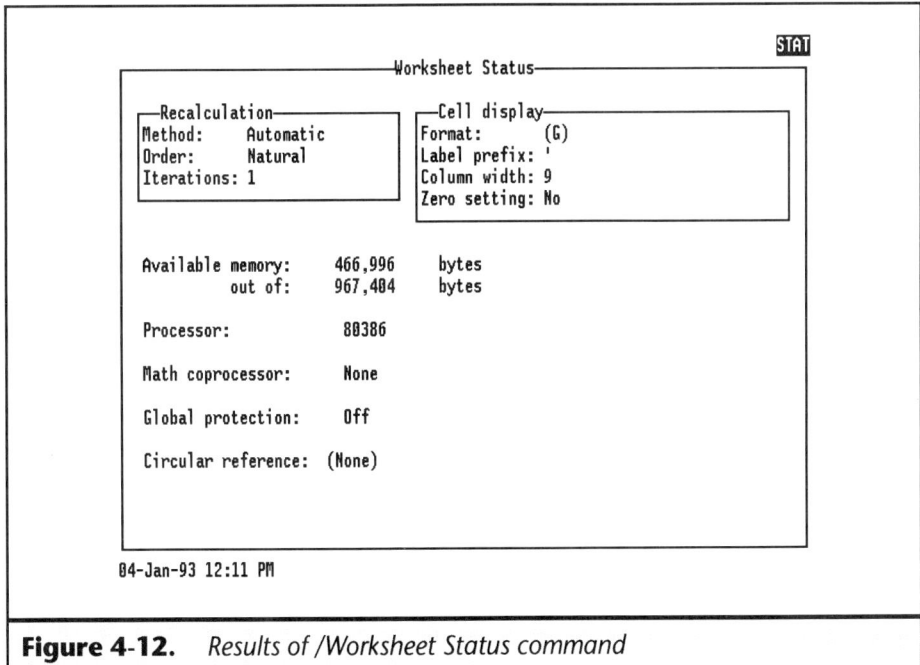

Figure 4-12. *Results of /Worksheet Status command*

been erased. When you press ENTER after typing **/Worksheet Column Hide**, the column where the cell pointer is located will be hidden. You may also use the RIGHT ARROW and LEFT ARROW keys to specify a range of columns before pressing ENTER.

Figure 4-13 shows a worksheet before Hide is invoked. To hide columns C and D, place the cell pointer in column C and type **/Worksheet Column Hide** followed by a decimal point (.), the RIGHT ARROW, and ENTER. The same worksheet will then look like Figure 4-14. Note that columns C and D have disappeared. The data in the two hidden columns can still be accessed in formulas.

TIP: Use /Range Format Hidden to eliminate any range from display, and thus display a group of cells as blank. This allows you to hide the information in a row or rectangle on the worksheet.

The /Worksheet Column Display command redisplays hidden columns. It displays the column letters of the formerly hidden columns with asterisks next to them, as shown in Figure 4-15. After typing the command, you can move the cell pointer to the column you want to redisplay and press ENTER, or you can select a range if you want to redisplay adjacent columns.

Figure 4-13. *Worksheet before hiding columns*

Chapter 4: Changing the Appearance of the Worksheet Display

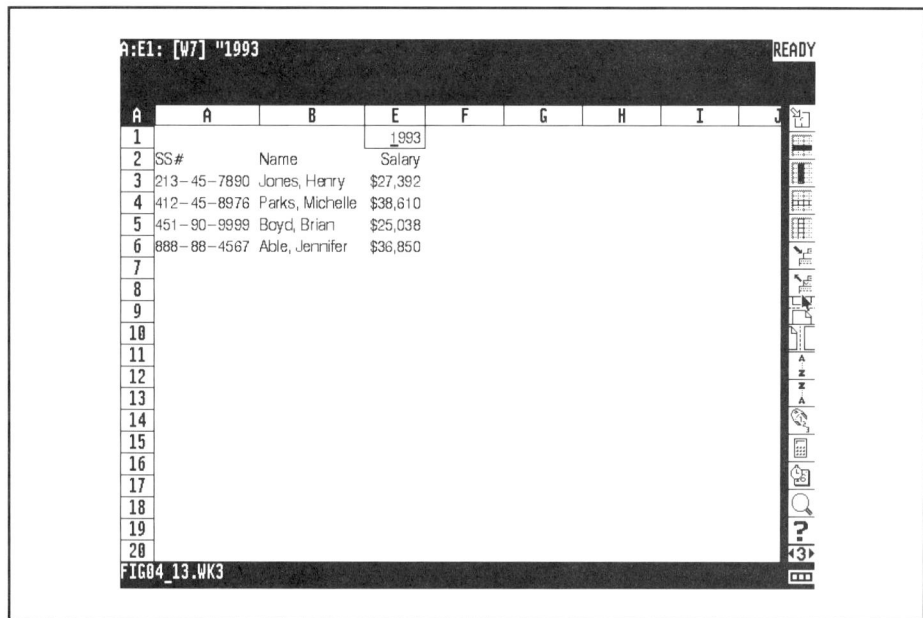

Figure 4-14. Worksheet after hiding columns C and D

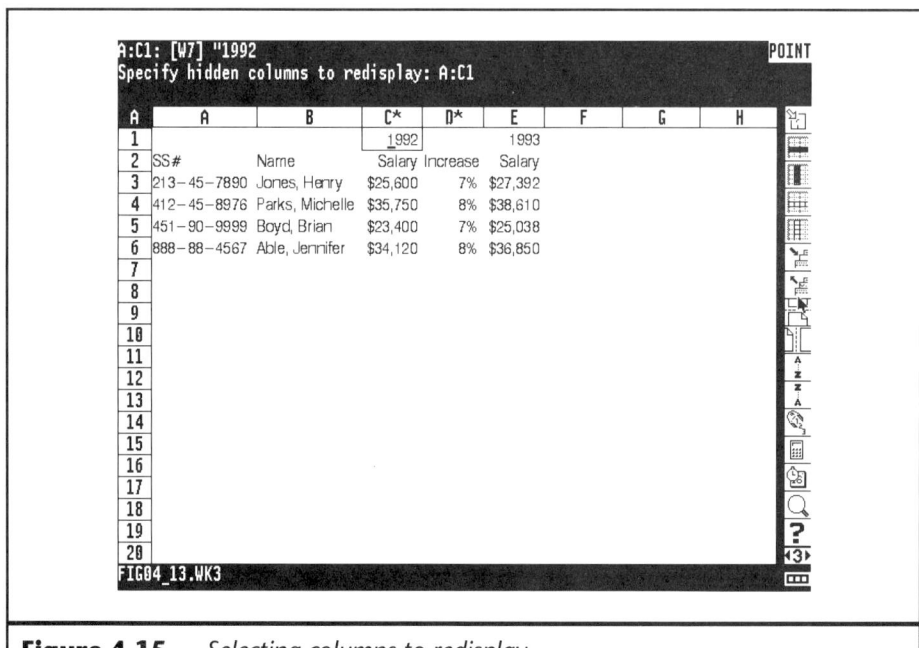

Figure 4-15. Selecting columns to redisplay

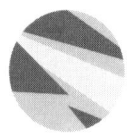

TIP: /Worksheet Column Hide and /Worksheet Delete Column have very different results. When you hide a column it is only eliminated from the display temporarily. When you delete a column, the column and its contents are permanently removed from the worksheet. Other columns are renamed with the letter from the deleted column—but its entries are lost unless you have a retrievable copy of the model on disk.

Column-Range

If you need to change the width of four or five consecutive columns, Column Set-Width or Reset-Width must be executed once for each column that you wish to change. However, Release 3 offers an additional, far more efficient approach: you can use the /Worksheet Column Column-Range command to change multiple columns at one time. Figure 4-16 shows a model where the width of columns D through G was changed to 3. This was accomplished by entering **/Worksheet Column Column-Range Set-Width**, highlighting the columns to change, pressing ENTER, typing a **3**, and pressing ENTER. Using /Worksheet Column Set-Width would have required four separate command entries.

The Reset-Width option resets the column width for the range of affected columns to the default global column width. You can enter **/Worksheet Status** to check the current setting before making a change if you wish.

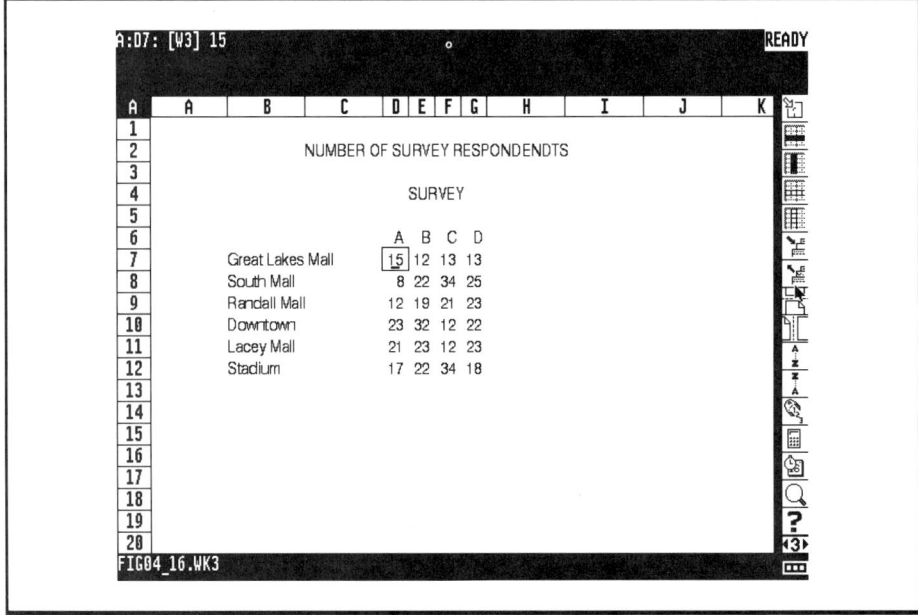

Figure 4-16. Worksheet with columns D, E, F, and G using a width of 3

Hiding Sheets

Release 3 offers the /Worksheet Hide command to allow you to remove sheets from display and then redisplay them. You can use this command for one or more consecutive sheets at once. For example, you may have a worksheet with five sheets (sheets A through E). If you want to work with sheets A, D, and E, moving between them frequently, you will want to hide sheets B and C. To hide sheets B and C, move to sheet B and enter **/Worksheet Hide Enable**. Expand the range to include sheet C by typing a period (.); then press CTRL-PGUP followed by ENTER. Your screen will now display sheets A, D, and E, as shown in Figure 4-17. Once sheets are hidden, you cannot move the cell pointer to them, even with the F5 (GOTO) key.

The /Worksheet Hide command is also a good option when you want to eliminate confidential or proprietary data from view. An alternative measure is to use /Worksheet Global Format Hidden to hide all the data on a worksheet. When you want to display the hidden sheets, select /Worksheet Hide Disable and select a range containing the sheets to display.

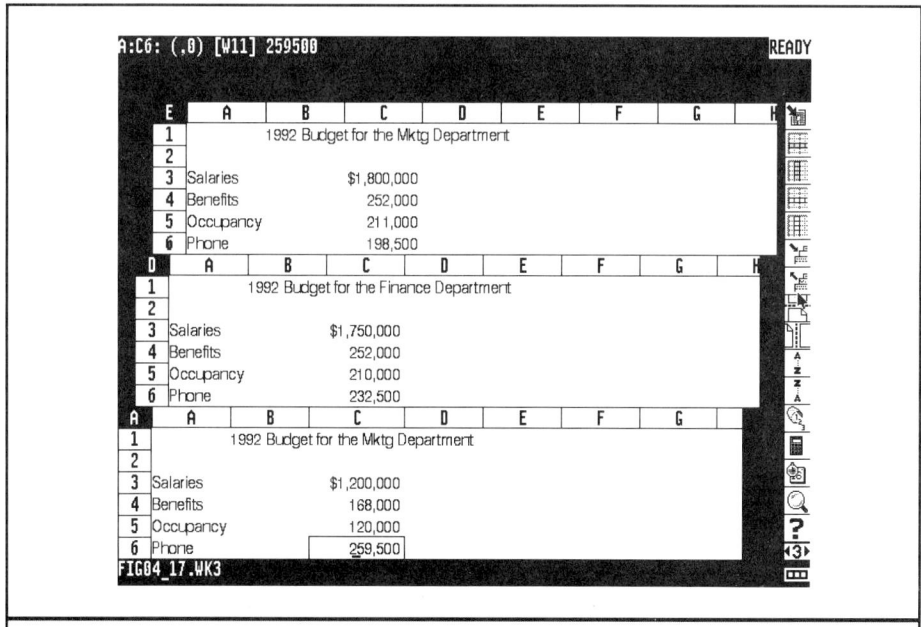

Figure 4-17. *Worksheet file after hiding sheets*

Global Commands

Global commands affect the entire worksheet. Every row, every column, and every cell in each row and column are affected by the changes you make with the /Worksheet Global command options, although most of the Global options will affect only numeric cell entries. When you invoke GROUP mode first, the global change affects not only every cell in the current sheet but every sheet in the current file. The options available under the Global menu are shown here:

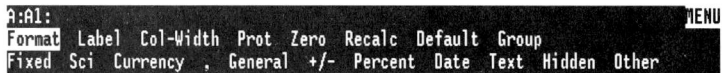

In this chapter you will have the opportunity to use Col-Width, Format, Zero, and Default. Additional Global options will be described in Chapter 5, "Basic Worksheet Commands."

Column-Width

Changing the column width for the entire worksheet with the /Worksheet Column option would take much too long. You could use /Worksheet Column Column-Range, but if you want to affect every column, it is more efficient to use a global change. In addition, a global change will be documented on the status screen, so it is easy to see the width that is currently selected. 1-2-3 allows you to change the width of every column on the worksheet with one command: /Worksheet Global Col-Width. With this option you can make all the columns on your worksheet any width from 1 to 240, instead of the default setting of 9 positions.

Since this command will affect the entire worksheet, there is no need to position your cell pointer before invoking it. The example in Figure 4-18 shows columns of numbers, all of which contain fewer than the default setting of 9 positions. Shrinking the size of the columns would allow you to display more information on the sheet. By typing **/Worksheet Global Col-Width 5** and pressing ENTER, you could change the display to match the one shown in Figure 4-19.

The /Worksheet Column command takes precedence over the Global Col-Width command. You could use both commands if you had a worksheet where all but one column could be narrow. /Worksheet Global Col-Width could set the narrow width for the entire worksheet. You would then move your cell pointer to the column requiring the wider width, type **/Worksheet Col Set-Width**, and specify the wider width needed for that column only.

Chapter 4: Changing the Appearance of the Worksheet Display

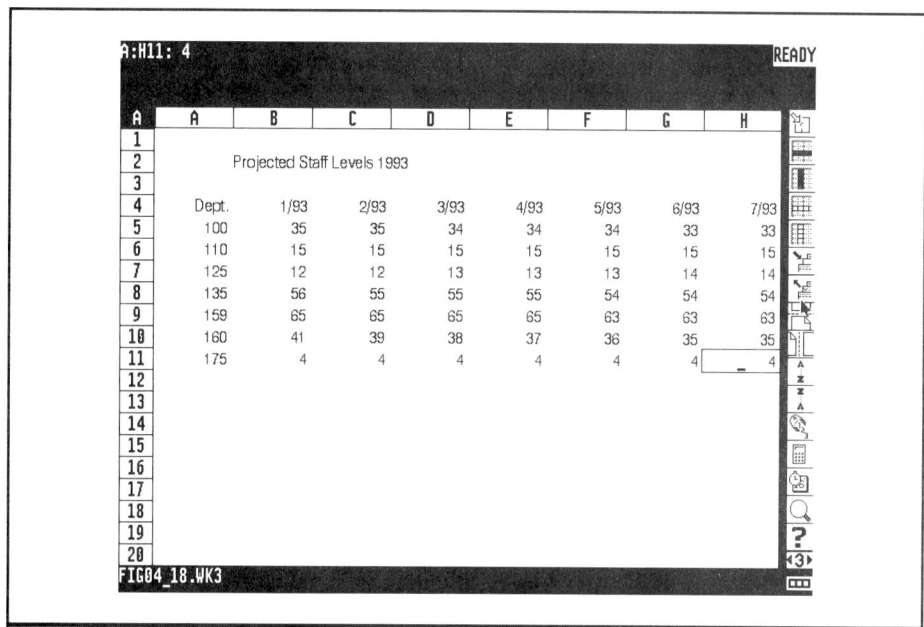

Figure 4-18. Worksheet using a default column width of 9

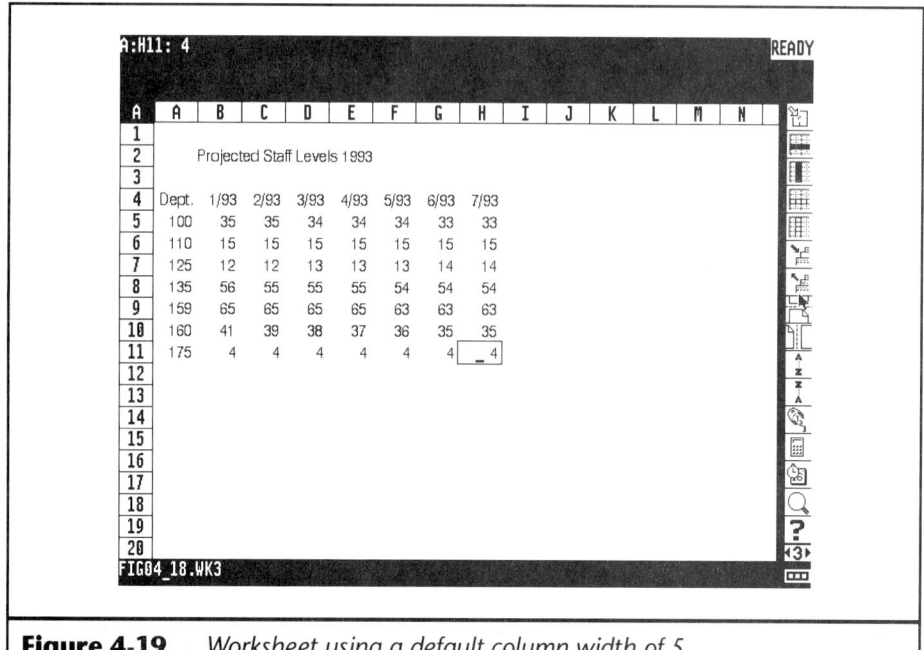

Figure 4-19. Worksheet using a default column width of 5

Format

Format can also be changed on a global basis. The default setting is General format, but if you want all your entries to be in Currency, Percent, Scientific, or any of the other available formats, every worksheet cell can be reformatted with the /Worksheet Global Format command and the format specification of your choice. Figure 4-20 displays a worksheet created with the General format setting. The appearance of this worksheet can be markedly improved by use of a single command, /Worksheet Global Format Currency. After the initial command sequence, type **0** to indicate zero decimal places and press ENTER. The newly formatted worksheet looks like Figure 4-21.

Any one of the options listed in the "Format Options" box can be used. Some formats require more worksheet space than others, however. If the display turns to asterisks when you change your format, you will have to widen your columns to accommodate the new format. As you will learn later in the chapter, a /Range Format command always takes precedence over a /Worksheet Global Format change.

Using the GROUP mode while making a formatting change causes the change to affect all sheets in the active file. If you choose Currency in the active sheet, all the sheets in the current file will have a format of Currency. Sheets added to the file at a later time will automatically assume the characteristics of

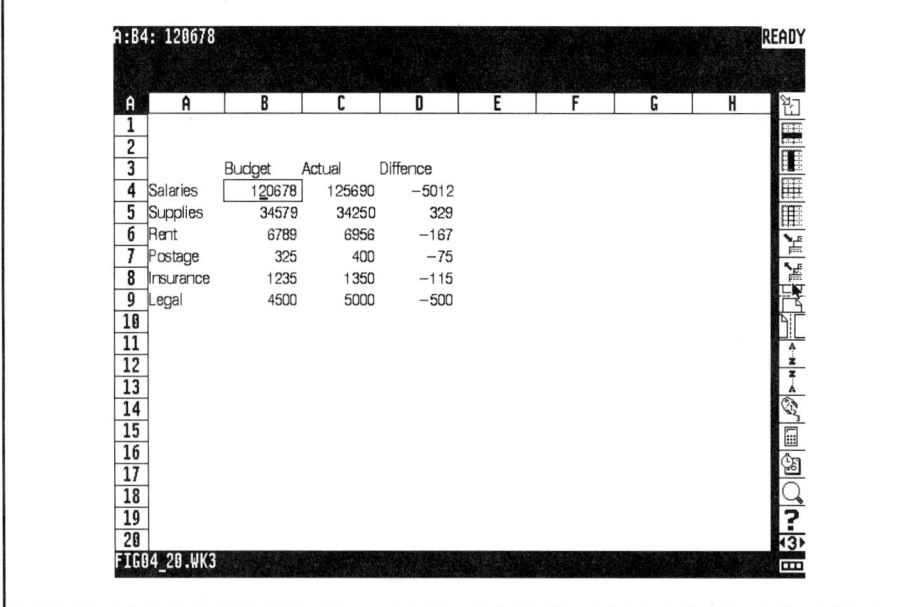

Figure 4-20. *Worksheet using the General format*

Chapter 4: Changing the Appearance of the Worksheet Display

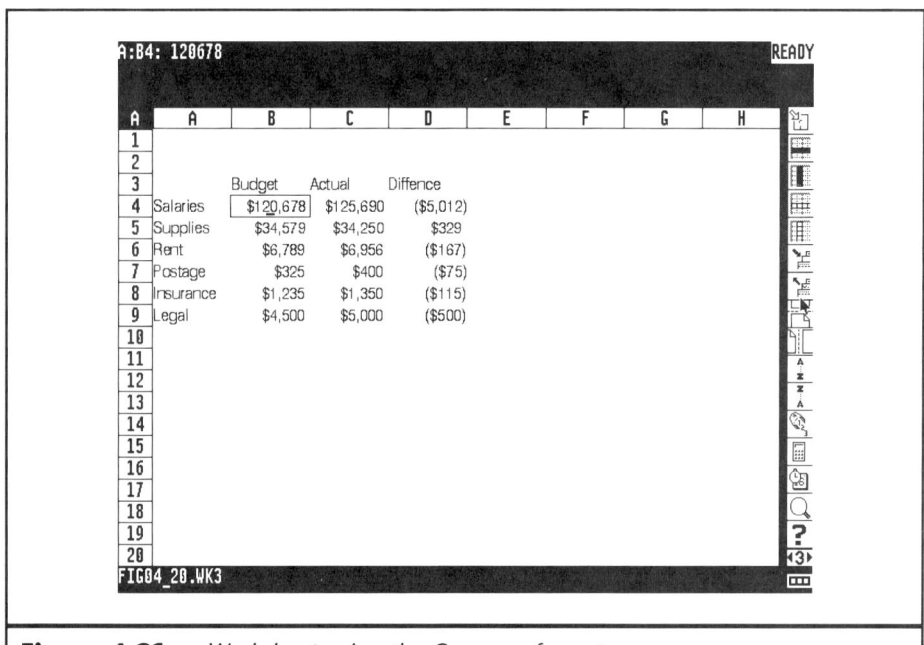

Figure 4-21. *Worksheet using the Currency format*

the existing sheets. Also when you first invoke GROUP mode, the format, column width, and zero suppression characteristics of the active sheet affect all the sheets in the file.

Zero Display

You can choose how zero values are displayed on the worksheet. In the past, a zero value always resulted in a cell containing a 0. The zero value options in Release 3 can hide zero values, display zero values, or display a label in every zero location on the worksheet. The zero values remain the same, as they can be referenced for calculations; but any cell with a zero value can appear, be hidden, or appear as a label.

To suppress the display of zeros on the worksheet, use /Worksheet Global Zero Yes. To restore the display, use /Worksheet Global Zero No. To display the zero values as labels, use /Worksheet Global Zero Label and enter a label to display in place of zero values. The label will be right aligned unless you provide it with a different alignment prefix character.

Figure 4-22 shows a worksheet with the Zero option set to Yes; Figure 4-23 shows the same worksheet with Zero set to Label, and "None" as the label.

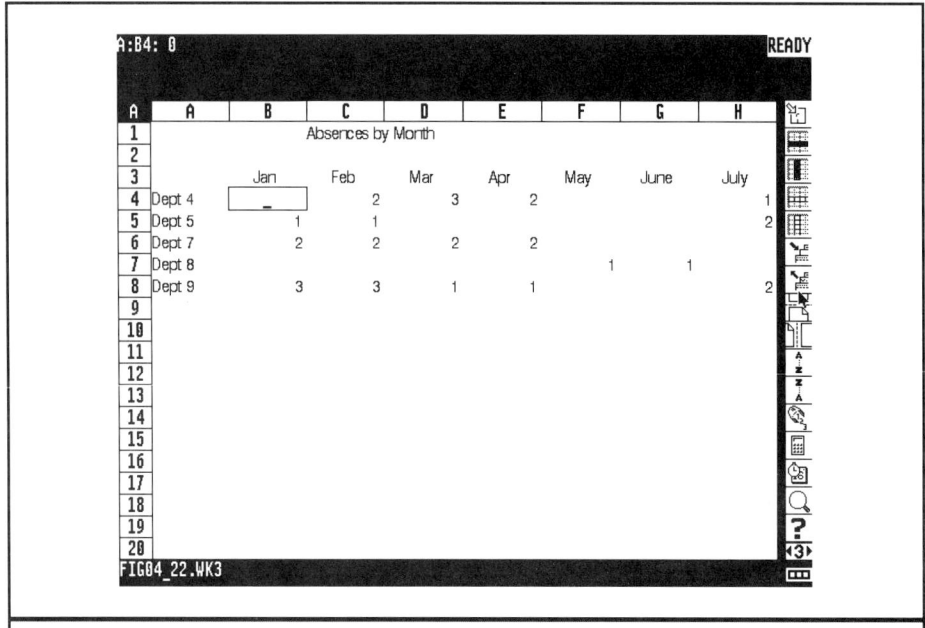

Figure 4-22. *Hiding zeros*

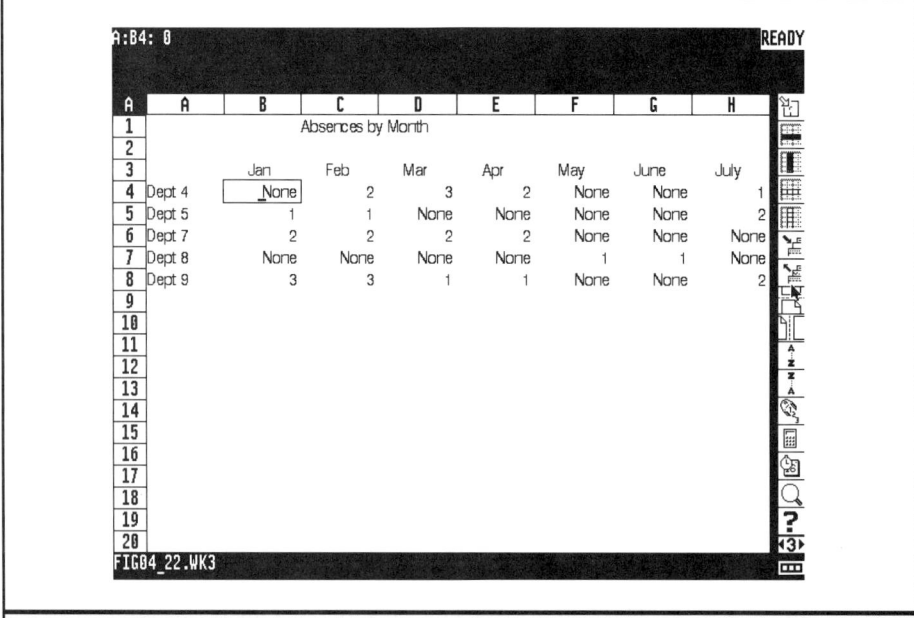

Figure 4-23. *Displaying labels instead of zeros*

Chapter 4: Changing the Appearance of the Worksheet Display

Format Options

This table provides a quick reference to the formatting features offered by 1-2-3.

Format	Entry	Display
Fixed 2 decimal places	5678 –123.45	5678.00 –123.45
Scientific 2 decimal places	5678 –123.45	5.68E+03 –1.23E+02
Currency 2 decimal places	5678 –123.45	$5,678.00 ($123.45)
, (Comma) 2 decimal places	5678 –123.45	5,678.00 (123.45)
General	5678 –123.45	5678 –123.45
+/–	4 –3 0	++++ – – – .
Percent 0 decimal places	5 .1	500% 10%
Date (D1)	31679	24-Sep-86
Time (T1)	.5	12:00:00 PM
Text	+A2*A3	+A2*A3
Other Automatic	$5 15-Aug-92	$5 15-Aug-92
Other Color Negative	–17	**–17***
Other Parentheses with Currency	–5	(–$5)
Other Label	123r7	'123r7

* The display is in color on a color monitor and in boldface on a monochrome monitor.

TIP: *Zeros may still appear in a worksheet, even when Global Zero is suppressing zeros or displaying them as labels. The worksheet will display zeros if it contains cells that appear as zero due to the cell's format. To convert these values to actual zeros, use the @ROUND function covered in Chapter 7, "1-2-3's Built-In Functions."*

Range Format Commands

Range format changes do just what their name implies: they change the format for a specified range of cells on the worksheet. Any of the valid ranges described in Chapter 3, "Entering Data in 1-2-3's Worksheet," can be affected. The range can be as small as one cell, or it can be a rectangle of cells on one or many sheets.

You can use /Range Format to change the format of any range from the current format setting. Any of the options in the Format Options box can be chosen.

If you preselect a range you can use the SmartIcons to apply a few numeric formats to the selected range. Currency, percent, and comma formats are available on the predefined palettes. Table 4-1 shows the numeric formats that are selectable from 1-2-3's predefined icon palettes, what they do, and the palette that you can use to select them.

Cells in the current selection that are already formatted in the same format as the icon will be reset to the global format setting. The cells will be reset if the format matches, even if the number of decimal places does not match. For example, if the cells you select are currently formatted as currency and you choose the % icon, they will be formatted as percent with two decimal places. If the cells are formatted as percent with one decimal place, they will be reset to the current global format, just as if you had selected /Range Reset for the cells.

TIP: Plan your format layout as you plan your worksheet design. You will not create well-designed models without adequate planning. As you lay out a worksheet design on paper, add color highlighting or some other indication of the formats you want to use. You can make the format changes as a first step in the model creation process.

Icon	Effect	Palette Number
$	Currency with 2 decimals	2
0,0	Comma for thousands separator with 0 decimals	2
%	Percent with 2 decimals	2

Table 4-1. *Numeric Format Palettes*

Chapter 4: Changing the Appearance of the Worksheet Display

Let's look at an example of the /Range Format command in action. The worksheet shown in Figure 4-24 has three different types of entries. Two of these worksheet entries have already been formatted, and one is in the process of being changed. To change the format of these cells, follow these steps:

1. Move your cell pointer to the upper leftmost cell in the range you wish to format. Placing the cell pointer in this location will allow you to specify the range using only the arrow keys.

2. Type **/Range Format**.

3. Select the Percent format from the menu, either by typing **P** or by pointing and pressing ENTER.

4. If the format requires a certain number of decimal places, either press ENTER to accept the default of two places, or enter the desired number of decimal places and then press ENTER. In our example, 1 was entered to replace the default.

5. 1-2-3 will request the range to format. Specify the range by using the RIGHT ARROW and DOWN ARROW keys to move to the lower rightmost cell you wish to format. If you are formatting just one cell, do not move the cell pointer. After all the cells to be formatted are highlighted, press ENTER, and they will be displayed with the new format. The worksheet will then look like Figure 4-25.

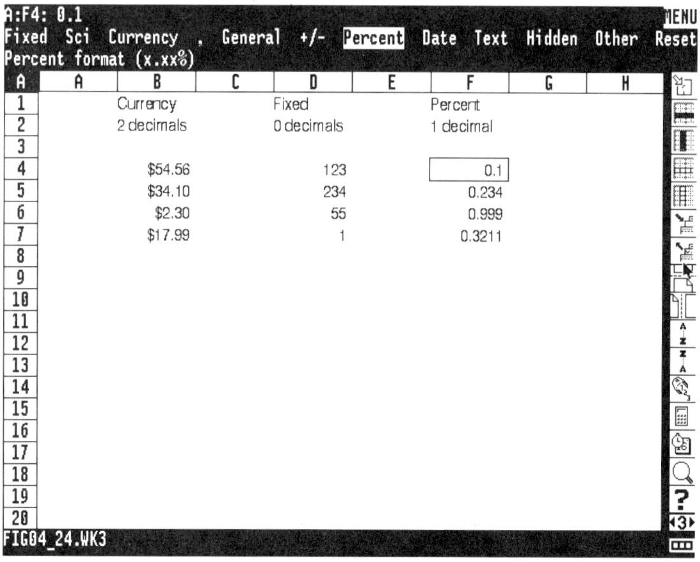

Figure 4-24. Worksheet with numbers in different formats

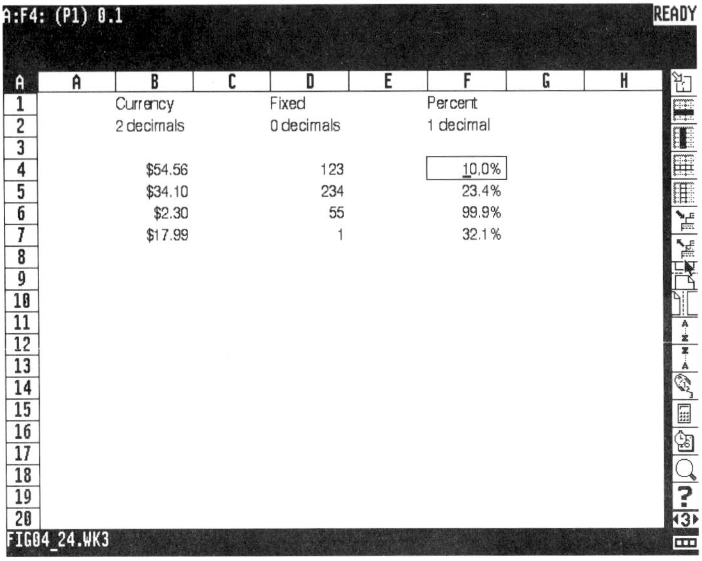

```
A:F4: (P1) 0.1                                              READY

     A         B         C         D         E         F         G         H
 1             Currency            Fixed               Percent
 2             2 decimals          0 decimals          1 decimal
 3
 4             $54.56              123                 10.0%
 5             $34.10              234                 23.4%
 6             $2.30               55                  99.9%
 7             $17.99              1                   32.1%
 8
 9
10
11
12
13
14
15
16
17
18
19
20
FIG04_24.WK3
```

Figure 4-25.   *Formatting Percent numbers*

Just as with /Worksheet Global Format changes, changes in format for a range of cells do not affect the internal storage accuracy of your numbers and calculated results. Suppose you decide to display an entry with no decimal places, but internally six or more places are stored. When that cell is used in a calculation, the full internal accuracy will be applied, because 1-2-3 maintains entries with an accuracy of approximately 18 decimal digits. Later, in Chapter 7, "1-2-3's Built-in Functions," you will learn a way to change the internal accuracy as well.

/Range Format commands always take priority over /Worksheet Global Format commands. You can use this fact to your advantage. Before constructing a new worksheet, plan its design. Determine which format will be used more than any other, and use /Worksheet Global Format to establish this format. Then, where necessary, use /Range Format commands to alter the format of individual cells or ranges.

The /Range Format commands have a feature that is not found in /Worksheet Global Format commands. Once a cell has been formatted with a /Range command, the top line in the control panel will show the format for the cell. (F2) means Fixed with two decimal places, (C0) means Currency with zero decimal places, and so on.

You can use the /Range Format commands with multiple sheet files in two ways. First, with the GROUP mode option, you can choose to make a format change on the current sheet and have it apply to every sheet in the file. Second, you can leave GROUP mode turned off and specify a range that spans sheets. In this second case, you might choose to format cells F2..H25 as Currency on sheets B, C, and D, by entering the range **B:F2..D:H25** in response to the prompt.

Using SmartIcons to Change the Numeric Format

You can change a worksheet quickly with the icon palettes if they happen to match your needs. If you are working with the worksheet shown in Figure 4-22, you will have an opportunity to use the three numeric format icons on the second palette. You can follow these steps to make the changes in Figure 4-26:

1. Move the cell pointer to B6, press F4, select B6..B9 as the range, and then press ENTER.

    You can also use the mouse to select the cells.

2. First make icon palette 2 active by clicking the arrows to the right of the palette number, and then select the icon to format with the thousands separator and zero decimal places (this is the icon with a comma and two zeros on it).

3. Select the range C6..C9, and then click the currency icon.

4. Select the range D6..D9, and then select the % icon.

    Your model will now match Figure 4-27.

Numeric Format Options

Each of the format options in this section, with the exception of Reset, can be used with either the /Worksheet Global Format or the /Range Format command. Since Reset is used to reverse a /Range Format command by changing the range back to the global setting, this option is not needed on the Worksheet Global Format menu. The following format options are summarized for you in the "Format Options" box shown earlier in the chapter.

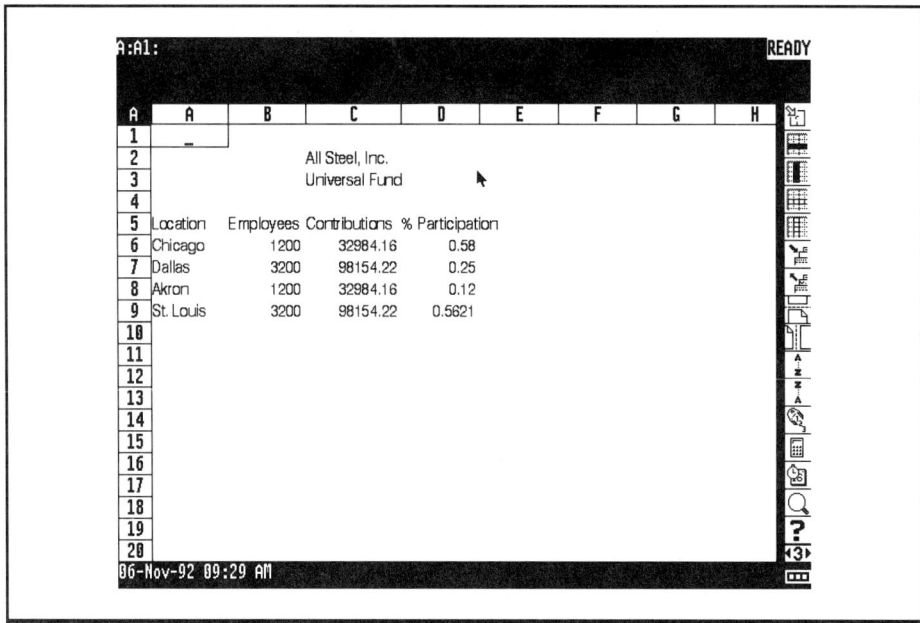

Figure 4-26. *Selected range to use for formatting*

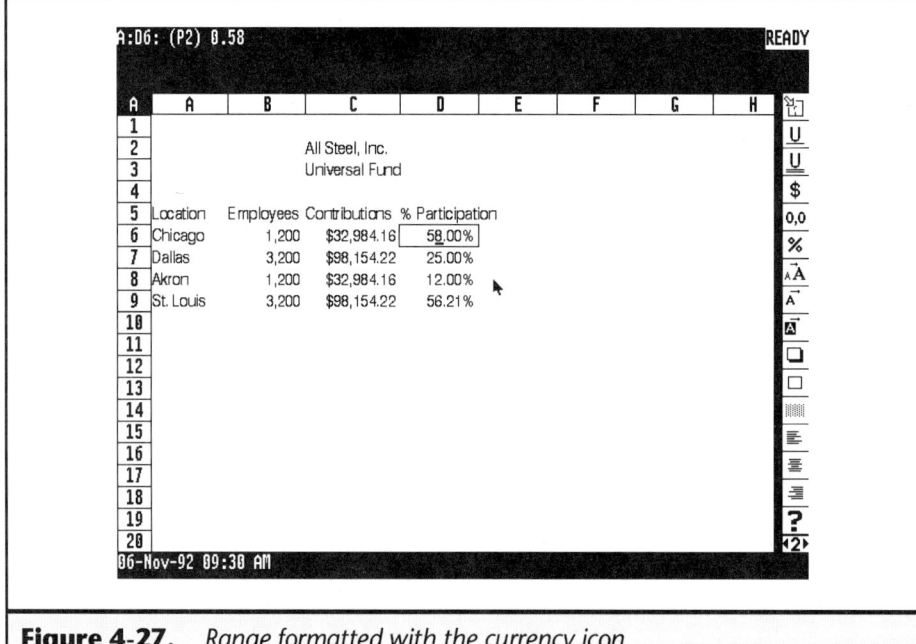

Figure 4-27. *Range formatted with the currency icon*

Fixed Format

The Fixed format lets you choose the number of places to the right of the decimal point that you wish to display. Like General format, it does not display dollar signs or commas.

If you use the Fixed format option and the numbers you enter or calculate with formulas do not contain a sufficient number of decimal places, zeros will be added. For example, if you enter **5.67** in a cell that you formatted as Fixed with four decimal places, your entry will display as 5.6700. The zeros used for padding are always added to the right. With Fixed format you may select from 0 to 15 decimal places. If the column is not wide enough, asterisks will appear. Leading zero integers are always added for decimal fraction numbers.

If, conversely, you enter or calculate numbers with more decimal places than have been specified, they will be rounded to the appropriate number of decimal places. Any number of 5 or above will be rounded upwards by 1-2-3. The following table may help you remember the action 1-2-3 will take in various circumstances.

Entry	Fixed 0	Fixed 2	Fixed 4
7.23	7	7.23	7.2300
8.54	9	8.54	8.5400
3.5674	4	3.57	3.5674
.98	1	0.98	0.9800

After you apply a Fixed format to a range of cells, the control panel will display an indicator like (F0), (F2), or (F4). The number following the F (for Fixed) is the number of decimal places that you specified for your display.

The Fixed format option presents an appealing display when cells have many decimal numbers. This format is particularly useful when these decimal numbers are the result of formulas, since it permits numbers to be displayed with the decimals aligned, which General format does not.

Scientific Format

This format displays numbers in exponential notation. This option appears as Sci in the menu. You can choose from 0 to 15 decimal places in the first, or multiplier, portion of the expression.

The following table shows entries as they are made in a worksheet cell, and the display that results when each of several Scientific decimal settings is established for the multiplier.

Entry	Scientific 0	Scientific 2	Scientific 4
100550000	1E+08	1.01E+08	1.0055E+08
7896543	8E+06	7.90E+06	7.8965E+06
.00005678	6E–05	5.68E–05	5.6780E–05

The indicator for Scientific when the /Range Format command is used is an S combined with the number of decimals. It is displayed within parentheses in the same way the Fixed format indicator was. Thus, you will see (S0), (S2), (S4), and so on.

Scientific notation is useful when you need to display very large or very small numbers in a limited cell width. It is used primarily in scientific and engineering applications and would not be acceptable on most business reports.

Currency Format

The Currency format places a dollar sign ($) in front of each entry. It adds a comma separator between thousands and hundreds and between millions and thousands. This format shows negative numbers in parentheses. The Currency format is used frequently in business reports because of the many dollar figures shown in such reports.

From 0 to 15 decimal places can be specified for this format, although the most common settings are 0 for whole dollars, and 2 to show both dollars and cents. The default setting is 2. Thus, when you want to show dollars and cents, you only have to press ENTER after selecting Currency as either the /Worksheet Global Format or /Range Format options. With the /Range command, you also need to specify the size of the range to be formatted.

The /Worksheet Global Default Other International command can change the way the Currency option works. In the "Advanced Features" section near the end of this chapter, you will learn to use symbols for other currencies such as pounds and guilders, and to place the symbol either in front of or behind the currency amount. In addition, the symbols used for the comma separator and the decimal point can be changed to meet your needs in working with international currencies. Further, the parentheses around negative numbers can be changed to a minus sign.

Let's look at the impact on several numeric entries of using different Currency formats.

Entry	Currency 0	Currency 2	Currency 4
34.78	$35	$34.78	$34.7800
–123	($123)	($123.00)	($123.0000)
1234.56	$1,235	$1,234.56	$1,234.5600

The indicator for the Currency format is a C followed by the number of decimal places. Like the other format indicators, this will appear in parentheses in front of the cell entry in the control panel.

Comma Format

The Comma format is just like the Currency format, except that the dollar sign is not used in the Comma format. Just as with the Currency format, negative numbers are shown in parentheses and commas are added as separators.

From 0 to 15 decimal places can be shown with this format. Enter the number of decimal places when prompted with the default. If you wish to accept the default (2), just press ENTER.

Here is a sample of the displays created with the Comma format:

Entry	, 0	, 2	, 4
34.78	35	34.78	34.7800
−123	(123)	(123.00)	(123.0000)
1234.56	1,235	1,234.56	1,234.5600

A comma and the number of decimal places are used as the indicator for this format. Thus (,0), (,2), and (,4) represent this format with zero, two, and four decimal places, respectively.

The Comma format is frequently combined with the Currency format for financial statements. As in Figure 4-28, the top and bottom lines of a financial statement typically have the $ added, whereas the other numbers are shown in Comma format. The best strategy for producing this layout is to use /Worksheet Global Format followed by /Range Format Currency commands for the top and bottom lines of the display.

General Format

Since General is the default format, it is the one you have seen in the entries made on your worksheet until now. This format does not provide consistent displays as the other formats do, since it depends on the size of the number you enter. As you saw in Chapter 3, "Entering Data in 1-2-3's Worksheet," very large and very small numbers will display in Scientific format when General format is in effect. Some numbers will appear as they are entered, while others will be altered to have a leading zero added, or be rounded to a number of decimal digits that will fit in the cell width you have selected. This format also suppresses

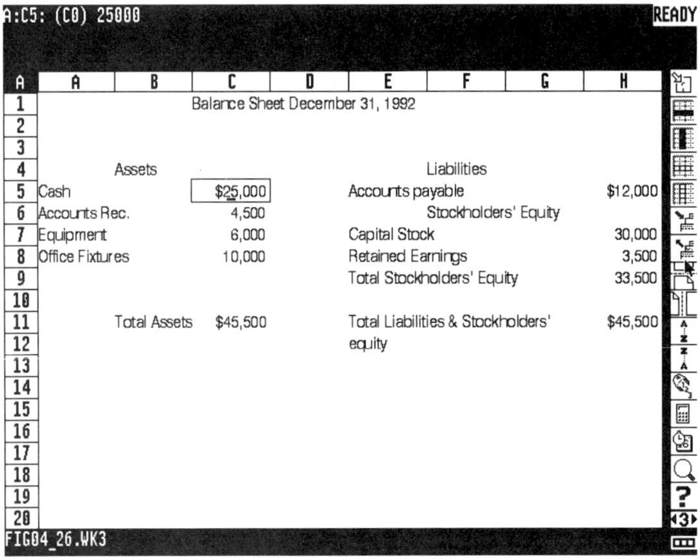

Figure 4-28. *Using Comma format to format numbers*

trailing zeros after the decimal point, so if you have used them, they will not appear in the display.

General format results in a display that has varying numbers of decimal places in the entries. There is also no way to establish the number of digits for the multiplier when the Scientific format option is used for very small and very large numbers.

Looking at the way various entries appear in General format will help you decide when it is an appropriate format for your needs.

Entry	General Display
10000000000	1.0E+10
2345678	2345678
234.76895432	234.769 (with Default font and Column-Width)

An indicator of (G) is used for General format. A numeric digit is not present, since the command does not expect you to decide the number of decimal digits to be shown.

Although it is the default worksheet setting, General format is seldom selected as the display of choice. For most applications you will want a more consistent display, even if it does require more room on the worksheet. This format would be particularly useful, however, if you were really short of space, since it automatically converts to Scientific notation when the entry becomes too large or small to fit in the cell width.

+/– Format

This is one of the most unusual formats available in 1-2-3. It creates a series of plus (+) or minus (–) signs as a representation of the size of the number in the cell, producing a sort of bar graph. These signs will change to asterisks if the size of the bar exceeds the column width. When the value of the cell is zero, a period (.) will display on the left side of the cell.

The +/– format creates the following horizontal displays from the entries shown:

Entry	**+/– Display**
0	.
5	+++++
–4	– – – –
–3.85	– – –

The indicator (+) will appear when the cell pointer is on any cell that has been formatted with the +/– format using the /Range Format command.

The +/– format can be used to create a series of small bars to show, for example, growth or decline in sales over a period of time. In this situation you may want to divide the sales figure by 100 or some other appropriate number, so that the result can be shown in a reasonable cell width. This approach has been used to create the bar graph shown in Figure 4-29.

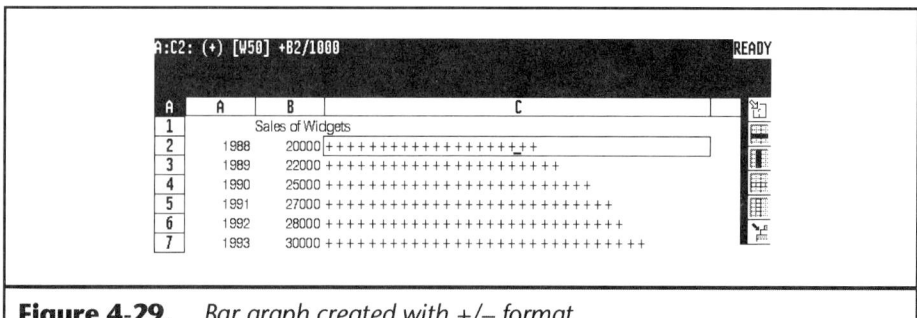

Figure 4-29. *Bar graph created with +/– format*

Percent

With the Percent format you can display percentages attractively, with the % symbol added to the end of each cell. You can choose any number of decimal places between 0 and 15. This format uses the indicator P followed by the number of decimal digits.

When the Percent format is applied, the number you have entered is multiplied by 100 before the % symbol is added. Thus, an entry of .1 becomes 10%, and an entry of 10 becomes 1000%. You can see why it is important to enter the correct decimal fraction for the percent you want.

In the Percent format the following entries will display as shown, depending on how many decimal places you specify:

Entry	0	2	4
5	500%	500.00%	500.0000%
–.089635	–9%	–8.96%	–8.9635%
.45	45%	45.00%	45.0000%
–1	–100%	–100.00%	–100.0000%
.12	12%	12.00%	12.0000%

The Percent format is used in many areas of business reports. Percentage growth rates, interest on loans, and sales increases all can be computed and formatted as percents.

Date/Time Format

This format is used to display date and time serial numbers as the dates and times they represent. The whole number portion of the entry represents the date, and the fractional portion of the entry represents the time.

Assuming that you entered **12-Jun-92** in each of several cells and generated the serial number 33767, here are the indicators and displays you would see with different Date formats:

Indicator	Format	Example
D1	DD-MMM-YY	12-JUN-92
D2	DD-MMM	12-JUN
D3	MMM-YY	JUN-92
D4	MM/DD/YY	06/12/92
D5	MM/DD	06/12

Chapter 4: Changing the Appearance of the Worksheet Display

When a cell contains both a date and time serial number (like the @NOW function creates), you will have to decide whether to apply a Date or a Time format, since both formats cannot be applied to the same cell. This means that although you place both a time and a date serial number in a cell, you will be able to see only one at a time. The one you see depends on the format you choose.

Time formats are accessed through the Date format option by selecting Time. There are four Time formats. Two use the A.M. and P.M. designations, and the other two are international formats that use a 24-hour day like military time. The indicators for times are D6 through D9, which represent the four time formats.

The effect of format selection on the display of time in worksheet cells can be seen in the table that follows.

Time Serial Number	HH:MM:SS A.M./P.M.	HH:MM A.M./P.M.	Long Intn'l	Short Intn'l
.25	06:00:00 A.M.	06:00 A.M.	06:00:00	06:00
.5	12:00:00 P.M.	12:00 P.M.	12:00:00	12:00
.75	06:00:00 P.M.	06:00 P.M.	18:00:00	18:00

Date and time entries are used in a variety of applications, such as to represent shipment receipts or line processing time. They can also be used to represent loan due dates, appointment dates, or order dates.

Text Format

Text format allows you to display actual formulas on the worksheet, rather than displaying the results of formula calculations, as will happen with any of the other formats. Using Text format causes a cell to display exactly what you enter. If your entry was a formula, 1-2-3 also remembers the result of the formula, and the results can be accessed with a reference to the cell.

When the cell pointer is on a cell formatted as text with a /Range command, the indicator (T) will appear in the upper line of the control panel. The cell displays the entry including any notes.

The Text format can be used to create a documentation copy of a worksheet, containing the actual formulas used in worksheet calculations. For example, to create a documentation copy of the worksheet shown in Figure 4-30, follow these steps.

1. Use /Worksheet Global Format Text to set the global format to Text. This will not completely change the display, because some of the entries have been formatted with /Range Format commands, which always override global settings.

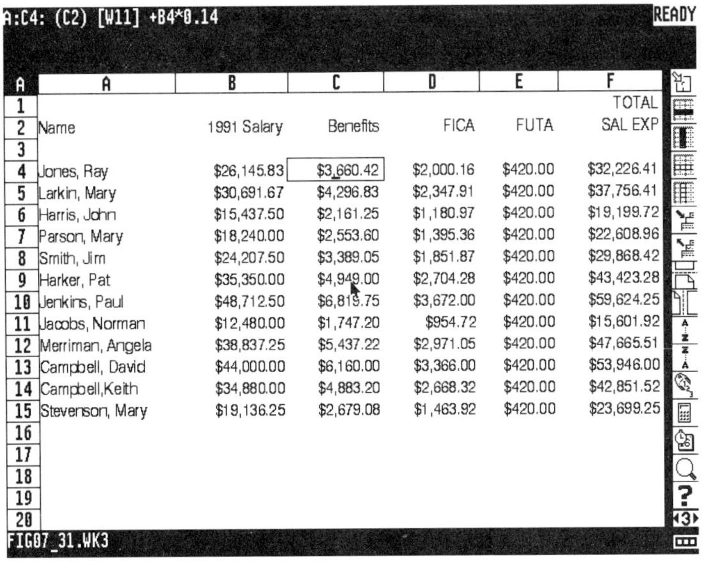
A:C4: (C2) [W11] +B4*0.14 READY

A	A	B	C	D	E	F
1						TOTAL
2	Name	1991 Salary	Benefits	FICA	FUTA	SAL EXP
3						
4	Jones, Ray	$26,145.83	$3,660.42	$2,000.16	$420.00	$32,226.41
5	Larkin, Mary	$30,691.67	$4,296.83	$2,347.91	$420.00	$37,756.41
6	Harris, John	$15,437.50	$2,161.25	$1,180.97	$420.00	$19,199.72
7	Parson, Mary	$18,240.00	$2,553.60	$1,395.36	$420.00	$22,608.96
8	Smith, Jim	$24,207.50	$3,389.05	$1,851.87	$420.00	$29,868.42
9	Harker, Pat	$35,350.00	$4,949.00	$2,704.28	$420.00	$43,423.28
10	Jenkins, Paul	$48,712.50	$6,819.75	$3,672.00	$420.00	$59,624.25
11	Jacobs, Norman	$12,480.00	$1,747.20	$954.72	$420.00	$15,601.92
12	Merriman, Angela	$38,837.25	$5,437.22	$2,971.05	$420.00	$47,665.51
13	Campbell, David	$44,000.00	$6,160.00	$3,366.00	$420.00	$53,946.00
14	Campbell,Keith	$34,880.00	$4,883.20	$2,668.32	$420.00	$42,851.52
15	Stevenson, Mary	$19,136.25	$2,679.08	$1,463.92	$420.00	$23,699.25
16						
17						
18						
19						
20						

FIG07_31.WK3

Figure 4-30. *Worksheet displaying results of formulas*

2. Use /Range Format Reset A1..F15 and ENTER to reset all the Range formats back to global settings.

3. Move your cell pointer to column D. Use /Worksheet Column Column-Range Set-Width, and press the RIGHT ARROW until column E is also selected, and press ENTER. Press ENTER to select 34 as the column width. Now you have a copy of the worksheet with all the formulas documented. It should look like Figure 4-31. Notice how the previously formatted numbers appear in the General format.

After you learn about saving files in Chapter 8, "Working with Files," you will want to make sure that you never save a documentation file under the same filename you used for your original file. If you do, you will lose all the formats and column widths that you worked so hard to establish for it. In Chapter 6, "Printing," you will learn how to print a documentation copy of your worksheet so you will have a paper to file away and refer to if your disk copies are ever damaged or destroyed.

Chapter 4: Changing the Appearance of the Worksheet Display

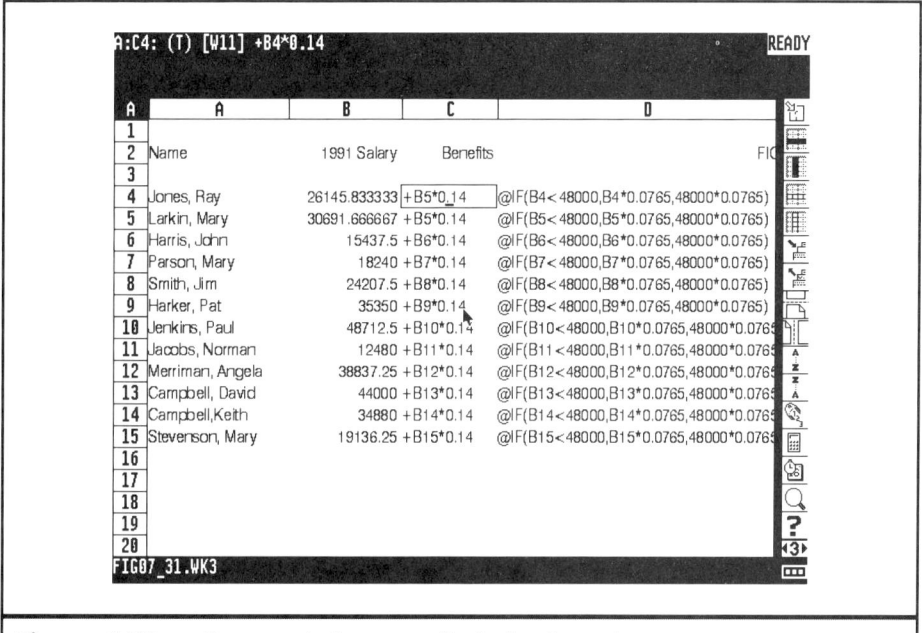

Figure 4-31. *Documentation copy displaying formulas*

Hidden Format

Hidden format causes a cell to display as a blank; that is, 1-2-3 will suppress the display of the cell. The cell's contents have not been lost, even though they do not appear on the worksheet. They are still stored internally and are accessed when you reference the cell in a formula. In fact, the contents of the cell will display in the control panel when you move your cell pointer to the cell. You can hide the contents further by enabling worksheet protection as discussed in Chapter 5, "Basic Worksheet Commands." When a worksheet is protected, 1-2-3 displays "PR" in the control panel when the cell pointer is on a hidden cell and does not display the cell entry.

With the Hidden format, all entries regardless of type will appear as blanks. The control panel indicator for a hidden cell, when the format is applied with a /Range command, is (H). In Figure 4-32, you see the cell pointer in a hidden cell, and the contents displayed in the control panel.

The main use of hidden cells is in macro applications. If the application is kept completely under macro control, the Hidden format could provide a measure of security. For more about macros, see Chapters 12 and 13.

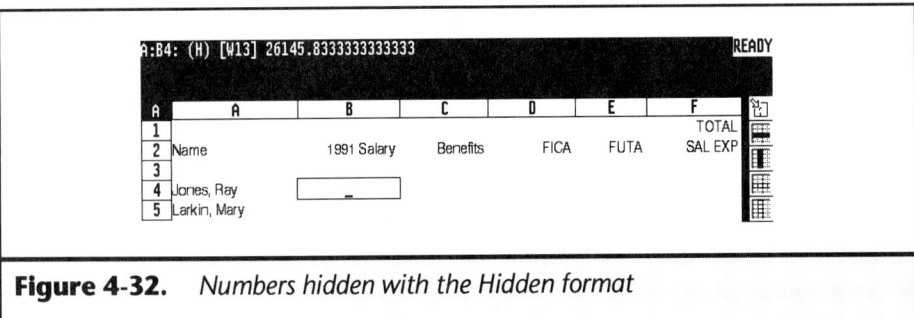

Figure 4-32. Numbers hidden with the Hidden format

Other Formats

Unlike the rest of the format options, the Other category provides access to a menu of four different format choices. The Other options essentially provide an extension to the options in the main Format menu, although each of the new formats is somewhat unique—providing either a temporary format, a format to be used with the existing formats, or a conversion to a label type entry.

Automatic

The Automatic format is the most powerful of all the formatting choices within 1-2-3. This format is a temporary format that will be converted to one of the other format types as soon as you make an entry in the cell. Automatic can supply the correct format for a variety of different data types. It allows you to make entries as you ultimately wish to see them, and uses the edit characters within your first entry in a cell to determine how the data will display. 1-2-3 then stores the data from your entry in a basic form.

A cell with an Automatic format can successfully handle Currency, Comma, Fixed, Percent, Scientific, Date, and Time formats. If you change a cell with an existing entry to Automatic, 1-2-3 will use the General format.

Figure 4-33 shows the effect of Automatic format in column B, assuming the entries in column A were entered exactly as shown. Column C shows how these entries are stored, and Column D shows the actual cell format after completing the entry shown in Column B. After you type your entry and press ENTER, the (A) for Automatic format is replaced by one of 1-2-3's other format entries.

TIP: Automatic format occurs only once for a cell. Once an entry is made into an Automatic format cell, 1-2-3 changes the cell's format to match the format of the entry. New entries made in the cell retain the cell format of the first entry. If you want to change the format, you must use the /Range Format command.

Chapter 4: Changing the Appearance of the Worksheet Display

```
A:A17: [W17]                                                          READY
   A         A              B             C              D
   1    Entry Typed    Automatic Format  Entry Stored   Format After Entry
   2               $5              $5             5           (C0)
   3            $5.45           $5.45          5.45           (C2)
   4               7%              7%          0.07           (P0)
   5            7.79%           7.79%        0.0779           (P2)
   6            5.678           5.678         5.678           (F3)
   7        8,125,145       8,123,145       8123145           (,0)
   8        5.695E+03       5.695E+03          5695           (S3)
   9         12:05PM        12:05 PM   0.50347222222222222    (D7)
  10           15:30           15:30   0.64583333333333333    (D9)
  11         3/15/90        03/15/90         32947            (D4)
  12       12-Mar-90       12-Mar-90         32944            (D1)
  13
```

Figure 4-33. *Effects of Automatic format*

Color

In many business models, negative numbers sound an alarm. Negative profits, cash flows, or sales trends need immediate attention. The Other Color Negative format can highlight these conditions with a different color while retaining the original format of the cell. Thus cells formatted as Currency, Comma, or Percent can have the added feature of a color that will change if they contain a negative number.

If your monitor does not support color display, 1-2-3 boldfaces entries to signify negative entries. You can quickly scan a worksheet for the variation in the display, and focus on situations requiring urgent attention. If you later decide to eliminate the color or highlighting from negative numbers, use the Other Color Reset option.

Label

This format adds a label indicator at the front of values entered after the format is applied. Existing value entries are not changed to labels. Cells formatted with the Other Label format have an (L) indicator in the control panel. This type of format is ideal for numbers that you do not want treated as values, such as social security numbers, zip codes, and phone numbers.

The effect of this format only applies to entries that you type. When 1-2-3 generates a series of entries with /Data Fill, the label prefix is not added, and the values display in General format.

The year numbers in the following worksheet are all generated after using the Other Label format on the range of cells where these numbers were to be entered. The current setting for global label prefix is used.

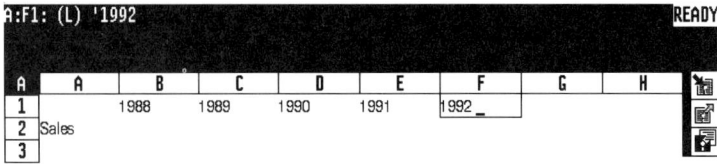

Parentheses

This format causes 1-2-3 to encase all numeric values in parentheses. The unique feature of this format is that it is supplemental to any existing format. A cell formatted as Currency will remain formatted as Currency while it is encased in parentheses, as in ($5). Likewise, cells formatted as Percent, Date, Time, or Scientific all retain their existing format. Even the format indicator in the control panel shows both formats, with Currency and Parentheses represented as (C0( )).

To add the Parentheses format to a range, select /Range Format Other Parentheses Yes and select the range. To remove the parentheses from entries, use Other Parentheses No.

TIP: Selecting a format option from the icon palette that matches the current format of your selection resets the format to the current global format setting. This is equivalent to choosing /Range Format Reset from the menu.

Wysiwyg Format Options Accessible with the SmartIcons

In addition to the icons for the numeric formats, the SmartIcons let you access some of Wysiwyg's format options in Release 3.4. The SmartIcons palettes are only available when Wysiwyg is loaded. The formatting changes that you make with these icons are visible on the worksheet immediately; however, they will only appear on your printed output if you use Wysiwyg to print your output. You can choose from options such as boldface, italics, shaded background, underlining with either a single or double line, drawing an outline, or changing the color. The full set of Wysiwyg options on the palettes is shown in Table 4-2.

Icon	Effect	Palette Number
B	Displays the selected cells as boldface	1, 7
I	Displays the selected cell as italics	1, 7
N	Removes formatting such as boldface, underlining, and italics	7
U	Underlines entries in the current selection	1, 2
U	Double underlines entries in the current selection	2
▢	Outlines the current cell or range and adds a drop shadow	2
□	Outlines the current cell or range	2
▦	Adds shading to the current cell or range	2
ₐA	Displays data in the next font size	1, 2
AA	Displays data in the next color	2
AA	Displays the background in the next color	2

Table 4-2. *Wysiwyg Options Available on the Icon Palettes*

You will learn all the details of what these features offer in Chapter 5, but you can use them now for some quick changes if you are already familiar with what boldface, italics, and other options do for text.

All of the SmartIcon palette options are applied the same way—the cells to be affected are selected and the icon option is chosen. You can remove any applied Wysiwyg format option from cells by selecting the cells and choosing the icon with an N (for Normal). A quick look at a few options will show how these changes can dramatically affect the worksheet shown in Figure 4-34.

Enlarging the Font Size

The font refers to the character style, size, and character set available to you. If you are using the full set of Wysiwyg features in Chapter 15, you will be able to change any of these features by selecting a different font. For now you will be able to use the SmartIcon palette to change the character size to the next largest size. You can choose this option repeatedly to increase the entries in the selected cells by more than one size.

To enlarge the heading for the worksheet shown in Figure 4-34, select B1..B2, then click the icon from palette 1 or 2 to enlarge the font. This icon is shown in Table 4-2 and is the icon that shows a smaller A progressing to a larger A.

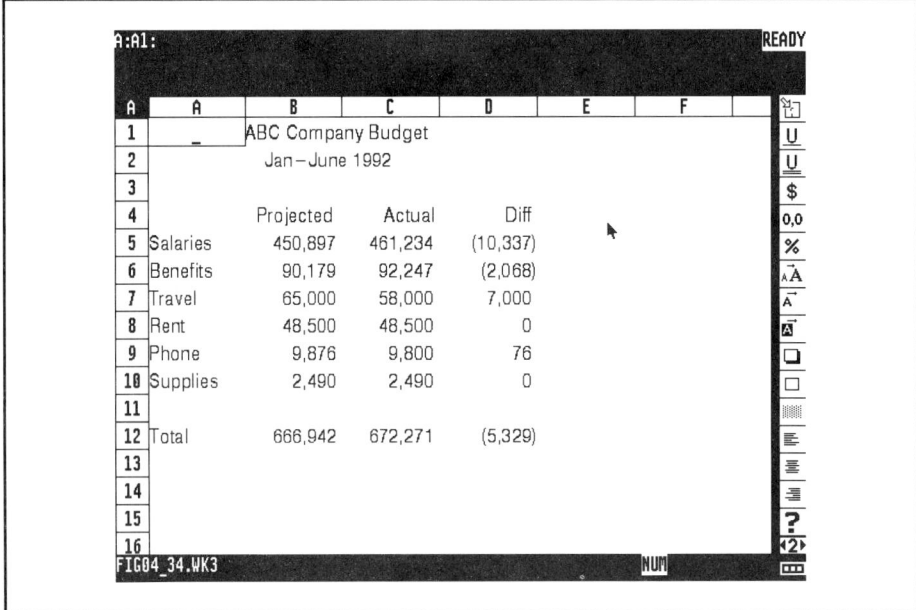

Figure 4-34. *Worksheet to be formatted with the Wysiwyg options*

Adding Bold

Adding bold to text makes it stand out from other text in the same report. You might want to add bold to the text at the tops of the columns, as in Figure 4-34, to make it stand out from column entries. Select the cells B4..D4, and then select the icon in palette 1 or 7 that has a large B on it to make the text boldface.

Adding Underline

When you select either single or double underlining, Wysiwyg underlines only the text within the entries in the selected range. If the cells that were boldfaced in Figure 4-34 are still selected, all you need to do to underline is select the icon with a U and a single underscore line in icon palette 1 or 2. With Wysiwyg you can add as many formatting options as you want by continuing to click the icons that represent them. If Undo is enabled you can always eliminate your last change. Without Undo enabled, you can select the icon representing Normal text (the icon with a large N) to remove all Wysiwyg formatting. You might also want to underline the last detail entry in each column. To do this you would select B10..D10, then click the underline icon from palette 1 or 2.

Outlining

When you outline a range, Wysiwyg will add lines around the perimeter of the range you select. In Chapter 15 you will see other variations of the outline feature; however, the icon palette offers only the full perimeter outline, either with or without a drop shadow effect. To add an outline around a complete row, select A12..D12, then select the outline icon from palette 2. This is the icon that looks like a rectangle.

Shading Cells

Shading adds a light grey scale to the selected range. It can be effective to set text off from other entries and is often used with the outline feature. To add grey shading to a complete row, all you need to do (if A12..D12 is still selected) is click the shading icon which follows the outline icon in palette 2. Figure 4-35 shows the worksheet from Figure 4-34 with all the Wysiwyg changes made from the palettes.

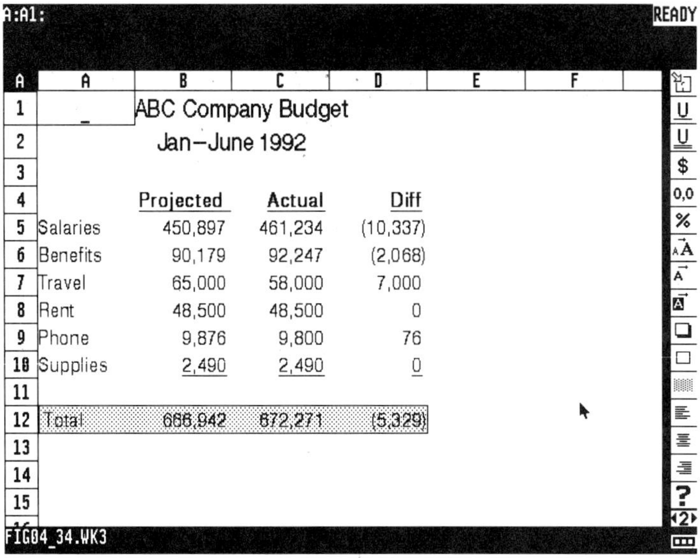

Figure 4-35. Document formatted with the Wysiwyg options

Advanced Features

The three options discussed in this section are not features you will need to change every day, like the other formatting options, but you may occasionally want to use them. One is the /Worksheet Global Default Other International option, which changes the way 1-2-3 handles punctuation, currency, date, and time displays, as well as negative numbers. A related command, /Worksheet Global Other Clock, alters the clock display format on your screen. The third feature, the justification options available under /Range Justify, manipulates a column of text-type entries in your worksheet. Let's look at each of these options in more detail.

Other International Format Options

The /Worksheet Global Default Other International command is the longest command sequence discussed so far. This command allows you to customize the display for numeric punctuation, currency, date, and time.

Chapter 4: Changing the Appearance of the Worksheet Display

Punctuation

The numeric punctuation indicators you can control are the point separator (that is, the decimal indicator in a number like 55.98), the thousands separator for numbers, and the argument separator in @functions and macro commands. The default point separator is a period (.), but you have the option of changing it to a comma (,). The default thousands separator is a comma, and can be changed to a period (.) or a space. The argument separator is initially set as a comma; it can be changed to a period (.) or a semicolon (;). The Punctuation options are not chosen individually, but rather in a threesome, as follows:

Option	Point	Argument	Thousands
A (default)	.	,	,
B	,	.	.
C	.	;	,
D	,	;	.
E	.	,	space
F	,	.	space
G	.	;	space
H	,	;	space

The next table shows how each choice affects the display of numbers, and the arguments for @functions like @SUM.

Punctuation Option	Numeric Entry in Current Format	Function Arguments
A (default)	$1,200.50	@SUM(D2,A8..A10)
B	$1.200,50	@SUM(D2.A8..A10)
C	$1,200.50	@SUM(D2;A8..A10)
D	$1.200,50	@SUM(D2;A8..A10)
E	$1 200.50	@SUM(D2,A8..A10)
F	$1 200,50	@SUM(D2.A8..A10)
G	$1 200.50	@SUM(D2;A8..A10)
H	$1 200,50	@SUM(D2;A8..A10)

International Currency

This option allows you to change the currency symbol from the standard $ to one of the international currency symbols found in the LMBCS codes. In addition, you may choose to place the symbol at the end of your entry rather than at the beginning, as in the default setting. Examples of currency symbols you may wish to use are those for Dutch Guilders, Pounds, Yen, and Pesetas. The Compose sequence for these entries is in Appendix B.

To change from $ to one of these symbols, invoke **/Worksheet Global Default Other International Currency**, and then use COMPOSE (ALT-F1) with the appropriate character sequence, followed by ENTER. The Compose sequence allows you to enter more than one character in a single position. To access it, hold down the ALT key while you press F1, then type the characters specified in the table. For Pounds you would type an **L** followed by =, for example. Once you select the currency character, 1-2-3 prompts you to determine whether you want the character to be a suffix or a prefix.

International Date

The international date formats—D4 and D5—can be altered with the Date option from the /Worksheet Global Default Other International command. The initial setting for the international date is MM/DD/YY. This can be changed to three other forms. The choices for this setting and how the setting will affect a sample date is as follows:

Option	Format	D4	D5
A	MM/DD/YY	09/24/92	09/24
B	DD/MM/YY	24/09/92	24/09
C	DD.MM.YY	24.09.92	24.09
D	YY-MM-DD	92-09-24	09-24

International Time

The appearance of the international time formats can be changed with this option. Format D8 shows hours, minutes, and seconds; format D9 shows only hours and minutes. The initial international time setting is HH:MM:SS. Each of the four options is indicated by a letter. The letters, time formats, and examples of the format with the time 12:30:25 P.M. are as follows:

Option	Format	D8	D9
A	HH:MM:SS	12:30:25	12:30
B	HH.MM.SS	12.30.25	12.30

Chapter 4: Changing the Appearance of the Worksheet Display

Option	Format	D8	D9
C	HH,MM,SS	12,30,25	12,30
D	HHhMMmSSs	12h30m25s	12h30m

Negative

The Worksheet Global Default International Negative option allows you to customize how negative numbers in the Comma or Currency format will be displayed. The default setting is to enclose these numbers in parentheses, but you can also use a minus sign. Once you select this command you can choose either parentheses or a minus sign to affect all the entries in the worksheet.

Update

Any changes made with /Worksheet Global Default Other International commands are in effect only for the current session. Next time you load 1-2-3, the original worksheet global default settings will be in effect. If you wish to make your changes permanent, invoke the **/Worksheet Global Default Update** command to save your custom settings. This will make your changes the new global default values, and they will be in effect the next time 1-2-3 is loaded into memory.

Clock Display

The clock display on your screen, when the current worksheet is not on disk, changes to the current filename as soon as you save the current file or retrieve a file that is stored on disk. If you would prefer to retain the clock display, you can change the setting for this option and 1-2-3 will display the clock at all times. You have several format options for the clock display. Use /Worksheet Global Default Other Clock, and select Standard, International, None, Clock, or Filename.

Standard is the default display for the clock. It displays the date in the long format: DD-MMM-YY. The time displays as HH:MM A.M./P.M. This display will only be used before a file is saved to disk or when the clock is active on the screen.

Selecting International changes the display of both date and time when they are on the screen. Time becomes the short international format, D9. Date displays in the long international format, D4.

Choosing None eliminates the time display or the filename from the screen. This is useful for applications where you do not wish to have part of the screen dedicated to a time and date display or filename.

The Clock option ensures that the clock display is always on the screen. It will use either Standard or International display, depending on your earlier selection.

Choosing Filename for the Clock display restores the filename display if you previously changed it to Clock. Filename is the default setting for this feature.

/Range Justify

The /Range Justify command readjusts text in label entries to fit within the width of one or more columns. 1-2-3 moves characters from one label entry to the next command.

With this command, you can enter one or more long labels in a column and then, after the entry is complete, decide how many columns wide the display of this information should be. The width of the display is determined by selecting a justify range. If that range is two cells wide, for example, the long labels will be redistributed so that they take up more rows but display only in two columns.

/Range Justify does not provide full word processing support, but it does allow you to write readable documentation on the screen, or write a short memo that references worksheet data. It frees you from having to concentrate on the length of your entry as you type. When all your data is typed in, 1-2-3 will adjust

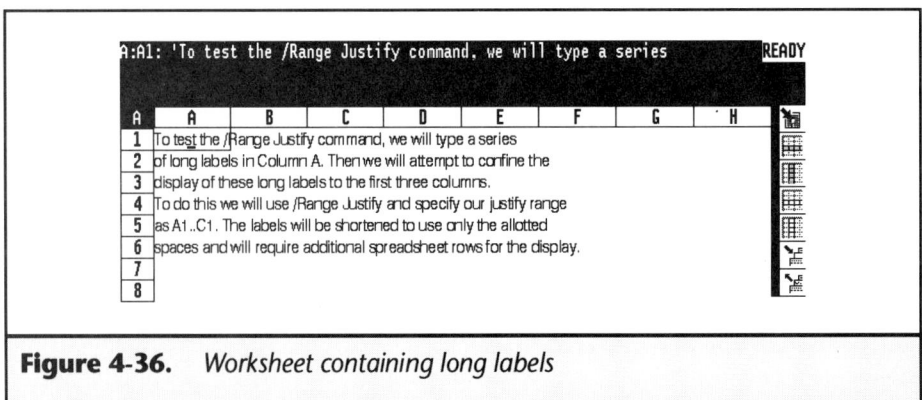

Figure 4-36. *Worksheet containing long labels*

Chapter 4: Changing the Appearance of the Worksheet Display

the line length according to your specifications. If you want additional word processing support, you can use the Text features of Wysiwyg, covered in Chapter 15.

Figure 4-36 contains an example of long labels entered into A1..A6 of the worksheet. The labels all have different lengths. Suppose you decide that the display should be confined to columns A through B. (The labels are entered in column A and will remain in that location; what you are changing is the space they borrow for display purposes.) To make the change, take the following steps:

1. Move your cell pointer to the beginning of the range you will use for display—A1 in the example.

2. Type **/Range Justify**.

3. Highlight the cells in the range A1..B1 with the RIGHT ARROW key.

4. Press ENTER. Your justified data should look like Figure 4-37.

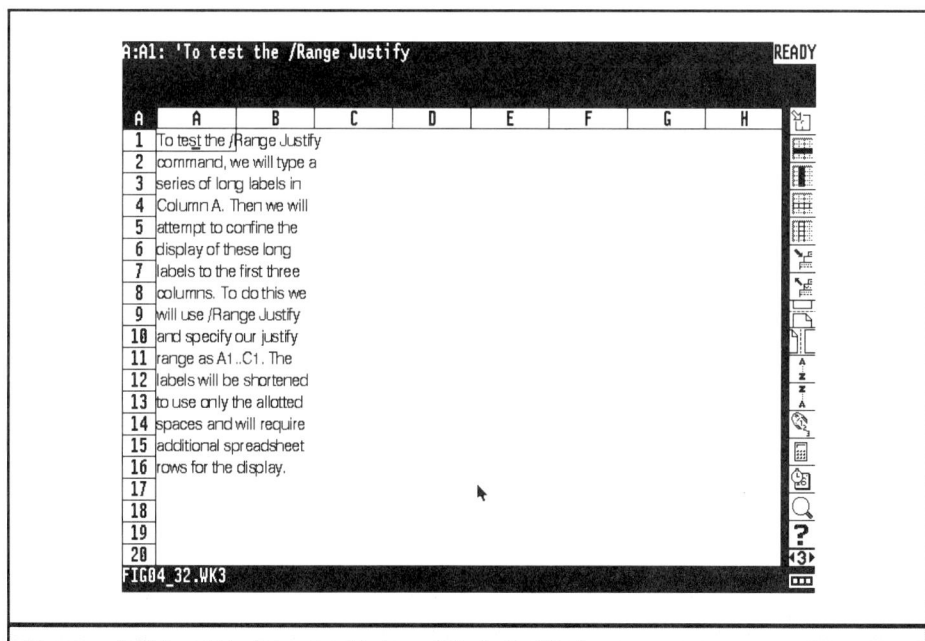

Figure 4-37. *Worksheet with long labels justified*

To make the display wider again, move your cell pointer to A1 and start the process over. For example, you might want to specify A1..F1 as the justify range. The first six columns would then be used for the display.

If there is information in column A, in cells after the end of the justify range, the /Range Justify command will displace that information as it expands the long label down the worksheet. Since the label was originally entered in column A, *only* the cell entries in column A will be displaced. Even if the justify range includes columns A..C, and there is information in the cells to the right of column A, it will not be displaced. For instance, a table in cells B10..C14 would be unaffected by the paragraph rearrangement shown in Figure 4-37. Instead, the label display in column A would be truncated in rows 10 through 14, just as it is when an entry to the right of any long label causes the label display to be truncated.

Command Reference

Worksheet Display

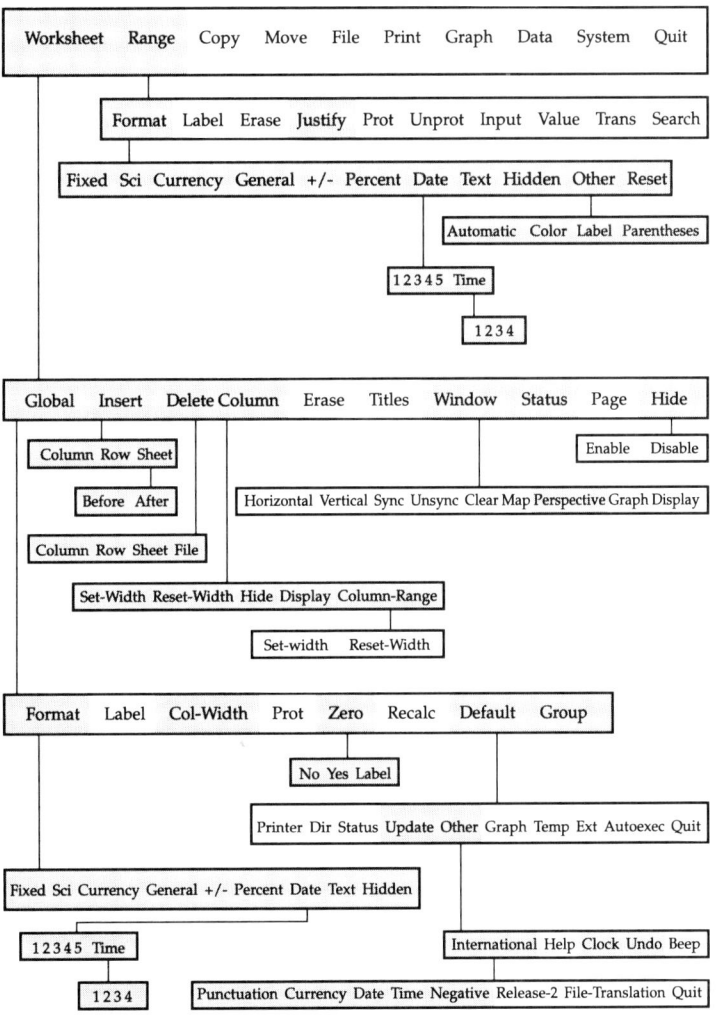

© 1989 Lotus Development Corporation. Used with permission.

/Range Format

Description

The /Range Format command allows you to determine the appearance of numeric entries on your worksheet. With this command you can change the specific display format for one or many cells in a contiguous range on the worksheet. You can choose the number of decimal places displayed (0 to 15) for most formats, and determine whether the numeric information is displayed as currency, a scientific notation, a date, a time, or one of several other options.

The display format you select will not affect the internal storage of numbers. You can elect to display a number with seven decimal places as a whole number, for example, but all seven places will be maintained internally.

Regardless of the format you choose, the column must be wide enough to display your selection. For all the formats, if the column is not wide enough, asterisks (*) will appear. For example, using a column width of 3 and attempting to format a number as Currency with two decimal places would result in a display of asterisks, because the $ and the decimal point require two positions.

Options

To employ the /Range Format command, enter **/Range Format** and select the option you wish to use. Then respond to 1-2-3's prompts concerning the number of decimal places (or the Date format) you desire. Finally, select the range of cells to be formatted by entering either the cell address, or a range name, or by highlighting the cells with your cell pointer.

FIXED   Fixed format allows you to display all entries with a specific number of decimal places. Two places are the default, but you may select any number between 0 and 15. Examples with three decimal places are .007, 9.000, and 4.156.

SCI   Scientific format displays numbers in exponential form, showing the power of 10 that the number must be multiplied by. This format allows you to concisely represent very large or very small numbers. From 0 to 15 places can be specified for the multiplier. Some examples with two decimal places are 6.78E–20, 4.11E+5, and 0.78E+8.

CURRENCY   Currency format will cause your entry to be preceded by a dollar sign ($). It will also insert a separator such as a comma between the thousands and hundreds positions. You may specify from 0 to 15 decimal places for this format; 2 is the default. Negative amounts will appear in parentheses. Examples with two decimal places are $3.40, $1,400.98, and ($89.95).

, (COMMA) Comma format is identical to the Currency format, except that Comma lacks the dollar sign ($). Comma format uses the thousands separator. You may specify any number of decimal places you want between 0 and 15; 2 is the default. Negative numbers are displayed in parentheses. Examples with two decimal places are 1,200.00, (5,678.00), and 45.00.

GENERAL General is the default format for 1-2-3. With it the leading zero integer will always appear, as in 0.78, but trailing zeros will be suppressed. If the number is very large or very small, it will appear in Scientific notation. Examples of numeric displays with the General format are 15.674, 2.7E+12, and 0.67543.

+/− +/− format produces a horizontal bar graph showing the relative size of numbers. Each integer is represented by a symbol. For example, −3 would be − − −, and 5 would be +++++. A period (.) is used to represent 0.

PERCENT Percent format displays your entries as percentages. Each entry will be multiplied by 100, and a % symbol will be added to the end. Because of this multiplication, you must enter percents as their decimal equivalent. For example, enter .05 for 5%. If you enter 5 and format the cell as Percent, it will display as 500%. You may specify from 0 to 15 decimal places; 2 is the default. Examples with two decimal places are 4.00%, 3.15%, and 1200.00%.

DATE The Date option provides a second menu of possibilities. From this second menu you can select specific formats for the date. The formats accessible through the Date option are:

D1	(DD-MMM-YY)	08-Sep-86
D2	(DD-MMM)	08-Sep
D3	(MMM-YY)	Sep-08
D4	(MM/DD/YY)	09/08/86*
D5	(MM/DD)	09/08*

*These formats can be changed to a number of other formats with the /Worksheet Global Default Other International command.

Time formats are accessed through the Date format. When you select Time from the Date options, a menu of four Time formats is presented. Two of the formats use the A.M. and P.M. designations, the other two are International formats that use a 24-hour day like military time. The formats available for the display of time in your worksheet cells are:

(D6) T1		HH:MM:SS A.M./P.M.	06:00:00 A.M.
(D7) T2		HH:MM	06:00 A.M.
(D8) T3		Long International	06:00:00*
(D9) T4		Short International	06:00*

*These formats can be changed to a number of other formats with the /Worksheet Global Default Other International command.

TEXT   Text format displays specified cells exactly as you have entered them. In the case of formulas, the formula rather than the result will be displayed.

HIDDEN   Hidden format causes the selected cells to appear blank on the screen. If you move your cell pointer to a hidden cell, the control panel will display the cell's contents. Cell entries with a Hidden format will not appear in the control panel if worksheet protection is enabled.

OTHER   The Other selection offers a number of Release 3 formatting options. Due to the significance of these options they are covered separately under the command /Range Format Other.

RESET   This option returns the specified range of cells to the default format setting. The only two options for eliminating a /Range format are to use /Range Format Reset, or apply a new /Range format. Erasing a range on the worksheet with /Range Erase does not affect the format of the cells in the range.

/Range Format Other

Description

The /Range Format Other command provides additional formatting options. The Automatic formatting option found in this group of commands also offers time savings in data entry.

Options

Like the /Range Format command, you must select an option, any additional selections required for the option, and the range to which the selected format applies.

AUTOMATIC   Existing values in a range formatted as Automatic will display in the General format, even if they were previously assigned another format. New entries will be formatted according to the style of the entry made. This feature supports Fixed, Scientific, Currency, Comma, Percent, Label, Date, and Time formats. New entries in the same cell assume the format established by the initial cell entry in that cell after the Automatic format is applied. This format stores as a label an entry containing non-numeric characters, even if the entry begins with numeric characters.

COLOR   This format option displays negative numbers in a different color or in a brighter intensity, or resets the color option to eliminate special treatment for negative numbers. The original format applied to the cell remains when the Color option is selected. The two Color options are Negative and Reset.

LABEL   This format adds a label prefix for new entries only. Existing entries are displayed in the General format without a label prefix added. Entries made with the /Data Fill command are not converted to labels, even if the Other Label format is in effect for the affected cells.

PARENTHESES   This format either encloses all numeric values in parentheses or removes parentheses added with this command. Like the Color option, this format retains the original format for the cell. The two options are Yes to add parentheses, and No to remove them.

/Range Justify

Description

The /Range Justify command lets you change the way a label is displayed. Once a label is entered (for instance, a long label entered in cell A1), you can use /Range Justify to redistribute the label so that it is displayed differently. The width of the display is determined by selecting a justify range, which may be one to several cells wide (the maximum is 512 characters) and one to several rows long.

   Information in cells to the right of a justify range is not displaced when you use /Range Justify. Instead, the display of a label in the justify range is truncated—even though the contents of the cells containing the label are not affected.

Options

You have the option of specifying one or more rows for the justify range. If you specify one row, 1-2-3 will include all labels from that row down to either the bottom of the worksheet or the first row that does not contain a label. Cells containing nonlabel entries below the justify range may be shifted up or down, depending on the space requirements for the justified labels.

If you specify more than one row with /Range Justify, you assume the burden of allowing sufficient space for the justification. If there is not enough space in the range you choose, you will see the error message "Justify range is full or line too long." With a selection of more than one row for the range, only the labels in the range down to the first nonlabel entry will be justified. Also, when you specify more than one row, cells outside the justify range will be unaffected.

NOTE: Do not use this command for cells that have been assigned range names. Although the contents of the cell may be displaced, the range name will still be assigned to the same cell.

/Worksheet Column

Description

The /Worksheet Column command allows you to change the characteristics of the worksheet columns. You can use the command to change the column width and to hide and display columns. When the GROUP mode indicator is on, all worksheets in the current file are affected by this command.

Options

SET-WIDTH   After choosing this option, either use the RIGHT and LEFT ARROW keys to change the column width of the current column, or type in the exact width desired for that column. Any width between 1 and 240 is acceptable. If you choose a column width narrower than the width of your data, formatted value data will display as asterisks.

RESET-WIDTH This option returns the width setting for the current column to the default setting—that is, either the initial default of 9, or the setting established with /Worksheet Global Col-Width if that command has been used.

HIDE This option affects the display and printing of worksheet data. You can hide one or many columns, depending on the range you specify for this command. The hidden columns will not appear on your display. They also will not be printed, even if the print range spans cells on both sides of them. These hidden columns only appear when 1-2-3 is in the POINT mode; an asterisk will appear next to the column letter.

Hide will not affect the data in the cells. At any time you can bring the data back into view with the Display option.

DISPLAY This option allows you to redisplay one or more hidden columns. Each hidden column will have an asterisk next to the column letter. The columns can be redisplayed either by highlighting a cell within each column you wish to redisplay, or by entering a range that includes the hidden columns you wish to redisplay.

COLUMN-RANGE This option allows you to change the width in one or more columns on the current worksheet. Column-Range functions the same as the /Worksheet Set-Width and Reset-Width commands, except that it allows you to work with more than one column. Any group of adjacent columns on the current worksheet can be changed. The two selections available for this choice are Set-Width and Reset-Width. After selecting either of these, select the range to change. Set the new width for the range of columns if you select Set-Width.

/Worksheet Delete

Description

The /Worksheet Delete command allows you to delete unneeded rows, columns, and sheets. You can also use this command to remove a file from memory. When GROUP mode is on, deleting rows or columns affects all sheets in the current worksheet file.

Options

The /Worksheet Delete command provides four options: Row, Column, Sheet, and File. The last option, File, is covered in Chapter 8, "Working with Files." You also have the option of deleting one or many rows, columns, or sheets with one execution of the command. The best approach is to place your cell pointer on the first column, row, or sheet to be deleted. Enter **/Worksheet Delete Row** or **/Worksheet Delete Column**, and then move your cell pointer to include at least one cell from each column, row, or sheet you wish to have deleted. Deletions from the middle of a range cause 1-2-3 to automatically adjust the range to compensate for the deletions.

/Worksheet Global Col-Width

Description

The /Worksheet Global Col-Width command allows you to change the default column width for every column on the worksheet. If the GROUP mode indicator is on, the global column width is changed in all active sheets in the current file.

Options

After entering /Worksheet Global Col-Width, either use the RIGHT ARROW and LEFT ARROW keys to change the column width, or type in the exact width desired. Any width between 1 and 240 is acceptable.

/Worksheet Global Default Other Clock

Description

This command lets you display the filename or the date and time in the status line.

Options

STANDARD This is the default setting used when the clock displays. It displays the date as DD-MMM-YY, and the time as HH:MM A.M./P.M.

INTERNATIONAL This option displays the date in the current long International format (month, day, and year will be shown), and the time in the current short international format (hours and minutes based on a 24-hour clock). The International format options are discussed in more detail under /Worksheet Global Default Other International.

NONE This option suppresses the filename or the date and time display in the status line.

CLOCK This option causes the clock to display at all times, overriding the default display of the filename.

FILENAME This is the default setting. It causes 1-2-3 to display the filename for file on disk. On a new worksheet that has not been saved, the clock continues to display.

/Worksheet Global Default Other International

Description

The /Worksheet Global Default Other International command allows you to customize the display for numeric punctuation, currency, date, and time. The Release-2 and File-Translation options for this command are covered in Chapter 8, "Working with Files," since they are used with saving and retrieving files.

Options

PUNCTUATION The numeric punctuation indicators you can control are the point separator (the decimal indicator in numbers like 55.98), the thousands separator for numbers, and the argument separator used in @functions. The default point separator is a period (.), but you have the option of changing it to a comma (,). The initial thousands separator is a comma; it can be changed to a period (.) or a space. The argument separator is initially set as a comma; it can be changed to a period (.) or a semicolon (;). The options are not chosen individually, but in a threesome after you select Punctuation. The options available are shown in the following table:

Option	Point	Argument	Thousands
A	.	,	,
B	,	.	.
C	.	;	,
D	,	;	.
E	.	,	space
F	,	.	space
G	.	;	space
H	,	;	space

CURRENCY   This option allows you to change the currency symbol from the standard $ to another international currency symbol. You can also use any LMBCS character. You have the further choice of placing the symbol at the end of your entry rather than at the beginning, as in the initial setting.

To change the currency indicator, invoke **/Worksheet Global Default International Currency**, and then type the currency character you want (the LMBCS characters are listed in Appendix B, "LMBCS Codes"). Then select Prefix to display the currency symbol before a number or Suffix to display the currency symbol after a number.

DATE   The International Date formats (D4 and D5) can be altered with the Date option under the /Worksheet Global Default Other International command. The fourth date format displays month, day, and year, and the fifth date format displays the month and day. The initial setting for the International Date (option A) is MM/DD/YY. This can be changed to three other options, as follows:

B	DD/MM/YY
C	DD.MM.YY
D	YY-MM-DD

TIME   The appearance of the International Time formats can be changed with this option. Format D8 shows hours, minutes, and seconds; format D9 shows only hours and minutes. The initial International Time setting (option A) is HH:MM:SS. The three options to which this setting can be changed are:

B	HH.MM.SS
C	HH,MM,SS
D	HHhMMmSSs

NEGATIVE   This option allows you to set 1-2-3 to use either minus signs or parentheses for negative numbers in the Comma and Currency formats.

/Worksheet Global Default Other Undo

Description

This command allows you to enable and disable 1-2-3's Undo feature (ALT-F4). When it is enabled, you can reverse (undo) the last command sequence. If Undo is disabled, the ALT-F4 (UNDO) key will have no effect on the worksheet.

Options

The Undo command has two options: Enable and Disable.

/Worksheet Global Default Update

Description

The /Worksheet Global Default Update command allows you to save changes you have made to 1-2-3's default global settings with the /Worksheet Global Default commands, so that the new settings will be available the next time you work with 1-2-3. The settings will be saved in the 123.CNF file on your 1-2-3 disk.

/Worksheet Global Format

Description

The /Worksheet Global Format command allows you to change the default display format for the entire worksheet. All numeric entries on the worksheet will use the format chosen with this command unless they have been formatted with the /Range Format command, which has priority over /Worksheet Global Format.

Options

The options for the /Worksheet Global Format command are the same options as for the /Range Format command (except Reset is not available). This includes the Release 3 options, which are further described under the /Range Format Other command.

/Worksheet Global Group

Description

This command allows you to determine whether or not you wish to work only with the current sheet, or with all of the sheets in the file. When GROUP mode is in effect, GROUP appears in the status line. With GROUP on, /Range Format, /Range Label, /Range Prot, /Range Unprot, /Worksheet Titles, /Worksheet Page, /Worksheet Column, /Worksheet Insert (Column or Row), and /Worksheet Delete (Column or Row) operate on all the sheets in the current worksheet file. The /Worksheet Global commands Col-Width, Format, Label, Prot, and Zero also affect all worksheets when GROUP is enabled.

GROUP mode also affects the movement of the cell pointer from sheet to sheet. While in GROUP mode, the cell pointer is moved to its same position in any new sheets displayed. Without GROUP mode on, the cell pointer is moved to the position it was in the last time the new sheet was viewed.

As soon as GROUP is activated, the global and range formats for the current worksheet are applied to all sheets in the file. The column widths are affected in the same manner.

Options

The two options for this command are Enable to activate GROUP mode, and Disable. When GROUP is disabled, only the current sheet is affected by commands. The default is for GROUP to be disabled.

/Worksheet Global Zero

Description

This command allows you to select how 1-2-3 displays cells that have a value equal to zero. The options let you display a zero, hide the zero, or display a label.

Options

The /Worksheet Global Zero Command presents three options: Yes, No, and Label. The default is No, which allows zero values to display. Choosing the Yes option will suppress the display of zero values. The Label option, which was new in Release 3.1, prompts you for a label (other than 0) that 1-2-3 will display for cells that have a zero value. With all of these options, the original value (a zero or a formula) still appears in the control panel when the cell is highlighted.

/Worksheet Hide

Description

This command allows you to hide and redisplay sheets in the active worksheet file. You can indicate a range of one or more adjacent sheets.

Options

This command's two options are Enable to eliminate the sheets from view and access, and Disable to make them available again. Once you select one of these options, you must select one cell from the adjacent worksheets that you want to hide or redisplay.

> NOTE: Changes made during GROUP mode affect hidden sheets. Also, a reference to a range that spans the hidden worksheets includes the appropriate cells in the hidden worksheets. Hidden sheets will not print.

/Worksheet Insert

Description

The /Worksheet Insert command can be used to add blank rows, columns, and sheets to your worksheet files. These blank areas can be used to improve readability or to allow for the addition of new information to your worksheet.

Inserts made to the middle of a range of cells will automatically expand the reference to the range name.

Options

This command provides three options: Row, Column, and Sheet. Columns are always added to the left of the cell pointer location or the range you specify. Rows are always added above the cell pointer or the range you specify. New sheets can be added before or after the current sheet. Select a range containing the number of columns or rows you want to add. After you select whether you want the new sheets before or after the current worksheet, 1-2-3 prompts you for the number of worksheets you want to insert. Enter a number between 1 and 255. 1-2-3 limits the total number of worksheets to 256.

/Worksheet Window Perspective

Description

This command allows you to view three consecutive sheets at one time. 1-2-3 automatically sizes the screen for the three sheets. To restore the display, use /Worksheet Window Clear for a permanent change, or ALT-F6 (ZOOM) for a temporary change.

CHAPTER 5

Basic Worksheet Commands

This chapter focuses on menu commands that will expand your productivity in using the worksheet. In the chapter you will learn additional commands on the Worksheet menus.

You will also use /Range commands—to name worksheet cells and create notes regarding their contents. Other /Range commands will help you find and optionally change entries within formulas or labels. /Range commands let you transpose data from a row layout to a column layout, or from a layout across worksheets to a row or column on another worksheet. You can also use /Range commands to establish a restricted input area.

The /Copy command and the /Move command will improve your skill at developing new worksheets. You will also be introduced to a variety of new Worksheet options that allow you to use your Worksheet data more effectively.

By the time you have finished reading this chapter, you will have experience with all the worksheet commands except the ones with a very specialized purpose. You will also know which SmartIcons to use to invoke these features if you are working with Release 3.4.

Working with Ranges

In Chapter 4 you learned to use some of the /Range commands to change the appearance of your worksheet. In this chapter you will expand your range options with commands that allow you to access cells through range names rather than cell addresses. You will also learn /Range commands that can change a worksheet column into a worksheet row. With Release 3, you can also change the layout of data that spans multiple sheets, transposing rows into columns, or taking data displayed across sheets and placing it in a single row or column of a single sheet. You will find out how to freeze formulas at their existing values for a large or small range of cells. You will be introduced to additional commands that alter the worksheet format, either erasing all entries for a range or changing the justification for labels stored in the range. Finally, you will learn how to use the new search features that locate matching entries in a formula or label.

Methods of Specifying Cell Ranges

You can tell 1-2-3 in a variety of ways which range you want to work with. With Release 3 you even have the option of preselecting the range. This is a useful technique when you need to work with the same range of cells with several different commands. You will learn more about methods for preselecting ranges later in the chapter.

To select a range after choosing a command that requires a range, press and hold the left button of your mouse while dragging across the cells that you want to include. If you have experience using a mouse, this can be the quickest approach to selecting a range. If you would prefer to use the keyboard to define your range, the easiest method is using the arrow keys to point to the desired range. Pointing and dragging offer the advantage of letting you visually verify the range you have chosen, since they highlight the range cells as you expand or contract the range. Pointing works only after a complete range is suggested. If a

Chapter 5: Basic Worksheet Commands

command references a single cell, type a period to turn the single cell address into a range, thereby locking the beginning of the range in place at this address. You can then expand the range to include additional cells by moving the cell pointer until you reach the end of the range you want.

In Figure 5-1, 1-2-3 suggests a range beginning at a location where you are using the /Range Format command from Chapter 4. If your cell pointer is positioned at the beginning of the range before you invoke the menu with a slash (/), you need only move with the arrow keys to highlight and complete the range, as shown here:

```
A:E5: [W11] 23450                                                    POINT
Enter range to format: A:E3..A:E5
  A     A        B         C         D         E         F     G     H
  1              Account Balances as of August 31, 1992
  2
  3              Cash                                   56980
  4              Accounts Receivable                    87450
  5              Accounts Payable                       23450
```

If you forget to position your cell pointer properly before invoking one of the /Range commands, you will have to unlock the beginning of the range before you can change it. To do this, press ESC and move the cell pointer to the desired location. You must again lock in the beginning of the range by entering a period before you begin to expand the range with the cell pointer movement keys. If the beginning of a range is not locked into place, 1-2-3 displays only the beginning of the range, as shown here:

```
A:E3: [W11] 56980                                                    POINT
Enter data range: A:E3
  A     A        B         C         D         E         F     G     H
  1              Account Balances as of August 31, 1992
  2
  3              Cash                                   56980
  4              Accounts Receivable                    87450
  5              Accounts Payable                       23450
  6
  7
```

If you then move to the end of the range without locking the beginning in place, only the last cell in the range is highlighted.

NOTE: You could also use the mouse to indicate the range by pointing to E3, then dragging the mouse to E5 with the left mouse button pressed.

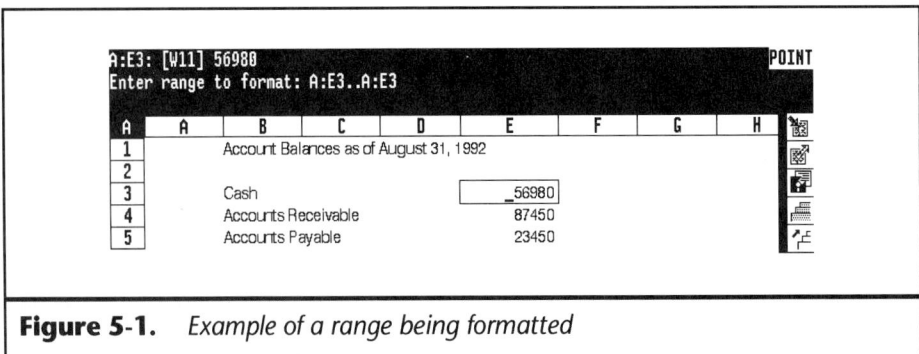

Figure 5-1. *Example of a range being formatted*

You can use other keys in combination with the arrow keys to save time when pointing out a range. For example, in Figure 5-2 the cell pointer is located in A1. When you invoke a command that suggests a range, it displays the range as A:A1..A:A1, indicating a single-cell range that begins and ends in cell A1 on sheet A. To select the complete rectangle of cells, in response to the prompt for the range, press END followed by RIGHT ARROW. This moves your cell pointer to the last entry on the right. To move to the bottom of the column, press END and DOWN ARROW. This will include all the filled cells in the selected range.

The END key can be used in other situations with a little planning. Let's say you want to format all the cells in row 3 but there are not entries in every cell. First move to the beginning of row 3 (cell A3), invoke **/Range Format Fixed**, and press ENTER. END and RIGHT ARROW will not work here because of the breaks in the entries. But if row 1 has entries in every cell and you press HOME to move to A1, and then END and RIGHT ARROW, you can then press the DOWN ARROW twice for the exact selection you wanted, as you can see in Figure 5-3.

Release 3 lets you specify multiple-sheet ranges that span two or more worksheets, although it is not possible to create one range that spans worksheet

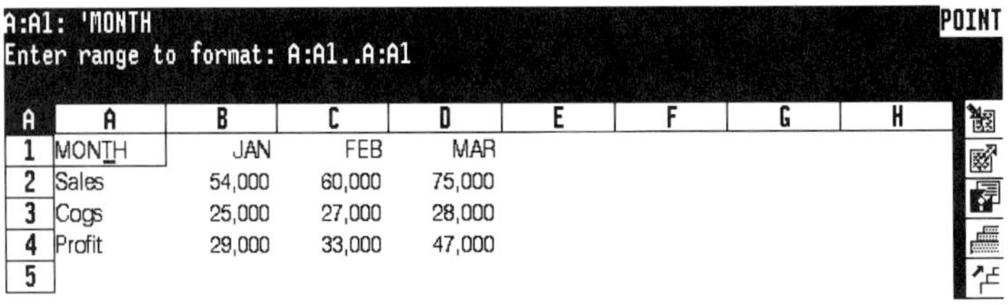

Figure 5-2. *Worksheet with the cell pointer in A1*

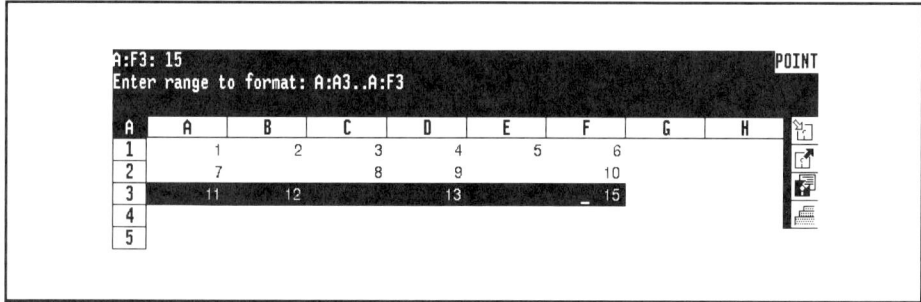

Figure 5-3. *Using other keys with the END and arrow key combinations*

files. Suppose you wish to format the range of cells B:B3..D:D10. First, move the cell pointer to cell B3 in sheet B. Invoke the **/Range Format** command. Assuming all the cells within the selected range contain data, you can use the END key method to highlight all the entries quickly. Press END followed by the RIGHT ARROW key. The range will now read B:B3..B:D3. Press the END key again, but this time follow it with DOWN ARROW. The range now reads B:B3..B:D10. For the last step, press the CTRL-PGUP key twice. The range now reads B:B3..D:D10. Press ENTER to finalize the range.

It is preferable to have 1-2-3 generate the cell addresses in a range whenever possible, but you always have the option of typing a cell reference in response to one of the range prompts. When you use the pointing method, 1-2-3 always adds the level numbers, even if the references are both on the same sheet. If you are typing the range yourself, you only need to type the cell addresses, unless the data is in another sheet or file.

When you type a single period in a reference (D4.D10) or when you type the complete entry, 1-2-3 will duplicate it so that two periods display (D4..D10). You can enter any two opposite corners of a rectangle of cells to specify a range. Normally, however, the upper left and the lower right corners are used for a single-sheet range (as in A2..F10). For a multiple-sheet range, use the upper left corner on the sheet with the lowest level and the lower right corner on the highest sheet, as in A:A2..G:F10. Remember, if you type a period after pointing to a range address, 1-2-3 will move the active corner (the corner containing the cell pointer) in the range, allowing you to expand or contract the range from a different side.

TIP: Some commands remember the last range they used. Commands like /Print and /Data Fill (described in Chapters 6 and 8, respectively) remember the range last used, and suggest it for the next use of the command. To change these suggested ranges you can use ESC to eliminate the range, or BACKSPACE to replace the cell pointer in its location before the command was invoked.

Naming Cell Ranges

In some respects, all worksheet cells automatically have names, since they have unique cell addresses by which they can be referenced. You are already familiar with column/row addresses such as A2, U7, or AX89 from a single-sheet perspective, and D:A2, D:F10, G:A2 from a multiple-sheet perspective. It is clear exactly what cell you mean when you use these addresses. If you leave out the sheet level indicator, 1-2-3 assumes you mean the current sheet. Although it is never wrong to add a sheet level, it is only required when the cells referenced are on another sheet. Likewise, a file reference is only required when you are referencing a range in another file.

However, though the location of the cell is evident, it is not clear what is contained in cells named A2, U7, or AX89. Is it the interest rate, the number of employees, or the Los Angeles Dodgers' batting average? It can take time to move the cell pointer every time you need to remember a particular cell's contents.

The /Range Name commands provide a solution for this dilemma. With these commands you can assign names to ranges of any size which provide meaningful information about the contents of the groups of cells they reference. If cell A10 contains sales for 1991, for example, you might assign it the name SALES_91. If cells B3..B25 contain all the expenses for a certain department, you might assign a range name like TOTAL_EXPENSES.

In Release 3, range names assume added importance. With the ability to access multiple worksheets in one file, it is more convenient to be able to access data in other sheets by using a name like SALES rather than remember that you stored it in M:D13..M:D42. This feature also makes it easier to link data across several files. Range names can only be assigned within active worksheet files (that is, files in memory), although you must use sheet or file indicators to assign names to sheets other than the current sheet.

1-2-3 allows you to assign any name to any range of cells, provided that the name does not exceed 15 characters. Once you assign a range name, you can use it the same way that you use a cell address. For example, you could create a formula for a profit calculation using assigned range names, such as +SALES_91–TOTAL_EXPENSES. Unlike Release 2, when you include a named range in the formula, 1-2-3 Release 3 keeps the range name in the formula, even when you edit. The box called "A Few Pointers for Creating Range Names" provides some additional tips on range names.

Release 3 provides many new range name options, including the ability to add a note for a range name. Since the named range can span many cells, the semicolon method used to add a note after a value or a formula will not work. Instead, you need to use the /Range Name Note command. Another option is support for undefined range names: you can finalize a formula even if it includes range name references that do not yet exist. If you delete an assigned range name used in a formula, 1-2-3 converts the range name reference to the corresponding range address. In conjunction with this feature, there is a /Range Name Undefine command that retains an existing range name but disassociates it from any specific range reference.

Assigning Range Names

There are two basic methods for assigning range names. Usually you will invoke the /Range Name Create command to enter your range names. In special cases where the name you want to use will be assigned to a single cell and already appears in an adjacent worksheet cell, you can use the /Range Name Labels command.

CREATING NEW NAMES The easiest way to name a range of cells is to move your cell pointer to the upper left corner of the range. If you are planning to create a name for a range that spans multiple sheets, you will also want to be in the first sheet in the range. After positioning the cell pointer, type **/Range Name Create**, type your range name, and press ENTER. If you want to name just one cell, simply press ENTER again. For a range larger than one cell, move your cell pointer to the lower right cell in the range and then press ENTER again. You can also select a range using the mouse.

Alternatively, you can leave your cell pointer on any worksheet cell, type **/Range Name Create**, type the range name, and press ENTER. You then type the cell coordinates corresponding to the range and press ENTER again. For example, consider the commands /Range Name Create SALES D:A1 and /Range Name Create EXPENSES B2..B6. In the first example, the range being named can be on another sheet in the active file. In the second example, the range must be in the current sheet of the active file since the sheet level is not supplied.

1-2-3 allows you to assign more than one name to a range. For example, suppose you have data in cells F4..F25 that represent expenses for 1991, and you name this range EXPENSES_91. Now suppose you wish to use these expenses to project next year's budget. You might then want to assign this same range of cells a name such as PREVIOUS_YR_EXP for use in your budget calculations. 1-2-3 permits you to assign both names.

The worksheet in Figure 5-4 offers several opportunities to use the /Range Name Create command. Suppose you want to name the cells containing the figures for Sales and Cost of Goods Sold (Cogs). To do this, place the cell pointer in B3 on the amount for sales, and enter **/Range Name Create**. In response to the request for a name, enter **SALES_91** and press ENTER. The next prompt wants the address of the range you are naming. Since the name is for just this one cell, simply press ENTER again. Now move the cell pointer to B4 and repeat the process, using the name COGS_91.

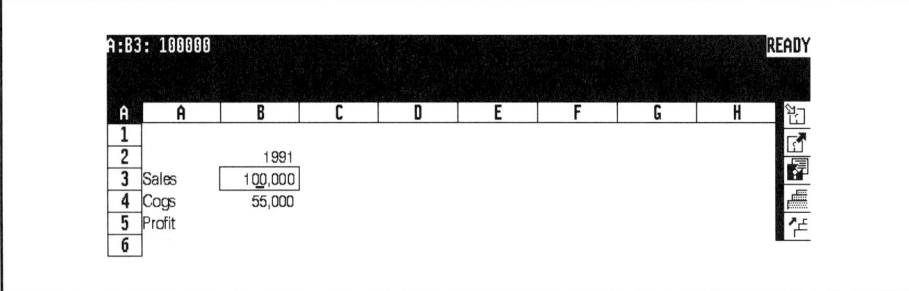

Figure 5-4. *A worksheet where range names can be used*

A Few Pointers for Creating Range Names

1-2-3 has few restrictions in range names, but it is helpful to add a few for the sake of clarity.

- 1-2-3 does not prevent you from using spaces in range names, but it is preferable not to use them. The name TOTAL SALES could be mistaken for two range names by someone just glancing at a formula, but TOTAL_SALES is clearly one name.

- You are also allowed to use arithmetic operators in range names, but they, too, can cause problems. TOTAL*SALES could be confusing as a range name; it might be interpreted as a request for an arithmetic operation that would multiply TOTAL by SALES.

- Another permitted type of name to avoid is a name that could be confused with a cell address, such as A3 or D4.

- Remember that numbers cannot be used as range names unless they are used in combination with letters. For example, SALES_86 is acceptable, but 56 is not acceptable as a range name.

- Do not name ranges with the same name as @functions, macro commands, or 1-2-3 key names.

- Do not start range names with numbers because they cannot be included in a formula.

To use these range names move the cell pointer to B5. Type + to start the formula. Press F3 (NAME) to display the range names in the worksheet file like this:

Notice the NAMES indicator that displays when 1-2-3 is listing range names. Highlight SALES_91 and press ENTER. 1-2-3 adds the range name SALES_91 to the formula to represent B3. Type – to continue the formula. Press F3 (NAME) and press ENTER to select COGS_91. Press ENTER to finalize the formula. Now the worksheet will look like this:

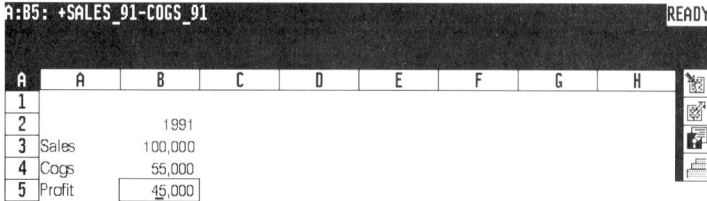

Once a name has been assigned to a cell or a range of cells, you may use this name anywhere you would use a cell or range reference. This means that you can use range names when formatting, copying, moving, printing, or graphing data, in addition to formula building. When you use a range name that refers to a multiple-cell range in a formula in which only single-cell references are allowed, Release 3.1 returns ERR.

TIP: 1-2-3 only replaces range references in formulas. If you use a cell address, like A1, in a formula and assign a name like SALES to the range A1..A1, 1-2-3 will not make a substitution. Since A1 is a cell address, not a range, 1-2-3 will not equate the two references, and the formula will continue to display A1. On the other hand, if you have a formula such as @SUM(B2..B10) and name the range B2..B10 as TOTALS, 1-2-3 will display the formula as @SUM(TOTALS).

USING EXISTING WORKSHEET LABELS TO CREATE RANGE NAMES The /Range Name Labels command can save you data entry time when assigning range names if conditions are right. First, the name you plan to use must already exist on the worksheet as a label entry. It must also be in a cell adjacent to the cell you plan to name. With this command you can assign a range name only to a single cell, so if you are naming a range of more than one cell, you must use the /Range Name Create command. One advantage of /Range Name Labels is that you can use it to assign several range names at once.

The cells in B3..B10 in Figure 5-5 can all have range names assigned with one execution of the /Range Name Labels command. To do this, position the cell pointer in A3 and enter **/Range Name Labels**. Since the range of cells you are naming is on the right of the labels, choose Right next. Finally, move the cell pointer to A10 and press ENTER. The range names you will create are CASH, MARKETABLE SECU, ACCOUNTS RECEIV, NOTES RECEIVABL, ACCOUNTS PAYABL, MORTGAGE PAYABL, NOTES PAYABLE, and STOCKHOLDERS' E. (These range names are truncated since 1-2-3 has a 15-character limit for range names.)

Deleting Range Names

Assigned range names use a small amount of 1-2-3's internal memory. If you are not using some of your old range names, consider deleting them to free up the space they use.

TIP: It is best to delete a range name as soon as you know it is no longer required, since later on you may forget whether you need it or not.

To delete a range name, enter **/Range Name Delete**. 1-2-3 will then present a list of all the assigned range names at the top of your screen just like when you press F3 (NAME). You have the option of typing the name to delete, or highlighting the name to delete. In either case, press ENTER after making your selection. You can also click on the name with the mouse. This action causes the

Figure 5-5. *A range suitable for /Range Name Labels*

selected range name to disappear permanently. Any formulas that use the deleted range name will have the range name replaced with the cell or range address that the range name represented.

Resetting Range Names

The /Range Name Delete option is ideal when you have only a few names to delete. If you have many names to delete, however, this option is slow. The /Range Name Reset command can speed up the process when you are deleting most or all of your range names. /Range Name Reset deletes all range names, so it is perfect for situations when you want to start fresh and create all new names. When you have a large number of names and want all but a few deleted, it may be quicker to delete them all and then use /Range Name Create to reenter the names you want to keep—rather than delete the names one by one with /Range Name Delete.

/Range Name Undefine also removes range names from the active list of range names. An important distinction between this command and /Range Name Delete is that formulas that use the undefined range name continue using the range name rather than the cell or range that the range name represents. These formulas will evaluate to ERR until the undefined range names are redefined. Also, the /Range Name Undefine command does not eliminate notes that may be attached to range names. If you use /Range Name Create at a later time to reinstate undefined range names, the notes will still be attached to the range names. If you use the Delete or Reset commands to remove a range name, the note is also deleted and will have to be reentered when you reinstate the range name.

Creating a Table of Range Names

One way of checking the range to which a range name is assigned is to list the names on the screen. The /Range Name Table command will build a table of range names and the cell addresses they identify. This table, built in any empty area of the worksheet, can serve as documentation for all the range names used in your worksheet.

Before executing the required command sequence, choose a good table location—one where you won't overwrite data or important formulas if the table is longer than you expect. You might even want to add a new sheet to the model with /Worksheet Insert Sheet and place the table there, rather than bothering to check the impact on existing model entries. When you are ready to create the table, enter **/Range Name Table** and respond to 1-2-3's prompt by typing in the table location. 1-2-3 permits you to supply just the upper left corner of the table range, and will then use as much space as it needs for the table. Figure 5-6 presents a table created with the /Range Name Table command. Note that the range names are listed in alphabetical order.

Using Filenames and Wildcard References with Range Names

Although range names like SALES or B:SALES are the most common form of reference used, you can also use a filename as part of the range name reference when you want to access a range in a file other than the current file. The standard double angle bracket notation << >> is used around the filename, as in <<C:\123R34\BUDGET.WK3>>SALES.

You can also use a question mark within the angle brackets as a wildcard, indicating a match regardless of the filename, and 1-2-3 will search all active files. Use the wildcard notation only when the range name is unique among the active files. If you enter this notation in a command or formula, 1-2-3 will display an error message if it does not find a match, or if it finds multiple matches. To look for the range name SALES in this manner, you would enter **<<?>>SALES** in a formula or a command that expects a range.

TIP: 1-2-3 does not convert wildcard references to range addresses when you delete the range name. Normally if you delete a range name, 1-2-3 converts formula entries that reference the deleted name to the appropriate range address. This does not occur when the formula reference is to a wildcard reference.

Figure 5-6. Output of /Range Name Table

Creating and Using Range Name Notes

You can attach notes to range names to describe the contents of the range, the individual entering the note, or the date and time it was entered. Since the range may include a number of cells, the note is not entered in a particular cell like the notes entered at the end of formulas or values. The /Range Name Note command displays a submenu that remains on the screen until you select the Quit option. This allows you to make multiple selections from the menu—creating, editing, and deleting notes without having to invoke the menu for each activity.

The /Range Name Note Create command allows you to enter a note for an existing range name. If a range name is undefined, you must define it before adding a note. A note can be as long as 512 characters, although the entire note does not display in the control panel on multiple lines the way a long cell entry does. Once you have created a note for a range name, you can also use the Create option to edit the note entry. Use the cursor control keys to move within the control panel line when you are editing. If you save the worksheet file after entering the note, it will be available for all future sessions.

To eliminate a note from a defined range name, invoke the /Range Name Note Delete command. Type the name of the range for which you want to delete the note, or highlight it in the list of defined range names. When the note is deleted, the range name is unaffected and is still assigned to the range.

If you want to eliminate all notes attached to all range names, use /Range Name Note Reset. This one command deletes all notes in the current file without prompting you to confirm your decision.

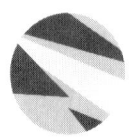

TIP: Remember to check the file you are in before using /Range Name Note Reset to delete all range notes. If Undo is not enabled, there is no way to restore notes you have Reset, unless you have a copy of the worksheet on disk that you can retrieve. To safeguard all of your hard work in note creation, check the active file to ensure that you are in the file you want to be in before invoking the Reset option.

You have learned that the /Range Name Table command creates a table of range names. /Range Name Note Table adds a third column to this table, to display any notes attached to the range names. /Range Name Note Table also lists undefined range names that have notes attached to them.

Practical Applications for Range Names

Assigning range names may seem like so much extra work that you may wonder why you should bother using them. For very small models they may not be worthwhile, but for larger ones—especially multiple-sheet models—range names offer a significant payback. They make formulas much more readable, for one thing. They also help prevent incorrect formula references, since you will see a descriptive name rather than a cryptic cell address. As data becomes farther removed from the formula location, the payback becomes greater, because you cannot see the data at the same time as the formula and verify the accuracy of the cell addresses used.

When range names are used, you will find that rows, columns, and sheets can be inserted in the middle of a range, and the range reference will be adjusted automatically. The references will also be updated if you delete rows, columns, or sheets from the middle of a range. If you want to see the updated references in a table, however, you will need to execute /Range Name Table or /Range Name Note Table again since neither command dynamically updates the worksheet.

Transposing Data

Sometimes you will want to rearrange a range of entries that you have made in a worksheet. You may have changed your mind about the best presentation method, or you may want to use an existing worksheet as the basis for a new worksheet but must reorganize the presentation to make this possible.

1-2-3 provides the /Range Trans (Transpose) command to permit you to change data entered horizontally across a row, to a vertical column presentation or vice versa. You can also reorganize in a number of different ways the information stored in a three-dimensional range. When you use the command on a two-dimensional range, it automatically transposes column data into a row, and row entries into a column, using a special copy process. When you use the command with three-dimensional ranges, a submenu of additional selections appears so you can specify exactly how you want the transposition to occur. The steps for transposing data are summarized in the box called "Steps for Transposing Data."

Since the /Range Trans command will operate on single or multiple rows or columns in single or multiple sheets, there are a wide variety of options to cover. Before using any of these options, you will want to be sure the formulas in any cells that you are transposing have up-to-date values. If CALC is showing at the bottom of your screen, press F9 (CALC) to recalculate the worksheet before beginning. Also, if the cells that you are transposing contain links to other files, you might want to refresh these links before starting (with /File Admin Link-Refresh).

To begin the transpose operation enter **/Range Trans**. Next, select a From range (the original location of your data) in response to 1-2-3's prompt, and press ENTER. For a single-sheet transposition, you can specify either a single row or column of entries, or a rectangular range of data. For a multiple-sheet transposition, the From range can be any range that spans sheets.

Chapter 5: Basic Worksheet Commands   159

Next you are asked to specify a To range (the new location). You can enter a range that has the opposite orientation but the same number of entries as the From range. However, the easiest approach is to enter the beginning cell of the To range and let 1-2-3 figure out the size of the range that it needs.

CAUTION: In specifying the To range in three-dimensional transpositions, make certain there are a sufficient number of open sheets to accommodate the requirements of the To range. For example, if your From range is A:A1..A:A12 and your To range will be B:A1..M:A1, have sheets B through M added before you make the transposition.

Steps for Transposing Data

Transposing data in your worksheet allows you to reorganize an entire application without reentering data. The steps you need to follow are:

1. Use F9 (CALC) and /File Admin Links-Refresh if you need to update calculations or links to external files.

2. Move the cell pointer to the first cell in the range you wish to transpose.

3. Enter **/Range Trans** and use the cursor movement keys to highlight the entire range containing entries that you want to transpose.

4. Highlight the first cell in the To range, and press ENTER. If both of your ranges are single-sheet ranges, the transposition will occur now. 1-2-3 implicitly performs a /Range Value command with the /Range Trans command, since it copies the values instead of the formulas to the To range.

5. If either range was a multiple-sheet range, select the type of change you want. The selections are

    ■ Rows/Columns to change the orientation of data within each sheet

    ■ Worksheets/Rows to change rows of data in several worksheets to a row on another worksheet

    ■ Columns/Worksheets to perform the same transition as Worksheets/Rows, except with a column orientation

NOTE: If you want to transpose a single-sheet range to a multi-sheet range, you must specify a To range that spans the correct number of worksheets.

With a single-sheet operation, 1-2-3 completes the transposition after the entry of the To range. However, with a three-dimensional transposition you must select how you want 1-2-3 to handle the process. The Rows/Columns option performs the same transpose operation as the single-sheet operation. Within each sheet, the data in the From range is reversed from a row to a column orientation in the To range and vice versa. With the Worksheets/Rows selection, the data in the first row of each worksheet's From range is copied to the first worksheet. Data from the second row in each worksheet is copied to the second worksheet, with the process continuing until all the rows in the From range have been transposed. With a Columns/Worksheets transposition the first column in the From range on each worksheet is copied to the first worksheet in the To range, and the data from the second column of each worksheet is copied to the second worksheet until all the columns in the From range have been transposed.

If some of the cells in the To range already contain data, their contents will be replaced as a result of the transposition operation. With Release 3, as formulas in a From range are copied to a To range, the resulting entries in the To range are always the converted value of the formula. Looking at examples for each of the options will help to clarify the operation of this command.

Single-Sheet Transposition

An example of original worksheet entries for a single-sheet transposition is shown here:

```
A:A1: 'Sales_90                                                      READY

A        A          B          C     D     E     F     G     H
1    Sales_90    $56,000
2    Sales_91    $65,000
3    Sales_92    $70,000
```

To complete the operation, enter **/Range Trans**, highlight A1..B3, and press ENTER. Highlight D1 as the beginning of the To range and press ENTER to complete the transposition. The results are shown horizontally in D1..F2.

```
A:A1: 'Sales_90                                                      READY

A        A          B          C     D         E         F         G     H
1    Sales_90    $56,000           Sales_90  Sales_91  Sales_92
2    Sales_91    $65,000           $56,000   $65,000   $70,000
3    Sales_92    $70,000
```

Multiple-Sheet Transpose Operations

Multiple-sheet transpose operations can either transpose several sheets as if you had performed several single-sheet transpose operations, or it can slice through a series of sheets and bring the data from a row or column of these sheets into one sheet.

The first sample multiple-sheet transpose operation shows a way to complete several row-to-column transitions without the need for separate requests. The data in Figure 5-7 shows a section from three different worksheets that displays discount percentages by customer type and amount purchased for three different regions. To change the orientation of these three individual tables and place Customer Type data across the top row rather than down the left-hand column, you can use the Rows/Columns option.

First, enter **/Range Trans**. Specify the From range as A:A3..C:E6 and press ENTER. Next, specify the To range as A:A10—the upper left corner of the range on the first sheet—and press ENTER. Although you may want the new orientation to replace the old data, you do not want to use overlapping From and To ranges. So first transpose the data; then you can move it to replace the old entries, to ensure

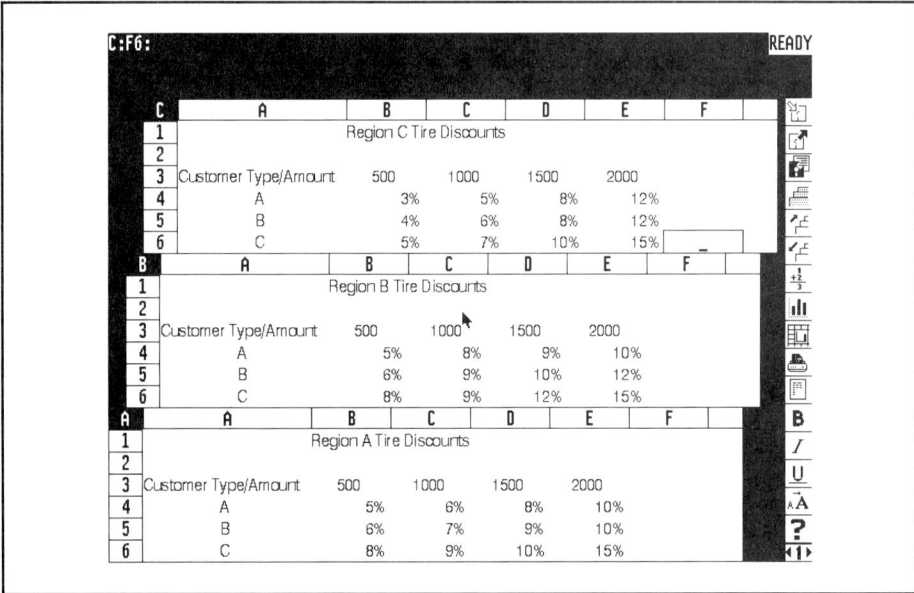

Figure 5-7. *Entries from three different worksheets*

an error-free operation. Select Rows/Columns from the menu and press ENTER. The worksheet now shows both sets of entries. The new entries are shown in Figure 5-8.

In the next example, a series of worksheets showing sales contest winners from three regions is shown in Figure 5-9. If you would like all the first-place winners in one list, second-place in another, and third in another, the Worksheets/Rows option can handle the task. The first step is setting up a form on the file to receive the data. Since sheets D, E, and F contain the data to be transposed, sheets A, B, and C can contain the new entries. These sheets were set up with headings in B2, and the words "Western Region," "Eastern Region," and "Southern Region" in C3..C5 of each sheet. After the preliminary setup, move the cell pointer to D:C3 and enter **/Range Trans**. Next, highlight D:C3..F:C5 and press ENTER. Specify the To range as A:D3 and Worksheet/Rows, planning for 1-2-3 to transpose the data so it displays on the sheets as shown in Figure 5-10.

The third type of multiple-sheet transposition that you might need is moving columns of data from several worksheets and placing corresponding columns on individual sheets. In Figure 5-11, there are three sheets that display the total sales information for three regions by year. In a set of consolidated reports by year, you might want to show all the 1990 data for all three regions on one sheet. Enter **/Range Trans**, highlight A:B3..C:D5 as the From range, and press ENTER. Highlight D:B3 as the To range, assuming that you want to use the prepared

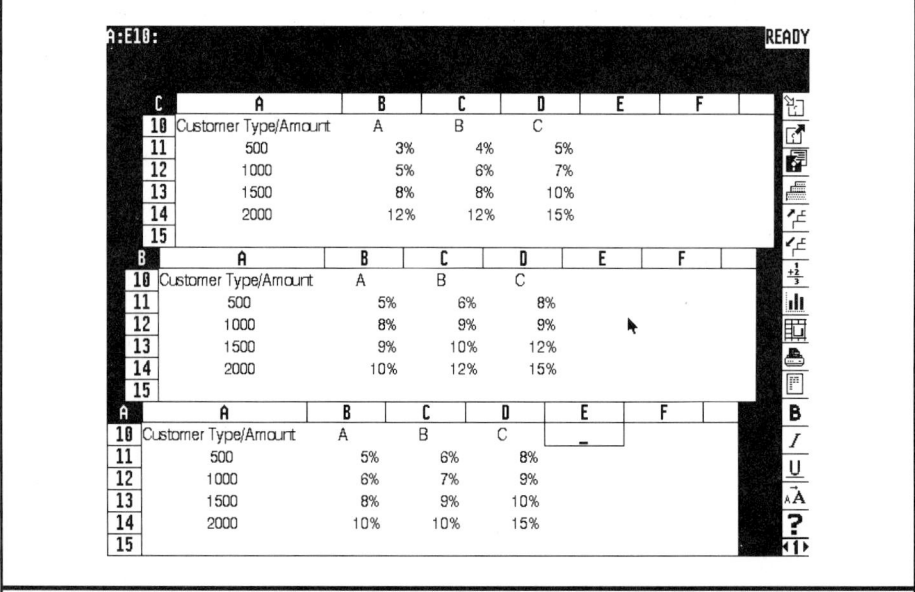

Figure 5-8. Entries from the three sheets in Figure 5-7 transposed in a new location

Chapter 5: Basic Worksheet Commands

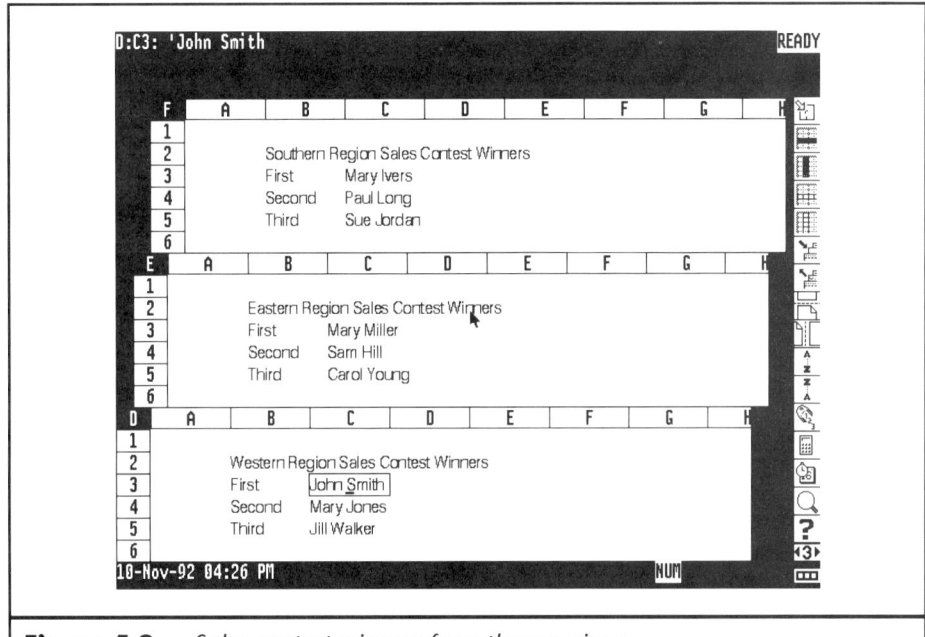

Figure 5-9. *Sales contest winners from three regions*

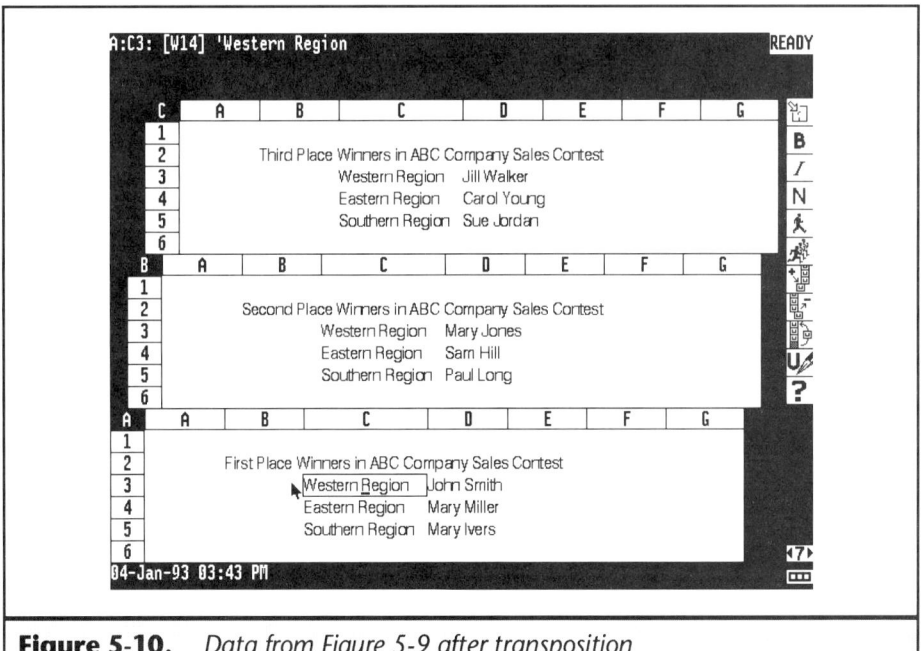

Figure 5-10. *Data from Figure 5-9 after transposition*

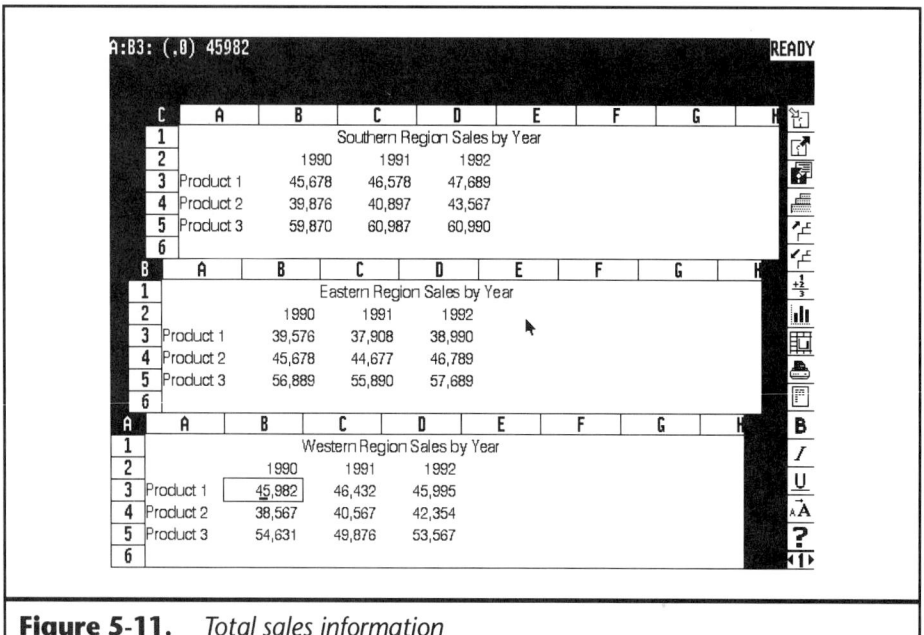

Figure 5-11. Total sales information

sheets in Figure 5-12 for the results. Then, select Worksheet/Columns and press ENTER to see the transposed data in Figure 5-13.

Converting Formulas to Values

At times during the model creation process, you may want to change some of your projections to fixed values, rather than allowing them to be revised each time the worksheet is recalculated. One example is the budgeting process. As you prepare a budget, you want to look at various possibilities. Once the budget is submitted, however, the projections you made are recorded and will serve as the target for your operation throughout the budget period. You may thus wish to freeze some of the formulas used to make the budget projection. 1-2-3 provides the perfect way to do this via the /Range Value command.

The /Range Value command copies the values produced by formulas to a new location. It copies only the values displayed in worksheet cells, not the formulas used to produce these values. Thus the original worksheet can still change as new values are entered for assumptions, but the copy will not be affected by changes in the assumptions. To use this command to freeze formula values, use the same range for From and To. Thus, the original formula values are replaced with fixed values.

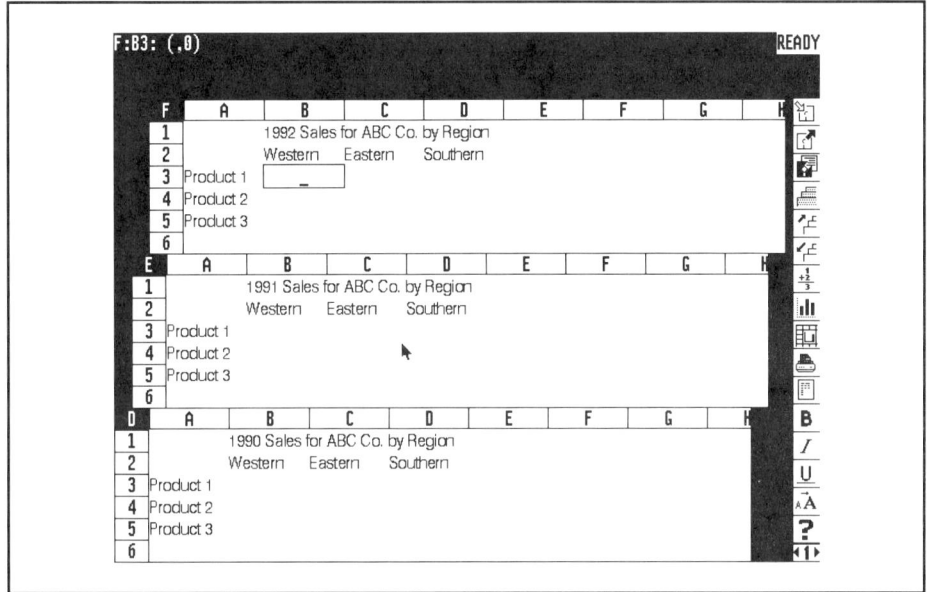

Figure 5-12. Sheets prepared for the transposed data

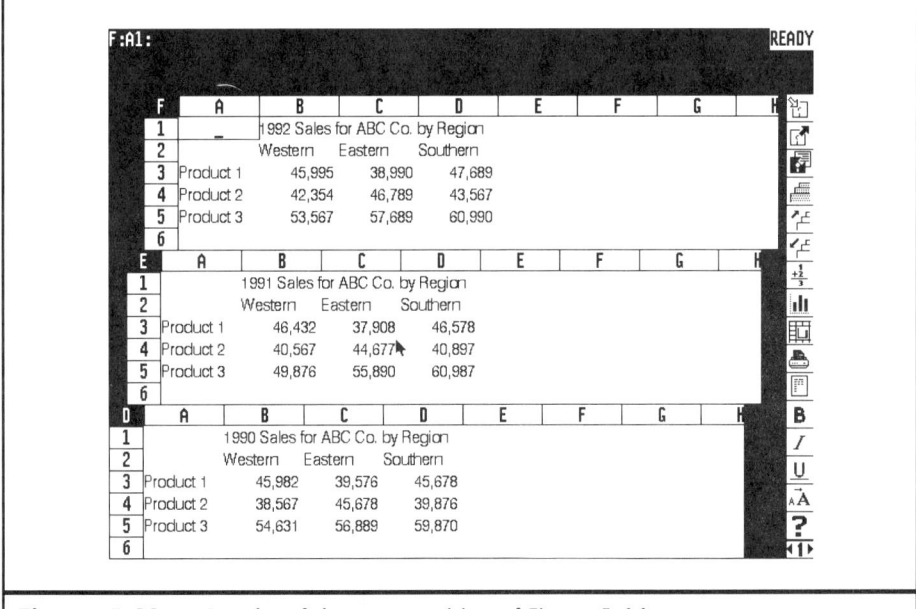

Figure 5-13. Results of the transposition of Figure 5-11

As an example of fixing values, the entry in B3 in the following worksheet displays in the worksheet cell as a number but as a formula in the control panel:

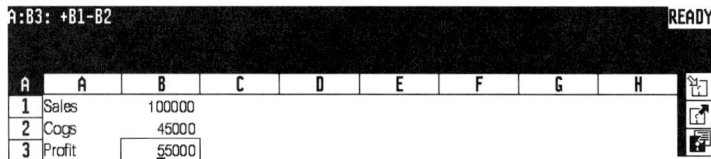

The same cell after using /Range Value, with B3 as a From and a To range, is now a value:

You will notice that the worksheet display is the same, but the control panel now shows the cell as containing a value, not a formula.

You can also use /Range Value on ranges that span worksheets if you have a multiple-sheet range that you wish to convert.

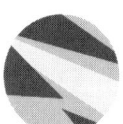

TIP: Be sure all your formula values are up to date before converting formulas to fixed values. If the CALC indicator appears at the bottom of your screen, press F9 (CALC) to update all formulas before proceeding. If you are referencing linked cells in shareable files, use /File Admin Links-Refresh to ensure the most recent values.

Changing the Justification of Labels

As a default, 1-2-3 begins labels at the left side of cells. You have already learned that you can change the alignment of an individual label by preceding it with a caret (^) for center justification or a double quotation mark (") for right justification. Using these options can be very time consuming, however, when you want to change the alignment of a whole range of cells.

The /Range Label command can handle this situation much more efficiently. You simply specify the range for which you want to change the labels and then execute the command. 1-2-3 ensures that existing label entries in the specified cells receive the correct label indicator. Neither entries made after /Range Label are entered nor nonlabel entries in the specified cells will be affected. New label entries will receive the default label prefix.

With this command you can select left, right, or center justification for an existing range of labels. Labels originally entered using the default label prefix of an apostrophe are left justified, as shown in column A of Figure 5-14. If you enter /Range Label and select Right to change the orientation of the labels to the right side of each cell, the results look like column C of Figure 5-14. Entering the command again and choosing Center causes each label to display in the center of the cell as shown in column E of Figure 5-14. The Left option could be used to change either of these results back to the original display format.

Release 3.4 offers SmartIcons on palette 2 that will allow you to change the alignment of the selected range. You can see by the lines in the icon whether right, left, or center alignment will be used. The icons look like this:

Erasing Cell Ranges

The /Range Erase command eliminates the entries in a range of cells. It does not matter whether the entries are numbers, labels, or formulas. Using this command will not affect the numeric format assigned to the cell, its width, or its protection status.

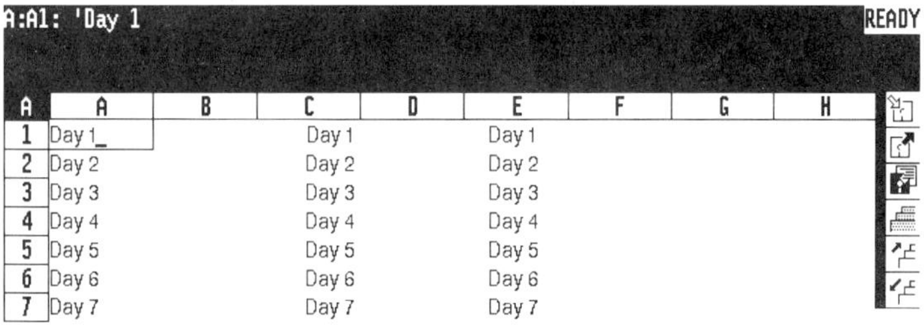

Figure 5-14. *Labels with various alignments*

Figure 5-15 shows a worksheet containing miscellaneous entries in F2..G6 that are no longer required. To remove these entries, move the cell pointer to F2 and type **/Range Erase**. Then move the cell pointer to G6 to extend the range, and press ENTER to achieve the results shown in Figure 5-16. Note that if worksheet protection has been enabled, the /Range Erase command will not work. If Undo is enabled, you can restore the entries removed with /Range Erase as long as no actions intervene between /Range Erase and the use of ALT-F4 (UNDO).

With Release 3.4's SmartIcons, you have another method for deleting the range's contents. You can select the range by using either the F4 (ABS) and the arrow keys, or the mouse. Then, select the trash can icon (shown below) from the fifth palette, deleting the contents of the cells in the range.

REMEMBER: You can also move to a cell and press the DEL key to remove the contents of just that cell.

Protecting Worksheet Cells

A completed worksheet often represents hours or days of work in planning, formula entry, and testing. Once you have created a well-planned and tested worksheet application, you will want to protect it from accidental keystrokes or

Figure 5-15. *Extraneous worksheet entries*

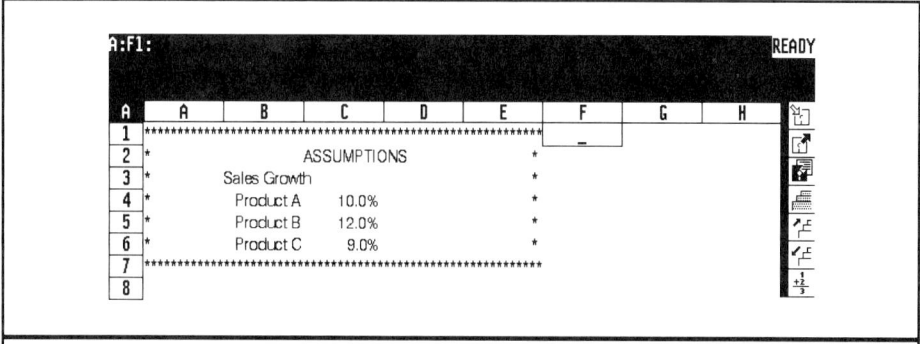

Figure 5-16. *Results of /Range Erase*

option selections that could cause you to overwrite formulas or other vital data. 1-2-3 provides features that will prevent this damage to important cells. These features can also make other users more comfortable in using models that you create for them, because they know they cannot destroy the models. You can protect individual cells with the /Range Prot, /Range Unprot, and /Worksheet Global Prot commands. You can also protect worksheet settings such as column widths, formats, and cell protection status with the /File Admin Seal command.

TIP: Watch your screen for information about the current Protection status. Use /Worksheet Status to see the Global Protection Status for the current file. Look in the control panel for "PR" to identify individual entries with a Protected status.

The Protection features of 1-2-3 let you determine which cells will be protected and which ones will accept entries. There is also an easy way to temporarily disable the Protection mechanism without changing a cell's basic definition as a protected or unprotected cell. Finally, 1-2-3 provides a command that is used in conjunction with Protection to restrict the cell pointer to a single input range on the worksheet.

TIP: Group input entries onto one sheet where possible. Rather than spread input entries across many sheets, gather them on an input form on one sheet if possible. This approach will save operator entry time, and also make it easy for you to apply Protection to the cells in all the other sheets and eliminate it from the entry cells on the input sheet.

1-2-3's Protection process requires that you first decide which worksheet cells you wish to have unprotected. All cells are protected as an initial default. If you wish to allow entries in certain cells, you can unprotect them with /Range

Unprot. You can then turn on the Protection features of the package, and these unprotected cells will still permit entries. Protection is turned on with a Global option under the Worksheet menu.

REMEMBER: The effect of GROUP mode applies to /Range Prot and /Range Unprot. Changes made to the Protection status of the current worksheet with GROUP mode on will apply to all the sheets in the file.

Deciding What Cells to Protect

1-2-3 establishes a default status of Protected for every worksheet cell. This might sound strange, since you can make an entry anywhere on a new worksheet. You can do that because the Protection features of the package are initially turned off. If you turn on the Protection features, the Protected status of each cell is energized, and 1-2-3 rejects any additional entries. It is therefore important to decide what cells should accept entries before you turn on Protection.

You might find it useful to think of 1-2-3's Protection feature as a fence placed around every cell. The fences do not protect the contents of cells in a new worksheet, since none of the fence gates are closed. The /Worksheet Global Prot Enable command will close all the gates, thereby protecting the contents of the cells. Cells that you do not wish to have protected should have their fences torn down with /Range Unprot. Then, when the gates are closed with /Worksheet Global Prot Enable, you can still change these cells, because a gate without a fence does not offer effective protection.

The /Range Unprot command is used to strip cell protection from a range of one or many cells. To unprotect a range, enter **/Range Unprot**, and either point to the limiting cells or enter the range. If you change your mind and decide that a cell should be protected again, you can use the /Range Prot command to restore Protection for the cell. Unprotecting a cell highlights it on a monochrome display, or changes the text's color on a color display. Removing Protection has no other effect on a cell unless the Global Protection features (discussed in the next section) are turned on. In addition, a "U" appears after the cell address in the top line of the control panel when the cell pointer is on the unprotected cell.

Enabling Worksheet Protection

As noted in the analogy established previously, the /Worksheet Global Prot Enable command "closes the gate" on every protected worksheet cell, ensuring that protected cells cannot be altered. It also places the entry "PR" in the control panel for every protected cell. Once Protection is enabled, any time you make an entry in a protected cell, 1-2-3 displays an error message when you try finalizing the entry. You can use the /Range Unprot command even after you enable Protection to allow you to make entries into cells.

You may need to turn Protection off after enabling it; if so, you can enter **/Worksheet Global Prot Disable**. This command allows you to temporarily suspend Protection so you can make a change to a formula, for example.

TIP: If you need more protection use /File Admin Seal. Anyone who knows how to enable Worksheet Protection also knows how to disable it or change the cells that are to be protected. Use /File Admin Seal to lock the current worksheet settings; a password is then required to unlock it.

Specifying an Input Range

The /Range Input command is used in conjunction with the Protection features. Once a worksheet is protected, the /Range Input command allows you to restrict cell pointer movement to unprotected cells within the input range. /Range Input is useful for focusing attention on the cells available for entry during data input. The steps for using this command are as follows:

1. Set up the worksheet with all needed labels and formulas. In other words, design your worksheet before restricting the cell pointer.

2. Remove Protection from the cells requiring data entry, using /Range Unprot.

3. Enable the Protection feature, using /Worksheet Global Prot Enable.

4. Enter **/Range Input** and select the range of cells in which you want to allow input.

Your screen will display the input range in the upper left corner. You can edit cells in the specified range or enter new data in them. You can also use ESC, HOME, END, ENTER, F1 (HELP), F2 (EDIT), BACKSPACE, or any of the arrow keys in completing your entries. The cell pointer will always remain within the input range, since that is the only area where entries can be made. While /Range Input is in effect, the END and HOME keys will move you to the end or the beginning of the input range. Pressing either ESC or ENTER without making an entry cancels the /Range Input command. This command is used in the macro environment to assist with automating applications, and is ideal for use with the input form capability of Release 3 (see Chapter 13, "Command Language Macros").

Sealing the Worksheet

To protect your data, you can seal the file reservation and worksheet settings. Sealing a reservation is described in Chapter 8, "Working with Files." Sealing a worksheet prevents changes to the worksheet settings, although it still permits changes to the data.

When a worksheet is sealed, a user can change only the cell pointer's position, the worksheet data, and the Window settings (described later in the chapter). Changing the Wysiwyg formatting is also prohibited. You can further limit which cells are changed by unprotecting cells where changes are allowed and then enabling Worksheet Protection before sealing the worksheet. Once the worksheet file is sealed, the Protection status cannot be changed, and only the unprotected data cells can be modified.

To seal a worksheet, select the /File Admin Seal File command. Next you must enter a password, which is the password you must later use to unseal the file. The password will display as asterisks as you type it. Passwords in 1-2-3 are limited to 15 characters, do not contain spaces, and are case sensitive. (A password entered in uppercase is different from a password entered in lowercase.) After pressing ENTER, you must enter the password again. This prevents a typing error from sealing you permanently from your worksheet. After you enter the password a second time and press ENTER, 1-2-3 returns to the READY mode. This assumes that you have entered the same password twice. Once in READY mode, you will want to use the /File Save command so that the file is sealed the next time you use it.

After you have sealed a file or reservation setting, you may want to remove the seal. To remove a seal, use /File Admin Seal Disable. 1-2-3 prompts you for the password. When you enter the same password that was used to seal the file and press ENTER, the file is unsealed. You can also use this command to change the password by disabling the seal and then reestablishing it with a new password.

Cutting and Pasting

Cutting and pasting can extend your productivity with 1-2-3 by allowing you to move or copy existing entries to new locations. You can thus restructure a worksheet to meet new needs without reentering data. You can also use the /Worksheet Insert and /Worksheet Delete commands from Chapter 4, "Changing the Appearance of the Worksheet Display," to add new rows, columns, or sheets and to eliminate rows, columns, and sheets that are no longer required.

Moving Information

Creating a worksheet can sometimes be a trial-and-error process, during which you attempt to obtain the most effective placement of data. 1-2-3 provides a /Move command that permits you to move a range of cells to another location on one of the sheets in the active file. The command requires that you specify both a From and a To range. The From range marks the original location of the data to be moved, and the To range is the new location you have selected. 1-2-3 will prompt you for these ranges when it is time to enter them. You can use any of the normal methods for specifying a range location, including range names, cell addresses, and pointing with either the keyboard or the mouse.

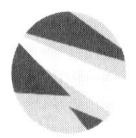

TIP: Use /Move to restructure worksheets created in Release 2 to utilize the multiple-sheet features of Release 3. If you have a number of different kinds of data in a Release 2 worksheet, you can reorganize it quickly. Use /Worksheet Insert Sheet to add the required number of sheets, and /Move to handle the remainder of the task.

It is easiest to specify the From range for the /Move command if you place your cell pointer on the upper left cell in the range to be moved before invoking the command. That is because 1-2-3 assumes that the current cell is the first cell in the range you wish to move. To expand this range, simply move the cell pointer in the direction you want; the beginning cell remains anchored in place. You can move a single-sheet range or a multiple-sheet range.

If you want to change the beginning of the range 1-2-3 suggests, press ESC or BACKSPACE to unlock the beginning of the range. Move your cell pointer to the upper left cell in the range you wish to move, type a period, and move to the end of the range, or drag a mouse across it. Alternatively, you can just type a new range when presented with 1-2-3's suggestion.

Unless you are typing the range reference, you must move your cell pointer for the To range — even if you position your cell pointer prior to executing the command. This is because 1-2-3 suggests the same range for To as it suggested for From. Since the suggestion for To is a single cell, you will not need to press ESC to unlock the beginning of the range. Just move to whatever beginning cell you wish for the To range, or enter the beginning cell from the keyboard. Only the beginning cell needs to be specified for To, even if many cells are being moved.

The /Move command can be used to move one or many worksheet cells. The example in Figure 5-17 shows a long label that is not in the center of the worksheet. To reenter the label in a more central location would be time consuming; you can move it more quickly with /Move. Place the cell pointer in A3 and enter **/Move**. Since the From range is the cell pointer location, press ENTER to accept the current cell address for the From range. Then move the cell pointer to C3, and press ENTER to accept C3 as the To range. Figure 5-18 presents

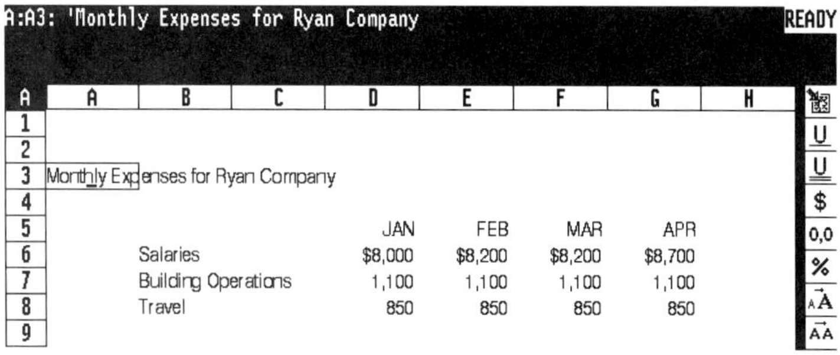

Figure 5-17. Long label to be moved

the worksheet after the move is complete. Although the label displays in multiple cells, you are able to move it by specifying only one cell each for the From and To ranges.

As another example, suppose that in the worksheet shown in Figure 5-19 you want to move the entries in cells A2..C15 to the right. These cells contain numbers, labels, and formulas. The formulas are formatted as text so that you can see how 1-2-3 adjusts formulas as you move them. To move all these entries at once, enter **/Move** and the From range A2..C15. When the To range is requested, enter **B2**. Only one cell is needed to tell 1-2-3 where to begin the To range; it will automatically use B2..D15 as the complete To range. Figure 5-20 shows the worksheet after the move, including the way in which the formulas

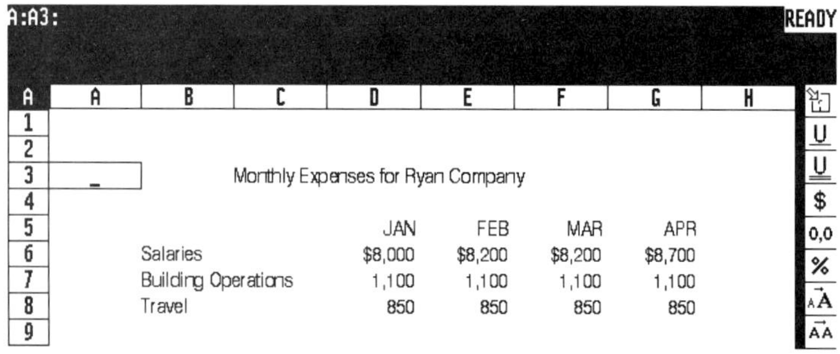

Figure 5-18. Result of moving the label

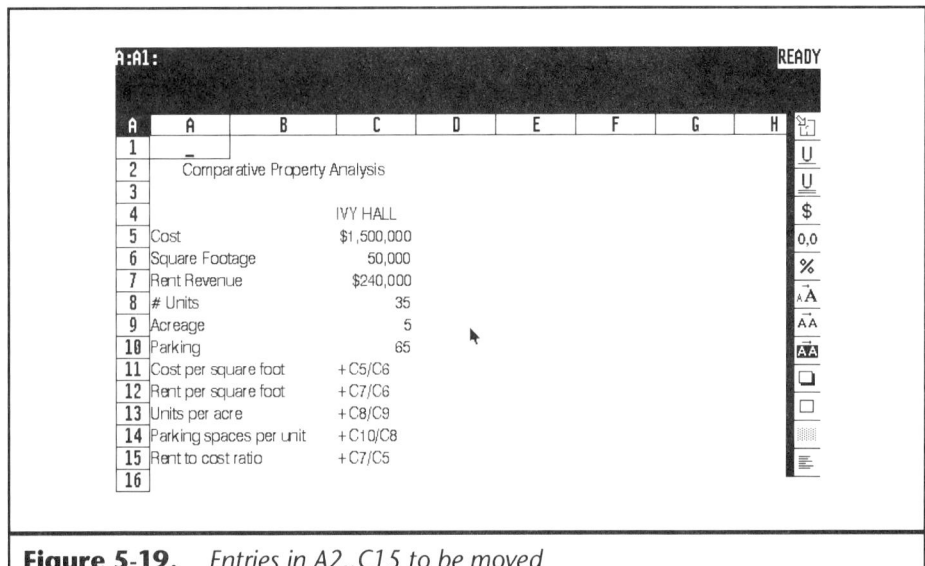

Figure 5-19. Entries in A2..C15 to be moved

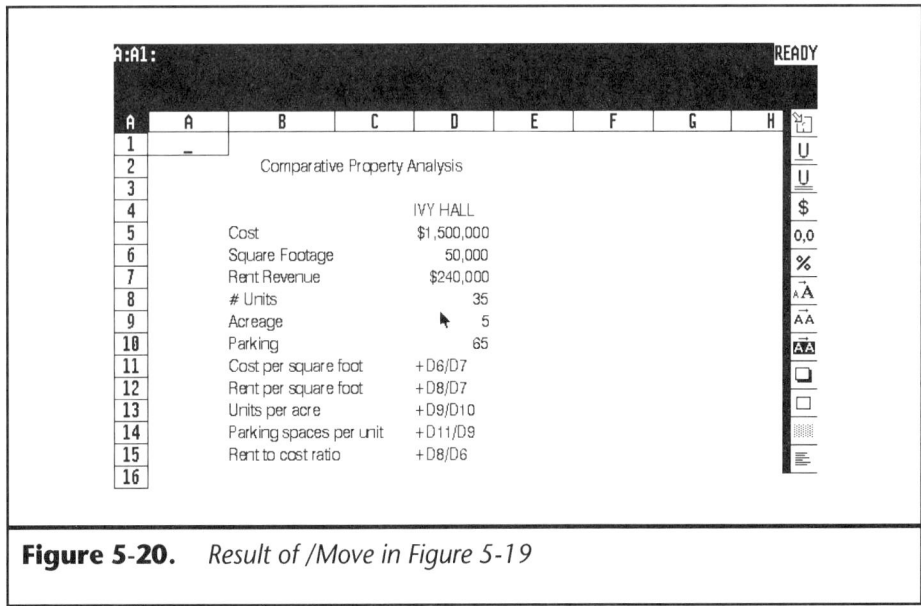

Figure 5-20. Result of /Move in Figure 5-19

have been adjusted to reflect the new locations of the cells referenced. Note also that there is an overlap between the From and To ranges. 1-2-3 is able to handle this.

NOTE: The /Move command moves not only the data in the From range, but the 1-2-3 numeric formats as well. In Figure 5-20, notice how the formulas moved to D11..D16 retain the Text format; however, Wysiwyg formatting is not moved by the /Move command. In Chapter 15 you will learn about the :Special Move command which moves both Wysiwyg formatting, and 1-2-3 data and formatting.

With Release 3.4 of 1-2-3, you have a SmartIcon which can be used for moving 1-2-3 data and both 1-2-3 and Wysiwyg formatting. You will need to select the From range before selecting the icon. After selecting the range, select the icon shown below from the fifth SmartIcons palette. Next, specify the To range either by pointing with the mouse or by using the keyboard, or by typing the To range or range name.

Duplicating Existing Entries

The copying features of 1-2-3 extend your productivity with the package more than any other single feature. /Copy permits you to enter a label, formula, or number in one cell and copy it to many new locations. This feature is especially valuable for formulas, since 1-2-3 is able to adjust the formulas to conform with their new locations. With the three-dimensional features, you can set up calculations for one business entity on one sheet and copy it to 5, 10, or 20 additional sheets, letting you enter data for other business entities immediately, without entering any formulas.

Copy Options

The /Copy command will perform its task in a variety of situations. You can copy the contents of one cell to another cell, or to a range of many cells. You can speed up the copying process by copying a range of cells to a second range of the same size. Lastly, this command can copy a range of cells to a second range whose size is a multiple of the original range. The data you are copying can be in the current sheet, another sheet in the current file, another active file, or a file on disk. The area to which you copy must be in any active file. Let's look at an example for each of these uses.

Suppose a label entry is placed in cell A1, like this:

```
A:A1: 'Cash                                                          READY

    A        B       C       D       E       F       G       H
1  Cash_
2
3
```

To copy this label to another cell, the easiest approach is to place your cell pointer on A1 before beginning. When you enter **/Copy**, 1-2-3 asks what you want to copy from. Since your cell pointer is already positioned on A1, just press ENTER. (If the cell pointer is not where you want it to be, press ESC before moving it to the correct From location.) After the From location is specified, 1-2-3's next prompt requests the To range. In the preceding illustration, to copy the label entry to B3, move the cell pointer to B3 in response to this prompt and press ENTER. The completed copy operation generates a second label in B3, like this:

```
A:A1: 'Cash                                                          READY

    A        B       C       D       E       F       G       H
1  Cash_
2
3           Cash
4
```

The next example will again start with the entry of "Cash" in A1, but this time the entry will be copied to many cells. The beginning of the operation is the same: place the cell pointer on A1 and enter **/Copy**. Press ENTER in response to the From range prompt. The entry is to be copied to D1..D51; therefore, when the prompt for a To range appears, move the cell pointer to D1. Enter a period to lock the beginning of the To range in place. Move the cell pointer down to D51, and then press ENTER. The result is the label copied into every specified cell from D1 down, like this:

```
A:A1: 'Cash                                                          READY

    A        B       C       D       E       F       G       H
1  Cash_                      Cash
2                             Cash
3                             Cash
4                             Cash
5                             Cash
6
```

Figure 5-21 shows a worksheet with labels in A3..A15. /Copy can be used to copy these labels to a second range of the same size and shape as the original. The best way to begin is to place the cell pointer in the upper left cell in the range, A3 in this example. Type **/Copy**. Then, instead of pressing ENTER, move the cell pointer to the bottom of the labels for the From range. Press ENTER, and 1-2-3 requests the To range. At this point, move the cell pointer to the top cell in the To range. Since 1-2-3 knows that the To range must match the From range in size and shape, you need specify only the upper left corner of the To range (in Figure 5-21, this is E3). Then press ENTER, producing the results shown in Figure 5-22. With just a few keystrokes, an entire range of label entries has been duplicated much faster than anyone could enter them.

The next use of /Copy is even more powerful, since it copies one row or column of entries to many rows or columns in one operation. Let's use the labels found in Figure 5-23. To copy them, place the cell pointer in A3 and enter **/Copy**. Move the cell pointer to A15 in response to a request for the From range, and press ENTER. This time the labels are to be copied into B3..B15, C3..C15, D3..D15, and E3..E15. When 1-2-3 requests the To range, therefore, move the cell pointer to the top of the first column where the labels will be copied, B3, and enter a period to lock the beginning of the range in place. Since 1-2-3 knows it is copying a partial column of labels that will extend down to row 15, it needs to be told only how far across the worksheet this partial column should be copied. To do this, move the cell pointer to E3 and press ENTER. The display in Figure 5-24 is produced with this operation.

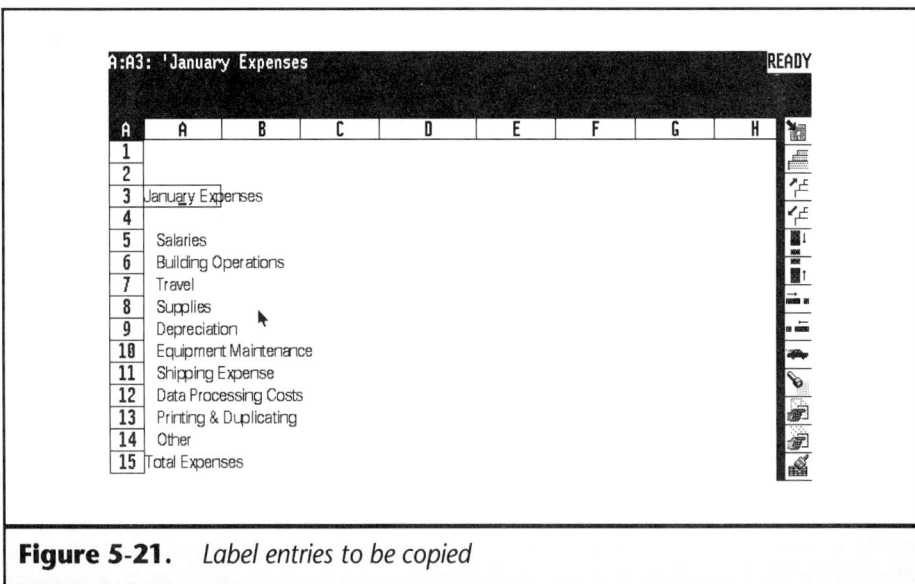

Figure 5-21. *Label entries to be copied*

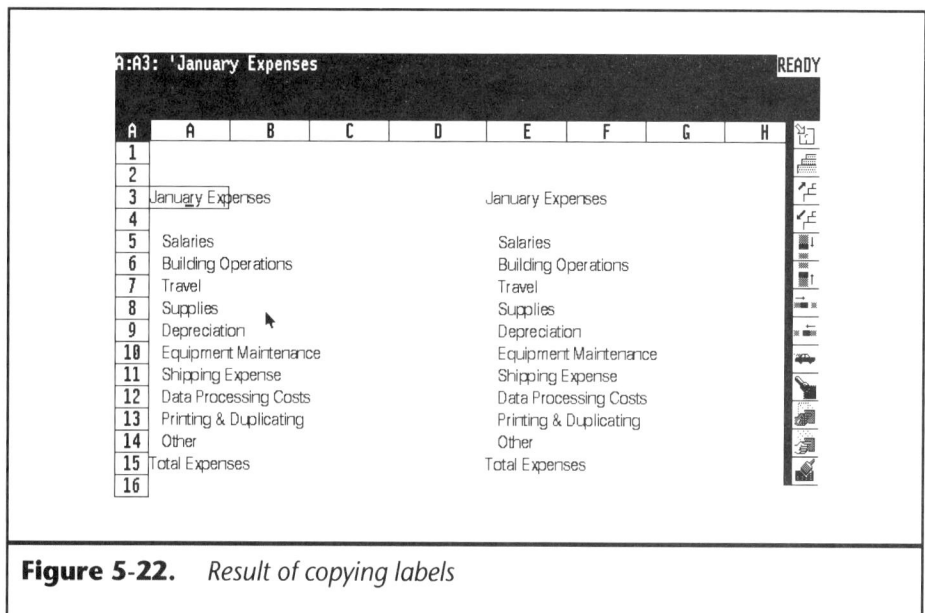

Figure 5-22.   *Result of copying labels*

The last option to be examined is copying entries in a rectangular range on one sheet to other sheets. First, enter **/Copy** and highlight the rectangle of cells to be copied. In Figure 5-25, this will be A:A1..A:G6. The cells without entries as yet

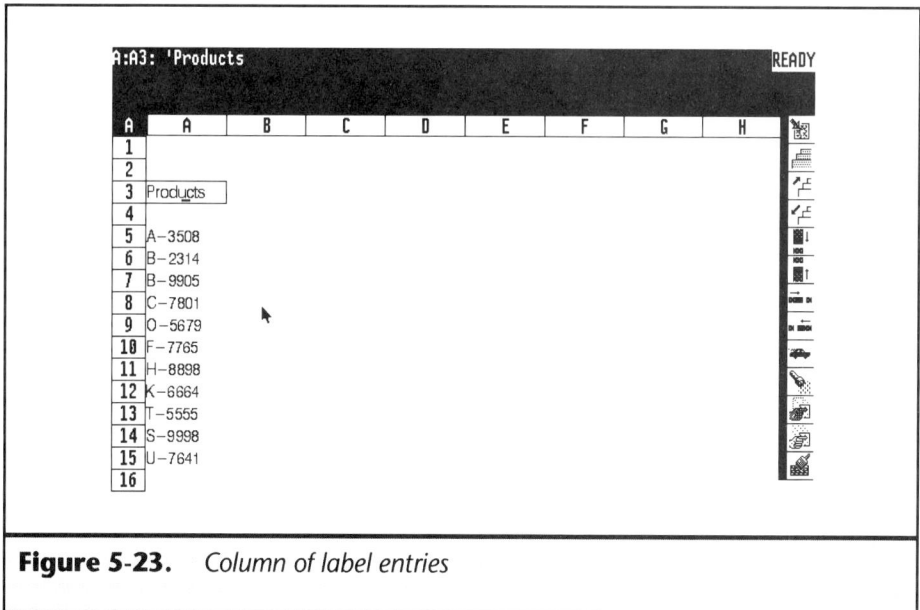

Figure 5-23.   *Column of label entries*

```
A:A3: 'Products                                                    READY

     A         B        C        D        E     F    G    H
 1
 2
 3  Products  Products Products Products Products
 4
 5  A-3508   A-3508   A-3508   A-3508   A-3508
 6  B-2314   B-2314   B-2314   B-2314   B-2314
 7  B-9905   B-9905   B-9905   B-9905   B-9905
 8  C-7801   C-7801   C-7801   C-7801   C-7801
 9  O-5679   O-5679   O-5679   O-5679   O-5679
10  F-7765   F-7765   F-7765   F-7765   F-7765
11  H-8898   H-8898   H-8898   H-8898   H-8898
12  K-6664   K-6664   K-6664   K-6664   K-6664
13  T-5555   T-5555   T-5555   T-5555   T-5555
14  S-9998   S-9998   S-9998   S-9998   S-9998
15  U-7641   U-7641   U-7641   U-7641   U-7641
16
17
```

Figure 5-24. *Result of copying to many locations*

are in this range; they are part of the range that includes the entries across the top and down the sides. Including the empty cells in this copy operation offers another advantage if you have used 1-2-3 range formats on the empty cells: the copy operation will copy the 1-2-3 range formats as well as the data. Specify the To range as B:A1..D:A1—or the first cell in each worksheet where you want this rectangle copied. Figure 5-26 shows part of the data copied to three new sheets.

Copying numbers works the same way as copying labels. Copying formulas can be even more valuable. Although the mechanics of copying formulas are the

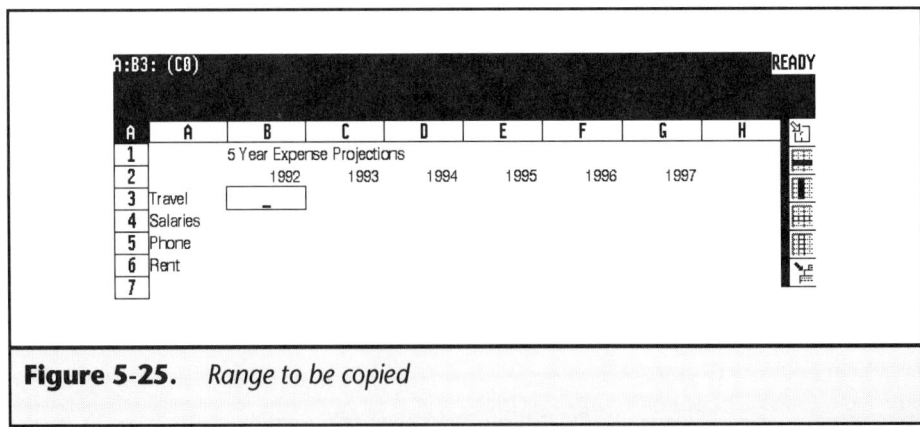

Figure 5-25. *Range to be copied*

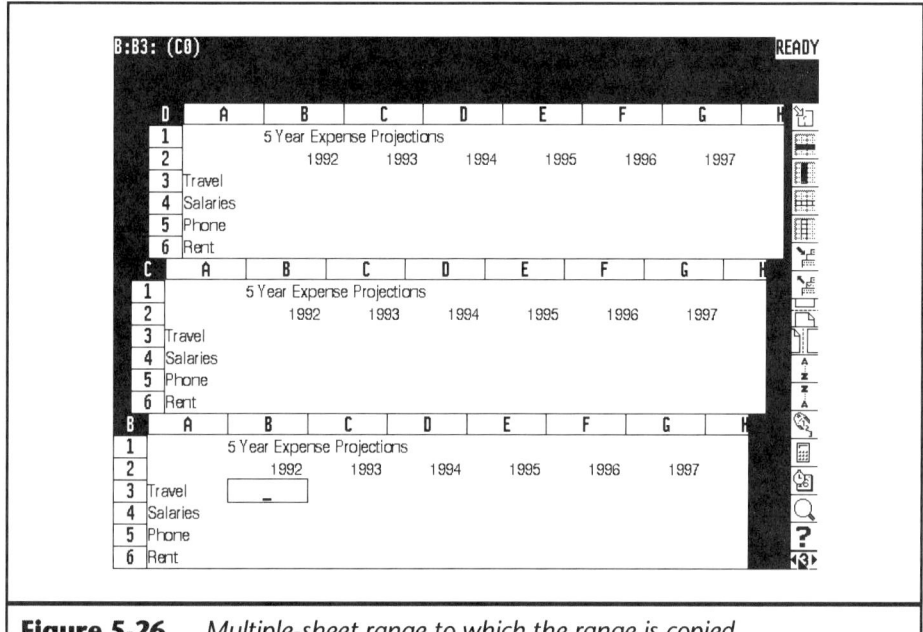

Figure 5-26. *Multiple-sheet range to which the range is copied*

same from your standpoint, it is important to understand exactly how 1-2-3 treats cell references when copying formulas.

Copying Formulas

Since copying formulas requires adjusting cell references, it is important to have a complete understanding of cell addressing. This topic was introduced in Chapter 4, "Changing the Appearance of the Worksheet Display," but will be expanded in this section to cover the three addressing options completely.

Relative References

Relative references are the addresses generated when you enter regular cell addresses into formulas. A19, D2, and X15 are all relative references, as are D:H5 and A:Z2. This is the normal reference style used with formulas in 1-2-3. When a formula is created with this reference style, 1-2-3 not only records the cell addresses for the formula, but also remembers their relative distance and direction from the cell containing the formula.

For example, when you enter the formula +A1+A2 in A3, 1-2-3 remembers facts that are not shown in the worksheet. Specifically, in the illustration presented here, 1-2-3 remembers the distance and direction that must be traveled to obtain each of the references in the formula.

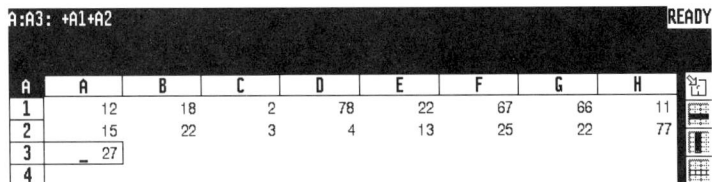

For A1, 1-2-3 knows that this reference is in the same column as the formula result, but is two rows above it. A2 is in the same column, one row above the result. This concept adds great power to the /Copy command. Let's say you want the same type of formula in B3, and you want it to add the values in B1 and B2 together. /Copy can handle this, since it remembers the directions for the formula's relative references.

To make this transfer, place the cell pointer on A3, enter **/Copy**, and press ENTER. Then move the cell pointer to B3 as the To location and press ENTER again. The formula is replicated into B3 and, in addition, adjustments are made that make the formula appropriate for B3, as shown here:

Let's try this again, but this time copy from B3 across the remainder of the row. Enter **/Copy** with the cell pointer on B3, and press ENTER. Move the cell pointer to C3 as the beginning of the To range, enter a period, move the cell pointer to H3, and press ENTER again. Figure 5-27 shows that the appropriate formulas were copied across the row.

Relative references can be used in formulas any time you want the formula adjusted during the copying process. Figure 5-28 shows another worksheet with a column of formulas. To copy the formulas, position the cell pointer on C3 and enter **/Copy**. Then move the cell pointer to C5, which expands the highlighting, and press ENTER. Move the cell pointer to D3, type a period, and move the cell pointer across to F3, before pressing ENTER to finalize the To range. Figure 5-29, which contains the results of the copying process, has been changed to a text format so that you can review 1-2-3's work in copying the formulas.

You can also use the same steps to copy to other worksheets. To copy the entries on sheet A to sheets B through D, select /Copy and A2..F8 as the From

Chapter 5: Basic Worksheet Commands

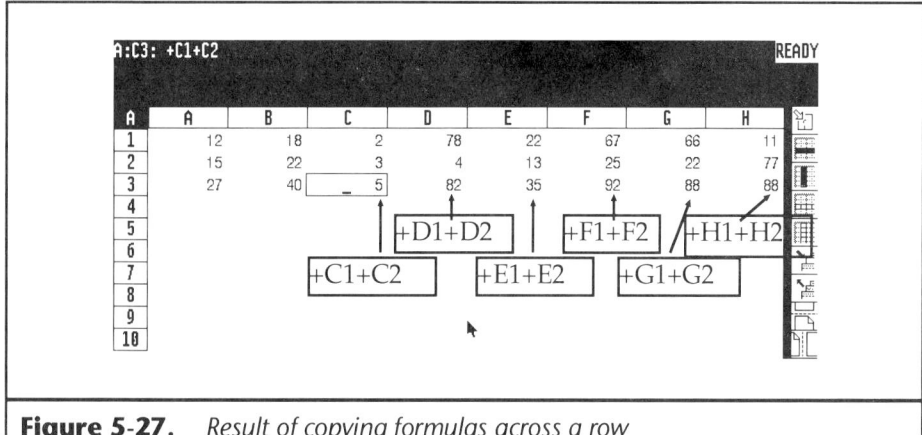

Figure 5-27. *Result of copying formulas across a row*

range. After pressing ENTER, select B:A2..D:A2 as the To range. When you press ENTER, 1-2-3 duplicates these entries on the other sheets. The formulas in sheets B through D will not include the sheet references since the values the formulas use are on the same sheet as the formulas.

Absolute References

Absolute references are references that you want held constant. In other words, you do not want these references to be adjusted when they are copied to a different location. This is the kind of reference you want for, say, a single interest rate, a specific value in an assumption block, or a table that is in a fixed location.

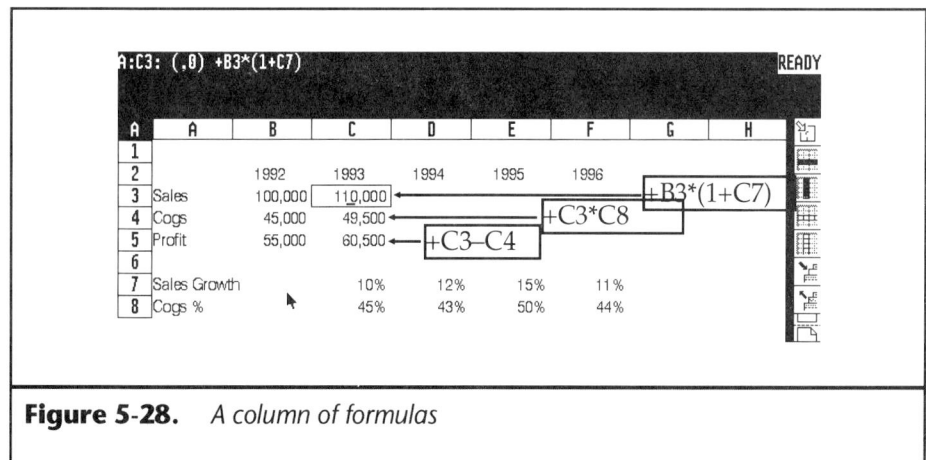

Figure 5-28. *A column of formulas*

```
A:C3: (T) [W12] +B3*(1+C7)                                              READY

   A    A         B           C            D           E          F       G
  1
  2              1992        1993         1994        1995       1996
  3  Sales    100,000    +B3*(1+C7)   +C3*(1+D7)   +D3*(1+E7)  +E3*(1+F7)
  4  Cogs      45,000    +C3*C8       +D3*D8       +E3*E8      +F3*F8
  5  Profit    55,000    +C3-C4       +D3-D4       +E3-E4      +F3-F4
  6
  7  Sales Growth                     10%          12%         15%        11%
  8  Cogs %                           45%          43%         50%        44%
  9
```

Figure 5-29. *Result of copying formulas, displayed as text*

Even when you copy this formula to other sheets, the sheet, column, or row portions of an absolute address are not updated.

Entering absolute cell references in formulas requires a little more work, because absolute references must have a $ in front of the column, the row, and the sheet portions of the address. $A:$A$A, $F$87, and $X$1 are all absolute references. 1-2-3 does not remember the relative direction and distance that must be traveled to obtain these values when they are used in a formula. Instead, it remembers the absolute cell address.

There are two ways to enter the $s during formula entry. You can type them wherever they are required, or you can have 1-2-3 enter them for you. For example, the worksheet in Figure 5-30 requires formulas that use both relative and absolute references, since there are varying Sales Growth rates but one fixed Cogs (cost of goods sold) percentage that applies to all years. The formulas that were already entered for the 1993 sales used only relative references. The formula for cost of goods sold (row 4) requires both a relative reference to sales for the current year, and an absolute reference to the Cogs % (cell C8). An absolute reference is required because the same Cogs % will be used for all years. The formula will be +C3*$C$8 for 1990, +D3*$C$8 for 1991, and so forth.

To enter this formula in cell C4 (it will later be copied to other cells in row 4), place the cell pointer in C4 and enter a +. The first cell reference needed in the formula is the 1993 Sales figure in C3, so use the UP ARROW to point to C3. Since you want to multiply this figure by the Cogs %, enter an *, representing multiplication, next.

Now, move the cell pointer to C8 to reference the Cogs %. If you needed a relative reference, you would press ENTER now, but since you want an absolute reference to this cell, $s are needed first. 1-2-3 will enter them for you from the POINT or EDIT mode if you press F4 (ABS). The first time you press this key, the

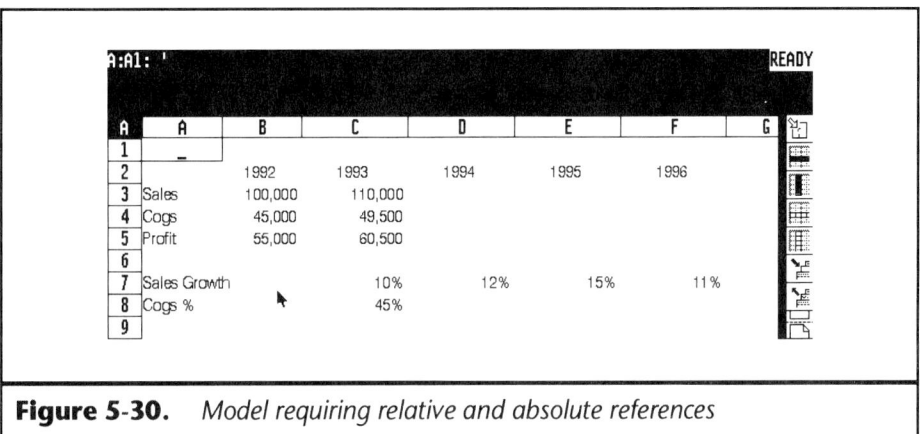

Figure 5-30. *Model requiring relative and absolute references*

reference becomes $A:$C$8. You can continue to press it to cycle through all the possibilities:

Absolute reference	$A:$C$8—first time
Mixed address	$A:C$8—second time
Mixed address	$A:$C8—third time
Mixed address	$A:C8—fourth time
Mixed address	A:$C$8—fifth time
Mixed address	A:C$8—sixth time
Mixed address	A:$C8—seventh time
Relative reference	C8—eighth time

The F4 (ABS) key will cycle through the possibilities again if you continue to press it.

Once the cell reference has the dollar signs added in all positions, press ENTER to accept it. If another arithmetic operation were required in the formula, typing the arithmetic operator would also have accepted the $ placement. (For instance, entering + to continue the formula would accept the $A:$C$8 reference.)

The formula +A:C3*$A:$C$8 is now entered, containing both an absolute and a relative reference. The result of the calculation is the same as if both relative references had been used. Only when the formula is copied to new locations will the difference become apparent. Before this is demonstrated, let's examine one more formula in Figure 5-30—the one needed to calculate the profit for 1990. This formula is simply +C3–C4, with both references relative.

All three years' formulas will be copied at once. To do this, move the cell pointer to the top cell in the range to be copied, C3, and enter **/Copy**. Move the cell pointer down twice to highlight the entire From range. Next move to D3 as the first location in the To range and enter a period. Then move across to F3, and press ENTER. Figure 5-31 shows the results of the copying process with the formulas formatted as text so that you can see how 1-2-3 has adjusted them as they are copied. If an absolute reference had not been used for the Cogs %, 1-2-3 would have attempted to increment the cell reference for each new formula, and blank cells would have been referenced for years beyond 1993.

As you can see from this example, you can combine relative and absolute references to create formulas that meet your exact needs.

Mixed Addresses

1-2-3 has one more reference type that extends the package features still further. This reference type is a *mixed address,* which combines relative and absolute features in one cell reference.

Since a cell address is composed of a sheet, a row, and a column reference, it is possible to make one component absolute while leaving the others relative. This gives you the flexibility, for example, to have the column portion of an address updated when a formula is copied across the sheet, while keeping the row portion of the same address constant when the formula is copied down the worksheet.

Figure 5-32 presents an application where the mixed addressing feature is useful. In this worksheet the 1992 figures are historic numbers, and all of the projections for subsequent years use these figures as base numbers. Sales projections for each product will use the appropriate growth factor from D4..D6. For Product A, for example, the sales figure from 1992 will be multiplied by 110%. This formula could be written in cell D11 as +C11*(1+D4). It would work

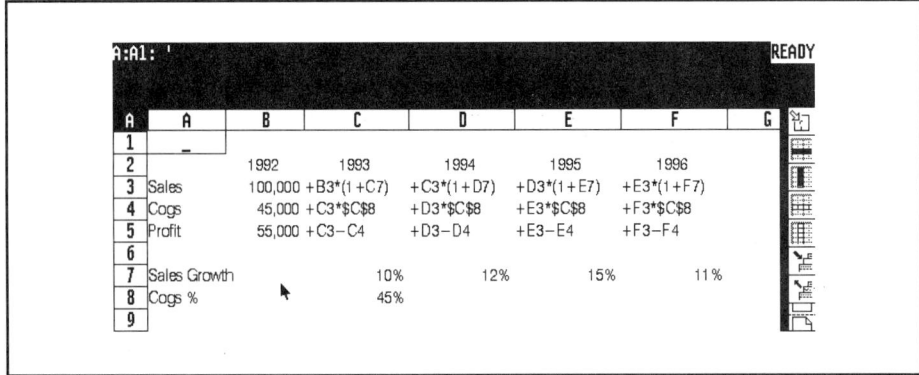

Figure 5-31. *Result of copying relative and absolute references (with formulas displayed)*

```
A:D11: +C11*(1+$D4)                                              READY

       A         B         C         D         E         F         G         H
  1   -----------------------------------------------------------------
  2   |              ASSUMPTIONS                            |
  3   |     Sales Growth                                    |
  4   |        Product A            10.0%                   |
  5   |        Product B            12.0%                   |
  6   |        Product C             9.0%                   |
  7   -----------------------------------------------------------------
  8
  9                         1992      1993      1994      1995      1996
 10  Sales                  ---------------------------------------------
 11    Product A          100,000   110,000   121,000   133,100   146,410
 12    Product B           50,000    56,000    62,720    70,246    78,676
 13    Product C           45,000    49,050    53,465    58,276    63,521
 14  Cost of Goods Sold    87,750    96,773   106,733   117,730   129,873
 15  Profit               107,250   118,278   130,451   143,892   158,734
 16
```

Figure 5-32. *An application of mixed addressing*

for this one year, but it would cause a problem when copied across to subsequent years, since D4 would be updated to E4, F4, and so on.

Using $D$4 in this formula would present another problem, since the Product A formulas could not be copied down for Product B and Product C. If an absolute reference were used for D4, the copied formulas could not reference D5 and D6. The ideal situation would be to freeze the column portion of the address, but allow the row portion to vary. Mixed addressing provides this capability. If the formula reference is written as $D4, only the column portion of the address will be absolute; the row portion will be allowed to vary during the copy process.

A little thought and planning is required to decide how to construct the address type you need. You might elect to just use a different formula for each of the product types. That is all right, but for twenty-five products rather than three, the mixed addressing feature really saves significant time, since it allows you to devise one formula to work for all situations.

The formula devised for D11 is +C11*(1+$D4). Mixed addressing allows this formula to be used for all the sales projections. First copy it down column D to D12 and D13. Then copy the range D11..D13 across to column E through column G. The formulas automatically created in E11..G13 are as follows:

    E11: +D11*(1+$D4)
    F11: +E11*(1+$D4)
    G11: +F11*(1+$D4)
    E12: +D12*(1+$D5)
    F12: +E12*(1+$D5)

G12: +F12*(1+$D5)
E13: +D13*(1+$D6)
F13: +E13*(1+$D6)
G13: +F13*(1+$D6)

Using mixed addressing, you can enter one formula and have 1-2-3 generate the other 11 formulas for you. Although mixed addressing is not useful in all models, its payback under appropriate circumstances is significant enough to make it a desirable part of your model building toolkit.

Using SmartIcon Options for Copying in Release 3.4

There are three different icons that will perform a copy operation for you. Two icons are related to the /Copy command and will copy entries and any related formatting. The other copy icon is designed to work with only the format of the current cell. This icon copies the current cell's format to the other cells in the selected range. You will want to familiarize yourself with what these three icons offer if you have 1-2-3 Release 3.4.

Specifying the To Location

You can use the Copy icon from palette 5 to specify the location where the cells selected can be copied. This icon looks like this:

To utilize this feature you would select the cells that you wish to copy with the F4 (ABS) key or the mouse. Next you would select the Copy icon from palette 5 and specify a To location to end the copy operation.

Copying the Contents of One Cell to Many Locations

Release 3.4 also has an icon palette option for copying the entry in the current cell to many locations within a preselected range. For example, if you had an entry in A2 and wanted to copy it to all the empty cells within the range A2..D15, one quick click would complete the copy operation if the range A2..D15 was selected before clicking the icon. The icon that you will use for this task is on icon palette 6 and looks like this:

Copying Cells Formats

The last copy operation does not have an equivalent command in 1-2-3's menu since there is no option in the menu for copying only the formats within cells. When you learn all the details about Wysiwyg in Chapter 15 you will find that you can use the Wysiwyg menu to duplicate the same operation. The SmartIcon palette option lets you copy the format of the current cell to all cells in the range. These formats can include numeric formats options such as fixed or currency but also includes Wysiwyg options such as boldface and italics. The cells where you are copying the formats to can have entries. These entries will not be affected by the copy operation except that the cells will take on the format of the current cell immediately.

The icon for copying the format from cells is on palette 5 if you have a VGA monitor and it looks like this:

To use this icon you must first select a cell that has the format that you want to use. In Figure 5-33 the only month shown with bold is Jan. You can apply the bold format to the other cells where these format attributes would improve the appearance of the display.

To make the changes you could select B5 then click the special copy icon. In response to the prompt you would select C5..G5, then all the month names would display as bold. If cell B5 had other attributes such as underline or italic, these other attributes would be copied at the same time. Figure 5-34 shows the model after the format is copied.

```
A:B5: {Bold} "Jan                                                    READY

     A            B        C        D        E        F        G
 1                            Innovation, Inc.
 2                           New Product Sales
 3                           Jan - June 1992
 4
 5               _ Jan      Feb      Mar      Apr      May      June
 6  Save-All Shower 23,400  25,740   28,314   31,145   34,260   37,686
 7  Faucet Save    34,500   36,225   38,036   39,938   41,935   44,032
 8  Waterless Cleaner 47,800 50,668  53,708   56,931   60,346   63,967
 9  Rain-saver      9,800    9,996   10,196   10,400   10,608   10,280
10
```

Figure 5-33. Worksheet with Jan formatted with bold

Using 1-2-3's Search and Replace Features

Through /Range Search, Release 3 offers you the ability to search for character strings within formulas and labels. This feature is especially useful in a large worksheet where you need to locate a particular entry with no knowledge of its cell address. The area that you search can span sheets in a multiple-sheet file if you are uncertain which sheet you want to search. With the Find option you can find the first occurrence of your entry, or continue to search through a specified range of the worksheet file. You can use /Range Search to search formulas, labels, or both.

The /Range Search command offers a Replace option in addition to its Find features. With the Replace option, you supply a replacement string which 1-2-3

```
A:B5: {Bold} "Jan                                                    READY

     A            B        C        D        E        F        G
 1                            Innovation, Inc.
 2                           New Product Sales
 3                           Jan - June 1992
 4
 5               _ Jan      Feb      Mar      Apr      May      June
 6  Save-All Shower 23,400  25,740   28,314   31,145   34,260   37,686
 7  Faucet Save    34,500   36,225   38,036   39,938   41,935   44,032
 8  Waterless Cleaner 47,800 50,668  53,708   56,931   60,346   63,967
 9  Rain-saver      9,800    9,996   10,196   10,400   10,608   10,280
```

Figure 5-34. Bold format copied to other headings

uses as a substitute for the character string you find within matching entries. This feature is useful if you need to replace cell references or range names in a large range of formula entries. You can replace the first occurrence or all occurrences. If you prefer, you can proceed through the selected range, finding one occurrence at a time.

TIP: You may want to replace matching entries one at a time until you are certain that the search string you entered is matching correctly. This isn't necessary if you need to change all occurrences of A:$D$9 to D:$A$9, because you will probably only find correct matches. But, if you want to change the A in A:$D$9 to D, searching for A and replacing it with D could be a disaster if you choose All. Entries like AB10 would be changed to DB10, and all A's in range names would be changed to D's. As a rule, be as specific as possible when performing a replace.

Using Search

The /Range Search command lets you locate a string of characters in a range of formulas or labels. If the range you choose spans sheets, 1-2-3 will be able to scan many sheets much quicker than you can. You might want to scan a large range of data for a vendor name, or a range name that you are considering deleting. When looking for a range name, you will want to use the Formulas option for this command, to scan only the cells with formula entries. When looking for text stored in a label cell, you can restrict your search to cells that contain labels.

To find the name Campbell in the data in Figure 5-35, enter **/Range Search** and highlight the cells that contain name entries. This range might be the cells that are visible, or it could include a much longer column or additional columns on other sheets. After selecting the appropriate range, press ENTER. Type **campbell**; since upper- and lowercase are equivalent in a search string, you do not need to capitalize your entry. Select Labels, and then Find from the next menu. The first occurrence of the cell containing the first occurrence of the string will be highlighted. Select either Next to look for additional occurrences or Quit to end the Find operation.

Using Replace

The Replace option not only locates strings but allows you to replace them with other entries. The data in Figure 5-35 can be used again for this example. Let's say you want to change the second occurrence of the last name Campbell to Camper. You could find the entry, quit, and then change it; or you can use Replace. Begin a Replace operation in the same way by entering **/Range Search**,

```
A:A1: [W12] 'Last Name                                                    READY

   A        A            B              C          D          E         F      G
   1  Last Name    First Name          SS#    Job Code    Salary   Location
   2  Wilkes       Caitlin        124-67-7432      17      $15,500      2
   3  Campbell     David          213-76-9874      23      $23,000     10
   4  Parker       Dee            659-11-3452      14      $19,800      4
   5  Hartwick     Eileen         313-78-9090      15      $31,450      4
   6  Preverson    Gary           670-90-1121      21      $27,600      4
   7  Smythe       George         560-90-8645      15      $65,000      4
   8  Justof       Jack           431-78-9963      17      $41,200      4
   9  McCartin     John           817-66-1212      15      $54,600      2
  10  Campbell     Keith          569-89-7654      12      $32,000      2
  11  Deaver       Ken            198-98-6750      23      $24,600     10
  12  Caldor       Larry          459-34-0921      23      $32,500      4
  13  Miller       Lisa           214-89-6756      23      $18,700      2
  14  Patterson    Lyle           212-11-9090      12      $21,500     10
  15  Hawkins      Mark           215-67-8973      21      $19,500      2
  16  Larson       Mary           543-98-9876      23      $12,000      2
  17  Samuelson    Paul           219-89-7080      23      $28,900      2
  18  Lightnor     Peggy          560-55-4311      14      $23,500     10
  19  Kaylor       Sally          312-45-9862      12      $32,900     10
  20  Stephens     Tom            219-78-8954      15      $17,800      2
```

Figure 5-35.   *Section of large worksheet*

highlighting the range containing the name entries, and pressing ENTER. Next, type **Campbell** and press ENTER. Select Labels followed by Replace. Type **Camper** and press ENTER. The first occurrence of Campbell is not the one you want to replace, so select Next to move to the next occurrence without changing the current entry. The second occurrence highlighted is the one you want, so select Replace to complete the change. Since there are no additional entries, you are finished. You can press ESC to return to READY mode.

Other menu options for Replace are All to change all the records at once, and Quit to return to READY mode when you do not wish to make further changes.

Making Other Worksheet Changes

Several additional features bring advanced capabilities to worksheet preparation. In this section you will look at options that allow you to change label justification for the entire worksheet, to erase the complete worksheet with one command, and to change the beep that occurs when you make a mistake.

Changing Default Label Justification for the Worksheet

The default worksheet setting for labels provides left justification for every label entry. This means that an apostrophe will be generated as the first character of every label entry. As you learned in Chapter 3, "Entering Data in 1-2-3's Worksheet," you always have the option of centering a label entry by typing the label alignment character yourself.

1-2-3 offers further flexibility with the /Range Label command, which lets you change the justification of label entries that are already in cells. But if you want all of your labels to default to a new justification, neither the single entry method nor the Range option is exactly right. For such circumstances, 1-2-3 provides the /Worksheet Global Label command to change the default label prefix for every new worksheet entry. To make the change, enter **/Worksheet Global Label** and select the left, right, or center justification you want from the menu.

With the /Worksheet Global Label command, existing entries are unaffected, but new entries will have the new label prefix. Just the opposite is true with /Range Label. With both options you should remember that numeric and formula entries are unaffected by changes made to the label prefix.

Erasing the Worksheet

1-2-3 provides a command to erase the entire contents of the worksheet currently in memory. This feature is useful when you have made so many mistakes that you want to wipe the slate clean and start over again, or when you have saved all your completed worksheets on disk and want to begin a new application without having to delete each worksheet individually.

When you enter **/Worksheet Erase** to request this feature, 1-2-3 prompts you to select between Yes and No. Selecting Yes erases all worksheet files. Selecting No cancels the command. This confirmation step is provided because of the dramatic effect of Erase. If you have not saved any of the open worksheets since the last change made to them, Release 3 will prompt you a second time to confirm that you want to erase the worksheet, noting that you will be losing the changes you have made. This gives you a second chance to cancel the command, and save the changes you have made to the worksheet. If you want to erase one worksheet file when several are open, you will want to use the /Worksheet Delete File command covered in Chapter 8, "Working with Files."

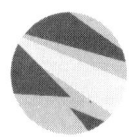

CAUTION: Your only hope for restoring the effect of /Worksheet Erase is with ALT-F4 (UNDO), and only then if your Undo feature is enabled at the time of the erase operation and there have been no intervening actions. In other words, once you have erased a worksheet, there is no way to bring the contents of memory back without Undo, unless you have saved a copy of the worksheet on disk.

You will notice that the cell pointer is initially positioned over the No option on the confirmation screen, so if you accidentally press ENTER without looking, you will not lose your worksheet files. To erase the worksheets you will have to take an action, either typing **Y** or pointing to the Yes option before pressing ENTER.

TIP: /Worksheet Erase has a more dramatic effect in Release 3 than in earlier releases. When you used /Worksheet Erase in prior releases, it did erase all of memory. However, since memory could only contain one worksheet, your risk was minimized somewhat if you accidentally executed the command. With Release 3, you might erase 15 files with one execution of this command.

Controlling the Beep Option

The default setting for 1-2-3 causes your computer to sound a bell when you make an error or execute 1-2-3's {BEEP} macro instruction. This sound is designed to alert you to an error situation, but it can be disabled if you would prefer not to hear it.

To change the setting for Beep in the current session, enter **/Worksheet Global Default Other Beep No**. You can enable it again later with the Yes option of this same command. If you wish to make this change permanent, enter **/Worksheet Global Default Update**; 1-2-3 will alter the file 123.DCF that contains the default parameters for each new session. To check the status of the current Beep or other default settings, enter **/Worksheet Global Default Status**. You cannot change any of the options from this screen.

Recalculating the Worksheet

1-2-3's recalculation abilities provide the power behind its formula features. A new improved calculation method offers minimal, intelligent, background recalculation. The essence of these adjectives is that 1-2-3 no longer recalculates the entire worksheet every time a new entry is made in a worksheet cell. It only recalculates the formulas affected by the new entry and has the intelligence to determine which cells are affected. Recalculation now takes place as a background activity, so that you can continue with your other worksheet tasks while 1-2-3 is updating the worksheet formula results.

Some tasks—like printing, changing formulas to values with /Range Value, or altering the layout of entries with /Range Trans—should only be done when the recalculation has completed. You can watch for this to occur by waiting for the CALC indicator to disappear from the bottom of the screen. Or press F9 (CALC) to cause 1-2-3 to do the calculations in the foreground. The latter approach is better, since you cannot proceed until 1-2-3 finishes, and all of your machine's resources are dedicated to the recalculation effort. All the recalculation options are accessed through the /Worksheet Global Recalc command.

Default Recalculation Settings

1-2-3's recalculation features have three different setting categories, all selected from the following /Worksheet Global Recalc menu:

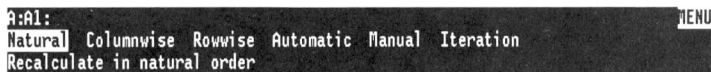

One group of commands controls the order in which the worksheet formulas will be reevaluated. The second group determines whether recalculation will be automatic or only upon request. The last recalculation option specifies how many times each formula will be reevaluated during recalculation.

Order of Recalculation

The default setting for recalculation order is Natural. This means that 1-2-3 will examine each worksheet formula for dependencies on other formulas, and determine which formulas must be calculated first to provide the results needed by the formulas to be reevaluated next. This Natural recalculation order set a new standard for other spreadsheets when it was first introduced. Before then the only options were Rowwise or Columnwise recalculation.

Rowwise recalculation evaluates all the formulas in row 1, then all the formulas in row 2, and so on. The problem with this method is that if a formula in row 1 references a value in a row farther down the worksheet, the earlier formula will reference a value from a prior recalculation. The same type of problem occurs with Columnwise recalculation, when early columns reference values farther to the right that have not yet been recalculated. These deficiencies in recalculation methods made 1-2-3's Natural recalculation order a welcome addition.

Timing of Recalculation

The default setting for a new worksheet is Automatic recalculation. This means that any new number, changed number, or new formula will cause 1-2-3 to recalculate all worksheet formulas affected by your change. The time needed for this recalculation depends on the number and complexity of the worksheet formulas and the number of formulas affected by your change. Since 1-2-3 recalculates in the background, you will be able to continue with other tasks, although part of your computer's resources will be dedicated to the recalculation. If you have a whole series of entries to make and are not concerned with the impact of each individual entry, you can use Manual recalculation, so that 1-2-3 does not do any recalculations until you request them.

Iterations of Recalculation

The default setting for the number of iterations for a recalculation is once. This means that each formula requiring recalculation is computed once each time the worksheet is recalculated. If you set this number higher than one, 1-2-3 will perform multiple recalculation when the order of calculation is Rowwise or Columnwise, or if there is a circular reference with Natural recalculation order.

Changing the Recalculation Settings

If you do not want the default settings, each of the three categories of recalculation options can be changed. The various recalculation options and appropriate circumstances for their use are summarized in the box called "Recalculation Options and Potential Pitfalls."

Order of Recalculation

If you want recalculation done in Rowwise or Columnwise order, rather than Natural order, you can obtain these options by entering the commands **/Worksheet Global Recalc Rowwise** or **/Worksheet Global Recalc Columnwise**, respectively. You might want to use the other recalculation orders when you import data from another worksheet package. If you bring a model created with a package like VisiCalc into 1-2-3, you might want to retain the recalculation order used with the original model.

Timing of Recalculation

To turn off Automatic recalculation, enter **/Worksheet Global Recalc Manual**. When the Manual option is in force, the worksheet will not recalculate unless you turn Automatic back on, or press the F9 (CALC) key. The Manual option can speed up your data entry, since you can enter everything before requesting a recalculation.

Iterations of Recalculation

In calculations that involve a circular calculation pattern, one iteration is not sufficient. This is because each calculation depends on the result of some other calculation, with the final result referring back to one of the earlier calculations. In situations like this, 1-2-3 is not able to identify a clear recalculation sequence for the formulas. Multiple calculations are required so that each will approximate the correct answer more closely.

Increasing 1-2-3's iterative count can solve the problem with circular references. This increase means that 1-2-3 will recalculate circular reference more than once each time the worksheet is automatically calculated or the F9 (CALC) key is pressed.

REMINDER: When a circular reference occurs in a 1-2-3 worksheet, the CIRC indicator appears in the right side in the Status Line at the bottom of the screen.

An example of a circular reference requiring iteration for resolution is shown in the formulas in Figure 5-36. When the formulas are first entered, C3 displays as 0 and C5 displays as 200. Since these two formulas are dependent on each other, each recalculation refines the accuracy of the result. The results after several recalculations with the F9 (CALC) key appear in the worksheet as shown in Figure 5-37. Slight changes continue to occur over the next several recalculations, until a final approximation is reached. All of these calculations could have been performed the first time the worksheet was calculated if the iteration count had been set higher.

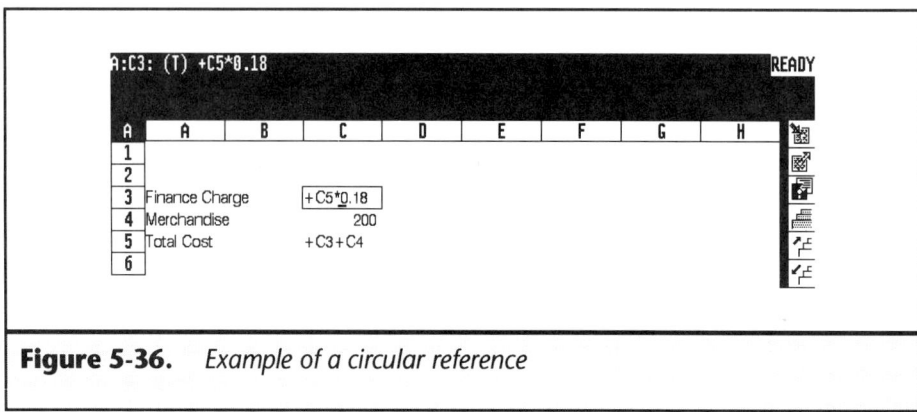

Figure 5-36. *Example of a circular reference*

Modifying the Screen Display

1-2-3 has several screen display options that are especially useful for large worksheets. One option allows you to lock the titles or descriptive labels at the side or top of your screen so that you can look at data in remote parts of the worksheet and still have these labels in view. Another feature lets you split the screen vertically or horizontally and use each section as a window into a different part of the worksheet. The third option allows you to create a map of the worksheet in order to easily identify cells that contain formulas, values, and labels.

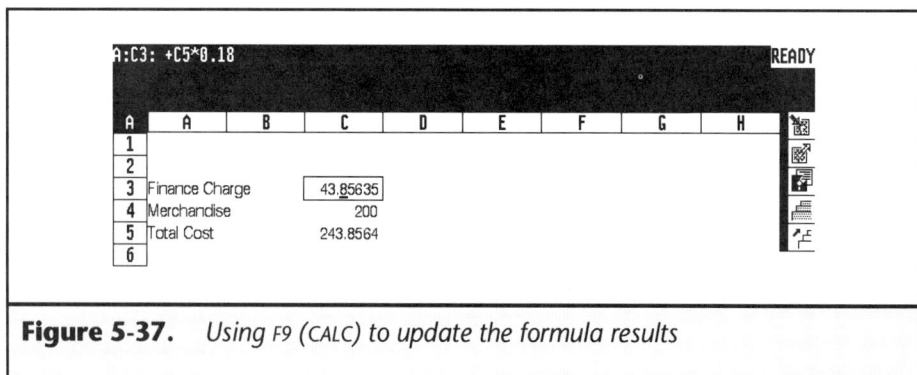

Figure 5-37. *Using F9 (CALC) to update the formula results*

Recalculation Options and Potential Pitfalls

The recalculation options control three different features of recalculation. Each of these settings remains in effect until changed, or until a file is loaded into memory with /File Retrieve or /File Open. Here are the specific options, along with a few tips for their use:

NATURAL   This option controls the order in which formulas are recalculated. This is the default setting, and makes 1-2-3 responsible for determining which formula to evaluate first. You can change to either Rowwise or Columnwise recalculation.

ROWWISE   This option disables the Natural recalculation sequence and switches to recalculation by rows. Row 1 is calculated from left to right, then row 2, and so on beginning on sheet A of the worksheet. The potential problem with this approach is early references that refer to values not yet recalculated.

COLUMNWISE   This option disables the Natural recalculation sequence and switches to recalculation by columns. Column 1 is calculated from top to bottom, then column 2, and so on from left to right on the worksheet. Again, the potential problem with this approach is early references to values not yet recalculated.

AUTOMATIC   This option, which causes the worksheet to recalculate automatically after every worksheet entry, is the default setting. You can stop the Automatic recalculation by invoking /Worksheet Global Recalc Manual.

MANUAL   This option turns off the Automatic recalculation feature. The worksheet will not recalculate with this option in effect unless you use F9 (CALC). You can restore Automatic recalculation with /Worksheet Global Recalc Automatic.

ITERATIONS   The normal setting for this option is 1, meaning that each formula is recalculated once during every worksheet recalculation. Circular references and other applications requiring iterative calculations to refine approximations require the iteration count to be set higher. The highest number 1-2-3 will accept is 50.

Freezing Titles

The /Worksheet Titles command presents a menu with the options Both, Horizontal, Vertical, and Clear. With these options you can elect to freeze titles at the top of your screen, the side of your screen, or both. The command is position dependent in that it freezes titles that are above and to the left of the cell pointer location at the time you invoke the command.

Once titles are frozen on the screen, you will not be able to use the arrow keys to move into these cells. If you need to make spelling corrections or other changes in these cells, you can use the F5 (GOTO) key. Pressing this key and specifying a cell in the frozen title temporarily brings two copies of the titles to the screen, as shown here:

```
A:A1:                                                           READY

   A       B         C        D         E       F       G       H
1                       New Employees By Department
2 DEPT.   1992      1991     1990      1989    1988    1987    1986
1                       New Employees By Department
2 DEPT.   1992      1991     1990      1989    1988    1987    1986
3         100        51       66        83      82      73      53      43
4         120        33       93        31      38      29      12      71
```

This double title will disappear when you scroll away from the title area.

TIP: GROUP mode will cause title changes to apply to all sheets in the active file. If GROUP mode is on, titles will be frozen at the same time in all active models.

Freezing Horizontal Titles

If you choose /Worksheet Titles Horizontal, the titles above the cell pointer will be frozen. Figure 5-38 presents a section from a worksheet with many entries. If you move your cell pointer toward the bottom of the entries, the top lines will scroll off. The remaining numbers are difficult to interpret without the column headings in row 1.

To freeze the labels in row 1, move the cell pointer to A2 on the original screen and select /Worksheet Titles Horizontal. Now, when the cell pointer is moved down the worksheet, the titles remain visible, as shown in Figure 5-39. Notice that the figure starts with row 1, which displays the horizontal titles, but the data displayed is from row 4 to 22.

```
A:A1: "Part_No.                                            READY

   A    A        B      C       D    E    F    G    H
   1   Part_No.  Cost Warehouse
   2    1502    $0.25    3
   3    1234    $1.70    4
   4    2134    $1.25    3
   5    5678    $2.35    2
   6    8543    $2.45    1
   7    6752    $5.90    2
   8    3412    $9.99    3
   9    2134    $7.50    3
  10    5432    $6.25    3
  11    8765    $0.59    2
  12    6667    $3.35    4
  13    5567    $2.00    5
  14    5543    $1.00    2
  15    4435    $2.25    2
  16    4432    $3.45    2
  17    7789    $7.80    3
  18    8876    $0.79    1
  19    9931    $2.00    1
  20    4452    $1.50    4
09-Nov-92 03:31 PM                                        NUM
```

Figure 5-38. *Worksheet with many entries down the sheet*

```
A:A22: 1133                                               READY

   A    A        B      C       D    E    F    G    H
   1   Part_No.  Cost Warehouse
   4    2134    $1.25    3
   5    5678    $2.35    2
   6    8543    $2.45    1
   7    6752    $5.90    2
   8    3412    $9.99    3
   9    2134    $7.50    3
  10    5432    $6.25    3
  11    8765    $0.59    2
  12    6667    $3.35    4
  13    5567    $2.00    5
  14    5543    $1.00    2
  15    4435    $2.25    2
  16    4432    $3.45    2
  17    7789    $7.80    3
  18    8876    $0.79    1
  19    9931    $2.00    1
  20    4452    $1.50    4
  21    3311    $1.75    5
  22    1133    $1.00    2
09-Nov-92 03:33 PM                                        NUM
```

Figure 5-39. *Titles remain on the screen after freezing*

Freezing Vertical Titles

Worksheets that are wider than the screen are candidates for freezing titles vertically. Doing so will allow you to move across the screen into columns far to the right of the normal display, and still have identifying labels visible on the left side of the screen. You freeze titles vertically simply by moving your cell pointer to the right of the titles you want frozen and entering **/Worksheet Titles Vertical**.

Freezing Titles in Both Directions

You may want to freeze in both directions when the worksheet is both longer and wider than the screen, and has descriptive titles at both the top and the left side of the screen. Figure 5-40 presents a portion of a worksheet with many entries. To freeze the titles in both directions, move the cell pointer to cell B3, which is to the right of the side titles and below the top titles, and then enter **/Worksheet Titles Both**. When the cell pointer is moved to J24, causing information to scroll off the top and left of the screen, both sets of titles are still visible, as you can see in Figure 5-41.

	A	B	C	D	E	F	G	H
1				New Employees By Department				
2	DEPT.	1992	1991	1990	1989	1988	1987	1986
3	100	51	66	83	82	73	53	43
4	120	33	93	31	38	29	12	71
5	130	20	28	95	25	39	78	35
6	140	88	59	0	33	53	73	56
7	145	23	31	32	7	22	39	27
8	150	84	18	72	59	47	76	78
9	160	64	89	62	55	26	21	54
10	175	85	22	27	93	46	37	17
11	180	5	92	17	8	60	73	98
12	190	21	36	41	76	6	9	57
13	195	5	65	14	91	83	5	39
14	200	0	85	41	48	87	13	32
15	210	62	45	11	60	61	19	52
16	220	31	23	39	65	31	20	30
17	225	61	5	38	42	18	74	64
18	228	50	47	85	1	49	49	57
19	230	33	96	73	46	9	77	70
20	235	21	99	70	73	82	4	2

Figure 5-40. *Worksheet with extra width and depth*

```
A:J24: @SUM(J3..J22)                                              READY

     A       D           E         F       G       H       I       J
 1              New Employees By Department
 7    145      32          7        22      39      27      59      36
 8    150      72         59        47      76      78      43      80
 9    160      62         55        26      21      54      42      92
10    175      27         93        46      37      17      50      45
11    180      17          8        60      73      98      15      87
12    190      41         76         6       9      57      94      16
13    195      14         91        83       5      39      23      87
14    200      41         48        87      13      32      94      16
15    210      11         60        61      19      52      23      87
16    220      39         65        31      20      30      94      44
17    225      38         42        18      74      64      19      28
18    228      85          1        49      49      57     100      23
19    230      73         46         9      77      70       6       9
20    235      70         73        82       4       2      57      62
21    240       9          7        88      34      36      18      43
22    245       5         28         1       9      76      51      28
23
24  TOTAL      845        937       910     775     994     820     902
25
```

Figure 5-41. *Titles frozen in both directions*

Clearing Titles

/Worksheet Titles Clear eliminates any titles that you have frozen. This command is not position dependent. It will remove the titles regardless of your cell pointer location.

Adding a Second Window

Having two windows in your screen display—available with /Worksheet Window—allows you to look at information in two completely different areas of the current worksheet file at the same time. When you learn how to open additional worksheet files in Chapter 8 "Working with Files," you can use the second window to display a different worksheet file. You can split the screen into two vertical or horizontal sections and then move your cell pointer within either window to bring whichever cells you choose into view.

There are also several special views of the worksheet available with the Window option, including the /Worksheet Window Map that provides a view of the types of data within the worksheet. The /Worksheet Window Perspective command described in Chapter 4 allows you to look at three sheets in the same file or three files at once. In Chapter 11, "Working with 1-2-3's Graphics Features," you will learn about another /Worksheet Window command that displays a graph on your screen at the same time as other worksheet entries.

If you decide to divide the screen into horizontal or vertical windows, the size of each window depends on the cell pointer location at the time the split is requested. The split is placed to the left of or above the cell pointer location, based on whether the split is vertical or horizontal.

The command to split the worksheet is /Worksheet Window, which produces the following menu:

```
A:A1:                                                                    MENU
Horizontal  Vertical  Sync  Unsync  Clear  Map  Perspective  Graph  Display
Split the screen horizontally at the current row
```

In addition to the Horizontal and Vertical options, the /Worksheet Window command has options that decide whether movement in one window will cause a corresponding shift of information in the second window. These options are Sync and Unsync.

Splitting the Screen Horizontally

A horizontal screen split is appropriate when you need the entire screen width to show two different sections of a worksheet report. To split the screen horizontally, move the cell pointer to a location within the row immediately below the desired split location. For example, Figure 5-42 shows the cell pointer positioned in row 12. When you enter **/Worksheet Window Horizontal**, the

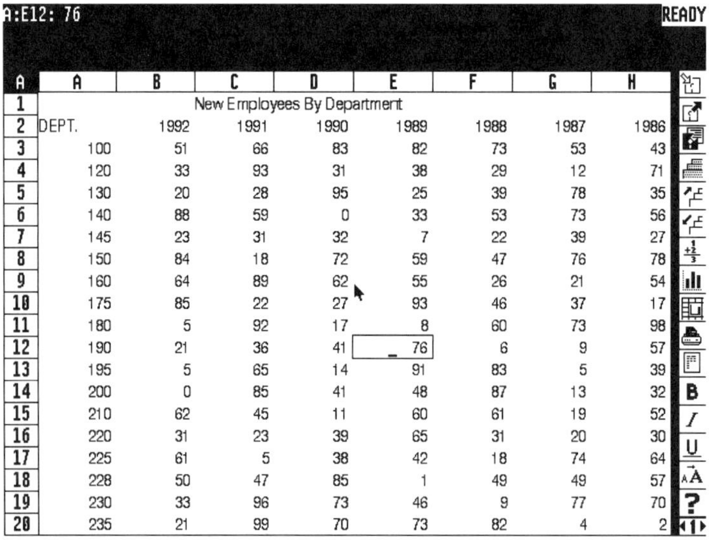

A:E12: 76								READY
	A	B	C	D	E	F	G	H
1			New Employees By Department					
2	DEPT.	1992	1991	1990	1989	1988	1987	1986
3	100	51	66	83	82	73	53	43
4	120	33	93	31	38	29	12	71
5	130	20	28	95	25	39	78	35
6	140	88	59	0	33	53	73	56
7	145	23	31	32	7	22	39	27
8	150	84	18	72	59	47	76	78
9	160	64	89	62	55	26	21	54
10	175	85	22	27	93	46	37	17
11	180	5	92	17	8	60	73	98
12	190	21	36	41	76	6	9	57
13	195	5	65	14	91	83	5	39
14	200	0	85	41	48	87	13	32
15	210	62	45	11	60	61	19	52
16	220	31	23	39	65	31	20	30
17	225	61	5	38	42	18	74	64
18	228	50	47	85	1	49	49	57
19	230	33	96	73	46	9	77	70
20	235	21	99	70	73	82	4	2

Figure 5-42. *Cell pointer positioned for horizontal window split*

screen splits into two different windows, with the size of the two windows being dictated by the cell pointer location at the time of the request. Figure 5-43 shows the result of the split in our example. F6 (WINDOW) can be pressed to move the cell pointer into the second window.

Once the screen is split, you can use the arrow keys to move the cell pointer around in either window. You can also move the second window to a different sheet while the first window remains on the original sheet.

Splitting the Screen Vertically

A vertical screen split is appropriate when you would like the full length of the screen to show sections of the worksheet but do not require the full width. Cell pointer position at the time of the request will again determine the size of the two windows. The split will occur to the left of the column in which the cell pointer is located.

You can split the worksheet shown in Figure 5-42 into two vertical windows at the cell pointer location. To produce this split, position the cell pointer in column E and enter **/Worksheet Window Vertical**. If you then press the F6 (WINDOW) key and move the cell pointer to column I, the display shown in Figure 5-44 will be produced. Notice that, just as with the Horizontal option, the cell pointer can be moved into the second window with F6 (WINDOW). Each time F6 (WINDOW) is pressed, the cell pointer will move into the opposite window.

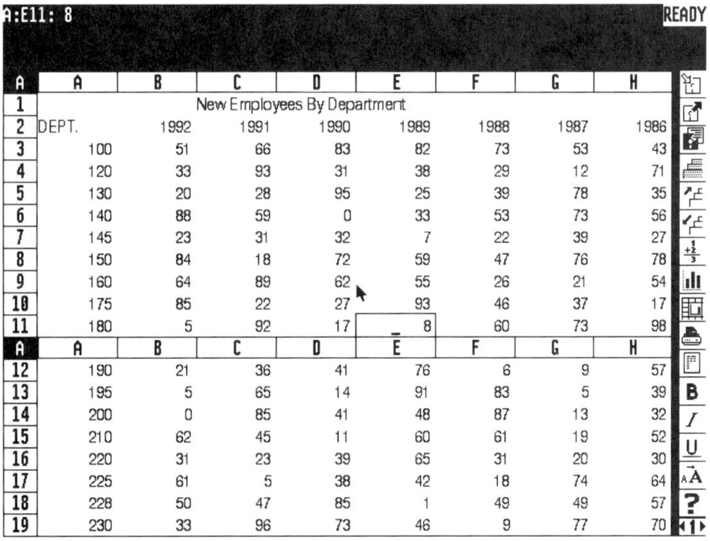

Figure 5-43. *Horizontally split screen*

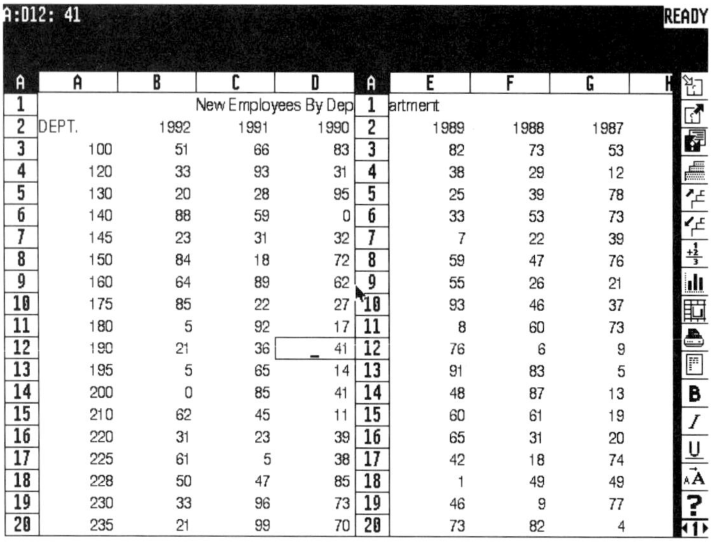

```
A:D12: 41                                                        READY

    A      A       B       C       D       A      E       F       G      H
    1              New Employees By Dep    1    artment
    2    DEPT.    1992    1991    1990    2    1989    1988    1987
    3            100      51      66      83   3      82      73      53
    4            120      33      93      31   4      38      29      12
    5            130      20      28      95   5      25      39      78
    6            140      88      59       0   6      33      53      73
    7            145      23      31      32   7       7      22      39
    8            150      84      18      72   8      59      47      76
    9            160      64      89      62   9      55      26      21
   10            175      85      22      27  10      93      46      37
   11            180       5      92      17  11       8      60      73
   12            190      21      36      41  12      76       6       9
   13            195       5      65      14  13      91      83       5
   14            200       0      85      41  14      48      87      13
   15            210      62      45      11  15      60      61      19
   16            220      31      23      39  16      65      31      20
   17            225      61       5      38  17      42      18      74
   18            228      50      47      85  18       1      49      49
   19            230      33      96      73  19      46       9      77
   20            235      21      99      70  20      73      82       4
```

Figure 5-44. *Vertically split screen*

Creating Windows with a Mouse

You can use the mouse to create windows if you are using Wysiwyg. To create horizontal windows with the mouse, point to the worksheet letter. Next, hold down the left mouse button and drag the mouse down to where you want the worksheet split into windows. As you drag the mouse down, 1-2-3 draws a line to indicate where the worksheet will be split into windows. When you release the left mouse button, 1-2-3 will split the screen into two windows using the line's location for where the screen is split. To create vertical windows the steps are the same, except that you drag the mouse to the right, instead of down, to indicate where you want the worksheet split.

Moving in Both Windows at Once

1-2-3's default setting has its two windows synchronized. This means that if you move in one window, the other window automatically scrolls to match it. With horizontal windows, moving the cell pointer from column A to column Z in one window causes the other window to automatically scroll to match. With vertical windows, moving from row 1 to row 120 in one window automatically updates the other window to display row 120, as well.

Moving in One Window at a Time

Sometimes you will want information, such as a table, to remain stationary while you move in the other window. You can make this change from either window using /Worksheet Window Unsync. With Unsync, the contents of the two windows are totally independent. If you choose, you can show the same information in both windows. To return to a synchronized mode, invoke **/Worksheet Window Sync**. This causes the two windows to move in tandem again. The Sync and Unsync options also affect window movement when a three-sheet perspective view is used.

Clearing the Second Window

When you decide to return to a single window display, you can enter **/Worksheet Window Clear**. If the screen was split horizontally, the returning single window obtains its default settings from the top window. If the screen was split vertically, the settings for the left window are used. If you are using Wysiwyg and a mouse, you can also close the windows by dragging the worksheet letter for the second window to be on top of the worksheet letter for the first window.

Using the Map Option to View Worksheet Information

As a worksheet grows large, it can be difficult to monitor all the entries it contains. Release 3's Map window can help you with this task by allowing you to audit the entries in the worksheet to determine if they contain numbers, labels, or formulas. This can be important. You might think that a model contains an entire column of formulas that add the data in each row. If you accidentally change a formula to a number, changes in the data will no longer update the total in this column.

Because the Map window narrows the display of the columns, many columns can be displayed on the screen at once. Label entries are displayed as double quotation marks ("), numbers are displayed as number signs (#), and formulas are displayed as plus signs (+). To invoke this view, enter **/Worksheet Window Map Enable**; to clear it again, press ESC.

Figure 5-45 shows a model with budget entries. These entries extend to column N, and are totaled in column O and at the bottom of each column. If one of the @SUM functions is accidentally entered as a number, the Map window will reveal the error. After entering **/Worksheet Window Map**, the display in Figure 5-46 is the result. You can see from this display that column O and row 13 do contain formulas in the required location, based on the "+" entries. If you encountered a "#" in any of these locations, you would need to explore the model further and make the required changes. While the map window is enabled, you

```
A:B8: (,0) [W11] 1050000                                              READY
```

	A	B	C	D	E	F
1					Budget for Division A	
2						
3		Jan	Feb	Mar	Apr	May
4	Salaries	$1,200,000	$1,218,000	$1,236,270	$1,254,814	$1,273,636
5	Benefits	168,000	170,520	173,078	175,674	178,309
6	Occupancy	120,000	121,800	123,627	125,481	127,364
7	Phone	259,500	263,393	267,343	271,354	275,424
8	Advertising	1,050,000	1,065,750	1,081,736	1,097,962	1,114,432
9	Utilities	19,000	19,285	19,574	19,868	20,166
10	Supplies	67,000	68,005	69,025	70,060	71,111
11	Postage	3,500	3,553	3,606	3,660	3,715
12						
13	Total	$2,887,000	$2,930,305	$2,974,260	$3,018,873	$3,064,157

Figure 5-45. Model with budget entries for an entire year

cannot make worksheet entries or use menu commands. When you want to return to the regular display, press ESC.

Displaying the Current Status of Worksheet Options

When you go back to a worksheet you used earlier, you may not remember all the options you chose for it. Conveniently, 1-2-3 lets you see the settings for all the worksheet options on one screen.

Enter **/Worksheet Status** to display the status of the options listed in Figure 5-47. With this command you can monitor the available memory, the existence of a math coprocessor to speed numeric calculations, the recalculation options, the default options for cell display, the global Protection status, and any cell causing a circular reference in the worksheet. The box called "A Closer Look at the Status Settings" provides a detailed look at the various status items listed. You cannot make changes to any of the options through the status display.

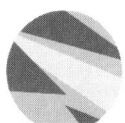

TIP: You can use both /Worksheet Status and /Worksheet Global Default Status to obtain a complete picture of 1-2-3's current settings, including selections, hardware, and system defaults.

Chapter 5: Basic Worksheet Commands   209

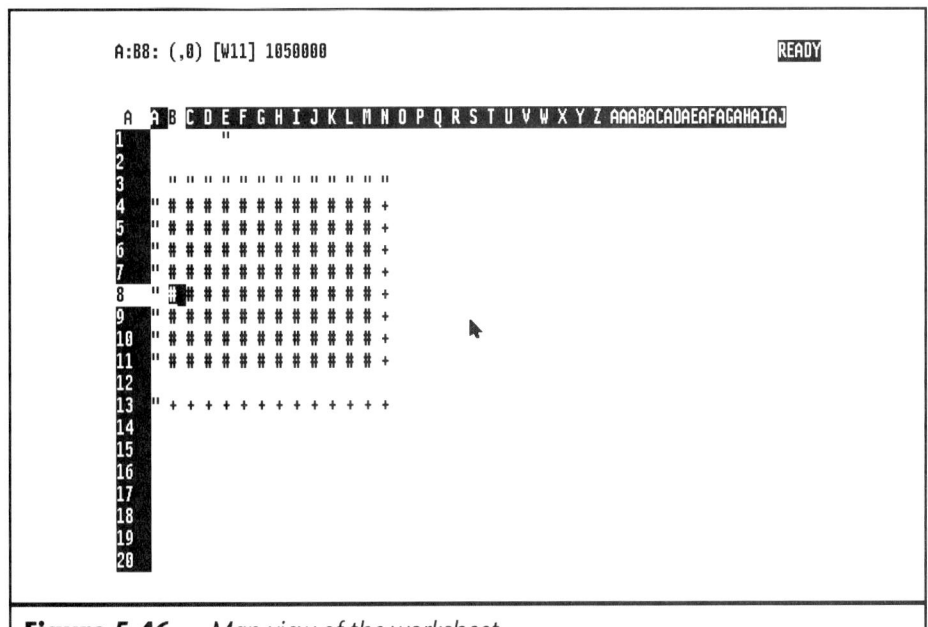

Figure 5-46.   *Map view of the worksheet*

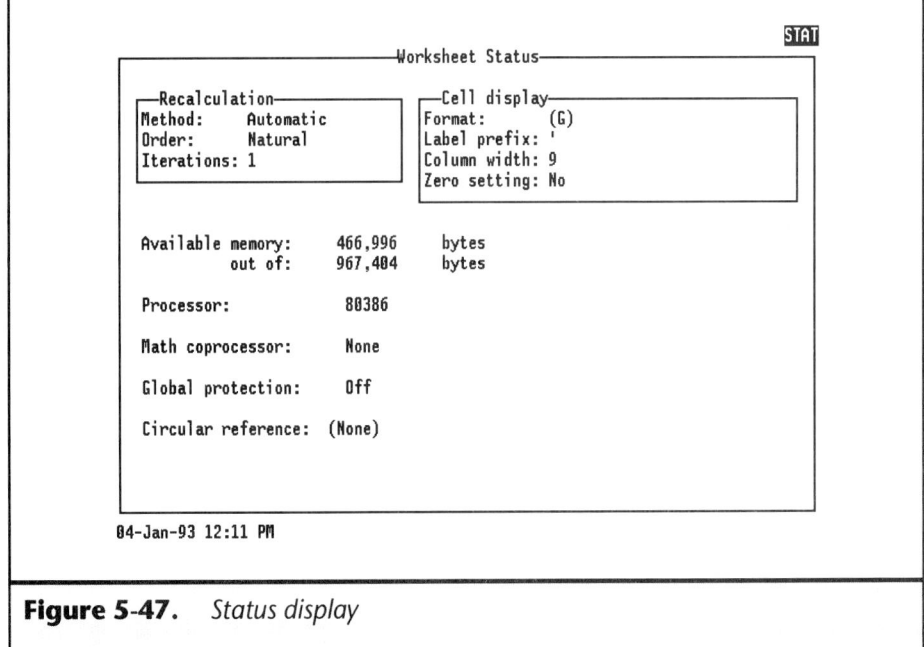

Figure 5-47.   *Status display*

A Closer Look at the Status Settings

There is a variety of information to monitor from the Status screen. Even though these settings are not individually selectable because they relate to different features of the worksheet, they can be regarded as options and are discussed here separately.

- **Available Memory** This portion of the display reports the amount of available memory you have used. This information helps you plan the remainder of your worksheet entries. When memory is almost full, you can split your worksheet in two.

- **Processor** This section reports the computer's resident processor. 1-2-3 automatically determines this display. Examples include 8088, 80286, and 80386.

- **Math Coprocessor** Release 3 supports the use of a math coprocessor chip. This section reports whether one of the supported chips is installed on your system.

- **Recalculation** This section reports on all the recalculation options. You can observe whether recalculation is set at Automatic or Manual. You can also monitor the current recalculation order to see whether it is set at Natural, Rowwise, or Columnwise. The current number of recalculation iterations set to occur is also displayed. To change any of the recalculation options use /Worksheet Global Recalc.

- **Circular Reference** This shows you the address of the first cell that is causing the CIRC indicator to appear at the bottom of your screen.

- **Cell Display** This section of the Status screen provides four different pieces of default information: the global format settings, the current label prefix, the column width, and whether zero suppression is on or off. These defaults can be changed through the /Worksheet Global commands.

- **Global Protection** The area of the Status screen shows whether global Protection is enabled or disabled. Changes to this setting can be made with /Worksheet Global Prot.

Command Reference

Basic Worksheet

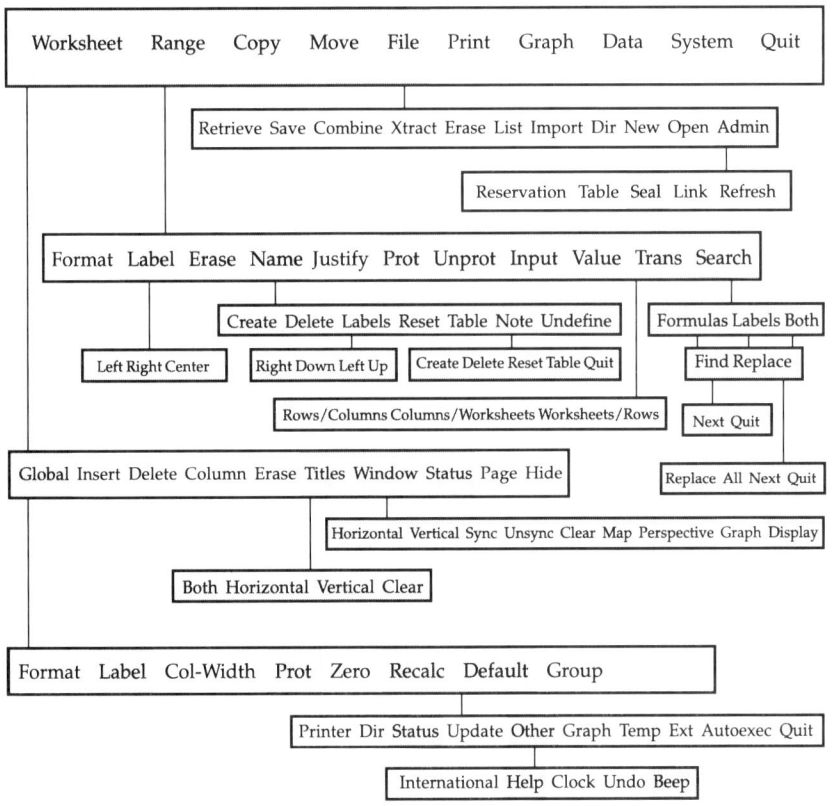

©1989 Lotus Development Corporation. Used with permission.

/Copy

Description

The /Copy command is the most powerful command 1-2-3 has to offer. It copies numbers, labels, and formulas to new locations on the worksheet. It copies the entries and any format assigned to the entries. If Wysiwyg is loaded, any Wysiwyg formats are also copied to the new location. This command can copy one cell or many cells in a range, to either a cell or a range. This command can copy information from any file, including files stored on disk into any active file.

Copying is a simple process that requires telling 1-2-3 only two things. First, it wants to know where to copy from. The From range can be one cell or many. Multiple cells to be copied can be arranged in a row, column, or rectangle on one or more sheets. The From range can be typed, referenced with a range name, or highlighted with the cell pointer.

Secondly you must tell 1-2-3 the To range. This defines whether you are making one or several copies, and specifies the exact location where you would like them placed. Each duplication of the From information requires only that the top left cell in the To range be entered. For example, to copy A1..A15 to B1..E15, you need only enter B1..E1 as the To range, since only the top cell in each copy is required. If you do not specify a sheet level or a file reference, the cells referenced are assumed to be in the current worksheet.

Options

The /Copy command supports four copying procedures:

- One cell to one cell
- One cell to many cells
- A range of cells to a range the same size as the original range
- A range of cells to a range whose size is a multiple of the original range. For example, a column of five cells can be duplicated in several additional columns of five cells.

Any of these options can be used with a single-sheet worksheet, a multiple-sheet worksheet, or with two different files. The specification of the From and To range determines what type of copying will take place.

/File Admin Seal

Description

The /File Admin Seal command seals a worksheet, which prevents changes to the file or to the reservation settings. When a file is sealed, only changes to the cell pointer's position, the worksheet data, and the window settings can be changed. You can combine this command with /Worksheet Global Prot Enable. Since a sealed file cannot have its protection status changed, enabling Protection before sealing the file prevents changes to all protected cells. When a reservation is sealed, the reservation setting cannot be changed. The file or reservation seal does not become permanent until the worksheet is subsequently saved with /File Save.

Options

This command has three options: File, Reservation-Setting, and Disable. The task each option provides is described here. Once an option is selected, 1-2-3 prompts for a password. Like passwords for the /File Save command described in Chapter 8, the password can be up to 15 characters and cannot contain spaces. Also, the password appears as asterisks and is case sensitive. When you enter a password for the File or Reservation-Setting options, you must enter the password a second time as a confirmation. This is the password you must use to unseal the file. It is different from the file password.

FILE   This option seals the file settings.

RESERVATION-SETTING   This option seals the reservation setting of the current worksheet file as described in Chapter 8, "Working with Files."

DISABLE   This option unseals the file and reservation settings for the current file.

/Move

Description

The /Move command moves a range of worksheet entries to any location on the worksheet. It moves the entries and any format assigned to the entries. If Wysiwyg is loaded, any Wysiwyg formats are also moved to the new location. /Move will adjust any formulas in the worksheet that refer to contents of the moved cells to correspond to the new location.

Options

This command permits you to move one or many cells to a new location. For example, you can move A2 to B3 by entering **/Move A2**, pressing ENTER, and then **B3** and pressing ENTER. To move a range of cells to a new location, you might enter **/Move A2..B6** and press ENTER, then enter a new destination like **D2** and press ENTER. With a multiple-sheet range, 1-2-3 will move the entire range, locating the contents of its upper leftmost cell (A2) in the designated To cell. You can use any of the options for specifying ranges, such as pressing F3 (NAME), pointing to the range, or typing the complete range address.

/Range Erase

Description

The /Range Erase command eliminates entries you have made in worksheet cells. Protected cells cannot be erased when worksheet Protection is enabled.

Options

The only options for this command are to specify a single cell or many cells in the range, and whether to type the range reference or highlight the included cells by pointing.

NOTE: *The /Range Erase command does not affect cell formats. A cell formatted as Currency is still formatted as Currency after /Range Erase is used. (To eliminate a format, use /Range Format Reset to return the range to the default setting.)*

/Range Input

Description

This command restricts cell pointer movement to unprotected cells. To use the command, first construct a worksheet and make sure the desired input cells are unprotected with /Range Unprot. Next, enter **/Range Input** and select a range of cells for the input area. 1-2-3 will only move to unprotected cells, skipping over protected ones. Remember that ranges must be rectangular; this command will not work on input cells scattered across the entire worksheet.

Options

While using the /Range Input command, you can employ many of the cell pointer movement keys to move among the unprotected cells in the selected area. HOME moves to the first unprotected cell, and END moves to the last unprotected cell. The arrow keys will move you within the selected range. ESC can be used to cancel an entry, but if you have not made an entry, it will cancel /Range Input. ENTER can be used to finalize entries, but if no entries have been made, it will cancel /Range Input. Selections cannot be made from the command menus, although some of the function keys are operational. These are F1 (HELP), F2 (EDIT), and F9 (CALC).

/Range Label

Description

The /Range Label command changes the justification (placement) of existing worksheet labels. Empty cells in the selected range are not affected by this command. These later entries will use the default worksheet setting.

Options

/Range Label has three options: Left, Center, and Right. These selections dictate the label indicator that will be used for existing cell entries. Left changes the label indicator to ' for all entries in the range, and left justifies them in the cells. Center places a ^ at the front of the labels and centers them in the cells. The last option, Right, places " at the beginning of the labels and right justifies them in the cells. After selecting one of the options, select the range to apply the new justification.

/Range Name Create

Description

The /Range Name Create command assigns names to cell ranges. Using names rather than cell addresses makes formulas easier to understand and helps you develop worksheet models that are self-documenting. Range names can be used anywhere cell addresses can be used.

Options

After entering **/Range Name Create**, you have two options: working with an existing range name or entering a new one. If you choose to work with an existing range name, you can select a name from the list of existing range names in the menu and have 1-2-3 highlight the cells that are currently assigned this name. At this point you can use ESC to undo the existing range name assignment and specify a new range name.

To establish a new range name, after entering **/Range Name Create**, type a new range name of up to 15 characters and press ENTER. Next, respond to 1-2-3's prompt for the range by pointing to or entering the range and then pressing ENTER. The range name you choose should be as meaningful as possible.

1-2-3 does not restrict you to a single name for a given range of cells. If a range is used for more than one purpose, you can assign multiple names to it by using /Range Name Create a second time.

/Range Name Delete

Description

The /Range Name Delete command deletes range names that are no longer needed. Each execution of this command removes a single range name and any note associated with the range name. To delete a range name, enter **/Range Name Delete**, point to the appropriate name in the list 1-2-3 provides, and press ENTER. Alternatively, type the name that you wish to delete after entering the command sequence.

/Range Name Labels

Description

The /Range Name Labels command assigns worksheet label entries as range names in certain situations. With this command, each label can be assigned as a name only to a single cell. Furthermore, the label must be in a cell adjacent to the cell you wish to assign the name to. If you choose a label that exceeds the 15-character limit for range names, the label will be truncated. The /Range Name Labels command is most useful when you have a column or row of labels and wish to assign each one to its adjacent cell as a range name. One execution of this command can assign all of the range names.

Options

The /Range Name Labels command has four options on a submenu. They let you tell 1-2-3 the direction in which to go for the cell needing assignment of the label. The choices are Right, Down, Up, and Left. After selecting one of the choices, select the range containing the labels to assign to the adjacent cells.

/Range Name Note

Description

The /Range Name Note command provides a number of options that allow you to create, modify, and view notes created for range names.

Options

There are five options for this command. Use Create and select a range name to enter or edit notes for any assigned range name. Each note can be a maximum of 512 characters. The Delete option deletes a note associated with a selected range name, although the range name itself is not affected. The Reset option deletes all the range name notes in the current file. The Table option creates a table of range names, their addresses, and associated notes after you provide the first cell 1-2-3 should use for the table. Quit returns you to READY mode.

/Range Name Reset

Description

The /Range Name Reset command eliminates all range names and any associated notes in a file at once.

/Range Name Table

Description

The /Range Name Table command lists all the range names in a file, and the range to which each name has been assigned.

Options

The only option you have with this command is to specify the upper left cell of the table. 1-2-3 will use as much space as required, and will overwrite worksheet entries if they are present in the cells used for the table.

/Range Name Undefine

Description

The /Range Name Undefine command "disconnects" the range address from a specified range name. The action does not affect any formula that uses the range name, although the formula will evaluate to ERR. The range name and note, if any, remain in the worksheet file. This allows you to redefine the range name, associating it with a new range of data that 1-2-3 immediately uses in any formula referencing that range.

Options

After entering this command, you must select or type the range name to undefine.

/Range Prot

Description

The /Range Prot command reprotects cells that you have unprotected with the /Range Unprot command. It allows you to change your mind and reestablish the

Protection features that are initially provided by 1-2-3 for every worksheet cell. Using the /Range Prot command has no apparent effect on a cell while the worksheet Protection features are turned off. Once Protection is turned on, cells that are protected will not accept entries of any type.

Since /Range Prot must be used in combination with /Worksheet Global Prot, you will also want to read the entry for that command.

Options

The only options for /Range Prot are ones for entering the range once you have requested the command. You can type the range address, use POINT mode to expand the cell pointer to include the entire range, or type the range name that you wish to use.

/Range Search

Description

The /Range Search command performs either a Search or a Replace operation. The command will search for a character string in either formulas or labels, and can optionally be used to replace the string with a new entry.

Options

After specifying the search range and search string, the first set of Search options lets you choose whether to search formulas, labels, or both. Next you tell 1-2-3 to find the string, or find it and replace it with another entry. If you choose Find, 1-2-3 looks for the first occurrence of your entry and highlights it. You can then continue to look for the next occurrence, or quit. If you choose Replace, 1-2-3 asks for the replacement string and highlights the first occurrence of the search string. You are then given the options to confirm this replacement, replace all occurrences of the search string, skip this replacement and move to the next matching string, or quit the Search and Replace operation.

This command skips hidden columns but includes cells with a Hidden format.

/Range Trans

Description

The /Range Trans command provides additional flexibility in restructuring a worksheet. It will copy data from column, row, or sheet orientation to another orientation. Unlike prior releases, Release 3 copies the value associated with any cell in the From range, rather than the formula. Earlier releases copied the formula, but would not adjust the formula's references.

Options

The options for this command select the entries to transpose and the type of transposition to make. First, select the range containing the cells to transpose and the first cell where the transposed entries should be copied. If both ranges use a single sheet, 1-2-3 makes a column/row transposition where the data that is in separate rows are in separate columns. If either range uses multiple sheets, 1-2-3 presents a second set of choices.

A submenu will appear that allows you to select from Rows/Columns, Worksheets/Rows, and Columns/Worksheets. The Rows/Columns option transposes the data on each sheet from a row to a column orientation. The Worksheets/Rows option copies the rows of the worksheets in the From range to the worksheets in the To range. The last option, Columns/Worksheets, converts column entries from the worksheets in the From range to the worksheets in the To range.

/Range Unprot

Description

The /Range Unprot command changes the cell protection characteristics of a range of cells. Using this command will allow entries in the selected cells after Worksheet Protection features are enabled.

Unless the /Range Unprot command is used, all worksheet cells have a status of Protected. This means entries cannot be made in the cells once the Worksheet Protection features are enabled. To remove the Protected status from a group of cells, simply enter **/Range Unprot**, and specify the range to unprotect.

Options

The only option for this command is to select the range to unprotect. You can type the range address, use POINT mode to expand the cell pointer to include the entire range, or type the range name that you wish to use.

/Range Value

Description

The /Range Value command copies the values displayed by formula cells without copying the formulas. The cells containing the values can be copied to a different range on the worksheet or to the location containing the original formulas. In both cases the cells that receive the data will not contain formulas; they will contain only the values resulting from the formulas.

Options

This command provides two options. When you enter **/Range Value** and specify the From range, you can specify a different To range in order to retain the original formulas and just make a copy of the values they contain. Or you can specify the same range for To and From, thus eliminating the original formulas and retaining just the values.

/Worksheet Erase

Description

/Worksheet Erase erases all the active files from memory. Unless you have Undo enabled, or have another copy of the worksheets stored on disk, you will not be able to retrieve the worksheets after using the /Worksheet Erase Yes option. This command returns all of the Wysiwyg settings for the worksheets to their defaults when Wysiwyg is loaded.

Options

The command presents a submenu with two options. One is Yes, indicating you want to proceed with the erasure of memory. The No selection is the default. The No option abandons the erase operation.

/Worksheet Global Default Other Beep

Description

This command enables or disables the computer bell that sounds when an error occurs, and when you execute the macro {BEEP} command.

Options

The two options for this command are Yes, which is the default and enables the beep, and No, which disables it.

/Worksheet Global Default Other Help

Description

This command sets the Help access method for earlier releases of 1-2-3. This command is only for compatibility and has no effect.

/Worksheet Global Default Status

Description

The /Worksheet Global Default Status command provides a screen snapshot of the worksheet settings made with /Worksheet Global commands. No changes to any of the settings can be made from this screen.

Options

In one sense there are no options for this command, since /Worksheet Global Default Status has no submenu. A variety of information is presented on the status screen, however. Even though the different items are not individually selectable, they can be regarded as options. All of the data listed are the results of selections made with other /Worksheet Global Default commands. When you press a key, 1-2-3 returns to the /Worksheet Global Default menu.

/Worksheet Global Label

Description

The /Worksheet Global Label command changes the default label prefix, and therefore the default justification (placement in the cell) for all new label entries on the worksheet.

Options

This command has three options: Left, Right, and Center. Left generates a ' as the label prefix; Right generates a "; and Center generates a ^ at the beginning of each label entry.

NOTE: The Global Label option takes a different approach from that of the /Range Label command, which changes the label prefix and justification for existing entries but does not affect new entries into cells within the range. Entries made after the employment of /Range Label use the default label prefix.

/Worksheet Global Prot

Description

The /Worksheet Global Prot command enables worksheet Protection for all worksheet cells that have a Protected status or disables Protection for the entire worksheet. The command works with the /Range Prot command to determine which worksheet cells are protected and which are unprotected.

Once Protection has been enabled, you will see "PR" in the control panel when your cell pointer is in cells that are protected. You will not be able to make entries in any protected worksheet cells. The color or highlighting created with the /Range Unprot command is maintained. With a color monitor, unprotected cells are highlighted in green, providing a "green light" signal that you can proceed with entries for that cell. Other cells remain their normal color. With a monochrome display, the unprotected cells are highlighted to indicate that you can make entries in these cells. Cell contents of Hidden format cells do not appear in the control panel while worksheet protection is enabled.

Options

This command has two options. The Enable option turns Protection on for the entire worksheet. Entering **/Worksheet Global Prot Enable** will prevent entries to cells that have a Protected status and allow entries only to those cells that have a status of Unprotected.

The second option is Disable. This option turns off Protection for the entire worksheet and permits entries to all cells. This command can be used to temporarily turn off Worksheet Protection so that you can modify a formula, erase or delete worksheet entries, or make new entries.

NOTE: While Protection is enabled, you can continue using 1-2-3 commands that do not affect the entries. This includes commands like /Range Format and /Range Unprot. If you want to protect the worksheet from these types of changes, seal the file with the /File Admin Seal command.

/Worksheet Global Recalc

Description

This command accesses all the recalculation options. With the use of /Worksheet Global Recalc you can affect the number of recalculations for a worksheet, determine whether the recalculation is automatic, and specify the order in which formulas are recalculated.

Options

The options for this command affect three different features of recalculation.

AUTOMATIC   This option causes the worksheet to recalculate automatically after every worksheet entry. With the efficient recalculation methods of Release 3, only the required recalculations are performed.

MANUAL   This option turns off the Automatic recalculation feature. When you use Manual recalculation, the worksheet is recalculated only when you press F9 (CALC).

NATURAL   This option gives 1-2-3 the responsibility for determining which formula to evaluate first.

ROWWISE   This option disables the Natural recalculation sequence and switches to recalculation by rows.

COLUMNWISE   This option disables the Natural recalculation sequence and switches to recalculation by columns.

ITERATIONS   The normal setting for this option is 1, meaning that every formula is recalculated once during every worksheet recalculation. It can be reset by typing in the number of iterations you want.

/Worksheet Status

Description

This command provides a screen snapshot of your current worksheet environment. It allows you to monitor available memory, as well as many of the default worksheet settings. No changes to any of the settings can be made from this screen.

Options

In one sense there are no options for this command, since /Worksheet Status has no submenu. A variety of information is presented on the status screen, however. The status screen indicates the amount of memory that you have used and the amount available; the processor; the math coprocessor; the recalculation method; the recalculation order; the number of iterations; the first cell that is part of a circular reference; whether protection is enabled; and the global settings for format, label prefix, column width, and zero display.

NOTE: This command is different from the /Worksheet Global Default Status command, which allows you to look at the default settings for each 1-2-3 session.

/Worksheet Titles

Description

The /Worksheet Titles command allows you to freeze label information at the top or left side of the screen. This is useful when you have a worksheet that is either wider or longer than the screen. Without the titles frozen on the screen, you would not see any descriptive information as you scrolled and moved through the worksheet.

The cell pointer movement keys will not move your cell pointer to the titles area once it is frozen on the screen. If you want to move there, you will have to use the F5 (GOTO) key. This will cause the title area to be shown on the screen twice. When you scroll away from this area, the double view of the titles will disappear from the screen.

Options

BOTH This option freezes information above and to the left of the cell pointer on your screen.

HORIZONTAL This option freezes information above the cell pointer on your screen.

VERTICAL This option freezes information to the left of the cell pointer on your screen.

CLEAR This option frees titles that have been frozen.

/Worksheet Window

Description

The /Worksheet Window command allows you to display the worksheet file in a different way. This has advantages for large worksheets where you cannot view the entire worksheet on one screen. You can view two different sections of the worksheet through two windows. When you split the worksheet area into two, the windows' size is controlled by the location of your cell pointer at the time you request the screen split. When the screen is split vertically, a dividing line will replace one of the worksheet columns; in a horizontal split, the dividing line will replace one of the rows. You can also split the worksheet area into three equally sized windows. You can move easily between windows with the F6 (WINDOW) key. F6 always moves you to the next window. You can use the windows to look at different files or sheets at once.

You can also use this command to switch between two different display drivers, or to display a graph and a worksheet on the screen at the same time. Another option provides a map of the types of entries in the cells.

Options

HORIZONTAL This option splits the screen into two horizontal windows. The dividing line is inserted immediately above the cell pointer.

VERTICAL This option splits the screen into two vertical windows. The dividing line is inserted immediately to the left of the cell pointer.

SYNC This option causes scrolling in the windows to be synchronized. That is, when you scroll in one window, the other windows will automatically scroll along with it. This is the default setting when you create a second window or display three windows with the Perspective option.

UNSYNC This option allows you to scroll in one window while the other windows remain stationary.

CLEAR This option returns the worksheet display to the default. When you clear a two-window screen, the window that remains is the top window when the split was horizontal, and the left window when the split was vertical.

MAP This option displays the worksheet with a Map view. Each column is two characters wide and displays " for cells containing labels, # for cells containing numbers, and + for cells containing formulas or annotated numbers.

PERSPECTIVE This option displays three windows sloped to the right. Each sheet uses one third of the screen.

GRAPH This option is covered in Chapter 11, "Working with 1-2-3's Graphics Features."

DISPLAY This option selects the display driver 1-2-3 uses. The selections for this option (1 and 2) are the same as the 1 and 2 for the Display drivers selected in the Install program.

NOTE: When Wysiwyg is loaded, you can create windows with a mouse only when the frame uses the enhanced or relief frame style (chosen with :Display Options Frame). To create a window, move the mouse pointer to the worksheet letter and drag the mouse, while holding down the left mouse button in the horizontal or vertical direction where you want the window split. As you drag the mouse, 1-2-3 draws a line to display where the window will split. When you release the mouse, 1-2-3 splits the worksheet into two windows at the selected location. You can also change the position of the split by dragging the worksheet letter of the second window to a new location. To close a second window, drag the second worksheet letter until it is on top of the first.

CHAPTER 6

Printing with 1-2-3 and Wysiwyg

Working with your models on the screen is great if you want to make changes and see their immediate impact. But when you have to go to a meeting and reference these same numbers, the screen in your office is no help. Fortunately, 1-2-3 Release 3 has extensive print features that allow you to create anything from a quick hardcopy of important figures to a professional-looking multi-page report.

Preparation for using the print features of 1-2-3 begins when you install 1-2-3. The installation process creates a driver configuration file that can speak the correct language for your particular printer.

If you have an early release of 1-2-3 without Wysiwyg you will find 1-2-3's print features adequate for your needs since you will not have a need to print with Wysiwyg's fancy formatting. If you are using Wysiwyg with 1-2-3 you can still use 1-2-3's print features to get a quick draft but you will want to use Wysiwyg for creating a final printout. In order to print your worksheet with your Wysiwyg formatting, you must print with Wysiwyg. If you print using 1-2-3, none of the Wysiwyg controlled formatting features will appear. These features include the fonts the characters use.

In this chapter you have an opportunity to work with the 1-2-3 and Wysiwyg commands related to printing. In addition to 1-2-3's Print menu commands, you will explore the /Worksheet Global Default Printer options and other 1-2-3 /Worksheet commands that affect printing. With these commands, you are able to set up default parameters, such as margins and page length, that are used every time you work with 1-2-3. By the time you finish the chapter, you should have mastered simple printing tasks and also be familiar with the more advanced print options that 1-2-3 provides. Besides printing with 1-2-3, you can print with Wysiwyg. Wysiwyg provides additional printing features beyond the capabilities of 1-2-3's Print menus.

Release 3 offers a number of features that give you additional options for printing worksheet reports. Support for *background printing* allows you to use your time for additional spreadsheet activities while 1-2-3 or Wysiwyg is printing completed worksheets in the background. You no longer have to sit and wait for print output to end before continuing your work on additional worksheet tasks. Also, 1-2-3 now lets you access additional printer features like font selection, line spacing, and character spacing through menu selections, instead of the setup strings required by earlier releases. You may want to use Wysiwyg for these features since Wysiwyg displays the data on your worksheet, as the data will print with Wysiwyg's :Print commands.

The Print Menus

Wysiwyg and 1-2-3 have very similar print features. With the later releases, however, you are going to want to do most of your printing with Wysiwyg because of its advanced spreadsheet publishing abilities. However, even with the later releases, you may find that 1-2-3 is the best choice for drafts or simple reports. The great advantage that 1-2-3 has over Wysiwyg when printing drafts is that 1-2-3 can be printed relatively quickly. Wysiwyg normally takes much longer because of the formatting codes. Both 1-2-3 and Wysiwyg have main print menus. 1-2-3's print menu appears after you select /Print and a printer destination. This main Print menu and its setting sheet is shown in Figure 6-1. The choices in the main Print menu are available regardless of the destination

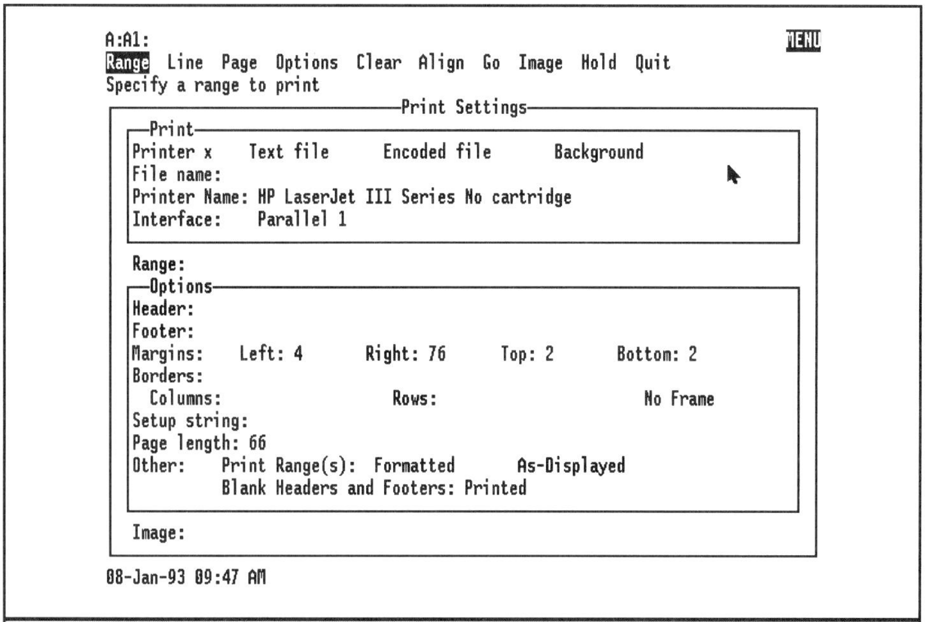

Chapter 6: Printing with 1-2-3 and Wysiwyg

```
A:A1:                                                              MENU
Range Line Page Options Clear Align Go Image Hold Quit
Specify a range to print
                           ┌─Print Settings─┐
 ┌─Print─────────────────────────────────────────────────────┐
 │ Printer x    Text file      Encoded file     Background   │
 │ File name:                                                │
 │ Printer Name: HP LaserJet III Series No cartridge         │
 │ Interface:    Parallel 1                                  │
 └───────────────────────────────────────────────────────────┘
 Range:
 ┌─Options──────────────────────────────────────────────────┐
 │ Header:                                                  │
 │ Footer:                                                  │
 │ Margins:    Left: 4      Right: 76     Top: 2   Bottom: 2│
 │ Borders:                                                 │
 │   Columns:              Rows:              No Frame      │
 │ Setup string:                                            │
 │ Page length: 66                                          │
 │ Other:    Print Range(s): Formatted      As-Displayed    │
 │           Blank Headers and Footers: Printed             │
 └──────────────────────────────────────────────────────────┘
 Image:

08-Jan-93 09:47 AM
```

Figure 6-1. *1-2-3's main Print menu and Print Settings setting sheet*

Printing with 1-2-3

The basic steps for printing with 1-2-3 are:

1. Type **/P** for the Print menu.
2. Type **P** for Printer, **F** for File, **E** for Encoded, or **B** for Background for the printing destination. If you select File, Encoded, or Background, type the name of the file and press ENTER.
3. Type **R** for Range and select the worksheet range you want to print. Press ENTER.
4. Make any other changes you want to make to the print settings.
5. Type **G** for Go. If you are printing to the printer, type a **P** for Page to advance to the next page.
6. Type **Q** for Quit.

1-2-3 Release 3.4: The Complete Reference

you select. The basic steps for printing with 1-2-3 are listed in the box "Printing with 1-2-3."

The Wysiwyg main Print menu is invoked by typing **:P**. When you invoke this menu, it looks like the one shown in Figure 6-2 which also shows the Wysiwyg settings sheet. The basic steps for printing with 1-2-3 are listed in the box "Printing with Wysiwyg."

With both 1-2-3 and Wysiwyg, the Print menus continue to remain on the screen until you select Quit. Pressing ESC is another way to exit. In 1-2-3, leaving the Print menu finishes the print job. If you are printing to a file, it closes the file. If you are printing to a network or a printer spooler, it directs the network or spooler to begin printing the output. Also, with both 1-2-3 and Wysiwyg, the settings sheet remains on the screen but you can press F6 (WINDOW) to remove it. With Wysiwyg, you can also use the :Print Info command to toggle between displaying and hiding the Wysiwyg Print Settings settings sheet.

Print Destination

The first choice you must make when you print is the destination of your printed output. In 1-2-3, you select the destination as soon as you select /Print. In

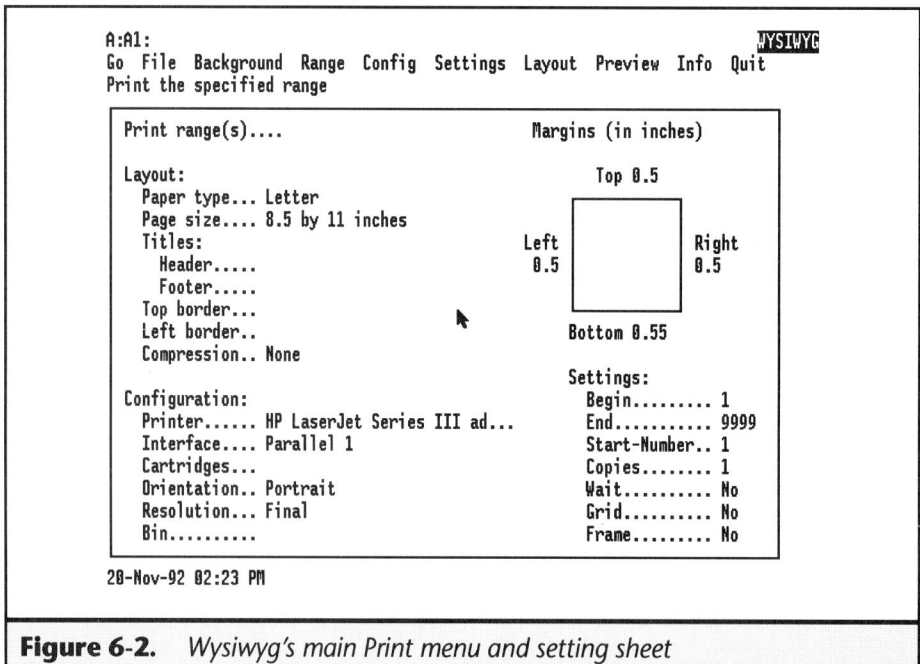

Figure 6-2. *Wysiwyg's main Print menu and setting sheet*

Printing with Wysiwyg

The basic steps for printing with Wysiwyg are:

1. Type **:P** for the Print menu.
2. Type **R** for Range and **S** for Set.
3. Select the worksheet range you want to print and press ENTER.
4. Make any other changes you want to make to the print settings.
5. Type **G** for Go to print to the printer or **F** for File or **B** for Background. If you select File or Background, type the name of the file and press ENTER.
6. Type **Q** for Quit.

Wysiwyg, you select the destination when you are ready to print the data. In either case, you must decide whether you want the information sent directly to your printer or written to a disk file. With 1-2-3, after you select the destination, you can then continue to select any of the Print options that tell 1-2-3 such things as the part of the worksheet you want to print, and the margins you want. With Wysiwyg, you select the options for the data you want to print and the print options such as margins first. Then you select the destination when you start the printing process by selecting Go, File, or Background.

To send the output directly to the printer, you select Printer after selecting /Print in 1-2-3 or Go from Wysiwyg's :Print menu when you are ready to print the selected information. The other options, at least temporarily, put the information in a file. When you select one of these options, you must supply a file name where the data is stored.

The File option in 1-2-3's /Print menu stores the data in a file without any formatting codes that are specific to your printer. You use this option when you want the data in a text file that you can subsequently bring into your favorite word processor or other program. These files will use a .PRN extension.

The Encoded option in 1-2-3's /Print menu and the File option in Wysiwyg's :Print menu stores the data in a file that includes the formatting codes that are specific to your printer. You use this option when you want to print the data in the file at a later time. To print an encoded file, use the DOS COPY command to copy the file to the printer (LPT1). These files will use a .ENC extension.

The Background option in 1-2-3's /Print menu and Wysiwyg's :Print menu stores the data in a file that includes the formatting codes that are specific to your printer. The difference is that this option creates a temporary file. Once the information is placed in the file, the BPrint utility handles sending the information to the printer as described below. After all the information is sent to the printer, the temporary file is deleted. Like encoded files, these files will use a .ENC extension.

Background Printing

Before Release 3, you had to wait until 1-2-3 finished printing before you could continue using the other features of 1-2-3. Release 3 uses *background printing,* that allows you to continue using 1-2-3 while worksheets are printed. As described above, 1-2-3 performs background printing by storing the information to print in a temporary file and sending portions of the file to the printer when 1-2-3 is not performing other tasks and the printer is capable of accepting more information.

1-2-3 stores each printing task as a print job in a queue. Documents are normally printed in the order they are created, but you can change the print order by assigning priority levels. During background printing, you have the option of temporarily or permanently halting the print jobs. If you temporarily suspend a print job, you can restart it.

In Release 3.4, if you plan to print into the background with either Wysiwyg or 1-2-3, you need to start the BPrint program before starting 1-2-3. Both 1-2-3 and Wysiwyg use the BPrint program for the background printing feature. To start BPrint, type **BPRINT** in the 123R34 directory and press ENTER. You cannot load BPrint into memory by selecting the /System command to access the DOS prompt. If you want to print in the background, but did not load BPrint first, you must exit 1-2-3, load BPrint and reload 1-2-3. In Release 3.4, if BPrint has not been loaded, then you receive an error message when you select Background from 1-2-3's /Print or Wysiwyg's :Print menu.

Assigning Priority Levels

As you create print jobs, you will want some worksheets printed before others. One way is to set the order that 1-2-3 prints your jobs is to request them in the order you want them printed. Another option for controlling the print order is assigning priority levels to the print jobs. 1-2-3 has three priority levels: High, Default, and Low. Within each priority level, 1-2-3 prints the print jobs in the order they are created. To assign a priority to the print job you are creating, use the /Print Printer Options Advanced Priority command. 1-2-3 first prints jobs with a priority of High, then Default, then Low.

Halting and Restarting Print Jobs

As 1-2-3 prints your document, you may need to stop the printing process temporarily or permanently. You may notice that the printer is about to run out of paper, or realize that the print output contains a mistake, or you want to stop printing so you can use another computer package. If you suspend printing, you can start printing again when you are ready.

To temporarily stop the printing, use the /Print Suspend command. This command stops 1-2-3 from sending more information to the printer. If the printer has a buffer, the printer will not stop immediately, since the printer usually has information stored that has not printed yet. The printer will stop when it prints the information that has already been transferred to its buffer.

Once you are ready to restart printing, the /Print Resume command will begin sending information to the printer at the point where 1-2-3 stopped sending information after you used /Print Suspend. /Print Resume is also used if 1-2-3 halts the printer due to a printer error, or if the printer uses a single sheet feeder. When 1-2-3 encounters a printer error or has finished printing a page on a single sheet feeder printer, 1-2-3 displays an error message in the status line. Unlike other error conditions, it does not prevent you from continuing to work with other 1-2-3 features.

There may be situations where you want to abort printing without the need to restart it. To permanently stop printing, use the /Print Cancel command. This command stops 1-2-3 from sending more information to the printer. If the printer has a buffer, the printer will stop when its buffer is empty. Unlike the /Print Suspend command, the /Print Cancel command removes all print jobs from the queue. You cannot restart the print jobs. After performing this command, you will want to realign the printer and use the /Print Printer Align command, so that subsequent print jobs are properly aligned.

Print Range

Whether you are printing to your printer or a disk file, you must decide what worksheet cells you want to print. You can print every cell that contains entries, or just a few. In either case, you must specify the range of cells to 1-2-3 or Wysiwyg. These cells can reside on one sheet, or several sheets in a multi-sheet file. You can even specify several areas in a worksheet file as separate print ranges—all with one Range command.

You specify the cells to print through the Range option in 1-2-3's or Wysiwyg's main Print menu. To see how this works, assume you want to print the model shown in Figure 6-3. If you have never printed this worksheet before, 1-2-3 and Wysiwyg will assume that the starting location for printing is the current cell pointer location. Therefore, you probably will want to position your

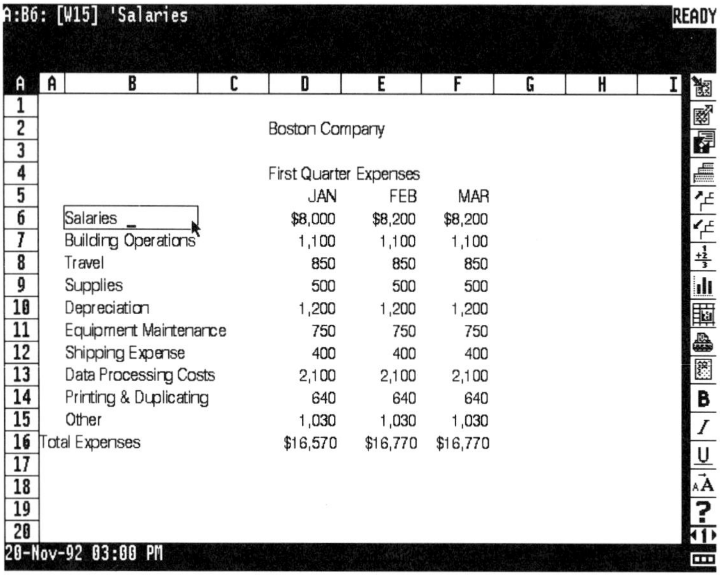

```
A:B6: [W15] 'Salaries                                                    READY

     A       B              C      D        E        F       G    H    I
 1
 2                                   Boston Company
 3
 4                                First Quarter Expenses
 5                                   JAN      FEB      MAR
 6        Salaries                  $8,000   $8,200   $8,200
 7        Building Operations        1,100    1,100    1,100
 8        Travel                       850      850      850
 9        Supplies                     500      500      500
10        Depreciation               1,200    1,200    1,200
11        Equipment Maintenance        750      750      750
12        Shipping Expense             400      400      400
13        Data Processing Costs      2,100    2,100    2,100
14        Printing & Duplicating       640      640      640
15        Other                      1,030    1,030    1,030
16        Total Expenses           $16,570  $16,770  $16,770
17
18
19
20
20-Nov-92 03:00 PM
```

Figure 6-3. *Worksheet data for printing*

cell pointer on A1 before telling 1-2-3 or Wysiwyg that you want to print. Once the cell pointer is in A:A1, type **/PP** for the 1-2-3 main Print menu or **:P** for the Wysiwyg Print menu.

To tell 1-2-3 the range to print, follow these steps:

1. Type **R** to select the Range option, and in Wysiwyg, select type **S** to select Set.

2. Lock the beginning of the range in place at A:A1 by typing a period.

3. Move to the end of the model by pressing the special key sequence of END followed by HOME.

4. Press ENTER to tell 1-2-3 or Wysiwyg that the range has been selected.

5. Assuming that all the default settings are acceptable, check to make sure the printer is turned on and the paper is aligned properly; then select Go. If you use the 1-2-3 Print menu, you should get the printout shown in Figure 6-4. If you used the Wysiwyg menu, you should get the printout shown in Figure 6-5.

```
                         Boston Company

                      First Quarter Expenses
                           JAN       FEB       MAR
    Salaries             $8,000    $8,200    $8,200
    Building Operations   1,100     1,100     1,100
    Travel                  850       850       850
    Supplies                500       500       500
    Depreciation          1,200     1,200     1,200
    Equipment Maintenance   750       750       750
    Shipping Expense        400       400       400
    Data Processing Costs 2,100     2,100     2,100
    Printing & Duplicating  640       640       640
    Other                 1,030     1,030     1,030
    Total Expenses      $16,570   $16,770   $16,770
```

Figure 6-4. *1-2-3's printout of the selected range*

	Boston Company		
	First Quarter Expenses		
	JAN	FEB	MAR
Salaries	$8,000	$8,200	$8,200
Building Operations	1,100	1,100	1,100
Travel	850	850	850
Supplies	500	500	500
Depreciation	1,200	1,200	1,200
Equipment Maintenance	750	750	750
Shipping Expense	400	400	400
Data Processing Costs	2,100	2,100	2,100
Printing & Duplicating	640	640	640
Other	1,030	1,030	1,030
Total Expenses	$16,570	$16,770	$16,770

Figure 6-5. *Wysiwyg's printout of the selected range*

NOTE: If you selected Background, Encoded, or File in 1-2-3's menu rather than Printer, selecting Go starts the process of writing your information to the disk. In Wysiwyg, you select the destination by selecting File or Background rather than Go to start the printing process.

The two examples in Figure 6-4 and 6-5 show some of the differences from printing using 1-2-3 and Wysiwyg. The Wysiwyg printout in Figure 6-5 uses the same font that appears in Figure 6-3. The 1-2-3 printout in Figure 6-4 uses the default printer font. While you can use the 1-2-3 /Print menu to change the font, you will not see the difference on the worksheet the way you do when you change the font in Wysiwyg and print using Wysiwyg's :Print menu. Also, when you print with Wysiwyg, the paper automatically advances to the next page. When you print with 1-2-3, you must use the Page command described below to advance to the next page.

These examples use the default margins and page length. Options to change these and other settings affecting the appearance of your printed output will be covered later in the chapter. Changes in the default settings would be made between steps 4 and 5 in the print procedure previously described.

When the selected range includes long labels that extend beyond their cells, you must include in the range the cells from which the labels borrow space. This keeps the labels from being truncated in the printout. For example, if G4 contains "Date of Report: March 17, 1993" and the cell width is 9, the label uses G4, H4, and I4 for its display. If all three cells are not included in the print range, 1-2-3 or Wysiwyg only print the portion of the label that appears in the selected range. Also, the default font for Wysiwyg is a proportional font so you can fit more than nine characters in a default width column. When you print using 1-2-3's menu, the font probably is a monospace font. As a result, the column that appears wide enough on your screen may not be wide enough when you print with 1-2-3's /Print menu.

REMEMBER: You can select a range with F4 (ABS) or the mouse before you select the 1-2-3 or Wysiwyg command to select the range to print. Also, in Release 3.4, if you preselect a range with F4 (ABS) or the mouse and then select the following icon, Wysiwyg will set the print range to print the selected data and print the data as if you selected both the :Print Range Set and :Print Go commands.

Changing the Print Range

There may be one additional step in the printing procedure if you have already printed a worksheet before, and now want to print a new area from it. When you select Range a second time in a worksheet, 1-2-3 or Wysiwyg remembers and highlights the last selected range. To select a new range, press ESC or BACKSPACE to change the range address to a single cell address. You can then reposition and anchor again before moving to the opposite corner of the range you want to print.

*TIP: When you select Range, 1-2-3 or Wysiwyg remembers and highlights the last selected range you printed. To expand or contract the print range, move the cell pointer to different corners of the range. To change the corner of the range that is most active, type a period; 1-2-3 will then move the active corner in a clockwise direction. (In some cases, the active corner will move in a counterclockwise direction.) The **active corner** determines the direction where expansion and contraction of the range occurs. The first cell address in the control panel is the anchored corner, and the second address is the corner that you can change.*

Printing Multiple Ranges

In Release 3, you can print multiple ranges. This feature is ideal when you want to print several different areas on a sheet or when you need to print data from several sheets.

To print more than one range, highlight the first range that you want to print. Then type a semicolon instead of ENTER. 1-2-3 or Wysiwyg finalizes the first range and repositions the cell pointer on the current cell so you can highlight another range. An example of using multiple print ranges to print is A1..G20;A45..G68. Once you select all the ranges that you want to print, press ENTER. 1-2-3 or Wysiwyg prints all of the specified ranges in the order they are specified. If you select Range again, 1-2-3 or Wysiwyg lists all of the selected ranges and highlights the last one for you to alter, if desired. You can edit the other ranges by pressing F2 (EDIT) to edit the range addresses.

Controlling the Printer from 1-2-3's Print Menu

1-2-3's Print menu provides several methods of controlling the paper in your printer. The three Print menu options involved are Line, Page, and Align. These commands are needed because 1-2-3 does not automatically advance to the top of a page when finished printing. Wysiwyg thinks of each page as a discrete unit. 1-2-3, since it does not include graphics, font changes or other advanced formatting features, counts your pages in lines, and prints one line at a time.

Advancing Printer Paper a Line at a Time

The /Print Printer Line command moves the paper in the printer up by one line. It acts just as if you used your printer's line feed button with your printer off line, with one important exception. The printer's line feed does not alter the internal line count that 1-2-3 maintains to determine when a new page is needed. The Line command, however, adds 1 to 1-2-3's internal line count, so it will stay in sync with the paper.

1-2-3 assumes that you have positioned your paper at the top of a form before turning your printer on. If you did not, printing starts on the same line on all pages as on your first page, since 1-2-3's line count does not change. The Align command, discussed shortly, can remedy this problem.

Advancing Printer Paper a Page at a Time

The /Print Printer Page command moves the paper in your printer to the top of the next form. When you select this command, 1-2-3 checks its internal line count to determine how many lines must be spaced to complete a full page and reach the top of the next page. The result is similar to pressing your printer's form feed button with your printer off line, except that the Page command prints a footer (if you define one) for the bottom of your page; form feed does not. Like Line, Page assumes that you started printing at the top of a form.

Using Align to Reset the Printer Line Count

The /Print Printer Align command is another page adjustment command. Rather than moving the paper in the printer, it resets the line count to zero to represent the top of a page, and resets the page number to 1. Every time you position your paper at the top of a new form with /Print Printer Page or the printer control buttons, you should also use Align to tell 1-2-3 to restart the line count for a new page. If you do not remember to use Align, your new page cannot be filled completely because 1-2-3 continues to use its existing line count even though it does not match the page currently in the printer.

Printing Options

You have had an opportunity to explore some of the default settings for print. In this section, you will learn how to tailor printing to the task at hand, making changes that affect only the current session or worksheet. This section focuses on features that both 1-2-3's and Wysiwyg's Print menus provide. These features include headers and footers, margins, borders, page size, and hiding columns and sheets to prevent data from appearing in printouts. To make changes to 1-2-3's printing options, select Options from the main Print menu to display this menu:

```
A:A1: [W3]                                                           MENU
Header Footer Margins Borders Setup Pg-Length Other Name Advanced Quit
Create a header
```

To make changes to Wysiwyg's printing options, select Layout from the main Print menu to display this menu:

```
A:A1: [W3]                                                          WYSIWYG
Page-Size Margins Titles Borders Compression Default Library Quit
1:Letter  2:A4  3:80x66  4:132x66  5:80x72  6:Legal  7:B5  Custom
```

The print option changes you make through 1-2-3's Print menu do not affect Wysiwyg and vice versa.

If you are printing to a file or to a print spooler in 1-2-3 and you want to make changes to the worksheet in the middle of printing the data, you do not want to return to READY mode using Quit from the main Print menu. When you select Quit you close any print job you are in the middle of creating. To return to the worksheet without terminating the transmission of all the information to the file or spooler, use the /Print Printer Hold command. This command returns you to the worksheet and holds the print job you are currently creating until you return to the 1-2-3 Print menu and finish it.

TIP: To temporarily change the appearance of a range before you print it, open a second window with /Worksheet Window. Modify the format and column widths in the second window. After printing the range from the second window, close it; 1-2-3 will retain the formatting selections from the first window.

Creating Headers and Footers

Headers and *footers* are lines of text printed at the top and bottom, respectively, of every page of your report. A header or footer may be, for example, a date, company name, report name, department, page number, or a combination of these elements. Except for page numbers, these elements are the same for each page.

Both 1-2-3 and Wysiwyg allow you to use a header or footer of 512 characters. You can divide both headers and footers into separate segments for the right, left, and center sections of each line. These capabilities mean you can place more than one information element in a header or footer. 1-2-3 and Wysiwyg require that all of the information for a header and footer fit on one line, so you must consider your line length when planning the contents of a header or footer.

In 1-2-3, headers and footers are specified through the /Print Printer Options Header and Footer commands. In Wysiwyg, headers and footers are specified through the :Print Layout Titles Header and Footer commands.

Header and Footer Special Characters

Several characters are essential to creating headers and footers: the vertical bar (|), the at sign (@), the pound sign (#), and the backslash (\).

The | , @, and # can be combined with each other and other text but not with the \. The cell referenced after the \ can contain the other special characters.

| The | character divides the header or footer into three sections. For example, if you enter the header **Accounting Department | Texas Company | Rpt: 8976**, the department name is printed at the left, the company name in the center, and the report identification at the right.

@   The @ character represents the current system date.

The # character represents the current page number. If you want the page number to start with a specific number, enter two # signs followed by the page number you want to start with.

\   This character can be placed in a header or footer, followed by a cell address. The header or footer will then use the contents of the cell referenced. For example, if A:A3 contains Acme Company - Toy Division | Page # | @, the header entry \A:A3 places Acme Company - Toy Division on the left side, the page number in the middle section, and the date at the far right.

Using Special Characters in a Header or Footer

Headers and footers can use four special characters. The special characters you can use in headers and footers are summarized in the box called "Header and Footer Special Characters."

To separate the information you are entering into each section of the header or footer, use the vertical bar character (|). Any spaces included between the vertical bars are counted as characters to be included in the heading, and they affect the alignment of the heading sections. For example, to create the heading shown in Figure 6-6, enter

Adams & Associates | | Rpt. No. 1234

If you want a heading only on the right side of each page, precede the header information with two vertical bars (| |).

The pound sign (#) represents the location where you want to add a page number. 1-2-3 begins with 1 and automatically increases the number for each page. With 1-2-3's Print menu, you will need to use /Print Printer Align when you print using # to make sure 1-2-3 starts counting with page 1, rather than with the page number after the last page printed. If you want to start with a different number, enter two # signs and the number you want to use.

Use @ to represent the location where you would like 1-2-3 to place the current date. 1-2-3 uses the system date, which is stored in your computer's memory. The only way to change this date is to access the DOS DATE command (using /System; see Chapter 8), enter a new date, and then use EXIT to return to 1-2-3.

The # and @ characters can be entered in any header or footer segment and can be combined with other text, such as **Page No:** or **Today's Date:**. As an example, if you enter the header **Today's Date: @ | Page# | Rpt. No. 1234**, the resulting header will look like the top of Figure 6-7.

```
Adams & Associates                                  Rpt. No. 1234


Description              Life    Cost  Dept        Type       Inv Code
IBM Selectric Typewriter    5    $980  Accounting  Office        54301
Royal Typewriter            5    $950  Training    Office        54455
Swivel Chair               10    $345  Check       Furniture     54789
TI Calculator               7    $100  Audit       Office        54177
Walnut Desk                15  $1,200  Cash        Furniture     54138
Xerox Copier                3  $2,500  Cash        Processing    54392
Xerox Copier                3  $2,800  Accounting  Processing    54999
```

Figure 6-6.   *A printout with a header*

```
Today's Date: 17-Mar-93         Page 1              Rpt. No. 1234

Description              Life    Cost  Dept        Type        Inv Code
IBM Selectric Typewriter  5     $980  Accounting  Office         54301
Royal Typewriter          5     $950  Training    Office         54455
Swivel Chair             10     $345  Check       Furniture      54789
TI Calculator             7     $100  Audit       Office         54177
Walnut Desk              15   $1,200  Cash        Furniture      54138
Xerox Copier              3   $2,500  Cash        Processing     54392
Xerox Copier              3   $2,800  Accounting  Processing     54999
```

Figure 6-7. *A printout with a header that includes the date and page number*

TIP: *To automatically date-stamp every page of output you create, use @ to represent the current date in either a header or footer on every worksheet printed.*

If you need to use different headers and footers when printing different sections of a worksheet, the easiest approach is to store the complete header or footer in a worksheet cell. Rather than typing the long header or footer entry with each change, you can instead reference the cell address for the appropriate header or footer after selecting the menu option. Use \ and a cell address to represent the referenced cell's contents.

Since 1-2-3 updates the information in the header each time it uses it, referencing a cell instead of retyping the contents provides the current contents of the cell. An example of the backslash in a footer entry is **A28**. In this example, each time 1-2-3 prints the footer, it checks the current value of cell A28 and uses that value in the footer. The referenced cell can include the header and footer special characters. If you enter a backslash and a cell address for the header or footer, you cannot use the other special characters in the entry. For example, **A28** | **Date:** @ is unacceptable.

Margins

The /Print Printer Options Margins command in 1-2-3 and the :Print Layout Margins command in Wysiwyg controls the amount of white space at the top, bottom, and sides of your printed document. A graphic representation of the page layout, including margins is seen in Figure 6-8. If you are printing a narrow range of cells, for example, you might want to increase the side margins settings to center the output on the paper. On the other hand, if you want to spread a great deal of data across a page, you might want to use very small margin settings.

```
           Payroll Report                                  Date: 21-May-93


                         Last Year's                  This Year's
           Name            Salary  Inc. Mo.   % INC      Salary    Benefits
           Alpen, Patrick  $35,000    10      4.00%     $35,350     $4,949
           Arbor, Jim      $23,000     4      7.00%     $24,208     $3,389
           Bunde, Norman   $12,000     1      4.00%     $12,480     $1,747
           Campbell, Keith $32,000     1      9.00%     $34,880     $4,883
           Campbell, David $40,000     1     10.00%     $44,000     $6,160
           Denmore, Mary   $18,900    11      7.50%     $19,136     $2,679
           Farper, Vincent $40,000     1     10.00%     $44,000     $6,160
           Fork, Angela    $36,900     4      7.00%     $38,837     $5,437
           Guest, Norman   $12,000     1      4.00%     $12,480     $1,747
           Guest, Samuel   $45,000     2      9.00%     $48,713     $6,820
           Guiness, Carl   $35,000    10      4.00%     $35,350     $4,949
           Harker, Steve   $35,000    10      4.00%     $35,350     $4,949
           Harper, Angela  $36,900     4      7.00%     $38,837     $5,437
           Harris, Kevin   $15,000     6      5.00%     $15,438     $2,161
           Harvey, Jim     $23,000     4      7.00%     $24,208     $3,389
           Hitt, Anne      $18,000     9      4.00%     $18,240     $2,554
           Jacobs, Norman  $12,000     1      4.00%     $12,480     $1,747
           Jenkins, Paul   $45,000     2      9.00%     $48,713     $6,820
           Jones, Ray      $25,000     2      5.00%     $26,146     $3,660
           Just, Alexander $25,000     2      5.00%     $26,146     $3,660
           Kaylor, Angela  $36,900     4      7.00%     $38,837     $5,437
           Kiger, Keith    $32,000     1      9.00%     $34,880     $4,883
           Kommer, John    $15,000     6      5.00%     $15,438     $2,161
           Korn, Charles   $35,000    10      4.00%     $35,350     $4,949
           Larkin, Susan   $29,000     3      7.00%     $30,692     $4,297
           Litt, Norman    $12,000     1      4.00%     $12,480     $1,747
           Merriman, Angela $36,900    4      7.00%     $38,837     $5,437
           Morn, Arthur    $35,000    10      4.00%     $35,350     $4,949
           Nest, William   $45,000     2      9.00%     $48,713     $6,820
           Parden, Christina $29,000   3      7.00%     $30,692     $4,297
           Parson, Adele   $18,000     9      4.00%     $18,240     $2,554
           Piltman, Carol  $18,000     9      4.00%     $18,240     $2,554
           Polk, Danielle  $18,900    11      7.50%     $19,136     $2,679
           Rensler, Jane   $12,000     1      4.00%     $12,480     $1,747
           Rolf, John      $15,000     6      5.00%     $15,438     $2,161
           Sarper, Angela  $36,900     4      7.00%     $38,837     $5,437
           Smith, Greg     $23,000     4      7.00%     $24,208     $3,389
           Stanbor, Jim    $23,000     4      7.00%     $24,208     $3,389
           Stark, Nancy    $18,900    11      7.50%     $19,136     $2,679
           Stedman, David  $40,000     1     10.00%     $44,000     $6,160
           Stephens, Paul  $45,000     2      9.00%     $48,713     $6,820
           Stevenson, Sharon $18,900  11      7.50%     $19,136     $2,679
           Stone, Mary     $29,000     3      7.00%     $30,692     $4,297
           Stone, Ray      $25,000     2      5.00%     $26,146     $3,660
           Tolf, Miles     $15,000     6      5.00%     $15,438     $2,161
           Tone, Agnes     $29,000     3      7.00%     $30,692     $4,297
           Trundle, Howard $15,000     6      5.00%     $15,438     $2,161
           Umber, Edward   $45,000     2      9.00%     $48,713     $6,820


                                       Page 1
```

Figure 6-8.   *The page layout*

The four Margin options are Left, Right, Top, and Bottom. In 1-2-3, these options get their default values from settings specified with /Worksheet Global Default Printer. In 1-2-3 a fifth option, None, sets the top, bottom, and left margins to 0 and the right margin to 10000. This option is for printing a worksheet to an unencoded file that will later be imported into another program.

With Wysiwyg you define margins in inches. On the standard letter sized paper, 8 1/2 inches by 11, the usual margins are 1 inch on each side. The worksheet itself only prints in the 7 1/2 by 10 inch area in the middle, evenly surrounded by the margins. The margins, as you can see, measure how far in from the edge of the paper the printing can start.

1-2-3 defines top and bottom margins as the number of lines it cannot use on a page. 1-2-3 uses left and right margins to determine the width of the paper in terms of characters of the default printer font. 1-2-3 does not need to know the actual physical width of the paper. It only needs to know where it can print characters. For the left margin, you tell 1-2-3 how many character spaces from the left edge of the paper you want the first character to appear. For example, for a one inch left margin, you would set a left margin of 10, since ten characters of the default font fit in one inch. To calculate the right margin, decide how many characters you want to print on a line. Add that number to the left margin count and enter the sum as the right margin. 1-2-3 does not care how many characters spaces are left between the last character and the right edge of the paper. It only wants to know where to put the first character in the line, and how many characters it can print for each line.

To change any margin setting, simply type the new number after specifying the appropriate Margins option. In 1-2-3, you can also press the RIGHT ARROW and LEFT ARROW keys to expand and contract these settings, just as you can with the column width settings. The changes you make to the margin settings are saved with the worksheet.

Borders

You can include the identifying information found at the top of columns and at the left side of rows in your worksheet on every printed page of a report. These cells are called *borders* since they border the data in the worksheet. The information in the borders might be account names or other identifying descriptions. When you print borders you print descriptive information on each page of a multi-page report rather than at the top and sides of the first page only. The descriptive information may be in columns, rows, or both. The print range is then printed to the right or below the border information.

This feature is useful if you have used the months of the year as column heads across the worksheet, for example, and have more data than can fit on one printed page. You can print the worksheet with these column heads at the top of each page, if the row containing the months is specified as a border. Similarly, if your report is wider than it is long, you can print the information found at the far left of your worksheet on every page of your report. In Figure 6-9, you can see a report that is two pages wide, listing expenses for the Boston Company for the

	Boston Company					
	First Quarter Expenses			Second Quarter Expenses		
	JAN	FEB	MAR	APR	MAY	JUNE
Salaries	$8,000	$8,200	$8,200	$8,700	$8,700	$7,500
Building Operations	1,100	1,100	1,100	$1,100	$1,100	$1,100
Travel	850	850	850	$850	$850	$850
Supplies	500	500	500	$500	$500	$500

	Third Quarter Expenses			Fourth Quarter Expenses		
	JULY	AUG	SEPT	OCT	NOV	DEC
Salaries	$7,500	$10,000	$10,000	$10,000	$10,000	$10,000
Building Operations	$1,100	$1,100	$1,300	$1,300	$1,300	$1,300
Travel	$850	$850	$850	$850	$850	$850
Supplies	$500	$500	$500	$500	$500	$500
Depreciation	$1,200	$1,200	$1,200	$1,200	$1,200	$1,200
Equipment Maintenance	$750	$750	$750	$750	$750	$750
Shipping Expense	$400	$400	$400	$400	$400	$400
Data Processing Costs	$2,100	$2,100	$2,100	$2,100	$2,100	$2,100
Printing & Duplicating	$640	$640	$640	$640	$640	$640
Other	$1,030	$1,030	$1,030	$1,030	$1,030	$1,030
Total Expenses	$16,070	$18,570	$18,770	$18,770	$18,770	$18,770

Figure 6-9. *Two pages of print output using a border at the left edge*

year. Without the border, the information on the second page would quickly become confusing. When you include the first column as a border on the second page, you make the report much easier to understand.

In Wysiwyg, borders are set with :Print Layout Borders then Left for the border on the left or Top for the border on the top. In 1-2-3 you will set borders with /Print Printer Options Borders then Columns for the border on the left or

Border Rules

The Borders option allows you to print descriptive information on each page of a multi-page report. The descriptive information may be in columns, rows, or both. To include a row or column in a border, you only have to select one cell from a row or column to select the entire row or column. When 1-2-3 or Wysiwyg prints the range, it prints the rows and columns from the border that apply to the rows and columns of the print range. For example, a worksheet can have a print range of A:B2..M:L24 and use column A and row 1 as the border. When 1-2-3 or Wysiwyg prints B:B2..B:H24 (the portion of the worksheet on sheet B that can fit across the page), it prints B:A1..B:A24 as the column border and B:A1..B:H1 as the row border.

Rows for the border on the top. Using Borders to print your worksheets are summarized in the box "Border Rules."

Column Borders

The /Print Printer Options Borders Columns or :Print Layout Borders Left command is used when you have more columns than will fit across one page, and the worksheet has labels or other information in a column or columns on the left side of the worksheet that are needed to identify data printed on subsequent pages of your report. Selecting these columns as borders causes the columns to print on each page of the report.

The expense worksheet containing monthly figures shown in Figure 6-10 serves as an example. If the print range A1..O16 is used, the descriptive account names will only appear with the first months printed. However, if you specify these account names as a column border, you can print them on each page. To do this, after selecting Borders, select Columns for 1-2-3 or Left for Wysiwyg. In response to the prompt for columns, enter the range **A1..C1**. Then when you print the worksheet, begin your print range with D1. (If you begin it with A1, the account name column information will be printed twice.) The multi-page printout should look like Figure 6-9.

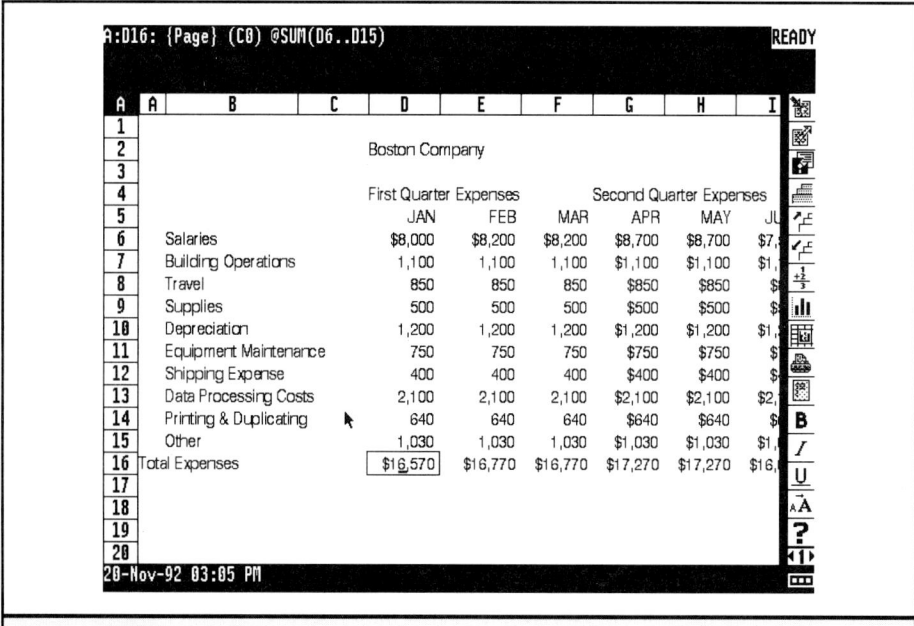

Figure 6-10. *Worksheet to use the border columns*

Row Borders

The /Print Printer Options Borders Rows or :Print Layout Borders Top command is used when the identifying data you want repeated on each page is located in rows at the top of your worksheet. Use this option if there are more rows of data to print than will fit on one page. First enter the command. Highlight a cell at the top of the border range, and anchor it with a period (.); then highlight a cell in the last row you want to use as a row border, and press ENTER. Once you have defined the border, change the range to omit the border rows so those rows do not print twice.

The example shown in Figure 6-11 has headings in row 1, and many rows of data below it. To have the entries in row 1 repeated for both pages of a printout, you need to select row 1 as a border row. To do this, after selecting Borders, select Rows for 1-2-3 or Top for Wysiwyg. In response to the prompt for rows, enter the range **A1..A1**. Then when you print the worksheet, begin your print range with A2. (If you begin it with A1, the contents of row 1 would appear twice on the first page.) The beginnings of the two pages looks like Figure 6-12.

Adding a Frame

1-2-3's and Wysiwyg's Print menu supports the addition of row numbers and column labels as a frame around the range of print data. When a frame is added with the /Print Printer Options Border Frame command or the :Print Settings Frame Yes command, 1-2-3 or Wysiwyg supplies row numbers above and column letters to the left of the printed range. Figure 6-13 shows a printed worksheet that uses a frame. You can use a frame in combination with row and column borders or separately. This option can be used to document a worksheet by changing the default format to Text, and then printing the worksheet with a frame. To remove a frame, use the /Print Printer Options Borders No-Frame

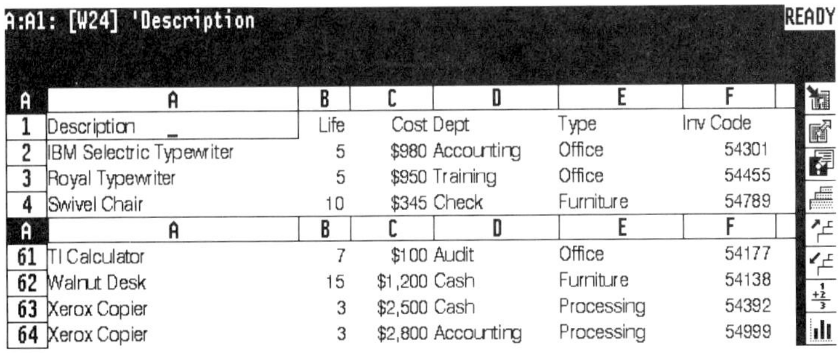

Figure 6-11. *Purchases worksheet for multi-page printout*

```
Date: 17-Mar-93              Page 1              Rpt. No. 1234

Description        Life      Cost Dept        Type       Inv Code
 I
 R    Date: 17-Mar-93              Page 2              Rpt. No. 1234
 S
      Description         Life      Cost Dept        Type       Inv Code
      TI Calculator         7       $100 Audit       Office       54177
      Walnut Desk          15     $1,200 Cash        Furniture    54138
      Xerox Copier          3     $2,500 Cash        Processing   54392
      Xerox Copier          3     $2,800 Accounting  Processing   54999
```

Figure 6-12. *Printout using border rows*

command or the :Print Settings Frame No command. You can also add grid lines to a Wysiwyg printout like the ones in Figure 6-13 by selecting the :Print Settings Grid Yes command. These grid lines are removed by selecting :Print Settings Grid No.

Page Size

Neither Wysiwyg nor 1-2-3 can check your printer to determine what size paper is loaded for use. You must tell Wysiwyg or 1-2-3 the size of paper that you will print on so the correct amount of information fits on each page. If you print on a

	A	A	B	C	D	E	F	G	H
1									
2					Boston Company				
3									
4					First Quarter Expenses			Second Quarter Expe	
5					JAN	FEB	MAR	APR	MAY
6			Salaries		$8,000	$8,200	$8,200	$8,700	$8,700
7			Building Operations		1,100	1,100	1,100	$1,100	$1,100
8			Travel		850	850	850	$850	$850
9			Supplies		500	500	500	$500	$500
10			Depreciation		1,200	1,200	1,200	$1,200	$1,200
11			Equipment Maintenance		750	750	750	$750	$750
12			Shipping Expense		400	400	400	$400	$400
13			Data Processing Costs		2,100	2,100	2,100	$2,100	$2,100
14			Printing & Duplicating		640	640	640	$640	$640
15			Other		1,030	1,030	1,030	$1,030	$1,030
16			Total Expenses		$16,570	$16,770	$16,770	$17,270	$17,270

Figure 6-13. *A printout showing the grid and the frame*

legal sheet of paper, with a smaller paper size defined, the full size of the paper will not be used. If you try printing on the smaller paper with the legal paper size defined, your data will run off the edge of the paper.

In 1-2-3, you set the page size by the page length and the margins. You have already learned how to set the left and right margins by setting start and stop points relative to the left side of the page. The page length is the number of lines that could be printed on a sheet of paper assuming every line was used. With the default options in effect and five lines printed per inch, only 45 lines are printed when the page length is the default of 66. This is because lines 1, 2, 65, and 66 are reserved for top and bottom margins. Line 3 is for the header and lines 4 and 5 are blank to make space between header and text. Similarly, line 64 is for a footer and lines 62 and 63 for space. Lines 6 through 51 are used for printing your worksheet data.

You can change the number of lines per page that 1-2-3 prints by using the /Print Printer Options Pg-Length command and entering the new number of lines that 1-2-3 should count for each page. Some printers, such as the Hewlett-Packard LaserJet, can print only 60 lines per page. You will know if you need to change the page length when the page breaks occur at different points on each page. If you change the number of lines per inch that fit on a page by using a setup string or the /Print Printer Advanced Options command, you will also have to enter the new number of lines for the /Print Printer Options Pg-Length command.

Wysiwyg specifies page size in terms of inches, just as you probably do. You can choose from one of seven standard paper sizes, or specify the measurements of a custom paper size for Wysiwyg, so you can use unusual sizes. To tell Wysiwyg the paper size you have in the printer, select the :Print Layout Page-Size command. After selecting this command, you can choose from one of eight options listed here:

No.	Name	English	Metric
1	Ltr	8 1/2" x 11"	216mm x 279mm
2	A4	8.268" x 11.693"	210mm x 297mm
3	80 x 66	8" x 11"	203mm x 270mm fanfold
4	132 x 66	13.2" x 11"	335mm x 270mm fanfold
5	80 x 72	8" x 12"	203mm x 305mm fanfold
6	Legal	8 1/2" x 14"	216mm x 356mm
7	B5	6.929" x 9.843"	176mm x 250mm
	Custom		

If you select Custom, type the width of the paper you are using and press ENTER. Then, type the length and press ENTER. Wysiwyg continues using the same paper size until you select another page size option.

Using Hidden Columns and Sheets To Affect the Print Range

If you want to print more than one range from a worksheet, one method is to select the ranges and then print them. The second range prints immediately after the first range as shown in Figure 6-14. You will notice that the columns in the second range do not have descriptive information preceding them.

In many instances, it is not possible to fit all the information in your worksheet across one printed page. You can solve this problem by using the /Worksheet Column Hide feature, discussed in Chapter 4, "Changing the Appearance of the Worksheet Display," to choose which columns to print, effectively extending the print features. Figure 6-15 presents part of a worksheet,

```
                                    Boston Company

                                    First Quarter Expenses
                                       JAN       FEB      MAR
            Salaries                 $8,000    $8,200   $8,200
            Building Operations       1,100     1,100    1,100
            Travel                      850       850      850
            Supplies                    500       500      500
            Depreciation              1,200     1,200    1,200
            Equipment Maintenance       750       750      750
            Shipping Expense            400       400      400
            Data Processing Costs     2,100     2,100    2,100
            Printing & Duplicating      640       640      640
            Other                     1,030     1,030    1,030
     Total Expenses                  $16,570   $16,770  $16,770
     Second Quarter Expenses
        APR       MAY      JUNE
      $8,700    $8,700    $7,500
      $1,100    $1,100    $1,100
        $850      $850      $850
        $500      $500      $500
      $1,200    $1,200    $1,200
        $750      $750      $750
        $400      $400      $400
      $2,100    $2,100    $2,100
        $640      $640      $640
      $1,030    $1,030    $1,030
     $17,270   $17,270   $16,070
```

Figure 6-14. *Two print ranges printed consecutively*

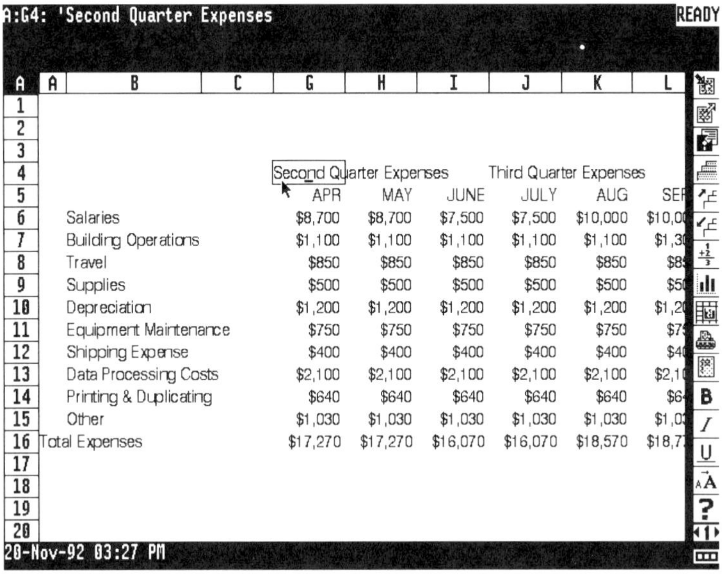

Figure 6-15. Worksheet with hidden columns

the result of using /Worksheet Column Hide to eliminate columns D through F. Choosing /Print Printer Range A1..I16 and then Go creates the printed report shown in Figure 6-16.

```
                         Second Quarter Expenses
                            APR      MAY     JUNE
      Salaries           $8,700   $8,700   $7,500
      Building Operations $1,100  $1,100   $1,100
      Travel               $850     $850     $850
      Supplies             $500     $500     $500
      Depreciation       $1,200   $1,200   $1,200
      Equipment Maintenance $750    $750     $750
      Shipping Expense     $400     $400     $400
      Data Processing Costs $2,100 $2,100   $2,100
      Printing & Duplicating $640   $640     $640
      Other              $1,030   $1,030   $1,030
Total Expenses          $17,270  $17,270  $16,070
```

Figure 6-16. Printed output with hidden columns

Using hidden columns is one way to print a second range with descriptive information. It is also useful when some columns contain data that you do not need in your report. You can also use the /Worksheet Hide command to hide sheets within a range that you do not want to print.

Wysiwyg Printing Features

1-2-3 Releases 3.1 and 3.4 come with the Wysiwyg add-in. This add-in adds professional spreadsheet publishing abilities that you will want to include in your printouts. Besides the basic printing features described above, Wysiwyg has additional printing features that 1-2-3 does not offer. You will want to spend some time learning how you can use these features to make your output look better. These features include adding page breaks, previewing, compressing the printout, and selecting the printer.

When you print with Wysiwyg, you will notice that the range you select to print has a dotted box around it. This dotted box shows the currently selected Wysiwyg print range. When the range is divided into several pages on a printout, the range will also be divided into the data that appears on each page by the dotted lines. You may also notice that when you move to a row that appears at the top of a page or to a column that appears in the first column of the page, the control panel contains {Page}. When you select a cell that is the upper left corner of the data that appears on the page, the control panel shows you the page number of the current cell (as it will print), as well as the total number of pages in the selected print range.

Adding Manual Page Breaks

One command which can influence the appearance of your document is found on the :Worksheet menu rather than the :Print menu. When you want to insert manual page breaks in Wysiwyg to tell Wysiwyg where you want to start a new page, you must position the cell pointer at the location where you want the page break, then select the :Worksheet Page command. This command presents four options. You can select Row to insert a horizontal page break, Column to insert a vertical page break, or Delete to remove page breaks from your worksheet. Since the :Worksheet Page menu is sticky, the fourth option is Quit, which you can select to return to Ready mode.

The exact position of the page break is determined by the cell pointer location and your selection of Row or Column. When you select Row, a horizontal page break is inserted above the row that your cell pointer is in. This is the same page break added when you select this icon in Release 3.4:

Chapter 6: Printing with 1-2-3 and Wysiwyg 255

This page break means that the row that your cell pointer is positioned in when you select this command is the first row of the new page. When you select Column, the vertical page break appears on the left of the current cell, making the column which your cell pointer is in the first column in the new page. This is the same page break added when you select this icon in Release 3.4:

In Figure 6-17, you can see Wysiwyg's page break markers, which are dotted lines. The cell pointer has not been moved since the page breaks were inserted, so that cell will appear in the upper left corner of that page of the printout.

When you want to delete the page breaks inserted with Wysiwyg, you select :Worksheet Page Delete after positioning your cell pointer so that the page break you want to delete is above or to the left of the cell pointer. Any page breaks to the left of or above the cell that the cell pointer is positioned in are deleted.

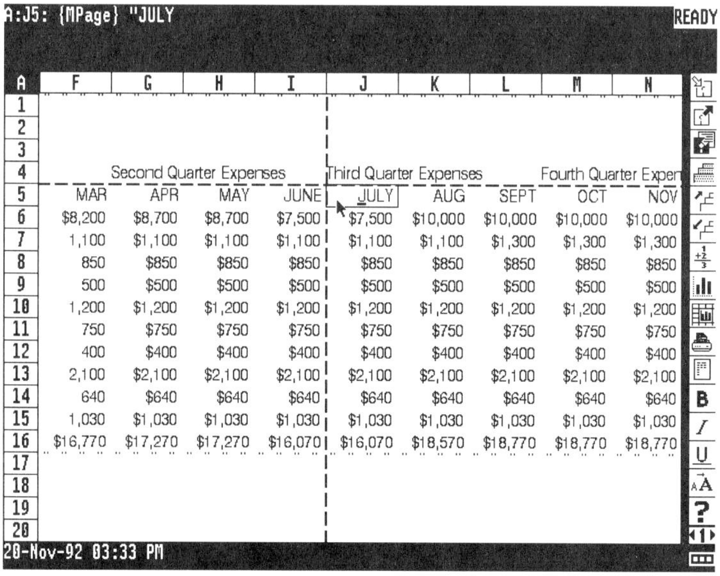

Figure 6-17. *Wysiwyg's page breaks are marked*

Previewing Your Printed Output

After setting the print range, you can preview how the page will print. You might want to do this to check that you selected all the page layout settings correctly. When you choose the command :Print Preview, Wysiwyg displays a graphic representation of the page you will print like the one in Figure 6-18. This includes the data that appears in the print range, titles, borders, and other features. While looking at the previewed output, pressing any key displays the next page if the print range spans multiple pages, or returns to the Wysiwyg Print menu (after the final page is shown). You can also preview the preselected worksheet range by selecting this preview icon in Release 3.4:

Compressing Your Printout

At times, you may find that you want to change the amount of space that your worksheet and the graphics added to it take on the printed page. You might find

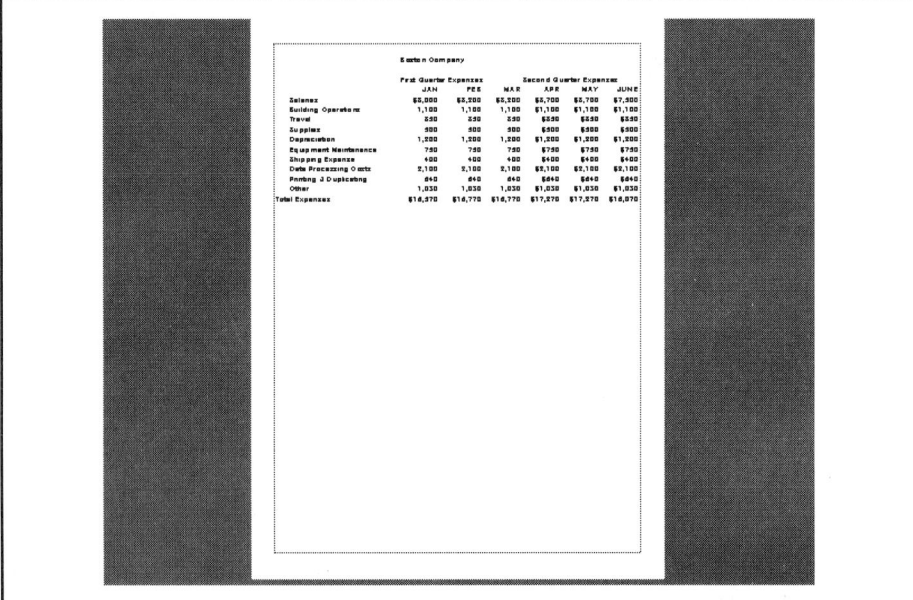

Figure 6-18. *The Print Preview screen*

that you want to get all of the information used to create a graph on the same page as the graph. To fit all of the information on one page, you can change the font size and other options to control how much room the data takes on the printed page, or you can change the compression with which the print range is printed. By using the :Print Layout Compression command, you can reduce or enlarge the size of the print range, not by including or excluding cells, but by shrinking or expanding the characters and graphs within the print range. When you alter the compression rate, you define the percentage that Wysiwyg either reduces or expands your data. You can see in Figure 6-19 how the worksheet shown in Figure 6-10, which required two pages to print, is compressed to fit on one page.

You can choose either Automatic or Manual compression. When you choose Automatic, Wysiwyg compresses the print range to print on a single page. Wysiwyg can only reduce the print range by a factor of seven. If you want to print a range to be more than seven times as large as the current page, you will need to rearrange the data, or use a larger page.

When you select the Manual option you can set the rate of compression precisely. The degree of compression is expressed in percentages. Therefore, 100 means that the text is not compressed at all. Numbers larger than 100 enlarge the print range so that it uses more room than normal on your page. Numbers smaller than 100 reduce the printed size of the print range. You can specify a compression rate between 15 and 1000, which equals 15% to 1000%.

Restoring Default Print Layout Settings

As you customize the page layout settings of a print range, you override the original default settings. The original default settings are designed to be useful for most people most of the time. When you want to return to the default settings, you do not have to reset each of the page layout features individually.

Boston Company												
	First Quarter Expenses			Second Quarter Expenses			Third Quarter Expenses			Fourth Quarter Expenses		
	JAN	FEB	MAR	APR	MAY	JUNE	JULY	AUG	SEPT	OCT	NOV	DEC
Salaries	$8,000	$8,200	$8,200	$8,700	$8,700	$7,500	$7,500	$10,000	$10,000	$10,000	$10,000	$10,000
Building Operations	1,100	1,100	1,100	$1,100	$1,100	$1,100	$1,100	$1,100	$1,300	$1,300	$1,300	$1,300
Travel	850	850	850	$850	$850	$850	$850	$850	$850	$850	$850	$850
Supplies	500	500	500	$500	$500	$500	$500	$500	$500	$500	$500	$500
Depreciation	1,200	1,200	1,200	$1,200	$1,200	$1,200	$1,200	$1,200	$1,200	$1,200	$1,200	$1,200
Equipment Maintenance	750	750	750	$750	$750	$750	$750	$750	$750	$750	$750	$750
Shipping Expense	400	400	400	$400	$400	$400	$400	$400	$400	$400	$400	$400
Data Processing Costs	2,100	2,100	2,100	$2,100	$2,100	$2,100	$2,100	$2,100	$2,100	$2,100	$2,100	$2,100
Printing & Duplicating	640	640	640	$640	$640	$640	$640	$640	$640	$640	$640	$640
Other	1,030	1,030	1,030	$1,030	$1,030	$1,030	$1,030	$1,030	$1,030	$1,030	$1,030	$1,030
Total Expenses	$16,570	$16,770	$16,770	$17,270	$17,270	$16,070	$16,070	$18,570	$18,770	$18,770	$18,770	$18,770

Figure 6-19. *One page of a printout that uses two pages when uncompressed*

Instead, select the :Print Layout Default Restore command. When you select this command, all of the page layout options are reset to the default settings.

You can also use several commands for resetting individual print layout features. When you want to remove a header, a footer, or both, select the :Print Layout Titles Clear, then select Header, Footer, or Both for the setting you want to remove. When you want to clear the borders, you can select the command :Print Layout Borders Clear. When you select this command, you can choose to clear the contents of either the Top, Left, or Both borders. Select :Print Layout Compression Clear when you want to remove any compression setting from the print range.

If you must frequently customize the page layout in the same fashion, you may prefer to change the default settings to match how you print with 1-2-3 worksheets. When you change the defaults, the new settings you specify appear each time you start 1-2-3, and are the settings restored when you select the :Print Layout Default Restore command. To change the defaults, first create the set of page layout settings that you would like to use as the default. Then select :Print Layout Default Update. The current settings become the default settings.

Creating a Layout Library File

The :Print Layout Library lets you create, retrieve, or erase a file that contains settings for the layout features. By creating such a layout library file, you can standardize the appearance of your printed worksheets and reports by using the same settings for all of your printed worksheets. When you retrieve a layout library file, all of the print layout settings become the settings saved in the file.

To create a layout library file, specify all the page layout settings. Then select the :Print Layout Library Save command. Type the name for the layout library file and press ENTER. Do not add a filename extension since Wysiwyg adds a .AL3 extension to mark it as a layout library file.

When you want to retrieve a layout library file, select the :Print Layout Library Retrieve command. Highlight the name of the file that you want to retrieve and press ENTER. You can delete a layout library file by selecting the :Print Layout Library Erase command and then selecting the name of the file you want to delete.

Setting Printer Configurations

The :Print Config menu commands control the printer that you use for printing the currently selected print range. With these commands, you can specify which type of printer you are using, the port to which the printer is attached to your computer, any font cartridges or cards your printer might have installed, the orientation of the printing, and the bin from which the printer is pulling the paper. By configuring the printer, you make maximum use of the printer features available to you. The :Print Config menu is a sticky menu, so you need to select Quit to return to the :Print menu.

Choosing a Printer

The first step in configuring a printer is selecting the printer you are using. When you select a printer, you are selecting the printer driver file that Wysiwyg uses in printing. The printer driver file includes all the codes that Wysiwyg uses to tell the computer what to do. If you select the wrong print driver, Wysiwyg and the printer are speaking different languages to each other, which means your printout will be garbled, at best.

Use the :Print Config Printer command to select the printer driver that you want to use. As you highlight the different numbers, the printer the number represents is described on the next line. Select the number for the printer you are using. The printer drivers available are the ones that you installed when you installed 1-2-3 and Wysiwyg. If you find that the printer driver for the printer that you are using is not installed, you must exit 1-2-3, and load 1-2-3's install program at the DOS prompt.

TIP: In 1-2-3 Release 3.4 you can create an Encapsulated Postscript file (.EPS file) by installing the Postscript EPSF driver, then selecting it before printing to a file. You can use this .EPS file with any of the desktop publishing programs.

Setting the Printer Interface

After determining and selecting the type of printer you are using, you need to tell Wysiwyg where it is. Wysiwyg locates a printer by the port to which the printer is attached. When you select the :Print Config Interface command, you are presented with eight selections defining the port or DOS device where your printer may be attached.

A port is the place where a cable from your computer attaches to your printer. Ports are either parallel or serial. LPT DOS devices point to parallel ports and COM DOS devices to serial ports. Usually printers are attached to parallel ports. A DOS device, such as LPT1 or COM2 is like a signpost that points the way to the physical port. You want to select the port where your printer is connected to your computer through a cable.

Installing Font Cartridges and Cards

If you want even more fonts to work with, many printers have slots where you can insert a cartridge or card that contains the programming for a font. These cartridges are then used as a font resource for that printer. With Wysiwyg, you can specify which font cartridges your printer has installed so that you can use the fonts installed in printing your worksheet. If you do not tell Wysiwyg which cartridges are installed, Wysiwyg does not have access to the fonts of those cartridges.

Select either the :Print Config 1st-Cart or the :Print Config 2nd-Cart command to select the font cartridges you have installed. After you select either of these commands you are presented with a series of font cartridge files and must select one. If the cartridge that you have installed in your printer is not on the list of cartridge files, you need to consult the documentation that came with the cartridge to find out how to install it.

Choosing an Orientation

Usually, text is printed across the short width of the paper. This orientation is called portrait, because painted portraits are usually longer than they are wide. You may want to print so that the top edge is the longest edge of the paper. This is landscape orientation because landscapes usually require more width than height. You can see the difference between these orientations in Figure 6-20. Worksheets are often printed with landscape orientation when you want to fit more columns on a single sheet.

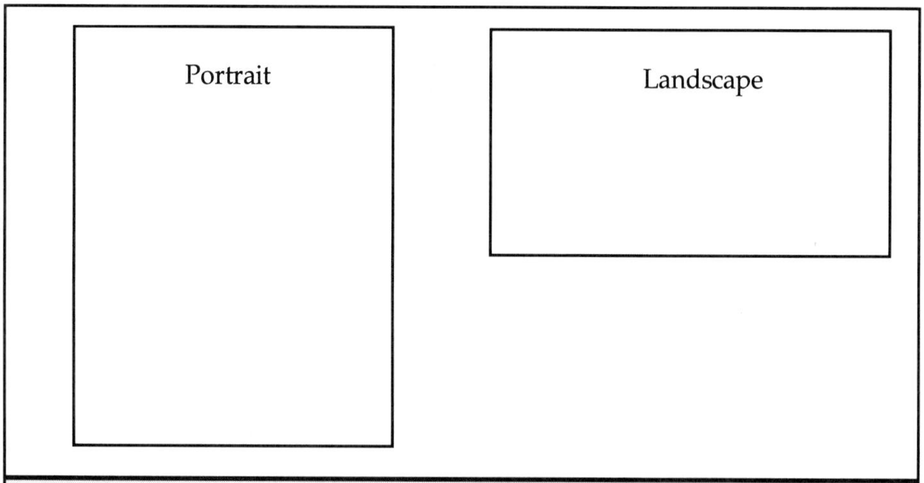

Figure 6-20. *Portrait and Landscape orientations*

The :Print Config Orientation command controls the orientation used when you print. This option is limited by your printer and whether it is capable of printing in the landscape mode. When you want to change the printing orientation, you select the :Print Config Orientation command, and select either Portrait or Landscape.

Selecting a Bin

When your printer has multiple paper feeding trays, you can select which paper feeding mechanism your printer uses when you print with Wysiwyg. To set the way a printer with multiple options receives its paper, select :Print Config Bin. You are presented with five options: Reset, Single-Sheet, Manual, Upper-Tray, and Lower-Tray. If your printer has only one paper-feeding mechanism, you have no reason to change this setting.

Select Single-Sheet when you want to use a single sheet paper feeder. Select Manual when you want to feed each page separately to the printer. If your printer has multiple trays which hold paper, you can specify which tray the paper comes from by selecting either Upper-Tray or Lower-Tray. When you select Reset, the bin setting is cleared.

Selecting a Resolution

If your printer has different quality levels, you can select the one Wysiwyg will use with the :Print Config Resolution command. For this command, you can select Final to use the best quality or Draft to use a lower quality but which often prints faster. Some printers only have one resolution, so changing this setting has no effect.

Print Settings

In addition to the print layout settings, Wysiwyg offers you several other ways to customize the printing process. You can control the page number of the first page that you are printing, or print a specific page from a multi-page print range. You can also choose to print multiple copies of the worksheet. You can tell the printer to wait at the end of each page for the next page. These features are accessed through the :Print Settings menu.

If you change your mind about the settings you have made with the :Print Settings command, select the :Print Settings Reset command. This command resets all of the :Print Settings menu commands to their default settings.

Controlling Multi-Page Print Ranges

Sometimes you may find that you do not want to redefine your print range, but instead want to print a limited number of pages from a multi-page print range. You may discover this need while printing sections of a large worksheet when each section needs to be printed separately for different reports. It may be easier to control which pages print than change the print range each time that you want to print.

To set the first page of the print range that you want to print, select the :Print Settings Begin command and type the number of the first page from the group of pages in the print range you want to print. After pressing ENTER, you can select End to set the last page of the print range that you want to print. For this command, type the number of the last page from the group of pages in the print range you want to print and press ENTER.

When printing begins, Wysiwyg divides the print range into pages and only prints pages in the range set by Begin and End. The page numbering, if used on these pages, reflects the entire number of pages in the print range, so if you start printing page 3, the # for the page number in a header or footer is replaced with a 3.

Setting the First Page Number

You can select the page number that is assigned to the first page in the current print range. If you are printing pages from 1-2-3 to include in a report partially created on a word-processor, you may want to start with a number other than 1 in order to keep it consistent with the page numbers of the word-processed portion of the reports. You may do this for reports where you are combining a lot of explanatory material with the worksheets and graphs.

Use the :Print Settings Start-Number command to define the page number of the first page of the currently selected print range. When you select this command, type the page number for the first page of the print range. Remember to count from this number if you choose the first and last page that you want to print from the print range.

Printing Multiple Copies

Usually, you print one copy of a worksheet and then photocopy the rest of the copies that you need. You may find it easier to print multiple copies. If you are printing with a color plotter or a color laser printer, this may be the only way to make color copies, unless you have a color copier as well. Select the :Print Settings Copies command. You are prompted to enter the number of copies that you want to print. You can enter a number between one and ninety-nine for the number of copies to print at once.

1-2-3's Printing Features

Wysiwyg and 1-2-3 have very similar print features. With the later releases, however, you will want to do most of your printing with Wysiwyg because of its advanced spreadsheet publishing abilities. However, even with the later releases, you may find that 1-2-3 is the best choice for drafts or simple reports. The great advantage that 1-2-3 has over Wysiwyg when printing drafts is that 1-2-3 can print relatively quickly. Wysiwyg normally takes much longer because of the formatting codes. This section deals exclusively with 1-2-3's printing features that are different from the Wysiwyg printing features.

Page Breaks

1-2-3 can add page breaks to a worksheet to control the way a large print range is divided into pages. By setting manual page breaks, you can keep information on one page without having to print different sections of the worksheet separately. With 1-2-3, you can only create horizontal page breaks.

The /Worksheet Page command makes it possible to split the printing of your reports wherever you want. /Worksheet Page causes 1-2-3 to insert a blank line, adding a page indicator, i.e. double colons (::), at the cell pointer location. A page break can be manually added by entering |:: on a blank row. (The /Range Erase or /Worksheet Delete Row commands can be used to erase an unwanted page break.) 1-2-3 ignores anything in the row after the page break. A page break created by 1-2-3 might look like this:

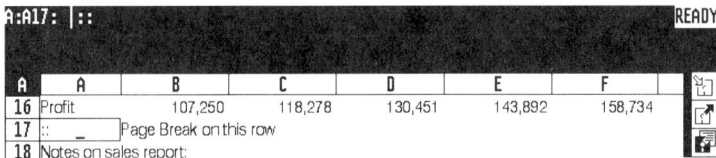

When you print this worksheet, 1-2-3 prints the data in rows 1..16 on one page. The next page starts with the contents of row 18. The printout will never show the entry in B17. The page breaks you add with 1-2-3 are ignored by Wysiwyg.

Other Options

The /Print Printer Options Other command allows you to decide whether information will be printed with or without formatting that has been added to the text. It also allows you to print formulas rather than the information displayed on your screen. A Release 3 option is to suppress 1-2-3's automatic use of the top and bottom three lines for headers and footers; you can employ this when you don't intend to have a header and footer.

Printing What You See on the Screen

The default setting, /Print Printer Options Other As-Displayed, causes your printed report to contain the same information you see on the screen if you do not have Wysiwyg attached. This means the results of formulas are printed just as they are displayed on the screen. The 1-2-3 formats in effect on your screen display are used for the printout, as will the column width for the current active window. In short, you have a duplicate of the worksheet portion of the screen display not including Wysiwyg formatting, except that you are not restricted to screen size for your printout. You are restricted to the limitations of the established page size, however.

Printing Cell Formulas

In Chapter 4, "Changing the Appearance of the Worksheet Display," you learned how to display formulas in cells by using the /Range Format Text command. To print a Text format worksheet like the one described in Chapter 4, you could use the As-Displayed option, since the formulas are already displayed. Alternatively, you can use 1-2-3's built-in formula printing option. With this option you do not have to change the format and width of cells as you did in Chapter 4, because the package does not print the formulas in the shape of the worksheet. Instead, it prints the formulas one per line down the page.

If an entire large worksheet is involved, the documentation produced by this approach can be quite a long list. However, this is an excellent way to print the formulas for a smaller range of cells, because it involves so little work on your part. All you have to do is select your print range and then choose Options Other Cell-Formulas. Quitting the Options menu and selecting Go from the Print menu produces a formula listing like the one in Figure 6-21. The formulas print according to the row they are in, with the order being A1, B1, C1, A2, B2, C2, and so on.

TIP: You can also print the notes you have added to cells. When you use the Cell-Formulas option, 1-2-3 includes notes added to both value and formula cells. Printing cell contents with this command bypasses the column width limitation to display lengthy formulas and notes.

```
A:A5: [W18] 'Alpen, Patrick
A:B5: (C0) [W12] 35000
A:C5: 10
A:D5: (P2) 0.04
A:E5: (C0) [W13] ((C5-1)*(B5/12))+((12-(C5-1))*(1+D5)*(B5/12))
A:F5: (C0) [W11] +E5*0.14
A:A6: [W18] 'Arbor, Jim
A:B6: (C0) [W12] 23000
A:C6: (F0) 4
A:D6: (P2) 0.07
A:E6: (C0) [W13] ((C6-1)*(B6/12))+((12-(C6-1))*(1+D6)*(B6/12))
A:F6: (C0) [W11] +E6*0.14
```

Figure 6-21. *Cell-formulas printout*

Using Format Options for Printing

Like As-Displayed, Formatted is another default setting in the Options Other menu. It uses page breaks, headers, footers, and any other 1-2-3 formatting you have done to create a professional report. Formatting is used almost every time a report is printed on a printer. Select this option after using the Unformatted option when you want 1-2-3 to return to formatting the output.

Eliminating Formatting from Output

When you write files to disk for use with another program, you often do not want print formatting added. The page breaks, headers, and footers will only need to be removed when you import the file into another program. Choosing the Unformatted option alleviates this problem by causing the files to be written without formatting. This means that 1-2-3 ignores page breaks, headers, footers, and top and bottom margins.

Usually this option is confined to printing to an unencoded file. It might also be used when you print a list that barely runs over to the next page. You might prefer to keep such a list together, even if it prints over the page perforation. You could do this by choosing /Print Printer Options Other Unformatted.

Suppressing Blank Headers

When your worksheet does not need a header or footer, you can reclaim the blank lines 1-2-3 reserves for headers and footers, and use them as additional lines for printing worksheet entries. Execute /Print Printer Options Other Blank Header, and select Suppress. This command tells 1-2-3 to use the two lines on each page that are reserved for the header and footer, and the four blank lines that precede them and follow them, for worksheet data. If you later want to again include the blank lines for the header and footer, select the /Print Printer Options Other Blank-Header Print command.

Saving Print Settings

When a worksheet file is saved, the print settings associated with this file are also saved. Saving a worksheet after setting its margins, setup strings, and other options ensures that you will not have to reenter these settings the next time you use the file. Release 3 adds other features that let you assign a name to a group of 1-2-3 print settings. These print settings names can also be saved with the file. You can have more than one set of print settings, allowing you to switch between groups of print settings.

To save the current worksheet's print settings, you must first assign a print settings name. Use the /Print Printer Options Name Create command and provide a name of up to 15 characters that does not include spaces. To use a named set, execute the /Print Printer Options Name Use command and specify the print settings name to use. This command first removes the current print settings before incorporating the settings you have selected.

To modify the settings associated with a print settings name, use /Print Printer Options Name Use to activate the print settings, modify the settings you want to change with /Print commands, and save the print settings again using the same name. To remove a single print settings name, use /Print Printer Options Name Delete, and specify the print settings name to remove. To remove all print settings names, use /Print Printer Options Name Reset.

To quickly list the print settings names associated with a worksheet file, use /Print Printer Options Name Table, and select a blank area of a worksheet. 1-2-3 will create a single column table that lists each print settings name in a separate row.

Using Printer Features

Most printers have a variety of special features that you can use if you "speak the language" of the printer. 1-2-3 can speak the language of the most popular printers. Some of the requests the printer understands are available in 1-2-3 through the /Print Printer Options Advanced command; they include boldface, compressed print, orientation, and color. Other printer features are accessed through 1-2-3 using *setup strings*.

Using Menu Commands for Printer Features

Your printer may have features like compressed print, the option of printing six or eight lines to the inch, boldface printing, and enlarged print. These common options are available through the /Print Printer Options Advanced command. These options assume that the printer you direct 1-2-3 to use matches the printer that is attached to your system. Since the Options Advanced option adds printer-specific codes to the print output, you will want to avoid sending codes that your printer will not interpret properly. If you do, the printed worksheet will not look like you expect it to. When an option you select with /Print Printer Options Advanced is not available, 1-2-3 makes the closest possible substitution. The /Print Printer Options Advanced commands have no effect when you are printing to a .PRN file.

The /Print Printer Options Advanced command has three options that access printer features: Layout, Fonts, and Color. The Layout option controls the character width (pitch), number of lines printed per inch (line-spacing), and whether 1-2-3 rotates the printed output by 90 degrees (orientation). The Fonts option selects the font, or character style, 1-2-3 uses to print the range, header and footer, border, and frame. When you use this option, 1-2-3 prompts for the area you are printing, and a font selection. Then it lists the numbers 1 through 8 representing the different fonts, along with a description of the font in the line below. The Color option controls the color 1-2-3 uses to print the worksheet.

These three options were only available in releases of 1-2-3 prior to Release 3 with the use of setup strings or external utilities. Since these features apply either to the entire worksheet or to a general area, a worksheet can still incorporate setup strings to change the formatting within a range or another area. These features can be combined. Since Wysiwyg is an integral part of 1-2-3 Release 3.4, you will use the Wysiwyg features to change fonts, attributes, and row heights rather than use these commands. The /Print Printer Options Advanced command does not show on the worksheet how the commands you select will affect the printed output's appearance.

Figure 6-22 shows a worksheet that uses /Print Printer Options Advanced Fonts Header/Footer 2. With this command, the header and footer appear in bold, which is font 2, while the rest of the worksheet uses the first font.

```
Today's Date: 17-Mar-93           Page 1                    Rpt. No. 1234

Description                Life   Cost Dept        Type        Inv Code
IBM Selectric Typewriter     5    $980 Accounting  Office         54301
Royal Typewriter             5    $950 Training    Office         54455
Swivel Chair                10    $345 Check       Furniture      54789
```

Figure 6-22. *Printing with a different font using 1-2-3's Print menu*

Using Setup Strings for Printer Features

Not all printer features can be added using the /Print Printer Options Advanced command. If you want to use these features, you must use setup strings. Since each printer has its own "language," or directions that tell the printer what to do, to use setup strings you must look up the printer commands that invoke the features you want. Look for a set of decimal codes assigned to that printer's features.

If you want the printer codes to affect all of your output, enter them through the /Print Printer Options Setup command. A sample of a printer code you might enter looks like \027\E, which is the Hewlett-Packard LaserJet Series II printer code to reset the printer. Setup strings entered with this command are sent to the printer after you select Go but before the data to print is sent. If you want to affect the printing of only a small area of the worksheet, you will need to embed the code in worksheet cells.

You can put these printer codes in worksheet cells. The advantage is that you can change print characteristics more than once while printing a worksheet. Place these entries in blank rows since 1-2-3 will ignore the rest of the row when you print the range. Setup strings in a worksheet cell must be preceded by two vertical bars (| |). For example, to embed \027(s3B in a cell, enter | |**\027(s3B**.

If you want to boldface the contents of a row in a worksheet, in the first cell of the row before the one to boldface you need to enter the printer command to boldface, and in the first cell in the row after the one to boldface, you need to enter the printer command to turn off boldfacing. Assuming you are using a Hewlett-Packard LaserJet printer with printer commands of \027(s3B and \027(s0B to turn boldfacing on and off, the beginning of the worksheet looks like this:

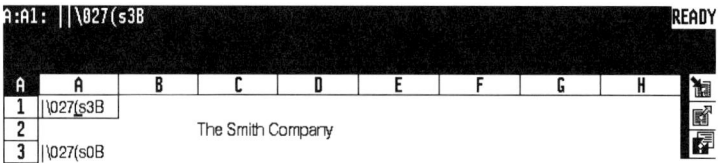

Since Wysiwyg commands provide the most frequently used printer features, you will probably use the Wysiwyg menu rather than setup strings. Wysiwyg commands do not need to be told the setup strings required to invoke the feature.

Clearing Print Settings

The Clear options let you eliminate some or all of the special print settings you have used for a report and return to the default settings. The six options presented from the Clear menu are All, Range, Borders, Format, Image, and Device. Since Image is used to print graphs, it is covered in Chapter 11, "Working with 1-2-3's Graphics Features."

Clearing All Settings

The All option restores the default for all of your print settings, including print range, borders, setup strings, and margins. If you want to be more selective, you can use one of the other options.

Clearing Range Settings

The Range option eliminates only a print range specification made earlier for the worksheet. Other print options are not affected.

Clearing Border Settings

The Borders option cancels the specification of any rows or columns as borders, and removes any frame. Other print options are not affected.

Clearing Format Settings

The Format option returns margins, setup strings, layout, fonts, colors, and page length to their default values, but does not affect a range or borders.

Clearing Device Settings

The Device option returns the device name and interface to the default value. This option is used when a different printer is selected.

Selecting a Printer

You may have several reasons for using a different printer. Perhaps you are printing to an encoded file that you will print later using a different computer. Another reason for selecting a different printer is that you have more than one printer attached to your computer. Since 1-2-3 includes printer codes designed to match the printer, it is important that 1-2-3 knows which printer to use.

Before you can select the appropriate printer for 1-2-3 to use, you must include the printer as one of the selectable options when you install 1-2-3. If the printer you want is not available in 1-2-3's Install menu, refer to Appendix A, "Installing 1-2-3," for instructions on adding a printer to 1-2-3's selection of printers. The printer's default settings are affected by the /Worksheet Global Default Printer command described later.

Selecting a Printer Device

To switch to a different printer, use the options for the /Print Printer Options Advanced command. The Device Name option lets you determine which printer selected from the Install menu 1-2-3 will use. The Device Interface option allows you to specify the printer interface. The default setting is 1; this is the appropriate setting for a parallel printer adapter. Eight other settings are possible. If you select a serial port, 1-2-3 will prompt you to specify the baud rate.

Automatic Line Feed

The /Print Printer Options Advanced AutoLf command determines whether 1-2-3 needs to generate a line feed after every carriage return. Select No, indicating that your printer does not generate line feeds, or Yes, indicating that it does. If your printer output looks the way you want it to, you do not have to change this setting. If 1-2-3 is generating extra line feeds, you will want to set this setting to Yes. If line feeds are missing and all of the data is printed on a single line, change this setting to No.

Pausing Between Pages

Use the /Print Printer Options Advanced Wait command to specify whether the printer uses single sheets or continuous feed paper. The No option indicates that the printer uses continuous feed paper and does not need to pause after printing each page. Yes means the printer uses single sheet paper, and 1-2-3 must pause after printing each page until you insert the next page and tell 1-2-3 to continue with the /Print Resume command.

Global Printer Defaults

It takes little effort to get a printed copy of your worksheet, because 1-2-3 does much of the preliminary work for you by setting up default values for many of the print options. These default values are available whenever you load 1-2-3. Sometimes, however, you want to change the defaults. You learned in the previous section how to make changes that apply to just one particular worksheet; this section shows how you can make permanent changes to the defaults.

The command you need to change the default values is not found in the Print menu. It is /Worksheet Global Default Printer, which presents the following menu:

```
A:A1:                                                             MENU
Interface AutoLf Left Right Top Bottom Pg-Length Wait Setup Name Quit
Select printer interface
```

Changing these options to values that meet your particular daily needs saves time; you do not have to change print options every time you load 1-2-3. Notice the Quit option at the end of this menu, which indicates that this is another menu that remains displayed until you eliminate it with Quit.

Printer Interface

The Default Printer Interface option allows you to specify the default printer interface. The default setting is 1 for a parallel interface; this is the appropriate setting for a parallel printer adapter. Eight other settings are possible. The first three are as follows:

- 2   Serial 1 for a serial printer (one with an RS232 interface)
- 3   Parallel 2 for a second parallel printer
- 4   Serial 2 for a second serial printer

You must specify additional information concerning your network configuration, such as baud rate, when selecting a serial interface. The remaining five options (LPT1 through LPT3 and COM1 and COM2) are DOS devices that your system can assign to printers.

Automatic Line Feed

The Default Printer AutoLf option determines whether 1-2-3 needs to generate a line feed after every carriage return. The two options are No, indicating that your printer does not generate line feeds, and Yes, indicating that it does. If your printed output looks the way you want it to, you do not have to worry about this setting. If extra line feeds are being generated, you must set this option to Yes. If line feeds are missing, change it to No.

Margins

The Left, Right, Top, and Bottom options available after selecting /Worksheet Global Default Printer establish default margins on the four sides of a page. The default settings are 4 for the Left margin, 76 for the right margin, and 2 for the top and bottom margins. You can select Left or Right to change the default to any number from 0 to 1000. You can select Top or Bottom to change the default to any number from 0 to 240.

Page Length

The default setting for Default Printer Pg-Length is 66. This is the correct setting for 8 1/2-by-11-inch paper, assuming printing at 6 lines per inch. You can change the default to any number from 1 to 1000.

Paper Feeding

The Default Printer Wait option indicates whether you want to wait for a paper change at the end of each sheet. The default setting is No, which is appropriate for continuous feed paper. Use the Yes setting when you print on single sheets.

Printer Setup

As you saw earlier in this chapter, setup strings are special codes you can transmit to your printer to access its special features. The default setting is no setup string, but if you use certain features regularly, such as double strike or compressed print, you can add the appropriate setup string to your printer's default settings. You may also want to use a default setup string to reset the printer so that any changes made to the printer, such as changing the fonts (even when made by other spreadsheet packages) are undone. Use the /Worksheet Global Default Printer Setup command and enter the setup string.

1-2-3 does not have a menu under this option because of the wide variations from model to model in printer codes. Your printer manual supplies the codes that turn on and off specific printer features.

Choosing Your Printer

The Default Printer Name option allows you to specify the name of the printer you want to use if you have more than one. The menu is customized during installation to include the names of your installed printers.

Exiting the Default Printer Menu

The Quit option is the last /Worksheet Global Default Printer menu choice. Aside from repeatedly pressing ESC, Quit is the only way out of the menu.

Saving Global Default Settings

Changing the Default Printer options does not automatically produce a permanent modification. You must first quit the Default Printer menu and choose Update from the previous menu. Update stores the default options in your configuration file, called 123R34.CNF, in your 1-2-3 directory.

Command Reference

Printing

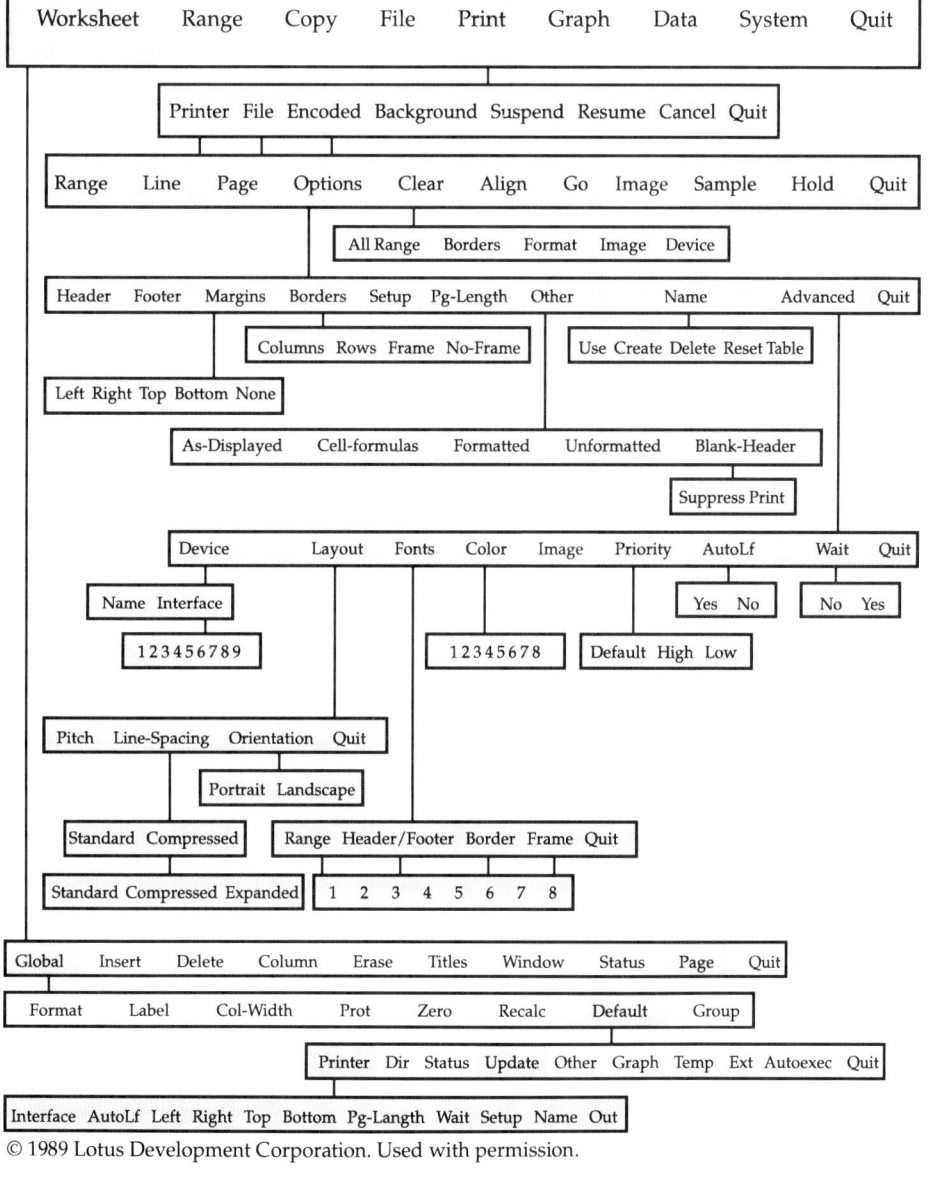

© 1989 Lotus Development Corporation. Used with permission.

/Print Background

Description

The /Print Background command sends the printed output to an encoded file and then prints it from the background. This command is used when you want to print your worksheet and then continue working with 1-2-3 while your printer prints. Before you can use this command, you must load BPrint from the operating system.

Options

Once you select this command, you must enter a filename that 1-2-3 will use to store the printed worksheet. 1-2-3 will add an .ENC extension to this filename. After 1-2-3 finishes printing, 1-2-3 deletes the temporary file. If you select an existing file, you have the Cancel and Replace choices. All of the /Print Printer options are also available when you choose /Print Background. This includes the range you print and the other printing options. 1-2-3 does not actually start background printing until you select Quit to tell 1-2-3 that you are finished.

/Print Cancel

Description

The /Print Cancel command cancels all print jobs, resets the page alignment, and resets the page number to 1. This command is used to stop print jobs either before they start or while printing is in progress. Since this command removes all print jobs from 1-2-3's memory, it is not for temporarily halting the printing process. To temporarily halt printing, use the /Print Suspend command.

Options

There are no options for this command. Since this command resets the top of the page, realign the paper before printing again.

/Print Encoded

Description

The /Print Encoded command prints a report to a file on the disk. Unlike the /Print File command, /Print Encoded includes printer formatting codes specific to your printer, and can also include graphs. This command is useful if your printer is not available. The resulting file with an .ENC extension is not designed to be read by other computer packages. You can use the DOS COPY command to print the encoded file. For example, COPY BUDGET.ENC LPT1 requests that DOS print the file on the printer device LPT1. You can also use the DOS PRINT command to achieve the same results.

Options

Once you select this command, you must enter a filename that 1-2-3 will use to store the printed worksheet. 1-2-3 will add an .ENC extension if you do not provide one. All of the /Print Printer options are also available when you choose /Print Encoded. You can select print ranges and apply any of these other options to them.

/Print File

Description

The /Print File command allows you to print a report to a disk file. This command is useful at times when your printer is not available. It can also be used to prepare data for other programs that manipulate 1-2-3's print output. The file created by this command does not include the printer codes that control printing features. This command also cannot accommodate graphs. To print graphs and include printer codes in a file, use the /Print Encoded command.

Options

Most of the /Print Printer options are also available when you choose /Print File. You can select print ranges and apply any of these other options to them.

/Print Printer

Description

This command is used whenever you wish to print information from a worksheet file on your printer. Since 1-2-3 contains default values for most of the Print parameters, printing can be as simple as specifying a print range. When you need greater sophistication or would like to tailor a report to your exact needs, you have a variety of options to work with.

Options

The /Print Printer command has the same options as the /Print Encoded command. You can make simple selections like specifying the range of worksheet cells to print, or you can include more sophisticated information, such as a set of printer control codes to meet your exact print style needs. You can change margins, choose rows or columns that you want to appear on all pages of a report, print the worksheet cells as they display, or print the formulas behind them.

/Print Printer Align

Description

This command will set 1-2-3's internal line count to zero. 1-2-3 then assumes that the printer is aligned at the top of a page. Any entries after this point will begin to add to the new line count. Before you perform this command, you should check that the paper is at the top of the page in the printer.

/Print Printer Clear

Description

This command can be used to eliminate special print settings, and return the specified print settings to their defaults. For example, if you have added a setup string, header, footer, and borders to a report, and want to print it again without these special features, the Clear option saves you time by eliminating the added settings. Without Clear, you would have to reexecute each of the commands for the special settings and delete the entries you made.

Options

The options for /Print Printer Clear let you decide whether you want to clear all or some print settings.

ALL   This option eliminates all the special entries made through the Print menus. The current print range is canceled. Borders, headers, and footers are all eliminated. Margins, page length, and setup strings are returned to their default settings.

RANGE   This option cancels only the current print range.

BORDERS   This option clears both row and column borders.

FORMAT   This option resets the margin, page length, graph settings, and setup string to the default setting found under /Worksheet Global Default Printer.

IMAGE   This option clears a graph selected to be printed.

DEVICE   This option returns the printer name and interface to default.

/Print Printer Go

Description

This command tells 1-2-3 to begin transmitting the print range to the printer (if Printer was selected), or to your disk drive (if File, Encoded, or Background was selected). If you are printing to a file, the file is not fully saved until you select the Quit option or press ESC to return to the READY mode. If you are printing to a printer in a network or to a spooler, the network or spooler will not start printing the print job until you select the Quit option or press ESC to return to the READY mode.

Options

There are no options for this command. If you are printing a large file while using large files, 1-2-3 may run out of memory. If this happens, remove some of the worksheets and files from the current session, and then use the /Print Resume command.

/Print Printer Hold

Description

This command returns to the READY mode and remembers all of the /Print command settings for the current print job. This command allows you to temporarily return to a worksheet to make a modification before printing. To complete the print job, return to the Print menus.

1-2-3 permanently halts the current print job if the /Print Cancel or the /Print Printer Options Advanced Device Name command is performed. The print job also ends if a /Print command sends a print job to a different destination. For example, if the /Print Printer command is sending the current print job to the printer and the /Print Printer Hold command temporarily pauses the current print job description, 1-2-3 cancels the current print job if the /Print Encoded command is performed. This command does not affect the job 1-2-3 is printing.

NOTE: If you are using a print spooler that starts each print job on a new page, use this command to print multiple print jobs on the same page, rather than returning to the READY mode with the Quit option or by pressing the ESC key.

/Print Printer Line

Description

This command is used to generate a line feed. It allows you to print two ranges with only one line between them, by entering Line after printing the first range, then selecting the second range and printing it. Line adds 1 to 1-2-3's internal line count.

 *NOTE: This command offers an advantage over using the printer's line feed button. Since the Line command increments 1-2-3's internal line count by one, it keeps the printing of a page in sync with the page's physical length.*

/Print Printer Options

Description

This command provides access to all the bells and whistles 1-2-3 offers for printing. Through the submenu this option presents, you can make many modifications to the appearance of a report.

Options

The Options menu includes choices for Header, Footer, Margins, Borders, Setup, Pg-Length, Other, Name, Advanced, and Quit. These options will be covered individually in the sections that follow.

/Print Printer Options Advanced

Description

This command accesses many of the new print features available with Release 3. The submenu for this command provides access to all the features your printer can offer, including whether 1-2-3 uses line feeds, the colors 1-2-3 uses, which device 1-2-3 prints to, which font 1-2-3 uses to print the worksheet, graphic image options, layout options, priority options, whether 1-2-3 pauses after each page, and returning to the Options print menu. The selections that are available will depend on your printer.

Options

This command has nine choices: AutoLf, Color, Device, Fonts, Image, Layout, Priority, Quit, and Wait.

DEVICE   This option selects which printer 1-2-3 uses for printing the selected range. After Device is selected, 1-2-3 displays Name and Interface. Name displays a list of numbers with the printers they represent on the third line in the control panel. Each of the printers is defined during installation. Interface displays the numbers representing the different output ports. If you select a serial port, 1-2-3 prompts you for the baud rate.

The selections made with this command are saved with the worksheet file, so the next time a range is printed, it uses the same device. To use another printer without saving the settings with the worksheet, change the default printer with the /Worksheet Global Default Printer Name command.

LAYOUT   This option determines the line spacing, the orientation, and the pitch (or width) of each character. It also includes Quit, which returns to the Options Advanced menu.

For Line-Spacing, you must specify Standard or Compressed. On several printers these settings are equivalent to 6 lines per inch and 8 lines per inch, although the actual results depend upon the printer.

For Orientation, 1-2-3 has the two options of Portrait (the default), and Landscape. This option lets you rotate the direction 1-2-3 prints, if this feature is available on your printer.

The Pitch option controls the number of characters per inch 1-2-3 fits on a line. The choices are Standard, Compressed, and Expanded. Changing the pitch automatically changes the number of characters for the left and right margins, to adjust for the changing size.

FONTS   This option lets you select the font for a specific section of the output. After Fonts is selected, you may choose Border, Frame, Header/Footer, or Range as the areas for which you can select a font. Select one of these areas, and 1-2-3 lists the numbers representing the different fonts; font descriptions appear in the third line of the control panel.

The actual fonts available depend upon your printer. If the printer cannot print the selected font, it substitutes its best approximation or uses standard characters. This option does not affect graphs. Changing the font can change the number of characters that will fit across a printed page. Selecting Quit returns to the Options Advanced menu.

COLOR   This option selects the color of a print range. 1-2-3 can print each range in a separate color, if the printer supports multiple colors. After choosing this option, select the color for the range. The color selected does not affect graphs.

IMAGE   This option is covered in Chapter 11, "Working with 1-2-3's Graphics Features."

PRIORITY This option assigns a priority level to the current print job: Default, High, or Low. If the current job has a High priority, it is printed after previous jobs with High priority, but before other jobs with Default or Low priority. If the current print job has a Default priority, it is printed after previous jobs except those with a Low priority. If the current print job has a Low priority, it is printed after all previous jobs. Within each priority level, the jobs are printed in the order they are created.

AUTOLF This option determines whether 1-2-3 prints a line feed at the end of each line. This setting only needs to be changed if the selected print device is different from the default printer, and the selected printer uses a different line feed setting. Change this setting to No if the printed output contains unwanted blank lines after each line of output. Change it to Yes if the output is printed on the same line.

WAIT This option determines whether 1-2-3 pauses after printing each page, to wait for single sheet feeding. Continuous feed printers that use a sheet feeder or continuous feed paper will have this set to No. Set it to Yes when the printer must pause after printing each page for a new page to be inserted. After each page, 1-2-3 pauses and displays a message to insert a new sheet, and then prints the next page after you execute the /Print Resume command.

QUIT This option returns to the /Print Printer Options menu.

/Print Printer Options Borders

Description

The Borders option allows you to print a frame, or specified rows or columns as borders on every page. When rows and columns are used as a border, you first select either Rows or Columns, and then specify the range of cells you wish to have appear as a border on each page. Be careful not to include the border rows or columns in your print job's print range; otherwise, they will be printed twice. Choosing the Frame option adds incremental row numbers and column letters as a frame for the borders.

Options

You have the choice of using either rows or columns as borders, and also of adding a frame containing the worksheet column letters and row numbers.

ROWS   Use this option when you have a report that is too long for one page. Select the rows you wish to print as borders on the second and subsequent pages, to provide descriptive information on each page.

COLUMNS   Use this option when your report is too wide for one sheet of paper, and when the left of your worksheet contains identifying information that applies to all pages. You can duplicate the selected column of information at the left side of each page.

FRAME   Use this option to include the incremental column letters above the columns of your printed worksheet, and the row numbers to the left of your rows. This option is useful for documenting worksheets. You can display the frame along with the worksheet contents using the Text format so the formulas appear.

NO-FRAME   Use this option to remove a frame added with the /Print Printer Options Border Frame command.

NOTE: If you accidentally select the Borders option, the current row or column will become a border, depending on whether you choose Rows or Columns. You can easily undo the damage with the command /Print Printer Clear Borders.

/Print Printer Options Footer

Description

This command allows you to add one line of up to 512 characters at the bottom of each page of a report. The footer text cannot extend for more than one line. Typical footer contents are date, report name or number, company name or department, and page number. 1-2-3 allows you to have three different entries for the footer line.

Options

The three Footer options allow an entry to be placed at the left, center, or right section of the footer. Entries are separated by the vertical bar character. Use a bar to separate each of the sections, even if they are not used (in other words, a single footer entry at the right should be preceded by two bars).

You also have the option of using #, \, and @ in your footer. The # represents the current page number; the \ followed by a cell address represents the contents of the referenced cell; and @ represents the current date.

NOTE: If you include the page number in your footer, you will have to exit the Print menu or use the /Print Align command before printing a second time. Otherwise, 1-2-3 will start the second printing of the report with the next page number, rather than beginning again with page 1. Also, you must use the /Print Printer Page command once 1-2-3 has finished printing the print job to include the footer on the last page.

/Print Printer Options Header

Description

This command allows you to add one line of up to 512 characters at the top of each page of a report. The header text cannot extend for more than one line. Typical header contents are date, report name or number, company name or department, and page number. 1-2-3 allows you to have three different entries for the header line.

Options

Header options allow an entry to be placed at the left, center, or right section of the header. Entries are separated by the vertical bar character. Use a bar to separate each of the sections, even if they are not used (in other words, a single header entry at the right should be preceded by two bars).

You also have the option of using #, \, and @ in your header. The # represents the current page number; the \ followed by a cell address represents the contents of the referenced cell; and the @ represents the current date.

NOTE: If you include the page number in your header, you will have to exit the Print menu or use the /Print Align command before printing a second time. Otherwise, 1-2-3 will start the second printing of the report with the next page number, rather than beginning again with page 1.

/Print Printer Options Margins

Description

This command allows you to control the amount of blank space at the top, bottom, and sides of a printed page. If you do not make an entry for Margins, the default values will be used.

Options

There is a Margins option for each of the four areas where you can control the amount of blank space on a printed page. The None option removes the margin settings made with the other Margin options.

LEFT The default setting for the left margin is 4 spaces. You can enter any number from 0 to 1000 to establish a new setting. Make sure the value you enter for the left margin is less than the value entered for the right margin, since it is the difference between these two values that determines how many characters will print in a line of your report.

RIGHT The default setting for the right margin is 76. You can enter any number between 0 and 1000 to change this margin setting. Make sure the value you enter for the right margin is greater than the value entered for the left margin, since it is the difference between these two values that determines how many characters will print in a line of your report.

TOP The default setting for the top margin is 2. You can change it to any number from 0 to 240.

BOTTOM The default setting for the bottom margins is 2. You can change it to any number from 0 to 240.

NONE This option sets the top, bottom, and left margins to 0, and the right margin to 1000.

/Print Printer Options Name

Description

This command is for creating named print settings that are saved with the worksheet file. The options are used to create, delete, list, and use print settings. Saved, predefined print settings can be selected and used to create additional groups of print settings. You can access the print settings with a single command, rather than having to redefine them each time you need them.

Options

This command has five options: Use, Create, Delete, Reset, and Table.

USE   This option selects a print settings name, and the print settings stored with the print settings name. It removes the print settings currently defined for the worksheet.

CREATE   This option assigns a name to the current group of print settings and saves them with the worksheet. You are prompted for a name of up to 15 letters, numbers, and symbols (except <<). If you provide an existing print settings name, the current settings are saved under that name, and the settings previously stored under that name are deleted.
   To change the print settings currently assigned to a name, select Name Use, enter the print settings name, change the settings with /Print commands, and then select Create and specify the same print settings name.

DELETE   This option deletes a selected print settings name and the print settings stored with the name.

RESET   This option deletes all of the selected print settings names and the print settings stored with the names.

TABLE   This option lists the print settings names in the current worksheet file. 1-2-3 will prompt you for a cell location for the table. The table uses a single column, with as many rows as the file has print settings names.

/Print Printer Options Other

Description

This command provides three very different sets of features. First, it lets you decide whether output should be the information as displayed in worksheet cells, or the formulas behind the display. Second, this command lets you determine whether print or file output should be formatted or unformatted. The Unformatted option is especially useful if you are attempting to take 1-2-3 data into another program, since the file will be stripped of headers and other special formats. Third, you can use this command to print additional worksheet data in place of the lines that would otherwise be printed for the header and footer.

Options

The Options Other command has five options: As-Displayed, Cell-Formulas, Formatted, Unformatted, and Blank-Header. The As-Displayed and Cell-Formulas pair of options provides opposing actions, as does the Formatted and Unformatted pair.

AS-DISPLAYED This is the default option. It causes your printout to match the screen display in the active window, in terms of cell values, format, and width. If you want to change the displayed printout, you can set up a second window (see Chapter 5, "Basic Worksheet Commands"), make width and formatting changes to this window, and print from there. After printing, the second window can be cleared.

CELL-FORMULAS This option causes the cell formulas, rather than their results, to be displayed. The formulas are shown one per line down the page.

FORMATTED This option prints the output with all of your formatting options, such as headers, footers, and page breaks. This is normally the way you want your output to appear when you send it to a printer.

UNFORMATTED This option strips all the formatting from your data. In other words, information is written to the output device without page breaks, headers, or footers. This option is useful when you are writing the output to a file for use by another program, or when you want the printer to ignore page breaks.

BLANK-HEADER This option prints three blank lines instead of a header and footer, or omits these three lines if the header and footer are not provided. This option has two selections. Select Print, the default, when you want 1-2-3 to include three blank lines in place of absent header and footer contents. Select Suppress when you want 1-2-3 to omit these three lines when a header and footer are not specified. When Suppress is selected, 1-2-3 uses the header and footer lines for the worksheet data.

/Print Printer Options Pg-Length

Description

This option determines the number of lines in a page of printed output. The default is 66, but 1-2-3 will accept entries from 1 to 1000. (There are not actually 66 lines of printed output on a default page. Remember that top and bottom margins, headers, footers, and the two blank lines below the header and above the footer must be subtracted from the page length to determine the number of print lines.)

Options

The only option for this command is to enter a page length between 1 and 1000.

/Print Printer Options Quit

Description

Use this command to exit from the Options menu. Since this menu stays displayed for you to make your option selections, you need Quit to make an exit when you have finished.

/Print Printer Options Setup

Description

This command allows you to transmit a setup string of control codes to your printer, so you can use the special features the printer offers. These special features may include enlarged, compressed, emphasized, or boldface printing, as well as different numbers of lines to be printed per inch. The control codes should be used to activate printer features that are unavailable from 1-2-3 menus. 1-2-3 does not automatically adjust the other printer settings for changes made with control codes. For example, if the control code setup string activates a different font, 1-2-3 does not adjust the margins to accommodate the different size of the characters.

Options

The options available for this command are dictated by the features your printer supports. A few of the options for the Hewlett-Packard LaserJet Series II and their respective setup strings are as follows:

```
\027(s3B  = Start boldface print
\027(s0B  = Stop boldface print
\027&dD   = Start underline
\027&d@   = Stop underline
```

The decimal codes you will need for setup strings can be found in your printer manual. When entering them into 1-2-3, precede each code with a backslash, and a zero if necessary, as in the example.

/Print Printer Page

Description

This command advances the paper to the top of the next form. This keyboard command makes it unnecessary to touch the printer. The command prints a footer if one has been specified.

/Print Printer Quit

Description

This command is used to exit the Print menu and place you back in READY mode. Since the Print menu stays displayed while you make selections, you need Quit to leave it. Even after printing, you will not return to READY mode until you have chosen Quit. Pressing the ESC key produces the same result.

This menu option ends the print job. For network environments and spoolers, it will tell the network or the spooler that the print job is completed and that printing can begin. If used after /Print File, /Print Encoded, or /Print Background, this command closes the file printed.

/Print Printer Range

Description

This command determines how much of the worksheet will be printed. Any valid range of cells can be specified, from one cell to the entire worksheet. 1-2-3 will decide how much of the range can be placed on one page, based on the margin and page length settings, and will carry the remainder of the range over to additional pages.

Options

The only option for this command is to specify a range. The format used for ranges is cell address..cell address, where the cell addresses specified are at opposite corners of the range of cells to be printed. For example, if you wanted to print cells A1 through D10, you could specify the range as A1..D10, D10..A1, D1..A10, or A10..D1. Any hidden columns included in the range are not printed.

This command can print ranges spanning multiple worksheets if the worksheet letter is included before the cell addresses. To print multiple ranges, separate the range addresses and names with the argument separator (a comma or semicolon), such as in SALES;A2..B12. The range should include the cells used by label cells to display their contents. Named graphs included in the range must be preceded with an asterisk (*).

/Print Quit

Description

This command leaves the 1-2-3 Print menus and returns to the READY mode.

/Print Resume

Description

This command restarts printing jobs that were temporarily suspended with the /Print Suspend command, or a printer error, or when 1-2-3 is waiting for the next sheet of paper when /Print Printer Options Advanced Wait or /Worksheet Global Default Printer Wait is set to Yes. This command also clears a printer error message if a printer error caused the printing suspension.

/Print Suspend

Description

This command temporarily halts the current print job. Use the command when you need to adjust the printer, or to realign computer paper that is jamming. Many printers have a buffer that holds data waiting to be printed, so there may be a delay between executing this command and actual suspension of printing.

/Worksheet Global Default Printer

Description

This command allows you to change the default printer settings. These settings determine the way a document prints if you have not made particular specifications for it through the Print menu. They also determine the default interface between 1-2-3 and your printer. Changes made with this command are not permanent unless you save them with /Worksheet Global Default Update.

Options

This command has eleven options. Each of these options have parallel options in the Print menus.

INTERFACE This option determines the type of connection between your printer and 1-2-3. There are three basic options with several choices: parallel connection, serial connection, or connection through a local area network. The available options are as follows:

(1) Parallel 1(default setting)
(2) Serial 1
(3) Parallel 2
(4) Serial 2
(5) DOS device LPT1
(6) DOS device LPT2
(7) DOS device LPT3
(8) DOS device COM1
(9) DOS device COM2

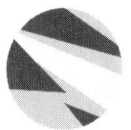

NOTE: If you select one of the serial interface options, 1-2-3 will also ask you to specify a baud rate (the transmission speed it supports). For 110 baud you will have to set your printer at 2 stop bits, 8 bits, and no parity. For speeds other than 110, 1 stop bit will be sufficient.

AUTOLF This option specifies whether your printer automatically issues line feeds after carriage returns. Installation sets this to correspond with your printer. If you are getting double spacing on everything you print, set AutoLf to Yes. If your paper is not advancing as it should, change this setting to No, indicating that the printer does not automatically print line feeds.

LEFT This setting for the left margin has a default value of 4, but you can change it to any number between 0 and 1000.

RIGHT This setting for the right margin has a default value of 76, but you can change it to any number between 0 and 1000.

TOP This option for the top margin has a default value of 2, but will accept values between 0 and 240.

BOTTOM This option for the bottom margin has a default setting of 2, but will accept values between 0 and 240.

PG-LENGTH   The default page length is 66, but it can be changed to any value between 1 and 1000.

WAIT   This option allows you to set the default for continuous feed or single sheet paper. The initial value is No, indicating continuous feed paper. If you change it to Yes for single sheets, 1-2-3 waits after each page is printed.

SETUP   This option specifies a setup string of control characters to be sent to your printer before every print request. The default is blank, indicating no print control codes. You may supply any valid control codes up to 512 characters in length. The control codes can be obtained from your printer manual. Precede each code with a backslash (\), and also a zero if necessary to make a three-digit code.

NAME   If you installed more than one printer for 1-2-3, this option allows you to specify the printer to use. The default value is the first printer selected during installation.

QUIT   This option exits the Worksheet Global Default Printer menu.

/Worksheet Global Default Update

Description

This command saves entries and changes made with the /Worksheet Global Default Printer command to a file called 123R34.CNF. This file will be loaded every time you bring up the 1-2-3 package.

/Worksheet Page

Description

This command inserts an empty row into the current worksheet and puts a page break symbol (::) in the current column of the new row. Before you execute this command, position the cell pointer in the first row that you want on the new page. This command is equivalent to entering a page break symbol on an empty row manually. 1-2-3 ignores worksheet contents on the same row with the page break symbol. To remove the page break symbol, delete the row, erase the cell, or change the cell's contents.

:Print Background

Description

This command prints your worksheet in the background using Wysiwyg so you can continue to work on other tasks. When you print in the background, Wysiwyg stores the printed information temporarily in a file. Before you can use this command you must execute the BPrint program from DOS.

Option

Your only option for this command is the filename you enter where Wysiwyg temporarily stores the information to be printed. Wysiwyg will add an .ENC extension. If you specify an existing filename, you must select between Cancel and Replace. After you select the name of the file, Wysiwyg will start sending the information to the file. When Wysiwyg has sent all of the information in the file to the printer, Wysiwyg deletes the temporary file.

:Print Config

Description

This command changes print configuration options like printer interface, font cartridges, print orientation, and the print bin used.

Options

PRINTER   This option selects a printer to use from the list of printers chosen during installation.

INTERFACE   This option selects the connection between the computer and the printer. Select a number between 1 and 9, representing Parallel 1, Serial 1, Parallel 2, Serial 2, LPT1, LPT2, LPT3, COM1, or COM2.

1ST-CART   This option chooses the first font cartridge.

2ND-CART   This option chooses the second font cartridge.

ORIENTATION This option selects whether the printer prints in Portrait mode, which is standard, or Landscape mode, which rotates your print output 90 degrees to print it sideways.

RESOLUTION This option controls the quality of graphics output. You can choose from Final quality and Draft quality.

BIN This option selects the bin the printer retrieves the paper from for printers with multiple-sheet feed options.

QUIT Returns you to the :Print menu.

:Print File

Description

This command prints your worksheet using Wysiwyg to disk rather than to the printer. To print the resulting file, use the DOS COPY command. You do not need 1-2-3 or Wysiwyg to handle printing from disk.

Option

The only option for this command is the filename you enter. Wysiwyg adds .ENC as the extension for the file. If you specify the name of an existing file, you must select from Cancel or Replace. Once you select the name of the file, Wysiwyg starts sending information to the file; you do not need to select Go as you do when printing with 1-2-3.

:Print Go

Description

This command tells Wysiwyg to start printing to the printer.

:Print Info

Description

This command removes or displays the Wysiwyg print status settings sheet. You can also perform this command by pressing F6 (WINDOW).

:Print Layout Borders

Description

This command changes the border columns and border rows. These columns and rows will appear on each page printed.

Options

TOP This option chooses border rows for the top of the printed pages. Select a range containing the rows to use.

LEFT This option chooses border columns for the left of the printed pages. Select a range containing the columns to use.

CLEAR This option removes existing border columns and rows.

QUIT This option returns you to the :Print Layout menu.

:Print Layout Compression

Description

This command sets whether or not to compress the output when it is printed.

Options

NONE This option prints with no compression.

MANUAL This option lets you manually define the extent of expansion or compression. Enter a number less than 100 to compress the output, or a number greater than 100 to expand the output.

AUTOMATIC This option compresses the output to fit an entire print range on a page. It uses manual page breaks to determine how much data fits on each page.

:Print Layout Default

Description

This command changes the current page layout or default page layout.

Options

RESTORE This option replaces the current settings with the default ones.

UPDATE This option replaces the default settings with the current ones.

:Print Layout Library

Description

This command maintains a library of page layouts on disk. This allows you to use the same page layout in several worksheets.

Options

RETRIEVE   This option replaces the current page layout with a layout saved to disk. Select a page layout library.

SAVE   This option stores the current layout in a file. Enter a name for the page layout library. If the name you specify already exists, you must choose Cancel or Replace to specify if you want to replace the existing file with the current layout.

ERASE   This option permanently removes a layout from the library.

:Print Layout Margins

Description

This command changes any of the margins on the page layout.

Options

You can specify which of the margins you want to change by selecting Left, Right, Top, or Bottom and then entering the distance you want for the margin. You can also choose Quit to return to the Layout menu.

:Print Layout Page-Size

Description

This command specifies the dimensions of the paper you will use for output.

Options

The options for this command select the following predefined page sizes:

1	Letter size (8 1/2 x 11 inches)
2	International A4 size (8 1/4 x 11 11/16 inches)

3	80 column by 66 line listing size (9 1/2 x 11 inches)
4	132 column by 66 line listing size (14 7/8 x 11 inches)
5	80 column by 72 line listing size (9 1/2 x 12 inches)
6	Legal size (8 1/2 x 14 inches)
7	International B5 size (6 11/16 x 9 27/32 inches)
Custom	This option defines a custom page size. Enter the length and width followed by "in" for inches, "mm" for millimeters, or "cm" for centimeters.

:Print Layout Titles

Description

This command creates or removes a header or footer for the top or bottom of every page of output.

Options

HEADER   This option supplies the header that appears at the top of every page. Enter the header using the same rules as for headers in 1-2-3.

FOOTER   This option supplies the footer that appears at the bottom of every page. Enter the footer using the same rules as for footers in 1-2-3.

CLEAR   This option removes an existing header or footer, or both.

QUIT   This option returns you to the :Print Layout menu.

:Print Preview

Description

This command previews how the print range will appear when printed. After viewing the preview, press any key to display the next page or, on the last page, return to the :Print menu.

:Print Quit

Description

This command returns you to the READY mode.

:Print Range

Description

This command clears or sets a range for printing.

Options

SET   This option selects the print range. Select any range to print the same way you select a range to print with the /Print Printer Range command.

CLEAR   This option eliminates the setting of the range to print.

:Print Settings

Description

This command controls how Wysiwyg prints the print range.

Options

BEGIN This option specifies the first page to print.

END This option specifies the last page to print.

START-NUMBER This option specifies which page number to use on the first page.

COPIES This option specifies the number of copies to print.

WAIT This option pauses the printer before pages (Yes) or restores continuous printing (No).

GRID This option chooses whether grid lines that indicate cell boundaries are printed (Yes) or omitted (No).

FRAME This option decides whether to print the frame of the worksheet (Yes) or not to (No).

RESET This option restores the default print settings.

QUIT This option returns you to the :Print menu.

:Quit

Description

This command returns you to the READY mode.

:Worksheet Page

Description

This command specifies the exact location for a page break. Otherwise, Wysiwyg breaks output into pages when pages are full.

Options

ROW   This option ends a page at the current row.

COLUMN   This option ends the page at the current column.

DELETE   This option removes the page break previously inserted at the current location.

QUIT   This option returns you to the READY mode.

CHAPTER 7

1-2-3's Built-In Functions

1-2-3's built-in functions provide ready-made formulas for a wide variety of specialized calculations. Since the formulas are already designed and tested, you can have instant reliability when you include them in your models. The built-in functions also allow you to perform calculations like square root and cosine, extending your range of formulas beyond those you can create with the formula operators covered in Chapter 3.

The 104 functions in Release 3 are grouped into eight categories. The categories are database, statistical, date and time, financial, mathematical, logical, special, statistical, and string. Each of these groups except the database functions will be covered in this chapter. Since the database functions require a knowledge of 1-2-3's data management features, they will be covered in Chapter 9. The remaining functions will be covered by category. Table 7-1 provides a list of 1-2-3's built-in functions and the category to which each belongs for quick reference.

Function	Type
@@(cell)	Special
@ABS(number)	Math
@ACOS(number)	Math
@ASIN(number)	Math
@ATAN(number)	Math
@ATAN2(x,y)	Math
@AVG(list)	Statistical
@CELL(attribute string,range)	Special
@CELLPOINTER(attribute string)	Special
@CHAR(code)	String
@CHOOSE(number,list)	Special
@CLEAN(string)	String
@CODE(string)	String
@COLS(range)	Special
@COORD(worksheet,column, row,absolute)	Special
@COS(number)	Math
@COUNT(list)	Statistical
@CTERM(interest,future value,present value)	Financial
@D360(start date,end date)	Date & Time
@DATE(year,month,day)	Date & Time
@DATEVALUE(date string)	Date & Time
@DAVG(input field,criteria)	Database
@DAY(serial date number)	Date & Time
@DCOUNT(input field,criteria)	Database
@DDB(cost,salvage,life, period)	Financial

Table 7-1. *List of Functions*

Function	Type
@DGET(input field,criteria)	Database
@DMAX(input field,criteria)	Database
@DMIN(input field,criteria)	Database
@DQUERY(function,list)	Database
@DSTD(input field,criteria)	Database
@DSTDS(input field,criteria)	Database
@DSUM(input field,criteria)	Database
@DVAR(input field,criteria)	Database
@DVARS(input field,criteria)	Database
@ERR	Special
@EXACT(string1,string2)	String
@EXP(number)	Math
@FALSE	Logical
@FIND(search string,entire string,starting location)	String
@FV(payment,interest,term)	Financial
@HLOOKUP(code to be looked up,table location, offset)	Special
@HOUR(serial time number)	Date & Time
@IF(condition to be tested, value if true,value if false)	Logical
@INDEX(table location,column number,row number [,worksheet number])	Special
@INFO(attribute string)	Special
@INT(number)	Math
@IRR(guess,range)	Financial
@ISERR(value)	Logical
@ISNA(value)	Logical
@ISNUMBER(value)	Logical
@ISRANGE(string)	Logical
@ISSTRING(value)	Logical
@LEFT(string,number of characters to be extracted)	String
@LENGTH(string)	String

Table 7-1. *List of Functions (continued)*

Function	Type
@LN(number)	Math
@LOG(number)	Math
@LOWER(string)	String
@MAX(list)	Statistical
@MID(string,start number, number of characters to be extracted)	String
@MIN(list)	Statistical
@MINUTE(serial time number)	Date & Time
@MOD(number,divisor)	Math
@MONTH(serial date number)	Date & Time
@N(range)	String
@NA	Special
@NOW	Date & Time
@NPV(discount rate,range)	Financial
@PI	Math
@PMT(principal,interest,term of loan)	Financial
@PROPER(string)	String
@PV(payment,periodic interest rate,number of periods)	Financial
@RAND	Math
@RATE(future value,present value,number of periods)	Financial
@REPEAT(string,number of times)	String
@REPLACE(original string, start location, # characters, new string)	String
@RIGHT(string,number of characters to be extracted)	String
@ROUND(number to be rounded,place of rounding)	Math
@ROWS(range)	Special
@S(range)	String
@SECOND(serial time number)	Date & Time

Table 7-1. *List of Functions* (continued)

Function	Type
@SHEETS(range)	Special
@SIN(number)	Math
@SLN(cost,salvage value,life of the asset)	Financial
@SQRT(number)	Math
@STD(list)	Statistical
@STDS(list)	Statistical
@STRING(number,number of decimal places)	String
@SUM(list)	Statistical
@SUMPRODUCT(list)	Statistical
@SYD(cost,salvage value,life, period)	Financial
@TAN(number)	Math
@TERM(payment,interest,future value)	Financial
@TIME(hour,minute,second)	Date & Time
@TIMEVALUE(time string)	Date & Time
@TODAY	Date & Time
@TRIM(string)	String
@TRUE	Logical
@UPPER(string)	String
@VALUE(string)	String
@VAR(list)	Statistical
@VARS(list)	Statistical
@VDB(cost,salvage,life,startperiod,end-period, [depreciation-factor], [switch])	Financial
@VLOOKUP(code to be looked up,table location, offset)	Special
@YEAR(serial date number)	Date & Time

Table 7-1. *List of Functions (continued)*

With Release 3.4 you can enter two @functions with SmartIcons. Both icons sum values; the first one sums values on a single sheet only, and the other sums values across sheets. If you define macros for entering other @functions, you can always use the instructions in Chapter 14 for entering other @functions with user icons.

All the built-in functions follow the same basic format. Each has a special keyword or name that tells 1-2-3 which function you wish to use. Most also require *arguments* that define your exact requirements for the function in a particular situation. The basic format rules for functions are as follows:

- Every function begins with an at sign (@).

- The @ sign is followed by a function name or keyword. When entering this name, you must match 1-2-3's spelling exactly. Either upper- or lowercase can be used, although function names will be shown in uppercase throughout this chapter.

- It is important never to use spaces within a function. You must always write @SUM(A5,A15..A17), not @SUM (A5, A15..A17) or @SUM(A5, A15..A17). If you accidentally include a space, 1-2-3 may remove it, return ERR, or prompt you to edit the function—depending on the space's location.

There are also a few general rules that apply to all function arguments. They are as follows:

- Function arguments must be encased in a set of parentheses.

- Functions that require no arguments do not require parentheses. One example is @RAND, which generates a random number between 0 and 1. The other seven functions that do not require arguments are @PI, @TRUE, @FALSE, @ERR, @NA, @NOW, and @TODAY.

- When a function is used as an argument for another function, you must use a second set of parentheses, because each function must have its arguments enclosed within parentheses. To use the result of @SUM in an @ROUND function, for example, enter the functions like this:

    @ROUND(@SUM(A2..A10),2)

- In most cases functions will require arguments to be separated by commas. (The separator character can be changed with /Worksheet Global Default International Punctuation, as described in Chapter 4, "Changing the Appearance of the Worksheet Display.") These arguments can be numeric values, cell addresses, string values, or special codes. The exact requirements for each function will be covered in the expanded description of the function in this chapter.

Different functions require different types of arguments and use them in different ways. Here are some of the format rules that pertain to different function types and uses:

- Some functions, such as @SUM, expect a list of arguments that can be entered in any order. @SUM will add together all the entries in its argument list to produce a sum, for example. If you wanted to sum the values in B1..B10, D4, and D7, you could enter the function as @SUM(B1..B10,D4,D7), @SUM(D7,B1..B10,D4), or any other order of the three entries within the parentheses.

- Arguments that must be provided in a specific order cannot be reordered without causing erroneous results. The @ROUND function is one example. It requires two arguments, the number to be rounded and the position. The latter argument tells 1-2-3 how many places from the decimal to round the number. The function must always be written as @ROUND(number,position), with the numbers or references substituted in the function. If you enter the function as @ROUND(position,number), you will cause an error.

- Arguments that require a specific argument type cannot have another type substituted without causing an error. For example, the @TRIM function removes leading, trailing, and consecutive spaces from a string and requires a string as an argument. An error will result if any argument other than a string is provided.

- For arguments requiring string values, enclose the actual values in double quotation marks—for example, "this is a string". For string arguments you can also enter a cell address (C3), a range name (SALES), or a string formula (+B3&"Company Report"). If you need to review string arithmetic, reread the "String Formulas" section in Chapter 3, "Entering Data in 1-2-3's Worksheet."

- If a function requires a range as an argument, you can specify the range with a range address (A2..A10), a range name (SALES), or a combination (SALES,A2..A10). If the function expects a range and you enter a single cell reference, 1-2-3 may not return the value you expect as it does not always convert the single cell address to a range.

- Functions requiring numeric values will accept them in many formats. You can use actual values (876.54), cell addresses (A2), range names (SINGLE_CELL), formulas (2*A3), functions (@PI), and combinations of the other options (@PI*3+SUM(D2..D4)+NUMBER).

- Some function arguments can use values from other files. To include values from other files as part of the function, enter two less-than (<<) signs (also called opening angle brackets), the filename with file extension, and two greater-than (>>) signs (or closing angle brackets) before the cell address from the other file. An example is @SUM(<<MONTHTOT.WK3>>SALES), which adds all the values in the SALES range from the MONTHTOT.WK3 worksheet.

- Most functions that support range arguments can use ranges that span multiple worksheets within a file. To select a range that uses multiple worksheets, include the first worksheet letter in the range's beginning address, and the last worksheet letter in the range's ending address. In the following example, the function @SUM(B:G5..M:G15) adds all of the values in the range G5 to G15 for all worksheets from B to M. Some functions require that a referenced range not span worksheets. The @HLOOKUP and @VLOOKUP functions are examples of functions that are limited to one worksheet for the table range. The example in the description of @VLOOKUP shows how to bypass this restriction.

You will see examples of these various kinds of functions and arguments in use as you proceed through the examples in this chapter. You may want to read through the descriptions of all the function groups, or you may prefer to concentrate on particular categories that meet an immediate need. The descriptive paragraphs at the beginning of the section on each function category provide an overview of the types of formulas offered by the functions in the group. The description of each individual function will cover its format, its arguments if any, and its use. The functions in each category are covered in alphabetical order.

Date and Time Functions

The date and time functions access, create, and manipulate the serial numbers 1-2-3 uses to represent dates and times. For example, you can use date and time arithmetic in your models to determine elapsed time for a production process, to learn whether a loan is overdue, or to age your accounts receivable.

Some of the date and time functions generate serial numbers (@DATE, @NOW), while others expect them as arguments (@DAY, @YEAR). For those functions that expect serial numbers as arguments, entering both an integer and fractional serial number for a function expecting a date will cause 1-2-3 to ignore the fractional part of the entry. The integer number portion would be ignored if a serial time number was expected. If only the integer portion is entered, the value .0, representing midnight, will be used for the time.

@D360

The @D360 function computes the number of days between two dates, based on a 360-day calendar year.

Format

@D360(*beginning date,ending date*)

Arguments

beginning date the starting date of a period. This is a date serial number, which is entered directly or referenced.

ending date the ending date of a period. This is a date serial number, which is entered directly or referenced.

Use

This function is used to determine the number of days between two dates, using a 360-day calendar year. A 360-day calendar year assumes 12 months of 30 days apiece. This function is used primarily for financial applications, which use a 360-day calendar in the computations.

   A common application is the calculation of interest payments. For example, if you deposit $100,000 in a bank from April 1 to August 16, you may want to know how much interest you will earn if the bank pays 9% interest based on a 360-day year. The entry +100000*@D360(@DATE(91,4,1),@DATE(91,8,15))/360*.09 will return 3350, which is the interest your money earns. You need to know the difference in days using a 360-day year rather than a 365-day year because the bank uses a 360-day year in its interest calculations. If you use the formula +100000*(@DATE(91,8,15)–@DATE(91,4,1))/365*.09 to calculate the interest using a 365-day year, the interest amount is $3353.

@DATE

The @DATE function allows you to create a serial date number when you supply the date components.

Format

@DATE(*year,month,day*)

Arguments

year a number between 0 and 199. 1900 is represented by 0, 1989 by 89, and 2099 by 199.

month a number from 1 through 12.

day a number from 1 through 31. The number must be valid for the month chosen. Since month 9 (September) has only 30 days, for example, 31 is an invalid value for the day when 9 is used for the month.

Use

The @DATE function can be used anywhere you wish to enter a serial date number on a worksheet. Any date used in arithmetic calculations must be in serial form. Figure 7-1 shows an application for the @DATE function. In this example, the charge for each video rental is determined by the number of days a patron has had the video. The date the video was checked out is entered in column C, and the date it was returned is entered in column D. The two serial dates are subtracted, and the result is multiplied by the daily charge of $2.25 to determine the amount the patron should pay—resulting in the formula (D5–C5)*2.25 (see Figure 7-2). The formulas are stored in column E.

A Date format is applied to the range of entries in columns C and D, and Currency format is applied to the range of entries in column E. You can also enter a date in the DD-MMM-YY, DD-MMM, or Long International Date format. 1-2-3

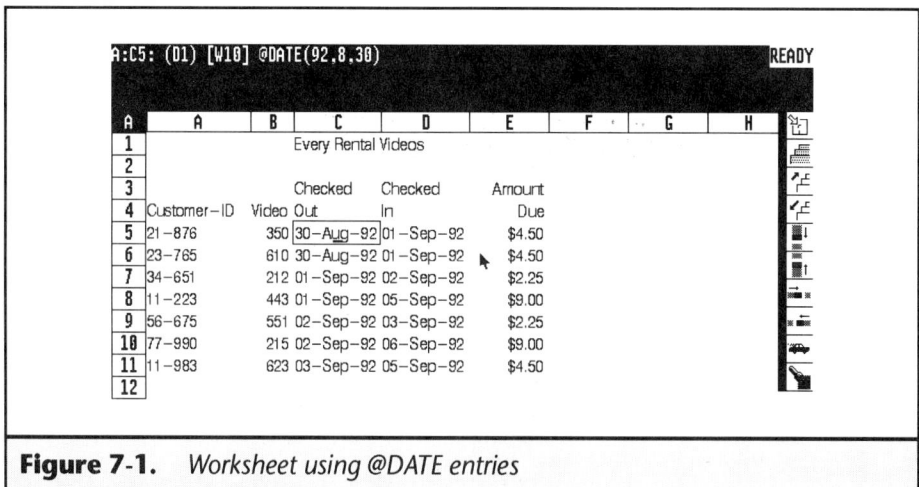

Figure 7-1. *Worksheet using @DATE entries*

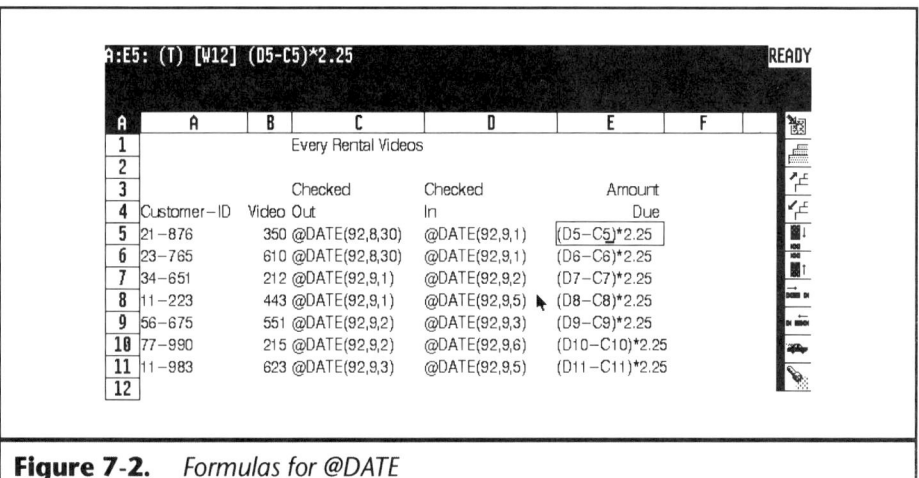

Figure 7-2. *Formulas for @DATE*

automatically converts entries entered in one of these formats to date serial numbers.

NOTE: 1-2-3 assigns a serial number to February 29, 1900, even though 1900 was not a leap year. This will cause problems only when you are using dates between January 1, 1900, and March 1, 1900.

@DATEVALUE

The @DATEVALUE function returns a serial date number when you supply a date string in one of the five Date formats.

Format

@DATEVALUE(*date string*)

Arguments

date string   a string argument in quotes, or a cell reference containing a date in one of the five acceptable Date formats.

Three of the acceptable Date formats are fixed, and two are dependent on the format chosen with /Worksheet Global Default Other International Date. Acceptable date string formats for September 29, 1991, are "29-Sep-91", "2-Sep", "Sep-91", and "29.09.91" if D4 (Date format 4) is set at DD.MM.YY; "9/29/91" if D4 is set at MM/DD/YY; "29/09/91" if D4 is set at DD/MM/YY; and "91-09-29" if D4 is set at YY-MM-DD. Acceptable D5 (Date format 5) options are similar except that only the month and day are shown, for example, "09-29".

Use

The @DATEVALUE function is used when you want to perform arithmetic with dates that have been entered in string format. For example, if you were to enter **@DATEVALUE("23-Oct-89")** in a cell, 32804 would be returned. You could then use this value in a formula. Figure 7-3 provides an example of a model using the @DATEVALUE function. It solves the same problem as the model for video charges in Figure 7-1, except that it uses the @DATEVALUE function and string date formats in the function arguments. The formulas to subtract the two dates are located in column E and follow the format of (@DATEVALUE(D5)– @DATEVALUE(C5))*2.25, as you can see in the control panel of Figure 7-3.

@DAY

The @DAY function is used to extract the day number from a serial date number.

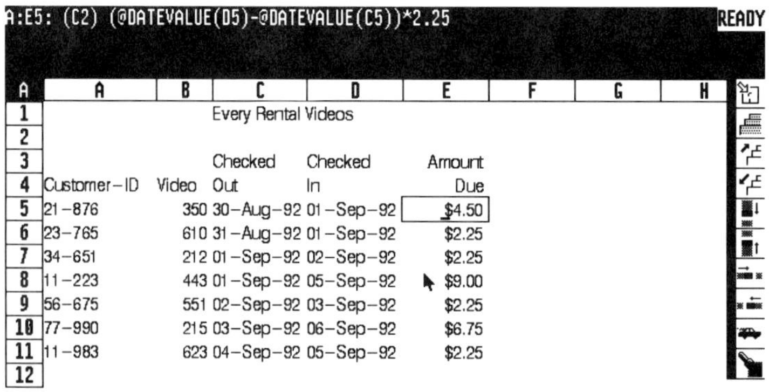

Figure 7-3. *Using @DATEVALUE to work with label (string) dates*

Format

@DAY(*serial date number*)

Arguments

serial date number   the serial date number of the desired date, which must be between 1 and 73050 to stay within the acceptable range of January 1, 1900, to December 31, 2099.

Use

This function is used whenever you are interested in only the day portion of a date. Used with @DATE, the @DAY function would be recorded as @DAY(@DATE(91,12,14)) and would return 14. Used with @DATEVALUE, it might be @DAY(@DATEVALUE("24-Dec-91")) and would return a value of 24.

As a sample use for this function, suppose you want to extract the day from a loan origination date so you can use it to generate payment due dates. @DAY can do this. The dates in Figure 7-4 are generated with @DATE, using a day generated with @DAY. The cell must be formatted with one of the Date formats, or the serial date number will display. The advantage of this approach is that the same date formulas could be used for all loans, as only the day numbers will vary. Naturally you would have to make some allowance for February and days 29 through 31. This could be handled with the @IF function, covered later in this chapter.

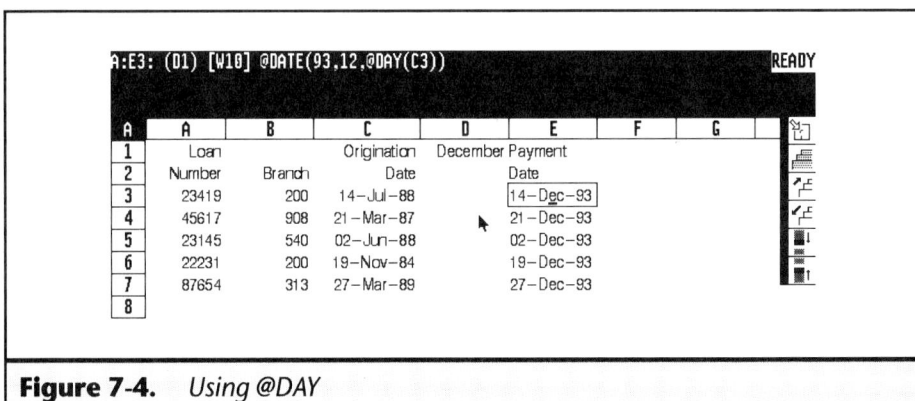

Figure 7-4.   *Using @DAY*

@HOUR

The @HOUR function extracts the hour from a serial time number, using a military time representation. For example, @HOUR(.75) will equal 6:00 P.M. or 18:00.

Format

@HOUR(*serial time number*)

Arguments

serial time number a decimal fraction between 0.000 and 0.9999 *Serial time number* can be entered as a fraction or a decimal number. It can be generated by @TIME, @TIMEVALUE, or @NOW.

Use

This function is used whenever you wish to work with only the hour portion of a time entry. The function will always return a value between 0 and 23. Used with @TIME, which creates a serial time number when provided with arguments of hour, minute, and second, the function might read @HOUR(@TIME(10,15,25)) and would return 10.

If you were interested in recording the delivery hour for packages received, you might capture the time at receipt and use the @HOUR function to access the specific hour. Figure 7-5 provides an example of using the @HOUR function for this purpose.

@MINUTE

The @MINUTE function extracts the minute from a serial time number.

Format

@MINUTE(*serial time number*)

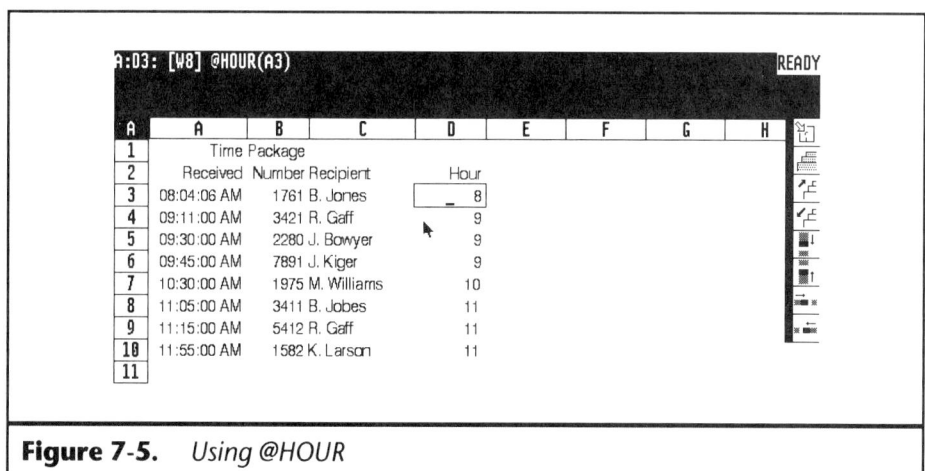

Figure 7-5. *Using @HOUR*

Arguments

serial time number   a decimal fraction between 0.000 and 0.9999. *Serial time number* can be entered as a fraction, a decimal number, a cell reference, or a function.

Use

This function is used whenever you wish to work with only the minute portion of a time entry. The function will always return a value between 0 and 59. Used with @TIME, which creates a serial time number when provided with arguments of hour, minute, and second, the function might read @MINUTE(@TIME(10,15,25)) and would return 15.

If you were managing a radio station and were interested in recording the exact minutes when you received calls for hourly radio contests, you could use the @MINUTE function to handle the task. Certain types of contests might generate many calls and immediate winners, whereas other types could be announced throughout the hour before a winner called in with the correct answer. You might want to capture the time of receipt of the winning calls. Figure 7-6 shows the use of the @MINUTE function for this purpose.

@MONTH

The @MONTH function extracts the month number from a serial date number.

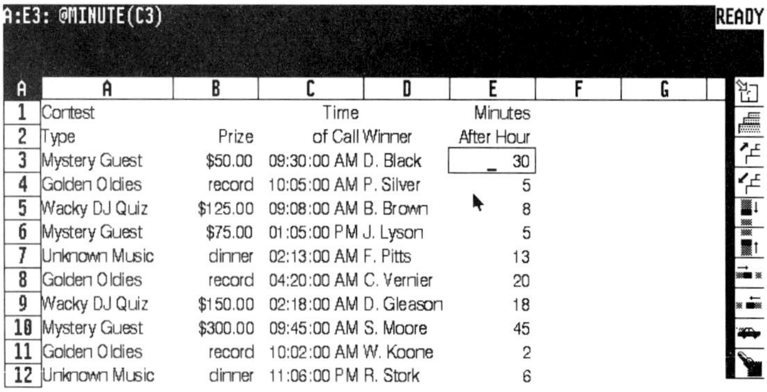

```
A:E3: @MINUTE(C3)                                                    READY

     A              B          C             D          E        F    G
 1  Contest                   Time                    Minutes
 2  Type            Prize      of Call      Winner    After Hour
 3  Mystery Guest   $50.00     09:30:00 AM  D. Black     30
 4  Golden Oldies   record     10:05:00 AM  P. Silver     5
 5  Wacky DJ Quiz   $125.00    09:08:00 AM  B. Brown      8
 6  Mystery Guest   $75.00     01:05:00 PM  J. Lyson      5
 7  Unknown Music   dinner     02:13:00 AM  F. Pitts     13
 8  Golden Oldies   record     04:20:00 AM  C. Vernier   20
 9  Wacky DJ Quiz   $150.00    02:18:00 AM  D. Gleason   18
10  Mystery Guest   $300.00    09:45:00 AM  S. Moore     45
11  Golden Oldies   record     10:02:00 AM  W. Koone      2
12  Unknown Music   dinner     11:06:00 PM  R. Stork      6
```

Figure 7-6. *Using @MINUTE*

Format

@MONTH(*serial date number*)

Arguments

serial date number the serial date number of the desired date, which must be between 1 and 73050 to stay within the acceptable range of January 1, 1900 to December 31, 2099. The *serial date number* can be generated by another function such as @NOW, @DATEVALUE, or @DATE.

Use

This function is used whenever you are interested in only the month portion of a date. Used with @DATE, the @MONTH function would be written @MONTH(@DATE(91,12,14)) and would return 12. Used with @DATEVALUE, it might be @MONTH(@DATEVALUE("24-Dec-91") and return a value of 12.

One sample use for this function would be to extract employees' vacation months from historic data, so you could monitor vacation schedules to plan for temporary help. You could use this function to extract the month from the vacation start date. The dates in columns D and E in Figure 7-7 are used to extract the month number. The advantage of this approach is that the same date formulas can be used for all vacations, as only the month numbers will vary.

```
A:F6: [W12] @MONTH(D6)                                                    READY

       A           A         B        C       D         E          F       G
       1                                                       31-Dec-93
       2                                                       02:08:19 PM
       3                           1992 Vacation Schedule
       4                     YEARS           VACATION  VACATION  VACATION
       5    EMPLOYEE         SERVICE  DEPT.  START     STOP      MONTH
       6    G. Brown         5        100    15-Jun-92 29-Jun-92      6
       7    M. Wilson        2        200    03-Jul-92 10-Jul-92      7
       8    N. Staunton      10       100    02-Jun-92 23-Jun-92      6
       9    H. Mailer        3        100    21-Jul-92 28-Jul-92      7
       10   B. Wyler         25       200    03-Aug-92 31-Aug-92      8
       11   K. Wilmer        2        100    22-Jun-92 29-Jun-92      6
       12   D. Jason         5        200    01-Apr-92 15-Apr-92      4
       13
```

Figure 7-7. *Using @NOW as a date and time stamp*

@NOW

The @NOW function is used to stamp a worksheet cell with the current system date and time. The function does not require any arguments and is simply entered as @NOW.

Use

The @NOW function can be used whenever you wish to place the current date or time in a worksheet cell. The integer portion of the serial number generated will be the current date, and the decimal fraction will be the time.

@NOW will appear as a date if formatted with one of the Date format options, and will display as time if formatted with one of the Time formats. @NOW will be recalculated when the worksheet containing it is loaded into memory, and every time the worksheet is recalculated thereafter.

Figure 7-7 shows a worksheet where two cells, F1 and F2, have @NOW entered in them. One is formatted as a date and the other as a time. Including these cells in the print range when a report is printed will date and time stamp the report so you can always identify the most recent copy of the report.

Using F2 (EDIT) followed by F9 (CALC), then pressing ENTER, will freeze the serial date and time number placed in a cell by @NOW, changing it to a fixed value.

@SECOND

The @SECOND function extracts the second from a serial time number.

Format

@SECOND(*serial time number*)

Arguments

serial time number a decimal fraction between 0.000 and 0.9999. *Serial time number* can be entered as a fraction, a decimal number, a cell reference, or a function.

Use

This function is used whenever you wish to work with only the second portion of a time entry. The function will always return a value between 0 and 59. If cell A3 contains a serial time number representing 11:08:19, @SECOND(A3) will equal 19. Used with the @TIME function, the @SECOND function might read @SECOND(@TIME(10,15,25)) and would return 25.

@TIME

The @TIME function allows you to create a serial time number when you supply the time components.

Format

@TIME(*hour,minute,second*)

Arguments

hour a number between 0 and 23. Midnight is represented by 0 and 11:00 P.M. by 23.

minute   a number between 0 and 59.

second   a number between 0 and 59.

Use

This function is used anywhere you want to enter time on a worksheet. When time is entered with this function, you will be able to perform arithmetic operations with the time value, since it will be stored as a serial time number. You can also enter a time by simply typing in the time, because any of 1-2-3's Time formats make times appear, except for the Short International format of HH.MM. 1-2-3 automatically converts the entries entered in one of these formats into time serial numbers.

Figure 7-8 presents a worksheet that uses the @TIME function to record the time vehicles are brought in for repair, and the time the work on each is completed. Entering both sets of numbers makes it easy to perform calculations with the time values, and the /Range Format Date Time command allows you to choose a suitable Time display format. Column E contains a formula that calculates the difference between the time each car was brought in for repair and the time it was completed, for example, +D5–B5. Using the Short International format under /Range Format Date Time allows you to show just the hours and minutes (represented by the decimal fraction) for the difference between the two time values.

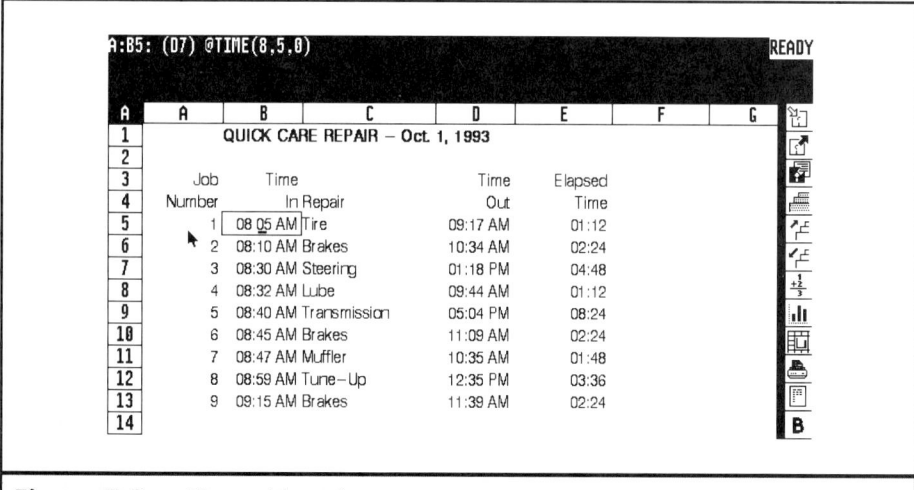

Figure 7-8.   *Time arithmetic*

@TIMEVALUE

The @TIMEVALUE function returns the serial time number, given the string value of the time.

Format

@TIMEVALUE(*time string*)

Arguments

time string   a single string value conforming to one of the acceptable Time formats and enclosed in double quotation marks.

"HH:MM:SS AM/PM" is acceptable, since it conforms to the D6 (Date Format 6) format, which is the first Time format option; "HH:MM AM/PM" is acceptable, since it conforms to the D7 format, which is the second Time format option. Formats D8 and D9 have more than one option and are changeable through the /Worksheet Global Default International Time command. The acceptable formats for D8 and D9 will depend on which format is in effect. Chapter 4, "Changing the Appearance of the Worksheet Display," provides additional information about Time formats.

Use

This function is used whenever you wish to generate a serial time number from a string value. For example, suppose an entry in your worksheet was originally entered as a string, but you decide you want to use it in a calculation of elapsed time. The @TIMEVALUE function makes this possible. It has the same capability as the @TIME function, but accepts a string for input rather than three separate numeric values for hour, minute, and second. As an example, you might enter @TIMEVALUE("2:14:14 PM"), which gives the value 0.5932175926. This value could then be used in a time formula.

The same worksheet used in Figure 7-8 is reproduced for the @TIMEVALUE example, except that all the times are entered as labels. For example, the entry in D5 is '09:17 AM. This means that the formula in column E will have to be changed, since two label values cannot be used to determine a difference. The formula is changed to use @TIMEVALUE, as shown in cell E5 of Figure 7–9. The entry in this cell is @TIMEVALUE(D5)\-@TIMEVALUE(B5), and the cell is formatted in the Short International Time format.

```
A:E5: (D9) @TIMEVALUE(D5)-@TIMEVALUE(B5)                              READY

     A         B            C              D          E      F    G
 1              QUICK CARE REPAIR — Oct. 1, 1993
 2
 3           Job      Time                   Time    Elapsed
 4          Number    In Repair              Out      Time
 5             1    08:05 AM Tire          09:17 AM   01:12
 6             2    08:10 AM Brakes        10:34 AM   02:24
 7             3    08:30 AM Steering      01:18 PM   04:48
 8             4    08:32 AM Lube          09:44 AM   01:12
 9             5    08:40 AM Transmission  05:04 PM   08:24
10             6    08:45 AM Brakes        11:09 AM   02:24
11             7    08:47 AM Muffler       10:35 AM   01:48
12             8    08:59 AM Tune-Up       12:35 PM   03:36
13             9    09:15 AM Brakes        11:39 PM   14:24
14
```

Figure 7-9. *Working with time labels*

@TODAY

The @TODAY function is used to stamp a worksheet cell with the current system date. The function does not require any arguments and is simply entered as @TODAY. It contains the integer portion of the @NOW function.

Use

The @TODAY function can be used whenever you wish to place the current date in a worksheet cell. The advantage of the @TODAY function over the @NOW function is @TODAY's efficiency with regard to minimal recalculation. 1-2-3 only recalculates the @TODAY function when a file containing the function is retrieved, when the date changes, or the cell is edited. The @NOW function is constantly updated since the time serial number portion of the function constantly changes.

@TODAY creates a date serial number that appears as a date if formatted with one of the Date format options. This feature can prevent the problem of not being able to tell which one of several printed reports is the most current. If the @TODAY function is entered somewhere in every worksheet and always included in your print range, you can always identify the most recent copy of a report. As an example, a worksheet can have the following heading:

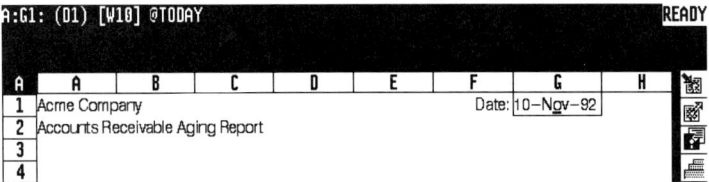

In this worksheet, G1 contains @TODAY, and the result is formatted as a date. Including this cell in the print range when a report is printed will date stamp the report.

Using F2 (EDIT) followed by F9 (CALC), then pressing ENTER, will freeze the serial date number placed in a cell by @TODAY, changing it to a fixed value.

For a similar effect as the @TODAY function provides, but with the added bonus of a date format, click the date icon that looks like this:

When you use this SmartIcon, 1-2-3 enters a date and time serial number for the current date or time in the cell. It also applies a format of MM/DD/YY unless you set /Worksheet Global Default Other International Data to a different date format. This date and time serial number will not change as the date changes.

@YEAR

The @YEAR function extracts the year number from a serial date number.

Format

@YEAR(*serial date number*)

Arguments

serial date number   the serial date number of the desired date, which must be between 1 and 73050 to stay within the acceptable range of January 1, 1900, to December 31, 2099. The *serial date number* can be generated by another function such as @NOW, @DATEVALUE, or @DATE.

Use

This function is used whenever you are interested in only the year portion of a date. Used with @DATE, the @YEAR function would be recorded as @YEAR(@DATE(91,12,14)) and would return 91. Used with @DATEVALUE, it might be @YEAR(@DATEVALUE("24-Dec-91")) and return a value of 91.

One sample use for this function would be to determine the start year for each of a group of employees. You can reference the date of hire and extract the year number, for an easy reference to the anniversary year, shown in Figure 7-10.

Financial Functions

The primary use of 1-2-3's financial functions is for investment calculations and other calculations concerned with the time value of money. For example, you can use them to monitor loans, annuities, and cash flows over a period of time. A second group of financial functions calculates depreciation. With these functions you can quickly compare the effects of different depreciation methods.

Since many of the financial functions deal with interest rate calculations, you will want to be aware of the two acceptable ways of entering interest rates for these calculations. You can always enter a percent as a decimal fraction, for example, .15 for 15%. Your other option is to enter the percent with the percent sign and have 1-2-3 convert your entry to a decimal fraction for internal storage. For example, 15% would be stored as .15.

Many of the financial functions require a term and a rate as arguments. It is important that the same unit of time be used for both arguments. If a term is expressed in years, an annual interest rate should be used. If a term is expressed in months, a monthly interest rate should be used.

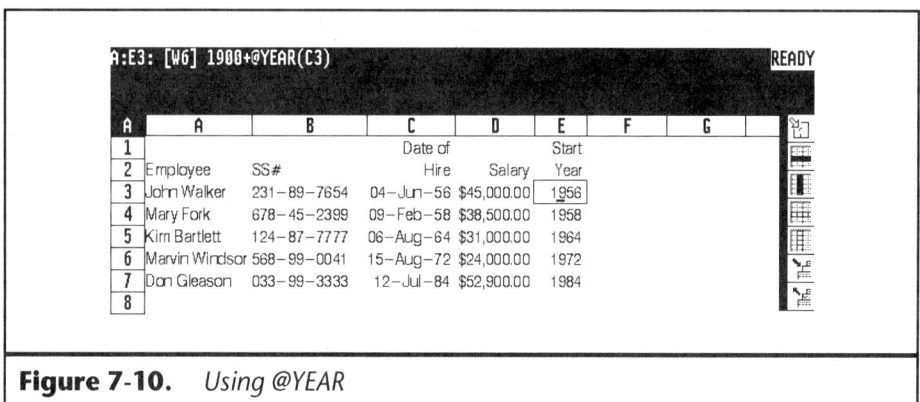

Figure 7-10. *Using @YEAR*

@CTERM

Given a present and a future value for an investment, as well as a fixed interest rate, @CTERM will compute the number of time periods it will take to reach the future value.

Format

@CTERM(*interest,future value,present value*)

Arguments

interest
: the fixed interest rate per compounding period. It can be expressed as a percent or a decimal fraction within the function, or it can be stored in a cell and referenced with the cell address or a range name. It can also be computed with a formula from within the function.

future value
: the value the investment will have at some point in the future. The objective of the @CTERM function is to determine the point at which an investment will reach a specified future value. This argument must be a value or a reference to a cell containing a value.

present value
: the current value of the investment. This argument must be a value or a reference to a cell containing a value.

Use

The @CTERM function can provide a quick answer when you want to know how long it will take an investment to grow to a certain value. The formula used by the function is as follows:

$$\frac{\text{natural log(future value/present value)}}{\text{natural log(1 + periodic interest rate)}}$$

As an example, if you have $5000 to invest today and feel you can get an 11% return on your money, you might want to know how long it would take to triple your money at that rate. The formula, @CTERM(11%/12,15000,5000), will provide the answer, assuming the compounding occurs monthly. The result is 120.3971 months or 10.03309 years.

@DDB

The @DDB function calculates depreciation expense for a specific period using the *double declining balance method*.

Format

@DDB(*cost,salvage,life,period*)

Arguments

cost	the amount you paid for the asset. This argument must be a value or a reference to a cell containing a value.
salvage	the value of the asset at the end of its useful life. This argument must be a value or a reference to a cell containing a value.
life	the expected useful life of the asset; that is, the number of years needed to depreciate the asset from its cost to its salvage value. Normally expressed in years, this argument, too, must be a value or a reference to one.
period	the specific time period for which you are attempting to determine the depreciation expense. Normally the number of the year for which you are calculating depreciation expense, this argument must be a value or a reference to one.

Use

The @DDB function gives you a figure for depreciation expense, using an *accelerated depreciation method* (one that allows you to write off more depreciation expense in the early years of an asset's life). The asset will no longer be depreciated when its book value (that is, cost minus total depreciation to date) equals its salvage value.

The formula used in the calculation of double declining balance depreciation is as follows:

$$\frac{\text{book value for the period} * 2}{\text{life of the asset}}$$

1-2-3 makes adjustments in the calculations to ensure that total depreciation is exactly equal to the asset cost minus the salvage value. Unlike the @VDB function, the @DDB function does not switch to straight-line depreciation when straight-line would be equal or greater.

Figure 7-11 shows the use of this function to determine the proper depreciation expense for each year in an asset's five-year life. The cost of the asset was $11,000, and its salvage value is $1000.

@FV

The @FV function computes the future value of an investment based on the assumption that equal payments will be generated at a specific rate over a period of time.

Format

@FV(payment,interest,term)

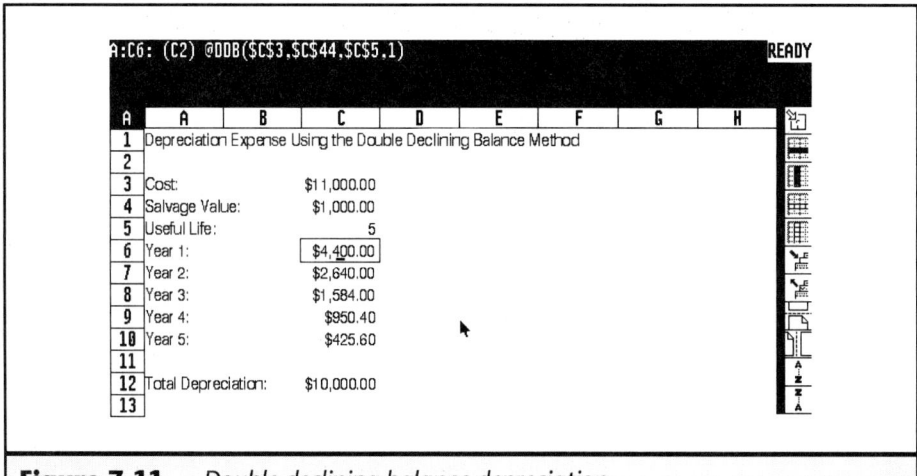

Figure 7-11. Double declining balance depreciation

Arguments

payment the amount of the equal payments for the investment. This argument must be a value or a reference to a value.

interest the periodic interest rate earned by the investment. This argument must be a value or a reference to a value.

term the number of periods for the investment. This argument must be a value or a reference to a value.

Use

This function is designed to perform calculations for an ordinary annuity. It uses the formula

$$\text{payment} * \left(\frac{(1 + \text{periodic interest rate})^n - 1}{\text{periodic interest rate}} \right)$$

where *n* is the number of periods.

You can use the @FV function to calculate the value for an ordinary annuity. Assuming that you plan to deposit $500 a month for each of the next 36 months, and will continue to receive interest on this money at a constant rate of 12% compounded monthly, you would enter the formula @FV(500,1%,36) to display the result of $21,538.43.

This example is based on the premise that interest is paid at the end of the month and that your next contribution is always made on the last day of the year.

The @FV function can be adapted to work with an annuity due (payment is made on the first day of the period), which uses the formula @FV(payment,interest,term)*(1 + interest). Using the same example, your formula is @FV(500,1%,36)*(1+1%). This formula would return $21,753.82.

This is appropriate for a situation where you must make contributions on the first day of the year. Assuming you make annual payments of $5000 at the beginning of each year, and they earn interest at a rate of 10%, the value at the end of ten years would be represented by @FV(5000,10%,10)*(1+10%). This formula would return $87,655.83, the value of your annuity after ten years.

@IRR

The @IRR function calculates the internal rate of return on investments.

Format

@IRR(*guess,range*)

Arguments

guess an estimate of the internal rate of return. Although any number between 0% and 100% will probably work, you will encounter situations where the correct internal rate of return cannot be closely approximated. If you think the internal rate of return for an investment is between 15% and 25%, 20% is a good guess to start with. A series of cash flows that alternate between positive and negative will result in more than one internal rate of return. The guess you make will affect which of the values is returned. Thirty iterations are the default for this function. If 1-2-3 cannot approximate the result to within 0.0000001 after thirty attempts, ERR will result.

range the range of cells containing the cash flows to be analyzed. Negative numbers in this range are considered outflows, and positive numbers are inflows. The first number in the range is expected to be negative, since it is the cost of the investment opportunity.

Use

The @IRR function is used whenever you wish to find the rate that will equate the initial investment with the expected future cash flows generated by the investment. Cash flows must be at equal intervals. If the cash flows are a mixture of positive and negative values, the @IRR function may find multiple internal rates of return. In this case, 1-2-3 returns the internal rate of return closest to the guess.

Figure 7-12 shows the @IRR function being used to analyze the stream of Projected Cash Flows shown in A2..A7. As required, the first number in the range is negative, signifying the cost of the investment opportunity. A guess of 12% was placed in D2. The /Range Format Percent command formatted the entries as percent in D2 and E2. The formula for the internal rate of return is placed in E2 as @IRR(D2,A2..A7). In this example, the function returns 19.58%.

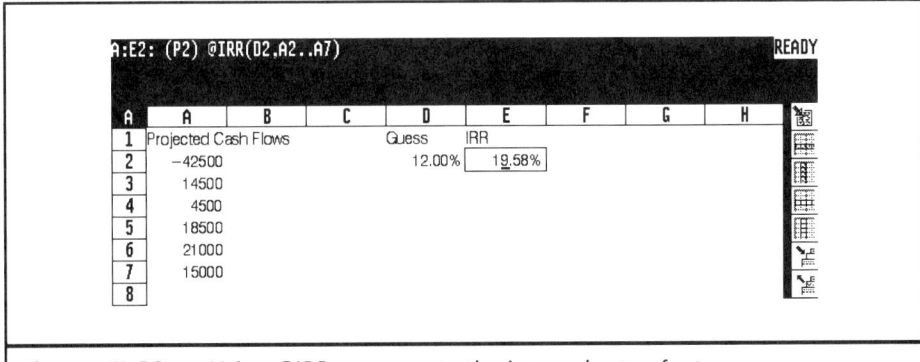

Figure 7-12. *Using @IRR to compute the internal rate of return*

@NPV

The @NPV function computes what you should be willing to pay for a projected stream of cash flows, given your desired rate of return.

Format

@NPV(*discount rate,range*)

Arguments

discount rate   a fixed periodic interest rate used to discount expected cash flows, to project their worth in today's dollars.

range   the series of cash flows to be discounted. These cash flows do not have to be equal, but they must be evenly spaced over a period of time (monthly, quarterly, and so forth). They are assumed to occur at the end of a period; the first cash flow will be received at the end of the first period.

Use

This is one of the most frequently used functions in 1-2-3, since it deals with the time value of money.

Figure 7-13 presents a sample use of @NPV. The expected cash flows are shown in B2..G2. You will notice from the column headings that these cash flows are to be received monthly. Yet the interest rate in D4 is expressed as an annual rate. Make note of this discrepancy between the time periods of the interest rate and the payments. The difference can be resolved by changing the interest rate to a monthly figure in the function argument. The formula for the calculation is @NPV(D4/12,B2..G2). It produces a result of $57,396.93, indicating that if the discount rate is 15%, you should be willing to pay up to $57,396.93 for this investment.

NOTE: *This function is not designed to handle situations where you make an immediate or up-front payment, although you could easily construct a formula to do this. Since the initial payment is already in today's dollars, there is no need to discount it. Your initial outflow can be subtracted from the result of the @NPV function. Using the data shown in Figure 7-13 and assuming the initial cost is $20,000, the formula is @NPV(D4/12,B2..G2)–20000 and the result is $37,396.93.*

Figure 7-13. *Net present value calculations*

@PMT

The @PMT function will calculate the appropriate payment amount for a loan when given the principal, interest rate, and term.

Format

@PMT(*principal,interest,term of loan*)

Arguments

principal a numeric value representing the amount borrowed. It can be provided as a number or as a cell address, formula, range name, or other function.

interest a numeric value representing the interest rate. It can be provided as a numeric constant in the formula or as a cell reference, formula, or range name.

term the number of payments in the loan term. If monthly payments will be made on a loan spanning several years, multiply the years of the term by 12 and use the product for this argument. It can be expressed as a fraction, a formula, a range name, or a cell address.

It is extremely important that the same unit of time be used for both the term and the interest rate. An annual interest rate means a term of a number of years, whereas a monthly interest rate indicates a term consisting of a number of months.

Use

This function can be used wherever you want to calculate the amount of a loan payment. This function makes it easy to calculate your own personal loan tables. Given a specific range of values for the principal and interest rate, you can look at a range of payment amount options and see which are possible given your current monthly income.

Figure 7-14 provides an example of a payment table. Interest rates are entered across row three. Cells A4..A20 are used for hypothetical principal amounts.

Only one payment formula must be entered; the rest can be copied. @PMT($A4,B$3/12,240) is entered in B4. The $s in the arguments are required to

```
A:B4: (C2) @PMT($A4,B$3/12,240)                                          READY

      A          B          C          D          E          F          G          H
 1   LOAN                              INTEREST RATE
 2   AMOUNT
 3               9.00%      9.50%      10.00%     10.50%     11.00%     11.50%     12.00%
 4   $100,000    $899.73    $932.13    $965.02    $998.38    $1,032.19  $1,066.43  $1,101.09
 5   $105,000    $944.71    $978.74    $1,013.27  $1,048.30  $1,083.80  $1,119.75  $1,156.14
 6   $110,000    $989.70    $1,025.34  $1,061.52  $1,098.22  $1,135.41  $1,173.07  $1,211.19
 7   $115,000    $1,034.68  $1,071.95  $1,109.77  $1,148.14  $1,187.02  $1,226.39  $1,266.25
 8   $120,000    $1,079.67  $1,118.56  $1,158.03  $1,198.06  $1,238.63  $1,279.72  $1,321.30
 9   $125,000    $1,124.66  $1,165.16  $1,206.28  $1,247.97  $1,290.24  $1,333.04  $1,376.36
10   $130,000    $1,169.64  $1,211.77  $1,254.53  $1,297.89  $1,341.84  $1,386.36  $1,431.41
11   $135,000    $1,214.63  $1,258.38  $1,302.78  $1,347.81  $1,393.45  $1,439.68  $1,486.47
12   $140,000    $1,259.62  $1,304.98  $1,351.03  $1,397.73  $1,445.06  $1,493.00  $1,541.52
13   $145,000    $1,304.60  $1,351.59  $1,399.28  $1,447.65  $1,496.67  $1,546.32  $1,596.57
14   $150,000    $1,349.59  $1,398.20  $1,447.53  $1,497.57  $1,548.28  $1,599.64  $1,651.63
15   $155,000    $1,394.58  $1,444.80  $1,495.78  $1,547.49  $1,599.89  $1,652.97  $1,706.68
16   $160,000    $1,439.56  $1,491.41  $1,544.03  $1,597.41  $1,651.50  $1,706.29  $1,761.74
17   $165,000    $1,484.55  $1,538.02  $1,592.29  $1,647.33  $1,703.11  $1,759.61  $1,816.79
18   $170,000    $1,529.53  $1,584.62  $1,640.54  $1,697.25  $1,754.72  $1,812.93  $1,871.85
19   $175,000    $1,574.52  $1,631.23  $1,688.79  $1,747.16  $1,806.33  $1,866.25  $1,926.90
20   $180,000    $1,619.51  $1,677.84  $1,737.04  $1,797.08  $1,857.94  $1,919.57  $1,981.96
10-Nov-92 05:02 PM                                                       NUM
```

Figure 7-14.   *Creating a payment table*

keep part of the cell addresses from changing as the formula is copied. $A4 indicates that the column for the reference is absolute, although the row can change. The reverse is true of B$3: the row can change, but the column is constant. B$3 is divided by 12 to convert the annual interest into a monthly interest. The term is 20 years, which equates to 240 monthly periods. The formula can be copied to accommodate the remaining places in the table. You will need to widen some of the columns in order to fit the currency display in the cells.

NOTE: Financial institutions calculate payment amounts in a number of ways. The formula used by the @PMT function is

$$\text{principal} * \frac{\text{interest}}{1 - (\text{interest}+1)^{-n}}$$

where n is the number of payments.

@PV

The @PV function determines the present value of an investment, assuming a fixed periodic interest rate and a series of equal payments over a period of time.

Format

@PV(*payment,periodic interest rate,number of periods*)

Arguments

payment — the amount of the equal payments, expressed as a value or a reference to a cell containing a value. Only one value may be referenced, since payments are assumed to be equal.

periodic interest rate — the periodic interest rate used to discount the cash flows. This argument must be a value or a reference to a cell containing a value.

number of periods — the term over which the payments will be generated. This argument must be a value or a reference to a cell containing a value.

Use

The @PV function is used whenever you wish to determine today's value of money to be received in the future. You can use the function to assess what you should be willing to pay for an investment today, given that it will return a certain amount of money in future periods. You can also use the function to evaluate a lump-sum payment as compared to future periodic payments if you have this option on the sale of a property or the receipt of prize money.

As an example, assume that you have the option of taking a one-time cash payment of $500,000 versus monthly payments of $5000 for the next 20 years. To compare the two options you must look at the present value of the future cash flows. This means you must make an assessment of the rate of return you would receive for investing the $500,000 lump-sum payment today. This example assumes that you could get 12% annually but compounded monthly. The present value then becomes @PV(5000,1%,240). The result indicates that the best decision (without considering the effect of taxes) is to choose the lump-sum payment, since the present value of the monthly payments is $454,097.

@RATE

The @RATE function determines the periodic interest rate that must be earned to increase a specified present value to a future value over a specific term.

Format

@RATE(*future value,present value,number of periods*)

Arguments

future value	the value of the investment at the end of a specified growth period. This argument must be a value or a reference to a value.
present value	the current value of an investment. This argument can contain a numeric value, a formula, or a reference to one of those two options.
number of periods	the compounding periods over which the investment will grow. This argument must be a value or a reference to a value.

Use

The @RATE function is used to determine the periodic interest rate that is required to realize a desired growth rate. If you give the number of periods in months, you get a monthly rate. You can convert this to an annual rate by multiplying by 12.

Suppose you invested $5000 in a bond maturing in eight years; you could use the @RATE function to calculate the rate of return. This example assumes that the maturity value is $10,000 and that the interest is compounded monthly. The required formula is @RATE(10000,5000,8*12). The rate of return is .72%, a monthly rate. To annualize it, multiply by 12 to obtain 8.7%.

@SLN

The @SLN function computes the straight-line depreciation for one period in an asset's life. Straight-line depreciation has the same amount of depreciation each year of the asset's life.

Format

@SLN(*cost,salvage value,life of the asset*)

Arguments

cost	the amount paid for the asset. This number can be included in the function or stored in a cell and referenced with an address or range name.
salvage value	the remaining value of the asset at the end of its useful life. This number can be included in the function or stored in a cell and referenced with an address or range name.
life of the asset	the number of years of useful life, or the time required to depreciate the asset to its salvage value. This number can be included in the function or stored in a cell and referenced with an address or range name.

Use

The @SLN function can be used whenever you wish to depreciate an asset evenly over its useful life, so that the depreciation expense will be the same for all years. The formula used by the function is as follows:

$$\frac{cost - salvage\ value}{life}$$

As an example, if you purchase a $12,000 machine and estimate its salvage value to be $2000 at the end of its five-year life, you can use @SLN to calculate its depreciation expense. The formula is @SLN(12000,2000,5), which returns $2000.

@SYD

The @SYD function computes depreciation expense for an asset using the sum-of-the-years'-digits depreciation method. This is an accelerated depreciation method that depreciates an asset more in the early years of its life.

Format

@SYD(*cost,salvage value,life,period*)

Arguments

cost	the amount paid for the asset. This number can be included in the function or stored in a cell and referenced with an address or range name.
salvage value	the remaining value of the asset at the end of its useful life. This number can be included in the function or stored in a cell and referenced with an address or range name.
life	the number of years of useful life, or the time required to depreciate the asset to its *salvage value*. This number can be included in the function or stored in a cell and referenced with an address or range name.
period	within the useful life of the asset, the year for which you wish the depreciation expense calculated. This number can be included in the function or stored in a cell and referenced with an address or range name. It should not be greater than the *life* of the asset.

Use

The @SYD function lets you calculate the sum-of-the-years'-digits depreciation expense for any period in the life of an asset. The formula used by the function is

$$\frac{(\text{cost–salvage})*(\text{life–period for depreciation expense} + 1)}{(\text{life}*(\text{life} + 1)/2)}$$

The worksheet in Figure 7-15 shows the sum-of-the-years'-digits depreciation expense for an asset that was purchased for $12,000 and has a $2000 salvage value. The cell pointer points to the formula for the depreciation expense in the first year. This calculation uses the formula @SYD($D$3/$D$4/$D$5). The worksheet shows the depreciation expense for the other four years, as well. The only difference in the remaining formulas is in the last argument, which indicates the period for which depreciation expense is being calculated.

@TERM

The @TERM function returns the number of payment periods required to accumulate a given future value if the payment amount and interest rate remain fixed.

Format

@TERM(*payment,interest,future value*)

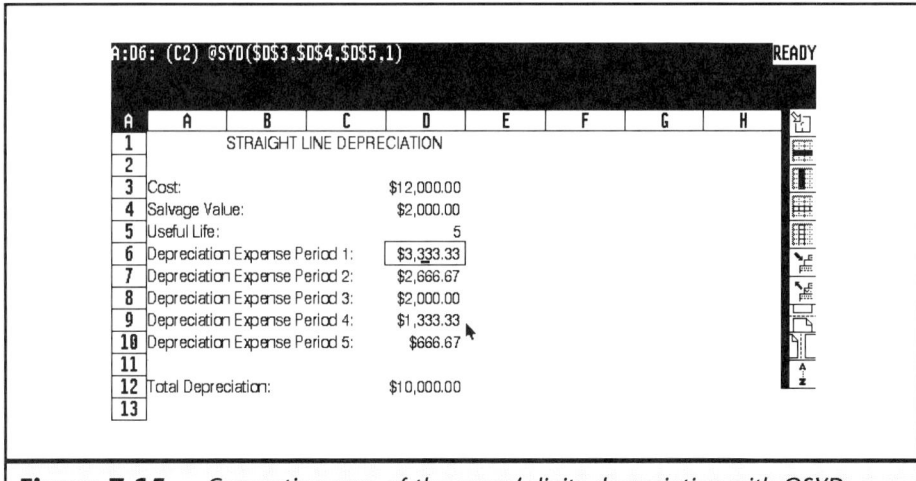

Figure 7-15. *Computing sum-of-the-years'-digits depreciation with @SYD*

Arguments

payment a fixed periodic payment, stored as a number in the function, or in a cell that can be referenced by the function.

interest the fixed interest rate per compounding period. It can be expressed as a percent or decimal fraction within the function, or stored in a cell and referenced with the cell address or a range name. It can also be computed with a formula from within the function.

future value the value of the investment at some point in the future. This argument must be a value or a reference to a cell containing a value.

Use

The @TERM function is used to calculate the number of periods required for an ordinary annuity to reach a given value. For example, it permits you to determine how long it will take to save for a dream vacation home or luxury yacht, assuming you set aside a fixed amount at the end of each month.

The formula behind 1-2-3's calculations is

$$\frac{\text{natural log }(1 + (\text{future value}*\text{interest}/\text{payment}))}{\text{natural log }(1 + \text{interest})}$$

As an example, suppose you set $350 aside at the end of each month for the purpose of accumulating a $25,000 down payment on a vacation home. If the funds are placed in a money market fund paying 10.25% annual interest, @TERM will calculate the time that is required to accumulate the down payment. The formula is @TERM(350,.1025/12,25000) and returns 56 months.

NOTE: *This function differs from the @CTERM function in that you must provide the payment amount, not the present value. @CTERM focuses on the number of growth periods required for an investment to reach a specific value, while @TERM is concerned with the number of payment periods for an ordinary annuity. To calculate the term of an annuity due, you would need to use the formula @TERM(payment,interest,future value)/(1+interest).*

@VDB

The @VDB function calculates depreciation expense for a specific period using a variable declining balance method. This function differs from @DDB in that the last function argument contains the percentage, allowing you to control the percentage used in the calculation. With @DDB, the percentage is always 200%. With @VDB, you decide the percentage used in comparison to straight-line depreciation. Also, this function can switch to straight-line when straight-line would be equal or greater. Finally, this function can compute depreciation for periods other than a year at a time.

Format

@VDB(*cost,salvage,life,start-period,end-period,[depreciation-factor],[switch]*)

Arguments

cost	the amount paid for the asset. This argument must be a value or a reference to a cell containing a value.
salvage	the value of the asset at the end of its useful life. Like the *cost,* this argument must be a value or a reference to a cell containing a value.
life	the expected useful life of the asset; that is, the number of years needed to depreciate the asset from its *cost* to its *salvage value.* Normally expressed in years, this argument also must be a value or a reference to one.
start-period	the starting period in the asset's life for which you are attempting to determine the depreciation expense. Normally the beginning of the year for which you are calculating depreciation expense, this argument must be a value or a reference to one, which is between 0 and the value of life. Fractional values represent fractional parts of a year.
end-period	the ending period in the asset's life for which you are attempting to determine the depreciation expense. Normally the number of the year for which you are calculating depreciation expense, this argument must be a value or a reference to a value that is between the start-period and life. The difference between start-period and end-period is the time span for which this function computes depreciation.

depreciation-factor	the percentage of straight-line depreciation that the function uses. If this optional argument is not provided, 1-2-3 uses 200%, which calculates the same result as the @DDB function.
switch	a 1 or a 0 that selects whether this function switches to straight-line depreciation when straight-line depreciation is higher. If this function uses a 0 or omits this optional argument, this function switches when straight-line depreciation is greater, which can occur in the later years of the asset's life.

Use

The @VDB function calculates variable declining depreciation expense, using an accelerated depreciation method (one that allows you to write off more depreciation expense in the early years of an asset's life). The asset will no longer be depreciated when its book value (that is, cost minus total depreciation to date) equals its salvage value.

1-2-3 makes adjustments in the calculations to ensure that total depreciation is exactly equal to the asset's cost minus the salvage value. @VDB automatically switches to straight-line depreciation when that method provides greater depreciation.

Figure 7-16 shows the use of this function to determine the proper depreciation expense for each year in an asset's five-year life. Since the asset was purchased in the middle of the year, it is depreciated over six years with the first and sixth year taking half a year of depreciation. The cost of the asset was $11,000 and its salvage value is $1000. This function uses a 1.5 depreciation factor to calculate depreciation using a 150% declining-balance depreciation rate. Notice how the variable declining-balance depreciation method switches to straight-line when straight-line is higher, which occurs in year 4.

Mathematical Functions

1-2-3's mathematical functions perform trigonometric and other numeric calculations. Their primary use is in engineering, manufacturing, and scientific applications.

The angles that some of the functions work with are all expressed in radians, a unit of measure that equates the radius and arc length. If you prefer to work

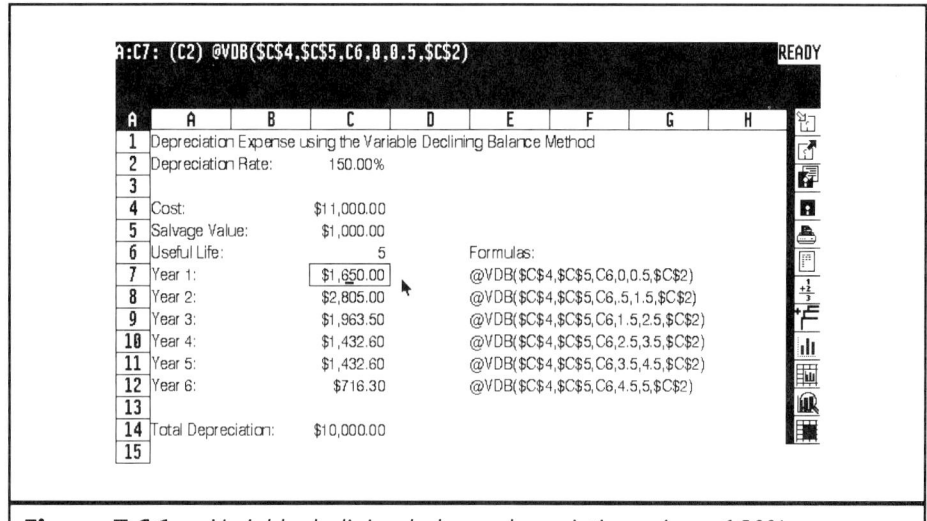

Figure 7-16. *Variable declining-balance depreciation using a 150% depreciation rate*

with angles in degrees, multiply radians by 180/@PI to produce the conversion. All angles that you enter for the @SIN, @COS, and @TAN functions should be expressed in radians. If they are in degrees, multiply by the inverse of the conversion factor (that is, @PI/180) to change degrees into radians.

@ABS

The @ABS function returns the positive or absolute value of a number.

Format

@ABS(*number*)

Arguments

number   any value, including references to a cell containing a value. If a string is used for *number*, an error will result.

Use

The @ABS function is used whenever you are interested in the relative size of a number and do not care whether it is positive or negative. A good example might be the need to monitor cash overages and shortages in the registers of a retail establishment. Consistent cash overages and shortages indicate a cash control problem that should be corrected. If you monitored both overages and shortages, adding their + and – signs, they might cancel each other out. Looking at the absolute value of the overages and shortages, however, provides a look at the total amount of the differences.

Figure 7-17 provides a look at a restaurant's cash overages and shortages by adding absolute values. If @ABS had not been used, the positive and negative numbers would have partially canceled each other, making the cash differences seem less of a problem.

@ACOS

The @ACOS function returns the inverse cosine (arccosine) when you provide the cosine of an angle.

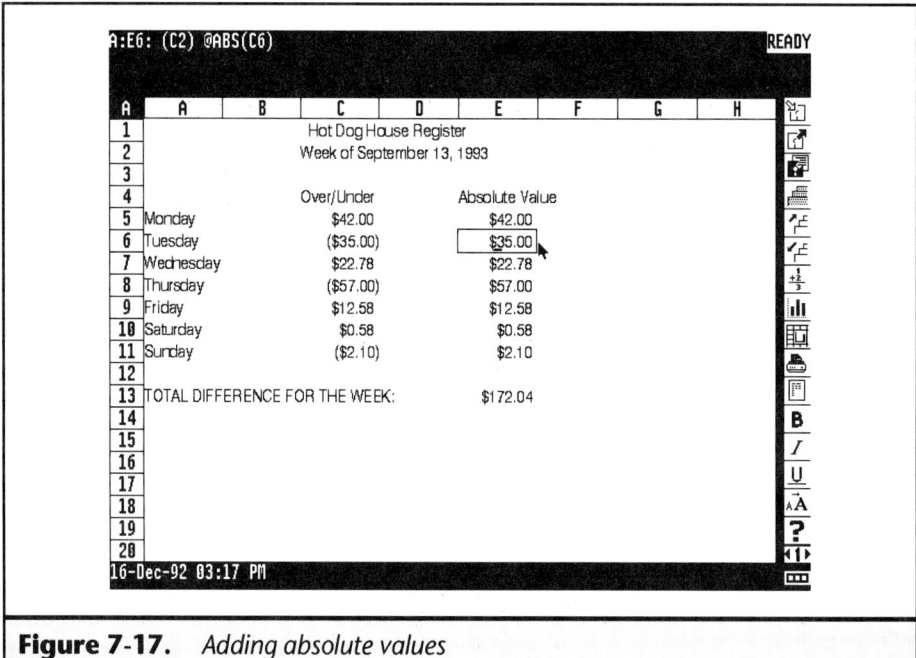

Figure 7-17. *Adding absolute values*

Format

@ACOS(*number*)

Arguments

number   the cosine of an angle, which can be in the range of –1 to 1. This numeric value can be provided within the function or through a reference to a cell or range. If you provide a number outside the allowable limits, ERR will be returned.

Use

The @ACOS function is used when you know the cosine of an angle but want to know the angle in radians. If you prefer the angle measurement in degrees, you can multiply the result of this function by 180/@PI.

Suppose you were at the top of a cliff in a lighthouse 100 feet above water and wanted to know the angle needed to make a projectile reach a boat approximately 200 feet away (see Figure 7-18). You could find the cosine of the angle by performing the following calculation:

cos of angle = 100/200
cos of angle = .5
@ACOS(.5)*180/@PI = 60 degrees

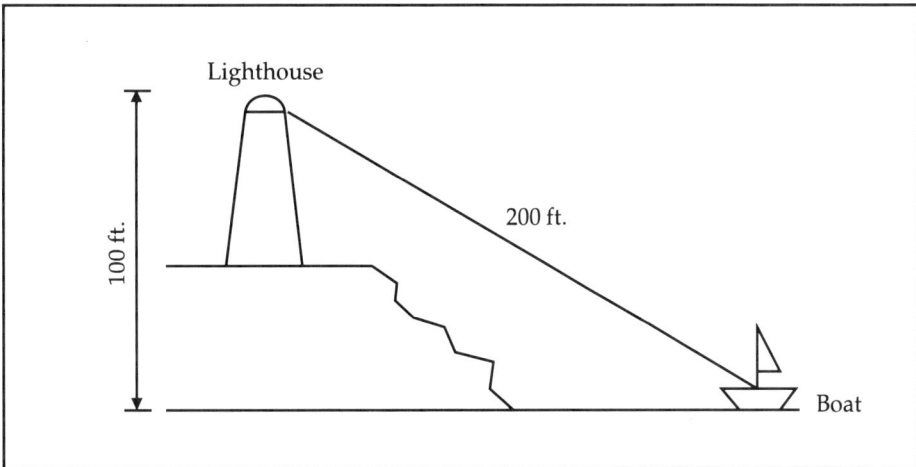

Figure 7-18. *Calculating the angle from the lighthouse to the boat*

@ASIN

The @ASIN function is used to determine the arcsine or inverse sine of an angle.

Format

@ASIN(*number*)

Arguments

number   the sine of an angle, which can be in the range of –1 to 1. This numeric value can be provided within the function or through a reference to a cell or range. If you provide a number outside the allowable limits, ERR will be returned.

Use

The @ASIN function returns an arcsine between @PI/2 and –@PI/2 and represents an angle in quadrant 1 or 2.

As an example, you can use the @ASIN function to determine the angle of a platform that will be used to roll a barrel into a truck. A diagram of the truck bed and platform is shown in Figure 7-19. The bed of the truck is three feet from the

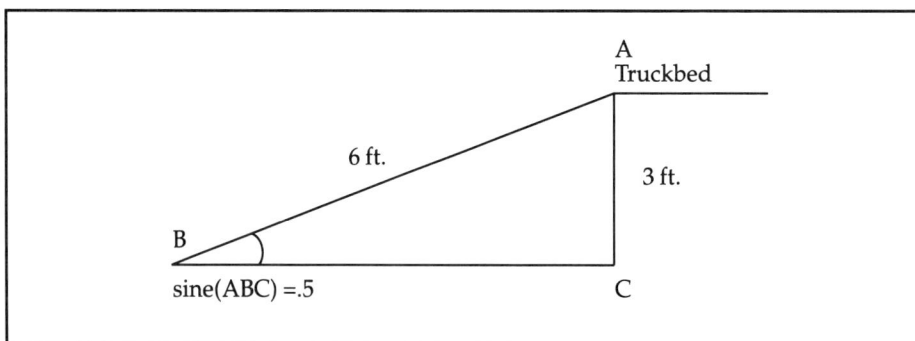

Figure 7-19.   *Using a ramp to get merchandise into a truck*

ground, and the platform used to roll the barrel is six feet long. The sine of the angle between the board and the ground is equal to 3/6 or .5, and @ASIN(.5)*180/@PI equals 30 degrees.

@ATAN

The @ATAN function calculates the arctangent or inverse tangent of an angle for use in trigonometric problems.

Format

@ATAN(*number*)

Arguments

number   the tangent of an angle, which can be in the range of −1 to 1. This numeric value can be provided within the function or through a reference to a cell or range. If you provide a number outside the allowable limits, ERR will be returned.

Use

The @ATAN function returns an arctangent between @PI/2 and −@PI/2 and represents an angle in quadrant 1 or 4.

This function can be used to solve many trigonometric problems. For example, suppose you are playing a championship game of pool and need to pass a ball from point A through point B in the diagram shown in Figure 7-20. The @ATAN function will determine the angle at which you should hit the ball.

The location of the ball is three inches from the bumper, and the location of the pocket in relationship to the bumper is four inches. The tangent between the pocket and the bumper is equal to 4/3 or 1.333333. @ATAN(1.333333) is .927295 radians. When this is multiplied by 180/@PI, it provides 53.13 degrees.

@ATAN2

The @ATAN2 function returns the 4 quadrant arctangent, or the angle in radians whose tangent is *y/x*.

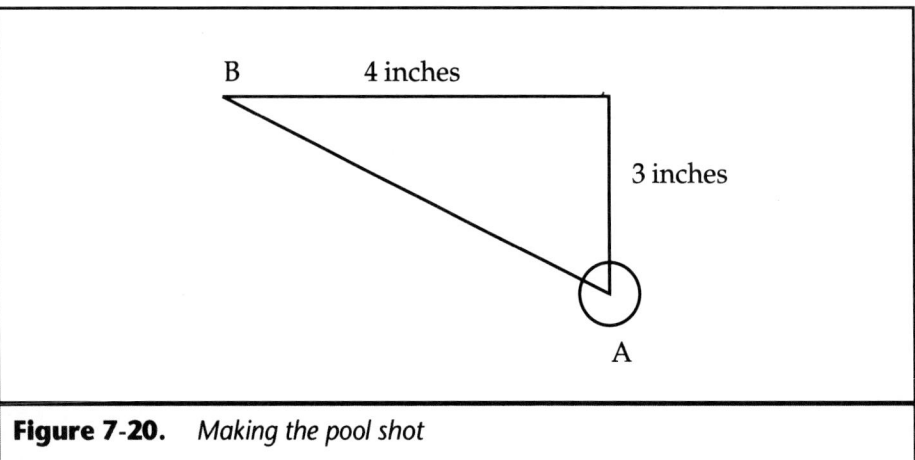

Figure 7-20. *Making the pool shot*

Format

@ATAN2(*x,y*)

Arguments

x the *x* coordinate of the angle, expressed as a number or a reference to a cell containing a number.

y the *y* coordinate of the angle, expressed as a number or a reference to a cell containing a number.

Use

The @ATAN2 function is used to solve trigonometric problems where you want to differentiate angles found in the first and third quadrants from those found in the second and fourth quadrants. Figure 7-21 shows the values of @ATAN2 for the different quadrants. @ATAN2(1,.5) returns .463647 radians.

@COS

The @COS function returns the cosine of an angle.

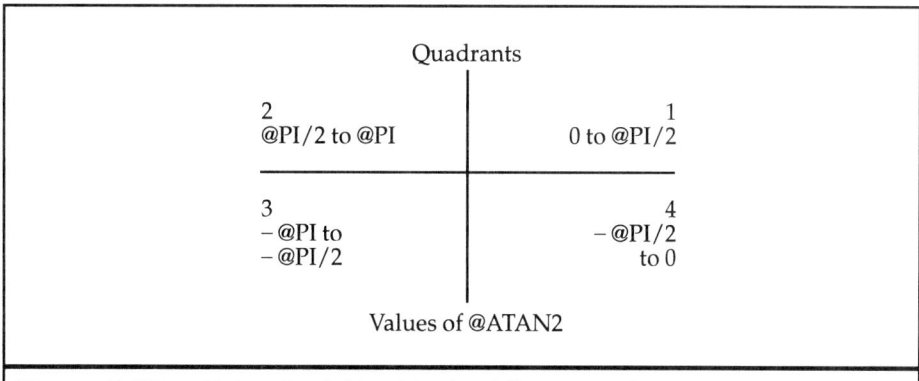

Figure 7-21. *Values for @ATAN2 in the different quadrants*

Format

@COS(*number*)

Arguments

number   a number representing the radians in an angle.

Use

The @COS function is used when you have an angle in radians and want to determine the cosine of that angle. This number can assist you in making other determinations, such as distances and other angles. Thus, a surveyor can use the @COS function to determine the length of a side of a plot of land in the shape of a right triangle (see Figure 7-22).

The longest side of the plot of land is 50 feet. There is a 60-degree angle at the point of the lot where the surveyor is standing. He would like to know the length of the side on his left (the adjacent side, in mathematics terminology). He constructs the formula COS (60°) = x/50. The @COS(60*@PI/180) function returns .5, which can be used to solve for x of 25. @PI/180 was needed because the angle was supplied in degrees.

@EXP

The @EXP function raises the base *e* (2.718282) to a specific power.

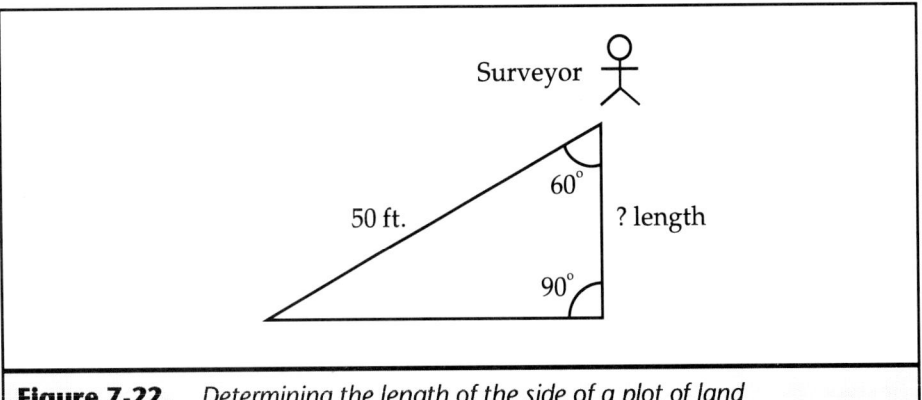

Figure 7-22. Determining the length of the side of a plot of land

Format

@EXP(*number*)

Arguments

number the power to which you want to raise *e*. This argument must be a numeric value or a reference to one. *Number* cannot exceed 230 if you wish to display it; it can be as high as 11356 if you just plan to store the number for later calculations.

Use

@EXP is the inverse of @LN and is used whenever you wish to raise *e* to a specific power. Here are several examples:

@EXP(1) equals 2.718282
@EXP(10) equals 22026.46
@EXP(@LN(5)) equals 5

@INT

The @INT function allows you to truncate the decimal places in a number to produce a whole number.

Format

@INT(*number*)

Arguments

number   any value whose integer portion you wish to use. Any digits to the right of the decimal point in the *number* will be truncated.

Use

This function is used whenever you wish to eliminate the decimal portion of a number. It can determine the number of complete batches finished by a production line, for example. In this situation, partial batches may not be of interest, since they would not be ready for shipment. Similarly, if you needed to calculate the number of items that could be produced from a given amount of raw materials, partial items would be of no interest. In both examples, you would not want the number rounded; you would simply want to truncate the decimal portion of the number to look at the number of units. This can be handled with @INT.

The worksheet in Figure 7-23 shows the use of @INT in calculating the number of wallets that can be created from different sized pieces of cowhide.

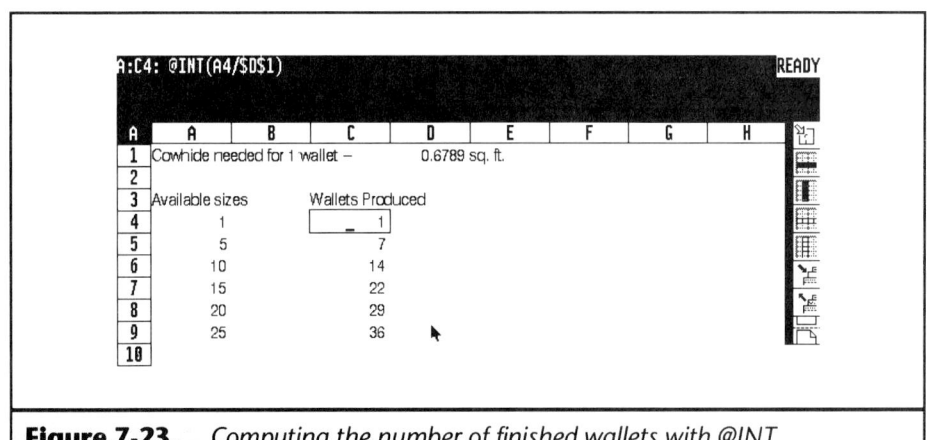

Figure 7-23.   *Computing the number of finished wallets with @INT*

Partial wallets are not of interest, since one hide will not necessarily match another.

@LN

The @LN function returns the natural log of a number.

Format

@LN(*number*)

Arguments

number   any value greater than zero. If *number* is less than zero, ERR will be returned.

Use

Natural logarithms are logarithms to the base *e*, where *e* is approximately 2.718282. @LN is the inverse of @EXP, which means that you can incorporate *e* in any calculation with @EXP(1). @LN(@EXP(4)) equals 4, and @EXP(@LN(8)) equals 8. The primary use of logarithms is to make complex calculations less complex. A few examples follow:

@LN(9) equals 2.197224
@LN(1.5) equals 0.405465

@LOG

The @LOG function computes the base 10 logarithm of a number.

Format

@LOG(*number*)

Arguments

number   any value greater than zero. If *number* is less than zero, ERR will be returned.

Use

Like natural logs, base 10 logs are primarily used in scientific or other complex calculations where the rules of logarithms can be used to simplify the math involved. The results returned by 1-2-3 from a few examples of @LOG are as follows:

@LOG(10) equals 1
@LOG(100) equals 2
@LOG(190) equals 2.278753

@MOD

The @MOD function returns the modulus or remainder when a number is divided by a divisor number.

Format

@MOD(*number,divisor*)

Arguments

number   any positive or negative number or a reference to one.
divisor   any number other than zero used to divide *number*, as in *number/divisor*.

Use

The @MOD function, which provides the remainder from dividing *number* by *divisor,* is useful in a variety of situations, although creativity is often required to see the applications. For example, this function can be used in conjunction with the date functions covered earlier in the chapter to determine the day of the week. @MOD(@NOW,7) will return a value between 0 and 6, since the @MOD function returns the remainder from a division. If the result is 0, the day is Saturday, and if the result is 6, the day is Friday. Each of the other days is represented by one of the other numbers between 0 and 6.

@PI

The @PI function returns an approximation of the constant π, or 3.14159265. The format of the function is simply @PI, since the function does not require any arguments.

Use

@PI is used frequently in geometric problems involving circumference and area. The circumference of (the distance around) a circle is 2*@PI*radius. Given a circle with a radius of 5 inches, you could find the circumference of 31.4 using the formula 2*@PI*5.

@RAND

The @RAND function generates random numbers between 0 and 1. The format of the function is simply @RAND; it has no arguments.

Use

This function is useful for generating test data for simulations. Each time the worksheet is recalculated, the @RAND function will take on a new value. You can create rows and columns of a worksheet with this function to generate data for queuing theory problems or other applications. Each @RAND will be a different number, since 1-2-3 uses 15 decimal digits for these numbers.

The worksheet in Figure 7-24 shows numbers generated with the @RAND function. You can control the range of the random number by multiplying the result by a number or adding a number to it. Multiplying @RAND by a factor raises the upper limit to the number you are multiplying by; for example, @RAND*100 provides random numbers between 0 and 100. Adding a fixed number to @RAND raises the lower limit; for example, @RAND*100+50 generates random numbers between 50 and 150.

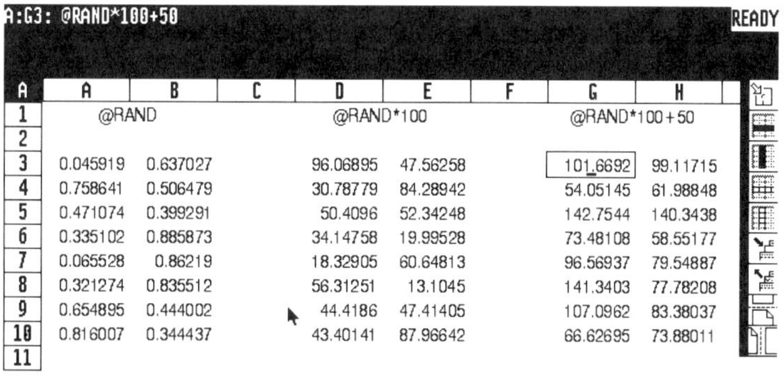

```
A:G3: @RAND*100+50                                          READY

  A     A        B       C      D         E      F     G         H
  1       @RAND                    @RAND*100          @RAND*100+50
  2
  3     0.045919  0.637027        96.06895  47.56258      101.6692   99.11715
  4     0.758641  0.506479        30.78779  84.28942       54.05145  61.98848
  5     0.471074  0.399291        50.4096   52.34248      142.7544  140.3438
  6     0.335102  0.885873        34.14758  19.99528       73.48108  58.55177
  7     0.065528  0.86219         18.32905  60.64813       96.56937  79.54887
  8     0.321274  0.835512        56.31251  13.1045       141.3403   77.78208
  9     0.654895  0.444002        44.4186   47.41405      107.0962   83.38037
 10     0.816007  0.344437        43.40141  87.96642       66.62695  73.88011
 11
```

Figure 7-24. *Using @RAND*

@ROUND

The @ROUND function is used to round a number in internal storage to a specified number of decimal places.

Format

@ROUND(*number to be rounded,place of rounding*)

Arguments

number to be rounded — any value or reference to a value that you want rounded to a specific number of places.

place of rounding — the number of places to the right or left of the decimal point where rounding should occur. A digit of five or higher after the place where 1-2-3 will round the number will cause the number to the left to be increased by one. Using zero for the place of rounding indicates that you want to round to the nearest whole number. Positive numbers indicate rounding to the right of the decimal point, with each higher number moving further to the right. Negative numbers indicate rounding to start at the tens position and move further to the left. For example, Figure 7-25 shows the number 12345.678123 rounded to varying numbers of decimal places in column B, using the formulas in column C.

```
A:C3: (L) '@ROUND($A$3,5)                                            READY

    A           B          C         D       E      F     G
1              Rounded   Formula Used
2   Number     Number    for Rounding
3   12345.678123 12345.67812 @ROUND($A$3,5)
4               12345.6781  @ROUND($A$3,4)
5               12345.678   @ROUND($A$3,3)
6               12345.68    @ROUND($A$3,2)
7               12345.7     @ROUND($A$3,1)
8               12346       @ROUND($A$3,0)
9               12350       @ROUND($A$3,-1)
10              12300       @ROUND($A$3,-2)
11              12000       @ROUND($A$3,-3)
12              10000       @ROUND($A$3,-4)
13
```

Figure 7-25. *Using @ROUND*

Use

1-2-3 will allow you to display numbers in rounded form, if you specify the number of decimal places you wish to see using the Format options (/Worksheet Global Format or /Range Format). However, the full accuracy of the original number, with all its decimal places, is maintained internally. This can cause displayed column totals to seem inaccurate, because the numbers in the column are displayed as rounded while the internal number has greater decimal accuracy. When all this additional decimal accuracy is summed, it can make the total at the bottom of the column disagree with the display of the detail numbers being summed.

The worksheet in Figure 7-26 shows this discrepancy in column E. The figures in column E are a product of column C and column D, but are displayed as Currency with zero decimal places. The column E figures alone suggest that the total should be $7041, not the $7042 that is shown. The difference of 1 is due to the rounding discrepancy. To solve this problem, more than just a product formula is required. The formula will become an argument for the @ROUND function, which will round the product to the nearest whole number (for example, @ROUND(C2*D2,0). This makes the internal product agree with the display, and the sum at the bottom of the column will match the displayed numbers, as you can see in Figure 7-27.

Often a complex worksheet model will require that the @ROUND function be used with many of the formulas in the worksheet. To use it, follow the same procedure as shown in the preceding example, making each formula an argument for the @ROUND function.

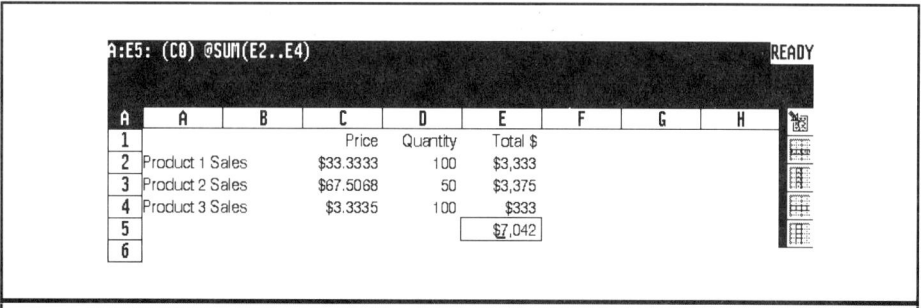

Figure 7-26. *Discrepancy caused by displaying rounded numbers*

@SIN

The @SIN function returns the sine of an angle.

Format

@SIN(*number*)

Arguments

number   a number representing the radians in an angle.

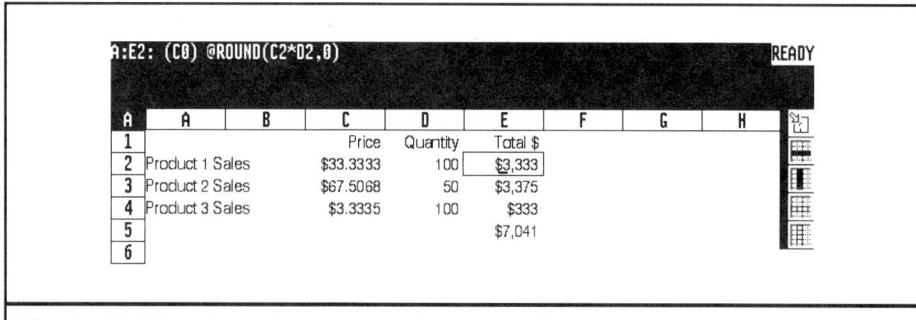

Figure 7-27. *Rounding numbers to prevent discrepancy*

Use

The @SIN function is used when you have the measurement of an angle in radians and want to determine the sine of the angle. You can use this information to help you make other determinations regarding physical aspects of a problem, such as length or other angles. The example that follows provides one potential application.

The diagram in Figure 7-28 shows terrain containing a large swampy area that blocks a road crew from traversing the path from point C to point B. They know that the distance from A to C is 100 meters. If they can determine the distance from B to C, they will be able to use that number in the Pythagorean theorem to determine the distance from A to B. Their entire distance traveled to avoid the swamp would be C to A, then A to B. The angle ABC is 30 degrees.

To calculate the distance from C to B, the crew could use the formula SIN(30)=100/x. Using the @SIN function to determine the sine of 30, @SIN(30*@PI/180) would return .5. The @PI/180 converts 30 degrees to the appropriate number of radians. The distance then is 100/.5, or 200 meters. Using the Pythagorean theorem, $a^2=b^2+c^2$, they get $200^2=100^2+s^2$. This means 40,000 equals 10,000, plus the unknown side squared. The side is thus equal to the square root of 30,000, which they can find with @SQRT(30,000). This function returns 173.2, so the distance from A to B is 173.2 meters.

@SQRT

The @SQRT function will determine the square root of any positive number.

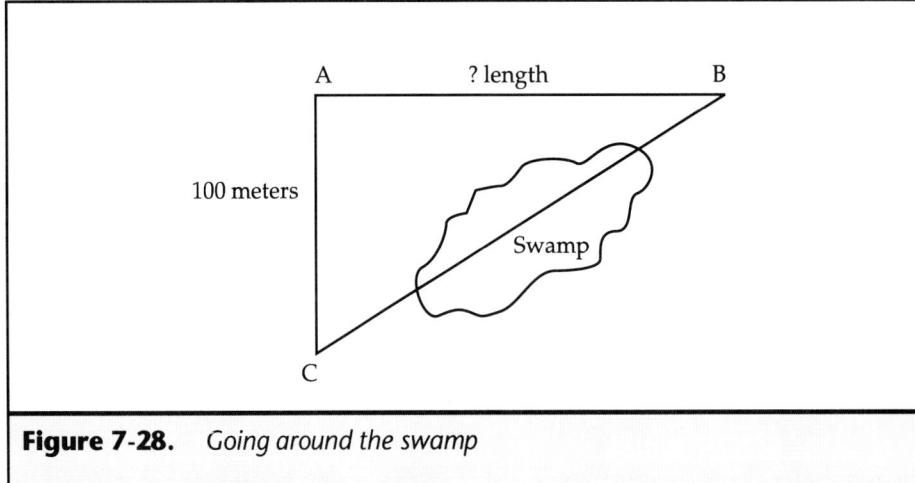

Figure 7-28. *Going around the swamp*

Format

@SQRT(*number*)

Arguments

number any positive integer included in the function, or stored in a cell and referenced with a cell address or range name. If *number* is negative, ERR will be returned.

Use

A number of statistical calculations, the Pythagorean theorem, and economic order quantity all require square root calculations. The following are a few examples of the way the square root function operates.

@SQRT(9) equals 3
@SQRT(64) equals 8
@SQRT(100) equals 10

@TAN

The @TAN function returns the tangent of an angle.

Format

@TAN(*number*)

Arguments

number a number representing the radians in an angle.

Use

The @TAN function returns the tangent, a value useful in solving trigonometric problems. The diagram in Figure 7-29 requires the @TAN function to determine

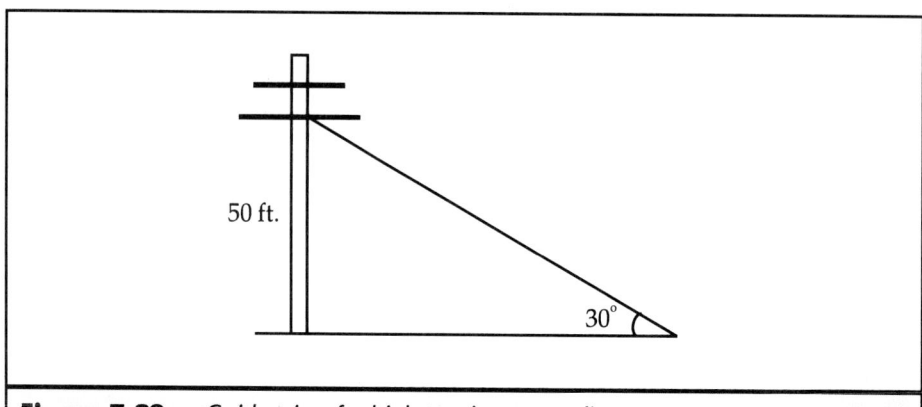

Figure 7-29. Guide wires for high tension power lines

the distance of guide wires for high tension power lines. The electric company has high tension wires at the top of a pole 50 feet high and wants to install guide wires from the top of the pole at a 30-degree angle with the ground. The tangent function can be used to determine the distance away from the high tension wires that the guide wires should be attached. The tangent of 30 must be calculated, and, since the angle was measured in degrees, it must also be converted to radians. The formula thus becomes @TAN(30*@PI/180). The height of 50 feet is divided by the result of .5774 to provide a distance of 87 feet.

Logical Functions

1-2-3's logical functions allow you to build conditional features into your models. These functions return logical (true or false) values as the result of condition tests that they perform. A value of 0 means false, and a value of 1 means true.

Some of the logical functions are used when ERR (error) and NA (not available) appear as a result of a formula. Both of these values are regarded as numeric and can be tested. This is a particularly important feature because of the ability of NA and ERR to ripple through all the formulas on a worksheet. As an example, if NA is used to flag a missing grade for a student, that student's average will be shown as NA, and when statistics for all students are combined, the totals will also take on the value NA. The functions @ISERR, @ISNA, @ISNUMBER, and @ISSTRING allow you to check for ERR and NA values and stop their effect on the remainder of the worksheet cells, by replacing ERR and NA with a value of zero.

Chapter 7: 1-2-3's Built-In Functions

The logical functions frequently use logical operators. For example, @IF(A2<>5,3,6) uses a simple operator, and the logical function @IF(A1=1#AND #B3=7,5,2) uses a complex operator. These operators were explained in Chapter 3, "Entering Data in 1-2-3's Worksheet."

@FALSE

The @FALSE function always returns the logical value 0, permitting you to use it to avoid ambiguity in formulas. @FALSE does not use any arguments.

Use

The @FALSE function is a substitute for the number 0 in formulas. It may seem a lot quicker to type 0 than to type @FALSE, but the function is self-documenting and indicates that you want to set up a logical false condition. As an example, consider @IF(A3=10,"A3 is equal to 10",@FALSE). If A3 is equal to 10, the string "A3 is equal to 10" will be stored in the cell. If A3 is not equal to 10, a 0 will be stored there.

The worksheet in Figure 7-30 shows @FALSE and its counterpart @TRUE used to determine if the number of items ordered equals the number billed. The formula in D3 checks the numbers ordered and billed for equality, and places @TRUE or @FALSE as the value in the cell accordingly. @FALSE displays as 0 and @TRUE as 1. You can then add these 0s and 1s to determine how many discrepancies were in the orders. Use the @COUNT function to get an item count for the number of entries in C3..C6, which is 4. This function is placed in C7 as @COUNT(C3..C6). @SUM is then used to total the 0s and 1s, returning 3, in D7. Lastly, G9 contains a formula that subtracts D7 from C7 (+C7–D7). The value produced is 1, indicating a discrepancy between number ordered and number billed for one product.

@IF

The @IF function permits you to test a logical condition to determine the appropriate value for a cell.

Format

@IF(*condition to be tested,value if true,value if false*)

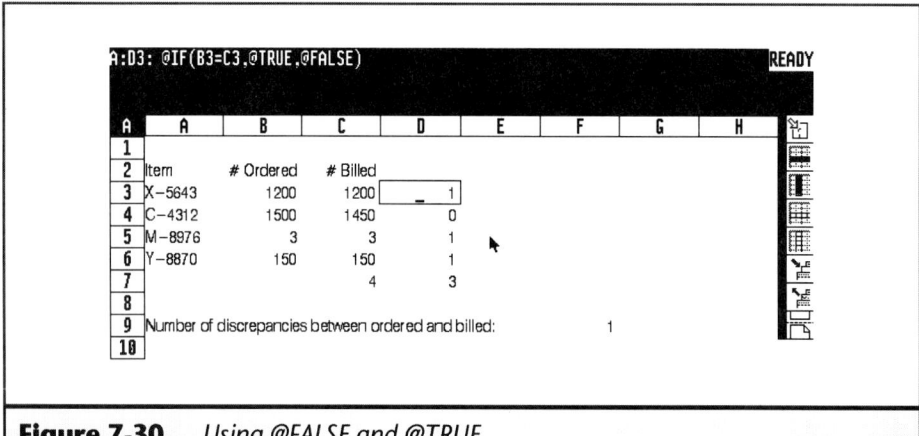

Figure 7-30. *Using @FALSE and @TRUE*

Arguments

condition to be tested any logical expression that can be evaluated as true or false. Examples of expressions are A1="B", A1>=4, D2=H3, and A2+D3<85. The second expression returns a value of true only if A4 contains a value greater than or equal to 4. The logical @IF statement can also work with compound conditions joined by #OR# and #AND#. When this condition is met, the cell containing the @IF takes on the value for true conditions (1); otherwise, it takes on the value for false (0).

value if true the value the cell containing the @IF statement will assume if the condition is true. This can be either a value or a label. When labels are included in the @IF statement, they must be enclosed in double quotation marks. If they are stored in a cell, they can be referenced with a cell address or range name. String formulas are also acceptable as labels. Value entries can be numbers, formulas, or references to cells containing numbers or formulas.

value if false the value the cell containing the @IF statement will assume if the condition is false. All the conditions listed under *value if true* also apply here.

Use

@IF is one of the most powerful built-in functions because it allows you to get around the limitation of having only one entry in a cell. Now you can set up two different values for a cell and determine which one to use, based on other conditions in your worksheet. You can use this function to establish two discount levels, commission structures, payroll deductions, or anything else requiring more than one alternative.

1-2-3 allows you to nest conditions several levels deep, that is, use a second @IF statement for the true and/or false value in the original @IF. As an example, you might want to determine whether a purchase is made by cash or credit and have a code of 1 for cash, assuming that entries without a 1 are credit sales. Once the type of sale is determined, you might want to check the amount of the sale to see if it is over the minimum for a discount. The statement might be coded as

@IF(TYPE=1,@IF(SALE>1000,.05,.02),@IF(SALE>2500,.04,.01))

if TYPE and SALE were named ranges. Regardless of the value for TYPE or SALE, the cell will contain a discount amount, but the amount will depend on the value of both variables. The following chart shows the appropriate discounts.

Type = 1	Discount
Sale > 1000	.05
Sale < = 1000	.02
Sale < = 1000	.02
	.02
Type <> 1	
Sale > 2500	.04
Sale < = 2500	.01

Another example is a calculation of total salary expenses that uses the logical @IF function to determine allowances for FICA/MEDICARE and FUTA taxes. The model is shown in Figure 7-31. The FICA/MEDICARE formula in column D is the first column that puts the @IF function to work. It has a condition that compares the projected salary to a $48,000 FICA cap (that is, the highest amount of salary on which an employer would pay FICA/MEDICARE tax). If the projected salary is less than $48,000, FICA tax will be calculated as the salary times 7.65%. If, however, the salary is equal to or greater than the cap amount, FICA tax will be paid on $48,000 at the rate of 7.65%.

The FUTA calculation, for unemployment tax, follows a similar pattern. The formula in W4 is

@IF(T4<7000,T4*.06,7000*.06)

This states that the FUTA tax will be 6% of salary if the salary is less than $7000, but will be paid on the cap amount of $7000 if the salary exceeds that amount.

@ISERR

The @ISERR function checks for a value of ERR in a cell. It returns 1 if the cell contains an ERR, and 0 if it does not.

Format

@ISERR(*value*)

Arguments

value a value, formula, or reference to a cell value.

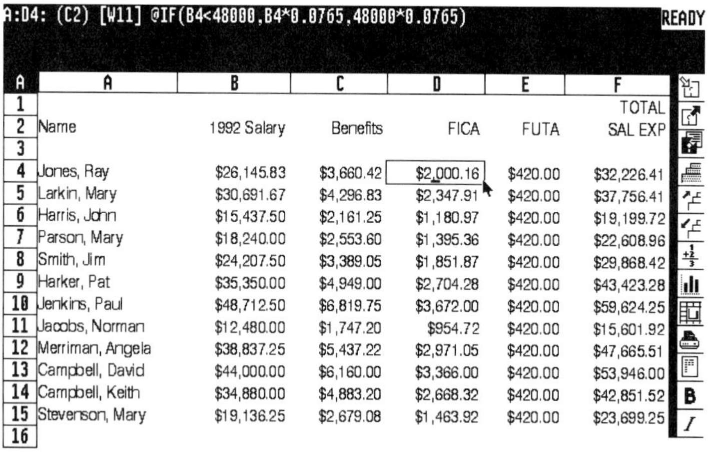
A:D4: (C2) [W11] @IF(B4<48000,B4*0.0765,48000*0.0765) READY

A	A	B	C	D	E	F
1						TOTAL
2	Name	1992 Salary	Benefits	FICA	FUTA	SAL EXP
3						
4	Jones, Ray	$26,145.83	$3,660.42	$2,000.16	$420.00	$32,226.41
5	Larkin, Mary	$30,691.67	$4,296.83	$2,347.91	$420.00	$37,756.41
6	Harris, John	$15,437.50	$2,161.25	$1,180.97	$420.00	$19,199.72
7	Parson, Mary	$18,240.00	$2,553.60	$1,395.36	$420.00	$22,608.96
8	Smith, Jim	$24,207.50	$3,389.05	$1,851.87	$420.00	$29,868.42
9	Harker, Pat	$35,350.00	$4,949.00	$2,704.28	$420.00	$43,423.28
10	Jenkins, Paul	$48,712.50	$6,819.75	$3,672.00	$420.00	$59,624.25
11	Jacobs, Norman	$12,480.00	$1,747.20	$954.72	$420.00	$15,601.92
12	Merriman, Angela	$38,837.25	$5,437.22	$2,971.05	$420.00	$47,665.51
13	Campbell, David	$44,000.00	$6,160.00	$3,366.00	$420.00	$53,946.00
14	Campbell, Keith	$34,880.00	$4,883.20	$2,668.32	$420.00	$42,851.52
15	Stevenson, Mary	$19,136.25	$2,679.08	$1,463.92	$420.00	$23,699.25
16						

Figure 7-31. *Calculating FICA with the logical @IF*

Use

The @ISERR function is most often used in conjunction with the @IF function, to prevent ERR values from "rippling" through a worksheet. The rippling occurs because any formula that references a cell with ERR will have a result of ERR.

The worksheet in Figure 7-32 shows ERR for one of the prices in column A. This ERR entry could have been generated by placing ERR in the cell, or it could be the result of an incorrect formula. When this cell is referenced to supply the unit cost for multiplication, it causes ERR to appear in column C. Again, when the sum is taken in C8, ERR will be the result, since one of the cells in the sum range contains ERR.

To prevent ERR from rippling through the worksheet like this, use the @ISERR function in conjunction with @IF, as shown in column D of the worksheet in Figure 7-32. This allows you to confine ERR to one location.

@ISNA

The @ISNA function allows you to check for a value of NA in a cell. It returns 1 if the cell contains NA, and 0 if it does not.

Format

@ISNA(*value*)

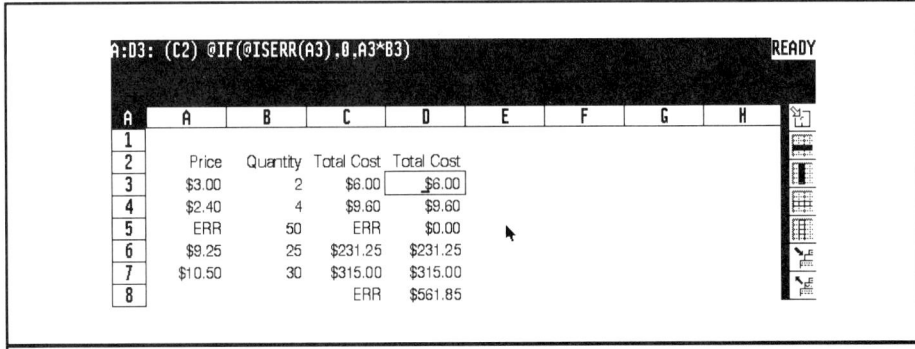

Figure 7-32. *@ISERR preventing ERR from rippling through a worksheet*

Arguments

value normally this is a reference to a cell value, although it may be a formula or a numeric value.

Use

This function is most often used in conjunction with the @IF function in order to prevent NA values from "rippling" through all your worksheet formulas.

In some worksheets @NA is used to represent missing data. Any formula that references a cell with a value of NA will produce a result of NA. If you would like to prevent the NA value from carrying forward in this way, you can use @ISNA to check for the value NA and substitute a zero or some other value, or you can display an error message to show that the value is missing.

Figure 7-33 presents a sample use of the @ISNA function combined with @IF. The @IF function checks the condition @ISNA(D3). If D3 is equal to NA, the condition will be considered true because @ISNA will evaluate as 1. On a true condition, the error message "MISSING UNIT PRICE" will display. If D3 is not equal to NA, column E will contain the result of column C times column D.

@ISNUMBER

The @ISNUMBER function allows you to check for a numeric value in a cell. @ISNUMBER returns 1 if the cell contains a number, and 0 if it does not.

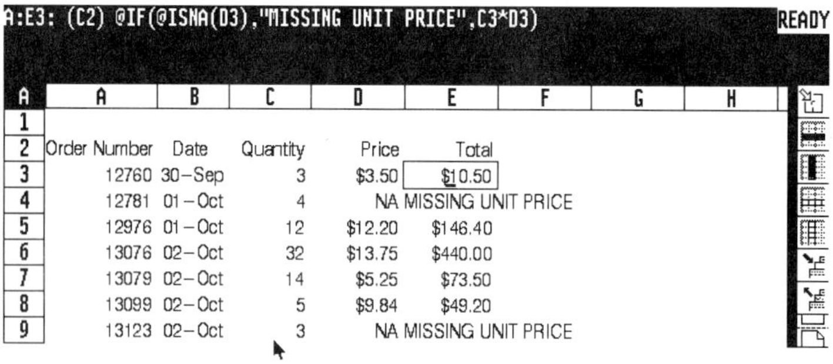

A:E3: (C2) @IF(@ISNA(D3),"MISSING UNIT PRICE",C3*D3) READY

A	A	B	C	D	E	F	G	H
1								
2	Order Number	Date	Quantity	Price	Total			
3	12760	30-Sep	3	$3.50	$10.50			
4	12781	01-Oct	4	NA	MISSING UNIT PRICE			
5	12976	01-Oct	12	$12.20	$146.40			
6	13076	02-Oct	32	$13.75	$440.00			
7	13079	02-Oct	14	$5.25	$73.50			
8	13099	02-Oct	5	$9.84	$49.20			
9	13123	02-Oct	3	NA	MISSING UNIT PRICE			

Figure 7-33. *Checking for missing data*

Format

@ISNUMBER(*value*)

Arguments

value   normally this is a reference to a cell value, although it may be a formula or a numeric value.

Use

This function is most often used in conjunction with the @IF function to check whether data entries are of the proper type. As an example, an entry of @ISNUMBER(56) in a worksheet cell would return 1, whereas @ISNUMBER("56") would return 0. When you use a formula with this function, the function returns a 1 or 0 depending on whether the formula returns a 1 or 0.

As an example, suppose you want to check C7 to ensure that a zip code was entered as a numeric value. You should use the formula @IF(@ISNUMBER(C7)," ","ERROR - Entry must be numeric"). This formula states that if the entry in C7 is numeric, this formula displays a blank string. If the cell contains a non-numeric value, an error message will appear. This allows the operator to quickly find errors.

@ISRANGE

The @ISRANGE function lets you determine if a defined range name exists. The function returns 1 if the current file contains the specified range name assigned to an address, and 0 if it does not, or if the range name is not assigned an address.

Format

@ISRANGE(*string*)

Arguments

string   the name of the range you want to find. It can be entered directly without quotes, or referenced with a cell address that contains a string representing the range name you want to check.

Use

This function is normally combined with @IF, to test for the presence of a range before using it in a calculation or command.

Figure 7-34 shows the first worksheet in a file used to summarize data. If the range the formula will add does not exist, the @IF function displays a message to alert you to the missing range.

@ISSTRING

The @ISSTRING function allows you to check for a string value in a cell. It returns 1 if the cell contains a string, and 0 if it does not.

Format

@ISSTRING(*value*)

Arguments

value   normally this is a reference to a cell value, although it may be a formula or a string.

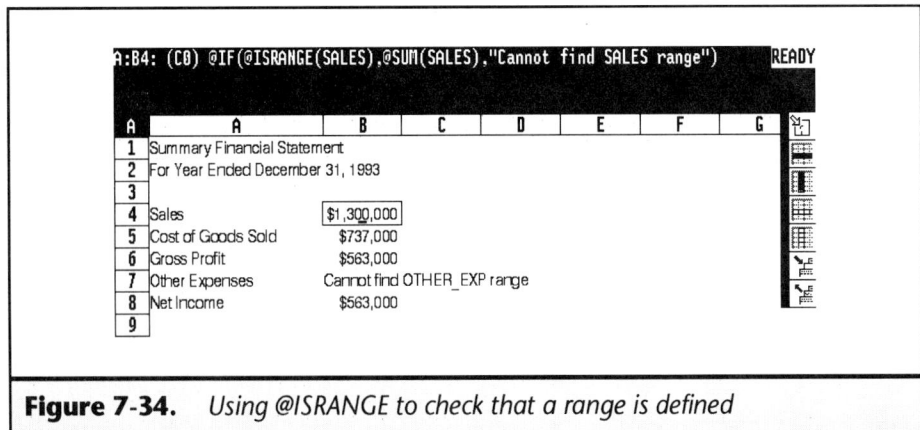

Figure 7-34.   *Using @ISRANGE to check that a range is defined*

Use

This function is normally used in conjunction with @IF, to test for a string entry during data entry. @ISSTRING("John") will return 1, whereas @ISSTRING(56) will return 0. Since ERR and NA are regarded as numeric values, @ISSTRING(ERR) or @ISSTRING(NA) returns 0. You can combine the @IF and @ISSTRING functions, as in

@IF(@ISSTRING(C2)," ","Entry is invalid - it is numeric")

This formula states that if the entry in C2 is a string, the formula returns a blank label. If the cell contains something other than a string value, an error message will appear. This type of error check can allow the operator to glance quickly for error flags, rather than having to study entries individually.

@TRUE

The @TRUE function always returns the logical value 1, making this function useful in avoiding ambiguity in formulas. The format of the function is @TRUE; it does not use any arguments.

Use

The @TRUE function is a substitute for the number 1 in formulas. It may seem a lot quicker to type a 1 than to type @TRUE, but the function is self-documenting and indicates that you want to set up a logical true condition. Here is an example:

@IF(A3=10,@TRUE,"A3 is not equal to 10")

The worksheet in Figure 7-35 shows @TRUE and its counterpart @FALSE used to determine if the number of items ordered equals the number billed. The formula in D3 checks the numbers ordered and billed for equality, and places @TRUE or @FALSE as the value in the cell accordingly. @TRUE displays as 1, @FALSE as 0. You can then add these 0s and 1s to determine how many discrepancies were in the orders. Use the @COUNT function to get an item count for the number of entries in C3..C6, which is 4. Then use @SUM to total the 0s and 1s, returning 3 in D7. Lastly, G9 contains a formula that subtracts D7 from C7 (+C7–D7). The value produced is 1, indicating a discrepancy in one of the orders.

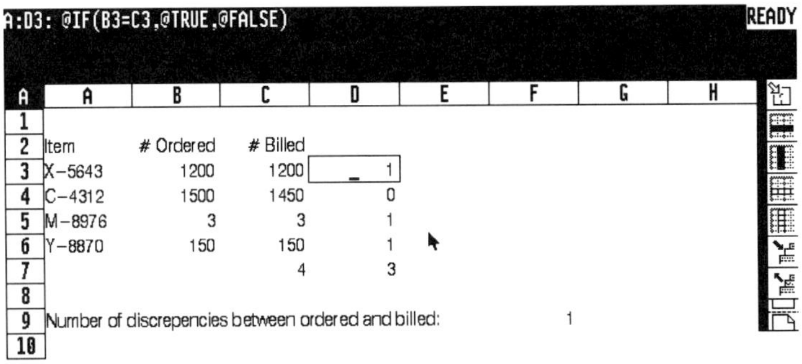

Figure 7-35. *Using @TRUE*

Special Functions

1-2-3's special functions perform advanced calculations that do not fit neatly into any of the other categories. Some of them extend the capabilities of the logical features by providing a table lookup feature, and the ability to choose a value from a list of options. Others can be used to trap errors, create addresses, or determine the number of rows, columns, or sheets in a range of cells. Still others are able to closely examine the contents of worksheet cells or the current 1-2-3 session, providing information about the cell value or other attributes. There is a smorgasbord of sophisticated features that can add power to your models. You will want to examine the functions in this category one by one, gradually adding each of them to your repertoire of 1-2-3 skills.

@@

The @@ function provides an indirect addressing capability that lets you reference the value in a cell pointed to by the cell referenced in the argument of @@.

Format

@@(cell)

Arguments

cell   the address of a cell containing a string value that looks like a cell address, such as R10, Z2, or B3; or a range name, such as SALES or PROFIT; or a string formula that will create a string that looks like an address, such as "A"&"A"&"1"&"3", which creates AA13.

Use

The indirect referencing capabilities of the @@ function permit you to set up various values as key variables, and easily change the one you wish to use. The function also provides a way to store file links in .WK1 format.

The worksheet in Figure 7-36 uses @@ to determine which of the key variable values to use. The model shows the annual sales and commissions for a sales staff. Base commission rate for the company is set at 7%, but if it has a profitable year, the company wants the ability to increase the commission percentage. The @@ function provides an easy way to do this. You will notice that the formula in C2 is @@($A$10)*B2. A10 in turn contains a reference to one of the commissions in E1..E5. The referenced entry must be a string variable in the form of a cell address. It is currently E4, so the commission is calculated using an 11% rate. Changing the commission to another rate merely requires a change to A10.

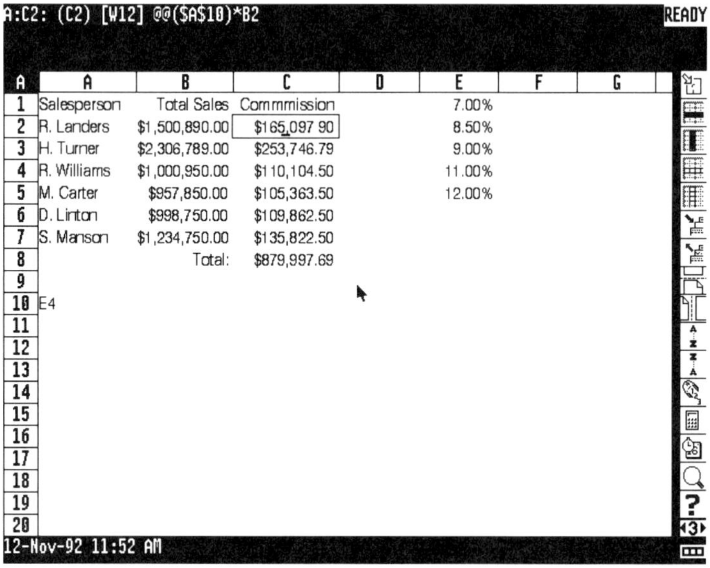

```
A:C2: (C2) [W12] @@($A$10)*B2                                      READY

     A           B            C          D       E       F     G
 1  Salesperson  Total Sales  Commission                7.00%
 2  R. Landers   $1,500,890.00  $165,097.90             8.50%
 3  H. Turner    $2,306,789.00  $253,746.79             9.00%
 4  R. Williams  $1,000,950.00  $110,104.50            11.00%
 5  M. Carter      $957,850.00  $105,363.50            12.00%
 6  D. Linton      $998,750.00  $109,862.50
 7  S. Manson    $1,234,750.00  $135,822.50
 8                     Total:   $879,997.69
 9
10  E4
11
12
...
20
12-Nov-92 11:52 AM
```

Figure 7-36.   *Using @@ function to select commission rate*

Figure 7-37. Worksheet after changing @@ function's argument

You can see in the worksheet in Figure 7-37 that when the entry in A10 is changed to E2, all the commissions are recalculated. Note that a lowercase *e* can be used to reference the cell address.

TIP: The @@ function may require F9 (CALC). 1-2-3 will return a 0 from @@ if you use the function to refer to a location that contains a formula. Pressing F9 (CALC) eliminates the problem by forcing 1-2-3 to recalculate the worksheet.

@CELL

The @CELL function allows you to examine characteristics of any worksheet cell, including the format, content, address, and other detail settings.

Format

@CELL(*attribute string,range*)

Arguments

attribute string   a character string corresponding to one of the attributes the @CELL function can check, or a reference to a cell containing one. If the characters are included in the function, they must be enclosed in double quotation marks. Acceptable *attribute strings* and the values they return are in the table that follows.

range   a single- or multiple-cell range, such as A3..A3 or A2..D10. If you enter a single-cell address, 1-2-3 converts it to a range address. If the range refers to multiple cells, only the upper left cell will be used.

Attribute String	Result
address	the address of the current cell; for example, $K$3
color	a 1 if the cell is formatted to display negative numbers in a different color, or a 0 otherwise
col	a number between 1 and 256, representing the column number
contents	the contents of the cell
coord	the cell address that includes the worksheet letter; for example, $A:$K$3
filename	the name and path of the cell's worksheet file
format	the current format of the cell. Choose from: A for Automatic C0-C15 for Currency with 0 to 15 decimal places D1 for DD-MMM-YY D2 for DD-MMM D3 for MMM-YY D4 for MM/DD/YY, DD/MM/YY, DD.MM.YY, or YY-MM-DD D5 for MM/DD, DD/MM, DD.MM, or MM-DD D6 for HH:MM:SS AM/PM D7 for HH:MM AM/PM D8 for HH:MM:SS, HH.MM.SS, HH,MM,SS, or HHhMMmSSs (all 24-hour) D9 for HH:MM, HH.MM, HH,MM, or HHhMMm (all 24-hour) F0-F15 for Fixed with 0 to 15 decimal places

format (cont.)	G for General H for Hidden L for Label format P0-P15 for Percent with 0 to 15 decimal places T for Text S0-S15 for Scientific with 0 to 15 decimal places Blank if the cell is empty ,0-,15 for Comma with 0 to 15 decimal places + for +/- format ( ) for Parentheses format - for Color format
prefix	label prefix for the cell. The label prefix ^ will appear for centered entries, ' for left justified entries, " for right justified entries, \ for repeating labels, ¦ for non-printing label, and blank for an empty or numeric cell.
protect	Protection status of the cell, with 1 representing Protected and 0 representing Unprotected
row	a number between 1 and 8192 representing the row number
sheet	a number between 1 and 256 representing the worksheet letter
type	the type of data in the cell. The value types are b for blank, v for numeric, and l for label.
width	a number between 1 and 240 representing the current cell width

Use

The @CELL function is primarily used in macros, though you may use it any time you wish to examine the contents of a cell closely. It can be combined with the @IF function to test for certain situations and take appropriate actions.

Figure 7-38 provides a look at many of the @CELL options. The main entry for examination is in A1. @CELL functions are stored in column C and are shown again in column E as formulas so you can compare the entry and the results. The formula in C1 reads @CELL("contents",A1..A1) and returns the contents of 123.45, the exact number entered without the addition of formatting characters. The entry in A11 allows you to check the prefix of a label entry. C11 contains the formula @CELL("prefix",A11..A11) and returns a^ , indicating center justification for the entry.

@CELLPOINTER

The @CELLPOINTER function allows you to examine attributes of the cell where the cell pointer is located. If you move the cell pointer and recalculate, new results will be computed.

Format

@CELLPOINTER(*attribute string*)

Arguments

attribute string   a character string corresponding to one of the attributes the @CELLPOINTER can check, or a reference to a cell containing one. If the characters are included in the function, they must be enclosed in double quotation marks. Acceptable *attribute strings* and the values they return are the same as listed in the tables for @CELL.

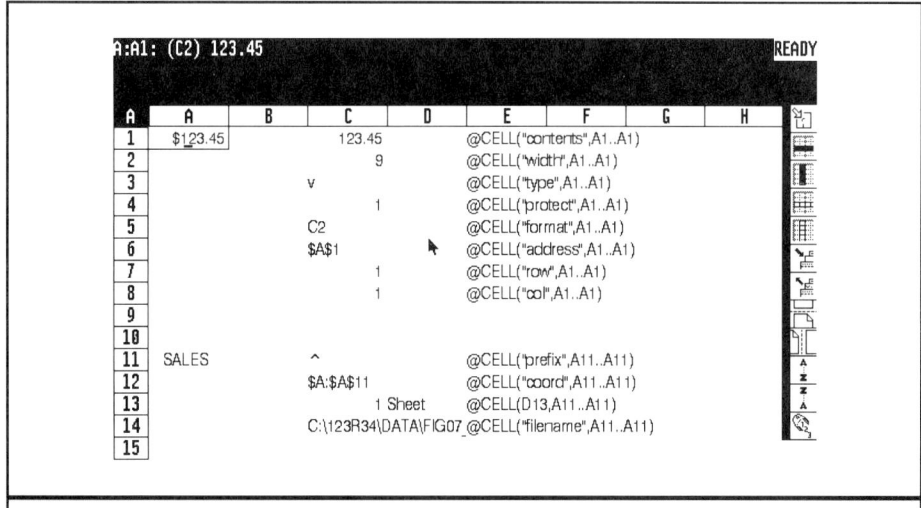

Figure 7-38. *Using @CELL for a close-up look at a cell*

Use

The @CELLPOINTER function is primarily used in macros, though you may use it any time you wish to examine the contents of a cell closely. It can be combined with the @IF function to test for certain situations and take appropriate actions.

Figure 7-39 provides a look at most of the @CELLPOINTER options. Since the cell pointer is located in A1, the results of @CELLPOINTER provide information about A1. If you were to move the cell pointer to a new location and recalculate the worksheet with F9 (CALC) or make another entry, you would get updated results. The @CELLPOINTER functions are stored in column C and are shown again in column E as formulas, so you can compare the entry and the results. For example, the formula in C1 reads @CELLPOINTER ("address") and returns $A$1, the address of the current cell.

@CHOOSE

The @CHOOSE function allows you to select a suitable value from a list of values.

Format

@CHOOSE(*number,list*)

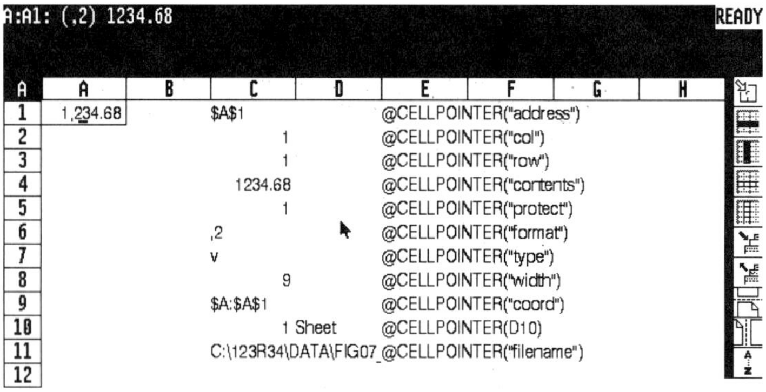

Figure 7-39. *Examining the current cell with @CELLPOINTER*

Arguments

number   the position number in the list of the value that you wish to use. The first value in the list has a position number of 0. This argument can be a number, formula, or a reference to either. *Number* must be smaller than the number of values in the list. If *number* is not a whole number, 1-2-3 uses only the whole number portion for the argument.

list   a group of numeric or string values that are not limited in number, except that the @CHOOSE function must occupy no more than 512 characters. 1-2-3 lets you mix string and numeric values in one *list*.

Use

The @CHOOSE function is ideal when you have a set of codes in your data that are consecutive, and limited in number. Since every number used to find a number in the list must have a value in the list, the number of values in the list must range from 0 to the largest number used to find a value in the list. For example, if you had codes of 1, 20, 300, and 750, @CHOOSE could not be used; you would have to turn to @VLOOKUP or @HLOOKUP. With consecutive and limited codes, however, @CHOOSE can provide a quick solution for supplying varying values.

Here are a few examples of the @CHOOSE function and the values it returns:

@CHOOSE(0,"Bill","Sally","Tom") equals Bill
@CHOOSE(1,"Bill","Sally","Tom") equals Sally
@CHOOSE(2,B10,A3,C2/4,A3*B4) equals the value C2/4
@CHOOSE(INTEREST,.09,.15,.08,.11) equals .15 when INTEREST equals 1.

The worksheet in Figure 7-40 shows the @CHOOSE function being used to determine a shipping cost from a warehouse location. Warehouse 1 adds $5.00 shipping charges, warehouse 2 adds $10.00, warehouse 3 adds $15.00, warehouse 4 adds $3.00, and warehouse 5 adds $20.00.

The Warehouse codes are in column A. The Item numbers are in column B. The Quantity and Unit Prices are in columns C and D respectively. The calculation for shipping cost requires the @CHOOSE formula. A dummy value must be used for warehouse 0, since all @CHOOSE lists start with 0. A $0 shipping charge will therefore be included in the list. The function is then recorded in E2 as @CHOOSE(A2,0,5,10,15,3,20). The formula is copied down column E and the column is formatted as Currency. Total Cost in the model,

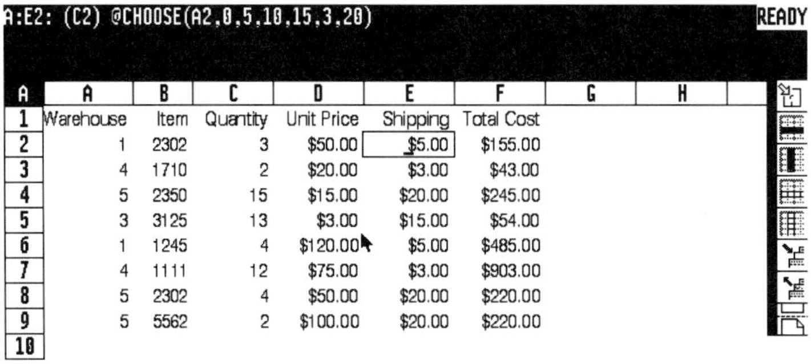

```
A:E2: (C2) @CHOOSE(A2,0,5,10,15,3,20)                              READY

     A         B      C         D         E         F       G    H
1  Warehouse  Item  Quantity  Unit Price Shipping Total Cost
2      1      2302     3       $50.00     $5.00    $155.00
3      4      1710     2       $20.00     $3.00     $43.00
4      5      2350    15       $15.00    $20.00    $245.00
5      3      3125    13        $3.00    $15.00     $54.00
6      1      1245     4      $120.00     $5.00    $485.00
7      4      1111    12       $75.00     $3.00    $903.00
8      5      2302     4       $50.00    $20.00    $220.00
9      5      5562     2      $100.00    $20.00    $220.00
10
```

Figure 7-40. *Choosing the correct value*

shown in Column F, is simply the entry in column C times the entry in column D plus the Shipping cost from column E.

@COLS

The @COLS function is used to determine the number of columns within a specified range.

Format

@COLS(*range*)

Arguments

range a cell range in the format A2..F7 or A:A2..G:F7, or a range name.

Use

This function is used primarily with range names. For example, you may have a range of cells containing employee information across the columns. By knowing how many columns there are in the range, you can tell how many employees are listed. A few more examples may help you understand this function.

@COLS(A2..H3) equals 8
@COLS(EMPLOYEES) equals 26 when EMPLOYEES refers to the range A3..Z10

@COORD

This function creates a cell address from the function arguments you provide.

Format

@COORD(*worksheet,column,row,absolute*)

Arguments

worksheet	a number ranging from 1 to 256 representing the worksheet number. The number 1 corresponds to worksheet A, and the number 256 corresponds to worksheet IV.
column	a number ranging from 1 to 256 representing the column number. The number 1 represents column A, and the number 256 corresponds to column IV.
row	a number between 1 and 8192 representing the row number.
absolute	a number between 1 and 8 indicating whether the resulting cell address creates an absolute, mixed, or relative cell reference. The values have the following meanings:

Value	Type of Cell Reference	Example
1	Absolute	$B:$K$3
2	Mixed (worksheet and row absolute)	$B:K$3
3	Mixed (worksheet and column absolute)	$B:$K3
4	Mixed (worksheet absolute)	$B:K3
5	Mixed (column and row absolute)	B:$K$3
6	Mixed (row absolute)	B:K$3
7	Mixed (column absolute)	B:$K3
8	Relative	B:K3

Use

This function is primarily used in macros and as the argument for other functions, although you may use it at any time to create an address. It is often used as the argument for the @@ function.

Figure 7-41 shows detail expense entries for expense codes 1001 and 1002 in sheets B and C. Other sheets contain entries for the company's remaining expense codes. Sheet A allows you to enter the month, year, and expense type for which you want information. In A:B6, the @COORD function uses these values to create a cell address that references the data tables contained in the other worksheets. The @@ function uses this address and returns the value in the cell.

@ERR

The @ERR function is used to return the value ERR in a cell and any other cells that reference the cell. The format of the function is @ERR; it has no arguments.

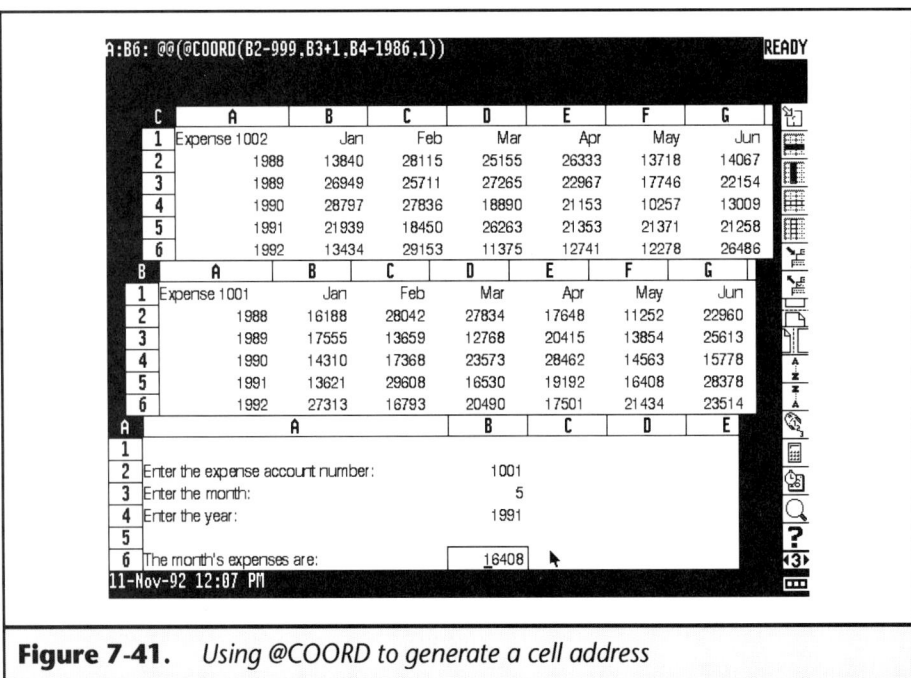

Figure 7-41. *Using @COORD to generate a cell address*

Use

This function is used to flag error conditions. For example, if you combine it with @IF, you can use it to verify that two totals are equal. If the two values are not equal, the cell containing the formula can be flagged with ERR. Such a formula might look like this:

@IF(A1=D2,0,@ERR)

Another situation where @ERR is useful is in verification of data input. An appropriate formula might be @IF(A6<500,0,@ERR). In this formula ERR will appear if A6 is greater than or equal to 500. Any cells that reference the cell containing @ERR will also be given a value of ERR.

NOTE: 1-2-3 generates ERR on its own when errors are made in the entry of, or in one of the arithmetic operations in a formula. The effect of both ERR conditions is the same, even though they are generated in different ways.

@HLOOKUP

The @HLOOKUP function allows you to search a table for an appropriate value to use in your worksheet. The distinction between this function and the @VLOOKUP function is that @HLOOKUP stores its table across the worksheet in a horizontal orientation, whereas @VLOOKUP uses a vertical orientation for table values.

Format

@HLOOKUP(*code to be looked up,table location,offset*)

Arguments

code to be looked up — the entry in your worksheet that will be compared against the table entry. When numeric values are used, 1-2-3 looks for the largest value in the table that is not greater than the *code*. When string values are used, the search is for an exact match.

table location a range containing one or more rows on a worksheet. A table is composed of a set of *codes* and one or more sets of return values in adjacent cells. It can be placed in any area of your worksheet. While the table does not have to be on the current worksheet, the table is limited to a single worksheet. The top row in the range will contain the *codes*, and the subsequent rows will contain return values.

offset a number that determines which row should be consulted for the return value when a matching code is found. The first row beneath the row of codes has an *offset* of 1, the second an *offset* of 2, and so on. Negative *offset* numbers will cause ERR to be returned, as will *offset* numbers that exceed the range established in the table location. If desired, you may use an *offset* of 0 to return the comparison code.

The process 1-2-3 uses for determining the value to be returned is as follows:

- The specified code is compared against the values in the top row of the table.
- The largest value in the top row of the table that is not greater than the code is considered a match. If the code to be looked up in the table is 3.5, the value adjacent to 3 or less is returned.
- Offset is used to determine which value in the row that contains the matching table cell will be returned. If offset is 0, the matching code value itself is returned. If offset is 1, the value below the matching value is returned, and so on.
- A code with a value less than the first value in the top row of the table will return ERR.
- A code value greater than the last value in the first row of the table is considered to match the last value.
- If you are using label entries for codes and have label entries in the top row of the table, only exact matches will return table values.

Building a table with numeric codes requires that they be in ascending sequence. They are not required to be consecutive numbers, however; nor do the gaps between numbers have to be of a consistent size. With label entries, the codes do not have to be in any special sequence within the table.

Use

Tables are a powerful feature, useful for everything from tax withholding amounts to shipping rates. They are especially valuable because they allow you to look at potential changes in discount or commission structures, with only a few changes to table values and no alterations in your worksheet formulas.

Figure 7-42 shows a table located in cells C3..F7. The following codes will return the values shown from the table, assuming the offsets listed were provided.

Code	Offset	Return Value
4.5	1	22
11	2	2
15	3	77
0	1	11
99	1	44
4.5	0	4.5
11	1	22
15	2	3
102	1	44
−1	1	ERR

Figure 7-43 provides an example of a purchase discount model for a wholesale store that has a minimum $100 order amount. The model relies on @HLOOKUP to compute the purchase discount. The table is placed in B11..F14, with the comparison codes in B11..F11. The discount rates depend on both the amount of the purchase and the purchase type. Purchase type 1 corresponds to

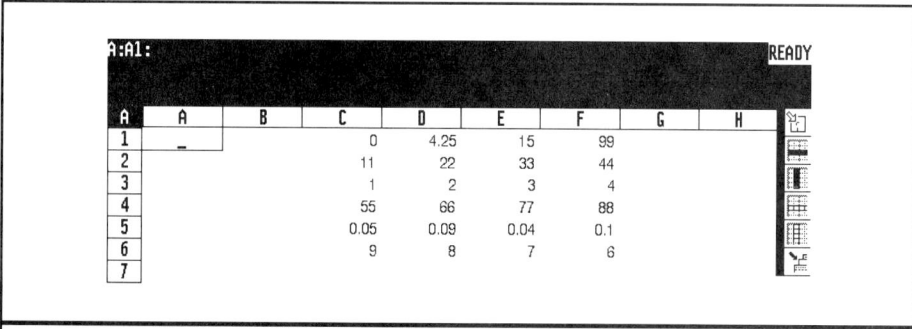

Figure 7-42. *Sample horizontal table*

```
A:D3: (C2) @HLOOKUP(C3,$A:B$11..$F$14,B3)*C3                    READY
```

	A	B	C	D	E	F	G	H
1	Customer	Purchase	Purchase		Net			
2	ID Number	Type	Amount	Discount	Due			
3	23-789	3	$500.00	$15.00	$515.00			
4	12-987	2	$100.00	$3.00	$103.00			
5	56-435	2	$175.00	$5.25	$180.25			
6	54-345	3	$980.00	$29.40	$1,009.40			
7	23-567	1	$1,200.00	$96.00	$1,296.00			
8	12-333	1	$6,000.00	$540.00	$6,540.00			
9	21-999	3	$10,000.00	$500.00	$10,500.00			
10								
11			100	500	1000	5000	10000	
12		1	5.00%	7.00%	8.00%	9.00%	10.00%	
13		2	3.00%	4.00%	5.00%	5.00%	6.00%	
14		3	3.00%	3.00%	3.00%	5.00%	5.00%	
15								
16								

Figure 7-43. *Horizontal table lookup*

cash and carry, which requires the lowest overhead and provides the highest discount structure. Purchase type 2 is cash, but requires delivery and uses a lower discount structure. The lowest discount structure of all is for credit sales. The purchase type is used as the offset code to access the proper row of the table. The comparison code in the table is chosen based on the Purchase Amount in column C.

The formula required to find the first discount is @HLOOKUP (C3,$B$11..$F$14,B3)*C3. This formula looks up the code in C3 in a table located in B11 through F14. The $s indicate absolute addresses for the table range, and thus permit the formula to be copied down the worksheet for calculation of the remaining discounts. The offset for the table is B3, the purchase type. The value returned is multiplied by the purchase amount to compute the discount. For this first entry, this is 3% times $500, or $15. The Net Due is obtained by subtracting the discount (D3) from the purchase amount (C3). The remaining entries are obtained by copying from D3..E3 to D4..D9.

TIP: Compare the code against the 0 column of the table when you need an exact match. Remember that 1-2-3 returns a matching value for numeric codes even if there is not an exact match. So, if you only want to use the value returned by @HLOOKUP or @VLOOKUP when the match is exact, compare it against the values with an offset of 0. Your formula might look like @IF(B7=@HLOOKUP(B7,$TABLE,0), @HLOOKUP(B7,$TABLE,1),"No exact match").

@INDEX

The @INDEX function allows you to retrieve a value from a table of codes by specifying the row, column, and worksheet number of the table you wish to access.

Format

@INDEX(*table location,column offset,row offset*[*,worksheet offset*])

Arguments

table location	the location of the table of codes to be accessed by this function. Unlike the lookup functions, @INDEX does not use a comparison value to access the codes. You must specify a row and column address to obtain the code of your choice.
column offset	the number of the column in the table from which you want to obtain a code. The leftmost column in the table range is column 0, with the numbers increasing by 1 for each column to the right that you move. The *column offset* that you specify must be within the valid range established for the table. If the number you supply is not a whole number, the decimal portion will be truncated.
row offset	the number of the row in the table from which you wish to obtain a code. The upper row in the table is row 0. The *row offset* specified must be in the relevant range for the table. If it is not a whole number, the decimal portion of the number will be truncated.
worksheet offset	the number of the worksheet in the table from which you want to obtain a code. If the *worksheet offset* is not provided, the function uses the first worksheet in the table. The first worksheet in the table range is worksheet 0, with the numbers

worksheet offset (cont.)   increasing by 1 for each worksheet the table uses. The worksheet that you specify must be within the valid range established for the table. If the number you supply is not a whole number, the decimal portion will be truncated.

Use

The @INDEX function can be used whenever your data values are used to access the proper row and column of a table. This type of function works well for quoting insurance rates, shipping charges, and any other calculation where you can specify the exact code you need from the table.

With Release 3, @INDEX can use tables from multiple worksheets. Figure 7-44 shows a formula that uses the @INDEX function to determine the shipping and insurance costs. Each shipping zone has its own table. For each item, the @INDEX function selects the worksheet it needs based on the shipping Zone, the

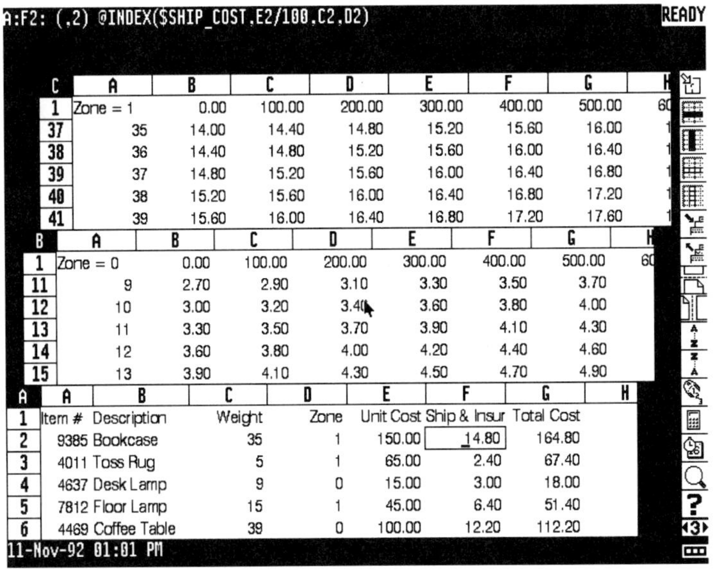

Figure 7-44.   *@INDEX using a multiple worksheet table*

Weight, and the Unit Cost. Since the Unit Cost is divided by 100, the function truncates the noninteger portion. The function returns the number at the intersection of these three values.

@INFO

The @INFO function returns information about 1-2-3 and the operating system. Many of the options return information that is also listed by the /Worksheet Status command.

Format

@INFO(*attribute string*)

Arguments

attribute string   a character string corresponding to one of the attributes the @INFO function can check, or a reference to a cell containing one of these strings. If the characters are included in the function, they must be enclosed in double quotation marks. Acceptable *attribute strings* and the values they return are as follows:

Attribute String	Result
directory	current directory
memavail	computer memory available
mode	current mode. The mode indicators are
	0 WAIT
	1 READY
	2 LABEL
	3 MENU
	4 VALUE
	5 POINT
	6 EDIT
	7 ERROR
	8 FIND

Attribute String	Result	
	9	FILES
	10	HELP
	11	STAT
	12	NAMES
	99	Any mode not listed above
numfile	current number of active files	
origin	cell address of the cell in the upper left corner in the worksheet containing the cell pointer	
osreturncode	value returned by the most recent /System command or {SYSTEM} macro command	
osversion	current operating system version	
recalc	current method of recalculation (automatic or manual)	
release	current release of 1-2-3	
system	current operating system name	
totmem	computer memory, including the memory used by 1-2-3 and the worksheets, and the remaining memory available	

Use

This function is primarily used in macros, although you may use it any time you wish to learn about the system. It can be combined with the @IF function or {IF} macro command to test a situation, such as insufficient memory before performing a task. You can respond to the condition test with an appropriate action. 1-2-3 updates this function each time you press F9 (CALC) or make another entry.

Figure 7-45 provides a look at the @INFO options. Column A contains the @INFO command using different attribute strings. The formulas are repeated to the right, and formatted as text.

@NA

This function causes NA, meaning "not available," to appear in the cell where this function is entered, as well as in all cells that reference it. The format for the function is @NA; it has no arguments.

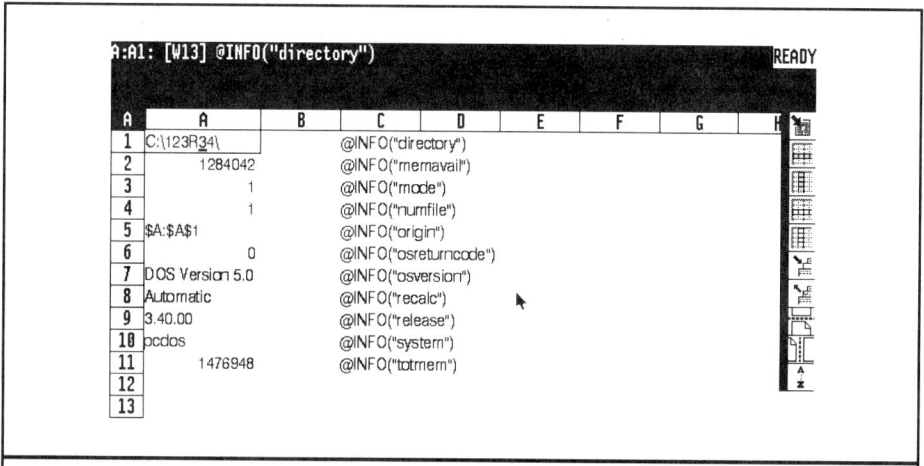

Figure 7-45. *@INFO providing information about the current 1-2-3 session*

Use

The @NA function is used when data is not available for entry in a cell. It serves as a flag for data that must be entered before correct model results can be computed. NA in one worksheet cell can ripple through a worksheet, since every cell that references a cell containing NA will also contain NA.

The NA function would be useful for an instructor recording student grades. All students who missed an exam would have NA, rather than a score, recorded. Figure 7-46 shows the effect on the grade point average for students with missing grades. At the end of the semester, the instructor can change all grades that are still NA to 0.

NOTE: The label NA entered in a cell is not equivalent to entering @NA, which produces a numeric rather than a label entry.

@ROWS

The @ROWS function is used to determine the number of rows within a specified range.

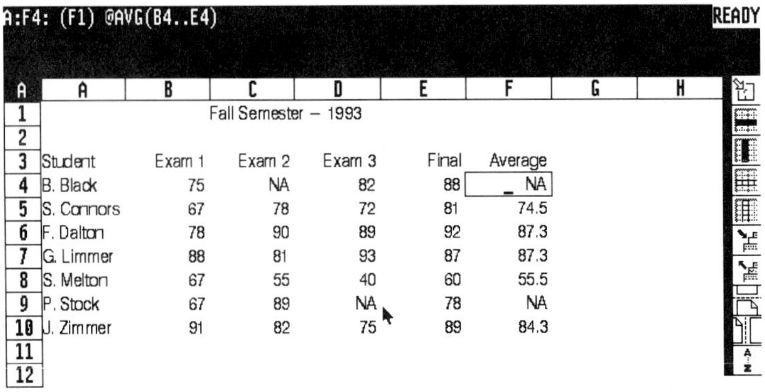

Figure 7-46. *The impact of NA on formulas*

Format

@ROWS(*range*)

Arguments

range   a cell range in the format A2..F7, or a range name

Use

This function is used primarily with range names. For example, you may have a range of cells containing order information with the orders listed down the worksheet. If all the order information were included in one range named ORDERS, you could obtain the number of orders with the function @ROWS(ORDERS). A few other examples may help to show how this function works.

@ROWS(A2..H3) equals 2
@ROWS(EMPLOYEES) equals 8 when EMPLOYEES refers to
the range A3..Z10

@SHEETS

The @SHEETS function is used to determine the number of worksheets within a specified range.

Format

@SHEETS(*range*)

Arguments

range   a cell range in the format A:A2..G:F7, or a range name.

Use

This function is used primarily with range names. For example, you may have a file containing a named range spanning a number of worksheets, with each worksheet containing the financial information for a division. After checking the number of worksheets in the named range, you know if you have the worksheets for all of the divisions. As you add worksheets between the beginning and end of a range, 1-2-3 automatically expands and contracts the range size. These examples may help you understand this function:

@SHEETS(A:A1..L:K72) equals 12
@SHEETS(DIVISION) equals 20 when the range called DIVISION uses 20 worksheets.

@VLOOKUP

The @VLOOKUP function allows you to search a table for an appropriate value to use in your worksheet. The distinction between this function and the @HLOOKUP function is that @VLOOKUP stores its table down the worksheet in a vertical orientation, whereas @HLOOKUP uses a horizontal orientation for table values.

Format

@VLOOKUP(*code to be looked up,table location,offset*)

Arguments

code to be looked up the entry in your worksheet that will be compared against the table entry. When numeric values are used, 1-2-3 looks for the largest value in the table that is not greater than the *code*. When string values are used, the search is for an exact match.

table location a range containing one or more columns on the worksheet. A table is composed of a set of *codes* and one or more sets of return values in adjacent cells. It can be placed in any area of your worksheet. While the table does not have to be on the current worksheet, the table is limited to a single worksheet. The left column in the range will contain the *codes,* and the subsequent columns will contain return values.

offset a number that determines which column should be used for the return value when a matching code is found. The first column to the left of the column of *codes* has an *offset* of 1, the second an *offset* of 2, and so on. Negative *offset* numbers will cause ERR to be returned, as will *offset* numbers that exceed the range established in the table location. If desired, you may use an *offset* of 0 to return the comparison code from the first column of the table.

Figure 7-47 shows a table in A2..D8. The codes are in A2..A8, and the return values are in B2..D8. The process 1-2-3 uses for determining the value to be returned is as follows:

- The specified code is compared against the values in the left column of the table.

- The largest value in the left column of the table that is not greater than the code is considered a match. If the code to be looked up in the table is 3.5, the value adjacent to the 3 is returned.

```
A:A1: 1                                                          READY
      A       B       C       D       E       F       G       H
 1     1      5      0.05     12
 2     3     10      0.07      5
 3     5     15      0.09     21
 4    15     20      0.11     14
 5    20     25      0.12     13
 6    35     30      0.13     21
 7    50     35      0.15     17
 8
```

Figure 7-47. *Sample vertical table*

- Offset is used to determine which value in the column that contains the matching table cell will be returned. If offset is 0, the matching code value itself is returned. If offset is 1, the value to the right of the matching value is returned, and so on.

- A code with a value less than the first value in the left column of the table will return ERR.

- A code value greater than the last value in the first column of the table will be considered to match the last value.

- If you are using label entries for codes and have label entries in the left column of the table, only exact matches will return table values.

Building a table with numeric codes requires that they be in ascending sequence. They are not required to be consecutive numbers, however; nor do the gaps between numbers have to be of a consistent size. With label entries, the codes do not have to be in any special sequence within the table.

Use

Tables are a powerful feature, useful for everything from tax withholding amounts to shipping rates. They are especially valuable because they allow you to look at potential changes in discount or commission structures, with only a few changes to table values and no alterations in your worksheet formulas.

The @VLOOKUP and @HLOOKUP functions cannot access multiple worksheets for the lookup tables. However, you can bypass this obstacle by combining the @CHOOSE command with the @VLOOKUP and @HLOOKUP commands.

Figure 7-48 shows three worksheets. The first one contains employee payroll information, including basic tax information. Column F contains a formula which uses @VLOOKUP to find the Gross Pay in a table, and @CHOOSE to select which sheet in the table to use. Federal Tax in G3 is computed with this formula:

@VLOOKUP(F3,@CHOOSE(D3—1,<<TAXES.WK3>>SINGLE,<<TAXES.WK3>>MARRIED,E3+1).

The table is a three-dimensional table that is stored in the file TAXES.WK3. Each worksheet contains a table for a different filing status, and each column in each worksheet contains the federal tax for a different number of dependents. Each row in each worksheet starts with a pay level that the @VLOOKUP function uses to select a row in the table. @VLOOKUP can use only a single worksheet table. Therefore, you must use a function like @IF or @CHOOSE to select the table in the taxes worksheet 1-2-3 uses.

When 1-2-3 computes the results for the @VLOOKUP function, it uses the table that @CHOOSE selected based on the employee's filing status. Each table is

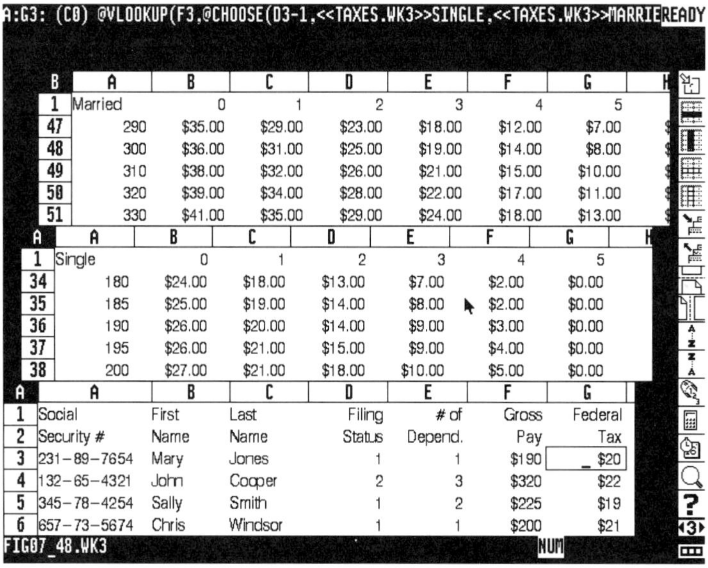

Figure 7-48. @VLOOKUP using @CHOOSE to select the worksheet containing the right table

named. Since these tables are in the TAXES.WK3 file, the range names are preceded by <<TAXES.WK3>>. Once the @VLOOKUP function knows which table to use, it looks for the highest value in the first column of the table (column A) that does not exceed the gross pay in column F. Then the function moves to the column chosen by the number of dependents. The intersection of the table, column, and row contains a number, which the function returns. As an example, for Mary Jones, the first employee, the @CHOOSE function embedded in the @VLOOKUP function in G3 uses the value in column D (filing status) to determine that @VLOOKUP will use the table stored in the named range SINGLE in the TAXES.WK3 file. Next, 1-2-3 searches column A in SINGLE for the highest entry that does not exceed 190. When 1-2-3 finds 190 in row 36, the @VLOOKUP function returns the value in the third column of the table since the offset is the number of dependents plus one. This process is similar to the @INDEX function, except 1-2-3 searches for the gross pay in the table's first vertical column rather than including a row number in the function.

Statistical Functions

1-2-3's statistical functions perform their magic on lists of values. Frequently these lists are a contiguous range of cells on the worksheet. They can also be a series of individual values or a combination of range and individual values. Blank ranges can be included within the list, but all the values in the blank range will count as 0s. When a range has multiple cells, 1-2-3 will ignore cells containing blanks. If a single blank cell is used in the list, 1-2-3 will assign a 0 to the cell.

The majority of the statistical functions work only with numeric values. @COUNT is the exception, since it counts the number of nonblank cells in a list and will also accept string values.

@AVG

The @AVG function finds the average of a list of values.

Format

@AVG(*list*)

Arguments

list any set of numeric values. They can be individual cell references, individual values, or a range of cells. You can also combine the options in one *list*. Examples of this function are @AVG(A2..A9,D4,L2) and @AVG(D4..D15). Note that the components in the *list* are separated by commas.

Use

You can use the @AVG function and the worksheet in Figure 7-49 to calculate the average bid amount received from vendors. The vendor bids are shown in B4..B11, and the formula is entered in B13 as @AVG(B4..B11). The result is 5837.25.

@COUNT

The @COUNT function determines the number of nonblank entries in a list. A cell that contains only a label prefix will still count as a nonblank, even though the cell displays as a blank.

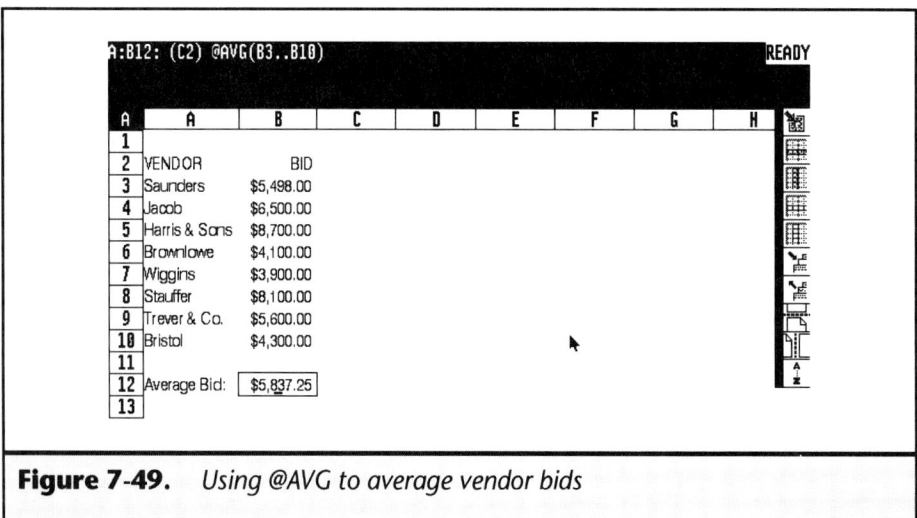

Figure 7-49. *Using @AVG to average vendor bids*

Format

@COUNT(*list*)

Arguments

list   any set of values. They can be individual cell references or a range of cells, although individual cell references may distort your results and should be avoided. A single cell reference increases the count by one, even if the cell is blank. You can also combine the two options in one *list*. Examples are @COUNT(A2..A9,D4,L2) and @COUNT(D4..D15). Note that the components in the *list* are separated by commas.

Use

The @COUNT function does not require numeric data. It will count all the nonblank entries in a list, regardless of whether they are values or characters. You can use the worksheet in Figure 7-49 to count the number of bids using the formula @COUNT(B4..B11) and returning a result of 8.

@MAX

The @MAX function searches a list of values and displays the largest value in the list.

Format

@MAX(*list*)

Arguments

list   any set of numeric values. They can be individual cell references, individual values, or a range of cells. You can also combine the options in one *list*. Examples of this function are the lists @MAX(A2..A9,D4,L2) and @MAX(D4..D15). Note that the components in the *list* are separated by commas.

Use

You can use the @MAX function and the worksheet in Figure 7-49 to obtain the highest bid in a group of vendor bids. Your formula would be @MAX(B4..B11) and would return 8700.

@MIN

The @MIN function searches a list of values and displays the smallest value in the list.

Format

@MIN(*list*)

Arguments

list any set of numeric values. They can be individual cell references, individual values, or a range of cells. You can also combine the options in one *list*. Examples are the formulas @MIN(A2..A9,D4,L2) and @MIN(D4..D15). Note that the components in the *list* are separated by commas.

Use

You can use the @MIN function and the worksheet in Figure 7-49 to find the lowest bid in a group of vendor bids. The bids are located in B4..B11, and the minimum is found with the function @MIN(B4..B11). The result is 3900. If you entered additional vendor bids, they would be included in the calculation.

@STD

The @STD function is used to determine the population standard deviation of a set of values, or how much variation there is from the average of the values. It is the square root of the variance.

Format

@STD(*list*)

Arguments

list any set of numeric values. They can be individual cell references or a range of cells. You can also combine the two in one list. Examples are @STD(A2..A9,15,L2) and @STD (D4..D15). Note that the components in the list are separated by commas. Blank cells within the list will be ignored, but label entries will be assigned a value of 0. Including both label entries and single cell references in this list can cause a problem, because @STD uses a count of the entries as part of its calculation.

Use

The @STD function determines the standard deviation when you have access to the values for the entire population—that is, all the values for the entire group you are studying. If you are measuring the deviation in the weight of packages filled in a plant, for example, population would refer to all packages filled, not just a sample. If you are working with only a sample of the population, use the @STDS function.

The purpose of the standard deviation calculation is to determine the amount of variation between individual values and the mean. Suppose, for example, that you determine the average age of your employees to be 40. This could mean that half of your employees are 39 and the other half 41, or it could mean that you have employees whose ages range from 18 to 65. The latter case shows a greater standard deviation because of the greater variance from the mean.

The @STD function is biased, since it uses a count as part of its calculations. Specifically, it uses the following formula:

$$\sqrt{\frac{\sum (x_i - \text{AVG})^2}{n}}$$

where x_i is the ith item in the list and n is the number of items in the list.

As an example, suppose that the Commemorative Bronze Company has made 50 replicas of antique bronze cash registers and wants to determine the standard deviation in the weight of these products. The worksheet in Figure 7-50 shows the list of weights and the formula for the standard deviation.

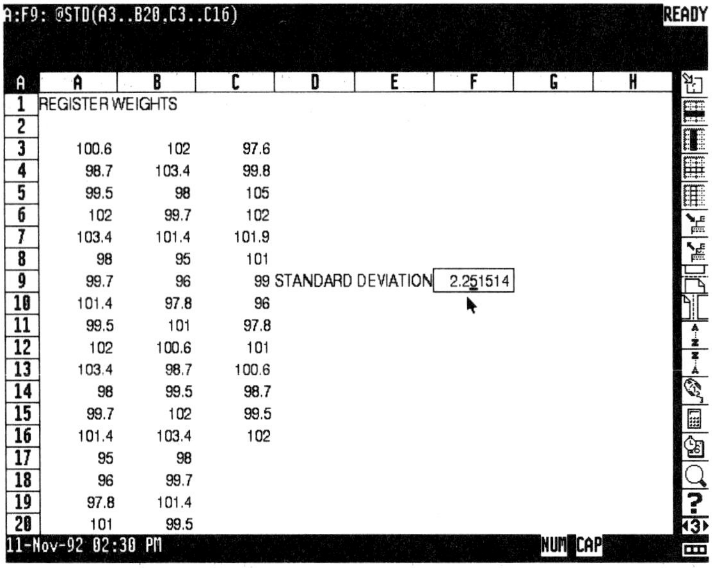

Figure 7-50. Using @STD to measure the fluctuations in register weights

@STDS

The @STDS function determines the sample standard deviation of a set of values, for a sample of a population. If the entire population is included in the values, the @STD function is used.

Format

@STDS(*list*)

Arguments

list   any set of numeric values. They can be individual cell references or a range of cells. You can also combine the two in one list. Examples are @STDS(A2..A9,15,L2) and @STDS(D4..D15). Note that the components in the list are separated by commas. Blank cells within the list will be ignored, but label entries will be assigned a value of 0. Including both label entries and single cell references in this list can cause a problem, because @STDS uses a count of the entries as part of the calculation.

Use

The @STDS function determines the standard deviation when you have access to the values for a sample of a population. For example, if you are measuring the customer responses to a survey, you are using a sample population unless all of your customers respond to the survey.

The purpose of the standard deviation calculation is to determine the amount of variation between individual values and the mean. For example, suppose the companies in a product survey have average sales of $500,000. If the standard deviation is $50,000, you know that most of your customers have approximately the same sales volume. If the standard deviation is $400,000, you know that your customer base includes companies with a wide range of sales volumes. You can use this information to target your advertising to the appropriate companies.

The @STDS function uses the $n-1$, or unbiased, method. The function performs this formula:

$$\sqrt{\frac{\Sigma (x_i - AVG)^2}{(n-1)}}$$

where x_i is the ith item in the list and n is the number of items in the list.

The difference between the results of the @STD and @STDS functions increases as the number of measurements decreases—making it critical to select the proper function. As an example, suppose you wanted to know the sample standard deviation for the cash registers with the weights in A3..C3. The formula would be @STDS(A3..C3) and the result would be 2.247962. Using @STD with the same data would return 1.835453.

@SUM

The @SUM function totals a list of numeric values.

Format

@SUM(*list*)

Arguments

list   any set of numeric values. They can be individual cell references, individual values, or a range of cells. You can also combine the options in one list. Examples are @SUM(A2..A9,D4,L2) and @SUM(D4..D15). Note that the components in the list are separated by commas.

Use

The @SUM function is used to obtain a total wherever you have more than two values to add together. It is much more efficient than using addition on each individual component. For example, you can enter **@SUM(B4..B11)** in place of +B4+B5+B6+B7+B8+B9+B10+B11. The other advantage offered by @SUM is that when you insert a row or column into the middle of the @SUM range, the range will automatically be adjusted for the extra entry without changing the formula.

One of the Release 3 features is combining multiple worksheets into one file. The statistical functions—particularly the @SUM function—will frequently use this new feature, because worksheets can now combine figures from multiple worksheets and files. Figure 7-51 shows a worksheet that sums the yearly total from each of the monthly worksheets. To create a yearly report, another worksheet is added before January's worksheet, and the formula @SUM(B5..M5) is copied from B5 to all of the cells in worksheet A that contain numeric values. If you want to combine worksheets from files instead, include the filename before the field names in the summation formula.

TIP: Make it easy to expand your @SUM range reference. Include a cell with a label entry like '---------- at the top and bottom of a column of label entries, and reference these cells as the first and last range entries. This allows you to insert a row at the top or bottom of the range without affecting the accuracy of the computation.

Release 3.4 provides two icons that apply the @SUM function; one that can quickly sum both rows and columns, and a second which can sum across worksheets. The first icon looks like this:

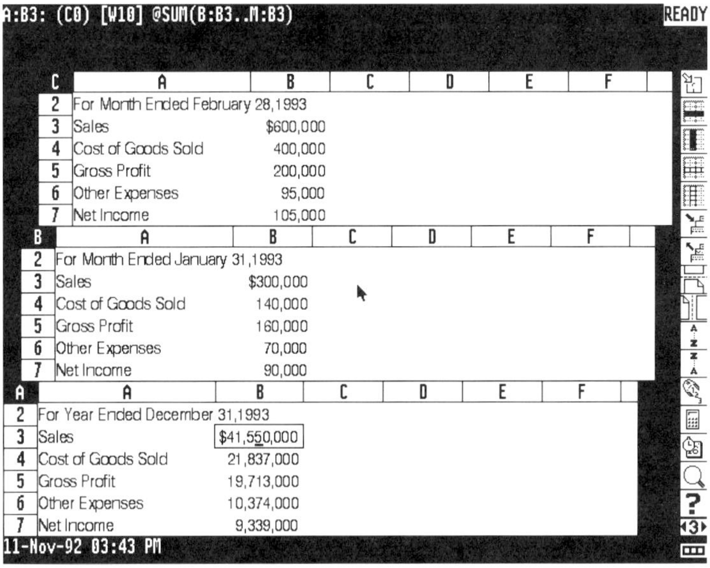

Figure 7-51. *Using @SUM to add across worksheets*

Getting used to the way this SmartSum icon works requires a little practice. Using it seems a bit tricky at first because it is so flexible in that it can sum the highlighted cells or cells adjacent to the highlighted cells. Just as when you enter @SUM yourself, the cells containing the result are not automatically formatted to match the detail entries.

The SmartSum icon can total the adjacent values in a single row or column. To get it to create a total, select the cell where you want this total to appear. It must be in the same row or column as the detail, but it is possible to leave a blank row or column for separation. For example, if you wanted to total the entries in column C of Figure 7-47, you could select cell C9 or C10 depending on whether or not you wanted a blank space between the last detail entry and the total for the column. If you wanted to total all four columns in Figure 7-47, you would select A9..D9 or A10..D10 to accomplish this in one step. Use the same techniques to select rows to sum.

To total both rows and columns in one step, you can select a range which includes the blank cells where you want the totals stored. You can also include an extra blank row or column to separate the total from the detail. 1-2-3 always stores the sum in the last column or row of your selection. In Figure 7-47, this would require you to select A1..E9 before selecting the SmartSum icon.

The second SmartSum icon, shown below, sums across worksheets and is somewhat more limited than the first SmartIcon. The second SmartSum icon enters an @SUM function in the selected cell, which sums the value filled cells directly beneath the selected cell. For example, this SmartIcon could be used to create the sum entries in Figure 7-51. To sum all sales for the year, place the cell pointer in B3 in worksheet A, and then select this SmartSum icon.

TIP: There is a trap to be aware of when using these SmartIcons options: you cannot successfully include blank cells in the selected range. 1-2-3 totals only the entries in the cells after the blank row or column. For example, if you were to separate June and July sales figures with a blank worksheet, the sum in Figure 7-52 would only include figures from January to June.

@SUMPRODUCT

The @SUMPRODUCT function multiplies the values in corresponding cells and returns their total.

Format

@SUMPRODUCT(*list*)

Arguments

list any set of numeric values contained in specified ranges or range names. Each range in the list must contain the same number of cells. An example is @SUMPRODUCT(C3..C8,E3..E8). Note that the components are separated by commas. The range must have the same orientation. For example, you cannot use A1..C1 with A2..A4 in this function.

Use

@SUMPRODUCT is used to compute a cross product of numbers. An example of computing a cross product is shown in Figure 7-52, in which the products on an order form are listed. The total for the entire order is computed after the last item. @SUMPRODUCT multiplies each item quantity by its price and adds it to the shipping cost. The shipping cost is the quantity times the weight times the shipping cost per pound. Once the cost for each item is computed, @SUMPRODUCT adds the totals for all of the items for the order. Using the @SUMPRODUCT function reduces the number of formulas the worksheet requires in order to compute the total cost. This function is also used to double-check worksheets that perform the same computations using multiplication and the @SUM function. The formula in C6 is equivalent to +C3*D3+C3*F3+C4*D4+C4*F4.

@VAR

The @VAR function computes the population variance of values in a population, or the amount the individual population values vary from the average. The variance is equal to the standard deviation squared.

Format

@VAR(*list*)

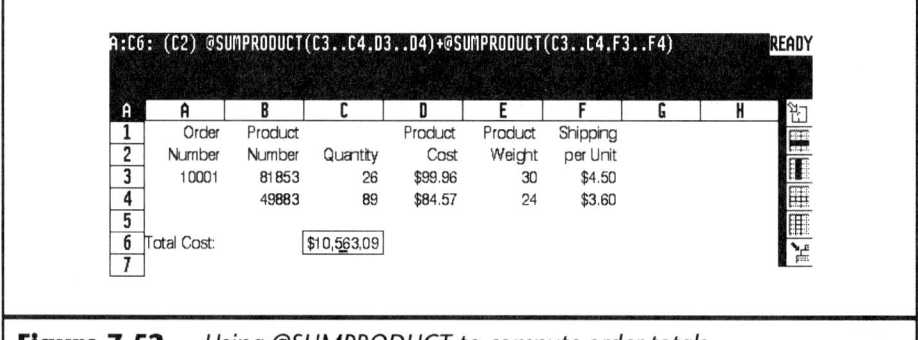

Figure 7-52.   Using @SUMPRODUCT to compute order totals

Arguments

list   any set of numeric values. They can be individual cell references or a range of cells. You can also combine the two in one list. Examples are @VAR(A2..A9,15,L2) and @VAR(D4..D15). Note that the components in the list are separated by commas. Blank cells within the list will be ignored, but label entries will be assigned a value of 0. Including both label entries and single cell references in this list can cause a problem, because @VAR uses a count of the entries as part of its calculation.

Use

The @VAR function determines the variance when you have access to the values for the entire population—that is, all the values for the entire group you are studying. If you are measuring the deviation in the weight of packages filled in a plant, for example, population would refer to all packages filled, not just a sample. If you are working with only a sample of the population, use the @VARS function.

The purpose of the variance calculation is to determine the amount of variation between individual values and the mean. Suppose, for example, that you determine the average age of your employees to be 40. This could mean that half of your employees are 39 and the other half 41, or it could mean that the ages range from 18 to 65. The latter case shows a greater variance because of the greater dispersion from the mean.

The @VAR function is biased, since it uses a count as part of its calculation. Specifically, it uses the following formula:

$$\frac{\sum (x_i - \text{AVG})^2}{n}$$

where x_i is the ith item in the list and n is the number of items in the list. The number of items is critical in determining whether to use @VAR or @VARS. When n is equal to the total population, use @VAR; when n represents a sample of the population, use @VARS.

As an example, suppose a worksheet like Figure 7-53 contains product survey information. Each of the questions has an answer between 1 and 5. For each of the questions, the worksheet shows the average and the variance. For the first question, the variance is small, which means that most of the responses are close to the average of 3.27. For the second question, the variance is high; the responses fluctuate more around the average than the first question responses.

@VARS

The @VARS function determines the sample variance of a set of values, for a sample of a population. If the values include the entire population, use the @VAR function.

Format

@VARS(*list*)

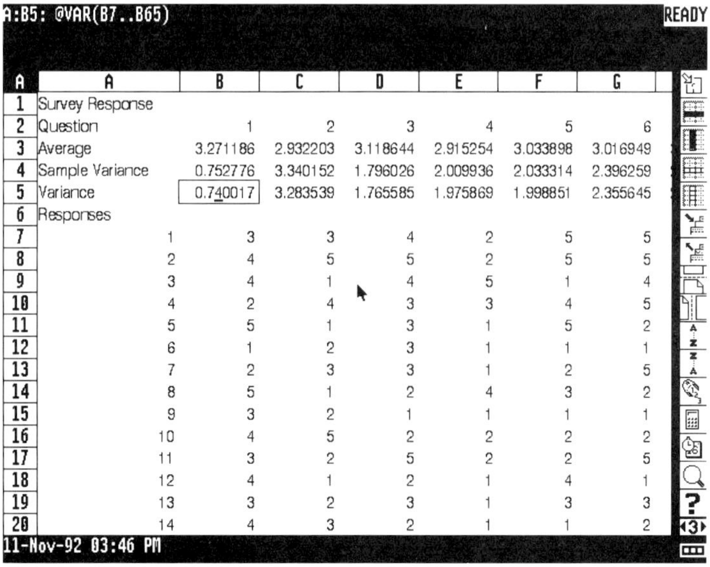

A	A	B	C	D	E	F	G
1	Survey Response						
2	Question	1	2	3	4	5	6
3	Average	3.271186	2.932203	3.118644	2.915254	3.033898	3.016949
4	Sample Variance	0.752776	3.340152	1.796026	2.009936	2.033314	2.396259
5	Variance	0.740017	3.283539	1.765585	1.975869	1.998851	2.355645
6	Responses						
7	1	3	3	4	2	5	5
8	2	4	5	5	2	5	5
9	3	4	1	4	5	1	4
10	4	2	4	3	3	4	5
11	5	5	1	3	1	5	2
12	6	1	2	3	1	1	1
13	7	2	3	3	1	2	5
14	8	5	1	2	4	3	2
15	9	3	2	1	1	1	1
16	10	4	5	2	2	2	2
17	11	3	2	5	2	2	5
18	12	4	1	2	1	4	1
19	13	3	2	3	1	3	3
20	14	4	3	2	1	1	2

Figure 7-53. *Using @VARS to measure the variance in survey responses*

Arguments

list any set of numeric values. They can be individual cell references or a range of cells. You can also combine the two in one list. Examples of this are @VARS(A2..A9,15,L2) and @VARS(D4..D15). Note that the components in the list are separated by commas. Blank cells within the list will be ignored, but label entries will be assigned a value of 0. Including both label entries and single cell references in this list can cause a problem, because @VARS uses a count of the entries as part of the calculation.

Use

The @VARS function determines the variance when you have access to the values for a sample of a population. For example, if you are measuring the customer responses to a survey, you are using a sample population unless all of your customers respond to the survey.

The purpose of the variance calculation is to determine the amount of variation between individual values and the mean. For example, suppose the companies in a product survey have average sales of $500,000. A variance of 2.5 billion indicates that more of your customers have approximately the same sales volume than if the variance is 160 billion. The variance values accentuate the variances among a set of values. You can use this information to target your advertising to the appropriate companies.

The @VARS function uses the $n-1$, or unbiased, method. The function performs this formula:

$$\frac{\sum (x_i - AVG)^2}{(n-1)}$$

where x_i is the ith item in the list and n is the number of items in the list.

Like the @STD and @STDS functions, the difference between the results of the @VAR and @VARS functions increases as the number of measurements decreases. As an example, suppose a worksheet like Figure 7-53 contains product survey information. Each of the questions have an answer between 1 and 5. For each of the questions, the worksheet shows the average and the variance. For the first question, the variance is small, which means that most of the responses are close to the median of 3.27. For the second question, the variance is high; the responses fluctuate more around the average than the first question responses. The difference between the variances in rows 4 and 5 is the effect of measuring a sample of the population versus measuring all of the population.

String Functions

String functions provide a variety of character manipulation formulas that give you flexibility in rearranging text entries. You can work with an entire entry and change its order, or you can use just a piece of a cell entry.

1-2-3's string functions often work with the individual characters in a text string. The numbering system that 1-2-3 uses for the characters in a string may not be what you expect. The character at the far left of a string is regarded as character 0, not character 1. The numbering proceeds with 1, 2, and so on, moving to the right in the character string. Understanding these positions within a string is very important, since you will want to be sure you are working with the right characters. String position numbers can range from 0 through 511, since a 512-character string is the largest that 1-2-3 can work with.

String position numbers must always be expressed as positive integers. A negative integer causes 1-2-3 to return ERR. Using a number with a decimal causes 1-2-3 to drop the decimal and use only the whole number portion of the value. No rounding occurs; for example, 1-2-3 truncates a value of 5.6 to 5 when it is used as a position number in a string. The following shows the positions for entries within a label.

```
T h i s   i s   a   s  t  r  i  n  g
0 1 2 3 4 5 6 7 8 9 |  |  |  |  |  |
                    10 11 12 13 14 15
```

It is also important to note that the label indicator that begins a string is not assigned a position number. An empty or null string has a length of 0 positions. A cell with a null string contains no entry except a label indicator. It is not the same as a blank cell without a label indicator.

When you use string values as arguments in a string function, you must enclose them in double quotation marks. These same entries referenced by a cell address will not require quotation marks, however. For example, if you want to use the character string "This is a string" in the @RIGHT string function to return the last 6 characters on the right, and the entry is stored in D10, you could use @RIGHT(D10,6); but if you put the string itself in the function, it would have to be written as @RIGHT("This is a string", 6).

Some string functions will produce numeric results equating to a position in a string, while others will produce a string value. You will want to become familiar with the workings of string functions before you indiscriminately combine the results of two string functions. Many of the examples in this section will combine several string functions, however, since this is the way string functions are most commonly used.

@CHAR

The @CHAR function is used to return a character that corresponds to a Lotus Multibyte Character Set (LMBCS).

Format

@CHAR(*code*)

Arguments

code any numeric value from 1 to 6143. Decimal fractions will be truncated; only the whole number portion of the entry will be used. Numbers less than 1 or greater than 4095 will return ERR.

Use

The @CHAR function converts an LMBCS code to a displayable and printable character. LMBCS codes above 127 produce foreign currency symbols, accent marks, and other special characters. If the character represented by the code number you specify cannot be displayed on your monitor, a blank or a character resembling the desired character will be substituted. Codes below 32 are returned as the characters for LMBCS codes 257 through 287. Codes above 511 cannot be printed or displayed; 1-2-3 displays these characters as a shaded rectangle. Here are a few examples:

@CHAR(40) equals (
@CHAR(49) equals 1

The primary use for this function is to compose characters from within a macro or a string formula.

@CLEAN

The @CLEAN function removes characters from a string that have values of less than 32. These include some special characters that you can import into the worksheet with /File Import.

Format

@CLEAN(*string*)

String is a string in quotes, or a cell or range address, or a name that contains a string.

Use

The following example shows the original strings and the strings this function returns:

@CLEAN("☺ This is ● text") equals This is text

@CODE

The @CODE function returns the Lotus Multibyte Character Set (LMBCS) code number of the first character in the function argument.

Format

@CODE(*string*)

Arguments

string   any character sequence up to 512 characters. If the characters are included in the function, they must be enclosed in double quotation marks. They can also be stored in a cell and referenced with a cell address or range name. Numeric characters can be used as long as they are preceded by a label prefix. This function uses only the first character in the string.

Use

This function finds its primary application in macros working with composed characters. The purpose of the function is to convert characters to their LMBCS code. Characters using the Wysiwyg font Xsymbols 12 point will return the LMBCS code of the character the symbol displays in the other fonts. A few examples of @CODE are as follows:

@CODE("$") equals 36
@CODE("V") equals 86
@CODE("@") equals 64

NOTE: Uppercase and lowercase characters have different codes. For example, an uppercase A *is code 65, but a lowercase* a *is code 97.*

@EXACT

The @EXACT function allows you to determine whether two string values are exactly equal.

Format

@EXACT(*string1,string2*)

Arguments

string1 any character sequence that does not exceed 512 characters. If the string is included in the function, the total length of the formula cannot exceed 512 characters, so the string will be restricted to a size that fits within this limitation. If used, the string must also be enclosed in double quotation marks.

string2 any character sequence that does not exceed 512 characters. If the string is placed in the function, the total length of the formula cannot exceed 512 characters, so the string will be restricted to a size that fits within this limitation. If used, the string must also be enclosed in double quotation marks.

Use

The @EXACT function returns 1 when the two strings match exactly, and 0 when they do not. Everything about the two strings must be the same, including blank spaces and capitalization, or 0 will be returned. Although this function can be used by itself, it is normally used with condition tests (that is, with @IF).

Several examples of @EXACT are

@EXACT("Mary Brown","MARY BROWN") equals 0
@EXACT("2144","2144") equals 1
@EXACT(2144,"2144") equals ERR, since string1 is a numeric value
@EXACT(A10,"MARY BROWN") equals 1 if A10 contains MARY BROWN

NOTE: Use @IF and the equal operator (=) if you do not want to consider case difference. For example, @IF("Tom Jones"="tom jones","True", "False") will return True, since the case difference is not considered.

@FIND

The @FIND function permits you to search a character string to find out if a substring (search string) appears within it. If the search string is found, the function returns the starting location of this string.

Format

@FIND(*search string,entire string,starting location*)

Arguments

search string   a character sequence or a reference to a cell containing one. When the characters are included in the function, they must be enclosed in quotation marks. The maximum length of the

search string (cont.)	search string must be less than or equal to the entire string to be searched. Since @FIND is case sensitive, the search string must exactly match a portion of the entire string.
entire string	a character sequence or a reference to a cell containing one. When the characters are included in the function, they must be enclosed in quotation marks. The maximum length of this string is 512 characters.
starting location	the position in the entire string where you wish to begin your search. Remember that the leftmost character in the string is character 0. The maximum starting location can be one less than the number of characters in the entire string.

Use

The @FIND function is used whenever you wish to locate a string within a string. It can be used to identify the location of the blank space between a first and last name, for example. This information, when combined with other string functions, lets you reverse the name entry so that the last name appears first in the cell. ERR is returned when your starting location number is negative or greater than the last position of the entire string, or when the search string is not found.

Several examples of @FIND are as follows:

@FIND("-","ABF-6785",0) equals 3
@FIND("-","213-46-2389",4) equals 6
@FIND("-","ABF-6785",8) equals ERR

@LEFT

The @LEFT function allows you to extract a specified number of characters from the left side of a string.

Format

@LEFT(*string,number of characters to extract*)

Arguments

string
a sequence of characters included in the function, either by enclosing them in double quotation marks or by a reference to a cell address or range name containing the characters.

number of characters to extract
a number representing the characters to be extracted from the string. If you want to extract the first three characters, for example, this number would be 3.

Use

The @LEFT function lets you extract one or many characters from a string. It can be used alone or in combination with other string functions. Some examples are

@LEFT("Lotus 1-2-3",5) equals Lotus
@LEFT("12:30:59",4) equals 12:3
@LEFT("   ABC COMPANY",7) equals ABC preceded by four leading spaces
@LEFT("John Smith",@FIND(" ","John Smith",0)) equals John

@LENGTH

The @LENGTH function returns the number of characters in a string.

Format

@LENGTH(*string*)

Arguments

string
a group of characters that can be included in the function (if they are enclosed in double quotation marks), or placed in a cell and referenced. You can also use a string formula as the string. Numeric entries are not allowed and will return ERR.

Use

This function can be used to determine the length of an entry you wish to manipulate, to verify input data, or to determine the length of a line. This function is frequently used in combination with other string functions such as @MID, @RIGHT, @LEFT, and @FIND when restructuring label entries. The following examples should clarify the results produced by @LENGTH:

Function	Length
@LENGTH("sales")	5
@LENGTH("profit "&"and loss")	15
@LENGTH(A2) where A2 contains abc	3

@LOWER

The @LOWER function converts strings to lowercase.

Format

@LOWER(*string*)

Arguments

string   a group of characters that can be in any case, such as upper-, lower-, or mixed upper- and lowercase. The characters can be included in the function if they are enclosed in double quotation marks, or they can be placed in a cell and referenced. You can also use a string formula as the *string*. Numeric entries are not allowed and will return ERR.

Use

This function is valuable when data from several sources must be combined and data entry was not done in a consistent manner. @LOWER is one of the functions that permit you to change the appearance of data without reentering it. You can use it to place all data in lowercase format. Figure 7-54 shows several examples of using the @LOWER function (in column C).

Chapter 7: 1-2-3's Built-In Functions   419

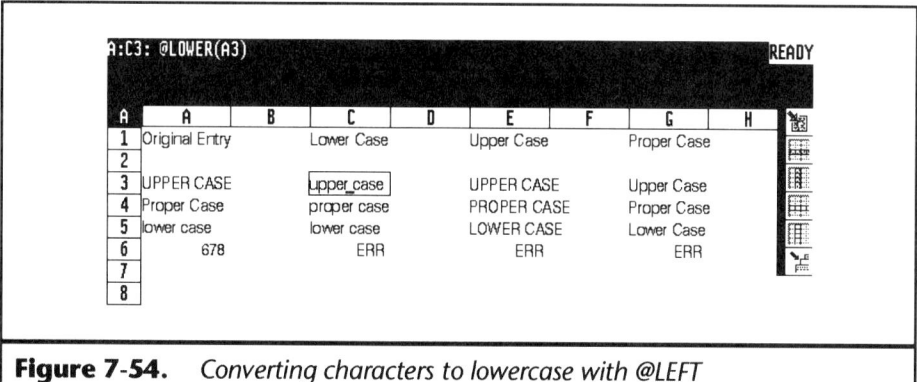

Figure 7-54. *Converting characters to lowercase with @LEFT*

@MID

The @MID function extracts characters from the middle of a string when you specify the number of characters to extract and the starting location.

Format

@MID(*string,start number,number of characters*)

Arguments

string — a group of characters that can be included in the function (if they are enclosed in double quotation marks) or placed in a cell and referenced. You can also use a string formula as the string. Numeric entries are not allowed and will return ERR.

start number — a number representing the first character position you wish to extract from the string. When you choose this number, remember that the leftmost position in the string is position 0. *Start number* should not be negative. If *start number* is greater

start number (cont.) than the number of positions in the string, an empty string will be returned. @MID("ABC",0,1) returns 1 character from the 0 position in the string: "A".

number of characters a number representing the number of characters you wish to extract from the string. This number can be stored in a cell and referenced by the function through a cell address or range name. When this argument is 0, an empty string is the result. You can set this number at 512 if you do not know how many characters are in the string and you want to extract all of them.

Use

The @MID function can be used whenever you wish to extract a portion of a string. The function offers complete flexibility: you can start anywhere in the string and extract as few or as many characters as you wish. Examples are

@MID("abcdefghi",3,3) equals def
@MID("123"&"456",1,512) equals 23456

The worksheet in Figure 7-55 shows @MID used with @LENGTH and @FIND to reverse a name entry. The formula uses the location of the "," plus 2 to identify the beginning of the first name. The number of characters in the first name is the length of the entire entry less the location of the ",". This is concatenated with a space and the last name. The last name consists of the characters on the left up to the ",". Creating the correct formula may require a little trial and error if you are not familiar with string functions, but once you have worked it out, you can copy it down the column to reverse all the name entries.

@N

The @N function returns the numeric value of a single cell.

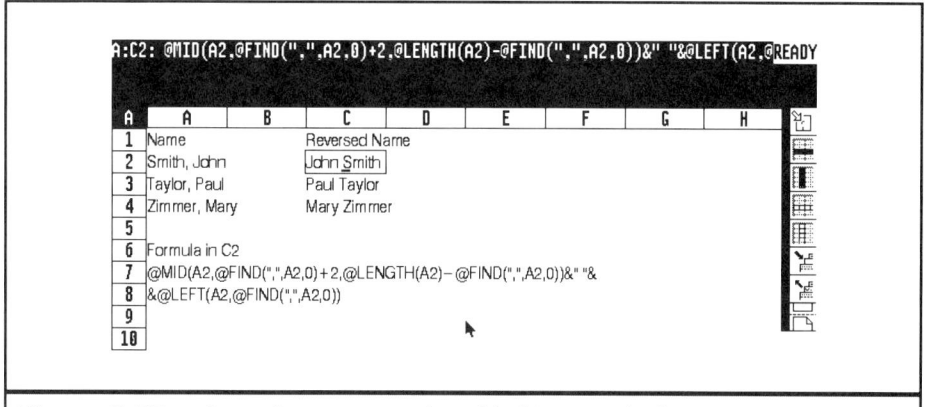

Figure 7-55. Reversing name entries with @MID and other string functions

Format

@N(*range*)

Arguments

range   a reference to a range, using either the cell addresses (for example, R2..U20) or a range name. Even though this function uses only the upper left cell of the range, the argument must still be in range format, that is, A2..A2.

Use

The @N function returns the value of the upper left cell in a range. If the cell contains a label, a 0 will be returned. The @N function is useful in macro applications to examine data in a cell. It is also a quick way of excluding label data from your calculations.

The following worksheet shows an example of @N. In this particular example, the range is a single cell.

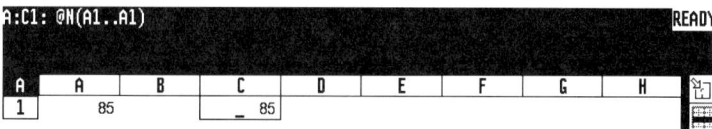

@PROPER

The @PROPER function converts strings to proper case (a format where the first letter of each word is capitalized).

Format

@PROPER(*string*)

Arguments

string   a group of characters that can be in uppercase, lowercase, or mixed upper- and lowercase. The characters can be included in the function (if they are enclosed in double quotation marks), or they can be placed in a cell and referenced. You can also use a string formula as the *string*.

Use

This function is valuable when data from several sources must be combined and data entry was not done in a consistent manner. @PROPER is one of the functions that permit you to change the appearance of data without reentering it. @PROPER(A2&" "&B3), where A2 contains JOBBARD MILLING COMPANY and B3 contains east dallas division, will return Jobbard Milling Company East Dallas Division. Every word in each string was converted to proper case (lowercase with initial capital). The worksheet in Figure 7-54 shows several additional conversions. Entries are made in column A, and @PROPER formulas are used to obtain the remainder of the display in column D.

@REPEAT

The @REPEAT function is used to duplicate a character string a specified number of times.

Format

@REPEAT(*string*,*number of times*)

Arguments

string a series of characters enclosed in quotation marks or a reference to a cell containing a string. The string can be one character or many, as long as the final string does not exceed 512 characters.

number of times a numeric value indicating the number of times to repeat the string.

Use

The @REPEAT function can improve the appearance of a worksheet by creating dividing lines. @REPEAT is in one sense similar to the backslash (\) character, since it repeats characters. It differs because \ is restricted to filling a single cell, whereas @REPEAT can extend across many worksheet cells. You can use the @REPEAT function in place of the +/− format when you do not want to change the column width. Figure 7-56 shows the @REPEAT function used to repeat a character so the resulting string is wider than the column. If you used a formula like +B3/1000 and the +/− format, you would have to widen column C so that 1-2-3 would not display the column as asterisks.

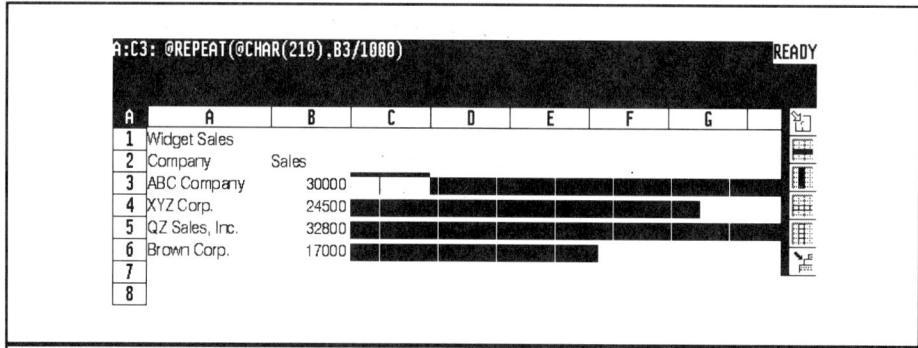

Figure 7-56. *Using @REPEAT to duplicate a label*

@REPLACE

The @REPLACE function replaces characters in a string with other characters.

Format

@REPLACE(*original string,start location,# characters,new string*)

Arguments

original string	a series of characters enclosed in quotation marks or a reference to a cell containing a string. The string can be one character or many. It must specify the complete string entry you wish to work with.
start location	the position number in the original string where you want the replacement to begin. Remember that the first character in the original string is position 0. If *start location* is greater than the length of the *original string*, the new string is added at the end.
# characters	the number of characters to remove from the original string. When *# characters* equals 0, the *new string* is inserted without removal of any part of the *original string*. When *# characters* is the same as the number of characters in the *original string*, the entire string is replaced.
new string	a series of characters enclosed in quotation marks or a reference to a cell containing a string. The string can be one character or many. When *new string* is an empty string, that is, "", @REPLACE simply deletes characters from the *original string*.

Use

The @REPLACE function enables you to make changes to a string without retyping the original string. For instance, you can use this function to manipulate a part number into a warehouse location, or an account code into a department number. Sample uses include:

@REPLACE("Department 100",11,3,"200") equals Department 200
@REPLACE("Commissions for: ",17,0,"Mary Brown") equals
Commissions for: Mary Brown
@REPLACE("AX/1265",2,1,"–") equals AX–1265
@REPLACE("AX/1265",0,7,"–") equals –

NOTE: To use this function to change text data entered incorrectly, first enter the function in an empty area of the worksheet, referencing the data to be corrected. You will need to restructure the data in a different location before copying it back, and you will want to be sure you do not overlay important data in the process of doing so. After the formulas are entered, you can freeze the values in the cells with F2 (EDIT) followed by F9 (CALC). You can then transfer them with /Move. Alternatively, you can use /Range Value to freeze the formulas as values and copy them all in one step. After verifying the accuracy of the data, you can erase the work area that originally contained the formula.

@RIGHT

The @RIGHT function allows you to extract a specified number of characters from the right side of a string.

Format

@RIGHT(*string,number of characters to extract*)

Arguments

string   a sequence of characters included in the function by enclosing them in double quotation marks, or by referencing a cell address or range name containing the characters.

number of characters to extract   a number representing the characters to be extracted from the string. If this number is greater than the number of characters in the *string*, the entire string will be extracted.

Use

The @RIGHT function lets you extract one or many characters from the right side of a string. It can be used alone or in combination with other string functions. Some examples of the function are

@RIGHT("Lotus 1-2-3",5) equals 1-2-3
@RIGHT("1:30:59",5) equals 30:59
@RIGHT("ABC COMPANY   ",8) equals Y with seven trailing spaces

@S

The @S function returns a value as a string.

Format

@S(*range*)

Arguments

range   a reference to a range using either cell addresses (such as R2..U20) or a range name. Even though this function uses only the upper left cell of the range, the argument must still be in range format (A2..A2).

Use

The @S function is used to return the value of the upper left cell in a range. If the cell contains a number, a blank cell is returned. This action can prevent the error condition that occurs if strings and numbers are mixed in one formula. If you have any doubt about the contents of a cell you are combining with a string, you can use @S, which will convert the contents of the cell to an empty string entry if it contains a number. For example, using @S in the formula @LEFT(@S(A1)) ensures that the formula will not return ERR even if A1 contains a value.

@STRING

The @STRING function converts numeric values to strings and allows you to specify the number of decimal places to be used for a string.

Format

@STRING(*number,number of decimal places*)

Arguments

number a numeric value or reference to a numeric value.

number of decimal places the number of decimal places to be used when the string is created from the *number*. If the *number* is longer than the specified *number* of places, rounding will occur. If the *number* is shorter, zeros will be used for padding.

Use

The primary use of this function is to permit the combination of numeric values with strings in a string formula. If @STRING is not used to convert numbers first, ERR is returned by any such string formula. The @STRING function uses the Fixed format with the number of places you specify to create the resulting string. The @STRING function ignores formatting characters such as commas and dollar signs. Several examples of @STRING are

@STRING(1.6,0) equals the string 2
@STRING(12,4) equals the string 12.0000
@STRING(2.3E+04,2) equals the string 23000.00

+"The total is "&@STRING(@SUM(B4..B11)) equals the string "The total is 46698" if the sum of B4..B11 is 46698

@TRIM

The @TRIM function allows you to strip away extraneous blanks from a string entry.

Format

@TRIM(*string*)

Arguments

string   a sequence of characters included in the function by enclosing them in double quotation marks or by referencing a cell address or range name containing the characters.

Use

This function is used to remove trailing, preceding, and multiple internal blanks from a string. It lets you clean up existing entries on a worksheet and establish a consistent format for data storage. @TRIM can be used with string formulas as well as strings. The examples that follow include both types of entries.

    @TRIM("   Sales") equals Sales
    @TRIM("January "&" Fuel Allowance") equals January Fuel Allowance

Note that @TRIM retains one space between strings joined by an ampersand (&).

@UPPER

The @UPPER function will convert initial-capped, lowercase, and mixed upper- and lowercase character strings to all uppercase.

Format

@UPPER(*string*)

Arguments

string   a group of characters that can be initial-capped, or in lower- or mixed upper- and lowercase. The characters can be included in the function (if they are enclosed in double quotation marks), or placed in a cell and referenced. You can also use a string formula as the *string*.

Use

This function is valuable when data from several sources must be combined and data entry was not done in a consistent manner. @UPPER is one of the functions that permit you to change the appearance of data without reentering it. @UPPER(A2&" "&B3), where A2 contains Jobbard Milling Company and B3 contains east dallas division, returns JOBBARD MILLING COMPANY EAST DALLAS DIVISION. All of every word in each string is converted to uppercase. The worksheet in Figure 7-54 shows several additional conversions. Entries are made in column A, and @UPPER formulas are used to obtain the remainder of the display in column G.

@VALUE

The @VALUE function is designed to convert a string that looks like a number into an actual numeric value.

Format

@VALUE(*string*)

Arguments

string a sequence of characters included in the function by enclosing them in double quotation marks, or by referencing a cell address or range name containing the characters. The sequence of characters must look like a number. Acceptable examples are 345.674, 345.1E8, 7, and 7/8 (a fraction). If *string* references an empty string, 0 will be returned.

Use

This function converts strings that look like numbers into actual numeric values so they can be used in calculations. The function removes any leading or trailing blanks from the string. Here are a few examples:

@VALUE("   23.98") returns the number 23.98
@VALUE(Z10) returns 0 if Z10 is blank, and ERR if Z10
contains a label such as abc

CHAPTER 8

Working with Files

The worksheets discussed so far have all been stored in part of your computer's random access memory (RAM). RAM offers the advantage of instant availability for information stored in it. Changes, additions, and deletions to information stored in RAM can be accomplished very quickly. The disadvantage of RAM storage is that it is very volatile. Losing the power to your computer for even a brief instant causes everything stored in RAM to be permanently lost.

A more permanent means of storage is clearly required and this normally is done with disk files. The 1-2-3 program itself is a file. That is why it is permanently available on your disk. If the program is lost from memory, you can restore it by reloading it from your disk.

This chapter will focus on the data files that contain information on the applications you have created on 1-2-3. You will learn how to save, retrieve, and delete files. You will also learn to combine files, and to perform other file management operations.

Naming and Using Files

1-2-3 uses disk files for the permanent storage of all information. These files can be maintained on either hard or floppy diskettes. They can be transferred from one disk to another by saving the worksheets to several disks with the /File Save command or by using operating system commands. Because 1-2-3 runs under DOS, the conventions established by DOS for the naming of files must be followed. A comprehensive discussion of rules for filenames and file storage can be found in your DOS manual.

Filenames and File Types

The 1-2-3 program creates three types of data files: worksheet files, graph files, and print files. 1-2-3 automatically appends a suffix to each filename that allows you to distinguish one file type from another. In addition, 1-2-3 has many files of its own that are part of the program and its various features.

DOS imposes an eight-character limit on filenames, and a three-character limit on filename extensions. A period (.) is used to separate the filename from the extension.

A filename and extension can contain letters, numbers, and many symbols. 1-2-3 automatically changes lowercase characters in your filename entries to uppercase. Symbols are permitted only if the specific release of your operating system allows them. Release 3 of 1-2-3 accepts any LMBCS character as long as your operating system supports the use of the character. Although 1-2-3 allows spaces in the filename if the operating system allows it, some versions of DOS prohibit spaces in filenames. An underscore (_) is a better way to separate filenames into words. Some examples of valid filenames are SALES, REGION_1, EMPLOYEE, and SALES_85.

If your operating system only accepts a maximum of eight characters for a filename, and you enter a filename longer than that, 1-2-3 automatically truncates the filename after the eighth character. Thus, SALES_REGION_1 becomes SALES_RE, which would be indistinguishable from truncated versions of SALES_REGION_2, SALES_REGION_3, and other filenames with the same characters in the first eight positions.

1-2-3 distinguishes file types by the extension added to the filename. The 1-2-3 program files and the files you create have different extensions to indicate the type of data stored in the file. The three most common types of files and their extensions are as follows:

File Type	Extension
Worksheet	.WK3 (Release 3)
	.WK1 (Release 2)
	.WKS (Release 1A)
Print	.PRN (unencoded)
	.ENC (encoded)
Graph	.CGM
	.PIC

You also have the option of supplying your own extension for any file type. If you supply this extension when you create a file, you must supply it every time you access that file. If you use 1-2-3's default extensions, the package will supply them for you at all times.

Subdirectories

You can create subdirectories for the storage of files. Subdirectories create logical rather than physical divisions for the hard disk, and manage the files within a particular directory so it is easy to find related files. The concept of subdirectories is similar to the filing system you may have developed to manage the large number of memos and other paper information you probably receive. Just as you would not throw all this paper in one desk drawer and expect to find something in it with ease, you do not want to randomly place all your files on the hard disk without the organization structure that subdirectories provide.

Using subdirectories lessens the time required for file retrieval because 1-2-3 does not have to search the directory for the entire hard disk to determine the file's location. Since Release 3 of 1-2-3 requires a hard disk, you are probably already using subdirectories for your other applications.

The first directory on your hard disk is automatic and is called the Root directory. You can store files in the Root directory, or you can create subdirectories immediately beneath it. The latter approach is better since it places all your files within the control of a subdirectory. Your operating system provides a command like MD or MKDIR to create new directories at any level within the directory structure.

Within a directory, each filename and extension combination must be unique. You may have two files named BUDGET on the disk, as long as they have different filename extensions. You can use the same filename on a hard disk more than once as long as the files are in different subdirectories. For example, you can have the filename BUDGET.WK3 in the subdirectory ACCT and the subdirectory FIN. The contents of these files may be the same or different. Even if the files originally contain the same data, they are two separate physical files, and an update to one does not affect the other file.

If you are using subdirectories, 1-2-3 must know the drive and the pathname in order to find a file. The drive designation is the drive letter followed by a colon; for example, A:, B:, or C:. The pathname tells 1-2-3 what directory the file is in. Higher level directories are always listed first. \SALES indicates that the file is in the first-level directory SALES, whereas \SALES\REGION\ONE indicates that the file is several levels down from the top directory in a subdirectory called ONE. If you are not familiar with the ins and outs of subdirectories, review your DOS manual for more information on this subject.

The File Menu Options

File is one of the options on 1-2-3's main menu. Most of the commands that manipulate files are options on the File submenu, which is shown in the following illustration. Let's look at each of these menu options in detail.

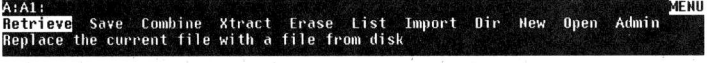

Saving a File to Disk

Any worksheet model in RAM must be saved to a disk file if it is to be available in later 1-2-3 sessions. Use the /File Save option to place a copy of the current worksheet on your disk. You will use this command to save a new worksheet, and to save an updated, existing worksheet.

If the current worksheet file has not been saved before, when you invoke /File Save, 1-2-3 will display a default filename. The default filename is FILE0001 or the next highest available default file number. You can accept this filename, or enter a new name in response to 1-2-3's prompt, and press ENTER.

If the file has already been saved in the current session, or if it is a file that you retrieved from disk, 1-2-3 will suggest that it be saved again under the same name. If you agree, press ENTER. When prompted to confirm this decision, select Replace if you want the current worksheet to replace the existing file. If you want to create a backup copy of the worksheet, select Backup to create a backup with a .BAK extension. If you decide not to save the file, select Cancel to return to READY mode. With Release 3.4, you can also use the File Save Icon, shown below, for saving files. This icon duplicates the effect of selecting the /File Save command.

TIP: Create a Backup version to retain the original and revised versions of a worksheet. When you use /File Save Backup, 1-2-3 saves the original file with the extension .BAK, and saves the current version with the extension .WK3—providing access to both versions of the worksheet.

1-2-3 automatically appends .WK3 to the filename. This assumes that the extension set by the /Worksheet Global Default Ext Save command is .WK3. You can choose any file suffix you wish, but you must then be prepared to reenter this suffix every time you access the file. For example, you can add a .WK1 extension if you want the file translated to a Release 2 format.

Whether you are saving a new or updated file, you may choose to name it with an existing filename. At the /File Save name prompt, press ESC. 1-2-3 will then provide a file list like the following:

```
List    ..  ◄  ►  ▲  ▼   A:   B:   C:                           FILES
Enter name of file to save: C:\123R34\DATA\*.WK3
ARTINDEX.WK3      BALANCE.WK3      BASS.WK3       BUDGET.WK3
```

Point to the name you want, and press ENTER.

Once you select a name, 1-2-3 displays the following prompt:

```
A:A1:                                                            MENU
Cancel  Replace  Backup
Cancel command: leave existing file on disk intact
```

This prompt asks if you wish to cancel the request, replace the file on the disk with the current contents of memory, or back up the original worksheet first before replacing the file on the disk with the current contents of memory. This is the same prompt that appears when you are saving an updated file using the same filename. This prompt is needed because each disk or subdirectory can have only one file with a particular name. When you reuse a name, only the last data you saved will be in the file when you attempt to retrieve it.

You can save a file to a different drive or directory by specifying the drive and directory designation along with the filename, for example, C:\SALES\REGION\FILE1. If you need to add or delete characters in the current filename and path specification, use the LEFT and RIGHT ARROW to move around.

1-2-3 makes it so easy to save files that you will want to save frequently. If your system goes down, you can then retrieve the most recently saved version of the file; it is easier to reconstruct what was lost if it has not been too long since the last save.

Retrieving a File from Disk

The /File Retrieve command permits you to retrieve a file from your disk. When 1-2-3 loads a worksheet file into RAM memory, it first erases the information currently in RAM memory. If you have not saved that information on disk, there is no way to bring it back. To retrieve a worksheet in Release 3.4, you can use the File Retrieve SmartIcon, shown below, which duplicates the effect of selecting /File Retrieve.

When you enter this command, 1-2-3 searches the current disk or subdirectory and lists all the files with a .WK3 (Release 3), .WK1 (Release 2), or .WKS (Release 1A) suffix. As shown here, 1-2-3 displays up to four names across the third line of the control panel.

You can use the RIGHT ARROW key to move across the display, scrolling across to additional filenames until you finally cycle through all of them and move back to the beginning of the subdirectory. Using the LEFT ARROW key moves you back toward the beginning of the list.

Other options available with the pointer control keys are as follows:

HOME	Moves the pointer or highlight to the beginning of the file list
END	Moves the pointer or highlight to the end of the file list
DOWN	Presents the next four options in the file list
UP	Presents the previous four options from the file list

If you wish to see all the filenames at once, press F3 (NAME). You will see a list like the one in Figure 8-1. Moving your pointer to a particular filename causes the control panel to display the date and time that file was saved, and its size. You can choose a file by pressing ENTER, or cancel the full display by pressing F3 (NAME) a second time.

To retrieve a file in another directory, type the complete pathname for the file. Pressing ESC twice removes the displayed pathname specification. You can also retrieve a file with an extension other than .WK3 by specifying the extension along with the filename.

Another option is pressing BACKSPACE at the 1-2-3 prompt to display the files in the parent directory of the current one. To select a subdirectory of the current directory, highlight it in the file list (directory names are at the end) and press ENTER to list its worksheet files.

```
List    ..  ◄  ►  ▲  ▼  A:  B:  C:                        FILES
Enter name of file to retrieve: C:\123R34\DATA\*.WK*
         ARTINDEX.WK3   19-Nov-92    05:12 PM      35975
ARTINDEX.WK3    BALANCE.WK1     BASS.WK3         BUDGET.WK3
EMPLOYEE.WK3    F644APPD.WK3    FIG01_03.WK3     FIG01_08.WK3
FIG01_11.WK3    FIG02_04.WK3    FIG03_02.WK3     FIG03_03.WK3
FIG03_04.WK3    FIG03_05.WK3    FIG04_01.WK3     FIG04_02.WK3
FIG04_03.WK3    FIG04_05.WK3    FIG04_07.WK3     FIG04_08.WK3
FIG04_10.WK3    FIG04_13.WK3    FIG04_16.WK3     FIG04_17.WK3
FIG04_18.WK3    FIG04_20.WK3    FIG04_22.WK3     FIG04_24.WK3
FIG04_26.WK3    FIG04_27.WK3    FIG04_28.WK3     FIG04_34.WK3
FIG05_01.WK3    FIG05_02.WK3    FIG05_03.WK3     FIG05_04.WK3
FIG05_05.WK3    FIG05_07.WK3    FIG05_09.WK3     FIG05_11.WK3
FIG05_14.WK3    FIG05_15.WK3    FIG05_17.WK3     FIG05_20.WK3
FIG05_21.WK3    FIG05_23.WK3    FIG05_25.WK3     FIG05_27.WK3
FIG05_28.WK3    FIG05_32.WK3    FIG05_33.WK3     FIG05_37.WK3
FIG05_38.WK3    FIG05_43.WK3    FIG06_01.WK3     FIG06_04.WK3
FIG06_05.WK3    FIG06_10.WK3    FIG07_01.WK3     FIG07_02.WK3
FIG07_03.WK3    FIG07_04.WK3    FIG07_05.WK3     FIG07_06.WK3
FIG07_07.WK3    FIG07_08.WK3    FIG07_09.WK3     FIG07_10.WK3
FIG07_11.WK3    FIG07_12.WK3    FIG07_13.WK3     FIG07_14.WK3
FIG07_15.WK3    FIG07_16.WK3    FIG07_17.WK3     FIG07_23.WK3
FIG07_24.WK3    FIG07_25.WK3    FIG07_27.WK3     FIG07_30.WK3
FIG07_31.WK3    FIG07_32.WK3    FIG07_33.WK3     FIG07_34.WK3
20-Nov-92 10:40 AM
```

Figure 8-1. *Complete filename display generated with F3 (NAME)*

Retrieving Files with a Mouse

When you have the Wysiwyg add-in loaded as you do by default with 1-2-3 Release 3.4, you can use a mouse to select a file to retrieve.

The List option in the first line of the control panel is equivalent to pressing F3 (NAME) to switch the display of filenames between the control panel and the full screen. You can use the triangles to move the highlight to the next filename in the direction of the triangle. The top line also includes .. to let you switch to the parent directory. The A:, B:, and other drive letters let you quickly change the directory that lists the worksheet files. To retrieve a listed file, point to the file you want with the mouse and double click the filename with the left mouse button.

Retrieving Files on a Network

When you retrieve a file on a network you have other considerations since another user may also be using the file that you want. With worksheet files on a network, only one person is allowed to make changes. Otherwise, the changes made by one person could be undone by another. The privilege to alter a worksheet is called the *file reservation*. 1-2-3 is initially set to get the reservation for the file when you retrieve it. If someone else has the reservation, you cannot have it until they relinquish it. When 1-2-3 cannot provide the reservation, it displays an extra prompt asking if you want the file without the reservation. If you select No, the /File Retrieve command is canceled. If you select Yes, 1-2-3 will retrieve the file, but you cannot save it using the same filename; you can save it using a different filename. 1-2-3 indicates that you cannot save the file using the same name by displaying RO for read-only in the status line. You will also see the RO indicator when a worksheet is set to obtain its reservation manually rather than automatically, or when you release a reservation so someone else can modify the file.

Once you have a reservation, you can release it by selecting /File Admin Reservation Release. Since you will not have the reservation after this command, it is important that you save any changes you want to keep before performing this command. On the other hand, you can try obtaining a reservation when you do not have one by selecting /File Admin Reservation Get. When you perform this command, 1-2-3 attempts to get the reservation. If the reservation is available, the file has not changed since you retrieved it, and you have write access to the file, the RO indicator disappears. If the reservation is not available, the worksheet stored in the file is different from the one you retrieved, or you do not have write access to the file, the RO indicator will not disappear. *Write access* is a privilege granted by the network administrator that allows you to save your changes.

You can set 1-2-3 to obtain the reservation automatically or manually with the /File Admin Reservation Setting command. When you enter this command, you can select Automatic, which means 1-2-3 tries to obtain the reservation when the worksheet is loaded, or Manual, which means 1-2-3 tries to obtain the reservation only when you use the /File Admin Reservation Get command. This setting is saved with the file and it applies to every person who uses the worksheet file. If you want to make the change to the reservation setting permanent, use the /File Admin Seal Reservation command. After entering this command, you must type a password and press ENTER twice. (Entering passwords is described in the next section.) Once the reservation setting is sealed, you can change it only by unsealing it with the /File Admin Seal Disable command and entering the password that you used to seal the file. The reservation is also sealed when you seal the worksheet with the /File Admin Seal File command, which is discussed in Chapter 5, "Basic Worksheet Commands."

Using Passwords with Files

Passwords are a form of protection for your files. When they are in effect, an operator cannot retrieve a file without first supplying the correct password.

Passwords are added to a file when it is saved. If you want to specify a password, after entering the filename press SPACEBAR and type a **p** before pressing ENTER as in NEWFILE P. 1-2-3 then prompts for the password, which can be up to 15 characters. When you type in the password, it is not displayed; each character is instead represented by an asterisk in the control panel, like this:

Your use of upper- and lowercase is recorded, and must be correctly duplicated when you access the file later. When you press ENTER, you will be prompted to enter the password again for verification. If the passwords entered on both occasions are not an exact match, 1-2-3 provides an error message to that effect. The second prompt for the password also offers a way to stop the addition of the password: simply press ESC. Once you have pressed ENTER for the final time, the password is added to the disk, and you will need to use it when you retrieve the file.

To access a file with a password, enter the command you wish to use in working with the file, such as **/File Retrieve**. 1-2-3 then generates a prompt for the password and waits for you to enter it. If you cannot reproduce the password exactly as it was originally entered, including the correct use of upper- and lowercase, 1-2-3 will not retrieve the file and will display an error message.

To change the password of a password protected file, save the file again. When 1-2-3 displays the filename followed by "[PASSWORD PROTECTED]", press the BACKSPACE key, then the SPACEBAR, and type a **p**. 1-2-3 will prompt you twice, for a new password, just as if you were adding a new password to a new file.

To remove the password of a password protected file, save the file again. When 1-2-3 displays the filename followed by "[PASSWORD PROTECTED]", press the BACKSPACE key and then ENTER.

Combining Information from Two Files

The /File Combine options allow you to bring information from other worksheet files into your current worksheet. With this capability you can produce budget consolidations, or build a new worksheet using components of several existing worksheet files. Unlike /File Retrieve, the Combine options do not erase what is in memory.

The three Combine options are Copy, Add, and Subtract. All three depend on the location of the cell pointer in the current worksheet for the actions they take. The Combine Copy option was essential in earlier releases because they did not support multiple-sheet files, or sheets referenced with external links. Although you can still use the /File Combine Copy command for many applications, you will want to consider the potential of links and multiple-sheet files as you work with applications that use several types of data. Alternatively, you can use the /File Combine Add and Subtract options to automatically perform arithmetic operations between the contents of the current file and the external file without the need for entering formulas.

Copying Information from a File to a Worksheet

The /File Combine Copy command allows you to replace the contents of current worksheet cells with the contents of cells in a disk file. The replacement begins at the cell pointer location in the current worksheet, and the extent of the replacement will depend on how many cells are being copied from the disk. Values, labels, and formulas can all be copied from the file on disk.

You have two options for determining the extent of the replacement. First, you can bring in an entire file. This operation takes each cell in the file that contains a value, label, or formula, and replaces an appropriate number of cells in the current worksheet to accommodate the imported data. The location of the cell(s) replaced is determined by the location of the cell pointer at the time of the Combine Copy request, and by the contents of the file to be incorporated.

Displacement of cells in the current file will match the dimensions of the replacement data, with the base point being the cell pointer location.

TIP: When using /File Combine in Release 3, make sure you have sufficient sheets in the current file for a three-dimensional range to be incorporated. Release 3 will support combining three-dimensional ranges, but the current worksheet must contain a sufficient number of sheets to support the Combine operation.

Suppose you have a file named HEADING that is stored on disk and looks like this:

Your current worksheet file looks like Figure 8-2. Position your cell pointer in B1 and enter **/File Combine Copy**. Choose the Entire-File option and specify the HEADING filename. The results should look like Figure 8-3. The /File Combine Copy command will overwrite the existing contents of cells starting at B1.

Figure 8-2. *Worksheet without heading entries at the top*

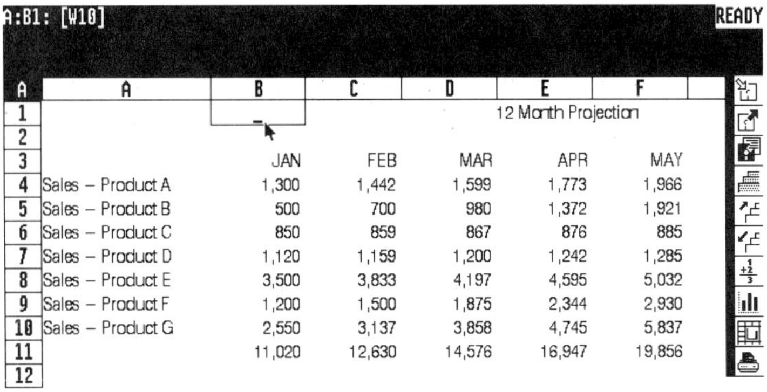

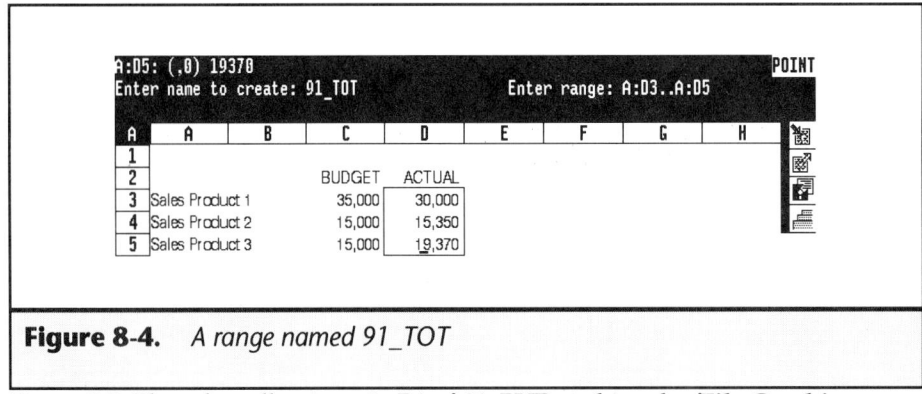

Figure 8-3. Heading entries added with /File Combine Copy

TIP: *If you only need to copy data once, and do not need to update the copy from the external file, use /File Combine, or /Copy with external file references. If you want to refresh the copied data, use a formula that contains external references. You can then update the links at any time with /File Admin Link-Refresh.*

If you do not need to copy an entire file, you can use /File Combine Copy's second option, Named/Specified-Range. This option will copy only the range of values that you specify. For example, suppose the highlighted range of cells named 91_TOT, as shown in Figure 8-4, is saved in a worksheet file called 91_BUD. You want to copy 91_TOT to the column headed 91 Sales on the worksheet shown in

Figure 8-4. *A range named 91_TOT*

Figure 8-5. Place the cell pointer in B4 of 91_BUD and invoke **/File Combine**

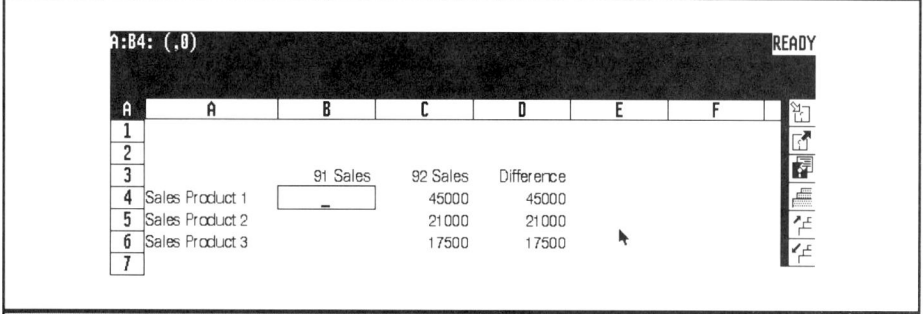

Figure 8-5. *Worksheet where the totals in the named range are needed*

Copy. Then select Named/Specified-Range and enter **91_TOT**, followed by the filename, **91_BUD**. The results should look like Figure 8-6.

TIP: Use range names with the /File Combine command, and name the ranges in the file you are combining. Range names are easier to remember. Also, if you give the same name to all the range names that you are combining, you only have to specify the filename each time you perform the /File Combine command.

Adding Information from a File to a Worksheet

The /File Combine Add command lets you add the values of cells in a disk file to corresponding cells in the current worksheet. The addition begins at the cell pointer location in the current worksheet and the extent of the addition depends on the arrangement of cells added from the disk. Only numeric values are

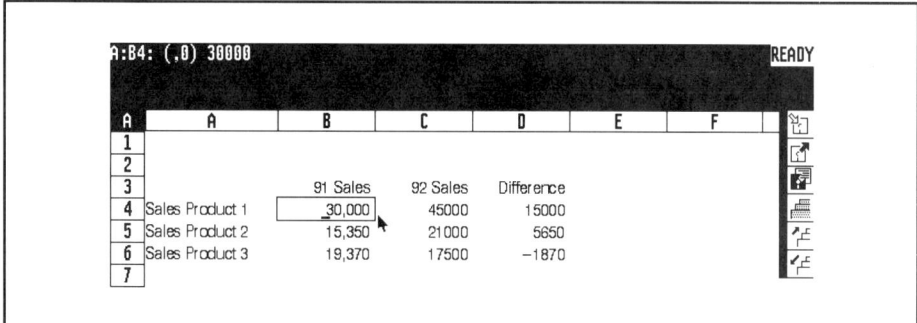

Figure 8-6. *Adding the named range to the existing worksheet with /File Combine Copy*

involved in the addition process. Labels in the incoming worksheet are ignored, formulas in the incoming worksheet are treated as values, and the label and formula entries in the current worksheet are retained for those cells. Unlike the Copy option, neither /File Combine Add nor /File Combine Subtract overlays the contents of existing worksheet cells.

You have two options for determining the extent of the addition. First, you can choose Entire-File. This operation will add each cell in the disk file that contains a value to the appropriate cell in the current worksheet. The location of the cells to which the disk file values are added is determined by the location of the cell pointer at the time of the Combine Add request, and by the amount of the displacement (that is, the location of the cell in relation to the beginning of the file) of the particular cell within the file. The same displacement is used to determine the cells that receive the added data, with the base point being the cell pointer location.

The second option is to choose Named/Specified-Range. In this case, only the cells in the selected range will be added. This will begin at the location of the cell pointer in the worksheet.

/File Combine Add provides one solution for budget consolidations. If you have files containing individual department or subsidiary budgets, the /File Combine Add command permits you to add all the figures into one consolidated budget. Figure 8-7 shows a portion of the budgets for each department in a

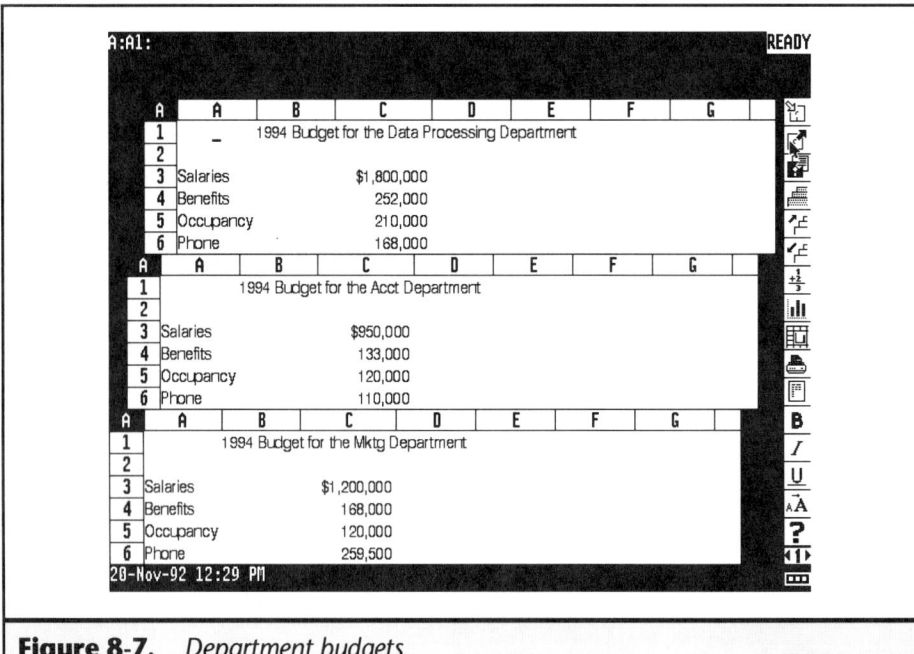

Figure 8-7. Department budgets

company. Notice that the format for all three is identical: this is required if you want to /Combine Add entire files. Add the three files one by one to the Total Budget worksheet (Figure 8-8). Since the entire file is being added in each case, place your cell pointer in A1 before invoking the /File Combine Add command. The final results are shown in Figure 8-9. The labels and formulas in the total budget worksheet do not change by adding the other worksheets. Any formulas in the worksheets that are added to the current one are converted to their values before being added to the current worksheet.

Subtracting Information in a File from a Worksheet

The /File Combine Subtract command allows you to subtract the values of cells in a disk file from corresponding cells in the current worksheet. The subtraction begins at the cell pointer location in the current worksheet, and the extent of the subtraction depends on the arrangement of cells from the disk that are being subtracted from the worksheet cells. Only numeric values are involved in the subtraction process. Labels and formulas are ignored, and the label and formula entries in the current worksheet are retained for those cells. /File Combine Subtract does not overlay the contents of existing cells.

You have two options for determining the extent of the subtraction. First, you can choose Entire-File. This operation will subtract each cell in the disk file that contains a value from the appropriate cell in the current worksheet. The location of the cells from which the disk file values are subtracted is determined by the location of the cell pointer at the time of the Combine Subtract request, and by

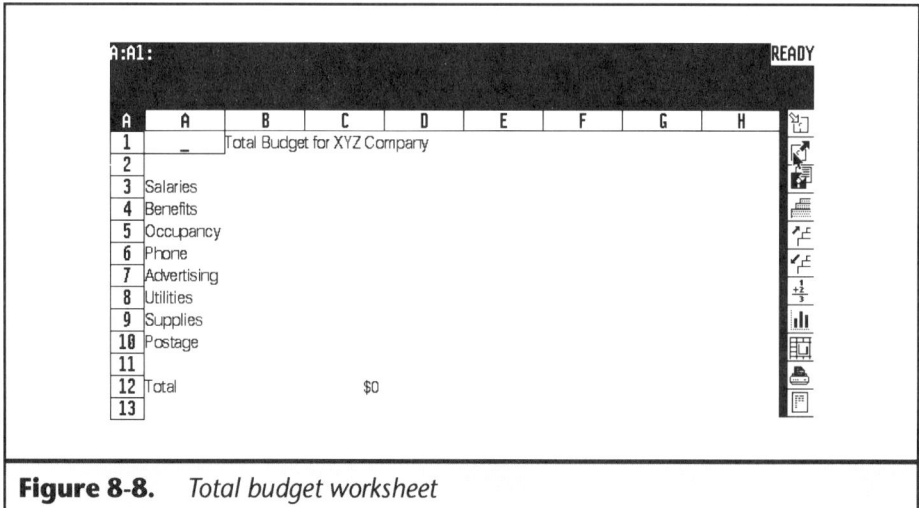

Figure 8-8.   *Total budget worksheet*

```
A:A1:                                                          READY

       A       B       C       D       E    F    G    H
   A
   1          Total Budget for XYZ Company
   2
   3  Salaries         $3,950,000
   4  Benefits            553,000
   5  Occupancy           450,000
   6  Phone               537,500
   7  Advertising       1,061,000
   8  Utilities            49,000
   9  Supplies            167,000
  10  Postage               5,900
  11
  12  Total            $6,773,400
  13
```

Figure 8-9. Result of /File Combine Add

the amount of the displacement of the particular cell within the file. The same displacement will be used to determine the cells that receive the subtracted data with the base point being the cell pointer location. If you choose Named/Specified-Range, only the cells in the selected range will be subtracted. This will begin at the location of the cell pointer in the worksheet.

The subtraction feature is useful after you have completed file consolidation with the /File Combine Add command. /File Combine Subtract allows you to see the effect of taking the budget figures for one department or subsidiary away from the total, thereby simulating the effect of closing it.

Saving Part of a Worksheet

The /File Xtract command permits you to save part of a worksheet. The specified section of the worksheet is saved as a .WK3 or .WK1 file, depending on the extension you provide. This feature is used for saving part of a worksheet file as a 1-2-3 Release 2 or 3 worksheet. It also lets you save sections of a worksheet for use in constructing new models, or when you have a file that is too large to save on one disk and you need to split it into more than one file. Settings established for the current worksheet are saved in the new file.

Worksheet sections are saved as either Formulas or Values. If you choose Values, 1-2-3 saves the values of the formulas in the extracted worksheet rather than maintaining the formulas in the new worksheet. If you choose Formulas, 1-2-3 saves formulas as they were entered, but not the value(s) referenced by the formulas unless they are in the range selected. The formulas in the range you select to extract are adjusted just as if you moved them to the new worksheet.

This means that relative, mixed, and absolute addresses are adjusted, although they will still be relative, mixed, or absolute addresses in the extracted worksheet. When labels are extracted, the result will be the same whether you select Formulas or Values, since labels do not reference other cells.

Extracting formulas that reference cells outside the extract range offers the biggest potential for error. For instance, you might extract E1..H12, and there might be a formula in E2 that refers to A1. When this reference is adjusted for the new file, it will refer to cell IS1, since the reference will be computed from A1 of the new worksheet. This cell will therefore not contain what you expected. This is because 1-2-3 adjusts the cell references in formulas as if you are using the /Move command.

When using the Values option, only calculated results and labels will be retained in the new file. All formulas will be replaced by the results of the formula calculations.

The procedure for using either option is to enter **/File Xtract** and choose either Formulas or Values. You will be prompted for the filename to use for storage; either type a name or choose one from the list of worksheet files on the disk. If you provide a .WK1 extension, 1-2-3 will save the file in a Release 2 format. You can also make the extracted file password protected by pressing the SPACEBAR after you name the file and typing a **p**. Then you must provide a password, as instructed for password protection with the /File Save command. Next 1-2-3 prompts you to supply the range of cells to extract by highlighting or typing the address, or supplying a defined range name.

If you choose an existing filename for the extracted file, you must confirm your choice with Replace or Backup. The Replace option erases the original file, and the Backup option renames the original file before storing the extracted data under the specified filename. The other option, Cancel, returns you to READY mode without saving the extract file.

Figure 8-10 shows a worksheet that contains formulas in column E. Suppose you extract the entries in column E and save them as Values. You then place this extract in another worksheet with /File Combine Copy. The result is shown in

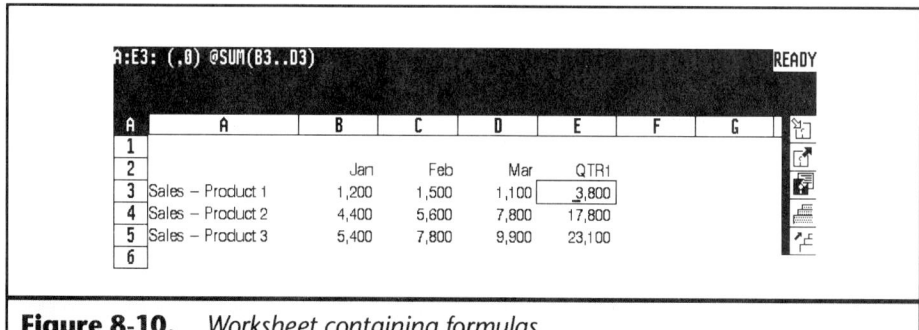

Figure 8-10. *Worksheet containing formulas*

Figure 8-11, where the formula entries from the previous worksheet appear as calculated values. If you did this again with the /File Xtract Formulas command, the formulas would become @SUM(IU3..A3), @SUM(IU4..A4), and @SUM(IU5..A5) as they were moved from E3..E5 in the first worksheet to A1..A3 in the extracted worksheet; and finally, B3..B5 in the worksheet where they are combined with the /File Combine Copy command.

Erasing Files from the Disk

From time to time you will have files that you no longer require. You can remove them from your disk with the DEL command under DOS, or you can eliminate them from within 1-2-3 with /File Erase. The advantage of /File Erase is that you are still in 1-2-3, so you can retrieve a file and look at it to make sure that you want to delete it.

The /File Erase command requires first that you specify the type of file you wish to erase. Choose from Worksheet, Print, Graph, or Other, and 1-2-3 then lists all the files of that type on the disk or in the current directory. 1-2-3 also lists the subdirectory names (if any) for the current directory. You can then change directories if you wish.

If you choose Worksheet, all .WK3, .WKS, and .WK1 filenames will be displayed. Select Print to see all files with a .PRN suffix. Graph will display files with the appropriate extension set by the /Worksheet Global Default Graph command. Other will cause 1-2-3 to display all the filenames on the current disk or in the current directory. With F3 (NAME), you can switch between listing the filenames in a single line or using the whole screen. To change the extension, press F2 (EDIT) and enter the extension of the files you want to see.

The /File Erase command offers wildcard features, just as DOS does. A ? can replace any single character in the filename, and an asterisk (*) specifies that any

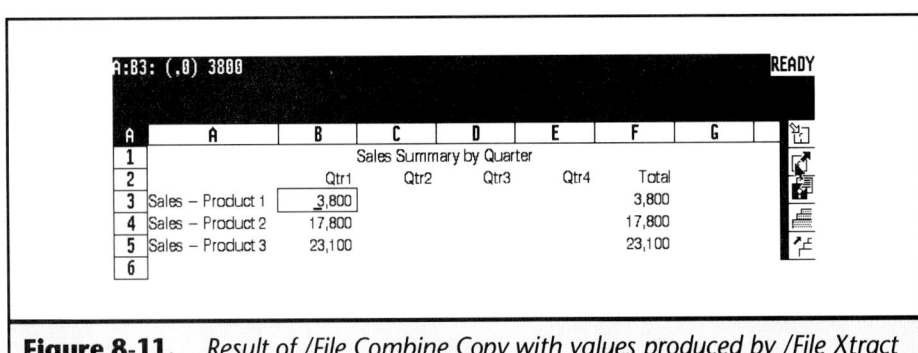

Figure 8-11. *Result of /File Combine Copy with values produced by /File Xtract*

characters will be accepted from that point to the end of the filename. For instance, J?N would match with JAN, JUN, JON, JEN, and so on. J* would match with all of these options, as well as names like JUNE, JANUARY, JOLLY, and JOINT.

After selecting the type of file, pick a filename from the display or enter a name yourself. Once the name is entered, 1-2-3 asks you to confirm your choice by responding with Yes. If you elect not to proceed, select No at the confirmation prompt.

Determining What Files Are on Your Disk

As your list of worksheet models and other 1-2-3 files grows longer, you may have trouble remembering all the files you have on a disk. You can always use the DOS DIR command to see a list of them, but you also have the option of using /File List from the 1-2-3 menu. Release 3 includes a feature for placing the file list on a worksheet.

Temporarily Listing Files

1-2-3's /File List command lists files on the screen and displays additional information about the highlighted filename. When you enter **/File List**, you are first presented with a menu of file type options. Choose from Worksheet, Print, Graph, Other, Active, or Linked, and 1-2-3 lists all the files of that type on the disk or in the current directory. 1-2-3 also lists the subdirectory names (if any) for the current directory. You can then use the cell pointer to change directories if you wish.

If you choose Worksheet, all .WK3, .WKS, and .WK1 filenames will be displayed, as shown in Figure 8-12. Select Print for all .PRN files. Graph displays files with the appropriate extension that has been set by the /Worksheet Global Default Graph command. Choose Other to see all the filenames on the current disk or in the current directory. To change the extension, press F2 (EDIT) and enter the extension of the files you want to see.

The option Active lists all the worksheet files currently open. Another option is Linked, which lists the files for which there are formula references in the current worksheet. Regardless of the file type selected, pointing to a filename in the list will display its size and the date and time it was last saved to disk. In addition, the Active option displays the number of worksheets in the file; the flag MOD or UNMOD indicating whether the file has been modified or not; and the flag RO if the file is a read-only file in a network environment. The Linked option also includes the pathname of the linked files.

```
List    ..  ◄  ►  ▲  ▼  A:   B:   C:                              FILES
Enter names of files to list: C:\123R34\DATA\*.WK*
              ARTINDEX.WK3   19-Nov-92      05:12 PM      35975
ARTINDEX.WK3       BALANCE.WK1       BASS.WK3         BUDGET.WK3
EMPLOYEE.WK3       EXTRACT.WK3       F644APPD.WK3     FIG01_03.WK3
FIG01_08.WK3       FIG01_11.WK3      FIG02_04.WK3     FIG03_02.WK3
FIG03_03.WK3       FIG03_04.WK3      FIG03_05.WK3     FIG04_01.WK3
FIG04_02.WK3       FIG04_03.WK3      FIG04_05.WK3     FIG04_07.WK3
FIG04_08.WK3       FIG04_10.WK3      FIG04_13.WK3     FIG04_16.WK3
FIG04_17.WK3       FIG04_18.WK3      FIG04_20.WK3     FIG04_22.WK3
FIG04_24.WK3       FIG04_26.WK3      FIG04_27.WK3     FIG04_28.WK3
FIG04_34.WK3       FIG05_01.WK3      FIG05_02.WK3     FIG05_03.WK3
FIG05_04.WK3       FIG05_05.WK3      FIG05_07.WK3     FIG05_09.WK3
FIG05_11.WK3       FIG05_14.WK3      FIG05_15.WK3     FIG05_17.WK3
FIG05_20.WK3       FIG05_21.WK3      FIG05_23.WK3     FIG05_25.WK3
FIG05_27.WK3       FIG05_28.WK3      FIG05_32.WK3     FIG05_33.WK3
FIG05_37.WK3       FIG05_38.WK3      FIG05_43.WK3     FIG06_01.WK3
FIG06_04.WK3       FIG06_05.WK3      FIG06_10.WK3     FIG07_01.WK3
FIG07_02.WK3       FIG07_03.WK3      FIG07_04.WK3     FIG07_05.WK3
FIG07_06.WK3       FIG07_07.WK3      FIG07_08.WK3     FIG07_09.WK3
FIG07_10.WK3       FIG07_11.WK3      FIG07_12.WK3     FIG07_13.WK3
FIG07_14.WK3       FIG07_15.WK3      FIG07_16.WK3     FIG07_17.WK3
FIG07_23.WK3       FIG07_24.WK3      FIG07_25.WK3     FIG07_27.WK3
FIG07_30.WK3       FIG07_31.WK3      FIG07_32.WK3     FIG07_33.WK3
20-Nov-92 01:01 PM
```

Figure 8-12. *List of all the worksheet files on a disk*

Listing Files on a Worksheet

1-2-3's /File Admin Table command creates a table in the worksheet containing a list of files and related information. When you enter **/File Admin Table**, you are presented with a menu of file type options. Choose from Worksheet, Print, Graph, Other, Active, or Linked. The types of files and the information listed for each option match the /File List command, except for the Active option. With the Active option, the next to last column contains a 1 to indicate the file has changed since it was retrieved, or a 0 if it has not changed. The last column contains a 1 if you have the reservation or a 0 if you do not. 1-2-3 displays a prompt of the files it will list, such as C:\123R34*.WK?. By editing the pathname, directory, and filename indicator in this prompt, you can determine which files 1-2-3 will include in the table. The selected directory can include the ? and * wildcard characters. For example, if you want all worksheet files that begin with the letter P, change the prompt to **C:\123R34\P*.WK***.

Once you select the type of files you want to list, 1-2-3 prompts for the location of the table. Either highlight the cell, or type the cell address or range where you want to place the upper left corner of the table. The table will contain as many rows as are needed by the files to be listed, and four to seven columns depending upon the file type selected. The table will write over the worksheet's current contents, so be sure to select an area where the table has plenty of room. Figure 8-13 shows a table created with the /File Admin Table Active command.

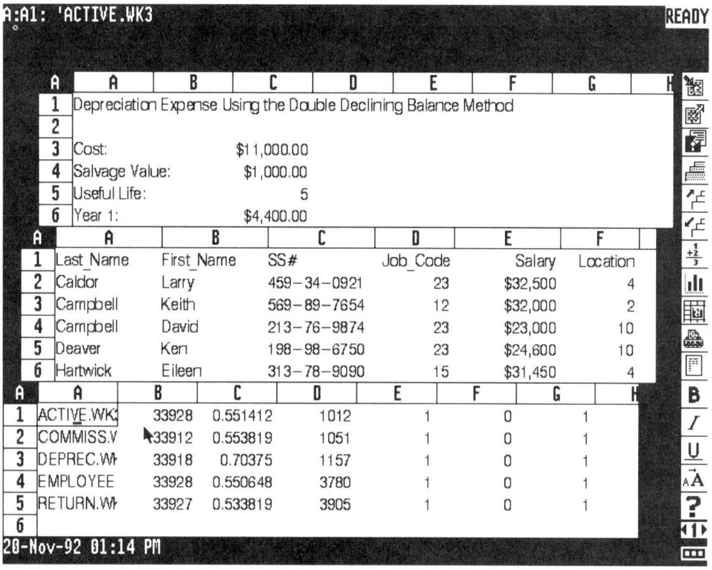

Figure 8-13. *Table created with the /File Admin Table Active command*

Adding Text Files to the Worksheet

The /File Import command allows you to transfer to your worksheet the data from a word processing program or other package that generates standard ASCII text input. You must be sure that the word processor does not include special characters in the file. (Most word processors have an option to eliminate special characters from the text file.) A standard ASCII text file is created by 1-2-3 every time you use the /Print File command.

The 1-2-3 program looks for filenames that have the extension .PRN. If the file you want to import does not, you can rename the file so it has a .PRN extension, using the DOS RENAME command or enter your own extension at 1-2-3's prompt for the filename. Move the cell pointer to the first cell where you want the text imported. Then select /File Import Text or /File Import Numbers and type or highlight the name of the file to import.

There are two basic options for importing text data into a 1-2-3 worksheet: Text and Numbers. These options determine how the data will be placed in the worksheet. Use the Text option when you want to import the entire file. The Numbers option is useful when you want to strip away everything but numeric values, or when you are importing data that is in a delimited format (each piece of data is separated by commas).

When you import data as Text, each line of the word processor document will become one long, left justified label. You will thus end up with a column of long labels. Once the data is imported, you can use /Data Parse (covered in Chapter 10, "Using Data Management Features in the Worksheet Environment") to split the labels into individual pieces. You can also use /Range Label if you wish to change the alignment of the long labels on the worksheet.

The Numbers option is for importing delimited data files. If you use the Numbers option, characters enclosed in double quotation marks, as well as all numbers, will be imported. Blanks and characters not in quotation marks will be eliminated in the import process. Each number in a line of the text file will generate a numeric cell entry, and each quote-enclosed label will create a left justified label cell. Entries from the same line of a text file will produce entries in the same row of the worksheet, proceeding from left to right of the row with each new entry. Commas separate each piece of data in each line in the imported file.

1-2-3 imposes a size limit on the imported file of 8192 lines. The maximum number of characters in a line is 512 when you are using the Text option. With the Numbers option you can have 512 characters for each entry. This means every comma delimited entry that is enclosed in quotes can contain 512 characters, since 1-2-3 will place each number in a separate field. In contrast, when text is imported the entire entry is placed in one field.

Figure 8-14 shows text entered into a Dos Editor file, NDOC.PRN. You have two choices for importing the information into 1-2-3. If you place your cell pointer in A1 and use /File Import Text, the results in Figure 8-15 are produced. The columns are not neatly aligned in Figure 8-15 because Wysiwyg is loaded into memory and is using a proportionally spaced font, in which characters take a different amount of space, depending on their natural width. This means that the words cannot align identically because all of their letters do not require the same amount of space. You will notice in the display of A1 that each of the

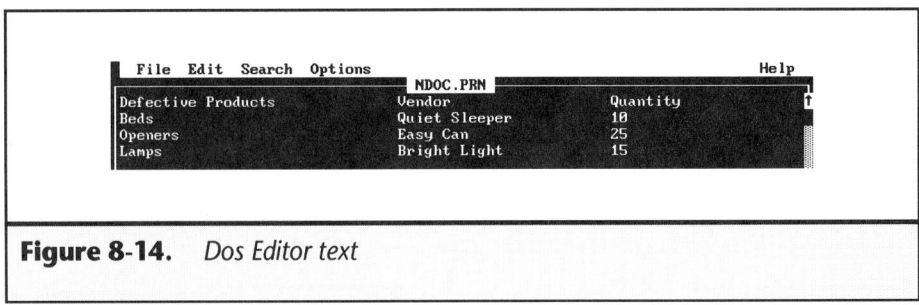

Figure 8-14. Dos Editor text

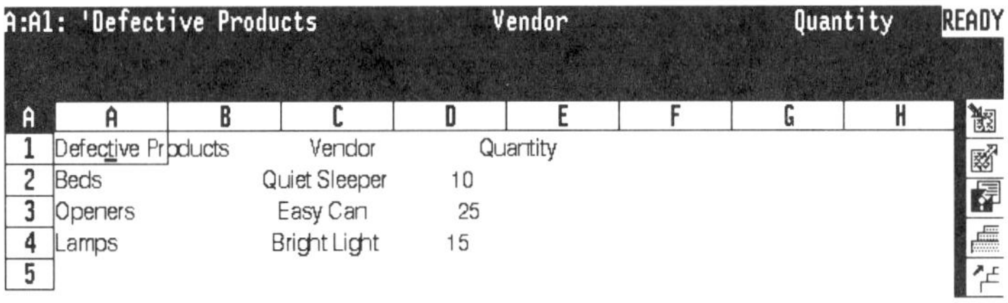

```
A:A1: 'Defective Products        Vendor           Quantity      READY

A      A             B        C         D       E      F      G      H
1   Defective Products      Vendor           Quantity
2   Beds                 Quiet Sleeper    10
3   Openers              Easy Can         25
4   Lamps                Bright Light     15
5
```

Figure 8-15.   */File Import with Text*

entries is a long label with the entire line in the one label. If you chose the Numbers options, the output in Figure 8-16 would result. In this instance only the numbers from the Quantity column are transferred, since the label entries were not enclosed in quotes. A delimited file containing the same data looks like Figure 8-17. When you import this file with /File Import Numbers, defective products and product names are imported into column A, vendor information is imported into column B, and quantity information is imported into column C.

When 1-2-3 imports text, it uses the setting of the /Worksheet Global Default Other International File-Translation command. This command's default of Country uses the ASCII code page that the computer is set for. To use code page 850, select International.

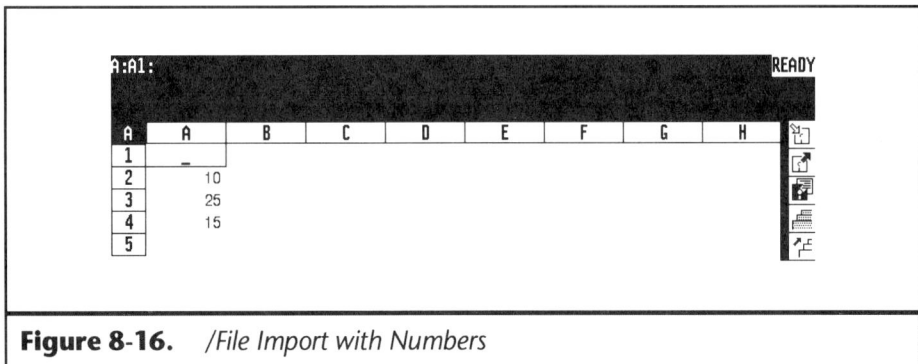

Figure 8-16.   */File Import with Numbers*

```
         "Defective Products", "Vendor", "Quantity"
         "Beds", "Quiet Sleeper", 10
         "Openers", "Easy Can", 25
         "Lamps", "Bright Light", 15
```

Figure 8-17.   *A delimited text file*

Changing the Current Directory

The /File Dir command permits you to change the disk drive or directory for your current 1-2-3 session. When you enter **/File Dir**, 1-2-3 displays the existing directory. You can press ENTER to accept it, or type a new directory or pathname. If you just want to reach a lower level directory, you can type the new level into the existing directory listing.

Working with Multiple Files

In Release 3 you can open multiple files in memory at the same time. Chapter 4, "Changing the Appearances of the Worksheet Display," described how you can have a single worksheet file that contains multiple worksheets. When you have multiple files open in memory, you can move between them just as you can with multiple sheets in the same file. You can copy between files to transfer information from one file to another, but you cannot specify ranges that span files.

You can add new files to 1-2-3's memory, delete files from 1-2-3's memory, and use commands that use data from other commands. 1-2-3 allows you to open as many files simultaneously as you like—as long as the total number of worksheets in all active files does not exceed 256. With multiple files, an *active* file or worksheet is a file or worksheet that 1-2-3 has in its memory. The *current* file or worksheet is the one that contains the cell pointer.

Opening and Closing Multiple Files

When you use one file at a time, you open a file with the /File Retrieve command, and remove it with another /File Retrieve command or the

/Worksheet Erase command. To use multiple files, you need to open a file without removing the current files. Release 3's /File Open command opens a file without affecting the other files in memory. With Release 3.4, you can use the File Open SmartIcon shown below, rather than the menu for opening files. Using this icon, you can open files without removing other files currently in memory.

When you use /File Open, 1-2-3 prompts you to determine if you want to open the file before or after the current one. For example, assume you have the worksheet files in Figure 8-18 and you are currently in the YEARLY worksheet file (the second worksheet in the perspective view). If you add the BUDGET file before the YEARLY file, 1-2-3 changes the order of the files to SUMMARY, BUDGET, and YEARLY. If you add the BUDGET file after the YEARLY file, 1-2-3 changes the order of the files to SUMMARY, YEARLY, and BUDGET. When you select Before or After, 1-2-3 inserts the new file before or after the current file rather than the current worksheet. For example, let's say the SUMMARY.WK3

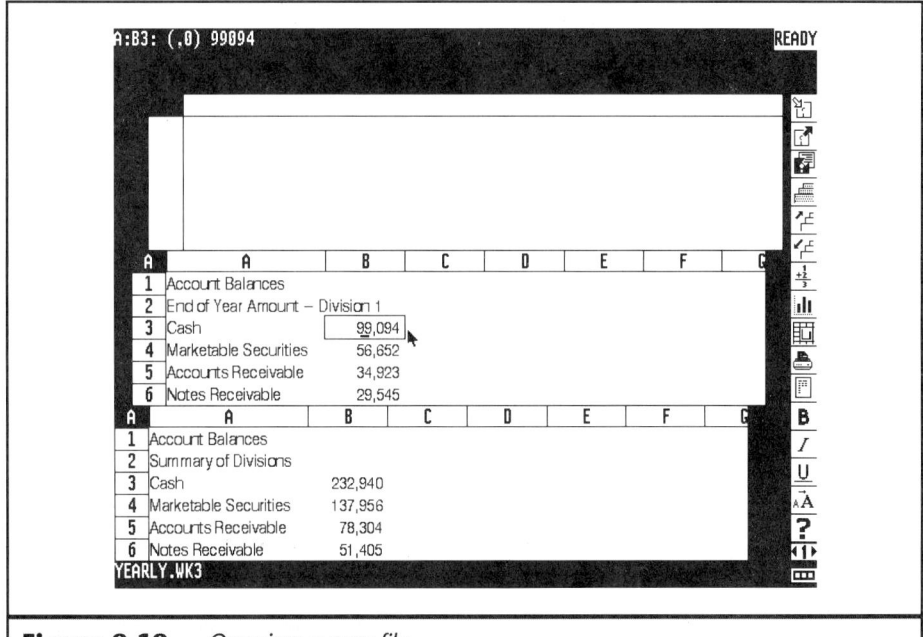

Figure 8-18. *Opening a new file*

file has three worksheets, and the B worksheet is current. Adding a file before the current file places the opened file before worksheet A of SUMMARY; adding a file after the current file places the opened file after worksheet C of SUMMARY.

Another option for opening a file while keeping other files in memory is to open a new file. You can do this by using either the /File New command or the File New SmartIcon shown below, which duplicates the /File New command.

The /File New command also has Before and After options that determine whether the new file is placed before or after the current file. Once this choice is made, 1-2-3 prompts for a filename. Like the /File Save command, /File New displays a default filename (FILE0001.WK3 or a higher number). You can enter a new filename or accept the default, and press ENTER. This filename appears in the status line when the file is active. The disk file for the new file is empty until the /File Save command saves its contents.

Once another worksheet file is opened, you can continue to use any of 1-2-3's worksheet features that you can use in single worksheets. To move between files without continually pressing CTRL-PGUP and CTRL-PGDN, try the keys in Table 8-1.

When you have multiple files open, 1-2-3 functions a little differently when some commands are executed. The worksheet settings remain with the worksheet file that originated them. After you open multiple worksheet files, changes that you make with Worksheet commands are saved with the worksheet that is current when the command is invoked. The /File Save command displays [ALL MODIFIED FILES] as the filename to save. Accepting this option saves all files that you have changed since the last /File Save command. If you press F2

CTRL-END-HOME	Moves to the cell last highlighted in the first active file.
CTRL-END-END	Moves to the cell last highlighted in the last active file.
CTRL-END-CTRL-PGUP	Moves to the cell last highlighted in the next active file.
CTRL-END-CTRL-PGDN	Moves to the cell last highlighted in the previous active file.

Table 8-1. *Keys for Moving the Cell Pointer Between Files*

(EDIT) with this prompt on the screen, 1-2-3 changes the filename prompt to the current file. Each file allows a range name to be used once, but you can use a single range name in each of the files if you choose.

When you are finished with and have saved a worksheet, you may want to remove it from 1-2-3's memory so you can load other files. To remove an active worksheet file, use the /Worksheet Delete File command. This command removes the current worksheet from 1-2-3's memory. Remember: the contents of this worksheet file are not saved unless you save it with the /File Save command. The /Worksheet Delete File command does not affect any files on the disk. To replace the current file use the /File Retrieve command. 1-2-3 will leave the other active files intact.

Using Multiple Files in Commands

Most 1-2-3 commands can use ranges from different files. For most commands, the file the command uses must be active.

In some cases, the file can be active or be on the default directory—specifically, when you are naming the From ranges for the /Copy, /Range Trans, and /Range Value commands. As an example, assume you want to copy the values in the TOTAL range in a YEARLY worksheet file, to the current worksheet. Use the /Range Value command to copy the values. When 1-2-3 prompts for the From range, enter **<<C:\123R34\YEARLY.WK3>>TOTAL**. When you press ENTER to select the current cell as the To range, 1-2-3 copies the values from the TOTAL range in the YEARLY.WK3 file starting at the current cell.

TIP: Use range names, rather than cell addresses as From ranges. Since 1-2-3 does not adjust cell references to an external file if you move them, you will want to use range names, which are automatically adjusted for their new location in the external file.

External File Links

Release 3 allows you to establish links between the current worksheet and data stored in cells or ranges on disk. You can use this feature to reference data in another file, and 1-2-3 will update the copy of the data that you reference. In previous releases of 1-2-3, if you wanted to use the data from another worksheet, you could use /File Xtract to extract it from the other worksheet, and /File Combine to combine it with the current worksheet. Another option was directly copying the data with /File Combine, using a named range in the other file. In both scenarios, you needed to continue using /File Combine to refresh the imported data when the data in the other file changed. You can also create links to external files, and 1-2-3 updates their values every time you use the /File Admin Link-Refresh command.

To refer to a value in another worksheet file, the cell address, range address, or range name is preceded by the filename surrounded by the file delimiter. (1-2-3 uses double angle brackets (<< >>).) 1-2-3 assumes the file is in the current directory unless a path is provided. If you want to include values from a file that you have not saved yet, you should include an empty file reference. Make sure you fill in this empty reference later, as 1-2-3 will not complete it for you.

1-2-3 also supports a wildcard feature that allows you to access a specified range name in any open file. If you use ? as the file reference for a range name's source, 1-2-3 uses the range name in all active files. You cannot include the wildcard ? filename specification with a cell address; if you do, 1-2-3 returns ERR.

TIP: If a file is linked to other files, include the pathname. By including the pathname, the worksheet can find the values it needs even when another directory is current. If 1-2-3 cannot find the file in the current directory, the formula containing the link to an external file returns ERR.

Figure 8-19 shows a formula that computes the yearly total for a company with multiple divisions. Each division has its own worksheet file. The first worksheet of each file contains the summary information for the entire year. The summary worksheet for the entire company adds the different ranges for each of the division's summary worksheets. The formula uses range names rather than cell addresses so that 1-2-3 can adjust the range names if they are moved.

When you have links between files (especially inactive ones), you will want to check that the numbers are still the most current values. This is a

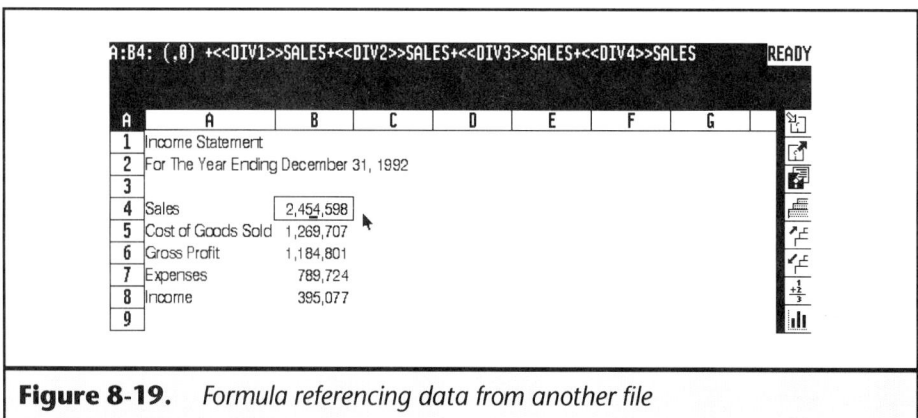

Figure 8-19. *Formula referencing data from another file*

recommended step before you print the worksheet, or before you extract values from it to use in another worksheet file. To recalculate values from other files, use the /File Admin Link-Refresh command. With this command, 1-2-3 rechecks all formulas in your current worksheet that refer to values in other files. 1-2-3 only checks values from other files when the formulas are entered, when the /File Admin Link-Refresh command is performed, or when the cell containing a reference to an external file is edited.

Other Ways to Work with Files

1-2-3 provides several commands and features, in addition to those on the File menu, that are useful in working with files.

Creating a Worksheet File That Loads Automatically

1-2-3 provides the ability to automatically load a specific worksheet file every time you bring up 1-2-3. The only requirement for creating this special worksheet is that you name it AUTO123 and place it in the default directory.

With this feature you can create a worksheet that contains help information for your application, and that documents the names of files to retrieve for different applications, to give one example. When you learn about macros in Chapters 12 and 13, you will see further applications for this capability. It allows you to start an application with no intervention from the operator, which eliminates any possibility for error. As soon as 1-2-3 is brought up, the application is started. Creating an automatically executing macro requires a setting of Yes for the /Worksheet Global Default Autoexec command.

Changing the Default Directory Permanently

The /File Dir command is used to change the disk drive or directory for the current 1-2-3 session. To change the default directory permanently, use /Worksheet Global Default Dir followed by /Worksheet Global Default Update to save your changes in the file 123R34.CNF.

The /Worksheet Global Default Dir command allows you to change the default disk drive or directory that 1-2-3 uses when saving or retrieving data files. If you do not change the default directory, it remains specified as the directory where you installed 1-2-3. To change the default directory, enter **/Worksheet Global Default Dir** and then the directory you want to use. After you press ENTER, this directory will be in effect for the remainder of your 1-2-3 session.

To make the change to the default directory permanent, enter **/Worksheet Global Default Update**. This saves any changes made through the Default options, and ensures they will be available for your next 1-2-3 session. The changes are saved in 1-2-3's configuration file, called 123R34.CNF.

Changing the Default Directory for Temporary Files

1-2-3 sometimes creates temporary files. These files are stored in memory if there is room, and written to disk with the extension .TMP if there is no room in memory. Temporary files are created when you are printing a copy of a worksheet in memory. The default location for these files is in your main 1-2-3 directory, which will be the file server when you are running 1-2-3 on the network. You can improve performance by having temporary files written to your own system rather than the file server. To do this use the /Worksheet Global Default Temp command to change the directory where the temporary files reside.

TIP: When working on a network, do not attempt to write the temporary files to a read-only directory. Choose a location on your own system. If you must choose another location on the file server, at least be certain not to select a read-only directory.

Setting the Default File Extension

You can set the file extensions for 1-2-3 to use with the /File commands. To set the default extension, enter **/Worksheet Global Default Ext**. To select the default extension for the /File New, /File Save, and /File Xtract commands, select Save and enter a three-character extension. To select the default extension for the /File Admin Table Worksheet, /File Combine, /File Erase, /File List, /File Open, and /File Retrieve commands, select List and enter the three-character extension 1-2-3 should use. You can use these two options to set 1-2-3 to work only with

.WK3 or .WK1 files. The change becomes permanent if you select /Worksheet Global Default Update.

Using Operating System Commands

Release 3 allows you to access DOS commands from within 1-2-3, through the /System command. You can use DOS commands while still retaining your worksheet in memory. The only requirement for using /System is that COMMAND.COM be in the 1-2-3 directory or a directory 1-2-3 can access through DOS's PATH command.

Let's say, for example, that you plan to import a file to the worksheet but forgot to assign it a suffix of .PRN. You can use /System to leave 1-2-3 temporarily and use the DOS RENAME command. Likewise, if you attempt to save a file and the disk is full, you can use /System to access DOS and format a floppy disk, while keeping your current worksheet in memory.

To access DOS commands, enter /**System**. At the DOS prompt, enter the DOS command of your choice. Caution: keep in mind that commands like PRINT, which cause DOS to overlay memory, will erase your worksheet data. Any memory-resident DOS command, such as DIR or COPY, can be used with no problem. However, DOS commands such as GRAPHICS and MODE that require a program to be permanently loaded in memory can cause problems. FORMAT is an externally stored program, but it does not remain permanently resident and thus can be used without problems.

Since 1-2-3 Release 3 adds DOS extenders that allow you to access all of your memory, you may even be able to run some of your other software from this temporary exit. Just be certain that you save your worksheet files before trying this, until you are certain that a specific package will execute smoothly and then let you return to 1-2-3 without having damaged the program or the worksheet in memory.

The /System command displays the DOS header shown in Figure 8-20. You can enter your DOS commands as usual. When you are finished with DOS, enter **EXIT**; you will return to your 1-2-3 worksheet exactly where you left off.

Translating Files from Other Programs

1-2-3 has several options for translating data from one format to another. 1-2-3 includes a separate program, called Translate, to translate file formats that 1-2-3 commands cannot handle. 1-2-3 also has individual translation programs that

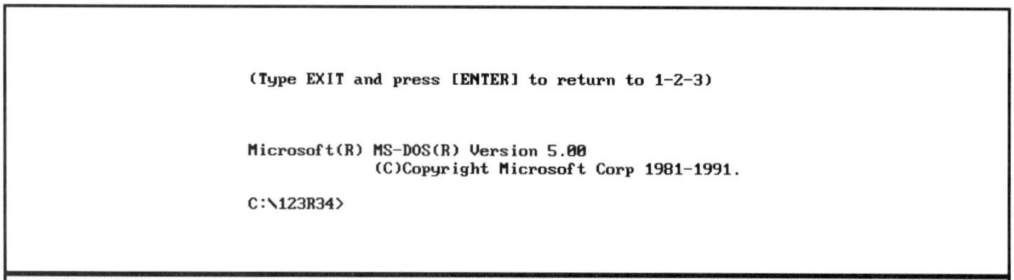

```
              (Type EXIT and press [ENTER] to return to 1-2-3)

           Microsoft(R) MS-DOS(R) Version 5.00
                       (C)Copyright Microsoft Corp 1981-1991.

           C:\123R34>
```

Figure 8-20.   *DOS header*

you can use instead of the menu-driven Translate Program. Some of the 1-2-3 commands can also translate data.

1-2-3's Translate Program

The 1-2-3 Translate Program is part of the Lotus Access System. It provides the ability to translate 1-2-3 files to other file formats, and files from other programs to the 1-2-3 format. Translate can be accessed directly from DOS or through the Lotus Access System. To use it you must first quit 1-2-3 with /Quit Yes or /System.

Select Translate from the Lotus Access System, or enter **trans** at the DOS prompt. When working with Translate, you first have to select the format to translate from. A list of Release 3's From format options is shown in Figure 8-21.

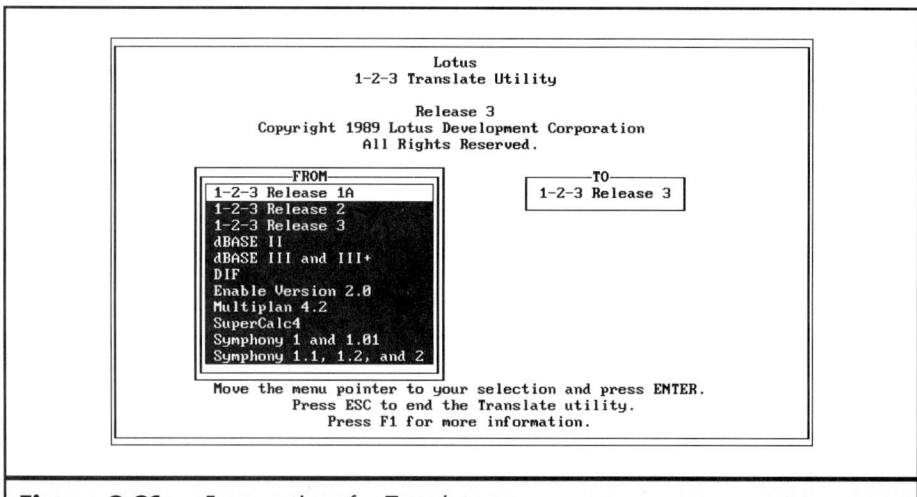

Figure 8-21.   *From options for Translate*

After making this selection, you are prompted to choose from the list of To formats shown in Figure 8-22. Translate displays a message if the formats you choose do not need translation. You do not need to translate Release 1A files in order to use them with Release 3. Nor do you need to translate Symphony files for use with Release 3 of 1-2-3, or Release 2 files for use with Release 3. However, converting to an earlier version of 1-2-3 eliminates new features from the files.

Once you select the To and From data formats, 1-2-3 prompts for the filename in the current directory that you want to translate. You can enter the filename directly, or select it from the list provided. Translate assumes that the translated file (the To file) will have the same filename, with an appropriate extension for the new data format. You can use asterisks and question marks to translate multiple files, such as BUDGET*.WK3 or *.DBF. When you translate multiple files, Translate uses some settings, such as orientation (DIF format), for all of the files. If the file already exists, Translate asks you if you want to write over the existing file. Select Yes to write over the file, or No to abort the translation and return to the file selection list.

If you are translating from 1-2-3 Release 3 to another format, Translate asks you if you want to translate all the sheets in the file. If you select All Worksheets, 1-2-3 uses the first six letters of the filename you provided and adds two characters for the worksheet letter, to form the new filename. For example, translating TAXTABLE.WK3 with four worksheets to TAXTABLE.WK1 creates the TAXTAB0A.WK1, TAXTAB0B.WK1, TAXTAB0C.WK1, and TAXTAB0D.WK1 files. If you select One Worksheet, Translate prompts you for the worksheet letter while displaying the default of "A." When you translate from Release 3, the file cannot be password protected. Also, if the file was created with /File Xtract, you must load it and save it with /File Save before translating it.

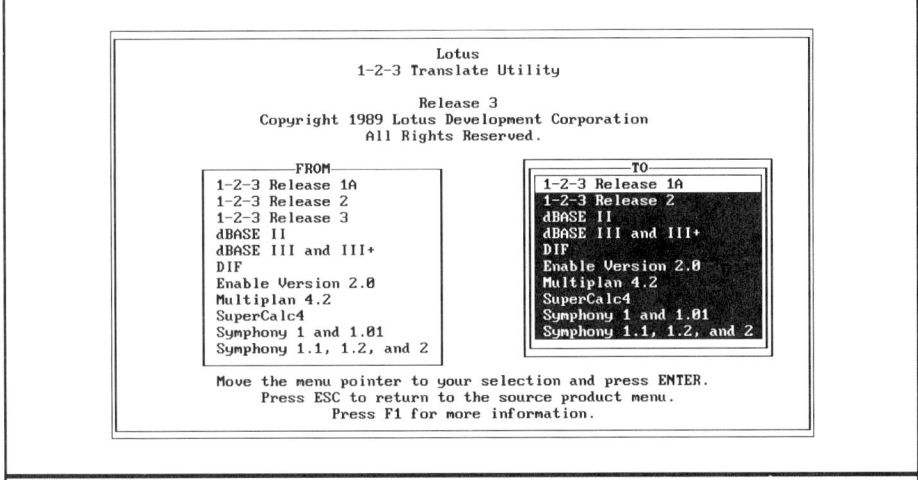

Figure 8-22. *To options for Translate*

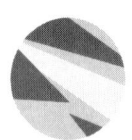

TIP: The first six letters of a file to be translated should be unique, because 1-2-3 uses these six letters, plus two characters for the worksheet letter, when it translates multiple worksheets. Let's say you translate INVENT.WK3 and INVENTRY.WK3 with three worksheets each. 1-2-3 translates the INVENT.WK3 file as INVENT0A, INVENT0B, and INVENT0C with the appropriate extension. Then it translates the INVENTRY.WK3 file also as INVENT0A, INVENT0B, and INVENT0C with the same extension, and writes over the first set (INVENT.WK3) of worksheets. To prevent this, you can use a different name for one of the output files, such as INV.WK3. Translate will then translate the worksheets to the INV0A, INV0B, INV0C, INVENT0A, INVENT0B, and INVENT0C files.

If you are translating to DIF format, Translate prompts for a row or column orientation. If you are translating to a dBASE II, dBASE III, or dBASE III+ format, Translate asks if you want to translate a named range or the entire file. If you select Named Range, you must enter a range name when Translate prompts for one.

Finally, Translate prompts if you want to continue. Select Yes to translate the file, or No to return to the initial Translate menu. Once you instruct Translate to continue, Translate converts the file and returns a message telling you that it did or did not successfully translate the file. To exit the Translate Program, press ESC until Translate asks if you want to leave, and select Yes.

When Translate translates a file, it only converts the features that are common to both data format types. For example, when Release 3 converts to Release 2, it truncates Release 3 labels larger than 512 characters to 240-character labels in Release 2.

When you translate to Release 2 or Symphony, Translate prompts you to select between Labels or Add-ins to determine how Release 3 @functions and link formulas are treated. Select Add-ins to have the translated file treat Release 3 @functions and link formulas as add-in functions; select Labels to store them as labels. Other limitations of translating Release 3 worksheet files into Release 2 worksheets are covered later in the section "Translating with 1-2-3 commands."

Translation Programs

The individual translation programs are included with the 1-2-3 files. Using these files directly, instead of through the Translate Program, reduces steps and allows you to incorporate the translation programs into a batch file. 1-2-3 has translation programs for each of the data formats handled by the Translate Program. Each translation program translates 1-2-3 files to another format, and files from another program to the 1-2-3 format. The translation programs can be accessed directly from DOS. To use them, you must quit 1-2-3 with /Quit Yes.

At the DOS prompt, enter the name of the translation program you want, the input data file, the output data file, and any flags the translation program uses. The box called "Translation Programs" names the translation programs and tells when you use each one. The individual translation programs use file extensions to determine the data formats of the input and output files. If the default extensions do not match your filenames and extensions, you must rename your files before translating them. You can use asterisks and question marks to translate multiple files, such as BUDGET*.WK3 or *.DBF.

The flags used by each translation program consist of the responses to the prompts you see when you use Translate Program to translate files. Flags consist of a hyphen, followed by one or more letters. The -c flag (used by the TRANDIF translation program) transposes the row/column orientation that the DIF files use. The -l# flag (used by all translation programs except TRANSYLK) selects the worksheet letter of the Release 3 input file being translated. The -o flag (used by any translation program) overwrites any existing file with the same name. The -p flag (used by TRANDB2 and TRANDB3 translation programs) names the range of the input worksheet file that the program translates.

Translating with an individual translation program has the same limitations as translating through the Translate Program. For example, if you are translating from 1-2-3 Release 3 to another format, the file cannot be password protected. If the Release 3 file was created with /File Xtract, you must load it and save it with /File Save before translating it. If you are translating multiple worksheets from a Release 3 file, the translation program follows the same filename conventions of

Translation Programs

File	Use
TRANDB2	Translates 1-2-3 Release 3 to dBASE II, and vice versa.
TRANDB3	Translates 1-2-3 Release 3 to dBASE III or dBASE III+, and dBASEIII or dBASEIII+ to 1-2-3 Release 3.
TRANDIF	Translates 1-2-3 Release 3 to DIF format files, and vice versa.
TRANSYLK	Translates Multiplan Release 1 and 2 to 1-2-3 Release 3, and vice versa.
TRANWKS	Translates 1-2-3 Release 3 to 1-2-3 Release 1A, 2, and 2.01, and Symphony.
TRANENE2	Translates Release 3 files to Enable.
TRANSUP4	Translates Release 3 files to SuperCalc4.

the Translate Program—that is, using the first six letters of the name and adding two letters for the worksheet letter.

When a translation program translates a file, it only converts the data that the output file format accepts. For example, when Release 3 converts to dBASE III+, the TRANDB3 program converts Release 3 formulas to the formula results, and puts the results in the output file.

Translating with 1-2-3 Commands

Some data formats do not need to be translated with the Translate Program because 1-2-3 can translate the data with the /File commands. The /File Retrieve command can retrieve 1-2-3 Release 1A, 2, and 3 files, as well as Symphony (any release). When Release 3.4 retrieves a Release 1A or Symphony file, it loads the data into memory and creates a file with the same name and a .WK3 file extension. Since this .WK3 file is empty, 1-2-3 will delete it if you do not save the file. Release 3.4 cannot save files in a Release 1A or Symphony format. The /File Save command can save files in a Release 2 or Release 3 format by using the file extension to tell 1-2-3 which format to use to save the data. If the worksheet does not contain any Release 3 specific features, 1-2-3 saves a file with a .WK1 extension in Release 2 format. If most of the files you are using and saving are Release 2 format, use the /Worksheet Global Default Ext Save and /Worksheet Global Default Update commands to set the default extension to .WK1.

When 1-2-3 retrieves a Release 2 file, it follows the setting of the /Worksheet Global Default Other International Release-2 command. This command has two options. The LICS option enables the LICS character set that Release 2 uses for Compose key characters, to create special characters such as foreign letters. The ASCII option is for Release 2 files created with the ASCII No-LICS driver available with Release 2.01. You will need to change this setting to ASCII if you load a Release 2 file and special characters in the file do not appear correctly.

When 1-2-3 saves a .WK1 file that has Release 3 features, 1-2-3 makes several conversions. 1-2-3 truncates long labels after 240 characters. Formulas with more than 240 characters are stored intact up to 2000 characters; however, if you edit the formula, 1-2-3 Release 2 will truncate the formula after 240 characters. Release 3 @functions become add-in @functions and evaluate as NA. 1-2-3 deletes range name notes and formula annotations. New command settings that Release 3 saves with the file disappear in the Release 2 worksheet file. Once 1-2-3 makes these conversions, it displays an error message telling you that some information is lost. The /File Save command cannot convert a Release 3 file to a Release 2 file if it contains multiple worksheets. The /File Xtract command can translate a worksheet by selecting the used portion of a worksheet for the extract range, as long as it is not a range that spans sheets in a three-dimensional file.

Command Reference

Files

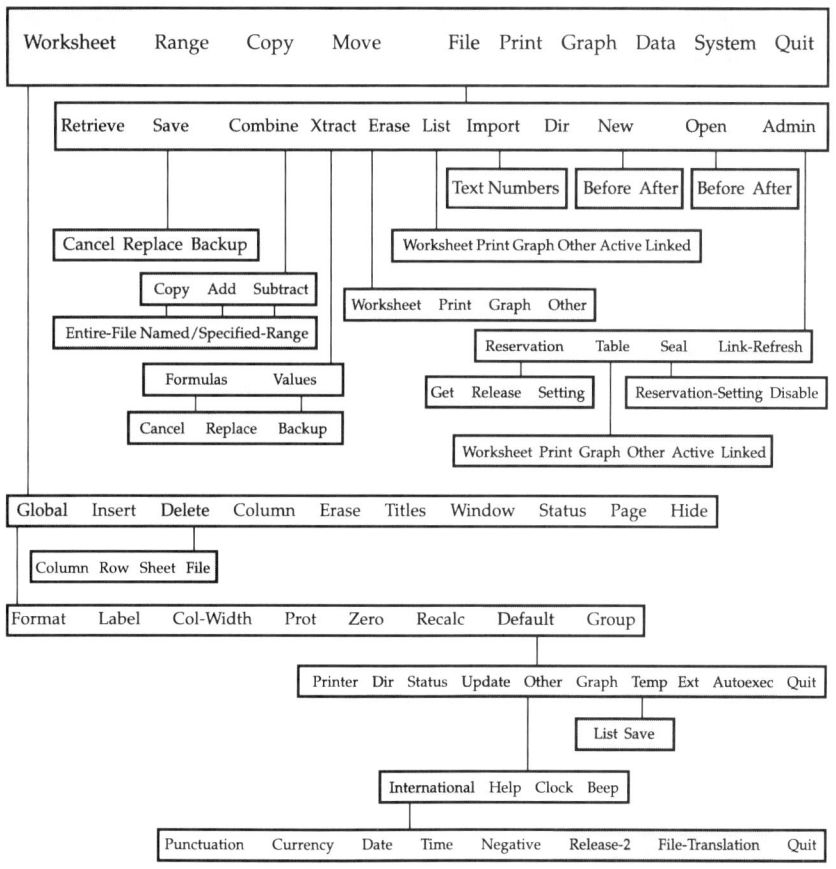

©1989 Lotus Development Corporation. Used with permisstion.

/File Admin Link-Refresh

Description

This command recalculates formulas in the current worksheet that have active links to other files.

/File Admin Reservation

Description

This command gets the file reservation, releases the file reservation, or sets when the file reservation is obtained. A file reservation is permission from the operating system to save the modified file over the original. File reservations are important in networks where more than one user may want the file. Only one person may have the file reservation. You can tell if you have the file reservation because RO for read-only appears in the status line when you do not have it.

Options

The options for this command manipulate the file reservation setting.

GET This option attempts to obtain the file reservation if you do not already have it. If 1-2-3 can obtain the file reservation for the current worksheet file, the RO indicator will disappear. If 1-2-3 cannot obtain the file reservation, the RO indicator remains. Possible reasons for not being able to obtain the file reservation include someone else using the file, the file changing since you retrieved it, and not having write access to the file.

RELEASE This option releases the file reservation so someone else can get it. Since you cannot save the file using the same name, make sure to save the worksheet before selecting this option.

SETTING This option controls when 1-2-3 obtains the reservation for the file. You can select Automatic (the default) to obtain the reservation when you retrieve the file, or Manual to obtain the reservation only when you use the Get option. The choice you make is saved with the file and applies each time you use the file.

/File Admin Seal Reservation-Setting

Description

This command seals the reservation setting made with the /File Admin Reservation-Setting command. Once you seal the reservation setting, you can unseal it only with /File Admin Seal Disable, providing the password you used to seal the file.

Options

The only option for this command is the password you enter. Like other passwords, the password can be up to 15 characters and cannot include spaces. The password distinguishes between upper- and lowercase. You must enter the password twice as a check that you are entering it correctly.

/File Admin Table

Description

This command creates a table that lists all the files of the specified type in the current directory. The table is four columns wide (seven columns for listing active files) and as many rows long as the directory has file entries. This command can select which files it lists.

Options

This command has six options to select the type of files in the table. The table includes the filenames and extensions, the date serial number when the file was saved last, the time serial number when the file was saved last, and the size. The Active option also includes three other columns. The Worksheet, Print, Graph, and Other options can further limit which files 1-2-3 lists by modifying the filename skeleton. Once you select the type of files 1-2-3 will list in the table, you must specify where you want 1-2-3 to put the information. This area must be unprotected and blank so that the table does not overwrite worksheet information.

WORKSHEET This option lists the worksheet files with the file extension set by the /Worksheet Global Default Ext List command.

PRINT This option lists the .PRN files. To list the encoded files, type ***.ENC** when 1-2-3 displays the file skeleton.

GRAPH This option lists the graphic image files with the file extension set by the /Worksheet Global Default Graph command.

OTHER This option lists all files.

ACTIVE This option lists the active files. The table created with this option contains three additional columns. The first extra column contains the number of worksheets in each file. The second extra column contains a 1 if the file has changed since it became active, or a 0 otherwise. The third extra column contains a 1 if you have the reservation in a network environment or a single user environment, or a 0 otherwise. A 1 in this column allows you to update this file.

LINKED This option lists the files to which the current file is linked by formula references. The first column of the table created with this option contains the pathname with the filename.

/File Combine Add

Description

The /File Combine Add command permits you to add some or all of the values from a worksheet file to current worksheet values. The addition process uses the cell pointer location as the upper leftmost cell to be combined with the first cell in the worksheet or range you are adding. Only cells that are blank or contain values are affected by this process. Cells that contain formulas or labels are unaffected.

The Add option is useful when you are performing a budget consolidation. You can begin with a total budget worksheet that contains nothing more than labels and a few total formulas. As long as all departmental budgets are in exactly the same format as the total worksheet, you can use /File Combine Add once for each worksheet file to produce a budget consolidation. This command can incorporate data from Release 1A, 2, and 3 files.

Options

Like the other /File Combine options, Add permits you to combine an entire file or a named range. In either case, it begins the combination at the cell pointer location. The cells in the combined range must have the format of the incoming data.

ENTIRE-FILE   With this option, every value cell in the worksheet file is added to a cell in the current worksheet. Cell A1 in the file is added to the cell where the cell pointer rests in the current worksheet. Remaining values will be added to the cell with the proper displacement from the current cell pointer location.

When you select Entire-File, the names of the worksheet files on the current disk (in the current directory if you are using a hard disk) are displayed. You can either point to one of the filenames or enter another filename you wish to use. 1-2-3 assumes that the file has a .WK3 file extension, unless you provide another one or select a filename from the list that has a different extension. Likewise, you can access files on a different drive or in a different directory if you supply the complete pathname.

NAMED/SPECIFIED-RANGE   With this option, only the cells in the selected range are combined with the cells in the current worksheet, starting at the current cell pointer position. 1-2-3 asks you to specify a range address or name, and then the file that contains this range. The range name you specify must be valid for the filename specified. The rules for entering the filename are the same as for Entire-File.

/File Combine Copy

Description

The /File Combine Copy command permits you to replace some or all of the values from the current worksheet with values (including formulas and labels) from a worksheet file. The copying process uses the cell pointer location in the current worksheet as the upper leftmost cell to be replaced with the first cell in the worksheet or range you are copying. Unlike /File Combine Add, current worksheet cells containing formulas and labels are affected by /File Combine Copy. They will be overwritten by the copied information.

The Copy feature is useful when you would like to copy headings and values from an existing worksheet to one you are currently creating. Although formulas can also be copied, you must be sure that the values they require are also copied, or an error could result.

Options

Like the other /File Combine options, Copy permits you to combine an entire file or a named range. The Entire-File and Named/Specified-Range options are described under the /File Combine Add command. In either case, Copy begins the replacement at the cell pointer location.

/File Combine Subtract

Description

The /File Combine Subtract command permits you to subtract some or all of the values from a worksheet file from the current worksheet values. The subtraction process uses the cell pointer location as the upper leftmost cell to be combined with the first cell in the worksheet or range you are subtracting. Only cells that are blank or contain values are affected by this process. Cells that contain formulas or labels are unaffected.

The Subtract option is useful when you are performing a budget consolidation. You can begin with a total budget worksheet. Then, to see the effect of closing one of a company's departments or subsidiaries, you can subtract the file containing its budget projections from the total. All subsidiary budgets must be in exactly the same format as the total worksheet, however.

Options

Like the other /File Combine options, Subtract permits you to combine an entire file or a named range. The Entire-File and Named/Specified-Range options are described under the /File Combine Add command. In either case, Subtract begins the combination at the cell pointer location. The cells in the combined range must have the format of the incoming data.

/File Dir

Description

The /File Dir command allows you to check or change the current Root directory that 1-2-3 is using for file storage and retrieval. With Release 3, the default directory is the subdirectory containing the 1-2-3 files, unless another directory has been set as the default. The /File Dir command lets you make a change only for the current session. If you wish to change the default directory permanently, use /Worksheet Global Default Dir followed by /Worksheet Global Default Update to save your change.

Options

With this command, you can simply review the current directory setting or change it. To review the setting, simply press ENTER after you have seen the /File Dir display.

To change the directory for the session, first decide if you want to change the complete directory that is designated, or to stay in the same directory and just change the subdirectory. You can change the drive, the directory, and the subdirectory with this command. To change the drive, type the drive designator followed by a backslash, for example, **B:**. To change the path as well, type the pathname at the same time, as in **B:\123R34\SALES**. To change the directory, enter or edit the entry so that it contains the new directory information.

/File Erase

Description

The /File Erase command is used to remove one or more files from the disk.

Options

First choose the type of file or files you wish to remove from the disk. With Release 3, your options are the following:

Worksheet	Worksheet files with the file extension set by the /Worksheet Global Default Ext command
Print	Print files with the .PRN file extension
Graph	Graph files with the file extension set by the /Worksheet Global Default Graph command
Other	Files with any file extension

Once you specify the file type you wish to delete, 1-2-3 lists all the files of that type that are on the current drive or directory. You can point to the file you wish to delete, or type in the filename. If the file you wish to delete is on a different drive or in a different directory, press F2 (EDIT) and change the drive designator and pathname to the path containing the file. After you select the file you want to delete, 1-2-3 prompts for a confirmation. Select Yes to delete the file, or No to cancel the command.

/File Import

Description

The /File Import command permits you to load information from a print file into the current worksheet at the cell pointer location. Standard ASCII files that do not exceed 8192 lines can be imported.

Options

/File Import offers two options, allowing you to bring either a column of long labels (Text option) or a combination of numbers and labels (Numbers option) into the worksheet. Once you have selected Text or Numbers, 1-2-3 lists the .PRN files in the current directory. To list files with a different extension, type *. followed by the extension you want, and press ENTER. After a filename is selected, 1-2-3 imports the file and places the data starting at the cell pointer's location.

TEXT   This option brings each line of the imported text file into the worksheet as a single long label. /Data Parse can then split files imported as text into separate entries, rather than one long label (see Chapter 10 for more information). This option imports up to 512 characters from each line into the worksheet.

NUMBERS   This option searches the imported file for numbers and for text entries enclosed in quotes. Each number is placed in a worksheet cell as a value, and each text entry in quotes is placed in a cell as a left justified label. If more than one number or enclosed text entry is found in a line of the text file, more than one column of the worksheet will be used. When the next line of the imported file is processed, entries will begin again the same column as the cell pointer.

NOTE: Special characters added by some word processors can cause problems. Most word processors have an option that excludes these special characters to produce a standard ASCII file.

/File List

Description

The /File List command lists all the files of the specified type in the current directory. This command creates a temporary listing, rather than the permanent listing the /File Admin Table command creates.

Options

With Release 3, you have six /File List choices:

Worksheet	Worksheet files with the file extension set by the /Worksheet Global Default Ext command
Print	Print files with the .PRN file extension
Graph	Graph files with the file extension set by the /Worksheet Global Default Graph command
Other	Files with any file extension
Active	All the active files
Linked	Files to which the current file is linked by formula references

Once you have specified the file type, 1-2-3 displays the filenames of all files of the selected type. For each filename you highlight, 1-2-3 displays the date serial number when the file was last saved, the time serial number when the file was last saved, and the file size, at the top of the list. In addition, the Active option also displays the number of worksheets in the file; the flag "MOD" or "UNMOD" to indicate if the file has been modified or remains unchanged; and "RO" if the file is read only in a network environment. The Linked option includes the pathname of the linked files.

/File New

Description

This command creates a blank worksheet file and inserts it into the current worksheets. Use /File New to insert a blank worksheet file that is separate from the other worksheet files in memory. After executing the command, the cell pointer is at A1 of the new file. The new file has the name you provide when you perform this command and the default file extension specified by the /Worksheet Global Default Ext Save command.

Options

This command has two options, Before and After, which identify the new worksheet file's location relative to the current file. You cannot insert a new worksheet file between the worksheets in another file. When 1-2-3 prompts for a filename and displays the default filename (FILE followed by the next highest number), enter a filename but only provide an extension if you want to override the default extension.

/File Open

Description

The /File Open command loads a file from disk into the memory of your computer. This command is used to open additional multiple files in memory. The other files in 1-2-3's memory remain in place. You can open a file from the current disk or directory, or from a different one if you specify the pathname. If you want a file from the current directory, you can select it from the list 1-2-3 displays. A file extension only needs to be provided if the file does not have the default file extension specified by the /Worksheet Global Default Ext Save command. 1-2-3 can retrieve files with .WKS (1-2-3 Release 1A), .WRK (Symphony), .WR1 (Symphony), .WK1 (1-2-3 Release 2), and .WK3 (Release 3) extensions.

You can open password-protected files by supplying the correct password when 1-2-3 prompts you. The opened file uses the recalculation and window settings in effect when the file is opened but 1-2-3 remembers the file's original settings when it saves the file.

Options

This command has two options, Before and After, which determine the opened worksheet file's location relative to the current file. You cannot insert a worksheet file between the worksheets in another file. If the file you want to open is used in a network environment and 1-2-3 cannot get the file reservation for you, 1-2-3 displays a Yes or No selection. Select Yes if you want read-only access to the file, or No to cancel the command.

/File Retrieve

Description

The /File Retrieve command loads a file from disk into the memory of your computer. The current worksheet file is erased by the loading of the new file.

Options

You can retrieve a file from the current disk or directory, or from a different one if you specify the pathname. You can retrieve password-protected files by supplying the password when 1-2-3 prompts you. 1-2-3 can retrieve files with extensions of .WKS (1-2-3 Release 1A), .WRK (Symphony), .WR1 (Symphony), .WK1 (1-2-3 Release 2), and .WK3 (Release 3). If the file you are retrieving is used in a network environment and 1-2-3 cannot get the file reservation for you, 1-2-3 displays a Yes or No selection. Select Yes if you want read-only access to the file, or No to cancel the command.

/File Save

Description

The /File Save command allows you to save the current worksheet and any settings you have created for it to a worksheet file. If 1-2-3 has multiple worksheet files in memory, it offers you the option of saving all modified files.

Options

The first time the file is saved, 1-2-3 displays a default filename of FILE*nnnn*.WK3, where *nnnn* is a number beginning at 0001 and incrementing by one as each filename is used. You can save the worksheet file to the current disk by accepting the default name, or entering another filename and pressing ENTER. If you wish to use a disk or directory different from the current one, you must specify the complete pathname.

If the file is already saved on the disk, 1-2-3 will prompt you with the existing filename. Press ENTER to accept it. The next prompt is a choice between Cancel, Replace, or Backup. Cancel stops the /File Save command and returns you to READY mode. Replace places the current contents of memory on the disk under the existing filename, erasing what was stored in the file previously. Backup copies the previous version of the file to a separate file with the same filename and a .BAK file extension, before saving the current version.

If 1-2-3 has multiple files in memory when you enter /File Save, it displays "[ALL MODIFIED FILES]" as the filename. Press ENTER to save all files modified since the last /File Save command. If you want to save only the current file, press F2 (EDIT) to convert "[ALL MODIFIED FILES]" to the current filename. From this point, you can modify or accept the current filename and press ENTER. If you want to save a file other than the current file, switch to the worksheet in the file you want to save.

This command also allows you to add a password to a file when it is saved. Once a file is saved with a password, you cannot retrieve the file unless you supply the password. After typing the name of the file to be saved, press the SPACEBAR and type **p**. 1-2-3 will prompt you for a password up to 15 characters long. After you enter it, a prompt will ask you to verify it by entering it again. Passwords are case sensitive, so be sure you enter the password in the upper- or lowercase letters that you want for this password. If you wish to abort the password procedure, instead of verifying the password, you can press ESC several times to return to READY mode, without saving the file or adding a password.

To change the password, press BACKSPACE to remove "[PASSWORD PROTECTED]" when 1-2-3 displays the filename. Then press the SPACEBAR and type a **p**. 1-2-3 will prompt you for the new password just as if you were adding the password for the first time. To remove password protection from a file, press the BACKSPACE to remove "[PASSWORD PROTECTED]" from the display, and then press ENTER.

This command can save the file in a Release 2 format if you name it with a .WK1 file extension, or set the default extension to .WK1 with the /Worksheet Global Default Ext Save command. For a worksheet to be saved in the Release 2 format, it cannot contain any Release 3 specific features, since the Release 3 features are lost when 1-2-3 translates the file to the Release 2 format. Some of the lost features include function arguments that are new to Release 3, formula notes, and undefined range names. Also, if labels are longer than 240 characters, they will be truncated.

NOTE: A file with the name AUTO123 will be retrieved every time you load 1-2-3, as long as it is in the default directory as determined by the /Worksheet Global Default Dir command.

/File Xtract

Description

The /File Xtract command allows you to save a portion of the current worksheet in another worksheet file. Settings established for the current worksheet, such as graph and print settings and range names, are saved in the new file.

Options

The /File Xtract command allows you to save either values or formulas from the range specified.

FORMULAS This option saves current worksheet formulas, as well as labels and values, in the worksheet file.

VALUES This option saves numbers and labels in the worksheet files. Formulas are evaluated to determine the numbers for saving, but the formulas are not saved. When you copy the values, check to see if the values need to be recalculated, or that links to external files need to be refreshed.

After entering /File Xtract and choosing Formulas or Values, select the filename from the menu or enter a new name. Next, enter a range of cell addresses or a range name. If the filename is new, press ENTER to complete the process.

If you are using an existing filename, 1-2-3 asks if you wish to cancel the request; back up the existing file to a .BAK file before replacing the existing file with the contents of the range selected; or replace the existing file with the contents of the range selected. If you supply a .WK1 file extension, 1-2-3 saves the extracted file in Release 2 format, assuming the selected range encompasses only one worksheet. After you have selected the file to hold the extract, specify the range to be extracted, by entering either a range name or range address.

This command also allows you to add a password to an extracted file. For more information on this feature, see /File Save in the Command Reference section in this chapter.

/System

Description

The /System command allows you to use the operating system commands without quitting 1-2-3. This means you can access some of the operating system commands while your 1-2-3 worksheet remains in memory.

Options

Any operating system command that does not overlay memory can be used with /System. Afterwards, EXIT returns you to your worksheet.

/Worksheet Delete File

Description

The /Worksheet Delete File command removes an active file from 1-2-3's memory. This command allows you to remove one file from the active files without affecting the other files. This command does not affect any files saved to disk.

Options

Your only option for this command is to select one of the active worksheet files to remove from memory from the list 1-2-3 provides.

/Worksheet Global Default Autoexec

Description

This command causes 1-2-3 to automatically run autoexecute macros (named \0) when a file containing these macros is retrieved or opened.

Options

This command has two options. If the Yes option is selected, 1-2-3 automatically runs the autoexecute macros when it reads a file that contains one. If the No option is selected, 1-2-3 does not automatically run any macros.

/Worksheet Global Default Dir

Description

Use this command to specify the directory that you want 1-2-3 to automatically look in for your files. Unless you change it, the default is the directory containing the 1-2-3 files.

Options

Normally, when you enter /Worksheet Global Default Dir, you will specify a new default directory. A second option is to clear the existing entry without entering a new one. In this case 1-2-3 will use the directory that was current when 1-2-3 was loaded, as the default for file storage and retrieval.

NOTE: To make this directory change permanent, use /Worksheet Global Default Update to save the new default to the 123R34.CNF file.

/Worksheet Global Default Ext

Description

Use this command to set the default worksheet file extension that 1-2-3 assigns for various /File commands.

Options

This command has two options: List and Save. Each option set the default extension for different file commands.

LIST   This option sets the default file extension for /File Admin Table Worksheet, /File Combine, /File Erase, /File List, /File Open, and /File Retrieve. The default is .WK*, which includes .WKS, .WK1, and .WK3.

SAVE   This option sets the default file extension for the files created by /File New, /File Save, and /File Xtract.

/Worksheet Global Default Other International File-Translation

Description

This command determines how Release 3 converts characters that the /File Import command imports into Release 3 worksheets.

Options

This command has two options. The Country option uses the IBM character set selected by the Country configuration. The International option uses code page 850, and is only selected when a text file is created on a computer that uses code page 850.

/Worksheet Global Default Other International Release-2

Description

This command determines how Release 3 converts characters from Release 2, which has the option of using LICS or ASCII.

Options

This command has two options. The LICS option uses the LICS character set that is the Release 2 default. The LICS characters include Compose key sequences to create special characters such as foreign letters. The ASCII option is for Release 2 files created with the ASCII No-LICS driver.

/Worksheet Global Default Temp

Description

This command determines the default directory that 1-2-3 uses for temporary files in such tasks as printing. Temporary files have a .TMP extension and are deleted when you exit 1-2-3.

Options

The only option for this command is selecting the directory where 1-2-3 will store these temporary files.

/Worksheet Global Default Update

Description

This command allows you to save any changes that you have made to the Worksheet Global Default settings, to the 123R34.CNF file.

Translate Program

Description

The Translate Program allows you to exchange data files between 1-2-3 and other popular programs. It is available from the Lotus Access System menu. You must quit 1-2-3 with /Quit Yes to use Translate. If you entered **123** to open 1-2-3, you will need to enter **trans** to start the Translate Program.

Options

You have two types of options for the Translate Program. You can select from a list of source file formats (From options), and a list of target file formats (To options).

The From options are as follows:

1-2-3 Release 1A
1-2-3 Release 2
1-2-3 Release 3
dBASE II
dBASE III and III+
DIF (VisiCalc and others)
Enable Version 2.0
Multiplan 4.2
SuperCalc4
Symphony Release 1.0 and 1.01
Symphony Release 1.1, 1.2, and 2

The To options are as follows:

1-2-3 Release 1A
1-2-3 Release 2
dBase II
dBase III and III+
DIF (VisiCalc and others)
Symphony Release 1.0 and 1.01
Symphony Release 1.1, 1.2, and 2
MultiPlan 4.2
Enable Version 2.0
SuperCalc4

NOTE: You will not need to translate Symphony files and earlier releases of 1-2-3 for use with Release 3 of 1-2-3. This is because the /File Retrieve command automatically translates these files when it retrieves them.

When you translate one format to another, the Translate Program only translates the features common to both the source and target file types. If you are translating a 1-2-3 Release 3 file to another format, you can select which worksheet you are translating. If you translate all of them, the Translate Program translates each worksheet to a different file by replacing or adding the last two filename characters, to indicate the worksheet letters. If you are translating a file to a DIF format, you must specify the orientation as row or column. If you are translating a file to dBASE II, III, or III+, you can select between a named range or the entire file. If you select Range, you must provide the range name when Translate prompts for that information.

THE COMPLETE REFERENCE

PART TWO
1-2-3's Advanced Features

CHAPTER 9

Data Management

In one sense, all the work you have done with 1-2-3 up to this point can be considered data management, because it has all involved the management of information recorded on the worksheet. But data management, as defined by 1-2-3, is a special term that refers to the formalized process of design, entry, and retrieval of information from a database.

The world of data management has its own terminology. A

database, for example, is a collection of all the information you have about a set of things. These things can be customers, orders, parts in inventory, employees, or anything else. If you created a database of employee information, for example, you would want it to contain information about each of your employees. All the information about one employee would be one *record* in the database. A record is composed of all the pieces of information you have about one thing in the set, such as one employee. These individual pieces of information in a record are referred to as *fields*. Fields you might want to have in each record in an employee database could include name, address, job classification, date of hire, social security number, department, benefits, and salary. When you design a new database, you need to decide what fields will be included in each record.

This chapter describes the /Data commands that permit organization and retrieval of information from 1-2-3's worksheets. You will also read about Lotus' exciting DataLens capability that lets you access external databases created with popular packages like dBASE, just as easily as if they were part of another worksheet file.

The next chapter will examine the /Data commands that add power to the calculations you do on the worksheet. Some of the commands covered in Chapter 10 serve a dual purpose. They work when information management is your only requirement, but they can also lend assistance when your objective is the more traditional use of the worksheet for calculations. In the next chapter you will find some hints on using these data management techniques with traditional worksheet applications.

The 1-2-3 Database

A 1-2-3 database is a range of cells on a worksheet. It can be in any area of the worksheet, but the field names, that is, the names you use to categorize data, must run across the top row of the range. The records in the database that contain data for each field are placed in the rows immediately following the row of field names. Figure 9-1 presents a section of an employee database in A1..F20. The field names are located in A1..F1, and the first database record is located in A2..F2.

As a database manager, 1-2-3 has both strengths and weaknesses compared to other packages. You may find it helpful to look at some ways in which 1-2-3's features differ from those of its competitors.

- The data in your 1-2-3 database is all stored in memory while you are working with the database. Unlike other packages that must read data from the disk when you need it, 1-2-3 provides unprecedented quick response to requests for resequencing records and finding those that match specific criteria. This feature does require that you have sufficient

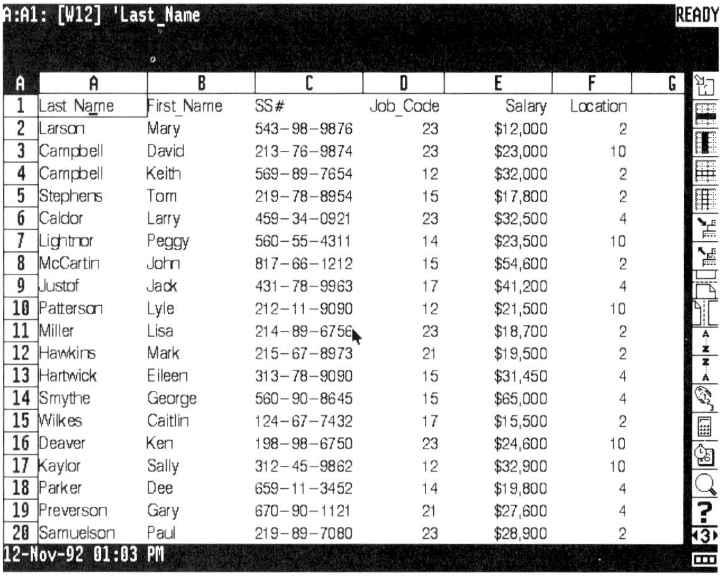

Chapter 9: Data Management

Figure 9-1. *Portion of an employee database*

	A	B	C	D	E	F
1	Last_Name	First_Name	SS#	Job_Code	Salary	Location
2	Larson	Mary	543-98-9876	23	$12,000	2
3	Campbell	David	213-76-9874	23	$23,000	10
4	Campbell	Keith	569-89-7654	12	$32,000	2
5	Stephens	Tom	219-78-8954	15	$17,800	2
6	Caldor	Larry	459-34-0921	23	$32,500	4
7	Lightnor	Peggy	560-55-4311	14	$23,500	10
8	McCartin	John	817-66-1212	15	$54,600	2
9	Justof	Jack	431-78-9963	17	$41,200	4
10	Patterson	Lyle	212-11-9090	12	$21,500	10
11	Miller	Lisa	214-89-6756	23	$18,700	2
12	Hawkins	Mark	215-67-8973	21	$19,500	2
13	Hartwick	Eileen	313-78-9090	15	$31,450	4
14	Smythe	George	560-90-8645	15	$65,000	4
15	Wilkes	Caitlin	124-67-7432	17	$15,500	2
16	Deaver	Ken	198-98-6750	23	$24,600	10
17	Kaylor	Sally	312-45-9862	12	$32,900	10
18	Parker	Dee	659-11-3452	14	$19,800	4
19	Preverson	Gary	670-90-1121	21	$27,600	4
20	Samuelson	Paul	219-89-7080	23	$28,900	2

memory to hold your entire database at once, however. You will need a large memory capacity, a fairly small database, or both.

- 1-2-3's data management commands are similar to its worksheet commands, which makes them easy for you to learn. By contrast, other packages may require a significant time investment to master their command structure.

- Most data management packages create formatted screens to enter or review one record at a time. With Release 3 macros, you have the capability to easily design a formatted screen for use with your database.

- Release 3 permits the entry of up to 8191 records in one database table in a worksheet. You can create multiple database tables in a file by putting them on different worksheets. You can combine these database tables in 1-2-3 functions and database commands. The practical limit to a database size is the amount of memory available, since the entire database resides in memory. These limits are sufficient for many applications, but some other database products allow an unlimited number of records.

- 1-2-3 can accommodate up to 256 fields in one database. Some packages allow more and others less.

- 1-2-3 permits each field to have up to 512 characters. Some packages allow more and others less.

Setting Up a Database

The first step in designing a 1-2-3 database is to create a list of fields you want your database to contain. Once you have all the field names recorded, estimate the number of characters that each field will require for storage and the number of records in your database. Add the number of characters for each field plus four additional characters per field to get a record total, and then multiply by the number of records. If the potential number of records exceeds 1-2-3's limits, you will have to find another alternative, such as splitting your file into two sections. Similarly, if the number of records times the length of one record exceeds the available memory in your system, you will not want to proceed with the design process unless you can use multiple subfiles in your application.

Choosing a Location for the Database

The next step is to select an area of the worksheet for storing the database. Here are some considerations to keep in mind as you select a location.

- To allow your database to expand with additional records, choose an area below calculations and other fixed information in your worksheet.
- If you plan to put more than one database in the worksheet, place them on separate sheets so that each database can expand without running into the other databases.
- If you have sufficient memory and have two databases in one worksheet, you might want to start one database in A1, and the other one to the right of and beneath the last record in the first database. This allows you to use the /Worksheet Delete and /Worksheet Insert commands to delete and insert records in either database without affecting the other.
- If you want to include other information in the worksheet file with the database entries, place the other information on a separate worksheet in the file. By keeping the database table separate from other information, you can prevent changes made to the database table—like row insertions and deletions—from affecting other data in the file.

Entering Field Names

Record your selected field names across the top row of the database area. Following these rules for field names will help you create a workable database.

- Make sure you record field names in the same order in which they appear in the form you plan to use for data entry. This will minimize the time required for entry.

- Each field name is placed in one cell, and must be unique.

- The names you choose for your fields will be used with some of the other database features. Therefore, choose meaningful names, but not names so long that reentry in other places will lead to misspellings.

- Do not enter spaces at the end of field names. It will not be apparent that you included them, and the names will not match with later entries for other data management features that do not include trailing spaces.

A layout of field names for an employee database might look like this:

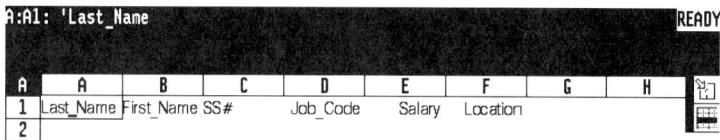

Entering Information

The first database record should begin immediately beneath the row of field names. Do not leave blank lines or use special symbols as divider lines. You can use Wysiwyg formatting to draw divider lines, using the :Format Lines command that you will learn about in Chapter 15.

All entries in corresponding fields of like records should be of the same type. For example, if a field contains numeric data, the value for that field should be numeric in every like record in the database. Mixing numeric values and labels in a single field causes the two types of data to be separated when records are sorted and when you attempt to select a subset of the records. It is acceptable to leave a field blank within a particular record if you lack data. Figure 9-1 presents an employee database after 19 records have been entered.

As your database grows longer, the field names at the top of your screen will scroll off the screen. You can prevent this by using the /Worksheet Titles Horizontal command to lock the field names in place on your screen. If you have forgotten how this command works, go back to Chapter 5, "Basic Worksheet Commands," for a quick review.

TIP: To ensure that the data in each field is of the same type, use the /Worksheet Window Map Enable command. 1-2-3 shows the data type of each of the cells. If you have forgotten how this command works, review it in Chapter 5.

If a database becomes too large to fit on a single worksheet, an alternative is to split the records into multiple database tables in different worksheets. For example, if a customer database is too large for one worksheet, the customers with last names beginning with A through L may be in the first worksheet's data table, and customer names beginning with M through Z may be in the second worksheet's data table.

Making Changes

Entries in a database can be changed with any of the techniques you have used on regular worksheets. An entry can be retyped to replace its current value. The F2 (EDIT) key will insert, delete, and replace characters within an entry.

You can use /Worksheet Insert to add a blank row for a new record or add a blank column for another field. The /Worksheet Delete command can be used to remove records or fields. Bear in mind, though, that the entire worksheet is affected by both of these commands; it is important to assess potential damage to areas outside the database. One good strategy is to save the file before using insertion or deletion commands. Then, if you have a problem, you can restore the file from disk. A better strategy is placing the database table on a worksheet by itself so the changes that you make to the database do not affect other data. Also, the /Copy command can be used to copy field values from other database records.

Sorting Your Data

1-2-3 provides extremely fast sort features because of the storage of the database in RAM. Any change in sequence can take place at the speed of transfer within RAM, which is considerably faster than sorting records from disk.

All the options you will need to specify the records to be sorted, specify the sort sequence, and tell 1-2-3 to begin the sort are located under the /Data Sort command. The submenu for this command looks like this:

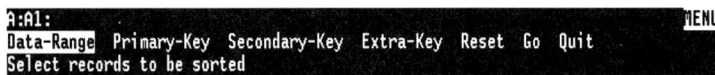

The steps for resequencing your data using the various Sort options are summarized in the box called "Steps for Sorting Your Data."

Determining What Data to Sort

You can sort all the records in your database or just some of them, depending on the range you specify. Always be sure to include all the fields in the sort, because excluding some fields causes those fields to remain stationary while the remainder of a record is resequenced. If you ever plan to return your records to their original entry sequence after a sort, you will need to include a field for record number in the record. A sequential number can be placed in this field at the time of entry.

To set the range for the sort, enter **/Data Sort Data-Range**. Then specify the range for the database. Be sure you *do not* include the row of field names. If you do, they will be sorted along with the record values. For the data in Figure 9-1, the data range is A2..F20, which includes all of the records and all of the fields, but omits the field names in the first row.

With Release 3, you can sort multiple worksheets. When you select multiple worksheets with a multiple-sheet range, 1-2-3 sorts each worksheet separately. Sorting does not move records between worksheets.

Specifying the Sort Sequence

1-2-3 permits you to specify multiple sort keys. In all cases the primary key will control the sequence of the records. The secondary key will be ignored, even when you specify one, except where duplicate examples of the primary key occur. In this situation, the secondary key will be used to break the tie. When records contain the same data for the primary and secondary keys, 1-2-3 then uses the extra keys to break the tie. You can specify up to 253 of these extra keys. For all sort keys, you may select whether the values are sorted in ascending or descending order.

Another setting also affects the sort order. This is the collating sequence, which is selected in the Install program. As discussed in Appendix A, "Installing 1-2-3," there are three options for a collating sequence: Numbers First, Numbers Last, and ASCII. The "Effect of Collating Sequence on Sorting" box describes these options in further detail. To make a change, you must reenter Install and select a different collating sequence.

Choosing a Primary Sort Key

To specify a primary key, enter **/Data Sort Primary-Key** and point to a cell containing data for a particular field within the database. This field (column) becomes your primary sort key. If you prefer, you can type the cell address instead of pointing. In either case you will next be prompted to choose the sort

> ## Steps for Sorting Your Data
>
> Sorting is a quick and easy process, but it requires a sequence of commands from the Data Sort menu. The steps and commands to use are as follows:
>
> 1. Enter **/Data Sort** and choose Data-Range.
> 2. Highlight (specify) all records and fields to be sorted, but do not include the field names within the range.
> 3. Select Primary-Key from the Sort menu.
> 4. Highlight any data value within the column you wish to use to control the sort sequence.
> 5. If you expect duplicate primary keys within your database, choose Secondary-Key from the Sort menu.
> 6. Highlight any data value within the column that you wish to use as the tie breaker if there are duplicate primary keys.
> 7. If you expect duplicate primary and secondary keys within your database, choose Extra-Key from the Sort menu.
> 8. Enter the number of the extra key or accept 1-2-3's default value and press ENTER.
> 9. Highlight any data value within the column that you wish to use as the tie breaker if there are duplicate primary and secondary keys.
> 10. Repeat Steps 7 through 9 for each extra key that you want.
> 11. Select Go from the Sort menu to have 1-2-3 resequence your data.

order (A for ascending order and D for descending order). When you choose A, the collating sequence you selected with Install will be used. When you choose D, the sequence will be reversed. Enter the letter for the choice you want, like this:

```
A:A1: [W12] 'Last_Name                                          EDIT
Primary sort key: A:A4          Sort order (A or D): A
```

Note that a default sort order may already be present on your screen. This is the order you chose for your previous sort. To keep this default, press ENTER in response to the prompt.

Setting the sort sequence does not automatically resequence your data. You also have to specify the data range and then select Go from the Sort menu.

> ### Effect of Collating Sequence on Sorting
>
> The order of your data after a sort is partly dependent on the collating sequence. This sequence is specified during the Install program. Sort order in the three possibilities for ascending sequence is as follows:
>
> - **Numbers last** Blank cells; label entries beginning with letters in alphabetical order; label entries beginning with numbers in numeric sequence; labels beginning with special characters; values.
>
> - **Numbers first** Blank cells; labels beginning with numbers in numeric sequence; labels beginning with letters in alphabetical order; labels beginning with special characters; values.
>
> - **ASCII** Blank cells; labels in ASCII order; values. Capitalization will affect the sort order with this choice.
>
> Sorting in descending order reverses the order.

Choosing a Secondary Sort Key

The secondary sort key serves as a tie breaker. For example, in the case of an employee file where last name has been specified as the primary sort key, you may wish to use first name as the secondary key, to handle instances where more than one employee has the same last name. Within the group of duplicate last names, records are then sorted by first name.

Set the secondary key by entering /**Data Sort Secondary-Key**, and either pointing to a cell containing a data value for the field you want to sort by, or by typing the cell address. Then specify A for ascending or D for descending sort order, as you did with the primary key. Again, the default sequence will be the last order you selected. (Thus, if you selected A last time, the default will be A.) If you wish to keep the current setting, press ENTER in response to this prompt.

Choosing Extra Sort Keys

The extra sort keys in Release 3 serve as additional tie breakers when records contain identical data in their primary and secondary sort key fields. Since 1-2-3 permits up to 253 extra keys, you can select up to 255 different sort keys. For example, in a large employee database, you may have more than one employee with the same first and last names. You may want to add the social security number as an extra key.

Specify an extra key by entering **/Data Sort Extra-Key**. 1-2-3 prompts for the extra sort key number by displaying the lowest unselected extra sort key number. You can either accept this number or enter your own. Next, 1-2-3 prompts for the field (column) containing the extra sort key. Either point to a cell containing a data value for the field by which you want to sort, or type the cell address. Specify A for ascending or D for descending sort order, as you did with the primary and secondary keys. The default sequence will be the last order you selected. If you wish to keep the current setting, press ENTER in response to this prompt.

Starting and Stopping the Sort

With the data range and (at a minimum) a primary key selected, you are ready to resequence your data. Simply select Go from the Sort menu after completing these other steps, and your data will be sorted in the specified order. 1-2-3 is very quick. With a small database, the sort will be complete as soon as you lift your finger after selecting Go.

Figure 9-1 presents an employee database with the records in random sequence. Suppose the data range is selected as A2..F20, using /Data Sort Data-Range. Next the Last Name field (A2) is selected as the primary key, with A for ascending sort order. A secondary key of First Name (B2) is then chosen, with D for descending sort order. Once Go is selected from the Data Sort menu, the records will be placed in the new sequence shown in Figure 9-2. Notice that the two records with a last name of Campbell are sequenced by first name.

If you decide to leave the Sort menu without completing the sort operation, you will need to use /Data Sort Quit to get rid of the "sticky" Sort menu. You do not need this command after a normally completed sort, since /Data Sort Go automatically returns you to READY mode after sorting the data.

Starting Over

Once you have made choices for a sort, 1-2-3 will use these settings as a default. Making a new selection for the data range or either of the sort keys will replace the default. If you want to first eliminate your settings to make sure that you have to reset the data range and primary key before sorting again, you can use /Data Sort Reset. This option eliminates default settings for data range, primary sort key, secondary sort key, and extra sort keys.

Sorting with the SmartIcons

In Release 3.4, you can use 1-2-3's SmartIcons to sort in either ascending or descending sequence. The icons you can use look like this:

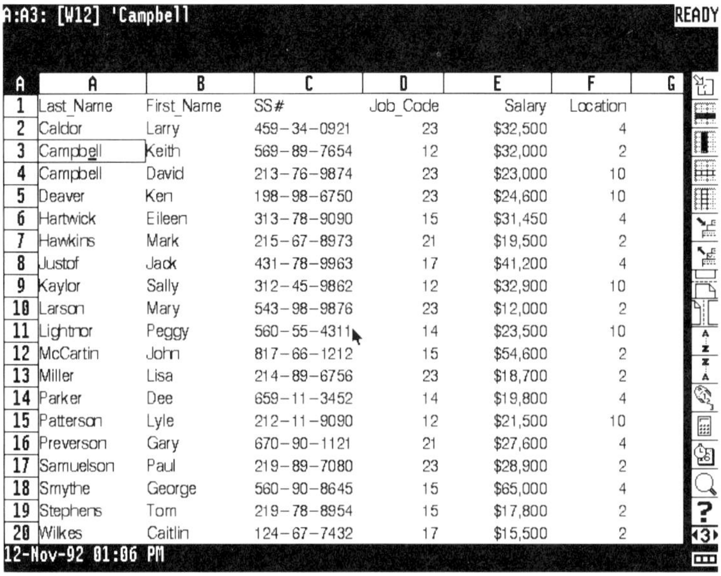

Figure 9-2. *Resequenced employee records*

	A	B	C	D	E	F
1	Last_Name	First_Name	SS#	Job_Code	Salary	Location
2	Caldor	Larry	459-34-0921	23	$32,500	4
3	Campbell	Keith	569-89-7654	12	$32,000	2
4	Campbell	David	213-76-9874	23	$23,000	10
5	Deaver	Ken	198-98-6750	23	$24,600	10
6	Hartwick	Eileen	313-78-9090	15	$31,450	4
7	Hawkins	Mark	215-67-8973	21	$19,500	2
8	Justof	Jack	431-78-9963	17	$41,200	4
9	Kaylor	Sally	312-45-9862	12	$32,900	10
10	Larson	Mary	543-98-9876	23	$12,000	2
11	Lightnor	Peggy	560-55-4311	14	$23,500	10
12	McCartin	John	817-66-1212	15	$54,600	2
13	Miller	Lisa	214-89-6756	23	$18,700	2
14	Parker	Dee	659-11-3452	14	$19,800	4
15	Patterson	Lyle	212-11-9090	12	$21,500	10
16	Preverson	Gary	670-90-1121	21	$27,600	4
17	Samuelson	Paul	219-89-7080	23	$28,900	2
18	Smythe	George	560-90-8645	15	$65,000	4
19	Stephens	Tom	219-78-8954	15	$17,800	2
20	Wilkes	Caitlin	124-67-7432	17	$15,500	2

When you choose either of these icons, 1-2-3 looks at the location of the cell pointer to determine the size of the database table that should be sorted. The database table is the contiguous area of cells that includes all database fields and records. If you want to omit the top row, such as when you sort a database that includes the field names, select the range to sort with F4 (ABS) or the mouse before choosing either icon. 1-2-3 also determines the column to use as a sort key by looking at the column of the selected cell. It will use either ascending or descending sequence depending on which icon you choose.

Generating a Series of Values

The /Data Fill command can save you considerable time when you are preparing a worksheet model. Use it to generate a series of dates, invoice numbers, purchase order numbers, new account numbers, or identification numbers for new employees, for example. You can combine this feature with sorting records to create record numbers for a database. Whenever you need to enter a series of data with evenly spaced values in either ascending or descending sequence, /Data Fill can handle the task. The /Data Fill command is often used in conjunction with some of the other Data commands covered in this and the next chapter. For example, the next chapter introduces /Data Distribution and /Data Table, which often use the /Data Fill command to generate a numeric series with regular intervals.

To use /Data Fill, place your cell pointer in the upper left cell of the row or column in which you want the series generated, and select /Data Fill. Next, enter the range you wish to use for the series. 1-2-3 will then prompt you for the first number in the series (the start value) and suggest the default value of 0. You can press ENTER to accept this value or enter another number. The prompt for the increment is next. To accept the default of 1, press ENTER again; alternatively, enter any positive or negative number for the increment before pressing ENTER. 1-2-3's last prompt is for a stop value. As long as the default stop value of 8191 is greater than or equal to your planned stop value, you can just press ENTER and allow 1-2-3 to determine a stop value, based on the size of the range and other values you have supplied. If 8191 is not large enough, enter a new stop value before pressing ENTER.

For example, suppose you need to enter the data for a group of consecutively numbered invoices. Rather than entering the invoice numbers, you can use the /Data Fill command to create them for you. To enter invoice numbers in cells A2..A20 of a worksheet, place your cell pointer in A2 to begin and enter **/Data Fill**. When 1-2-3 prompts for a range, select A2..A20. For the start value, enter **1004**, representing the first invoice number that you want to enter. For the increment, enter **1**.

Remember that there are two situations that stop generation of entries in a fill series. You must ensure that the range is large enough, and the stop value is high enough. 1-2-3 stops generating values as soon as either condition is exceeded. Consider what happens if you accept the default stop value of 8191. This number exceeds the start value, and it also far exceeds the range, so the range is what stops the generation of fill values. The results are shown in Figure 9-3. If you entered 1009 as the stop value, your results would be quite different, since the stop value would have been reached before the end of the range. In this case, the /Data Fill command would only fill A2..A7.

TIP: If you want /Data Fill to fill every cell in the range, make the stop value sufficiently larger than what you expect the last value in the fill range to be.

Adding Record Numbers for Sorting Records

1-2-3 does not have an "unsort" feature. Once you have changed the sequence of your records, there is no command that will automatically restore them to their original sequence unless you can use Undo. There is a solution to this dilemma, however, if you plan ahead. You can add a record number field to each record, containing a sequential number based on when the records are added to the

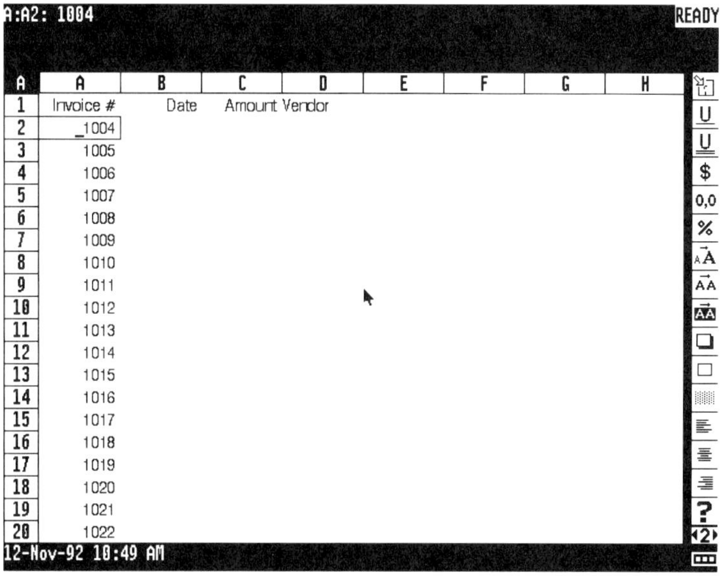

Figure 9-3. Result of /Data Fill

database. To return sorted records to their original entry order, you could then simply re-sort based on record number.

You can get 1-2-3 to do the work of sequential record number assignment by using /Data Fill. You have already learned how this command will generate any series of numbers that have even increments, if you specify the start, stop, and increment values you wish to use.

A look at the command in action with the employee database from previous examples will clarify the steps required for this use. Suppose a blank column has been inserted at the left of the employee database for record sequence numbers, and the field name, Sequence, was entered in A1. Record numbers can be used in this field to keep track of the original entry order for the employee records. To make /Data Fill supply the numbers, follow these steps:

1. Move the cell pointer to A2, the upper leftmost cell in the range where the numbers will be generated.

2. Enter **/Data Fill** and specify the fill range as A2..A20, either by pointing or by typing the range reference.

3. At the prompt, enter **1** for the start value.

4. The next prompt is for the step or increment value (that is, the amount to add to each value to generate the next number). Enter another **1**.

5. The last prompt is for the stop value—the highest number that can be in the series. You could enter a 19, since this will be the last value in the range. However, as long as the default stop value is not less than the stop value you want, you can let 1-2-3 generate the exact stop value, based on the range and increment you have supplied. To do this, accept the default of 8191 by pressing ENTER, as shown. You can always use this method when 8191 is greater than the last value in your series. 1-2-3 will stop when it fills the range. Your entries will look like this:

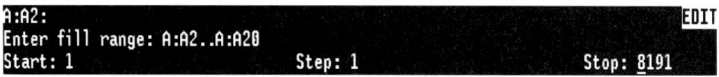

The result of the /Data Fill operation is shown in Figure 9-4.

You can use the paint can icon on the SmartIcons palette to fill a selected range with a series of numbers. With a VGA monitor, the icon is on palette 5 and looks like this:

Selecting this icon fills the selected range with numbers starting with the number entered in the first cell. If you have not defined a Data Fill operation within the current session, 1-2-3 will place a 0 in the first cell and increase each succeeding value by 1.

Using /Data Fill with Dates and Times

Release 3 features make the /Data Fill command easier to use with dates and times. One of these features is 1-2-3's recognition of dates and times if they are entered in one of 1-2-3's date and time formats (except Short International format for dates). This lets you enter dates and times as start and stop values making it much easier to generate the required date and time serial numbers than by computing them or using @functions.

Another feature in Release 3 for /Data Fill is the addition of step value options; these are used for the generation of date and time entries. For dates, if the step value contains:

- An integer or an integer followed by a D, 1-2-3 increases the date value in daily increments

- An integer followed by an M, 1-2-3 increases the step value in monthly increments

- An integer followed by a W, 1-2-3 increases the step value in weekly increments

- An integer followed by a Q, 1-2-3 increases the step value in quarterly increments

- An integer followed by a Y, 1-2-3 increases the step value in yearly increments

For example, a step value of 2M increments the date serial numbers in two-month increments.

For times, if the step value contains:

- An integer followed by an S, 1-2-3 increases the time value in second increments

- An integer followed by MIN, 1-2-3 increases the step value in minute increments

- An integer followed by an H, 1-2-3 increases the step value in hour increments

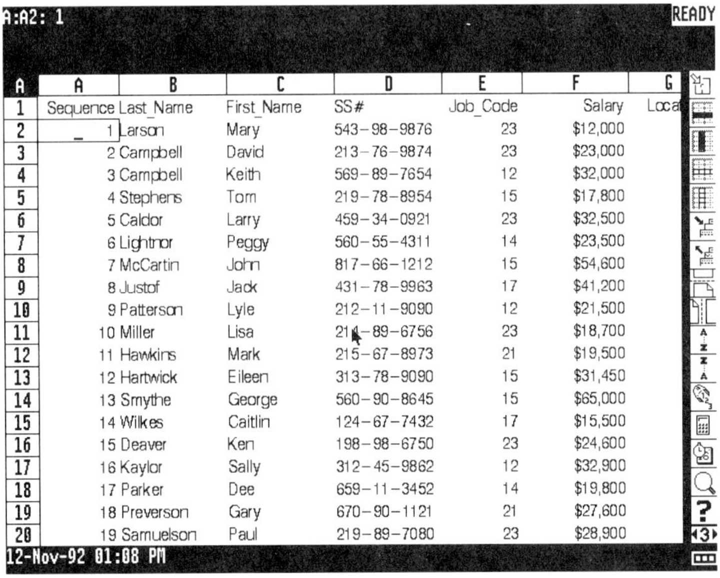

	A	B	C	D	E	F	G
1	Sequence	Last_Name	First_Name	SS#	Job_Code	Salary	Loca
2	1	Larson	Mary	543-98-9876	23	$12,000	
3	2	Campbell	David	213-76-9874	23	$23,000	
4	3	Campbell	Keith	569-89-7654	12	$32,000	
5	4	Stephens	Tom	219-78-8954	15	$17,800	
6	5	Caldor	Larry	459-34-0921	23	$32,500	
7	6	Lightnor	Peggy	560-55-4311	14	$23,500	
8	7	McCartin	John	817-66-1212	15	$54,600	
9	8	Justof	Jack	431-78-9963	17	$41,200	
10	9	Patterson	Lyle	212-11-9090	12	$21,500	
11	10	Miller	Lisa	214-89-6756	23	$18,700	
12	11	Hawkins	Mark	215-67-8973	21	$19,500	
13	12	Hartwick	Eileen	313-78-9090	15	$31,450	
14	13	Smythe	George	560-90-8645	15	$65,000	
15	14	Wilkes	Caitlin	124-67-7432	17	$15,500	
16	15	Deaver	Ken	198-98-6750	23	$24,600	
17	16	Kaylor	Sally	312-45-9862	12	$32,900	
18	17	Parker	Dee	659-11-3452	14	$19,800	
19	18	Preverson	Gary	670-90-1121	21	$27,600	
20	19	Samuelson	Paul	219-89-7080	23	$28,900	

Figure 9-4. *Output from /Data Fill*

For example, a step value of 30S increments the time serial numbers in thirty-second increments.

A third feature in Release 3 is the way 1-2-3 format values are generated by /Data Fill. If the range selected for /Data Fill uses the Automatic format, 1-2-3 will automatically format the cells as dates and times using the format of the start, step, and stop values. If the range selected for /Data Fill does not use a date or time format, 1-2-3 displays the time or date serial number using the format established for the range.

For example, suppose you need to enter a series of dates that are each seven days apart. If the first date you need is January 3, 1990, you can enter **@DATE(90,1,3)** or **03-Jan-90** and get a serial date number of 32876. Assuming you want to enter the dates in cells A2..A20 of the current worksheet, place your cell pointer in A2 to begin, and enter **/Data Fill**. Next, select A2..A20 as the data range to fill. For the start value, enter **03-Jan-90**. Enter **1w** for the increment and **45000** for the stop value. Since you check the date serial number for the beginning entry you can be certain that 45000 is larger than the last number required to fill the range. The results are shown in Figure 9-5, which has a column width of 10 and an Automatic format. If you entered 33000 as the stop value, your results would have been quite different, since the stop value would have been reached before the end of the range.

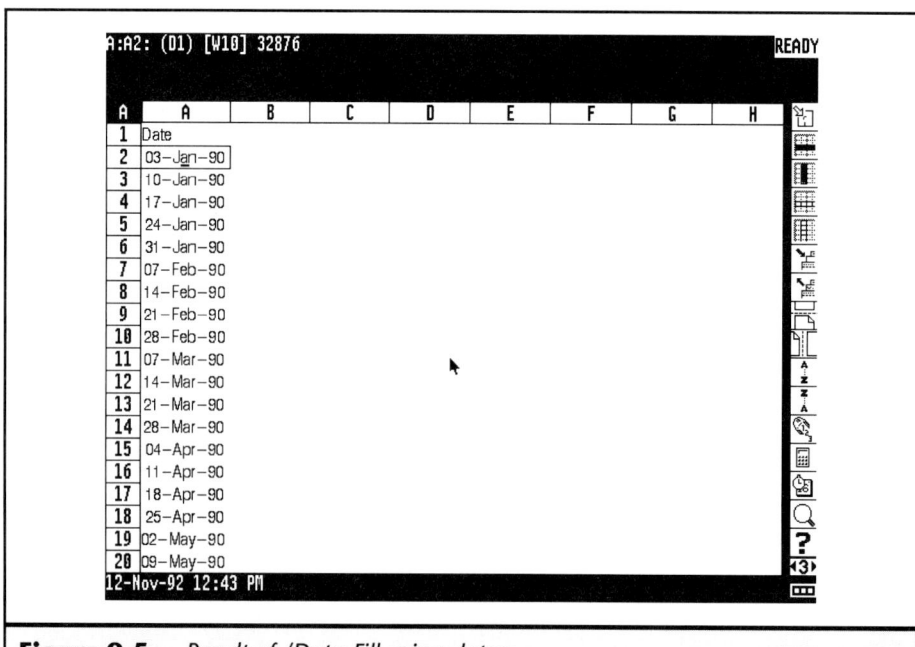

Figure 9-5. *Result of /Data Fill using dates*

Searching the Database

As your database grows large, it becomes increasingly important to selectively review the information it contains. 1-2-3's /Data Query commands provide the ability to work selectively with information in your database and thus offer an exception reporting capability; that is, information can be brought to your attention if it is considered to be outside an established norm. You can also use the selective review feature to clean up your database, or to create reports in response to unexpected requests.

All the commands required to review information selectively are found in the /Data Query menu shown here:

```
A:A1:                                                                    MENU
Input Criteria Output Find Extract Unique Del Modify Reset Quit
Specify ranges or external tables that contain records to manipulate
```

You will need to use at least three of the /Data Query commands to make a selection. Your database must be specified with /Data Query Input, and your selection criteria identified with /Data Query Criteria before you can select a specific action for the Query command to perform. In addition, database records and selection criteria must be entered on the worksheet before you enter a Query command that uses them. The steps required for using /Data Query commands are summarized in the "Steps for Using /Data Query Commands" box. Let's examine each of the Query options in detail.

Telling 1-2-3 Where Your Data Is Located

When you use the Query options, 1-2-3 must know where your field names and data records are located. Contrary to the case with /Data Sort, you *must* include the field names when you specify the range. These field names will be matched against the field names in the selection criteria area to ensure that selections are correct.

The command by which you specify the location of the database is /Data Query Input. After you enter this command, you can point to your data range or type the required cell references. In both cases, be sure to include the field names, as shown in the selection in Figure 9-6. Release 3 lets you select input ranges that are in active files, inactive files, and external tables (which are discussed later in the chapter). If you are planning to insert or replace records with the /Data Query commands, you must use an active file for the input range.

Specifying the Desired Records

To determine what records from the database will be used to fill your query request, 1-2-3 checks the criteria you specify against each record in the selected database range. Records that do not meet the criteria are not used.

```
A:F20: 2                                                    POINT
Enter input range: A:A1..A:F20

      A           B           C         D         E         F      G
 1  Last_Name   First_Name   SS#        Job_Code  Salary    Location
 2  Larson      Mary         543-98-9876      23  $12,000        2
 3  Campbell    David        213-76-9874      23  $23,000       10
 4  Campbell    Keith        569-89-7654      12  $32,000        2
 5  Stephens    Tom          219-78-8954      15  $17,800        2
 6  Caldor      Larry        459-34-0921      23  $32,500        4
 7  Lightnor    Peggy        560-55-4311      14  $23,500       10
 8  McCartin    John         817-66-1212      15  $54,600        2
 9  Justof      Jack         431-78-9963      17  $41,200        4
10  Patterson   Lyle         212-11-9090      12  $21,500       10
11  Miller      Lisa         214-89-6750      23  $18,700        2
12  Hawkins     Mark         215-67-8973      21  $19,500        2
13  Hartwick    Eileen       313-78-9090      15  $31,450        4
14  Smythe      George       560-90-8645      15  $65,000        4
15  Wilkes      Caitlin      124-67-7432      17  $15,500        2
16  Deaver      Ken          198-98-6750      23  $24,600       10
17  Kaylor      Sally        312-45-9862      12  $32,900       10
18  Parker      Dee          659-11-3452      14  $19,800        4
19  Preverson   Gary         670-90-1121      21  $27,600        4
20  Samuelson   Paul         219-89-7080      23  $28,900        2
12-Nov-92 01:09 PM
```

Figure 9-6. *Selecting an input range*

When entering criteria on the worksheet, keep in mind two things. First, criteria must be positioned on the worksheet in an out-of-the-way location that will not interfere with the expansion of the database. This action must be taken in READY mode, not from within /Data Query, because once you select /Data Query, you cannot make entries on the worksheet. Second, 1-2-3 needs to be told where the criteria are stored, by means of the /Data Query Criteria command.

Location of Criteria

When you use one of the /Data Query commands that requires the use of search criteria, you must use the /Data Query Criteria command to tell 1-2-3 the location of the criteria. (Remember that the criteria themselves must be entered before you select /Data Query.) Unlike Release 2, Release 3 allows you to leave blank areas in the criteria range without producing wildcard matches with every record in the database table. Entering criteria and telling 1-2-3 where they are located with /Data Query Criteria will not show you the matching records, however. A number of other commands can display the matching records, copy them to a new area, or delete them from your database; these commands are explained later in the chapter.

Chapter 9: Data Management

> ## Steps for Using /Data Query Commands
>
> The /Data Query commands allow you to access selected records in your database. Obtaining the results you desire involves some preliminary work, as well as a number of /Data Query options. The required steps are as follows:
>
> 1. Enter the Query criteria on your worksheet.
>
> 2. If you plan to use the Extract, Unique, or Modify options, enter the field names you will be copying in the output area of your worksheet.
>
> 3. Enter **/Data Query Input** from the Query menu and specify the range for your database, including field names.
>
> 4. Enter **/Data Query Criteria** from the Query menu and specify the location of your criteria.
>
> 5. If you plan to use Extract, Unique, or Modify, enter **/Data Query Output** and specify the location of your output area.
>
> 6. Select the /Data Query option you wish to use: Find, Del, Extract, Unique, or Modify.
>
> 7. If you choose Find, press ESC after you have finished browsing in your file, and then Quit to exit the /Data Query menu.

You can choose any location you desire for your search criteria. A popular location is to the right of the database; this allows the criteria area to be expanded to the right, and does not interfere with the expansion of your database. If your database occupies columns A through M, for example, you may wish to begin your criteria in column R. This allows for the expansion of the database by four new fields before the criteria would have to be moved.

With Release 3, you have the option of putting your criteria on a separate worksheet or a separate file. With this approach, you don't have to plan for expansion or modifications. 1-2-3 does not support search criteria that span sheets and will not allow a multiple-sheet range for the criteria.

Types of Criteria

You can use a variety of different ways to specify which records in the database you wish to query. You can use values that match your database entries exactly; you can use 1-2-3's wildcard characters to specify only a portion of the entry you are looking for; or you can specify formulas. For matches other than formulas, the name of the field in the database you are searching must appear above the specific entry you are searching for. For formula matches you can use any field name, although for documentation purposes it is best to use the name of the field referenced in the formula.

For example, if you want to search the last name field in an employee database to find all records with a last name of Smith, your criteria area might look like this:

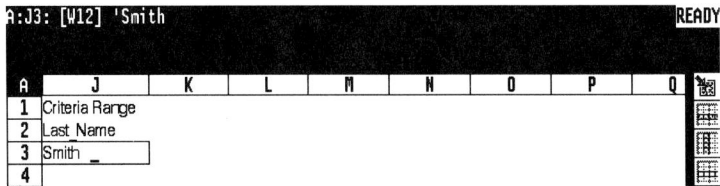

Note that the criteria area is J2..J3. The entry in J1 is documentation. The search value is placed immediately underneath the field name in the criteria area. The field name in the criteria area must be an exact match with the field name in your database. A space at the end of one or the other, or a misspelling, can cause a problem. The safest approach is to copy the field name from its location above the data to the criteria area where you wish to use it.

NOTE: 1-2-3 is case sensitive to field names when the collating sequence used in sorting is set to ASCII.

In Release 3, you can leave blank criteria areas without jeopardizing Query operation results. You can include columns with field names but no criteria beneath them; 1-2-3 will still find the records that you want rather than the wildcard matching that occurred in previous releases.

TIP: Copy database field names from the database table to the criteria range, so the spacing and the upper- and lowercase arrangement of the field names in the criteria match the database table.

VALUES To search for numeric values in your records, record the desired field name in the criteria area. Underneath this field name enter the value for which you are searching. The criteria value need not have the same format as the values you are looking for. In a search based on the following criteria area, only records for Job Code 23 would match.

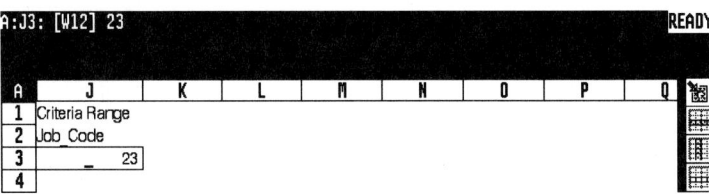

LABELS If you want to match label entries, you can enter them in the criteria exactly as they appear in your database, under the name of the field you wish to search. For example, entering **Last_Name** in the criteria area and placing **Jones** beneath causes 1-2-3 to select records that contain Jones in the last name field.

1-2-3 has two special characters that are useful when specifying label criteria. These characters are the asterisk (*) and the question mark (?).

The * at the end of a criteria entry indicates that if the first part of the criteria entry matches a database record, any characters from the location of the * to the end of the database entry should be accepted in the match. The following criteria would search the Last Name field for all records beginning with Sm.

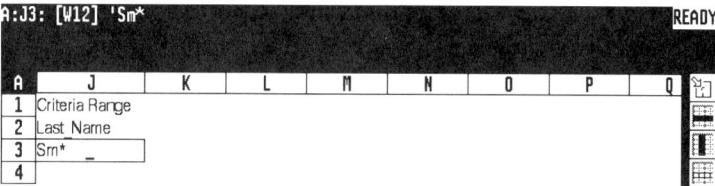

Smith would match, as would Smithfield, Smothers, and Smeltman. The ? replaces any one character in an entry. The question mark says that you do not care what character comes at that location in the data entry, as long as all the other characters match exactly. The following criteria tells 1-2-3 that you do not care what character is located in the second position of the Last_Name field, as long as *B* is the first character, and *tman* the third through the sixth characters of the database entry.

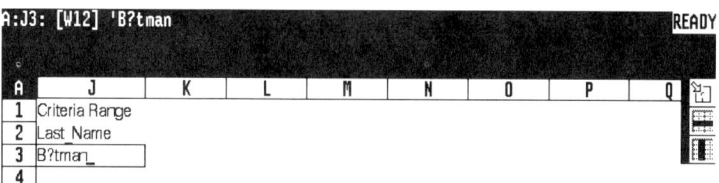

Bitman, Butman, Batman, Botman, and Betman would be among the matching entries if records containing these names were in the database. All entries longer than six characters, such as Bitmanson, would be rejected.

FORMULAS The ability to create formulas to serve as search criteria offers additional query power. You can use formula comparisons to check for records that contain values with a specific range, and you can even use string formulas in your criteria. When you enter a formula as criteria, the formula will display as 0 or 1, depending on whether it evaluates to true or false for the first database record. You may want to format the cell of the criteria area as Text, so it will display as the formula you entered.

When you create formulas as search criteria, it is not important that the field name used in the criteria area match with the field referenced in the formula, although for clarity it is always best to use the proper field name. As you construct your formulas to compare values in the database against a specific value, always reference the first value for the field in the database, or the field name.

In the example in Figure 9-6, to find all values in a Salary field located in column E that are greater than $25,000, you might use this criteria formula.

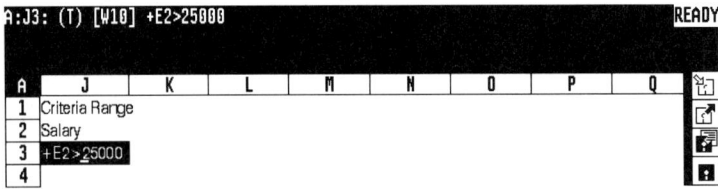

The cell referenced is E2, since that contains the first value in the salary field. Always use a relative reference when referring to database fields. When you format criteria cells as Text, the formulas will display exactly as you enter them. You could also enter the previous formula as **+SALARY>25000**, since 1-2-3 will substitute the field values for the field name. Another shortcut approach is an entry like >25000.

If you need a criteria formula that compares a database field against a value located elsewhere in the worksheet, use an absolute reference as the reference outside the database. Let's say you want to compare the salaries in Figure 9-6 against the average salary amount stored in J10. The criteria in Figure 9-7 will identify all records where the salary exceeded the average by $3,000.

 *TIP: You may need to start a criteria with a less than (<) symbol. Be aware that when you type a less than symbol in the READY mode, 1-2-3 activates the menus. This feature accommodates foreign language keyboards, where the slash (/) is in an awkward position. So, to start a formula for a criteria range with a less than symbol, type a label prefix before typing the <.*

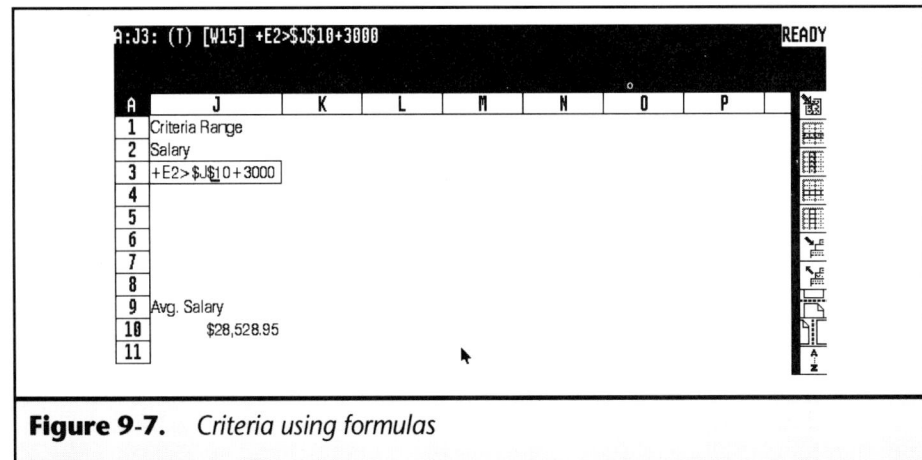

Figure 9-7. *Criteria using formulas*

The complex operators #AND#, #OR#, and #NOT# can also be used in formula criteria. Suppose you wish to determine if a salary is less than or equal to $25,000 or greater than or equal to $50,000, for example. The proper criteria formula to use is shown here:

If you use the #AND# operator, the conditions on both sides of the operator must be true for the record to be selected. If you use #OR#, either condition may be true for the record to be selected. #NOT# negates the condition that follows it. When you use a complex operator, you must include the field names or the cell address for the first record. In the previous example, you could not use the criteria formula <=25000#OR#>=50000. A criteria like this would look for the string <=25000#OR#>=50000 in the salary column.

COMPOUND CRITERIA Whenever you use more than one field in the criteria area, you are using compound criteria. 1-2-3 allows up to 256 fields to be used for search criteria at one time. These criteria must be joined by implied "and's" and "or's."

If two criteria values are placed on the same line beneath their separate field names, they are joined by an implied "and." The following criteria, for example, will select records where the job code is equal to 23 *and* the salary is less than $16,000.

Notice that the field names in the criteria area are placed in adjacent cells. Note also that the criteria types do not have to be the same; one criterion is a formula, and the other a value. A database record must meet both criteria to be selected.

If one criteria value is placed one row below the other, the two criteria are joined by an implied "or." Perhaps you want records with a job code of 23 or a salary of less than $16,000. The criteria shown here will select records meeting *either* of these conditions:

Highlighting Selected Records

Once you have defined your search area and criteria, 1-2-3's /Data Query Find command will highlight records that match the criteria you have defined. The records are highlighted one at a time, beginning at the top of the database. Table 9-1 lists the keys you can use to move through the selected records.

Finding records requires a few preliminary steps. You must have defined your database, including the field names, with /Data Query Input. You must also have entered your search criteria on the worksheet or in a separate area

Key	Action
DOWN ARROW	Moves to the next record in the input range that meets the criteria. If the cell pointer is on the last record that meets the criteria, 1-2-3 beeps.
UP ARROW	Moves to the previous record in the input range that meets the criteria. If the cell pointer is on the first record that meets the criteria, 1-2-3 beeps.
LEFT ARROW	Moves one field to the left in the selected record. If the cell pointer is on the first field, 1-2-3 beeps.
RIGHT ARROW	Moves one field to the right in the selected record. If the cell pointer is on the last field, 1-2-3 beeps.
HOME	Moves to the first record in the input range that meets the criteria.
END	Moves to the last record in the input range that meets the criteria.
ESC	Ends the /Data Query Find operation and returns to the Data Query menu.
ENTER	Ends the /Data Query Find operation and returns to the Data Query menu.
F2(EDIT)	Switches to EDIT mode for the current field in the selected record. Pressing F2 (EDIT) again or ENTER saves your edits and returns to the /Data Query Find operation. Pressing ESC cancels the edits and returns to the /Data Query Find operation.
F7 (QUERY)	Reexecutes the most recent query operations or ends the /Data Query Find operation and returns to the READY mode.

Table 9-1. *Cell Pointer Movement Keys for Use with /Data Query Find in Database Records*

before requesting the Query commands, and then defined the criteria with /Data Query Criteria. Figure 9-8 shows a database that has been defined with /Data Query Input as A1..E10. The following criteria are established in J1..J3 to locate records for the Accounting Department:

Figure 9-9 shows the first record matching the criteria highlighted on the screen.

The /Data Query Find option is a good one if you need a quick answer to a question concerning data you have stored in your database. The drawback to using it is that all the matching records are not listed at once and cannot be printed out. If you need to do either of these things, you will want to use the /Data Query Extract and /Data Query Unique commands.

Writing Selected Records on the Worksheet

1-2-3 provides three commands that make a copy of selected records and fields from your database to another area of the worksheet. You can add headings to these new areas to create an instant report that can be shared with others. Before you can have 1-2-3 copy database information, however, you must prepare an output location.

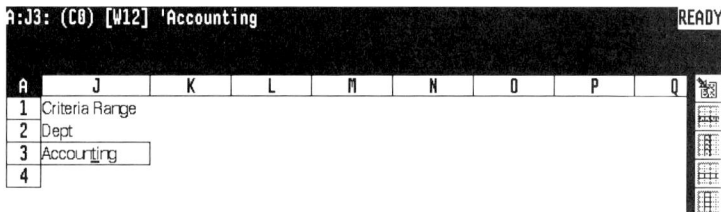

Figure 9-8. *Asset records*

```
A:A2: [W25] 'FTY Computer                                            FIND
       A              B         C              D        F
  1  Description     Life      Cost Dept      Type
  2  FTY Computer    5         $980 Accounting Office
  3  Dover Typewriter 5         $850 Training  Office
  4  Swivel Chair    10        $345 Check     Furniture
  5  KL Calculator   7         $100 Audit     Office
  6  Walnut Desk     15        $1,200 Cash    Furniture
  7  Lanver Copier   3         $2,500 Cash    Processing
  8  Lanver Copier   3         $2,800 Accounting Processing
  9  Computer Table  5         $300 Training  Furniture
 10  File Cabinet    10        $450 Audit     Furniture
 11
 12
```

Figure 9-9. *Finding records for a specific department*

Defining an Output Area

First decide on a location and prepare it to receive data. The bottom of the existing database is a commonly selected location. Just make sure you leave some blank rows at the bottom of the database to allow for expansion, or you may find yourself moving the output area around to acquire more space. With Release 3, you have the option of placing your output on a separate worksheet or a separate file. This allows both the input and output areas to be as large as 8192 records if you have sufficient memory, and lets you place your output in a location where a growing database will not interfere. You should not have any information below the output range, since the cells below it are erased before 1-2-3 copies matching records to the output range.

With the location selected, enter the names of the fields you wish to copy from matching records. They need not be in the same sequence as the fields in your database, and you do not have to include every field.

TIP: Use the /Copy command to copy field names from the database table directly to the output range, so the spacing and letter case of the field names in the criteria match the database table exactly. Once you have all the field names, you can delete field names of the fields you do not want in the output range.

Once the field names are placed in the output area, you are ready to define its location to 1-2-3. This is done with /Data Query Output. If you define the output area as consisting of only the row containing the field names, 1-2-3 will use the range from the field names to the bottom of the worksheet for writing records that match. If the output area is in a worksheet that contains other data, it is important that you do not put additional worksheet data below the field names, since 1-2-3 erases the entire range before copying records to the output range.

You can also specify the range for the output area to include the number of blank rows beneath the row of field names. If you use this approach, 1-2-3 will stop copying matching database records when the specified output area becomes full. In this case, 1-2-3 only erases the selected range before copying matching records. For example, if you select B:A1..B:F10 as the output range, 1-2-3 will only copy the first nine records it finds (it uses the first line for the field names). If 1-2-3 cannot fit all the selected records into the output range, it displays an error message in the status line.

Extracting All Matches

To extract matching records, enter **/Data Query Extract** once you have set up the criteria and output areas on your worksheet, and defined the database, criteria, and output to 1-2-3. Since so many preliminary steps are required before using this command, let's review them in order, using the database in Figure 9-8 as an example.

1. Add selection criteria to the worksheet, as shown here:

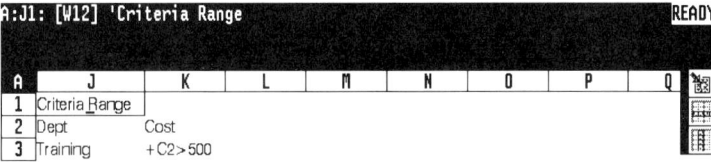

2. Set up the output area on the worksheet to look like this:

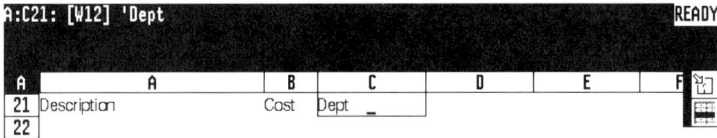

3. Enter the **/Data Query Input** command to define the database as located in A1..E10.

4. Since the /Data Query menu remains displayed, all you have to enter is **Criteria** in order to define the criteria location as J2..K3.

5. Define the output area next by entering **Output**, and specifying its location of A21..C21 at the prompt.

6. Enter **Extract**, and the following output will be produced.

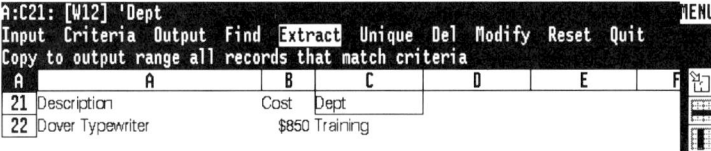

If you want to turn extracted records into a report, you need only add a report title at the top of the extract area and then print the worksheet range containing the heading and the extract.

Adding Computed and Aggregate Columns to the Output Range

An output range can also include computed and aggregate columns. A *computed column* contains values that are calculated based on values in the database. An *aggregate column* calculates values based on groups of database records. Aggregate columns use the @AVG, @COUNT, @MIN, @MAX, or @SUM functions. Computed columns use any valid formula.

An example of a computed column is shown in Figure 9-10, which uses the database shown in Figure 9-8 and criteria that match all records with Furniture in the Type field. This column computes each asset's straight-line depreciation by dividing the cost by the life. The formula in H21 describes the calculation performed in the column. It is entered as a formula and may be formatted as text as in this example. You can use any valid formula that does not include one of the functions used for an aggregate column. Just like entering formula criteria, you can reference database fields either by using the field name (as in Life and Cost in this example) or by using the cell address of the cell to use, as in +C2/B2. You do not have to include the fields used by the calculation in the output range. This example also shows how the fields can be in a different order in the output range from their order in the database.

An example of an aggregate column is shown in Figure 9-11, which uses the database shown in Figure 9-8 and criteria that match all records. This column computes the total cost of all purchases for each department. Using an aggregate column groups matching records into unique groups based on the other fields in the output range, in this case the Dept field. The formula in G21 is entered as a formula and may be formatted as Text as in this example. Just like computed columns, you can reference database fields either by using the field name, as in

```
A:H21: (T) [W15] +COST/LIFE                                    READY

    A    F          G              H           I      J      K
   21   Dept      Description    +COST/LIFE
   22   Check     Swivel Chair        34.5
   23   Cash      Walnut Desk         80
   24   Training  Computer Table      60
   25   Audit     File Cabinet        45
```

Figure 9-10. *Example of a computed column*

```
A:G21: (T) [W15] @SUM(COST)                                    MENU
Input Criteria Output Find Extract Unique Del Modify Reset Quit
Specify ranges or external tables that contain records to manipulate
   A     F         G         H         I         J         K
21 Dept     @SUM(COST)
22 Audit            450
23 Cash            1200
24 Check            345
25 Training         300
```

Figure 9-11.   *Example of an aggregate column*

Cost, or by the cell address of the first cell to use, as in C2. You do not have to include the field used by the aggregate column in the output range.

Extracting and Replacing Records

Release 3 includes a /Data Query Modify command that you can use to modify records by copying matching records to the output range, modifying them, and then copying them back to the database. /Data Query Modify Extract differs from /Data Query Extract in that Modify Extract remembers the extracted records' position in the original database. You can use this command when you want to edit an extracted group of records, and then use the /Data Query Modify Replace command to replace the records in the database with the modified records from the output area.

To extract the matching records, enter **/Data Query Modify Extract** once you set up the criteria and output areas on your worksheet, and define the database, criteria, and output to 1-2-3. 1-2-3 only copies the fields for each record that are in the first row of the output range. Since several steps are required to extract and replace records, let's again use the data in Figure 9-8 to review them in order.

1. Add selection criteria to the worksheet, using the same criteria that you used for the /Data Query Extract command example.

2. Set up the output area on the worksheet to match the output range you used for the /Data Query Extract command example.

3. Enter the **/Data Query Input** command to define the database as located in A1..E10.

4. Since the /Data Query menu remains displayed, all you have to enter is **Criteria** in order to define the criteria location as J2..K3.

5. Define the output area next by entering **Output**, and specifying its location of A21..C21 at the prompt.

6. Enter **Modify Extract**, and the following output will be produced. 1-2-3 then returns to the Data Query menu.

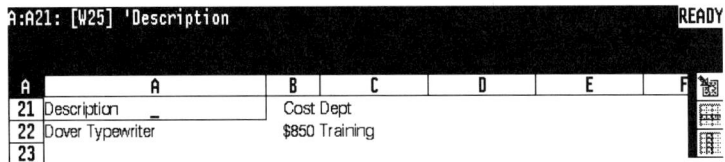

7. Select Quit to return to READY mode.

8. Edit the data in the extract range; change the Cost of the Typewriter to $950.

9. Enter **/Data Query Modify Replace**. The final output shows $950 for the cost of the Dover typewriter in the database. While /Data Query Find may be quicker for one record, when you have many records you will find the /Data Query Modify commands easier to use. Select Quit to return to READY mode.

If you decide not to replace the records, use the /Data Query Modify Cancel command. This command instructs 1-2-3 to forget the original record positions the extracted records had in the database.

Writing Only Unique Records

The Unique option is very similar to Extract in that it writes records to the output area. However, it writes only unique records to this area, so if two selected entries are an exact match, only one will be written. Uniqueness of records is determined by the fields written to the output area.

Be aware that the number of records written to the output area can be affected by the number of fields you plan to write there. If two records are alike in five of the six fields you plan to write to the output area, they are unique; yet, if you select fewer fields, the same two records may well match and therefore not be unique.

For instance, consider the following criteria:

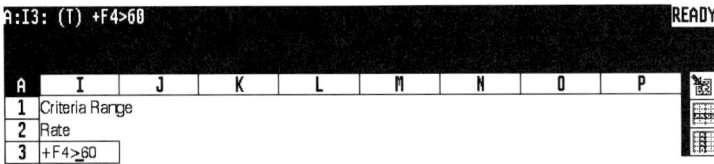

and the database records shown in Figure 9-12. 1-2-3 produced the output shown below when Unique was selected from the Data Query menu. Note that the

```
A:A1: [W16]                                                    READY

    A        A           B        C         D      E      F    G    H
    1                  CLIENT BILLINGS - SEPTEMBER
    2
    3   Customer       Type Phone          Location  Hours  Rate
    4   STR Rentals         5 231-4567     Dallas    10.5   75
    5   XCV Company         3 341-4545     Chicago    5.0   60
    6   Tower College       5 431-9092     New York  15.0   85
    7   Lower Rentals       3 498-2123     Dallas    20.0   60
    8   Nelson Products     4 213-9845     Albany     3.0   60
    9   Tower College       5 431-9092     New York  30.0   85
   10   Lower Rentals       3 498-2123     Dallas     2.0   60
   11   Nelson Products     4 213-9845     Albany    14.0   60
   12   XCV Company         3 341-4545     Chicago   15.0   60
   13   Tower College       5 431-9092     New York  22.0   85
   14   Lower Rentals       3 498-2123     Dallas     7.0   60
```

Figure 9-12. *Database used with /Data Query Unique*

Tower College record appears only once, even though several qualifying records for it exist in the database.

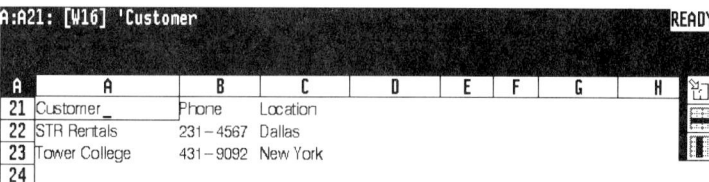

Adding Selected Records to the Database

The /Data Query Modify Insert command copies records from one database to another. Modify Insert requires that the output range contain both the field names and the records to add. This command adds all records in the selected output area to the bottom of the input area. Blank rows are excluded in this copy operation. If you do not want all the records added, you must remove unwanted records from the selected output area.

As an example, suppose you have the database tables in Figure 9-13. You can add the records in the database on sheet A to the database on sheet B with the /Data Query Modify Insert command. Define the input range as B:A1..B:E10, and the output range as A:A1..A:E3. When you perform the /Data Query Modify Insert command, 1-2-3 copies all of the records in the output range to the database (the input range). Figure 9-14 shows the records added to the input range. Only the data in the fields common to both the input and output ranges are copied.

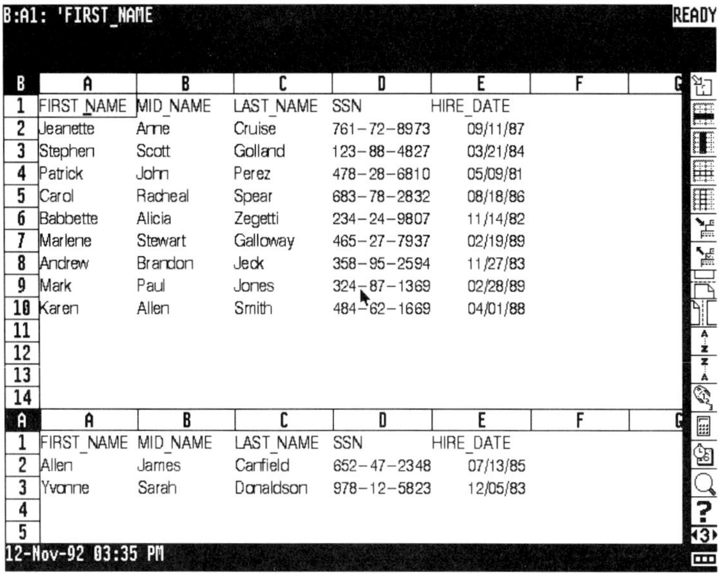

Figure 9-13. *Using Modify Insert to add records*

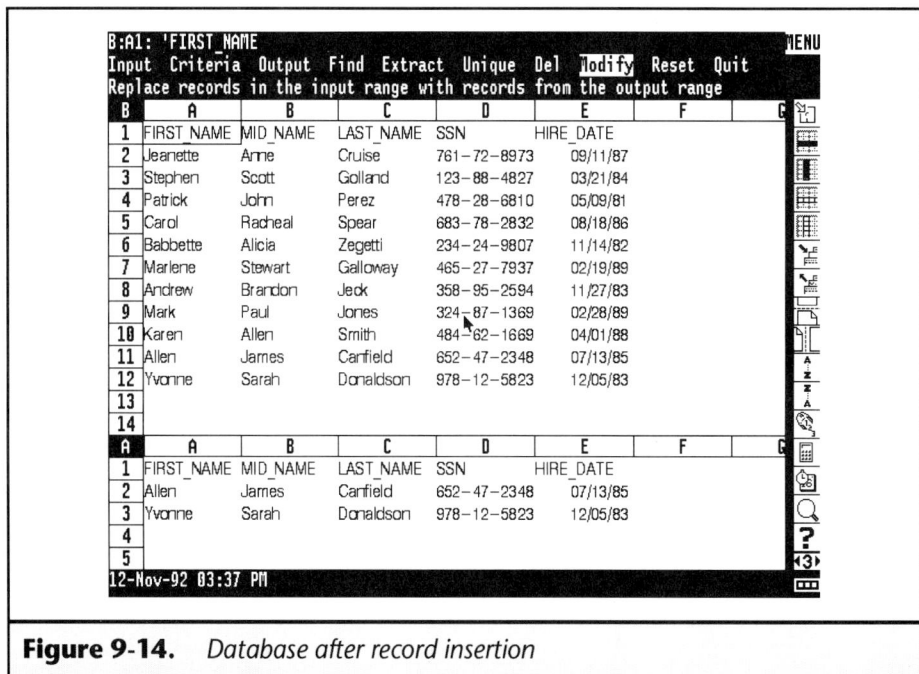

Figure 9-14. *Database after record insertion*

Deleting Selected Records from the Database

/Data Query Del is a powerful yet dangerous command. In one easy process it can purge outdated records from your database—but if you make a mistake in entering your search criteria, it can also purge records you still need. You would be wise to test your criteria with Find or Extract before selecting the Del option.

If you specified the criteria to match records that have a rate of 60 and the input range as the database in Figure 9-12, and then chose the Del option and selected Delete for confirmation, only the following records would remain in the database:

```
A:A1: [W16]                                                          MENU
Input Criteria Output Find Extract Unique [Del] Modify Reset Quit
Delete all records that match criteria
        A              B          C         D        E    F    G    H
1                     CLIENT BILLINGS — SEPTEMBER
2
3   Customer         Type Phone           Location    Hours Rate
4   STR Rentals           5 231 – 4567    Dallas      10.5   75
5   Tower College         5 431 – 9092    New York    15.0   85
6   Tower College         5 431 – 9092    New York    30.0   85
7   Tower College         5 431 – 9092    New York    22.0   85
```

TIP: Look at database records before you delete them. Use /Data Query Find or /Data Query Extract to view records the /Data Query Del command is going to delete. This step prevents you from deleting records that you want to keep.

Resetting Selection Options

All of the Query specifications can be eliminated with the /Data Query Reset command. This includes the input range, the criteria specification, and the output range if you specified one.

Quitting the Query Menu

When you want to leave the /Data Query operation, choose Quit from the Query menu to return to READY mode. This allows you to make new entries for criteria and perform other tasks. To return to /Data Query after making changes, you can reenter through the menu. Alternatively, if you want to use the same choices for Input and Criteria and would like to perform the same query operation as the last one you performed (Find, Unique, Del, or Extract), you have an easier option. Simply press F7 (QUERY), and another query will be executed.

Adding a Second Database

With Release 3, you can include more than one database table in the input range. Using multiple ranges can change the way you use some of the /Data commands, allowing you to design applications or worksheets containing multiple database tables. Multiple input ranges are not allowed for the /Data Query Modify commands.

To select multiple input ranges, you must separate the range names or addresses with the default argument separator. This is a comma unless you select another one with the /Worksheet Global Default Other International Punctuation command. Since a semicolon is always a valid argument separator you may prefer to use that character. An example is A:A1..A:G60;B:A1..B:K100. You may want to use range names instead since they are easier to use.

To join the two databases, you need a join formula. A *join formula* describes the fields in each database that link records from one database to another. For example, when you use the employee and payroll databases, the social security numbers can link the records from the two databases together. To create a join formula, enter a criteria such as +PAYROLL.SSN=EMPLOY.SSN. This tells 1-2-3 that the records from the two databases match when a social security number from the PAYROLL database matches a social security number in the EMPLOY database. You need to include the database names in the join formula only when the field names are the same. If the social security number in the PAYROLL database is called SOC_SEC_NUM, the join formula will be +SOC_SEC_NUM=SSN. You will also need to include the database address or name in the output range when you use a field name that appears in more than one database.

External Databases

With Release 3, you can link to databases from other packages while you continue using 1-2-3. Lotus has developed a special facility known as DataLens that allows you to link with these external databases.

You can use this feature to access data from another database that you do not want to enter into 1-2-3. It will access databases that are much too large to bring into a worksheet file. When this is the case, 1-2-3's /Data External commands let you manipulate the external file like a database table in an active 1-2-3 file.

To use an external database, 1-2-3 must have a DataLens driver for the external package. 1-2-3 includes a sample DataLens driver file for dBASE III+, which does not have all of the external database features implemented, as well as the dBASE IV, Paradox, and SQL Server drivers. Other drivers will become available through Lotus or the database program manufacturers. The steps you need to take to access the database are summarized in the box called "Steps for Using an External Database."

Opening an External Database

The first step in using an external database is opening the file from 1-2-3. To open the file, enter the /Data External Use command. 1-2-3 prompts you for the table to use. The name for the table includes the name of the driver, and the path and filename of the database. The first selection is the name of the DataLens driver. 1-2-3 lists the selections it uses and then prompts you for the database name. (For dBASE III+, you must provide the path to the dBASE file and the database name.) 1-2-3 displays the default directory for the database name. You can either accept this, select another listed one, or press ESC and type one. 1-2-3 prompts you for the table name. You can select a listed table or database filename, or press ESC and type a table or database filename. Finally, 1-2-3 prompts you for the range name for referring to the external database table. 1-2-3 displays a prompt of the table name, unless the name starts with a $ or !, contains a period, or could be interpreted as a cell address. You can accept the default or enter a new range name before pressing ENTER. If the external program requires a password or user name for access to it, 1-2-3 will prompt for a password or user name before establishing the connection.

You do not need a copy of the other database management program on your system to access its files, if you have 1-2-3 and the proper DataLens driver on your system. This means you can use databases that have been created on other machines. If you are primarily using an external database with 1-2-3, consider placing the external database file in the 1-2-3 default directory.

As an example, suppose you want to use the data in the dBASE III file shown in Figure 9-15, which displays the Browse screen. Assume that this file is called INVOICES.DBF and it is in the dBASE directory on drive C. First, enter **/Data External Use**, and then select Sample. Next, enter **C:\DBASE** before pressing ENTER. When 1-2-3 lists the dBASE files in the C:\DBASE directory, select INVOICES. The prompt looks like this:

When you press ENTER to select the INVOICES database file, 1-2-3 prompts you for a range name to assign to the table, and it displays INVOICES as the default range name. Press ENTER to accept the range name.

Once you establish a connection between a table in an external database and 1-2-3, you can use the external data table in 1-2-3 /Data Query commands, formulas, and database functions. When you use the external database in 1-2-3, you will refer to it using the range name assigned by the /Data External Use

```
        Records   Organize   Fields   Go To   Exit
        INVOICE VENDOR            ITEM_DESCR         QUANTITY AMOUNT  PAID
        K1037   National Hardware Paint Brushes           400  438.57 Y
        Q9259   Machine Tool & Die 3/8 HP Drill           100 4944.89 Y
        L6572   Dutch Hardware    Whitney Punch            50  750.58 N
        Y7858   National Hardware Metal Files             150   78.74 Y
        R4362   Baker Hand Tools  Sanding Disks           500  159.98 N
        H2963   Cedar Woods, Inc. Clear Polyurethane      100  549.37 Y
        P9248   Baker Hand Tools  Wood Round Rasps        175  139.42 Y
        N2934   Machine Tool & Die 1/4 HP Table Saw        75 8426.24 N
        U8252   Dutch Hardware    C Clamps                200  221.58 N
```

Figure 9-15.   *INVOICES.DBF file from dBASE III*

command. The number of links you can create to external databases is limited by your computer's memory.

Steps for Using an External Database

The /Data External commands let you access records in external database tables. Before you can use an external database table, you must create a link between 1-2-3 and the external database table. The required steps are as follows:

1. Enter **/Data External Use**.

2. Enter or highlight the name of the DataLens driver and press ENTER.

3. Enter or highlight the path and press ENTER. (For SQL, this is the path to the SQL tables.)

4. Enter or highlight the filename and press ENTER. (For SQL, this is the SQL table.)

5. Enter a range name, or accept the default range name that 1-2-3 uses to refer to the external database table. The default is the name from Step 4 unless the table name starts with a $ or !, contains a period, or could be interpreted as a cell address. Press ENTER. Select Quit to return to READY mode.

6. Select this database table as the input range for /Data Query operations by selecting /Data Query Input. When 1-2-3 prompts for an input range, press F3 (NAME) and select the range name entered in Step 5. Press ENTER to finalize the input range.

If you establish links with database files on a different directory, you can add the directory containing the database files to your directory list. To do this, edit the LOTUS.BCF file in a text editor and add a line at the end of the file:

DB="database files path" DN="Driver name that uses this path" DD="description";

For example, to add the dBASE directory, enter **DB="C:\DBASE" DN="dBASE" DD="dBASE files"** so that 1-2-3 will display C:\DBASE as one of the possible selections. The description appears when you highlight the pathname for the database and press F3 (NAME) for a full screen list.

If the external database contains characters that are not displaying correctly, such as A appearing as a graphics character, 1-2-3 is not using the correct translation character set. To change the translation character set, use the /Data External Other Translation command. 1-2-3 will display the available character sets. If the external program only has one character set, 1-2-3 automatically sets this option for you; it will appear as if 1-2-3 is doing nothing. Most of the time, 1-2-3 selects the appropriate character set for you.

Listing Information About External Databases

Once you have created links to an external database, you can obtain information from it. Use the /Data External List Tables and /Data External List Fields commands.

The /Data External List Tables command lists the tables in an external database. This command is used with SQL databases. SQL database names are pathnames and each file in that directory is a table in the database. This command lists the table names or the filenames in one column; a second column lists the owner's names, if any, or NA; the third column lists the table descriptions if they have one, or NA if they do not. When you execute this command, 1-2-3 first prompts for a range in which to write the list. Figure 9-16 shows a list of external tables created with this command.

/Data External List Fields lists a table definition of an external database that has already been selected with the /Data External Use command. You can use this feature if you plan to create a database or table similar to one you have already created. This command lists, in columns, the field names, widths, lengths, column labels, and descriptions. If a field lacks any of this information, 1-2-3 displays NA. When you execute /Data External List Fields, 1-2-3 prompts for the range name of the external database you want to use, and then for the first cell to use for recording the fields list. The list uses as many rows as the external database has fields. Figure 9-17 shows a list of fields for the EMPLOYEE database, created with this command.

```
A:A1: 'INVOICES                                              MENU
Use List Create Delete Other Reset Quit
List the tables in an external database or the fields in an external table
   A         B      C      D      E      F      G      H
1 INVOICES   NA     NA
2 BENEFITS   NA     NA
3 CITY       NA     NA
4 CITY_NUM   NA     NA
5 DATES      NA     NA
6 EMPLOYEE   NA     NA
7 FINGOODS   NA     NA
8 TAXES      NA     NA
9 YEARS      NA     NA
```

Figure 9-16. *List of external database tables*

Once you are finished with the Data External menus, you can return to the READY mode by selecting Quit.

TIP: Use the /Data External List Fields command to list the field names in the external database table that you want to use with /Data Query commands. Once you have the table definition, you can use the /Copy or the /Range Transpose command to copy the field names to the criteria and output ranges. Then you can erase the table definition. This ensures that the field names in the search criteria are correct.

Using External Databases

Once you have created a link to an external database, you can start using its data in 1-2-3 commands. In /Data Query commands, you can specify an external database as an input range by entering its name as assigned by the /Data External Use command. To look at the database's records, use the /Data Query

```
A:A1: [W11] 'FIRST_NAME                                     READY

   A          B         C    D    E    F    G    H
1 FIRST_NAME Character  10   NA   NA   NA
2 MID_NAME   Character  10   NA   NA   NA
3 LAST_NAME  Character  15   NA   NA   NA
4 SSN        Character  11   NA   NA   NA
5 HIRE_DATE  Date       8    NA   NA   NA
```

Figure 9-17. *Employee database table definition*

Extract, /Data Query Modify Extract, and /Data Query Unique commands to copy the records to a worksheet. To copy records from an external database table, specify it as the input range name. To copy records to the external database table, specify it as the output range name.

Release 3 can also perform commands in the other database management program if you are familiar with the required command syntax for the program. To do this, use /Data External Other command. 1-2-3 will prompt for the database driver, the external database directory, and the database management command. (This feature is not available with the Sample DataLens driver provided with 1-2-3.)

When you include the external database values in @functions and formulas, 1-2-3 updates their values according to the /Worksheet Global Recalc command and the /Data External Other Refresh command. When both these commands are set to automatic, 1-2-3 reexecutes the last issued /Data Query and /Data Table commands, updates worksheet formulas, and updates database @functions at the interval selected with /Data External Other Refresh Interval. This command sets the number of seconds between 1-2-3 external database updates. When /Worksheet Global Recalc is set to automatic and /Data External Other Refresh is set to manual, /Data Query and /Data Table commands are only updated each time the commands are executed. The functions and formulas are updated according to the setting in /Worksheet Global Recalc.

Closing an External Database

After you have finished using an external database, you will want to close it. This breaks the connection between 1-2-3 and the database. To close an external database, use the /Data External Reset command. 1-2-3 will prompt you for the range name assigned by /Data External Use to the external database table. Select the range name for the table that you want to close. If the table you select is the only one in the database file, as with dBASE databases, 1-2-3 closes the file. If the closed database file is the only one using a particular driver, 1-2-3 removes the driver from memory.

As an example, suppose you want to close the database table in INVOICES.DBF that you have established with the /Data External Use command. First, enter **/Data External Reset**. Then select the range name INVOICES. Once you press ENTER to select the INVOICES range name, 1-2-3 breaks the connection to the INVOICES.DBF file. If this is the only dBASE III database open, 1-2-3 removes the dBASE driver from memory.

Creating an External Database

You can create an external database rather than storing all your database information within 1-2-3. This feature is frequently used for transferring information between external databases, or for transferring information from 1-2-3 database tables to external databases. 1-2-3 can serve as the conduit for moving information from one database to another, if there is no built-in link between the two database packages and if 1-2-3 supports interface with both of them. You can also use this feature to transfer 1-2-3 data to another database package, to take advantage of its unique reporting or query features.

To create an external database, you must create an input table definition, create the structure in the external table, and copy information to the external table. The following examples for creating an external database table use the data in the 1-2-3 worksheet shown in Figure 9-18.

Selecting Records for the New External Database Table

Before copying records to an external database, select the records that you want to put into the new database table. These records determine the structure of the new database table. Use the /Data Query Input command to select the records. The input range can be a database table in an active worksheet file or in an external database. For the data in Figure 9-18, the input range is A1..E12.

Creating a Table Definition

The first step in creating an external table is assigning a range name to the new table and creating a table definition. This defines the database structure that the new table uses. The format of the table is identical to the fields listing created by

	A	B	C	D	E	F
1	FIRST_NAME	MID_NAME	LAST_NAME	SSN	HIRE_DATE	
2	Allen	James	Canfield	652-47-2348	07/13/85	
3	Jeanette	Arne	Cruise	761-72-8973	09/11/87	
4	Yvonne	Sarah	Donaldson	978-12-5823	12/05/83	
5	Stephen	Scott	Golland	123-88-4827	03/21/84	
6	Patrick	John	Perez	478-28-6810	05/09/81	
7	Carol	Racheal	Spear	683-78-2832	08/18/86	
8	Babbette	Alicia	Zegetti	234-24-9807	11/14/82	
9	Marlene	Stewart	Galloway	465-27-7937	02/19/89	
10	Andrew	Brandon	Jeck	358-95-2594	11/27/83	
11	Mark	Paul	Jones	324-87-1369	02/28/89	
12	Karen	Allen	Smith	484-62-1669	04/01/88	

Figure 9-18. *EMPLOYEE database*

the /Data External List Fields command. The steps performed to create a table definition vary depending on which external database product you are using. Refer to the DataLens documentation for your particular database. If you return to the READY mode without creating the new table, you must execute the /Data External Create Name command again.

CREATING A TABLE DEFINITION IN A 1-2-3 WORKSHEET If the external database that you want to create is unlike other external database structures or 1-2-3 database tables, perform these steps:

1. Move to an empty area in a worksheet that has at least six columns and as many rows as the new database table will have fields.

2. Put the field name in the first column, the field type in the second column, the field width in the third column, the field label in the fourth column, the field description in the fifth column, and the field creation string (if any) in the sixth column. The format of the data must match what the database driver expects.

3. Repeat Step 2 for each field that you want in the created external table, using a new row for each field. An example of a table definition is shown in Figure 9-17.

TIP: Use the /Data External List Fields command to create a sample table definition that you can refer to as you create another table definition. Referring to a sample prevents errors due to lack of information or an inappropriate format.

4. Enter the **/Data External Create Name** command, and specify the database driver and external database you want to create. Then type the new table name and press ENTER. If the database driver requires an owner name for the database, enter the owner's name before the table name. When 1-2-3 prompts for the range name for the new table, press ENTER to accept the suggested table name or type a new table name before pressing ENTER. 1-2-3 will prompt for a table definition string. Either enter the table definition string and press ENTER, or press ENTER to omit it (since some databases, such as dBASE, do not use them).

5. Enter **/Data External Create Definition Use-Definition** and select the table definition that you created. For the table in Figure 9-17, the range is A1..E5.

6. Select Go to create the new table. This creates the external database but does not add any records to it. Because selecting Go establishes a link to the new database, you can use the /Data Query commands to copy data into it.

CREATING A TABLE DEFINITION FROM AN EXISTING DATABASE TABLE
The /Data External Create Definition Create-Definition command can create a table definition from a 1-2-3 database table or an external database table. First name the new table with /Data External Create Name. When you execute this command, you must select a database driver and the external database. Then type a table name and press ENTER. If the database driver requires an owner name for the database, enter the owner's name before the table name.

Next, 1-2-3 prompts for the range name for the new table. It then prompts for a table definition string. If the database driver uses one, type the table definition string. Press ENTER to accept your entry, if any. To create the table definition, select Definition Create-Definition, press F3 (NAME), and select the 1-2-3 database table or enter the range name of the external database. Select a range for 1-2-3 to place the table definition. This area must have at least six columns, and as many rows as the 1-2-3 database table or external database table has fields.

When you create a table this way using a 1-2-3 database table, 1-2-3 uses the field names in the top row as the table definition field names, the data types in the second row of the data table as the table definition field types, and the column widths as the field widths. When you create a table this way using an external database table, 1-2-3 uses the field names, field types, and field widths from the external database table. With both types of database tables, 1-2-3 may not assign field widths to fields containing values, depending upon the database driver selected by the /Data External Create Name command. Figure 9-17 shows a table definition.

Once you create a table definition, you can create an external database by selecting Go and returning to the READY mode. This creates the external database but does not add any records to the new database. Since selecting Go establishes a link to the new database, you can use the /Data Query commands to copy data to the new database. If you need to return to the READY mode before creating the table, select Quit. When you are ready to create the table, you must enter the /Data External Create Name and Definition commands again. You can make changes to the table definition from READY mode.

Copying Records to the New Database Table

Once you have created the external database table, you can copy records to it. Define the new table range name as the output range with the /Data Query Output command, and you can copy in all desired records using **/Data Query Extract**. To limit which records 1-2-3 copies, use criteria specified with the /Data Query Criteria command. The criteria selected must follow all of the criteria rules discussed earlier in the chapter. For example, to copy the database records in Figure 9-18 to the EMPLOYEE database created with the structure shown in Figure 9-17, select C:A1..C:E12 as the input range, criteria that match all records, and the EMPLOYEE database as the output range. When you select /Data Query Extract the records will be copied to the external database.

Deleting External Database Tables

Just as you can use 1-2-3 to create external database tables, you can also delete them with 1-2-3. This permanently removes the table from the disk. (This feature is not available with the Sample DataLens driver.)

To delete an external database table, use /Data External Delete. This command does not require a connection between 1-2-3 and the external database table. When you execute this command, 1-2-3 prompts for the name of the table, just as with the /Data External Use command. Select the table name that you want to delete and then select Yes as a confirmation.

As an example, suppose you want to delete the INVOICES.DBF database table. First, enter **/Data External Delete**. Then select dBASE as the driver. Next, select C:\DBASE for the external database name (which is the directory for dBASE III files). When 1-2-3 lists the dBASE files, select the database name INVOICES. Once you press ENTER to select the INVOICES file, select Yes to confirm that you want to delete the file. 1-2-3 deletes the file from the disk.

The Database Statistical Functions

1-2-3's database statistical functions are a special category of functions designed to coordinate with the other data management features. Using criteria you enter on your worksheet, they can perform a statistical analysis on selected records in your database. The criteria used is identical to the criteria for the /Data Query commands, except that you may have many active criteria areas. In fact, it is possible to set up a criteria area for each database statistical function that you use.

Each of the database statistical functions has a D immediately following the @ in the function name to show that it is a database function. The characters following the D indicate the exact task the function performs, and also correspond to the name of one of the statistical functions covered in Chapter 7, "1-2-3's Built-In Functions."

All of the database statistical functions except @DQUERY have the same arguments. The first is the location of the database (including the field names), which is a range name or address. If multiple databases are used, they are separated by commas or semicolons. The second argument is the field used to select which field is used to perform the calculation. It is either the number of the column or the field name in quotes. If you use the field column number, the first column is 0, the second column is 1, and so on. The third argument is the range address or name containing the criteria.

@DAVG

The @DAVG function obtains an average of a selected group of database records.

Format

@DAVG(*input,field,criteria*)

Use

Use the @DAVG function whenever you wish to obtain an average of the values in a field, in a selected group of records in the database. The database and the criteria in Figure 9-19 are used with the @DAVG function in the formula @DAVG(A1..F12,4,A15..A16) to calculate an average salary for employees in job code 23 of $21,550. Note that the database is defined as being located in A1..F12. The field the function uses is the Salary field, and the criteria used in the selection are located in A15..A16.

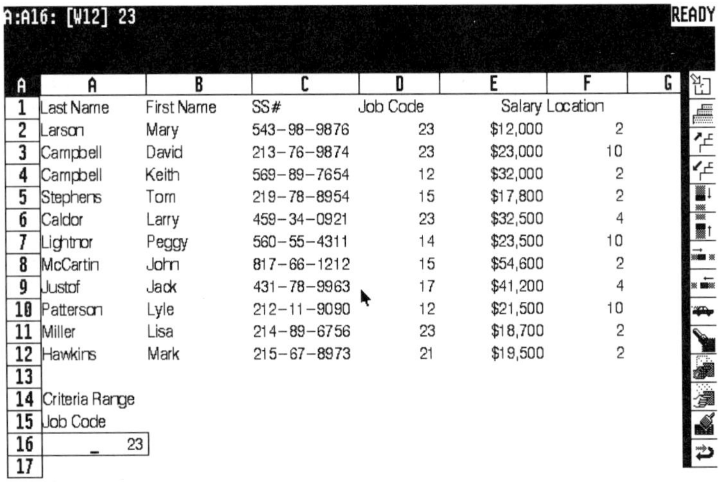

A	A	B	C	D	E	F
1	Last Name	First Name	SS#	Job Code	Salary	Location
2	Larson	Mary	543-98-9876	23	$12,000	2
3	Campbell	David	213-76-9874	23	$23,000	10
4	Campbell	Keith	569-89-7654	12	$32,000	2
5	Stephens	Tom	219-78-8954	15	$17,800	2
6	Caldor	Larry	459-34-0921	23	$32,500	4
7	Lightnor	Peggy	560-55-4311	14	$23,500	10
8	McCartin	John	817-66-1212	15	$54,600	2
9	Justof	Jack	431-78-9963	17	$41,200	4
10	Patterson	Lyle	212-11-9090	12	$21,500	10
11	Miller	Lisa	214-89-6756	23	$18,700	2
12	Hawkins	Mark	215-67-8973	21	$19,500	2
13						
14	Criteria Range					
15	Job Code					
16	23					
17						

A:A16: [W12] 23   READY

Figure 9-19. *Database used by database statistical functions*

@DCOUNT

The @DCOUNT function counts a selected group of database records.

Format

@DCOUNT(*input,field,criteria*)

Use

Use @DCOUNT function whenever you wish to obtain a count of the records in the database that match your selection criteria. The database and criteria in Figure 9-19 are used with the @DCOUNT function in the formula @DCOUNT(A1..F12,4,A15..A16) to count the four salary entries for records with a job code of 23. Note that the database is defined as being located in A1..F12. The offset to refer to the Salary field is 4, and the criteria used in the selection are located in A15..A16. Since @DCOUNT counts only records with a nonblank entry in the specified field, choose carefully the field that you count. For example, some records need not have a location assignment, but all records should have a salary.

Another use of @DCOUNT is to determine the size of the output range. For example, assume you want to determine how many rows you need in an output range for a /Data Query Extract command that you are using on an external database with the range name INVOICES. In a cell enter **@DCOUNT(INVOICES,"INVOICE",G1..G2)** as in the following worksheet:

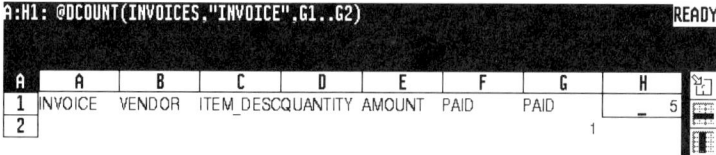

The formula in H1 returns 5 as the number of rows the output range needs below the field names. This function uses the criteria range G1..G2. The field names in the criteria range match the field names in the external database table.

@DGET

The @DGET function returns a value for a record that meets a set of criteria. If more than one record fits the criteria, it returns ERR.

Format

@DGET(*input,field,criteria*)

Use

Use the @DGET function whenever you wish to obtain a value from a particular record that matches your selection criteria. The database (sheet C) and criteria (B:C1..B:C2) in Figure 9-20 are used with the @DGET function to return the social security number of the employee with the last name of Canfield. Note that the database is defined as being located in C:A1..C:E12, the SSN field of the record that the function finds is returned, and the criteria used in the selection are located in C1..C2. This function returns the expected result since only one record matches the criteria. If more than one record matched, this function would return ERR.

@DMAX

The @DMAX function obtains the maximum value in a field within a selected group of database records.

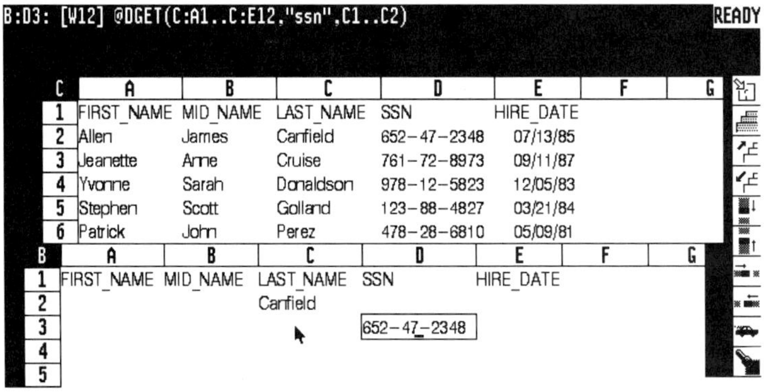

Figure 9-20. *Using @DGET*

Format

@DMAX(*input,field,criteria*)

Use

Use the @DMAX function whenever you wish to obtain the maximum (highest) value in a field for records in the database that match your selection criteria. The database and the criteria in Figure 9-19 are used with @DMAX(A1..F12,4,A15..A16) to determine the maximum salary of $32,500 for employees with a job code of 23. Note that the database is defined as being located in A1..F12. The field used is the Salary field, and the criteria used in the selection are located in A15..A16.

@DMIN

The @DMIN function obtains the minimum value in a field within a selected group of database records.

Format

@DMIN(*input,field,criteria*)

Use

Use the @DMIN function whenever you wish to obtain the minimum (lowest) value in a field for records in the database that match your selection criteria. The database and the criteria in Figure 9-19 are used with @DMIN(A1..F12,4,A15..A16) to determine the minimum salary of $12,000 for employees with a job code of 23. Note that the database is defined as being located in A1..F12, the Salary field is used, and the criteria used in the selection are located in A15..A16.

@DQUERY

The @DQUERY function sends a command to an external database management program. This function performs a command in another program without leaving 1-2-3. (This function cannot be used with the Sample DataLens driver.)

Format

@DQUERY(*function*,*ext-arguments*)

Arguments

function   a command in another database management program. This argument is a string, a cell reference, or a formula that evaluates to a string.

ext-arguments   the arguments the external command uses.

Use

Use the @DQUERY function to execute a command in an external database management program. This function is usually combined with criteria for 1-2-3 database features. 1-2-3 calculates @DQUERY when the /Data Query Delete, /Data Query Extract, /Data Query Modify Extract, or /Data Query Unique commands are executed. The database and criteria in Figure 9-21 are used with the @DQUERY function to locate the employees in the EMP_BENE external database that participate in the company's medical, dental, and long-term disability plans. The /Data Query commands use EMP_BENE as the input range, A9..H10 as the criteria, and A13..H13 as the output range. "SIGN" is a dBASE

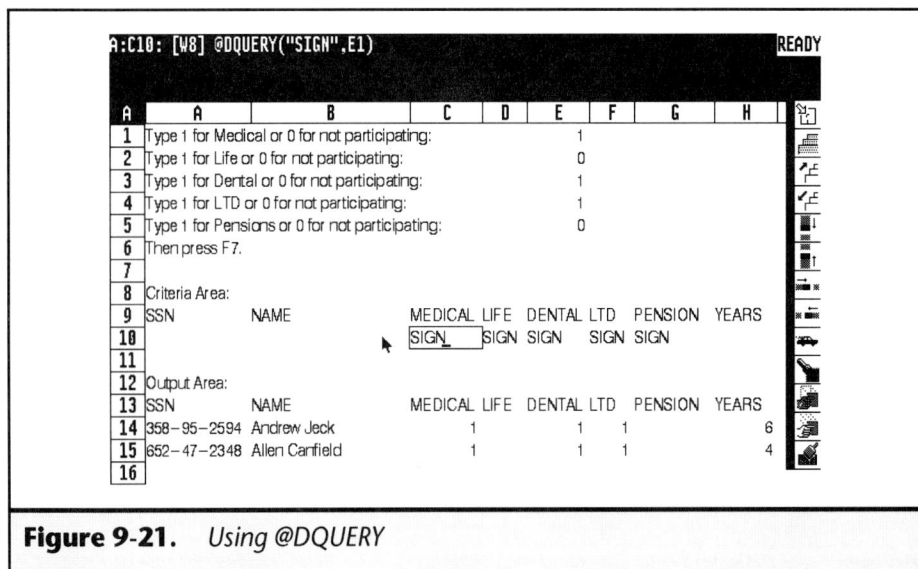

Figure 9-21. *Using @DQUERY*

function that returns a 1 if the field contains a positive number, a −1 if the field contains a negative number, or a 0 if it contains a 0.

@DSTD

The @DSTD function is used to determine the standard deviation of a set of values, or how much variation there is from the average of the values. The values used in this calculation will be from selected records in the database. The standard deviation is the square root of the variance.

Format

@DSTD(*input,field,criteria*)

Use

Use the @DSTD function to determine the standard deviation when the selected records comprise the entire population you are measuring. If you are working with only a sample of the population, use the @DSTDS function.

The purpose of the standard deviation is to determine the amount of variation between individual values and the mean. If you determine that the average age of your employees is 40, this could mean that half of your employees are 39 and the other half 41, or it could mean that you have employees whose ages range from 18 to 65. The latter case shows a greater standard deviation, due to the greater variance from the mean.

The @DSTD function is biased, and it uses a count as part of the standard deviation calculation. The following formula is used:

$$\sqrt{\frac{\sum (X_i - \text{AVG})^2}{n}}$$

where X_i is the ith item in the list, and n is the number of items in the list.

The formula @DSTD(A1..F12,4,A15..A16) and the database in Figure 9-19 return the result of 7438.581854, which is the standard deviation of salaries for employees in job code 23.

@DSTDS

The @DSTDS function is used to determine the standard deviation of a set of values, or how much variation there is from the average of the values for a sample of the population. The values used in this calculation will be from selected records in the database. The standard deviation is the square root of the variance.

Format

@DSTDS(*input,field,criteria*)

Use

Use the @DSTDS function to determine the standard deviation when the selected records comprise a sample of the population you are measuring. If you are working with the entire population, use the @DSTD function.

The purpose of the standard deviation is to determine the amount of variation between individual values and the mean. If you determine that the average age of your employees is 40, this could mean that half of your employees are 39 and the other half 41, or it could mean that you have employees whose ages range from 18 to 65. The latter case shows a greater standard deviation, due to the greater variance from the mean.

The @DSTDS function is unbiased. The following formula is used:

$$\sqrt{\frac{\sum (X_i - \text{AVG})^2}{n-1}}$$

where X_i is the ith item in the list, and n is the number of items in the list.

The formula @DSTD(A1..F12,4,A15..A16) and the database in Figure 9-19 return the result of 8589.334472, which is the standard deviation of salaries for employees in job code 23 when this group is treated as a sample of the population.

@DSUM

The @DSUM function obtains the total of values in a field within a selected group of database records.

Format

@DSUM(*input,field,criteria*)

Use

Use the @DSUM function whenever you wish to total up the values in a field for records in the database that match your selection criteria. The database and criteria in Figure 9-19 are used with the function @DSUM(A1..F12,4,A15..A16) to determine the total of salaries ($86,200) for employees with a job code of 23. Note that the database is defined as being located in A1..F12, the Salary field is selected to total, and the criteria used in the selection are located in A15..A16.

@DVAR

The @DVAR function computes the variance of values in a population, or the amount that the individual population values vary from the average. The records used in the computation are selected from the database with your criteria.

Format

@DVAR(*input,field,criteria*)

Use

Use the @DVAR function to determine the variance when the selected records comprise the entire population you are measuring. If you are working with only a sample of the population, use the @DVARS function.

The purpose of the variance is to determine the amount of variation between individual values and the mean. If you determine that the average age of your employees is 40, this could mean that half of your employees are 39 and the other half 41, or it could mean that you have employees whose ages range from 18 to 65. The latter case shows a greater variance, due to the greater dispersion from the mean.

The @DVAR function is biased, and it uses a count as part of the variance calculation. The following formula is used:

$$\frac{\sum (X_i - \text{AVG})^2}{n}$$

where X_i is the ith item in the list, and n is the number of items in the list.

The formula @DVAR(A1..F12,"Salary",A15..A16) and the worksheet in Figure 9-19 return the result of 55332500, which is the variance for salaries of employees with a job code of 23.

@DVARS

The @DVARS function computes the variance of values in a population, or the amount that the individual sample values vary from the average. The records used in the computation are selected from the database with your criteria.

Format

@DVARS(*input,field,criteria*)

Use

Use the @DVARS function to determine the variance when the selected records represent a sample of the entire population you are measuring. If you are working with the entire population, use the @DVAR function.

The purpose of the variance is to determine the amount of variation between individual values and the mean. If you determine that the average age of your employees is 40, this could mean that half of your employees are 39 and the other half 41, or it could mean that you have employees whose ages range from 18 to 65. The latter case shows a greater variance, due to the greater dispersion from the mean.

The @DVARS function uses the unbiased method. The following formula is used:

$$\frac{\sum (X_i - AVG)^2}{n-1}$$

where X_i is the ith item in the list, and n is the number of items in the list.

The formula @DVARS(A1..F12,"Salary",A15..A16) and the worksheet in Figure 9-19 return the result of 112437971.5, which is the variance for salaries of employees with a job code of 23.

Command Reference

Data Management

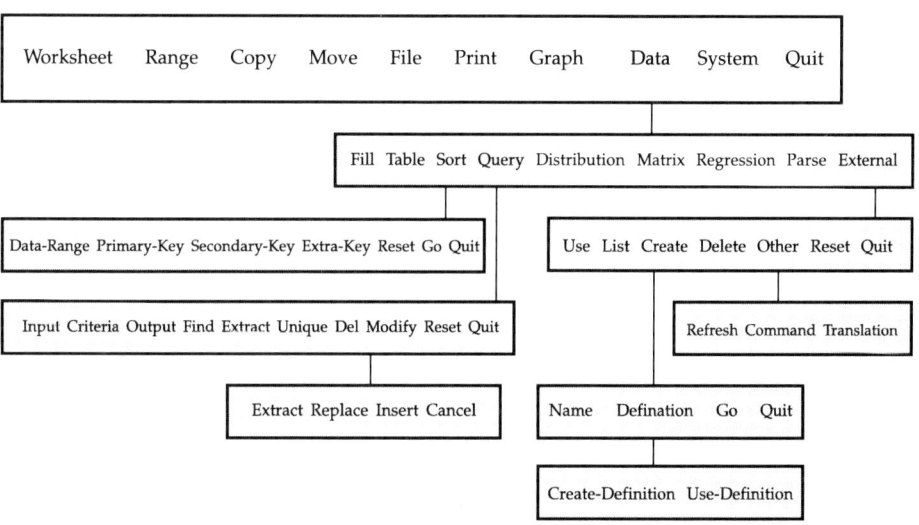

©1989 Lotus Development Corporation. Used with permission.

/Data External Create Definition

Description

The /Data External Create Definition command creates or selects a table definition used to create an external database. The command options select the table definition's source.

Options

This command has two options that select the source of the table definition.

CREATE-DEFINITION   This option creates a table definition from a 1-2-3 database table or an external database table. When you select this option, you are prompted for the 1-2-3 database table address, or a range name for a 1-2-3 database table or external database table. A 1-2-3 database table address or range name must include the field names and at least one database table record.

Then this command prompts for the first cell of the range in which to place the table definition. This table uses six columns, and as many rows as are needed by the database table fields. If the input table is a 1-2-3 database table, this command creates a table with the names appearing in the first row of the table as the field names, the data types of the second row determining the field types, and the column widths setting the field widths. To modify the table after creating it, select Quit from the Data External Create menu to return to the READY mode.

USE-DEFINITION   This option selects a worksheet range that contains a table definition. When you use this option, 1-2-3 prompts for the range that contains the table definition. You can point to the range, or type the range address or name directly.

/Data External Create Go

Description

This command creates a new external database table named with the /Data External Create Name command, using the table definition defined with the /Data External Create Definition command. This command only creates the database structure; it does not copy any records to the table. /Data External Create Name and /Data External Create Definition must be executed before this command.

/Data External Create Name

Description

This command names the external database that the /Data External Create Go command creates and defines the 1-2-3 range name that will refer to the table.

Options

When you execute this command, 1-2-3 prompts for you to select the table name consisting of the database driver, the database name, and the table name. In some cases you may have to provide a user name and password. Next 1-2-3 prompts for the 1-2-3 range name that other 1-2-3 commands and functions will use. Finally, 1-2-3 prompts for a table creation string. If the database driver that you are using requires one, enter it; otherwise, press ENTER. This command must be performed before the other /Data External Create commands.

/Data External Create Quit

Description

This command leaves the Data External Create menus and returns to the READY mode. 1-2-3 forgets the settings made with the /Data External Create Name and /Data External Create Definition commands. You must reexecute these to create an external database.

/Data External Delete

Description

The /Data External Delete command removes a table from an external database. This command can be executed without establishing a connection with the /Data External Use command. The /Data External Delete command's actions may be limited by the database administrator restricting your access to the database, or if the database driver does not permit you to delete an external table. The /Data External Delete command may prompt you for a user name and password if the database management program requires this information. When you execute this command, 1-2-3 prompts you to select the driver, the database name, and the table name.

Options

The only option for this command is to select Yes to confirm that you want to delete the external database or No to cancel this command.

/Data External List

Description

The /Data External List command lists the fields in a table, or tables in a database; the list is displayed in a worksheet range.

Options

This command has two options for the listed information: Fields and Tables. Select one of these options, and 1-2-3 prompts you to select the driver and the database name from a displayed list. If you select Fields, 1-2-3 lists the table names and prompts you to select one. In both cases, you can either select or type in your entry. Once 1-2-3 has the list specifications, it prompts you for a worksheet location for the list.

The command's output has six columns if the Fields option is selected, and three columns if the Tables option is selected. Both options use as many rows as are necessary to list all the fields or tables. It writes this information over any worksheet contents in the selected output area.

FIELDS This option lists in a worksheet the field names, data type, width, column label, description and field creation strings for a database table that is connected with the /Data External Use command. NA's appear for the column labels and descriptions when the database management program does not support column labels and descriptions.

TABLES This option lists in a worksheet the table names, owner's name, and table descriptions in a selected external database. NA's appear for the table descriptions if the database management program does not support owner names or table descriptions. These table names are not the 1-2-3 range names the /Data External Use command assigns.

/Data External Other Command

Description

/Data External Other Command can execute a command within the database management program that the /Data External Use command has loaded.

Options

When you select this command, 1-2-3 lists the driver and name of the external databases to which the /Data External Use command has connected. Select the one you want or enter a different one. Then, enter the command from the external program that you want to execute, or a cell address containing a label with a command. The command must match the database management program's syntax rules. The features this command can perform are detailed in the specific DataLens driver documentation.

/Data External Other Refresh

Description

The /Data External Other Refresh command determines when 1-2-3 reexecutes the most recent /Data Query and /Data Table commands, and updates worksheet formulas and database @functions.

Options

AUTOMATIC   This option causes 1-2-3 to reexecute the last issued /Data Query and /Data Table commands, and update worksheet formulas and database @functions, at the interval selected with the Interval option.

INTERVAL This option sets the interval for 1-2-3's reexecution of the most recent /Data Query and /Data Table commands, and update of worksheet formulas and database @functions. The default is 1 second, but the setting can range between 0 and 3600 seconds. If the time needed to perform these recalculations and updates is greater than the interval, the worksheet will continually be recalculated and updated. This interval remains set until the end of the 1-2-3 session or another interval is selected.

MANUAL This option causes 1-2-3 to reexecute the last issued /Data Query and /Data Table commands, and update worksheet formulas and database @functions, on a manual basis. The /Data Query and /Data Table commands update their most recent results. The formulas and functions are recalculated as set according to the /Worksheet Global Recalc command.

/Data External Other Translation

Description

The /Data External Other Translation command selects the character set 1-2-3 uses when it transfers data to and from a table in the external database. This command is only used when the information copied from the external table contains inappropriate characters. Most of the time, 1-2-3 selects the appropriate character set for you. When you use this command, 1-2-3 displays the available character sets. If the database management program only has one character set, 1-2-3 automatically sets this command for you. In this case, it appears as if 1-2-3 is doing nothing.

Options

The options for this command are to select a database driver and an external database from which you want to select a character set, and then to select the character set you want to use.

/Data External Quit

Description

The /Data External Quit command permits you to exit the sticky Data External menu.

/Data External Reset

Description

This command breaks a connection between a table in an external database and 1-2-3. Any further references to the external file may result in errors.

Options

When you execute this command, 1-2-3 prompts you for the range name of the external table from which you are disconnecting. If the range name selected is the only table connected to 1-2-3, this command closes the external database file. If the range name selected is the only external table connection established for a particular driver, this command removes the driver from 1-2-3's memory.

/Data External Use

Description

This command establishes a connection between 1-2-3 and a table in an external database. A 1-2-3 range name is assigned to the external database for other commands and functions to use. You can connect multiple external database tables by using this command for each table. Once a connection is established between 1-2-3 and the external table, you can refer to the table in most of 1-2-3's database functions and commands. To look at the records in the external database, you must copy them to a worksheet with /Data Query commands.

When 1-2-3 connects to an external table, it loads a driver that connects with the database management program. This driver also lets you execute the commands and functions of the database management program from within 1-2-3.

Options

When you execute /Data External Use, 1-2-3 prompts you to select the driver, the database name, and the table name. You can either select a highlighted one or type in your own entry. Then 1-2-3 prompts for a range name; the table name is suggested as the default, unless it starts with a $ or !, contains a period, or looks like a cell address. You can accept the default or enter a new range name before pressing ENTER. Like all range names, it must be unique within the 1-2-3 file. If the database management program requires a user name and password, you must also enter this information.

/Data Fill

Description

The /Data Fill command allows you to produce an ascending or descending list of numbers separated by the same interval. The following series can all be generated with /Data Fill:

```
1 2 3 4 5 6 7 8 9 10 11 12 13 14 15 16
5001 5006 5011 5016 5021 5026 5031 5036
90 88 86 84 82 80 78 76 74 72 70 68 66
03-Jan-92 10-Jan-92 17-Jan-92 24-Jan-92 31-Jan-92
```

Options

When you use /Data Fill, you must specify the range of cells to hold the numeric series. The /Data Fill options include a start value, a stop value, and an increment or step value. The start value is the beginning number in your sequence and has a default of 0 or the value most recently entered. The stop value is the last value in your sequence: its default is 8191 or the value most recently entered. The increment (step) value is the distance between each pair of numbers in the series; its default is 1 or the value most recently entered. Any of these values can be either positive or negative.

The values can also include functions, such as @DATE(91,12,13); formulas, such as +@YEAR(@TODAY)+1900; or a cell address, range address or range name that evaluates to a value, such as A1, which may contain the number 30. If you provide a range name or range address, 1-2-3 uses the cell value in the upper left corner of the range.

When /Data Fill is used for dates, 1-2-3 offers additional features for the start, step, and stop values. To include a date as a start or stop value, you can enter it in any one of 1-2-3's date formats, except Short International. If the step value contains:

- An integer or an integer followed by a D, 1-2-3 increases the date value in daily increments

- An integer followed by a W, 1-2-3 increases the step value in weekly increments
- An integer followed by an M, 1-2-3 increases the step value in monthly increments
- An integer followed by a Q, 1-2-3 increases the step value in quarterly increments
- An integer followed by a Y, 1-2-3 increases the step value in yearly increments

For example, a step value of 2M increments the date serial numbers in two-month increments.

When the /Data Fill function is used for times, 1-2-3 offers some new features for the start, step, and stop values. To include a time as a start or stop value, you can enter it in any one of 1-2-3's time formats. If the step value contains:

- An integer followed by an S, 1-2-3 increases the time value in second increments
- An integer followed by MIN, 1-2-3 increases the step value in minute increments
- An integer followed by an H, 1-2-3 increases the step value in hour increments

For example, a step value of 30S increments the date serial numbers in thirty-second increments.

NOTE: If the range selected for the /Data Fill command uses the Automatic format, 1-2-3 will automatically format the cells as dates and times using the format of the start, step, and stop values you specify.

/Data Query Criteria

Description

The /Data Query Criteria command lets you specify the location of the criteria you have entered on the worksheet for database record selection. Criteria must already be entered on the worksheet when you issue this command.

Options

The only option you have with this command is the method you use to specify the criteria range. Pointing, typing the cell addresses, and using a range name are all acceptable methods of specifying the two-dimensional range.

/Data Query Del

Description

The /Data Query Del command searches database records for specified criteria and deletes all the records in the input area that match the criteria. The database records must first be specified with /Data Query Input, and the criteria must already be entered on the worksheet and specified with /Data Query Criteria. This command works only on one data table at a time.

Options

The only option for this command is to select Delete to confirm that you want to delete the matching records or Cancel to cancel this command.

NOTE Since the /Data Query Del deletion process is permanent, be sure to save your file to disk before using the command. This way you can always retrieve the file if you make a mistake in specifying your criteria and delete too many records. Another protective strategy is to use your criteria to extract records (with /Data Query Extract) before using the same criteria for a deletion.

/Data Query Extract

Description

The /Data Query Extract command searches database records for specified criteria, and writes all records from the input area that match your criteria to an output area on the worksheet. Preliminary steps that must be completed before using this command are these:

- The database records to be searched must first be specified with /Data Query Input.
- The criteria for extraction must be entered on the worksheet and specified with /Data Query Criteria.
- An output area must be specified with /Data Query Output. This area must be large enough to hold all the extracted records, and must be out of the way of your other data.

/Data Query Find

Description

The /Data Query Find command searches database records for specified criteria, and highlights one at a time all records from the input area that match those criteria. Before using this command you must specify the database records to be searched, with /Data Query Input. You must also enter the search criteria on the worksheet, and identify them with /Data Query Criteria. This command only works on one data table at a time. It cannot work with external tables.

Options

Your options for this command include using the arrow keys to move between matching records and between fields. You can press HOME and END to move to the first and last matching record. To change an entry, move the cell pointer to the entry and make a new entry or press F2 (EDIT) and alter the current one. You can end FIND mode by pressing ENTER or ESC to return to the Data Query menu or by pressing F7 (QUERY) to return to the READY mode.

/Data Query Input

Description

The /Data Query Input command is used to specify the location of the database. Database records should already be entered on a worksheet when you issue this command.

Options

The only option you have with this command is the method you use to specify the input range. Pointing, typing the cell addresses, and entering a range name are all acceptable methods. The input range can include multiple input ranges or external tables. To include multiple tables, type the argument separator (default is a comma) after highlighting an input range; then specify the next input range. If you specify an external table, use the name assigned with the /Data External Use command. The /Data Query Extract command can use an input range from an active file, a file on disk, or an external table. The /Data Query Modify Insert and /Data Query Modify Replace commands can use an input range from an active file or an external table.

NOTE: The input range should always include the field names at the top of your database.

/Data Query Modify Cancel

Description

The /Data Query Modify Cancel command cancels the actions taken by other /Data Query Modify commands and returns you to the READY mode. Once this command is executed, the /Data Query Modify Replace command has no effect.

/Data Query Modify Extract

Description

The /Data Query Modify Extract command copies records from the input range set by /Data Query Input that meet the criteria set by /Data Query Criteria, to the output area set by /Data Query Output. This command only copies the fields for each record that are in the first row of the output range. Unlike /Data Query Extract, /Data Query Modify Extract remembers the copied records' location in the input range so that you can modify and replace the extracted records in the database.

/Data Query Modify Insert

Description

The /Data Query Modify Insert command copies records from the output range set by /Data Query Output, to the input area set by /Data Query Input. This command only copies the fields for each record that are in the first row of the output range.

/Data Query Modify Replace

Description

The /Data Query Modify Replace command replaces records in the input range set by /Data Query Input, using records in the output area set by /Data Query Output. This command is used to replace records extracted with the /Data Query Modify Extract command after the extracted records in the output range are edited. This command only copies the fields for each record that are in the first row of the output range.

This command replaces formulas in the input range with their value from the output range. You can prevent this from occurring by changing the name of the field in the output range to a temporary name.

/Data Query Output

Description

The /Data Query Output command permits you to specify the location of the area you plan to use to store information extracted from a database. The field names for the data you extract must already be entered on the worksheet when you issue this command. The other task this command performs is specifying the location of the records to be added to the input range with /Data Query Modify Insert.

Options

You have two options with this command: specifying the entire output area or just the top row. You also have a number of options for specifying the range for the output area.

If you specify a one-row output range that includes only the field names, 1-2-3 will use as many rows as it needs for writing data in the columns selected for the output range. If you specify a multiple-row output range, 1-2-3 will stop extracting records when your output range is full. Options for specifying the range are pointing, typing the cell addresses, and entering a range name. The output range can be in the current file, an active file, or an external table.

/Data Query Quit

Description

This command permits you to exit the sticky /Data Query menu.

/Data Query Reset

Description

This command will clear the range specifications for Input, Criteria, and Output made with the /Data Query commands or /Data External commands.

/Data Query Unique

Description

The /Data Query Unique command copies records from the input range that match the criteria. Unlike the /Data Query Extract command, this command only includes the first record when several identical records exist. The output is sorted according to the field values in the output area. Preliminary steps that must be completed before using this command are as follows.

- The database records to be searched must first be specified with /Data Query Input.
- The criteria for search must be entered on the worksheet and specified with /Data Query Criteria.

- An output area must be specified with /Data Query Output. This area must be large enough to hold all the selected records and must be out of the way of your other data.

/Data Sort Data-Range

Description

The /Data Sort Data-Range command permits you to specify the location of the records you plan to sort. Database records should already be entered on the worksheet when you issue this command.

Options

The only option you have with this command is the method you use to specify the input range. Pointing, typing the cell addresses, and entering a range name are all acceptable methods of specifying the range.

NOTE: The sort range should not include the field names at the top of the database. If you accidentally include the field names, they will be sorted.

/Data Sort Extra-Key

Description

The /Data Sort Extra-Key command permits you to select additional fields within the database to serve as tie breakers whenever there is more than one primary and secondary key with the same value. When this situation occurs, the sort operation uses the extra keys to provide a sequence for the records containing the duplicate entries. As an example, you may have an employee file with the location field selected as the primary key and job code selected as the secondary key. When you encounter more than one employee with the same job code and location, and have selected last name as the first extra key, the employees with the same location and job code will appear in a sequence determined by their last names.

Options

You can specify any nonblank within a field and whether to use ascending or descending sort order.

/Data Sort Go

Description

The /Data Sort Go command tells 1-2-3 to sort the records. Before this command is executed, the database must be defined with the /Data Sort Data-Range command. The primary key and any additional sort keys must also be specified.

/Data Sort Primary-Key

Description

The /Data Sort Primary-Key command permits you to sort your database records into a new sequence, by selecting a field to control the resequencing. Enter the address of a nonblank cell within the field that you wish to use for controlling the sort sequence.

Options

You can specify either ascending or descending sort order.

/Data Sort Quit

Description

This command lets you exit the sticky Data Sort menu.

/Data Sort Reset

Description

The /Data Sort Reset command cancels the current settings for the primary, secondary, and extra keys, and the data range.

/Data Sort Secondary-Key

Description

The /Data Sort Secondary-Key command permits you to select a field within the database to serve as a tie breaker whenever there is more than one primary key with the same value. When this situation occurs, the sort operation uses the secondary key to provide a sequence for the records containing the duplicate entries. As an example, you may have an employee file with the last name field selected as the primary key. When you encounter three employees with the last name of Smith, and have selected first name as the secondary key, the three Smiths will appear in a sequence determined by their first names.

A secondary key is selected in the same manner as a primary key. Any nonblank cell within a field can be specified as the secondary key.

Options

You can specify either ascending or descending sort order.

CHAPTER 10

Using Data Management Features in the Worksheet Environment

In Chapter 9, "Data Management," you learned how to use the data management features of 1-2-3 to build your own database of information. In this chapter you will discover ways that data management commands can assist you with calculations and other worksheet tasks. You will see some of the same commands used in Chapter 9, such as /Data Sort, but they will be presented in a new light. You will also explore more sophisticated features that allow you to handle tasks like regression and sensitivity analysis. These features will introduce new commands, such as /Data Table and /Data Regression, including all of the Release 3 Data Table features.

Performing Statistical Analyses with /Data Commands

The statistical options that are part of the /Data commands allow you to perform sophisticated analyses of your data. You can perform a regression analysis, create a frequency distribution, or prepare a sensitivity analysis.

Sensitivity Analysis

The /Data Table options allow you to quickly substitute a range of values in one or more cells referenced by formulas and to record the results of worksheet calculations at the same time. In other words, /Data Table automates the "what-if" analysis you may have been doing with the package as you plugged in new individual variable values and tried to remember the results from previous iterations. The advantage of this automated approach is that 1-2-3 will do all the work, plug in the values, and remember the results for you. The results will be recorded in a table, as you might guess from the command's name.

The /Data Table command provides five options: a one-way table, a two-way table, a three-way table, a labeled table, and a reset option that eliminates settings you have made through any of the other choices.

One-Way Data Tables

A one-way data table allows you to choose a set of values for one variable and record them in a worksheet column. Above and to the right of this column of values you place formulas to be evaluated for each value of the variable. The results are recorded below the formulas to form a complete table.

Let's look at two examples of a one-way table. The first will be used with the worksheet data shown in Figure 10-1. This worksheet computes commissions using the quarterly sales figure for each salesman times the commission percentage in D1. If you were considering changing the commission percentage, you might be interested in what you would have paid out if that commission structure existed in prior periods. You could plug individual values one by one

Chapter 10: Using Data Management Features in the Worksheet Environment

```
A:C5: (C0) [W11] +B5*$D$1                                    READY
```

	A	B	C	D	E	F	G
1		Sales Commissions Assuming a		1.50% Commission			
2							
3			Quarterly				
4	Salesperson		Sales	Commission			
5	Rich Roberts		$1,200,987	$18,015			
6	Jana Jolson		$2,134,567	$32,019			
7	Mike Moore		$1,987,600	$29,814			
8	Harriet Harm		$3,278,965	$49,184			
9	Tom Tom		$3,456,123	$51,842			
10	Rita Roberts		$2,134,987	$32,025			
11	Paul Peters		$1,897,626	$28,464			
12	Kira Kolson		$1,750,890	$26,263			
13	Herb Horst		$2,345,910	$35,189			
14	Fran Folly		$3,890,152	$58,352			
15	Ivan Imers		$3,186,450	$47,797			
16	Wilma Walker		$2,134,567	$32,019			
17	Norm Nait		$1,678,932	$25,184			
18	Eva Edens		$540,900	$8,114			
19							
20	TOTAL		$31,618,656	$474,280			

```
13-Nov-92 06:34 PM
```

Figure 10-1. *Commission schedule*

into D1 and monitor the effect on the total commission calculation in C20, but it is faster to have 1-2-3 do the work for you.

The first step is to set up the framework for the table. This step must be completed before you enter /Data Table. Record the values you want to substitute for D1 in a column. The example in Figure 10-2 uses I4..I19, but any empty location can be selected. If you are using values in even increments, you can have /Data Fill generate these values for you. The next step in the setup process is to record the formula or formulas you wish to evaluate, placed one column to the right of the values and one row above them. In this example, to evaluate total commission, a reference to C20 will suffice. This entry is made in J3. After entering +C20, you can format the cell as Text to display the formula. The table at this time looks like the display in Figure 10-2. After completing these two preliminary steps, you are ready to use the /Data Table command.

Move your cell pointer to I3, the blank cell to the left of the formulas and immediately above the values. Enter **/Data Table** and select 1 for a one-way table. Select the range I3..J19 for the table location. You can use cell addresses, pointing, or a range name for this task.

1-2-3's next prompt is for the input cell. This is the cell into which you want to plug the values from the commission percentage column, one by one. For our example this will be D1. When you press ENTER, 1-2-3 takes the first value in the

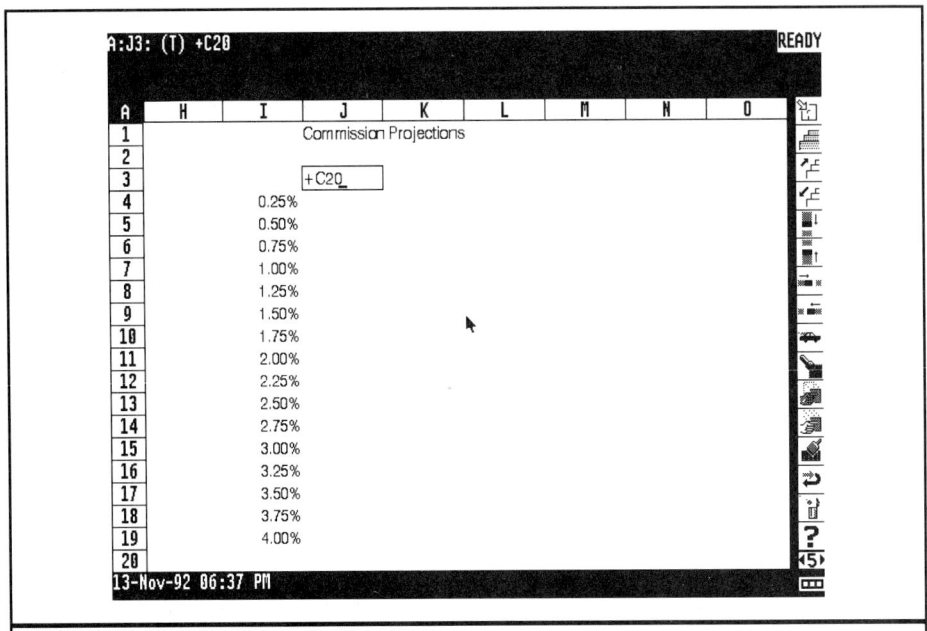

Figure 10-2. Outline of a one-way table

input column and plugs it into D1 in the model. After the first calculation is completed, 1-2-3 records the result in the table and repeats the process for each of the remaining values. Figure 10-3 shows the level of total commissions at a variety of percentages. Be aware that if you change the formulas in your model, the table is not updated to reflect these changes. To update the table values, issue the /Data Table command again or press F8 (TABLE).

Now let's look at a second example of a one-way table, this time using more than one formula. Figure 10-4 shows the model and the completed table. The model projects sales, cost of goods sold, and profit, using a 9% fixed growth rate for sales, and 45% as the cost of goods sold percentage. Suppose you want to look at the impact on sales, costs, and profits of variations in the sales growth factor. Place the variable values in A11..A20. References to the cells containing the formulas you wish to evaluate are placed in B10..D10, as +G4, +G2, and +G3. Using /Data Table 1, define the table as being in A10..D20 and the input cell as C7. This range must include the formulas in the top row and the input values in the leftmost column. The results are shown in cells B11..D20 of the figure.

TIP: Use F8 (TABLE) to recalculate tables instead of executing the /Data Table command each time you want to update the values of the formulas. Pressing this key reexecutes the last /Data Table command.

Chapter 10: Using Data Management Features in the Worksheet Environment 563

```
A:J4: (C0) 79046.64                                              READY
```

		H	I	J	K	L	M	N	O
1				Commission Projections
2				
3				+C20
4			0.25%	$79,047
5			0.50%	$158,093
6			0.75%	$237,140
7			1.00%	$316,187
8			1.25%	$395,233
9			1.50%	$474,280
10			1.75%	$553,326
11			2.00%	$632,373
12			2.25%	$711,420
13			2.50%	$790,466
14			2.75%	$869,513
15			3.00%	$948,560
16			3.25%	$1,027,606
17			3.50%	$1,106,653
18			3.75%	$1,185,700
19			4.00%	$1,264,746
20				

13-Nov-92 06:40 PM

Figure 10-3. Commission table output

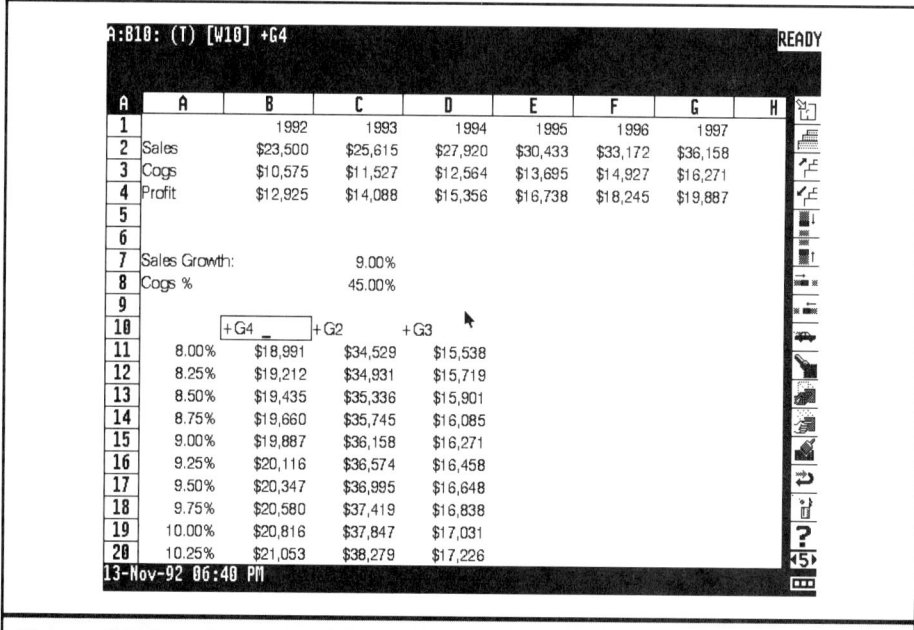

Figure 10-4. One-way table with multiple formulas

Two-Way Data Tables

The /Data Table 2 command allows you to build a table in which you supply input values for two variables, instructing 1-2-3 to apply these values when recalculating the worksheet and recording the result of one of the worksheet formulas in the table. This kind of table is referred to as a two-way table. It differs from a one-way table in its use of two sets of variable values and its ability to record the results of only one formula. This command allows you to see to which variable the formula being evaluated is most sensitive.

Like the one-way table, the two-way table requires a significant amount of preliminary work. The example uses a two-way table with the model in Figure 10-5 for payment calculations. The payment calculation is dependent on the amount borrowed, the interest rate, and the term of the loan. The amount borrowed may vary, since it will be equal to the cost of the new home minus the equity from the sale of the existing home. While holding the loan term constant, you can use /Data Table 2 to vary both the equity received from the sale of an existing home, and the interest rate.

Values for the first input variable (the interest rate) are stored in one column of the worksheet. If the values are spaced at equal intervals, /Data Fill can be used to generate the column of values. Values for the second input value (equity) are placed one row above the top value for input variable 1 and one cell to the right. The values for the second input variable are placed across the row. A formula or a reference to one is then placed in the cell at the top of the column used for input variable 1 and in the same row as the input variable 2.

In the payment example in Figure 10-6, column H is used for the values for input variable 1. Values are in H2..H17, beginning with 9%, adding increments of .25%, and ending with 12.75%. The equity figures start in I1 with 75000 and proceed at increments of 2500, ending with 90000 in O1. Cell H1 contains the formula reference, +D8, representing the payment calculated. If you want this cell to display as a formula, format the cell as Text with /Range Format Text.

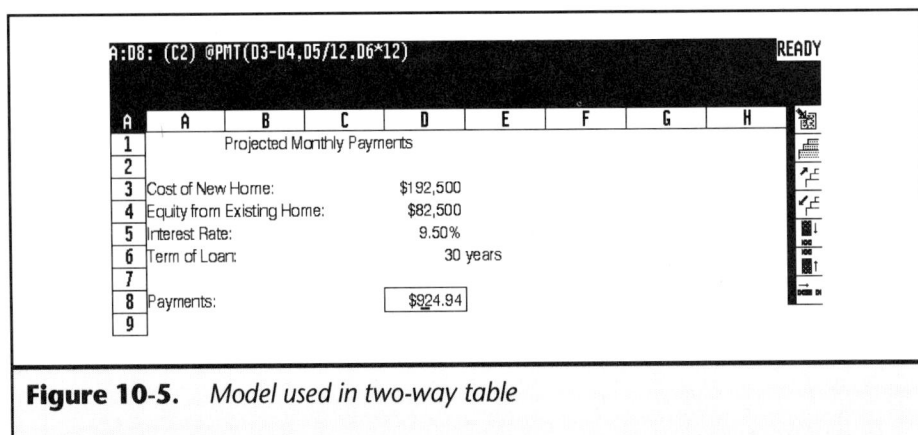

Figure 10-5.   *Model used in two-way table*

```
A:I2: (C0) 945.431574910119711                                          READY

     A    H        I        J        K        L        M        N        O
 1  +D8       $75,000  $77,500  $80,000  $82,500  $85,000  $87,500  $90,000
 2   9.00%     $945     $925     $905     $885     $865     $845     $825
 3   9.25%     $967     $946     $926     $905     $884     $864     $843
 4   9.50%     $988     $967     $946     $925     $904     $883     $862
 5   9.75%    $1,010    $988     $967     $945     $924     $902     $881
 6  10.00%    $1,031   $1,009    $987     $965     $943     $921     $900
 7  10.25%    $1,053   $1,031   $1,008    $986     $963     $941     $919
 8  10.50%    $1,075   $1,052   $1,029   $1,006    $983     $960     $938
 9  10.75%    $1,097   $1,074   $1,050   $1,027   $1,003    $980     $957
10  11.00%    $1,119   $1,095   $1,071   $1,048   $1,024   $1,000    $976
11  11.25%    $1,141   $1,117   $1,093   $1,068   $1,044   $1,020    $996
12  11.50%    $1,164   $1,139   $1,114   $1,089   $1,065   $1,040   $1,015
13  11.75%    $1,186   $1,161   $1,136   $1,110   $1,085   $1,060   $1,035
14  12.00%    $1,209   $1,183   $1,157   $1,131   $1,106   $1,080   $1,054
15  12.25%    $1,231   $1,205   $1,179   $1,153   $1,126   $1,100   $1,074
16  12.50%    $1,254   $1,227   $1,201   $1,174   $1,147   $1,121   $1,094
17  12.75%    $1,277   $1,250   $1,223   $1,195   $1,168   $1,141   $1,114
```

Figure 10-6. *Two-way table for payment calculation*

With all these preliminaries accomplished, you enter **/Data Table** and choose 2 from the submenu. The first prompt asks for the location of the table, which is H1..O17. The next prompt asks for the cell to use for the first input value, which is D5. Then answer the next prompt with D4, the second input cell. All these locations can be entered as a range, as a range name, or by pointing. After you respond to this last prompt, 1-2-3 provides the results shown in Figure 10-6.

You can use this table of results to determine the monthly payment as long as the interest rate and the amount of money borrowed are in the ranges established for the table. Locate in column 1 the interest rate you feel you can obtain for a loan; then use that row to determine your payments at different levels of borrowing. Similarly, you can use the column for any given borrowing level and determine your payments, based on one of the interest rates in column 1.

Three-Way Data Tables

The /Data Table 3 command allows you to build a three-dimensional table in which you supply input values for three variables; 1-2-3 then applies these values when recalculating the worksheets and recording the result of one of the worksheet formulas in the table. This kind of table is referred to as a three-way table. It differs from a one- or two-way table in its use of three sets of variable values and its ability to record the results of only one formula. Also, a three-way table uses a separate worksheet for each value of the third input variable.

Like the other tables, the three-way table requires a significant amount of preliminary work. The example uses a three-way table with the model in Figure 10-7 for the present value of annuity calculations. The present value of an annuity is dependent on the amount paid each period, the interest rate, and the number of periods. By adding the loan term as a third variable, you can use /Data Table 3 to vary the periodic payment, the interest rate, and the number of periods.

Values for the first input variable are stored in one column of the data table. If the values are spaced at equal intervals, /Data Fill can be used to generate the column of values. Values for the second input value are placed one row above the top value for input 1 and one cell to the right. The values for the second input variable are placed across the row. Again, evenly spaced values make /Data Fill the ideal choice for making the entries.

Once the first and second input variables are stored in the usual way in the first worksheet of the data table, you can add worksheets to the file for each value of the third variable. Each of the worksheets must use the same rows and columns for the data table. The /Worksheet Insert Sheet command can add all of the worksheets in a single command. Then the values for the first and second variables can be copied in with the /Copy command. Finally, each of the third variables must be entered in the upper corner of the data table in separate worksheets, at the intersection of the column and row of data values already entered for the first two variables.

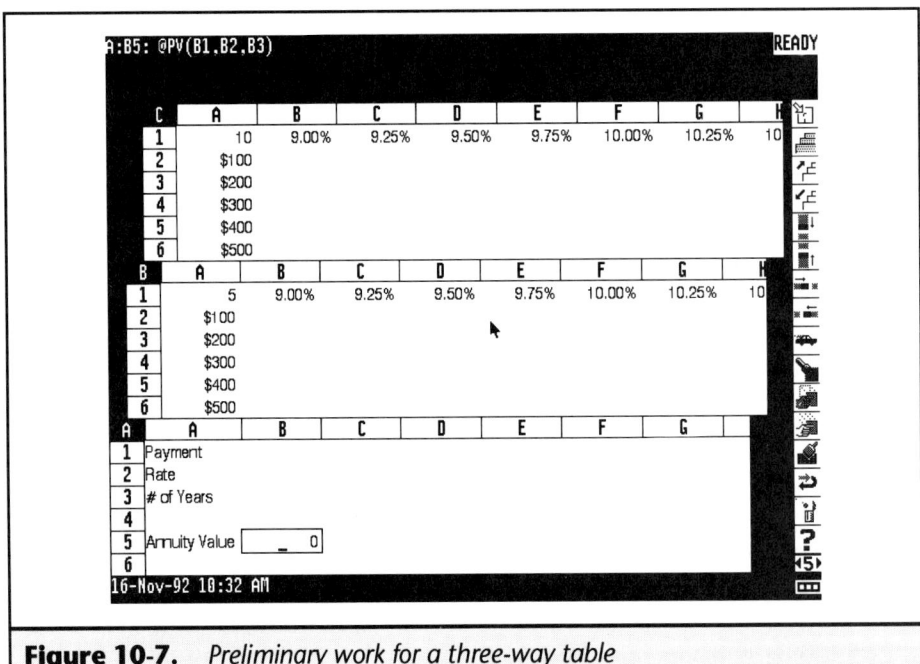

Figure 10-7. *Preliminary work for a three-way table*

A worksheet formula or a reference to one must be placed in a cell outside the data table. This formula is used to supply the table entries as the values of the variables change. Other formulas can exist on the worksheet, but one formula is singled out, and its results provide the entries within the table. This formula does not refer to the table cells, but to other formulas or input cells where the variable values in the table will be substituted.

An input cell must be defined for each dimension of the table. The values in the table are plugged into these input cells one by one, and the results of each iteration are captured and stored in the table cells. Systematically, each input cell is assigned new values from the table shell, with the /Data Table command returning the formula results for each of the values of the three variables. This input cell is formatted with /Range Format Text to display as a formula. Unlike /Data Table 1 and /Data Table 2, with /Data Table 3 the formula the command evaluates is outside of the data table.

Let's pull this all together using the annuity example in Figures 10-7 and 10-8. Use the first worksheet for the input variables and the formula for the data table. The formula is stored in B5 of sheet A.

The data table is located in B:A1..F:K6. In the data table, A2..A6 in each worksheet contains the input values for variable 1 (the periodic payment) beginning with $100, adding increments of $100, and ending with $500. B1..K1 in each worksheet is for the input values for variable 2 (the interest rate) beginning with 9%, adding increments of .25%, ending with 11.25%. Once these values are created in worksheet B, the /Copy command can copy the row and column values from B:A1..B:K6 to C:A1..F:A1. A1 in each worksheet is for the input values for variable 3 (the number of periods) beginning with 5, adding increments of 5, and ending with 25. Variable 3 is the only value that changes in each worksheet.

With all these preliminaries accomplished, enter **/Data Table** and choose 3 from the submenu. The first prompt asks for the location of the table; highlight B:A1..F:K6 and press ENTER. (Or enter a range or a range name.) The next prompt asks for the cell containing the formula to be evaluated for each set of values in the data table. In the annuity example, highlight A:B5 and press ENTER. Next, 1-2-3 prompts for the input cell to use for the first input value. In this example the input cell is A:B1, which you can point to or enter as a range name or address. The same procedure works for A:B2, the second input cell, and A:B3, the third input cell. After you respond to this last prompt, 1-2-3 provides the results shown in Figure 10-8.

You can use this table of results to determine the present value of annuities for various payment amounts, interest rates, and payment periods. Move to the worksheet containing the desired number of payment periods in the upper left corner, and look down the column of the table that has the interest rate you want for an annuity, to determine what the annuity is worth. Similarly, you can look across the row for a particular payment amount and determine the present value at various interest rates.

Figure 10-8. Three-way table

TIP: When you are selecting variables for a three-way table, use the variable with the fewest values as the third input variable. Since each third input cell value creates a table on a different worksheet, using a third variable with many values can fill the computer's memory quickly.

Using Labeled Data Tables in Sensitivity Analysis

Release 3 provides labeled tables for the features you can access with the /Data Table command. The /Data Table Labeled command surpasses the limits of the other /Data Table commands. For example, /Data Table 1 requires that the input values be stored in the first column of the data table. With /Data Table Labeled, you can create one-way tables with the input values in a column, a row, or on multiple worksheets. Also, the /Data Table Labeled command allows you to:

- Include blank rows, columns, and worksheets between the input values and the results, and among the results.

Chapter 10: Using Data Management Features in the Worksheet Environment

- Include more labels than in the other data tables in order to document the table so it is easier to understand.
- Evaluate multiple formulas.
- Include formulas within the data table that operate on the data table results. This feature can be used to add some of the numbers generated by the table.
- Include more than three variables by having multiple variables for a column, row, or worksheet that are assigned different input values.

This command can create one, two, and three-way tables.

The /Data Table Labeled command requires the most preliminary work of all the /Data Table commands. Since creating a labeled table requires several steps, reviewing the steps will help you understand this command. The following paragraphs show you how to create a simple one-way labeled table, and a more complicated three-way table. The steps for creating a labeled table are summarized in the box titled "Creating a Labeled Table."

Creating a Simple Labeled Table

One feature of the /Data Table Labeled command is the ability to create one- and two-way tables that have a different orientation from /Data Table 1 and /Data Table 2 tables. Another advantage of the /Data Table Labeled command is how it can create tables that manipulate more values than the other tables can. The preliminary work of a labeled table that uses these features is shown in Figure 10-9. This table computes the net profit and the after-tax profit using assumptions about the sales growth rate, the cost of goods sold (COGS) percentage, and operating expenses. The formulas (A18..B18) and the income statement (B10..B14) appear using the Text format; the data in rows 3 and 4 are formatted using the Percent format; and row 5 is formatted as Currency.

Figure 10-9 is a one-way table that substitutes three values for each cell in the data table it calculates. For each Guess column, the table substitutes the sales growth rate, the COGS percentage, and the operating expenses in the input cells, and computes net profit and after-tax profit. Since only column variable values are used, this is still a one-way table.

To use this table with the /Data Table Labeled command, it must have several additional features shown in the figure. First, the input cells must be selected, in this case, E17..E19. Each of these input cells are labeled.

Next the formulas must be created and labeled. This table has two formulas, Net Profit and After Tax Profit. You must enter the formula's name in the cell above it; this is the *formula range*. The formula name, or label, tells 1-2-3 when to use each formula in the data table. In Figure 10-9, the table uses the Net Profit formula to compute row 7, and the After Tax Profit formula to compute row 8.

Creating a Labeled Table

A number of steps are required to create a labeled table. They are as follows:

1. Select the input cells you want to use for the formulas and enter labels next to them.
2. Enter the formulas that you want evaluated in the table. List the formula name on one row and the formula itself in the cell below.
3. Select an area in the worksheet file that you want to use for the data table.
4. Enter the values that you want plugged in as column variable values; place them above or below where you want 1-2-3 to fill in the values. If you have multiple column variable values, they must be in adjacent rows.
5. Enter the values that you want plugged in as row variable values; place them to the right or to the left of where you want 1-2-3 to fill in the values. If you have multiple row variable values, they must be in adjacent columns.
6. Enter the values that you want plugged in as sheet variable values; place them outside of the area reserved for the data table. The sheet variable values must be in the same cell in each sheet.
7. Enter the formula label above or below the data table, or to the left or right of the data table. If the formula label is above or below the data table, it must stretch across all columns the formula will use for input values. It can be stretched by adding the label-fill character (a hyphen) to the beginning and end of the formula label.
8. Enter **/Data Table Labeled Formulas**. Select the formula range created in Step 2; then select the formula label range selected in Step 7.
9. Select the Across option if you have entered column variable values. Specify the cells entered in Step 4. For each row in the column variable values, 1-2-3 prompts for confirmation and the input cell.
10. Select the Down option if you have entered row variable values. Specify the cells entered in Step 5. For each column in the column variable values, 1-2-3 prompts for confirmation and the input cell.
11. Select the Sheets option if you have entered worksheet variable values. Specify the cells entered in Step 6. For each cell in the worksheets, 1-2-3 prompts for confirmation and the input cell.
12. Choose Go to create the table.

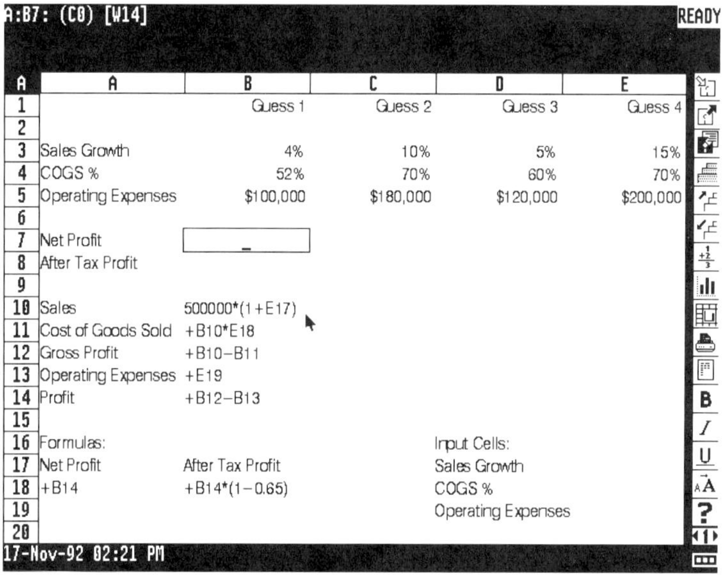

Chapter 10: Using Data Management Features in the Worksheet Environment

Figure 10-9. Preliminary work for a labeled table

The names of these formulas in rows 7 and 8 are called the *formula label range*. The formula label range appears above or below the table to indicate which formulas the columns use, or to the left or right of the table to indicate which formulas the rows use. The formulas can reference any cell outside of the data table. As the figure shows, you can add blank rows to a labeled table.

With the preliminary work finished, you are ready to create the table with the /Data Table Labeled command. 1-2-3 presents a new menu like this:

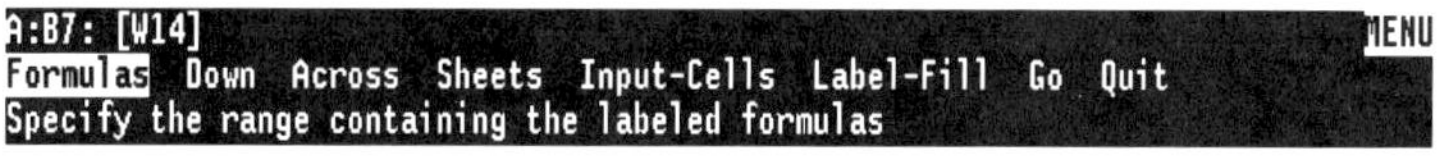

You can select the worksheet cells 1-2-3 uses for the labeled data table by following these steps:

1. Select Formulas. 1-2-3 prompts for the formula range, which is A17..B18; this includes the formula name in the first row and the formula in the second.

2. Then 1-2-3 prompts for the formula label range, which is A7..A8; this is the formula name that tells 1-2-3 which formula to use for each row.

3. Since this table has input variables stored across columns, select Across next. When 1-2-3 prompts for the column variable range, enter **B3..E5**.

4. Once 1-2-3 knows the column variable range, it prompts for confirmation of the first row in the column range, and wants to know the input cell for this row. For the Sales Growth variables, 1-2-3 displays B3..E3; the input cell is E17.

5. Next 1-2-3 prompts for confirmation of B4..E4 as the second row in the column range (COGS percentage) and wants to know the input cell for this range, which is E18.

6. Then 1-2-3 asks you to confirm B5..E5 as the third row in the column range (Operating Expenses) and wants to know the input cell for this range, which is E19.

7. Since this finishes your selections, select Go to have 1-2-3 generate the table.

The results are shown in Figure 10-10. You do not need to define a data table range, since this command uses all cells where formulas and variable ranges intersect.

```
A:B7: (C0) [W14] 149600                                                    READY

     A              A              B              C              D              E
  1                              Guess 1        Guess 2        Guess 3        Guess 4
  2
  3  Sales Growth                   4%            10%             5%            15%
  4  COGS %                        52%            70%            60%            70%
  5  Operating Expenses         $100,000       $180,000       $120,000       $200,000
  6
  7  Net Profit                 $149,600       ($15,000)       $90,000       ($27,500)
  8  After Tax Profit            $52,360        ($5,250)       $31,500        ($9,625)
  9
 10  Sales              500000*(1+E17)
 11  Cost of Goods Sold +B10*E18
 12  Gross Profit       +B10-B11
 13  Operating Expenses +E19
 14  Profit             +B12-B13
 15
 16  Formulas:                                   Input Cells:
 17  Net Profit         After Tax Profit         Sales Growth
 18  +B14               +B14*(1-0.65)            COGS %
 19                                              Operating Expenses
 20
17-Nov-92 03:22 PM                                                          NUM
```

Figure 10-10.   Table after /Data Table Labeled command

TIP: Use /Copy or /Range Transpose to copy the formula names into formula label ranges. Since the /Data Table Labeled command does not calculate formulas properly if the formula name is misspelled, use /Copy or /Range Transpose to copy the exact formula names from the formula range to the data table.

Creating a Three-Way Labeled Table

Like the prior example, you can create more advanced tables with the /Data Table Labeled command. The steps you perform to create a three-way table, using the example in Figure 10-11, will show more of the features of this command. Figure 10-11 computes the monthly payment and yearly taxes on a number of houses. An extra computation in the middle of the table computes the average house payment.

SETTING UP THE INPUT CELLS AND FORMULAS First, you must label the input cells the table uses. The first input is in B1, the second is in B2, and the third is in B3. Each of these input cells is labeled for documentation purposes. Notice that the second input cell can contain either the interest rate or the tax

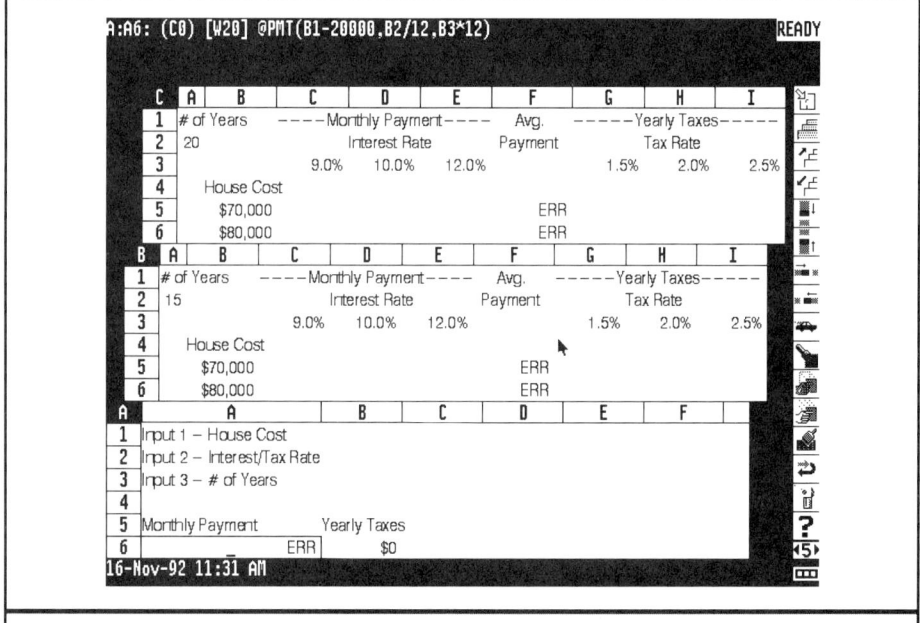

Figure 10-11. *Preliminary work for a three-way labeled table*

rate. You can use an input cell for multiple types of data when the table uses multiple formulas. In this example, all of this information is contained in the first worksheet to keep it separate from the data table. Also, by having multiple worksheets in perspective, you can see the results of two of the worksheets in the data table, as well as the formula and input cells.

Once the input cells are decided and labeled, the formula range can be added. For each formula range, you must enter the formula name and below it the formula. The formula must reference the cell values outside the data range. The first formula, Monthly Payment, assumes that a $20,000 down payment is made on the house so the amount borrowed is $20,000 less than the house cost. The second formula, Yearly Taxes, multiplies the house cost by the tax rate.

SETTING UP THE DATA TABLE After you have the input cells and the formulas, you can create the labeled data table. For the example in Figure 10-11, the table uses worksheets B through E. Cell A2 in each worksheet contains the number of years the monthly payment calculation uses. Unlike /Data Table 3 tables, values for input cells that span worksheets can be placed outside the data table if the value is in the same cell in each worksheet. In the example in Figure 10-11, the entries in B5..B10 in sheets B and C were supplied by /Data Fill, with a start value of 70000, a step value of 10000 and a stop value of 120000. While the house cost entries look identical to column entries for the other /Data Table commands, the /Data Table Labeled command allows blank lines in the column. The House Cost label in B4 is ignored, since it is above the first row input value.

The columns in Figure 10-11 look different from other /Data Table commands because the formula label range is combined with the column variable values. The columns determine the formulas that 1-2-3 performs based on formula name range, as well as providing another set of values for an input cell. For the columns headed with Monthly Payment, 1-2-3 evaluates the Monthly Payment formula for each of the possible values listed in row 3.

The formula names in C1 are stretched across all of the columns that use the formula, by using the label-fill character specified with the /Data Table Labeled Label-Fill command. The default is a hyphen. By filling in the formula label range with this character, you can stretch the label to cover all the columns that you want to use the formula. The Yearly Taxes label in G1 also uses the label-fill character to stretch the formula name across columns G through I.

When the formula label range contains other types of data, such as blanks, other labels, or values, 1-2-3 skips that column in the data table. For example, in Figure 10-11, 1-2-3 skips column F because it contains a label that is not a formula name. When 1-2-3 skips a row, column, or worksheet in a data table, you can fill that row, column, or worksheet with another type of data. For example, cell F5 contains the formula @AVG(C5..E5), which is copied to the other cells in column F. The /Data Table Labeled command does not write over the @AVG functions, and 1-2-3 recalculates the averages based on the values in the data table. The Interest Rate and Tax Rate column headings below the formula names are also

Chapter 10: Using Data Management Features in the Worksheet Environment

ignored, because they are above the column input values. You can use this area to add documentation to the table.

Once the row and column input variables and labels are entered, you can add worksheets to the worksheet file for the other # of Years values, and copy the first data table to the other worksheet areas. One option is to enable the GROUP mode so all of the formatting and column widths of the first data table are automatically applied to the other worksheet. In the example in Figure 10-11, the /Worksheet Insert Sheet After 4 command inserted four worksheets after the first one, although the last 2 do not appear in the figure. The formulas and input cells are determined and labeled. Next, the GROUP mode is enabled. As the data values and labels for the first worksheet in the data table are created, the formatting and column widths are automatically applied to the other sheets in the file. Once the table is created in worksheet B, it is copied to worksheets C through E. Then the values of A2 on the various sheets are updated with the /Data Fill command to establish # of Years values, starting with 15 and ascending by increments of 5. Finally, GROUP mode is disabled, and the width of column A in worksheet A is enlarged.

Using the /Data Table Labeled Command

You have really worked hard to accomplish all the preliminary steps, but the payoff is at hand! 1-2-3 will now supply all the calculations for the tables.

1. Enter **/Data Table** and choose Labeled from the submenu.

2. Select Formulas. 1-2-3 prompts for the formula range, which is A:A5..A:B6. This includes the formula name in the first row and the formula in the second. Then 1-2-3 prompts for the formula label range which is B:C1..B:I1. This range displays the formula names used across all the columns in the data table, including the columns the data table skips. 1-2-3 only needs to know the formula label range for the first data table.

3. Since this table uses input values stored in a column, select Down. When 1-2-3 prompts for the row variable range, enter **B:B5..B:B10**. Once 1-2-3 knows the row variable range, 1-2-3 wants to know the input cell for the row variable range. In this example, it is A:B1.

4. Since this table has input values stored in a row, select Across. When 1-2-3 prompts for the column variable range, enter **B:C3..B:I3**. 1-2-3 knows that the /Data Table Labeled command omits column F because it does not have a formula name in the formula label range. Next 1-2-3 wants to know the input cell for the column variable range; in this example, it is A:B2.

5. Since this table has input variable values that span worksheets, select Sheets. When 1-2-3 prompts for the worksheet variable range, enter **B:A2..E:A2**. Then, for the worksheet variable range, enter **A:B3**.

6. Since selecting the row variable range, column variable range, and worksheet variable range is all you need to tell 1-2-3 about the data table, select Go, and 1-2-3 generates the table. The results are shown in Figure 10-12.

After you create a labeled table, you may want to perform the table calculations again if you change a variable value. For example, you may want to change the first interest rate to 8%. To make this change, enter **.08** in B:C3 and copy it from B:C3 to C:C3..E:C3. To recompute the table, use the /Data Table Labeled Go command, or press F8 (TABLE).

If you want to change one of the table values, use the /Data Table Label Input-Cells command. When you execute this command, 1-2-3 prompts for the row variable range and its input cell; the column variable range and its input cell; and the worksheet variable range and its input cell. For each of these prompts, 1-2-3 displays the current selection. You can accept it or make a new selection.

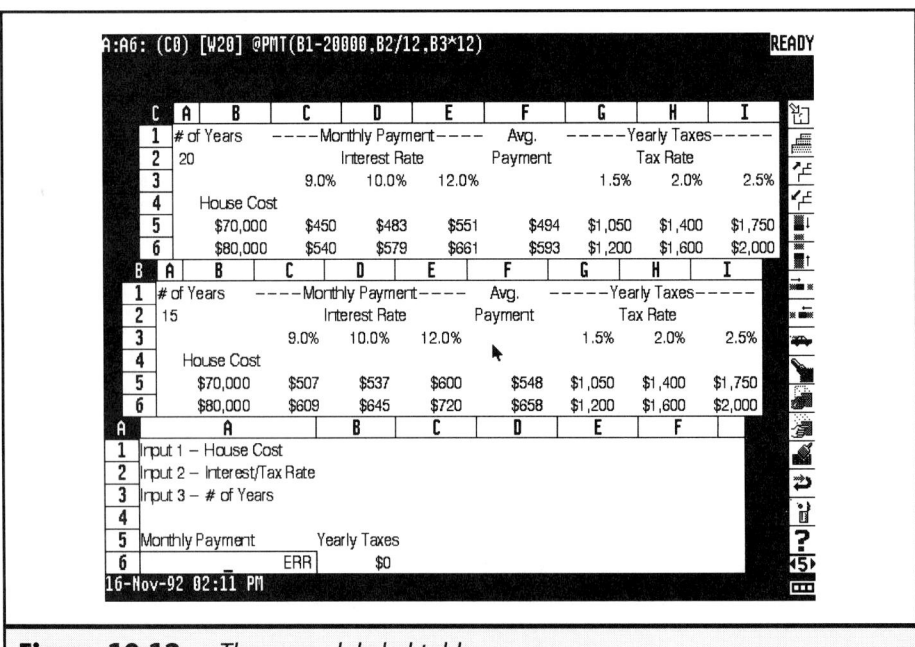

Figure 10-12. *Three-way labeled table*

Adding Blank Columns, Rows, and Worksheets to the Data Table

One of the advantages of the /Data Table Labeled command is its capacity to insert blank columns, rows, and worksheets into the data table to improve readability. To insert a blank row in a data table, skip the row when you are entering the row variable range. The same applies for skipping columns and worksheets.

Figure 10-13 shows the previous data table after a few modifications. The column containing Avg. Payment is deleted, and a column is added between the 10% and 12% figures. Since column E does not have a value in the column value range, the table leaves column E blank. Also, the column headings in row 2 are deleted to show more of the data table; and a row is inserted between the $70,000 and $80,000 house costs. Since this row does not have a value in the row variable range, the table leaves this row blank. Finally the 20 in C:A2 is erased. Since this worksheet does not have a variable for the worksheet variable range, the table skips worksheet C in the data table, although it used worksheets D and E.

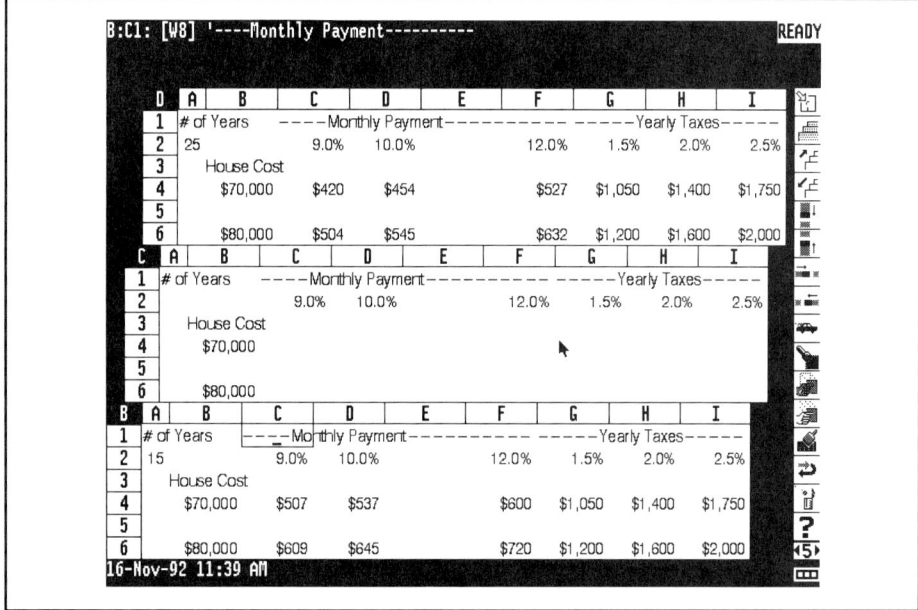

Figure 10-13. *Blank columns, rows, and worksheets in a labeled table*

Using /Data Table with Database Statistical Functions

The /Data Table command can also be used effectively with the database statistical functions covered in Chapter 9. For example, you can use the command's variable values to supply different criteria values to be used with the database functions. These values may be numeric or label entries, depending on the search criteria you are using.

The database this example will use is shown in Figure 10-14. It contains employee records for a variety of locations and job codes. Let's use the /Data Table 2 command to systematically vary the values for these two variables and obtain an employee count for each job code at each location.

The table is created in B22..E28, as shown in Figure 10-15. In B23..B28, job code values 12, 14, 15, 17, 21, and 23 are listed. Location codes are in C22..E22 as 2, 4, and 10. The formula in B22 is @DCOUNT(A1..F20,0,J2..K3). The first argument references the database. The second references the first column of the database, which contains the last name. That field is a good choice because it is unlikely to be missing from any record. The third argument references a criteria area that you must set up by entering Job Code and Location in J2 and K2, respectively. Then specify the two cells immediately below these, J3 and K3, as

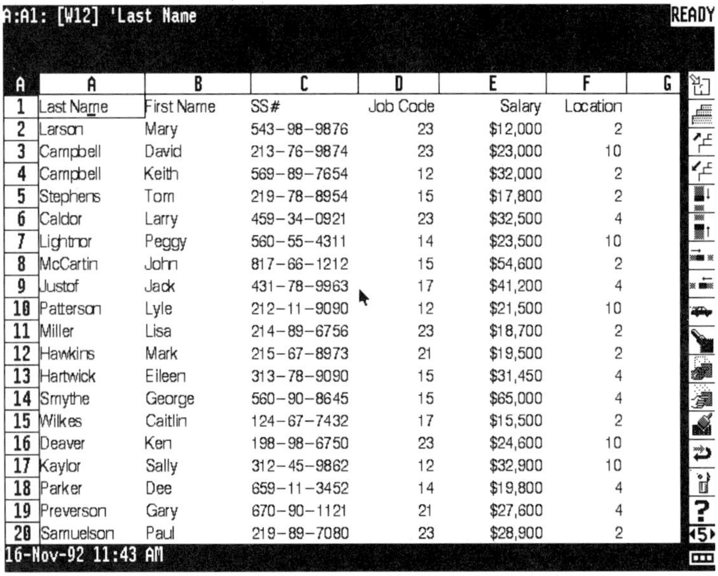

A:A1: [W12] 'Last Name READY

A	A	B	C	D	E	F	G
1	Last Name	First Name	SS#	Job Code	Salary	Location	
2	Larson	Mary	543-98-9876	23	$12,000	2	
3	Campbell	David	213-76-9874	23	$23,000	10	
4	Campbell	Keith	569-89-7654	12	$32,000	2	
5	Stephens	Tom	219-78-8954	15	$17,800	2	
6	Caldor	Larry	459-34-0921	23	$32,500	4	
7	Lightnor	Peggy	560-55-4311	14	$23,500	10	
8	McCartin	John	817-66-1212	15	$54,600	2	
9	Justof	Jack	431-78-9963	17	$41,200	4	
10	Patterson	Lyle	212-11-9090	12	$21,500	10	
11	Miller	Lisa	214-89-6756	23	$18,700	2	
12	Hawkins	Mark	215-67-8973	21	$19,500	2	
13	Hartwick	Eileen	313-78-9090	15	$31,450	4	
14	Smythe	George	560-90-8645	15	$65,000	4	
15	Wilkes	Caitlin	124-67-7432	17	$15,500	2	
16	Deaver	Ken	198-98-6750	23	$24,600	10	
17	Kaylor	Sally	312-45-9862	12	$32,900	10	
18	Parker	Dee	659-11-3452	14	$19,800	4	
19	Preverson	Gary	670-90-1121	21	$27,600	4	
20	Samuelson	Paul	219-89-7080	23	$28,900	2	

16-Nov-92 11:43 AM

Figure 10-14. *Employee database*

Chapter 10: Using Data Management Features in the Worksheet Environment

```
A:B22: (T) [W23] @DCOUNT(A1..F20,0,J2..K3)                        READY

       A            B              C        D        E
  21                                      Location
  22         @DCOUNT(A1..F20,0,J2..K3)      2        4       10
  23                      12
  24    C                 14
  25  J  O                15
  26  O  D                17
  27  B  E                21
  28                      23
```

Figure 10-15. *Table range selected*

input cells. Initially these input cells will be blank, but as the /Data Table 2 command executes, it will supply values for criteria to compute the selective counts of database records.

With all the preliminary work accomplished, enter **/Data Table 2** and specify the table location as B22..E28, the first input cell as J3, and the second input cell as K3. 1-2-3 will then produce the output in Figure 10-16. From this table you can tell how many employees in each job code work at each location.

Regression Analysis

The /Data Regression command is used to perform a simple regression with one independent variable, or a multiple regression with as many as 75 independent variables. You can have up to 8192 observations (that is, values) for each of your

```
A:B22: (T) [W23] @DCOUNT(A1..F20,0,J2..K3)                        READY

       A            B              C        D        E
  21                                      Location
  22         @DCOUNT(A1..F20,0,J2..K3)      2        4       10
  23                      12                1        0        2
  24    C                 14                0        1        1
  25  J  O                15                2        2        0
  26  O  D                17                1        1        0
  27  B  E                21                1        1        0
  28                      23                3        1        2
```

Figure 10-16. *Table created using database table*

variables. All variables must have the same number of observations, however; you cannot have 8192 values for one independent variable, and 50 values for the dependent variable or another independent variable.

The purpose of this statistical technique is to determine whether changes in the independent variables can be used to predict changes in the dependent variable. This potential interrelationship is described quantitatively with *regression analysis*. Details of the theory behind regression analysis can be found in any business statistics book.

The first step in using regression analysis is recording the values for the dependent and independent variables in columns on your worksheet. Figure 10-17 shows the dependent variable—the sales of Product A—in column A. You can use regression analysis to see whether the independent variables for which you have historic data for the same period had an impact on the sales figures for the period. If these variables do seem to have a relationship to the values for sales, you may be able to predict sales for future periods—if you know the values for the other independent variables during the future periods.

Suppose the two independent variables selected are Disposable Income and Advertising Expense. Disposable Income is in column B, and Advertising Expense is in column C.

You are now ready to enter **/Data Regression**. When you do, the following menu will be displayed.

```
A:A1: "Sales                                                          MENU
X-Range  Y-Range  Output-Range  Intercept  Reset  Go  Quit
Specify independent variables (X range)
```

You will need to make a number of selections from this menu. These are summarized for you in the box called "Creating a Regression Analysis." Your first step is to select the independent variables with the X-Range option. You can

	A	B	C
1	Sales	Disposable	Advertising
2	Product A	Income	Expense
3	110,000	25,000,000	9,000
4	135,000	31,000,000	9,500
5	205,000	53,000,000	12,500
6	215,000	58,000,000	13,000
7	125,000	42,000,000	9,000
8	175,000	43,000,000	11,000
9	210,000	63,000,000	11,000
10	250,000	67,000,000	12,000

Figure 10-17. *Regression variables*

Creating a Regression Analysis

A number of steps are required to create a regression analysis. They are as follows:

1. Enter values for the dependent and independent variables in worksheet columns.

2. Enter **/Data Regression**.

3. Choose the X-Range option to select the range containing the independent variables.

4. Choose the Y-Range option to select the column containing the dependent variable.

5. Choose an output range of nine rows and at least four columns. The number of columns should be equal to the number of independent variables plus two.

6. Select the Intercept option and choose Zero for a zero intercept, or Compute if you wish 1-2-3 to compute the intercept. If you have not previously done a regression with a 0 intercept during the current session, you can omit this entry if you wish the intercept to be computed, since Compute is the default.

7. Choose Go to create the regression output.

specify up to 16 columns of values, with as many as 8192 total entries in the columns. This example will use B3..C10. You can use a range name, cell addresses, or the pointing method to inform 1-2-3 of your choice.

Your next selection is Y-Range. This selection, used to specify the dependent variable, would be A3..A10 in our example. This can be specified as a range name or cell addresses, or by pointing.

Output-Range is your third selection. You can specify the upper left cell in the range or the complete range. If you choose to explicitly specify the range, keep in mind that it must be at least nine rows from top to bottom, and two columns wider than the number of independent variables, with a minimum width of four columns. If you choose to specify only the left corner, be sure that the space under and to the right of that cell is free, or 1-2-3 will overwrite existing data with your regression results. A21 was chosen for our example.

The fourth menu choice is Intercept. If you wish to have 1-2-3 compute the Y intercept, you can leave this choice blank, since Compute is the default. If you want the intercept set to zero, select Zero rather than Compute.

Once the preliminary setup is finished, enter **Go** to have 1-2-3 tabulate the regression statistics. The result of the regression for our two variables when 1-2-3 computes the intercept is shown in Figure 10-18. After your analysis is finished, you can use the Reset option to remove previous settings for the command. The Quit option allows you to exit the /Data Regression menu.

In general, the higher the R value, the greater the correlation, although you will want to be aware of the number of observations and the degrees of freedom when determining the reliability of your results. All this is explained in more detail in a book on statistics. The results shown in our example include a computed intercept of – 60493.6; a standard error of the estimated Y values; R squared (if you want to know what R is, use @SQRT with R squared as the argument); the number of observations for your variables; the coefficients or slopes for the independent variables; and the standard error for the X coefficients.

You can use the same variable values to do two simple regressions. The variable with the highest R squared value will have the closest relationship to the dependent variable. Figure 10-19 presents two regression output areas. The upper regression output is for disposable income, and the lower regression output is for advertising dollars. The R squared value for disposable income is higher, which indicates that disposable income is a better predictor of sales than advertising dollars. Since the R squared value in Figure 10-18 is higher than either output in Figure 10-19, you can assume that both variables together are stronger predictors than either one individually.

You can also use the regression output to help you determine estimated Y values and the best fitting regression line. The formula you would use to estimate the Y values is as follows:

Constant + Coefficient of X1 * X1 + Coefficient of X2 * X2

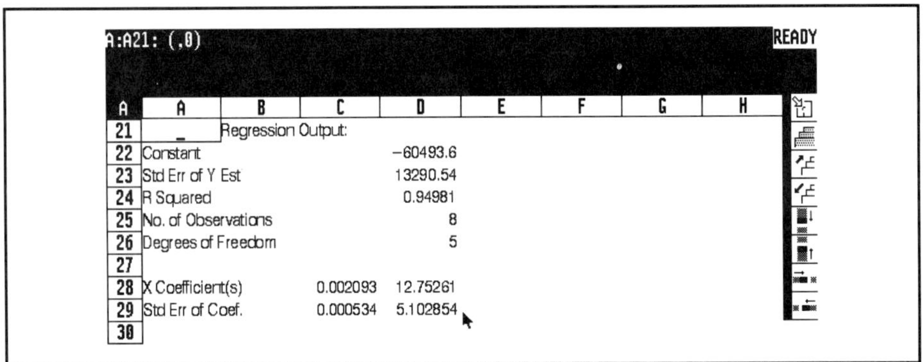

Figure 10-18. *Multiple-regression analysis*

Chapter 10: Using Data Management Features in the Worksheet Environment

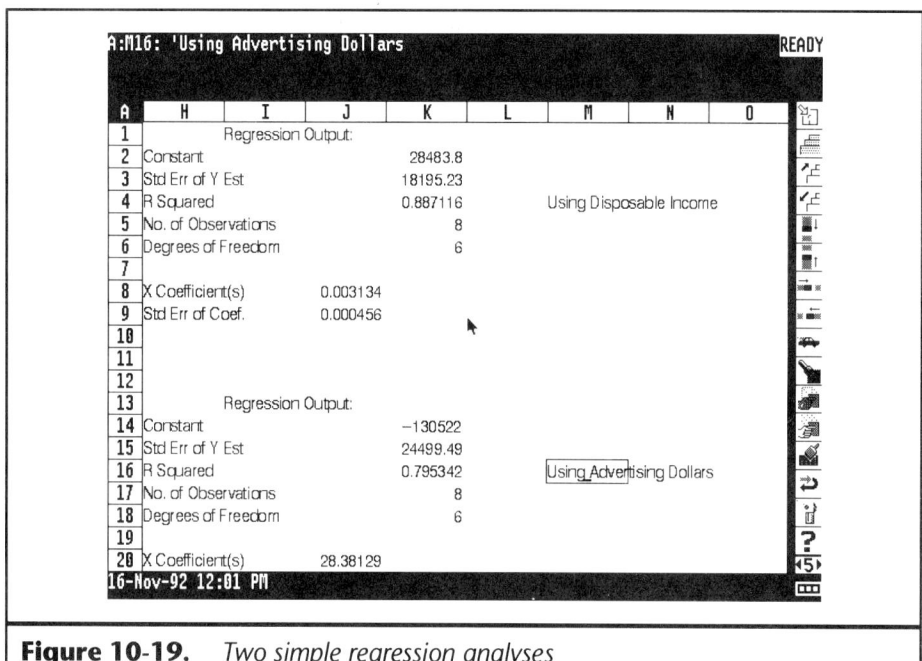

Figure 10-19. *Two simple regression analyses*

You can use this formula to project sales values, assuming that historic relationships are being maintained.

Frequency Distribution

A *frequency distribution* allows you to count the number of values that fall within specific categories. With the /Data Distribution command features that 1-2-3 provides, you can set up whatever intervals (bins) for categorizing your data that you want. 1-2-3 will then count the number of entries that fall within each of these intervals.

The frequency distribution table is set up prior to using the command by placing the value categories in a location where the column to the right of the categories, and the table cells below the last interval, are blank. Or you can use a separate worksheet to store the bins. The two cells at the bottom of the table location must be blank to record frequencies greater than the largest specified frequency. All category entries must be numeric and in ascending sequence.

When you enter **/Data Distribution** and tell 1-2-3 the locations of the data to be categorized and of the frequency table, 1-2-3 will place each data entry within the range you selected into the smallest category that is equal to or greater than the value in your data. In other words, it will add 1 to the frequency count for

```
A:C20: (C0) [W11] +B20*0.015                                    POINT
Enter values range: A:C3..A:C20

    A              B           C        D      E          F      G
1                Quarterly              Frequency Distribution
2  Salesperson    Sales    Commission
3  Rich Roberts  $1,200,987  $18,015          10000
4  Jana Jolson   $2,134,567  $32,019          15000
5  Mike Moore    $1,987,600  $29,814          20000
6  Harriet Harm  $3,278,965  $49,184          30000
7  Tom Torn      $3,456,123  $51,842          35000
8  Rita Roberts  $2,134,987  $32,025          40000
9  Paul Peters   $1,897,626  $28,464          45000
10 Kira Kolson   $1,750,890  $26,263          50000
11 Herb Horst    $2,345,910  $35,189          55000
12 Fran Folly    $3,890,152  $58,352          60000
13 Ivan Imers    $3,186,450  $47,797
14 Wilma Walker  $2,134,567  $32,019
15 Norm Nait     $1,678,932  $25,184
16 Eva Edens       $540,900   $8,114
17 Abe Avens    $1,235,243  $18,529
18 Lona Linhurst $5,162,900  $77,444
19 Vern Vern    $2,134,750  $32,021
20 Betty Bollen $1,900,765  $28,511
16-Nov-92 12:07 PM
```

Figure 10-20. *Commission data*

that bin. With bin values of 3, 7, and 10, a value of 4 would be counted in bin 7. Each time a value is counted for a category, it increments that category's counter by 1. 1-2-3 ignores labels and cells that are empty. Cells containing @ERR are counted in the last bin and cells with @NA are counted in the first bin.

Figure 10-20 presents a worksheet that contains commission data in C3..C20. The categories for the frequency count are located in E3..E12. These are arbitrary settings and could have been any set of ascending numbers. The area to the right of these categories is blank, as are cells E13 and F13 immediately below the category area. The /Data Distribution command has already been entered, and cells C3..C20 are highlighted in response to 1-2-3's prompt for the range of values requiring categorization. When you press ENTER, 1-2-3 prompts you for the location of the frequency table or bin range. This is E3..E12. You may enter just the column bin values, or the entire table area as your range. Press ENTER, and the completed table in Figure 10-21 appears. You can interpret the first entry in the table as meaning that there was one entry less than or equal to 10,000. The last "1" in F13, says that there was one entry greater than the largest bin of 60,000.

/Data Distribution provides a quick way to condense data. It is ideal when you want an overall picture of the data within a category. You can also show the result of a frequency distribution in a bar chart or line graph very effectively.

Frequency distribution can be performed for a category of numeric values, or on the results of a formula calculation like the one found in our example. The frequency count is not updated as changes occur in the data that was

Chapter 10: Using Data Management Features in the Worksheet Environment

```
A:F3: 1                                                    READY

    A         A            B          C      D     E         F      G
    1                   Quarterly               Frequency Distribution
    2  Salesperson      Sales    Commission
    3  Rich Roberts   $1,200,987   $18,015        10000       1
    4  Jana Jolson    $2,134,567   $32,019        15000       0
    5  Mike Moore     $1,987,600   $29,814        20000       2
    6  Harriet Harm   $3,278,965   $49,184        30000       5
    7  Tom Torn       $3,456,123   $51,842        35000       4
    8  Rita Roberts   $2,134,987   $32,025        40000       1
    9  Paul Peters    $1,897,626   $28,464        45000       0
   10  Kira Kolson    $1,750,890   $26,263        50000       2
   11  Herb Horst     $2,345,910   $35,189        55000       1
   12  Fran Folly     $3,890,152   $58,352        60000       1
   13  Ivan Imers     $3,186,450   $47,797                    1
   14  Wilma Walker   $2,134,567   $32,019
   15  Norm Nait      $1,678,932   $25,184
   16  Eva Edens        $540,900    $8,114
   17  Abe Avens      $1,235,243   $18,529
   18  Lona Linhurst  $5,162,900   $77,444
   19  Vern Vern      $2,134,750   $32,021
   20  Betty Bollen   $1,900,765   $28,511
  16-Nov-92 12:08 PM
```

Figure 10-21. *Frequency output*

categorized, however. If the data is changed, /Data Distribution must be executed again to update the frequency table.

TIP: If the bins are the same interval apart, use /Data Fill to quickly create the bins the /Data Distribution command uses.

Matrix Arithmetic

Matrices can be used to solve problems of econometric modeling, market share, and population study. 1-2-3 offers both matrix multiplication and matrix inversion options. The word *matrix* indicates a tabular arrangement of data—something that is quite easy to arrange on a worksheet. Both matrix options allow you to perform sophisticated calculations on the data in these tabular arrangements, without the need for complicated formulas. Although many of the mathematical applications are beyond the scope of this book, two different examples are presented. Thus if matrix algebra is a requirement of your application, you will want to know how to invoke these capabilities from 1-2-3.

Matrix Multiplication

One of the applications of matrix multiplication is to streamline formulas where you must multiply a set of variables by another set of variables and add the result of each multiplication together, which is just like the @SUMPRODUCT function except that the second of the two ranges involved is transposed. To illustrate this type of application, consider four different products for which you are trying a number of advertising spots. Each advertising option has a price, and varying numbers of ads are placed for each of the products, in various time slots.

Using conventional formulas, determining the total advertising costs for one product would involve multiplying the cost of advertising in time slot 1 times the number of these slots that you purchased. This process must be repeated for each of the advertising slots, each time multiplying the number of slots for the product times the cost of advertising once in that slot. When the cost for each advertising slot has been determined, the values are added together to determine a total advertising cost for the first product. This must be repeated for each of the products. This is a cumbersome process, even when the number of products and potential advertising slots are small.

Matrix multiplication can provide a solution if you can construct your problem according to the rules that matrix operations must follow. After reviewing the rules, you will have an opportunity to see them applied to the advertising problem just discussed.

Matrix Multiplication Rules

There are a few rules of matrix multiplication that you must follow. The restrictions are a combination of matrix algebra rules and the limitations of matrices used in 1-2-3. Each of these rules must be met.

- Matrix multiplication involves multiplying the values in one matrix by the values in a second matrix. The order in which the multiplication is expressed is critical. Multiplying matrix A by matrix B is not equivalent to multiplying matrix B by matrix A.

- Matrix order is determined by the number of rows and columns in the tabular arrangement of the matrix entries. A matrix with x rows and y columns is an x-by-y matrix. When matrices are multiplied, the number of columns (the y) for the first matrix must be equal to the number of rows in the second matrix (the x). The easiest way to test this rule is to write the order of the matrices next to each other, as in 5-by-4 and 4-by-6. When the two inner numbers are the same, as in this example, the matrices are compatible and can be multiplied. Rewriting this as 4-by-6 and 5-by-4

Chapter 10: Using Data Management Features in the Worksheet Environment

produces a set of matrices that are not compatible, which demonstrates that the order in which the two matrices are multiplied is critical.

- The maximum size matrix that 1-2-3 can multiply is 256-by-256.

- Matrices cannot have blank cells and must have a zero inserted in any cell that is blank before you invoke the matrix command.

Entering the Advertising Matrix

In the advertising problem there are four different products and five different advertising spots. The number of advertising spots for each product is arranged in a 4-by-5 matrix in B11..F14 of the worksheet shown in Figure 10-22. The costs of the spots are arranged in a 5-by-1 matrix in A2..A6. In order for the two matrices to be compatible, the data must be arranged in a 5-by-1 table rather than a 1-by-5 table. It is expected that results will be stored in B17..B20, and appropriate labels are entered around the worksheet to label all the entries.

The /Data Matrix Multiply command is invoked and the first matrix is highlighted, as shown in Figure 10-22. The next prompt is for the second matrix in A2..A6. Finally, the /Data Matrix Multiply command prompts for the output range. Select B14 and 1-2-3 will use this cell for the first cell of the output range.

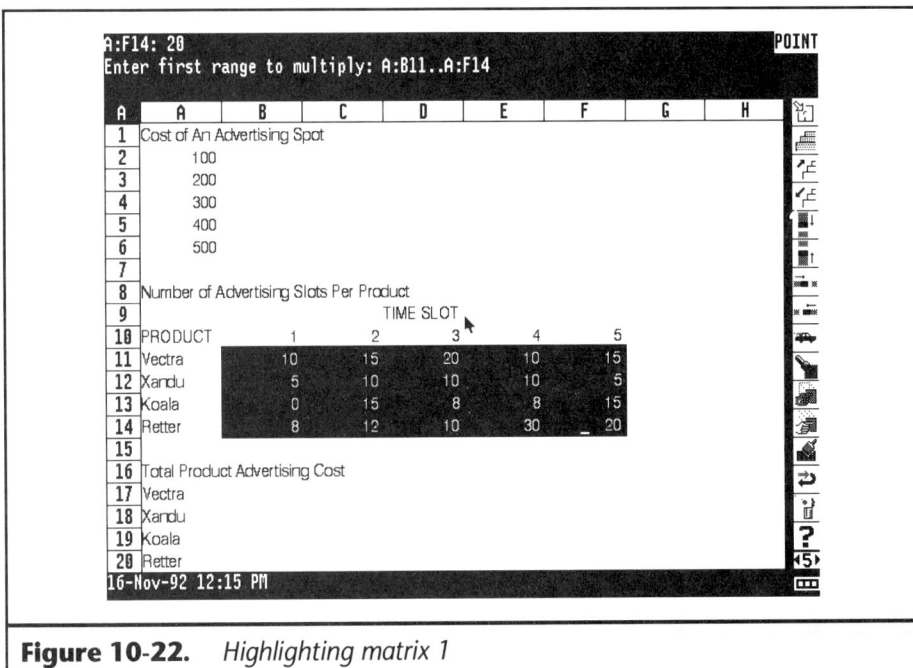

Figure 10-22. *Highlighting matrix 1*

The results are placed in B17..B20, as shown in Figure 10-23. The $21,500 represents the total advertising done for the Vectra product. It is obtained as the matrix operation multiplies B11*A2, C11*A3, D11*A4, E11*A5, and F11*A6, and then adds each of these products together. A similar process occurs for Xandu, Koala, and Retter. All this is accomplished without the need for writing a formula.

Matrix multiplication is quite an operation and can be a real time-saver if it fits your application. One drawback is that the results are not automatically updated when a value in either matrix is changed. To do this updating, you would have to execute /Data Matrix Multiply again. A second potential drawback is that matrices are more difficult to document than formulas, and understood less than formulas by most business users. Despite the drawbacks, matrices are a great tool to have for many applications.

Release 3 includes an @SUMPRODUCT function, which you can use to multiply matrices. Figure 10-24 shows the same advertising mix problem set up to use the @SUMPRODUCT function. There are two differences between the worksheets in Figures 10-23 and 10-24. The first matrix is transposed with the /Range Transpose command and the results of the multiplied matrices in Figure 10-24 are formulas. If you change one of the values in the matrices, 1-2-3 will immediately update the values in Figure 10-24 but in Figure 10-23 you must use the /Data Matrix Multiply command again.

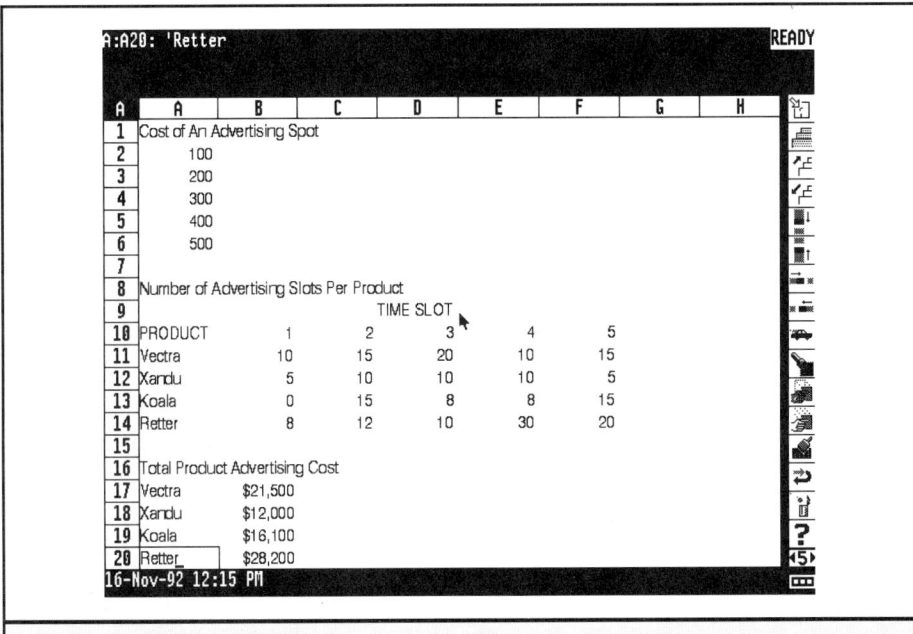

Figure 10-23.   *Result of /Data Matrix Multiply in B17..B20*

```
A:B14: (C0) @SUMPRODUCT(B8..F8,$A$3..$E$3)                              READY

     A        B           C          D          E          F        G        H
 1  Cost of An Advertising Spot Per Time Slot
 2              1           2          3          4          5
 3            100         200        300        400        500
 4
 5  Number of Advertising Slots Per Product
 6                                TIME SLOT
 7  PRODUCT     1           2          3          4          5
 8  Vectra     10          15         20         10         15
 9  Xandu       5          10         10         10          5
10  Koala       0          15          8          8         15
11  Retter      8          12         10         30         20
12
13  Total Product Advertising Cost      Formula in Column B
14  Vectra   $21,500                    @SUMPRODUCT(B8..F8,$A$3..$E$3)
15  Xandu    $12,000                    @SUMPRODUCT(B9..F9,$A$3..$E$3)
16  Koala    $16,100                    @SUMPRODUCT(B10..F10,$A$3..$E$3)
17  Retter   $28,200                    @SUMPRODUCT(B11..F11,$A$3..$E$3)
```

Figure 10-24. *Using the @SUMPRODUCT function to multiply matrices*

Matrix Inversion

Matrix inversion is more difficult, but its potential is even greater. The mathematical concepts behind it are difficult to explain, but in essence they involve the creation of a matrix which, when multiplied by your original matrix, will result in an identity matrix.

An *identity matrix* is one where all of the elements are zero, except one element in each row, which is a 1. The 1 is in a different location in each row. It is easy to remember the location of the 1 for each row, since it is a location identified by the row number. That is, in row 1 the 1 will be in element one; in row 2 the 1 will be in the second element; and so on. You can only convert square matrices (matrices with the same number of columns and rows). 1-2-3 will let you invert matrices up to 80 columns by 80 rows.

If all this seems confusing, you do not really have to understand it all to use the concept, so don't be too concerned. A traditional application for matrix multiplication also uses matrix inversion. It is the same product-mix problem that you solved so often in college algebra. Seeing the solution probably makes you wish you had a copy of 1-2-3 during your college algebra days, when you were trying to solve these with simultaneous equations.

Product-mix problems come in all flavors. Normally there is a limited amount of certain resources, and you have to decide how much of each product to produce. In the sample problem (Figure 10-25), you must determine how much Green Slime and Red Goo should be produced. Green Slime requires two units of Goop, and eight units of Gunk. Red Goo takes six units of Goop, and five

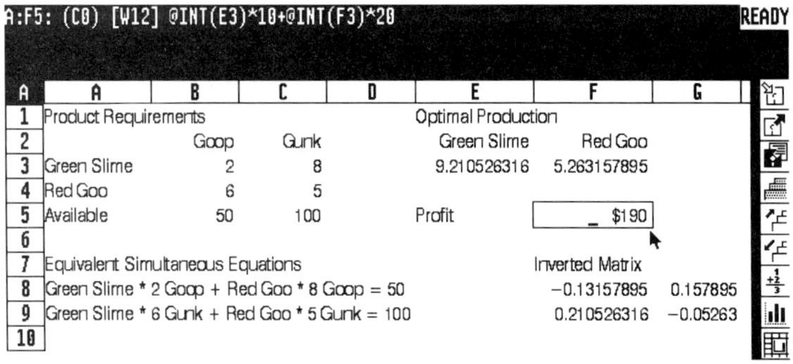

```
A:F5: (C0) [W12] @INT(E3)*10+@INT(F3)*20                                READY

    A              B         C         D         E              F           G
 1  Product Requirements                         Optimal Production
 2                 Goop      Gunk                Green Slime    Red Goo
 3  Green Slime    2         8                   9.210526316    5.263157895
 4  Red Goo        6         5
 5  Available      50        100                 Profit              $190
 6
 7  Equivalent Simultaneous Equations            Inverted Matrix
 8  Green Slime * 2 Goop + Red Goo * 8 Goop = 50                −0.13157895   0.157895
 9  Green Slime * 6 Gunk + Red Goo * 5 Gunk = 100                0.210526316  −0.05263
10
```

Figure 10-25.   *Matrix inversion solving simultaneous equations*

units of Gunk. There are 50 units of Goop available, and 100 units of Gunk. The matrix operations allow you to optimize your use of these two raw materials.

First, the data of Green Slime and Red Goo are entered in a 2-by-2 matrix. This matrix is inverted to create another 2-by-2 matrix, which will be used in solution. The original matrix is stored in B3..C4, the /Data Matrix Invert command is invoked, and this area is highlighted. F8..G9 is used for the output.

The 2-by-1 matrix in B5..C5, which contains the available units of each resource, is multiplied by the resulting 2-by-2 inverted matrix. The result is a new matrix, which is stored in F3..G5 and contains the optimal production for each of the products. Since the profit from Green Slime is $10 a unit and the profit from Red Goo is $20 a unit, the whole units produced for each product are multiplied by respective unit profit figures. The @INT function is used to access the whole units for the final formula, which is placed in F5. All of the arbitrary locations used in this example are shown in Figure 10-25, which includes the results and the equivalent simultaneous equations that you would use to solve the problem algebraically.

If you are interested in learning more about applications of matrix inversion, you will want to look for a reference on linear programming. If you are currently using linear programming, you will be delighted to have these handy techniques incorporated into 1-2-3's features. If you do not need this type of problem-solving tool, keep it in mind in case such a need arises at a later time.

Splitting Long Labels into Individual Cell Entries

The /File Import command can be used to bring information from an ASCII text file into your 1-2-3 worksheet, as described in Chapter 8, "Working with Files."

Chapter 10: Using Data Management Features in the Worksheet Environment

However, it imports this information as a column of long labels, which may not be what you want. Fortunately, the /Data Parse command allows you to split these long labels into various components. These individual pieces can be labels, numbers, or serial time or date numbers.

Using /Data Parse is a multistep process. The steps are summarized for you in the box called "Splitting Text Entries into Cell Values." The options in the /Data Parse submenu are as follows:

To use /Data Parse, place your cell pointer on the first cell in the column that needs to be parsed and enter **/Data Parse**. When the command options are presented, select Format-Line and choose Create from its submenu. 1-2-3 will then insert a blank row above your cell pointer and create a format line that shows how it will split the label into component pieces.

Splitting Text Entries into Cell Values

After importing text into your worksheet, you may need to use /Data Parse to split long labels into individual entries. Follow these steps after using /File Import:

1. Move your cell pointer to the top of the column containing the labels to be parsed, and enter **/Data Parse**.

2. Choose the Format-Line option, and then Create to have 1-2-3 generate a suggested format line.

3. If the generated formatted line requires changes, choose Format-Line Edit and make your changes.

4. Select the Input-Range option and choose the column of labels to be altered; include the format line in the range.

5. Select the Output-Range option, and choose the top left cell in a blank area large enough to hold the output, or else specify a range large enough to hold each of the parsed entries. The width of this area is determined by the number of individual fields in the output. The length is the same as the number of labels being parsed.

6. Select Go.

The characters used in the format line generated by 1-2-3 are as follows:

D marks the first character of a date block.

L marks the first character of a label block.

S marks the first character of a block to be skipped during the parse operation. This character is never generated by 1-2-3, but you can enter it manually through the Edit option.

T marks the first character of a time block.

V marks the first character of a value block.

\> indicates that the block started by the letter that precedes this character is continued. The entry that began with the letter will continue to be placed in one worksheet cell until a skip or another letter is encountered.

* represents a blank space immediately below the character. This position can become part of the block that precedes it.

The pattern established in the format line will be followed in the parsing operation to determine where to split the labels and what type of data is needed for each block. Although you can generate a format line in multiple locations within your column of labels, you will need some consistency in the format of the column in order for this command to be useful.

If you are not pleased with the format line generated by 1-2-3, you can edit it with /Data Parse Format-Line Edit. After you select Edit, the SmartIcons disappear and the graphical appearance of your screen changes. The format line and the lines of text below it now display in a monospace font. A monospace font means every character occupies the same amount of space. Now the format line characters align with the characters below which the format line character will parse. You can add, replace, or delete any part of the format line after entering the Edit option. When you press ENTER to accept the edited format line, the display returns to normal and you will see the SmartIcons again.

Once the format has been established, the remaining steps for using /Data Parse are quite easy. Choose Input-Column, and then either highlight the cells to be parsed or type in the address of this column of label entries. Be sure to include the format line in the range. Then select Output-Range and enter the upper left cell. 1-2-3 will determine the space requirements of the output range, overwriting data if necessary. With the first three menu options set, choose Go to have 1-2-3 restructure the long labels into individual cell entries according to the pattern established by the format line.

The other two options in the Parse menu are Reset and Quit. Reset eliminates any settings you have established for the parsing operation. Quit removes the sticky Parse menu and returns you to READY mode. (Pressing ESC does the same thing.)

A few examples will help clarify the workings of /Data Parse. In this illustration, the entries in A1..A3 are long labels.

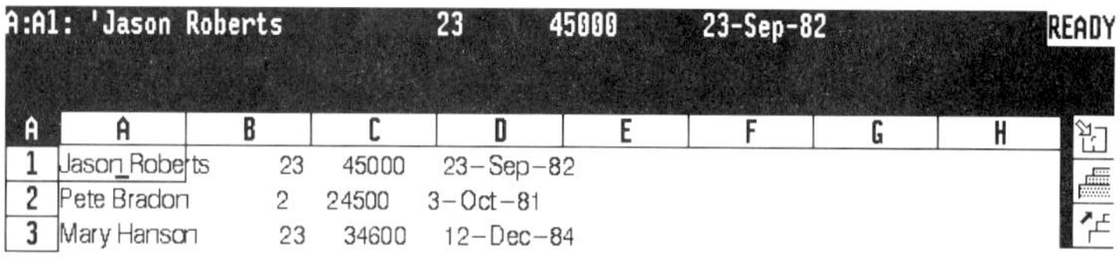

Chapter 10: Using Data Management Features in the Worksheet Environment

Although at first glance the components of each line may appear to be in separate cells, the control panel shows that each line is in fact a single label entry. The steps to parse these labels are as follows:

1. Move the cell pointer to A1 and enter **/Data Parse Format-Line Create**. 1-2-3 will generate a format line like the one in Figure 10-26. Notice that first names and last names have been treated as separate entries because of the space between them.

2. Choose Input-Column and select A1..A4.

3. To duplicate our example, choose A9 as Output-Range.

4. Select Go, and the output shown in Figure 10-27 is produced.

If you do not want the two name components treated as separate entries, choose Format-Line Edit. Then change the format line to agree with the one in Figure 10-28, and issue Go. You will notice that the entry "Jason Roberts" is now placed in A9. The display is initially truncated due to the column width, but you can change this easily with /Worksheet Column Set-Width.

Sequencing Worksheet Data

Although the /Data Sort commands were designed primarily for use in the data management environment, they can sometimes be used successfully when your

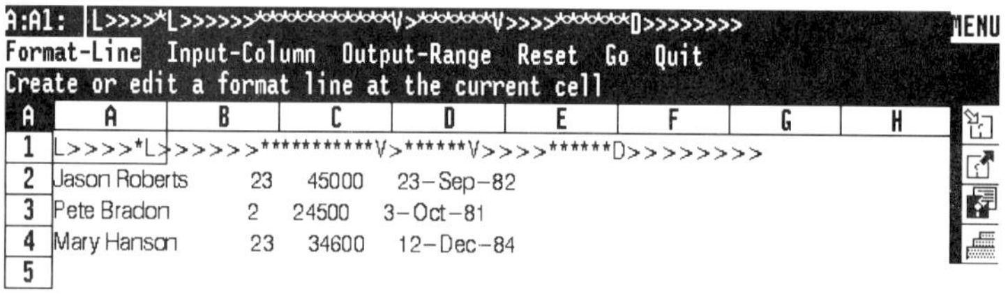

Figure 10-26. *Format line for parsing data*

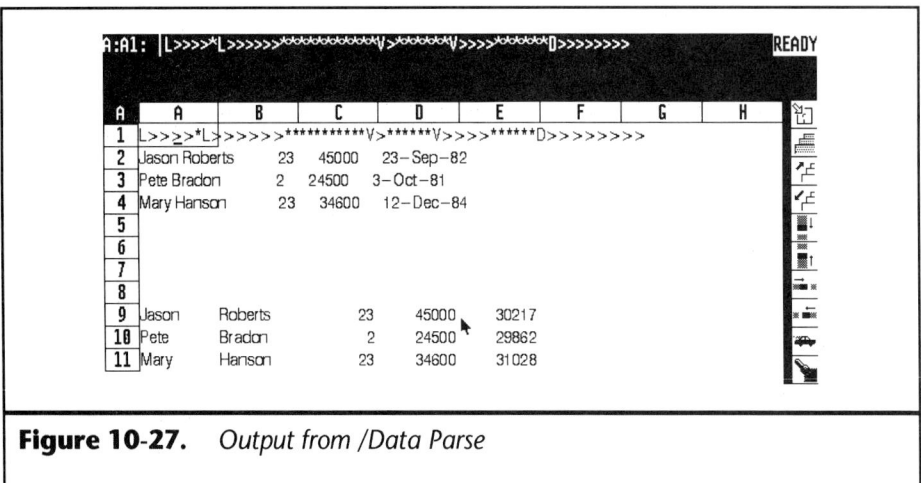

Figure 10-27. *Output from /Data Parse*

worksheet contains data used solely for calculations. Let's look at an example of a successful and an unsuccessful sort for a worksheet application. If you are not familiar with the /Data Sort command, review its features described in Chapter 9, "Data Management," before using it with your worksheet data.

Before using /Data Sort, you will need to assess whether your worksheet is organized so that sorting the data will not cause problems with your formulas. It would be advisable to save a copy of your worksheet file to disk prior to the sort, just in case you make a mistake and sort formulas that cannot be shuffled without causing an error. Naturally, if you notice the problem right away, ALT-F4 (UNDO) will be the easiest solution. If you enter a command or two before you notice the problem, you will appreciate the backup copy you saved to disk.

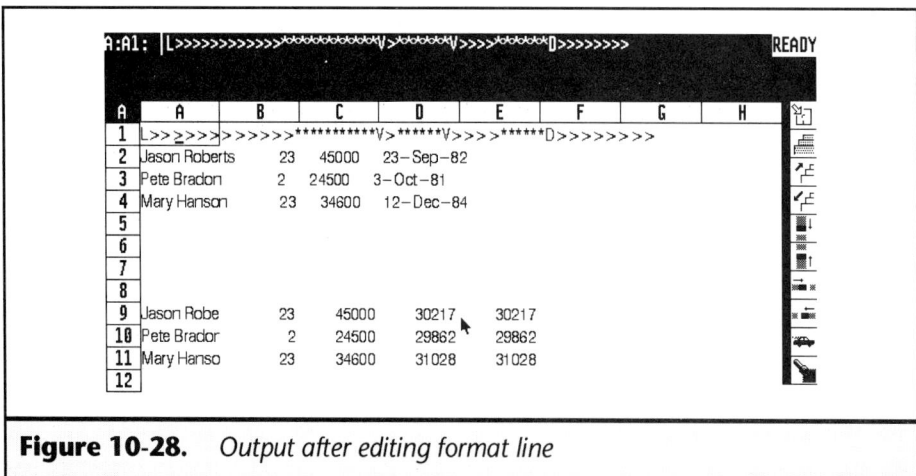

Figure 10-28. *Output after editing format line*

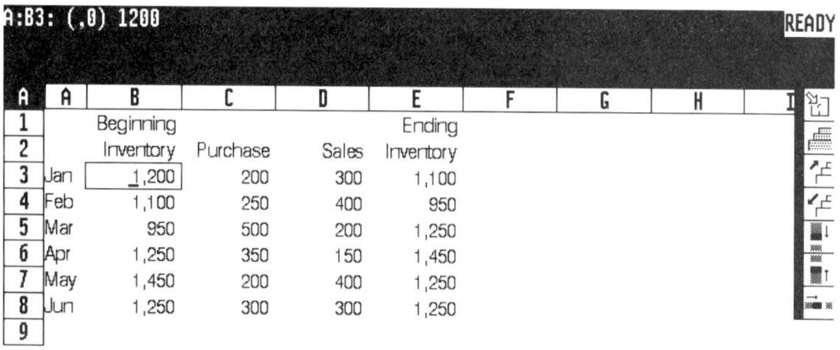

Chapter 10: Using Data Management Features in the Worksheet Environment

```
A:B3: (,0) 1200                                              READY

     A      B        C       D        E       F    G    H
  1       Beginning                Ending
  2       Inventory Purchase Sales Inventory
  3 Jan    1,200     200     300    1,100
  4 Feb    1,100     250     400      950
  5 Mar      950     500     200    1,250
  6 Apr    1,250     350     150    1,450
  7 May    1,450     200     400    1,250
  8 Jun    1,250     300     300    1,250
  9
```

Figure 10-29. *Inventory database*

As a worksheet is sorted, the rows of your model will be placed in a different order. As long as the formulas within each row reference only other variables in that row, the sort will not cause a problem. When formula references point outside the row, however, errors can occur. Look at the inventory calculations for six months in Figure 10-29; you will see that for each month the new beginning inventory is equal to the inventory at the end of the last period. To obtain the beginning inventory figures, the formula in each month references the appropriate address in the previous month (that is, the prior line of the model). These formulas are shown in Figure 10-30. If you wanted to sequence the data by the Sales figure rather than by month, you might decide to try the /Data Sort command. You would use /Data Sort Data-Range and then specify the range as

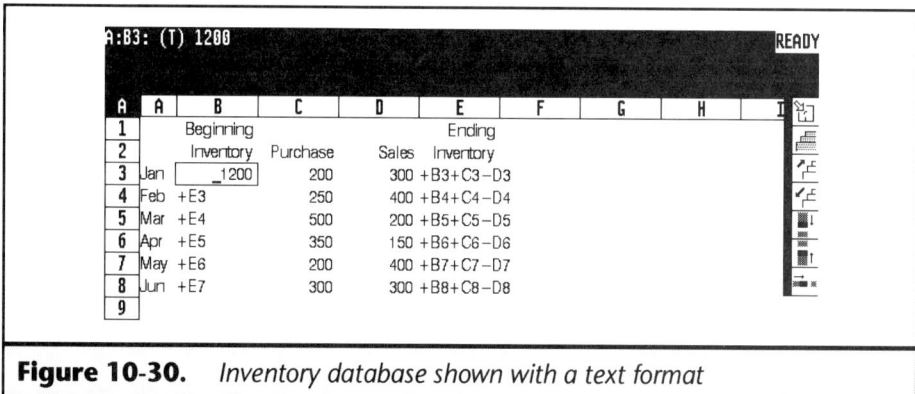

Figure 10-30. *Inventory database shown with a text format*

```
A:B3: (,0) +E2                                                    READY

    A     B         C       D       E        F    G    H
 1        Beginning                  Ending
 2        Inventory  Purchase  Sales  Inventory
 3  Feb   Inventory    250     400   (150)
 4  May   (150)        200     400   (350)
 5  Jan   1,200        200     300   1,100
 6  Jun   1,100        300     300   1,100
 7  Mar   1,100        500     200   1,400
 8  Apr   1,400        350     150   1,600
```

Figure 10-31. *Sorted inventory database*

A3..E8. You would select a primary key of D2 (Sales) and then choose Go. The results shown in Figure 10-31 indicate a problem with the references to previous lines.

To avoid this problem, you have two options for sorting the original inventory data. First, you can use /Range Value to freeze the values in column B before sorting. Your other option is to use /File Extract Values to save the portion you want to sort as another file that can be retrieved and sorted separately.

Figure 10-32 shows another worksheet that, at first glance, may appear to have the same kind of problem with the formula in F6. The formula references a table located outside the row of the worksheet. You will notice, however, that the formula references the table with absolute addresses. References that are absolute will not change when the sort is performed, so these rows can be sorted without being changed. When /Data Sort is entered and a data range of A6..I13

```
A:E6: (C2) [W10] @VLOOKUP(B6,$K$7..$L$9,1)*D6                           READY

    A            B        C       D        E         F        G         H
 1
 2
 3           LODGING   TRAVEL    #     LODGING/                      TOTAL
 4  LOCATION  CLASS     COST   TRIPS   MEALS   AIRFARE    MISC.      COST
 5
 6  Dallas      1        2      12    $420.00  $3,600.00  $420.00   $4,440.00
 7  Akron       2        2       2     $90.00    $600.00   $90.00     $780.00
 8  Chicago     3        1       3    $150.00    $750.00  $150.00   $1,050.00
 9  Denver      2        2      12    $540.00  $3,600.00  $540.00   $4,680.00
10  Phoenix     2        3       5    $225.00  $1,750.00  $225.00   $2,200.00
11  Atlanta     2        2       4    $180.00  $1,200.00  $180.00   $1,560.00
12  New York    3        2       6    $300.00  $1,800.00  $300.00   $2,400.00
13  Portland    2        4       3    $135.00  $1,500.00  $135.00   $1,770.00
```

Figure 10-32. *Travel worksheet*

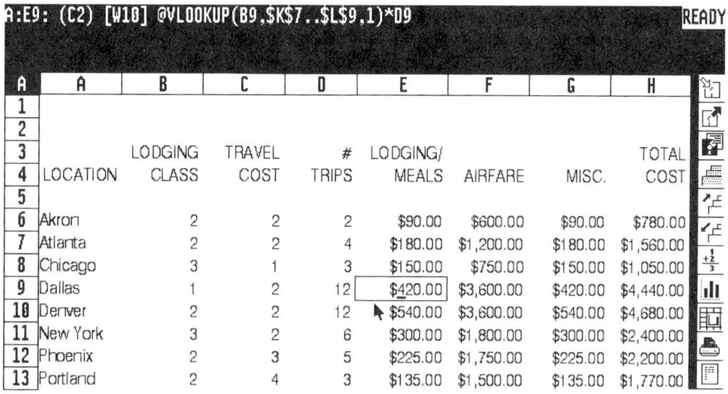

```
A:E9: (C2) [W10] @VLOOKUP(B9,$K$7..$L$9,1)*D9                READY
```

	A	B	C	D	E	F	G	H
1								
2								
3		LODGING	TRAVEL	#	LODGING/			TOTAL
4	LOCATION	CLASS	COST	TRIPS	MEALS	AIRFARE	MISC.	COST
5								
6	Akron	2	2	2	$90.00	$600.00	$90.00	$780.00
7	Atlanta	2	2	4	$180.00	$1,200.00	$180.00	$1,560.00
8	Chicago	3	1	3	$150.00	$750.00	$150.00	$1,050.00
9	Dallas	1	2	12	$420.00	$3,600.00	$420.00	$4,440.00
10	Denver	2	2	12	$540.00	$3,600.00	$540.00	$4,680.00
11	New York	3	2	6	$300.00	$1,800.00	$300.00	$2,400.00
12	Phoenix	2	3	5	$225.00	$1,750.00	$225.00	$2,200.00
13	Portland	2	4	3	$135.00	$1,500.00	$135.00	$1,770.00

Figure 10-33.   *Sorted travel worksheet*

is specified, with a primary key of A6 for location, the results in Figure 10-33 are produced.

Another situation to watch for is data placed at the side of the data range, like a new field for the database. This data will not be moved, since /Data Sort will move only the specified data range.

Command Reference

Data Analysis

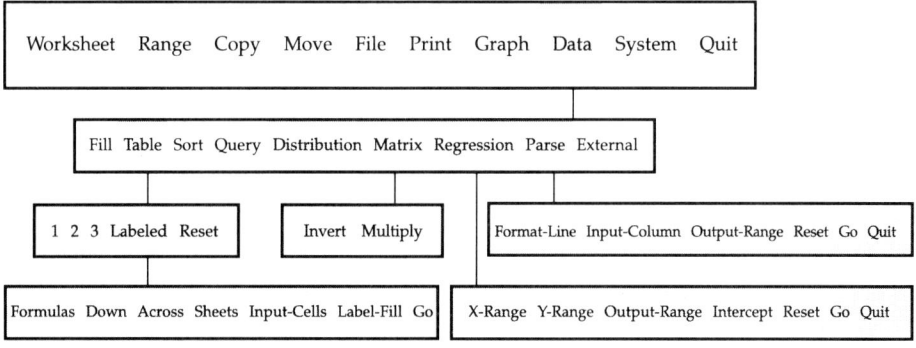

©1989 Lotus Development Corporation. Used with permission.

/Data Distribution

Description

The /Data Distribution command permits you to create a frequency distribution table from the values in a range on your worksheet. This table will tell you how many values in the range fall within each of the intervals you establish. An area of an active worksheet must be set aside to record the frequency intervals (bins) against which your data are analyzed. The frequency for each bin is placed in an adjacent column.

Using the /Data Distribution command requires some preliminary work. First, you must select a location on your worksheet for the bins. 1-2-3 will use the column to the right of the bins for the frequency numbers for each interval, and the row immediately below the last bin for a count of all the values that exceed the last bin value. Second, the values you place in the bins must be in ascending sequence from the top to the bottom of the column you are using.

Here is an example of the way 1-2-3 assigns values to the bins. If you create bin values of 5, 10, and 20, the first bin will contain a count of the values in your list that are less than or equal to 5; the second bin will contain a count of values greater than 5 and less than or equal to 10; and the third bin will hold values greater than 10 and less than or equal to 20. 1-2-3 creates a fourth bin for a count of all values greater than 20. This command ignores blank cells or cells containing labels. Cells containing @ERR are counted in the last bin and cells containing @NA are counted in the first bin.

Once /Data Distribution has classified the values in the specified range, a change in one of the values will not cause a reclassification. To reclassify data after a change, you must use /Data Distribution again. This time you only have to press ENTER in response to 1-2-3's prompts, since 1-2-3 will suggest the same ranges used previously.

Options

The only options you have with this command are the size of the intervals you enter in the bin range, and the number of values in the values range.

/Data Matrix

Description

The /Data Matrix command allows you to multiply and invert matrices. Matrices are tabular arrangements of data with a number in each cell. They are specified by their size. The number of rows is specified before the number of columns. Thus, a matrix with 5 rows and 6 columns is a 5-by-6 matrix. A square matrix has the same number of rows as it has columns.

With 1-2-3's matrix multiplication and inversion options you can solve problems relating to market share, projecting receivable aging, inventory control, and other modeling problems for the natural and social sciences. The specifics of the theory behind matrix operations are not examined in this volume.

Options

The /Data Matrix command provides options for two algebraic matrix operations: multiplication and inversion.

MULTIPLY   This option multiplies the individual components of two matrices according to the rules for matrix arithmetic. It assumes that only two matrices will be multiplied and that the number of columns in one matrix is equal to the number of rows in a second matrix. 1-2-3 can multiply matrices up to 256 rows by 256 columns.

When the Multiply option is chosen, 1-2-3 prompts you for the location of the two matrix ranges. You can type the cell addresses, reference the matrices with range names, or use the pointing method for specifying the ranges. When prompted for the output range, you can choose to enter the complete range or a reference to it, or just enter the upper left cell.

INVERT   This option inverts any square matrix according to the rules for matrix algebra. 1-2-3 prompts you for the range of the matrix to invert and the output range. When prompted for the output range, you can enter the complete range or a reference to it, or just the upper left cell. 1-2-3 can invert matrices up to 80 rows by 80 columns.

/Data Parse

Description

The /Data Parse command creates shorter, individual field values from the long labels stored in worksheet cells. You will need to use this command after you use /File Import to bring long labels from text files created by your word processor or other program into a column of cells. This column of long labels is limited to descriptive use or a string formula unless /Data Parse is used to split the long labels into individual fields. Then you can also use the results in numeric formulas and graphs.

Assuming some consistency in the format of the labels, /Data Parse can divide each label into a row of individual values, including label, value, date, and time entries. 1-2-3 makes a suggestion for splitting the label into its individual components, but you have the option of changing this recommendation.

Options

FORMAT-LINE   This is the most important option in the /Data Parse command, since it determines how 1-2-3 will split the long labels into individual cell entries. You can use it to create a new format line or edit an existing one.

The Create option under Parse Format-Line creates a format line above the cell pointer location at the time you make the selection. Position your cell pointer one cell above the first long label in your column to be parsed before entering /Data Parse Format-Line Create, to ensure that the format line is positioned correctly.

1-2-3 places letters and special symbols in the format line to present its interpretation of the way the long label should be split. The letters and symbols used are as follows:

- D   marks the first character of a date block.
- L   marks the first character of a label block.
- S   marks the first character of a block that is to be skipped during the parse operation. This character is never generated by 1-2-3, but you can enter it manually through the Edit option.
- T   marks the first character of a time block.
- V   marks the first character of a value block.
- \>   indicates that the block started by the letter that precedes this character is continued. The entry that began with the letter will continue to be placed in one worksheet cell until a skip or another letter is encountered.
- *   represents a blank space immediately below the character. This position can become part of the previous block.

After 1-2-3 creates a format line, you can use the Edit option to make changes in it if you wish. 1-2-3 only lets you enter valid format line characters.

INPUT-COLUMN   This is the location for the column of long labels imported from an ASCII text file. The range you specify should include the format line.

OUTPUT-RANGE This is the location you wish to use for the individual entries generated from the long label. You can enter the upper left cell in an area of the worksheet large enough for the output. 1-2-3 will determine how much space is required and will write over cells containing worksheet data if it needs the space.

RESET This option eliminates the settings for input or output area, so you can start over.

GO The Go option tells 1-2-3 that you have created and verified the accuracy of the format line and have defined the location of the input and output areas. It causes the long labels to be parsed according to the specifications given, and returns to the READY mode.

QUIT This option leaves the Data Parse menu without parsing the data.

/Data Regression

Description

The /Data Regression command allows you to perform a statistical analysis to see whether two or more variables are interrelated. This command allows you to use from 1 to 75 independent variables for your regression analysis. It will estimate the accuracy with which these independent variables can predict the values of a specified dependent variable.

As an example, your dependent variable may be the sales of hot chocolate at a football concession stand. You may wish to look at outdoor temperature and pregame ticket sales as possible predictors of the number of cups of hot chocolate that will be sold at a game. These two factors would be your independent variables. By applying regression analysis to historic data for the three variables, you can determine how effective the independent variables are as predictors of the dependent variable. When the regression analysis has been completed, 1-2-3 will display the number of observations, the Y intercept or constant, the standard error of estimated Y values and X coefficients, R squared, the X coefficients, and the degrees of freedom.

As with many of the other data commands, using /Data Regression involves a few preliminary steps. Your dependent and independent variable values must be placed in columns on the worksheet. Each column must have the same number of entries, and all of them must contain numeric values. You can have a maximum of 8192 values; this is one value for each row of the worksheet. After these preliminary steps are completed, use the /Data Regression options to complete your analysis.

Options

The /Data Regression submenu has the following options.

X-RANGE   This is the column or columns (75 maximum) that contain the values for your independent variables. Enter cell addresses or a range name, or point with your cell pointer to highlight the selected area.

Y-RANGE   This is the column containing the values for your dependent variable. Enter a range name or cell addresses, or point to the selected column.

OUTPUT-RANGE   This is the area that will contain the results of the analysis. It must be at least nine rows deep and four columns wide, and it must be at least two columns wider than the number of independent variables you are using. You have the option of specifying the entire range or just the upper left corner. If you use the latter approach, 1-2-3 will decide the size of the area to use for the output of the regression analysis. Any existing data in the cells of the output range will be overwritten.

INTERCEPT   This is the Y intercept. You have the option of having 1-2-3 compute this value or setting it to zero. Compute is the default setting.

RESET   This option eliminates all the settings you have established for /Data Regression.

GO   This option completes the regression analysis after you have chosen X-Range, Y-Range, Output-Range, and Intercept.

QUIT   This option exits the Data Regression menu and returns you to READY mode.

/Data Sort

Description

This command allows you to sequence information in worksheet cells. The command is covered fully in Chapter 9, since its primary application is for data management. It is mentioned again here because there are selected instances where it can be used in the worksheet environment. These are described in this chapter.

Options

The options for /Data Sort are covered in Chapter 9.

/Data Table 1

Description

The /Data Table 1 command allows you to use different values of a variable in formulas. This command provides a structured "what-if" feature that substitutes various values in your formulas and records the result of each value.

The /Data Table 1 command builds what is called a one-way table. The table will have one set of input values running down its left side. It can evaluate many formulas.

/Data Table 1 requires that you set up a table area in your worksheet. The purpose of the table is to structure the values that you want to plug into an input cell one by one, while recording the impact of these values on the formulas that are also part of the table. To set up the table, place the input values you wish to use in a column in a blank area of your worksheet. The row of formulas you wish to have evaluated must begin one row above the first input value and one column to the right. You may place new formulas in these cells, or you may reference other cells in the worksheet that contain the desired formulas. For example, to have a formula in A3 evaluated, place +A3 in one of the cells in this formula row. You may also wish to format the formula cells as text for documentation purposes.

The two sets of entries just discussed create the framework for the table. The column of value cells forms the left edge of the table, with the last entry determining the bottom edge of the table. The row of formulas forms the top of the table, with the last entry in the row marking the right edge.

After the initial setup, you are ready to respond to 1-2-3's prompts to define the location of your table and the cell you wish to reference for input.

Options

After your table is defined, tell 1-2-3 the location you have selected for the table. The best way to do this is to position your cell pointer at the upper left edge of the table before you enter the /Data Table 1 command. The table should be a rectangular area that includes all the formulas and all the values you are concerned with. You can use cell addresses, a range name, or the pointing method to communicate the table location.

Next, 1-2-3 asks you what worksheet cell you want to use as an input cell. This is the cell into which 1-2-3 will place the input values from the table column, one by one. Using a given value for the input cell, 1-2-3 evaluates each of the table formulas and places the formula result in the column beneath the formula, on the row for the input value being used.

When 1-2-3 has used each of your values, the table will be complete with formula results. Depending on the size of your table, this takes up to several minutes. When 1-2-3 has completed the table, the input cell still has its original value; 1-2-3 makes its substitutions behind the scenes without affecting the cell entry. A change to a value in the input table does not cause the table to recalculate. To get recalculation, you must reuse **/Data Table**, or press F8 (TABLE). If you wish to reset the table location and input cell before using the command again, use /Data Table Reset to eliminate your previous settings.

/Data Table 2

Description

The /Data Table 2 command allows you to pick any two cells on the worksheet that contain numeric variable values and set up substitution values for these cells, so that the impact of the changes can be measured in the result of a particular worksheet formula. This feature provides a structured approach to "what-if" analysis, in which 1-2-3 does most of the work.

The /Data Table 2 command produces a table that is similar to a one-way table, except that you can substitute values for two variables at once and evaluate only one formula. It allows you to see whether the formula result is more sensitive to changes in variable one or variable two, which provides an easy-to-use sensitivity analysis feature.

/Data Table 2 requires that you set up a table area in your worksheet. The purpose of the table is to structure the values that you want to plug into the two input cells one by one, while recording the impact of these values on the result of a formula that is also part of the table. To set up the table, place the input values for the first variable you wish to use in a column in a blank area of your worksheet. The values for the second variable you wish to use must begin one row above the first input value and one column to the right; place these values across the row. You can use the /Data Fill command to supply them if the increment between values is evenly spaced.

The formula you wish to have evaluated for each value of the input variable is placed in the blank cell at the intersection of the row and column of variable values. You may enter either an actual formula or a reference to a worksheet cell containing a formula. For example, to have a formula in A3 evaluated, place +A3 in the formula cell. You may also wish to format the formula cell as text for documentation purposes.

The two sets of entries just discussed create the framework for the table. The column of value cells forms the left edge of the table, with the last entry determining the bottom edge of the table. The row of value entries forms the top of the table, with the last entry in the row marking the right edge. To have 1-2-3 complete the table entries for you, enter **/Data Table 2** and respond to 1-2-3's requests for specifications.

Options

After your table is defined, tell 1-2-3 the location you have selected for the table. To facilitate this process, position your cell pointer at the upper left edge of the table before entering the /Data Table 2 command. The table should be a rectangular area that includes the formula and all the values with which you are concerned. You can use cell addresses, a range name, or the pointing method to communicate the table location.

Next, 1-2-3 asks you what worksheet cell you want to use as an input cell for the column of values you entered. This is the cell into which 1-2-3 will place the input values from the table column, one by one. 1-2-3 then asks what input cell will be used for the row of values. 1-2-3 then evaluates the formula shown at the upper left corner of the table, using each of the possible value combinations for input cell 1 and input cell 2.

When 1-2-3 has used each of your values, the table will be complete with formula results. Depending on the size of your table, this takes up to several minutes. When 1-2-3 has completed the table, the input cell still has its original value; 1-2-3 alters the values of the input cell only internally. A change to a value in the input table does not cause the table to recalculate. To get recalculation, you must reuse /Data Table, or press F8 (TABLE). If you wish to reset the table location and input cells before using the command again, use /Data Table Reset to eliminate your previous settings.

/Data Table 3

Description

The /Data Table 3 command allows you to pick any three cells on the worksheet file that contain numeric variable values and set up substitution values for these cells, so that the impact of the changes can be measured in the result of a particular worksheet formula. This feature provides a structured approach to "what-if" analysis, in which 1-2-3 does most of the work. This command creates data tables that use multiple worksheets.

The /Data Table 3 command produces a table that is similar to one- and two-way tables, except that you can substitute values for three variables at once and evaluate only one formula. It allows you to see whether the formula result is more sensitive to changes in variable one, variable two, or variable three, which provides an easy-to-use sensitivity analysis feature.

/Data Table 3 requires that you set up a table area in your worksheet. The purpose of the table is to structure the values that you want to plug into the three input cells one by one, while recording the impact of these values on the result of a formula that is outside of the table. To set up the table, place the input values for the first variable you wish to use in a column in a blank area of your worksheet. The values for the second variable you wish to use must begin one row above the first input value and one column to the right; place these values across the row. The value for the third variable should be in the upper leftmost cell (usually A1) in each worksheet that is part of the data table. You can use the /Data Fill command to supply these values if the increment between values is evenly spaced.

The formula you wish to have evaluated for each value of the input variables is placed outside of the data table. You may enter either an actual formula or a reference to a worksheet cell containing a formula. For example, to have a formula in A3 evaluated, place +A3 in the formula cell. You may also wish to format the formula cell as text for documentation purposes.

The three sets of values just discussed create the framework for the table. The column of value cells forms the left edge of the table, with the last entry determining the bottom edge of the table. The row of value entries forms the top of the table, with the last entry in the row marking the right edge. The first worksheet with a value in the upper left corner of the data table is the front of the table; the last worksheet containing a third input value determines the back of the table. To have 1-2-3 complete the table entries for you, enter **/Data Table 3** and respond to 1-2-3's requests for specifications.

Options

After your table is defined, tell 1-2-3 the location you have selected for the table. To facilitate this process, position your cell pointer at the first value for the third input variable, which is the upper left edge of the table in the first worksheet, before entering the /Data Table 3 command. The table should be a rectangular area that includes all the values with which you are concerned. You can use cell addresses, a range name, or the pointing method to communicate the table location.

Next, 1-2-3 asks you for the address of the cell containing the formula. Once 1-2-3 knows where the formula is, it asks for the worksheet cell you want to use as an input cell for the column of values you entered. This is the cell into which 1-2-3 will place the input values from the table column, one by one. 1-2-3 then asks what input cell will be used for the row of values. Finally, 1-2-3 prompts for the input cell for the third input value that is in the upper left cell in each worksheet's table. 1-2-3 will evaluate the formula, using each of the possible value combinations for input cell 1, input cell 2, and input cell 3.

When 1-2-3 has used each of your values, the table will be complete with formula results. Depending on the size of your table, this takes up to several minutes. When 1-2-3 has completed the table, the input cell still has its original value; 1-2-3 alters the values of the input cell only internally. A change to a value in the input table does not cause the table to recalculate. To get recalculation, you must reuse /Data Table, or press the F8 (TABLE) key. If you wish to reset the table location and input cells before using the command again, you can use /Data Table Reset to eliminate your previous settings.

/Data Table Labeled

Description

The /Data Table Labeled command allows you to create "what-if" tables that can contain multiple variables and evaluate multiple formulas. This command has the fewest limitations of the /Data Table commands. /Data Table Labeled can create one- and two-way data tables with a different orientation from those of /Data Table 1 and /Data Table 2. Labeled data tables can have blank columns, rows, and worksheets. You can leave these areas blank or fill them with labels, values, or formulas that use the data in the data tables. The /Data Table Labeled command substitutes variables entered in rows, columns, or worksheets and returns the value of one or more formulas to the data table. You can have multiple input values for each set of column, row, or worksheet variables.

/Data Table Labeled requires that you set up an input cell area, a formula range, and a data table area in your worksheet file. The input cell is the cell that the command will substitute for the values in the data table. The formula range contains the formula name in one row, and the formula underneath.

The table contains input values stored in a column, row, and one or more worksheets. Where the specified values meet, 1-2-3 computes a value and treats the intersecting cell as part of the data table. If a cell does not intersect with the selected column, row, and worksheet, 1-2-3 does not include it in the data table. This cell is skipped when the table values are calculated; it can contain any data, and the /Data Table Labeled command will not interfere with it. To set up the table, enter values for an input cell in a column, a row, or the same cell in multiple worksheets. The values for the column variable range and the row variable range cannot be in the same row or column. You can use one, two, or all three of these variable ranges. This command does not order the variable ranges.

To make the data table and input area easier to read, document the values in the table using cells that the command will not use. To supply the data values for column, row, and worksheet variables, you can use the /Data Fill command if the increment between values is evenly spaced.

Select the formula that the /Data Table Labeled command uses by entering the formula name above the row variable values in the column. To select the formula for column variable values, enter the formula to the left of the data table. The formula name above or to the right of the data table is referred to as the formula label range. The formula name can be stretched to cover multiple cells by adding the label-fill character (a hyphen by default).

To have 1-2-3 complete the table entries for you, enter **/Data Table Labeled** and respond to 1-2-3's requests for specifications.

Options

FORMULAS This option selects the formula range and formula label range. The formula range contains both the row with the formula names, and the row with the formulas. The formula label range is the formula name that appears next to or above the data table indicating which formulas 1-2-3 evaluates for the data table. You can use cell addresses, a range name, or the pointing method to communicate the formula range and the formula label range locations.

ACROSS This option selects the column variable values and the input cell the /Data Table Labeled command uses to evaluate the formulas. You can use cell addresses, a range name, or the pointing method to communicate the column variable values. Then press ENTER to confirm each row in the column variable values and select an input cell for each row. 1-2-3 repeats this step for each row in the column variable values.

DOWN This option selects the row variable values and the input cell the /Data Table Labeled command uses to evaluate the formulas. You can use cell addresses, a range name, or the pointing method to communicate the row variable values. Then press ENTER to confirm each column in the row variable values and select an input cell for each column. 1-2-3 repeats this step for each column in the row variable values.

SHEETS This option selects the sheet variable values and the input cell the /Data Table Labeled command uses to evaluate the formulas. You can use cell addresses, a range name, or the pointing method to communicate the sheet variable values. Then press ENTER to confirm each cell for the worksheets in the sheet variable values and select an input cell for each cell. 1-2-3 repeats this step for each cell in the sheet variable values.

INPUT CELLS This option prompts for the variable values and input cells for the row, column, and worksheet variables. For each of these prompts, 1-2-3 displays the current selection. You can accept or change the selection.

LABEL-FILL This option selects a label-fill character for the formula label range and column variable range.

GO This option generates the table and returns 1-2-3 to the READY mode. For each cell at an intersection of a selected worksheet, row, and column variable, 1-2-3 substitutes the column, row, and worksheet variable values in the input cells and puts the result in the cell. Depending on the size of your table, this can take up to several minutes. When 1-2-3 completes the table, the input cell still has its original value, since 1-2-3 only alters the values of the input cell internally. A change to a value in the input table does not cause the table to recalculate. To recalculate table entries, use /Data Table or the F8 (TABLE) key. If you wish to reset the column, row, and worksheet variable ranges, or the formula range and formula label ranges before using the command again, you can use /Data Table Reset to eliminate your previous settings.

/Data Table Reset

Description

The /Data Table Reset command eliminates the settings you have established for the table location and input cell. Since 1-2-3 will suggest the previous setting the next time you use the command, Reset is convenient when the next table location or input cell setting is far removed from the last use. If you select /Data Table before cancelling your previous settings, you must then press ESC and move your cell pointer to the new location in order to establish new settings. Once Reset is used, your cell pointer will remain in its current location.

CHAPTER 11

Working with 1-2-3's Graphics Features

The graphics features of 1-2-3 allow you to display your worksheet information in a format that is easy to interpret. Rather than presenting all the specific numbers, graphs summarize the essence of your data, so that you can focus on general patterns and trends. When you notice something that warrants further analysis, you can return to the supporting worksheet numbers and look at them more closely.

1-2-3's graphics features are popular because they do not require that data be reentered. Indeed, you can use data already entered for your worksheet—without any changes at all. Nor do you need to transfer data to another program or learn a new system in order to print a graph. 1-2-3's graphics menus are just like the other 1-2-3 menus, so you need only learn a few new 1-2-3 commands in order to use the graphics features. They are an integral part of 1-2-3, available from the main menu. After creating your worksheet model, you simply make a few more menu selections to project the data onto a chart.

If you have a color monitor or a graphics card, you will be able to view your graph or chart on the screen. If you have only a monochrome monitor without a graphics card, you will not be able to view your graph, but you can create graphs and print them.

This chapter explores the various options available through the /Graph command, including all of the Release 3.4 features that expand 1-2-3's graphics ability. The chapter also covers other 1-2-3 commands that affect graphs, such as printing and displaying a worksheet and a graph at the same time. This chapter also covers the Wysiwyg add-in that has other features you may want to use with your graphs. These features include adding a graph to a worksheet range and adding other graphic elements to your graphs.

Creating an Automatic Graph

A quick method for creating a graph is to create an automatic graph, which you can do if your worksheet data is in the proper format. 1-2-3 attempts to create an automatic graph when the /Graph View command is executed, or the F10 (GRAPH) key is pressed, and you have not selected worksheet data to graph.

1-2-3 can create two types of automatic graphs: a rowwise and a columnwise automatic graph. Columnwise and rowwise refer to how 1-2-3 divides the data into data ranges to graph. When you create an automatic graph, 1-2-3 uses the first column or row of the data as the X range, which appears at the bottom of the graph in the X axis. The subsequent columns or rows become the data ranges graphed against the X range. 1-2-3 stops using the worksheet data for the graph when it selects the seventh data range (X and A through F), or when it encounters two blank rows or columns that mark the end of the worksheet data to graph. Once you create an automatic graph, 1-2-3 keeps the data ranges from the automatic graph in its graphics settings. This feature permits you to add enhancements to the automatic graph.

A *columnwise automatic graph* is the default automatic graph. To create a columnwise automatic graph, the data to be graphed must look like the data in Figure 11-1. The worksheet data that 1-2-3 will graph must have two blank rows and columns on all sides to isolate the data to graph from the remaining worksheet data. The edges of the worksheet can serve as one or two of these borders. The automatic graph will use the labels in A5..A16 as the X axis labels. Each column to the right of the labels will become an additional data range. To display this data as an automatic graph, move the cell pointer to the first label

Chapter 11: Working with 1-2-3's Graphics Features 615

Figure 11-1. Data for columnwise automatic graph

(A5), and press F10 (GRAPH). Figure 11-2 shows the automatic line graph for the worksheet in Figure 11-1. 1-2-3 creates a line graph with this data because a graph type is not selected.

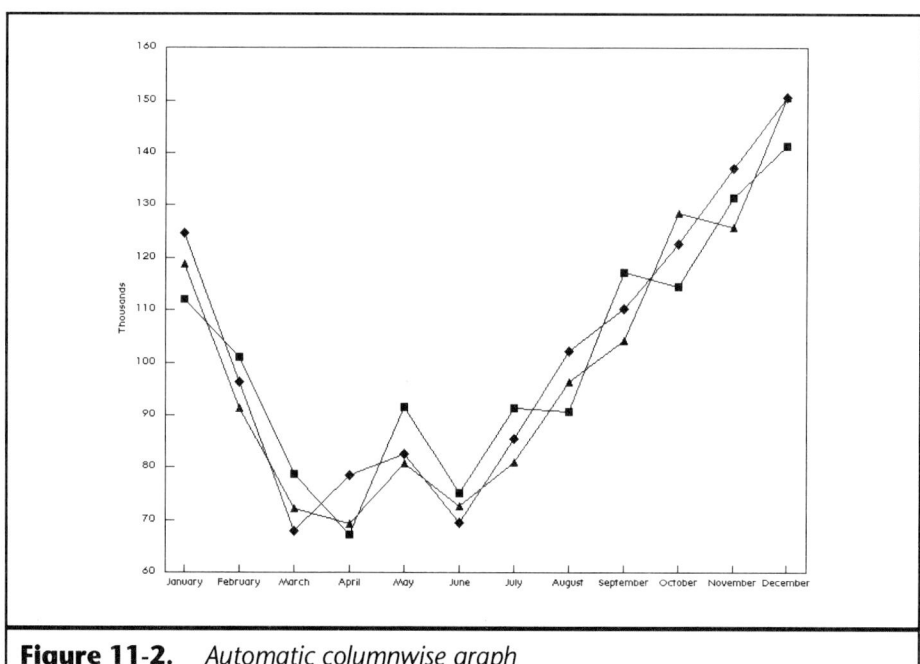

Figure 11-2. Automatic columnwise graph

The other type of automatic graph is a *rowwise automatic graph*. This option tells 1-2-3 to divide the worksheet data into data ranges for a graph by rows instead of columns. You can choose this option by invoking the /Worksheet Global Default Graph Rowwise command. After executing this command and returning to READY mode, move the cell pointer to the first cell you want to include in the graph. For the data in Figure 11-3, it is D2. A rowwise automatic graph uses the first row for the values along the X axis, and the subsequent rows as the other data ranges. The worksheet has two blank columns, B and C, so 1-2-3 does not include the salespeople's names in the graph. To display this data as an automatic graph, view the graph using the /Graph View command, which is equivalent to the F10 (GRAPH) key. Figure 11-4 shows the automatic graph for the worksheet in Figure 11-3. If you want to return the automatic graph type to columnwise, use the /Worksheet Global Default Graph Columnwise command.

Automatic graphs use the current selected graph type. Since a line graph is the default, creating an automatic graph without selecting a graph type results in a line graph, as in the Figure 11-2 and 11-4 examples. If you do select a graph type, 1-2-3 uses your selection to create the automatic graph data.

Viewing Graphs and Worksheets Simultaneously

As mentioned for automatic graphs, you can view a graph by simply pressing F10 (GRAPH), or by using the /Graph View command. Release 3 has a feature that allows you to see the worksheet and the current graph at the same time. This is the /Worksheet Window Graph command, which splits the screen at the cell pointer's position and uses the left half to show the current worksheet and the right half to show the current graph.

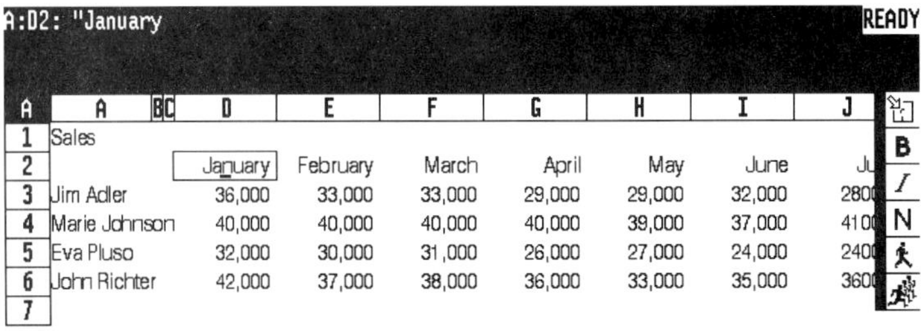
A:D2: "January READY

A	A	BC	D	E	F	G	H	I	J
1	Sales								
2			January	February	March	April	May	June	Ju
3	Jim Adler		36,000	33,000	33,000	29,000	29,000	32,000	280
4	Marie Johnson		40,000	40,000	40,000	40,000	39,000	37,000	410
5	Eva Pluso		32,000	30,000	31,000	26,000	27,000	24,000	240
6	John Richter		42,000	37,000	38,000	36,000	33,000	35,000	360
7									

Figure 11-3. *Data for rowwise automatic graph*

Chapter 11: Working with 1-2-3's Graphics Features

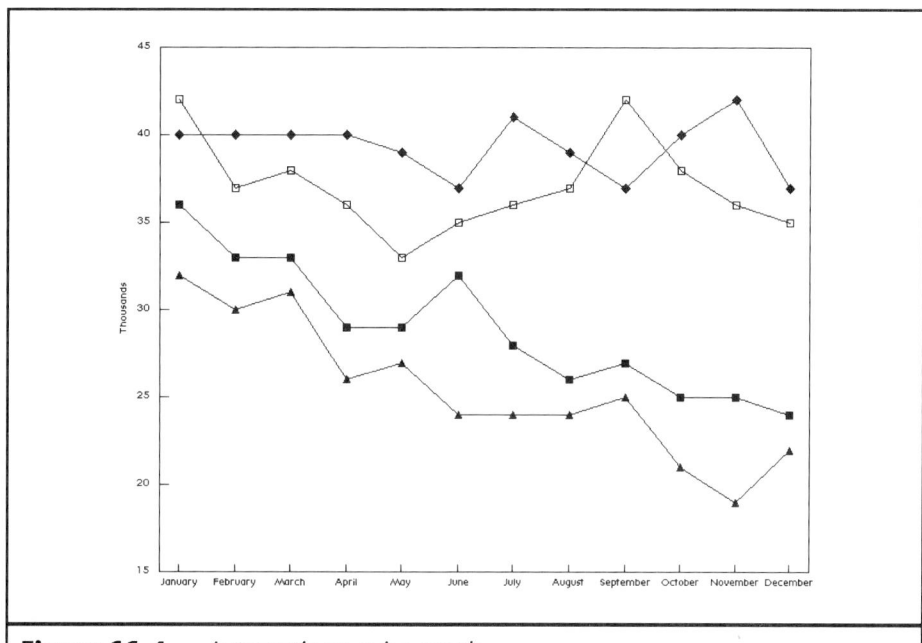

Figure 11-4. *Automatic rowwise graph*

When you execute this command, the cell pointer determines where 1-2-3 splits the screen. To split the worksheet in Figure 11-2 into a worksheet and a graph window, move the cell pointer to column E or the column where you want to split the worksheet area. When the /Worksheet Window Graph command is executed for this worksheet, the screen looks like Figure 11-5. Note that the cell pointer remains in the worksheet so you can continue working on the worksheet. 1-2-3 automatically incorporates any changes in the worksheet that affect the graph. You can still use F10 (GRAPH) or /Graph View to display the graph using the entire screen.

In a split-screen, the graph window remains until another /Worksheet Window command is executed or another file is retrieved. If the worksheet does not have a defined graph when a Graph window is created, the Graph window appears blank. 1-2-3 will create an automatic graph in the blank Graph window if you move the cell pointer to the first cell in the graph data and press F10 (GRAPH) or execute /Graph View. When you return to the READY mode, the automatic graph will appear in the Graph window.

TIP: Another way to display both the graph and the worksheet at the same time is to use Wysiwyg to add the graph to the worksheet, as discussed in the Wysiwyg Graph Printing Features section of this chapter, or in Chapter 15 on the Wysiwyg add-in.

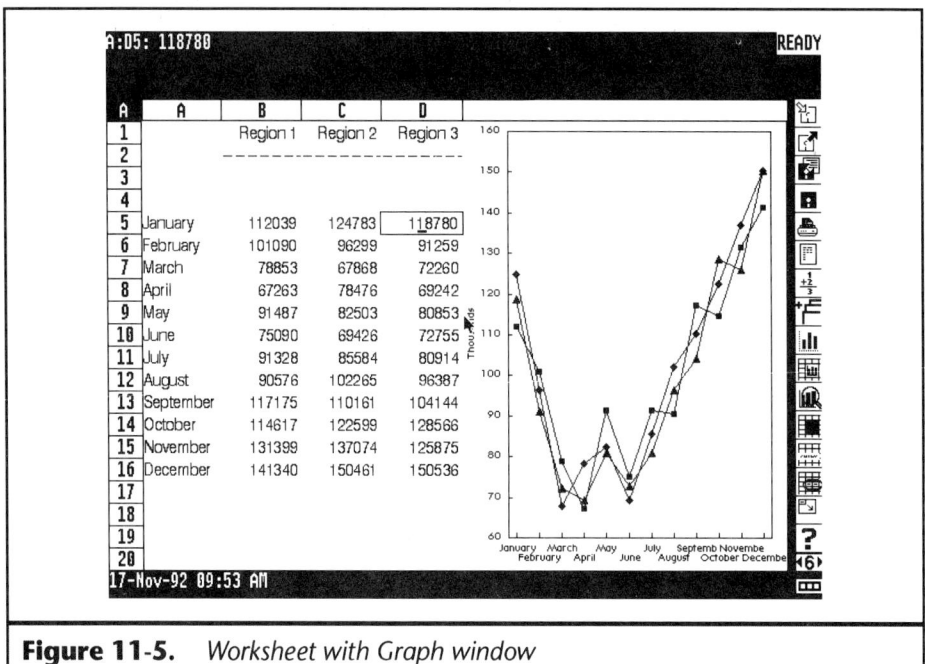

Figure 11-5. *Worksheet with Graph window*

Creating Graphs

Most of the options you need to create, modify, display, and save graphs are located under the /Graph command, available from 1-2-3's main menu. When you select /Graph, you will be presented with a menu that looks like this:

Under Type, this menu presents the options for selecting the type of graph you wish to generate. The specific data to be shown in your graph is accessed through options X, A through F, and Group. You can use the Options selections to enhance your graph. Various other selections permit you to view, save, and name your graph. You can always view your graph by using the /Graph View command. Another option is to press F10 (GRAPH) at any point, including while you are using other /Graph commands. Once the graph is displayed, pressing any key returns you to where you had been before you viewed the graph. 1-2-3 always displays the most current changes to the graph when you view it.

1-2-3 Release 3.4 displays a setting sheet beneath the /Graph menu. This setting sheet shows you the options you have selected for the current graph. A different setting sheet appears when you alter options such as titles and scales. This setting sheet displays all of your choices in one place, making it easy for you to see the changes to your graph while you are making them.

Selecting a Graph Type

To create a graph for the first time, you will need to make several menu selections. These specify the type of graph you wish to see, and tell 1-2-3 which data to show in the graph.

1-2-3 offers a choice of seven different types of graphs, as shown in the following menu, which appears when you select Type from the main Graph menu.

You can easily change from one type of presentation to another by returning to the Type menu and choosing another graph type. The Type options include basic graph types like line and bar, as well as additional options available through the Features selection. This flexibility allows you to look at your data in a number of presentation formats, and select the one that seems to show the data most effectively.

Figure 11-6 presents an example of each of the different graph types. A description of each graph type, along with some suggested uses, is found in the box called "Graph Types for Every Need." By combining the basic graph types with Release 3's Features options, you can create an entire graphics presentation with a different type of graph on each of your slides. The Features options let you rotate the X and Y axes, stack the data ranges, assign data ranges to a second Y axis, display data ranges as percentages of the total, modify the frame of the graph, add a drop-shadow to the graph range, display the graph as three-dimensional, and add a table of the graphed data to the graph.

To select any of the graph types from the menu, simply point to the graph type you want and press ENTER. Alternatively, you can type the first letter of the selection or use the mouse. If you do not select a graph type, 1-2-3 uses a line graph.

Labeling the X Axis

After selecting the graph type, you must define the data to be shown on your graph. The X option in the main Graph menu is used to specify a range of cells

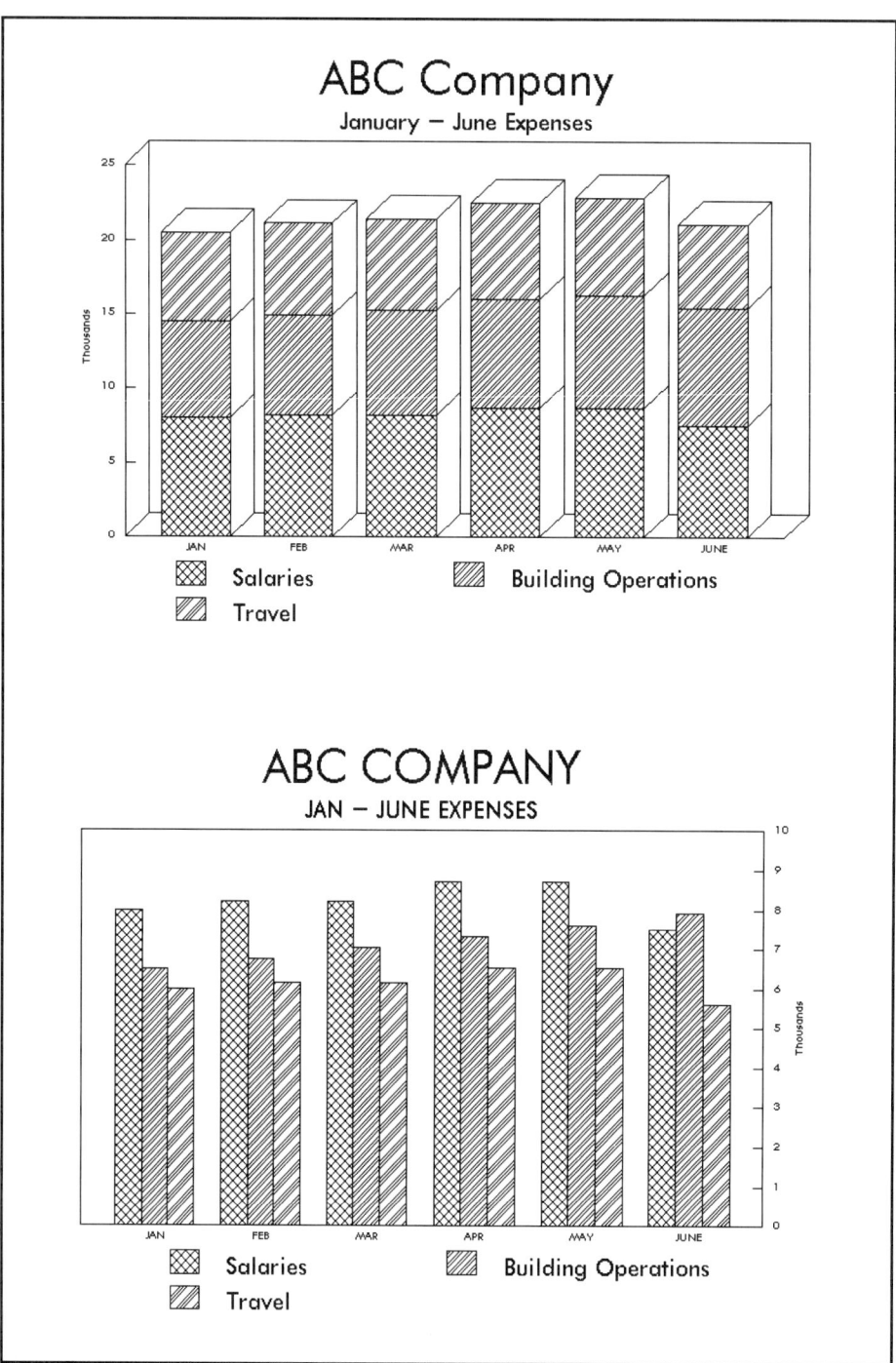

Figure 11-6. *The seven graph types—stacked bar with drop-shadow (top) and bar (bottom)*

Chapter 11: Working with 1-2-3's Graphics Features

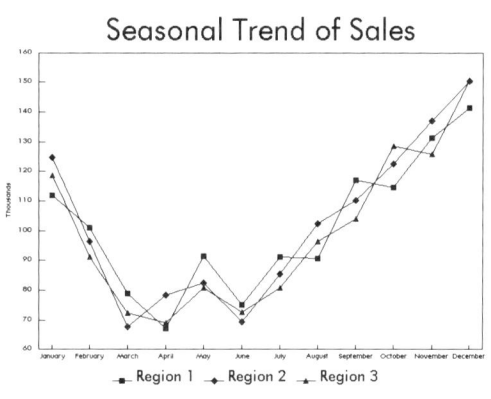

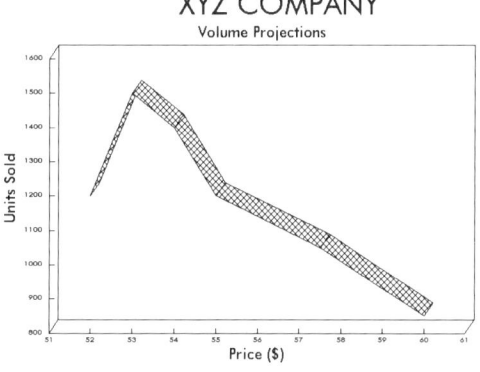

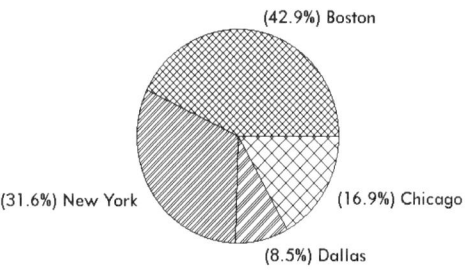

Figure 11-6. *The seven graph types* (continued)—*line (top), XY with drop-shadow (middle), and pie (bottom)*

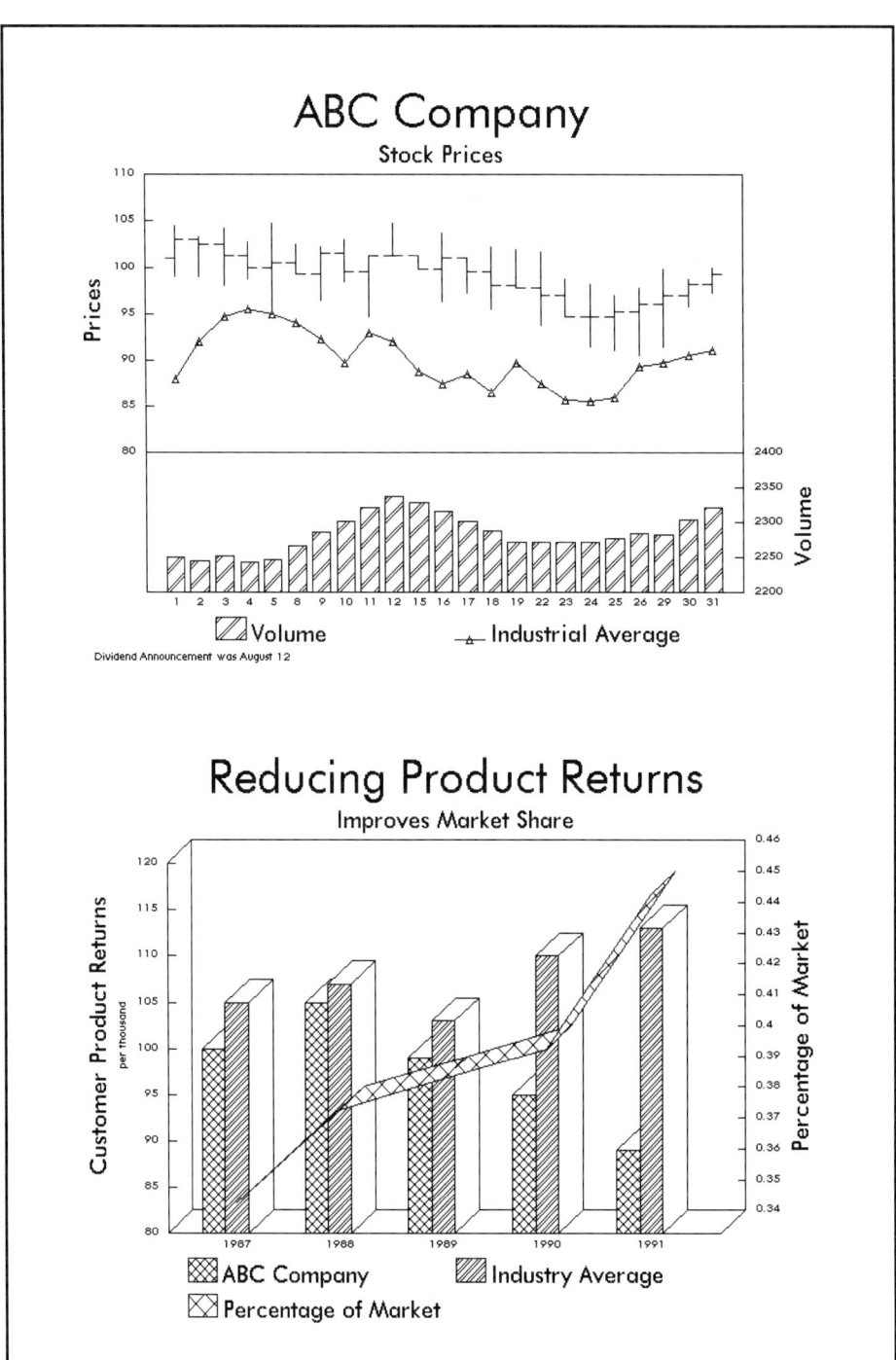

Figure 11-6. *The seven graph types (continued)—HLCO (top) and mixed with drop-shadow (bottom)*

Graph Types for Every Need

The variety of graph types allows you to find a type suitable for presenting almost any kind of data. Here is a description of each type and some suggested uses.

BAR   A bar graph represents the data points in your series with bars of different heights. Although any data can be plotted on a bar graph, it is especially appropriate for comparing the values in several series.

LINE   A line graph shows the points of your data ranges plotted against the Y axis. The points in a range may be connected with a line, shown as symbols, or both. The line graph is an excellent choice for plotting trend data over time, such as sales, profit, or expenses.

STACKED BAR   A stacked bar graph places the values in each series on top of each other for each point on the X axis. The total height of a bar thus represents the total values in all the series plotted for any given point. A stacked bar graph is effective for displaying total levels, as well as component levels. Contribution to total company profit of the various subsidiaries could be shown effectively on a stacked bar graph, for example.

PIE   A pie chart shows one range of values. The size of the pie wedge represents each value's percentage of the total. A pie chart is effective for showing the relative size of different components. Pie charts are effective for analyzing different kinds of expenses, or the contribution to profit from different product lines, for example.

XY   An XY graph plots the values in one series against those in another. An XY graph could be used to plot age against salary, machine repairs by age, or time against temperature, for example.

HLCO   An HLCO chart shows the high, low, close, and open values. For each set of data values for each X axis value (such as each day you are recording stock prices), the HLCO graph has a line from the high to the low value. A projection to the left indicates the open value and a projection to the right indicates the close value. Additional ranges appear as a bar graph below this graph, or as a line graph shown with the high, low, close, and open values. This graph type is for graphing financial commodities or statistical results.

MIXED   A mixed graph shows up to three data ranges as a bar graph and up to three data ranges as a line graph. The bar graph and line graph are on top of each other. Mixed graphs can be used to graph profit from different divisions against sales from different divisions.

containing labels to be placed along the points on the X axis, for all graphs except XY and pie charts. These labels may mark the points of the graph for years, months, or other data values. For the worksheet in Figure 11-3, the cells containing the words "January" through "December" were selected as the range after choosing /Graph X. The words in the X range are placed along the X axis, as shown in Figure 11-4. While the graph in Figure 11-4 is an automatic graph, X axis labels will appear the same whether you use them in an automatic graph or add them with the /Graph X command.

For pie charts, the X range is used to label the sections of the pie. It might list regions, expense categories, or something similar. X range data for a pie chart must be in the same sequence as the data you provide for the A range, which gives the values for the chart.

For XY charts, the X range data is plotted against corresponding Y values provided by the ranges A through F. Again, use /Graph X to specify the range of cells that contains the entries you wish to use for the X axis. For this type of chart, the entries should be values rather than labels. If an XY type is selected for an automatic graph, 1-2-3 uses the worksheet data differently. The XY graphs skip rows or columns containing labels and use the first numeric row or column as the first data range (the X axis).

If the range you select for X contains too many characters, 1-2-3 will use two rows, with half of the labels on one row and half on the next row, creating a display like the one shown here:

If the X values are too long for two rows, 1-2-3 truncates them if they are labels, or displays them as asterisks if they are values. The X axis can be made easier to read by using fewer or shorter names. Or you can use /Graph Options Scale Skip and enter a skip factor that will cause 1-2-3 to skip some of the labels in the range. A skip factor of 3 will cause every third label in the X range to be used for labeling, for example.

The Y Axis

In contrast to the X axis, the Y axis is labeled automatically once you have selected the data you wish to show on your graph. If 1-2-3 needs to represent your data values in thousands or millions to place them on the graph effectively, it will make the conversion and label the Y axis appropriately.

Selecting Data for a Graph

1-2-3 permits you to show up to six sets of data values on all graph types except the pie chart. A set of data values might represent the sales of a product for a period of months or years, or the number of rejects on a production line for each of the last 16 weeks, to give two examples. Any series of values can be used, as long as they all pertain to the same subject, and are organized according to the points labeled on the X axis. The six different sets of data values are specified for the chart in ranges A through F. To expand our two examples, they might represent sales figures for six different products, or production line rejects from six different factories.

Pie charts are special in that they show what percentage each value is of the total. They therefore would not be appropriate for multiple sets of data. With a pie chart, you use only the A range for your data values. As mentioned earlier, you use the X range to label the sections of the pie. 1-2-3 can use the B and C ranges to change the appearance of the pie "slices"—as discussed later in the chapter.

The High-Low-Close-Open (HLCO) graph is another special type of graph because it automatically decides how different ranges are treated. An HLCO graph expects a high-to-low range for each value of X. It is designed for financial applications, such as following the price of a stock. The A range is the high value for each X value; the B range is the low value for each X value. The C range is the closing value, and the D range is the opening value for the X values. The E range is graphed as a second graph below the first one. The F range is a line graph combined with the A through D ranges.

Using the example of tracking a bond price, the X range contains the dates for which you are tracking the bond price. The A range contains the highest sell values for the bond during each day; the B range contains the lowest sell values. The C range contains the closing value of the bond, and the D range contains the opening value of the bond. The E range contains the numbers of shares traded, and the F range contains the average stock price for the industry.

The A through F options on the main Graph menu represent the six possible ranges of data values to be shown on a graph. If you plan to show only one set of data values, choose A and specify the range of cells containing the numeric values you wish to have plotted on the graph. With Release 3, you have the option of including cells from other worksheets and other worksheet files. If you wish to show other sets of data in the graph, select as many of the other range letters as are appropriate, and specify the range of data you wish assigned to each. Remember that you do not have to show all your worksheet data on a graph; you can select just those data ranges that are most important. For example, you may have Sales, Cost of Goods Sold, and Profit data on your worksheet, but you may elect to graph just the Profit data.

Figure 11-7 shows the unit sales of four products for the Boston, New York, Dallas, and Chicago regions of a company. To create a graph from this data, enter **/Graph** to invoke the Graph menu, and then select Type. If you want to see the data for Product 1 as a pie chart, choose Pie. Next, select A for the first data range and specify B5..B8 as the range containing the data. You can specify this range by entering a range name, or pointing after moving to the beginning of the range and locking it in place with a period, or typing the range reference. Select X next, and specify A5..A8 as the X axis range.

Multiple Data Ranges in a Graph

A feature of Release 3 is the ability to define the data groups for multiple data ranges at once. This reduces the number of steps required to create a graph. The Group option in the Graph menu selects all the data ranges at once.

For example, assume that you want to create a line graph using the data in Figure 11-7. Enter **/Graph Group**; 1-2-3 then prompts for the range that you want to divide into data ranges for the graph. You can enter the range by typing a range address, typing a range name, or pointing to the cells. Next, 1-2-3 asks if you want to divide the data for the graph according to columns or rows. For the data in Figure 11-7, you can select A5..E8 as the range and divide it by columns. This makes A5..A8 the X range, B5..B8 the A range, C5..C8 the B range, D5..D8 the C range, and E5..E8 the D range. The city names will be placed along the X axis. The sales for each product are thus assigned to different data ranges in the line graph.

An alternative approach would be to select B4..E4 as the range and divide it by rows. This makes B4..E4 the X range, B5..E5 the A range, B6..E6 the B range, B7..E7 the C range, and B8..E8 the D range. In this case, the product names are

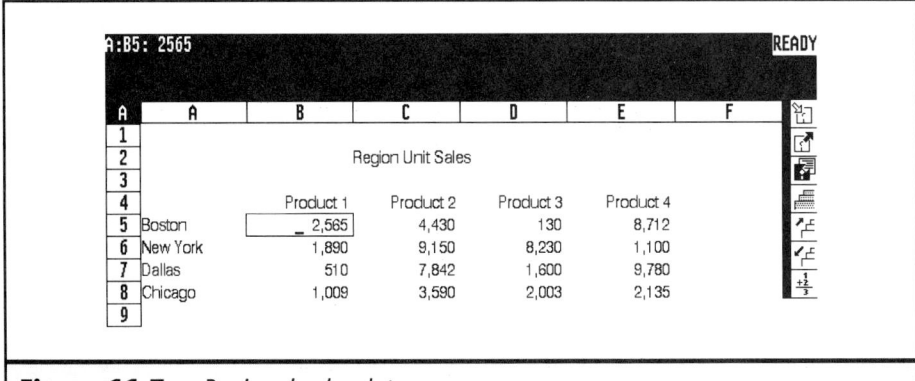

Figure 11-7. *Regional sales data*

placed along the X axis, and the sales for each city are plotted as different ranges in the line graph.

Enhancing the Basic Graph Type

While Release 3 has only seven basic graph types, there are many enhancements that make it seem as though you have more. Some of the changes you can make to the basic graph types are: rotating the axes, stacking data ranges, adding a second Y axis, controlling the graph's frame, adding a three-dimensional effect, adding a data table, adding a drop-shadow to the graph's frame, and displaying the data ranges as a percentage of the total. These features are available through the Graph Type Features menu, which is shown here.

```
A:A1:                                                                    MENU
Vert Horiz Stacked 100% 2Y-Ranges Y-Ranges Frame Drop-Shadow 3D Table Quit
Draw the graph upright
```

Setting the Orientation of the Axes

All the graphs, except pie charts, start with the X axis on the bottom of the graph and the Y axis on the left side of the graph. You can switch these two axes and make the Y axis horizontal and the X axis vertical. To rotate the axes, select Horiz (Horizontal in Releases 3.0 and 3.1) from the Graph Type Features menu. Figure 11-8 shows a graph without the axes rotated. After rotation, the appearance and emphasis of the graph is quite different, as shown in Figure 11-9. If you decide you want the X axis on the bottom of the graph again, use the /Graph Type Features Vert (Vertical in Releases 3.0 and 3.1) command.

Stacking the Data Ranges

The Stacked bar graph type option creates a graph with the values placed on top of each other, instead of next to each other, or in the same area like in a line graph. Previous releases of 1-2-3 supported stacked bar graphs, but with Release 3 you can also stack the values for the other graph types. When the Stacked option is selected, 1-2-3 prompts for a Yes or No selection. If you select Yes, 1-2-3 stacks the data range values for bar, line, mixed, and XY graphs. To discontinue stacking, enter **/Graph Type Features Stacked** and select No.

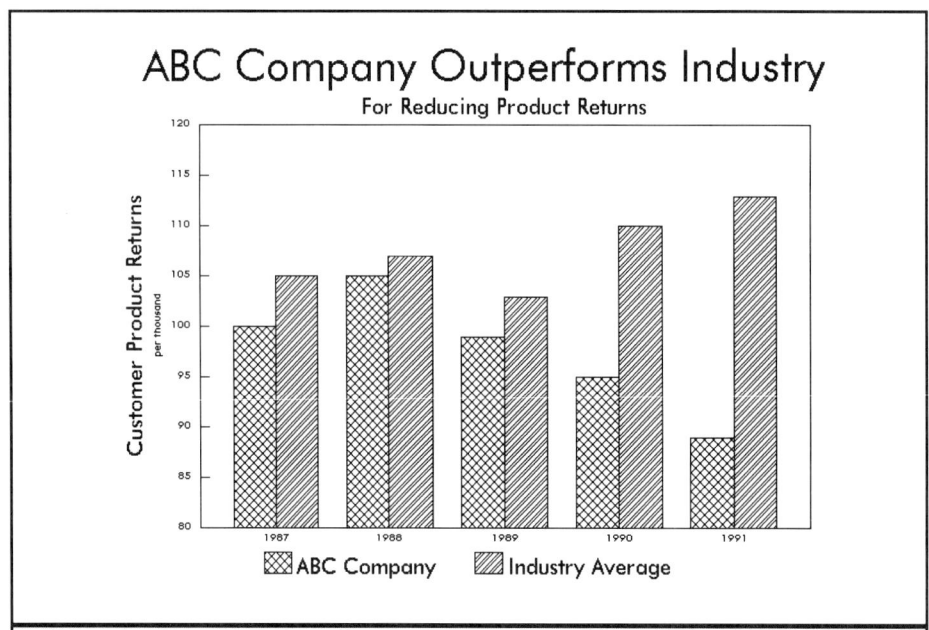

Figure 11-8. *Vertical graph*

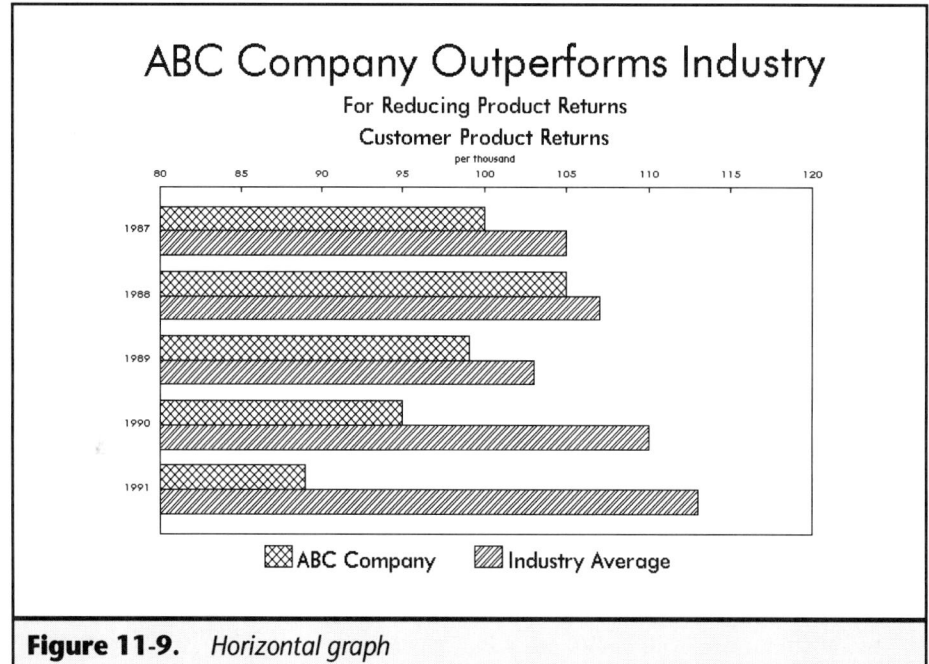

Figure 11-9. *Horizontal graph*

Figure 11-10 shows a line graph with stacked values. 1-2-3 first graphs the A data range, and then the B data range. The value of the B data range determines the distance between the A data range and the B data range.

Displaying Data Ranges As Percentages

In releases of 1-2-3 prior to Release 3, if you wanted to graph the data values as a percentage of the whole, you had to first create a table in the worksheet to compute the percentage for each value, for example, as shown in Figure 11-11. With Release 3, you can display data values as percentages of the total value, without this extra work.

To use this special display for a bar, line, mixed, stacked bar, or XY graph, select 100% from the Graph Type Features menu. When this option is selected, 1-2-3 prompts for a Yes or No selection. If you select Yes, 1-2-3 displays the data values as the percentage of their total value; the Y scale shows the percentages. Figure 11-12 shows a 100% bar graph.

If you create this same graph in Release 2, you must use the data in the range B11..E15 from Figure 11-11. With the 100% feature, you can use the data in the B4..E8 range, saving the time required for the additional computation and the worksheet space for other entries.

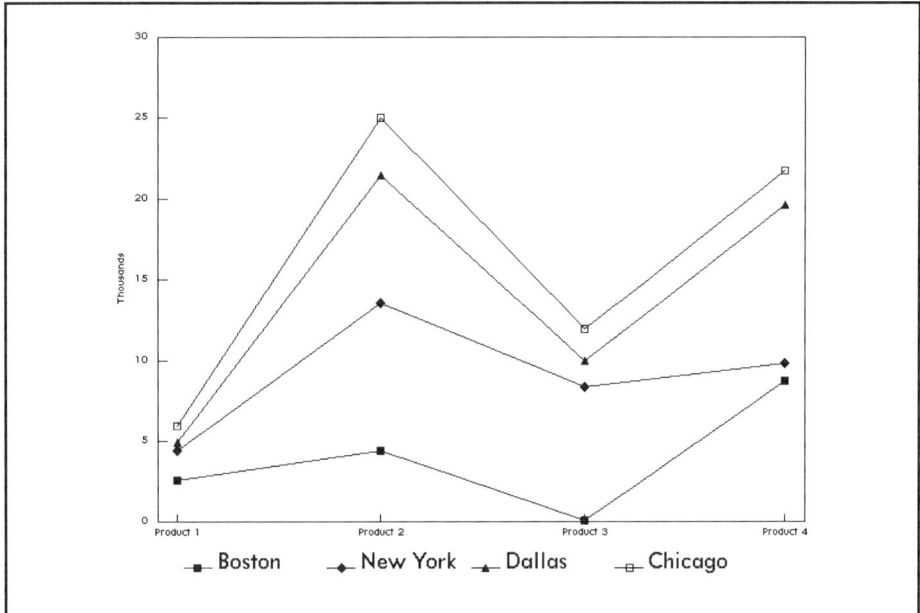

Figure 11-10. *Stacked data ranges on a line graph*

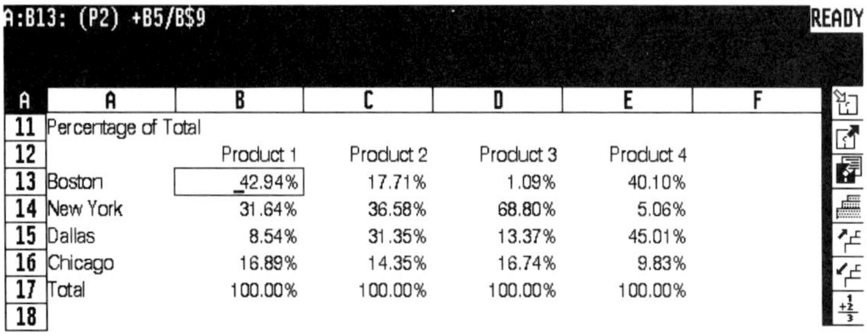

```
A:B13: (P2) +B5/B$9                                            READY

     A         A         B         C         D         E        F
 11  Percentage of Total
 12                   Product 1  Product 2  Product 3  Product 4
 13  Boston            42.94%    17.71%     1.09%     40.10%
 14  New York          31.64%    36.58%    68.80%      5.06%
 15  Dallas             8.54%    31.35%    13.37%     45.01%
 16  Chicago           16.89%    14.35%    16.74%      9.83%
 17  Total            100.00%   100.00%   100.00%    100.00%
 18
```

Figure 11-11.   *Worksheet for 100% graph*

To return to the default setting of not showing the data in percentages, enter **/Graph Type Features 100%** and select No.

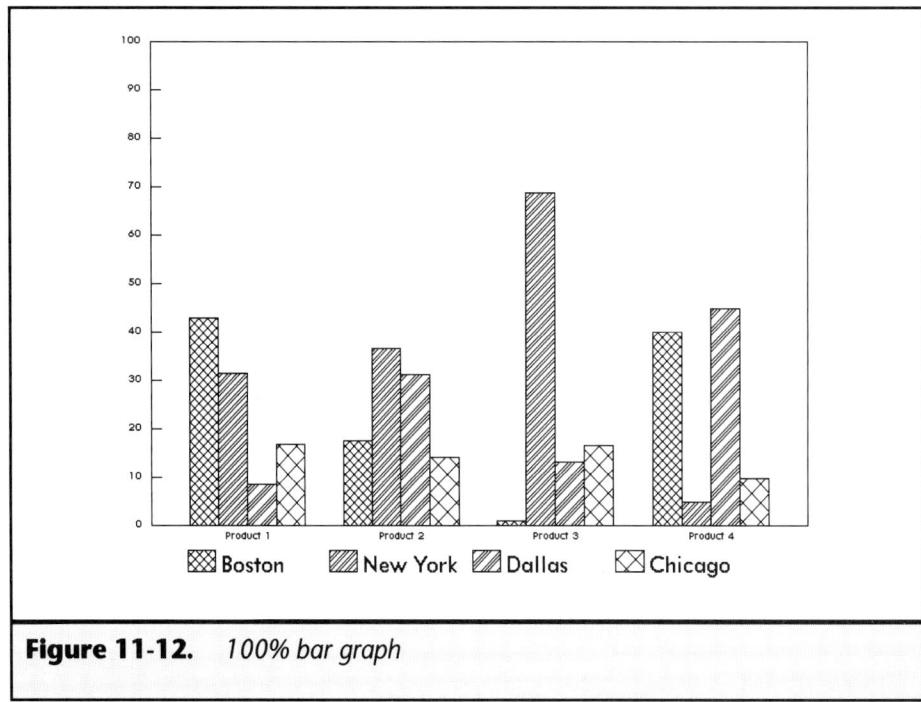

Figure 11-12.   *100% bar graph*

Using Two Y Axes

Initially, a graph uses a single Y range. However if you are graphing different types of data together, one Y axis may not allow you to combine the data on one graph. You may want to include two axes—one for each measurement. Creating a second Y axis is as simple as assigning data ranges to the second axis, since 1-2-3 automatically creates the second axis when you assign data ranges to it.

To assign data to the second axis, select 2Y-Ranges under the Features option. 1-2-3 will prompt you for the graph ranges to assign to the second axis. Point to the range letter and press ENTER, or type the range letter to be assigned to the second Y axis. You can continue assigning ranges to the second Y axis, select the 2Y-Ranges Graph option to assign all ranges to the second Y axis, or select Quit to return to the Graph Type Features menu. If you then decide to reassign a range to the first Y axis, select Y-Ranges and execute the same steps that you would execute with the 2Y-Ranges selection. If a graph does not have any ranges assigned to the second axis, the second axis does not appear.

Figure 11-13 shows a mixed graph with two axes. A mixed graph frequently uses one Y axis for the bar graph values and the other Y axis for the line graph values. The HLCO graph automatically assigns the E range to the second Y axis.

If you rotate the X and Y axes for a graph that has two Y axes, 1-2-3 puts the first Y axis on top and the second Y axis on bottom. For example, if you rotate the

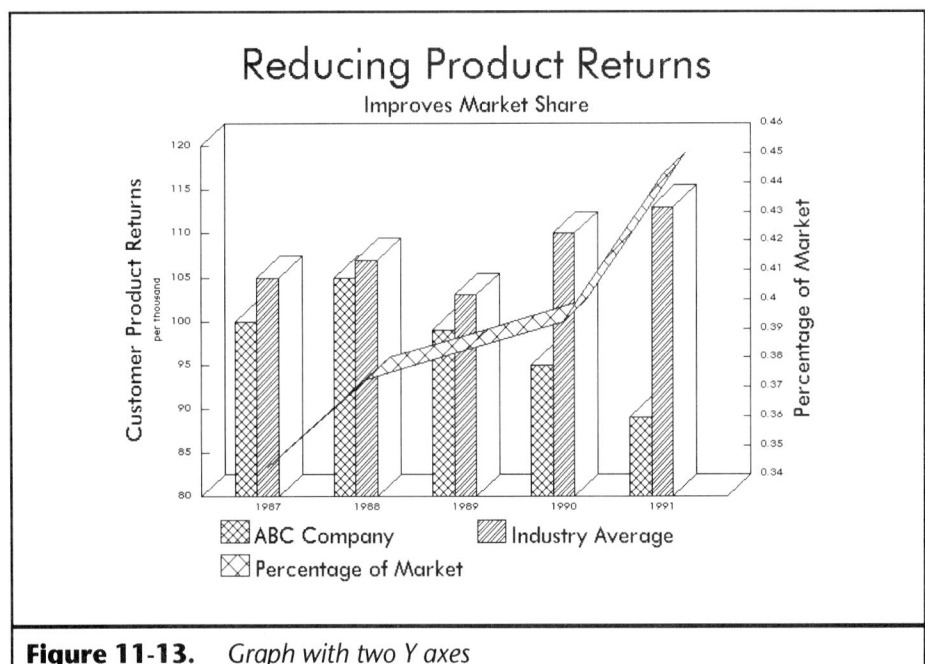

Figure 11-13. *Graph with two Y axes*

axis in the graph in Figure 11-13, the top axis will dislay thousands and the bottom axis will display percentages.

Changing the Appearance of Graph Elements

Two graphics features new to 1-2-3 Release 3.4 allow you to radically alter the appearance of graphs by lending a 3D look to them. The 3D option affects bar graphs by making them into three-dimensional graphs. The Drop-Shadow option adds drop-shadows to elements of the graph, turning line graphs into ribbons, and giving pie charts a three-dimensional appearance.

To add drop-shadows to graph elements such as lines, bars, and pies, select Drop-Shadow, and then Yes. Figure 11-14 shows the line graph of Figure 11-10 with the drop-shadow effect. This option can be used to give this three-dimensional appearance to any type of graph except the HLCO graph.

The 3D option changes only bar graphs. When you use the Drop-Shadow option with bar graphs, the bars are given the drop-shadow as shown in Figure 11-15. When you use the 3D effect, the bars are arranged in a three-dimensional fashion, as shown in Figure 11-16.

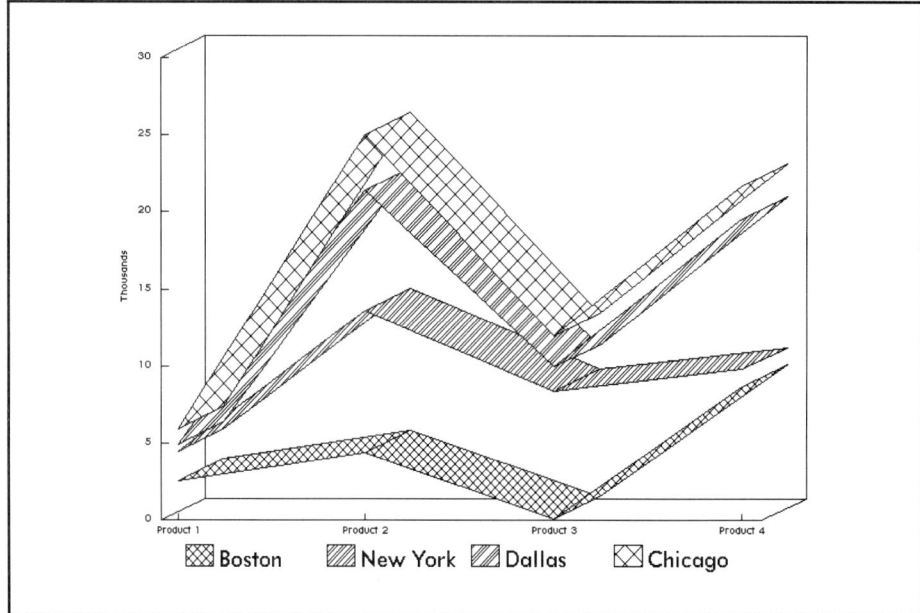

Figure 11-14. *Stacked data ranges on a line graph with drop-shadow*

Chapter 11: Working with 1-2-3's Graphics Features 633

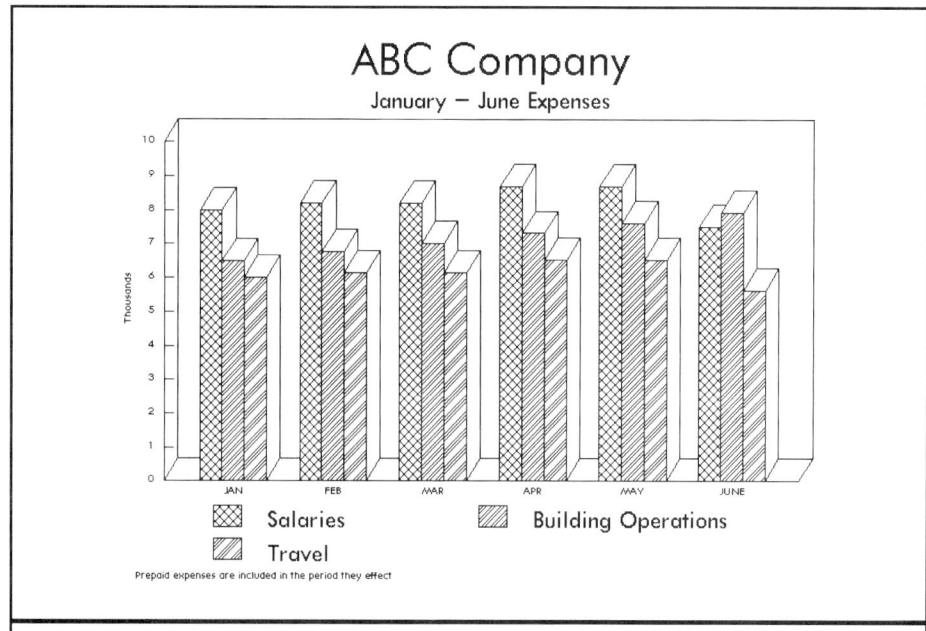

Figure 11-15. *Bar graph with drop-shadow*

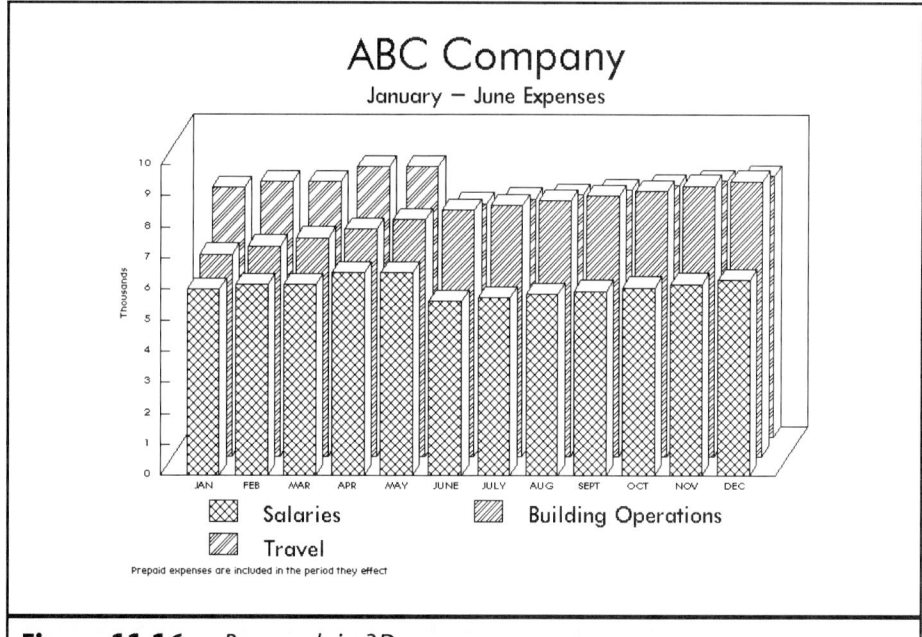

Figure 11-16. *Bar graph in 3D*

TIP: You may find it necessary, when creating a bar graph using the 3D feature, to reorder the data ranges so that a range with smaller numbers does not disappear behind ranges with larger numbers. In Figure 11-16, you can see that the order of the ranges has been reversed for this reason.

Adding a Data Table

With 1-2-3 Release 3.4, you can add a data table below the graphs you create. The data table displays the actual numbers used to create the graph. This feature can be used to create a concise presentation of the information you have graphed, especially when the graph is presenting many pieces of information. Figure 11-17 shows a data table added to a graph.

Changing the Frame's Appearance

A graphics feature new to 1-2-3 Release 3.4 gives you the ability to control the frame, which is the line that appears around the outside of the graph area. There

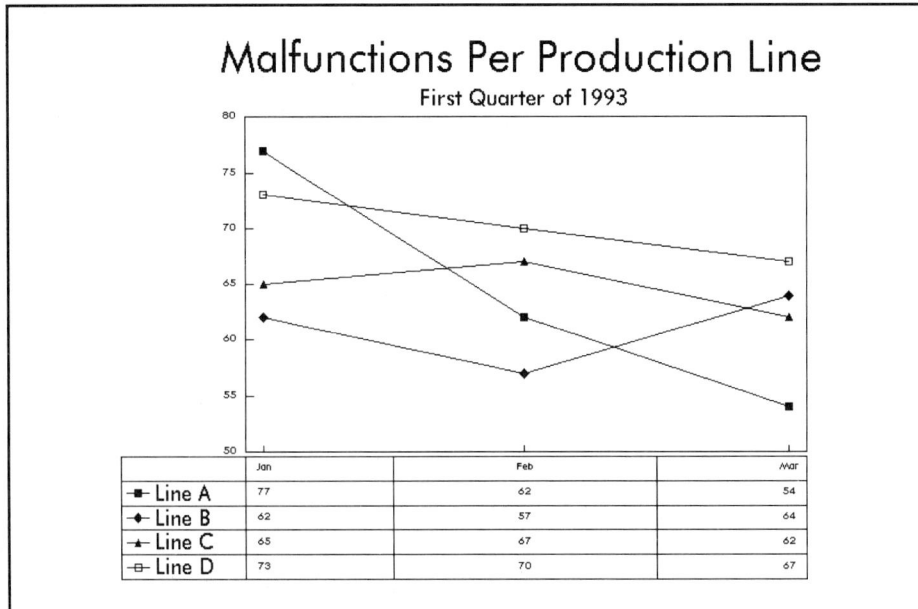

Figure 11-17.   *Line graph with data table*

is no frame with pie charts. When you select Frame from the /Graph Type Features menu, you see this menu:

From this menu you can choose to display all, some, or none of the sides of the frame. Select Quit to exit this menu.

Using the QuickGraph Icon

With Release 3.4 of 1-2-3, you have access to a second shortcut for creating graphs. By using the QuickGraph icon from the SmartIcons icon palette, you can speed up the process of creating graphs with only simple enhancements.

Before selecting the QuickGraph icon, you should select the range cells that contain the data and the X-axis labels that you want to use in the graph. After selecting this range, select the QuickGraph icon from the SmartIcons palette. You can select this icon by clicking on it with the mouse, or by pressing CTRL-F10 and moving to the icon using the arrow keys before pressing ENTER.

When you select the QuickGraph icon, the QuickGraph dialog box opens as in Figure 11-18. From this dialog box, you can select the graph type, whether the data series are in rows or columns, the orientation of the chart, and whether you are using colors and 3D effects.

To select the type of graph, select one of the option buttons under Type in the QuickGraph dialog box. To choose whether the data ranges are in rows or columns on the spreadsheet, select one of the option buttons under Data Ranges in in the dialog box. Select Vertical or Horizontal under Orientation to set the orientation of the graph.

If you would like to have 3D effects with your graph, select the 3D-effect on check box. If you would like to use colors instead of hatch marks to indicate the separate data series, select the Colors on check box.

When you are finished selecting the settings for your graph, select the OK button or press ENTER. 1-2-3 shows you the current graph for the worksheet. Using the QuickGraph features is easier than using the 1-2-3 Graph menu

```
             ┌──── QuickGraph Settings ────┐
             │                              │
             │  Type            Data ranges in
             │  (*) Line        (*) Columns
             │  ( ) XY          ( ) Rows
             │  ( ) Bar
             │  ( ) Stacked bar Orientation
             │  ( ) Pie         (*) Vertical
             │  ( ) HLCO        ( ) Horizontal
             │  ( ) Mixed
             │  ( ) Area        [ ] 3D-effect on
             │                  [ ] Colors on
             │
             │              »  OK  «   Cancel
```

Figure 11-18.   *QuickGraph dialog box*

commands. Use the QuickGraph to get graphs that you want to be able to review quickly, and save 1-2-3's Graph commands for custom graphs.

Enhancing the Basic Display

Once you are sure that your data can be shown effectively with the graph type you selected, you will most likely want to make some changes to improve its appearance. 1-2-3 offers plenty of enhancement options, from colors and hatch patterns, to exploding a pie chart, to adding titles and legends on any type of graph. Most of the commands needed to produce graph enhancements are shown on the Graph Options menu, which follows; others are options on the main Graph menu.

```
A:A1: 'Jan                                                        MENU
Legend Format Titles Grid Scale Color B&W Data-Labels Advanced Quit
Create data-range legends
```

Pie Chart Options

Normally the B graph data range is used to specify a second set of data for your graph. With a pie chart, however, the B range can be used to specify the color or hatch pattern for the individual pieces of the pie. The B range offers code numbers from 1 through 14 representing different colors or hatch patterns. For example, Figure 11-19 shows the hatch patterns 1-2-3 uses for each of the 14 hatch pattern values. These hatch patterns are useful for a monochrome display, and for printing to a printer that cannot print colors. The same numbers (1 through 14) represent available colors when 1-2-3 can display or print the graph in color.

In a pie chart, the B data range assumes a special function, in addition to determining color or hatch mark patterns: it can also be used to explode or hide a section from the pie. Any pie slice can be exploded by adding 100 to the color or hatch pattern code number for the slice. A pie segment can be hidden by designating a negative, instead of a positive hatch or color pattern number.

Figure 11-20 shows the same data found in Figure 11-7, except that an extra column is added for the hatch pattern codes to be specified as the B data range. These codes are stored in F5 through F8; each set of data values to be shown in the pie chart has a hatch pattern code. When the B range is selected and F5..F8 is used as the range, the pie chart will change the hatch patterns it uses, as you would see if you chose View again.

Figure 11-21 shows the pie chart exactly as it would appear in your display after the addition of these hatch pattern codes. Notice that the section for Dallas is pulled away from the center, or exploded; this is accomplished by using 103 for the B range value for this pie slice. Also, the segment for Chicago does not appear; it is hidden by using a negative number for the B range value.

Pie chart segments can also be displayed without their percentage values, using the C data range. To hide a percentage for any slice, put a zero in that segment's C range cell. Leave the other cells in the C range blank. For example,

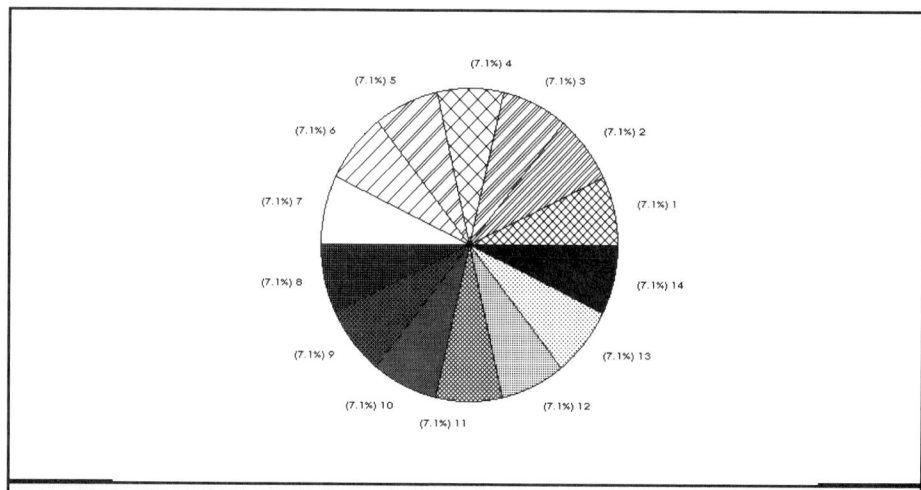

Figure 11-19.   *The 14 hatch mark patterns*

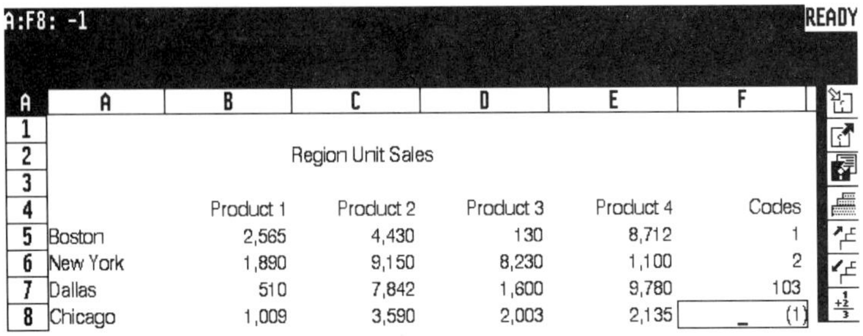

```
A:F8: -1                                                      READY

    A         B          C          D          E          F
1
2                     Region Unit Sales
3
4              Product 1   Product 2   Product 3   Product 4   Codes
5  Boston         2,565       4,430         130       8,712        1
6  New York       1,890       9,150       8,230       1,100        2
7  Dallas           510       7,842       1,600       9,780      103
8  Chicago        1,009       3,590       2,003       2,135       (1)
```

Figure 11-20.   Hatch mark pattern codes added in column F

using the data in Figure 11-20 and the graph in Figure 11-21, define a C range as G5..G8 and put a 0 in G5. Leave G6 through G8 blank. When 1-2-3 displays the graph, the percentage for Boston will not appear.

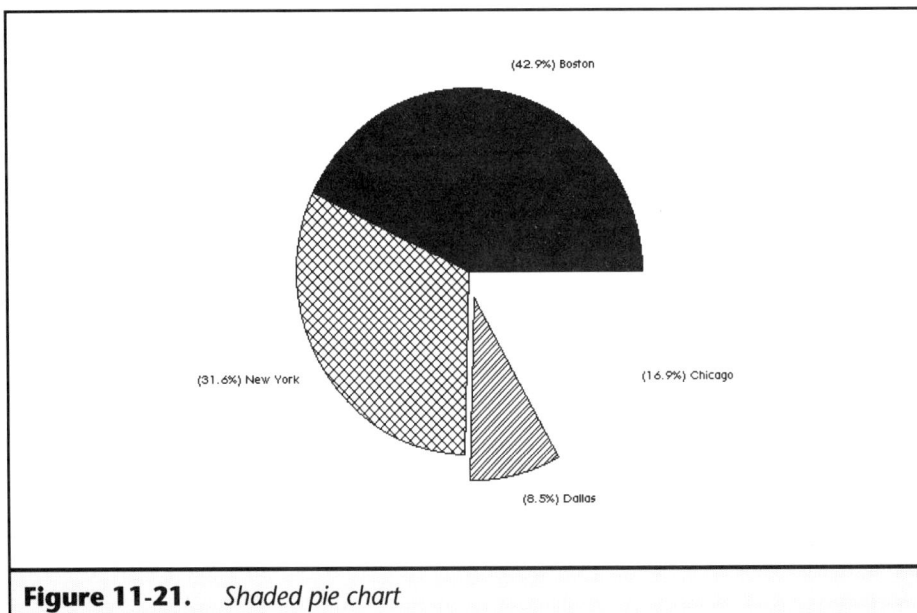

Figure 11-21.   Shaded pie chart

Selecting Colors for Graph Ranges

If your monitor can display graphs in color, or if your printer can print colors, you may want to select the colors 1-2-3 uses for the data ranges for all graph types.

To select the color for a data range, use the /Graph Options Advanced Colors command. When 1-2-3 prompts you for the data range that you want to select the colors for, select a range from A through F. Then, for each range, select a color from 1 to 8 or select Hide, or Range. If you select a number 1 through 8, 1-2-3 will display the range using that color. If you select Range, 1-2-3 prompts you to supply a predefined range containing color codes 1 through 14 for each of the graph data values just like F5..F8 in Figure 11-20, although negative numbers and adding 100 to the code has no effect. Selecting Range selects a color for each value in a range. Selecting Hide hides the data range in the graph, just like using a negative number in the Range of hatch marks.

The color associated with each color value depends on your monitor. The color the graph prints depends on your printer or plotter. If you are using a plotter, the actual colors depend on the pens in the plotter. If your printer cannot print colors, changing the color 1-2-3 uses when displaying the ranges has no effect on how the printer prints the graph.

Once you select a color or a color range, 1-2-3 returns to the menu, and you can select another data range for color customization. You may want to change a data range's color to make it appear different from the surrounding data ranges. You can assign different colors to a data range's values when you want to emphasize the values of a particular data range. To return to the previous menu, select Quit. The /Graph Options Advanced Colors command only selects colors for pie slices (the A range) when a B range is *not* selected.

Selecting Hatch Patterns for Graph Ranges

1-2-3 can also differentiate the appearance of graph data ranges using hatch patterns. Hatch patterns are line patterns 1-2-3 uses for pie slices, bars, and areas. 1-2-3 has fourteen different hatch patterns that are shown in Figure 11-19. 1-2-3 can select the hatch patterns for you, or you can select them using the /Graph Options Advanced Hatches command.

To select the hatch patterns for a data range, use the /Graph Options Advanced Hatches command. 1-2-3 prompts you for the data range for which you want to select the hatch pattern; select a range from A through F. Then, for each range, select a hatch pattern from 1 to 8 or select Range. When each hatch pattern number (1 through 8) is highlighted, 1-2-3 describes the selection on the following line. Select a number, and 1-2-3 will display the range using the corresponding hatch pattern.

Choose Range to select a hatch pattern for each value in a range. 1-2-3 will prompt you to supply a predefined range containing hatch pattern codes 1 through 14 for each of the graph data values. Figure 11-20 shows a range of codes that you can use, although negative numbers and adding 100 to a code has no effect for other graph types. (You can use the same range for both hatch pattern and color codes.) The graph will display and print using the same hatch pattern. If you are using a color monitor and displaying the graph in color, selecting hatch patterns displays the hatch patterns in color.

Once you select a hatch pattern or a hatch pattern code range, 1-2-3 returns to the menu. You may then select another data range. You may customize a data range's hatch pattern to make it appear different from the surrounding data ranges. You can assign different hatch patterns to a data range's values, to emphasize each one. The /Graph Options Advanced Hatches command can select the hatch patterns for pie slices (the A range) when you want to combine colors with hatch patterns, or if a B range is *not* selected for a monochrome display. To return to the previous menu, select Quit.

Adding Descriptive Labels

Figure 11-22 shows a bar graph created by selecting Bar from the Graph Type menu. This graph has been enhanced with titles at the top, values along the Y axis, X axis data labels, legends, and a note at the bottom. Adding this type of extra description to a chart makes it convey your message more effectively. Additional text options let you select the color, font, and size of the text.

The data used to create this graph is shown in Figure 11-23. Of the data in the worksheet, only Salaries, Building Operations, and Travel are selected to be shown. This was done by assigning the numeric values for January through June to the A, B, and C data ranges, respectively. The months are assigned to the X range. You can select all of the ranges at once by entering the /Graph Group command, selecting D4..I7 as the range, and selecting Rowwise to divide D4..I7 into graph data ranges according to rows.

Adding Legends

A legend provides a description for each of the ranges shown on a graph. (You saw an example in Figure 11-22.) If you create a line graph with symbols marking the data points in the range, the legend defines these symbols at the bottom of your chart. If you create a graph with hatch patterns, the legend defines each hatch pattern by placing a small box filled with the hatch pattern at the bottom of the chart, and adding a description next to the box.

Chapter 11: Working with 1-2-3's Graphics Features

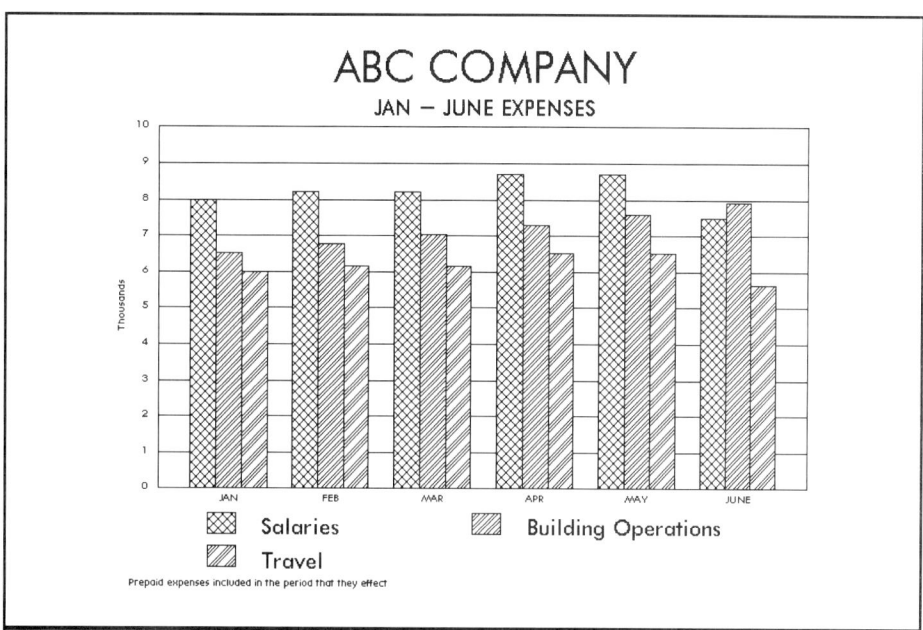

Figure 11-22. Bar graph with titles, legends, and horizontal grid lines added

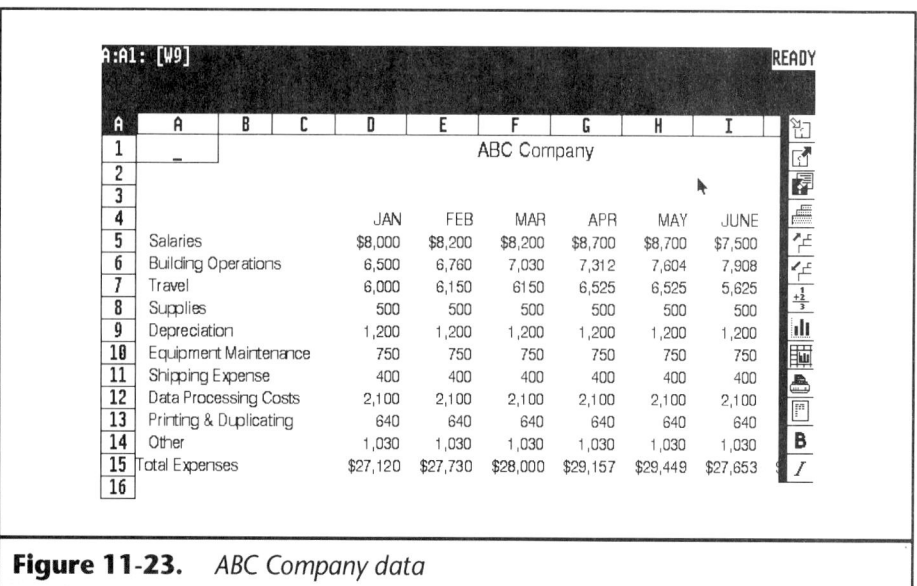

Figure 11-23. ABC Company data

Legends are added using the /Graph Options Legend command, which lets you select from A through F for the data ranges or Range to assign the legend for multiple ranges. Enter the letter corresponding to the data range for which you want to specify a legend. Or select Range if the text that you want for all of the legends is predefined in a range in the worksheet.

When you enter a range letter, 1-2-3 prompts you for the legend description to be stored for that data range. The legends used for Figure 11-22 were Salaries, Building Operations, and Travel for the A, B, and C ranges, respectively. If the legend you wish to use appears in a worksheet cell, you have an alternative entry method. Rather than typing the legend at the prompt, you can enter a backslash (\) and the address of the cell containing the legend data. For example, entering **\A5** tells 1-2-3 to use the text in cell A5 as the legend. While 1-2-3 does not limit the number of characters you can enter for a legend, the legend text that appears in the graph is limited by the amount of space used for the other legends.

If you select Range, 1-2-3 prompts you for the worksheet range containing the predefined legends. You can enter this range by typing a range address or name, or by pointing to the cells you want to use. For example, for the legends in Figure 11-22, you could have selected Range and entered A5..A7. 1-2-3 assigns the first cell as the A range legend, the second cell as the B range legend, and so on, until it runs out of cells or graph data ranges.

You can also add legends to pie charts, to label the first six slices. To label pie slices, select Legend Range and enter the range address containing the predefined legends for the pie slices. 1-2-3 assigns the first cell in the legend range to the first slice, and continues assigning cell contents to pie slices until it uses all the cells in the legend range, or the sixth pie slice is assigned a legend, or the last pie slice is assigned a legend.

TIP: Combine pie slice legends with hatch patterns. If you want to group pie slices in a pie chart, assign the same hatch pattern to each group. Also, have one slice of each group in the beginning of the data range. Then assign legends describing the group to the first pie slice of each group. The resulting graph will show each group with the same hatch pattern and the legend identifying the group. Each slice is still individually labeled using the X range labels.

Adding Titles

1-2-3 has seven title options, all accessible through the /Graph Options Titles command. Titles appear at the top of the chart, or along the X, Y, or second Y axis. Notes appear at the bottom of the graph.

The first title appears at the top of the graph. For example, the first line title of the graph in Figure 11-22 was generated by entering **/Graph Options Titles First**, and then **ABC COMPANY**. (If this label were already somewhere in your worksheet, you could enter a backslash (\) and a reference to the cell containing the label.)

A line for a second label is also reserved at the top of the graph. To place an entry in this location, enter **/Graph Options Titles Second**. The entry JAN—JUNE EXPENSES was typed at the prompt for the second line title in our example. This second title can also be supplied from the worksheet, with a backslash (\) and a reference to the cell address. Either method lets you enter a title up to 512 characters long, although the number of characters that are displayed and printed depends on the monitor's resolution and on the printer.

Titles can also be given to the X or Y axis. These labels normally describe the quantities being measured. The Y axis title might be Dollars and the X axis title might be Sales, for example. If you enter a value for the Y axis title, it is placed vertically on the graph to the left of the Y axis. An X axis title is placed horizontally below the X axis. A graph containing a second Y axis can also have a label on the second Y axis; enter **/Graph Options Titles 2Y-Axis** and the label text, or a backslash and a reference to a cell containing the label.

Release 3 allows you to add two lines of note text at the bottom of the graph. You can use these two lines to identify the data source or to add descriptions about what the data represents. For example, the note at the bottom of the example in Figure 11-22 is added by entering **/Graph Options Titles Note** and then the text for the note. A second line can be added with **Titles Other-Note**. If suitable text for a note is already in your worksheet, you can enter a backslash (\) and a reference to the cell containing the text.

Changing the Text Characteristics

Options in Release 3 let you select the color, font, and size of the text in a graph by using the /Graph Options Advanced Text command.

1-2-3 divides the text of a graph into three groups. The first text group includes the first title. The second group includes the second title, axes titles, and legend text. The third group includes the scale indicators, axes labels, data labels, and footnotes. The /Graph Options Advanced Text command can set the characteristics for any of these three groups. When this command is executed, 1-2-3 prompts you to specify the text group you want to change. Then it prompts for the text characteristic that you want to change. When you have set the text group's characteristics, select Quit to return to the previous menu.

SELECTING A FONT You can choose a particular font for a text group. The various fonts have characters with different sizes, shapes, and thicknesses. When you select the Font option, 1-2-3 prompts you for the font number (1 through 8) or Default, which uses the default for the text group. The default for the first text group is font 1, and the default for the second and third group is font 3. The font selections of 1 through 8 match the /Print Printer Options Other Advanced Fonts selections.

This Font option only changes how 1-2-3 *prints* the graph's text, since it always uses the same predetermined font for *displaying* the graph. 1-2-3 will only display the graph using the selected font if a utility program adds display fonts. The way the fonts print depends upon the printer.

SELECTING THE TEXT COLOR   If your monitor and printer can display and print graphs in color, you may want to experiment with the colors 1-2-3 makes available for displaying and printing graph text. You may also want to hide part of the text. The Color option either selects a color for the text group, or hides it. The color selections 1 through 8 match the /Graph Options Advanced Colors selections. The actual colors available depend on the monitor and printer. If your printer cannot print colors, changing the color option on 1-2-3 has no effect on how the printer prints the graph.

Choosing the Hide option hides the text group. This option works for both displaying and printing the graphs in color. On a monochrome printer or monitor, this command can only hide text groups.

SELECTING THE TEXT SIZE   You may wish to set the size of the text groups, for example, to enlarge some text groups so they are visible from a distance. This option selects the character size 1-2-3 uses for the text groups.

Choose this option, and 1-2-3 prompts for the character size (1 through 9) or Default, which uses the default for the text group. Since 1-2-3 only has three text sizes for displaying graphs, it displays graphs with the text sizes 1 to 3 as small-sized characters, text sizes 4 to 6 as medium-sized characters, and 7 to 9 as large-sized characters. The way the character sizes print depends on the printer and the font.

The default for the first text group is 7, the default for the second group is 4, and the default for the third group is 2. 1-2-3 automatically reduces the text size if it needs to fit more text on the graph, and then truncates text that still does not fit.

Adding Grid Lines

If you have a number of points on a graph, it may be difficult to identify the exact X and Y values for each point on the line. To make such identification easier, 1-2-3 allows you to add vertical and horizontal lines that originate at the axis markers and extend upward and to the right. These lines are called *grid lines*, since using them in both directions forms a grid pattern across your graph.

The menu for Grid is obtained by entering **/Graph Options Grid**. The Grid options can be used with all graph types except the pie chart, since grid lines across a pie chart would detract from your ability to interpret the graph. The

Grid menu contains five options. Choose Horizontal to add horizontal lines across the graph. This is especially effective for bar graphs, since it enables you to more accurately interpret the tops of the bars. Figure 11-22 presents a bar graph to which horizontal lines were added by entering **/Graph Options Grid Horizontal**.

Vertical bars extend upward from the X axis points. They are more effective on a line or XY graph than on a bar graph. They are added using **/Graph Options Grid Vertical**.

To add grid lines in both directions, enter **/Graph Options Grid Both**. Figure 11-24 shows a line graph with grid lines in both directions.

Since Release 3 graphs can contain two graph axes, you must specify which Y axis is to be used for grid lines when the graph uses Horizontal or Both grid line options. To select the Y axis for grid line use, enter **/Graph Options Grid Y-Axis**. 1-2-3 displays the selections Y Axis (the first Y axis), 2Y-Axis (the second Y axis), and Both.

You can remove grid lines without changing the rest of your graph, simply by entering the command sequence **/Graph Options Grid Clear**.

The grid lines start at a specific axis. If you rotate the axes, the grid lines rotate as well. For example, horizontal grid lines begin at the first or second Y axis. Rotating this graph also rotates the grid lines, so they will appear as vertical lines starting from the first or second Y axis.

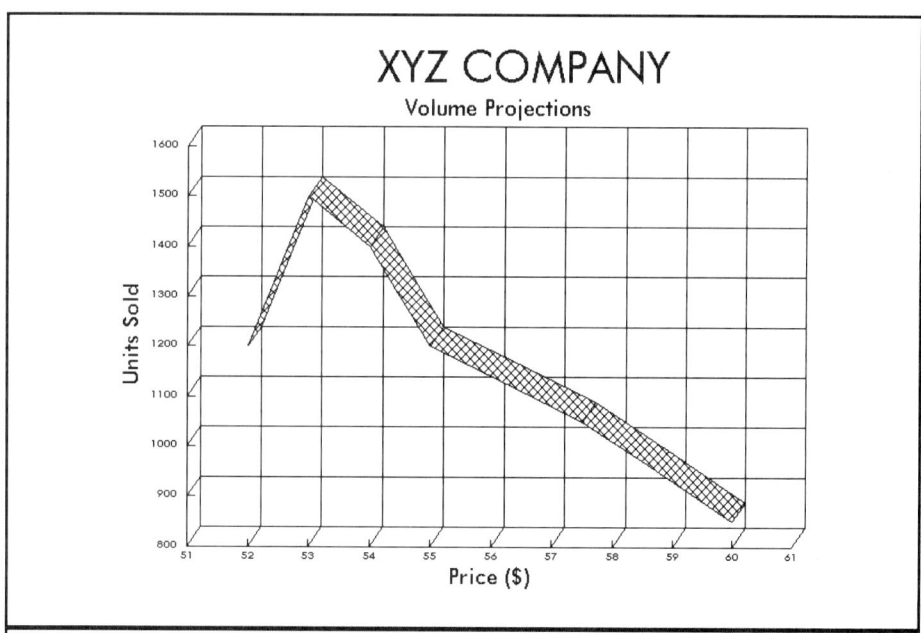

Figure 11-24. *Grid lines in both directions*

Choosing Line and Symbol Options

1-2-3 allows you to show line graphs and XY graphs in a variety of formats by using the options under /Graph Options Format. You can show the graph as a smooth line connecting the points, or as symbols marking the points with lines connecting them, or just as symbols. Or you can fill in the area between the data ranges with different hatch patterns. The options are Lines, Symbols, Both, Neither, and Area. Before you select a line and symbol option, you must first specify the range for the graph application, as either Graph (all ranges in the graph) or one of the range letters, A through F.

The first Format option, Lines, connects the points for a data range with a line. The points are not marked by symbols when this option is chosen. The Symbols option omits the line and just marks the data points with one of the six different symbols that 1-2-3 provides. The third option is Both. As the name implies, it provides both lines and symbols for your display. The last option, Neither, may seem useless, since it means that neither lines nor symbols are shown. However, it can be used with the Data-Labels option (described later in this chapter) to mark the points with actual data values. The default setting for /Graph Options Format is Both.

The Area Format option creates *area graphs.* An area graph stacks the data ranges and fills the area between the data ranges with a hatch pattern. Figure 11-25 shows an area graph.

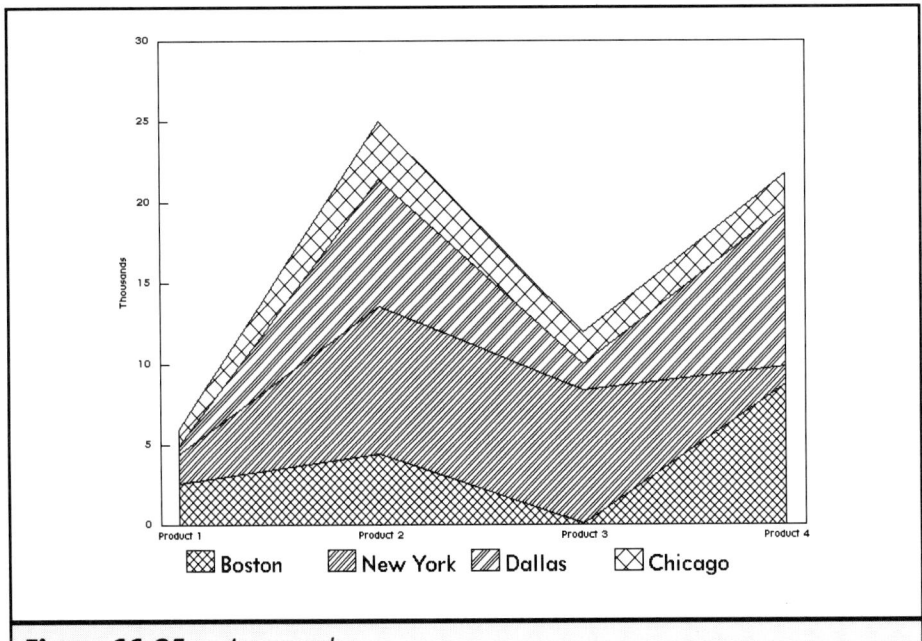

Figure 11-25.   *Area graph*

Choosing Color or Black and White

If you have a color monitor, 1-2-3 automatically displays the graphs in color. If you have a monochrome monitor, 1-2-3 automatically displays the graph in monochrome. You can change the way 1-2-3 displays your graph with /Graph Options Color and /Graph Options B&W.

Unlike previous releases of 1-2-3, with Release 3 you do not have to change a color graph display to B&W in order to print the graph using a printer that cannot print colors. 1-2-3 automatically translates color graphs to monochrome graphs so it can print them using a single color (black). You will want to change the display to color if you are using a monochrome monitor but are printing on a printer that can print colors. Since you cannot view a color graph on a monochrome screen, wait to change the graph display until after you have finished viewing the graph and are ready to print it.

The colors 1-2-3 uses depends on the monitor selected during the Install program. For example, if you are using a Color Graphic Adapter screen, 1-2-3 uses three colors. If you are using an Enhanced Graphic Adapter, 1-2-3 uses 16 colors.

Selecting Scaling Options

1-2-3's scaling options let you override the scaling selections that 1-2-3 makes when constructing a graph. You always have the option of letting 1-2-3 make the decisions, and you will seldom need to use the Scale option to improve upon the selections made by 1-2-3. You can use this command to change the scaling for the X, first Y, or second Y axis, or to specify a skip factor for X-axis data labels. The selections made for the X axis only affect XY graphs. /Graph Options Scale Skip was discussed earlier in this chapter in the section called "Labeling the X Axis."

Specify the scale to be changed by choosing /Graph Options Scale X-Axis, /Graph Options Scale Y-Axis, or /Graph Options Scale 2Y-Axis. The menu presented for any of these selections looks like this:

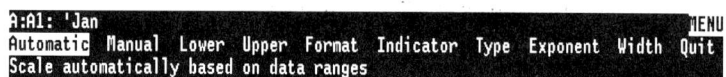

The Automatic option is the default setting. It is also the method for returning to automatic scaling after requesting Manual. 1-2-3 remembers the settings you have made for a manual axis in case you decide to switch to a manual axis later.

Manual permits you to decide what the upper and lower limits of your scale will be. If you choose this option, plan also to choose Upper and Lower to define the limits of your scale. With a manual setting, 1-2-3 does not display values outside the established limits. In a bar or stacked bar graph, 1-2-3 displays a bar stretching the height of the graph for values over the established limits and an empty space for values under the established limits. In a line graph, the line connecting the points discontinues at the top or bottom of the graph to indicate values outside the established limits.

The Format option on the Scale menu allows you to use any of the numeric formats on the scale markers for the X and Y axis. You can format the numbers as Currency, Percent, or any of the other formats acceptable for the /Range Format command covered in Chapter 4.

The Indicator option permits you to turn off the label indicator that specifies size, or create a new one. As an example, say you are showing sales in thousands of dollars, and 1-2-3 generates the label "Thousands" for use along the Y axis. If you do not wish this to appear, request Indicator None. If you want to use a different indicator, select Manual and enter the label you want as an indicator. You can reference a cell's contents by typing a backslash and the cell address. Yes is the default setting for this option.

With the Type option, you can select the type of scaling 1-2-3 uses for the axes. The two choices are Standard and Logarithmic; Standard is the default. Logarithmic increases the scale by powers of 10. You may want to change the type of scaling if you want to emphasize a trend. For example, Figure 11-26 shows a graph using the standard scaling. Since the numbers grow so rapidly, it

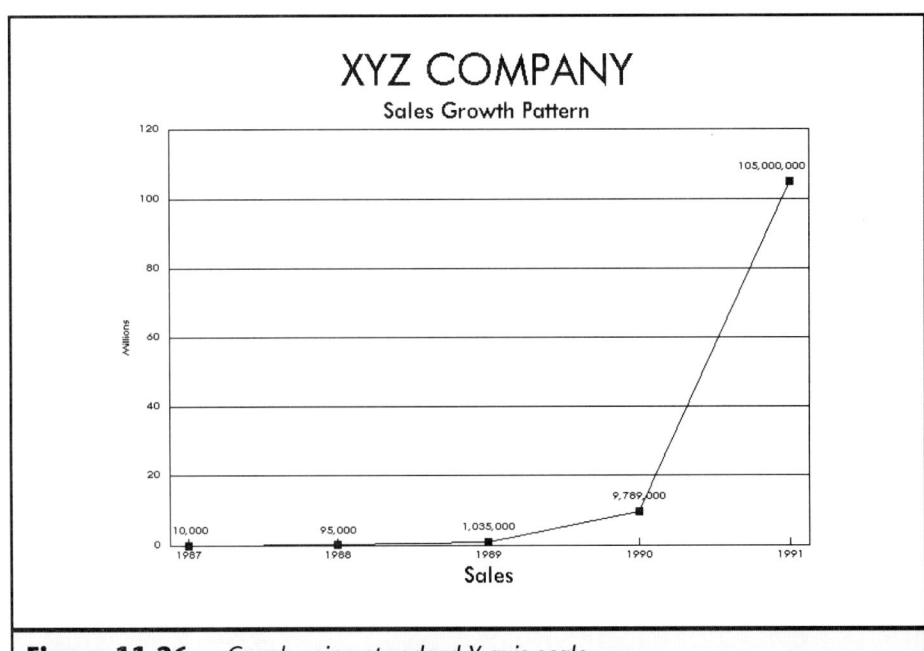

Figure 11-26.   *Graph using standard Y axis scale*

is difficult to see any trend. Figure 11-27 shows the same graph after the type of scaling is changed to logarithmic. This graph shows a more definite trend.

The Exponent option lets you set the order of magnitude for a scale. The default, Automatic, lets 1-2-3 determine if the data should be scaled by thousands, millions, or another power of 10. The other selection, Manual, allows you to select the power of 10 factor used to graph the numbers. 1-2-3 allows any integer between –95 and +95 as options for setting the order of magnitude.

The Width option permits you to set the width of the scale numbers. The default, Automatic, lets 1-2-3 determine the correct width for displaying the numbers. The other selection, Manual, lets you select the width. 1-2-3 prompts you for a number between 1 and 50 for the width. Numbers larger than the specified width appear as asterisks.

When you are finished with the Scale menu, enter **/Graph Options X-Axis** or **Y-Axis Quit**. This returns you to the Graph Options menu.

TIP: Use a manual axis scale indicator when the graph data produces an erroneous label. When a graph uses data with an order of magnitude other than 0, such as financial data listed in the thousands, you may want to change the scale indicator to reflect what the numbers actually represent. Select the Manual option for the indicator and enter an appropriate label, such as Thousands.

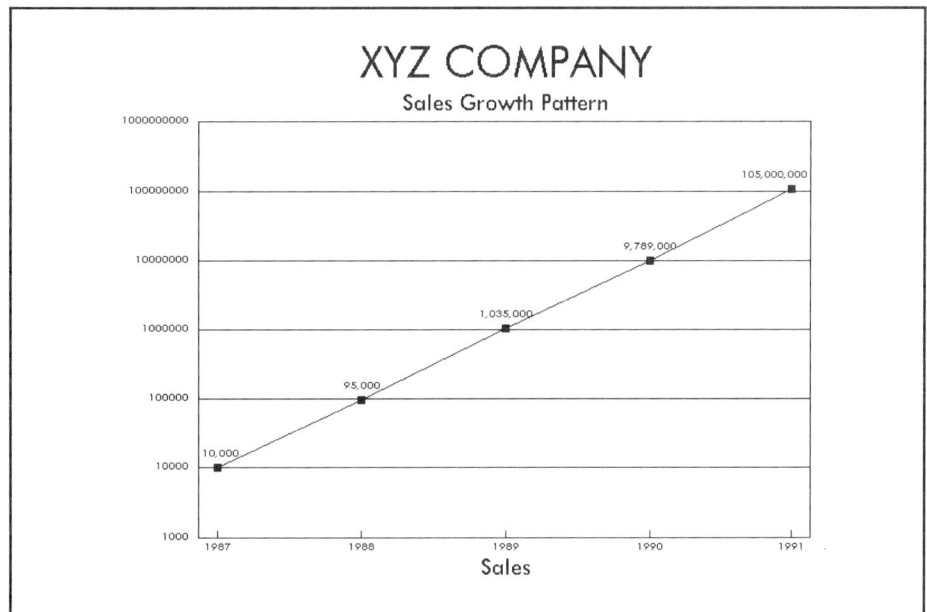

Figure 11-27. *Graph using logarithmic Y axis scale*

Using Data to Label Your Graph

You can use the contents of worksheet cells to label the points or bars in a graph. 1-2-3 lets you assign data labels to any one of the data ranges involved in your graph.

Simply choose /Graph Options Data-Labels; then enter the letter of your range choice (A through F). Or choose Group to enter the data labels for all the data ranges at once. Then 1-2-3 prompts you for a range containing the data labels. The labels range must contain as many cells as there are data points in the range or ranges to which you are assigning labels. Enter the labels range by typing the range address or the range name, or by pointing to the cells. If you are assigning data labels to multiple data ranges, you must choose whether 1-2-3 divides the cells into the data labels for each data range according to columns or rows.

After entering the range of cells containing the labels, you will need to choose the location for the data labels relative to your data points. Your options are Center, Left, Above, Right, and Below. Figures 11-26 and 11-27 present charts where labels are shown above the data points to provide a clear description of the datapoint. On bar graphs, the Center, Left, and Right selections produce the same result as Above. On stacked bar graphs, 1-2-3 puts the data inside the stacked bar regardless of the position selected.

To use data labels as the only marker on a graph, create a line graph. Then enter **/Graph Options Format Neither**, which will keep lines and symbols from being displayed. Then center the data labels at each point on the chart with **/Graph Options Data-Labels Center** to create a display like Figure 11-28.

Resetting Graph Options

After specifying particular options for a graph, you might change your mind about some of them. Individual labels can be erased by reentering the appropriate command and deleting the label from the prompt. As an example, if you wish to remove the first line title, "ABC COMPANY," enter **/Graph Options Title First** and delete the title "ABC COMPANY" from this entry. If a cell reference was used to supply the label, just delete the cell reference and backslash from the entry.

If you want to eliminate all the graph settings, however, use /Graph Reset Graph. This command eliminates all graph settings, including ranges. It lets you redefine a new graph from the beginning.

The Reset command also allows you to remove just some of the graph settings. The Graph Reset menu provides a number of options for removing particular settings. You can remove the X data range by choosing X, or any of the data ranges (A through F) by choosing the letter of the range you wish to

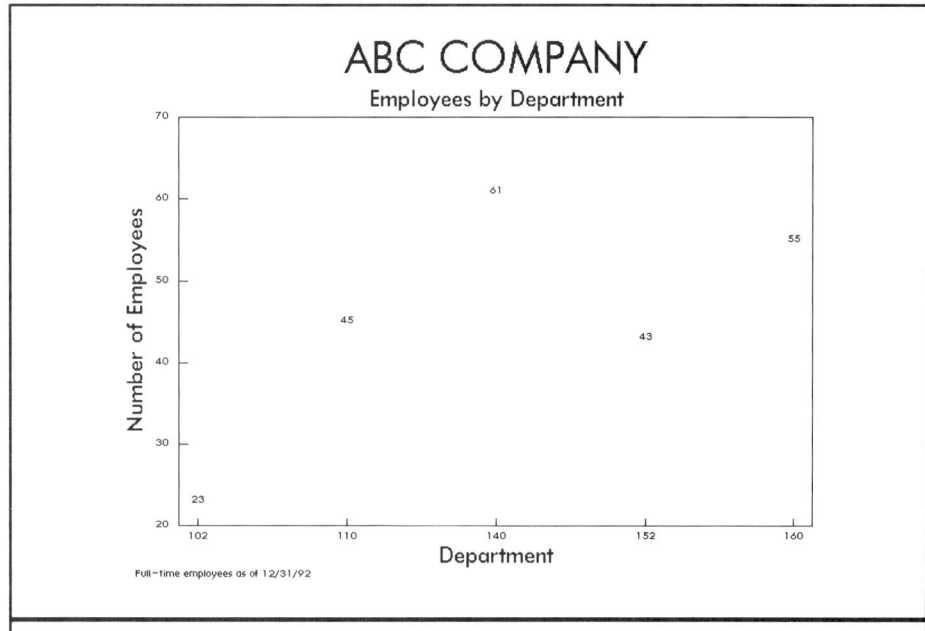

Figure 11-28. *Data labels displayed without lines or symbols*

eliminate. You can remove all of the ranges by choosing Ranges. To delete the selections made with the Graph Options menu, choose Options.

Since the Reset menu remains displayed after you make a selection (unless you select Graph), you will have to choose Quit or press ESC when you want to exit from this command.

Storing and Using Graphs

Each of the graphs created up to this point has been the current graph for the worksheet file. 1-2-3 limits the worksheet file to have only one current graph at a time. To include multiple graphs in your worksheet you must name a current graph before you create a new one. Once a graph is named, it can become the current graph at a later point. Another option for storing the graph once you create it is saving it to a file. 1-2-3 can save graphs to files that you can use with other software packages such as WordPerfect and Lotus Manuscript, or you can add the graphs to 1-2-3 worksheets with Wysiwyg.

Naming Graphs for Later Use

1-2-3 uses all the settings you enter for a graph to define the current graph. Since only one graph can be current at a time, you will lose the original settings if you start choosing different ones for a new graph. If you want to retain the definition of the current graph while you begin a new graph, first save the current one with /Graph Name Create. When 1-2-3 prompts you for the name of the graph to create, you can enter any name up to 15 characters in length. To eliminate all of the settings after saving the graph, use /Graph Reset Graph. You can then start defining a new graph, and, when the definition is complete, you can name it, too. When you save your worksheet, all the graph names and definitions will be saved along with the other data.

A graph whose settings have been saved can be used again. To use the settings of a named graph, enter **/Graph Name Use** and specify the name you assigned previously with /Graph Name Create. The settings that were current at the time the graph was saved will be activated, and 1-2-3 will display the named graph on your screen.

1-2-3's ability to name and save graphs lets you create a number of graphs in one worksheet file. You can define and name all the graphs you need for a single application. Then, when you update your worksheet figures, you can create an up-to-date slide show of graphic results by using and viewing each of the named graphs. You will not have to re-create the graphs, because their settings are saved with the worksheet.

Once you have created the graphs, you may need to list them. The /Graph Name Table command lists a worksheet's defined graphs in a table in the worksheet file. When you execute this command, 1-2-3 prompts you for a location to start the graph name table. Specify an area three columns wide, and with as many rows as the worksheet file has named graphs. The table will contain the graph names, the graph types, and the first title line, if any. Figure 11-29 shows a graph name table.

```
A:A21: [W17] 'PRODUCT_RETURNS                                        READY

     A                    B          C              D           E       F
21  PRODUCT_RETURNS     Line       Return from Product Sales
22  PRODUCT_SALES       Line       Sales by Product Line
23  REGION_SALES        Bar        Sales by Region
24  SALES               Line       Sales
25  STOCK               HLCO       Stock for Week of 11/21/92
26
```

Figure 11-29. *Table listing named graphs*

 *TIP: 1-2-3 does not keep the setting and option changes that you make to a named graph unless you save it again with the /Graph Name Create command. This command saves the named graph with the other worksheet data. To use this graph in another 1-2-3 session, save the worksheet file with /File Save.*

Deleting Graphs

The /Graph Name Delete command permits you to eliminate stored graph settings that you no longer need. When you enter this command, 1-2-3 prompts you with a list of all existing graph names. Selecting a name from the list or typing in a name causes all the settings for that graph to be eliminated. If you change your mind and wish to reproduce the graph, you must reenter all the options.

1-2-3 also provides a quick delete feature. Use it with caution, because it eliminates all saved graph names in the current file. If you do want to eliminate all the current graph names and their associated settings, enter **/Graph Name Reset**. Since 1-2-3 does not provide a confirmation step for this command, be sure you do not accidentally press **R** while working with the Graph Name menu.

 *TIP: Check the graphs in your file before you reset them. Unless Undo is enabled, you cannot recover named graphs that you have reset. If multiple files are open, observe which worksheet file is active before you execute the /Graph Name Reset command, so you do not accidentally delete the wrong file's graphs. A good habit is to list the graphs in the current worksheet file with the /Graph Name Table command before resetting them.*

Saving Graphs to an External File

The graphs created in a worksheet file are part of the worksheet file. The graphs in a worksheet file cannot be used in other programs, such as word processors. You can, however, extract a graph to an external file and use the external file in other programs. For example, once you have saved a graph to a .PIC file, you can incorporate it into a WordPerfect document.

Release 3 saves graphic images in two formats. One format is the PIC format, which stores graphs in the same format that earlier versions of 1-2-3 used. Several word processors with graphics capabilities can incorporate .PIC files into a document. Release 3 can also save the file in a Metafile format, which is used in some word processors (such as Lotus' Manuscript) to create sharper graphics images than are available in .PIC files. Metafile follows the ANSI standard for graphic images. The /Worksheet Global Default Graph command selects which format 1-2-3 uses to save graphs. When Metafile is selected, 1-2-3 saves the graphs with a .CGM file extension. When PIC is selected, 1-2-3 saves the graphs with a .PIC file extension. This command also sets the format of graph files 1-2-3 uses for the /File Erase Graph and /File List Graph commands.

Once you have selected the external graph file format, you are ready to save a file. To create a graphic image file, enter **/Graph Save**. Then provide a filename up to eight characters in length. 1-2-3 will save the current graph as a .PIC or .CGM file. If you enter an existing filename, 1-2-3 prompts you to choose between canceling the command or saving the graph over the existing file. If you want to save a graph other than the current graph, you must first make the desired graph current with /Graph Name Use.

A graph that is saved to an external file cannot be read by a worksheet file, although Wysiwyg can display the graph file in a worksheet range. Also, the external graphic image file contains the graph as it existed when you saved it. The graphic image file is not updated if you update the graph data.

Quitting the Graph Menu

The main Graph menu and several of its submenus remain on your screen until you choose the Quit option when you are finished with the menu. Your other option for quitting is to press ESC the number of times required to return to READY mode.

Printing Graphs

Release 3 lets you print your graphs directly from 1-2-3. With previous releases, you had to save the graph to a file, exit 1-2-3, and enter the PrintGraph program. With Release 3 this is not necessary; you can use the Print menus to print your graphs. You only need to learn a few new 1-2-3 commands, because the graphics features from the PrintGraph program are now set with the /Graph and /Print commands. You can also print your graphs in combination with worksheet ranges. In addition to printing directly to the printer, you can also print to an encoded file. 1-2-3 cannot print graphs to a text file.

1-2-3 must have the correct printer selected when 1-2-3 was configured. If it is not, you will need to return to Install and add the necessary drivers to the program. Appendix A provides instructions for this.

Selecting Graphs to Print

The first step in printing a graph is selecting the graph to print. You can use either the /Print Printer Image or the /Print Printer Range command.

If you only want to print a graph, use /Print Printer Image. Enter **/Print Printer Image** and indicate if you want to print the current graph or another named graph. When you select Current, 1-2-3 prints the graph that appears when you press F10 (GRAPH). When you select Named, 1-2-3 prompts you for the name of a graph to print, and provides a list of the named graphs in the active worksheet files. 1-2-3 will not start printing your graph until you select Go.

If you have multiple graphs to print, or you want to also include a worksheet range in the print range, you probably want to use the /Print Printer Range. Enter **/Print Printer Range** and specify the print range. (1-2-3 displays the last selected print range.) To include a graph in a print range, enter an asterisk followed by the graph name. When you select multiple graphs and multiple worksheet ranges, each graph name and worksheet range should be separated by a semicolon or the argument separator set with /Worksheet Global Default Other International Punctuation (by default, a comma). Some valid print ranges are *LINE;*LOG;*STAND and A1..G10;*LINE_GRAPH;A11..G25. When the print range includes multiple graphs and ranges, 1-2-3 prints them in the order specified by the /Print Printer Range command.

TIP: View the graph before printing it. This view displays most of the graph as it is set to print and gives you a last chance to check that the graph appears as you want it.

Print Menu Commands for Graphs

A few of the Print menu commands only apply to graphs, and were not covered in Chapter 6, "Printing." The /Print commands specific to graphs are for setting the rotation, the image size, and the density 1-2-3 uses to print graphs. These settings do not affect worksheet print ranges. The graph printing options are in the Print Printer Options Advanced Image menu, which has the selections Rotate, Image-Sz, Density, and Quit. Once you have finished with the Print Printer Options Advanced Image menu, select Quit to return to the previous menu level.

Selecting the Image Size

The Image-Sz option provides the settings for the size of the graphs. You may want to change the graph's size so it fits on the same page with other print ranges. When you execute this command, 1-2-3 presents three choices: Margin-Fill, Length-Fill, and Reshape. The first two keep the width-to-height ratio at 4:3.

- For Margin-Fill, 1-2-3 expands the graph to stretch across from the left to right margin, and adjusts the height so the width-to-height ratio remains the same. This is the default setting.

- For Length-Fill, you must provide the height that 1-2-3 uses to create the graph. 1-2-3 expands the graph from top to bottom to stretch down the number of lines on the page that you specify, and adjusts the width so the width-to-height ratio remains the same.

- The Reshape option prompts for the graph width and height that 1-2-3 stretches the graph to fill. This option changes the width-to-height ratio.

The Rotate option rotates the graph within the area specified by the Image-Sz option.

1-2-3 may change the graph's size within the area selected. For example, if you select Image-Sz Length-Fill and want the graph to occupy 33 page lines (about half a page), the graph will be about 7 1/3 inches wide. If you rotate the graph, the 5 1/2 inch graph length becomes the graph width. 1-2-3 keeps the same aspect ratio, and makes the graph's height 4 1/8 inches.

TIP: Do not change the image size drastically when you reshape a graph. If you alter the width-to-length ratio drastically, the graph will appear elongated or compressed. The image will appear correctly on the screen, but it will have a somewhat bizarre appearance when printed. Changes in the width-to-height ratio are especially noticeable in pie charts.

Rotating the Image

The Rotate option lets you rotate the graph within the area you selected with the Image-Sz option. Figure 11-30 shows a graph that is rotated and one that is not rotated. Both graphs are printed on the same page by printing them in separate print requests, and not forwarding the page after printing the first graph. The top graph uses a length-fill setting of 23 lines and the bottom graph uses a length-fill setting of 28 lines. To rotate a graph like the first one in the example, you could request Rotate Yes. No is the default setting for this option. It is the selection made for printing the first graph in Figure 11-30.

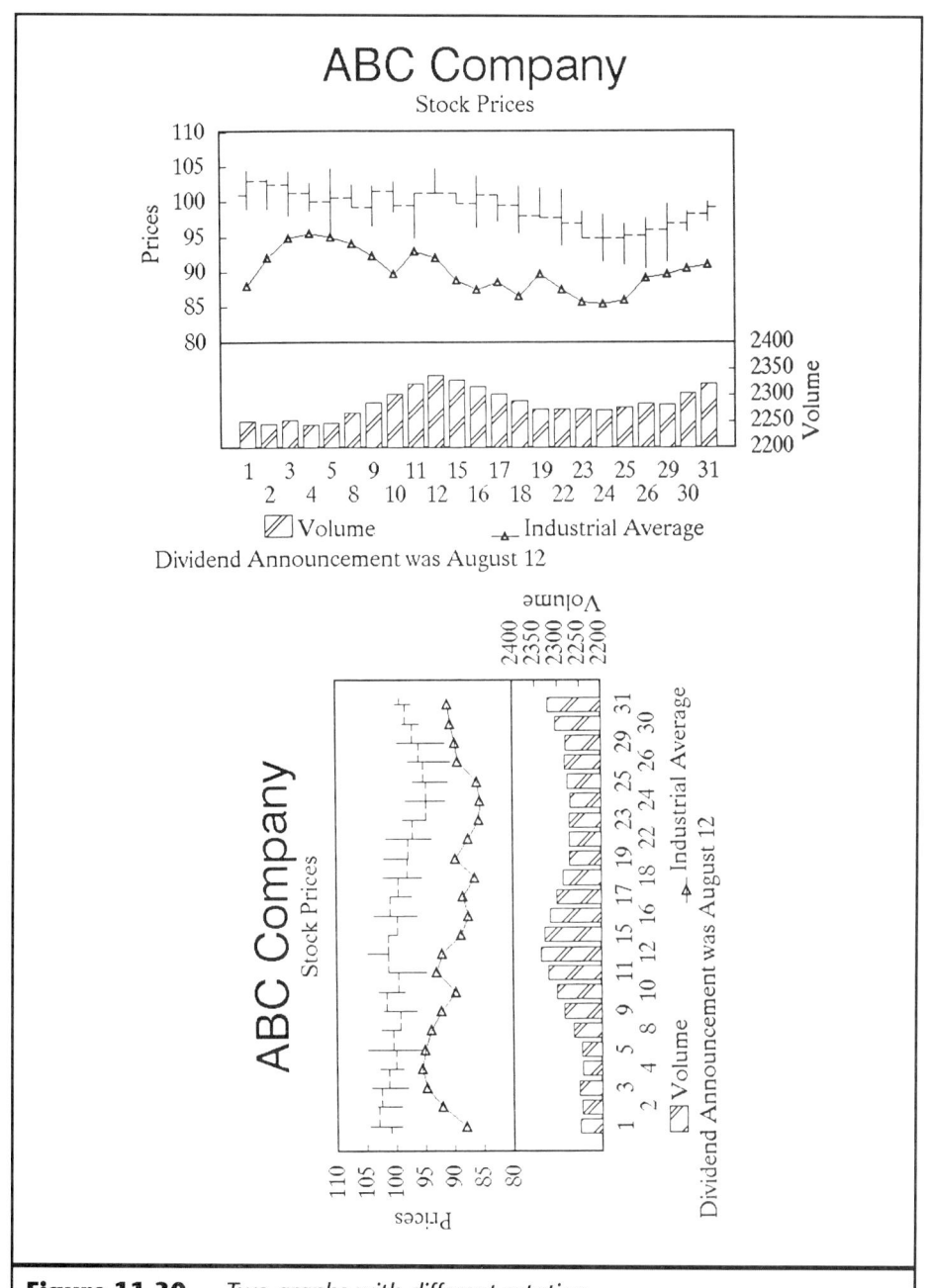

Figure 11-30. *Two graphs with different rotation*

Setting the Print Quality

Some printers can use different quality print levels. For example, a printer may have a draft print mode that prints quickly but does not produce the clearest image. The same printer may have a final print mode which takes longer to print but creates clearer images.

When you are creating your initial graphs, you may want to change to the draft print mode so you can print your graphs more quickly. Use the Density option to set the printer quality of the graphs. To print more quickly although not as clearly, request Draft. To print clearly although more slowly, request Final. When you execute this command using a printer that has only one print quality, the command has no effect.

Printing Selected Graphs

When 1-2-3 returns to the Print menus, you may need to make other menu selections before selecting Go to print the graph. Once you have selected the graph you want to print (with /Print Printer Image or /Print Printer Range), and used any needed /Print Printer Options Advanced Image options, you are almost ready to print your graph. The final steps involve the other /Print commands that you learned about in Chapter 6, "Printing."

For example, if you want different margins around the graph, you must use the /Print Printer Options Margins command to set the margins the graph uses. Table 11-1 lists several /Print commands that you will use with graphs to control the output.

Finally, after you select the graphs and all their options, 1-2-3 will begin printing when you choose the Go option from the Print Printer menu. Because Release 3 uses background printing, you can start creating your next print job as soon as Go is selected.

Moving Beyond 1-2-3's Graph Features

With Release 3's many graphics features, you may not need any further enhancements. In Chapter 15, "Using the Wysiwyg Add-In," you will learn how you can display graphs on a worksheet range. You can display the current graph, named graphs, or images stored in .PIC and .CGM files. Other options let you create your own graphics and add enhancements to an existing graph or graphic. An advantage of using Wysiwyg is that you can preview the output before you

Chapter 11: Working with 1-2-3's Graphics Features

Command	Task Performed
/Print Encoded	This command prints to a disk file containing printer-specific codes.
/Print Printer	This command prints to the printer.
/Print Printer Align	This command starts a new page at the printer's current position.
/Print Printer Clear	This command eliminates some or all of the print settings.
/Print Printer Go	This command starts printing to the printer or to a disk file.
/Print Printer Line	This command generates a line feed.
/Print Printer Options Advanced Device	This option selects which printer 1-2-3 uses.
/Print Printer Options Advanced Priority	This option assigns a priority level to the current print job.
/Print Printer Options Footer	This command adds a footer to the bottom of each page.
/Print Printer Options Header	This command adds a header to the top of each page.
/Print Printer Options Margins	This command sets the amount of blank space at the top, bottom, and sides of a printed page.
/Print Printer Options Name	This command handles named print settings that are saved with the file.
/Print Printer Options Pg-Length	This option determines the number of lines in a page of output.
/Print Printer Page	This command advances the paper to the top of the next form.
/Print Printer Range	This command determines which graphs and worksheet ranges are printed.
/Print Printer Sample	This command prints a sample worksheet and graph using the current print settings.

Table 11-1. *Print Commands Used with Graphs*

print it. The Wysiwyg add-in also has worksheet enhancements that give worksheets and graphs a more professional look.

If you want to explore other possibilites, there are two other Lotus packages that support 1-2-3's graph definitions and offer additional enhancements. Lotus Graphwriter II offers a production feature for graphs, allowing you to define each graph once and then produce it periodically as your 1-2-3 worksheet files are updated for the current period. Although the package offers some additional graphics features, its greatest contribution is its ability to store information on all the graphs you need from many worksheet files and to produce them for you automatically, grouping up to 100 charts in one production run.

The Lotus FreeLance Plus package provides graphics enhancements of a different sort. It lets you further customize graphs using arrows, a corporate logo, or tailoring the composite of any element of the graph. As an example, you can customize a corporate headcount report created with 1-2-3, to show the company logo. You can also change the bars representing the headcount to be composed of people figures stacked one on top of the other, where the total number of people in the stack represents the relative size of the data entry.

Command Reference

Graphics

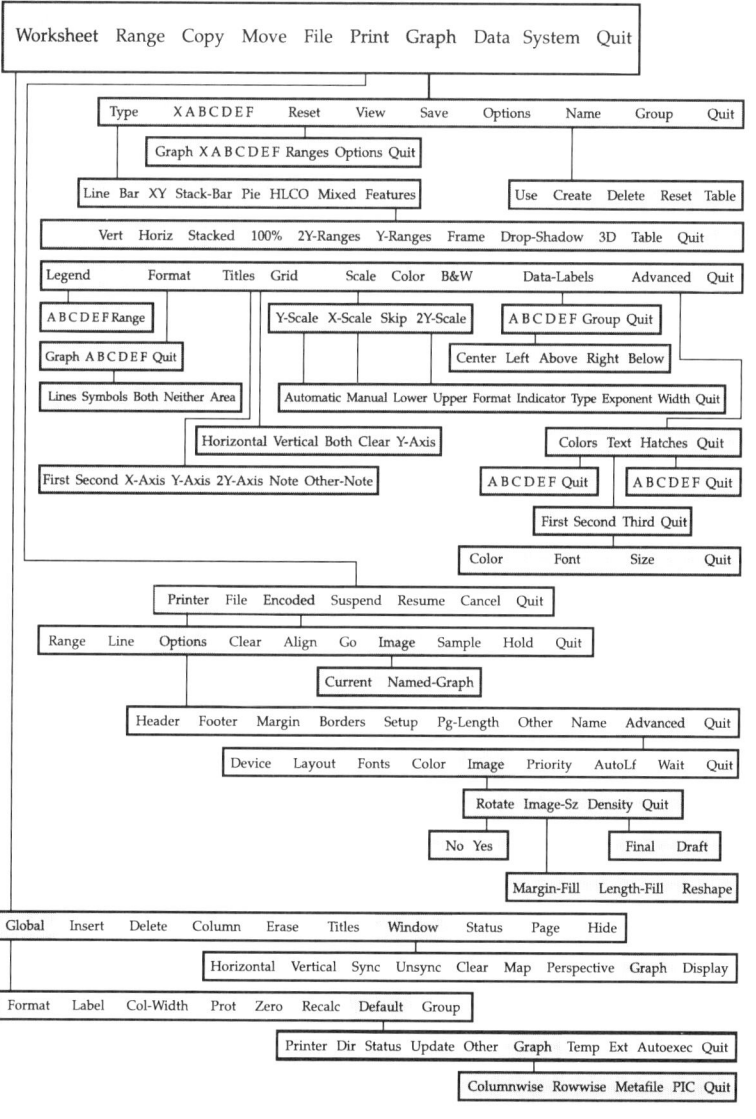

©1989 Lotus Development Corporation. Used with permission.

/Graph A B C D E F

Description

This is actually six different commands. Each one assigns one data range to be displayed on a graph. For instance, you would enter **/Graph A** and then specify the first graph data range, by entering or pointing to the range, or entering a range name.

Options

These commands allow you to use from one to six data ranges in your graph. To use all six data ranges, enter each of the range letters from A through F one by one and reference the data you want assigned to each one. The data can be in any worksheet, including in a separate worksheet file. If you are using only one data range (in a pie chart, for example), assign it to option A.

/Graph Group

Description

This command is used instead of /Graph A B C D E F when the data for the graph is in adjacent cells. This command assigns the first row or column as the X range, the second row or column as the A range, the third row or column as the B range, and so forth until the command runs out of worksheet data or graph data range names. When this command is executed, 1-2-3 prompts for the worksheet data that you want divided into graph data ranges. You can enter the range addresses a range name, or point to the cells you want to include.

Options

This command has two options, Columnwise and Rowwise which determine whether the worksheet data is divided into graph data ranges according to columns or rows.

/Graph Name Create

Description

The /Graph Name Create command assigns a name to the current set of graph settings and stores them with your worksheet. If you want this name and its settings available during your next 1-2-3 session, be sure to save the worksheet with /File Save. This command is used for creating a new named graph, and for saving the updates made to a named graph.

Options

Your only option for this command is the name you select. The name follows the rules for range names rather than filenames; you can use up to 15 characters. If you want to save the graph in another worksheet file, include the filename delimiters (<< >>) and the worksheet filename before the graph name.

NOTE: 1-2-3 does not warn you if you select a name that has already been assigned to another graph. If you do this, it will overwrite the existing settings with the current settings without asking you.

/Graph Name Delete

Description

The /Graph Name Delete command removes unneeded graph names one by one from the worksheet. Since this process frees up some memory space, it is wise to purge graph names and their associated settings when you no longer need them.

Options

Your only option for this command is the name you select to delete. 1-2-3 lists the current graph names below the prompt. You can select one of these names or type a name.

/Graph Name Reset

Description

This command removes all graph names and their settings from a worksheet file. Since there is no cautionary prompt before the deletion, you risk losing all your graph definitions if you accidentally choose Reset from the Graph Name menu. Be careful not to accidentally press R when you are working within the /Graph Name command.

/Graph Name Table

Description

This command creates a worksheet table that lists the named graphs in the current file. For each named graph it also lists the graph type and first line title, if any.

Options

The only option for this command is the location of the table the command creates. When this command prompts you for a location for the graph name table, enter or point to any cell in an active file where you want the table. This command creates the table starting at the selected cell, writing over existing information.

/Graph Name Use

Description

The /Graph Name Use command allows you to choose a graph name from the list associated with the current worksheet file. The graph selected becomes the current graph and appears on the screen.

Options

You can either type the graph name or point to it in the list that 1-2-3 displays.

/Graph Options Advanced Colors

Description

The /Graph Options Advanced Colors command specifies the color for a data range, or hides a range. If the printer can print colors, this command sets the colors the printer uses. If this command is not used to select the colors, 1-2-3 uses the colors 2 through 7 for the ranges A through F.

Options

When this command is executed, it displays the letters A through F, representing the six data ranges for which you can select colors. After you enter the data range, you can select one of the options discussed below. Then 1-2-3 returns to the Graph Options Advanced Colors menu. Select Quit to return to the Graph Options Advanced menu.

1 — 8 This option selects the color for the entire range that you named. The actual colors available depend on the monitor.

HIDE This option hides the data range selected. To redisplay a hidden range, assign a color to the range.

RANGE Use this option to select the colors for the individual data values in a range. When this option is selected, 1-2-3 prompts you for the cells containing the color range. You can enter the color range by entering the range address or a range name, or by pointing to the cells. The color range contains as many cells as the data range, and contains color code values 1 to 14. The first value in the color range sets the color of the legend for the data range. If the graph is a pie chart, 1-2-3 only uses the settings for this command when a B range is not selected and the graph is displayed in color.

/Graph Options Advanced Hatches

Description

The /Graph Options Advanced Hatches command specifies the hatch pattern for a data range in area, bar, stacked bar, HLCO, and mixed graphs, or for data values in pie charts. If the printer cannot print colors, this command selects the hatch patterns the printer uses. If this command does not select the hatch patterns, 1-2-3 uses the hatch patterns 2 through 7 for the ranges A through F. When this command is combined with /Graph Options Advanced Colors, it displays (and prints if possible) the hatch patterns in colors.

Options

The options for this command are identical to those for the /Graph Options Advanced Colors command, except that this command does not have a Hide option.

/Graph Options Advanced Quit

Description

The /Graph Options Advanced Quit command leaves the Graph Options Advanced sticky menu and returns to the Graph Options menu.

/Graph Options Advanced Text

Description

The /Graph Options Advanced Text command selects the color, fonts, and sizes of text for various locations in a graph. This command divides the text in a graph into three groups. The first group includes the first line of the graph title. The second group includes the second line of the graph title, the axis titles, and the legend text. The third group includes the scale indicators, axes labels, data labels, and footnotes.

Options

When this command is executed, it prompts for the text group for which you want to set the text color, font, or size. Once the data range is selected, this command has the following options.

COLOR   This option specifies the color for the text group or hides it. The selections of 1 through 8 match the color selections of the /Graph Options Advanced Colors command. The actual colors available depend on the monitor. Choose the Hide selection to hide the text group. Hide works whether the graph displays in color or monochrome.

FONT   This option specifies the font for the text group. When this option is selected, 1-2-3 prompts for the font number (1 through 8) or Default, which uses the default for the text group. The default for the first text group is font 1; the default for the second and third groups is font 3. The selections of 1 through 8 match the /Print Printer Options Other Advanced Fonts command. This option only changes how 1-2-3 prints the graph's text, since it always uses the same predetermined font for displaying the graph. The way the fonts print depends upon the printer.

SIZE   This option selects the character size 1-2-3 uses for the text groups. When this option is selected, 1-2-3 prompts for the size number (1 through 9) or default, which uses the default for the text group. The default for the first text group is 7, the default for the second text group is 4, and the default for the third text group is 2. Since 1-2-3 only has three text sizes for displaying graphs, it displays graphs with the text sizes 1 to 3 as small-sized characters, text sizes 4 to 6 as medium-sized characters, and 7 to 9 as large-sized characters. The way the character sizes print depends on the printer and the font. 1-2-3 automatically reduces the text size if it needs to fit more text on the graph, and truncates what still does not fit.

QUIT   This option returns to the Graph Options Advanced Text menu.

/Graph Options B&W

Description

This command displays graphs in one color. To differentiate between the bars on a bar chart, 1-2-3 automatically adds hatch mark patterns when the B&W option is in effect. To print a graph in color, even when the monitor is monochrome, you must use the /Graph Options Color command. If the printer can only print in one color, you do not need to change the color setting to print the graph.

/Graph Options Color

Description

This command displays your graphs in color. If your printer cannot print the graph in color, 1-2-3 converts the colors to hatch patterns automatically.

/Graph Options Data-Labels

Description

The /Graph Options Data-Labels command permits you to add specific labels to a range of data points. 1-2-3 will obtain these data labels from the range of worksheet cells you specify.

Options

1-2-3 prompts for the name of the data range to which you want to assign labels; the range choices are A through F, or Group. If Group is selected, this command assigns data labels one by one to data ranges A through F until the command runs out of label data or graph data ranges. When you specify the data range name, you are prompted for the range containing the data labels. The labels range should contain the same number of cells as the data values selected for the graph data range. After you enter the labels range, the command prompts for the labels' placement relative to the data point. For line graphs, the choices are Center, Left, Above, Right, and Below; for bar graphs, the choices are Above and Below. The other selections are equivalent to Above. When you are finished assigning data labels, select Quit to return to the Graph Options menu.

NOTE: *In a line graph, you can use data labels as the only markers for your data points. To do this, choose /Graph Options Format Neither to remove lines and symbols.*

/Graph Options Format

Description

The /Graph Options Format command lets you select the type of line or XY graph you will create. You can also choose whether data points are shown as symbols, connected with a line, marked with both symbols and a line, or neither. An additional option makes a line graph an area graph.

Options

Your first choice is the range that the format will apply to. Specify Graph as the range if you want your selection used for all ranges on the graph. Or select a specific data range by entering a letter from A through F. Then select among the following options:

LINES This option shows the data points connected by a line without marking the data points.

SYMBOLS This option shows only symbols, with no connecting line. 1-2-3 uses a different symbol for each of the ranges.

BOTH This option shows both the symbols and a connecting line.

NEITHER This option shows neither lines nor symbols. This option is used in conjunction with the Data-Labels option when you center a data label to mark a point and do not want any other marking on the graph.

AREA This option creates the graph with lines. It fills the space between the lines (for each data range and the X axis) with a different color or hatch pattern. If more than one data range is formatted, 1-2-3 stacks the data—even if /Graph Type Features Stacked is set to No. An area graph treats negative numbers as 0.

/Graph Options Grid

Description

The /Graph Options Grid command adds vertical lines, horizontal lines, or both to a graph. These lines start at the markers on the X or Y axis and extend upward or to the right, depending on whether you choose Vertical, Horizontal, or Both. Additional options clear the existing grid lines or set the origination point for horizontal grid lines. The lines can greatly aid in the interpretation of points on the graph.

Options

The options for /Graph Options Grid determine whether the grid lines are generated in one or both directions.

HORIZONTAL This option adds horizontal lines that extend across from the Y axis. These lines are effective with bar graphs, since they help you interpret the value for the top of each bar. Horizontal grid lines originate from the Y axis, the second Y axis, or both, depending upon the Y-Axis setting.

VERTICAL This option adds vertical lines that start at the X axis and extend upward. They are most effective with an XY or line graph; they tend to detract from the clarity of a bar graph.

BOTH This option adds lines in both directions at once. The lines form a grid pattern on the graph. Horizontal grid lines will originate from the Y axis, the second Y axis, or both depending upon the Y-Axis setting. Vertical lines start at the X axis.

CLEAR This option eliminates grid lines that you have added to a graph.

Y-AXIS This option determines whether the horizontal lines created with the Horizontal or Both options originate from the first Y axis, the second Y axis, or both. The default is the first Y axis.

NOTE: *Rotating the graph axes rotates the grid lines. If a graph is rotated, this command starts grid lines from the X and Y axis as set with this command, although the horizontal line setting appears vertical and the vertical line setting appears horizontal.*

/Graph Options Legend

Description

This command displays legends at the bottom of your graph to describe the data represented by the different graph data ranges.

Options

You can choose any one of the ranges (A through F) each time you request this command. If you select Range, you will select the legends for all data ranges. You can either type in a legend or reference a cell address containing the legend you wish to use. With the Range option, you must select a legend range containing up to six legends for the six data ranges. While this command does not limit the number of characters that you can enter for a legend or in a cell referenced for the legend, the practical limit on the legend size is based on what 1-2-3 can fit in the graph. The number of characters a legend can contain depends on the number of legends, and the amount of text in each legend.

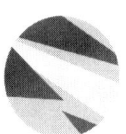

NOTE: The /Graph Options Legend Range command can also be used to assign legends to the first six pie slices in a pie chart. The first cell in the legend range is assigned to the first slice. One by one, cell contents are assigned to pie slices until all the cells in the legend range are used, or the sixth pie slice is assigned a legend, or the last pie slice is assigned a legend.

/Graph Options Quit

Description

The /Graph Options Quit command leaves the /Graph Options sticky menu and returns to the /Graph menu.

/Graph Options Scale Skip

Description

This command permits you to remove the congestion that can occur when you assign labels to be displayed along the X axis. The skip factor you specify lets you use only some of the labels in the range. If you specify a skip factor of 3, for example, only every third label will be used.

Options

You can specify any number from 1 to 8192 for the skip factor. The default is 1, meaning that 1-2-3 uses every label in the range.

/Graph Options Scale X-Scale

Description

This command permits you to let 1-2-3 choose the scale for the X axis or, alternatively, to choose the scale yourself. These options only affect XY graphs.

Options

The options for the /Graph Options Scale X-Scale command are as follows.

AUTOMATIC This setting is the default. It lets 1-2-3 determine the proper lower and upper range of the X axis.

MANUAL This option informs 1-2-3 that you want to determine the scale range.

LOWER This is the lower limit or the smallest value that can be shown on your scale. You must define it when you select Manual.

UPPER This is the upper limit or the highest value that can be shown on your scale. You must define it when you select Manual.

FORMAT   This option allows you to select a display format (Currency, Percent, or the like) for the numeric values represented on the scale.

INDICATOR   This option permits you to turn off the size indicator for the scale or create your own. The default is Yes, allowing 1-2-3 to display indicators like "Thousands." Another choice, None, hides the indicator. The third choice, Manual, prompts for a different indicator, which you can type in or specify with a backslash and a cell address containing the text you want as the indicator.

TYPE   This option selects a linear or logarithmic scale for the X axis. The default is Standard, or linear. Select Logarithmic when you want the scale increments to increase by the power of 10. For example, the first increment is 1, the second increment is 10, and the third increment is 100.

EXPONENT   This option selects an order of magnitude for a scale. The order of magnitude is the power of 10 by which you multiply the numbers in the X axis to determine the values they represent. For example, if the scale has an exponent of 6, the numbers on the X axis scale must be multiplied by one million (10 to the sixth power) to determine the number they represent. This option has two selections. When Automatic is selected, 1-2-3 automatically determines the appropriate exponent for the graph. When Manual is selected, 1-2-3 prompts for the power of 10 for the exponent. 1-2-3 accepts any number between –95 and +95. If the order of magnitude is not 0, 1-2-3 adds an indicator that appears if /Graph Options Scale X-Scale Indicator is set to Yes.

WIDTH   This option sets the maximum width of the X axis scale numbers. This option has two selections. Automatic lets 1-2-3 set the width for the X axis scale numbers. Manual prompts you for a number between 1 and 50 for the X axis scale number width. 1-2-3 displays the scale numbers as asterisks when the width is insufficient for the scale numbers, or when the scale numbers would extend for more than one-third of the graph's area.

QUIT   This option returns you to the Graph Options menu.

/Graph Options Scale Y-Scale

Description

This command permits you to let 1-2-3 choose the scale for the Y axis or, alternatively, to choose the scale yourself.

Options

The options for the /Graph Options Scale Y-Scale command are identical to the options for the /Graph Options Scale X-Scale command.

/Graph Options Scale 2Y-Scale

Description

This command permits you to let 1-2-3 choose the scale for the second Y axis or, alternatively, to choose the scale yourself.

Options

The options for the /Graph Options Scale 2Y-Scale command are identical to the options for the /Graph Options Scale X-Scale command.

/Graph Options Titles

Description

This command permits you to add titles to your graph to improve its clarity and readability. Your titles will be limited to the characters 1-2-3 can fit on the graph. Referencing a stored title requires that you enter a backslash (\) and a cell address containing the title.

Options

You can add titles at the top of your graph, along the axes, or at the bottom of your graph with the options available. Your choices are as follows:

FIRST The label you enter after this choice will be centered at the top of your graph.

SECOND Your label entry for this option will be centered and placed immediately below the label shown by the First option.

X-AXIS This option places a title below the X axis.

Y-AXIS This option places your entry vertically to the left of the Y axis.

2Y-AXIS This option places your entry vertically to the right of the second Y axis.

NOTE: This option places your entry below the graph, starting at the left side of the graph area.

NOTE: This option places your entry below the text entered for the Note option.

/Graph Quit

Description

This command exits the Graph menu and returns you to the worksheet in READY mode.

/Graph Reset

Description

The /Graph Reset command cancels graph settings in a worksheet file that you selected in a previous session.

Options

You can choose to cancel all or some of the graph settings with the options for this command. Your choices are as follows:

GRAPH This option cancels all graph settings and returns to the Graph menu.

X This option cancels the X data values.

A-F Choosing one of this set of letter options cancels the data range for the letter selected.

RANGES This option cancels the data ranges and data label settings for the X, A, B, C, D, E, and F data ranges.

OPTIONS This option cancels the selections made with /Graph Options commands.

QUIT This option tells 1-2-3 that you have canceled all the settings you want to eliminate and returns you to the previous menu.

/Graph Save

Description

The /Graph Save command saves the current graph picture in a .CGM or .PIC file separate from your worksheet. The file this command creates can be used by other programs. The extension this command uses is set by the /Worksheet Global Default Graph command.

Options

After selecting this command, you have the choice of entering a filename or choosing one from the list that 1-2-3 presents. If you choose to use an existing .CGM or .PIC filename, 1-2-3 prompts you to confirm that you do want to reuse (and therefore overwrite) that file, or else to cancel your request.

/Graph Type

Description

The /Graph Type command lets you pick from seven different formats for displaying your graph data. You can easily change from one format to another without any alterations other than selecting another type. If you do not select a graph type, 1-2-3 uses a line graph. Use the other selections in this command to add graph enhancements. By selecting a graph type without selecting graph data, and then moving the cell pointer to the upper left corner of the data that you want to graph, you can create an automatic graph if your data is in the proper format. To view the automatic graph, press F10 (GRAPH) or use the /Graph View command.

Options

This command provides seven basic graph types, and a Features option to add other enhancements to the basic graph. These options are as follows:

LINE   This graph plots the points of a data range and connects them with a line. The default is to use both symbols and a line on the graph. Symbols mark each point, and a line joins the data points. Up to six separate lines, displaying six data ranges, can be generated on one graph. A line graph can also become an area graph (one that fills the area between the data values with a color or hatch pattern) if you select the Area option under the /Graph Options Format command.

BAR   This graph uses up to six sets of vertical bars to represent the data ranges selected. 1-2-3 uses hatch mark patterns or colors to distinguish the different data ranges.

XY   This graph pairs X range values with values from the A through F data ranges. With this kind of graph, 1-2-3 generates a numeric scale for the X, as well as the Y axis.

STACKED-BAR   For one data range, a stacked bar graph will appear the same as an ordinary bar graph. Graphing several data ranges lets you compare them differently. Rather than adding the second set of bars to the right of the first, the stacked bar graph option stacks the second set on top of the first, the third on top of the second, and so on. The total height of a bar thus indicates the total of the values for that category. The different bars in a stack are distinguished by hatch patterns or colors.

PIE   A pie chart is used to compare the size of each of several categories relative to the whole. Each category shown in the pie will be represented by a wedge whose size is proportional to its value compared with the values for the other categories shown in the chart. Only one set of data, the A range, can be shown. A B range can be used to indicate colors or hatch patterns, wedges that are hidden, or wedges that are exploded.

HLCO   An HLCO chart creates a High-Low-Close-Open graph used to graph financial commodities over time. For each set of data values (such as each day you are recording stock prices), the HLCO has a line from the high to the low value. A projection to the left indicates the open value; a projection to the right indicates the close value. 1-2-3 uses the A data range as the high values, the B data range as the low values, the C data range as the close data range, and the D data range as the open data range. The E range appears as a bar graph below the HLCO graph for the A, B, C, and D ranges, and is assigned to the second Y axis. The F range is graphed as a line graph with A through D ranges. An HLCO graph must have at least an A and B range, or an E and F range. While this graph is primarily for financial commodities, it can also be used for graphing ranges such as statistical data showing the high, low, and average values for X range values.

MIXED A mixed graph displays the A, B, and C data ranges as bar graphs, and the D, E, and F data ranges as line graphs. The bar graph data uses different hatch patterns or colors to distinguish the data ranges; the line graph data uses lines and symbols to indicate the data ranges. The colors, hatch patterns, lines, and symbols can be changed with the /Graph Options commands.

FEATURES This option is not a graph type. It creates variations of the other basic graph types. The Vert (Vertical) feature orients the graph axes so the X axis is horizontal and the Y axes are vertical; this is the default orientation. The Horiz (Horizontal) feature orients the graph axes so the X axis is vertical and the Y axes are horizontal. The Stacked feature, if set to Yes, stacks the data ranges of line, bar, mixed, and XY graphs on top of each other; the default is No. The 100% feature displays the data values as the percentage of their total value, and the Y axis markings as percentages, if set to Yes; the default is No. The 2Y-Ranges feature assigns ranges to the second Y axis range. The Y-Ranges feature assigns ranges to the first Y axis range. For both 2Y-Ranges and Y-Ranges you must select a graph range (A-F) or all of the graph ranges (Graph). Ranges belong to the first Y axis unless assigned to the second Y axis. When you select Frame, you can choose to display an entire frame (All), remove the graph's frame (None), or delete the sides where you do not want the frame to appear. Drop-Shadow adds a shadow to the bars, pies, or lines that appear on the graph when you select Yes, and removes the effect when you select No. 3D adds a three-dimensional effect to bar graphs. Table adds a data table below the graph presenting the data when you select Yes, and removes this effect when you select No. Selecting Quit returns you to the /Graph Type Features menu; selecting Quit again returns to the Graph menu.

/Graph View

Description

The /Graph View command displays the graph that you have defined by selecting data ranges and a graph type. If you have not defined data to graph and you invoke /Graph View, 1-2-3 attempts to create an automatic graph using the worksheet data, starting with the cell pointer's position. If 1-2-3 cannot create an automatic graph, the screen appears blank when you select this command. To return to the Graph menu when you are through with the View option, press any key. You can also view the graph by pressing F10 (GRAPH). Using the F10 (GRAPH) function key lets you see the graph at any time, including while you are using other Graph menus. Pressing any key returns you to where you were before you pressed F10 (GRAPH).

NOTE: If your 1-2-3 package is installed for a graphics device that your monitor cannot support, your screen will appear blank when you invoke /Graph View. To correct the problem, go back to the installation process described in Appendix A, "Installing 1-2-3." Similarly, if you attempt to use the package on a system without graphics support, entering /Graph View will cause the screen to appear blank. In both cases you can press any key to return to the Graph menu.

/Graph X

Description

The /Graph X command is used to label the points on the X axis for a line or bar graph. For a pie chart, the X values provide labels for the pie segments; for an XY chart they provide values to plot against the Y values. The labels assigned to the points must be stored in worksheet cells and specified with a range name or a range address, or by pointing to the cells you wish to use.

Options

There are no options for this command. If the labels you choose contain too many characters, 1-2-3 uses two rows to display the X labels, alternating the X labels between the rows. If the labels still have too many characters, 1-2-3 truncates the X labels. You can use /Graph Options Scale Skip to tell 1-2-3 not to use every label.

/Print Printer Image

Description

This command selects a graph to print. Once a graphics image is selected, you can use the other /Print commands to control how 1-2-3 prints the graph. Most of the /Print commands have the same effect for graphs as for worksheet ranges. If the current printer cannot print graphs, 1-2-3 leaves the space for the graph blank. Once a graph is selected to print, 1-2-3 keeps the graphics image in memory so you can print the graph again without reselecting it. Graphs can be printed to encoded files and to the printer, but not to text files.

Options

This command has two options: Current and Named-Graph. The Current option prints the current (active) graph. The Named-Graph option prompts you for a graph name and displays the named graphs in the current worksheet file. You can select a listed graph name or type a different one.

NOTE: You can also print a graph by entering an asterisk and the graph name after invoking the /Print Printer Range command. This option is for printing a combination of worksheet ranges and graphs.

/Print Printer Options Advanced Image Density

Description

This command sets the density of the points that 1-2-3 uses to print the graph. This command sets the printer quality, in order to change the speed at which the printer prints the graphs.

Options

This command has two options: Final and Draft. Final prints a higher quality graph, but takes longer. Draft prints a lower quality graph, but prints more quickly. If a printer can only print using one quality level, this command has no effect.

/Print Printer Options Advanced Image Image-Sz

Description

The /Print Printer Options Advanced Image Image-Sz command determines the size of the printed graph. The graph can be sized according to the height or width, while maintaining the same height-to-width ratio. This command can also set the height and width, which can change the height-to-width ratio.

Options

This command has three options: Length-Fill, Margin-Fill, and Reshape. If the values for the height and width exceed the printer's capabilities, 1-2-3 automatically resizes the graph to fit within the printer's width. The graph's default width-to-length ratio is 4:3, although the Reshape option will change it.

LENGTH-FILL This option expands the graph down to fill the graph length you specify, and adjusts the width to have the same length-to-width ratio. This option prompts you for the number of standard lines that the graph should use. Entering a number greater than the page length will use the number of lines per page for the graph, and will center the graph horizontally and vertically on the page.

MARGIN-FILL This option expands the graph to fill the area between the left and right margins. This option adjusts the length to have the same length-to-width ratio. 1-2-3 centers the graph horizontally on the page. This option is the default.

RESHAPE This option expands the graph to fill the length and width you specify. This option changes the length-to-width ratio. You are prompted for the number of standard lines and the number of characters across that the graph should use. Entering a higher number than can fit on a page will center the graph horizontally and vertically on the page.

/Print Printer Options Advanced Image Quit

Description

This command returns you to the /Print Printer Options Advanced menu.

/Print Printer Options Advanced Image Rotate

Description

The /Print Printer Options Advanced Image Rotate command rotates the entire graph. This is different from the /Graph Type Features Vertical and /Graph Type Features Horizontal commands which select the orientation of the X axis and the Y axes in a graph. If a graph is rotated, 1-2-3 changes the image size, since the width and length of the graph are perpendicular to the width and length of the paper. If the printer cannot rotate graphs, this command has no effect.

Options

When the No option is selected (the default) the top of the graph is parallel to the top of the page. When the Yes option is selected, the top of the graph is parallel to the left side of the page.

/Worksheet Global Default Graph

Description

This command provides two different sets of features. First, it lets you decide the default graphic image file extension. This is the extension used by the /Graph Save, /File List Graph, and /File Erase Graph commands. Second, this command lets you determine how 1-2-3 uses worksheet data to create automatic graphs.

Options

This command has five options: Columnwise, Rowwise, Metafile, PIC, and Quit. The first four options form two pairs, with each member of the pair having an effect opposite to that of the other.

COLUMNWISE   This option divides a worksheet data range into graph data ranges for automatic graphs according to columns. This is the default.

ROWWISE   This option divides a worksheet data range into graph data ranges for automatic graphs according to rows.

METAFILE   This option sets the default graphic image file extension to .CGM and saves graphic images in a Metafile format.

PIC   This option sets the default graphic image file extension to .PIC and saves graphic images in a picture file format. This is the default.

QUIT   This option returns to the Worksheet Global Default menu.

/Worksheet Window Graph

Description

This command splits the display screen vertically at the cell pointer position. In the left half, 1-2-3 displays the current worksheet. In the right half, 1-2-3 displays the current graph. As the worksheet data changes, 1-2-3 updates the graph concurrently. The Graph window remains in effect for all worksheets and active files until another /Worksheet Window, or /File Retrieve, or /Worksheet Erase command is executed.

NOTE: Creating a Graph window does not create an automatic graph. To create an automatic graph, you must position the cell pointer and use the /Graph View command or F10 (GRAPH) key. When you return to the worksheet, the automatic graph will appear in the Graph window.

CHAPTER 12

Keyboard Macros

Many people are intimidated by macros because they have tried unsuccessfully to work with them. Macros, however, are a powerful and flexible feature of 1-2-3. They can be quite simple to master if you use a step-by-step approach and learn the most basic macros first, before attempting the more sophisticated variety. The Release 3 keystroke recorder feature and other macro enhancements make mastery of macros easier than ever. You will also be able to improve your success ratio if you follow the procedures for creating macros outlined in this chapter and Chapter 13, "Command Language Macros."

With 1-2-3 Release 3.4, you can assign macros to user icons. 1-2-3 provides 12 user icons to use in palette 8, or to add to the custom palette. This allows you a quick way to access any macro with the SmartIcons palette.

Types of Macros

1-2-3's *keyboard alternative macros* can be used to automate printing, formatting, or any other task that is accomplished with menu selections. This type of macro provides an alternative to typing from the keyboard. Keyboard macros are good to begin with if you are new to macros, since they contain familiar keystroke commands. They can also provide a wealth of time-saving features. If you follow the instructions in this chapter, you will find yourself creating keyboard alternative macros that are successful the first time you try them.

The second type of macro uses commands beyond menu selections. These commands are available as keyword options from 1-2-3's macro command language. With *command language macros* you can read and write records to a file, create your own menus, utilize iterative loops, and alter the order in which commands are processed. 1-2-3's command language is a full programming language that functions like other programming languages, to allow you to develop complete applications. With Release 3.4 macro commands, you can create data entry forms for your 1-2-3 database applications. Chapter 13 will cover all the features of 1-2-3's command language.

Both types of macros can be stored in the worksheet file where they are used, or in a separate file if you want to create a library of macros for use with many worksheets. At a minimum, macros should be placed on a separate sheet of the file to minimize the risk of change due to alterations in the remainder of the worksheet entries. With Release 3.4, you can easily build macro library files that support many applications. Since 1-2-3 can access macros in any sheet in memory, you can open a macro library at the beginning of a session and utilize it throughout.

Keyboard Macros

Like all macros, a keyboard alternative macro is nothing more than a column of label entries that have a name assigned to them. The contents of the labels are the sequence of keystrokes that you want 1-2-3 to execute for you.

After all your label entries are stored in a column, you will name the top cell in the column with the /Range Name Create or the /Range Name Labels command. You can use any name for a macro, as long as it conforms to the rules of range names and falls within the 15-character limit. The special names

The ABCs of Keyboard Macros

1. Plan the task you want the macro to perform.

2. Erase the keystroke recorder with ALT-F2 (RECORD) Erase. Execute the steps required for your task and enter ALT-F2 (RECORD) Copy. To copy the keystrokes to your macro, move to the first entry in the recorder screen, press the TAB key, move to the last keystroke, and press ENTER. Move to a cell at the top of an empty column in the worksheet and press ENTER. (If you prefer, you can simply type the macro keystrokes you want into a series of labels in a column of worksheet cells.)

3. Edit the label entries in the macro column and make any required changes.

4. Record the macro name one cell to the left of the top cell in the macro column. Use the backslash key and a single letter if you want to execute the macro with a single key combination. Or you can use any valid range name.

5. Use /Range Name Labels Right to apply the name to the macro.

6. Save the worksheet containing the macro.

7. Execute the macro using the ALT key plus the macro letter name, like **\s**. If you used a range name, use ALT-F3 (RUN) or the Run Macro SmartIcon, highlight the name, and press ENTER.

---

consisting of a backslash and a single letter that were required in earlier releases are still accepted. These special names allow you to execute a keyboard macro by pressing the ALT key in combination with the letter used as the macro's name, but these letters are not very descriptive.

To execute a macro without the special backslash-letter combination name, press ALT-F3 (RUN) or click this Run Macro SmartIcon.

Highlight the macro name in the list or type the name. You will need to press ENTER to start macro execution. With Release 3.4, you can make macros even easier to use. You can assign macro code to a user icon while entering the keystrokes, or you can access code already stored on the worksheet. The steps for creating and executing keyboard macros are summarized for you in the box entitled "The ABCs of Keyboard Macros."

TIP: Avoid macro names that duplicate cell addresses, existing range names, and 1-2-3's keywords. Stay away from macro names like A10, @SUM, and {DOWN}. With so many other meaningful names from which to select, it is easy to avoid names that will cause confusion.

Recording the Keystrokes

There are several options for storing macro keystrokes in Release 3. You can type them in a cell as label entries, or you can use the entries in 1-2-3's buffer, which records your keystrokes. To utilize any of the 512 characters that 1-2-3 records in the keystroke recorder, you must first copy them to a cell or play them back directly from the buffer. First, you will look at the typing alternative. You will need this technique to modify existing macros, and the procedure will give you an appreciation for the work that the new keystroke recorder does for you.

Typing the Required Keystrokes

When you want to store a menu request in a macro, begin the sequence with an apostrophe, so it will be treated as a label. This prevents 1-2-3 from executing a menu request immediately. Then enter the keystrokes. Indicate the request for a menu command with a slash, and record each of the menu commands by entering the first letter of the menu choice. For instance, to enter the keystrokes necessary to view a Worksheet Status screen, type **'/ws** or **'/WS** in the cell (case is not important).

TIP: If you make a mistake throughout a long macro repeatedly, the quickest correction method is the Replace option of /Range Search.

In addition to specifying menu selections, you will sometimes have to indicate an ENTER key press. The ENTER key is represented in a macro by the tilde mark (~).

Filenames or range names should be entered in full. As an example, to store the characters needed to retrieve a file named SALES from the default drive, enter **'/FRSALES~** or **'/FRsales~** in the macro cell. Although you can use all upper- or lowercase for the keystroke entries, a consistent combination can help to clarify range names, filenames, cell addresses, and menu selections.

TIP: Beware of missing tildes. The single most frequent cause of mistakes in macros created by novice users is missing tildes. After recording the correct menu selections, it is easy to forget that you press ENTER at certain points when executing a command sequence from the keyboard. Even one missing tilde will cause the macro to malfunction.

To correct a macro once it is entered, you can use the F2 (EDIT) key with the cell pointer on the cell containing the macro code. Since the macro code is nothing more than a label entry, special techniques are not required for making changes.

Recording Special Keys

There are a number of special keyboard keys, like the function keys and cell pointer movement keys, that you will want to include in your macros. These keys and the macro keywords that stand for them are listed in the box called "Special Keys in Macro Commands." Note that all the keywords are enclosed in curly brackets or braces ({ }). Several of these keys are for Release 3's ability to work with multiple worksheets and multiple files. Whether you use the keystroke recorder feature to enter your macros or type them in, you will need to be familiar with the effect of each of these keys so that you can make intelligent modifications to existing macros.

There is no keyword for the NUM LOCK or SCROLL LOCK key, because it must be requested from outside a macro. CAPS LOCK is not represented either, since cell entries are typed right into a macro and you have your choice of typing either uppercase or lowercase letters. Case is also unimportant in operator entries made while a macro is executing, unless you are storing these entries on the worksheet and have preference for the case of the entry. Other keys not supported are ALT-F1 (COMPOSE), PRINT SCREEN, ALT-F2 (RECORD), ALT-F3 (RUN), ALT-F4 (UNDO), and the SHIFT key.

TIP: Check the spelling of the special key names carefully. In a macro, your entries must be exact. A small mistake is just as serious as a large one, since 1-2-3 only recognizes entries that exactly match the defined set of options.

Cursor Movement Keys

1-2-3 has macro commands for all of the different keystrokes you can use to move the cell pointer to any cell. You can also repeat keystrokes either by repeating the macro keyword, as in {UP}{UP}{UP}, or by using the repeat factor, which is a number in the keyword, as in {UP 3} or {U3}. All three representations

Special Keys in Macro Commands

1-2-3 has a macro keyword to represent each of the special keyboard keys, except for NUM LOCK, SCROLL LOCK, CAPS LOCK, ALT-F1 (COMPOSE), ALT-F2 (RECORD), ALT-F3 (RUN), ALT-F4 (UNDO), SHIFT, and PRINT SCREEN.

Cell Pointer Movement Keys	Keywords
UP ARROW	{UP} or {U}
DOWN ARROW	{DOWN} or {D}
RIGHT ARROW	{RIGHT} or {R}
LEFT ARROW	{LEFT} or {L}
HOME	{HOME}
END	{END}
PGUP	{PGUP}
PGDN	{PGDN}
CTRL-RIGHT or TAB	{BIGRIGHT}
CTRL-LEFT or SHIFT-TAB	{BIGLEFT}
CTRL-END CTRL-PGUP (next file)	{NEXTFILE}, {NF}, or {FILE}{NS}
CTRL-PGUP (next sheet)	{NEXTSHEET} or {NS}
CTRL-PGDN (prev sheet)	{PREVSHEET} or {PS}
CTRL-END CTRL-PGDN (prev file)	{PREVFILE}, {PF}, or {FILE}{PS}
CTRL-END (file)	{FILE}
CTRL-HOME (first cell)	{FIRSTCELL} or {FC}
CTRL-END HOME (first file)	{FIRSTFILE}, {FF}, or {FILE}{HOME}
END CTRL-HOME (last cell)	{LASTCELL} or {LC}
CTRL-END END (last file)	{LASTFILE}, {LF}, or {FILE}{END}

Editing Keys	
DEL	{DEL} or {DELETE}
INS	{INS} or {INSERT}
ESC	{ESC} or {ESCAPE}
BACKSPACE	{BACKSPACE} or {BS}

Function Keys	
F1 (HELP)	{HELP}
F2 (EDIT)	{EDIT}
F3 (NAME)	{NAME}

Function Keys (continued)	**Keywords**
F4 (ABS)	{ABS}
F5 (GOTO)	{GOTO}
F6 (WINDOW)	{WINDOW}
F7 (QUERY)	{QUERY}
F8 (TABLE)	{TABLE}
F9 (CALC)	{CALC}
F10 (GRAPH)	{GRAPH}
ALT-F6 (ZOOM)	{ZOOM}
ALT-F7 (APP1)	{APP1}
ALT-F8 (APP2)	{APP2}
ALT-F9 (APP3)	{APP3}
ALT-F10 (ADDIN)	{ADDIN} or {APP4}
Special Keys	
Input from keyboard during macro	{?}
ENTER key	~
Tilde	{~}
{	{{}
}	{}}
/ or <	/, <, or {MENU}

have the same effect; they all move the cell pointer three cells above its current location.

The END and arrow key combination is supported in macros. You can enter {END}{RIGHT} to have the macro move the cell pointer to the last occupied cell entry on the right side of the worksheet.

All of the special entries that relocate the cell pointer to different sheets or files are also supported. The entries {NEXTFILE}, {NF}, and {FILE}{NS} move the cell pointer to the next file. The cell pointer will be placed in the first cell in the current file if you enter {FIRSTCELL} or {FC}.

Function Keys

With the exception of ALT-F1 (COMPOSE), ALT-F2 (RECORD), ALT-F3 (RUN), and ALT-F4 (UNDO), all the function keys can be represented by the special macro keywords listed in the box, "Special Keys in Macro Commands."

Edit Keys

In addition to F2 (EDIT), which places you in the EDIT mode, there are several special keys that you use when correcting worksheet entries. When you are in EDIT mode, the macro commands for keys behave in the same way as when you press the keys in EDIT mode. You can use {DEL} or {DELETE} and {BS} or {BACKSPACE} to remove a character at a time. Like arrow keys, you can include repeat factors such as {DELETE 4}. The keywords {ESC} or {ESCAPE} can remove an entry from a cell and delete a menu default, such as a previous setup string, so you can make a new entry.

To remove existing data from the Edit line use {CLEARENTRY} or {CE}. Although it is similar to {ESC}, there are important differences. This command is unique because it is the only keystroke command that does not have a single keyboard equivalent. When there is one entry in the Edit line, {CE} functions identically to {ESC} and eliminates the entry. When you would have to press ESC several times, you can use {CE} once to remove the entire entry. An example is the /File Save command, where you would have to press ESC several times to remove the existing entry.

The {CE} instruction is also handy when you are not certain if there is an entry on the Edit line. Where {ESC} returns 1-2-3 to the previous command level, {CE} always remains in EDIT mode. Compare {ESC} and {CE} in the context of the /Print command, and the difference is clearer. If a macro includes the entry /PPR, there may or may not be a range highlighted on the screen. If there is one, {ESC} will unlock the range and show the beginning of the range as a cell reference. If there is no range, {ESC} places you in the main Print menu. The {CE} entry remains in the Print Range prompt regardless of whether there are any entries. With {CE} you can proceed to enter a new range. With {ESC} your ability to do so is dependent on the existence of a predefined range.

Other Special Keys

As mentioned earlier, the tilde represents ENTER. To use a macro to place an actual tilde in a cell, type {~}. To use a macro to place curly brackets (braces) in a cell, enter either {{} or {}}. These features can be useful in a macro that builds another macro.

The symbol {?} can be used in a macro to let 1-2-3 know that you want the operator to input something from the keyboard. 1-2-3 will then wait for the entry to be made and ENTER to be pressed. Chapter 13 covers two additional methods for indicating keyboard input that offer greater sophistication, in that they allow you to present a message to the operator regarding the data you wish to have entered.

Typing a Keyboard Macro

The following procedure for entering a macro is not the fastest way, but it should more than pay for itself in time savings during the testing and debugging phase, as you are trying to get your macro to execute correctly.

- The first step in creating a keyboard macro is planning the task you wish to accomplish. Without a plan, you are not likely to create a macro that is well organized and successful.

- After you have made your plan, test it by entering the proposed keystrokes for immediate execution by 1-2-3. As you enter each keystroke directly into the menus, record it on a sheet of paper. Later you will learn to capitalize on these written entries and actually turn them into the macro code. For now, you will want to type at least a few for a firsthand look at what each keystroke represents.

- If the menu selections handled your task correctly, use your sheet of paper as a script when you record the keystrokes as labels in the macro cells.

- Choose a location on your worksheet, or a macro library worksheet for recording your macro. With Release 3, you might want to use a separate worksheet in the current file, or even a separate file; Release 3 can access all the macros in memory as long as they each have a unique name.

- Where possible, use range name references rather than cell addresses as you build your macro. 1-2-3 will adjust to a change in the range name location, but it will not adjust for changes in the location of cell addresses.

- You can record up to 512 keystrokes in one label cell, but it would not be advisable to do so, since you could never read the entire entry at one time without editing the cell. At the other extreme, you can enter each single keystroke of the entry in a separate cell of the column. 1-2-3 will read down the column until it reaches a blank cell. However, this second approach is also not advisable because you would need so many cells to create even a short macro. The best approach is to select some reasonable upper limit for the number of characters to be entered in one macro cell and then, within that limit, move to a new cell whenever you reach a logical breaking place in your keystroke entries.

- Use file references if you need to refer to cells or ranges outside the current worksheet.

TIP: Remember to enter all your macro instructions as labels. Start them with a label indicator if the first character is a number or one of these characters: / + − @ . # $.

Using the Keystroke Recorder Feature

Release 3's automatic keystroke recorder can save you a significant amount of time in macro entry. It makes the creation of macros easy, because you can execute a task without needing to remember the representations for the special keys; 1-2-3 will record the proper entries. The special keyboard buffer that 1-2-3 uses can hold up to 512 characters. You can create longer macros, but you must copy the keystrokes from the buffer before the limit is exceeded and begin recording a new group of keystrokes to add to the macro.

Copying Recorder Entries to the Worksheet

There is no need to invoke the macro recorder; it automatically, continually records your keystrokes. However, it is a good idea to empty the buffer if you know that you are beginning to record a macro. At any time during a macro session, you have the option of converting any or all of the last 512 keystrokes to macro entries.

Before looking at the buffer, let's make a few entries so you will have at least a few keystrokes recorded, even if you just started your 1-2-3 session. First, enter **/Range Format Currency** and press ENTER twice. Next, enter **/Worksheet Column Set-Width 18** and press ENTER. As you know, these entries have formatted the current cell as Currency and extended the width of the current column to 18.

To work with these entries in the keyboard buffer, press the ALT-F2 (RECORD) key to see the menu that includes Playback, Copy, Erase, Step, and Trace. If you select the Copy option, you will see the last keystrokes (up to 512) entered in the current session. They may look something like the entries in Figure 12-1, depending on the type of entries that you have made.

Notice that the recorder translates your menu selections to uppercase and uses the abbreviated form for the keyword wherever possible. Range names and cell addresses are in lowercase, since the recorder does not convert these entries

```
A:A1: (C2) [W18]                                                           EDIT
Press TAB to anchor cursor, then highlight keystrokes to copy:
/WS{ESC}/WG{ESC 3} {ESC 3}{HELP}{R}{D 3}~{D}{L}~{R}~{R}{L}~{ESC 3}/FNA{CE}C:\123
R34\DATA\FILE0001.WK3~/FNA{CE}C:\123R34\DATA\FILE0002.WK3~{PS}{FILE}{PGUP}{NS}/{
HELP}{ESC 3}{HELP}{D 3}{R}~~{R}~{ESC}{GOTO}A4~/{ESC 2}/FR{R}~/WDF{R 2}~/{ESC}{HE
LP}{D 3}{R}~{PGDN}~{R}~~~{ESC}/WWC/RFC~~/WCS18~_
```

Figure 12-1. *Keystrokes stored with macro keystroke recorder*

to uppercase for you. You can use the arrow keys, the END key, and the HOME key to move within the recorder screen. You will also notice that any commands, movements, and icons you have selected with the mouse are entered in the recorder as if you used the keyboard to make the selections.

Despite any preceding entries you have made, you should be able to see the entries representing the /Range and /Worksheet commands you just entered. Move the cursor to the / that precedes the *R* representing the /Range command (the second / from the end of the last line). Press the TAB key to mark this keystroke as the place where you want to begin copying keystrokes. Use the RIGHT ARROW key to move to the final tilde (~) and press ENTER. Supply an address on any active sheet where you want 1-2-3 to record these keystrokes. 1-2-3 uses the width of the range address to select the width of the cells copied to the worksheet and as many rows as are necessary to store all of the keystrokes. Be sure that the column below the specified cell is empty, since 1-2-3 will write over any entries they contain. After pressing ENTER to finalize, the entries are copied.

Figure 12-2 shows a large number of keystrokes copied by the recorder feature. Notice how the keystrokes are split up into manageable groups. While each cell's contents are in the output range's first column, the contents use the width selected by the number of columns you chose for the range.

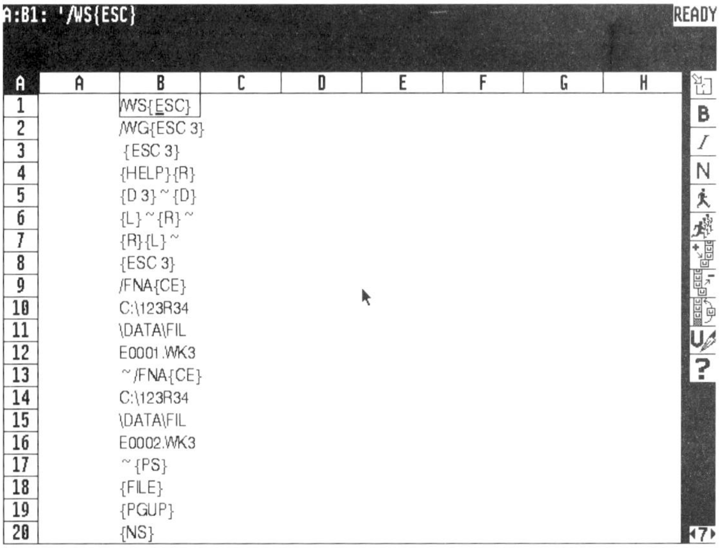

Figure 12-2. *Recorded keystrokes copied to a worksheet*

TIP: Keywords in a macro are easier to understand when they are spelled out. Use /Range Search with the Replace option to locate entries like {D} and change them to {DOWN}. You can even develop a macro that will handle this task if you specify the search range it should use.

Other Recorder Menu Options

Other options on the keystroke recorder menu include Erase, which empties the buffer. Invoke the recorder feature with ALT-F2 (RECORD) and select Erase. Remember to do this before beginning a sequence of keystrokes you plan to record as a macro. The Playback feature allows you to reexecute the keystrokes in the buffer. After selecting Playback, move the cursor to the first keystroke to play back, press TAB, highlight the last keystroke to play back, and press ENTER. Playback allows you to perform keystrokes without storing them as a macro in a worksheet. You can use this feature to perform repetitive keystrokes that you do not want to make into a macro.

Step turns on the STEP mode of execution, so that each macro instruction executes at your request as you press the SPACEBAR. You will see an indicator at the bottom of the screen telling you when STEP mode is on. To turn off STEP mode, enter ALT-F2 (RECORD) a second time and choose Step again. In prior releases of 1-2-3, pressing ALT-F2 alone controlled STEP mode, since there was no recorder feature. In Release 3.4 you can use the SmartIcon that looks like this to turn on STEP mode:

Trace turns on the macro tracing which shows the macro instructions as 1-2-3 performs them. This menu command is only available in Release 3.4. When you run a macro with Trace mode on, the status line contains the macro instructions and highlights the currently executed instruction.

Naming Your Macro

Once you have entered or copied all the macro keystrokes, you are ready to name your macro. Before doing this, position your cell pointer on the top cell in the macro, since this is the only cell that will be named. Then enter **/Range Name Create**. At the prompt for the range name, enter a backslash and any single alphabetic character before pressing ENTER if you want to be able to execute the macro with a single key combination. An alternative is to type any valid range name and press ENTER to execute the macro with the ALT-F3 (RUN) option. Since you positioned your cell pointer before requesting the /Range command, simply press ENTER in response to the prompt for the range address. When you save the worksheet, the macro and its name will be saved as well and will be available whenever you retrieve the worksheet.

The naming conventions for 1-2-3's macros allow you to create an unlimited number of macros. You can also create 26 unique macro names using the backslash and the letters of the alphabet, such as \t; these macros can be executed with the ALT key in combination with the letter used in the macro name. 1-2-3 does not distinguish between upper- and lowercase characters in a macro name.

TIP: Choose a special character or letter as the first entry in all macro names. When you use the F3 (RUN) option, 1-2-3 displays a list of all valid range names. To help distinguish macro names from other range names, start all of them with the same character. Using a special symbol like # will place them at the front of the list.

You can obtain a list of all your current macro names and the range addresses to which they are assigned with the /Range Name Table command. Enter **/Range Name Table** and respond to 1-2-3's prompt for a table range by entering the address of the upper left cell in any blank section of the worksheet where 1-2-3 can write the macro name assignments. This command is described more fully in Chapter 5.

Documenting Your Macro

As you create a macro, you are aware of the name you have assigned to it and the function of each of its steps. A month from now, however, when you look again at the macro cells, it may take some thought to remember what you were attempting to accomplish. It is therefore a wise move to document information like the macro name and the function of each step on the worksheet as you create the macro. The time investment in this extra step will more than pay for itself later on.

A good documentation strategy is placing the macro name in the cell immediately to the left of the top macro cell. If the macro is named Currency, type **currency** in the cell immediately to the left of the top macro cell. If the macro is named \a, you would enter **'\a** in the cell to the left of the macro's first instruction. (The ' is needed to prevent 1-2-3 from interpreting the backslash as the repeating label indicator and filling your cell with the letter a.) The cell to the left of your top macro cell is an especially appropriate choice because, if you have already placed the macro name there before actually naming the macro range, you can use the /Range Name Labels Right command to name the macro cell without typing the name in again. In other words, you can type the macro steps, then type the macro name in the empty cell to the left of the macro, leave the cell pointer on the name, enter **/Range Name Labels Right**, and press ENTER.

A good area to use for documenting macro instructions is a column of cells to the right of the instructions. Depending on the length of your macro entries, you can widen the column containing the macro instructions or move several cells to the right of the macro column for the documentation entries. A brief description of every command will make each step's function clearer and will save a significant amount of time if it is necessary to modify the macro later. Figure 12-3 shows a macro with documentation entries for the individual macro instructions.

Executing Your Macro

Once you have entered and named a macro, you can use it whenever you wish from READY mode or within a command. Macros can supply entries like graph titles or print headers. If your macro requires the cell pointer to be positioned in a certain cell, put the cell pointer there before executing the macro. The cell pointer does not need to be on the macro cell to execute the macro.

If the macro is named with a backslash-letter combination, you can execute the macro in several ways. The short-cut approach is to press the ALT key and, while the key is pressed, touch the letter key that you used in your macro name; then release both keys.

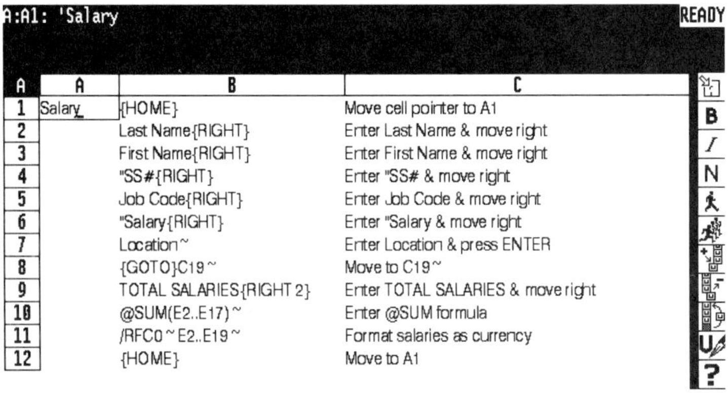

A	A	B	C
1	Salary	{HOME}	Move cell pointer to A1
2		Last Name{RIGHT}	Enter Last Name & move right
3		First Name{RIGHT}	Enter First Name & move right
4		"SS#{RIGHT}	Enter "SS# & move right
5		Job Code{RIGHT}	Enter Job Code & move right
6		"Salary{RIGHT}	Enter "Salary & move right
7		Location~	Enter Location & press ENTER
8		{GOTO}C19~	Move to C19~
9		TOTAL SALARIES{RIGHT 2}	Enter TOTAL SALARIES & move right
10		@SUM(E2..E17)~	Enter @SUM formula
11		/RFC0~E2..E19~	Format salaries as currency
12		{HOME}	Move to A1

Figure 12-3. *Macro with documentation*

Chapter 12: Keyboard Macros

The other approach can be used regardless of the macro's name. Press the ALT-F3 (RUN) key or click the Run Macro SmartIcon, and 1-2-3 displays the names of all the range names in the current file, including macro names, and the names of other open files. Selecting a filename in the list displays a new list of range names and macro names located in the newly selected file. Highlight the name you want to use and press ENTER; or type the desired name.

TIP: Save the worksheet where you recorded the macro before trying it. If the macro contains mistakes, saving it will prevent you from losing your work if the macro writes over its own instructions or locks up your system. If the macro sheet contains other entries, you might want to use the /File Save Backup feature to maintain the integrity of the existing file until after macro testing.

Assigning Macros to User Icons

In Release 3.4, there are two ways that you can customize 1-2-3's SmartIcons palettes. In Chapter 14 you will learn how to change the icons which appear on the first palette. This allows you to put all of the frequently used icons together on one palette. Another option is to assign macro instructions to any of the twelve user icons represented by U1 through U12. You can use this feature to store frequently needed text. This text would be typed automatically if you selected the icon. You can also use this feature to develop a custom formatting macro that meets your exact needs.

The steps to assign macros to user icons are summarized in the box titled "Assigning a Macro to a User Icon." After assigning a macro to any of these user icons you can use them just as you would any other icon, invoking the macro

Assigning a Macro to a User Icon

1. Select Edit User icon from the seventh SmartIcons palette.
2. Select Previous Icon or Next Icon to select the user icon to modify.
3. Select the Icon Description text box.
4. Type a description of up to 72 characters.
5. Select the Macro Text text box.
6. Type the macro instructions you want to attach up to 512 characters.
7. Select OK.

they represent or assigning one of them to your custom palette. Later, in Chapter 14, you will learn how you can edit the icon's appearance so it looks like the macro task it represents.

Defining a User Icon from Keyboard

You can use the Edit User icon on the seventh palette to define any of the twelve user icons labeled U1 through U12. This Edit User icon looks like this:

After selecting the Edit User icon, the Assign Macro to U1 dialog box shown in Figure 12-4 appears. Select Previous Icon or Next Icon until the 1 in the dialog box title becomes the number for the user icon you want to modify.

You can supply a description of as many as 72 characters in the Icon Description text box. Just as other icons display text in the control panel when they are highlighted, user icons will display this text when they are highlighted.

Next, type the macro instructions in the Macro Text text box. You can use as many as 512 characters to represent any menu command or keystroke. The menu representations can be for 1-2-3 as well as Wysiwyg or other attached add-ins. In Chapter 14, you will learn how you can change the appearance of the icons and the palette in which the icons display.

To complete the user icon's definition, select OK and you return to READY mode. You can cancel the request by selecting Cancel. You can reset the current user icon definition by choosing Reset Macro.

Figure 12-4. *Assign Macro to dialog box*

As an example of changing a user icon, you can type **Formats a range as currency with 0 decimal places** for the Icon Description and **/rfc0~** for the Macro Text. Select OK, and when you click this user icon, you will format the current cell or range using the currency format and 0 decimal places. When you click the icon with the right mouse button, you will see the Icon Description's text in the control panel.

Define a User Icon's Macro with Stored Keystrokes

You can add the macro instructions you have stored on a sheet to the icon's Macro Text text box. This feature lets you try out a macro before assigning it to a user icon, or use an existing macro for a user icon's macro text. Once added in this way, the macro instructions are added to the dialog box and are only updated by editing the contents of the icon's Macro Text text box. In other words, the icon's macro instructions do not change as you revise the macro instructions on the worksheet.

To obtain macro instructions from the worksheet, define the user icon as described above with one exception. Rather than selecting Macro Text text box and typing the macro instructions, select the Get Macro from Sheet button. Specify the range containing the macro code or the name that you have assigned to the range. If you have stored macro instructions in F3..F6 and have named these \c, you can either type **F3..F6** or **\c** for the range.

Modifying the Definition of a User Icon

Once you attach macro instructions to a user icon, you must use the same basic procedure to modify them as you did when you first defined them. The steps that you will follow are:

1. Select the Edit User icon.

2. Select Previous Icon or Next Icon to select the user icon to modify.

3. Select the Icon Description text box and make any changes to the icon's description.

4. Select the Macro Text text box and modify the text in the box to make any additions or corrections.

5. Select OK to return to 1-2-3's READY mode.

Debugging a Macro Assigned to a User Icon

If the macro that you attached to a user icon is not working the way you want, you will need to copy it to the worksheet in order to use STEP mode in testing it. The method you will use to complete the copy is as follows:

1. Select the Edit User icon.
2. Select Previous Icon or Next Icon to select the user icon to modify.
3. Select Copy Macro to Sheet, specify an empty range on the worksheet, and then select OK.

Creating a Macro Library

A macro library is simply a worksheet file that contains all of your macros. With Release 3 you can really use this concept effectively, since the macros and the files they work on can be different—as long as the macros are in an active file.

Your separate macro library file can be in any worksheet in the file. You might want to start in sheet A at the beginning of the file, since the file will not contain other types of data. You can also group the macros, using different sheets to group a single type of macros—like formatting macros, data entry macros, and print and graph macros. An organized storage method makes it easy to find the macro when you need it for use, or when it is time to make modifications. If you decide to create some specialized macros in a worksheet file with a model or a database, you will want to store the macros on a separate sheet. This minimizes the risk of damage to the macro when changes are made to the application area of the file.

If you use the macro library concept, you must load the library into memory before using any of its macros. If your application file is already in memory, you can use the /File Open command.

When you wish to add a new macro to your library file, make the macro library file the current file. Enter the new macro, and it will be available in all your other active files. Save the macro library file under its original filename. To add a macro from another worksheet to the library, use the /File Xtract command to extract the macro from the other sheet, saving it to another file temporarily. Then retrieve your macro library file and use the /File Combine Copy command to place the new macro in the library. This approach also works for copying a single macro from the macro library to any of your other worksheets. Be sure to copy the entire macro, including the documentation to the right and left of the macro. Then, when you use /File Combine, you can specify the Named/Specified-Range option and copy in just the one macro. You will need to name the macro again once it is on the new worksheet, since the range name used for the macro on the disk file will not be copied.

TIP: Be careful of multiple-sheet and external file references. Cell or range addresses consisting of nothing more than column and row references are always assumed to reference the current sheet. To reference a different sheet, use the level indicator, as in B:A10. Even with a level indicator, the reference is assumed to be in the current file. To reference an external file, use the angle brackets around the filename, as in <<ACCT.WK3>>B:A10.

Debugging Macros

The debugging process involves testing and correcting macros to ensure that you obtain the desired results. One of the most common mistakes made when creating keyboard macros is forgetting to enter the tilde mark to represent each time the ENTER key needs to be pressed.

1-2-3 has a STEP mode that executes a macro one keystroke at a time so you can follow its progress and spot any area of difficulty. STEP mode is available from the Record menu activated with ALT-F2 (RECORD). Once you activate the menu you can highlight Step and press ENTER, or type an **S**. Step is a toggle operation, so selecting Step a second time turns STEP mode off again. When this mode is operational, you will see "STEP" on the bottom line of your screen.

When the STEP indicator is on, any macro you invoke will be executed one instruction at a time. Press the SPACEBAR whenever you are ready to move on to the next instruction. While the macro is executing, "SST" will appear in place of STEP at the bottom of the screen.

To stop a malfunctioning macro, press the CTRL and BREAK keys simultaneously. This cancels macro operation immediately, and presents an ERROR indicator at the upper right corner of the screen. Pressing ESC will return you to READY mode so you can make corrections to your macro.

The other debugging feature is the Trace mode which displays the executing macro instructions in the status line. Trace mode is activated from the Record menu by pressing ALT-F2 (RECORD). From the Record menu, select Trace. Trace is a toggle operation; when you select Trace a second time, you will no longer see the executing macro instructions in the status line. Trace mode does not have an indicator; you only know that it is on when you run a macro. When you run a macro, the status line includes a segment of the macro's instructions, along with the macro instruction 1-2-3 is performing highlighted as shown here:

```
A:B2 Last Name{RIGHT}
```

STEP and Trace modes are often combined since 1-2-3's execution speed is so fast that you would not be able to follow along if you used Trace mode with the normal macro execution speed.

Automatic Macros

1-2-3 has a unique feature that allows you to create an automatic macro for a worksheet. Every time a worksheet containing an automatic macro is retrieved, 1-2-3 immediately executes this macro. This feature has more application with the advanced macro commands discussed in Chapter 13. However, there may be situations where you want to execute, say, a /File Combine or a /Range Erase command as soon as a worksheet is retrieved. 1-2-3 also can suspend execution of automatic macros; you will want to be familiar with this command, too.

Creating an Automatic Macro

The only difference in creating an automatic macro and a normal executable macro is in the macro name. There can be only one automatic macro on a worksheet, and it must have the name \0 (backslash zero).

Figure 12-5 shows an automatic macro designed to erase a range of input cells used by an @PMT function every time the worksheet is retrieved. That way, each new operator can enter new values for the principal, interest rate, and term. To create this macro, place your instructions into a column of worksheet cells on the sheet that will trigger its execution, and assign the special \0 name to the name cell. Then save the worksheet file with /File Save. The next time the worksheet is retrieved, the macro executes immediately.

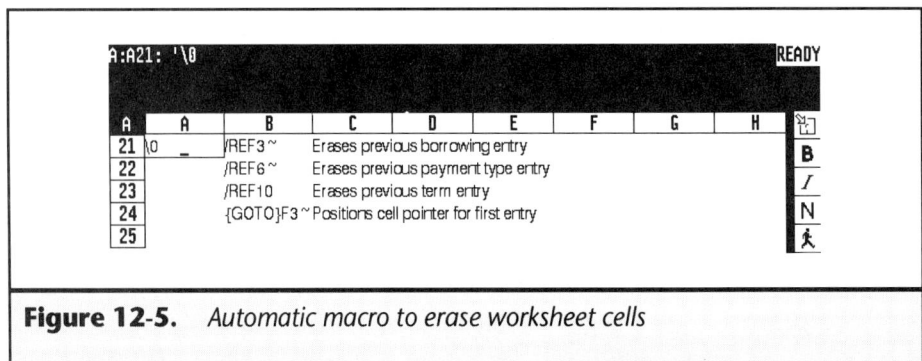

Figure 12-5. *Automatic macro to erase worksheet cells*

TIP: An automatic macro executes when you retrieve the worksheet file with the automatic macro. An automatic macro must be stored in the file whose retrieval you want to trigger execution of the macro.

Disabling Automatic Macros

If you change the setting for /Worksheet Global Default Autoexec to No, 1-2-3 will not execute automatic macros when you retrieve a file that contains one. When you first install 1-2-3, the default setting for this command is Yes. To make a permanent change to this setting, you have to use /Worksheet Global Default Update to save the change to the configuration file.

With Release 3's multiple file capabilities, you can have nested macros. For instance, if an executing macro in file A contains an instruction that opens file B, and file B contains an automatic macro, the setting for /Worksheet Global Default Autoexec determines which macro will execute next. If the setting is No, the macro in File A will continue. If the setting is Yes, the automatic macro in File B will begin execution.

Ready-to-Use Macros

The macros in the following paragraphs are ready to use; they are complete macros designed to perform the tasks described. Since it is likely your data will be located in files, sheets, or cells different from the data on the worksheets used to create these examples, you probably will have to make minor modifications to the cell addresses referenced in the macros. Each macro description will include guidelines for its use, and a section on potential modifications.

The same conventions have been used for all the macros. The name used for the macro is shown in the first column to the left of the top cell in the macro. The macro is written in the second column as labels. A description is placed in the third column. Uppercase characters are used for the all the macro entries, including menu selections, responses to menu prompts, filenames, special key indicators such as {HOME} and {ESC}, and range names.

Worksheet Macros

Many repetitive worksheet tasks are candidates for macros. Examples are changing the global format, checking the worksheet status, moving between worksheets or between files, and changing default settings like the printer interface. You can even have a macro do some of your typing in worksheet cells. For example, you can create a macro that enters the months for you. You can have a macro make changes to an entry to enhance it, or to fix existing errors.

A Macro to Display Formulas

1-2-3 prints the formulas behind your worksheet results when you specify /Print Printer Options Other Cell-Formulas, but it creates one line of printed output per cell. If you would like to display or print out formulas while maintaining the integrity of your worksheet design, you will have to change the format of each formula cell to text. The steps involved can be placed in a macro to simplify the task.

```
     A        B          C
1    \t       /WGFT      Request global format as text
2             /RFR       Request range format reset
3             A1..Z60~   Specify range as A1..Z60 in current sheet
```

The instructions in the first line request /Worksheet Global Format Text. Next, this macro uses /Range Format Reset to make all the cells conform to the global format setting of Text. This is followed by a range that contains all the entries on the worksheet with which the macro is designed to work.

GUIDELINES FOR USE It is important that you save your worksheet before executing this macro. You will not want to save your worksheet afterward, since all your regular formats will have been superceded.

MODIFYING THE MACRO You may want to add an instruction at the beginning to save your current worksheet file, so that you do not lose your established formats. The only risk with this addition is that you might execute the macro a second time and overlay your existing file with the Text formatted version.

Another option is adding the commands necessary to print the file. These instructions could be placed at the end of the macro. You could add a /Worksheet Erase command after the /Print commands so that the text formatted version is not saved to disk after the macro ends. You could also add a command to increase the column width so that complete formulas can display. You can alter the macro to select the range with a specification of {CE}{HOME}.{END}{HOME}. This approach selects A1 as the first cell in the range, and the last cell in the sheet is used as the last cell in the range.

A Macro to Insert Blank Rows

You can create macros that will add and delete blank rows for you. When you use the worksheet for calculations and printed reports, use the macro that inserts blank rows.

The macro that follows will insert blank rows.

```
    A           B               C
1   INSERT      /WI             Request /Worksheet Insert
2               R               Specify Rows
3               {DOWN}{DOWN}~   Move down to insert 3 rows
```

The macro as shown adds three blank rows, but it can easily be modified to add any number you choose. The first macro instruction, in B1, requests /Worksheet Insert. The next instruction specifies that rows rather than columns should be inserted. The third instruction expands the insertion to three rows. You can use the shortcut approach for moving the cell pointer and write this instruction as {DOWN 2}~.

GUIDELINES FOR USE   This macro requires that you place your cell pointer where you want to insert the blank rows, since they are added above the cell pointer. When you invoke the macro, the cell pointer row is shifted down to make room for the new rows. Just as with a keyboard entry of the same command, your formulas are adjusted to reflect the addition, but insertions at the top or bottom of a range do not expand the range.

MODIFYING THE MACRO   By changing the entry in B2, you could create a macro that inserts columns or sheets. If you choose to add sheets, an additional modification will be required to indicate that you want the sheets inserted either before or after the current sheet by including a *B* or an *A* after an S in B2. You may also wish to modify the last instruction, to allow for the addition of extra rows, columns, or sheets. A third option is to end the macro after line 2 and allow the operator to specify the number of rows, columns, or sheets to be added.

A Macro to Change the Global Default Directory

When you are working with completed worksheet models, you may want your directory set at drive C if all your completed models are stored on the hard drive. If you have a number of new models to create and wish to store them on a floppy disk, you may want the directory set at drive B. You may also wish to change the directory if you use 1-2-3 on two systems that have different configurations.

Changing the drive with a macro eliminates the need for remembering the command path required.

The following macro changes the existing directory to drive B:\.

	A	B	C
1	CHG_DIRB	/WG	Request /Worksheet Global change
2		D	Specify a Default change
3		D	Specify Directory
4		{CE}	Clears existing directory entry
5		B:\~	Sets new directory
6		Q	Quits default menu without saving

The first instruction requests a /Worksheet Global change. A default change and directory change are specified in the next two instructions. B4 causes the macro to remove the current directory setting. The instruction in B5 generates the new directory setting and finalizes it, and the last instruction leaves the Default menu and returns to READY mode.

GUIDELINES FOR USE   When you change the directory, both the old and the new directories must be available on the system you are using to change the settings. If you are changing the directory to a floppy drive, place a data disk in the drive before executing the macro, since 1-2-3 attempts to read the directory for the selected device. You can also use this macro to change the subdirectory for model storage and retrieval if you are using a hard disk.

MODIFYING THE MACRO   B5 is the instruction you are likely to want to modify in this macro. B5 should contain the pathname of the device and directory you plan to use for data storage. As an example, if you are currently using drive A and want to change to a subdirectory on drive C, you might change this instruction to read C:\123\Dallas\Sales\.

A Macro to Set the Window to Perspective and Move to the First Sheet

When you are working with multiple sheets or files, Release 3's Perspective window makes it easier to work with your data. If you change frequently from a consolidation sheet to one of the detail sheets, you might want several macros to handle some of these changes for you. For example, this macro creates a Perspective view and then moves to the first sheet:

	A	B	C
1	\w	/WWP	Use perspective window
2		{FS}	Move to the first sheet

The first instruction sets the screen to a three-window perspective, and the second moves the cell pointer to the first sheet in the current file. Although the macro only saves a few keystrokes, it can still save time if you need to execute the task frequently. Having the required keystrokes in a macro also frees you from having to remember anything other than the name of the macro.

GUIDELINES FOR USE   You can use this macro regardless of the sheet you are on when you decide you need to see a Perspective view. You can also use this macro when the current worksheet only contains one sheet, and other files are open in memory, since the other worksheet files will display in the other windows.

A Macro to Change the Global Printer Default Setup

When you install your 1-2-3 package, you have the option of installing more than one printer. You may have both a dot matrix and a letter quality printer coupled to your system. You may want to use the letter quality printer for printing most worksheets, and the dot matrix for printing graphs or quick drafts of a model.

If you want to change the default printer that 1-2-3 uses when you request /Print, but your second printer is cabled to another port, you will have to change both the printer requested and the interface. The printer will be the device requested, and the interface specification will tell 1-2-3 whether you have it cabled to a serial or parallel device, or wish to access one of the operating system devices on your local area network.

A macro for changing the default printer is as follows:

	A	B	C
1	\s	/WG	Request /Worksheet Global change
2		D	Specify Default
3		P	Choose Printer
4		I1	Set Interface to parallel 1
5		N1	Set Name to first printer installed
6		S{CE}\027E~	Create default setup string
7		Q	Quit printer default menu
8		Q	Quit default menu

The first line requests a /Worksheet Global change. The next two lines tell 1-2-3 that you wish to use the Default Printer option. The instruction in B4 tells 1-2-3 to set the Interface option to the first parallel interface. The Name option is selected next, and the first name in the list of printers is specified.

It is possible to change other default print settings at the same time you change the specified printer. Although you can now select many print options from 1-2-3's Print menus where setup strings were required in earlier releases, there are still many setup strings that are not part of the menus. For instance, in this macro, the {CE} first removes any existing default setup string and then supplies the setup string \027E, which resets a Hewlett-Packard LaserJet printer. The last two instructions quit the Default Printer submenu and the Default menu.

GUIDELINES FOR USE   Before creating this macro, you will need to know the name and interface for the printer you want to use. The printer names you use in the macro depend on the options you selected during installation. You cannot access printer types that were not installed, since the necessary driver files will not be available. If you plan to use a new printer device, you must go back to the installation program and add it there.

MODIFYING THE MACRO   B4 would be modified to I2 or I4 if you planned to use a serial connection for your printer. For a serial printer, you would also need a macro instruction to select the baud rate. If you wanted a different setup string, you would modify the string in B6.

You could also expand this macro to include a change to the default settings for other print characteristics, such as margins and page length. If you wanted to have these new settings available the next time you used the package, you would have to add a command to select the Global Default Update option after exiting the Default Printer menu. Then you could save your changes to the file 123R34.CNF.

A Macro to Handle Data Entry Errors

Macros can be used to correct a variety of data input errors. They are especially valuable since 1-2-3 gives you access to all the string functions.

For example, if you had employees' names entered in the following format in your database:

Jeff Jones

it would be considered "proper case," since only the first letter of each word is capitalized. Some string functions such as @EXACT, @HLOOKUP, and @VLOOKUP are case sensitive, so if someone else updates your database and enters names as BOB BROWN or bill smith, you are likely to have trouble with these functions. It could be time consuming to make corrections so that all the entries match in format. However, you can create a macro that will change any entry into proper case. It is shown in Figure 12-6.

The macro begins by preparing to edit the current cell. It then moves to the first position and deletes the label indicator in the first position. The @PROPER function is entered, followed by a (and ", since the string entry from the current cell must be enclosed in double quotes. The instruction in B4 moves the cell pointer to the end of the entry. The last instruction adds the " at the end and follows it with a). Before finalizing the entry, the macro calculates the formula so it can be stored in the cell as a label rather than as a formula.

GUIDELINES FOR USE   This macro is position dependent. It changes only the label entry at the cell pointer location to proper case. You must move the cell pointer and reexecute the macro to change additional cells.

MODIFYING THE MACRO   If you want your data in uppercase, you can use the @UPPER function in place of @PROPER. For lowercase, use @LOWER. You can also modify the macro to round numbers by changing @PROPER(" in B3 to @ROUND and changing ") in B5 to ,0), which will round numbers to the nearest whole number.

A Macro to Enter a Worksheet Heading

If you need to create a whole series of worksheets that use the same heading, you can place the heading instructions in a macro and use the macro in each worksheet. Since the macro is designed to begin the heading at the cell pointer location, the headings need not start in the same position in each worksheet.

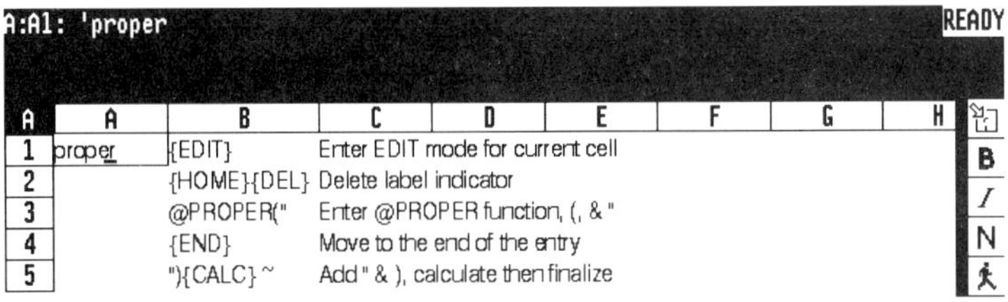

```
A:A1: 'proper                                                    READY

    A        B              C           D          E       F    G    H
1  proper   {EDIT}         Enter EDIT mode for current cell
2           {HOME}{DEL}    Delete label indicator
3           @PROPER("      Enter @PROPER function, (, & "
4           {END}          Move to the end of the entry
5           "){CALC}~      Add " & ), calculate then finalize
```

Figure 12-6.   *Proper case macro*

The following macro places headings for the quarters of the year across a worksheet:

```
        A          B              C
1   heading    ^QTR1{RIGHT}   Enter QTR1 and move 1 cell right
2              ^QTR2{RIGHT}   Enter QTR2 and move 1 cell right
3              ^QTR3{RIGHT}   Enter QTR3 and move 1 cell right
4              ^QTR4{RIGHT}   Enter QTR4 and move 1 cell right
5              ^TOTAL~        Enter TOTAL and press ENTER
6              {END}{LEFT}    Move to the leftmost entry
7              {DOWN}         Move down 1 cell
```

Each of the first four macro instructions center justifies one of the quarter headings in a worksheet cell, and moves one cell to the right. The instruction in B5 places the heading TOTAL in a cell and finalizes the entry with ENTER. The cell pointer is then moved to the left of this section of the worksheet. It will be on the first heading if the cell to its left is blank, or it will be in column A. The last instruction moves the cell pointer down one cell.

GUIDELINES FOR USE   The macro places the first heading at the cell pointer location and moves to the right with subsequent entries, so it is important that you position your cell pointer before executing the macro.

MODIFYING THE MACRO   The macro can be modified to create any series of headings, like the months of the year, weeks of the month, multiple years, or account numbers. All you need to change are the headings themselves. You can easily modify the label prefix that begins each heading entry as well, if you wish different justification.

This macro can be modified to create account names down a column. The only difference is that the cell pointer would be moved down after each entry and the caret symbol (^) for center justification would not be used.

Range Macros

You can create macros for all the /Range commands you use frequently. They can be either open-ended macros or closed ones. An open-ended macro is one that returns control to the operator before the range is selected. Closed macros are more limited in their application, since they function only under one particular set of circumstances. If you are developing macros for yourself, open-ended macros add flexibility. If you are developing them for someone else and want to maintain as much control over the application as possible, try closed macros.

A Macro to Create a Range Name Table

The /Range Name Table command lists all the range names and their cell addresses in a table on your worksheet. This table is not updated automatically as you add new range names, however; you must execute the command sequence again to have 1-2-3 update the table. A macro can easily handle this task for you.

The short macro needed reads as follows:

```
   A    B          C
1 \z   {GOTO}G5~  Position cursor at range table
2     /RNT~       Request /Range Name Table at current location
```

The first instruction in the macro positions the cell pointer in the upper left corner of the area where you wish your table to appear—cell G5, in this example. The second instruction requests the /Range Name Table command.

GUIDELINES FOR USE   Before executing this macro, make sure the area to the right and below G5 (or wherever you send the cell pointer) is empty, since the macro overwrites any data that is stored there. If you plan to print the table of range names, you will always want to execute this macro before printing, to ensure that your table of names is current.

File Macros

You can automate any of the /File commands with a macro. Although /File Save and /File Retrieve do not require a significant number of keystrokes, they are still possible candidates for a macro because they are used so frequently. Other /File commands, such as Combine and Xtract, also can be automated. This may cut down on typing errors, since the same keystrokes are executed each time.

A Macro to Save Files

A /File Save does not require many keystrokes, but it should be done frequently so you do not risk the loss of your data. A macro can be created to save your file with one keystroke, as follows:

```
     A     B      C
1    \s    /FS    Request /File Save
2          ~      Specify existing file name
3          R      Replace file
```

The first line of the macro invokes the /File Save command. The tilde (~) in line 2 indicates that you want to retain the file's existing name. The final line tells 1-2-3 to replace the file on disk with the current contents of memory.

GUIDELINES FOR USE   This macro is designed to save a file that has been saved previously. It cannot be used if you want to use a new name for the file.

MODIFYING THE MACRO   The macro can easily be modified to allow your input of the filename. Simply use an input statement between line 1 and line 2 of the macro. If you prefer, a predetermined filename can be placed in the macro in the same location.

A Macro to Retrieve Files

The /File Retrieve macro that follows calls a new file into memory. The worksheet file that is active when you execute this macro will no longer be resident in memory when the retrieve operation is completed. Such a macro is normally used as part of a larger macro that chooses the task you wish to have performed and retrieves the appropriate file.

A Retrieve macro might look like this:

```
     A     B        C
1    \r    /FR      Request /File Retrieve
2          SALES~   Specify SALES file
```

The first line of the macro issues the request to retrieve a file. The second line contains the filename and the tilde (~) to finalize the filename entry.

GUIDELINES FOR USE The macro erases the active worksheet file when the macro is executed. If you made changes to the current worksheet, you will want to save it before executing this macro.

MODIFYING THE MACRO You can modify the macro to add a /File Save before the /File Retrieve. You can also change the name of the file being saved.

If you want, you can modify the macro so it has a name of \0. This causes it to do an immediate retrieve of a second file as soon as the first one is retrieved. In this situation you will probably want to add some other macro instructions at the beginning, to perform a few tasks in the current file before retrieving the new file.

A Macro to Extract Files

The /File Xtract command is used to save a section of a worksheet in a separate worksheet file. This process can be used to transfer end-of-period totals to a new worksheet for the next period, for example. If you need to extract files frequently, consider the time-saving features of a macro that does the job.

Our macro is as follows:

	A	B	C
1	extract	/FXV	Request value extract
2		TOTALS~	Specify filename TOTALS
3		YEAR_END_TOTAL~	Enter range name to extract
4		R	Select replace

The first line contains a request to perform a /File Xtract Values operation to save the values from the original file. The next step contains the name of the file in which you want the new material saved. In this macro, the filename is TOTALS. The next instruction tells 1-2-3 what to place in the new file; you can specify a range address or a range name. This macro uses the range name **year_end_total**. The *R* in the last instruction tells 1-2-3 to replace the TOTALS file with the current contents of **year_end_total**.

GUIDELINES FOR USE This macro operates on two assumptions. First, it assumes that the range name **year_end_total** has already been created. Second, it assumes that the file TOTALS has already been created, since it requests that 1-2-3 replace it.

MODIFYING THE MACRO The macro can be modified easily to use a range address rather than a range name for the extract area. The filename used can also be modified. Either of these can be entered by the operator while the macro is executing if you use an input instruction.

A Macro to Combine Files

The /File Combine command allows you to add data from files on disk to the current worksheet, without erasing the current worksheet as a /File Retrieve operation would do. A macro to handle the combining operation is shown in Figure 12-7. The final product of the macro is shown in Figure 12-8, where each figure represents the combined totals of each of the four company regions.

Each of the detail worksheets contains a 1 in column H in the row number that corresponds to the region number. After the macro has added all four regions to the consolidated company template, the four cells in column H should each contain a 1, as they do in Figure 12-8. These 1's are your confirmation that each detail sheet has been combined with the total worksheet only once, since each detail sheet has a 1 in a different location. In addition to saving keystrokes, this macro ensures that the combining process is handled consistently and accurately. When you are entering /File Combine commands from the keyboard to consolidate many worksheets, it is easy to forget which combining operations have been completed.

After moving to A1 to ensure correct cell pointer placement, the macro executes the /File Combine instructions that follow. The four Combine instructions are the same except for the filenames being combined. Each requests a /File Combine Add Entire-File operation for the appropriate region file.

GUIDELINES FOR USE The region files are assumed to be in the current directory at the time you execute this macro. Each of the region files is also assumed to have a format identical to that of the file in memory. The region file

```
A:A21: 'combine                                                      READY


     A       B            C       D          E          F      G    H
21  combine  {HOME}               Move to A1
22           /FCAEREGION1~        Request file combine add for Region1
23           /FCAEREGION2~        Request file combine add for Region2
24           /FCAEREGION3~        Request file combine add for Region3
25           /FCAEREGION4~        Request file combine add for Region4
```

Figure 12-7. *Macro to combine files*

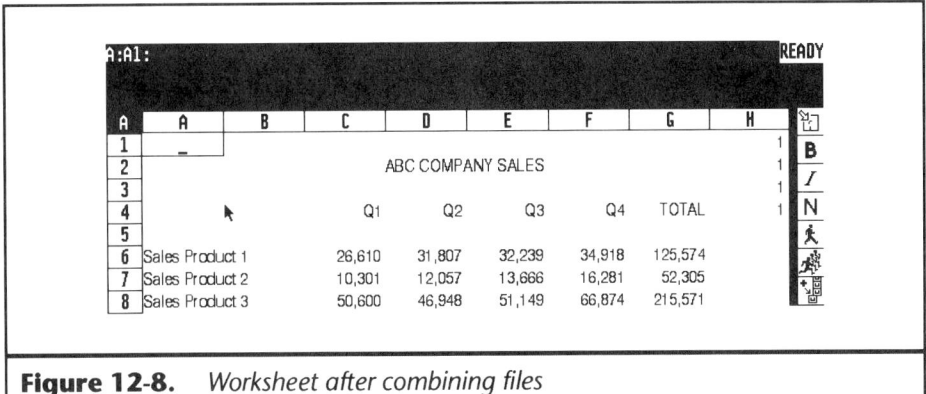

Figure 12-8. *Worksheet after combining files*

should contain a 1 in column H in the row that corresponds to the region number (rows 1 through 4). As previously noted, these serve as flags to indicate that each region has been combined into the total worksheet. This is a good strategy to use with /File Combine Add even when you are not using a macro.

MODIFYING THE MACRO The macro can be modified to combine any number of files. Although each of the region files is combined with the Add option in this case, you can easily change the macro to use the Subtract option instead.

After you learn to add more sophistication to macros in Chapter 13, you may want to return to this macro and make it check for the 1's in column H using the {IF} and {BRANCH} instructions.

With 1-2-3's ability to handle multiple sheets in one file, you might want to revise the macro to load the detail for each region on a separate sheet in the file and use formulas that span sheets to create the consolidation report.

Print Macros

Since 1-2-3 can retain only one set of print specifications at a time, and since many worksheets contain more than one printed report, you may find that you are reentering print specifications each month as you print your worksheet reports. This wastes time and can lead to errors that might require the reprinting of a report.

You can avoid such problems by using macros to record the commands needed to print your reports. Once you have worked out the details, a macro can print as many reports as you like with one keystroke. Also, since the macro is tested, you will not have to reprint reports because of errors in print specifications.

A Macro to Create Printed Reports

Most of your reports are likely to be sent directly to the printer. It is possible that the margins, setup strings, header, and other specifications for the printed page may differ between two reports printed from the same worksheet. If you store the different print specifications in a macro, you need only position your paper at the top of a form and turn your printer on. 1-2-3 can handle everything else.

The macro shown here will print two different reports from one worksheet.

	A	B	C
1	\p	/PP	Request print
2		RA1..C15~	Specify range
3		OML20~	Request options and left margin of 20
4		MR55~	Request right margin of 55
5		MT15~	Request top margin of 15
6		H¦¦Today's Date:@~	Create header with date
7		Q	Quit options
8		G	Print
9		PA	Page & align
10		RA1..H20~	Specify range
11		OML5~	Left margin 5
12		MR75~	Margin right 75
13		Q	Quit options
14		G	Print
15		PA	Page & align
16		Q	Quit print

The first instruction in the macro tells 1-2-3 that you want the /Print commands and would like your output sent directly to the printer. The first print range, A1..C15, is requested in B2.

The Options changes come next. The first request is to change the left margin to 20. Next, the right margin is set to 55. The top margin is set to 15. B6 specifies the header to be used at the top of each page of the report. There is no entry on the left or in the center of the header, so the line contains only two vertical bars to mark the positions. The rightmost portion of the header contains the constant "Today's Date:". It also contains an @ sign, which will cause 1-2-3 to substitute the current date. Since this is the last change through the Options menu, a *Q* is used to quit this menu. Printing is requested with the *G* for Go in the next cell.

The Page and Align request will be processed as soon as 1-2-3 finishes printing. This request causes 1-2-3 to page to the top of the next form and align its internal line count with the appropriate setting for a new page.

B10 contains the first instruction for the second report. Since the Print menu remains on the screen until you choose Quit, there is no need to make a new request for this menu. The first Options request for the second report is found in B11. The left margin is set at 5 and the right margin is set at 75.

B13 quits the Options menu. The second report is printed by the G in B14. Page and Align are issued again to position the paper and 1-2-3's line count for your next print request, and the Print menu is exited with the Q in the last macro instruction.

GUIDELINES FOR USE The critical success factor for use of the macro is positioning your paper before turning your printer on. The position of your paper when you turn on your printer is where 1-2-3 assumes the top of the form to be. The macro assumes that the paper is at the top of a form when you start.

MODIFYING THE MACRO You will want to modify this macro to conform to the specific ranges you need to print your report. These instructions are found in B2 and B10; they can be edited to supply a new range. Depending on the range you select and your exact printing requirements, you may need to modify Options parameters such as margins and setup strings. You may also wish to add print options besides those listed in this macro. If you have additional reports to create, you can insert their specifications on new lines ahead of line 16. This way you will be able to have one macro print all your reports.

You can also modify this macro to clear all the print options between reports, depending on how much your specifications change from report to report. If they stay almost the same, you might prefer to change just one or two options by including the appropriate commands and new values in your macro. On the other hand, if there are substantial changes, you might want to include /Print Printer Clear All in the macro. This could be accomplished by adding CA (for Clear All) after the G in B8.

A Macro to Store Print Output in a File

If you have never printed to a file, you may wonder why anyone would want to store printed output on a file. There are several good reasons. First, your printer may be out for repair, and you may want to save the printed output until later. Or you may simply want to continue with your current task and wait until later to print. Perhaps you want to use the worksheet data in another package, and you need to supply that program with print output stored on a .PRN file.

The macro presented here will write worksheet formulas to a file with one formula per line. The macro reads as follows:

	A	B	C
1	formulas	/PF	Request print to file
2		FORMULAS~	Write to file FORMULAS
3		RA1..C20~	Specify range A1..C20
4		OO	Request Options Other
5		U	Request Unformatted
6		OC	Request Other Cell-Formulas
7		Q	Quit Options menu
8		G	Write requested file
9		CA	Clear all print specifications
10		Q	Quit Print menu

The first line in the macro requests the Print menu and selects File as the output destination. B2 contains the filename that will be supplied in response to 1-2-3's prompt. The range to be printed is shown next and includes the cells in A1..C20.

The Options menu is requested next, and the Other selection from this menu is chosen. Unformatted output is requested to remove any formatting specifications in the current print settings. While still in the Options menu, the macro requests Other again, and Cell-Formulas is chosen to print each cell in the range on a line by itself and print the formulas. B7 contains a request to quit the Options menu, and the next instruction writes the output to disk. All print specifications are cleared with the CA in B9, and the Print menu is exited via the Q in B10.

GUIDELINES FOR USE   When your computer writes to disk files, it writes data to the disk in blocks. When you request Go, most of your print output is written to the disk. It is not until you request Quit from the Print menu that you can be sure that all of your output is written to the file, however. Also, the end-of-file indicator is not placed in the file until after you choose Quit. Be sure to quit the Print menu with Quit rather than pressing ESC, and make sure you leave your disk in the drive until after quitting, to ensure that all your data is in the file.

MODIFYING THE MACRO   This macro will work for any set of reports. You should eliminate the request for Other Cell-Formulas from B6 if you want the worksheet printed as displayed rather than as the formulas the macro requests. The range in B3 can be modified to print other reports.

If you want to print multiple reports to one file, you can begin the range specification process again after B8 or B9, depending on whether or not you want the existing print parameters cleared. If you want the output in a second file, place your second request after B10, and begin again with /Print File so you can request a new filename.

Graph Macros

Graphs normally require numerous settings. You have to add titles, data labels, grid lines, legends, and other options to create appealing graphs. You can save time and reduce errors by capturing the required keystrokes in a macro and making it available for use with departmental budgets or other worksheets where a number of managers are using the same formats.

A Macro to Create a Bar Graph

The following macro is designed to work with the sales worksheet used with the /File Combine macro example shown earlier in the chapter (Figure 12-8). It can be used for any of the regional budgets or the total company worksheet. The only change you may wish to make is in the first line title.

The macro looks like this:

```
      A        B           C
1   graph    /GRG         Request graph and reset all options
2            TB           Select bar type graph
3            XC4..F4~     X range for labels below axis points
4            AC6..F6~     First data range
5            BC7..F7~     Second data range
6            CC8..F8~     Third data range
7            OGH          Select horizontal grid lines from Options menu
8            TF\D2~       First line title from D2
9            TY$ Sales~   Y axis title
10           LAProduct 1~ Legend for first product
11           LBProduct 2~ Legend for second product
12           LCProduct 3~ Legend for third product
13           CQ           Request color and quit options
14           V            View graph
```

The macro begins in line 1 with a request for the Graph menu. This instruction also resets all the graph values. A bar graph is selected in the next instruction, after which the ranges for the different series used to create the graph are specified. The labels below the X axis will be the entries in cells C4..F4. The next three instructions assign values to data ranges A, B, and C.

The Graph Options menu is requested next, and horizontal grid lines are added by the instruction in B7. The first line title is set to use the contents of cell

D2. A Y axis title of "$ Sales" is entered next. Legends for data ranges A, B, and C are then added. Color is requested as the last option, and the Options menu is exited. The graph is viewed with the "V" in B14.

GUIDELINES FOR USE   This macro can be used every time you update your worksheet. Of course, if you have just displayed a graph and simply want to see it again, the F10 (GRAPH) key is a quicker approach, since the graph specifications will not be changed. This macro is useful when you are in a new 1-2-3 session and find that someone else has been using the graphics features and has deleted the definition of your graph.

MODIFYING THE MACRO   This macro can be modified to save the graph specifications under a graph name. A second, shorter macro could issue a /Graph Name Use command to make the specifications current at a later time.

The macro can also be modified to specify settings for any type of graph you wish. You can use as many options as you need to enhance your basic data.

Data Macros

Macros can also save you time when used to automate functions in the data environment. Most of the /Data commands require that you make a number of selections before you complete your task. Some, like /Data Table, require that you complete preliminary steps before requesting the command. Also, since you must reissue the /Data commands if you want a sort, data table, frequency analysis, regression analysis, or /Data Fill operation performed again, you could be executing them frequently. With the macro approach, you can enter them once and check their accuracy, then store them in worksheet cells and use them as much as you want.

A Macro to Create a Data Table

A data table can perform a sensitivity analysis for you by systematically plugging values into your input variables. Before you ask 1-2-3 to perform this analysis, you must build a table shell on the worksheet. Since a macro to do this is a little more complicated than our other macros, you will want to take a look at the worksheet in Figure 12-9 before you study the next macro listing. Projections for Products A and B use the growth rates in D10 and D11 and the previous years' sales to project future periods. Product C is calculated as a percentage of Products A and B sales. The completed table is shown in Figure 12-10.

The rules for working with tables are found in Chapter 10; you will want to look at this chapter if you are not familiar with the /Data Table command. The

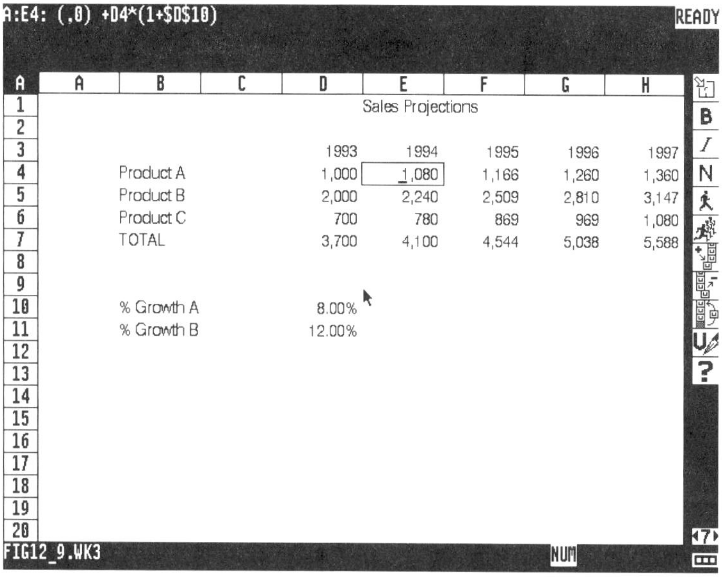

```
A:E4: (,0) +D4*(1+$D$10)                                           READY
```

	A	B	C	D	E	F	G	H
1					Sales Projections			
2								
3					1993	1994	1995	1996	1997
4		Product A			1,000	1,080	1,166	1,260	1,360
5		Product B			2,000	2,240	2,509	2,810	3,147
6		Product C			700	780	869	969	1,080
7		TOTAL			3,700	4,100	4,544	5,038	5,588
8								
9								
10		% Growth A			8.00%			
11		% Growth B			12.00%			

Figure 12-9.   *Worksheet for use with /Data Table*

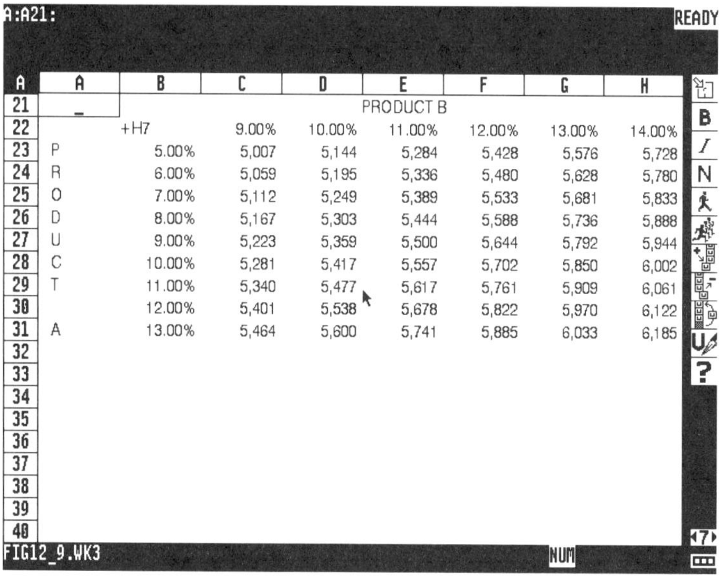

```
A:A21:                                                             READY
```

	A	B	C	D	E	F	G	H
21					PRODUCT B			
22		+H7	9.00%	10.00%	11.00%	12.00%	13.00%	14.00%
23	P	5.00%	5,007	5,144	5,284	5,428	5,576	5,728
24	R	6.00%	5,059	5,195	5,336	5,480	5,628	5,780
25	O	7.00%	5,112	5,249	5,389	5,533	5,681	5,833
26	D	8.00%	5,167	5,303	5,444	5,588	5,736	5,888
27	U	9.00%	5,223	5,359	5,500	5,644	5,792	5,944
28	C	10.00%	5,281	5,417	5,557	5,702	5,850	6,002
29	T	11.00%	5,340	5,477	5,617	5,761	5,909	6,061
30		12.00%	5,401	5,538	5,678	5,822	5,970	6,122
31	A	13.00%	5,464	5,600	5,741	5,885	6,033	6,185

Figure 12-10.   *Completed table*

table in our macro is calculated by having 1-2-3 substitute the values in B23..B31 for the growth of Product A in D10 each time the table performs a new calculation. The percentages in row 22 will be substituted as new growth factors for Product B. The table contains the result of the formula in H7, which is the total sales in 1997.

The first macro instruction is found in B1 of another sheet, as shown here:

	A	B	C
1	\t	/DF	Request Data Fill
2		A:B23..A:B31~	Set fill range
3		.05~	Enter start value
4		.01~~	Enter increment & accept stop value
5		/DF	Request Data Fill
6		A:C22..A:H22~	Set fill range
7		.09~	Enter start value
8		.01~~	Enter increment & accept stop value
9		/DT2	Request Data Table 2
10		A:B22..A:H31~	Set range
11		A:D10~	Set input value 2
12		A:D11~	Set input value 1
13		{GOTO}A:A21~	Move cell pointer to view table

This starting location may seem to conflict with the table data, except that the table macro is on sheet B but the macro is executed on sheet A. This first instruction requests /Data Fill to start building the shell for the table. A fill range is established with the second instruction. Then a start value of .05 and an increment of .01 are specified. When the stop value prompt is displayed, the second tilde in B4 will accept the default, since it is greater than the stop value needed.

The second /Data Fill operation supplies the values across row 22. A start value of .09 is used, along with the same increment as the first range. The default stop value is accepted again.

The request for the /Data Table 2 command is made in B9. The table location is defined in B10 as B22..H31. The first input value is the value for the growth factor for Product A, stored in D10. The second input value is the growth factor for Product B, which is stored in D11. When this second input value is entered, the macro calculates the new values for H7 and places them in the table.

GUIDELINES FOR USE This macro is designed to handle most of the table setup, as well as the call for /Data Table to do the calculations. The only tasks it does not perform are the entry of the formula in cell B22 on the sheet containing the table, and the formatting of the table cells. This is to ensure that the values you want are always placed in the table as input values. Be sure not to store information in the cells the table uses, since executing the macro would overlay these cells.

MODIFYING THE MACRO The macro can be modified to create a table of a different size or with different input values generated by the /Data Fill operation. You could also modify the instructions in B3, B4, B7, and B8 to contain {?}, so that the operator can enter the fill parameters, and therefore the input values, every time the macro is executed.

You can also modify the macro to handle the remaining preliminary steps for preparing the table. It would be easy to include instructions for the entry of the formula in B22 on the table sheet and the /Range Format statements required to display the table as shown.

A Macro to Sort a Database

Sorting a database requires the definition of the data range. This does not have to be done every time you sort, but it must be done if you have added a new field or new records to your database. Since it is easy to forget to do this, you can have a macro handle this precautionary step to ensure that you do not sort just a section of your database.

The database this example will use is shown in Figure 12-11. Notice that the names are in random sequence. The macro will sort the file into sequence by last name and use the first name as a secondary key.

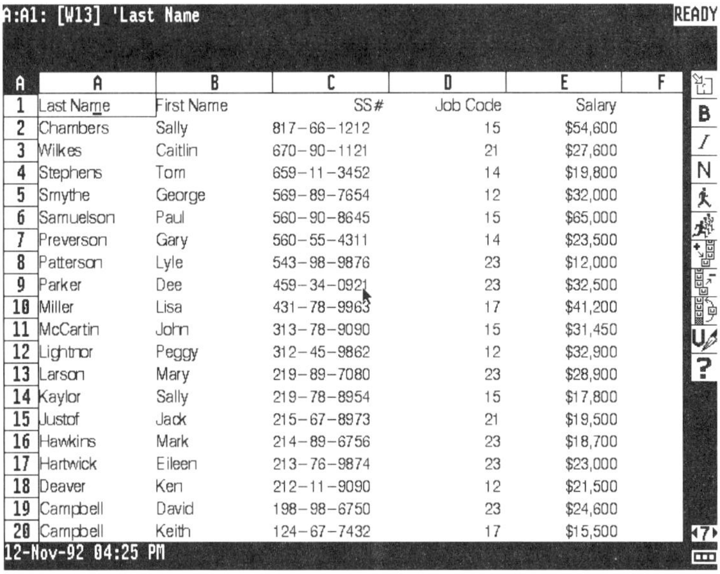

#	A Last Name	B First Name	C SS#	D Job Code	E Salary
1	Last Name	First Name	SS#	Job Code	Salary
2	Chambers	Sally	817-66-1212	15	$54,600
3	Wilkes	Caitlin	670-90-1121	21	$27,600
4	Stephens	Tom	659-11-3452	14	$19,800
5	Smythe	George	569-89-7654	12	$32,000
6	Samuelson	Paul	560-90-8645	15	$65,000
7	Preverson	Gary	560-55-4311	14	$23,500
8	Patterson	Lyle	543-98-9876	23	$12,000
9	Parker	Dee	459-34-0921	23	$32,500
10	Miller	Lisa	431-78-9963	17	$41,200
11	McCartin	John	313-78-9090	15	$31,450
12	Lightnor	Peggy	312-45-9862	12	$32,900
13	Larson	Mary	219-89-7080	23	$28,900
14	Kaylor	Sally	219-78-8954	15	$17,800
15	Justof	Jack	215-67-8973	21	$19,500
16	Hawkins	Mark	214-89-6756	23	$18,700
17	Hartwick	Eileen	213-76-9874	23	$23,000
18	Deaver	Ken	212-11-9090	12	$21,500
19	Campbell	David	198-98-6750	23	$24,600
20	Campbell	Keith	124-67-7432	17	$15,500

Figure 12-11. *Unsorted database*

The macro shown here begins in B:B1 with a request for /Data Sort Data-Range.

	A	B	C
1	sort	/DSD	Request Data Sort Data-Range
2		{CE}	Clear entry of existing data range
3		{FIRSTCELL}{DOWN}	Set A:A2 as beginning of the range
4		.	Lock beginning of range
5		{END}{DOWN}	Move to last entry in first field
6		{END}{RIGHT}~	Move to last field on right
7		PA:A2~A~	Set last name as primary ascending key
8		SA:B2~A~	Set first name as secondary ascending key
9		G	Complete sort
10		{HOME}	Move to A:A1 to view sorted records

Here the macro is stored on a different sheet from the data. Since the range is set from the previous use, {CE} is needed to unlock the beginning of the range. The cell pointer is moved to A:A1 with the CTRL-HOME key, and then down one row to A2. This cell is locked in place as the beginning of the sort range by typing a period. The cell pointer is moved to the last entry in the column and then is moved across to the last column to complete the range specification.

A2 is defined as the primary key, on which the records will be sorted in ascending sequence. The secondary key is B2, the first name, which will also be applied in ascending sequence. The "G" in B9 on the macro sheet requests that the sort begin. The macro ends by moving to A1 so you can review your results.

GUIDELINES FOR USE The macro makes one assumption about the worksheet. The macro assumes that the first and last data fields will have values for every record. The instructions in B5 and B6 would not work if some of the fields were blank.

MODIFYING THE MACRO The macro can be modified to sort on any field. You can enter the range address for the macro, though this approach would require modification to the macro as the database expands.

CHAPTER 13

Command Language Macros

Command language macros are even more powerful than the keyboard alternative macros described in the last chapter. Command language macros allow you to perform repetitive tasks with ease, and automate applications so that even novice users can handle complex worksheet tasks. They also allow you to use features that are not part of the 1-2-3 menu structure.

The macro command set in Release 3 provides a number of new options—especially in support of data management activities. Although the Release 1A /X macro commands are still supported in Release 3 for compatibility, you should not use the /X commands since 1-2-3 has macro commands that perform the same functions and are more descriptive. You can alter the execution flow of a macro by branching to a new location. You can also create your own custom menus patterned after 1-2-3's.

Command language macros are not for everyone, however. They are built with 1-2-3's command language, which is essentially a programming language. As with any programming language, you are likely to have moments of frustration and exasperation as you strive to make 1-2-3 understand your needs. To be successful in creating command language macros, you must be willing to work at the detail level in defining your needs exactly. You will need blocks of uninterrupted time so you can concentrate fully on these details. Finally, you will need persistence to stick with the task until the macro works correctly. Given these efforts, you can learn to create macros you will be proud of.

This chapter is designed to provide strategies for creating command language macros with as little pain as possible. The first part of the chapter offers some general strategies for creating macros, and discusses specific techniques used by programmers working in other programming languages to ensure the correct operation of their programs. Since the 1-2-3 macro command language is also a programming language, you are likely to find some of these techniques helpful when writing your macros. The second section of this chapter describes each macro command separately. It provides a description and a working example that incorporates the macro command.

Differences Between Command Language Macros and Keyboard Macros

Command language macros are entered in the same way as the keyboard variety covered in Chapter 12. Like keyboard macros, they are label entries stored in a column of worksheet cells. Just as you needed to follow rigid rules when entering a keyboard menu selection sequence, you also have to follow rules when entering instructions from 1-2-3's macro command language. The command keyword and any arguments it requires must always be enclosed in curly braces { }—for example, {BRANCH A9}. Arguments must always be entered in the prescribed order.

How will you know when to use command language macros and when to use keyboard macros? It is really quite easy. When a keyboard macro will work, use it. When you want to accomplish things that menu commands cannot handle, however, it is time to look beyond keyboard macros.

Your first command language macros may use only a few statements, as in the following macro, which enters a series of @PMT functions all the way down a column.

```
1   \d           {LET z1,0}
2   top          {IF z1=5}{BRANCH finish}
3                @PMT(
4                {?}
5                ,
6                {?}
7                ,
8                {?}
9                )~
10               {DOWN}
11               {LET z1,z1+1}
12               {BRANCH top}
13  finish       {QUIT}
```

After you master the simpler variety of command language macro, you can begin to think of more sophisticated tasks you would like to delegate to 1-2-3. Many of these will require the use of command language instructions, but they are likely to employ the familiar built-in functions, formulas, and menu options, as well. As long as you are working with the 1-2-3 package, you will want all its features at your disposal.

Constructing and Using Command Language Macros

A command language macro normally consists of a number of detailed steps that must be executed in a logical order. When you communicate instructions to another person, you can often be less than fully specific and still get the desired results. That is because human beings can interpret directions and make assumptions about the exact way a task should be performed. If someone knows your way of doing business and has worked for you in the past, his or her interpretations and assumptions about the way you want a particular task done are likely to be correct.

When you ask a computer to do your bidding, however, there will be no interpretation and no assumptions. You will get exactly what you ask for, whether or not it is what you want. If you leave out a step or provide the steps in the wrong sequence, you will get results different from what you expect.

Since you can't change the way computers do their processing, you must learn to set up tasks in a way that a computer can handle. You need to create a road map showing what you want the computer to do for you. If you create this road map on paper, it will be easy to separate logic and syntax. *Logic* refers to the steps in the task you wish the computer to perform, and *syntax* refers to the detailed instructions in the 1-2-3 macro command language, and the arguments they need to execute successfully. If you do not have all the logic of your macro worked out, you will never be able to solve the problem by entering specific instructions. You need to know where you are going and the general route you plan to follow before you start.

Planning Command Language Macros

You can use a variety of techniques to map out your logic flow. Programmers frequently use *flowcharts* or *pseudocode* (statements written in something like computer code but without concern for precise syntax) to map out their programs. The following subsections describe these techniques in more detail. You can use one of them, or you can develop your own technique. The important thing is to completely think through the steps needed to complete your tasks before you get involved with the command language syntax. If you attempt to tackle both logic and syntax at once, and your macro does not work, you will not know where to begin the correction process.

Flowcharts

Flowcharts are diagrams of the detailed logic in a macro or other program; they are constructed with special symbols. These symbols are joined with lines to form a pictorial representation of the logic flow. A standard set of symbols is used so that any programmer can understand a flowchart created by another individual. In fact, a programmer often asks another programmer to review the flowchart of a problem solution before it is coded, to help identify logic errors early in the testing process.

In most flowcharts, the diamond represents a decision to be made, the small circle is a connector, the parallelogram marks input and output operations, and the rectangle indicates arithmetic operations and other processes. Figure 13-1 presents a flowchart using these symbols. It describes the logic required to combine a variable number of region files into one worksheet. This would allow

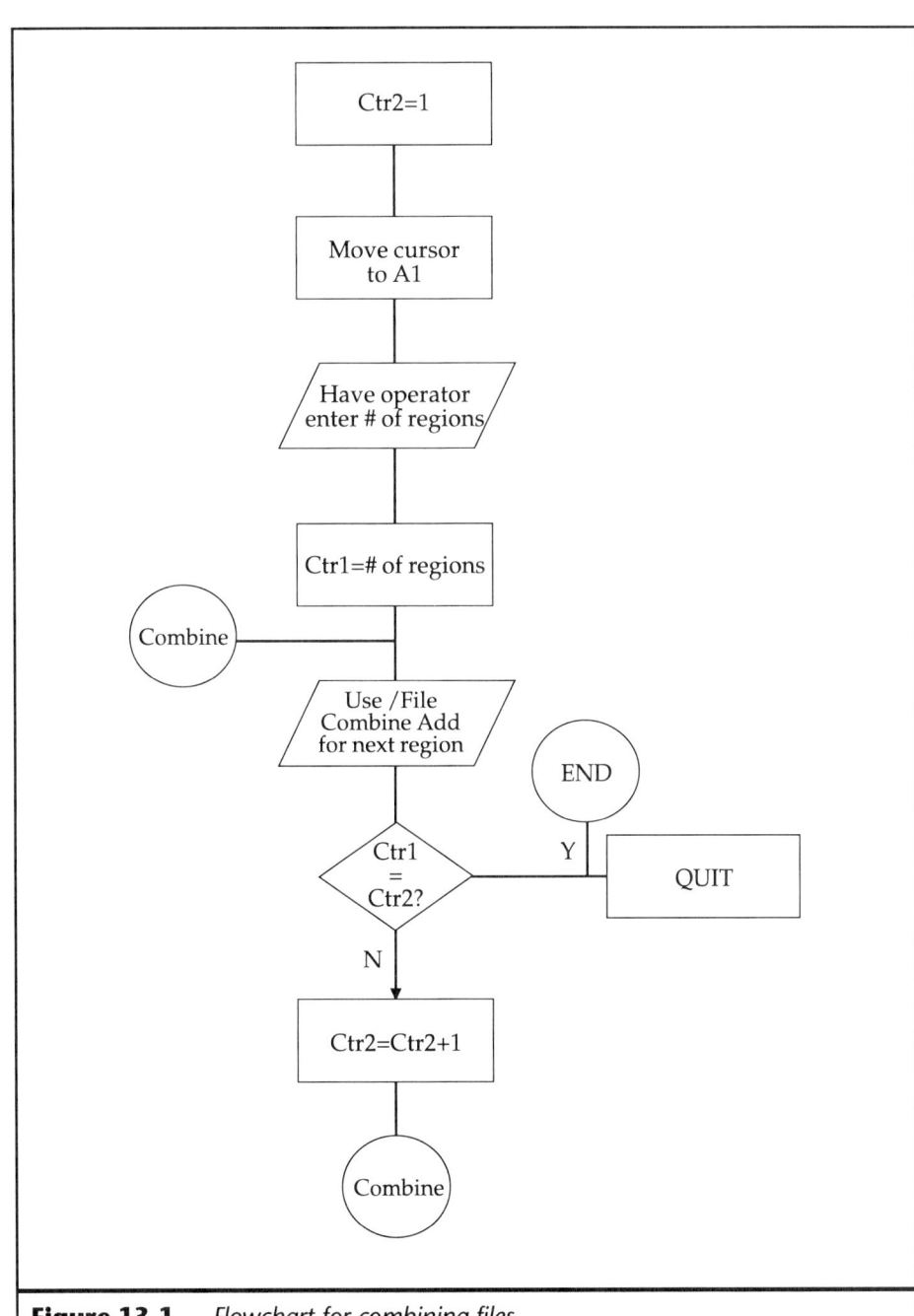

Figure 13-1. *Flowchart for combining files*

someone to create division or total company reports with one worksheet. Ctr1 and Ctr2 are counters.

If you use flowcharts for mapping your program logic, there is no need to buy a special flowchart template to create the special symbols. Drawing them by hand is just as effective. You can even use a different set of symbols if you prefer.

Pseudocode

Pseudocode is a shortcut method of documenting your logic with everyday English words. It is quicker to use than flowcharts, since there are no figures to be drawn, and it is closer to the final form of program code that you will use. When writing pseudocode, don't concern yourself with spelling, grammar, or complete sentences; phrases are best, in fact, as long as they are clear.

The following lines of pseudocode describe the same process that is pictured in the flowchart in Figure 13-1. The first column represents labels that the macro uses to branch to. The second column shows the steps the macro performs.

	Initialize Ctr2 to 1
	Position cell pointer
	Enter number of regions to combine
	Set Ctr1 = # of regions
Combine	Use /File Combine Add
	If Ctr1 = Ctr2 branch to End
	Add 1 to Ctr2
	Branch to Combine
End	Quit

Strategies for Designing Complex Macros

A three- or four-line command language macro is no more difficult to create than a keyboard macro. It is so small that you can keep track of its entire logic flow mentally. More sophisticated command language macros, however, need more careful structuring and planning.

Branching Versus Straight-Line Code

It is easy to create macro code that branches all over the place; programmers refer to this as "spaghetti bowl" code. It usually results from lack of planning.

New instructions are simply added as the programmer thinks of them. If there is not enough room to insert all the instructions needed, the program branches away to a blank location and then branches back again to execute the remaining instructions. The result is confusion. It may be faster to code a program or a macro in this fashion, but making it work correctly is something else again.

Straight-line code is at the opposite end of the spectrum. Wherever possible, it proceeds from the top to the bottom of the logic flow without branching. Of course, branching need not be forbidden entirely. A little common sense can go a long way in creating macros that are both workable and correct. Straight-line code, however, offers the advantage of allowing you to read from the top to the bottom of the code and get a picture of what it is accomplishing.

Main Code and Subroutines

You can write a large macro that contains, say, 400 instructions, and list them consecutively down a column on your worksheet. To get a picture of what this macro is designed to accomplish, one would have to read all 400 lines of code. A better approach is to separate your macros into a mainline code section and subroutines. Properly planned, this structure combines the advantages of branching and straight-line code.

A manageable upper limit for the length of the main section is considered to be 50 lines. Detail tasks are taken out of this section and placed in subroutines, which are referenced by instructions in the main section. Because the main section is short, it can be scanned quickly to learn the essence of the macro. This form of organization also makes it easier to test the macro a section at a time and thereby trace errors to particular sections of code.

When a main program calls a subroutine, the subroutine instructions will be executed until a {RETURN} is encountered or the end of the subroutine is reached. At that time, control will return to the main program that called the subroutine. The instruction immediately following the subroutine call will be executed next. A subroutine call is always indicated by enclosing the subroutine name in curly braces. To call a subroutine named Print, for example, you would enter **{Print}**.

The following example shows how a main program and its subroutines might be structured.

Main Routine

    . . .
    . . .
    {update}
    {print}

```
Subroutines
update
            . . .
            . . .
            . . .
            . . .
            {RETURN}
    print
            . . .
            . . .
            {RETURN}
```

The ... entries represent macro instructions appropriate for the routines. Note that with this structure, you can read down the main code and see that an update operation will be performed, followed by a print operation. You need not read the precise instructions in either subroutine to understand the program's basic structure.

When you call a subroutine, you can pass arguments to it. This allows you to tailor the routine to each particular situation. Passing arguments to a subroutine requires that the arguments be included in the instruction that calls the subroutine. In addition, the subroutine must contain a {DEFINE} instruction that provides a storage location for each argument passed to it. Release 3 supports a maximum of 31 arguments for each subroutine.

When it encounters a {RETURN} statement, 1-2-3 returns to the subroutine calling location and executes the instruction immediately following the subroutine call. If 1-2-3 encounters a second subroutine call before a {RETURN} instruction, it begins executing the code in the second subroutine. Adding various levels of subroutine calls within a macro is referred to as *stacking* or *nesting* subroutine calls. The number of levels of stacked subroutines that you can use is limited by available memory, although you may reach a practical limit well before you run out of memory.

TIP: Limit nested subroutines to three levels. It can be difficult to decipher the logic of a program when it contains nesting of subroutines that exceed three levels.

You can have a main program that calls the same subroutine multiple times and passes different arguments to it each time. For example, you might want to print your worksheet with three different setup strings, using an argument to pass a setup string to the print subroutine. Your main program might appear as follows:

{print k1}
{print k2}
{print k3}

Each time a call is executed, whatever is stored in the specified cell (that is, K1, K2, K3) is passed to the subroutine.

The print subroutine would require a storage place for only one argument, since only one argument is passed to it each time it is executed. Assuming Setup was defined as a range name, the print subroutine might appear like this:

print {DEFINE Setup:*string*}
. . .
. . .
{RETURN}

Setup is defined as a string argument; it will contain the values of K1, K2, and K3 from each execution of the Print routine. You must include a location argument in the {DEFINE} command for each argument passed by the subroutine call.

The location arguments in a {DEFINE} command support the addition of *:string* or *:value*. If you use *:string*, 1-2-3 will store the argument that is passed to the location argument as a left aligned label. When *:value* is used, 1-2-3 stores the entry if it is a number, or evaluates the argument if it is a formula. When a cell address or range name is supplied as an argument, 1-2-3 evaluates the cell reference and stores the contents based on the type of entry it finds. The way the result is stored depends on the type of formula evaluated. String formulas return labels, and numeric formulas return numbers. If you omit the argument, 1-2-3 uses *:string*.

Entering Command Language Macros

Having mapped out a plan for your macro, you are ready to begin entering actual code. Command language macros are entered in the same manner as keyboard alternative macros. As with keyboard macros, you can enter them in a separate file to create a macro library or as part of a file that contains worksheet or data management entries. If you enter them within an existing file, consider using a separate sheet. If a separate sheet does not meet your needs, it is a good idea to place command macros in an out-of-the-way location that has room for a blank column on both sides of the macro instructions column. Then you can use the column to the left of the macro for the macro name and any range names you might assign to different sections of the macro. You might want to consider a location diagonally opposite from your data. This way, if you insert rows or columns in the data portion of the sheet, the macro will not be affected.

You can use either upper- or lowercase for macro commands, argument names, cell address references, keyboard commands, and macro names. You must follow the command syntax exactly, using the curly braces around each command entry, and the exact spelling for each command keyword.

You can have 1-2-3 do some of the work for you: type the curly brace { once, and press F3 (NAME) twice. 1-2-3 will list all the macro key names and commands; you can highlight the one you want, and press ENTER to have 1-2-3 add it for you. Since most of the commands expect arguments to define the specific use of the command, a space is left after the keyword, and each of the arguments is entered with commas as separators. You must then supply the proper type of data for each type of argument. Although you can use the specified type of entry within the macro, you can also use range names, cell addresses, or an appropriate formula to supply the necessary argument information. A closing brace follows the last argument entry.

Arguments that are literal strings sometimes require quotation marks around them. Quotation marks are needed when the string contains 1-2-3's separator characters (a comma, a semicolon, a colon, or a period).

Each cell in the column where you make your macro entries can contain up to 512 characters, since each macro instruction is entered as a label. It is not recommended that you use entries that even approach this upper limit, however. Forty or fifty characters is a reasonable upper limit if you want your macros to be readable. You must complete each macro instruction in the same cell where you begin entering it.

Naming Command Language Macros

Command language macros are named in the same fashion as keyboard macros. You can name the macros either by using a backslash and a letter, or by using a range name. The first cell of the macro is named with the /Range Name Create or /Range Name Labels Right command. 1-2-3 will execute all the macro instructions until it encounters a {QUIT} command or a non-label cell.

Creating a Macro Shell

If you like, you can code all your macro instructions at once. It often works better, however, to code just the major instructions first. As an example, if you have a macro that branches to one of four principal subroutines depending on operator input, first code only the instructions to process the operator's input and the beginning instructions for each of the four subroutines. At the beginning of each subroutine, place an instruction that informs you that you have reached that particular routine. In this manner you can check out the upper-level logic of your macro without investing time in creating detailed code. This kind of "framework" code is called a *macro shell*.

This approach to program construction is referred to as top-down programming. It can save considerable time by allowing you to detect major logic problems before you proceed with detailed coding. If a problem occurs, there will be far fewer instructions at this point to change or move.

You might construct a shell that consists of little more than subroutine calls and instructions to display messages, for example. You can use a "dummy" input statement with the {GETNUMBER} or {GETLABEL} command with the sole purpose of displaying a message on the screen. The {INDICATE} instruction is another option to inform you of a macro's progress.

This method speeds up your testing process significantly, since you can test the program's basic logic by invoking each subroutine and checking the special message it displays. Once you check the execution flow, you can add the detailed code needed to complete the subroutines.

Figure 13-2 provides an example of this shell structure. Here, each subroutine contains only an instruction to let you know that you have arrived at that location in the macro. Once this program pattern checks out as correct, you can add instructions for each routine.

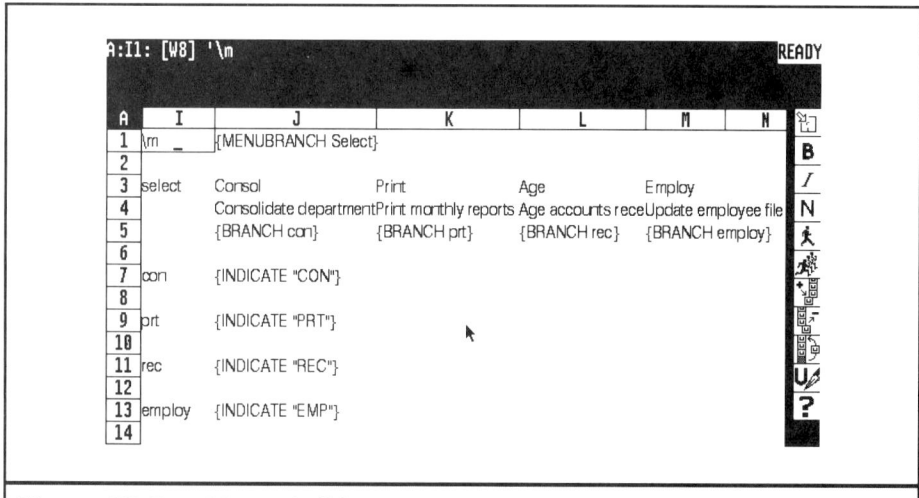

Figure 13-2. *Macro shell for a menu*

Creating Interactive Macros

Interactive macros are macros that change as they are executed. They can change logic flow in response to entries by the operator. They can even change entries in instructions, such as filenames.

Macros That Respond to Operator Input

As you look through the various macro commands in this chapter, you will find several that accept operator input. These include {?}, {GETLABEL}, {GETNUMBER}, {GET}, and {LOOK}. You can use the information obtained from these entries to control {BRANCH} instructions and subroutine calls, as well as other processing within the macro.

Dynamically Altered Macros

Dynamically altered macros store information that is input or calculated during execution as part of the macro itself.

For example, in a file retrieve instruction, you might want to change the file retrieved depending on the application you are working on. To do this, use a menu selection to determine the application and have this instruction alter the following macro instruction sequence:

```
/fr
blank
~
```

In this example, the macro cell that contains the word "blank" would actually be an empty cell. You want to have the macro make an appropriate entry in this cell, using either a {PUT} or a {LET} instruction. Thus the macro would be altering itself to perform the exact action you want.

Documenting Command Language Macros

Macro documentation consists of comments added to the worksheet to explain the macro. Its main purpose is to make each macro step clear to someone who was not involved in the macro's creation. However, you also are likely to find it helpful when you look back at a macro you wrote, say, three months previously. All of the examples in this chapter include documentation to the right of the macro instructions. Be as brief as possible when documenting a macro, but make sure you clearly describe all formulas or other entries that might not be clear to you or another user at a later time.

If you are like most people, you probably will not want to bother with the documentation step. Learn to think of documentation as a worthwhile investment that can save you time in the future, and make it possible to delegate the maintenance of your applications to others as you move on to new responsibilities. A few extra minutes spent documenting a macro when you have just finished creating it can pay off in hours of time saved later.

Testing Command Language Macros

Do not assume that a macro will work correctly unless you have tested it. A multiple-step testing process is the most efficient and will ensure that your macro works under all conditions. Here are macro testing guidelines.

1. Your first test should be an easy one. If the macro performs calculations, use even numbers so you can check its answers mentally. If you choose a complicated number, you might make arithmetic mistakes yourself while testing it.

2. If your macro is an iterative one (one that is executed numerous times), test only two or three iterations of its cycle. This saves time and makes it easier to check results.

3. Next try to see what the macro does with exceptions or unusual conditions that occur only sporadically.

4. Check for error conditions next. If the macro prompts you for the number of times you wish to execute a certain routine, respond with –25. If it asks for a number of vacation days, respond with 560. If it asks for a salary increase, respond with 1500%. See whether it responds to the error conditions as you would expect.

5. If your macro fails at any step along the way, correct the error condition and go back to the first step for a quick recheck after the change. Never assume that a change to one part of a macro will not affect another part. It often does, and the only way you will know for sure is to test it.

6. If your macro will be used by others, involve them in the testing process. No one knows better the type of data that will be entered into the macro than the person who will use the program every day. This approach will also help you discover if you have to change the macro because you have misinterpreted the user's needs. For instance, you may have allowed for

the entry of an invoice amount, whereas the user expected the macro to compute a total invoice amount based on entry of detail figures.

7. If you are designing a macro to work in multiple files, you must test its operation in more than one file.

TIP: Turn on the Undo feature with /Worksheet Global Default Other Undo Enable, before testing a macro. Then you can press ALT-F4 (UNDO) to eliminate all the effects of the macro if it causes errors in the worksheet.

Executing Command Language Macros

Executing a completed command language macro is easy. Just like a keyboard macro, simply press the ALT key and the letter key of the macro's name simultaneously. An alternative is to press ALT-F3 (RUN) or click the Run Macro icon, and select the name of the macro you want to execute. Like the keystroke macros introduced in the last chapter, you can create command language macros that run when you click a user-defined icon. The macro instructions for these icons are added the same way you add keystroke alternative macro instructions to an icon. You may want to test the macro on a worksheet first, then copy the macro instructions to the icon's Macro Text text box. Remember that you are limited to 512 characters for macro instructions for each user icon. There are several other things you should be aware of before executing a macro, however.

Using Undo While Running Macros

As indicated in the last Tip, if you run a macro with Undo enabled, you can press ALT-F4 (UNDO) to cancel all the effects of the macro on the worksheet. Undo eliminates the effect of menu selections and macro commands within the normal scope of its capabilities; that is, the action of Undo is confined to the worksheet and cannot eliminate file save and print operations that have been completed. If 1-2-3 does not have sufficient memory to run the macro with Undo turned on, it will prompt you before turning Undo off.

Updating the Worksheet

As you begin using macros, you will find that some of the macro commands update worksheet cells. They do not always update these cells immediately, and sometimes the worksheet must be recalculated before the update takes place. For some commands, pressing the ENTER key may be sufficient to cause the updating. You will want to follow these commands with a tilde (~) if immediate update is critical to the successful execution of the macro. Other commands require that the worksheet be recalculated.

The following commands will update the worksheet if you follow them with a tilde (~) or {CALC}:

{CONTENTS}	{LOOK}
{DEFINE}	{ONERROR}
{FILESIZE}	{PUT}
{FOR}	{READ}
{GET}	{READLN}
{GETLABEL}	/XL
{GETNUMBER}	/XN
{GETPOS}	

Stopping a Macro

Unless you have disabled the BREAK key by including {BREAKOFF} in your macro, you can interrupt a macro in midstream simply by pressing CTRL-BREAK. This displays an ERROR indicator on the screen. If you then press ESC, you can leave the macro and return to READY mode. {BREAKOFF} is described in the "Macro Commands" section of this chapter.

Macro Commands

Syntax of Macro Commands

1-2-3's command language has two separate types of macro commands: commands without arguments and commands with arguments. Both types include a keyword in braces. Subroutine calls are exceptions to these rules. See the box named "The Macro Language Commands" for a list of macro commands and their functions.

The format of a macro command without arguments is nothing more than a keyword enclosed in braces. Examples are {RETURN}, {RESTART}, and {QUIT}.

The format of a macro command with arguments consists of the keyword followed by a blank space and a list of arguments separated by commas. As with

@function arguments, no spaces are allowed between or within arguments. The entire command entry is enclosed in braces. Here are two examples:

```
{GETLABEL "Enter your name:",A2}
{FOR Counter,1,20,1,Loop}
```

The following discussion describes all the arguments for each command and specifies which of the arguments are optional as indicated by the brackets ([ ]).

Conventions for Macros in This Chapter

The same conventions have been used for all the example macros whenever possible. The macro name and subroutine name are shown in the first column to the left of the top cell in the macro. The macro instructions are written in the second column as labels, except for menu macros, which extend to the right into additional columns. The columns on the sheets where the macros were entered were widened to allow for the complete display of each element. When possible, documentation has been placed in the third column.

Lowercase characters are used for menu selections and responses to menu prompts. Filenames, command keywords, and special key indicators, such as {HOME}, {ESC}, {IF}, and {MENUBRANCH} are shown in uppercase. Range names, which also serve as subroutine names, are shown in lowercase. When used within the text, these names are boldfaced to indicate their special use. Arguments in the text are shown in italics.

The macro commands in the sections that follow are grouped according to the categories in which they are placed in your 1-2-3 manual: commands that affect the screen, commands that interact with the keyboard operator, commands that control the flow of execution within a macro, commands that affect data entry, and commands that access file data. For each command you will find a description, format rules, descriptions of arguments (if any), suggestions for use, and an example. Special setup procedures are also described, if any are required.

Macro Commands that Affect the Screen

Macro commands that affect your screen can handle such tasks as updating the worksheet and control panel. If the macro commands display as they execute, you have an indication of where the macro is at any particular moment, but the macro's quick progress can cause a flicker as the screen is updated. These macros also provide the ability to create your own mode indicator, and to sound your computer's bell to get the operator's attention.

The Macro Language Commands

Macro Command	Function	Type of Macro
{?}	Accepts keyboard input	Interactive
{APPENDBELOW}	Appends one or more rows of data below an existing database	Data
{APPENDRIGHT}	Appends one or more columns of data to the right of an existing database	Data
{BEEP}	Sounds bell	Screen
{BLANK}	Erases cell or range	Data
{BRANCH}	Changes execution flow to a new routine	Flow
{BREAKOFF}	Disables BREAK key	Interactive
{BREAKON}	Restores BREAK key	Interactive
{CLOSE}	Closes an open file	File
{CONTENTS}	Stores the numeric contents of a cell as a label in another cell	Data
{DEFINE}	Specifies location and type of arguments for a subroutine call	Flow
{DISPATCH}	Branches to a new location indirectly	Flow
{FILESIZE}	Determines number of bytes in a file	File
{FOR}	Loops through a macro subroutine multiple times	Flow
{FORBREAK}	Cancels current {FOR} instruction	Flow
{FORM}	Allows you to use a form for input. Can monitor keystrokes and execute subroutines	Interactive
{FORMBREAK}	Cancels current {FORM} instruction	Interactive
{FRAMEOFF}	Turns off the worksheet frame	Screen
{FRAMEON}	Restores the worksheet frame	Screen
{GET}	Halts macro to allow single-keystroke entry	Interactive
{GETLABEL}	Halts macro to allow label entry	Interactive
{GETNUMBER}	Halts macro to allow number entry	Interactive
{GETPOS}	Returns the pointer position in a file	File
{GRAPHOFF}	Removes a graph displayed by {GRAPHON}	Screen
{GRAPHON}	Displays a graph or makes a set of graph settings active	Screen
{IF}	Causes conditional execution of command that follows	Flow
{INDICATE}	Changes mode indicator	Screen
{LET}	Stores a number or label in a cell	Data
{LOOK}	Checks to see if keyboard entry has been made	Interactive
{MENUBRANCH}	Executes a custom menu and branches to a new set of macro instructions	Interactive

The Macro Language Commands (*continued*)

Macro Command	Function	Type of Macro
{MENUCALL}	Executes a custom menu as a subroutine	Interactive
{ONERROR}	Branches to an error processing routine	Flow
{OPEN}	Opens a file for read or write access	File
{PANELOFF}	Eliminates control panel updating	Screen
{PANELON}	Restores control panel updating	Screen
{PUT}	Stores a number or label in one cell of a range	Data
{QUIT}	Ends the macro and returns to READY mode	Flow
{READ}	Reads characters from file into a cell	File
{READLN}	Reads a line of characters from a file into a cell	File
{RECALC}	Recalculates formulas in a range row by row	Data
{RECALCCOL}	Recalculates formulas in a range column by column	Data
{RESTART}	Clears subroutine pointers	Flow
{RETURN}	Returns to the instruction after the last subroutine call or {MENUCALL}	Flow
{*routine*}	Calls the subroutine specified by *routine*	Flow
{SETPOS}	Moves file pointer to a new location in the file	File
{SYSTEM}	Executes an operating system command	Flow
{WAIT}	Waits until a specified time	Interactive
{WINDOWSOFF}	Suppresses window updating	Screen
{WINDOWSON}	Restores window updating	Screen
{WRITE}	Places data in a file	File
{WRITELN}	Places data in a file and adds a carriage return/line feed at the end	File

{BEEP}

The {BEEP} command sounds your computer's bell.

FORMAT   The format for the {BEEP} command is

{BEEP [*number*]}

where *number* is an optional argument to set the tone of the bell. The *number* argument can have any value from 1 to 4, with 1 as the default when no number is specified.

Chapter 13: Command Language Macros

USE You can use the beep to alert the operator to an error, indicate that you expect input, show periodically that a long-running macro is still functioning, or signify the conclusion of a step.

TIP: Switching the Beep tone off with /Worksheet Global Default Other Beep causes this macro instruction to have no audible effect.

EXAMPLE In this example, it is used to indicate that an input instruction follows.

```
{BEEP 3}
{GETNUMBER "Enter your account number",F2}
```

This {BEEP} instruction will cause the computer's bell to ring with tone 3 right before the input message is displayed.

NOTE: When you use a tone argument other than 1 through 4, 1-2-3 divides the number by 4 and uses the remainder for the tone value.

{FRAMEOFF}

The {FRAMEOFF} command allows further customization of the screen by turning off the display of the worksheet frame. This macro command has no effect with Wysiwyg's graphics mode display; however, you can hide the frame with Wysiwyg's :Display Options Frame None command.

FORMAT The format for the command is {FRAMEOFF}. This command has no arguments.

USE This command allows you to create a help display or data entry form without the distraction of the frames containing column letters and row numbers. The frame will not be restored to the display until a {FRAMEON} instruction is encountered or the macro ends.

EXAMPLE The screen in Figure 13-3 is created with text entries and format commands. The {FORM} command displays the form and controls input within the defined input area. If the {FRAMEOFF} command is added to the macro code before executing the {FORM} command, the row and column headings are eliminated and the screen looks like Figure 13-4.

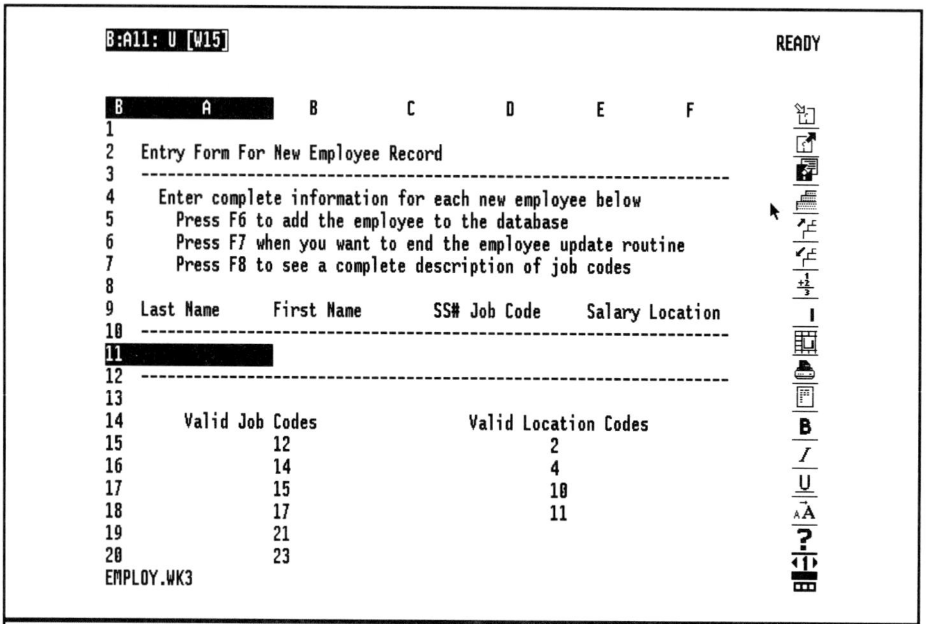

Figure 13-3. Data entry form with a frame

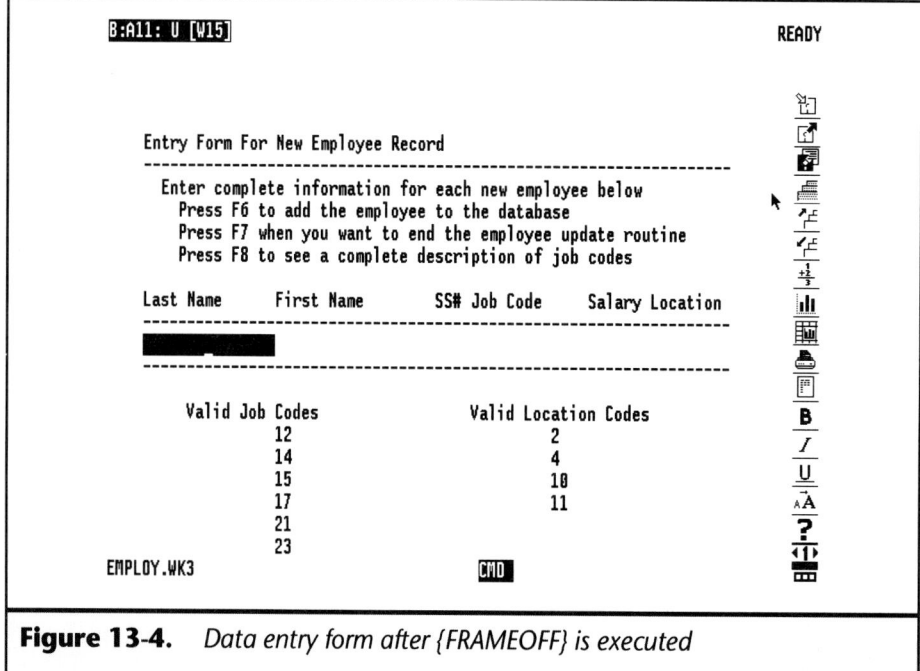

Figure 13-4. Data entry form after {FRAMEOFF} is executed

{FRAMEON}

The {FRAMEON} command allows you to restore the display of the worksheet row and column frame after it has been disabled with {FRAMEOFF}. This macro command has no effect with Wysiwyg's graphics mode display since the frame display is controlled by Wysiwyg's :Display Options Frame command.

FORMAT   The format of the command is {FRAMEON}. This command has no arguments.

USE   You can use the {FRAMEON} command to restore the display of the frame when a task requiring cell pointer positioning is required. You might remove the frame to display a help screen or a data entry form. If the next required task is completing data entry in a group of cells, you might want to restore the frame.

EXAMPLE   The following code illustrates the restoration of the frame after the execution of the {FORM} command:

```
         A              B                    C
1     addrec         {FRAMEOFF}       Eliminate frame
2                    {FORM custadd}   Use custom form for add
3                    {FRAMEON}        Restore frame
```

Setup   You must create the range name **custadd** before invoking this macro. The range should have its Protection status removed, as this is the area where entries can be made on the form.

{GRAPHOFF}

The {GRAPHOFF} command eliminates from the screen the graph display created with the {GRAPHON} command.

FORMAT   The format of the command is {GRAPHOFF}. The command has no arguments.

USE   You can use this command to eliminate the effect of a {GRAPHON} command that you executed. You may display a graph with {GRAPHON} for a fixed amount of time or allow the user to make an entry that will remove it. Either way, when you want the graph eliminated from the screen, use {GRAPHOFF}.

EXAMPLE   The following macro code will display and remove a graph:

	A	B	C
1	dispgrph	{GRAPHON pie1}	Display pie graph
2		{WAIT @NOW+@TIME(0,0,20)}	Wait 20 seconds
3		{GRAPHOFF}	Remove pie graph

The graph will remain on the display for the 20 seconds generated by the {WAIT} instruction. Next, it will be removed with the {GRAPHOFF} command.

{GRAPHON}

The {GRAPHON} command makes a specific graph current and displays this graph or the current set of graph definitions on the screen.

FORMAT   The format of this command depends on the specific action desired. {GRAPHON} with no arguments displays the current graph on the screen. To make another graph current and display it on the screen, the format of the command is {GRAPHON *named-graph*} where *named-graph* is a set of graph definitions. Another format of this command is {GRAPHON *named-graph*,nodisplay}. Although the named graph is still made current, it is not displayed on the screen.

USE   You can use this command to display a graph on the screen for the user. Since the macro continues to process commands, you can use other instructions and make customization changes available without the user needing to know the commands required to make enhancements to the graph.

You can also use this command to make a set of graph specifications current, yet not display them immediately. This allows you to provide a menu of options for the user that will affect the graph. When the selections are made, you can issue the {GRAPHON} command again without the *nodisplay* argument, and the graph will display with the changes made from the user's selections.

EXAMPLE   You can use this command to create a slide show of graphs. The following example displays four graphs for 30 seconds each:

	A	B	C
1	slides	{GRAPHON pie1}	Displays graph pie1
2		{WAIT @NOW+@TIME(0,0,30)}	Wait 30 seconds
3		{GRAPHON bar1}	Displays graph bar1
4		{WAIT @NOW+@TIME(0,0,30)}	Wait 30 seconds

```
5            {GRAPHON pie2}              Displays graph pie2
6            {WAIT @NOW+@TIME(0,0,30)}   Wait 30 seconds
7            {GRAPHON bar2}              Displays graph bar2
8            {WAIT @NOW+@TIME(0,0,30)}   Wait 30 seconds
```

These graphs continue to appear until a {GRAPHOFF}, another {GRAPHON}, a {?}, an {INDICATE}, or other macro command displays a prompt or menu in the control panel (like {GETLABEL}, {GETNUMBER}, {MENUBRANCH}, or {MENUCALL}).

{INDICATE}

The {INDICATE} command provides the ability to customize the mode indicator in the upper right corner of the screen.

FORMAT   The format of the {INDICATE} command is

{INDICATE [string]}

where *string* is any character string. The string supplied is displayed in place of 1-2-3's regular indicator. Using an empty string, that is, {INDICATE ""}, removes the indicator from the control panel. Using no string, that is, {INDICATE}, returns the indicator to the default. Although the normal mode indicators are limited to a few characters, with {INDICATE} your only limit is the number of characters that will fit in the control panel.

USE   The indicator you select with this command will remain until you use the command again to establish a new setting. The setting will continue beyond the execution of the macro. If you set the indicator to be FILE, FILE will remain on the screen even if you are in READY mode. Remember to include {INDICATE} without an argument at the end of any macro that has used this instruction. Doing so will restore 1-2-3's normal indicator display at the conclusion of the macro.

The {INDICATE} command is useful when you are designing automated applications. If you have a series of menu selections for the operator to use, you can have an {INDICATE} instruction for each path that will supply a string related to the selection the operator has made. This command is also useful in testing macro shells. Each subroutine can be represented initially by nothing more than an {INDICATE} with a suitable character string, to allow you to check the logic flow. If you have a budget subroutine, for example, you might represent it in your shell with {INDICATE "BUDGET SUBROUTINE"}.

EXAMPLE The macro shown here will change the mode indicator several times.

```
       A              B                        C
1     \i       {INDICATE "SETUP"}      Change indicator to SETUP
2              /wcs15~                 Change column width to 15
3              /rfc0~{DOWN 5}~         Format as currency 0 decimals
4              {INDICATE "SPLIT"}      Change indicator to SPLIT
5              {DOWN 5}                Move down 5 cells
6              /wwh                    Create horizontal window
7              {INDICATE}              Eliminate indicator setting
```

The first step in the macro changes the indicator to SETUP. The macro then performs worksheet commands to set up the worksheet with a new column width adjustment and Currency format.

The instruction in B4 changes the indicator to SPLIT. A horizontal second window is then created. Finally, the {INDICATE} command is used without an argument to return to the default setting of READY mode when the macro ends. Without this last instruction, the mode indicator would still read SPLIT after the macro executed.

You may want to try this macro in STEP mode, since it does not remain in any one mode for very long. You will just see the indicators flash on the screen briefly, unless you slow the macro down.

{PANELOFF}

The {PANELOFF} command prevents 1-2-3 from redrawing the control panel while the command is in effect.

FORMAT The format for the {PANELOFF} command is

{PANELOFF} or {PANELOFF clear}

When the second form is used, the control panel and status line are cleared before freezing.

USE This command reduces the flicker that can occur when macro instructions are executed. It is also useful if you do not want the operator to be aware of the exact instructions being executed. Even if the operator turns the STEP mode on to slow down the operation of the instructions so they can be read, the control panel and status line are not updated while {PANELOFF} is in effect. This command affects only the execution of menu commands, since 1-2-3 does not use the control panel for advanced macro commands like {BRANCH} and {IF}. Control panel and status line updating starts when 1-2-3 performs a {PANELON} command or the macro ends.

EXAMPLE The following macro lets you determine whether you want the control panel updated as you execute the macro.

```
        A                    B
1      \p            {GETLABEL "Update Control Panel?",update}
2                    {IF update="Y"}{BRANCH yes}
3                    {PANELOFF}
4                    {BRANCH finish}
5      yes           {PANELON}
6      finish        {GOTO}d1~
7                    /RFC2~~
8                    /WCS12~
9                    {GOTO}f3~
10                   /rfp3~{DOWN 3}~
```

This macro lets you see the effect of updating the panel instead of disabling it. The first instruction expects a Y if you want to update the control panel and an N if you do not. The entry you make is stored in a range (cell) called **update**, which is checked by the {IF} statement in B2. If the entry in Update is a Y, control passes to B5. If it is any other value, control passes to B3, where {PANELOFF} disables updating of the control panel. B4 branches to the subroutine called **finish** to bypass the instruction that turns the control panel on. The remainder of the macro moves the cell pointer to D1, then invokes a /Range Format and a /Worksheet Column Set-Width command. The cell pointer is moved to F3, and another format instruction is issued.

SETUP In addition to entering the macro instructions and naming the macro \p, you must select a cell to contain the response to the {GETLABEL} instruction. This cell should be assigned the range name **update**. Range names must also be assigned to two sections of the macro. B5 is assigned the range name **yes**, and B6 is assigned the range name **finish**. You may wish to enter these labels in column A as documentation and assign the names with /Range Name Labels Right.

{PANELON}

The {PANELON} command restores the default setting of having 1-2-3 update the control panel with each instruction executed.

FORMAT The format for the {PANELON} command is

{PANELON}

This command has no arguments.

USE This command is useful when you want to reactivate control panel updating in the middle of a macro.

EXAMPLE The example for the {PANELOFF} instruction shows the effect of both {PANELOFF} and {PANELON} on the control panel.

{WINDOWSOFF}

The {WINDOWSOFF} command freezes the entire screen, with the exception of the control panel and status line, until 1-2-3 performs a {WINDOWSON} command or the macro ends.

FORMAT The format for the {WINDOWSOFF} command is

{WINDOWSOFF}

The command has no arguments.

USE Using this command reduces the flicker that occurs on the screen with each new macro instruction executed. Without this command, you see the screen flicker as ranges are selected, the cell pointer is moved, and entries are generated for worksheet cells. This flicker can be annoying to the operator and is best eliminated. Eliminating window updating also reduces execution time for long macros, since it means that 1-2-3 does not have to redraw the screen every time you move the cell pointer or manipulate data.

Like {PANELOFF}, {WINDOWSOFF} is also useful when you do not want the operator to be aware of each activity performed. You can change the mode indicator to WAIT, and then resume window updating (with {WINDOWSON}) at an appropriate point in the macro.

EXAMPLE The following macro will allow you to monitor the effects of updating the window or freezing it during the execution of the macro.

```
        A                       B
   1    \w        {GETLABEL "Do you want the window updated?",update}
   2              {IF update="Y"}{BRANCH yes}
```

```
3            {WINDOWSOFF}
4            {BRANCH finish}
5    yes     {WINDOWSON}
6    finish  {GOTO}d1~
7            /rfc2~~
8            /wcs~
9            {GOTO}f3~
10           /rfp3~{DOWN 3}~
```

With just one entry in response to a prompt message you can change the window updating option, enabling you to see the difference between updating and freezing.

The first instruction expects a Y if you want to update the screen while the macro executes and an N if you do not. The entry you make is stored in the cell range **update**, which is checked by the {IF} statement in B2. If the entry is a Y, control passes to B5, where {WINDOWSON} is executed. If it is any other value, control passes to B3, where {WINDOWSOFF} disables updating of the window portion of the screen. B4 branches to the subroutine called **finish** to bypass the instruction that turns window updating on. The remainder of the macro moves the cell pointer to D1, then invokes a /Range Format and a /Worksheet Column Set-Width command. The cell pointer is moved to F3, and another format instruction is issued.

Using this macro with the two alternative responses shows you what both ways look like to the user. You can then select the approach you think would be most appropriate for your application.

SETUP   In addition to entering the macro instructions and naming the macro \w, you must select a cell to contain the response to the {GETLABEL} instruction. This cell should be assigned the range name **update**. Range names must also be assigned to two sections of the macro. B5 is assigned the range name **yes**, and B6 is assigned the range name **finish**. You may wish to enter these labels in column A as documentation and assign the names with /Range Name Labels Right.

{WINDOWSON}

The {WINDOWSON} instruction returns to the default setting of having the screen updated with each instruction.

FORMAT   The format of the {WINDOWSON} command is

{WINDOWSON}

This command has no arguments.

USE   You would use this command when you want to reactivate screen updating. It could be inserted near the end of a macro to have the screen updated with the current results.

EXAMPLE   The example found under {WINDOWSOFF} provides a look at the {WINDOWSON} command.

Interactive Macro Commands

{?}

The {?} command is actually an advanced macro instruction, although it was introduced in Chapter 12, "Keyboard Macros." As you know, it is used to allow the operator to enter information from the keyboard.

FORMAT   The format for the {?} command is

   {?}

This command has no arguments.

USE   The {?} command is useful when you need to obtain a few pieces of information from the operator. If you have more extensive needs, {GETNUMBER} and {GETLABEL} are more useful, since they allow you to supply prompts as part of the instruction, to clarify the exact information you want.

If you do use the {?} instruction, you can precede it with an instruction to place a prompt message in the current cell, as follows:

   Enter your department number~

   {?}

The number entered by the operator would replace the message placed in the current cell by the previous instruction.

EXAMPLE You can use the {?} macro command to enter a series of values, such as the entries needed for the @PMT function. You can include a loop to add several @PMT formulas. The macro would appear as follows:

```
       I        J                      K
 1   \d      {LET a1,0}            Initialize A1 to 0
 2   top     {IF a1=10}{QUIT}      Check for max value in counter
 3           {LET a1,a1+1}         Increment counter
 4           @PMT(                 Enter first part of function
 5           {?}                   Pause for the entry of principal
 6           ,                     Generate comma separator
 7           {?}                   Pause for the entry of interest
 8           ,                     Generate comma separator
 9           {?}                   Pause for the entry of term
10           )~                    Generate close and finalize
11           {DOWN}                Move cell pointer down 1 cell
12           {BRANCH top}          Begin loop again
```

This macro shows how the {?} can be enhanced with the use of other instructions to produce multiple formulas rather than a single entry.

SETUP In addition to entering the macro instructions and a macro name assignment of \d, you will need to assign the range name **top** to J2 of the macro. Assign these range names to the appropriate cells with either /Range Name Create or /Range Name Labels Right.

{BREAKOFF}

The {BREAKOFF} command is used to disable the BREAK key function, thereby preventing the interruption of a macro.

FORMAT The format of the {BREAKOFF} command is

{BREAKOFF}

This command has no arguments.

USE Normally, CTRL-BREAK can be used to stop a macro. It will display ERROR as a mode indicator. When you press ESC, you can proceed to make changes to the worksheet from READY mode. However, when you have designed an automated application and want to ensure its integrity by maintaining control throughout the operator's use of the worksheet, you can disable the Break feature by placing {BREAKOFF} in your macro. Be sure you have tested the macro before doing this, since a macro that contains an infinite loop and {BREAKOFF} can be stopped only by turning off the machine.

EXAMPLE   Since the {BREAKOFF} command disables the ability of the CTRL-BREAK sequence to stop a runaway macro, it can be dangerous. It is even more dangerous in a \0 macro that executes automatically, since there is then no way to interrupt the macro.

This may be exactly what you want if you have enabled the Protection feature and wish to ensure that the operator's entries are restricted to the cells you choose. With Worksheet Protection, you can prevent accidental destruction to the contents of cells, but you cannot prevent malicious destruction, since an operator can turn Protection off. However, if you allow worksheet updating only through a controlled access macro with /Range Input statements, disable Break, and save the file at the end before erasing the worksheet, the operator cannot do anything other than what you have established. The only problem is that your access also is limited but a solution to that problem will be presented later, after a discussion of what is needed to lock the operator out of illegal changes.

The macro reads as follows:

```
        A                B
23   \0           {BREAKOFF}
24                {GETLABEL "Update employee names?",r1}
25                {IF r1<>"Y"}{BRANCH address}
26                /ria2..b20~
27   address      {GETLABEL "Update employee addresses?",r2}
28                {IF r2<>"Y"}{BRANCH phone}
29                /ric2..f20~
30   phone        {GETLABEL "Update employee phone numbers?",r3}
31                {IF r3<>"Y"}{BRANCH salary}
32                /rig2..g20~
33   salary       {GETLABEL "Enter password to update salaries",r4}
34                {IF r4=z1}{BRANCH update}
35   end          {BREAKON}{QUIT}
36
37   update       /rih2..h20~
38                {BREAKON}{QUIT}
```

The first instruction, in B23, contains {BREAKOFF}, but you should not add this until you have tested the macro. From here the macro controls the updating of various sections of an employee database. Certain fields cannot be changed, others can be changed as desired, and salaries are updatable only with the correct password.

The {GETLABEL} instruction in B24 checks to see if the operator wishes to update the section of the database that includes employee names. If the response is Y, the macro proceeds to the /Range Input instruction in B26. The names in the database for our example are located in worksheet columns A and B, and this instruction allows the operator to change any of them.

If the operator does not wish to alter any names and responds with N, the **address** section of the macro is executed next. Again the operator will respond to the {GETLABEL} prompt, and if updates are needed, a new Range Input instruction is established.

The next section is **phone**, which allows the updating of phone numbers in the same manner. When the operator is finished with this section, **salary** is next. This section functions a little differently, in that the {GETLABEL} instruction expects a password. This password must match the one stored in cell Z1. Since BREAK is disabled, the operator must know the password, because it is impossible to interrupt the macro to look at the contents of Z1. If the operator's entry matches Z1, the macro branches to **update** and allows updates to the section of the worksheet where salaries are stored. In our example, this is H2..H20, but of course it could be changed to any appropriate range.

{BREAKOFF} is then canceled with {BREAKON} before the macro ends, although this is not mandatory, since ending a macro automatically disables {BREAKOFF}. This macro leaves the worksheet vulnerable to unauthorized changes after the update is completed, because the worksheet is still on the screen. To prevent this, the two {BREAKON}{QUIT} instruction sequences can be replaced with **/fsemploy~r/wey** to both save the worksheet and erase memory. If you do this, you have forever locked both the operator and yourself out of this worksheet unless Undo is enabled.

A fix for this problem is to store another password in a different cell and request the password right before the /File Save. If the password is entered correctly, {BREAKON} is executed and another instruction asks if you have further changes.

SETUP There are a number of steps to be completed in addition to the entry and naming of the macro.

- The cells where you wish to allow entries must be unprotected with /Range Unprot.

- Range names of **address**, **phone**, **salary**, **end**, and **update** must be assigned to B27, B30, B33, B35, and B37, respectively.

- The password to allow salary updates must be stored in Z1.

{BREAKON}

The {BREAKON} command restores the BREAK key function so that you can press CTRL-BREAK to interrupt a macro.

FORMAT The format of the {BREAKON} command is

{BREAKON}

This command has no arguments.

USE You may elect to disable the BREAK function during part of a macro and then restore its operation for a later section, for printing or data entry. BREAK is always restored at the end of a macro.

EXAMPLE The example found under {BREAKOFF} contains an explanation and example of the {BREAKON} instruction. {BREAKON} is the default setting, and is needed only to restore the default after using {BREAKOFF}.

{FORM}

The {FORM} command suspends macro execution, allowing you to enter data in an unprotected range. Although the concept is similar to /Range Input, {FORM} offers more flexibility because you may define either included or excluded keystrokes. You may also define keys that will invoke subroutines during the execution of the {FORM} instruction.

FORMAT The format of the command is

{FORM *input-location[,call-table][,include-list][,exclude-list]*}

Input-location is a range that contains the unprotected cells where you want to make entries. Normally *input-location* is an area on a form which you have designed for data entry purposes. Since {FORM} is frequently used with {APPENDBELOW} in adding records to a database, the *input-location* is likely to be a row.

Call-table allows you to equate keystrokes like function keys or other entries to a subroutine. It is supplied as a range address or range name. The entries in this range are expected to be placed in two adjacent columns. The first column lists the keystroke, and the column to the immediate right of the keystroke contains the subroutine commands that will be executed in response to the keystroke. The keystroke entries are case sensitive; *A* is a different request from *a*. These assignments are only effective while the form is active.

The remaining two arguments are also optional. When you choose to use *include-list*, do not specify *exclude-list* since 1-2-3 will ignore it. You can use *include-list* when you wish to limit the keys that can be used while the form is active. Any key not listed will be disabled. You can include typewriter keys, pointer movement keys, and function keys in the list. *Include-list* is specified as a cell address or range name where these keystrokes are stored. The *exclude-list* allows you to list the keys that you wish to be inactive. Any keys not in this list are enabled. Keys in the list will not function. The *exclude-list* argument is provided as a cell address or range name where these keys are stored. Like *call-list*, both *include-* and *exclude-list* are case sensitive.

USE You can use the {FORM} command to improve data entry. Rather than entering information directly into a database, with the distraction of the records above your entry, you can make your entry on a form and then transfer it to the database with {APPENDBELOW}. The {FORM} command offers other options, like specifying a table of subroutine calls. Or you may take the approach of allowing all keyboard entries during input by not using either an *include-* or an *exclude-list*; this makes all keys available to you. The keys will function as they do when /Range Input is being used.

EXAMPLE Figure 13-5 shows a form that was developed for entering new employee information. The range A11..F11 was unprotected with /Range

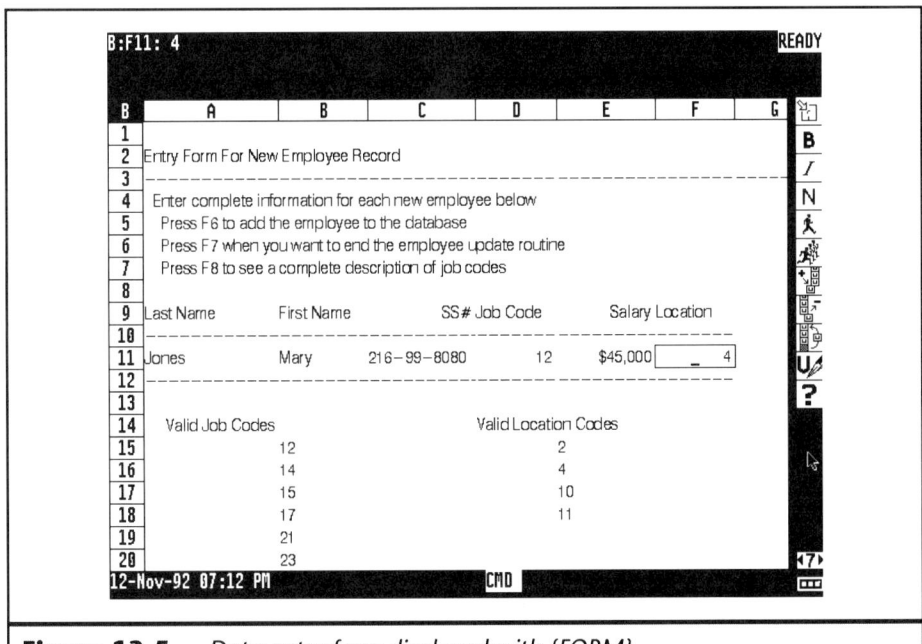

Figure 13-5. *Data entry form displayed with {FORM}*

Unprot. This selects the cells you can change with the {FORM} macro command or during a /Range Input command. These unprotected cells display in another color on a color monitor or are highlighted on a monochrome display. The input range B:A1..B:F11 is named **newrec**.

Next, the macro code in Figure 13-6 is entered. The first instruction activates the form and allows for input in the range **newrec**. Subroutines which you want invoked can be defined with an optional argument *call-table*. For this instruction the call table is a two-column range named **subrtns** located in K4..L6. The keys are recorded using standard macro representation like {WINDOW} for the F6 key. Actions assigned to each of these keys are noted on the form for the operator, and they are placed in the table. The optional argument for *include-list* is not supplied, so an extra comma is used to separate *exclude-list* from *call-table*. The *exclude-list* is named **exclkeys**. It is located in K8. The keys in this list will not be operational when {FORM} is active.

TIP: Be careful not to make your exclude-list *an* include-list. *Remember the extra comma separators to replace unused optional arguments. If you forget this comma, 1-2-3 will misinterpret your {FORM} command entries.*

If the user presses F6 (WINDOW), F7 (QUERY), or F8 (TABLE), special actions occur. F6 appends the input information to the area below the database named **employdb**. It then blanks the range named **newrec** and waits for you to enter the data for the next record. F7 (QUERY) stops the {FORM} command with {FORMBREAK} so that 1-2-3 performs the macro instructions in K2, which saves the file and quits the macro. F8 (TABLE) displays a special help screen stored in **help10** for 10 seconds and returns to the form entry.

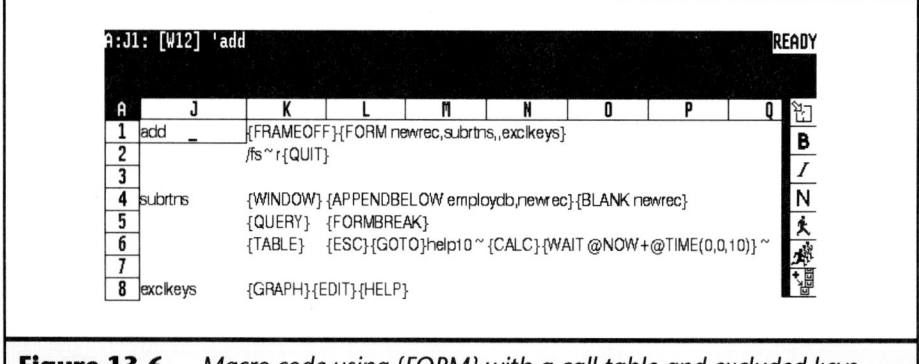

Figure 13-6.   *Macro code using {FORM} with a call table and excluded keys*

SETUP In addition to naming the macro before invoking it, the example requires establishment of the range names **newrec**, **subrtns**, and **exclkeys**.

{FORMBREAK}

The {FORMBREAK} command halts the {FORM} command and continues executing the macro with the instructions in the worksheet cell below the {FORM} command.

FORMAT The format of this command is {FORMBREAK} with no arguments.

USE This command is used either as part of the call-table in a {FORM} command or in an {IF} command to determine when the current {FORM} command will end.

EXAMPLE The {FORM} example also contains an example of a {FORMBREAK} instruction to end the {FORM} command when the user presses F7 (QUERY).

{GET}

The {GET} command is designed to accept the entry of a single character from the keyboard.

FORMAT The format of the {GET} command is

{GET *location*}

where *location* is the storage location for the single character you enter from the keyboard. Your entry can be an alphabetic character, a numeric digit, or any other key, including one of the special function keys such as F9 (CALC) or F2 (EDIT).

USE This command provides another option for keyboard input. It offers an advantage over commands like {?}, {GETLABEL}, and {GETNUMBER} in that it can restrict the keyboard response to a single character. However, it lacks the ability to display a prompt message as {GETNUMBER} and {GETLABEL} can. {GET} is the ideal solution for situations where you wish to build your own full-screen menu and expect a one-letter code for each selection.

EXAMPLE The screen in Figure 13-7 presents a full-screen menu that offers selections in Smith Company's accounting application. Letter selections represent a budget update, aging of receivables, and other accounting functions.

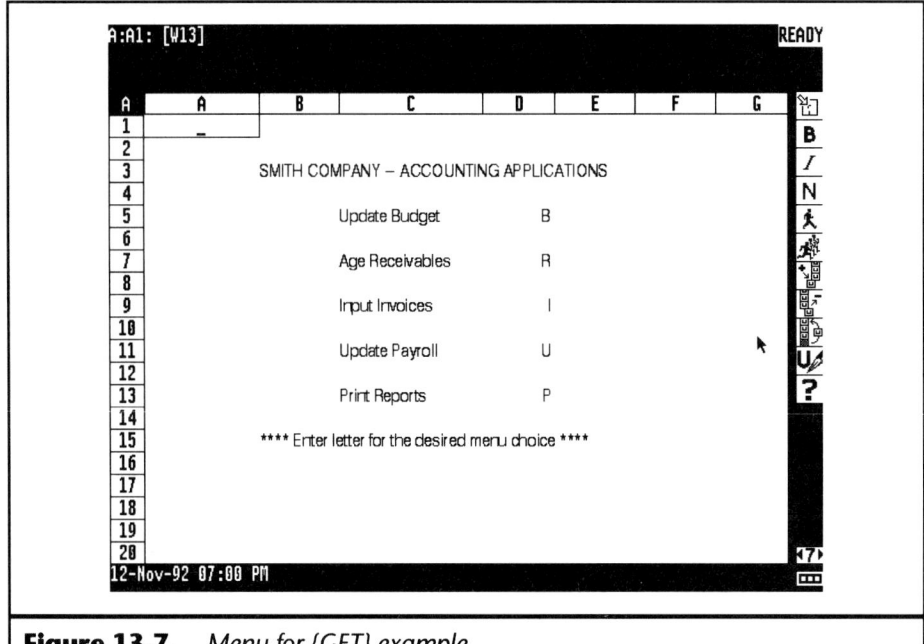

Figure 13-7. Menu for {GET} example

Instructions at the bottom of the screen tell the operator to enter the letter representing a menu choice.

The following macro works with this menu.

```
        J          K
1       \g         {BLANK a20}
2                  {INDICATE}
3                  {GOTO}a1~
4                  {GET choice}
5                  {IF choice="B"}{BRANCH budget}
6                  {IF choice="R"}{BRANCH rec}
7                  {IF choice="I"}{BRANCH inv}
8                  {IF choice="U"}{BRANCH payroll}
9                  {IF choice="P"}{BRANCH report}
10                 {INDICATE "ERROR"}
11                 {LET a20,"Incorrect entry, re-execute macro"}{CALC}
12
13      budget     {GOTO}q1~
14                 {GETLABEL "Budget routine",z1}
15                 {CALC}
```

The macro begins with a {BLANK} instruction that makes sure A20 has been erased. This cell must be erased because it will be used to present an error message to the operator when incorrect entries have been made. You must start each new selection process with no entry in this cell.

The {INDICATE} instruction in line 2 ensures that the mode indicator is in its default state, without any previous displays in this area of the screen. Again, this is necessary so that the mode indicator can be set to ERROR if an incorrect response is made.

The cell pointer is next moved to A1 to allow the display of the entire screen. The {GET} instruction accepts a single-character response and stores it in a cell that has previously been assigned the range name **choice**.

The next five instructions check the value of **choice** and then branch to appropriate subroutines. Only one subroutine is shown in the listing, but they all follow the same pattern. They have been established as shell routines that do nothing more at this time than move the cell pointer and display a message letting the operator know what routine has been reached. These shells can be expanded later to include a full set of instructions to do the appropriate processing.

If none of the branches is taken, this means that the operator entered an unacceptable character. When this happens, the mode indicator is set to ERROR in line 10, and an error message is placed in A20 with the {LET} instruction, which assigns a string value to A20.

{GETLABEL}

The {GETLABEL} command is used to permit the entry of a character string from the keyboard in response to a prompt message.

FORMAT The format for the {GETLABEL} command is

{GETLABEL *prompt-message,location*}

The argument *prompt-message* is a string that must be enclosed in double quotation marks if it contains a character that can be used as an argument separator (a comma, colon, semicolon, or period), or a cell reference, range name, or formula that produces a string. The string displays in the control panel. Its length is limited to the 72 characters at the top of the control panel. If you supply a longer string, it scrolls off the screen.

The argument *location* is a cell address or range name where the information entered from the keyboard is stored. Up to 80 characters will be accepted as input. If a range is supplied for the argument, the character string entered is stored in the upper left cell of the range.

USE The {GETLABEL} command stores your entry as a left justified label in the location specified. This feature makes the command appropriate for numeric entries, as well, when you want them placed at the left edge of the cell so they can be read as macro keystrokes.

EXAMPLE Figure 13-8 shows a screen that might be used to capture data entry information. The following instructions are an extract from a macro that might be used with this data entry screen.

```
         J             K
1        \e            {GOTO}A1~
2                      {GETLABEL "Enter Name (Last, First)",d3}
3                      {GETLABEL "Enter Street Address",d5}
4                      {GETLABEL "Enter City",d7}
5                      {GETLABEL "Enter State",d9}
6                      {GETLABEL "Enter Zip",d11}~
```

The first macro instruction moves the cursor to A1. Then the {GETLABEL} instruction presents a prompt and stores the response in C3. The remaining instructions all follow the same pattern, providing a prompt for each new piece of information required and storing it in a cell. At the end of these instructions, you might wish to add further instructions to move this data to the next available database record within the worksheet or perform some additional manipulations with the data.

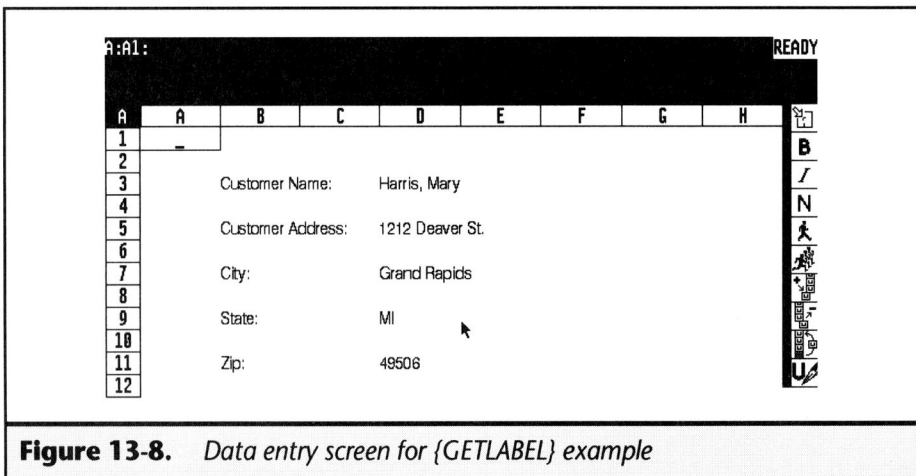

Figure 13-8. *Data entry screen for {GETLABEL} example*

 NOTE: *{GETLABEL}* is equivalent to the Release 1A /XL command. To use the /XL command, enter **/XLprompt~location~** where prompt is the message displayed in the control panel and location is the cell address or range name where the entry is stored.

{GETNUMBER}

The {GETNUMBER} command is used to permit the entry of numeric information from the keyboard in response to a prompt message.

FORMAT   The format for the {GETNUMBER} command is

   {GETNUMBER *prompt-message,location*}

The argument *prompt-message* is a string that must be enclosed in double quotation marks if it contains a character that can be used as an argument separator (, : ; or .) or a cell reference, range name, or formula that produces a string. The string displays in the control panel. Its length is limited to the 72 characters at the top of the control panel. If you supply a longer string, it scrolls off the screen.

The argument *location* is a reference to a cell, range, or range name where the information entered from the keyboard is stored. A numeric value, formula, or range name referencing a numeric value can be entered. If a range is supplied for the argument, the numeric value entered is stored in the upper left cell of the range.

USE   You can use the {GETNUMBER} command to store an entry as a value rather than as a label that {GETLABEL} stores.

EXAMPLE   The following macro is another macro that can be used to enter a built-in function like @PMT.

```
         H          I
1    \d         {LET p1,0}
2               {GETNUMBER "How many would you like to enter?",p2}
3    top        {IF p1=p2}{BRANCH end}
4               {LET p1,p1+1}
5               @PMT(
6               {?}
7               ,
8               {?}
```

```
9               ,
10              {?}
11              )~
12              {DOWN}
13              {BRANCH top}
14    end       {QUIT}
```

This macro uses the {?}, which does not provide prompts. You can still choose the number of iterations you want, however. The first instruction initializes a counter. Next, the number of iterations is determined by requesting input from the operator. The iterative section or loop begins with the label **top**. An {IF} instruction checks for equality between the counter and the number of iterations requested. If they are equal, a branch to **end** executes a {QUIT} to stop the macro.

Until the equal condition is reached, the macro stays within the loop and enters the @PMT function in worksheet cells. The operator provides the function arguments and the macro adds the fixed characters needed for each function. At the end of the loop, the cursor is moved down a cell, and control branches to the top of the macro.

*NOTE: {GETNUMBER} is equivalent to the Release 1A /XN command. To use the /XN command, enter /**XN**prompt~location~ where prompt is the message displayed in the control panel and location is the cell address or range name where the entry is stored.*

{LOOK}

The {LOOK} command checks the keyboard buffer for characters and places the first character in this buffer as an entry in the range identified by the *location* argument. It is similar to {GET}, except that with {LOOK} the operator can type the entry ahead and the macro will still find it.

FORMAT   The format of the {LOOK} command is

   {LOOK *location*}

where *location* is a cell address or range name used to store the character from the type-ahead buffer. If {LOOK} finds the buffer blank, it erases the *location* cell.

USE   {LOOK} does not suspend macro execution while waiting for an entry, as the {GET} instruction does. Normally you will use {LOOK} within a loop, allowing a certain amount of time for an entry before canceling the instruction. You may or may not wish to update the file before canceling.

EXAMPLE The following macro uses the {LOOK} instruction to process a menu request from the same application designed for {GET} earlier in this section.

```
            I                   J
 1   \1                 {INDICATE}{GOTO}a1~
 2                      {LET time,@NOW}
 3   keep_looking       {LOOK selection}
 4                      {IF selection<>""}{BRANCH process}
 5                      {IF @NOW<(time+@TIME(0,10,0))}{BRANCH keep_looking}
 6                      {INDICATE "ERROR"}
 7                      {LET a20,"No selection made - Reexecute macro"}
 8                      {QUIT}
 9
10   process            Macro instructions to process menu selection
```

Unlike the example with {GET}, this macro does not wait beyond a specific amount of time. It uses a loop to control the time it will wait if the selection is not in the type-ahead buffer.

The macro begins by setting the indicator to its default setting and moving the cursor to A1. It then places the current date and time in a cell named **time**.

The next instruction begins the loop for checking the type-ahead buffer. {LOOK} is executed and stores the first character from the type-ahead buffer, if present, in **selection**. The next instruction, in line 4, checks to see if anything has been placed in **selection**. If anything is stored there, the macro branches to **process**. If the cell is empty, the macro continues to the {IF} instruction in line 5. This {IF} instruction compares the current time against the time stored at the beginning (in **time**) plus an acceptable wait interval. For this example, the wait time was set at 10 minutes. If the current time is less than 10 minutes after the beginning time, the macro continues to look for an entry by branching to the **keep_looking** subroutine. If the chosen time interval has elapsed, the macro sets the indicator to ERROR and displays an error message in A20. Alternative strategies might be to save the file, clear memory, and quit 1-2-3. The **process** section of this macro is not shown, but would contain instructions similar to those in the {GET} example shown earlier.

SETUP The example macro requires that cells for the storage of variables be named **time** and **selection**. The range names **keep_looking** and **process** must be assigned to locations in the macro as shown.

{MENUBRANCH}

The {MENUBRANCH} command allows you to branch to a location containing information required to build a customized menu. Once this branch occurs, the macro executes instructions based on your menu selections.

FORMAT   The format of the {MENUBRANCH} command is

{MENUBRANCH *location*}

where *location* is a cell address or range name that represents the upper left cell in the area for menu storage. This area must be a minimum of three rows deep and two columns wide. You may have up to eight columns of menu information.

USE   Information for the customized menu must be organized according to specific rules.

- The top row of the menu area will contain the menu selection words that you wish to use. Each of these words should begin with a different character, just as in 1-2-3's menus. This allows the operator to enter the first letter of an option to represent its selection, or to point to the option. Menu selection words are entered one to a cell. You may use up to eight cells across, providing eight menu options.

- The second row of the menu area contains the expanded description for each menu choice that will display when you point to the menu selection. As you make one label entry in each cell and move across, it is likely that the entries will appear truncated, since they are long labels. Although you will want to keep your descriptions brief, do not be concerned about this apparent overlap. Place each expanded description in the appropriate column for the menu choice.

- Place the remainder of the macro instructions appropriate for each choice in the column with the menu item and expanded description. Begin these instructions in the cell immediately under the expanded description, and extend as far down the column as you need. You may include a branch to a subroutine.

EXAMPLE   Figure 13-9 shows a menu. There are four different selections in the menu, and it is duplicated four times in the figure so that you can see the expanded description for each of the four choices.

The macro that created this custom menu is shown in Figure 13-10. The macro begins with the {MENUBRANCH} instruction and has all the menu options stored at a location named **select**. The cell J3 is the one to which this

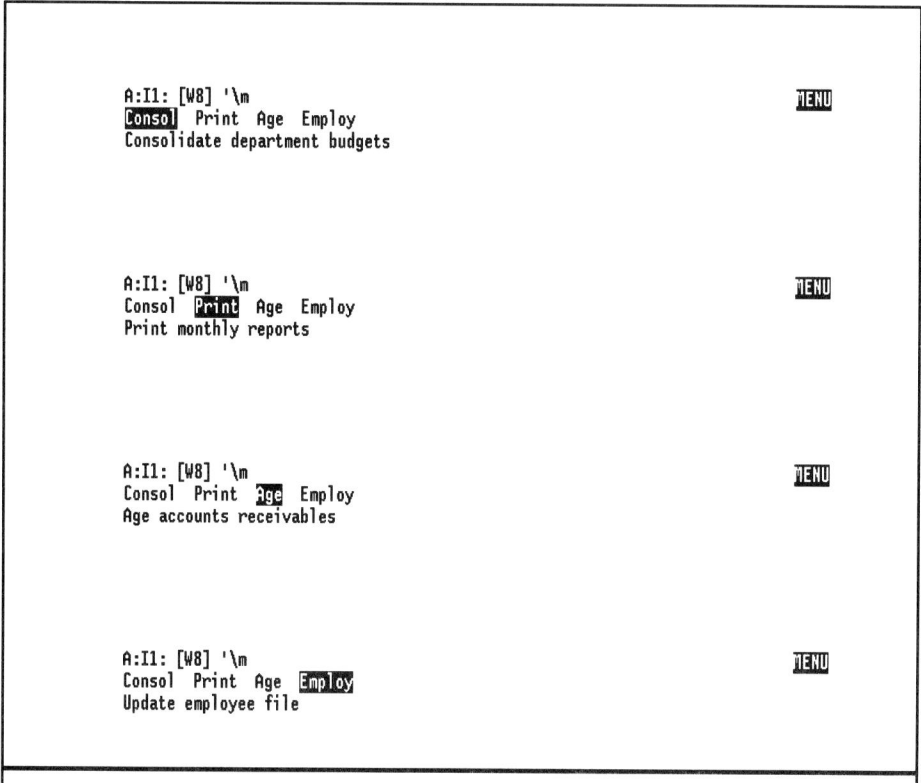

Figure 13-9. Custom menu with expanded descriptions

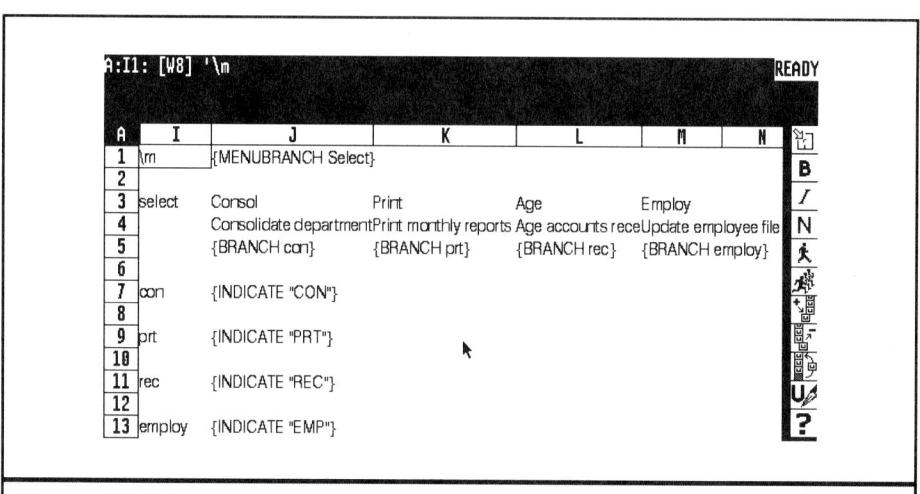

Figure 13-10. Macro for creation of custom menu

name was attached, although the menu selections and descriptions extend down from there and to the right.

The menu selections shown in J3..M3 are the words "Consol," "Print," "Age," and "Employ." As required, each word begins with a different letter. The expanded descriptions appear in cells J4..N4. They are as follows:

J4	Consolidate department budgets
K4	Print monthly reports
L4	Age accounts receivables
M4	Update employee file

As you enter the second through the fourth descriptions, it will appear that you are writing on top of previous ones, but you need not be concerned. Each description is stored as a label in the appropriate cell.

The last step in creating a menu macro is to fill in the cells underneath the descriptions with all the instructions for each choice. In our example, these instructions occupy only row 5, but the entries could extend down in the columns to row 50 or longer.

In this macro, each option has a branch to a different subroutine. At this point the routines are simply shells to allow you to check the logic. The only action taken in each shell is to change the indicator to the entry specified.

SETUP   The entire menu section must be entered before a macro like this can be tested. It is the only example of a macro that can extend across as many as eight columns. Actually, it is eight individual macros in adjacent columns.

All the names listed in column I must be assigned to the respective cells in column J. /Range Name Labels Right is the easiest way to handle this task.

NOTE: {MENUBRANCH} is equivalent to the Release 1A /XM command. To use the /XM command, enter /XMlocation~ where location is the cell address or range name where the menu starts.

{MENUCALL}

The {MENUCALL} command displays a custom menu as does {MENUBRANCH}, but it executes the menu as a call rather than as a branch. This affects the execution flow at the end of the menu processing. With {MENUBRANCH}, the macro ends when the code for the selected option completes. With {MENUCALL}, control returns to the statement following {MENUCALL} in the main code for the macro, and execution begins again at that location.

FORMAT   The format of the {MENUCALL} command is

   {MENUCALL *location*}

where *location* is a cell address or range name that represents the upper left cell in the area for menu storage. This area must be a minimum of three rows deep and two columns wide. You may have up to eight columns of menu information.

USE   The {MENUCALL} command is used when you want to continue executing the macro instructions directly beneath the {MENUCALL} macro instruction. The structure of the menu and the rules it must follow are identical to the structure and rules described for the {MENUBRANCH} command.

EXAMPLE   An example of {MENUCALL} would be exactly the same as the one for {MENUBRANCH}, except that you would expect to see statements after {MENUCALL} in the main code. These would be executed after the menu processing had completed.

{WAIT}

The {WAIT} command will halt the execution of a macro until a specified time.

FORMAT   The format of the {WAIT} command is

   {WAIT *time_serial_number*}

where *time_serial_number* is a decimal value that represents the serial time number for the time of day when you wish execution to continue.

EXAMPLE   You can use the {WAIT} command to delay a macro's execution for several seconds or minutes. To do this, the *time-serial-number* used by {WAIT} can be computed by adding a time value to the value computed with @NOW to create a fixed delay. You may, for example, want to display information on the screen for 30 seconds to allow time for it to be read, like this:

   {WAIT @NOW+@TIME(0,0,30)}

This adds 30 seconds to the current time and waits until that time is reached before continuing execution. While 1-2-3 is waiting, the mode indicator will say WAIT.

The macro shown as an example for the {LOOK} command also uses the {WAIT} command to delay macro execution.

Macro Commands that Affect Flow of Execution

{BRANCH}

The {BRANCH} command allows you to move the flow of execution in your macro to a new location.

FORMAT   The format of the {BRANCH} command is

{BRANCH *location*}

where *location* is a cell address or a range name that tells 1-2-3 the location of the next instruction to be executed. If you specify a range name that refers to a range of cells, 1-2-3 will begin execution with the keystrokes in the upper left cell of the range.

USE   {BRANCH} is frequently used with a condition test to change the flow of execution. As an example, you might have the following entry in your macro:

```
     {IF A1>10}{BRANCH end}
     ...
     ...
end  {QUIT}
```

In this case you may have been using A1 as a counter, and when A1 exceeds 10, your task is finished. This sequence of instructions would then branch to **end** and execute the {QUIT} instruction stored there.

EXAMPLE   The following listing is an excerpt from a macro that combines the data in four files.

```
      A                    B
1    \c         {GETLABEL "Begin combine?",h21}
2               {IF h21<>"Y"}{BRANCH stop}
3               {HOME}
4               /fcaeREGION1~
```

```
5                  /fcaeREGION2~
6                  /fcaeREGION3~
7                  /fcaeREGION4~
8     stop         {CALC}
```

The excerpt begins by asking the operator whether to proceed with the consolidation. The logical {IF} in the next line checks for any value other than Y and uses the {BRANCH} instruction to alter the execution flow to **stop** if such a value is found. Stop recalculates the worksheet and ends the macro.

Assuming a Y was entered, the cursor is moved to the Home position, and the four files are combined with the /File Combine Add Entire-File command. The worksheet is then recalculated, and the macro ends.

*NOTE: This is equivalent to the Release 1A /XG command. To use the /XG command, enter /**XGlocation~** where* location *is the cell address or range name of the next macro instruction to execute.*

TIP: {BRANCH} is frequently confused with {GOTO}, but they are not the same. {GOTO} repositions the cursor without affecting the execution of the macro. {BRANCH} alters the macro's execution flow but does not move the cursor.

{DEFINE}

The {DEFINE} command allocates space for arguments to be passed to subroutines and establishes the type of information they will contain.

FORMAT   The format of the {DEFINE} command is

{DEFINE *location1:type1,location2:type2,...locationn:typen*}

The argument *location* is a cell where the value being passed to the subroutine is to be stored. This cell can be specified with a cell address or a range name. If you specify a range name that references a group of cells, the upper left cell in the range will be used for storage.

The argument *type* tells 1-2-3 whether value or string data is to be passed to the subroutine. *Type* may be entered as either value or string, like this:

{DEFINE price:value,supplier:string}

where **price** and **supplier** are range names that will be used for passing the arguments to the subroutine. **Price** will contain value data, and **supplier** will contain strings. String is the default type.

EXAMPLE   Examples of the {DEFINE} command are included in the "Main Code and Subroutines" section at the beginning of the chapter and also later in the chapter under the {*routine*} macro command.

{DISPATCH}

The {DISPATCH} command allows you to use the contents of a cell to determine the branch location.

FORMAT   The format of the {DISPATCH} command is

{DISPATCH *location*}

where *location* is a cell address or a range name that refers to a single cell. This cell in turn must contain a cell address or a range name of another cell. {DISPATCH} will read this information from the cell and branch to the location represented by its contents.

USE   This command is useful when you need to set up a variable branching situation based on the contents of data fields or other worksheet results. It differs from the {BRANCH} command in that {BRANCH} immediately executes the instructions in the cells beginning at *location*, whereas {DISPATCH} first reads the location cell to determine the final branch location at which it will execute instructions.

EXAMPLE   The macro shown here provides an example of {DISPATCH}.

```
        A                    B
1      \d         {IF due_date>@NOW}{LET routine,"not_due"}
2                 {IF due_date<=@NOW}{LET routine,"over_due"}
3                 {CALC}{DISPATCH routine}
4
5      not_due    {LET a18,"Account not yet due"}
6
7      over_due   {LET a18,"*** Account Overdue***"}
```

The macro is designed to take two different paths, depending on whether the date in **due_date** is greater than today's date. The first instruction checks due_date against @NOW. If **due_date** is greater, it places the value **not_due** in the cell named **routine**. If the opposite condition is true, the value **over_due** is placed in **routine**.

The worksheet is calculated to place these values in **routine**, so you can see them display if you use the STEP mode for this macro. {DISPATCH} is the next instruction. It reads the entry in **routine** and then branches to the appropriate location. Again the two subroutines have been set up in the example as shells, but they can be expanded easily to handle whatever tasks you require.

{FOR}

The {FOR} command permits you to execute the code at a given location numerous times through a loop that it establishes.

FORMAT The format of the {FOR} command is

{FOR *counter,start,stop,increment,starting_location*}

The argument *counter* is a location within the worksheet that the {FOR} instruction can use to count the number of iterations performed. {FOR} initializes this location with the value you specify for *start*.

The argument *start* is the initial value for counter.

The argument *stop* is the end value for *counter. Counter* will never exceed this value.

The argument *increment* is the amount that should be added to *counter* for each iteration of the loop.

The argument *starting_location* is a cell address or range name that specifies the location of the routine to be executed repetitively.

None of these values should be altered from within the subroutine. *Start, stop,* and *increment* are maintained internally by 1-2-3.

USE You have seen examples earlier in this chapter of loops created without the {FOR} statement. Using {FOR} can make looping tasks easier, since it automatically handles initialization of the counter, increments it with each iteration, and checks for the last execution of the loop. When you create an iterative process outside of {FOR}, you must manage these tasks yourself.

The rules used by {FOR} in processing a loop are as follows:

- Before each pass through the loop, {FOR} compares *counter* and *stop*. If *counter* is less than or equal to *stop*, the loop is processed. If *counter* is greater than *stop*, control passes to the instruction following {FOR}.

- At the end of the *starting-location* routine or at a {RETURN}, control passes to the top of the loop. At this time, *counter* is increased by *increment*.
- If *stop* is less than *start,* the loop is not executed. A loop with an *increment* of 0 is an infinite loop; it can be stopped only by pressing CTRL-BREAK.
- If {QUIT} or {FORBREAK} is used at the end of the loop rather than {RETURN}, the loop ends.

EXAMPLE The following macro is designed to enter a column of numbers from the numeric keypad and to sum the numbers once they are entered. An arbitrary limit of 20 numbers was established, but if you want to stop sooner, enter **z**.

The macro instructions are as follows:

```
      A                B
1    \f          {FOR counter,1,20,1,numbers}
2                /re~
3                @SUM(
4                {UP}{END}{UP}.{END}{DOWN}
5                )~
6
7    numbers     {?}~
8                {IF @CELLPOINTER("contents")="z"}{FORBREAK}
9                {DOWN}
```

The first instruction sets up the loop with an initial value of 1, an *increment* of 1, and a *stop* value of 20. A cell named **counter** is used to store the number of iterations performed, and **numbers** is the location of the code that begins the loop.

Numbers will be executed next. In every iteration, it will expect you to enter a value. You may use the numeric keypad if you disable the movement keys with NUM LOCK.

The next instruction checks to see whether the current cell contains a z. If it does, the {FOR} loop ends (via {FORBREAK}), regardless of the number of iterations completed, and control returns to line 2. If a z was not entered, the cell pointer moves down one cell. The *counter* is incremented by 1, and the loop begins again.

When control returns to B2, the current cell is erased. It will either be blank already or contain a z, depending on how the loop ended. The @SUM instruction is added to this cell. The complete list of numbers you entered will then be added and the @SUM function finalized.

SETUP The range name **numbers** must be assigned to B7. You must also assign a range name to *counter.* Before executing the macro, position your cell pointer in the desired location for the column of numbers to be entered, and turn on NUM LOCK, since this cannot be done from the macro.

{FORBREAK}

The {FORBREAK} command cancels processing of a {FOR} loop before the stop value is reached.

FORMAT   The format of the {FORBREAK} command is

   {FORBREAK}

This command has no arguments.

USE   Normally {FORBREAK} is used in conjunction with an {IF} statement that checks the value of a variable and, on a certain condition, exits the loop. As an example, say you want to process a loop 20 times, or until the account balance is zero. {FORBREAK} can be executed based on a test of the account balance.

EXAMPLE   The {FOR} example also contains an example of a {FORBREAK} instruction that can end the loop early, based on the contents of a cell.

{IF}

The {IF} command will conditionally execute the command on the same line with {IF}.

FORMAT   The format of the {IF} command is

   {IF *condition*}

where *condition* is any expression with either a numeric or a string value.

USE   The statement on the same line as the {IF} statement is treated as a THEN clause: "IF the expression is true, THEN the instruction following is executed." Any numeric expression is considered true as long as it is not the numeric value zero. A false condition, blank cells, ERR, NA, and string values all evaluate as zero.
   The instructions on the line after {IF} are regarded as the ELSE clause. Normally the THEN clause contains a {BRANCH}; otherwise, the macro executes the instructions in the ELSE clause after completing the THEN instructions.

EXAMPLE   The macro shown here provides an example of the {IF} command.

```
       A     B                          C
 1    \h    {GOTO}i1~                  Move cell pointer to read directions
 2          {GET k1}                   Get type
 3          {IF k1="C"}{LET c15,i20}   Check Budget Year/Set heading
 4          {IF k1="P"}{LET c15,i19}   Set heading for previous year
 5          {GOTO}b16~                 Move to B16
 6          ^QTR 1                     Enter ^QTR 1
 7          {RIGHT}^QTR 2              Move right and enter ^QTR 2
 8          {RIGHT}^QTR 3              Move right and enter ^QTR 3
 9          {RIGHT}^QTR 4              Move right and enter ^QTR 4
10          {RIGHT}^TOTAL              Move right and enter ^TOTAL
11          {END}{LEFT}                Move to end on left
12          {DOWN}                     Move down 1 cell
```

This macro establishes a heading for a budget report and uses the {IF} command to determine which budget year to print at the top of the report.

At the beginning of the macro the cell pointer is moved to cell I1, where directions are displayed. Then {GET} waits for a single-character entry of *C* for current or *P* for previous.

The {IF} statements in lines 3 and 4 check the character entered to determine the proper heading to use; then it is placed in C15. The statement following each {IF} on the same line will be executed only if the condition shown for that {IF} is true.

The macro then proceeds to complete the remainder of the heading after the year is entered. The year is selected by the {IF} command as described in the previous paragraph. At the end of the macro, the cell pointer is positioned immediately beneath the first quarter heading to be ready for the operator's first entry.

SETUP   The macro expects to find headings for the previous and current budget years in I19 and I20, respectively.

NOTE: {IF} is equivalent to the Release 1A /XI command. To use the /XI command, enter **/XIcondition~keystrokes-for-true-condition**. *Enter the* condition *to evaluate and the keystrokes to execute if the condition is true.*

{ONERROR}

The {ONERROR} command allows you to intercept errors, or process them yourself, during macro execution.

Chapter 13: Command Language Macros

FORMAT   The format of the {ONERROR} command is

{ONERROR *location*[,*message-location*]}

The argument *location* is the location to which 1-2-3 branches for error processing when an error is encountered.

The argument *message-location* is a cell containing the message that 1-2-3 displays at the bottom of the screen when an error occurs. This argument is optional, but if you do not supply it, you will not be able to determine what type of error occurred.

USE   Since the {ONERROR} command is not effective until 1-2-3 has executed it within the flow of the macro, you will want to place it near the beginning of your macro. It remains in effect until either another {ONERROR} command is executed, an error is encountered, CTRL-BREAK is pressed, or the macro ends. Since CTRL-BREAK registers as an error, you can use {ONERROR} to intercept Break requests without using {BREAKOFF}. Once {ONERROR} is used to intercept an error, it will not normally be available again in the same macro. If you want to reinstate {ONERROR} after using it, the routine at *location* should contain another {ONERROR} command.

EXAMPLE   The following macro shows the macro and message 1-2-3 uses when an error occurs. This macro automatically executes when the file is retrieved. The {ONERROR} command directs 1-2-3 to execute the macro starting at the cell called **start_over** if an error occurs while 1-2-3 executes the {Update_pay} macro. If an error occurs, 1-2-3 displays the message in the cell labeled **message** for ten seconds before retrieving the file again so you can start over. This type of error processing would occur when you want an all-or-none transaction processing. If the macro cannot perform all of the changes and save the modified file, it does not save any changes. In a payroll example, you would not want to perform payroll computations for only half of your employees. You would want to make the computations for all of them or none of them.

	A	B	C
1	\0	{ONERROR start_over,message}	If error, restart
2		{update_pay}	Updates payroll
3		/fs~r	Saves results
4			
5	start_over	{WAIT @NOW+@TIME(0,0,10)}	Displays message
6		/frPAYROLL~	Retrieves the file
7			
8	message	Unable to complete process, starting over	

{QUIT}

The {QUIT} command is used to terminate a macro.

FORMAT The format of the {QUIT} command is

{QUIT}

This command has no arguments.

USE The {QUIT} command can be used as a value at the end of a condition test, for example, {IF a1>10}{QUIT}. When the condition evaluates as true, the macro, including all its subroutines, will end.

EXAMPLE The following is a macro that uses the {QUIT} command to stop the macro's execution. This macro will continue executing until the current cell no longer contains a label, making the {IF} command false. The instructions in B2..B6 are the same ones you saw in the previous chapter as an example of a keyboard macro to handle data entry errors.

```
         A                      B
1  proper      {IF @cellpointer("type")<>"l"}{QUIT}
2              {EDIT}
3              {HOME}{DEL}
4              @proper("
5              {END}
6              "){CALC}~
7              {D}~{BRANCH proper}
```

NOTE: {QUIT} is equivalent to the Release 1A /XQ command. To use the /XQ command, enter /XQ.

{RESTART}

The {RESTART} command cancels the execution of the current subroutine and eliminates all pointers to routines that called it, so it cannot return.

FORMAT The format of the {RESTART} command is

{RESTART}

This command has no arguments.

USE When you include this command anywhere within a called subroutine, it will immediately cancel the call, complete the routine, and continue executing from that point downward. All upward pointers to higher-level routines are canceled.

EXAMPLE The following is a macro that uses the {RESTART} command. The first {IF} command redirects the macros's execution to the **no_password** subroutine if the variable "password" is not equal to "money". In the **no_password** subroutine, the first instruction is {RESTART}. The {RESTART} command prevents 1-2-3 from returning to the macro instructions in the body of the **update_pay** macro. Instead, only the macro commands which appear in the **no_password** subroutine are performed; then the macro is ended.

```
           A                         B
1  update_pay    {IF password<>"money"}{BRANCH no_password}
2                ...
3                {GETLABEL "Do you want to edit the worksheet?",answer}
4                {IF answer<>"Y"}{RETURN}
5                ...
6
7  no_password   {RESTART}
8                {GOTO}H1~
9                {WAIT @now+@time(0,0,20)}
10               /wey
```

{RETURN}

The {RETURN} command is used to return from a subroutine to the calling routine. It is used in conjunction with {MENUCALL} and {*routine*}. A blank cell or one containing a numeric value has the same effect as {RETURN} when it is encountered in a subroutine.

FORMAT The format for the {RETURN} command is

{RETURN}

This command has no arguments.

USE Placing {RETURN} anywhere in a called subroutine sends the flow of control back to the instruction following the one that called the subroutine. Unlike {RESTART}, {RETURN} does not cancel upward pointers. Check the example under the {routine} command for further information on the use of {RETURN}.

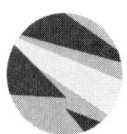

TIP: Do not confuse {RETURN} with {QUIT}. {RETURN} continues processing after returning to the calling routine. {QUIT} ends the macro. With {QUIT}, no further instructions are processed.

NOTE: {RETURN} is equivalent to the Release 1A /XR command. To use the /XR command, enter /XR.

{routine}

This command calls the subroutine it specifies. Its format is different from that of all the other macro commands, in that it contains no keyword, but only the argument *routine* and any optional value arguments you may choose to use.

FORMAT The format of the {routine} command is

{routine [argument1][,argument2]...[,argumentn]}

The *routine* is a range name assigned to a single cell. This name must not be the same as any of the function key or movement key names, such as {UP}, {EDIT}, or {CALC}.

The *arguments* are optional values or strings passed to the subroutine. They must have corresponding entries in a {DEFINE} statement.

EXAMPLE The following macro provides an example of the use of a subroutine call.

```
         A              B
1       \r       {GETNUMBER "How many items did you buy?",k1}
2                {LET counter,0}
3                {LET k5,0}{LET k6,0}
4                {purchase k1}
5                {INDICATE "DONE"}
6                {GOTO}q1~The total purchased is :~
7                {RIGHT 3}+k6~/rfc2~~
8                {QUIT}
9
```

```
10   purchase    {DEFINE k2:value}
11               {IF counter=k2}{BRANCH end}
12               {GETNUMBER "Enter Purchase Amount",k5}
13               {LET k6,k6+k5}
14               {LET counter,counter+1}
15               {BRANCH purchase}
16   end         {RETURN}
```

This macro allows you to enter as many purchase amounts as you wish, and totals them for you.

The first instruction prompts you for the number of items purchased. This number is stored in cell K1. The next two instructions do some housekeeping by zeroing counters that the macro will use.

The subroutine call is in line 4. Notice that the optional argument is used to pass the value in K1 to the subroutine.

The subroutine that begins in line 10 first uses a {DEFINE} statement to set aside K2 for the information passed to it, and declares this information to be a numeric variable. It uses **counter** to loop within the subroutine until **counter** is equal to the number of purchases specified. Until that time, it increments cell K6 by the purchase amount each time, increments **counter** by 1, and then branches back to the top of the subroutine.

When all purchases are processed, the subroutine branches to **end**, where a {RETURN} statement is located. This statement returns control to line 5 in the main routine. The mode indicator is then changed to DONE, and the total amount purchased is displayed.

NOTE: *This is equivalent to the Release 1A /XC command. To use the /XC command, enter* **/XClocation~** *where* location *is the cell address or range name of the routine to execute.*

{SYSTEM}

The {SYSTEM} command allows you to temporarily suspend your work with 1-2-3 and execute an operating system command.

FORMAT   The format for the {SYSTEM} command is

{SYSTEM *command*}

The argument *command* is the name of a batch file or an operating system command or a string formula that evaluates to a command or a batch filename. The entry should be enclosed in quotation marks unless it is a range name or cell address where this information is stored.

USE   You can use this command any time you want to suspend 1-2-3's execution to run operating system commands. When running under DOS you should not attempt to invoke a memory resident program with this method since it may overlay some of 1-2-3's memory space and not allow you to resume execution of the macro. When the operating system command completes execution, the macro execution will resume.

EXAMPLE   You can format a new disk during macro execution with an entry of {SYSTEM "FORMAT A:"}. After formatting disk A (you will first need to press ENTER when DOS prompts you to enter a blank disk), 1-2-3 will perform the next macro instruction, which may copy files to the disk. You can use the @INFO function to confirm that the disk formatted correctly. @INFO("osreturncode") returns 0 when the disk formats correctly.

Macro Commands that Manipulate Data

The macro commands in this section allow you to manipulate values and strings stored in worksheet cells. You can use these commands to blank out a section of the worksheet or store a value or string in a cell. Commands from this section can also be used to recalculate the worksheet in row or column order.

{APPENDBELOW}

The {APPENDBELOW} instruction allows you to add information across a row in a worksheet to the end of an existing database. It extends the range of the database to include the extra row that it adds.

FORMAT   The format of {APPENDBELOW} is

   {APPENDBELOW *target-location,source-location*}

Target-location is a range or range name that references an existing database. *Source-location* is the range of entries across a row or rows, for one or more records, to be added to the existing database. The number of rows in the source location cannot exceed the number of available rows in the worksheet below the target location. This command will not execute if it will write over existing entries.

USE You can use this command to enter new records in a database. It is normally used in conjunction with /Range Input or {FORM} to add the information as a new record in the database. It can also be used to join the contents of two database tables with an identical format.

EXAMPLE Figure 13-11 shows an employee database with 19 records. You can use a custom input form and have 1-2-3 automatically add new records to the end of this database; Figure 13-12 shows the Entry Form that was designed for this purpose. The form in the example was invoked with {FORM} and will accept entries in much the same way as /Range Input. When the user presses F6 (WINDOW), the {FORM} instruction executes an {APPENDBELOW} instruction, which adds the new record to the database. 1-2-3 will automatically expand the **employdb** range name, which contains the database and is used by the {APPENDBELOW} command to include the added records. The Unprotect attribute moves to the database with the new entry and causes it to appear in a different color or highlighted depending on your monitor.

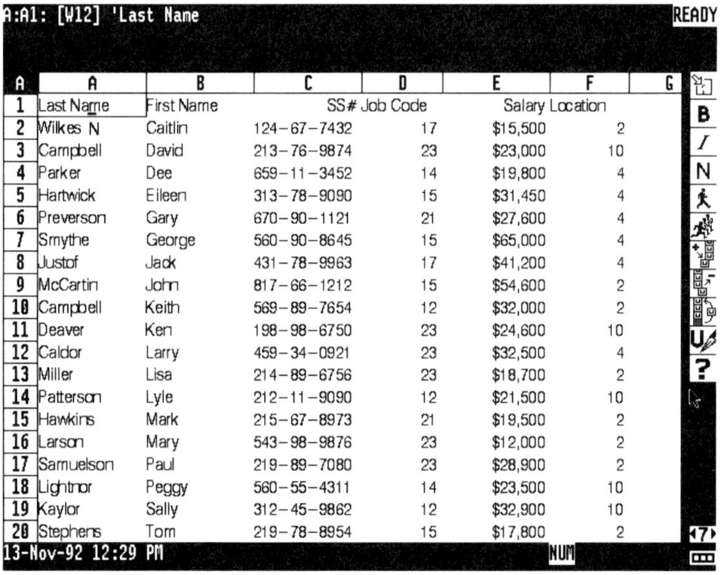

A:A1: [W12] 'Last Name READY

A	A	B	C	D	E	F
1	Last Name	First Name	SS#	Job Code	Salary	Location
2	Wilkes N	Caitlin	124-67-7432	17	$15,500	2
3	Campbell	David	213-76-9874	23	$23,000	10
4	Parker	Dee	659-11-3452	14	$19,800	4
5	Hartwick	Eileen	313-78-9090	15	$31,450	4
6	Preverson	Gary	670-90-1121	21	$27,600	4
7	Smythe	George	560-90-8645	15	$65,000	4
8	Justof	Jack	431-78-9963	17	$41,200	4
9	McCartin	John	817-66-1212	15	$54,600	2
10	Campbell	Keith	569-89-7654	12	$32,000	2
11	Deaver	Ken	198-98-6750	23	$24,600	10
12	Caldor	Larry	459-34-0921	23	$32,500	4
13	Miller	Lisa	214-89-6756	23	$18,700	2
14	Patterson	Lyle	212-11-9090	12	$21,500	10
15	Hawkins	Mark	215-67-8973	21	$19,500	2
16	Larson	Mary	543-98-9876	23	$12,000	2
17	Samuelson	Paul	219-89-7080	23	$28,900	2
18	Lightnor	Peggy	560-55-4311	14	$23,500	10
19	Kaylor	Sally	312-45-9862	12	$32,900	10
20	Stephens	Tom	219-78-8954	15	$17,800	2

13-Nov-92 12:29 PM NUM

Figure 13-11. *Employee database with 19 records*

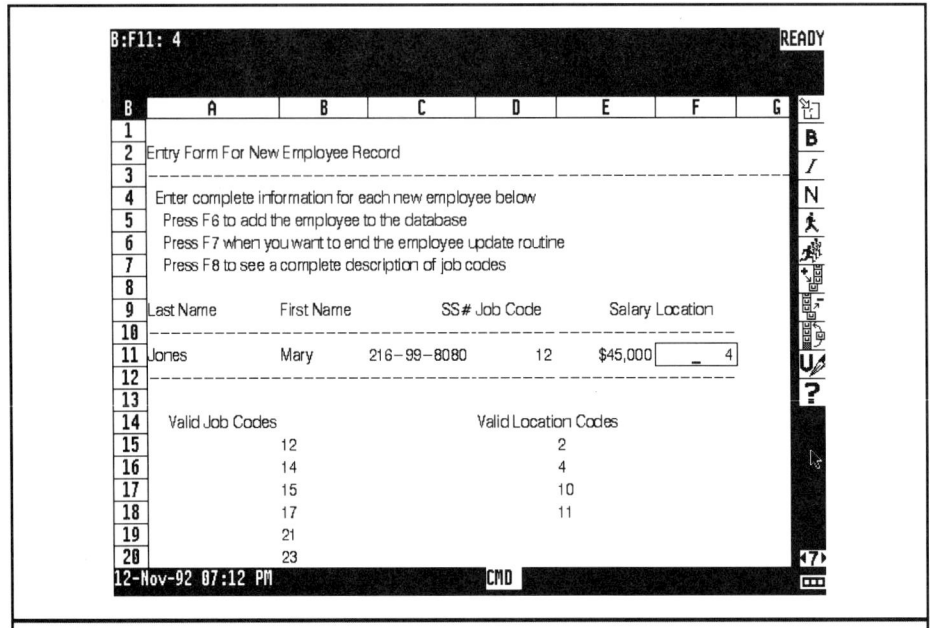

Figure 13-12. Entry form for new employee record

{APPENDRIGHT}

The {APPENDRIGHT} command is used to add fields of data to an existing database. It will extend the range of the database to include the new columns of information.

FORMAT   The format of the {APPENDRIGHT} command is

{APPENDRIGHT *target-location,source-location*}

where *target-location* is a range name that references an existing database. *Source-location* is a range name referring to one or more columns that you want to append to the right edge of the existing database. The number of columns in the source location should not exceed the number of columns to the right of the target location. 1-2-3 will not write over existing entries when executing this command.

USE   If you have two databases that are in the same table sequence and contain information about identical objects, you can use {APPENDRIGHT} to add several columns of one database to another, and maintain a single database. You might want to add information from the employee benefits database to the salary database, for example.

EXAMPLE Figure 13-11 shows records from an employee database. Other information on the exact same employees is recorded in the personnel database on a sheet in another file (Figure 13-13). Notice that the employees are listed in the same order in both files. You can use {APPENDRIGHT} to join the last two columns of information in the personnel database to the employee database.

Figure 13-14 shows the result of joining the two database tables with {APPENDRIGHT} (columns D through F are hidden). If the employee database is named **employdb** and the personnel database is named **personnel**, you can use the append instruction {APPENDRIGHT employdb,personnel} to handle the task. After the {APPENDRIGHT} command is performed, the **employdb** database and range name will include A1..I20.

As a precaution, you might want to initially append all three personnel database columns, as shown in Figure 13-14. Then add a formula temporarily to verify that the two columns of social security number entries are identical. You might use a formula like @IF(C2=G2,"","SS#'s DO NOT MATCH ERROR"). This formula could be copied down another column of the combined worksheet to verify a match on all records. Assuming no errors displayed, column G could be deleted and the database size would automatically readjust. The column range containing the @IF formula could also be deleted.

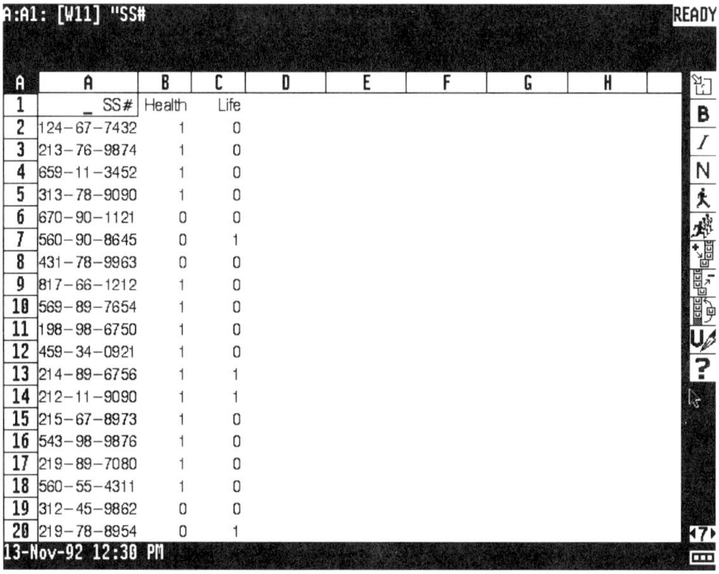
A:A1: [W11] "SS# READY

A	A	B	C	D	E	F	G	H
1	SS#	Health	Life					
2	124-67-7432	1	0					
3	213-76-9874	1	0					
4	659-11-3452	1	0					
5	313-78-9090	1	0					
6	670-90-1121	0	0					
7	560-90-8645	0	1					
8	431-78-9963	0	0					
9	817-66-1212	1	0					
10	569-89-7654	1	0					
11	198-98-6750	1	0					
12	459-34-0921	1	0					
13	214-89-6756	1	1					
14	212-11-9090	1	1					
15	215-67-8973	1	0					
16	543-98-9876	1	0					
17	219-89-7080	1	0					
18	560-55-4311	1	0					
19	312-45-9862	0	0					
20	219-78-8954	0	1					

13-Nov-92 12:30 PM

Figure 13-13. *Personnel information*

```
A:G1: [W12] "SS#                                                    READY

   A    A            B            C              G          H      I       J
   1  Last Name    First Name         SS#            SS#    Health  Life
   2  Wilkes       Caitlin      124-67-7432   124-67-7432     1      0
   3  Campbell     David        213-76-9874   213-76-9874     1      0
   4  Parker       Dee          659-11-3452   659-11-3452     1      0
   5  Hartwick     Eileen       313-78-9090   313-78-9090     1      0
   6  Preverson    Gary         670-90-1121   670-90-1121     0      0
   7  Smythe       George       560-90-8645   560-90-8645     0      1
   8  Justof       Jack         431-78-9963   431-78-9963     0      0
   9  McCartin     John         817-66-1212   817-66-1212     1      0
  10  Campbell     Keith        569-89-7654   569-89-7654     1      0
  11  Deaver       Ken          198-98-6750   198-98-6750     1      0
  12  Caldor       Larry        459-34-0921   459-34-0921     1      0
  13  Miller       Lisa         214-89-6756   214-89-6756     1      1
  14  Patterson    Lyle         212-11-9090   212-11-9090     1      1
  15  Hawkins      Mark         215-67-8973   215-67-8973     1      0
  16  Larson       Mary         543-98-9876   543-98-9876     1      0
  17  Samuelson    Paul         219-89-7080   219-89-7080     1      0
  18  Lightnor     Peggy        560-55-4311   560-55-4311     1      0
  19  Kaylor       Sally        312-45-9862   312-45-9862     0      0
  20  Stephens     Tom          219-78-8954   219-78-8954     0      1
13-Nov-92 12:31 PM
```

Figure 13-14.   *Result of joining two tables with {APPENDRIGHT}*

{BLANK}

The {BLANK} command is functionally equivalent to /Range Erase; it erases a range of cells on the worksheet.

FORMAT   The format of the {BLANK} command is

{BLANK *location*}

where *location* is a range of cell addresses or a range name associated with one or more worksheet cells.

USE   This command can be used to clear data from previous uses of the worksheet. You might want to clear a data entry area with this command. The difference between the {BLANK} command and /Range Erase is that the {BLANK} command does not have to be started from READY mode. Therefore, you can use it while you are doing something else.

EXAMPLE   Figure 13-15 presents a data entry screen to be used with a macro. The screen shown contains the data from the previous entry, which may confuse

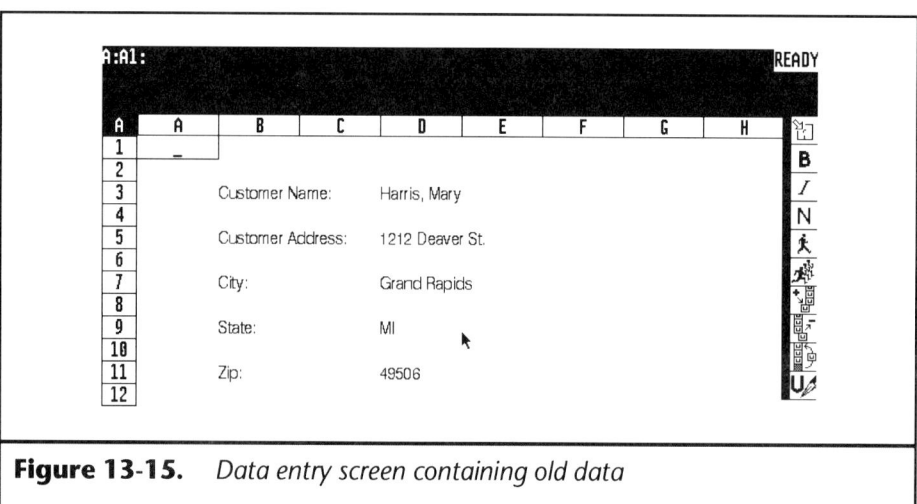

Figure 13-15. *Data entry screen containing old data*

an operator ready to enter a new record. To clear the screen, add these lines of code to an existing macro, placing them so they will be executed following the processing of the current record.

```
        P                  Q
1       \b                 {BLANK d3..d11}
2                          {CALC}
```

The lines are shown with a macro name, so they could be executed from the keyboard without incorporating them into another macro if desired. The first line requests that the range D3..D11 be erased. The second line calculates the worksheet to ensure that these cells are blanked immediately.

{CONTENTS}

The {CONTENTS} command stores a numeric value in a cell as a label with a specified format.

FORMAT The format for {CONTENTS} is

{CONTENTS *destination,source,[width],[format]*}

The argument *destination* is the location where you wish the label to be stored. You may specify it as a cell address or a range name.

The argument *source* is the location of the value entry you want stored in *destination* as a string (label). You may specify this location as a cell address or a range name.

The argument *width* is an optional argument unless you choose to specify *format*, in which case *width* is required. *Width* determines the width of the string entry. If you do not specify width, it is obtained from the *source* location.

The argument *format* is an optional argument that allows you to determine the exact manner in which the *source* value is formatted in the destination string. Table 13-1 lists the values you can select for this argument.

EXAMPLE   If you ever want to display the formula behind a cell at a given location, the {CONTENTS} command allows you to do this. Let's say that the

Code	Format
0 to 15	Fixed format with 0 to 15 decimal places
16 to 32	Scientific format with 0 to 15 decimal places
33 to 47	Currency ($) format with 0 to 15 decimal places
48 to 63	Percent (%) format with 0 to 15 decimal places
64 to 79	Comma (,) format with 0 to 15 decimal places
112	+/– format
113	General format
114	Date format 1 (DD-MMM-YY)
115	Date format 2 (DD-MMM)
116	Date format 3 (MMM-YY)
117	Text display
118	Hidden
119	Date format 6 (HH:MM:SS AM/PM)
120	Date format 7 (HH:MM AM/PM)
121	Date format 4 - Long International date display
122	Date format 5 - Short International date display
123	Date format 8 - Long International time display
124	Date format 9 - Short International time display
127	Default numeric display format for the worksheet

Table 13-1.   *Codes and Associated Formats for the {CONTENTS} Command*

source location is D1, and it contains the formula +Z1*Z3, although 30 displays in the cell. The formula behind D1 can be displayed in D5 with the following macro statement:

{CONTENTS D5,D1,9,117}~

In this statement, D5 represents the *destination* location and D1 represents the *source*. A *width* of 9 is established, and the *format* represented by 117 is selected. The number 117 specifies Text display, so the formula behind D1 will display in D5. Remember that it is no longer a formula but a label once it is stored in the *destination* location.

{LET}

The {LET} command permits the assignment of a number or a string to a location on the worksheet.

FORMAT   The formats for the {LET} command are

{LET *location,number*}

or

{LET *location,string*}

The argument *location* is the address or range name of the cell in which you wish to store the value or label. If you specify *location* as a range, only the upper left cell in the range will be used.

The argument *number* is a numeric value or a formula that evaluates to a numeric value.

The argument *string* is a string or a string formula.

USE   This command is useful whenever you wish to control the value in a worksheet cell. It can be used with a loop to increment a counter. Since it can be used with either strings or values, it is extremely flexible. Here are several examples.

- {LET a1,10} stores 10 in cell A1.
- {LET a1,a1+1} increments cell A1 by 1.
- {LET a1,"ABC "&"COMPANY"} places ABC COMPANY in cell A1.

You also have the option of using an indicator for numeric values that tells 1-2-3 whether you wish them treated as numbers (values) or as strings. The examples that follow show the proper format:

- {LET a1,5+1:value} places a 6 in cell A1.
- {LET a1,5+1:string} places '5+1 in cell A1.

EXAMPLE The {LET} command can be used to initialize and increment a counter when you want to set up your own loops. The following shell shows the format of a loop using {LET} in this way.

```
\s          {LET counter,1}
top_loop    {IF counter>stop}{BRANCH end_loop}
            ...
            ...
            ...
            {LET counter,counter+1}
            {BRANCH top_loop}
end_loop    {QUIT}
```

If you choose to build your own loop rather than use the {FOR} instruction, you will always need to initialize your counter, increment it, and test it to see that it is within an acceptable range. In this example, **stop** is a range name used to contain the ending value for this range.

{PUT}

The {PUT} command allows you to put a value in a location within a range. Unlike {LET}, which accepts only a cell address, {PUT} lets you select a row and column offset within a range.

FORMAT The formats for the {PUT} command are

{PUT *location,column,row,number*}

or

{PUT *location,column,row,string*}

The argument *location* is a range of cells identified by cell addresses or a range name.

The argument *column* is the column number within the *location* range. The first column in the range is column 0.

The argument *row* is the row number within the *location* range. The first row in the range is row 0.

The argument *number* is the value you wish to have stored at the specified *location*.

The argument *string* is the string you wish to have stored in the specified *location*.

USE This command is similar to {LET} but has additional flexibility, since it lets you store values within a range. A few examples and their results follow:

- {PUT a1..b5,0,3,4} places a 4 in cell A4.
- {PUT a1..b5,1,0,3} places a 3 in cell B1.
- {PUT a1..b5,0,15,0} causes an error, since a row number of 15 is not within the range specified.

EXAMPLE This command could be used to supply the values for a table. You might have entries like this in your macro:

- {PUT table,0,0,100}~
- {PUT table,0,1,d5/2}~

The tilde at the end of each instruction causes the table entry to be updated immediately.

NOTE: The row and column offsets must be within the range you establish with the location argument. When they are not, an error occurs. This error cannot be processed with {ONERROR}.

{RECALC}

The {RECALC} command recalculates the formulas within the range you specify, proceeding row by row within this range.

FORMAT The format for the {RECALC} command is

{RECALC *location*[,*condition*][,*iteration*]}

The argument *location* is the range of the worksheet that you wish to have recalculated.

The optional argument *condition* specifies a condition that must be true before the *location* range selected is no longer recalculated. As long as the condition is false, 1-2-3 will continue to recalculate the worksheet. This argument is used in conjunction with *iteration,* which specifies a maximum number of iterations.

The optional argument *iteration* specifies the number of times that formulas within the location range will be recalculated as long as *condition* is false. When *condition* is true, recalculation stops, even though you may not have used all the iterations. With each iteration the count is reduced by 1. When it is zero, no further recalculations will occur.

USE   When you use {CALC}, the entire worksheet is recalculated. This can be unnecessarily time-consuming if you need just a section of it recalculated. The {RECALC} and {RECALCCOL} commands are designed for this purpose. Use {RECALC} when the area you are recalculating is below and to the left of the cells referenced by the formulas in this area. Use {RECALCCOL} when the area you are recalculating is above and to the right of the cells referenced by the formulas in this area. If the formula is *both* above and to the left of cells with new values, you must use {CALC} and recalculate the entire worksheet.

EXAMPLE   If you have a macro that changes the value of cell AB10 and you are interested in the value of cell Z12, which is affected by AB10, you can use a {RECALC} instruction in your macro, as follows:

   {RECALC z1..ab12}

1-2-3 will recalculate row by row to obtain the correct result of AB10 and thus for Z12. You can also add a condition and iteration count to this instruction:

   {RECALC z1..ab12,z3>20,10}

The recalculation of the specified range will now continue until either Z3 is greater than 20, or 10 iterations are performed.

{RECALCCOL}

The {RECALCCOL} command recalculates the formulas within the range you specify, proceeding column by column within this range.

FORMAT   The format for the {RECALCCOL} command is

   {RECALCCOL *location[,condition][,iteration]*}

The argument *location* is the range of the worksheet that you wish to have recalculated.

The optional argument *condition* specifies a condition that must be true before the *location* range selected is no longer recalculated. As long as the condition is false, 1-2-3 will continue to recalculate the worksheet. This argument is used in conjunction with *iteration,* which specifies a maximum number of iterations.

The optional argument *iteration* specifies the number of times that formulas within the location range will be recalculated as long as *condition* is false. When *condition* is true, recalculation stops, even though you may not have used all the iterations. With each iteration the count is reduced by 1. When it is zero, no further recalculations will occur.

USE When you use {CALC}, the entire worksheet is recalculated. This can be unnecessarily time consuming if you need just a section of it recalculated. The {RECALC} and {RECALCCOL} commands are designed for this purpose. Use {RECALC} when the area you are recalculating is below and to the left of the cells referenced by the formulas in this area. Use {RECALCCOL} when the area you are recalculating is above and to the right of the cells referenced by the formulas in this area. If the formula is *both* above and to the left of cells with new values, you must use {CALC} and recalculate the entire worksheet.

EXAMPLE {RECALCCOL} follows the same syntax rules as {RECALC}. Select one or the other depending on whether a row or a column order of recalculation fits best with your application. Refer to the example under {RECALC} for additional information.

Macro Commands that Handle Files

The file macro commands provide sequential file handling capabilities equivalent to the ones you find in the BASIC programming language. You can use these commands in macros to read and write records to text files. If you have never worked with files, you will want to review a section from a data processing text that overviews records, file size concepts, file input and output procedures, and other basic terminology connected with the use of files before you try to use these macros.

The commands in this section are interdependent. For example, it is not possible to use {READLN}, {READ}, {WRITE}, or {WRITELN} unless you have first opened the file with {OPEN}. Short examples dealing with the syntax are provided with each command. Examples showing commands used in context with other required commands are found under {WRITE}, {WRITELN}, {READ}, {READLN}, and {FILESIZE}.

{CLOSE}

The {CLOSE} command closes the file you opened with the {OPEN} command. You must close one file before opening a second one. If you use this command when there are no open files, 1-2-3 will ignore it.

FORMAT   The format for the {CLOSE} command is

{CLOSE}

This command has no arguments.

USE   You must use this command when you have finished working with a text file. The {READ} command has an example of using {CLOSE}.

{FILESIZE}

This command allows you to determine the number of bytes or characters in your file.

FORMAT   The format for the {FILESIZE} command is

{FILESIZE *location*}

where *location* is the cell address or range name of the cell where you want 1-2-3 to store the number representing the length of your file.

USE   The file must be open before you use this command. Remember, too, that the character for the end-of-file condition will be included in the count for {FILESIZE}. If you know the length of the records on the file, you can use {FILESIZE} to determine how many records the file contains.

EXAMPLE   The following macro uses the {FILESIZE} command:

```
        A              B
   22   \f          {OPEN "B:TEST.PRN",R}
   23               {FILESIZE g21}
   24               {CALC}
   25               {CLOSE}
```

The first step in the macro is to open the file, since a file must be opened before {FILESIZE} can be used. The entry in line 23 determines the number of bytes in the file and places this number in cell G21. A {CALC} is included to update the worksheet cell immediately, after which the file is closed.

{GETPOS}

The {GETPOS} command determines the current position in a file.

FORMAT   The format for the {GETPOS} command is

{GETPOS *location*}

where *location* is the address or range name of the cell where you wish the current position number stored. Remember that the first character in a file is considered position 0.

EXAMPLE   You can use this command to monitor your progress through a file, comparing the current position to the file size so that you do not attempt to read beyond the end of the file. After reading a record, you might include a {GETPOS} instruction, like this:

{READLN a10}
{GETPOS current}

You could then compare **current** and the result from the {FILESIZE} command and determine the number of records yet to read.

{OPEN}

The {OPEN} command allows you to open a file and specify whether you plan to read the file, write to it, or do both.

FORMAT   The format for the {OPEN} command is

{OPEN *file,access*}

The argument *file* is a string or range name referring to a single cell that contains a string or string formula that references the name of the file you want to open. The cell string has an upper limit of 64 characters and can include the entire pathname and subdirectory, as well as the filename extension.

The argument *access* is a single character that controls the type of access you have to the file. The possible code characters are as follows:

R means read-only. You cannot write to the file if your access mode is R.

W means write-only. This argument opens a new file or re-creates an existing file. You can't read from a file if the access mode is W.

M allows modifications to the file, permitting both read and write access. It can be used only on existing files.

A means append. This argument opens the existing file and adds data written to it at the end of the file. You can both read and write data.

USE If you wish to use an error routine in the event {OPEN} fails, you can place it on the same line as {OPEN} as a subroutine call—for example, {OPEN "SALES",R}{fix_err}.

{READ}

The {READ} command reads the number of characters specified into the location you define, starting at the file pointer's present location.

FORMAT The format for the {READ} command is

{READ *byte-count,location*}

The argument *byte-count* is the number of characters you wish to have read from the file, beginning at the current position in the file. If the number of bytes is larger than the number of remaining characters in the file, {READ} will take the amount of data remaining. *Byte-count* must be a numeric value or an expression that evaluates to one. The number should be between 0 and 512.

The argument *location* is the address or range name for the cell where you would like the string of characters to be stored. The data will be stored in this location as a left justified label.

EXAMPLE The following macro shows the use of the {READ} instruction:

```
        A              B
30      \r             {OPEN "B:TEST.PRN",R}
31                     {SETPOS 6}
32                     {READ 9,g22}
33                     {CALC}
34                     {CLOSE}
```

Chapter 13: Command Language Macros   803

The file is opened for reading in the first instruction. The file pointer is then set at 6, which would be the seventh character in the file. Nine bytes (characters) are read from the file and stored in cell G22. The worksheet is recalculated immediately to show this entry, after which the file is closed.

{READLN}

The {READLN} command copies a line of characters (a record) from a file and places it at the location specified.

FORMAT   The format for the {READLN} command is

   {READLN *location*}

where *location* is the cell address or range name that specifies the cell where you wish the line of data stored.

USE   The {READ} command works based on the number of bytes. {READLN}, by contrast, looks for a carriage return/line feed to know how many characters to read. Like {READ}, it uses the current file pointer position as the starting point and can be used with {SETPOS}.

EXAMPLE   The following macro will read one line from a text file.

```
        A                B
1      \z          {OPEN "B:TEST.PRN",R}
2                  {READLN place}
3                  ~
4                  {RIGHT}
5                  {CLOSE}
```

The file is first opened. {READLN} then reads the first line from the file and places these characters in **place**. A tilde rather than {CALC} is used to update the worksheet, since the tilde is just as effective and more efficient. The cell pointer is moved to the right, and the file is closed.

{SETPOS}

The {SETPOS} command positions the file pointer at the location you specify.

FORMAT   The format for the {SETPOS} command is

{SETPOS *number*}

where *number* is a numeric value or an expression that results in a numeric value that tells 1-2-3 which character you want the pointer set on. Remember that the first character in the file is considered to be position 0.

USE   1-2-3 does not prevent you from setting the pointer at a location beyond the end of the file. You should always use {FILESIZE} to ensure that this does not occur.

EXAMPLE   Given the following information stored in a file:

ABC Company, LaCrosse, MI

setting the pointer to 4 would place it on the C in "Company."

{WRITE}

The {WRITE} command places a set of characters in a file that you have opened.

FORMAT   The format for the {WRITE} command is

{WRITE *string*}

where *string* is a character string, an expression evaluating to a character string, or a range name assigned to a single cell that contains a string.

USE   When you use this command, 1-2-3 writes a string to the file at the current location of the file pointer. It then moves the pointer to the end of this entry to place it in position for writing the next set of characters.

EXAMPLE   If you have a column of worksheet cells that contains the days of the week, use this command to write this list of days of the week to a file. If you use {WRITE}, they will all be in one line (record) of the file.
   Assuming that you position your cell pointer at the top of the list, the macro that follows will write all seven names for you.

Chapter 13: Command Language Macros

```
        A           B
1      \z          {OPEN "B:TOGETH.PRN",W}
2                  {LET ctr,1}
3      top         {IF ctr>7}{BRANCH end}
4                  {WRITE @CELLPOINTER("contents")}
5                  {DOWN}
6                  {LET ctr,ctr+1}
7                  {BRANCH top}
8      end         {CLOSE}
```

The file is opened for write access in the first instruction. A counter is initialized in line 2. The first statement in the iterative loop of the macro checks the counter to see whether it is greater than 7. If it is, the macro ends by closing the file.

If the counter is not greater than 7, the loop continues. The contents of the current cell are written to the file using the built-in function @CELLPOINTER. The pointer is moved down, and **ctr** is incremented. The execution flow then branches to the top of the loop. The macro continues in this cycle until it has written all seven entries to the file.

Since entries are written sequentially on the same line, the result of using this macro would be

MondayTuesdayWednesdayThursdayFridaySaturdaySunday

assuming that the first cell contained Monday and the days proceeded in order throughout the week as you moved down the column.

SETUP The macro requires that the range names **top**, **end**, and **ctr** be assigned to appropriate cells. Also, the days of the week must already be in the worksheet, and your cell pointer must be positioned on the first one before you execute the macro.

{WRITELN}

The {WRITELN} command places characters in an open file. In contrast to {WRITE}, it adds a carriage return/line feed to the end of each character string written, so a new line or record is created in the file each time the command is used.

FORMAT The format for the {WRITELN} command is

{WRITELN *string*}

where *string* is a character string, an expression evaluating to a character string, or a range name assigned to a single cell that contains a string.

USE   When you use this command, 1-2-3 writes a string to the file at the current location of the file pointer. It then moves the pointer to the beginning of the next line to place it in position for writing the next set of characters.

Using {WRITELN ""} generates a carriage return/line feed at the current position in the file. You might want to build a record with a series of {WRITE} commands, and then use {WRITELN} to add a line feed before beginning the next record.

EXAMPLE   Let's look at two examples. The first writes a series of string literals to a file named DAYS. It reads as follows.

```
          A                B
1        \z        {OPEN "B:DAYS",W}
2                  {WRITELN "Monday"}
3                  {WRITELN "Tuesday"}
4                  {WRITELN "Wednesday"}
5                  {WRITELN "Thursday"}
6                  {WRITELN "Friday"}
7                  {WRITELN "Saturday"}
8                  {WRITELN "Sunday"}
9                  {CLOSE}
```

The file is first opened. Seven individual {WRITELN} statements are then used to write character strings to the file, after which the file is closed.

If you import the text file created with this macro into the worksheet with your cell pointer in Z1, Z1..Z7 will contain the following:

Monday
Tuesday
Wednesday
Thursday
Friday
Saturday
Sunday

Since each day was written to a separate line when the file was imported, each record is written to a different cell.

A second macro that achieves the same end results is this:

```
        A              B
1      \z       {OPEN "B:TOGETH.PRN",W}
2               {LET ctr,1}
3      top      {IF ctr>7}{BRANCH end}
4               {WRITELN ˅CELLPOINTER("contents)"}
5               {DOWN}
6               {LET ctr,ctr+1}
7               {BRANCH top}
8      end      {CLOSE}
```

This macro uses a loop construction and writes the days of the week, which are stored in worksheet cells, to the file. It follows the same format as the example discussed under {WRITE}, except that each day of the week appears in a separate line (record) of the file.

CHAPTER 14

Using 1-2-3's Built-In Add-Ins and Icons

You can give 1-2-3 additional features using add-ins. Add-ins are products provided by Lotus or other manufacturers which can provide additional functions to the 1-2-3 worksheet, macro commands, and special features such as spreadsheet publishing. Since 1-2-3 is loaded when you use them, these products add onto the features 1-2-3 provides. 1-2-3's functionality can be expanded by customizing the icons in the palette.

Release 3.4 includes five add-ins: Viewer, Backsolver, Auditor, Solver, and Wysiwyg. The Viewer add-in lets you look at files to select which worksheet to retrieve, which file to view, or lets you just browse through available files. The

Backsolver add-in works backwards through a series of formulas to calculate the initial value that returns a final result in another cell. The Auditor add-in provides worksheet auditing features such as following the path of cell values used in other formulas and finding other cells that are used by a formula. The Solver add-in finds the cell values that provide desired results in other formulas within limits that you have set. The Wysiwyg add-in provides advanced spreadsheet publishing features. You may have already used some of the Wysiwyg features mentioned earlier in this book, and you can learn all about Wysiwyg in Chapter 15, "Using Wysiwyg."

Most add-ins are made by other manufacturers and are compatible, which means that as you upgrade to Release 3.4, you should be able to use most of the add-ins you have acquired for prior releases. With some add-ins you may need to contact the add-in manufacturer and acquire an updated version of the program if it does not run with Release 3.4.

This chapter covers how you use 1-2-3's add-ins and the built-in add-ins of Release 3.4. Add-ins use the Add-In Manager, which is accessed by pressing ALT-F10 (ADDIN). Before you can use an add-in, you must install it according to its accompanying directions. The add-ins that accompany Release 3.4 are installed as part of 1-2-3's installation process, described in Appendix A. Finally, you will learn about working with the icons in the SmartIcons palettes.

Activating the Add-In Menu

The Add-In menu allows you to work with one or more separate add-in programs. You can activate the add-in menu by pressing ALT-F10 (ADDIN) to display the menu shown here:

These commands are used to load, unload, and invoke add-in programs. Loading an add-in is the first step, since it places the add-in in memory and makes it available to 1-2-3. With Release 3.4, Wysiwyg is automatically loaded and is immediately available in 1-2-3. You do not have to load this add-in. After selecting Load, select the add-in either from a list of current directory files with an .PLC extension, or from another directory. For example, to load Auditor, select AUDITOR.PLC. You are prompted as to whether you want to assign the add-in to a function key.

For add-ins with menus, assigning a key allows you to invoke the Add-In's menu quickly. You can select No-Key, 1, 2, or 3. The last three options represent the key combinations ALT-F7, ALT-F8, and ALT-F9, respectively. Usually, add-ins without menus—such as the ones that provide additional functions and macro commands—use the No-Key selection. For Wysiwyg, since the colon will invoke the Wysiwyg menu, you will want to select No-Key. Once you select how to invoke the add-in, 1-2-3 returns to the Add-In menu. The screen will change with some add-ins but not with others. To return to READY mode, select Quit.

Other Add-In Menu Commands

While Load and Quit may be the only add-in commands you need to use for add-ins with 1-2-3, you will want to learn how you can use the other commands on the Add-In menu. You can remove add-ins from memory, and activate, list, and select add-ins that 1-2-3 will load for you.

Some add-ins, like Wysiwyg, have their own menu. While Wysiwyg's menu is available by typing a colon, the menus for other add-in programs do not usually have a special key preassigned to invoke them. In this case, to invoke an add-in program, select Invoke from the Add-In menu and then the name of the add-in. If you selected 1, 2, or 3 instead of No-Key when you loaded the add-in, you can also invoke the add-in's menu by pressing ALT-F7, ALT-F8, or ALT-F9.

Each add-in uses part of your computer's memory. When you are using large worksheets, you may want to remove one or more add-ins from memory to leave more room for your worksheet files. To remove one add-in from memory, select Remove from the Add-In menu and then the add-in you want to remove from the list 1-2-3 presents. To remove all add-ins from memory, select Clear from the Add-In menu. You do not want to remove an add-in from memory if you are using it. For example, removing Wysiwyg from memory removes all of the Wysiwyg formats from the worksheet display. Also, any changes you make to the worksheet, such as inserting a column or row, will not be reflected in the Wysiwyg format file that stores the formatting information for the worksheet.

Another use of the Add-In menu is to list the add-ins that are loaded. To list add-ins, select Table and then @Functions, Macros, or Applications to select the type of add-ins you want to list. Applications are programs like Wysiwyg, while @Functions and Macros are add-ins that provide additional @functions and macro commands. After you select one of the three choices, you must select the first cell where 1-2-3 will list the add-ins. The table will have one column and as many rows as the number of loaded application, @function, or macro add-ins, plus one.

The final option of the Add-In menu is Settings. This option specifies the add-ins that 1-2-3 loads automatically. You can have 1-2-3 load add-ins when you load 1-2-3 by selecting System, or when you load the current worksheet file by selecting File. For example, you may want to use the Viewer add-in for most of your worksheets; therefore, you would load Viewer along with 1-2-3 by selecting

System. On the other hand, if you wanted to use the Solver add-in only with the current file, you would load it by selecting File from the menu.

To set the add-ins that 1-2-3 will load along with 1-2-3 itself or the current file, select Set, the add-in to load, and the key if any that it is assigned to. Since only one add-in can be assigned to each key, this means that up to three add-ins can have keys assigned and any other add-ins must have the No-Key selection. You can also select whether the add-in is automatically invoked after it is loaded. After adding a few add-ins, these selections might look like this:

```
A:A1:                                                                    MENU
Set Cancel Directory Update Quit
Specify an add-in file to read into memory with 1-2-3

     Program name        Auto-invoke              Key
1:   WYSIWYG             No
2:   AUDITOR             No                       1
3:   VIEWER              Yes                      2
```

You can remove an add-in that is set to automatically load by selecting Cancel and then the add-in's name. If the add-ins are in a different directory from the default directory, select Directory and supply the directory where the .PLC files are found. Directory is only available after selecting System, not File. To make the changes permanent, select Update after selecting System. Without selecting System and Update, the system and file add-ins you select are forgotten as soon as you leave 1-2-3. When you are finished, select Quit to return to the Add-In menu.

TIP: If you use an add-in only with a few specific worksheet files, use the ALT-F10 Settings File command to have the add-in loaded with the worksheet files that use them. Doing so means that you will have the features provided by the add-in, and that the memory the add-in needs will be available for worksheet data when the add-in is not in use.

The Viewer Add-In

Release 3.4 includes a Viewer add-in that makes viewing files, retrieving files, opening files, and creating external file links easier. The Viewer add-in is a scaled-down version of Lotus Magellan, which lets you view files of different formats.

To use the Viewer add-in, load the VIEWER.PLC file. The Viewer menu has four options: Retrieve, Open, Link, and Browse. Selecting Retrieve will retrieve a worksheet file you select to become the current worksheet. Selecting Open will open a worksheet file you select before or after the current worksheet. Selecting Link will create an external link formula for you based on the worksheet and cell you select. Browse allows you to look at different files and return to 1-2-3 where you left off when you are finished.

When you select Retrieve and the current worksheet has unsaved changes, 1-2-3 will prompt you if you want to retrieve the file and replace the current worksheet. When you select Link and the current cell has an entry, 1-2-3 will prompt you if you want to replace the entry in the current cell with the external link formula. You can select Yes to continue or No to return to READY mode. When you add a link formula, you are adding a formula that links to a single cell in another worksheet.

Once you select Retrieve, Open, Link, or Browse, Viewer displays the files of the current directory as shown in Figure 14-1. When you highlight a file on the left side of the screen, the file's contents will appear on the right side. If you

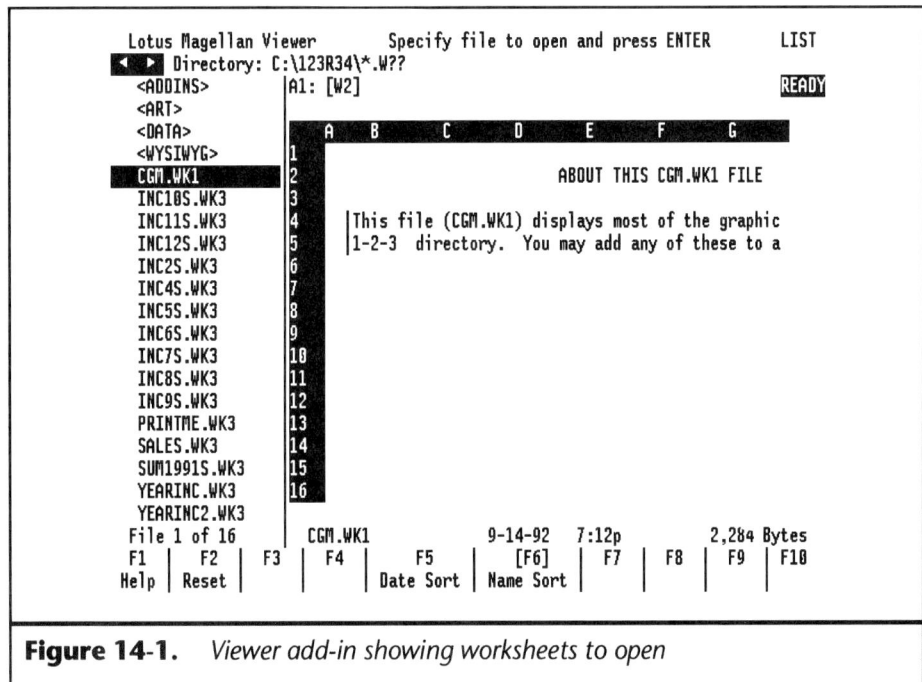

Figure 14-1. *Viewer add-in showing worksheets to open*

select Retrieve, Open, or Link, only worksheet files are listed; however, if you select Browse, all files are listed.

You can press the RIGHT ARROW key to move from the file list into the worksheet. When you are in the worksheet, you can use all of the keys you would use in 1-2-3 to move to different cells. The control panel displays the cell's contents and formatting information. Cells containing formulas display (formula) and the formula results. You cannot change a worksheet in the Viewer. If a file is password protected, you cannot see its contents. To return to the file list, press HOME and LEFT ARROW.

You can move the file list by pressing UP ARROW, DOWN ARROW, PGUP, or PGDN. You can also press HOME or END to move to the first or last file in the list. If you want to change the drive or directory of files that 1-2-3 displays, press LEFT ARROW or RIGHT ARROW. Pressing LEFT ARROW changes the directory of files displayed to the parent directory of the current one. Pressing RIGHT ARROW changes the directory of files displayed to the highlighted directory. You can only press RIGHT ARROW to change the directory when the highlight is on a directory name like <DATA> in Figure 14-1. You can press F2 to return to the default directory 1-2-3 uses. You can also use the F5 and F6 function keys to change the order in which the files are listed. Pressing F6 displays files in alphabetical order, which is the default. Pressing F5 displays files according to the date and time they were created.

If you are opening or retrieving a file with Viewer, press ENTER when the highlight is on the file you want. This is identical to the /File Open or /File Retrieve command, except that in this case you can visually check whether or not it is the file you want. If you are creating a link with Viewer, press ENTER when the highlight is on the file you want to use on the left side of the screen, and the cell pointer is on the cell you want on the right side. The Viewer add-in will create the external link formula for you using the selected worksheet and cell. Once this formula is created, you can add more operators and values to it. You cannot type a formula, however, up to the point you want a link to another file, and then use the Viewer to add the external file link. If you are browsing through files, press ENTER when you want to return to READY mode.

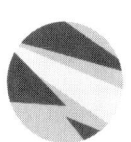

TIP: If you want to create a range of link formulas with Viewer, move the cell pointer to the first cell where you want the link formulas, activate the Viewer add-in, and select Link. Then select the worksheet containing the range of cells that you want to link, and move to the first cell of the range. Next, select the range by typing a period and pressing the arrow keys to cover the cells you want to link, and then press ENTER. For example, if you select the range B10..B13 in the Viewer add-in, the current cell in the current worksheet and the three cells below it will contain formulas that each link with B10, B11, B12, and B13 in the selected worksheet.

The Auditor Add-In

The Auditor add-in lets you follow the path of cells that formulas use and the path of formulas that 1-2-3 recalculates. Specifically, with the Auditor add-in, you can use the following features:

- Find cells that are used by another cell's formulas (precedents)
- Find cells that use another cell in its formulas (dependents)
- Find formulas in a range
- Find formulas in the order 1-2-3 recalculates them
- Find cells that are part of a circular reference
- Select whether the add-in highlights, lists in the worksheet, or moves to the cell that it finds

Like other add-ins, you must attach the Auditor add-in before you can use it. When you add the Auditor add-in, you will select the file AUDITOR.PLC. After you attach the add-in, you can invoke it to display the menu that is shown here:

```
A:A1:                                                               MENU
Precedents  Dependents  Formulas  Recalc-List  Circs  Options  Quit
Identify all cells that provide data for a specified formula cell
─────────────────────── Auditor Settings ───────────────────────
Audit all files in memory                    Audit Mode: HIGHLIGHT
```

Using the Auditor Add-In

To use the Auditor add-in, you must make three decisions. First, you must select how you want the Auditor add-in to indicate the cells that you want it to find. Second, you need to select the range of cells for the Auditor to search through to find the cells you want. You will need to select the audit range and how you want any cells found to be indicated only once, since these settings are retained until you unload the add-in. Finally, you must select the cells you want the add-in to find.

The first decision to make when you use the Auditor is how you want the add-in to display the information it finds for you. You have three choices: Highlight, List, or Trace. You can choose among these by selecting Options from the initial Auditor add-in menu, and then selecting one of the three.

The Highlight option changes the cells that you select to the same color used by unprotected cells. The cells you highlight remain highlighted until you select Reset Highlight from the Auditor's Options menu.

The List option lists the cell addresses and their contents in a worksheet range as labels. If you choose this option, after selecting an Auditor add-in command to indicate a group of cells, you will need to select a range where the add-in can write the information. Like the 1-2-3 /Range Justify command, this can either be a single cell that lets 1-2-3 write over any cells between the selected cell and the bottom of the worksheet, or it can be a complete range that limits the Auditor add-in to using only the selected cells before it displays a message that the range is full.

The third choice, Trace, lets you move from one selected cell to another using the arrow keys—much like when you use the 1-2-3 /Range Input command to move between unprotected cells in a range.

The second decision to make is which cells you want to include in the search. Initially, the Auditor add-in is set to use all open worksheets, but you can limit the worksheet range the Auditor uses by selecting Options Audit-Range and then selecting a specific range to narrow the search. If you later change your mind, you can select Options Reset Options which causes the Auditor to return to using all open worksheets for the audit range, and also highlights the cells you select to find.

The third decision you will make with the Auditor add-in involves which cells you want it to find. The menu option you select from the main Auditor menu (other than Quit and Options) selects the cells the add-in finds. To select the cells you want the Auditor add-in to find, select Precedents, Dependents, Formulas, Recalc-List, or Circs.

Finding Cells Used in a Formula

Finding the cells a formula uses can be made easier by using the Auditor, since it can highlight these cells, move to the cells, or list them in the worksheet. To find these cells, select Precedents. For example, using the worksheet in Figure 14-2, you can find the cells that are used in the formula in D11. (Figure 14-3 shows the same worksheet as Figure 14-2 formatted as text.) After you select Precedents, you must select the cell or range of cells containing the formulas (to limit the Auditor's search for the cells these formulas use).

The next step depends on how the Auditor indicates the cells it finds. If the Auditor highlights the cells it finds, the main Auditor menu displays after the cells are highlighted. If the Auditor moves to the cells it finds, at the first cell it displays a menu containing Forward, Backward, and Quit. Select Forward to move to the next cell the Auditor finds, select Backward to move to the previous cell, or select Quit to return to the Auditor menu.

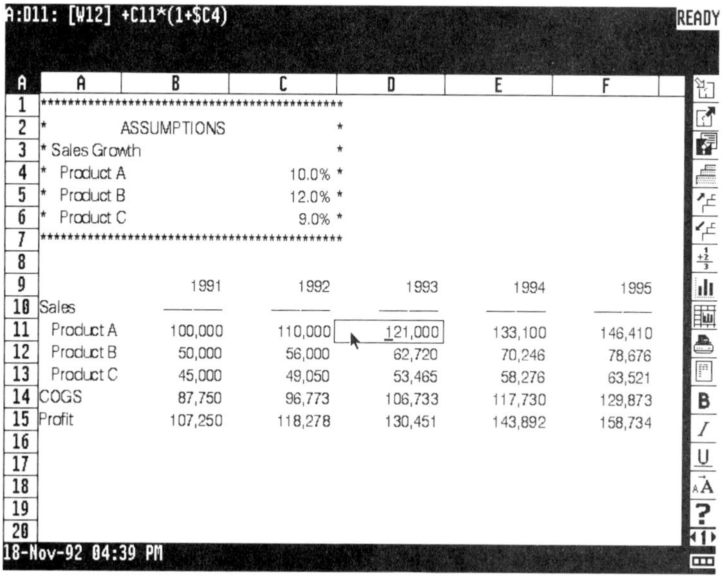

Chapter 14: Using 1-2-3's Built-In Add-Ins and Icons

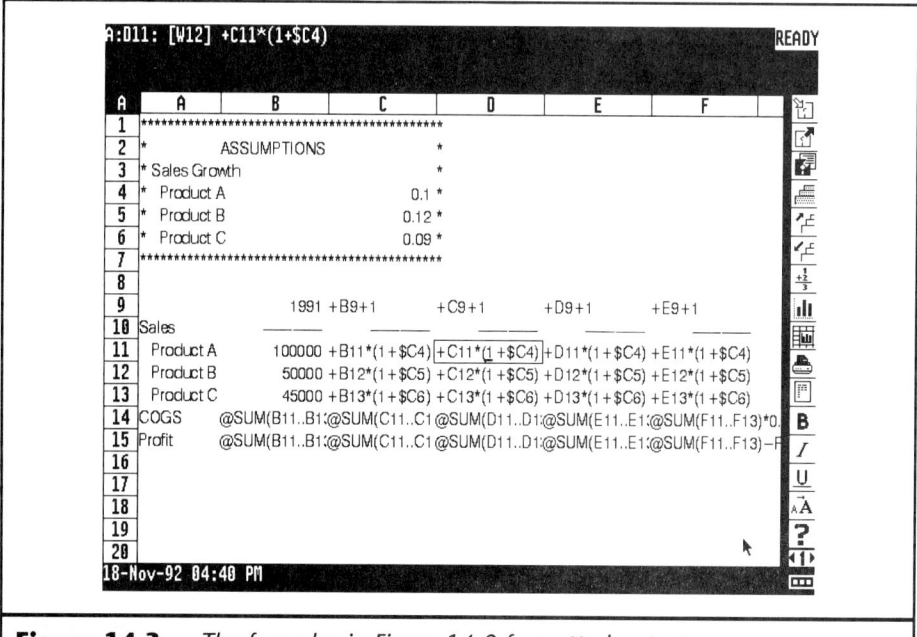

Figure 14-2. *A worksheet to use with the Auditor add-in*

Figure 14-3. *The formulas in Figure 14-2 formatted as text*

If the Auditor lists the cells it finds, the Auditor prompts you for where you want the list. Select a cell or range where the Auditor can list the cells it finds. 1-2-3 erases everything from the cell to the bottom of the worksheet in the same column before it writes the cells to the list. The list is one column wide and as many rows long as necessary. The list contains the cell addresses and the contents of the cells the Auditor finds. The first cell of the list describes the contents below it.

Using Figure 14-2 as an example, if you select D11 as the cell for which you want to find the precedents, the Auditor will find C4, B11, and C11.

TIP: You can limit the range that the Auditor uses to list the cells it finds by selecting a range. The Auditor then only erases the selected range before listing the cells it finds if the range is big enough. If the range is not big enough, the Auditor will display an error message. Also, the range you select should not contain any preexisting entries since the Auditor will not write over the range until you remove the previous entries. The only exception is when the range contains the list from a previous use of the Auditor to list cells.

Finding Formulas Used by a Cell

Finding formulas that use a cell as part of the formula can be difficult. Without the Auditor add-in, you must use the /Range Search command to find these cells. You can, however, find a formula that depends on another cell, so if you are planning to delete it, you will know which cells are affected. For example, you can use the Auditor to find which cells will be affected if you change Product A's growth in C4 of Figure 14-2 to 15 percent. To find these cells, select Dependents. Next, you must select the cell or range of cells containing the values for which the Auditor finds formulas that use these values.

Like finding formula precedents, the Auditor will highlight the cells, move to them (with the Forward and Backward menu options), or list them on the worksheet after you select a cell or range to put the list. If you use C4 as the cell you select after selecting Dependents, the Auditor will find C11..F11 and C14..F15.

Finding Formulas in a Range

Besides listing formulas using the /Print Printer Options Other Cell-Formulas command, you can also find them using the Auditor. You can use the Auditor when you are checking a worksheet to ensure that the cells you expect to contain formulas actually do. To find the cells that contain formulas, select Formulas. The Auditor will find the formulas in the Audit range and highlight them, move to them, or list them on the worksheet as the Auditor does for the Precedents and Dependents options.

For example, you can use the Auditor to list the formulas in the worksheet in Figure 14-2. When you select Formulas and select A21 for where the formulas will be listed, the results shown in Figure 14-4 will display.

Finding Formulas in the Order They Are Recalculated

If you are developing a complex model, you may want to know the order in which 1-2-3 recalculates the formulas. You can list formulas in the order 1-2-3 recalculates them using the Auditor by selecting Recalc-List. Depending on how you want the Auditor to indicate the cells it finds, the worksheet cells are either highlighted, traced, or listed. If you are listing cells, the first cell of the list describes recalculation order as well.

Finding Cells Used in Circular References

Besides using /Worksheet Status to find a circular reference, you can also use the Auditor to find these cells. Unlike /Worksheet Status, using the Auditor shows

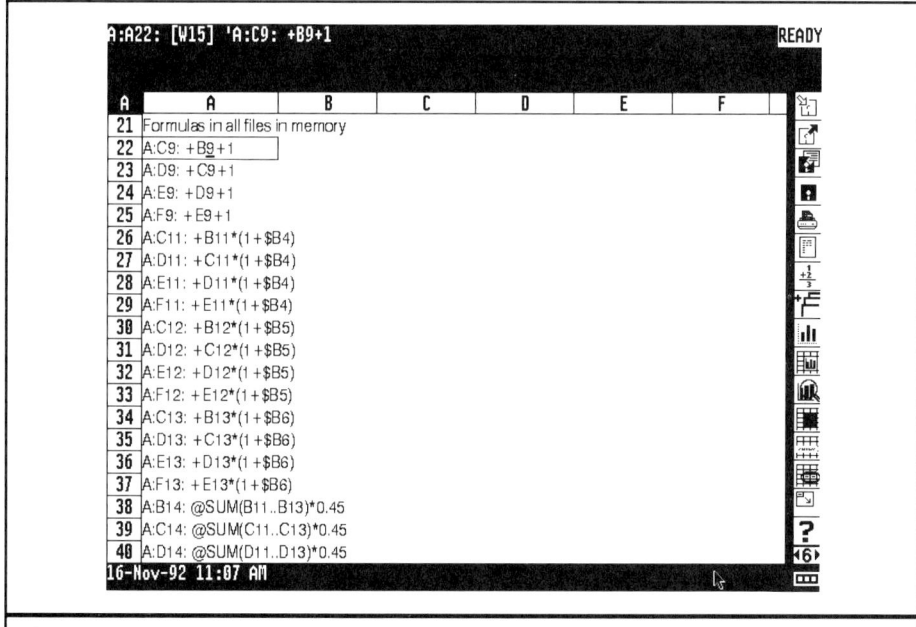

Figure 14-4. *The formulas list generated with the Auditor add-in*

all of the cell entries that are part of the circular reference. You find the cells that are part of a circular reference by selecting Circs. Depending on how you want the Auditor to indicate the cells it finds, the worksheet cells are either highlighted, traced, or listed.

The Backsolver Add-In

You may often want to proceed backwards from a final result to find a value or values that you need to achieve a specific result. The Backsolver add-in uses formulas to work backwards in this way. For example, given an affordable monthly payment, Backsolver can tell you the price of the house you can buy and still meet this payment.

You enter Backsolver problems directly on the worksheet, without special techniques. After you invoke Backsolver, you define the location of the required information, and Backsolver goes to work. Like other add-ins, you must attach the Backsolver add-in before you can use it. After selecting Load from the Add-In menu, you will select the file BSOLVER.PLC.

When you invoke Backsolver, a menu appears in the control panel as shown in Figure 14-5. You need to specify two locations and a setting before asking for a solution. In Figure 14-5, the formula calculates the monthly payment, depending on how large a mortgage you are taking on and how many total payments you are going to make. If you have a good idea of what you can afford to pay each month, you can calculate the maximum price of the house you can afford to buy.

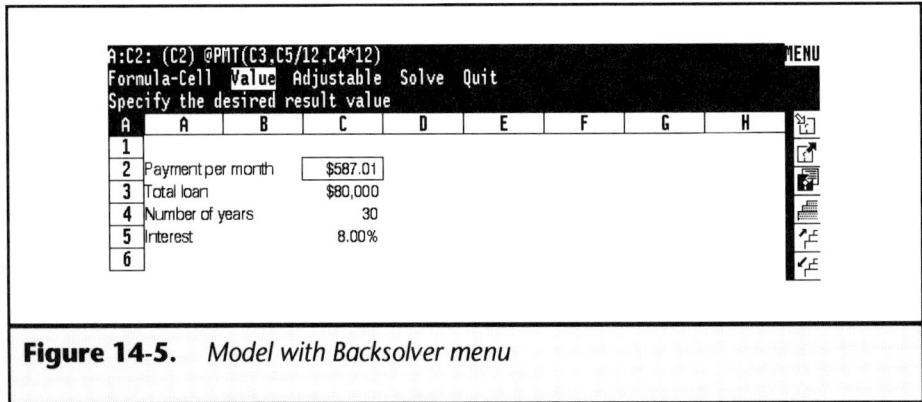

Figure 14-5.   Model with Backsolver menu

In this example, you would first create the model shown in Figure 14-5, setting up the formula and data that Backsolver will work with. Then you would invoke the loaded Backsolver add-in and follow these steps:

1. Select Formula-Cell from the Backsolver menu and specify C2 as the cell containing the formula.

    The Formula-Cell is the address of the formula you want to evaluate to find a specific value. You can specify the formula cell either by entering the name or range address of the cell or by pointing to the cell using the keyboard or a mouse. The formula cell must be adjusted by the cell specified as adjustable.

2. Select Value and type **550** as the amount you are willing to pay each month toward your mortgage.

    For Value, you want to enter the value that you want the Formula-Cell you selected in step 1 to equal.

3. Select Adjustable and then C3, the cell containing the total loan amount, as the value in the formula that can be adjusted.

    For Adjustable, you want to select the cell or cells you want to vary in order to produce the specified value in the Formula-Cell.

4. Select Solve.

    Backsolver will calculate that if you pay $550 a month toward a 30-year mortgage at 8 percent annual interest, you can afford a total mortgage of $74,956. Now you know what price range of houses you should be looking at. When you select Solve, if Backsolver succeeds in finding a value for the adjustable cells that results in the specified value in the formula cell, the value is substituted in the adjustable cells on the worksheet.

The Solver Add-In

The Solver add-in is like the Backsolver add-in in that you tell Solver what you expect to find and the add-in finds the initial values that returns the answer you want. The difference between Solver and Backsolver is how you place limits on the calculations and results. With Backsolver, the add-in uses the formulas between the formula cell and the adjustable cells to limit what the add-in returns

> ## Steps for Using Solver
>
> 1. Enter your model including all formulas, numbers, and labels.
> 2. Define your constraints on the worksheet using logical formulas.
> 3. Leave a place on the worksheet for adjustable cells entries.
> 4. If you plan to select a range for adjustable cells that includes blank cells, unprotect the cells where Solver can make entries and select /Worksheet Global Prot Enable.
> 5. Invoke the Solver add-in.
> 6. Select Define and Adjustable, then the range containing the adjustable cells. You cannot select blank cells as part of a range unless they are unprotected and worksheet protection is enabled.
> 7. Select Constraints and the cells containing the constraints.
> 8. If you wish to look for an optimal solution, select Optimal, then X Maximize or N Minimize, and then specify a cell to optimize.
> 9. Select Quit to return to the initial Solver menu.
> 10. Select Solve and Problem.

as an acceptable answer. With Solver, the add-in can adjust many more cells. Also, you can place limits on the returned values through the formulas on the worksheet and other formulas you add. These additional limits provide more control over the resulting values. For example, you can specify that the returned values must be within a range or that one value has a specific ratio to another. Solver is for when you are considering what-if proposals that Backsolver cannot handle because you want to define result criteria.

The Solver add-in is not automatically installed as part of 1-2-3. Since Solver requires that you have 2MB of memory to run, you may not be able to run Solver in 1-2-3 if your computer does not have this memory. Also, if you see a message that you are out of memory while trying to run Solver, you may want to try running Solver after removing Wysiwyg from memory (which also removes the SmartIcons). To run Solver, you will probably run the Install program from the floppy disks again to add the Solver add-in to your hard disk. Once Solver is installed, it is loaded into 1-2-3 and invoked just like the other add-ins. This add-in has the name SOLVER.PLC. The box "Steps For Using Solver" summarizes the definition of a Solver problem and its use in locating problem solutions.

Solver is limited to problems that are not too large for your personal computer memory and disk space, and that use @functions that you can use with Solver. When you create a problem that is too large, you will see a message that the problem must be simplified before Solver can solve it. Also, with very large problems, Solver may take longer that you want.

Entering The Basic Problem

Before you use Solver, you must enter the problem you want to solve with this add-in. You must complete all your worksheet entries before invoking Solver. Your model is constructed with familiar 1-2-3 entries with the only limitation being the use of certain @functions. The entries that are specifically needed for Solver are adjustable cells that Solver can change and constraints that place limits on Solver's solutions.

The problem you will enter into a 1-2-3 worksheet consists of the adjustable cells, the formulas these adjustable cells use, any formula you want to equal the highest or lowest value possible, and the constraints.

The adjustable cells are the cells you expect Solver to change as it locates acceptable answers. They are the same cells that you would change if you manually perform a series of "what-if" calculations affecting the model. The adjustable cells in the sales model in Figure 14-6 are located in D2..D5. Solver will alter the percentages indicating the difference between 1992 and 1993.

TIP: Disable the protection for adjustable cells with /Range Unprotect and then enable worksheet protection with /Worksheet Global Prot Enable. By enabling protection and unprotecting adjustable cells, you can select a larger range than the few cells containing the adjustable cells.

The other worksheet entries and formulas you enter depend on the calculations you would enter if you are performing your own what-if calculations. Figure 14-6 shows some entries that project next year's unit sales and profit depending on how different customer bases change from one year to the next. Increasing sales is one goal of the company, but since the value of sales varies by consumer group, you want the percentage of sales change to be in the customer groups that offer the most profit. An increase percentage is applied to the current sales for existing customers. The formula in C2 is +B2*(1+D2) and copied for the other customer groups. The profit in column F multiplies 1993 sales by the profit per unit sold. The total profit, in F6, is also the entry you want to make as large as possible. When you tell Solver the cell to optimize, you will select this cell. There are many possibilities for achieving this sales level, although some options may be more realistic as goals than others. These limitations are set through constraints.

```
A:E9: +D2>0.15                                                      READY

     A           B         C         D         E        F        G
1              1992 Sales 1993 Sales Increase Unit Profit Total Profit
2  Other manufacturers  125,694   125,694   0.00%     3      377,082
3  Direct to the consumer 175,900 175,900   0.00%     4      703,600
4  Resellers    235,000   235,000   0.00%     1      235,000
5  Government    87,500    87,500   0.00%     2      175,000
6  Totals       624,094   624,094                   1,490,682
7
8  Constraints
9  Sales to other manufacturers increases by 15% to 20%   0 +D2>0.15
10 Sales to other manufacturers increases by 15% to 20%   1 +D2<0.2
11 Sales directly to the customer increases by 6% to 7%   0 +D3>0.06
12 Sales directly to the customer increases by 6% to 7%   1 +D3<0.07
13 Sales to resellers increases by 0% to 10%              0 +D4>0
14 Sales to resellers increases by 0% to 10%              1 +D4<0.1
15 Sales to the government changes by -5% to 1%           1 +D5>-0.05
16 Sales to the government changes by -5% to 1%           1 +D5<0.01
17 Total sales is no more than 650,000 units              1 +C6<=650000
18
19
20
SOLVER.WK3
```

Figure 14-6. *Sales projection worksheet*

Constraints define the range for adjustable cells and place limits on acceptable solutions. Every constraint must be expressed as a logical formula that 1-2-3 evaluates as true or false. For example, you might enter +D2=.05. You can use any of the logical operators described in Chapter 2. You cannot use compound logical formulas when entering constraints. If C5 can only range from 0 to 5000, you must use two separate constraints: +C5>0 and +C5<5000. Solver won't accept +C5>0#AND#C5<5000. Often you'll need more than one constraint to control values for adjustable cells since you will want to place upper and lower limits on these cells. Figure 14-6 contains a description of the constraints for the sales problem. Each entry is recorded as a formula in column E. These formulas are also entered in column F for documentation purposes. The descriptive information in column A also serves as documentation. The objective is for Solver to identify combinations of adjustable cell entries where all of the constraints evaluate as a 1 for true.

TIP: If you want the adjustable values to be positive numbers, include constraints that prevent the adjustable cells from being less than 0. Examples of these types of constraints are +D7>0 and +D8>0.

Chapter 14: Using 1-2-3's Built-In Add-Ins and Icons

As you make your entries, you can add range names. For example, you can name the ranges or collections used for constraints and adjustable cells. This will make it easier to define these cells to Solver. If you are defining a collection of non-adjacent cells as adjustable cells you might want to unprotect the cells you want Solver to adjust and enable worksheet protection. This allows you to specify a range of cells that includes some where entries should be made. The non-adjustable cells in this range should be protected.

TIP: Range names offer another important advantage when you start creating Solver reports. These names will appear to label important cells in the report. If you choose not to use range names, place label entries on the worksheet. 1-2-3 will use these labels to identify entries in the report.

@Function Limitations

Several @functions cannot be used with Solver. When you try using one of the unacceptable @functions, you will see a message that a cell contains an unsupported @function or string. The @functions that you can use in Solver problems are:

@ABS	@INDEX	@SHEETS
@ACOS	@INT	@SIN
@ASIN	@IRR	@SLN
@ATAN	@ISNUMBER	@SQRT
@ATAN2	@LN	@STD
@AVG	@LOG	@STDS
@CHOOSE	@MAX	@SUM
@COLS	@MIN	@SUMPRODUCT
@COS	@MOD	@SYD
@COUNT	@NOW	@TAN
@CTERM	@NPV	@TERM
@DDB	@PI	@TRUE
@EXP	@PMT	@VAR
@FALSE	@PV	@VARS
@FV	@RATE	@VDB
@HLOOKUP	@ROUND	@VLOOKUP
@IF	@ROWS	

Invoking Solver

To invoke Solver, select Invoke from the Add-In menu and then Solver, or press the key combination you selected for this add-in when you loaded it. This displays the following menu:

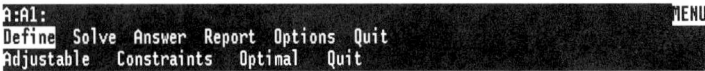

The first step when you see this menu is to tell Solver where you have made your entries by selecting Define. After you define where your entries are made, you are ready to tell Solver to start.

Defining The Model to Solver

After you select Define, you need to tell Solver the location of the adjustable cells, the constraints, and any cell whose value you want to make as large or small as possible. After you have made these selections, you will want to select Quit to return to the initial Solver menu.

To tell Solver which cells the add-in can change, select Adjustable. Next, specify a range containing the cells that Solver can change. Solver ignores blank cells, and cells containing either labels or formulas. The cells that you want Solver to alter must contain numbers. You will want to enter 0's in adjustable cells that do not yet contain numbers. If worksheet protection is enabled, the adjustable cells must be unprotected. For the example in Figure 14-6, the adjustable cell range is D2..D5.

To tell Solver the limits you are placing on the adjustable cells, select Constraints. Next, specify the range containing the logical formulas. These are the formulas that will all equal 1 when Solver finds sets of adjustable cell values. An entry in a constraint cell that is not a logical formula is ignored. Other unacceptable constraint entries are conflicting constraints, constraints that do not depend on adjustable cells, and constraints with compound logical operators like #OR#. You will know if you have any of these when you try to solve the problem. For the example in Figure 14-6, the constraint range is E9..E17.

You can select an optimal cell when you want Solver to find either the highest or lowest value in a cell while the adjustable cells meet all the constraints. The optimal cell can be an adjustable cell or a cell that depends on an adjustable cell. To select this cell, select Optimal, then either X Maximize or N Minimize for the largest or smallest value, respectively. Then select the cell you want to be the largest or smallest possible value. For the example in Figure 14-6, you want to select Optimal, X Maximize, and the cell F6. If you later change your mind, you can select Optimal and Reset.

Creating a Solution

After you describe the problem to Solver, you can tell Solver to start working by selecting Solve and Problem. Solver analyzes your problem and begins its search for answers. Solver searches for up to 10 combinations of adjustable cell values that meet all the constraints, unless you change the default value by selecting Options and Number-Answers, and then typing a new number. As Solver finds answers, the status line describes the number of answers found and the progress made so far.

When Solver finishes its search for solutions, the best set of adjustable values are placed in the worksheet, as shown in Figure 14-7. If Solver can find a solution, as many as 10 answers are available for review. If Solver is unable to find a solution, it will provide information about its attempt to find an answer. You can cycle through the answer values on your screen or can choose to obtain a current cell or table report.

If Solver cannot find any combination of values that meet all constraints, Solver will put its closest guess in the adjustable cells. When the problem has a flaw that prevents Solver from finding a solution, Solver displays a message explaining the reason. These reasons include invalid functions, and constraints that conflict with one another. When you run into these problems, you will need to correct the problem on the worksheet and request Solver to solve the problem again.

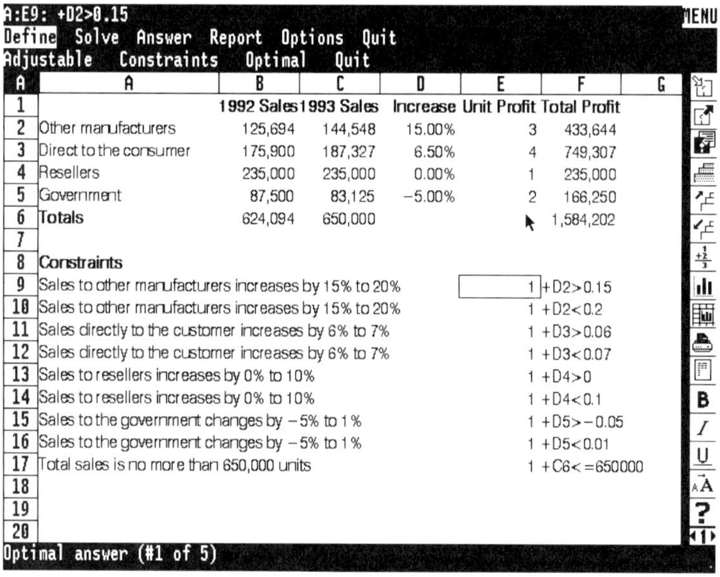

Figure 14-7. *Worksheet after finding optimal solution*

You may also see the message of "Guesses required." This occurs when the problem is too complicated. When this occurs, select Solve and Guess, and then supply guesses for the adjustable cells before you select Solve and Problem again.

Exploring The Answers

To explore the answers Solver finds, you can select Answer. The next menu contains Next, First, Previous, Last, Optimal, Reset, and Quit. These options enable you to select the answer displayed in the worksheet. Reset returns to displaying your initial worksheet values in the adjustable cells. If you requested an optimal solution, the first answer represents the optimal, or best, answer. Sometimes when there are additional solutions to explore, Solver is not always able to determine which answer is best. You can request Solve and Problem again to get the next group of sets of adjustable cell values that meet the constraints. Some problems will have more than ten sets of adjustable cell values that Solver will find which meet all the constraints. If you have less than ten sets of values when you solve the problem, you will not get any more sets of answers by trying to solve the problem again.

If Solver is unable to find an answer, you can use the Answer menu to review Solver's attempts at a solution. For each of Solver's attempts, at least one of the constraint cells will have a false value.

Solver Report Options

You can use Solver's report options to obtain additional information about answers or attempts that Solver makes to find answers. Each of these reports is created by selecting Report and the name of the report you want. Solver has these seven reports:

- Answer
- How Solved
- What-if Limits
- Differences
- Inconsistent Constraints
- Unused Constraints
- Cells Used

With some reports, you can choose to create an abbreviated current cell report within a small screen window or on a separate worksheet. Since each of

Solver's reports can be created as a table in a separate worksheet file, it is easy to print, graph, or store these reports. The current cell reports are summary offerings available in a report window for selected cells on the worksheet. Figure 14-8 shows an Unused report in a window. The remaining reports in this chapter are discussed in their table form.

The Answer Report

The Answer report provides information on the answers or attempts. It is useful when you want an overview of all the answers in a group. The report has either two or three sections, depending on whether or not you selected an optimal cell. The three sections are:

- **Optimal cell**   Displays the range of values for the optimal cells in the answers or attempts. Displays the value of the optimal cell in each answer.

- **Adjustable cells**   Displays the range of values for the adjustable cells as well as the value of each adjustable cell in every answer.

- **Cells used to solve**   Reports the range of values used in all cells in the problem. Provides the range of values and each answer for each cell.

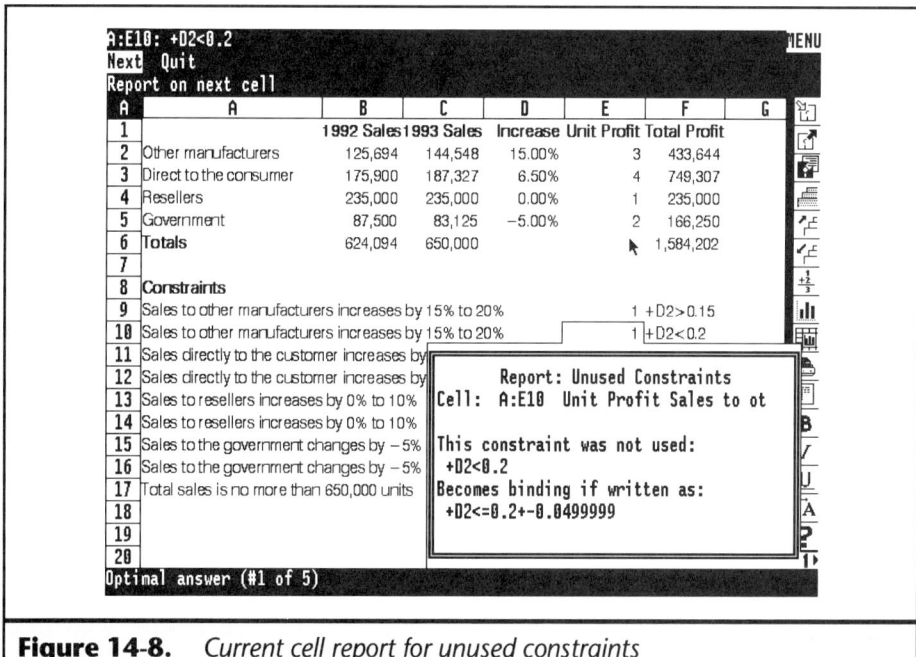

Figure 14-8.   *Current cell report for unused constraints*

The Answer report is created in a worksheet named ANSWER*n*, where *n* is the next sequential number that is not in the current directory. Figure 14-9 shows part of an Answer report. You can see in this section of the report how 1-2-3 uses nearby labels to identify unnamed cells used in the problem.

The How Solved Report

The How solved report summarizes the solution process. It covers guess cells, the optimal cells, binding constraints, inconsistent constraints, and adjustable cell values. It is available for the current answer or attempt. It shows the following information:

Cell	Provides a cell address
Name	Provides the name of the cell specified as Cell
Value	Provides the value of Cell for the current answer or attempt
Optimal answer	Reports the optimal answer if one is found
Optimal cell	Provides the cell address, name, and value
Adjustable cells	Reports on all adjustable cells in the current answer or attempt
Binding constraints	Reports on constraints that affect the current answer or attempt
Formula	Displays the logical formula for each constraint
Becomes binding	Shows how to change the logical formula to make it binding
Unused constraints	Reports on cells that do not affect the answer
Becomes satisfied	Displays the change needed in a constraint cell to make it true
Guessable cells	Reports on cells where a guess is needed
Unsatisfied constraints	Reports on cell where the constraints are false

The How solved report is created in a worksheet file named HOW*n*, where *n* is the next sequential number not in the current directory. Figure 14-10 provides a look at part of this report.

The What-if Limits Report

This report lists the range of highest and lowest values for all answers in a group. It also lists the range for a particular answer, assuming the other variables in the answer remain constant. You can use this report to determine how much you can

Chapter 14: Using 1-2-3's Built-In Add-Ins and Icons

```
A:A1: [W1] 'Solver Table Report - Answer table                READY

   A  B           C            D             E             F          G
  1  Solver Table Report - Answer table
  2  Worksheet: C:\123R34\DATA\SOLVER.WK3
  3  Solved: 17-Nov-92 07:27 PM
  4
  5  Optimal cell                              Answers
  6  Cell     Name         Lowest value  Highest value  Optimal (#1)    2
  7  A:F6     Total Profit To  1,580,710    1,584,202    1,584,202   1,583,3
  8
  9  Adjustable cells                          Answers
 10  Cell     Name         Lowest value  Highest value  Optimal (#1)    2
 11  A:D2     Increase Othe   15.00%       15.69%        15.00%       15.69
 12  A:D3     Increase Dire   6.00%        6.50%         6.50%        6.00
 13  A:D4     Increase Res    0.00%        0.37%         0.00%        0.00
 14  A:D5     Increase Gov   -5.00%       -4.00%        -5.00%       -5.00
 15
 16  Supporting formula cells                  Answers
 17  Cell     Name         Lowest value  Highest value  Optimal (#1)    2
 18  A:C2     1993 Sales O   144,548      145,421       144,548      145,42
 19  A:F2     Total Profit O   433,644      436,263       433,644      436,28
 20  A:C3     1993 Sales Di   186,454      187,327       187,327      186,45
ANSWER01.WK3
```

Figure 14-9.   *Answer table report*

```
A:A1: [W1] 'Solver Table Report - How solved                 READY

   A  B  C       D                    E                   F           G
  1  Solver Table Report - How solved
  2  Worksheet: C:\123R34\DATA\SOLVER.WK3
  3  Solved: 17-Nov-92 07:30 PM
  4
  5  Optimal answer (#1)
  6
  7  Answer #1 is one of 5 which satisfies all of the constraints.
  8
  9  This answer maximizes the value of cell A:F6 (Total Profit Totals).
 10
 11  For this answer, the optimal cell attained the following value:
 12
 13  Optimal Cell
 14  Cell     Name                  Value
 15  A:F6     Total Profit To       1,584,202
 16
 17  For this answer, Solver changed the values in the following adjustable cells:
 18
 19  Adjustable cells
 20  Cell     Name                  Value
HOW00001.WK3
```

Figure 14-10.   *How solved report*

change one adjustable cell without affecting the answer. The table version provides the following information:

Cell	Address of cell
Name	Range name or closest labels
Range for all answers	Range of values across answers
What-if limits	Range within which you can change values and not affect the current answer

This report is available in a worksheet file named LIMITSn, where n is the next unused sequential number. Figure 14-11 shows part of this report.

The Differences Report

The Differences report allows you to focus on the differences in any two answers that exceed a tolerance amount. After choosing the report, you can select any two answers and specify the difference amount. The fields presented in the report are:

Cell	Address of a cell
Name	Range name for the cell or the closest labels
Answer #	Cell value for the answer or attempt
Difference	Amount of the difference between the two answers
Difference %	Percent difference between the two answers

Figure 14-12 shows part of a Differences report created to report the difference between the first and second answers for values of more than 0. This report is created in a worksheet file named DIFFSn, where n is the next sequential number.

The Inconsistent Constraints Report

The Inconsistent constraints report provides information on why Solver could not find an answer for you. It highlights how you would need to change

Chapter 14: Using 1-2-3's Built-In Add-Ins and Icons

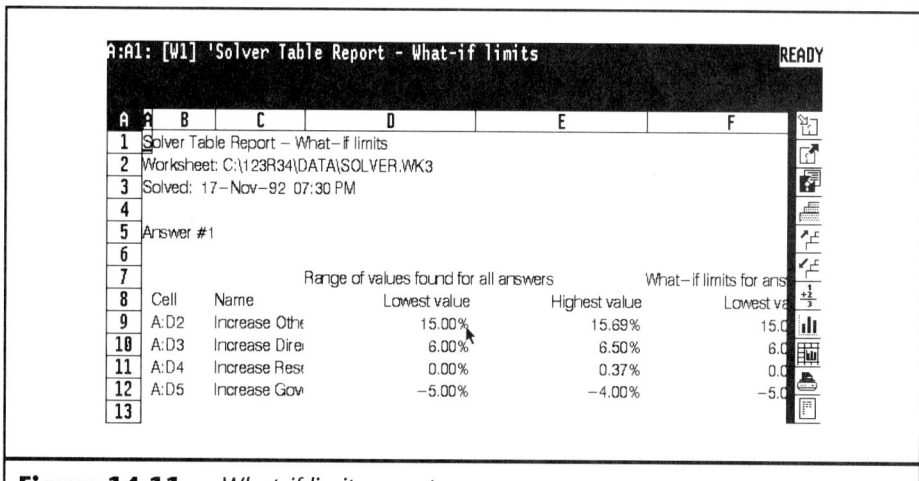

Figure 14-11. *What-if limits report*

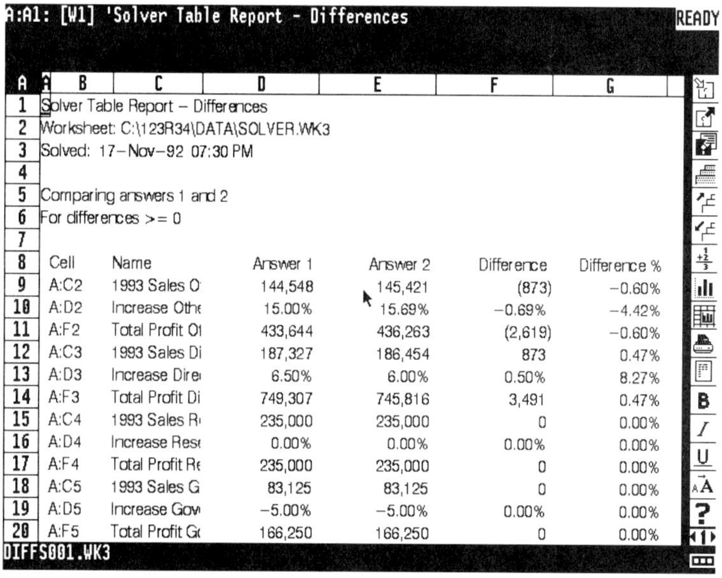

Figure 14-12. *Differences report*

constraints to find an answer. It lists all the constraints that return false, providing the following fields:

Cell	Address of a constraint cell
Name	Range name or closest labels
This constraint not satisfied	Current formula that returns false
Becomes satisfied if written as	Displays a formula for the constraint that would return true

The Inconsistent constraints table reports are stored as INCONSn, where n is the next sequential number. Figure 14-13 shows part of this report after editing one of the problem's constraints, making the problem unsolvable.

The Unused Constraints Report

The Unused constraints report provides information on constraints that Solver did not use in finding an answer. This means that the constraint is not currently binding on the problem solution. This often occurs when the upper or lower limits established for a variable are unrealistic given other constraints in the problem. For example, you might have a customer discount shown as a maximum of 50% but find that constraint is unrealistic if you also expect to make a profit. Solver makes a suggestion for how you might change the constraint to make it binding. Fields shown in the Unused constraints report include:

Cell	Address of the unused constraint
Name	Range name or nearest labels for the unused constraint
This constraint was not used	Logical formula used for the constraint
Becomes binding if written as	Rewritten constraint that would become binding

Figure 14-14 shows a portion of an Unused Constraint report. These are written in worksheets named UNUSEDn, where n is the next sequential number.

The Cells Used Report

This report indicates the cells that Solver uses. If these cells are not what you expected, there may be a problem with your problem definition. The data shown in the report is:

Optimal cell   Address and name of the optimal cell if one exists
Adjustable cells   Addresses and names of adjustable cells
Constraint cells   Addresses and names of constraint cells

Solver creates a worksheet named CELLS*n*, where *n* is the next sequential number. Figure 14-15 shows part of this report.

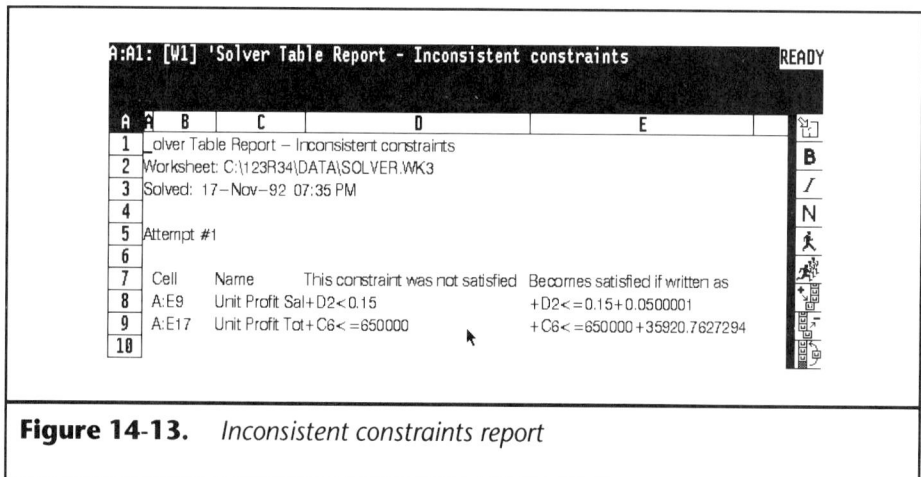

Figure 14-13.   Inconsistent constraints report

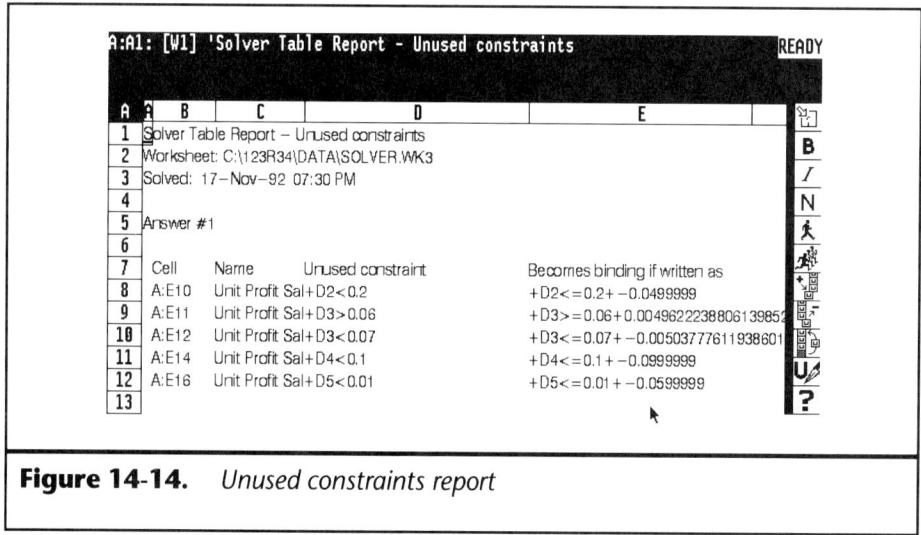

Figure 14-14.   Unused constraints report

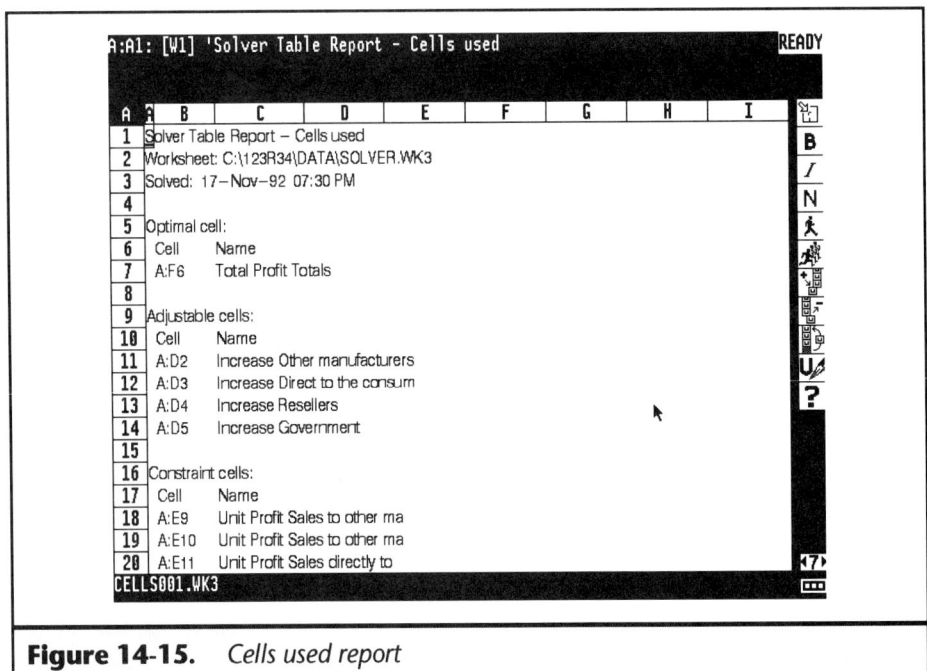

Figure 14-15. *Cells used report*

The @SOLVER Add-In Function

When Solver is loaded, you can use the @SOLVER function. @SOLVER is a special @function that returns information about Solver. This @function is recalculated whenever the worksheet is recalculated. You can use it to either run the @SOLVER add-in or return information about the Solver problem you are solving. The syntax of this function is @SOLVER(*query-string*). *Query-string* is a string that specifies the information you need about Solver. The eight options you can use for query-string are shown in Table 14-1.

@SOLVER is used primarily in macros to monitor the progress of Solver. An example of this function is @SOLVER("Numanswers") that would return 5 for the problem in Figure 14-6, since Solver found five combinations of answers.

Using Macros with 1-2-3 Add-Ins

Just as you can create macros with 1-2-3, you can create macros that load and use your 1-2-3 add-ins, such as Backsolver. Some add-ins can be used with macros while others cannot. You can try out your installed add-ins to learn the ones you can run through macros. Just as you use keystrokes for 1-2-3 instructions, you

Query-String	Return value	Meaning
Consistent	1	All constraints true
	2	One or more constraints false
	ERR	Solver inactive or no answer
Done	1	Done
	2	Currently solving
	3	Active but not solving
	ERR	Solver inactive
Moreanswers	1	All answers found
	2	More answers possible
	ERR	Solver inactive
Needguess	1	Guess not needed
	2	Guess needed
	ERR	Solver inactive
Numanswers	n	Number of answers
	ERR	Solver inactive
Optimal	1	Optimal answer
	2	Best answer
	3	Unbounded problem
	4	Optimal answer not requested
	ERR	Solver inactive
Progress	n	Percent complete
	ERR	Solver inactive, or solving has not begun
Result	1	One or more answers
	2	No answers found, but representative attempts are available
	ERR	Solver inactive

Table 14-1.   @Solver Query-Strings

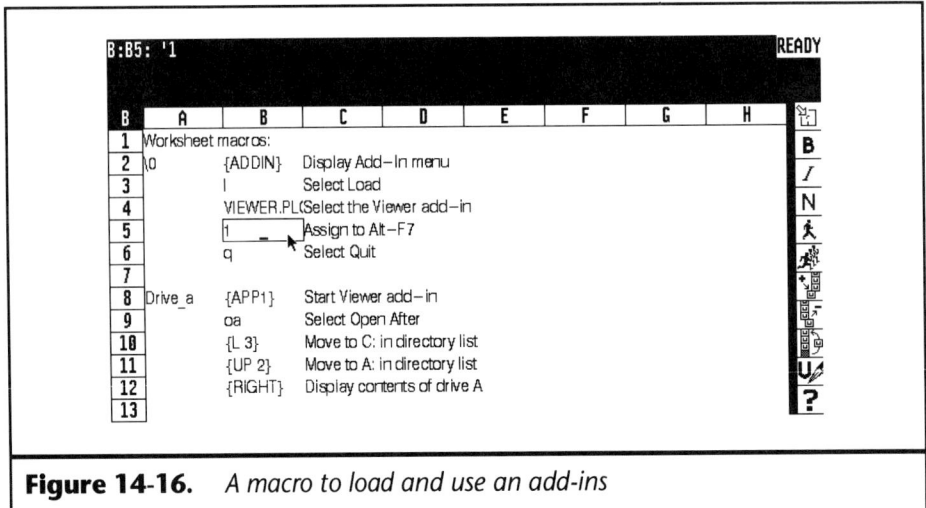

Figure 14-16. *A macro to load and use an add-ins*

can use the same method of storing keystrokes in 1-2-3 cells to run as macros. You can also use the keystroke recorder that you can see when you press ALT-F2 (RECORD). Figure 14-16 shows two macros. The **\0** macro loads the Viewer add-in; the **Drive_a** macro invokes the Viewer add-in and sets the add-in to display the contents of drive A to select the file to open.

If you want to invoke an add-in with a macro, you can use {APP1}, {APP2}, and {APP3} for the ALT-F7, ALT-F8, and ALT-F9 key combinations. You can also use {APP4} or {ADDIN}, and then an **I** for Invoke to invoke an add-in, especially those not activated by a key combination.

SmartIcons

SmartIcons add to the functionality of 1-2-3 by providing the most frequently used commands as pictures. These SmartIcons automatically load with 1-2-3 as part of Wysiwyg. When Wysiwyg is not loaded, these icons will not appear. The SmartIcons provide you with several palettes of icons that represent various things you can do with 1-2-3. Select an icon, using either the mouse or the keyboard, to carry out these options. The icons can apply formatting to a range of cells, quickly create a graph, delete rows or columns, and much more. The icons serve as a shortcut you can use to bypass the menu system, and they carry out certain procedures quickly.

The icons appear on the icon palette displayed at the right edge of the screen as you can see in Figure 14-16. Only a few of the icons appear on any one icon palette. The number of palettes you have depends on your monitor. For example, with a VGA monitor, you will have eight icon palettes. Beneath the icon palette, you can see the palette number, flanked by two arrows. The first icon palette is the custom palette. You can remove and copy icons to this palette, as well as move the icons around on the palette. The other palettes are set and cannot be altered.

Using the SmartIcons

You can use the icon palette with either the mouse or the keyboard. The icon palette is easier to use with the mouse, but the keyboard methods are still simple. To select a particular icon with the mouse, simply point the mouse pointer at the desired icon and click the left mouse button once. The icon is activated, and the assigned activity is carried out. To switch to another icon palette, click the left mouse button on the arrows on either side of the icon palette number beneath the icon palette, until the palette you want appears.

To use the keyboard, you have to invoke the icon palette and then use the arrow keys to select the desired icon. To invoke the icon palette, press CTRL-F10. After invoking the icon palette, you can select an icon by moving to it using the UP ARROW and DOWN ARROW keys and pressing ENTER. When you want to move from one palette to the next, use the LEFT ARROW and RIGHT ARROW keys.

Modifying the Custom Palette

Only the first palette, called the custom palette, can be customized. The other palettes are all set, both in contents and in order. You can remove or add icons to the custom palette and also move the icons around. You can customize the custom palette by using three icons that appear on the next-to-last palette.

Removing an Icon

Since the custom palette is full, you need to remove icons from this palette before you can add others. Removing an icon from the custom palette is as easy as selecting an icon to use. The first step is to select the Remove Icon icon from the next-to-last palette. This icon looks like this:

When you select this icon, the custom palette appears, and you are prompted to select the icon you want to remove. Select the icon as you normally would, either by clicking it with the mouse or by highlighting it with the UP ARROW and DOWN ARROW keys and pressing ENTER. The icon is then removed from the custom palette. Since all of the icons on the custom palette also appear on one of the other palettes, you can always replace any icons you remove from the custom palette. For example, if you wanted to remove the Font SmartIcon from the custom palette, you would follow these steps:

1. Click the arrows on the bottom of the palette until the next-to-last palette appears. If you are not using a mouse, press CTRL-F10 to activate the palette, and then press the RIGHT ARROW or LEFT ARROW key until the next-to-last palette appears.

2. Click the Remove Icon icon in the palette.

    If you do not have a mouse, press the UP ARROW or DOWN ARROW key to highlight this icon and press ENTER.

3. Select the Font icon from the custom palette.

You can either click the icon or press the UP ARROW or DOWN ARROW key to highlight this icon and press ENTER. The Font icon is the one containing two A's with an arrow between them. Now the palette is shorter because it contains one less icon. You can now add an icon to the first palette if you desire.

Adding an Icon

Adding an icon is just as easy as deleting one. You use the Add Icon icon from the next-to-last palette. The Add Icon icon looks like this:

After selecting this icon, you are prompted to select the icon you want to add to the custom palette. You can choose from among the icons which appear on other palettes. Select the icon as you normally would, either by clicking it with the mouse or by using either the LEFT ARROW or RIGHT ARROW key to highlight it, and then pressing ENTER. When you select the icon, a copy of it appears at the bottom of the custom palette. For example, you may want to copy the Outline SmartIcon to the custom palette. This icon uses Wysiwyg to create a line around the outside of the range selected. To add this icon to the custom palette, follow these steps:

1. Move to the next-to-last icon palette, as previously described.
2. Select the Add Icon icon using either the mouse or the keyboard.
3. Move to the palette on which the Outline icon appears (palette 2 for VGA monitors) and select it using either the mouse or the keyboard.

Moving Icons

You may want to move icons on the custom palette to make their placement more logical or to keep related icons together. When you want to move an icon, you use the Move Icon icon from the next-to-last menu. The icon looks like this:

The custom palette appears, and you are prompted to select the icon you want to move. Select the icon just like you select icons at any other point. You are then prompted to choose the place where you want to move the icon. Do so by selecting the icon currently in the position where you want the selected icon to be. The icon you first selected now appears in that position, and the icon you selected second and those beneath it move down one place to make room for your new choice. If you wanted, for example, to move the Outline icon to the top of the custom palette, you would follow these steps:

1. Move to the next-to-last icon palette, as previously described.
2. Select the Move Icon icon using either the mouse or the keyboard.
3. Select the Outline icon at the bottom of the custom palette.
4. Select the Perspective icon that is the fourth icon in the custom palette, using either the mouse or the keyboard.

    As you can see here, the Outline icon takes the place of the Perspective icon, and the Perspective icon and those below it all move down one place to make room.

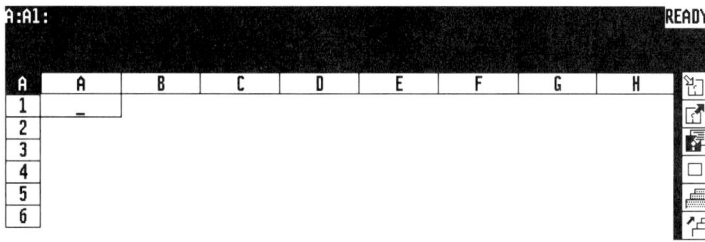

User Icons

The last palette that appears contains 12 user icons. You can assign macros to these icons. These macros are activated and perform their operations when the user icon is selected. The User Icon icon (the one with a U and a pencil point) assigns a macro to one of the 12 user icons that appear on your last palette. The steps for adding the macro instructions and description for a user icon are in Chapter 12, along with keyboard alternative macros. Once you add macro instructions to the user icons, you are ready to select them to perform the macro. You can also copy the user icons onto the custom palette, following the same steps you use to copy icons that are defined for 1-2-3 and Wysiwyg commands. The one feature about user icons you did not learn about in Chapter 12 is how you can change the appearance of the user icons.

Changing User Icons Pictures

You may want to change the user icons from displaying U1 through U12 to displaying a picture. You can edit these icons to change the image displayed on the icon so it looks like the task it represents. You need to use a mouse to change the icon's picture. To change the icon's picture, select the User Icon icon (the one with a U and the pencil point). Next, select Next Icon or Previous Icon until you are working with the user icon you want to change. Then select Edit Icon. This displays a window like the one in Figure 14-17. The grid represents the points on the icon's image you can change.

To change the icon, click the color below the grid for the icon. Then click the points in the grid where you want that color to appear. You can repeat this for each of the colors you want to use on the icon. If you want to remove the existing icon design, select Clean. When you are finished, select OK to have that icon use the modified picture. This picture will also appear in the custom palette if you have copied the user icon to that palette. Figure 14-18 shows an icon after editing it. Notice that you can see this icon appearing in the icon palette in Figure 14-18. If you want to return to the default of U1 through U12 for a particular user icon, select Default.

Another possibility for changing the icon's appearance is to use images stored in BMP files. These include files that you can create with Windows' Paintbrush. If you select Import and then the BMP file to use, the icon will use the image stored in the BMP file. Your only limit is that the BMP file must be small since the image can only be 32 by 32 dots in size.

Chapter 14: Using 1-2-3's Built-In Add-Ins and Icons 843

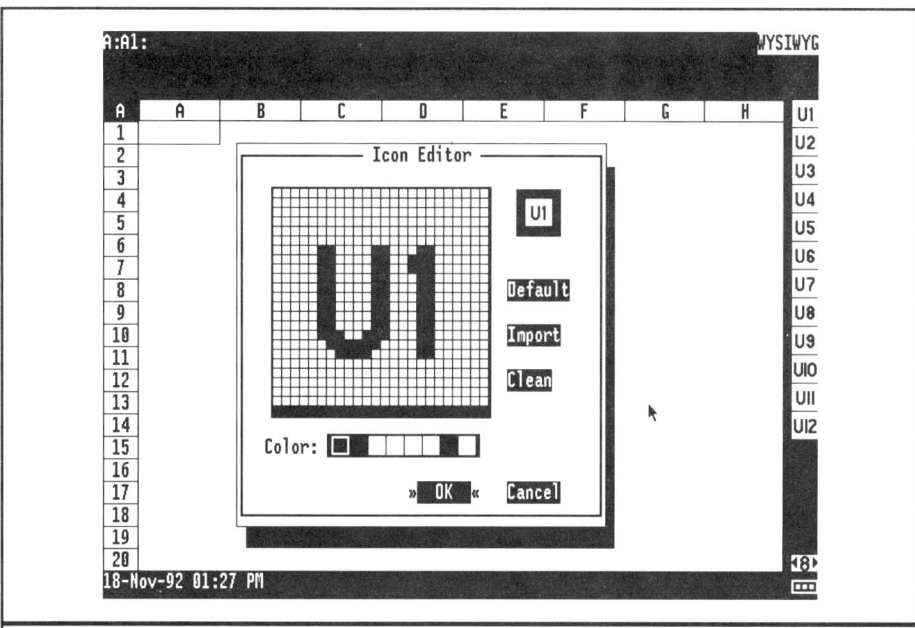

Figure 14-17. *Window for editing an icon's picture*

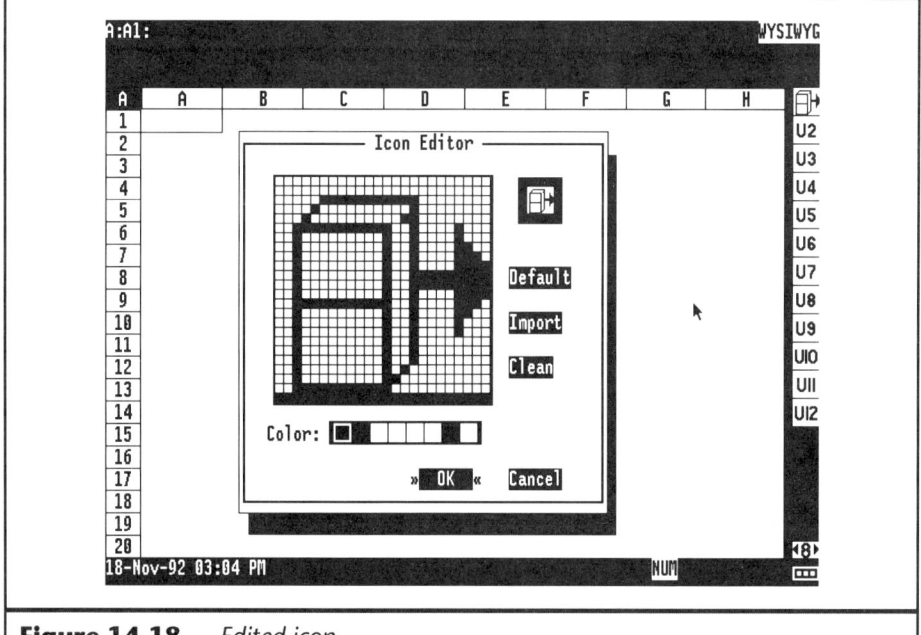

Figure 14-18. *Edited icon*

Command Reference

Add-In Menu

Add-In Menu

```
Load    Remove    Invoke    Table    Clear    Settings    Quit
        @Functions Macros Applications      System  File
        Set Cancel Directory Update Quit    Set Cancel Quit
```

Auditor Add-In

```
Precedents  Dependents  Formulas  Recalc-List  Circs  Options  Quit
            Highlight List Trace Audit-Range Reset Quit
                                              Highlight  Options
```

Backsolver Add-In Menu

```
Formula-Cell  Value  Adjustable  Solve  Quit
```

Solver Add-In

```
Define               Solve  Answer  Report              Options  Quit
Adjustable Constraints Optimal Quit                     Number-Answers
X Maximize  N Minimize  Reset
                              Answer How What-If Differences Inconsistent Unused Cells Quit
Problem Continue Guesses Quit
            Next First Previous Last Optimal Reset Quit
```

Viewer Add-In

```
Retrieve  Open  Link  Browse
Before  After
```

The Add-In Menu

ALT-F10 Clear

Description

This command frees all loaded add-ins from memory.

ALT-F10 Invoke

Description

This command activates the menu of an add-in that you have loaded into memory. If an add-in is not loaded, you cannot invoke it. Some add-ins do not use this command because the @functions or macro commands do not need to be invoked to be used or, as in Wysiwyg's case, the menu is activated by another method (a colon).

Options

The options for this command let you select the add-in to invoke.

NOTE: If you assign a function key to an add-in, you can invoke the add-in with the function key as well as with the menu.

ALT-F10 Load

Description

This command attaches add-in programs to use with 1-2-3. Add-ins extend the basic functionality of 1-2-3. A loaded add-in remains in memory until you remove it or end your 1-2-3 session.

Options

The options for this command are to select the add-in to load and the key to use to invoke the add-in. For the second set of options, you can choose No-Key to invoke the add-in by pressing ALT-F10 and selecting Invoke; or you can select 1, 2, or 3, assigning ALT-F7, ALT-F8, or ALT-F9 to be used to invoke the add-in.

ALT-F10 Quit

Description

This command leaves the add-in menu and returns you to READY mode.

ALT-F10 Remove

Description

This command frees a specific add-in from memory. If you have assigned the add-in to a function key, it is also freed and available for assignment to another add-in.

Option

The only option is to select the add-in to remove from memory.

ALT-F10 Settings

This command selects the default add-in directory as well as add-in programs to load when you start 1-2-3 or when a worksheet file is loaded.

Options

SYSTEM This option chooses the add-ins to load with 1-2-3 (Set), removes an add-in previously set from loading with 1-2-3 (Cancel), chooses a default add-in directory (Directory), saves the selected settings (Update), and returns to the Add-In menu (Quit). If you select Set, you must select the add-in to automatically load, whether the add-in is automatically started (you can only have one), and the function key assigned to the add-in.

FILE   This option chooses an add-in to load with the current file (Set), removes an add-in from loading with the current file (Cancel), and returns to the Add-In menu (Quit). Selecting Set prompts for the same information as Set for the System option.

ALT-F10 Table

This command creates a table of one column in the current file which lists the add-ins in memory.

Options

After selecting one of the three types of add-in options listed below, select the select the first cell on the worksheet where 1-2-3 will list the add-ins.

@FUNCTIONS   This option creates a table of add-in @functions loaded in memory.

MACROS   This option creates a table of add-in macro commands loaded in memory.

APPLICATIONS   This option creates a table of add-in applications loaded in memory.

Auditor Add-In Commands

The Auditor add-in provides commands that allow you to quickly identify potential problems in your worksheets.

Circs

Description

This command finds cells in the audit range which are part of a circular reference.

Option

The only option for this command is tracing through cells it finds or selecting where this add-in places the list of cells on the worksheet.

Dependents

Description

This command finds cells in the audit range which contain formulas that reference cells in a range you select. These are the formulas that depend on the cells in the selected range.

Options

After selecting this command, select the range of cells where you want to find formulas that use the selected cells. Next, the add-in highlights the cells, traces through the cells, or puts the list of cells on the worksheet (after you select where you want the list placed).

Formulas

Description

This command finds formulas in the audit range.

Option

The only option for this command is tracing through cells containing formulas, or selecting where this add-in places the list of cells and their formulas on the worksheet.

Options

Description

This command performs three functions. First, it sets how cells selected with other Auditor add-in commands are indicated. Second, this command sets the worksheet range that the other Auditor add-in commands use. Third, this command returns the Auditor add-in settings to their defaults.

Options

HIGHLIGHT   This option displays the cells that the Circs, Dependents, Formulas, Precedents, and Recalc-List commands find in a different color. The cells highlighted by the Auditor remain highlighted until you select the Options Reset Highlight command. Therefore, each time you use a new command, and the Auditor finds new cells to highlight, more and more cells will appear highlighted.

LIST   This option lists the cells that the Circs, Dependents, Formulas, Precedents, and Recalc-List commands find in a worksheet range. When you select one of these commands, you must select where you want the Auditor add-in to list the cells it finds in the worksheet. After selecting a cell, the Auditor will use the space from that cell to the bottom of the worksheet. The Auditor will not put anything in this range if it contains any entries unless the entries are the result of a previous Auditor command. The list this command creates will contain the cell addresses of the cells it finds, followed by their formulas. The first cell in the list will describe the Auditor command used and the audit range. If you use the Recalc-List command, it will display the current worksheet recalculation mode.

TRACE   This option moves to the cells that the Circs, Dependents, Formulas, Precedents, and Recalc-List commands find in a worksheet range. When you select one of the other Auditor commands, the Auditor will display a menu containing Forward, Backward, and Quit. Select Forward to move to the next cell the Auditor finds, select Backward to move to the previous cell the Auditor finds, and select Quit to return to the Auditor menu.

AUDIT-RANGE This option selects the range that the Circs, Dependents, Formulas, Precedents, and Recalc-List commands use to find cells. Select a range in the current worksheet to use. By default the Auditor add-in will use all open worksheets.

RESET This option resets the highlight or the other Auditor options. After selecting Reset, you can select Highlight to return all of the cells the Auditor add-in has highlighted to their original display. You can also select Options to return the report mode to Highlight and the audit range to all open worksheet files.

QUIT This option returns to the Auditor add-in's initial menu.

Precedents

Description

This command finds cells in the audit range which are used by formulas in a range you select. These are the cells that the formulas in the selected range depend on.

Options

After selecting this command, you must select the range of cells containing the formulas that you want to use to find the precedents. Next, the add-in highlights the cells, traces through the cells, or puts the list of cells on the worksheet after you select where you want the list to be placed.

Quit

Description

This command leaves the Auditor add-in and returns to 1-2-3 READY mode. Any cells highlighted by the Auditor will continue to be highlighted, as well as any previously highlighted cells which are still listed in the worksheet.

Recalc-List

Description

This command lists formulas in the audit range in the order 1-2-3 recalculates them. It takes into account the recalculation order selected with the 1-2-3 /Worksheet Global Recalc command.

Option

The only option for this command is tracing through cells in the order 1-2-3 will recalculate them, or selecting where this add-in places the list of cells and their formulas on the worksheet.

Backsolver Add-In Commands

Formula-Cell

Description

This command specifies the cell containing the formula that Backsolver is to use.

Option

The only option is selecting the cell that contains the formula.

Value

Description

This command specifies the value that you want the formula to equal after selecting Solve.

Option

The only option is typing the value you want the formula to equal.

Adjustable

Description

This command specifies the cells containing values that Backsolver can adjust, so that the formula-cell equals the value you enter.

Option

The only option is selecting the cell or cells containing values that Backsolver will alter when you select Solve.

Solve

Description

This command starts Backsolver calculating the values needed in the adjustable cell for the formula in the formula-cell to result in the specified value.

Quit

Description

This command leaves the Backsolver add-in and returns to READY mode.

Solver Add-In Commands

Define

Description

This command defines the problem you will solve with Solver. Use this command to tell Solver the location of the adjustable cells, the constraints, and any cell whose value you want to make as large or small as possible.

Options

ADJUSTABLE   Select the range containing the cells that you want Solver to adjust. These adjustable cells must contain values. If you want to limit the adjustable cells to a few cells in the range, unprotect those cells and enable worksheet protection.

CONSTRAINTS   Select the range containing the logical formulas that you want to all equal 1 when Solver finds a set of values for the adjustable cells. Solver ignores any entry in the range which is not a logical formula.

OPTIMAL   Select this option when you want a cell's value to be as large or small as possible after solving the problem. Select X Maximize to make the cell's value as large as possible, or N Minimize to make the cell's value as small as possible. Then, select the cell you want to optimize. If you change your mind about using an optimal cell, select this option again and Reset.

QUIT   This option returns to the main Solver menu.

Solve

Description

This command solves the problem you have defined. You cannot use this command until you have defined adjustable cells and constraints.

Options

PROBLEM This option finds the sets of values for the adjustable cells while making all constraints true and optimizing any optimal cell. After finding 10 sets of answers, Solver places the first set of adjustable cell values in the adjustable cells. If the problem cannot be solved, you will see a message indicating the problem. If the problem has no solution, Solver puts the best attempt in the adjustable cells.

CONTINUE This option continues finding the answers for the problem after Solver has been interrupted.

GUESSES This option lets you make guesses for the adjustable cells, then uses the guesses to find answers. For each of the adjustable cells, you can supply a guess.

QUIT This option returns to the main Solver menu.

Answer

Description

This command replaces the values of the adjustable cells, with one of the sets of values that Solver has calculated.

Options

NEXT This option sets the adjustable cell values to the next answer generated by Solver.

FIRST This option sets the adjustable cell values to the first answer generated by Solver.

PREVIOUS This option sets the adjustable cell values to the previous answer generated by Solver.

LAST   This option sets the adjustable cell values to the last answer generated by Solver.

OPTIMAL   This option sets the adjustable cell values to the best answer generated by Solver.

RESET   This option returns the adjustable cell values to their values when you invoked Solver.

QUIT   This option returns to the main Solver menu.

Report

Description

This command creates a report that returns information about the answers Solver has generated and the process completed to generate those answers.

Options

For each of the reports except Answer, you can select Cell or Table. Selecting Cell displays the report in a window on the screen for each cell involved in the report. You can go to the next cell in the report by selecting Next, or return to the initial Solver menu by selecting Quit. When you select Table, Solver opens a new worksheet and puts the report on that worksheet. The worksheet's name depends on the type of report.

ANSWER   This report lists information on the attempts of each answer. This report displays the range of values for the optimal cells, the range of values for the adjustable cells and the value of each adjustable cell, and the range of values used in all cells in the problem. When you select Table for this report, the report is in a worksheet named ANSWERn, where n is the next unused sequential number.

HOW   This report lists guess cells, the optimal cells, binding constraints, inconsistent constraints, and adjustable cell values for the current answer or attempt. When you select Table for this report, the report is in a worksheet named HOWn, where n is the next unused sequential number.

WHAT-IF   This report lists the range of highest and lowest values for all answers in a group, as well as the range for a particular answer assuming the other variables in the answer remain constant. When you select Table for this report, the report is in a worksheet named LIMITSn, where n is the next unused sequential number.

DIFFERENCES Where there is a difference between the two values in the answer sets, this report lists the different values, the difference between the values, and the percentage of the difference. You must supply the two answer values you want to compare and the amount of the differences to report. When you select Table for this report, the report is in a worksheet named DIFFSn, where n is the next sequential number.

INCONSISTENT This report lists constraints cells, current formulas, and how they must be modified to become consistent. This report only includes constraints that are false with the current answer attempt. When you select Table for this report, the report is in a worksheet named INCONSn, where n is the next unused sequential number.

UNUSED This report lists constraints cells, current formulas, and how they must be modified to become binding. This report only includes constraints that do not put limits on the current solution. When you select Table for this report, the report is in a worksheet named UNUSEDn, where n is the next unused sequential number.

CELLS This report lists the optimial cell, adjustable cells, and constraint cells used in the problem. When you select Table for this report, the report is in a worksheet named CELLSn, where n is the next sequential number.

QUIT This option returns to the main Solver menu.

Options

Description

This command lets you set options used by Solver.

Options

This command has only one option, Number-Answers. This option sets the number of answers Solver looks for when you solve the defined problem. The default is 10 but you can enter another number instead.

Quit

Description

This command leaves the Solver add-in and returns to READY mode.

Viewer Add-In Commands

Browse

Description

This command shows the files in a directory. When you press ENTER you return to READY mode in 1-2-3.

Options

From the viewer, you can change the files you are looking at. Pressing UP ARROW, DOWN ARROW, PGUP, PGDN, HOME, and END changes the file shown at the right. Pressing the RIGHT ARROW key moves into the highlighted file or the highlighted directory. Pressing the LEFT ARROW key moves out of a highlighted file or to the current directory's parent directory. While in a file, you can use the directional keys to move through the file just as you do in 1-2-3. You can press F2 to return to the default directory 1-2-3 uses. You can also press F5 for date order and F6 for alphabetical order to change the order of the listed files.

Link

Description

This command creates a formula in the current cell in 1-2-3. The current file contains an external file link to a cell in another worksheet file that you visually select.

Options

Once you see the file viewer, you have all the options for looking at the files and worksheet contents that are described for the Browse command. You want to select the cell in the worksheet file for the formula to use. When you press ENTER, you leave the viewer to return to 1-2-3. Assuming the current cell is empty, the Viewer add-in enters an external file link formula to the selected worksheet and cell. If the current cell has an entry, you must select Yes before the Viewer add-in enters the formula or No to cancel the formula entry.

Open

Description

This command opens a selected worksheet before or after the current worksheet file. Selecting a file to open with this add-in's command has the same results as 1-2-3's /File Open command.

Options

After you select Open, you must select Before or After to position the opened file relative to the current one. Once you see the file viewer, you have all the options for looking at the files and worksheet contents that are described for the Browse command. You want to select the worksheet file you want to open. When you press ENTER, you leave the viewer to return to 1-2-3 and open the file.

Retrieve

Description

This command retrieves a selected worksheet in place of the current worksheet file. Selecting a file to retrieve with this add-in's command has the same results as 1-2-3's /File Retrieve command.

Options

After you select Retrieve, if the current worksheet has changes that you have not saved, you must select Yes to continue or No to cancel retrieving a file. Once you see the file viewer, you have all the options for looking at the files and worksheet contents that are described for the Browse command. You want to select the worksheet file you want to retrieve. When you press ENTER, you leave the viewer to return to 1-2-3 and retrieve the file.

CHAPTER 15

Using the Wysiwyg Add-In

Wysiwyg is an acronym that stands for "what you see is what you get." 1-2-3's Wysiwyg is a spreadsheet publishing package that provides a completely new way to work with your spreadsheet information. Wysiwyg's features can significantly enhance the output that you produce with 1-2-3. You can add graphs to a worksheet range so that when you print the worksheet range you will print both the graph and the surrounding worksheet data. You can also use Wysiwyg to change the appearance of the worksheet data by adding features such as lines, boxes, boldface, italics, and different fonts. Wysiwyg not only uses the features of the printer to print your worksheet but also displays the worksheet as it will appear when printed.

Wysiwyg is an add-in that is included with 1-2-3 Releases 3.1 and 3.4. As you learned in Chapter 14, an *add-in* is a separate program that can be loaded with 1-2-3's Add-in commands to provide seamless integration to the product—without exiting 1-2-3 to start the other product. Add-ins can provide additional functions to the 1-2-3 worksheet, macro commands, or special features such as spreadsheet publishing. With Release 3.4, this add-in is automatically loaded with 1-2-3; you have been using Wysiwyg and may not have realized it.

Although Wysiwyg and 1-2-3 are separate products, the menu interface to the two is so similar that you will quickly learn how to use the Wysiwyg commands you want. The Wysiwyg menus and the 1-2-3 menus are available at the same time. This means that you can switch between altering the worksheet data with 1-2-3 and altering the worksheet appearance with Wysiwyg. Before you can use Wysiwyg with Release 3.1, you must load it into system memory. The procedure that you use to load Wysiwyg will work with any 1-2-3 Release 3.1 or 3.4 add-in. You will want to learn more about add-ins before exploring Wysiwyg features in detail. Add-ins are discussed in Chapter 14.

The Wysiwyg Interface

When Wysiwyg is loaded, the appearance of the screen looks exactly like the output that will be produced when you print the worksheet. The default background color of the Wysiwyg worksheet display is white. Also, all of the worksheet entries will use the Wysiwyg fonts instead of the font used by 1-2-3. When Wysiwyg is loaded, the control panel describes the special attributes added by Wysiwyg to the current cell after the cell address and before the 1-2-3 formatting information—such as cell protection, cell format, and column width.

Although the Wysiwyg screen looks very different from 1-2-3 without Wysiwyg, you can continue using 1-2-3 just as you used it before you loaded Wysiwyg. When you type a slash, you will see the 1-2-3 menu and you can continue working with the 1-2-3 commands. The Wysiwyg menu commands are available by typing a colon. The Wysiwyg commands let you change the appearance of the worksheet. These changes are not stored as part of the worksheet file but in a separate file with the same filename as the worksheet but with an .FM3 extension. When you retrieve a worksheet while Wysiwyg is loaded, Wysiwyg looks for a file with the same filename as the worksheet and an .FM3 extension to use for the Wysiwyg formatting information. When you save a file in 1-2-3, Wysiwyg also saves the Wysiwyg formatting in the file with the same filename and an .FM3 extension.

The screen when Wysiwyg is loaded has the same components as a 1-2-3 screen. One difference is the SmartIcons palette that appears on the right side as described in Chapter 2, "The Access System, Display, and Keyboard." Figure 15-1 provides a look at a screen after Wysiwyg is loaded and before Wysiwyg formatting changes are made to the worksheet. If you are using Release 3.4, this may look very familiar since Wysiwyg is set to automatically load with 1-2-3.

Just as in 1-2-3, the control panel comprises the top three lines of the screen. The only difference in the information displayed when Wysiwyg is loaded and when it is not loaded is that Wysiwyg displays descriptions about the Wysiwyg formats of the current cell next to the cell address. The formatting descriptions Wysiwyg will display may look something like this:

As you can see in the example, the entry is boldfaced, underlined, and uses the Swiss 24-point font. Information about the Wysiwyg formats is listed between the curly braces. A list of the format descriptions you may see is provided in Table 15-1.

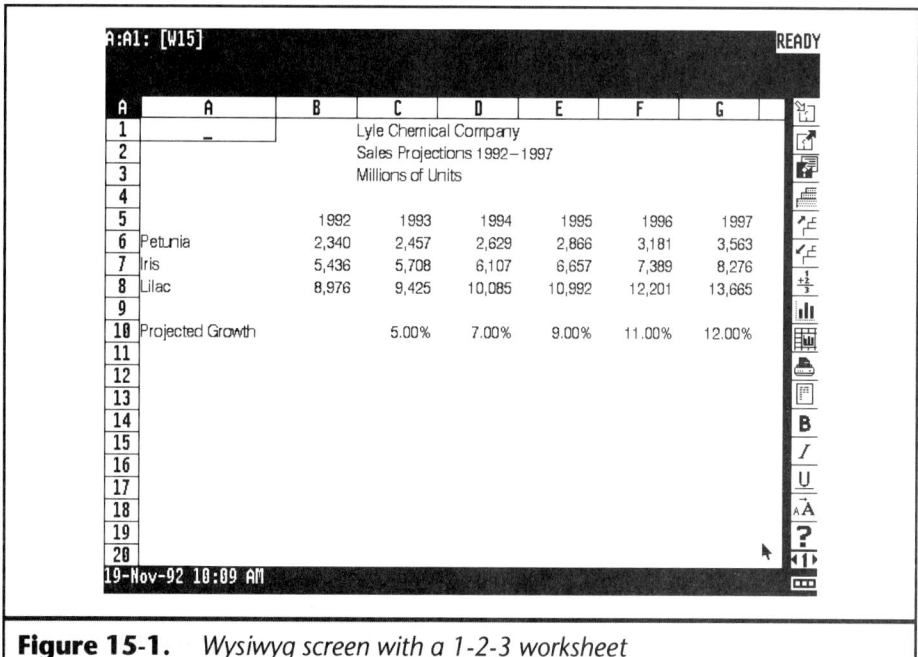

Figure 15-1. *Wysiwyg screen with a 1-2-3 worksheet*

Descriptions	Meaning
Bold	Cell's contents are boldfaced.
color1/color2	Color of text appears before the slash and background color is shown after the slash. If one of these two color choices uses the defaults, that part of the formatting description does not appear.
font	Font of cell is described in text. Examples are SWISS12, DUTCH14, and COURIER10.
Italics	Cell's contents are italicized.
LRTB	Lines appear on sides of cell. L indicates Left, R indicates Right, T indicates Top, and B indicates Bottom. These letters are combined to show which sides of the cells have lines, as in TL for a cell with a line at the top and left side.
S1, S2, or S3	Cell has light (S1), medium (S2), or dark (S3) shading.
U1, U2, or U3	Cell has single (U1), double (U2), or wide (U3) underlining.
Graph *name*	Cell is used by graph indicated by name.
Text	Cell is part of a text range.
MPage	Cell is at a manual page break.
Page	Cell is at an automatic page break.
H*points*	Height of row is set by the number of points.
Shadow	Cell is part of a range that has a shadow box drawn around it.
−	Negative numbers in the cell are shown in red.
named_style:	Cell uses named style format described by named_style.

Table 15-1. *Wysiwyg Format Descriptions*

You can invoke the Wysiwyg menu by typing a colon (:). Once the menu is on the screen, you can make a selection by using the arrow keys to highlight the desired selection and pressing ENTER. You can also type the first letter of any menu command or use the mouse to activate it. These are the same menu selection options for 1-2-3. If Wysiwyg presents another menu, you must make a second selection. In some cases it asks you to respond to a prompt to select an item from the list. Just as in 1-2-3, pressing ESC backs you out of the current activity by one menu level and CTRL-BREAK returns you to the READY mode.

Function keys work in the same way as they do with 1-2-3 alone. The only difference is F4 (ABS). As you will discover later, you can use F4 (ABS) to select a range for a Wysiwyg command before you activate the menu. Pressing F1 (HELP) displays help for Wysiwyg when the Wysiwyg menu displays, and help for 1-2-3 at other times.

Improving the Appearance of Worksheet Entries

1-2-3 has adequate print features if all you want is a simple printout of your worksheet. You can even use the /Print Printer Options Advanced commands to change the print attributes, such as the size and weight of the print. Now that most businesses have desktop publishing packages and access to word processing packages with desktop publishing features, the plain print achieved with 1-2-3's Print menus no longer seems state of the art.

Also, businesses have made major investments in printer technology. They have acquired laser printer and other sophisticated output devices and want to realize a full return on their investment in the output produced with this equipment. Although 1-2-3's Print menus allow you to use some of these features, 1-2-3 does not exploit print features to the fullest and is not as flexible as possible in allowing you to change the characteristics of the output on a cell-by-cell basis.

Wysiwyg is designed to improve the situation. It allows you to print financial numbers with the same pizzazz you use when creating a brochure or a sales presentation. The output you can create is equivalent to the desktop publishing output of word processing packages.

Using Different Fonts

A *font* is a typeface or character design of a particular style and size. Each typeface you select has an appearance that is different from other typefaces. The characters may be plain or may have many embellishments. Fonts without embellishments are referred to as *sans serif fonts*. Fonts with embellishments on the characters are referred to as *serif fonts*. Figure 15-2 shows the Dutch typeface, which is a serif font; the Swiss typeface, which is sans serif; and the Xsymbol font, which creates many characters that are not part of the standard character set. The Xsymbol characters are shown in a column in Appendix B, "LMBCS

Codes." Wysiwyg also has a Courier typeface, which is similar to the style that typewriters use. Depending on the printer you selected during installation, you may have other print styles supplied by your printer. You may also have fonts provided by other software that further increase the number of typefaces from which you can choose.

The size of a font is measured in *points*; each point is 1/72 of an inch. For example, a point size of 20 indicates that a character is twice as large as when the point size is 10. You can use point sizes between 3 and 72 points. Most users select 10 point for regular text, 5 point for fine print, and around 20 point for headings.

Choosing a Font Set

Each worksheet can use up to eight different fonts. You can use the eight default fonts that Wysiwyg initially provides or change them to other fonts. To see the current fonts, type :**FF** to select :Format Font. These eight fonts are assigned the numbers 1 through 8 and are shown in Figure 15-2 with examples of the different fonts. To leave this menu, you must assign a font to a range or select Quit. By default, all of the worksheet cells use font 1. You can use another font by

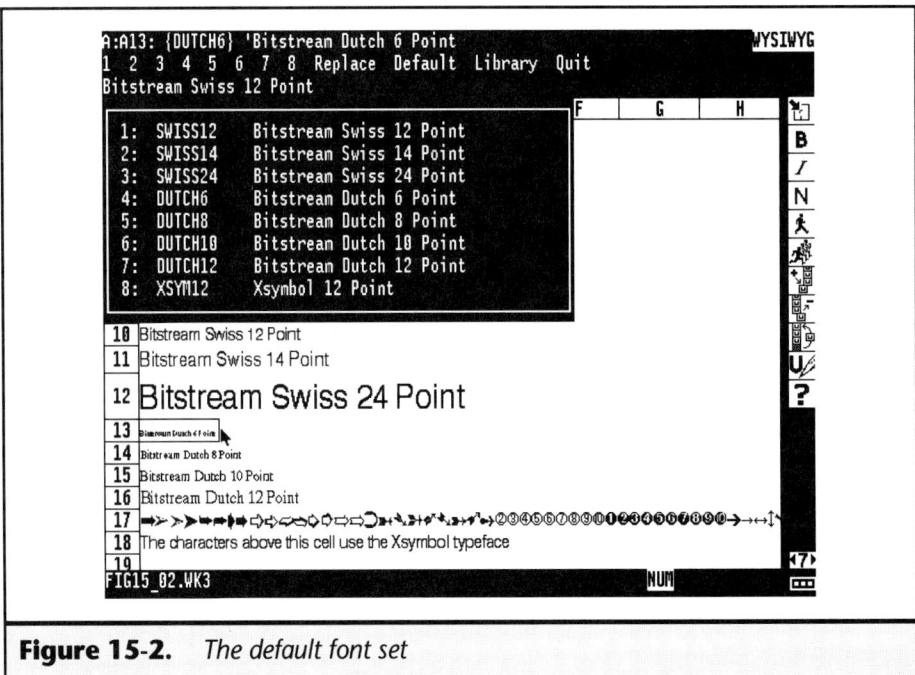

Figure 15-2. *The default font set*

selecting another font choice and telling Wysiwyg the ranges for applying the different font.

To change the font used by a range to another font in the selected font set, select :Format Font and the number of the font you want to use. For example, to change the font of C1 in Figure 15-1 to Swiss 24 point, move the cell pointer to C1, type **:** for the Wysiwyg menu, and type **F** twice to select Format and Font; then type **3** to select the third font. Wysiwyg prompts for the range to use with the font; press ENTER to select the current cell. Another option for selecting a range to format is to select the range before selecting the Wysiwyg command. This is especially useful if you will be using the same range for multiple Wysiwyg commands. For example, if you want to change the font of B5..G5 as well as boldface the text, move the cell pointer to B5 and press F4 (ABS). The control panel looks like this, indicating that you are selecting a range:

```
A:B5: (F0) 1992                                                    POINT
A:B5..A:B5
```

Press END and the RIGHT ARROW to select the range B5..G5. Now when you type **:FF2** to format the range with the second font, Wysiwyg will not prompt for a range, since a range is already selected. This will change the font of the range B5..G5. The range remains selected and you can then select the commands to boldface this range. When you move the cell pointer to a new location, this range will no longer be selected. Also, ranges that you select with F4 (ABS) are not automatically used for 1-2-3 commands. When you use a 1-2-3 command, you must supply a range each time 1-2-3 prompts for one. 1-2-3 will not use a range preselected with F4 (ABS).

With Release 3.4, you can select the Font icon to change the font used for the text in the selected range. To do so, first select the range you want to alter. Then select the Font icon shown below:

The range is now formatted for the next font from the current font library. The appearance of the entries depends on which font was current when you selected the Font icon.

You can use all eight fonts on a worksheet although this approach is not recommended. Too many fonts on one page distract the reader from the information presented. It creates a busy effect and detracts from the successful communication of information. Three different font sizes on one worksheet is a good guideline that should not normally be exceeded. You might use all eight fonts when you have several reports on the same worksheet and each report uses different fonts.

Changing the Available Fonts

While you can have only eight fonts in a worksheet, you can define which eight fonts the worksheet will use. You must give up the use of one of the existing fonts when you select a new font for the current set since there can never be any more than eight fonts in one set. You can enter :**Format Font Replace** and select the number of the font you wish to replace. Wysiwyg presents a list of all the typefaces—such as Swiss, Dutch, Courier, Xsymbol, or Other. If you select Other, you must select one of the typefaces in the list that Wysiwyg displays. Next, select the point size that you want by typing a number between 3 and 72. This updates the font listed below the :Format Font menu. Fonts in the worksheet that use the font you replaced will use its replacement. For example, if you change font 1, all worksheet cells that do not use another font will use the new font selected for font 1.

When you change the current font set, the change is effective immediately and stays in effect until you make another change or end the current session. The font settings are saved with the worksheet files that you use with them. If you want to change the default font set that is loaded at the beginning of each new Wysiwyg session you must select Default and Update to make the current font selections the defaults. At any time you can also elect to replace the current font set with the default font set by selecting :Format Font Default Restore. If you never change the default font set, the default font is the one shipped with Wysiwyg.

Creating a Library of Font Sets

Since each application may require a unique combination of fonts, Wysiwyg allows you to create a library of named font sets and retrieve any font set from this library. The library can consist of as many font sets as you need to meet a variety of printing needs. To make the current font set a library font file, enter :**Format Font Library Save** and a valid filename. These files have an .AF3 extension. When you want to make the fonts in a library font file the current font set, select :Format Font Library Retrieve and the name of the library font file. To remove a font set you no longer need, you can select :Format Font Library Erase and specify the name of a library font file.

Adding Boldface

If you want to highlight text in certain cells, you can add bold to these cells with the :Format Bold command. You can select the range to boldface before or after selecting the :Format Bold command. Selecting Set after :Format Bold adds boldface to the text in the range, and selecting Clear removes boldface from the text in the range. Figure 15-3 shows boldface added to B5..G5.

Instead of using the :Format Bold command with Release 3.4, you can use the Bold icon from the SmartIcons palette. First, select the range containing the text you want to boldface. Next, select the Bold icon shown here:

If the text is already formatted as bold, then selecting this icon removes bold from the selected range.

Adding Italics

If you want to emphasize the text in certain cells, Wysiwyg can help you by italicizing the contents of those cells. To do this, select the :Format Italics command. You can select the range to italicize before selecting this command, or after. If you select Clear, you remove the Italics format from the selected cells.

If you are using Release 3.4, you can use the Italics icon from the SmartIcons palette instead of selecting the :Format Italics command. To use this icon, first select the range of cells which you want to italicize. Then select the Italics icon shown here:

If the text is already italicized, then selecting this icon removes italics from the selected range.

Adding Underlining

Wysiwyg also allows you to add three styles of underlining to cells. Wysiwyg underlines only the text within a selected range; it does not place the underline marks under blank areas in the selected cells. To add underlining, select :Format Underline; then select Single, Double, Wide, or Clear. Single adds a narrow line below cell entries; Double adds two narrow lines below cell entries; Wide adds a wide line below cell entries; and Clear removes any underlining added with the three other options. Like other :Format commands, you can select the range to use with this command before you activate the menu to select :Format Underline or after you select Single, Double, Wide, or Clear. Figure 15-3 shows the Wysiwyg screen after single underlining was added to the heading in C1.

You can also use two of the SmartIcons with Release 3.4 as a shortcut when you are underlining text in a range. Select the range that includes the text that you want to underline. Then select either the Single Underline (top) or the Double Underline (bottom) icon shown below:

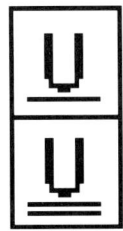

If you choose one of these two icons and the range is already formatted for that feature, the formatting is removed.

Adding Lines

Lines and boxes can help set off information in the worksheet from other entries. Wysiwyg has several different options for adding lines to a worksheet. Figure 15-4 shows a worksheet where the different types of lines are used. These lines are added by selecting :Format Lines and one of the options. Like other :Format commands, you can select the range to work with either before you select :Format or after you select one of the options for the lines to add. The Top, Bottom, Left, and Right options add lines to the top, bottom, left, and right sides of cells. Adding a line to the top of a cell is the same as adding it to the bottom of the cell above it. Adding a line to the right edge of a cell is the same as adding a line to the left edge of the cell in the next column. Selecting All adds lines to all four sides of the cells. Selecting Outline adds lines to the edge of the range selected. Each of these six options draws a single narrow line.

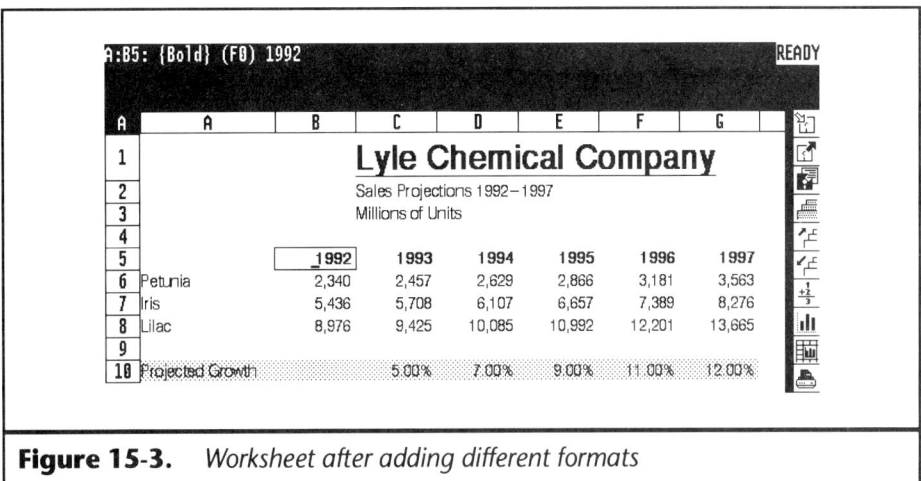

Figure 15-3. *Worksheet after adding different formats*

The Double and Wide options draw double lines and wide lines. If you select Double or Wide, you must also select from Top, Bottom, Left, Right, All, or Outline to indicate where you want the double or wide lines placed. You can remove some or all of the lines added with any of these options by selecting Clear and then Top, Bottom, Left, Right, All, or Outline to select the lines to clear. The last option, Shadow, draws a box with a shadow around a range (see the shadow box around A2..G4 of Figure 15-4). This box is added by selecting Set after selecting Shadow. To remove a shadow box, select :Format Lines Shadow Clear.

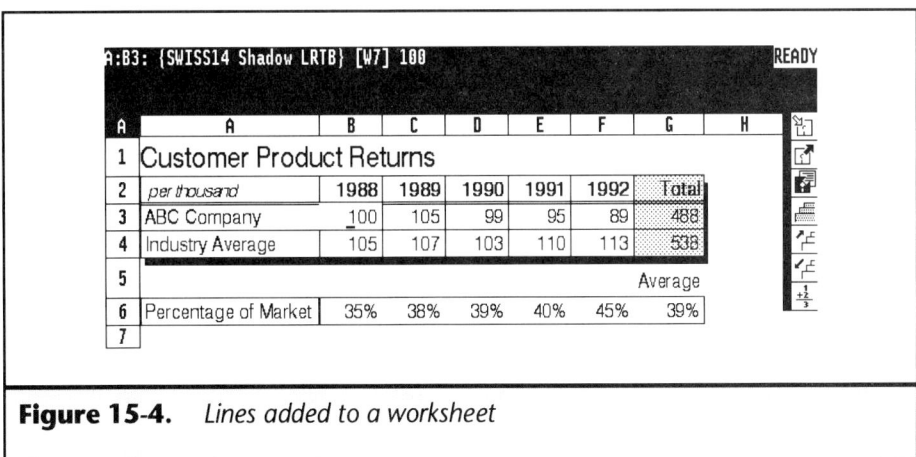

Figure 15-4. *Lines added to a worksheet*

If you are using Release 3.4, you will find two SmartIcons that can help you add lines to your worksheet. One is the Shadow icon (top) and the other is the Outline icon (bottom); the two are shown here:

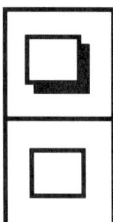

To use these icons, you need to select the range you want to affect, and then select the icon. When you select the Shadow icon, the selected range is outlined, and a drop-shadow appears at the bottom and right side of the outline. When you select the Outline icon, the entire range is outlined with a single, double, or wide line, or no line at all, depending on whether there had been any outline formatting previously applied to that range. Continued clicking on the Outline icon cycles through all of the options.

Adding Color

You can add color to your output if you have a printer or screen that supports colors. In addition you can also display negative numbers in a different color. You can use colors to emphasize information that needs more attention.

To set the color of a range, use the :Format Colors command. You can select the range to change either before selecting :Format or after completing the selections for one of the :Format Colors command options. By selecting the Text option, you are changing the color of the text that is stored in the selected range (even if the text extends into the display space of other cells). If you select the Background option, you are changing the background color of the cells (rather than the background color of the text). For these two options, your choices are Normal, Red, Green, Dark-Blue, Cyan, Magenta, and Yellow. Another option is to select Reverse, which switches the colors for the text and background. By selecting Negative, you can select Normal (which displays negative numbers using the normal color) or Red (which displays negative numbers in red). The final option, Quit, returns you to the READY mode.

If you are using Release 3.4, you can also change text and background color using icons from the SmartIcons palettes. First you need to select the range to be affected by this formatting. Then select either the Color Text (top) or Color Background (bottom) icon shown here:

Chapter 15: Using the Wysiwyg Add-In   **875**

When you select one of these icons, the color of either the text or the cell, depending on which icon you selected, changes to the next color on the list given above. Continued selection of the icon cycles through the other options.

Adding Shading

Shading can be used to create a backdrop for a graph or can be added to information enclosed within boxes. You can choose light, dark, or solid shading. In most cases light shading is more effective when the cells to be shaded contain data. It is much easier to read the text in the file when the shading is light. Figure 15-3 shows a worksheet that uses light shading to emphasize a range of data. To add shading, select :Format Shade and one of Light, Dark, Solid, or Clear to add or remove shading to or from a range. Select the range either before selecting :Format or after selecting one of the four options.

With Release 3.4, you can add shading using this Shade icon from the SmartIcons palette:

To add shading using this icon, first select the range that you want to shade, then select the Shade icon. When you select this icon, the selected range is shaded light, dark, solid, or not at all, depending on how the range was shaded before you selected the icon. Continuing to select this icon causes Wysiwyg to cycle through all of the options.

Removing Formats

Most of the format options that you select in Wysiwyg can be undone by the same command that added the format but by selecting a different option. If you have several formats that you want to remove, you may want to use the :Format Reset command and select a range to reset all Wysiwyg formats (unless you select a range before selecting :Format Reset). This command removes all Wysiwyg format enhancements and returns the font of the selected range to font 1. This command does not affect 1-2-3 formats and formats that are entered directly into a cell.

If you are using Release 3.4, you can use this Normal icon as a shortcut for removing all Wysiwyg formatting from a cell:

Simply select the range of cells from which you want to remove all Wysiwyg formatting. Then select the Normal icon. All Wysiwyg formatting is removed from the selected range. This does not include any formatting that is typed directly into the cell, such as the codes for bold and other formats described in the section "Adding Formats to Text in Entries," and does not affect any 1-2-3 formatting codes.

Using Named Format Styles

Besides adding each format you want individually, you can group a set of formats into a named style and apply the named style to a range, rather than applying the :Format commands that produce the formatting represented. As an example, suppose you are setting several ranges to use boldface and the sixth font. You can use the :Format Bold and :Format Font 6 commands to add the formatting to one range and use a cell from the range to define the named style. The next time you want to boldface and set the font to font 6 for a range, you can apply the named range and both formats will be applied automatically.

To define a named style, move the cell pointer to a cell containing the formats you want associated with a named style. Select :Named-Style Define and a number between 1 and 8 as the number you want to define. When Wysiwyg prompts for a cell to use for the definition, press ENTER to select the current cell, or select another cell to use. If you selected a range before selecting :Named-Style, Wysiwyg uses the first cell of the selected range. Next, type up to six characters for the name of the named style and press ENTER; then type up to 37 characters for a description and press ENTER.

To use a named style, move the cell pointer to the first cell where you want to apply it. Select :Named-Style and the number (1 through 8) of the named style you want to apply. The description of each format appears on the third line of the control panel screen. Finally, select the range that will use the named style (unless you selected a range before you selected :Named-Style).

As an example, you can define a named style that boldfaces and underlines text. First, go to a cell and press F4 (ABS) (so that Wysiwyg commands will automatically use this as the range); then select :Format Bold Set and :Format Underline Single. Next, select :Named-Style Define 1 to change the first named style. Press ESC to remove Normal; type **B&U** for the style name; press ENTER; type **Boldface and underline** for the description; and press ENTER again. To use this style, move the cell pointer to the first cell to use these two formats and select :Named-Style 1:B&U. Then select the range that you want to boldface and underline.

Using Text Ranges and Adding Formats to Text

With Wysiwyg you can treat a worksheet range as a text range, which allows you to use the range as if you are using a word processor. When you use text ranges, you can enter the text directly onto the worksheet and see how it will appear within the selected range. You can also use the text alignment options to alter the alignment of the text within the range. Another command you can use while working with text ranges lets you reformat the range, which is like reformatting a paragraph in a word processor. All of the :Text commands you use to work with text ranges will operate on all sheets in a worksheet file if GROUP mode is enabled. Other features of Wysiwyg that make it similar to a word processor are the formatting features described earlier for text within a label entry. For example, you can boldface and italicize parts of an entry.

Entering and Editing a Text Range

Creating and using a text range is as simple as selecting the range to treat as text, and entering or editing the text in the range. To select the range to use as a text range, select :Text Set and the range. The range should be as wide as you want the labels to extend in each line. You may also want to include additional rows so that the text has room to expand if needed. If the range you select is too small for the text you enter, you will see an error message, indicating that the text range is full. The text is actually stored in the first column of the range although the entries use the entire range to display. If the range already has entries, the entries will use the alignment of the first label in the range.

When you are ready to enter or edit text in the range, select :Text Edit. With a mouse you can also edit a text range by double clicking one of the cells in the text range with the left mouse button. Wysiwyg will suggest the text range that contains the cell pointer or the last text range edited. You can either accept this range or select a different range. When you are editing the text, your entries are made directly to the worksheet rather than in the control panel, as shown here:

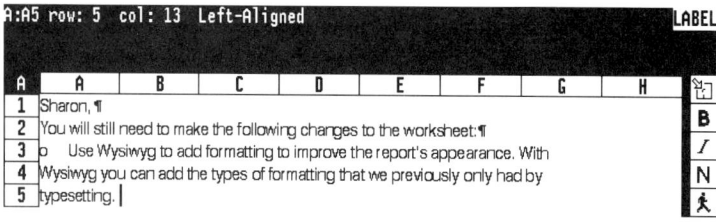

This means that if you make a mistake while entering text, you cannot press ESC to start over. Wysiwyg also handles word wrapping, which moves the cursor to the next line when the current line is full. While you are editing the text, the editing keys behave more like they do in a word processing package. Table 15-2 lists the editing keys that you can use while editing a text range. Figure 15-5 shows a text range. Notice how the control panel displays {Text} to indicate that the cell pointer is on a cell that is part of a text range. Later, when you learn how to add graphs to a worksheet range, you will find that the graphs change into shaded areas during editing and Wysiwyg wraps the text around the graph.

Changing the Alignment of a Text Range

After you have entered the text range, you may want to try some of the different alignments that Wysiwyg provides for text ranges. Unlike label prefixes, text range prefixes align the entries in a range rather than in a cell. To change the alignment of a text range, select :Text Align and then Left, Right, Center, or Even. The Left, Right, and Center options are like 1-2-3's alignment choices, enabling you to left justify, right justify, and center labels. The Even option adds spaces between words in the labels so that both the left and right sides are aligned for all lines except the last. After choosing one of the options, select the range of text to align. Figure 15-6 shows text ranges that use the different alignments.

Chapter 15: Using the Wysiwyg Add-In

Key	Effect
LEFT ARROW	Moves cursor one character left
RIGHT ARROW	Moves cursor one character right
DOWN ARROW	Moves cursor one line down
UP ARROW	Moves cursor one line up
CTRL-LEFT ARROW	Moves cursor to beginning of previous word
CTRL-RIGHT ARROW	Moves cursor to beginning of next word
CTRL-ENTER	Ends current paragraph (with a paragraph symbol) and starts a new one
DEL	Deletes character to the right of cursor
END	Moves cursor to the end of the line when pressed once and moves cursor to the end of the paragraph when pressed again
ENTER	Moves cursor to the next line
ESC	Stops editing text range and returns to READY mode
F3	Displays menu to add formats to a text range
HOME	Moves cursor to the beginning of the line when pressed once and moves cursor to the beginning of the paragraph when pressed again
INS	Switches between insert and overstrike mode
PGUP	Moves to top or upper screen of text range
PGDN	Moves to bottom or next screen of text range

Table 15-2. *Editing Keys for Editing a Text Range*

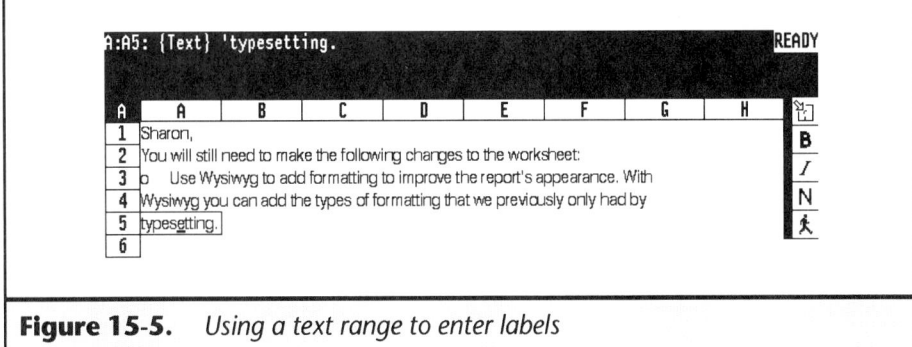

Figure 15-5. *Using a text range to enter labels*

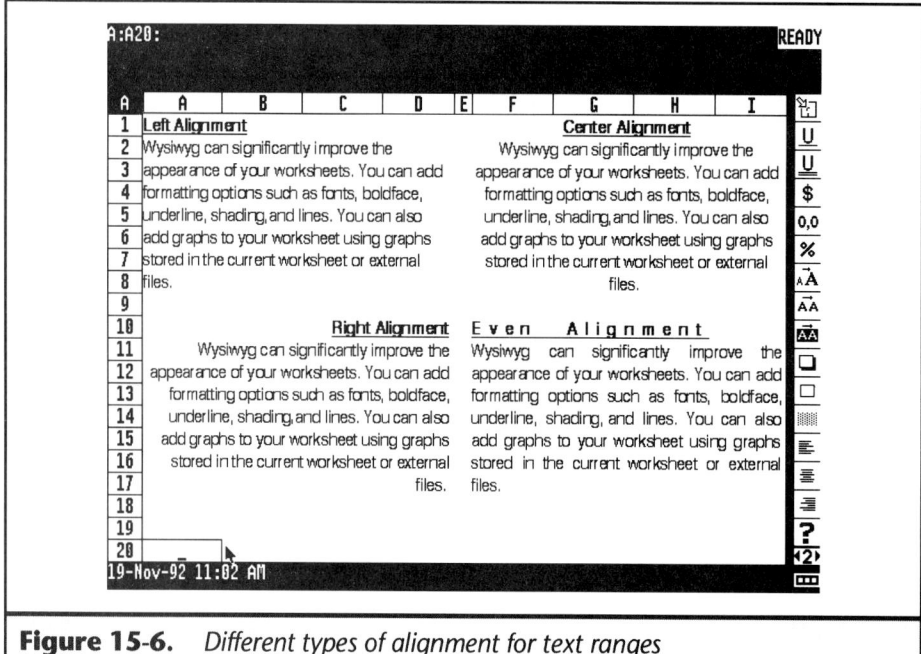

Figure 15-6. *Different types of alignment for text ranges*

You can create a Wysiwyg text range, or change the alignment of a text range by using the Text Align icon. Before selecting this icon, shown here:

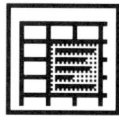

select either a range of cells in which you want to create a text range, or a range of cells which are already formatted as text. If the cell or range of cells which you select is not formatted for text, then selecting this icon formats them as text. If the cell is formatted as text but is empty, the text format is removed. If the cell is formatted for text and contains an entry, then the alignment of the text changes.

You can edit a text range by using the Text Edit icon. To do so, place the cell pointer in a cell within a text range, or select a range of cells and use the icon shown here:

If the range is not already a text range, the selected range will now become one and you can immediately begin editing text in it.

Reformatting a Text Range

As you are editing a text range, you may want to rearrange the text in it. This is especially the case when you are making an existing range of labels into a text range and you want to rearrange the labels to look like a paragraph. Also, as you edit the text in a text range, the text will no longer fit into each cell and you will want to readjust the text that appears in each label. A third use is if you use F2 (EDIT) to alter an entry in a text range. The :Text Reformat command reformats the text in a text range to use the worksheet area you select. After selecting :Text Reformat, select the range. Unlike the 1-2-3 /Range Justify command, you must select all the rows you want to reformat as well as the columns the text should be distributed over (assuming that the total width is less than 512 characters). Also unlike the /Range Justify command, the :Text Reformat command maintains your separate paragraphs.

Paragraphs are indicated by the paragraph symbol, which you add by pressing CTRL-ENTER to start a new paragraph; a blank line separating paragraphs; or a line that starts with a space. The :Text Reformat command also provides different results from the /Range Justify command since the :Text Reformat command takes into account the font size of the characters and any special formatting you add to the text (as described in the next section). Figure 15-7 shows a text range in two places, where the top shows the text as it was

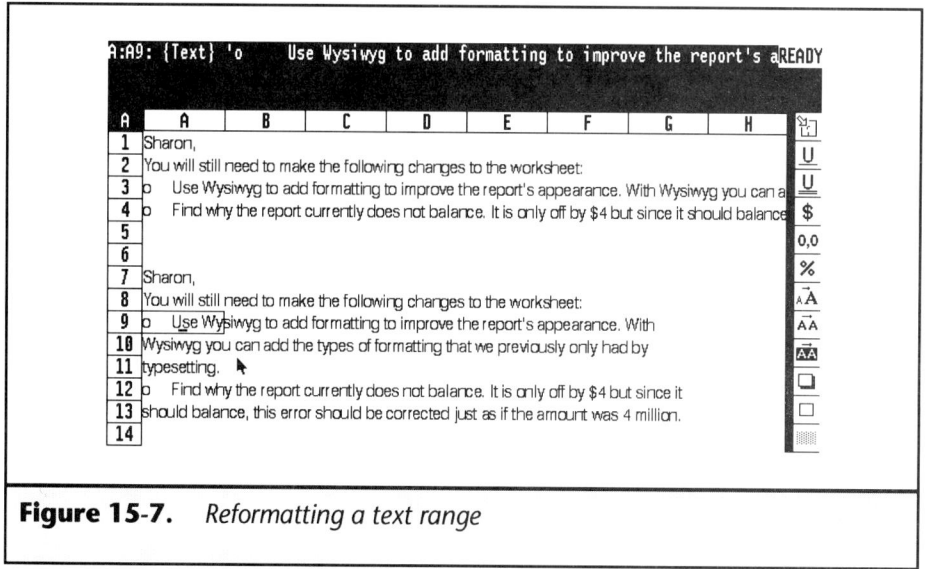

Figure 15-7. *Reformatting a text range*

before selecting :Text Reformat, and the bottom half has the :Text Reformat command applied to it.

Adding Formats to Text in Entries

Besides using formatting such as fonts, boldface, and italics with :Format commands that apply to entire cells, you can also use these formats within a cell entry. While these examples use text ranges as results, you can add formatting to text in text ranges or labels although the steps are slightly different.

To add formatting to text in a text range, position the cursor before the character where you want the format to begin and press F3. This displays a menu containing Font, Bold, Italics, Underline, Color, + (for superscript), − (for subscript), Outline, and Normal. To add one of these formatting options, select the format to add. If you select Font, you must also select a number between 1 and 8 that represents the font you want to use. If you select Color, you must then select from Normal, Red, Green, Dark-Blue, Cyan, Yellow, or Magenta. When you change a format option, Wysiwyg adds a formatting sequence that will appear in the control panel during READY mode when the cell is highlighted. When you add a format attribute, Wysiwyg adds the formatting sequence to the end of the cell entry that will cancel the formatting sequence. For example, if you change the font to font 4 in the middle of a cell in a text range, Wysiwyg adds the formatting sequence for font 4 in the middle of the cell and the sequence to stop using font 4 at the end of the cell. To end a format before the end of a cell, move the cursor to where you want the format to end, press F3, and select Normal.

The other method of adding formatting to text in a label is to directly enter the formatting sequences. This can be done either in a text range or when entering a label in EDIT or LABEL mode. To enter a formatting sequence, press CTRL-A and type one of the codes that appear in Table 15-3. These codes are case sensitive so you must use the same case that appears in the table. To stop using one of the formatting options, press CTRL-E and type the code you originally entered to add the formatting option. For example, suppose you want to boldface and underline "twenty percent" in

This report assumes twenty percent growth.

First, move the cursor to the first *t* in "twenty." Press CTRL-A and type **b** to add boldface, and then press CTRL-A and type **1_** to add underlining. Next, move to just after the *t* in "percent." Press CTRL-E and type **b** to stop boldface, and then press CTRL-E and type **1_** to stop underlining. The final result looks like this:

This report assumes **twenty percent** growth.

Code	Format Added
b	Boldface
d	Subscript
i	Italics
u	Superscript
x	Text is backwards (flipped on its x-axis)
y	Text is upside down (flipped on its y-axis)
1_	Single underlining
2_	Double underlining
3_	Wide underlining
4_	Outline around characters
5_	Strike through characters
1c to 8c	Text is in a different color; the numbers 1 through 8 represent the colors Normal (set with :Display Colors Text), Red, Green, Dark-Blue, Cyan, Yellow, and Magenta
1F to 8F	Font selected; the numbers 1 through 8 represent the eight fonts available with :Format Font
1o to 255o	Outline of characters; the higher the number the greater the distance between the sets of lines in the outline

Table 15-3. *Formatting Sequences*

When you edit this cell, this appears in the control panel:

```
A:A1: 'This report assumes ▲b▲1_twenty percent▲0b▲01_ growth.                EDIT
```

The ▲b, ▲1_, ▲0b, and ▲ 01_ are the formatting sequences that indicate when the formats should start and stop. You can remove formatting sequences by deleting them just as you delete other characters in an entry. Since these formatting sequences are part of the entry, you do not want to use cells containing them with the /Range Name Labels command or as part of a range you are sorting with the /Data Sort command.

Removing a Text Range

As you work with a worksheet that includes text ranges, you may need to remove some of them. For example, if a paragraph you added to the end of a report no longer applies, you may want to use /Range Erase to erase the entries and then tell Wysiwyg that you no longer want to use the range as a text range. To stop using a range as a text range, select :Text Clear and the range to clear. The :Text Clear command does not erase any worksheet data (including the text stored in each cell) or any formatting you have added to the labels. Once you use the :Text Clear command, any alignment set with :Text Align disappears and the labels in the range use the default alignment.

Copying, Moving, and Importing Formats

Besides adding Wysiwyg formats to worksheet cells, you can also copy and move them to new locations. The 1-2-3 /Copy and /Move commands will copy both the data and the Wysiwyg formats to a new location. Wysiwyg has :Special Copy and :Special Move commands with which you can copy and move Wysiwyg formats to new locations without copying or moving the worksheet data. These two Wysiwyg commands copy only Wysiwyg formats; they will not copy 1-2-3 formats, graphics (described later), or worksheet data. Wysiwyg also has commands that let you export and import Wysiwyg formats to and from format files. These commands let you apply formats from one range to other ranges.

The :Special Copy and :Special Move commands are similar to the 1-2-3 /Copy and /Move commands. After selecting either :Special Copy or :Special Move, select the range containing the Wysiwyg formats you want to copy or move. If you select a range before activating the Wysiwyg menu, Wysiwyg will use this range as the From range. Next, select the first cell of the range where you want the formats copied or moved. With :Special Copy, you can select an expanded range as the To range when you want to make several copies of the formats. As an example of the :Special Copy command, suppose you want to copy the font, boldface, and underlining in C1 of this worksheet:

```
A:C1: {SWISS24 Bold U1} 'Lyle Chemical Company                    READY

    A        B        C        D        E        F        G
1                     Lyle Chemical Company                              U
2                     Sales Projections 1992–1997                        U
3                     Millions of Units                                  $
```

To copy this format to C2..C3, select **:Special Copy**, press ENTER to use C1 as the From range, press the DOWN ARROW, type a period, press the DOWN ARROW again, and press ENTER to use C2..C3 as the To range. The resulting worksheet looks like this:

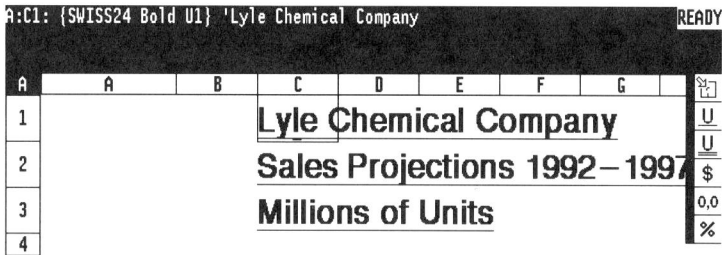

Another method of transferring Wysiwyg formats is to export them to or import them from another format file. The format files are the files with the .FM3 extension that Wysiwyg uses to store formatting descriptions for a worksheet. As an example, suppose you have two worksheet files that use the same formats. If you want to make the same changes to the formats in each file, you have to repeat the Wysiwyg commands twice. Another option is to make the changes in one of the two files. Once the changes are made, you can export the changed format file to the unchanged one or import the changed format file into the unchanged one.

To see how importing and exporting works, suppose you have the DIV_SALE and SALEPROJ worksheet files shown in Figure 15-8 and you want to apply the Wysiwyg formats from the SALEPROJ worksheet to the DIV_SALE worksheet. After saving both files, switch to the SALEPROJ worksheet file, select **:Special Export**, and type **DIV_SALE** as the name of the format file to export. The format file has the same name as the worksheet to which the formats apply. Another option (after saving the two worksheet files) is to switch to the DIV_SALE worksheet and select the :Special Import All command and SALEPROJ.FM3 as the format file to import. The result is shown in Figure 15-9.

When you import a format file, you can select whether you want to import all the Wysiwyg formats (All), just the named styles (Named-Styles), the font set (Fonts), or the graphs added to the worksheet (Graphs). The last option adds the graphs in the format file to the current worksheet rather than replacing the graphs in the current worksheet with the graphs in the imported format file. When you import and export graphs, graphs contained in the current worksheet and named graphs in the worksheet are not transferred, but their position and any enhancements are transferred. (Using Wysiwyg with named styles and graphs is covered later in the chapter.) When importing and exporting formats, the two worksheet files involved should have the same design, since the location of the imported or exported format is the same in both worksheets. If the design

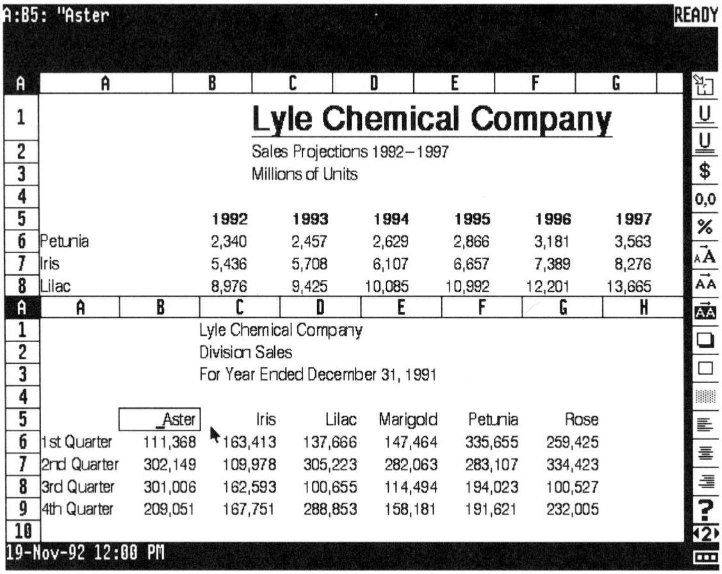

Figure 15-8. Worksheets with different formats

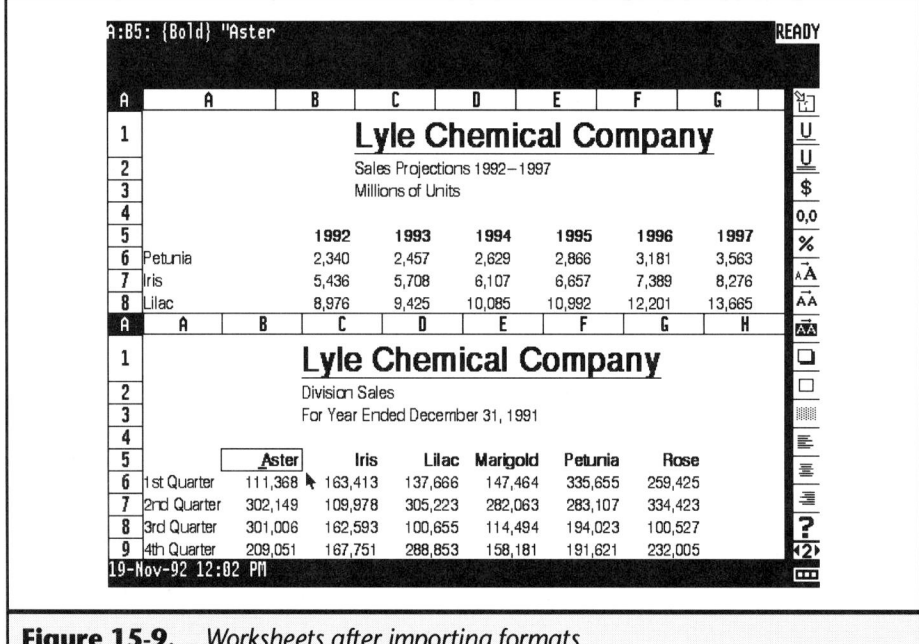

Figure 15-9. Worksheets after importing formats

of the worksheet is different, you may have the formats applied to different cells from those you intended.

These two commands can also use format files in other formats. While omitting a file extension in the filename defaults to using .FM3, you can also use .ALL to use an Allways format file or .FMT to use an Impress format file. These other format files are for working with other 1-2-3 add-ins that provide some of the spreadsheet publishing features available in Wysiwyg. When you use Allways or Impress format files, you can only import and export formatting features that are common between Wysiwyg and Allways or Impress. For example, if you export the formats to an Allways format file, you will notice these changes:

- Changes made with :Format Color Background, :Format Lines Shadow, :Display Colors, :Graph Settings Opaque, :Print Layout Compression, and :Print Settings Frame have no effect.

- Lines added with :Format Lines Double (Left, Right, and Top) and :Format Lines Wide are saved as single lines while lines added with :Format Lines Double Bottom are saved as double underlining.

- Named styles are lost.

- Only .PIC graphs added to a worksheet are recorded in the Allways format file.

- Graph enhancements made with :Graph Edit are removed.

- Text ranges are treated as labels.

Changing Column Widths and Row Heights

Column widths and row heights can be set in either of two ways. In 1-2-3, column widths can be set with the 1-2-3 /Worksheet Column commands or the Wysiwyg :Worksheet Column command. The :Worksheet Column command is just like the /Worksheet Column Column-Range command. When you select :Worksheet Column Set-Width, select the range of columns to change and then enter the number of characters wide you want the columns. The column widths are the number of characters wide (between 0 and 240), using the width of the characters of font 1 rather than the fonts that the entries in the columns use. The :Worksheet Column Reset-Width command returns a range of columns that you select to the global column width set by the /Worksheet Global Col-Width command.

Row heights are either set automatically by Wysiwyg to match the height of the text using the fonts you select or by the :Worksheet Row Wysiwyg command. When you select :Worksheet Row Set-Width, select the range containing the rows to change and enter the number of points for the new row height. You can also use the UP ARROW and DOWN ARROW to increment the row heights a point at a time. To use Wysiwyg's default row heights, which are based on the height of the fonts used in the row, select :Worksheet Row Auto and the range containing the rows to let Wysiwyg set the height. With both the :Worksheet Column and :Worksheet Row commands, if GROUP mode is enabled, the changes are applied to every worksheet in the worksheet file.

You can also use the mouse for changing row height and column width in Wysiwyg. Simply point the mouse to the line dividing the columns or rows. Drag the mouse. (This drags the line as well.) When you release the mouse, the row or column adjusts to fit where you moved the separation line.

Changing the Wysiwyg Display

Wysiwyg provides a number of options for altering the appearance of the display. These options change how 1-2-3 and Wysiwyg appear on the screen but do not change the appearance of the worksheet in the way that the :Format commands do. Most of the options affecting the display can be found under the menu option :Display. The options you select with the :Display commands do not affect your print output. They are designed to allow you to customize the presentation of information on the screen to meet your needs. When you are ready to leave the :Display menu to return to READY mode, you can select Quit.

The only 1-2-3 command that changes the screen appearance is the /Worksheet Window Display command. If you have selected two Display drivers in the Install program as described in Appendix A, "Installing 1-2-3," this command selects which of the two drivers 1-2-3 and Wysiwyg will use. For example, you can select one Display driver for color and another for monochrome. When you want to switch to the monochrome display, you can select /Worksheet Window Display 2. To return to the primary display driver, select /Worksheet Window Display 1.

Graphics Versus Text Mode

A big advantage of Wysiwyg is that it displays your spreadsheet as it will appear when you use Wysiwyg to print. This feature requires that your computer and monitor are capable of displaying graphics. Some monitors can display only text, which means that although you can alter the worksheet format and print it using Wysiwyg's features, the worksheet on the screen looks like the standard 1-2-3 screen.

If you have a graphics monitor you can choose how you want your worksheets displayed. Wysiwyg has three options. First, you can display it in text mode, which means that the worksheet does not appear as it will print. The text mode uses the standard 1-2-3 fonts, attributes such as boldface and underlining will not appear, and added graphs do not appear on the worksheet display. The control panel will continue to display the format descriptions of the formats that are applied to the cell. To use the text mode, select :Display Mode Text. To display Wysiwyg using the default graphics mode, select :Display Mode Graphics and the worksheet will appear as it will be printed. For graphics display modes, you have two choices: you can display the worksheet using colors or using only black and white. To use colors, select :Display Mode Color. To use only black and white, select :Display Mode B&W.

Changing Colors

If you are using a color monitor with Wysiwyg, you can select from a rainbow of colors for your display. You can set the color of the various worksheet components with the :Display Colors commands. These options let you select the color for the background, the text, the unprotected cells, the cell pointer, the grid, the frame (the border of row numbers and column letters), negative numbers, the lines that you add with :Format Lines, and the drop shadow added with :Format Lines Shadow. To change the colors used by the worksheet, select :Display Colors and an option from Background, Text, Unprot, Cell-Pointer, Grid, Frame, Neg, Lines, or Shadow. For these nine options you can select from Black, White, Red, Green, Dark-Blue, Cyan, Yellow, or Magenta. The Neg option changes only the color of the negative numbers that appear on the screen. Commands like :Format Color Negative and /Range Format Other Color change the color used to display and print negative numbers.

You can also change the eight colors. For example, you may want to use a lighter blue for the Dark-Blue selection. To change the colors that the eight color selections represent, select Replace and the color you want to change. Wysiwyg displays the color number of the current color, which is a number between 0 and 63. You can either type the number of the color you want or use the LEFT ARROW and RIGHT ARROW to switch through the numbers. When you finish replacing the colors you want, select Quit to return to the :Display Colors menu. The :Display Colors menu is a sticky menu; you must select Quit to return to the :Display menu.

Zooming In and Out

Wysiwyg has several different display sizes. You can zoom in to your worksheet to see the cells up close. You can zoom out to see how the worksheet appears without printing it. Like the other :Display menu commands, zooming in or out does not affect the printed output.

When you select :Display Zoom, you can choose from the options of Tiny, Small, Normal, Large, Huge, or Manual. Tiny displays the worksheet at 63% of its normal size; Small displays it at 87% of its normal size; Normal displays it at its normal size; Large displays it at 125% of normal size; and Huge displays it at 150% of its normal size. With Manual, you can enter a number representing the percentage of its normal size at which you want to view the worksheet. Enter a number between 25 and 400, where numbers below 100 display the worksheet entries smaller than their actual size and numbers greater than 100 display the worksheet entries larger than their actual size.

Another option for setting the size of the cell entries that appear on your screen is to set the number of rows that appear on the screen. When you change the number of rows that appear on your screen, you are changing the height of the displayed entries without changing their width. To set the number of worksheet rows that Wysiwyg displays, select :Display Rows and enter a number between 16 and 60 for the number of rows to display. Wysiwyg may actually display more or less depending on the graphics display card and the size of the default font.

With Release 3.4, you can select the Zoom icon from the SmartIcons palette to invoke this command. When you do so, the display changes to the next zoom setting, depending on how it is currently formatted. This means it will move from normal to large, from huge to tiny, or from small to normal. You will not have the option of setting the percentage of zoom manually if you use the Zoom icon.

Setting the Appearance of the Cell Pointer

Wysiwyg has two ways to indicate the cell pointer. The default is a solid rectangle. You can change this to an outline of the current cell, like the cell pointer in C2 shown in Figure 15-10. To change the cell pointer's appearance, select: Display Options Cell-Pointer. Next, select Solid to display the cell pointer as a solid rectangle or Outline to display the cell pointer as an outline around the current cell.

Setting the Appearance of the Worksheet Frame

Another change you can make to the Wysiwyg display is to change how the frame appears. The frame is the bar with the column letters and row numbers at the top and left of the worksheet. Wysiwyg has several options for how this frame will appear. To try the other frame display options, select :Display Options Frame. This command has five options: 1-2-3, Enhanced, Relief, Special, and None. 1-2-3 displays a frame similar to the 1-2-3 frame when Wysiwyg is not loaded, where there are no lines indicating where each column or row begins or ends. Enhanced is the default Wysiwyg frame that you see in most of this book's figures. The Relief option displays a frame that has a three-dimensional look as well as changing the cyan (light blue) on the screen to grey.

The Special option creates a frame that measures distances in terms of inches; centimeters; characters; or points and picas. If you select Special, you must select Characters, Inches, Metric, or Points/Picas. Selecting Characters creates a frame that indicates the number of characters across and lines down. Selecting Inches creates a frame that indicates the number of inches across and down. Selecting Metric creates a frame that indicates the number of centimeters across and down. Selecting Points/Picas creates a frame that indicates the number of points across and down. You can use the Inches and Metric options to determine how the worksheet will be placed on the page since Wysiwyg keeps track of the width of each column and the height of each row. Finally, None removes any frame

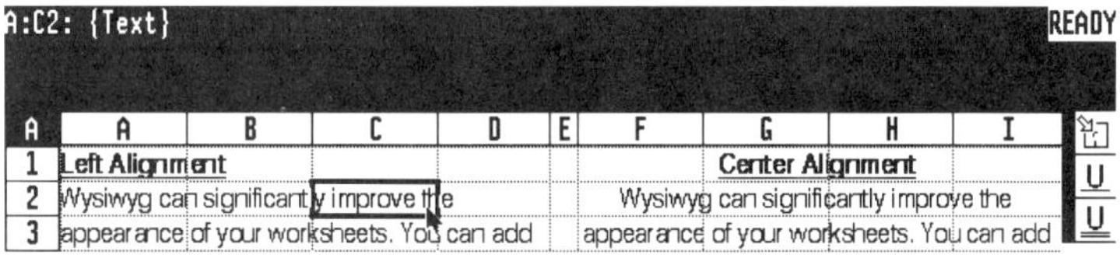

Figure 15-10. *Changing the display of the cell pointer*

created by the another option. Figure 15-11 shows some frames created by the different options.

Showing Grid Lines

In 1-2-3 the cells are divided into columns and rows, although 1-2-3 does not draw lines indicating the separate columns and rows. In Wysiwyg, you can use the default of not displaying lines to divide the columns and rows or you can add lines by selecting :Display Options Grid Yes. This adds grid lines that separate the cells on a 1-2-3 spreadsheet (as shown in Figure 15-10). If you later want to remove these lines, select :Display Options Grid No.

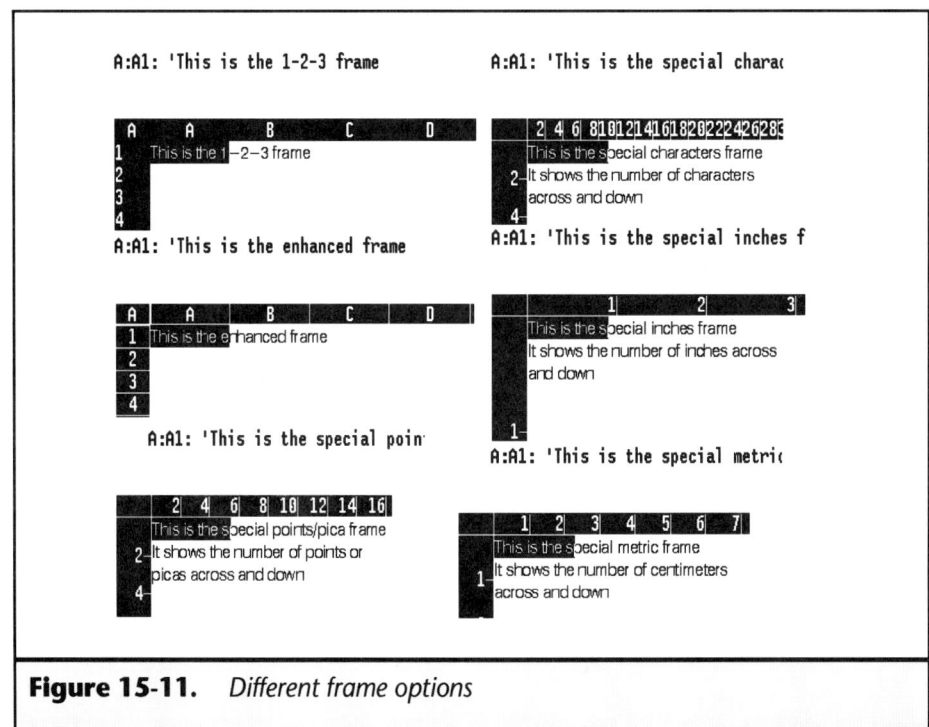

Figure 15-11. *Different frame options*

Showing Page Breaks

When you select a range to print, Wysiwyg draws dotted lines indicating how the range will be broken into pages. While you can use these dotted lines to guide you so that you have the desired information on each page, they can also be distracting. If you want to remove these dotted lines, select :Display Options Page-Breaks No. Later, if you want to display these page breaks, select :Display Options Page-Breaks Yes.

Setting the Display Intensity

Wysiwyg can also display your worksheet at a higher level of brightness. To use a brighter display, select :Display Options Intensity High. This changes Wysiwyg to use brighter versions of the display colors. When you want to return to the normal intensity, select :Display Options Intensity Normal. Some monitors have their own controls for making the display more or less intense. You may want to use the monitor knobs in place of these commands.

Setting the Directory Containing Font Files

Wysiwyg uses font files that are normally stored in the 1-2-3 Wysiwyg subdirectory. For Wysiwyg and 1-2-3 to display and print the worksheet with the correct fonts, it is important for Wysiwyg to know where the files are contained. If Wysiwyg cannot find the font files, it uses the 1-2-3 system font. To set where Wysiwyg can find these files, select :Display Font-Directory and enter the directory containing the font files.

Setting the Display Default

If you are frequently making the same changes to the Wysiwyg display, you will want to make these settings the defaults. You can use default settings to return all of the :Display command settings to their defaults after you have made numerous changes. To make the current display choices the new defaults, select :Display Default Update. If you want to replace the current display settings with the defaults, select :Display Default Restore. The default display settings are stored in the file called WYSIWYG3.CNF.

Using Wysiwyg for Your Graphs

Wysiwyg lets you work with graphs in your worksheet. You can use graphs saved in .PIC or .CGM files, graphs created with the /Graph commands, or empty graphs to which you can add your own enhancements. With Wysiwyg, you can add the graphs directly into a worksheet. By including a graph in the print range when you print with Wysiwyg, you can print the graph in the location where it appears on the worksheet. You can print your graphs on the same sheet of paper with text entries from the worksheet and choose exactly where the graph is placed on the page. Additional graphics features with Wysiwyg allow you to take these graphs (stored in separate files or in worksheets) and add enhancements. You can add text, lines, and freehand drawing. Unlike the :Format commands, the :Graph commands you use to work with graphics have sticky menus; you must select Quit to return to READY mode or the previous menu level.

Adding and Removing Graphs

The :Graph Add command is used to add graphs to a worksheet. Graphs are attached to a range of the worksheet and occupy space on the worksheet display. You can continue to make entries in these cells but unless you set the graph to display the contents beneath it, these entries will appear hidden.

Once you enter **:Graph Add**, you must select the type of graph you are adding. You can select Current, Named, PIC, Metafile, or Blank. If you select Current, you will add the current graph (the one you see when you press F10 (GRAPH)). If you select Named and one of the named graphs in the current worksheet, you will add the selected named graph. If you select PIC and one of the graph image files saved with a .PIC extension, you will add a graph that is saved in a .PIC file. If you select Metafile and one of the graphic image files saved with a .CGM extension, you will add a graph that is saved in a Metafile format. *Metafiles* are graphic image files that can be created from a variety of programs as well as with the 1-2-3 /Graph Save command. If you select Blank, you will add an empty graph. This last type is for when you want to start from scratch to create your own graphics.

You can specify the range for the graph by typing the range address or name or by highlighting the cells. Like the :Format commands, you can select the range before selecting :Graph Add, and Wysiwyg will use the selected range. Highlighting is the preferred approach since it lets you view the area the graph will occupy on the spreadsheet. Wysiwyg uses the range you select to determine the size and placement of the graph. The graph is expanded or contracted to fit into the selected range. Figure 15-12 shows part of two graphs that were added to ranges on the Wysiwyg screen. The second graph has a text range that is

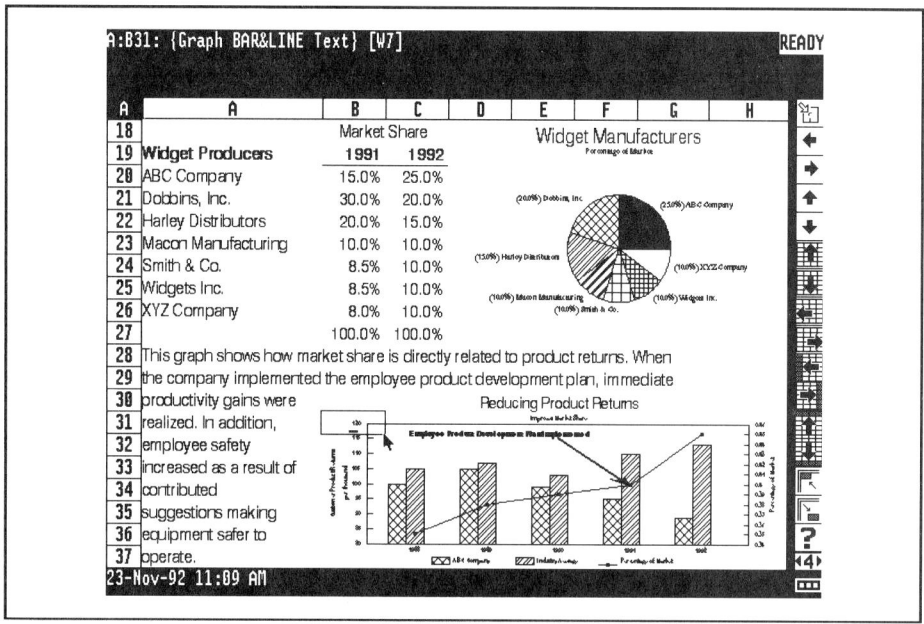

Figure 15-12. *Two graphs added to a worksheet*

wrapped around the graph, since the :Text Edit commands readjust the text so that it does not overwrite the graphic you are adding.

With Release 3.4, you can select the Add Graph icon from the SmartIcons palette as a shortcut for adding the current graph to the worksheet. Before selecting this icon, which is shown here:

select the range where you want the graph to appear. The current graph appears in the selected range of the worksheet.

You can remove a graph from the worksheet with the :Graph Remove command. After selecting this command, you must select a cell or range containing the graph to remove from the worksheet, or press F3 (NAME) and select the name of the graph you want to remove from the list Wysiwyg provides. You can also remove more than one graph by including more than one graph in the range you select for this command. Removing a .PIC or .CGM graph from a worksheet does not affect the copy of the graph stored on disk. Also, named graphs and the current graphs on the worksheet are still stored as part of the worksheet so that you can access them with the /Graph commands. Any worksheet data that is beneath a graph is untouched by this command; worksheet data that was hidden by a deleted graph will reappear. If you make any enhancements to the graph as described in the next section, these enhancements will be lost.

If you want to locate a graph quickly to check it before removing it or changing its settings you can use the :Graph Goto command. After selecting this command, select the name of the graph and press ENTER. This command moves you to the first cell that the graphic uses.

Changing the Graph Settings

Once you add a graph to a worksheet, the :Graph menu has several commands that let you alter the appearance of the graph. You can change the graph's position and size, change the graph that appears, make worksheet data display through the graph, and set when graphs are updated.

Changing the Graphic's Location and Size

Unlike the formatting added with the :Format commands—which can be moved with 1-2-3 commands such as /Move, /Worksheet Insert, and /Worksheet Delete—graphics do not change their size or location with 1-2-3 commands. The only 1-2-3 command that changes a graphic is /Worksheet Column, which changes the widths of the columns the graphic uses. Wysiwyg has several commands to change a graphic's location and size.

If you want to move a graphic, use the :Graph Move command. When you select this command, you must select the graphic to move, unless you selected a range containing the graphic to move before you started this command. You can either select a cell from the range that the graphic uses to display or press F3 (NAME) and select the name of the graphic to move. Next, Wysiwyg prompts for the new location. As with the /Move command, move the cell pointer to the first cell that you want for the new location of the graphic. The moved graphic uses the same number of columns and rows as the original, so the graph may be a different size if the column widths and row heights of the new worksheet area are different.

If you want to change the size of a graphic as well as changing the position, use the :Graph Settings Range command. When you select this command you must select the graphic to alter, unless you selected a range containing the graphic before you selected this command. You can either select a cell from the range that the graphic uses to display or press F3 (NAME) and select the name of the graphic. Wysiwyg displays the current selected range of the graphic. Like other 1-2-3 commands that prompt you with a range, you can expand or contract the range the graphic uses with the arrow keys. You can type a period to change which corner of the range is anchored. You can also press ESC or BACKSPACE to convert the range address to a single-cell address. Once you have a single-cell address, you can move to a new location and define another range for the graphic. When the range you want is highlighted, press ENTER to use the new range.

Other Graph Settings

The :Graph Settings command has several options for changing the appearance of a graphic. You can change the graph that appears in a graphic, and you can select whether underlying worksheet data appears, whether graphs appear on the worksheet, and when a graph is updated.

To display a different graph in the range established, use the :Graph Settings Graph command and select from Current, Named, PIC, Metafile, or Blank to select the graphic you want to appear in the window. If you select an option like PIC or Metafile, you must also specify the name of a new .PIC or .CGM file. If you select Named, you must select the name of the graph to display.

The :Graph Settings Display and :Graph Settings Opaque commands control the appearance of graphics. When you select :Graph Setting Display and select Yes or No, you are selecting whether a graphic in the worksheet appears on the screen as the graphic or as a shaded rectangle. Displaying a graphic as a shaded rectangle can make 1-2-3 and Wysiwyg run noticeably faster, since Wysiwyg does not constantly update the screen to draw the graphic. Selecting :Graph Settings Opaque selects whether worksheet data in the range a graphic uses to display shows through the graphic. Selecting Yes hides underlying worksheet data and selecting No displays the worksheet data. For both the :Graph Settings Display and :Graph Settings Opaque commands, you must select the range containing at least one cell from the graphic you want to change or press F3 (NAME) and select the name of the graphic.

When you add the current graph or a named graph to the worksheet, every time the current or named graph changes, Wysiwyg updates the graph in the worksheet. You can change when the graphs on the worksheet are updated with the :Graph Settings Sync command. When you select Yes, the default, Wysiwyg constantly updates the current and named graphs on the worksheet. When you select No, Wysiwyg updates a graph only when you retrieve the file or use the :Graph Compute command. The exception to retrieving the file is when recalculation is set to Manual, which means you must press F9 (CALC) to update the graph. After selecting one of the two options, you must select a cell from the graphic or press F3 (NAME) and select the name of the graphic. You can also change several graphics by including multiple graphics in the range you select for this command. If you select a range with one or more graphics before you select :Graph Settings Sync, Wysiwyg uses the graphics in the range for the command.

The :Graph Compute command tells Wysiwyg to update every graphic in the worksheet. Any current or named graphs are updated. All graphics from .PIC or .CGM files are reread into memory and updated on the worksheet.

Viewing Graphs

Wysiwyg has several options for looking at graphs besides adding them to a worksheet. You can use Wysiwyg to display a graph saved in a .PIC or .CGM file. You can also use Wysiwyg to display one of the graphics on the worksheet using the full screen.

To display one of the graphics in the current worksheet using the entire screen, select :Graph Zoom. Next, either select a cell from the range the graphic uses or press F3 (NAME) and select the name of the graphic from the list 1-2-3 provides. (You can also select a range containing the graphic before you select :Graph Zoom.) After viewing the graphic, press a key to remove the graphic and return to the :Graph menu.

To display a graphic stored in a .PIC or .CGM file, select :Graph View. Next, select PIC to view a file with a .PIC extension or Metafile to view a file with a .CGM extension, and then select the file to display. After viewing the graphic, press a key to remove the graphic and return to the :Graph menu.

Making Enhancements to Graphics

Wysiwyg includes a *graphics editing window* that you can use to edit and enhance graphics. You can use this to create drawings in blank graphs as well as to annotate existing graphs. The graphics editing window provides many of the graph features you expect in a full-blown graphics package. With Wysiwyg, as well as many other graphics packages, you will find it easier to edit graphics using a mouse, since it is easier to point to what you want in a graph with a mouse than to continually press the arrow keys.

The graphics editing window is accessed by selecting :Graph Edit and the graph to alter (unless you select a range containing the graph to alter before selecting :Graph Edit). With a mouse, you can also double click a cell that the graphic uses to display and Wysiwyg will display the graphic in the graphics editing window. Once you are in the graphics editing window, you can only exit the menu by selecting Quit. This means that if you are backing out of a command in the graphics editing window by pressing ESC you do not have to worry that you may press ESC too many times.

When you are in a graphics editing window, your screen looks like Figure 15-13. As this figure shows, Wysiwyg displays the graph on the screen with lines at the top and bottom indicating the limits of the graph size. This means that the lines will be different for each graphic you edit based on their relative sizes. In the graphics editing window, each item you can manipulate is called an *object*. A current graph, named graph, or image from a .PIC or .CGM file is considered a single object, although a graph has different pieces such as titles, axes, and data labels. If you want to change these components of the graph, you must use the 1-2-3 Graph menu.

A graphics editing window also includes a *bounding box* when you move or change the size of an object. It outlines the object you are changing to show you where the object will be moved or the new size of the object. When you work with objects, you must select them to let Wysiwyg know which object you want to change. An object is selected when it is marked with *selection indicators* like the selection indicators on the text in Figure 15-13. Most of the objects you work with are the graphic objects you add such as text or freehand drawings. You can also select the underlying graphic, which is the 1-2-3 graph or image in a .CGM file. Many of the :Graph Edit commands do not work with the underlying graphic although you can use :Graph Edit commands to change the colors and some other attributes.

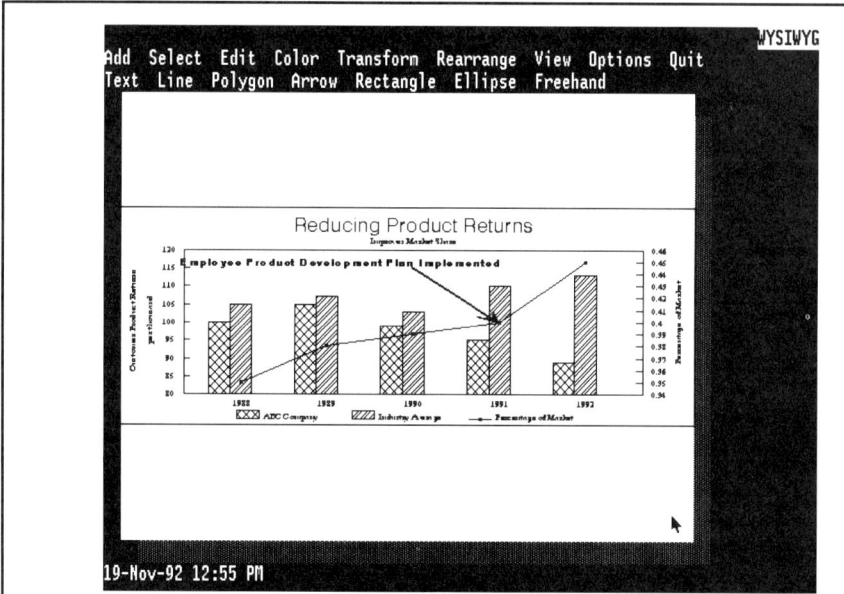

Figure 15-13.   *Graphics editing window*

Selecting Objects

There are several methods for selecting objects in the graphics editing window. The choice you will use depends on whether you are using a mouse and on the number of objects you want to select.

With a mouse you can move the cursor—which appears as a plus sign—to an object and click on the object. Selecting an object in this way deselects any previously selected objects. You can also deselect an object by clicking on a selected object. If you want to select multiple objects, move to the first corner of a box that you will draw to contain all of the objects to select. Then drag the mouse to draw a box containing all of the objects you want to select. When you release the mouse, the objects that are in the box you drew are selected. You can also select or deselect an object without affecting other selected objects by pressing SHIFT as you select or deselect an object.

Another method of selecting objects is to choose Select from the :Graph Edit menu. This displays another menu with the selections One, All, None, More/Less, Cycle, Graph, and Quit. Selecting One and pointing to the object to select deselects any other selected objects. You can use this option to select the underlying graphic (the current or named graph, or the image from the .PIC or .CGM file). Choosing All adds the selection indicators to all the objects except the underlying graphic in the graph. Choosing None deselects any selected objects. Choosing More/Less lets you select or deselect objects while keeping other objects selected or deselected. After selecting More/Less, point to an object to select or deselect and press the SPACEBAR. When all of the objects you want to use are selected, press ENTER. Choosing Cycle proceeds through all of the objects in the graphic each time you press a pointer movement key to change which object is marked with outlines of selection indicators. To select or deselect the object with the outlines of selection indicators, press the SPACEBAR. You can stop cycling through the objects by pressing ENTER. Choosing Graph selects the underlying graphic and deselects other objects.

Adding Objects to a Graphic

The graphics editing window lets you add several types of objects to a graphic. You can add arrows, ellipses, lines, polygons, rectangles, text, and freehand drawing. To add one of these items, select Add in the graphics editing window and the type of object you want to add. The type of object you add determines the information you must provide. These are the objects you can add and the information you must provide for each object:

- *Arrow*   Move the cursor to where you want the arrow to start and click the left mouse button or press the SPACEBAR. Move to the next point on the line that makes up the arrow and click the left mouse button or press the SPACEBAR. Finally, move to where you want the arrow to end and double click the left mouse button or press ENTER.

- *Ellipse*   Move the cursor to where you want the corner of the box that will define the ellipse. Next, move to draw the bounding box so that it is the size the ellipse will fill and press ENTER.

- *Freehand*   Move to where you want the freehand drawing to begin. Press the left mouse button and drag it to where you want the lines to be drawn. When you release the left mouse button you can draw another freehand line or double click the mouse to finish drawing.

- *Line*   Move the cursor to where you want the line to start and click the left mouse button or press the SPACEBAR. Move to the next point on the line and click the left mouse button or press the SPACEBAR. Finally, move to where you want the line to end and double click the left mouse button or press ENTER.

- *Polygon*   Move the cursor to where you want one corner of the polygon and click the left mouse button or press the SPACEBAR. Next, move to each corner of the polygon and click the left mouse button or press the SPACEBAR. Finally, move to the last corner of the polygon and double click the left mouse button or press ENTER. Wysiwyg draws a line between the first corner and the last corner of the polygon.

- *Rectangle*   Move the cursor to where you want one corner of the rectangle. Move to draw the bounding box so that it is the size of the rectangle and press ENTER.

- *Text*   Type the text you want to add, using formatting sequences if you want to add formatting to the text. You can also use the contents of a cell by typing a backslash and the cell address containing the text you want to use. After pressing ENTER, move to where you want the text and press ENTER or click the left mouse button.

You can add as many of each of the types of objects as you want. Wysiwyg also has a few features for adding objects. By pressing SHIFT as you select positions for the objects, you change ellipses to circles and rectangles to squares, and make lines use only 45-degree-angle increments. This means that you can use SHIFT to make sure that your lines are straight. Another special feature is available when you must select a position for an object. Besides moving the cursor with the mouse or the arrow keys, you can also type the x- and y-coordinates separated by a comma, as in **400,1600**. X- and y-coordinates can range between 0 and 4095 with 0,0 representing the lower left corner. You can use this feature to ensure that objects you are adding are aligned.

Changing the Appearance of Objects

Once you have added an object, you can make several changes to the object. You can change the colors it uses. For objects with lines, you can change the line width and style. For text objects, you can change the text, font, alignment, and magnification.

Changing the Color of Objects   By selecting Color in the graphics editing window, you can change the colors that the object uses. With graphs you have more color selections than with :Format Color. You can select Lines to change the color of the lines and the outlines in objects like rectangles and freehand drawings. For this option you can select from Black, White, Red, Green, Dark-Blue, Cyan, Yellow, Magenta, and Hidden. You can select Inside and one of the many colors from the palette that Wysiwyg displays to change the inside color of solid objects like rectangles. You can select Map to change up to 16 of the colors the underlying graphic uses. The underlying graphic uses colors labeled 1 through 9 and A through G. Select one of these letters or numbers and select a color to use. This option lets you change the colors of the underlying graphic without using the /Graph commands or needing to create the .PIC or .CGM files with different colors. You can select Background and then select one of the colors from the palette to change the color that is behind an object, such as the background behind text.

Changing the Appearance of Lines   You can make four types of changes to lines. You can change the line width, the line style, the arrowhead style for arrows, and the line smoothing. With these commands, you must either select the objects to change before entering the command or, if no objects are selected, you can select the objects to change after entering the command. To change the line width, select Edit Width and the description of the line width you want. To change the line style, select Edit Line-Style and the description of the line style you want. Initially, lines use the Very Narrow line width and a solid line.

You can also change the arrowheads on arrows. By selecting Edit Arrowheads, you can choose between Switch, One, Two, and None. Switch changes the end of the line where the arrowhead appears. One adds one arrowhead at one end of the line. Two adds arrowheads at both ends of the line. None uses no arrowheads so that the arrows look like lines.

With solid objects such as rectangles, polygons, some freehand drawings, and connected lines, you can smooth the lines so that the object has curves rather than angles separating the lines. To change the smoothing, select Edit Smoothing and then None, Tight, or Medium. None, the default, does not use any smoothing, Tight uses the smallest amount, and Medium uses the largest amount of smoothing. Figure 15-14 shows some objects that have different amounts of smoothing.

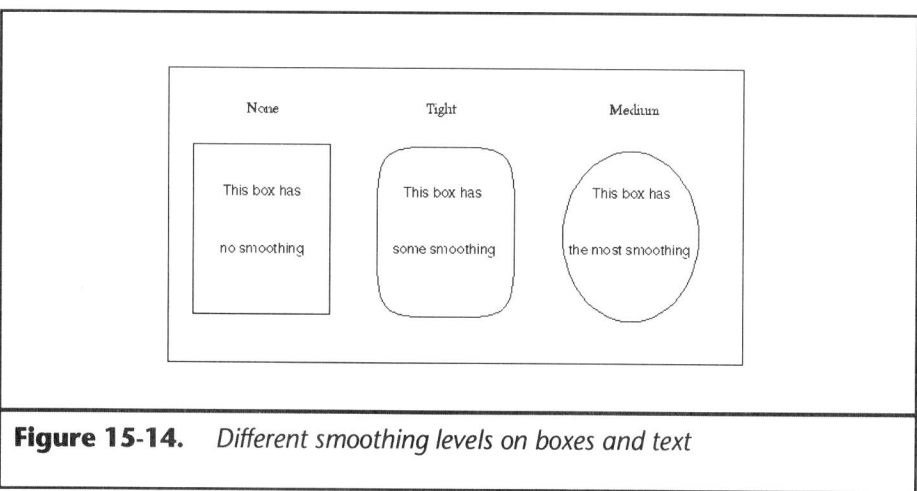

Figure 15-14. *Different smoothing levels on boxes and text*

Changing Text Objects   Wysiwyg has four commands for altering text objects that are not part of the underlying graphic. You can change the text in the text object, the alignment, the font, and the size. By selecting Edit Text, you can alter the text that is in the selected text object and press ENTER when you are finished. By selecting Edit Font, you can alter the font a text object uses from the default of font 1 to one of the eight fonts that are part of the current font set. By selecting Edit Centering, the text is aligned relative to the line area the text occupied when it was originally entered. By selecting Options Font-Magnification and a number between 1 and 1000, which represents the percentage of the text's normal size, you can expand or contract the size of all text in a graphic (including the text in the underlying graphic). By entering a number less than 100 you will shrink the text and by entering a number greater than 100 you will expand the text. You can also enter 0, which displays the text in the graphic using the original point size rather than the default Wysiwyg scaling. With each of the :Graph Edit commands (except Options Font-Magnification), you must either select the objects to change before entering the command or, if no objects are selected, you can select the objects to change after entering the command.

Changing the Graphics Editing Screen

Wysiwyg has two commands that change the appearance of the graphics editing screen without changing the graphic on the screen. You can add grid lines that indicate the cells by selecting Options Grid Yes. The resulting lines indicate the boundaries of each cell used to display the graph. You can hide these lines by selecting Options Grid No. You can also change the cursor to a larger cross or plus sign by selecting Options Cursor Big. By selecting Options Cursor Small, the cursor is returned to its default size.

Rearranging Graph Objects

Wysiwyg has many commands to help you change the position, size, and appearance of objects on the graph to customize the graph to look exactly as you want. With these commands, you must either select the objects to change before entering the command or, if no objects are selected, you can select the objects to change after entering the command. If you want to prevent an object from changing, select the object and then Rearrange Lock. Once an object is locked, it cannot be changed until you select Rearrange Unlock.

To move an object, you can select Rearrange Move. Wysiwyg draws a boundary box around the selected object that you can move. You can also move an object by selecting it and dragging the mouse from the initial location to where you want the object moved. If you press SHIFT while you move the object, you will only move the object in 45-degree increments. You can use this when you want to move an object up or down without moving it sideways.

You can also change the size of objects. To alter the size of an object, select Transform Size. Wysiwyg draws a boundary box around the selected object that you are resizing. You can move the lower right corner of the box to a new location to expand or contract the size of the selected object. The new size of the boundary box sets the size of the object in it. By pressing SHIFT while you change the object's opposite corner, the resized object will have the same height-to-width proportion as the original.

To copy an object, select Rearrange Copy and Wysiwyg creates a copy of the selected object next to the original. You can also copy objects by selecting them and pressing INS. The copied version of an object becomes the only selected object. Therefore, you can immediately use Rearrange Move to move it to a new location.

To delete an object, select Rearrange Delete. You can also delete objects by selecting the objects and pressing DEL. If you discover that you deleted the wrong object, select Rearrange Restore and the last object (or group of objects) is returned to the graphic.

As you add more objects, the overlaying objects are placed on top of each other. You can change which objects are on the top and bottom. To place an object to display on top of other overlaying ones, select the object and Rearrange Front. To move a selected object to the bottom, select Rearrange Back.

Wysiwyg has several commands that rotate and flip objects. To turn an object 90 degrees counterclockwise, select Transform Quarter-Turn. Each time you use this command the selected objects are rotated an additional 90 degrees. If you want to rotate an object by a different increment, select Transform Rotate and move the cursor in the direction you want the object rotated or type the number of degrees you want the object rotated. To flip an object so that it is backwards, select Transform X-Flip. To flip an object so that it is upside down, select Transform Y-Flip.

Another variation of rotating is skewing the object one way or another. You can change the vertical slant of an object by selecting Transform Vertical. This shifts the vertical sides of an object in different directions. You can change the horizontal slant of an object by selecting Transform Horizontal. This shifts the horizontal sides of an object in different directions. Figure 15-15 shows both types of skewing added to objects. You cannot use this feature with the underlying graphic. Also, selecting Transform Vertical for text changes the vertical position where each letter starts without changing the slant of the letters. Horizontal skewing has no effect. If you make changes with the Transform menu that you do not like, you can remove the effect of all Transform commands made while the same objects were selected by selecting Transform Clear.

Changing How Graphics Appear in the Graphics Editing Window

Wysiwyg has several commands that let you change the amount of the graphic that appears in the graphics editing window. You can use these commands to look at the graphic in greater detail. To look at the graph closer up, you can type

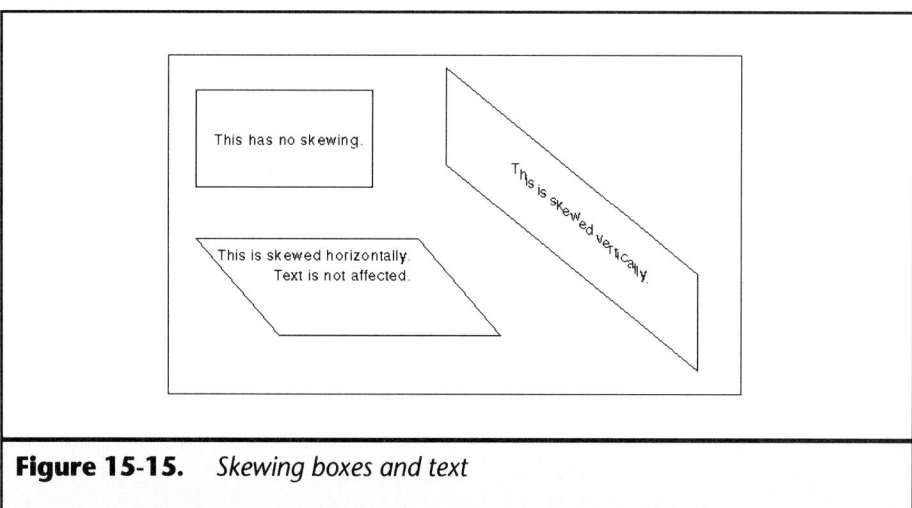

Figure 15-15.   *Skewing boxes and text*

+ or select View +. Each time you type + or select View +, Wysiwyg expands the graphic that appears in the graphics window. You can expand the graphic five times with + or View + as well as contract it by typing – or selecting View –. Another method of zooming into the graphic is the View In command. When you select the View In command, you must select a rectangle in the graphic that you want to see in greater detail. Wysiwyg blows up this selected area so that it is larger. You can return to displaying the entire graphic by typing + or selecting View + several times or by using the View Full command once.

When you are looking at a graphic closely, you may want to change the part of the graphic that appears in the graphics editing window. When you select View and then Up, Down, Left, or Right, Wysiwyg shifts the graphic a half screen in the direction you select. If you expect to move the graphic around in the graphics editing window frequently, you may want to use the View Pan command. When you select View Pan, you can utilize the View commands also available through the other View menu choices. You can type + and – to expand and contract the graphic and use the arrow keys to shift the part of the graphic that appears in the graphics editing window until you press ENTER to return to the main graphics editing window menu.

Printing with Wysiwyg

Wysiwyg offers many of the same print options as 1-2-3 but there are important additions. One important change is the additional formatting available through Wysiwyg's menu commands and formatting sequences, which exceed 1-2-3's Print menu commands. Also, Wysiwyg can maintain a library of layout sheets that are definition templates for a report or group of reports. By using Wysiwyg to print, you can also alter many of the configuration options and settings directly from the :Print menu. With its preview feature Wysiwyg can also show you how the output will appear.

As you use Wysiwyg's :Print menus, a status screen displays many of the print settings. Figure 15-16 shows the :Print menu and the setting sheet. You can always remove the setting sheet and display the worksheet below by selecting Info. Some of the commands like Go, File, Range, and Background should already be familiar since 1-2-3 has similar options. Range allows you to define the area of the worksheet to be printed. Printing does not take place until you have selected a print range with Range and started the print operation with the menu command Go or File. The File selection tells Wysiwyg that you want your output directed to an encoded file. This feature works similarly to the /Print Encoded command in 1-2-3. Other options that you select from the :Print menu will affect the printout written to disk. You will find other familiar options in some of the second-level print selections.

```
A:A1:                                                    WYSIWYG
Go File Background Range Config Settings Layout Preview Info Quit
Print the specified range

   Print range(s)....              Margins (in inches)

   Layout:                              Top 0.5
     Paper type... Letter
     Page size.... 8.5 by 11 inches
     Titles:                    Left            Right
       Header.....              0.5             0.5
       Footer.....
     Top border...
     Left border..                    Bottom 0.55
     Compression.. None
                                      Settings:
   Configuration:                       Begin......... 1
     Printer...... HP LaserJet III No cartri...  End........... 9999
     Interface.... Parallel 1           Start-Number.. 1
     Cartridges...                      Copies........ 1
     Orientation.. Portrait             Wait.......... No
     Resolution... Final                Grid.......... No
     Bin..........                      Frame......... No

   19-Nov-92 01:46 PM
```

Figure 15-16.   *Printing status sheet*

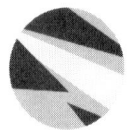

TIP: Wysiwyg formats will print only if you print with Wysiwyg, not 1-2-3. If you print a range with 1-2-3 that contains Wysiwyg formatting sequences, they will not print as planned.

The Basic Print Process

Printing in Wysiwyg can be easy if you want to use Wysiwyg's defaults. To print a worksheet with Wysiwyg, select :Print Range Set. This command selects the range to print. Like selecting ranges to print in 1-2-3, you can select multiple ranges by separating each range address with a comma. Also, any hidden columns or sheets are not printed. Unlike printing with 1-2-3, you cannot print graphs by including the graph name. You can, however, print a graph by printing a worksheet range that has a graph added with the :Graph Add command. Once you select the range to print, Wysiwyg adds dashed lines to the worksheet area, indicating where it will break the output into pages.

Wysiwyg displays in the control panel the page of the output where the cell highlighted by the cell pointer will appear. The control panel also displays the {Page} Wysiwyg format indicator when the cell pointer is on a cell where the range is divided into pages. You can use these page indicators to determine whether you want to add your own page breaks or to change the worksheet so that more worksheet data will fit on each page. If you want to remove the setting for the ranges to print, select :Print Range Clear. You will probably use the :Print Quit command to return to the READY mode and make final modifications to the worksheet range you want to print.

Once the range to print is selected, you can print the worksheet with Wysiwyg by selecting :Print Go. This command prints the worksheet to the printer. If you want to print the worksheet to a file, select :Print File and type the name of the file in which you want the output saved. This file will have an .ENC extension and will contain all of the information the installed printer needs to print the output as desired. Unlike 1-2-3, Wysiwyg will print to a file as soon as you select File, provide a filename, and press ENTER. Since Wysiwyg uses more graphics features than 1-2-3, these .ENC files will be much larger than the .ENC files you create with /Print Encoded. A file created with the :Print File command should only be printed to the same type of printer that is listed in the status screen, since each type of printer uses different printer codes.

If you want to see how your selected print range will look when it is printed, select Preview. This displays your worksheet as it will appear when printed, as shown in Figure 15-17. When the output prints on several pages, pressing any

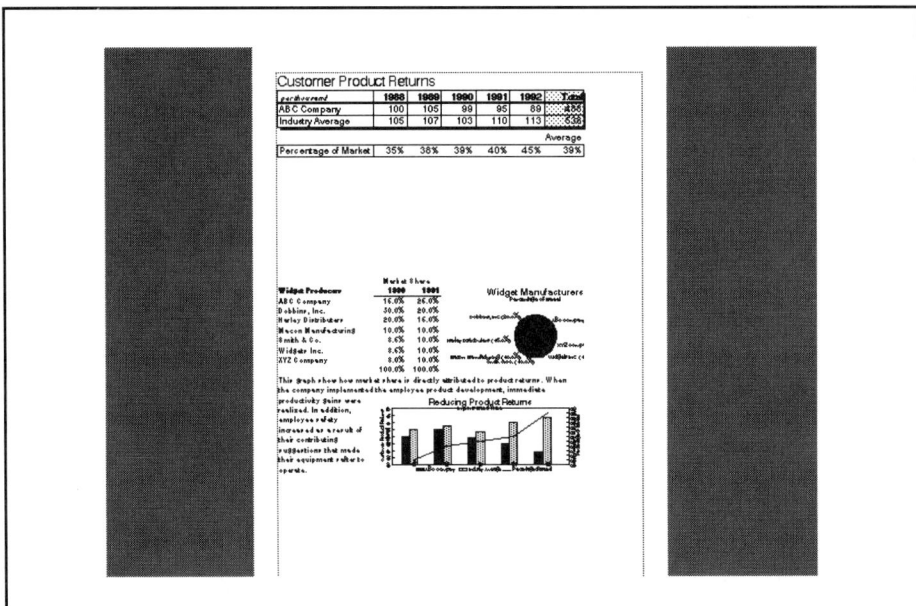

Figure 15-17.   *Previewing a worksheet to print*

key except ESC displays the next page. Pressing ESC or pressing any key when you are viewing the last page returns you to the :Print menu.

With Release 3.4, you can select the Page Preview icon from the SmartIcons palette as a shortcut for both setting a print range and previewing how the range will print. First, highlight the range that you wish to print or preview. Then select the Page Preview icon. You can view how the selected range will print, just as if you had selected Preview from the menu. Press any key to return to the worksheet. The range you selected is now set as a print range.

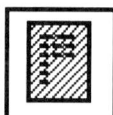

Adding Page Breaks

If you are not happy with the page breaks inserted by Wysiwyg, indicating where it will break your worksheet into pages, you can set your own manual page breaks. The page breaks that you set with Wysiwyg are different from the page breaks you set with 1-2-3. These page breaks are not interchangeable. Also unlike 1-2-3, you can add both column and row page breaks. To add a page break, move the cell pointer to the cell in the first column or row that you want on the next page. Select :Worksheet Page. To add a page break so that the current column is the first column on the new page, select Column. To add a page break so that the current row is the first row on the new page, select Row. When you add a page break, Wysiwyg displays a dashed line where the page break is located. When you have finished adding page breaks, select Quit to return to the READY mode. You can delete the page breaks by selecting :Worksheet Page Delete. When your cell pointer is positioned at the location of a page break, this command deletes page breaks at the current column and row.

TIP: If you do not want to see the dashed lines representing page breaks, select :Display Options Page-Breaks No.

With Release 3.4, you can select one of two icons from the SmartIcons palette to insert Wysiwyg page breaks. One icon inserts horizontal page breaks, and the other vertical page breaks. To insert a page break using the icons, position the cell pointer either in a cell in the row that you want to be the first row of the new page, or in the column that you want to be the first column of a new page. Then select the appropriate icon. A dashed line will appear indicating where the page break falls.

Layout Options

The :Print Layout commands control the page layout. These commands are similar to the commands found in 1-2-3's Print Options menu although there are a number of new additions. The :Print Layout menu is a sticky menu; you can select Quit or press ESC when you want to return to the :Print menu.

Setting the Page Size

Wysiwyg can print on any page size that your printer supports. You can select the page size with the :Print Layout Page-Size command. Your choices are 1:Letter (8 1/2" x 11"), 2:A4 (8.268" x 11.693"), 3:80X66 (8 1/2" x 11" fanfold), 4:132X66 (14" x 11" fanfold), 5:80X72 (8 1/2" x 12" fanfold), 6:Legal (8 1/2" x 14"), 7:B5 (6.929" x 9.843"), and Custom. If you select Custom, type the length and the width followed by "in" for inches, "mm" for millimeters, or "cm" for centimeters.

Setting Margins

By default Wysiwyg uses .5 inch for the top, left, and right margins and .55 for the bottom margin. You can change these margins by selecting :Print Layout Margins. For the four options Left, Right, Top, and Bottom, select the option to change and type the new margin followed by "in" for inches, "mm" for millimeters, or "cm" for centimeters. After setting the margins, select Quit to return to the :Print Layout menu. The total of the left and right margins must be less than the page width and the total of the top and bottom margins must be less than the page height.

Adding a Header or Footer

Just as in 1-2-3, you can add headers and footers to the page layout. To add a header or footer, select :Print Layout Titles and either Header or Footer. The header and footer must follow the same rules as in 1-2-3, which means that you can have up to 512 characters and you can use special characters such as #, @, |, and \. (The rules and examples for headers and footers are provided in Chapter 6, "Printing.") You can use formatting sequences to add formatting to a header or footer. The 512-character limit includes formatting sequences and special characters created with ALT-F1, which may use more than one character of memory. The header and footer in Wysiwyg are separate from the header and footer in 1-2-3. Therefore, when you first select :Print Layout Titles Header or Footer, you will not see any header or footer entered with the /Print Printer Options Header or Footer command. When you use a header or footer, Wysiwyg skips two lines between the header or footer and the worksheet data. To remove a header or footer, select Clear and then Header, Footer, or Both. You will also need to select Quit when you are finished with the :Print Layout Titles menu.

Border Options

Wysiwyg can also have border columns and rows that print on every page just like the 1-2-3 /Print Printer Borders command. This lets you maintain column and row headings on long and wide worksheets. To add borders select :Print Layout Borders. To add rows at the top of every page, select Top and a range containing cells from the rows you want to use. To add columns on the left of every page, select Left and a range containing cells from the columns you want to use. If you later decide that you do not want these border columns or rows, select Clear and then Top, Left, or All to select the borders to remove. When you have finished selecting the border columns and/or rows, select Quit to return to the :Print Layout menu. As with 1-2-3, you do not want to include the same columns and rows in the print range that you are using in the border because if you do they will print twice. You may want to look at the examples in Chapter 6, "Printing."

Compressing the Layout

One of Wysiwyg's unique features is the ability to compress or expand the printed output. You can compress the output to fit on one page or tell Wysiwyg by how much you want the output expanded or contracted. To change the compression of the output, select :Print Layout Compression. If you select

Automatic, Wysiwyg will compress the output so that it fits on one page. If the output range contains manual page breaks that you added with the :Worksheet Page command, Wysiwyg uses these page breaks to determine how each page should be compressed. You can also select Manual. If you select Manual, you must enter the percentage by which you want the output compressed as a number between 15 and 1000. Numbers less than 100 compress the output and numbers greater than 100 expand the output. For example, a Manual compression of 50 compresses the output to 50% of its original size while a compression of 500 expands the output to five times (500%) its original size. The third choice is None, which does not compress or expand the output. This choice is the default.

Creating a Library of Page Layouts

Wysiwyg allows you to create and maintain a library of page layouts. You can retrieve any layout and use it in your next print request. The :Print Layout Library commands are Erase, Retrieve, and Save. Like other Erase commands, this Erase option eliminates a page layout library file on disk.

The Save option allows you to specify a name for the current layout and save it to disk for later use. The Retrieve option reads the specified page layout from disk, making it the current layout. Its settings are used to define the print settings for the :Print Go command. Wysiwyg page layout libraries are stored in files with .AL3 extensions.

Setting the Page Layout Default

If you frequently use the same settings for the page layout, you will want to make these settings the defaults. Another use of a page layout default is to replace the current page settings with the page layout defaults that Wysiwyg has saved as part of its configuration file. To make the current page layout become the new default page layout, select :Print Layout Default Update. If you want to make the default page layout replace the current page layout settings, select :Print Layout Default Restore. The default page layout is stored in the file called LAYOUT3.CNF.

Changing Printing Configuration Options

You can change your print configuration from the Wysiwyg :Print menu with the :Print Configuration command. These configuration settings include font cartridges, printer interface, print bin, and orientation. When you are finished with the :Print Configuration menu, select Quit to return to the :Print menu.

The Printer and Interface options are frequently selected when you are using a different printer from the default selection. The Printer option selects the printer to use from a list of printers installed during 1-2-3 installation. The Interface option selects the connection between your computer and your printer. You can select from Parallel 1, Serial 1, Parallel 2, Serial 2, or the DOS devices LPT1, LPT2, LPT3, COM1, or COM2. These options present the settings of listed printers in the Name and Interface options of the 1-2-3 /Print Printer Options Advanced Device command. The settings for these options are saved with the file; therefore, if you plan to use the worksheet with other printers, you should select /Print Printer Clear Device so that Wysiwyg will use the default printer.

The Orientation options let you change the direction of print on the output page. Portrait output is standard with the lines of print running across the 8 1/2-inch sheet of paper. Landscape output uses the paper sideways and prints lines across the 11-inch width. By selecting Landscape, you can print your output sideways if your printer supports this.

The Resolution option allows you to use the different resolution options that your printer may support. Higher resolutions have better output quality, but are slower to print. You can select Final to print your worksheet using the best resolution, or Draft to quickly produce a lower quality resolution output.

If you are using a printer that supports font cartridges or font cards, you can tell Wysiwyg the cartridges that are installed so that you can use these fonts in Wysiwyg. By selecting 1st-Cart or 2nd-Cart and one of the font-cartridge or font-card files, the fonts will become available with the :Format Font Replace command. It is important that you select the correct font cartridge or font card files to get the results you want.

If your printer has multiple paper feeding options, you can select how paper is fed to the printer by selecting Bin. The Bin option has five choices: Reset, Single-Sheet, Manual, Upper-Tray, and Lower-Tray. Upper-Tray and Lower-Tray select which of two trays the printer takes paper from if the printer has two paper trays. Single-Sheet uses the printer's single-sheet feeder and Manual uses the printer's manual paper-feed option. Reset removes the setting made by one of the other four choices.

Altering Print Settings

The :Print Settings command lets you choose options for how Wysiwyg will print the range you select. This command has the options Begin, End, Start-Number, Copies, Wait, Grid, Frame, Reset, and Quit. The Reset option returns all settings for the other options to the default setup and Quit returns to the :Print menu.

If you are printing a report that you want to combine with other documents, you may want the page number to start with a different number than 1. By selecting Start-Number and typing a new number to begin numbering pages, you are setting the page number of the first page of the output.

After selecting a print range you may decide that you do not want to print the entire print range. This is especially true if you made a correction to the worksheet and you need to reprint only one page. Rather than redefining the print range, you can select :Print Settings Begin and type the number of the first page of the selected range to print. Next, select End and type the number of the last page of the selected range to print. These two options depend on the Start-Number option. For example, if you use 3 and 4 for the Begin and End options and start numbering pages with 3, Wysiwyg will print the first two pages of the selected range because these pages have page numbers that start with 3 and end with 4.

The Copies option lets you print more than one copy by entering a number other than 1. The Wait option is used for situations when you need to hand-feed sheets into your printer. Selecting Wait Yes causes Wysiwyg to wait until you insert a sheet of paper and choose /Print Resume to continue printing the next sheet.

The Frame and Grid options select whether Wysiwyg will print the worksheet frame and the grid. Selecting Yes for either of these options prints the selected option and selecting No (the default) omits the option. Unlike the other options for the settings commands, the settings for these two options are saved with the format file. The settings chosen for the other options are only in effect for the current session.

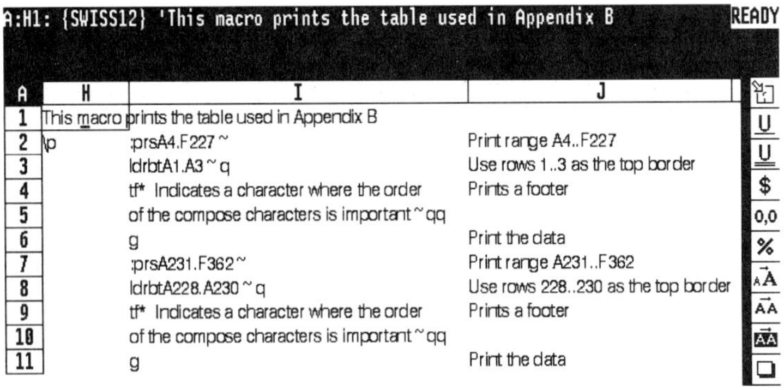
A:H1: {SWISS12} 'This macro prints the table used in Appendix B
READY
A
H
I
J
1 This macro prints the table used in Appendix B
2 \p :prsA4.F227~ Print range A4..F227
3 ldrbtA1.A3~q Use rows 1..3 as the top border
4 tf* Indicates a character where the order Prints a footer
5 of the compose characters is important~qq
6 g Print the data
7 :prsA231.F362~ Print range A231..F362
8 ldrbtA228.A230~q Use rows 228..230 as the top border
9 tf* Indicates a character where the order Prints a footer
10 of the compose characters is important~qq
11 g Print the data
U
U
$
0,0
%

Figure 15-18. *A macro to print in Wysiwyg*

Wysiwyg and GROUP Mode

Just as many 1-2-3 commands are affected by GROUP mode, Wysiwyg formats are also affected by GROUP mode. When GROUP mode is enabled, all of the :Format commands—as well as :Named-Style, :Special Copy, :Special Move, the :Text commands except :Text Edit, and all of the :Worksheet commands—affect every sheet in the worksheet file.

Using Macros with Wysiwyg

Just as you can create macros within 1-2-3, you can create macros that load and use Wysiwyg. You can represent any menu selection within Wysiwyg by including the first letter of the menu option. Figure 15-18 shows a macro that prints two ranges of a worksheet using Wysiwyg commands. Notice that this macro uses the colon to activate the Wysiwyg menu just as if you were making the menu selections yourself. This macro assumes that Wysiwyg is already loaded. If you want to invoke an add-in within a macro, you can use {APP1}, {APP2}, {APP3}, and {ADDIN} for the ALT-F7, ALT-F8, ALT-F9, and ALT-F10 key combinations to invoke Wysiwyg or any other add-in. You can also use F2 (RECORD) to record the keystrokes to use in the macro.

Command Reference

Wysiwyg

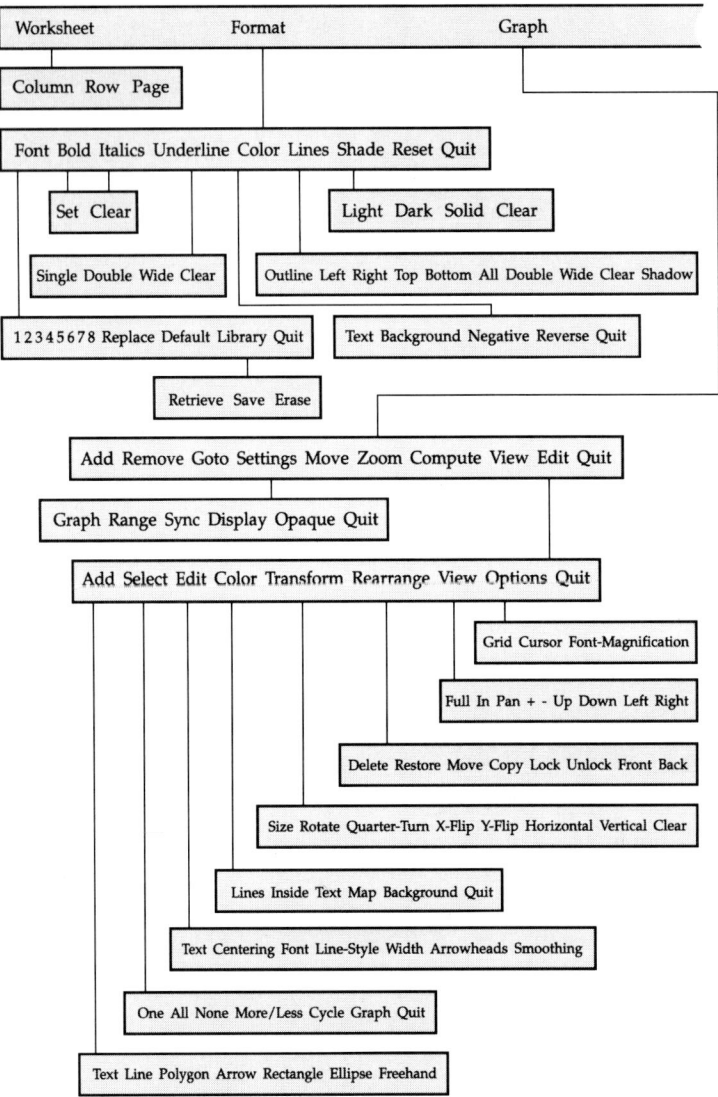

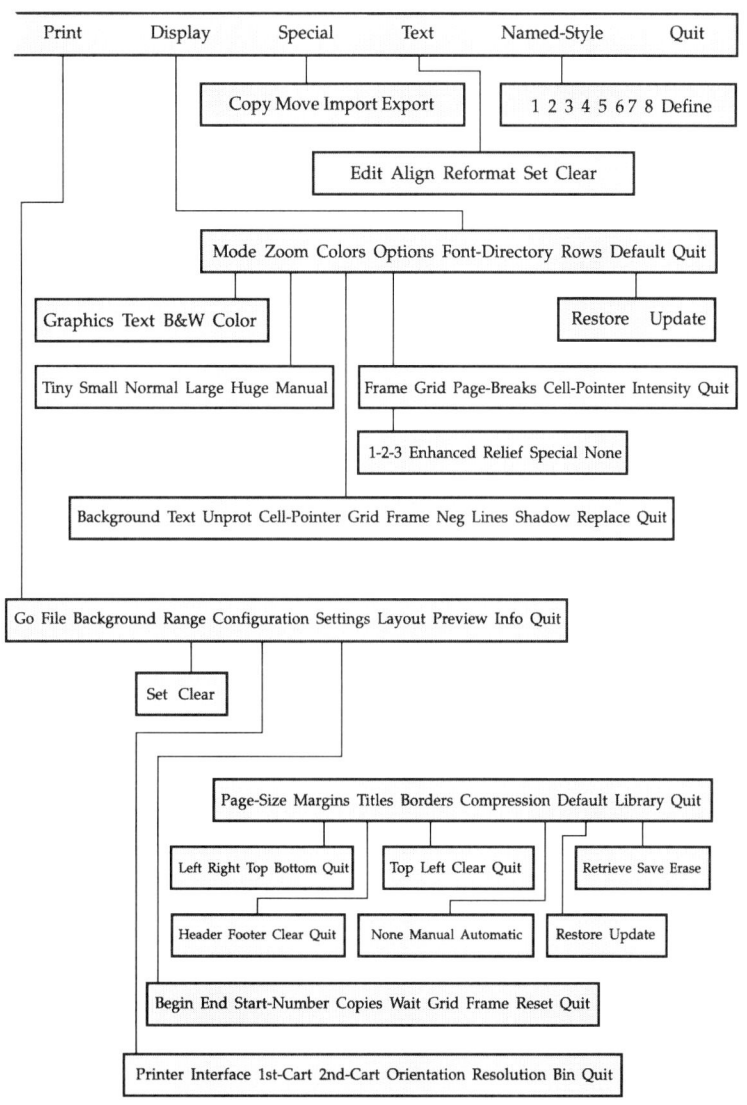

:Display Colors

Description

The :Display Colors command customizes the Wysiwyg display if you have a color monitor. The default display is black for the background, white for the worksheet area, and aqua for the cell pointer.

Options

This command has 11 different options. The eight default colors to choose from for these options are black, white, red, green, dark-blue, cyan, yellow, and magenta.

BACKGROUND   This option selects the color for the background.

TEXT   This option selects the color for the text.

UNPROT   This option selects the color for the unprotected cells.

CELL-POINTER   This option selects the color for the cell pointer.

GRID   This option selects the color for the grid lines.

FRAME   This option selects the color for the worksheet frame.

NEG   This option selects the color for negative values in the worksheet.

LINES   This option selects the color for the cell borders.

SHADOW   This option selects the color for drop-shadows.

REPLACE   This option selects the eight colors used by the other options. Select the color to change and either type a number between 0 and 63 or press the LEFT and RIGHT ARROW to adjust the color.

QUIT   This option returns you to the :Display menu.

:Display Default

Description

This command replaces the current display settings with the default settings or creates new default settings. The default settings are those used by Wysiwyg when you load it. This includes most of the settings made through :Display.

Options

RESTORE This option replaces the current display settings with the default settings.

UPDATE This option replaces the default display settings with the current display settings.

:Display Font-Directory

Description

This command chooses the directory that contains the Wysiwyg fonts.

Options

Your only option with this command is which directory to use.

:Display Mode

Description

This command selects between text and graphics modes, assuming your monitor can support both modes. In graphics mode you can see the output on the screen exactly as it prints. In text mode your display looks like the 1-2-3 display. The features selected still print but do not affect the appearance of the 1-2-3 display.

Options

B&W   This option sets the worksheet display to black and white graphics mode.

COLOR   This option sets the worksheet display to color graphics mode.

GRAPHICS   This option displays the worksheet as it will look when printed.

TEXT   This option displays the worksheet as it appears in 1-2-3 without Wysiwyg loaded.

:Display Options Cell-Pointer

Description

This command chooses the appearance of the cell pointer.

Options

SOLID   This option displays the cell pointer as a solid rectangle.

OUTLINE   This option displays the cell pointer as an outline.

:Display Options Frame

Description

This command chooses how the worksheet frame appears. Changing the frame does not change the column and row orientation of 1-2-3.

Options

1-2-3 This option displays the standard 1-2-3 worksheet frame, which has no lines separating the column and row headings.

ENHANCED This option displays the default Wysiwyg worksheet frame, which has lines separating the column and row headings.

RELIEF This option makes the worksheet frame appear as three-dimensional.

SPECIAL This option causes the worksheet frame to appear as a ruler indicating characters, inches, centimeters, or points/picas. Select Characters, Inches, Metric, or Points/Picas to select the type of ruler you want.

NONE This option hides the worksheet frame. Your screen will have no row and column headings.

:Display Options Grid

Description

This command makes the grid lines that mark the boundaries of each cell appear or disappear.

Options

The only options for this command are Yes and No. Yes displays the grid lines, while No hides the grid lines.

:Display Options Intensity

Description

This command determines the brightness level of the display screen.

Options

NORMAL   This option causes the screen to have normal brightness.

HIGH   This option causes the screen to have a high brightness level.

:Display Options Page-Breaks

Description

This command sets whether page breaks are displayed in the worksheet.

Options

This command has the options of Yes and No. Choosing Yes displays the page breaks, while choosing No hides the page breaks.

:Display Options Quit

Description

This command returns to the :Display menu.

:Display Quit

Description

This command leaves the :Display menu and returns to the READY mode.

:Display Rows

Description

This command chooses how many rows appear on the screen.

Options

The only option is the number of rows to display on the screen (between 16 and 60). The higher the number you choose, the smaller the size of the rows displayed.

:Display Zoom

Description

This command is used in graphics mode to change the size of the cells in the worksheet display. It makes the normal cell size either larger or smaller.

Options

TINY   This option displays cells at 63 percent of normal size.

SMALL   This option displays cells at 87 percent of normal size.

NORMAL   This option displays the cells in their actual size.

LARGE   This option displays the cells at 125 percent of normal size.

HUGE   This option displays the cells at 150 percent of normal size.

MANUAL   This option manually reduces or enlarges the cell size. You can choose a number from 25 to 400, where 400 is the largest cell size (400 percent of normal size).

:Format Bold

Description

This command either sets or removes boldface for a range of cells. To use this format while editing text press CTRL-A and type **b**, pressing CTRL-E when finished. You can select the range for the format either before selecting :Format Bold or after selecting an option.

Options

SET   This option adds boldface to the selected range.

CLEAR   This option eliminates any boldface from the range.

:Format Color

Description

This command specifies the colors of a range for both displaying and printing (if you have a color printer). To use this format within a cell, press CTRL-A and type **1c** (default color), **2c** (red), **3c** (green), **4c** (dark- blue), **5c** (cyan), **6c** (yellow), **7c** (magenta), or **8c** (reversed colors), pressing CTRL-E when you are finished.

Options

TEXT   This option chooses the color of a range of cells. You can choose from Normal (the default color), Red, Green, Dark-Blue, Cyan, Yellow, and Red.

BACKGROUND   This option chooses the color of the background of a range of cells. You can choose from Normal (the default color), Red, Green, Dark-Blue, Cyan, Yellow, and Magenta.

NEGATIVE   This option chooses the color of negative values in a range of cells. You can select Normal (the default color) or Red as the color for these cells.

REVERSE This option reverses the colors of the text and background of cells in the chosen range.

QUIT This option leaves the menu and returns you to the READY mode.

:Format Font

Description

The :Format Font command allows you to assign fonts to ranges and selects the fonts that are part of the current font set. When you select this command, a list of the eight current fonts appears on the screen. To use this format within a cell press CTRL-A and type **1F** (font 1), **2F** (font 2), **3F** (font 3), **4F** (font 4), **5F** (font 5), **6F** (font 6), **7F** (font 7), or **8F** (font 8), pressing CTRL-E when you are finished. You can also press CTRL-A and type **d** (subscript) or **u** (superscript) for other formats.

Options

1 THROUGH 8 This option assigns the selected font to a range that you select before entering the :Font Format command or after selecting a number between 1 and 8.

REPLACE This option replaces one of the fonts in the current font set with the fonts from the master directory. Select the number of the font to replace and the style desired; then type the point size and press ENTER.

DEFAULT This option replaces the current font set with the default font set or saves the current font set as the default. When you choose this option, you must choose Restore (which replaces the current font set with the default), or Update (which replaces the default font set with the current font set).

LIBRARY This option maintains the font libraries. It has three choices. Select Retrieve and a font library file with an .AF3 extension to replace the currently selected fonts with the fonts in the font library file. Select Save and enter a filename to save the current set of fonts as a font library file. Select Erase and a font library file to remove the file from the disk.

QUIT This option returns you to the READY mode.

:Format Italics

Description

This command adds or removes italics from a range of cells. To use this format within a cell, press CTRL-A and type **i**, pressing CTRL-E when you are finished. You can select the range for this command before entering the command or after selecting an option.

Options

SET   This option adds italics to a range of cells.

CLEAR   This option removes italics from a range of cells.

:Format Lines

Description

This command creates lines, boxes, or outlining around cells. You can use this command to create a box around a range of worksheet cells or to draw lines anywhere on the output. You can select the range this command uses before selecting :Format Lines or after selecting one of the options.

Options

OUTLINE   This option draws an outline around the range of cells.

LEFT   This option draws lines at the left edge of the cells in the range.

RIGHT   This option draws lines at the right edge of the cells in the range.

TOP   This option draws lines at the top of the cells in the range.

BOTTOM   This option draws lines at the bottom of the cells in the range.

ALL   This option draws a box around each cell in the range.

DOUBLE   This option adds double lines. Choose from Outline, Left, Right, Top, Bottom, or All for the location to draw the lines.

WIDE   This option draws wide lines. Choose from Outline, Left, Right, Top, Bottom, or All for the location to draw the lines.

CLEAR   This option removes any lines assigned to cells in the range. Choose Outline, Left, Right, Top, Bottom, or All to select the location of lines to remove.

SHADOW   This option adds (Set) or removes (Clear) a shadow from a range. A shadow is dark shading added to the bottom and right side of the range.

:Format Quit

Description

This command returns you to the READY mode.

:Format Reset

Description

This command removes all the formatting applied to a cell or range in one easy step. It removes boldface, underlining, shading, and lines. It establishes font 1 for the cell with the default display color.

Options

The only option for this command is the range you select to reset.

:Format Shade

Description

This command adds contrast to your display and printouts through the addition or removal of shaded backgrounds on any range of cells. You can select the range this command alters either before you select :Format Shade or after you select one of the options.

Options

LIGHT   This option adds light shading to the range.

DARK   This option adds dark shading to the range.

SOLID   This option adds solid shading to the range.

CLEAR   This option removes any shading already assigned to a range of cells.

:Format Underline

Description

This command adds different kinds of underlining to one or more cells. To use this format within a cell press CTRL-A and type **1_** (single underlining), **2_** (double underlining), or **3_** (wide underlining), pressing CTRL-E when you are finished. You can select the range this command affects either before you select :Format Underline or after you select one of these options.

Options

SINGLE   This option adds a single underline under all the text in the range selected.

DOUBLE   This option adds double underlining under all the text in the range selected.

WIDE   This option adds a wide underline under all the text in the range selected.

CLEAR   This option removes any underlining currently used in the specified range.

:Graph Add

Description

This command adds graphs to the worksheet. Wysiwyg sizes the graph to fit within the range that you specify. You can also change the range for the graph once it is placed to alter its size.

Options

After selecting one of these options and any graph or filename the option requires, you must select the worksheet range where Wysiwyg will display the graph.

CURRENT   This option adds the current graph to the worksheet.

NAMED   This option adds a named graph to the worksheet. Select a named graph from the list 1-2-3 provides.

PIC   This option adds a graph in a .PIC file to the worksheet. Select a .PIC file to add.

METAFILE   This option adds a graph in a .CGM file to the worksheet. Select a .CGM file to add.

BLANK   This option marks a worksheet range where you will eventually place a graph or create your own graphic image.

NOTE: Changing the row height and the column width of the cells within the range used by the graph alters its size as well.

:Graph Compute

Description

This command updates all graphs added to active worksheet files. This means that .PIC and .CGM graph files are read into the worksheet and 1-2-3 updates the current and named graphs to reflect changes in the graph settings or worksheet data.

:Graph Edit Add

Description

This command adds various items to a graph. You must select the graph to alter at Wysiwyg's prompt (you can press F3 (NAMES) to list the graph names) or select a cell from the range used to display the graph you want to alter.

Options

TEXT   This option adds text to this graph. Type the text you want to add (or type a \ and the address or range name of the cell containing the content you want to use), press ENTER, move the text to where you want it to appear, and press ENTER again. You can use CTRL-A formatting sequences to add formatting to the text.

LINE   This option adds a line to the graph. Move to the first point on the line, press the SPACEBAR, move to the ending position of the line, and press ENTER.

POLYGON   This option adds a polygon to the graph. Move to where you want a corner of the polygon and press the SPACEBAR. Continue moving to each corner and pressing the SPACEBAR. When you move to the last corner of the polygon press ENTER. Wysiwyg will draw the line for the last side of the polygon.

ARROW   This option adds an arrow to the graph. Move to the beginning point of the arrow, press the SPACEBAR, move to the ending position for the arrow, and press ENTER.

RECTANGLE This option adds a rectangle to the graph. Move to where you want the first corner of the box, press the SPACEBAR, move to the opposite corner of the box, and press ENTER.

ELLIPSE This option adds an ellipse or a circle to the graph. Move to where you want the first corner of the box that defines the ellipse's size, press the SPACEBAR, move to the opposite corner of the box, and press ENTER.

FREEHAND This option draws freehand lines on the graph. Move to the first point where you want to start drawing lines and press the SPACEBAR. As you move on the graph, Wysiwyg draws lines that follow your movements until you press ENTER.

NOTE: By pressing SHIFT *as you move on the graph, you can adjust the object you are drawing so that a rectangle becomes a square, an ellipse becomes a circle, and lines are drawn at 45-degree increments.*

:Graph Edit Color

Description

This command chooses from numerous colors for the graph and objects that have been added to the graph.

Options

The options for this command select the color used by a graph object or the entire graph. When using this command, you can either select the object before you select the command or after you select the color to be used by the object.

LINES This option selects the color for specific lines and outlines.

INSIDE This option selects the color to use to fill a specific object of the graph.

TEXT This option chooses a color for specific text.

MAP This option changes the graph's colors to different colors.

BACKGROUND This option selects the color for the background of the graph.

:Graph Edit Edit

Description

This command manipulates objects that are added to the graph. You can either select the object to edit before selecting this command or after making the choices for the selected option.

Options

TEXT This option edits text that has been added to the graph. Edit the text and press ENTER when you are finished.

CENTERING This option chooses the alignment for text that is added to the graph; either left, center, or right.

FONT This option changes the font of text in an object to one of the eight font choices determined with the :Format Font command.

LINE-STYLE This option changes the type of lines used by an object. Select from 1:Solid, 2:Dashed, 3:Dotted, 4:Long-Dashed, 5:Chain-Dotted, 6:Chain-Dashed, and 7:Hidden.

WIDTH This option changes the width of the lines used by an object. Select from 1:Very Narrow, 2:Narrow, 3:Medium, 4:Wide, and 5:Very Wide.

ARROWHEADS This option alters the direction that the arrow points (Switch), adds an arrowhead to a line (One), adds arrowheads to both ends of the line (Two), and removes arrowheads from lines (None).

SMOOTHING This option takes an object and replaces that object's angles with curves. The choices for this option vary the degree of smoothing of the lines. Select from None (objects appear without smoothing), Tight (some smoothing is present), and Medium (objects appear with the most smoothing possible).

:Graph Edit Options

Description

This command changes the size of all of the text in a graph, changes the cursor size, or adds or removes grid lines in the graph.

Options

GRID   This option adds (Yes) or removes (No) grid lines that indicate cell boundaries in the graph.

CURSOR   This option changes the size of the graphics editing window cursor. The cursor either appears as a small cross (if you choose Small) or a large cross (if you choose Big).

FONT-MAGNIFICATION   This option changes the text size of all of the text in a graph. You can choose a number between 0 and 1000 for the scaling factor. Numbers less than 100 decrease the font size and numbers greater than 100 increase the font size. Zero uses the point size chosen for the text without adjusting it for the graph size.

:Graph Edit Quit

Description

This command returns you to the READY mode in 1-2-3. This is the only way you can leave the :Graph Edit menu.

:Graph Edit Rearrange

Description

This command rearranges objects in a graph. For all of the options except Restore, you can select the object before or after selecting the command.

Options

DELETE   This option removes objects from the graph. You can also delete selected objects by pressing the DEL key.

RESTORE   This option restores the object that was last deleted.

MOVE   This option moves objects to a new location. Move the object to the new location and press ENTER.

COPY   This option copies objects in your graph next to the original. You can also copy objects by pressing the INS key.

LOCK   This option locks objects so that they cannot be altered.

UNLOCK   This option enables locked objects to be altered.

FRONT   This option places selected objects in front of other objects.

BACK   This option places selected objects behind other objects.

:Graph Edit Select

Description

This command selects objects to use with the :Graph Edit commands.

Options

ONE   This option selects one object to edit.

ALL   This option selects all the objects to edit except the underlying graph.

NONE   This option deselects all objects.

MORE/LESS   This option selects more or fewer objects to edit. Selecting an unselected object adds the object to the current selection. Selecting a selected object removes the object from the current selection.

CYCLE This option selects objects to edit by cycling through all of the objects. Press the arrow keys to cycle through the objects. Press the SPACEBAR to select the object and ENTER to finish selecting objects.

GRAPH This option selects the underlying graph but not the objects added to it.

QUIT This option returns you to the :Graph Edit menu.

:Graph Edit Transform

Description

This command changes the size and orientation of the selected objects. You can select the object to change either before or after selecting the command and one of its options.

Options

SIZE This option alters the size of the object.

ROTATE This option rotates an object around its axis.

QUARTER-TURN This option rotates the selected object by 90 degrees.

X-FLIP This option vertically flips the selected object.

Y-FLIP This option horizontally flips the selected object.

HORIZONTAL This option changes the size and slant of the object by changing the width of the object.

VERTICAL This option changes the size and slant of the object by changing the height of the object.

CLEAR This option cancels the :Graph Edit Transform commands performed on the selected objects.

:Graph Edit View

Description

This command changes the visibility of various portions of the graph in order to better view specific parts of the graph.

Options

FULL   This option displays the graph in its normal size.

IN   This option enlarges a portion of the graph so that it occupies all of the window. Select the two corners of a box containing the area of the graph you want to appear in the window.

PAN   This option displays selected sections of the graph by moving with the arrow keys to select the parts of the graph that appear.

+   This option displays the graph larger in the window.

−   This option displays the graph smaller in the window.

UP   This option shifts the graph upwards.

DOWN   This option shifts the graph downwards.

LEFT   This option shifts the graph to the left.

RIGHT   This option shifts the graph to the right.

:Graph Goto

Description

This command moves the cell pointer to the first cell on a worksheet that contains a graph.

Options

The only option for this command is to select the graph to go to from the list Wysiwyg provides.

:Graph Move

Description

This command moves any graph on the worksheet to a new location.

Options

The options for this command select the graph to move and the cell to contain the upper left corner of the graph.

NOTE: The 1-2-3 /Move, /Worksheet Insert, and /Worksheet Delete commands have no effect on the graph's position. The /Worksheet Column Width command will change the width of the columns Wysiwyg uses to display the graph.

:Graph Quit

Description

This command returns you to the READY mode.

:Graph Remove

Description

This command removes graphs that are on the worksheet. It does not affect any graph files on disk.

Options

The only option for this command is to select the graph to remove.

:Graph Settings

Description

This command alters several settings for a graph. You can select the graph to alter by moving the cell pointer to any cell the graph uses or by entering the graph name.

Options

GRAPH This option replaces a graphic with a different one. Select Current, Named, PIC, Metafile, or Blank and the graph name or filename if necessary.

RANGE This option changes the size of the range the graphic uses.

SYNC This option selects whether graphics are recalculated automatically. Select Yes or No.

DISPLAY This option displays the graphics (Yes) or displays them as shaded ranges (No).

OPAQUE This option hides the worksheet entries under the graph (Yes) or makes them visible (No).

QUIT This option returns you to the READY mode.

:Graph View

Description

This command displays a graph that is saved as a .PIC file or .CGM file.

Options

PIC This option displays a .PIC file for viewing. Select the .PIC file to view.

METAFILE This option displays a .CGM file for viewing. Select the .CGM file to view.

:Graph Zoom

Description

This command displays any graph in the current worksheet on the full screen.

Options

Your only option is to select a graph from the current worksheet.

:Named-Style

Description

This command formats a range by using a named style format. Wysiwyg named style formats are applied to a cell and have been assigned a name with which to format a range.

Options

1 THROUGH 8   These options assign the format of a named style to a range. Select the range for applying the format.

DEFINE   This option defines the eight named styles. Select the named style to change, select the cell containing the format that the named style represents, edit the six characters that will appear next to the number, and enter the style description that will appear in the control panel when the named style is highlighted.

:Print Background

Description

This command prints your Wysiwyg output in the background so you can continue to work on other tasks. When you print in the background, Wysiwyg stores the printed information temporarily in a file. Before you can use this command you must execute the BPRINT program from DOS.

Option

Your only option for this command is the filename you enter. Wysiwyg uses this filename temporarily to store the information to be printed. Wysiwyg will add an .ENC extension. If you specify an existing filename, you must select between Cancel and Replace. After you select the name of the file, Wysiwyg will start sending the information to the file. When Wysiwyg has sent all of the information in the file to the printer, Wysiwyg deletes the temporary file.

:Print Configuration

Description

This command changes print configuration options like font cartridges, printer interface, print bin used, and the print orientation.

Options

PRINTER   This option selects a printer to use from the list of printers chosen during installation.

INTERFACE   This option selects the connection between the computer and the printer. Select a number between 1 and 9, representing Parallel 1, Serial 1, Parallel 2, Serial 2, LPT1, LPT2, LPT3, COM1, or COM2.

1ST-CART   This option chooses the first font cartridge.

2ND-CART   This option chooses the second font cartridge.

ORIENTATION   This option selects whether the printer prints in Portrait mode, which is standard, or Landscape mode, which rotates your print output 90 degrees to print it sideways.

RESOLUTION   This option controls the quality of graphics output. You can choose from Final quality and Draft quality.

BIN   This option selects the bin the printer retrieves the paper from for printers with multiple-sheet feed options.

QUIT   Returns you to the :Print menu.

:Print File

Description

This command prints your Wysiwyg output to disk rather than to the printer. To print the resulting file, use the DOS COPY command. You do not need 1-2-3 or Wysiwyg to handle printing from disk.

Options

The only option for this command is the filename you enter. Wysiwyg adds .ENC as the extension for the file. If you specify the name of an existing file, you must select from Cancel or Replace.

:Print Go

Description

This command tells Wysiwyg to start printing to the printer.

:Print Info

Description

This command removes or displays the print status screen.

:Print Layout Borders

Description

This command changes the border columns and border rows. These columns and rows will appear on each page printed.

Options

TOP This option chooses border rows for the top of the printed pages. Select a range containing the rows to use.

LEFT This option chooses border columns for the left of the printed pages. Select a range containing the columns to use.

CLEAR This option removes existing border columns and rows.

QUIT This option returns you to the :Print Layout menu.

Print Layout Compression

Description

This command sets whether or not to compress the output when it is printed.

Options

NONE   This option prints with no compression.

MANUAL   This option lets you manually define the extent of expansion or compression. Enter a number less than 100 to compress the output or a number greater than 100 to expand the output.

AUTOMATIC   This option compresses the output to fit an entire print range on a page. It uses manual page breaks to determine how much data fits on each page.

:Print Layout Default

Description

This command changes the current page layout or default page layout.

Options

RESTORE   This option replaces the current settings with the default ones.

UPDATE   This option replaces the default settings with the current ones.

:Print Layout Library

Description

This command maintains a library of page layouts on disk. This allows you to use the same page layout in several worksheets.

Options

RETRIEVE   This option replaces the current page layout with a layout saved to disk. Select a page layout library.

SAVE This option stores the current layout in a file. Enter a name for the page layout library. If the name you specify already exists, you must choose Cancel or Replace to specify if you want to replace the existing file with the current layout.

ERASE This option permanently removes a layout from the library.

:Print Layout Margins

Description

This command changes any of the margins on the page layout.

Options

You can specify which of the margins you want to change by selecting Left, Right, Top, or Bottom and then entering the distance you want for the margin. You can also choose Quit to return to the Layout menu.

:Print Layout Page-Size

Description

This command specifies the dimensions of the paper you will use for output.

Options

1 THROUGH 7 These options select the following predefined page sizes:

1	Letter size (8 1/2 x 11 inches)
2	International A4 size (8 1/4 x 11 11/16 inches)
3	80 column 66 line listing size (9 1/2 x 11 inches)
4	132 column 66 line listing size (14 7/8 x 11 inches)
5	80 column 72 line listing size (9 1/2 x 12 inches)
6	Legal size (8 1/2 x 14 inches)
7	International B5 size (6 11/16 x 9 27/32 inches)

CUSTOM This option defines a custom page size. Enter the length and width followed by "in" for inches, "mm" for millimeters, or "cm" for centimeters.

:Print Layout Titles

Description

This command creates or removes a header or footer for the top or bottom of every page of output.

Options

HEADER This option supplies the header that appears at the top of every page. Enter the header using the same rules as for headers in 1-2-3.

FOOTER This option supplies the footer that appears at the bottom of every page. Enter the footer using the same rules as for footers in 1-2-3.

CLEAR This option removes an existing header or footer or both.

QUIT This option returns you to the :Print Layout menu.

:Print Preview

Description

This command previews how the print range will appear when printed. After viewing the preview, press any key to display the next page or, on the last page, return to the :Print menu.

:Print Quit

Description

This command returns you to the READY mode.

:Print Range

Description

This command clears or sets a range for printing.

Options

SET   This option selects the print range. Select any range to print.

CLEAR   This option eliminates the setting of the range to print.

:Print Settings

Description

This command controls how Wysiwyg prints the print range.

Options

BEGIN   This option specifies the first page to print.

END   This option specifies the last page to print.

START-NUMBER   This option specifies which page number to use on the first page.

COPIES   This option specifies the number of copies to print.

WAIT   This option pauses the printer before pages (Yes) or restores continuous printing (No).

GRID   This option chooses whether grid lines that indicate cell boundaries are printed (Yes) or omitted (No).

FRAME   This option decides whether to print the frame of the worksheet (Yes) or not to (No).

RESET   This option restores the default print settings.

QUIT   This option returns you to the :Print menu.

:Quit

Description

This command returns you to the READY mode.

:Special Copy

Description

This command copies any format options added to a range with Wysiwyg to another range.

Options

The options to copy work the same as 1-2-3's /Copy command options. They are not menu selections but selections of the size of the range you define for the From and To ranges. You can copy one cell to one cell, one cell to many cells, or many cells to many other cells.

:Special Export

Description

This command saves the formatting of the current worksheet to a file with an .FM3 (Wysiwyg), .FMT (Impress), or .ALL (Allways) extension.

Options

Your only option with this command is what to call the file. (If you name it after an existing file, you can either Cancel the request or Replace the existing file.) The extension of the file determines the format of the file this command creates. If you do not supply an extension, Wysiwyg uses .FM3.

:Special Import

Description

This command imports the worksheet format stored in a file with an .FM3 extension to the current worksheet. The imported format replaces all Wysiwyg formatting added to the current worksheet.

Options

After selecting one of these options you must select the name of the format file that you want to import.

ALL   This option replaces all formats, named styles, and graphics with the formats, named styles, and graphics in the file you select.

NAMED-STYLES   This option replaces the named styles with the named styles in the file you select.

FONTS   This option replaces the font set with the font set in the file you select.

GRAPHS   This option adds the graphics from the file you select to the current worksheet file.

:Special Move

Description

The :Special Move command moves formats assigned to a cell or range to another cell or range. The destination range adopts the formats of the source range and the source range formats are reset to the default format.

Options

You can specify any From and To ranges that you want to receive all of the Wysiwyg format options.

:Text

Description

This command works with worksheet ranges as text paragraphs.

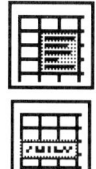

Options

EDIT This option lets you edit text in a text range as if you were using a word processor. Enter or edit the text and press ESC when finished.

ALIGN This option changes the alignment of text in a text range to Left, Right, Center, or Even (both sides of each line are aligned).

REFORMAT This option moves text from one cell to another in a text range so that the resulting range fits in the boundaries of the text range. Select the text range to reformat.

SET This option chooses a worksheet range to be a text range. Select the range to be part of a text range.

CLEAR This option stops treating a worksheet range as a text range. Select the range from which to remove the text range attribute.

:Worksheet Column

Description

This command changes the column width or resets the column to the global column width.

Options

RESET-WIDTH   This option returns the column width to the global column width set by 1-2-3. Select a range containing the columns to reset.

SET-WIDTH   This option sets the column width. Select a range containing the columns to change and enter the new column width.

:Worksheet Page

Description

This command specifies the exact location for a page break. Otherwise, Wysiwyg breaks output into pages when pages are full.

Options

ROW   This option ends a page at the current row.

COLUMN   This option ends the page at the current column.

DELETE   This option removes the page break previously inserted at the current location.

QUIT   This option returns you to the READY mode.

Worksheet Row

Description

This command sets the row height of any row within Wysiwyg. You can either allow Wysiwyg to make changes automatically based on font sizes of text or provide a specific height setting.

Options

SET-HEIGHT   This option sets the row height. Select a range containing the rows to change and enter a new row height in points.

AUTO   This option sets the row height to fit the largest text in the row. Select a range containing the rows to change.

THE COMPLETE REFERENCE

PART THREE

Appendixes

Appendix A

Installing 1-2-3

This appendix is an introduction to installing Lotus 1-2-3 Release 3.4 and its accessory programs on your system. It will cover 1-2-3 installation on various types of equipment. You will find detailed instructions to ensure that the installation process proceeds smoothly.

If your copy of 1-2-3 has already been installed by your computer dealer or someone else, you do not need to read this appendix. If your copy of 1-2-3 is still covered in shrink wrap, you need to install the package. You will find this appendix to be a valuable reference for the steps that you must take. It will also provide some information on various equipment options to help you make intelligent selections during the installation process.

Before beginning with specifics, this appendix will introduce the hardware options and the various system components. You cannot install 1-2-3 if you do not have at least some general knowledge about the system you are using. In order for the Install program to configure your copy of 1-2-3 to run with your specific hardware components, you must be able to tell the program what those components are.

Your Equipment

Release 3 has minimum system requirements that are different from it's 1-2-3 predecessors'. These releases require a minimum of 1MB RAM. Release 3.4 requires 2 MB of RAM when you use the Solver add-in. Most ATs that use 640K RAM for DOS applications have 1 MB of RAM that 1-2-3 can use. Release 3 can use expanded and extended memory, allowing you to take full advantage of the memory in PS/2s, as well as the memory added to ATs with cards like Intel's Above Board card.

Unlike many earlier versions of 1-2-3, 1-2-3 Release 3 must be run from a hard disk. The hard disk needs at least 3MBs of available space for the 1-2-3 files, and up to 6.5MBs of space for 1-2-3, the accessory programs and add-ins.

Release 3 also supports the addition of a math coprocessor. Both the 80287 and the 80387 coprocessor chips are supported and are automatically recognized once they are installed. Worksheet models with a significant number of calculations compute much more quickly with one of these chips added to the motherboard of your machine.

Before you can install 1-2-3, your computer must have DOS (the disk operating system) loaded. The operating system is the control program that resides in the memory of your computer, regardless of the software you are working with. It controls the interface between the various devices and establishes the format for data storage on disk. 1-2-3 Release 3.4 can use DOS version 3.0 or higher.

Monitors

Monitors can be described using two features. The first feature varies depending on whether the monitor can display multiple colors. Monitors come in two basic varieties, color and monochrome (one color).

The second feature of a monitor is its *resolution*. Resolution refers to how many dots of light your monitor can display across the screen—the more dots your monitor uses to fill the screen, the sharper the image it displays. The type of graphics adapter card in your computer, along with your monitor, determines the resolution. The different types of monitor resolution are described with letters like CGA (Color Graphics Adapter), EGA (Enhanced Graphics Adapter), VGA (Video Graphics Adapter), and Super VGA. When you install 1-2-3 you have to select the type of display you want based on the monitor's resolution and manufacturer.

Printers

1-2-3 can use a variety of output devices for creating printed copies of your 1-2-3 data. Some of these output devices include dot matrix printers, laser printers, and plotters.

To connect any of these output devices to your system, you also need a cable and an available port. It is possible to connect printers to both parallel and serial ports as long as they are compatible, but there are some special settings if you use a serial connection. First, you must set the printer's baud rate to control the speed of data transfer. At any baud rate except 110 you should also set 1 stop bit, 8 data bits, and no parity. With a speed of 110 there should be 2 stop bits. Once 1-2-3 is loaded, use the /Worksheet Global Default Printer Interface command, as described in Chapter 6, to select the baud rate that matches your printer's rate.

A plotter provides another option for producing graphs. With most devices you can use either paper or transparencies in your plotter with the appropriate pens to create the display medium of your choice. Since 1-2-3 supports only a limited number of plotters, you will want to ensure that the one you are considering purchasing is on the acceptable list; otherwise, it may not function with 1-2-3.

Installing 1-2-3

Installing Release 3.4 of 1-2-3 registers your disks with your name and company name, copies the program files to the hard disk, and tailors 1-2-3 to run with your specific hardware configuration. If 1-2-3 only ran with one type of hardware, this step would not be necessary. Since it is necessary, however, you should remember that it offers you an advantage: you can continue to use the package even if you change your hardware configuration to include a plotter, a new printer, or a different monitor.

When you purchase 1-2-3, the package you receive contains an envelope with several diskettes. These disks contain all of the files that 1-2-3 and its accessory programs need to run. You use these disks as you follow the steps to install 1-2-3 on your computer.

NOTE: These instructions assume DOS is already installed on your system. If this is not the case, install DOS before you install 1-2-3.

TIP: Make sure that you know what kind of monitor and printer you wish to use with 1-2-3 before starting to install it, so that you can respond appropriately to the installation questions.

1. To start the Install program, insert the Install disk into drive A. Type **A:** and press ENTER to make the drive current. (You can also do this with drive B.) Then type **INSTALL** and press ENTER to start the installation program. Press ENTER after viewing the opening screen.

2. 1-2-3 first requests your name and the name of your company for the installation procedure. On the first line enter your name and on the second, your company's. Press INS when finished. When prompted, press **Y** and ENTER to confirm the two names are correct.

3. Next, 1-2-3 prompts for the disk drive 1-2-3 will use and displays C. If you want to install 1-2-3 on a different hard disk drive, enter the drive letter. Press ENTER to accept the default or your new entry.

4. The program now prompts for the directory that 1-2-3 is installed into. Either use 1-2-3's suggested directory of \123R34 or supply a subdirectory name, and then press ENTER. If the directory exists and already contains files, you must press ENTER after reading the message box and specify a new directory. 1-2-3 program files cannot be installed in a directory that contains other files.

5. Next, you are prompted for the directory where the add-in files are to be installed. Either use 1-2-3's suggested directory of \123R34\ADDINS or supply a new subdirectory name, and then press ENTER.

6. Install prompts for the programs you want to transfer to your hard disk. This lets you select the parts of the 1-2-3 programs and accessory programs you want to install. Initially 1-2-3 and three add-in files (Auditor, Backsolver, and Viewer) are selected. As you highlight each option, you are shown how much disk space is required. At the top of the screen, a running total of the available space and the space required by the selected files is shown. Since the program files on the disk are compressed, you must use Install to transfer these programs to your hard

disk. You can add programs later by running Install again from drive A or B. To include or remove a program to be transferred to your hard disk, use the arrow keys to highlight a program and press the SPACEBAR (a cketk will appear to indicate selection). Press ENTER when you have selected the programs you want.

7. 1-2-3 prompts to see which add-ins you want loaded automatically when 1-2-3 is started. Highlight any one you want loaded and press the SPACEBAR to select it. Press ENTER when you are finished.

8. After you select the files to install, 1-2-3 starts copying files from the Install disk. The Install program prompts you for the next disk it needs when it has finished copying files to your hard disk. Replace the disk as Install requests and press ENTER.

9. Once Install has finished copying files to your hard drive, it displays an introductory screen for the second part of the installation process: specifying the equipment. Press ENTER to continue.

10. At the main Install menu, highlight the First Time Installation menu option and press ENTER.

11. Next, Install displays a screen describing what it has identified as the correct screen display. For most monitors, it is correct. Press ENTER to display the screen listing the available screen displays. Unless you know that the suggestion is incorrect, press ENTER to accept the suggestion. If you are certain that the suggestion is incorrect, highlight the correct display and press ENTER. Some monitor selections have a second menu that offers additional display options. Select the one you want and press ENTER.

12. Install next asks if you want to install a printer. Unless you do not have a printer, select Yes. In the next screen, select the printer manufacturer or one with which your printer is compatible by highlighting the name and pressing ENTER. Then highlight the model name from the list Install displays and press ENTER. If there are further options for your printer, highlight the appropriate options and press ENTER. In the last screen, select No unless you have another printer to set up.

13. After the printers are selected, Install asks you if you want to change the name of the driver set. If you select No, the installation program names it 123.DCF. If you select Yes, you must provide a filename for it.

14. Install now requests the last of the 1-2-3 program disks, and uses the files on this disk to copy only the information relevant to your printer and graphics card or monitor to the hard drive. When 1-2-3 is finished copying, it displays "Installation Successful." Press ENTER to acknowledge this screen.

NOTE: Although the message says installation is complete, there are still a few more steps. These steps generate the fonts that Wysiwyg will use.

15. Next, Install displays an introductory screen for the third part of the installation, generating fonts for you to use in your spreadsheet. Press ENTER after reading the introductory screen. Highlight Basic, Medium, or Extended for the set of fonts that you want to install and press ENTER. If you select Medium or Extended, Install asks if you want to generate the fonts immediately or wait to generate them. If you select Yes, the fonts are generated immediately. Once the fonts are generated, press any key to leave Install. You are now ready to run 1-2-3. If you are not generating the fonts immediately, you return to the Main Menu screen. At this point, you can select End Install Program Yes to return to the DOS prompt. With 1-2-3 installed, you can start the program by typing **123** and pressing ENTER.

Using Install After Installing 1-2-3

Once you have installed 1-2-3, you may continue to use the Install program. You use the Install program if you want to create more than one driver set with different hardware settings. You may need to change the hardware configuration to include another printer or screen display. You may also want to change the sort order that 1-2-3 uses for the /Data Sort command. You can also change certain Wysiwyg settings.

Using Install to change 1-2-3 settings requires that you start Install from the directory containing the 1-2-3 program files on your hard disk. You only start Install from a floppy disk when you want to add 1-2-3 or its accessory programs to your hard disk.

Creating More Than One Driver Set

If you use your Lotus software on more than one computer or if you frequently alter the configuration of your system, you may want more than one driver set. This allows you to switch from one driver set to another without having to change the installation parameters each time.

If you use more than one driver set, pick a meaningful driver name for each, such as 2MONITOR, PLOTTER, or HOME. You can use up to eight characters for

the filename. You must avoid using the following symbols: , . ; : / ? * = < > [ ] \ '
in the filename. Install adds a .DCF extension to the filename, as in COLOR.DCF.

Use the First Time Installation menu option to create each driver set. Save each driver set under a different name. You may want to store each driver set on a separate disk or in a different directory, if you want to use different drivers with the files in different drives or directories. To use a driver set other than 123.DCF, specify the path and filename of the driver set when you start 1-2-3, as in C:\123\BUDGET\HOME.DCF.

Modifying the Current Driver

To modify the existing 1-2-3 driver sets, select Change Selected Equipment from the installation menu. To select a driver set to change, select Make Another Driver Set Current and supply a driver set filename. If you do not select a driver set file, Install uses 123.DCF. Then select Modify the Current Driver Set. This displays a menu of settings you can change, namely, the screen, printer, and country settings.

Changing the Display

The display driver may need to be changed if you want to change the initial display driver. Several monitors can use more than one display driver. For example, if you are using a monitor with a VGA display, you may want to see how your graphs will look to someone with an EGA monitor. To change a display driver, select Change Selected Display. The Install program lists the possible selections, with a 1 next to the display driver that is currently selected. When you select a different driver, Install replaces the current selection with the new selection.

Changing the Printer

The printer driver may need to be changed if you change the printer or want to add another one. 1-2-3 allows up to 16 printer drivers. To add or change a printer driver, select the Change Selected Printer menu option. The Install program lists the possible printer manufacturers, with a 1 next to the printer manufacturer that is currently selected. To add another printer driver, select the printer driver you want to add. Then make the additional menu selections appropriate for the printer. This selects the printer driver that you added as the secondary printer driver. To remove a printer driver, select Change Selected Printer and press DEL after selecting the manufacturer and highlighting the model.

To select a printer driver from 1-2-3, use the /Worksheet Global Default Printer Name command. Then type the number that represents the selected driver. To select a printer driver for Wysiwyg, use the :Print Config Printer command. Then highlight the appropriate printer in the Printer List pop-up dialog box and press ENTER.

Changing the Sort Order

The Change Selected Country option allows you to change the collating sequence for the existing driver set. Install provides three options: ASCII, Numbers first, and Numbers last. The sort order for each option is as follows:

- ASCII   Blank cells, followed by labels and values in ASCII order. Capitalization affects the sort order of this option. This selection also makes functions case sensitive. This can have serious implications for formulas containing string functions that are used in computations or for the criteria area with /Data Query commands.
- Numbers last   Blank cells, label entries with letters in alphabetical order, label entries beginning with numbers in numeric sequence, labels beginning with special characters, and values.
- Numbers first   Blank cells, labels beginning with numbers in numeric sequence, labels beginning with letters in alphabetical order, labels beginning with special characters, and values.

To change the collating sequence, select Change Selected Country from the Modify Current Driver Set menu, and then select the sort order you want from the submenu.

Saving the Driver Files

Once you have changed your driver file's display, printer, and sort configurations, you need to save them so that the driver file will contain your new selections. To save the driver file, select the Save Changes menu option. When 1-2-3 displays the filename, edit it if you want the new settings saved with a different filename. When the filename is correct, press ENTER to save the updated changes. You will need to provide a 1-2-3 program disk for Install to transfer some files. When the new driver set file is saved, you are instructed to press F9 to return to the last menu, or press ENTER to leave Install. After pressing ENTER, you must select Yes to confirm that you want to leave Install.

Changing Wysiwyg Options

You can also change certain Wysiwyg options for 1-2-3. You can generate more fonts for Wysiwyg, add fonts from a disk, or switch the mouse buttons. To use these options, select Wysiwyg Options from Install's main menu.

Generate Fonts

After selecting this menu option, you can choose to generate the Basic, Medium, or Extended set of fonts for use with Wysiwyg. This is a simple way to add more fonts if you initially selected a minimal number.

Switch Mouse Buttons

This menu option allows you to select which mouse button will be used for selecting items on the screen. By default, it is the left button that is used for selecting, and clicking the right mouse button has the same effect as pressing ESC. Left-handed people will find that switching mouse buttons makes using the mouse much easier. To switch the buttons, highlight Right or Left and press ENTER.

Add Fonts

You can add fonts for use with 1-2-3 and Wysiwyg by using this menu option to transfer them from a floppy disk onto your hard drive. You will need to select the drive that will contain the fonts.

Installing 1-2-3 with Windows

You can use Release 3.4 with Windows. Windows allows you to switch between applications without having to exit one to get into another. To install 1-2-3 with Windows, you can either add the program to Windows yourself or have Windows do it for you. You will first need to install 1-2-3 as described earlier in this appendix.

To add the program to Windows yourself, activate the group window to which you want to add 1-2-3 and select New from the File menu. Select Program Item and select OK. In the next dialog box displayed, enter **1-2-3 Release 3.4** in the Description text box and **C:\123R34\123** in the Command Line text box. Now you can select OK to add the program item to the program group.

To have Windows add 1-2-3 for you, select Windows Setup from the Main group window. Select Set Up Applications from the Options menu. Select OK to search all directories or change the option selected to limit the search. After the search is completed, highlight Lotus 1-2-3, select it, and select the Add command button. Finally, select the OK command button and follow any remaining instructions that Windows displays on the screen.

Appendix B

The SmartIcons

The SmartIcons appear when Wysiwyg is loaded with 1-2-3 Release 3.4, and contain 94 icons that you can use to simplify various operations performed with 1-2-3 and Wysiwyg. Selecting a SmartIcon is like selecting a menu command in that the operation that the icon or menu command represents is carried out. You can use this appendix as a quick reference for the identification of the various SmartIcons.

The number of icons appearing on each icon palette is controlled by what type of monitor you have and whether Wysiwyg is attached. With a VGA monitor, you will have eight palettes of icons. The first of these is the custom palette, which can be individualized by selecting icons from other palettes. In the table below, the icons are divided by the palette where they would appear if you had a VGA monitor. If you are using another monitor, you will find that these icons are in a slightly different order. The File Save icon, which is described only once in this table, appears at the top of every palette, and the Help icon appears at the bottom of every palette. All of the icons appearing on the custom palette also appear on one of the other palettes. Here those icons are described by their position on the other palettes.

Palette 2

Graphic Icon	Description
	Saves the worksheet to a disk
U	Adds or removes single underlining
U	Adds or removes double underlining
$	Formats as currency or returns to the default format
0,0	Formats with a comma or returns to the default format
%	Formats as a percentage or returns to the default format
AA	Displays the text in the next font
AA	Displays the text in the next color
AA	Displays the background in the next color
	Adds or removes outlining with a drop-shadow
	Adds a single, double, or wide line outline
	Adds light, dark, or solid shading
	Left-aligns all the labels in the selected range
	Centers all the labels in the selected range
	Right-aligns all the labels in the selected range
?	Starts the Help system

Palette 3

Graphic Icon	Description
	Inserts one row above the selected range
	Inserts one column left of the selected range
	Deletes all rows in the selected range
	Deletes all columns in the selected range
	Adds a worksheet after the current sheet
	Deletes the current worksheet
	Inserts a horizontal Wysiwyg page break in the row
	Inserts a vertical Wysiwyg page break in the column
	Sorts a database in descending order
	Sorts a database in ascending order
	Fills the selected range with a series of values
	Recalculates all of the formulas
	Enters the current date and time
	Cycles through the standard zoom settings

Palette 4 Graphic Icon	Description
←	Moves the cell pointer one cell to the left
→	Moves the cell pointer one cell to the right
↑	Moves the cell pointer one cell up
↓	Moves the cell pointer one cell down
	Moves the worksheet display one screen up
	Moves the worksheet display one screen down
	Moves the worksheet display one screen to the left
	Moves the worksheet display one screen to the right
	Moves the worksheet display one column to the left
	Moves the worksheet display one column to the right
	Moves the worksheet display one row up
	Moves the worksheet display one row down
	Moves the cell pointer to cell A1
	Moves the cell pointer to the lower right corner of the active area

Appendix B: The SmartIcons

Palette 5

Graphic Icon	Description
	Switches between normal and perspective view
	Moves the cell pointer back one worksheet
	Moves the cell pointer forward one worksheet
	Moves the cell pointer down to the intersection of a blank and a filled cell
	Moves the cell pointer up to the intersection of a blank and a filled cell
	Moves the cell pointer right to the intersection of a blank and a filled cell
	Moves the cell pointer left to the intersection of a blank and a filled cell
	Prompts for the new location for the cell pointer
	Activates the Search feature
	Moves the highlighted range
	Copies the highlighted range
	Applies the Wysiwyg formats of the selected range
	With Undo enabled, cancels your last action
	Deletes the entries in the highlighted range

Palette 6

Graphic Icon	Description
	Retrieves a worksheet from a disk
	Opens a worksheet file without erasing the current worksheet file
	Creates and opens a new worksheet file
	Prints a range
	Previews print output
	Sums a preselected range
	Sums values on multiple sheets
	Displays the current range as a graph
	Places the current graph in the worksheet
	Displays the current graph
	Edits the text range the cell pointer is in
	Defines a range as text and cycles through alignment choices
	Adds a graph which circles the current range
	Duplicates the current cell

Palette 7

Graphic Icon	Description
B	Adds or removes bold
I	Adds or removes italic
N	Removes all Wysiwyg formatting
(running figure)	Turns on the STEP mode used for macros
(running figure with arrow)	Lets you choose a macro to run
(icon with +)	Adds an icon to the custom palette
(icon with −)	Removes an icon from the custom palette
(icon with arrow)	Moves an icon on the custom palette
U	Displays the descriptions of User icons

Palette 8

Graphic Icon	Description
U1	Runs the macro attached to the user icon. There are twelve of these icons, labelled U1 through U12.

APPENDIX C

LMBCS Codes

You can use the Lotus Multibyte Character Set (LMBCS) codes to create special characters within your worksheets. These special characters can create boxes or special letters used in various languages.

Creating LMBCS Codes

Use LMBCS codes to create characters unavailable on your keyboard. Each possible character has an LMBCS code. LMBCS characters are divided into groups of 256 characters. The first group, Group 0, omits the characters from 0 to 31. If you use them, 1-2-3 returns the characters for LMBCS codes 256 through 287.

Some monitors and printers cannot display all LMBCS characters. When a worksheet contains an LMBCS character that the monitor cannot display or the printer cannot print, 1-2-3 substitutes a different character for displaying and printing.

Table C-1 lists the LMBCS codes, the characters the codes create, and the key codes you use to create them.

Creating LMBCS Characters

You can create LMBCS characters five different ways. The method you use depends on the task you are performing when you want the LMBCS character.

- **Enter the character directly from the keyboard.** Many LMBCS characters such as letters, numbers, and common punctuation can be entered by pressing a key.

- **Use the ALT-F1 (COMPOSE) key.** Press ALT-F1 and type the Compose sequence. For example, to create a trademark symbol (™), press the ALT-F1 (COMPOSE) key and type a **T** and an **M**. 1-2-3 converts these entries into a trademark symbol.

- **Use extended Compose.** Press the ALT-F1 (COMPOSE) key twice and type the LMBCS group number, a hyphen, and the key code. For example, to create a trademark symbol (™), press the ALT-F1 (COMPOSE) key twice. Then type a **1** for the group number, a **-** and **118**. 1-2-3 converts these entries into a trademark symbol.

- **Use the @CHAR function.** Enter the appropriate LMBCS code for the function's argument. For example, to include the trademark symbol (™) in a note for a cell formula, enter **@CHAR(374)**. 1-2-3 converts the function into a trademark symbol. The @CHAR function is used within formulas especially when you cannot enter the character using another method, such as a double quote.

Lotus Multibyte Character Set (LMBCS) Codes for Group 0

LMBCS Code	Normal Character	Xsymbol Character	Compose Character	Key Code	Description of Normal Character
32				032	Space
33	!	♩		033	Exclamation point
34	"	⁝		034	Double quotes
35	#	⁝	+ +	035	Pound sign
36	$	♥		036	Dollar sign
37	%	♦		037	Percent
38	&	♚		038	Ampersand
39	'	⸰		039	Close quote
40	(	♣		040	Open parenthesis
41	)	♦		041	Close parenthesis
42	*	♥		042	Asterisk
43	+	♠		043	Plus sign
44	,	①		044	Comma
45	–	②		045	Minus sign
46	.	③		046	Period
47	/	④		047	Slash
48	0	⑤		048	Zero
49	1	⑥		049	One
50	2	⑦		050	Two
51	3	⑧		051	Three
52	4	⑨		052	Four
53	5	⑩		053	Five
54	6	❶		054	Six
55	7	❷		055	Seven
56	8	❸		056	Eight
57	9	❹		057	Nine
58	:	❺		058	Colon
59	;	❻		059	Semicolon
60	<	❼		060	Less than
61	=	❽		061	Equal sign

* Indicates a character where the order of the compose characters is important

Table C-1. *Lotus Multibyte Character Set (LMBCS) Codes*

Lotus Multibyte Character Set (LMBCS) Codes for Group 0

LMBCS Code	Normal Character	Xsymbol Character	Compose Character	Key Code	Description of Normal Character
62	>	⑨		062	Greater than
63	?	⑩		063	Question mark
64	@	①	aa or AA	064	At sign
65	A	②		065	A, uppercase
66	B	③		066	B, uppercase
67	C	④		067	C, uppercase
68	D	⑤		068	D, uppercase
69	E	⑥		069	E, uppercase
70	F	⑦		070	F, uppercase
71	G	⑧		071	G, uppercase
72	H	⑨		072	H, uppercase
73	I	⑩		073	I, uppercase
74	J	❶		074	J, uppercase
75	K	❷		075	K, uppercase
76	L	❸		076	L, uppercase
77	M	❹		077	M, uppercase
78	N	❺		078	N, uppercase
79	O	❻		079	O, uppercase
80	P	❼		080	P, uppercase
81	Q	❽		081	Q, uppercase
82	R	❾		082	R, uppercase
83	S	❿		083	S, uppercase
84	T	→		084	T, uppercase
85	U	→		085	U, uppercase
86	V	↔		086	V, uppercase
87	W	↕		087	W, uppercase
88	X	↘		088	X, uppercase
89	Y	→		089	Y, uppercase
90	Z	↗		090	Z, uppercase
91	[	→	((	091	Open bracket

* Indicates a character where the order of the compose characters is important

Table C-1. *Lotus Multibyte Character Set (LMBCS) Codes* (continued)

Appendix C: LMBCS Codes

Lotus Multibyte Character Set (LMBCS) Codes for Group 0

LMBCS Code	Normal Character	Xsymbol Character	Compose Character	Key Code	Description of Normal Character
92	\	→	//	092	Backslash
93	]	→	))	093	Close bracket
94			vv	094	Caret
95	_	⇒		095	Underscore
96	'	⇒		096	Open single quote
97	a	⇒		097	a, lowercase
98	b	➢		098	b, lowercase
99	c	➢		099	c, lowercase
100	d	➤		100	d, lowercase
101	e	⇒		101	e, lowercase
102	f	➡		102	f, lowercase
103	g	♦		103	g, lowercase
104	h	⇒		104	h, lowercase
105	i	⇨		105	i, lowercase
106	j	⇨		106	j, lowercase
107	k	⇔		107	k, lowercase
108	l	⇔		108	l, lowercase
109	m	⇨		109	m, lowercase
110	n	⇨		110	n, lowercase
111	o	⇨		111	o, lowercase
112	p			112	p, lowercase
113	q	⇨		113	q, lowercase
114	r	⊃		114	r, lowercase
115	s	➪		115	s, lowercase
116	t	➘		116	t, lowercase
117	u	➪		117	u, lowercase
118	v	➚		118	v, lowercase
119	w	➘		119	w, lowercase
120	x	➪		120	x, lowercase
121	y	➚		121	y, lowercase

* Indicates a character where the order of the compose characters is important

Table C-1. *Lotus Multibyte Character Set (LMBCS) Codes* (continued)

Lotus Multibyte Character Set (LMBCS) Codes for Group 0

LMBCS Code	Normal Character	Xsymbol Character	Compose Character	Key Code	Description of Normal Character
122	z	→		122	z, lowercase
123	{	↔	(-	123	Open brace
124	|	⇥	^/	124	Bar
125	}	⇨	-)	125	Close brace
126	~	⇒	- -	126	Tilde
127	⌂			127	Delete
128	Ç		C,	128	C cedilla, uppercase
129	ü		u"	129	u umlaut, lowercase
130	é		e'	130	e acute, lowercase
131	â		a^	131	a circumflex, lowercase
132	ä		a"	132	a umlaut, lowercase
133	à		a'	133	a grave, lowercase
134	å		a*	134	a ring, lowercase
135	ç		c,	135	c cedilla, lowercase
136	ê		e^	136	e circumflex, lowercase
137	ë		e"	137	e umlaut, lowercase
138	è		e'	138	e grave, lowercase
139	ï		i"	139	i umlaut, lowercase
140	î		i^	140	i circumflex, lowercase
141	ì		i'	141	i grave, lowercase
142	Ä		A"	142	A umlaut, uppercase
143	Å		A*	143	A ring, uppercase
144	É		E'	144	E acute, uppercase
145	æ		ae	145	ae diphthong, lowercase*
146	Æ		AE	146	AE diphthong, uppercase*
147	ô		o^	147	o circumflex, lowercase
148	ö		o"	148	o umlaut, lowercase
149	ò		o'	149	o grave, lowercase
150	û		u^	150	u circumflex, lowercase

* Indicates a character where the order of the compose characters is important

Table C-1. *Lotus Multibyte Character Set (LMBCS) Codes (continued)*

Lotus Multibyte Character Set (LMBCS) Codes for Group 0

LMBCS Code	Normal Character	Xsymbol Character	Compose Character	Key Code	Description of Normal Character
151	ù		u'	151	u grave, lowercase
152	ÿ		y"	152	y umlaut, lowercase
153	Ö		O"	153	O umlaut, uppercase
154	Ü		U"	154	U umlaut, uppercase
155	ø		o/	155	o slash, lowercase
156	£		L=l=L- or l-	156	British pound sterling symbol
157	Ø		O/	157	O slash, uppercase
158	×		xx or XX	158	Multiplication sign
159	ƒ		ff	159	Guilder
160	á		a'	160	a acute, lowercase
161	í		i'	161	i acute, lowercase
162	ó		o'	162	o acute, lowercase
163	ú		u'	163	u acute, lowercase
164	ñ		n~	164	n tilde, lowercase
165	Ñ		N~	165	N tilde, uppercase
166	ª		a_ or A_	166	Feminine ordinal indicator
167	º		o_ or O_	167	Masculine ordinal indicator
168	¿		??	168	Question mark inverted
169	®		RO or ro	169	Registered trademark symbol
170	¬		-]	170	End of line symbol/Logical NOT
171	½		12	171	One half*
172	¼		14	172	One quarter*
173	¡		!!	173	Exclamation point, inverted
174	«		<<	174	Left angle quotes
175	»		>>	175	Right angle quotes
176	▓			176	Solid fill character, light

* Indicates a character where the order of the compose characters is important

Table C-1. *Lotus Multibyte Character Set (LMBCS) Codes* (continued)

Lotus Multibyte Character Set (LMBCS) Codes for Group 0

LMBCS Code	Normal Character	Xsymbol Character	Compose Character	Key Code	Description of Normal Character
177	▓			177	Solid fill character, medium
178	▓			178	Solid fill character, heavy
179	│			179	Center vertical box bar
180	┤			180	Right box side
181	Á		A'	181	A acute, uppercase
182	Â		A^	182	A circumflex, uppercase
183	À		A`	183	A grave, uppercase
184	©		CO C0 co or c0	184	Copyright symbol
185	╡			185	Right box side, double
186	║			186	Center vertical box bar double
187	╗			187	Upper right box corner double
188	╝			188	Lower right box corner double
189	¢		c| c/ C| or C/	189	Cent sign
190	¥		Y= y= Y- or y-	190	Yen sign
191	┐			191	Upper right box corner
192	└			192	Lower right box corner
193	┴			193	Lower box side
194	┬			194	Upper box side
195	├			195	Left box side
196	─			196	Center horizontal box bar
197	┼			197	Center box intersection
198	ã		a~	198	a tilde, lowercase
199	Ã		A~	199	A tilde, uppercase

* Indicates a character where the order of the compose characters is important

Table C-1. *Lotus Multibyte Character Set (LMBCS) Codes* (continued)

Appendix C: LMBCS Codes

Lotus Multibyte Character Set (LMBCS) Codes for Group 0

LMBCS Code	Normal Character	Xsymbol Character	Compose Character	Key Code	Description of Normal Character
200	╚			200	Lower left box corner, double
201	╔			201	Upper left box corner, double
202	╩			202	Lower box side, double
203	╦			203	Upper box side, double
204	╠			204	Left box side, double
205	═			205	Center horizontal box bar double
206	╬			206	Center box intersection double
207	¤		XO or xo	207	International currency sign
208	ð		d–	208	Icelandic eth, lowercase
209	Ð		D–	209	Icelandic eth, uppercase
210	Ê		E^	210	E circumflex, uppercase
211	Ë		E"	211	E umlaut, uppercase
212	È		E'	212	E grave, uppercase
213	ı		i(space)	213	i without dot (lowercase)
214	Í		I'	214	I acute, uppercase
215	Î		I^	215	I circumflex, uppercase
216	Ï		I"	216	I umlaut, uppercase
217	┘			217	Lower right box corner
218	┌			218	Upper left box corner
219	■			219	Solid fill character
220	■			220	Solid fill character, lower half
221	¦		/(space)	221	Vertical line, broken
222	Ì		I'	222	I grave, uppercase

* Indicates a character where the order of the compose characters is important

Table C-1. *Lotus Multibyte Character Set (LMBCS) Codes* (continued)

Lotus Multibyte Character Set (LMBCS) Codes for Group 0

LMBCS Code	Normal Character	Xsymbol Character	Compose Character	Key Code	Description of Normal Character
223	■			223	Solid fill character, upper half
224	Ó		O'	224	O acute, uppercase
225	ß		ss	225	German sharp, lowercase
226	Ô		O^	226	O circumflex, uppercase
227	Ò		O`	227	O grave, uppercase
228	õ		o~	228	o tilde, lowercase
229	Õ		O~	229	O tilde, uppercase*
230	µ		/u	230	Greek mu, lowercase
231	þ		p-	231	Icelandic thorn, lowercase
232	Þ		P-	232	Icelandic thorn, uppercase
233	Ú		U'	233	U acute, uppercase
234	Û		U^	234	U circumflex, uppercase
235	Ù		U`	235	U grave, uppercase
236	ý		y'	236	y acute, lowercase
237	Ý		Y'	237	Y acute, uppercase
238	‾		^-	238	Overline character
239	´			239	Acute accent
240	-		-=	240	Hyphenation symbol
241	±		+-	241	Plus or minus sign
242	=		__ or ==	242	Double underscore
243	¾		34	243	Three quarters sign*
244	¶		!p or !P	244	Paragraph symbol
245	§		SO S0 so or s0	245	Section symbol
246	÷		:-	246	Divison sign
247	¸		''	247	Cedilla accent
248	°		^0	248	Degree symbol

* Indicates a character where the order of the compose characters is important

Table C-1. *Lotus Multibyte Character Set (LMBCS) Codes (continued)*

Lotus Multibyte Character Set (LMBCS) Codes for Group 0

LMBCS Code	Normal Character	Xsymbol Character	Compose Character	Key Code	Description of Normal Character
249	¨			249	Umlaut accent
250	•		^.	250	Center dot
251	^{1}		^1	251	One superscript
252	^{3}		^3	252	Three superscript
253	^{2}		^2	253	Two superscript
254	■			254	Square bullet
255				255	Null

Lotus Multibyte Character Set (LMBCS) Codes for Group 1

LMBCS Code	Normal Character	Xsymbol Character	Compose Character	Key Code	Description of Normal Character
256	Not used	Not used		000	Null
257	☺			001	Smiling face
258	☻			002	Smiling face, reversed
259	♥			003	Heart suit symbol
260	♦			004	Diamond suit symbol
261	♣			005	Club suit symbol
262	♠			006	Spade suit symbol
263	•			007	Bullet
264	◘			008	Bullet, reversed
265	○			009	Open circle
266	◙			010	Open circle, reversed
267	♂			011	Male symbol
268	♀			012	Female symbol
269	♪			013	Musical note
270	♫			014	Double musical note
271	☼			015	Sun symbol
272	►			016	Forward arrow indicator
273	◄			017	Back arrow indicator
274	↕			018	Up-down arrow

* Indicates a character where the order of the compose characters is important

Table C-1. *Lotus Multibyte Character Set (LMBCS) Codes* (continued)

Lotus Multibyte Character Set (LMBCS) Codes for Group 1

LMBCS Code	Normal Character	Xsymbol Character	Compose Character	Key Code	Description of Normal Character
275	‼			019	Double exclamation points
276	¶			020	Paragraph symbol
277	§			021	Section symbol
278	▮			022	Solid horizontal rectangle
279	↕			023	Up-down arrow, perpendicular
280	↑			024	Up arrow
281	↓			025	Down arrow
282	→			026	Right arrow
283	←		mg	027	left arrow
284	∟			028	Right angle symbol
285	↔			029	Left-right symbol
286	▲		ba	030	Solid triangle
287	▼		ea	031	Solid triangle inverted
288	¨		"(space)	032	Umlaut accent, uppercase
289	~		~(space)	033	Tilde accent, uppercase
290	°			034	Ring accent, uppercase
291	^		^(space)	035	Circumflex accent, uppercase
292	`		'(space)	036	Grave accent, uppercase
293	'		'(space)	037	Acute accent, uppercase
294	"		"^	038	High double quotes, opening
295	'			039	High single quote, straight
296	…			040	Ellipsis
297	–			041	En mark
298	—			042	Em mark
299	Not used			043	Null

* Indicates a character where the order of the compose characters is important

Table C-1. *Lotus Multibyte Character Set (LMBCS) Codes* (continued)

Lotus Multibyte Character Set (LMBCS) Codes for Group 1

LMBCS Code	Normal Character	Xsymbol Character	Compose Character	Key Code	Description of Normal Character
300	Not used			044	Null
301	Not used			045	Null
302	<			046	Left angle parenthesis
303	>			047	Right angle parenthesis
304	¨		(space)"	048	Umlaut accent, lowercase
305	~		(space)~	049	Tilde accent, lowercase
306	°			050	Ring accent, lowercase
307	^		(space)^	051	Circumflex accent, lowercase
308	`		(space)'	052	Grave accent, lowercase
309	'		(space)'	053	Acute accent, lowercase
310	„		"v	054	Low double quotes, closing
311	‚			055	Low single quote, closing
312	"			056	High double quotes, closing
313	▬			057	Underscore, heavy
314	Not Used			058	Null
315	Not Used			059	Null
316	Not Used			060	Null
317	Not Used			061	Null
318	Not Used			062	Null
319	Not Used			063	Null
320	Œ		OE	064	OE ligature, uppercase
321	œ		oe	065	oe ligature, lowercase
322	Ÿ		Y"	066	Y umlaut, uppercase
323	Not Used			067	Null
324	Not Used			068	Null
325	Not Used			069	Null

* Indicates a character where the order of the compose characters is important

Table C-1. *Lotus Multibyte Character Set (LMBCS) Codes* (continued)

Lotus Multibyte Character Set (LMBCS) Codes for Group 1

LMBCS Code	Normal Character	Xsymbol Character	Compose Character	Key Code	Description of Normal Character
326	╞			070	Left box side, double joins single
327	╟			071	Left box side, single joins double
328	▌			072	Solid fill character, left half
329	▐			073	Solid fill character, right half
330	Not Used			074	Null
331	Not Used			075	Null
332	Not Used			076	Null
333	Not Used			077	Null
334	Not Used			078	Null
335	Not Used			079	Null
336	╨			080	Lower box side, double joins single
337	╤			081	Upper box side, single joins double
338	╥			082	Upper box side, double joins single
339	╜			083	Lower single left double box corner
340	╛			084	Lower double left single box corner
341	╕			085	Upper double left single box corner
342	╖			086	Upper single left double box corner
343	╪			087	Center box intersection, vertical double
344	╫			088	Center box intersection, horizontal double
345	╡			089	Right box side, double joins single

* Indicates a character where the order of the compose characters is important

Table C-1. *Lotus Multibyte Character Set (LMBCS) Codes* (continued)

Appendix C: LMBCS Codes

Lotus Multibyte Character Set (LMBCS) Codes for Group 1

LMBCS Code	Normal Character	Xsymbol Character	Compose Character	Key Code	Description of Normal Character
346	╢			090	Right box side, single joins double
347	╜			091	Upper single right double box corner
348	╛			092	Upper double right single box corner
349	╝			093	Lower single right double box corner
350	╛			094	Lower double right single box corner
351	╧			095	Lower box side, single joins double
352	ij		ij	096	ij ligature, lowercase
353	IJ		IJ	097	IJ ligature, uppercase
354	fi		fi	098	fi ligature, lowercase
355	fl		fl	099	fl ligature, lowercase
356	'n		'n	100	n comma, lowercase
357	l·		l.	101	l bullet, lowercase
358	L·		L.	102	L bullet, uppercase
359	Not Used			103	Null
360	Not Used			104	Null
361	Not Used			105	Null
362	Not Used			106	Null
363	Not Used			107	Null
364	Not Used			108	Null
365	Not Used			109	Null
366	Not Used			110	Null
367	Not Used			111	Null
368	†			112	Single dagger symbol
369	‡			113	Double dagger symbol
370	Not Used			114	Null
371	Not Used			115	Null

* Indicates a character where the order of the compose characters is important

Table C-1. *Lotus Multibyte Character Set (LMBCS) Codes* (continued)

Lotus Multibyte Character Set (LMBCS) Codes for Group 1

LMBCS Code	Normal Character	Xsymbol Character	Compose Character	Key Code	Description of Normal Character
372	Not Used			116	Null
373	Not Used			117	Null
374	™		TM Tm or tm	118	Trademark symbol
375	ℓ		lr	119	Liter symbol
376	Not Used			120	Null
377	Not Used			121	Null
378	Not Used			122	Null
379	Not Used			123	Null
380	Kr		KR Kr or kr	124	Krone sign
381	⌐		-[	125	Start of line symbol
382	£		LI Li or li	126	Lira sign
383	Pt		PT Pt or pt	127	Peseta sign

* Indicates a character where the order of the compose characters is important

The LMBCS codes with numbers between 384 and 511 create the same characters as the LMBCS codes with numbers between 128 and 255. The characters with LMBCS codes between 384 and 511 have the same key codes as the characters between 128 and 255.

Table C-1. *Lotus Multibyte Character Set (LMBCS) Codes (continued)*

Index

+/- format, 111
@@, 372-374
@ABS, 345-346
@ACOS, 346-347
@ASIN, 348-349
@ATAN, 349
@ATAN2, 349-350
@AVG, 397-398
@CELL, 374-376
@CELLPOINTER, 377-378
@CHAR, 50, 412
@CHOOSE, 378-380
@CLEAN, 412-413
@CODE, 314-315
@COLS, 380-381
@COORD, 381-382
@COS, 350-351
@COUNT, 398-399
@CTERM, 328-329
@D360, 312-313
@DATE, 313-315
@DATEVALUE, 315-316
@DAVG, 532
@DAY, 316-317
@DCOUNT, 533
@DDB, 329-330
@DGET, 533-534
@DMAX, 534-535
@DQUERY, 535-537
@DSTD, 537
@DSTDS, 538
@DSUM, 538-539

@DVAR, 538-540
@DVARS, 540
@ERR, 382-383
@EXACT, 314-315
@EXP, 351-352
@FALSE, 363
@FIND, 315-316
@functions, 305-429
    complete list of, 306-309
    database statistical, 531-540
    date and time, 312-327
    entering, 63-66
    financial, 327-344
    logical, 362-371
    mathematical, 344-362
    new, 10
    special, 372-397
    statistical, 397-410
    string, 411-429
See also name of function
@FV, 330-331
@HLOOKUP, 383-386
@HOUR, 318
@IF, 363-366
@INDEX, 387-389
@INFO, 389-390
@INT, 352-354
@IRR, 331-332
@ISERR, 366-367
@ISNA, 367-368
@ISNUMBER, 368-369
@ISRANGE, 369-370
@ISSTRING, 370-371
@LEFT, 416-417
@LENGTH, 417-418
@LN, 354
@LOG, 354-355
@LOWER, 418

@MAX, 399-400
@MID, 419-420
@MIN, 400
@MINUTE, 318-319
@MOD, 355-356
@MONTH, 319-320
@N, 420-421
@NA, 390-391
@NOW, 321
@NPV, 333-334
@PI, 356
@PMT, 335-336
@PROPER, 422
@PV, 337
@RAND, 356
@RATE, 338
@REPEAT, 422-423
@REPLACE, 424-425
@RIGHT, 425-426
@ROUND, 357-358
@ROWS, 391-392
@S, 426
@SECOND, 322
@SHEETS, 393
@SIN, 359-360
@SLN, 339-340
@SOLVER add-in function, 836
@SQRT, 360-361
@STD, 400-401
@STDS, 402-403
@STRING, 427
@SUM, 64, 403-406
@SUMPRODUCT, 406-407, 588
@SYD, 340-341
@TAN, 361-362
@TERM, 341-342
@TIME, 322-323
@TIMEVALUE, 324

@TODAY, 325-326
@TRIM, 427-428
@TRUE, 371
@UPPER, 428-429
@VALUE, 429
@VAR, 407-409
@VARS, 409-410
@VDB, 343-344
@VLOOKUP, 393-397
@YEAR, 326-327

A

Absolute cell references, 66-67, 183-186
Access System, 22-24
Active corner (print ranges), 239
Active file, 454
Add-in menu commands, 810-812
    ALT-F10 Clear, 811, 846
    ALT-F10 Invoke, 811, 846
    ALT-F10 Load, 810-811, 846-847
    ALT-F10 Quit, 812, 847
    ALT-F10 Remove, 811, 847
    ALT-F10 Settings, 811-812, 847-848
    ALT-F10 Table, 811, 848
Advancing printer paper, 239-240
Aggregate column (databases), 516-517
Allways format files, 887
Arguments, function, 310-312
Arithmetic formulas, 57-60
Arithmetic, matrix. *See* Matrix arithmetic
Arithmetic operators used in 1-2-3, 58

Assigning macros to User icons, 701-704
Auditor add-in, 815-820
    using, 815-820
        finding cells used in a formula, 816-818
        finding circular references, 819-820
        finding formulas in a range, 818-819
        finding formulas in recalculation order, 819
        finding formulas used by a cell, 818-819
Auditor commands,
    Circs, 819-820, 849
    Dependents, 818, 849
    Formulas, 818-819, 849-850
    Options, 815-816, 850-851
    Precedents, 816-818, 851
    Quit, 851
    Recalc-List, 819, 852
AUTO123 file, 459
Automatic format, 7, 116
Automatic graphs, 614-616
Automatic macros, 706-707

B

Background printing, 11, 230, 234-235
Backsolver add-in, 820-821
Backsolver commands,
    Adjustable, 821, 853
    Formula-Cell, 821, 852
    Solve, 821, 853
    Quit, 853
    Value, 821, 852-853

Bar graph, 620, 623
    macro to create, 723-724
Beep, controlling, 194
Blank rows, macro to insert, 709
Borders, 246-249
    column borders, 248
    row borders, 249
    rules for, 247
Built-in @functions. *See*
    @functions

C

Cell pointer movement keys, 36-38
Cell ranges
    erasing, 167-168
    specifying, 70-73, 146-149
    valid and invalid, 70-71
    working with, 146-168
    See also Range names
Cell reference types, 66-67, 181-188
    See also Absolute cell references; Mixed cell references; Relative cell references
CGM files, 433, 653-654
Circular reference, 197
    finding circular references, 819-820
Clock display format options, 125-126
Collating sequence (printer driver), 495, 497, 962
Color format, 117
Column borders, 248

Column commands. *See*
    /Worksheet commands
Column widths
    changing, 88-91, 94
    changing for entire worksheet, 96-97
Columns
    deleting, 85-87
    hidden, 91-94
    inserting, 80-81
Columnwise automatic graph, 614-615
Combining files, 440-448
    macro for, 718-719
Comma format, 109
Command language macros, 687-728, 731-807
    constructing and using, 733-745
    designing, 736-739
    documenting, 742-743
    entering, 739-740
    executing, 744-745
    flowcharts for, 734-736
    and keyboard macros, 732-733
    logic and syntax, 734
    main code and subroutines, 737-739
    naming, 740
    planning, 734-736
    pseudocode for, 736
    stopping, 745
    testing, 743-744
    use of braces in, 732
    See also Macro commands
Command references
    add-in menu, 845-848

Index

basic worksheet, 212-227
data analysis, 600-611
data management, 542-557
files, 468-485
graphics, 662-684
printing, 276-303
worksheet display, 129-142
Wysiwyg, 920-953
Commands. *See* Command references; individual names of commands
Compound operators, 61
Compressed print
　1-2-3, 268
　Wysiwyg, 256-257
Computed column (databases), 516-517
Configuration, for installation, 956-3
Control panel, 25-28
/Copy, 176-190, 212
Copying formulas, 181-188
Correcting errors in entries, 68-70
Currency formats, 108-109, 123-124
Current directory, changing, 454
Current file, 454
Custom palette. *See* SmartIcons
Cutting and pasting, 172-175

D

Data analysis, 559-611
/Data Distribution, 583-585, 600
/Data External commands, 13, 522-531
　Create Definition, 528-531, 542

　Create Go, 529, 542
　Create Name, 527-531, 543
　Create Quit, 543
　Delete, 531, 543-544
　List, 544-545
　List Fields, 525-526
　List Tables, 525-526
　Other Command, 545
　Other Refresh, 527, 545-546
　Other Translation, 525, 546
　Quit, 546
　Reset, 527, 547
　Use, 523-525, 547-548
/Data Fill, 499-504, 548-549
Data management, 489-557
　new features, 11-13
/Data Matrix commands, 600-601
　Invert, 589-590
　Multiply, 586-588
/Data Parse, 590-593, 601-603
/Data Query commands,
　Criteria, 505-511, 549-550
　Del, 521, 550
　Extract, 515-516, 530-531, 550-551
　Find, 512-513, 551
　Input, 505, 551-552
　Modify Cancel, 518, 552
　Modify Extract, 517-518, 552
　Modify Insert, 519-520, 553
　Modify Replace, 517-518, 553
　new features, 11-13
　Output, 514-515, 553-554
　Quit, 521, 554
　Reset, 521, 554
　steps for using, 507
　Unique, 518-519, 554-555
Data ranges

displaying as percentages, 629-630
in graphs, 625-626
stacking, 627-629
/Data Regression, 579-583, 579-583, 603-604
/Data Sort commands, 593-597, 604-605
    Data-Range, 495, 555
    Extra-Key, 497-498, 555-556
    Go, 498, 556
    new features, 11-13
    Primary-Key, 495-496, 556
    Quit, 498, 556
    Reset, 498, 557
    Secondary-Key, 497, 557
/Data Table commands, 560-579
/Data Table 1, 560-563, 605-606
/Data Table 2, 564-565, 606-607
/Data Table 3, 13, 565-568, 607-609
    Labeled, 13, 568-579, 609-611
    Reset, 611
Data tables, 560-579
    macro to create, 724-727
Database statistical functions, 531-540
    using data tables with, 164-165
    See also individual function names
Databases
    choosing a location, 492
    entering field names, 492-493
    entering records, 493-494
    introduced, 489-490
    linking external, 522-531
    macro to sort, 727-728

making changes in, 494
    searching, 505-521
    setting up, 492-494
    sorting data, 494-499
DataLens utility, 110-119
Date and time options, international, 124-125
Date and time serial numbers, 55-56
Date and time functions, 312-327
Date/time format, 112-113
Dates and times
    entering, 55-56
    using /Data Fill for, 502-504
Default directory, changing, 459-460
    using a macro, 709-710
Defining User icons,
    from keyboard, 702-703
    with stored keystrokes, 703
Debugging macros, 705-706
    assigned to User icons, 704
Deleting rows and columns, 85-87
Deleting worksheets, 85-87
Delimited text file, 453-454
Display. *See* Screen Display
Directories
    current directory, 454
    default directory, 459-460, 709-710
DOS commands, accessing from 1-2-3, 461
Duplicating entries, 176-190

E

EDIT mode, 69-70
Entries, 47-49

Index

See also Label entries; Value entries; Numbers; Formulas
Erasing cell ranges, 167-168
Erasing files from disk, 448-449
Erasing worksheets, 193-194
Errors in entries
    correcting, 68-70
    macro to handle, 712-713
Extensions, file, 432-433
External file links, 7, 457-459, 522-531
    creating with Viewer, 812-814
Extracting files, macro for, 717-718

F

Field names, entering in a database, 492-493
Fields, database, 490
/File Admin commands
    Link-Refresh, 459, 468
    Reservation, 468
    Seal, 172, 213
    Seal Reservation-Setting, 469
    Table, 450, 469-470
/File Combine commands
    Add, 443-445, 470-471
    Copy, 440-443, 471-472
    Subtract, 445-446, 472
/File commands, 434-454
    Dir, 454, 472-473
    Erase, 448-449, 473-474
    Import, 451-453, 474-475
    List, 449-450, 475
    New, 456, 476
    Open, 454-455, 476-477
    Retrieve, 436-153, 477
    Save, 434-436, 477-479
    Xtract, 446-448, 479-480
    See also /File Admin commands; /File Combine commands
File links, 7, 457-459, 522-531
File macros, 715-719
File management, 431-485
File types, 432-433
Filenames, 432-433
Files
    combining, 440-448
    erasing from disk, 448-449
    importing, 451-453
    listing, 449-450
    loading automatically, 459
    naming and using, 432
    retrieving from disk, 436-439
    saving, 434-436
    using multiple, 454-456
    using passwords with, 439-440
Financial functions, 327-344
Finding cells used in a formula, 816-818
Finding formulas in a range, 818-819
Finding formulas in recalculation order, 819
Finding formulas used by a cell, 818-819
Fixed format, 107
Flowcharts for command language macros, 734-736
Fonts, 867-870
Footers, 241-244
    storing, 244

using special characters in, 242, 243-244
Format options, 105-118
    quick reference to, 101
Formatting worksheets, 75-142
Formulas
    adding notes to, 67-68
    arithmetic formulas, 57-60
    cell references in, 66-67, 181-188
    converting to values, 164-166
    copying, 181-188
    as database search criteria, 509-511
    entering, 57-67
    extracting from a worksheet, 446-448
    functions. *See* @functions
    logical formulas, 61-62
    macro to display, 708
    precedence of operators in, 59-60
    printing, 264
    and recalculation, 66
    rules for entering, 57
    string formulas, 62-63
    types of, 58
FreeLance Plus, 660
Freezing titles, 200-203
Frequency distribution, 583-585
Function key assignments, 35-36
Function keys in macro commands, 692-693, 693
Functions. *See* @functions

G

General format, 56-57, 109-111

/Graph commands, 662
    Group, 626-627, 662
    Quit, 675
    Reset, 650-651, 675-676
    Save, 653-654, 676
    Type, 619, 623, 676-678
    Type Features, 627-635
    View, 614, 679
    X, 619, 624, 679-680
    See also /Graph Name commands; /Graph Options commands; Graphs
Graph macros, 713-724
/Graph Name commands
    Create, 651-653, 663
    Delete, 653, 663
    Reset, 653, 664
    Table, 664
    Use, 651-653, 664-664
/Graph Options commands
    Advanced Colors, 639, 665
    Advanced Hatches, 639-640, 666
    Advanced Quit, 666
    Advanced Text, 643-644, 666-667
    B&W, 647, 667-668
    Color, 647, 668
    Data-Labels, 650, 668
    Format, 646, 650, 669
    Grid, 644-645, 669-670
    Legend, 640-642, 671
    Quit, 671
    Scale 2Y-Scale, 647-649, 673-674
    Scale Skip, 624, 672

Index

Scale X-Scale, 647-649, 672-673
Scale Y-Scale, 647-649, 674
Titles, 642-643, 674-675
Graph window, 616-617
Graphics, 613-684
Graphics editing window (Wysiwyg), 898-906
Graphs
   adding grid lines, 644-645
   adding legends, 640-642
   adding titles, 642-643
   area graph, 646
   axes orientation, 627
   bar graph, 620, 623, 723-724
   creating, 618-627
   deleting, 653
   displaying data as percentages, 629-630
   enhancing, 627-635
   frame options, 634-635
   HLCO graph, 15-16, 622, 623
   line graph, 621, 623
   mixed type graph, 15, 622, 623
   multiple data ranges in, 626-627
   naming, 651-654
   new features, 15-16
   pie chart, 621, 623, 636-638
   printing, 11, 654-660
   QuickGraph SmartIcon, 635-636
   resetting graph options, 650-651
   saving to an external file, 653-654
   selecting a graph type, 619, 623
   selecting colors for, 639
   selecting data for, 625-626
   selecting hatch patterns for, 639-640
   stacked bar graph, 620, 623
   stacking data ranges, 627-629
   storing and using, 651-654
   table of print commands for, 659
   three-dimensional, 632-634
   using two Y axes, 631-632
   using Wysiwyg for, 894-906
   viewing with worksheets, 616-617
   with data tables, 634
   XY graph, 621, 623
   See also /Graph commands; /Graph Name commands; /Graph Options commands; Wysiwyg add-in
Graphwriter II, 660
Grid lines (graphs), 644-645
GROUP mode, 5, 76-78
   and Wysiwyg, 915

H

Hardware, 4
   configuration, 956-957
Headers, 241-244
   storing, 244
   suppressing blank, 265-266
   using special characters in, 242-244
Help features, 31

Hidden columns, 91-94
    and print range, 252-254
Hidden format, 115
Hidden worksheets, 95
    and print range, 252-254
Hiding zeros, 99-101
High-Low-Close-Open (HLCO)
    graphs, 15-16, 622, 623
Horizontally split screen, 204-205

Icons. *See* SmartIcons
Identity matrix, 589
Importing files, 451-453
Impress format files, 887
Inserting rows and columns,
    80-81
Inserting worksheets, 80-84
Install program, 24
    using after installation, 24,
        960-963
    using to install 1-2-3 and
        add-ins, 957-960
Installing, 1-2-3 and Add-Ins,
    955-964
Interactive macros, 742
International format options,
    122-125
    currency formats, 123-124
    date and time formats,
        124-125
    Negative, 125
    Punctuation, 123
    Update, 125

Join formula (databases), 522
Justification, label. *See* Label
    justification

Key indicators, 29-31
Keyboard, 33-39
Keyboard macros, 687-728
    braces in, 691
    and command language
        macros, 732-733
    creating and executing,
        688-700
    debugging, 687-706
    documenting, 699-700
    executing, 700-701
    naming, 699
    new features, 16-17
    recording keystrokes,
        690-694
    recording special keys,
        691-694
    STEP mode execution, 698,
        705-706
    tildes in, 690
    typing, 695
    using the keystroke
        recorder, 16-17, 696-698
    using with Wysiwyg, 915
Keys, special, 35-40

L

Label entries, 47-52

and changing column
   width, 88-89
and label indicators, 48,
   50-52
repeating, 52-53
rules for, 50
See also Long labels
Label format, 117-118
Label indicators, 48, 50-52
Label justification, 50-52, 126-128
   changing, 50-52, 166-167
   changing the default, 193
Labeled data tables, 568-579
LAN package, 18
Line feeds, setting, 270, 271
Line graph, 621, 623
Linking files, 7, 457-459, 522-531
   with Viewer, 812-814
LMBCS codes, 49, 977-993
Loading,
   add-ins, 810-811
   1-2-3, 23-24
   Wysiwyg, 23, 864
Logical formulas, 61-62
Logical functions, 362-361
Logical operators, 61
Long labels
   displaying, 126-128
   splitting, 590-593
Lotus Access System, 22-24
Lotus FreeLance Plus, 660
Lotus Graphwriter II, 660

M

Macro commands, 745-807
   {?}, 758-759
   {APPENDBELOW}, 788-789
   {APPENDRIGHT}, 790-791
   {BEEP}, 748-749
   {BLANK}, 792-793
   {BRANCH}, 776-777
   {BREAKOFF}, 759-761
   {BREAKON}, 762
   {CLOSE}, 800
   complete list of, 747-748
   {CONTENTS}, 793-795
   {DEFINE}, 777-778
   {DISPATCH}, 778-779
   flow of operations, 776-788
   files, handling, 799-807
   {FILESIZE}, 800-801
   {FOR}, 779-781
   {FORBREAK}, 781
   {FORM}, 762-765
   {FORMBREAK}, 755
   {FRAMEOFF}, 749-750
   {FRAMEON}, 750-751
   {GET}, 765-767
   {GETLABEL}, 767-769
   {GETNUMBER}, 769-770
   {GETPOS}, 801
   {GRAPHOFF}, 751-752
   {GRAPHON}, 752-753
   {IF}, 781-782
   {INDICATE}, 753-754
   interactive, 758-776
   {LET}, 795-796
   {LOOK}, 734-771
   manipulating data, 788-799
   {MENUBRANCH}, 772-774
   {MENUCALL}, 774-775
   {ONERROR}, 782-783
   {OPEN}, 801-802
   {PANELOFF}, 754-755
   {PANELON}, 755-756

{PUT}, 796-797
{QUIT}, 784
{READ}, 802-803
{READLN}, 803
{RECALC}, 797-798
{RECALCCOL}, 798-799
{RESTART}, 784-785
{RETURN}, 785-786
{routine}, 786-787
{SETPOS}, 803-804
screen, affecting, 746-758
special keys in, 691-694
syntax of, 745-746
{SYSTEM}, 787-788
{WAIT}, 775-776
{WINDOWSOFF}, 756-757
{WINDOWSON}, 757-758
{WRITE}, 804-805
{WRITELN}, 805-807
Macro keystroke recorder, 16-17, 696-698
Macro library, 704-705
Macro shell, 740-741
Macros,
    assigning to icons, 701-704
    with add-ins, 836-838
See also Automatic macros; Command language macros; Keyboard macros; Macro commands; Ready-to-use macros; SmartIcons
Map windows, 8-9, 207-208
Margins, controlling, 244-246, 272
Mathematical functions, 344-362
Matrix, 585
Matrix arithmetic, 585-590
Matrix inversion, 589-590
Matrix multiplication, 586-588

Menus,
    1-2-3, 32-33
    Wysiwyg, 33
Mixed address, 186-188
Mixed cell references, 66-67, 186-188
Mixed graph type, 15, 622, 623
Mode indicators
    1-2-3, 26-28
    Wysiwyg, 28
Modifying User icons, 703
Mouse pointer movement, 40-43
/Move, 173-175, 213-214
Multiple files
    opening and closing, 454-456
    using in commands, 457
Multiple worksheets, 5-6, 46-47
    displaying levels, 26
    keys to use with, 38-40
    in memory at once, 5-6
    ranges in, 72-73
    transposing data on, 161-164

N

Negative number format options, 125
Network support, 18
Networks, retrieving files on, 438-439
New features for 3.4, 4
Numbers 52
    entering, 54-55
    changing column width to accommodate, 90
    displaying, 56-57
    rules for entering, 53-56
    size, 53-54

See also Format options;
Formulas; Values
Numeric keypad functions, 36-38

O

Object (graphics), 899
One-way data tables, 560-563
Operator precedence (in formulas), 59-60
Operators, in database search criteria, 509-511

P

Page breaks
    1-2-3, inserting, 263
    Wysiwyg inserting, 254-255
Page layout sample, 245
Page layout library, Wysiwyg, 258
Page length, 250-251
Page size, 250-251
Palettes. *See* SmartIcons add-in
Parentheses format, 118
Parsing data, 590-593
Passwords, using with files, 439-440
Pasting (and cutting), 172-175
Percent format, 102
Perspective windows, 5-6, 81-84, 87-88, 142
    macro to set, 710-711
Pie charts, 621, 623, 636-638
Points (font measurement), 868
Preview printing, 256
/Print commands
    Background, 276
    Cancel, 276
    Encoded, 277
    File, 277
    new features of, 11
    Quit, 292
    Resume, 235, 292
    Suspend, 235, 292
    See also /Print Printer commands; /Print Printer Options commands
Print destination, 232-235
Print macros, 719-722
/Print Printer commands, 278
    Align, 240, 278
    Clear, 268-269, 278-279
    Go, 279-280
    Hold, 280
    Image, 655, 680
    Line, 240, 280-281
    Page, 240, 290
    Quit, 290-291
    Range, 235-239, 291, 655
    See also /Print commands; /Print Printer Options commands
/Print Printer Options commands, 241-255, 263-270, 281
    Advanced, 263-270, 281-283
    Advanced Fonts, 282
    Advanced Image, 655-657
    Advanced Image Density, 681
    Advanced Image Image-Sz, 681-682
    Advanced Image Quit, 682
    Advanced Image Rotate, 682-683

Borders, 246-249, 283-284
Footer, 241-244, 284-285
Header, 241-244, 285
Margins, 244-246, 286
Name, 266, 287
Other, 263-266, 288-289
Pg-Length, 250-251, 289
Quit, 289
Setup, 268, 289-290
See also /Print commands;
/Print Printer commands
Print range, 235-239
and hidden columns and
sheets, 252-254
Print settings, 1-2-3
clearing, 268-269
macro to change, 711-712
saving, 266
Print settings, Wysiwyg, 261-262
first page number, 262
multi-page ranges, 262
multiple copies, 262
Printer device, selecting
1-2-3, 270
Wysiwyg, 259
Printer driver, modifying, 960-963
Printer driver sets
changing the collating
sequence, 495, 497, 962
creating, 960-963
Printer interface,
1-2-3, 271
Wysiwyg, 259
Printer paper, controlling from
the keyboard, 239-240
Print Preview, 256
Printing, 10-11, 230-303
assigning priority levels, 234

graphs, 11, 654-660
halting and restarting, 235
multiple ranges, 239
new features, 11
protecting cells, 168-172
Pseudocode in command
language macros, 736
Punctuation format options, 123

Q

Queries, database, 505-521

R

RAM, 431
/Range commands
Erase, 79, 167-168, 214
Format, 76-77, 102-118,
130-132
Format +/-, 111-112, 131
Format ,(comma), 109, 131
Format Currency, 108-109,
130-131
Format Date, 112-113,
131-132
Format Fixed, 107, 130
Format General, 109-111, 131
Format Hidden, 115, 132
Format Other, 116-118,
132-133
Format Percent, 112
Format Reset, 132
Format Sci, 107-108, 130
Format Text, 113-114, 132
Input, 171, 151-215
Justify, 126-128, 133-134

Label, 166-167, 215
Prot, 170-171, 218-219
Search, 8, 190-192, 219
Trans, 158-164, 219-220
Unprot, 170-171, 220
Value, 164-166, 221
See also /Range Name commands
Range macros, 714-715
/Range Name commands
Create, 151-154, 215-216, 688-689, 698
Delete, 154-155, 216
Labels, 153-154, 216-217, 688-689
Labels Right, 700
Note, 157, 217
Reset, 155, 217
Table, 155-156, 218, 699
Undefine, 218
See also /Range commands
Range names
applications for, 157-158
assigning, 153-154
assigning notes to, 8
creating, 151-154
creating a table of, 155-156
creating a table with a macro, 715
creating and using notes with, 157
deleting, 154-155
expanded support for, 7
resetting, 155
using, 150-158
using existing labels, 153-154
using filenames with, 156
See also Cell ranges

Ranges, cell. *See* Cell ranges
Ready-to-use macros, 707-728
data macros, 724-728
file macros, 715-719
graph macros, 723-724
print macros, 719-722
range macros, 714-715
worksheet macros, 707-714
Recalculating worksheets, 66, 194-197
Records
defined, 490
entering in a database, 493-494
numbered, 500-502
References. *See* Cell references; Absolute cell references; Mixed cell references; Relative cell references
Regression analysis, 579-583
Relative cell references, 66-67, 171-183
Repeating label entry, 52-53
Reports, macro to print, 720-721
Retrieving files from disk, 436-439
macro for, 716-717
Row borders, 249
Rows and columns
deleting, 85-87
inserting, 80-81
Rowwise automatic graph, 616

S

Sans serif fonts, 867
Saving files to disk, 434-436
macro for, 716

Saving part of a worksheet, 446-448
Scientific format, 53, 107-108
Scientific notation, 53
Screen display, 25-33
Searching a database, 505-521
Search and replace features, 8, 190-192
Sensitivity analysis, 146-165
   and labeled data tables, 568-579
Serial numbers, date and time, 55-56
Series of values, generating, 499-504
Serif fonts, 867
Setup strings (printing), 266-268
Sheets. *See* Worksheets
Skewing boxes and text, 905
SmartIcon add-in, 4, 31, 838-843, 969-975
   adding an icon, 840-841
   changing user icon pictures, 842-843
   modifying the custom palette, 839-842
   moving icons, 841
   removing an icon, 839
   selecting, 839
   using, 839
SmartIcons, 4, 31, 838-843, 969-975
   Add Graph, 895
   assigning macros to User icons, 701-704
   Background Color, 119, 874-875
   Bold, 119, 121, 871
   Comma format, 102, 105, 131
   Copy, 188-190
   Currency format, 102, 105, 130-131
   Data Fill, 502
   deleting rows, columns or sheets, 86, 135-136
   Drop-Shadow, 119, 874
   Edit Text, 880-881
   Font, 119-120
   inserting rows and columns, 81, 141-142
   inserting worksheets, 83, 141-142
   Italic, 119, 871
   Move, 176
   Normal, 876
   Outline, 119, 121, 874
   Page Breaks, horizontal and vertical, 909-910
   Percentage format, 102, 105, 131
   Perspective, 88
   Preview, 909
   QuickGraph, 635-636
   Retrieve File, 436
   Run Macro, 689
   Save File, 435
   Shading, 119, 121, 875
   SmartSum, 64-66
   Sort, ascending and descending, 498-499
   Step, 698
   Text Align, 880
   Text Color, 119, 874-875
   Underline, single and double, 119, 121, 872
   Undo, 79

User icons, 701-704, 842-843
Smoothing levels (graphics), 902-903
Solver add-in, 821-838
    @function limitations, 825
    @SOLVER add-in function, 836, 837
    answer report, 829-830, 831
    cells used report, 834-836
    creating a solution, 827
    exploring the answers, 828
    defining the model, 826
    differences report, 832, 833
    entering the basic problem for, 823-825
    how solved report, 830, 831
    inconsistent constraints report, 832-834, 835
    report options, 828-835
    steps for, 822
    unused constraints report, 834, 835
    what-if limits report, 830-832, 833
Solver commands
    Answer, 828, 855-856
    Define Adjustable, 826, 854
    Define Constraints, 826, 854
    Define Optimal, 826, 854
    Options, 857
    Report, 828-835, 856-857
    Solve, 827-828, 855-856
    Quit, 858
Sorting a database, 494-499
    adding record numbers, 500-502
    changing the sort order, 962
    macro for, 727-728

Sorting worksheet data, 593-597
Special functions, 372-397
Stacked bar graph, 620, 623
Starting
    add-ins, 810-811
    1-2-3, 23-24
    Wysiwyg, 23, 864
Statistical analysis, 560-590
Statistical functions, 397-411
Status line, 29-31
Status screen, 208-210
STEP mode, with macros, 698
String formulas, 62-63
String functions, 411-429
Subdirectories, 433-434
/System, 461, 480
System configuration, 956-957

T

Text format, 113-114
Text format worksheet, printing, 264
3-D worksheets, 5-6
Three-way data tables, 565-568
Tildes in macros, 690
Time functions, 312-327
Titles, freezing, 200-203
Translate program, 24, 461-466, 484-485
Transposing data, 158-164
    multiple-sheet, 161-164
    single-sheet, 160
    steps for, 159
Two-way data tables, 564-565

U

Undo feature, 10, 79-80
    using while running macros, 744
User icons. *See* SmartIcons

V

Value entries, 47-49, 52-68
    types of, 52
Values
    converting formulas to, 164-166
    generating a series of, 499-504
Vertically split screen, 205
View graph
    and worksheet, 616-617
    full-screen, 614, 679
Viewer add-in, 812-814
Viewer commands
    Browse, 813-814, 858
    Link, 813-814, 858-859
    Open, 813-814, 859
    Retrieve, 813-814, 860

W

Wildcards, 156
Windows
    adding a second window, 203-207
    Map windows, 8-9, 207-208
    perspective view, 5-6, 81-84, 87-88, 142

/Worksheet Column commands, 88-94, 134-135
    Column-Range, 94
    Hide, 91-94, 252-254
    Reset-Width, 88
    Set-Width, 88-87
    See also /Worksheet commands; /Worksheet Global commands; /Worksheet Global Default commands
/Worksheet commands
    Delete, 85-87, 135-136
    Delete File, 457, 480
    Erase, 79, 193-194, 221
    Hide, 95, 141
    Insert, 80-84, 141-142
    Insert Column, 80-81
    Insert Row, 80-81
    Insert Sheet, 81-84
    Page, 263, 294
    Status, 208-210, 225
    Titles, 200-203, 225-226
    Window, 203-207, 226-227
    Window, Graph, 14, 616-617, 684
    Window, Perspective, 81-84, 87-88, 142
    See also /Worksheet Column commands; /Worksheet Global commands; /Worksheet Global Default commands
/Worksheet Global commands, 96-101
    Col-Width, 96, 136
    Format, 76-77, 98-99, 101, 139-140

Group, 76-78, 140
Label, 193, 222-223
Prot, 169-171, 223-224
Recalc, 194-197, 224
Zero, 99-101, 140
See also /Worksheet
   commands; /Worksheet
   Column commands;
   /Worksheet Global
   Default commands
Autoexec, 481
Dir, 459-460, 481
Ext, 460-461, 482
Graph, 653, 683
Other Beep, 194, 221-222
Other Clock, 125-126,
   136-137
Other Help, 222
Other International, 122-125,
   137-138
File-Translation, 482
Other International
   Release-2, 483
Other Undo, 79-80, 139
Printer, 270-273, 292-294
Status, 222
Temp, 460, 483
Update, 139, 294, 460, 483
See also /Worksheet
   commands; /Worksheet
   Column commands;
   /Worksheet Global
   commands
Worksheet macros, 707-714
Worksheet
   changing the display,
      75-142, 198, 200-208
   correcting entry errors, 68-70

deleting, 85-87
entering data, 45-73
erasing, 193-194
formatting, 75-142
hiding, 95
inserting, 80, 81-84
layout of, 28-29
new options for, 4-9
recalculating, 194-197
structure of, 4-7, 46-47
types of entries, 47-68
See also Multiple worksheets
Wysiwyg add-in, 17, 863-953
   adding boldface, 871
   adding color, 874-875
   adding italics, 871
   adding lines, 872-874
   adding shading, 875
   adding underlining, 872
   attaching, 810-811
   changing column widths
      and row heights, 887-888
   changing the display,
      888-894
   choosing a font set, 868-870
   copying and moving
      formats, 884-887
   default font set, 868-869
   format descriptions, 865-866
   formatting sequences, 883
   formatting text in entries,
      882-883
   and GROUP mode, 915
   importing and exporting
      formats, 885-887
   interface, 864-867
   page breaks, 909-910

previewing a worksheet, 908-909
printing status sheet, 906-907
printing with, 906-860
types of objects available, 900-901
using fonts, 867-871
using for graphs, 462-474
using keyboard macros with, 861
using named format styles, 876-877
using text ranges, 877-884
working with objects, 898-906
Wysiwyg commands, 920-953
:Display Colors, 920
:Display Default, 893, 921
:Display Font-Directory, 893, 921
:Display Mode, 888-889, 921-922
:Display Options Cell-Pointer, 890-891, 922
:Display Options Frame, 891-892, 922-923
:Display Options Grid, 892, 903-904, 923
:Display Options Intensity, 893, 923-924
:Display Options Page-Breaks, 254-255, 893, 924
:Display Options Quit, 924
:Display Quit, 924
:Display Rows, 890, 925
:Display Zoom, 890, 925
:Format Bold, 871, 926
:Format Color, 889-890, 926-927
:Format Colors, 874-875
:Format Font, 868-870, 927
:Format Italics, 871, 928
:Format Lines, 872-874, 928-929
:Format Quit, 929
:Format Reset, 876, 929
:Format Shade, 875-876, 930
:Format Underline, 872, 930-931
:Graph Add, 894-896, 907, 931
:Graph Compute, 898, 932
:Graph Edit, 898
:Graph Edit Add, 932-933
:Graph Edit Color, 902, 933-934
:Graph Edit Edit, 902, 934
:Graph Edit Options, 935
:Graph Edit Quit, 898, 935
:Graph Edit Rearrange, 904-905, 935-936
:Graph Edit Select, 900, 936-937
:Graph Edit Transform, 904-905, 937
:Graph Edit View, 938
:Graph Goto, 896, 938-939
:Graph Move, 896-897, 939
:Graph Quit, 939
:Graph Remove, 940
:Graph Settings, 897-898, 940
:Graph View, 898, 905-906, 941
:Graph Zoom, 898, 941

:Named-Style, 876-877, 941-942
:Print Background, 295, 942
:Print Configuration, 258-261, 295-296, 912-914, 942-943
:Print File, 232-235, 296, 908, 943
:Print Go, 232-235, 296, 908, 944
:Print Info, 297, 890
:Print Layout Borders, 246-249, 297, 911, 944
:Print Layout Compression, 297-298, 911-912, 944-945
:Print Layout Default, 298, 912, 945
:Print Layout Library, 298-299, 912, 945-946
:Print Layout Margins, 244-246, 299, 910, 946
:Print Layout Page-Size, 250-251, 299-300, 910, 946-947
:Print Layout Titles, 241-244, 300-301, 911, 947
:Print Preview, 256, 301, 947
:Print Quit, 301, 908, 947
:Print Range, 235-239, 301, 908, 948
:Print Settings, 301-302, 913-914, 948-949
:Quit, 302, 949
:Special Copy, 884-887, 949
:Special Export, 885-887, 949-950
:Special Import, 885-887, 950
:Special Move, 884-887, 950-951
:Text, 951
:Text Align, 878-880
:Text Reformat, 881-882
:Text Set, 877-878
:Worksheet Column, 887-888, 951-952
:Worksheet Page, 254-256, 302-303, 909-910, 952
:Worksheet Row, 840, 952-953
See also Wysiwyg add-in

X

X axis, labeling (graphs), 619, 624
XY graph, 621, 623

Z

Zero display, 99-101

COMMAND CARD

WORKSHEET COMMANDS

/Worksheet Global
- Format
  - Fixed
  - Sci
  - Currency
  - , (General)
  - +/−
  - Percent
  - Date
    - Time
  - Text
  - Hidden
  - Other
    - Automatic
    - Color
    - Negative
    - Reset
  - Label
    - Parentheses
- Label
  - Left
  - Right
  - Center
- Col-Width
- Prot
  - Enable
  - Disable
- Zero
  - No
  - Yes
  - Label
- Recalc
  - Natural
  - Columnwise
  - Rowwise
  - Automatic
  - Manual
  - Iteration
- Default
  - Printer
  - Interface
  - AutoLf
  - Left

WORKSHEET COMMANDS
(continued)
  - Right
  - Top
  - Bottom
  - Pg-Length
  - Wait
  - Setup
  - Name
  - Quit
  - Dir
  - Status
  - Update
  - Other
    - International
      - Punctuation
      - Currency
      - Date
      - Time
      - Negative
      - Parentheses
      - Sign
    - Release-2
    - LICS
    - ASCII
    - File-Translation
      - Country
      - International
    - Quit
  - Help
  - Clock
  - Undo
  - Beep
  - Graph
  - Columnwise
  - Rowwise
  - Metafile
  - PIC
  - Quit
  - Temp
  - Ext
  - List
  - Save
  - Autoexec
  - Quit

WORKSHEET COMMANDS
(continued)
- Group
  - Disable
  - Enable
- /Worksheet Insert
  - Column
  - Row
  - Sheet
    - Before
    - After
- /Worksheet Delete
  - Column
  - Row
  - Sheet
  - File
- /Worksheet Column
  - Set-Width
  - Reset-Width
  - Hide
  - Display
  - Column-Range
    - Set-Width
    - Reset-Width
- /Worksheet Erase
- /Worksheet Titles
  - Both
  - Horizontal
  - Vertical
  - Clear
- /Worksheet Window
  - Horizontal
  - Vertical
  - Sync
  - Unsync
  - Clear
  - Map
  - Enable
  - Disable
  - Perspective
  - Graph
  - Display
    - 1
    - 2
- /Worksheet Status

WORKSHEET COMMANDS
(continued)
- /Worksheet Page
- /Worksheet Hide
  - Enable
  - Disable

RANGE COMMANDS

/Range Format
- Fixed
- Sci
- Currency
- , (General)
- +/−/Percent
- Date
  - Time
- Text
- Hidden
- Other
  - Automatic
  - Color
    - Negative
    - Reset
  - Label
    - Parentheses
  - Reset
- /Range Label
  - Left
  - Right
  - Center
- /Range Erase
- /Range Name
  - Create
  - Delete
  - Labels
  - Reset
  - Table
  - Note
    - Create
    - Delete
    - Reset
    - Table
    - Quit

RANGE COMMANDS
(continued)
- Undefine
- /Range Justify
- /Range Prot
- /Range Unprot
- /Range Input
- /Range Value
- /Range Trans
  - Rows/Columns
  - Worksheets/Rows
  - Columns/Worksheets
- /Range Search
  - Formulas
    - Find
      - Next
      - Quit
    - Replace
      - Replace
      - All
      - Next
      - Quit
  - Labels
    - Find
      - Next
      - Quit
    - Replace
      - Replace
      - All
      - Next
      - Quit
  - Both
    - Find
      - Next
      - Quit
    - Replace
      - Replace
      - All
      - Next
      - Quit

COPY COMMAND
- /Copy

MOVE COMMAND
/Move

FILE COMMANDS
/File Retrieve
/File Save
Cancel
Replace
Backup
/File Combine
Copy
 Entire-File
 Named-Range
Add
 Entire-File
 Named-Range
Subtract
 Entire-File
 Named-Range
/File Xtract
 Formulas
 Values
/File Erase
 Worksheet
 Print
 Graph
 Other
/File List
 Worksheet
 Print
 Graph
 Other
 Linked
 Active
/File Import
 Text
 Numbers
/File Dir
/File New
/File Open
 Before
 After
/File Admin
 Reservation
 Get

FILE COMMANDS
(continued)
 Release
 Setting
 Automatic
 Manual
 Table
  Worksheet
  Print
  Graph
  Other
  Active
  Linked
 Seal
  File
  Reservation-Setting
  Disable
 Link-Refresh

PRINT COMMANDS
/Print [P,E,B,F] Range
/Print [P,E,B,F] Line
/Print [P,E,B,F] Page
/Print [P,E,B,F] Options
 Header
 Footer
 Margins
  Left
  Right
  Top
  Bottom
  None
 Borders
  Columns
  Rows
 Frame
 No-Frame
 Setup
 Pg-Length
 Other
  As-Displayed
  Cell-Formulas
  Formatted
  Unformatted
  Blank-Header
  Suppress
  Print

PRINT COMMANDS
(continued)
 Name
  Use
  Create
  Delete
  Reset
  Table
 Advanced
  Device
  Name
  Interface
  Pitch
  Layout
   Standard
   Compressed
   Expanded
   Line-Spacing
  Orientation
   Standard
   Compressed
   Portrait
   Landscape
  Fonts
  Range
  Header/Footer
  Border
  Frame
  Quit
  Image
   Rotate
   Image-Sz
   Margin-Fill
   Length-Fill
   Reshape
   Density
   Draft
   Final
   Quit
  Priority
   Default
   High
   Low
   AutoLf

PRINT COMMANDS
(continued)
  Wait
  Quit
/Print [P,E,B,F] Clear
 All
 Range
 Borders
 Format
 Device
 Image
/Print [P,E,B,F] Align
/Print [P,E,B,F] Go
/Print [P,E,B,F] Image
 Current
 Named-Graph
/Print [P,E,B,F] Hold
/Print [P,E,B,F] Quit
 Print Suspend
 Print Resume
 Print Cancel
/Print Quit

GRAPH COMMANDS
/Graph Type
 Line
 Bar
 XY
 Stack-Bar
 Pie
 HLCO
 Mixed
 Features
  Vert
  Horiz
  Stacked
  100%
  2Y-Ranges
  Y-Ranges
  Frame
  Drop-Shadow
  3D
  Table
  Quit
/Graph X
/Graph A

GRAPH COMMANDS
(continued)
/Graph B
/Graph C
/Graph D
/Graph E
/Graph F
/Graph Reset
 Graph
 X
 A
 B
 C
 D
 E
 F
 Ranges
 Options
 Quit
/Graph View
/Graph Save
/Graph Options
 Legend
  A through F
  Range
 Format
  Graph
  A through F
  Quit
  Titles
   First
   Second
   X-Axis
   Y-Axis
   2Y-Axis
   Note
   Other-Note
  Grid
   Horizontal
   Vertical
   Both
   Clear
   Y
   2Y
   Both

GRAPH COMMANDS
(continued)

Scale
  Y-Scale
    Automatic
    Lower
    Upper
    Format
    Indicator
    Type
    Exponent
    Width
    Quit
  X-Scale
    Skip
    Same options as Y-Scale
  2Y-Scale
    Same options as Y-Scale
Color
B&W
Data-Labels
  A through F
  Group
    Columnwise
    Rowwise
  Quit
Advanced
  Colors
    A through F
    Quit
  Text
    First
    Second
    Third
    Quit
  Hatches
    A through F
    Quit
  Quit
/Graph Name
  Use
  Create
  Delete
  Reset
  Table

GRAPH COMMANDS
(continued)

/Graph Group
  Columnwise
  Rowwise
/Graph Quit

DATA COMMANDS

/Data Fill
/Data Table
  1
  2
  3
  Labeled
    Formulas
    Down
    Across
    Sheets
    Input-Cells
    Label-Fill
    Go
    Quit
  Reset
/Data Sort
  Data-Range
  Primary-Key
  Secondary-Key
  Extra-Key
  Reset
  Go
  Quit
/Data Query
  Input
  Criteria
  Output
  Find
  Extract
  Unique
  Del
    Cancel
    Delete
  Modify
    Extract
    Replace
    Insert
    Cancel
  Reset

DATA COMMANDS
(continued)

  Quit
/Data Distribution
/Data Matrix
  Invert
  Multiply
/Data Regression
  X-Range
  Y-Range
  Output-Range
  Intercept
    Compute
    Zero
  Reset
  Go
  Quit
/Data Parse
  Format-Line
    Create
    Edit
  Input-Column
  Output-Range
  Reset
  Go
  Quit
/Data External
  Use
  List
    Tables
    Fields
  Create
    Name
    Definition
      Create-Definition
      Use-Definition
    Go
    Quit
  Delete
  Other
    Refresh
      Automatic
      Manual
      Interval
    Command
    Translation
    Reset

DATA COMMANDS
(continued)

  Quit

SYSTEM COMMAND

/System

QUIT COMMAND

/Quit

ADD-IN MENU COMMANDS

Load
Remove
Invoke
Table
  @Functions
  Macros
  Applications
Clear
Settings
  System
    Set
    Cancel
    Directory
    Update
    Quit
  File
    Set
    Cancel
    Quit

WYSIWYG COMMANDS

:Worksheet
  Column
    Set-Width
    Reset-Width
  Row
    Set-Height
    Auto
  Page
  Row
  Column
  Delete
  Quit
:Format
  Font

WYSIWYG COMMANDS
(continued)

    1 through 8
    Replace
    Default
    Library
      Retrieve
      Save
      Erase
    Quit
  Bold
    Set
    Clear
  Italics
    Set
    Clear
  Underline
    Single
    Double
    Wide
    Clear
  Color
    Text
    Background
    Negative
    Reverse
    Quit
  Lines
    Outline
    Left
    Right
    Top
    Bottom
    All
    Double
    Wide
    Clear
  Shade
    Light
    Dark
    Solid
    Clear
  Reset
  Quit

WYSIWYG COMMANDS

:Graph
  Add
  Current
  Named
  PIC
  Metafile
  Blank
  Remove
  Goto
  Settings
    Graph
    Range
    Sync
    Display
    Opaque
    Quit
  Move
  Zoom
  Compute
  View
  Edit
    Add
      Text
      Line
      Polygon
      Arrow
      Rectangle
      Ellipse
      Freehand
    Select
      One
      All
      None
      More/Less
      Cycle
      Graph
      Quit
    Edit
      Text
      Centering
      Font
      Line-Style
      Width

WYSIWYG COMMANDS (continued)

      Arrowheads
      Smoothing
      Color
        Lines
        Inside
        Text
        Map
        Background
        Quit
      Transform
        Size
        Rotate
        Quarter-Turn
        X-Flip
        Y-Flip
        Horizontal
        Vertical
        Clear
      Rearrange
        Delete
        Restore
        Move
        Copy
        Lock
        Unlock
        Front
        Back
    View
      Full
      In
      Pan
      +
      -
      Up
      Down
      Left
      Right
      Top
      Bottom
      Quit
    Options
      Grid
      Cursor
      Font-Magnification
      Quit
  Quit
:Print
  Go

WYSIWYG COMMANDS (continued)

  File
    Cancel
    Replace
  Background
    Range
    Set
    Clear
  Config
    Printer
    Interface
    1st-Cart
    2nd-Cart
    Orientation
      Portrait
      Landscape
    Resolution
      Final
      Draft
    Bin
    Quit
  Settings
    Begin
    End
    Start-Number
    Copies
    Wait
    Grid
    Frame
    Reset
    Quit
  Layout
    Page-Size
    Margins
      Left
      Right
      Top
      Bottom
      Quit
    Titles
      Header
      Footer
      Clear
      Quit
    Borders
      Top

WYSIWYG COMMANDS (continued)

      Left
      Clear
      Quit
    Compression
      None
      Automatic
      Manual
    Default
      Restore
      Update
      Library
        Retrieve
        Save
        Erase
        Quit
    Preview
  Info
  Quit
:Display
  Mode
    Graphics
    Text
    B&W
    Color
  Zoom
    Tiny
    Small
    Normal
    Large
    Huge
    Manual
  Colors
    Background
    Text
    Unprot
    Cell-Pointer
    Grid
    Frame
    Neg
    Lines
    Shadow
    Replace
    Quit
  Frame

WYSIWYG COMMANDS (continued)

    1-2-3
    Enhanced
    Relief
    Special
    None
  Grid
  Page-Breaks
  Cell-Pointer
    Solid
    Outline
  Intensity
    Normal
    High
  Quit
  Font-Directory
  Rows
  Default
    Restore
    Update
  Quit
:Special
  Copy
  Move
  Import
    All
    Named-Styles
    Fonts
    Graphs
  Export
    Cancel
    Replace
    Text
  Edit
    Align
      Left
      Right
      Center
      Even
    Reformat
    Set
    Clear
    Named-Style
    1 through 8
    Define
    Quit